COLLECTED WORKS OF JOHN STUART MILL

VOLUME IX

The Collected Edition of the works of John Stuart Mill has been planned and is being directed by an editorial committee appointed from the Faculty of Arts and Science of the University of Toronto, and from the University of Toronto Press. The primary aim of the edition is to present fully collated texts of those works which exist in a number of versions, both printed and manuscript, and to provide accurate texts of works previously unpublished or which have become relatively inaccessible.

An Examination
of
Sir William Hamilton's
Philosophy
and of
The Principal
Philosophical Questions
Discussed in his Writings

by JOHN STUART MILL

Editor of the Text

J. M. ROBSON

Professor of English,
Victoria College, University of Toronto

Introduction by

ALAN RYAN

New College, Oxford University

UNIVERSITY OF TORONTO PRESS

ROUTLEDGE & KEGAN PAUL

© *University of Toronto Press 1979*

Toronto and Buffalo

Printed in Canada

ISBN 0-8020-2329-0
LC 63-25976

London: Routledge & Kegan Paul
ISBN 0 7100 0178 9

This volume has been published with the assistance of a grant from the
Social Sciences and Humanities Research Council of Canada

Contents

APPENDICES

Introduction

ALAN RYAN

I. REPUTATION OF THE WORK

AN EXAMINATION OF SIR WILLIAM HAMILTON'S PHILOSOPHY is not a
widely read work; nor is it very highly regarded, even by those who are
most attracted-to Mill's writings on philosophy. It contains some instructive set-pieces, which have preserved a sort of exemplary interest: Mill's
analysis of Matter in terms of "permanent possibilities of sensation," his
confessedly abortive analysis of personal identity in similarly phenomenalist terms, his analysis of free-will and responsibility, and his ringing
declaration that he would not bow his knee to worship a God whose moral
worth he was required to take on trust—all these still find their place in
contemporary discussions of empiricism. Mill's analysis of the nature of
judgment and belief perhaps engages the interest of those who hope to
explore the problems raised by *A System of Logic* in a secondary source.
But it is doubtful whether many readers who leave the *Logic* wondering
quite what Mill really thought about the epistemological status of arithmetic and geometry find themselves helped by reading the *Examination*; nor
does it add much to Mill's earlier account of causation, beyond the effective
demonstration that whatever rivals there were to Mill's account, Hamilton's was not one.

In part, the fallen position of the *Examination* is the result of the obscurity into which its target has fallen. If the *Examination* is not much read,
then Hamilton's edition of Reid's *Works*[1] is certainly not read now, as it
was in Mill's day, for Hamilton's elaborate "Dissertations on Reid." The
most recent discussion of Reid's philosophy, for example, treats Hamilton
as a late and somewhat eccentric contributor to the philosophy of common
sense.[2] Hamilton's *Lectures on Metaphysics and Logic*,[3] of whose repeti-

---

[1]Thomas Reid, *Works*, ed. Sir W. Hamilton, 6th ed. (Edinburgh: Maclachlan and Stewart,
1866).
[2]Selwyn Grave, *The Scottish Philosophy of Common Sense* (Oxford: Clarendon Press,
1960).
[3]Ed. John Veitch and Henry Longueville Mansel, 4 vols. (Edinburgh: Blackwood, 1859–
60).

tive and elementary character Mill was severely critical, were something of an embarrassment to their editors when they appeared after Hamilton's death. Now they are simply unreadable. The one accessible source for Hamilton's opinions is the volume of collected essays, *Discussions on Philosophy and Literature, Education and University Reform*,[4] in which he reprinted his contributions to the *Edinburgh Review*. Even those essays now attract the educational historian rather more than the philosopher; Hamilton's attack on the corruption and incompetence of early nineteenth-century Oxford excites more interest than his critique of Cousin's views on the Absolute.

To the destruction of Hamilton's philosophical reputation, Mill's *Examination* contributed a good deal. Mark Pattison, reviewing the *Examination* in *The Reader*, exclaimed:

The effect of Mr Mill's review is the absolute annihilation of all Sir W. Hamilton's doctrines, opinions, of all he has written or taught. Nor of himself only, but all his followers, pupils, copyists, are involved in the common ruin. The whole fabric of the Hamiltonian philosophy is not only demolished, but its very stones are ground to powder. Where once stood Sebastopol bidding proud defiance to rival systems is now

> a coast barren and blue
> Sandheaps behind and sandhills before.[5]

The enthusiasm with which Pattison contemplated the ruin of Sir William's followers may have had rather more to do with the academic politics of Oxford, in which Pattison and Hamilton's disciple H. L. Mansel were fiercely opposed to one another, than to any very exact appreciation of just which of Hamilton's doctrines had suffered just what damage. But, although Hamilton's friends and followers ignored Pattison's advice that they "had better erect a monument to him, and say nothing about Mr Mill's book,"[6] they could not restore Hamilton's status. Mill might not have shown that the intuitive school of metaphysics was inevitably doomed to obscurity and muddle, but it was generally held that he had shown Hamilton himself to be at best obscure, at worst simply incompetent.

Whether Hamilton was worth the expenditure of Mill's powder and shot is another question. W. G. Ward, writing some years after in the *Dublin Review*,[7] thought that Mill had done well to take on one representative figure of the anti-empiricist school and pursue him steadily through all the cruces of the argument between associationism and its opponents. But

---

[4]3rd ed. (Edinburgh: Blackwood, 1866). (1st ed., 1852; 2nd ed., 1853, used by Mill in the *Examination*.)

[5]Mark Pattison, "J. S. Mill on Hamilton," *The Reader*, V (20/5/65), 562.

[6]*Ibid.*, 563.

[7]William George Ward, "Mr. Mill's Denial of Necessary Truth," *Dublin Review*, n.s. XVII (Oct., 1871), 285–6.

Mark Pattison thought that the cracking of dead nuts just to make sure they were empty was a task which wearied both those who undertook it and those who watched them do it. It is, at the very least, doubtful whether Mill was wise to devote quite so much attention to Hamilton, for the *Examination* falls awkwardly between the twin tasks of providing a complete critical exposition of Hamilton's philosophy on the one hand and of providing an equally comprehensive defence of associationism on the other. In effect, Mill's defence of associationism is spread over the notes he supplied to James Mill's *Analysis of the Phenomena of the Human Mind*,[8] and over his reviews, as well as through the *Examination*. Whatever else may be said for this defence, its organization impedes the reader of the *Examination*, who is likely to resent having to recover Mill's views on perception, say, from an argument conducted at several removes from the issues, in which Mill complains of the injustice of Hamilton's attacking Thomas Brown for supposed misrepresentation of the views of Thomas Reid.[9] It also does something to account for the fact that the criticisms of Mill were criticisms of his positive claims on behalf of associationism more frequently than they were positive defences of Hamilton. Perhaps Mill should have ignored Hamilton altogether, and stuck to the positive task; he certainly left a great many openings for his critics, and might have been better advised to stop them up rather than triumph over Hamilton.

There are more serious problems than these in the way of the reader of the *Examination*. Mill's critique of Hamilton and Mansel was one engagement in the battle between empiricism and rationalism. But it was an engagement in which the combatants employed intellectual weapons which we find difficult to use. The argument between Mill and Hamilton is, in their terms, an argument about the nature and contents of "consciousness"; it is in some sense an argument about psychological issues. But whereas we now tend to draw a sharp distinction between the empirical inquiry into the mind and its powers which we call psychology, and the non-empirical inquiry into the possibility of knowledge or into the intelligibility of knowledge-claims which we now call philosophy, no such distinction appears in the *Examination*. Where we are tolerably sure that philosophical claims about the nature of space and time, or about the nature of perception, ought to be immune from empirical confirmation and disconfirmation, Mill and Hamilton were not. This difference does not make for difficulties with Mill alone; it means that the views of all other philosophers are "read" rather differently by Mill and Hamilton from the way it is natural to us to read

---

[8]James Mill, *Analysis of the Phenomena of the Human Mind*, 2 vols., 2nd ed., ed. J. S. Mill (London: Longmans, Green, Reader, and Dyer, 1869).

[9]E.g., *Examination*, 167ff. below. Subsequent references, which are all to the present edition, are given in parentheses in the text.

them. Thus, Kant's contribution to philosophy is treated as a contribution to psychology. Where, for instance, we might interpret Kant's account of the *synthetic a priori* as entailing that it is a sort of nonsense, though not strictly a grammatical or syntactical sort of nonsense, to suggest that there might be regions of space and time in which the laws of geometry or arithmetic do not apply, Hamilton plainly took the claim to be one about the incapacity of the mind to *conceive* non-Euclidean space or things which were not countable; and Mill was equally ready to understand Kant in this way, differing over the issue of whether our incapacity to conceive such a space or such objects was part of the original constitution of the mind or the result of experience. To some extent, therefore, readers of the *Examination* have to engage in a process of translation in order to feel at home with Mill's argument. Sometimes there are cases which seem to defy the process. Mill's discussion of how we might come to have the concept of space, for instance, is, as we shall see, very awkward if it is read as an empirical hypothesis about how the furniture of the mind might have been built; and it is more awkward still if it is read as what we now call philosophy.

Against such a background, the proper task of a critic is a matter for debate. Even if we can decently evade any obligation to show that the *Examination* is a neglected masterpiece, there is a good deal left to do. The task is partly historical and partly philosophical, and it is perhaps an instance of those cases where the history is unintelligible without the philosophy, as well as the other way about. Firstly, something has to be said about why Mill should have decided to write the *Examination* at all, and about the reasons for its immediate *succès* both *d'estime* and *de scandale*. Then, something must be said about the life and career of Sir William Hamilton, and at least a little about the role of Mill's other main antagonist, H. L. Mansel. Once the appropriate background in Mill's career has been filled in, and the main characters have been identified, I shall go on to provide a substitute for the extended analytical table of contents which was once (though it was not part of the *Examination*) such a useful feature of scholarly works. My account will be both expository and critical, and some at least of the distinctive philosophical views of Hamilton and Mansel will be there explored.

II. MILL'S MOTIVATION

WHY SHOULD MILL IN PARTICULAR have devoted himself to writing such a book as the *Examination*?[10] From his reading of the *Discussions* shortly

[10]See *Autobiography*, ed. Jack Stillinger (Boston: Houghton Mifflin, 1969), 161–2.

after its appearance, Mill had inferred that Hamilton occupied a sort of halfway house, subscribing neither to his own enthusiasm for the principle of the association of ideas nor to the excesses of post-Kantian Continental philosophy, in which, as Mill saw it, we were supposed to know intuitively all sorts of implausible things. Mill explains in his *Autobiography*, however, that his reading of Hamilton's posthumously published *Lectures* during 1861 alerted him to the fact (a fact confirmed by his subsequent study of the "Dissertations on Reid") that Hamilton was a much more committed and unrestrained intuitionist than he had previously supposed.[11]

As readers of the *Autobiography* will recall, Mill was very insistent that the struggle between the intuitionists and the school of "Experience and Association" was much more than an academic argument over the first principles of the moral sciences. In explaining why he had written the *System of Logic*, Mill had said that "it is hardly possible to exaggerate the mischiefs"[12] caused by a false philosophy of mind. The doctrine that we have intuitive and infallible knowledge of the principles governing either our own selves or the outside world seemed to him

the great intellectual support of false doctrines and bad institutions. By the aid of this theory, every inveterate belief and every intense feeling, of which the origin is not remembered, is enabled to dispense with the obligation of justifying itself by reason, and is erected into its own all-sufficient voucher and justification. There never was such an instrument devised for consecrating all deep seated prejudices.[13]

The *System of Logic* was in quite large part directed at William Whewell, and, up to a point, Mill was right to see Whewell as the defender of conservative and Anglican institutions—he was Master of Trinity, and Mill had refused to attend Trinity as a youth for obvious anti-clerical reasons.[14] The *Examination* is described in terms which suggest that Mill thought it necessary to return to the attack on the same front. The difference between the intuitionists and the associationists, he says,

is not a mere matter of abstract speculation; it is full of practical consequences, and lies at the foundation of all the greatest differences of practical opinion in an age of progress. The practical reformer has continually to demand that changes be made in things which are supported by powerful and widely spread feelings, or to question the apparent necessity and indefeasibleness of established facts; and it is often an indispensable part of his argument to shew, how those powerful feelings had their origin, and how those facts came to seem necessary and indefeasible.[15]

One might doubt whether there was any very close practical connection

[11]*Ibid.*
[12]*Ibid.*, 134.
[13]*Ibid.*
[14]But see Jerome B. Schneewind, *Sidgwick's Ethics and Victorian Moral Philosophy* (Oxford: Clarendon Press, 1977), 96n, where Whewell appears as a rather liberal churchman.
[15]*Autobiography*, 162.

between, say, a Kantian view of knowledge and conservatism on the one hand, and a Humean view and liberalism on the other. Certainly it is hard to imagine Hume welcoming the French Revolution, had he lived to see it, and it is not very difficult to construct radical political philosophies of a broadly intuitionist kind. Kant at least welcomed the French Revolution, even if he trembled before the execution of Louis XVI.[16]

But Mill had no doubt that some such connection did hold.

I have long felt that the prevailing tendency to regard all the marked distinctions of human character as innate, and in the main indelible, and to ignore the irresistible proofs that by far the greater part of those differences, whether between individuals, races, or sexes, are such as not only might but naturally would be produced by differences in circumstances, is one of the chief hindrances to the rational treatment of great social questions, and one of the greatest stumbling blocks to human improvement.[17]

He therefore decided that it was right to produce something more combative and controversial than a treatise on the associationist philosophy of mind. It was necessary to attack the chief exponent of the opposite view—hence what some readers will surely think of as the grindingly negative tone of a good deal of the *Examination*. Mill, in many ways, was ill-fitted to assault Hamilton in this fashion; he was too fair-minded to let Hamilton's case take its chances, and therefore encumbered his attack with enormous and tedious quantities of quotation from Hamilton. Yet at the same time he was so entirely unsympathetic to Hamilton that he rarely paused to wonder if some rational and useful case might be extracted from the confused jumble, which was all that Hamilton's writings eventually seemed to him to amount to. In a way, he could neither do his worst to Hamilton, nor could he do his best for him.

Yet the attack was a sort of duty, especially in view of the use made of Hamilton's philosophy of the conditioned by his pupil Mansel. H. L. Mansel's Bampton Lectures had aroused a good deal of indignation from the time of their delivery in 1858, and they went into several editions, with replies to critics appended to new editions. Mansel's aim had been something like Kant's—to limit the pretensions of reason to make room for faith. Accordingly, he had argued that we were obliged as a matter of faith to believe that God was everything that was good, although "good," as applied to the Almighty, was a term which was at best related only by analogy to "good" applied to a human being. Mill thought that this conclusion amounted to using Hamilton's doctrine to justify a "view of religion which I hold to be profoundly immoral—that it is our duty to bow down in worship

[16]*Kant's Political Writings*, ed. Hans Siegbert Reiss (Cambridge: Cambridge University Press, 1970), 144–6.
[17]*Autobiography*, 162.

before a Being whose moral attributes are affirmed to be unknowable by us, and to be perhaps extremely different from those which, when we are speaking of our fellow-creatures, we call by the same names."[18]

The implausibility of Mill's attempt to line up the progressives behind the doctrine of association and the reactionaries behind the doctrine of intuitive knowledge is neatly illustrated by his conjoining Hamilton and Mansel in this fashion. Their political allegiances were practically as far apart as it was possible to get. Mansel was politically a Tory, and was conservative in educational matters too. He was one of the most powerful defenders of the old tutorial arrangements that characterized teaching at Oxford and distinguished it from the Scottish and German universities. Hamilton, on the other hand, was a liberal in politics, thought the tutorial system beneath contempt, thought Oxford colleges entirely corrupt, and, had he been able, would have swept away the whole system in favour of something modelled on the Scottish system.

Mill's intention of provoking a *combat à outrance* was wholly successful. The *Examination* attracted much more attention than the *System of Logic* had done.[19] Mansel's long review of it, *The Philosophy of the Conditioned*—which only covered the first few chapters on the principle of the relativity of knowledge and the attack on his Bampton Lectures—came out within months. James McCosh produced a volume, *In Defence of Fundamental Truth*, intended to defend those parts of Hamilton's philosophy which were most characteristic of the Scottish philosophy of common sense. Within two years Mill was preparing a third edition of the *Examination* in which these and several other extended attacks were answered; the furore continued in the years before Mill's death, with the appearance in 1869 of John Veitch's *Memoir of Sir William Hamilton Bart.*, a pious defence of the opinions as well as the life of his old teacher, and W. G. Ward's further assault on associationism in the *Dublin Review* in 1871. The balance of the comments was undoubtedly hostile to Mill, less because of a widespread enthusiasm for the doctrines of Sir William Hamilton than because of a widespread fear that their rejection must lead to what McCosh almost invariably conjoined as "Humeanism and Comtism"—a mixture of atheism and dubious French politics. In this sense Mill's belief that he was fighting the pious and the conservative was absolutely right, for it was they—with the exception of some support from Herbert Spencer on the one topic of self-evidence—who were his hostile reviewers. Even then, some of the supposedly pious and the conservative were more in sympathy

---

[18]*Ibid.*, 163.

[19]*Examination*, ciii: "a host of writers, whose mode of philosophic thought was either directly or indirectly implicated in the criticisms made by this volume on Sir W. Hamilton, have taken up arms against it, and fought as *pro aris et focis*."

with Mill than with Hamilton. Two notable adherents were William Whewell, who, for all that he was Mill's victim on many occasions, had no doubt that Hamilton was an intellectual disaster who had set the course of speculation back by twenty years, and F. D. Maurice, who had been a harsh and persistent critic of Mansel for years.

It is difficult to know when this interest in the argument between Mill and Hamilton died.[20] From what evidence there is, it looks as though an interest in the *Examination* lasted so long as the *System of Logic* was still doing its good work in changing the philosophical syllabus in Oxford and Cambridge. But during the 1870s a new and in many ways more professional generation of philosophers became prominent, who had in one sense absorbed as much as they needed of Mill's work and, in another, were determined to clear away his intellectual influence. In Oxford at any rate, it was T. H. Green and F. H. Bradley who set the pace; and they were not inclined to defend Hamilton for the sake of refuting Mill, especially when their epistemological allegiances were Hegelian rather than patchily Kantian. So Bradley's *Ethical Studies* contains an extremely effective analysis of Mill's account of personal identity, but does not bother with the rest of the contest between the transcendental and empiricist analysis of the relations between mind and matter. And Green, though he applies to Mill the criticisms he develops against Hume, does not treat the *Examination* as the *locus classicus* of Mill's views. Thereafter, it seems that anyone much interested in Mill's philosophy would look into the *Examination* only for the range of topics mentioned at the beginning of this Introduction.

III. HAMILTON AND MANSEL

ALTHOUGH THE NAME OF HAMILTON is scarcely mentioned now, except in connection with his doctrine of the quantification of the predicate, it seems a proper estimate of his eminence in the first half of the nineteenth century to say that he and Mill were the two people in Britain whose names might occur to a philosophically educated foreigner who was asked to name a British thinker of any distinction. Sorley's *History of English Philosophy*, for instance, links the two names together in precisely this sense.[21] And it seems that if one had asked teachers in American universities during the middle years of the century what contemporary influences they felt from

---

[20]Rudolf Metz, *A Hundred Years of British Philosophy* (London: Allen and Unwin, 1938), Chap. i, gives a brief but lucid account of the final phases of the Scottish common-sense tradition.

[21]William Ritchie Sorley, *A History of English Philosophy* (Cambridge: Cambridge University Press, 1920), 240.

Britain, they would have talked of Hamilton and Mill—though a little later the influence of Spencer would no doubt have been, if anything, stronger.

Hamilton was born in Glasgow on 8 March, 1788, in one of the houses in Professors' Court, for his father was Professor of Botany and Anatomy. His father died when William was only two years old, but there is no evidence that the family suffered any financial difficulties in consequence, and Mrs. Hamilton's character was quite strong enough to ensure that the absence of the father's hand was not much felt.

After attending both Scottish and English schools and Glasgow and Edinburgh Universities, Hamilton began in 1807 a distinguished academic career at Balliol College, Oxford. In spite of his exceptional erudition and an epic performance in the final examination in Classics, as a Scot he received no offer of a fellowship, and returned to study law at Edinburgh, being admitted to the bar in 1813. His legal career was distinguished solely by a successful application (heard by the sheriff of Edinburgh in 1816) to be recognized as the heir to the Baronetcy of Preston and Fingalton.

If his nationality cost him the first opportunity of academic preferment, it was his Whig sympathies that scotched the second when, in 1820, he failed to succeed Thomas Brown in the Chair of Moral Philosophy in Edinburgh. The following year he obtained an underpaid and undemanding Chair in Civil History, but he made no mark in intellectual circles until 1829, when he began to contribute to the *Edinburgh Review*.

His first article, on Cousin, was an editor's nightmare, being late in arrival, much too long, and completely beyond the grasp of most of the readers of the *Review*.[22] But it was a great success with Cousin himself, and it served notice on the outside world that someone in the British Isles was abreast of European philosophy. It was for the *Edinburgh* that Hamilton wrote the most readable of his work: the two essays on "The Philosophy of the Conditioned" and on "Perception," his essay on "Logic" which contains (at least on Hamilton's reading of it) the first statement of the doctrine of the quantification of the predicate, and his condemnation of the intellectual and legal condition of the University of Oxford. It cannot be said that they were thought, even at the time, to be uniformly readable; Napier, the editor, was frequently reduced to complaining of the excessive length, the over-abundant quotations, and the archaic forms of speech which Hamilton indulged in.[23] But, as Mill's account would lead one to expect, it is these essays, reprinted in his *Discussions*, which show Hamilton at his best and most accessible. Even then, there are longueurs attributable less to the mania for quotation than to the combative manner of the author. The essay

[22]John Veitch, *Memoir of Sir William Hamilton* (Edinburgh: Blackwood, 1869), 146ff.
[23]*Ibid.*, 173–4.

on perception, for instance, is so grindingly critical of Thomas Brown that
the reader loses patience with the argument.

In 1836, however, academic justice was at last done. The Chair of Logic
and Metaphysics in Edinburgh fell vacant, and this time the City Council
elected him, by eighteen votes to fourteen. The composition of lectures for
the courses he was now obliged to give followed very much the same
pattern as his literary exploits—everything was done too late and too
elaborately; so in his first year Hamilton not infrequently worked until
dawn the night before delivering his lectures, and then took what rest he
could while his wife got the day's lecture into shape for delivery. Shortly
after the election, he embarked on his edition of the *Works* of Reid. This
was a characteristically acrimonious business, in which Hamilton started
work at the suggestion of Tait, the Edinburgh bookseller, then took offence
at the financial arrangements proposed by Tait (who seems to have expected a volume of Reid's writings with a short preface, rather than something with as much of Hamilton's erudition as Reid's thinking in it, and who
was not willing to pay for labours he had no wish to see anyone undertake),
and published the edition at his own expense in 1846.[24]

Hamilton's active career was relatively brief. In 1844 he suffered a
stroke, which did not impair his general intellectual grasp, but left him lame
in the right side and increasingly enfeebled. He had to have his lectures read
for him much of the time, although he managed to keep up a reasonably
active role in the discussion of them. He was, however, well enough to see
the republication of his earlier essays and to carry on a violent controversy
with Augustus De Morgan, both about their relative priority in the discovery of the principle of the quantification of the predicate, and about its
merits. De Morgan was vastly entertained by the violence of Hamilton's
attacks, both because he enjoyed the resulting publicity it conferred on his
own work and, so far as one can see, because he liked having an argument
with someone so uninhibited in his aggression as was Hamilton.[25] Others
were less sure: Boole, thanking Hamilton for the gift of a copy of the
Discussions, took the opportunity to say: "I think you are unjustifiably
severe upon my friend Mr De Morgan. He is, I believe, a man as much
imbued with the love of truth as can anywhere be found. When such men
err, a calm and simple statement of the ground of their error answers every
purpose which the interests either of learning or of justice can require."[26]
The effort was wasted twice over, seeing that Hamilton was unlikely to
become more moderate, and De Morgan was perfectly happy to be abused.

[24]*Ibid.*, 207–8.
[25]See Augustus De Morgan, *On the Syllogism, and Other Logical Writings*, ed. Peter Heath
(London: Routledge & Kegan Paul, 1966), xvii–xviii.
[26]Veitch, *Memoir*, 344.

Hamilton's health became worse after a fall during 1853, and he became less mentally active in the last two or three years of his life. Retirement, however, was impossible, since he could not live without the £500 a year that the Chair gave him.[27] Despite these outward difficulties, and the acerbity of his writings, all was not gloom and grimness. Hamilton's domestic life was strikingly happy; when he died on 6 May, 1856, he left behind a devoted family, loyal pupils, and a good many friends as well.

A matter of much more difficulty than establishing the outward conditions of his life is working out how Hamilton came to exercise such a considerable influence on the philosophical life of the country. He created enthusiastic students, of whom Thomas S. Baynes became the most professionally and professorially successful, but otherwise it seems to have been the weight of learning of a half-traditional kind which backed up the reception of his views. His innovations in logic, for instance, were produced in articles which were largely devoted to a minute chronicle of the fate of deductive logic in the fifteenth to seventeenth centuries. His views on perception, or on the relativity of knowledge, are always placed in the framework of an historical analysis of the sort which the higher education of the time encouraged. How much it assisted his, or anyone's, understanding of Kant to yoke him with Plato for the purposes of comparison and contrast is debatable, but the weight it added to his arguments looked to some of his audience very much like intellectual power rather than mere weight. He was more or less an intellectual fossil thirty years after his death, however. Sir Leslie Stephen's account of Hamilton in the *Dictionary of National Biography* presents him as an eccentric and pedantic leftover from the Scottish school of common sense. And Stephen's marginal comments in his copy of the *Discussions* display the exasperation Hamilton is likely to induce; at the end of "Philosophy of the Conditioned," the pencilled comment reads: "A good deal of this seems to be very paltry logomachy. His amazing way of quoting 'authorities' (eg Sir K. Digby, Walpole & Mme de Stael) to prove an obvious commonplace is of the genuine pedant. And yet he had a very sound argument—only rather spoilt."[28]

Henry Longueville Mansel was Hamilton's chief disciple in Oxford.[29] Born in 1820 he shone as a pupil first at Merchant Taylor's School and then at St. John's College, Oxford; and in 1843, with a double First in Mathematics and Classics, he settled down with great pleasure to the task of tutoring

---

[27]See *ibid.*, 286–93, for an account of Hamilton's vain attempts to secure an adequate pension.

[28]Marginalia in the copy of *Discussions*, 3rd ed. (Edinburgh and London: Blackwood, 1866), in the London Library, 38.

[29]For an account of Mansel's life, see John William Burgon, *The Lives of Twelve Good Men*, 2 vols. (London: Murray, 1888), II, 149–237.

clever undergraduates; he was regarded throughout the university as its best tutor. He held the first appointment as Waynflete Professor of Metaphysical Philosophy, and therefore counts R. G. Collingwood, Gilbert Ryle, and Sir Peter Strawson among his intellectual progeny. With his interest in Kant and his German successors, and his astringent, largely destructive approach to the subject he professed, he might almost be said to have set the boundaries of the subsequent style.

Mansel was a productive writer: his *Prolegomena Logica* appeared in 1851; his *Metaphysics*, which was an expansion of a substantial essay for the *Encyclopædia Britannica*, in 1860. He was most widely known as the author of *The Limits of Religious Thought*, the Bampton Lectures for 1858. This work was reprinted several times, and aroused a great deal of controversy, in which F. D. Maurice played an especially acrimonious role. Philosophically, Mansel was greatly indebted to Kant, but he was very hostile to Kant's theology and to Kant's moral philosophy alike. *The Limits of Religious Thought* was described by Mansel himself as

an attempt to pursue, in relation to Theology, the inquiry instituted by Kant in relation to Metaphysics; namely, *How are synthetical judgments à priori possible?* In other words: Does there exist in the human mind any direct faculty of religious knowledge, by which, in its speculative exercise, we are enabled to decide, independently of all external Revelation, what is the true nature of God, and the manner in which He must manifest Himself to the world . . .?[30]

The answer he gave was that there was no such faculty of religious knowledge, and that natural theology was quite unable to set limits to the nature and attributes of God. Moreover, he shared none of Kant's certainty that our moral faculty allowed us to judge supposed revelations by their consistency with divine goodness. What goodness is in the divinity is not a matter on which human reason is fit to pronounce.

Mansel was not only a productive writer; he wrote elegantly and lucidly. There are many reasons for wishing that it had been Mansel's *Metaphysics* which Mill had examined, rather than Hamilton's *Lectures*, and the clarity of Mansel's prose is not the least. Even in the pious context of the Bampton Lectures he is witty—replying to a critic who complains that Mansel's attack on rationalism in theology is an attempt to limit the use of reason, he says that it is only the improper use of reason he is rejecting: "All Dogmatic Theology is not Dogmatism, nor all use of Reason, Rationalism, any more than all drinking is drunkenness."[31] It was not surprising that progress

[30]Mansel, *The Limits of Religious Thought*, 4th ed. (Oxford: Clarendon Press, 1859), xliii.
[31]*Ibid.*, ix–x. He also enjoyed entertaining children with jokes and outrageous puns. Burgon says that on one occasion when Mansel was out driving with friends, a little girl in the party exclaimed that a donkey by the roadside seemed to have got its head stuck in a barrel. "Mansel was heard to murmur softly to himself,—'Then it will be a case of *asphyxia*.' " (Burgon, *Lives*

came quickly. In 1855 he was elected to the Readership in Moral and Metaphysical Philosophy, and in 1859 to the Waynflete Professorship. Mansel's wit and exuberance were, however, not matched by physical strength. His acceptance of the Chair of Ecclesiastical History in 1866 was a partial recognition of the need to conserve his energy, and a move to London as Dean of St. Paul's in 1868 more explicit recognition. Besides, by the mid-1860s he was finding the moderately reformed Oxford increasingly uncongenial to his conservative tastes. In 1871 he died suddenly in his sleep.

The contrasts between Mansel and Hamilton are so complete that it is difficult to know why Mansel was so devoted a follower of "the Edinburgh metaphysician"—for his devotion did indeed extend to employing Hamilton's logical innovations in rather unlikely contexts, and even to defending them against De Morgan.[32] What is evident so far is that Mansel required nothing much more than an ally against the pretensions of Absolute Idealism; but that judgment plainly understates the strength of his conviction. It is obviously preposterous to think of Mansel and Hamilton as sharing any *political* commitment which would account for such a degree of conviction. It is more reasonable to suppose that they shared something which one can only gesture towards by calling it a matter of religious psychology. Mansel genuinely seems to have thought that an acknowledgement of the limitations of human reason was a more reverent attitude towards the unknowable God than any attempt to look further into His nature, and he seems to have been impressed by a similar outlook in Hamilton:

True, therefore, are the declarations of a pious philosophy:—"A God understood would be no God at all;"—"To think that God is, as we can think him to be, is blasphemy."—The Divinity, in a certain sense, is revealed; in a certain sense is concealed: He is at once known and unknown. But the last and highest consecration of all true religion, must be an altar—'Αγνώστῳ Θεῷ—"*To the unknown and unknowable God.*"[33]

Hamilton's insistence that his doubts about Absolute knowledge are not only compatible with, but in some sense required by, Christian revelation is practically the theme of Mansel's Bampton Lectures. Between them and Mill there was a gulf, therefore, but one less political than Mill's *Autobio-*

---

of Twelve Good Men, II, 213.) And such outrages were not reserved for children alone; later when Mansel was showing a visitor the interior of St. Paul's, the man "complained of the heathenish character of the monuments. 'Just look at *that* now,'—(pointing to a huge figure of Neptune). 'What has *that* got to do with Christianity?' '*Tridentine* Christianity, perhaps,' suggested Mansel." (*Ibid.*)

[32]De Morgan, *On the Syllogism*, xxi.

[33]*Discussions*, 15n; cf. 34n–5n below.

graphy suggests. It was the gulf between Mill's utterly secular, this-worldly temperament and their sense of the final mysteriousness of the world. The harshness of Mansel's attack on the *Examination* in *The Philosophy of the Conditioned* reflects his resentment of this matter-of-fact approach to the world, a resentment which cannot have been soothed by the fact that in Oxford, as elsewhere, the staples of a Christian philosophy, such as Butler's *Analogy*, were losing ground to such textbooks as the *System of Logic*.[34]

IV. THE PHILOSOPHY OF THE CONDITIONED

THE OPENING SHOTS of Mill's campaign against Hamilton's philosophy are directed against "the philosophy of the conditioned." The burden of Mill's complaint against Hamilton is that his attachment to what he and Mill term "the relativity of knowledge" is intermittent, half-hearted, explained in incoherent and self-contradictory ways. He accuses Hamilton of both asserting and denying that we can have knowledge of Things in themselves, and of giving wholly feeble reasons for supposing that we cannot conceive of, particularly, the nature of space and time as they are intrinsically, but can nevertheless believe that they are genuinely and in themselves infinite. It is this part of Hamilton's philosophy that Mansel's essay on *The Philosophy of the Conditioned* had to endeavour to rescue; his Bampton Lectures on *The Limits of Religious Thought* hung on the negative claim that the human mind could not conceive of the nature of the Deity, so that He remained inaccessible to philosophical speculation, and on the positive claim that there was still room for belief in such an inconceivable Deity. Mansel's version of the philosophy of the conditioned was intended to repel the pretensions of philosophy in the sphere of religion. "Pantheist" philosophers of the Absolute, such as Hegel and Schelling, were unable to provide knowledge of an Absolute that might replace, or be recognized as the philosophically reputable surrogate of, the God of Christianity; less ambitious philosophers were shown to be unable to restrict the attributes of a Deity by the categories of human reason. As this account suggests, the Kantian overtones in Mansel's work are very marked, and, as we shall see, *The Philosophy of the Conditioned* gives a very Kantian interpretation of Hamilton.

Yet the oddity, or perhaps we should only say the distinctive feature, of Hamilton's philosophy on its metaphysical front was the combination of the critical philosophy of Kant with Reid's philosophy of common sense.

[34]Burgon, *Lives of Twelve Good Men*, II, 201.

Hamilton's position seems at first to be exactly that of Reid. He sided with Reid and common sense in holding that "the way of ideas" is suicidal, that any theory which presents the external world as a logical construction from the immediate objects of perception (construed as "ideas") simply fails to account for the world's true externality. In particular, he held, with Reid, that what we perceive are things themselves, not a representation of them, or an intermediary idea. Moreover, *some* of the properties which we perceive things to possess really are properties of the objects themselves, and not contributions of the percipient mind. The secondary qualities he was willing to recognize as not existing in the object itself, but primary qualities were wholly objective, not observer dependent. The knowledge we have of things, however, still remains in some sense relative or conditioned. The question is, in what sense?

It is at this point that the invocation of Kant's criticalism causes difficulties, for Hamilton could afford to take only a few details from Kant if he was not to run headlong against Reid. Above all, he wanted to side with Kant against Kant's successors, and to deny that we can know anything of the Absolute or the Unconditioned. He wanted, that is, to deny the possibility of a positive pre- or post-critical metaphysics, in which it was supposed to be demonstrated that Space and Time were in themselves infinite—or not. But he did not want to follow Kant in his "Copernican revolution"; or, rather, he could not have intended to do anything of the sort. For Hamilton did not think that the contribution of the percipient mind to what is perceived is anything like as extensive as Kant claimed. The implication for metaphysics of the "relative" or "conditioned" nature of human knowledge he certainly took to be what Kant claimed it to be:

The result of his examination was the abolition of the metaphysical sciences,—of Rational Psychology, Ontology, Speculative Theology, &c., as founded on mere *petitiones principiorum*. . . . "Things in themselves," Matter, Mind, God,—all, in short, that is not finite, relative, and phænomenal, as bearing no analogy to our faculties, is beyond the verge of our knowledge. Philosophy was thus restricted to the observation and analysis of the phænomena of consciousness; and what is not explicitly or implicitly given in a fact of consciousness, is condemned, as transcending the sphere of a legitimate speculation. A knowledge of the Unconditioned is declared impossible; either immediately, as an intuition, or mediately, as an inference.[35]

But he refused to draw Kant's conclusions about the subjectivity of space and time, and denied that the antinomies showed that they were only forms of intuition:

The Conditioned is the mean between two extremes,—two inconditionates, exclusive of each other, *neither of which can be conceived as possible*, but of

[35]*Discussions*, 16.

which, on the principles of contradiction and excluded middle, *one must be admitted as necessary*. On this opinion, therefore, our faculties are shown to be weak, but not deceitful. The mind is not represented as conceiving two propositions subversive of each other, as equally possible; but only, as unable to understand as possible, either of two extremes; one of which, however, on the ground of their mutual repugnance, it is compelled to recognise as true.[36]

In effect, Hamilton's view seems to have been that Reid and common sense were right in holding that what we perceive are real, material objects, located in an objective space and time, objectively possessed of (some of) the properties we ascribe to them, but that Kant was right in holding that those properties which we can ascribe to them must be adapted to our faculties, "relative" in the sense of being related to our cognitive capacities.

The question of the sense in which all our knowledge is thus of the relative or the conditioned is not quite here answered, however. For there remains a considerable ambiguity about the nature of this relativism, or relatedness. The simplest reading turns the doctrine of relativity into a truism. It amounts to saying that what *we* can know depends in part upon our perceptive capacities, and that beings with different perceptual arrangements from our own would perceive the world differently. In that sense, it is no doubt true that what *we* perceive of the world is only an aspect of the whole of what is there to be perceived. More philosophically interesting is an exploration of why we seem able to agree *that* we might in principle perceive the world quite otherwise than we do, but find it impossible to say much about *how* we might do so. Mill, however, pursues that topic no further than to its familiar sources in the questions asked by Locke—whether a man born blind could conceive of space, for instance (222ff.). Mill's chief complaint is that Hamilton confuses several senses of relativity together, when talking of the relativity of knowledge, and that the only sense he consistently adheres to is this truistic sense. In any real sense, says Mill, Hamilton was not a relativist:

Sir W. Hamilton did not hold any opinion in virtue of which it could rationally be asserted that all human knowledge is relative; but did hold, as one of the main elements of his philosophical creed, the opposite doctrine, of the cognoscibility of external Things, in certain of their aspects, as they are in themselves, absolutely (33).

When Hamilton attempts to reconcile this objectivist account with the doctrine of the relativity of knowledge, flat contradiction is only averted by retreat into banality:

He affirms without reservation, that certain attributes (extension, figures, &c.) are known to us as they really exist out of ourselves; and also that all our knowledge of

[36]*Ibid.*, 14–15.

them is relative to us. And these two assertions are only reconcileable, if relativity to us is understood in the altogether trivial sense, that we know them only so far as our faculties permit. (22.)

Mill was not the severest critic of Hamilton on this score. J. H. Stirling's critique of Hamilton's account of perception treats Hamilton's views with complete contempt. The contradiction between the objectivist account and the relativist account of our knowledge of the outside world is so blatant that Hamilton cannot have failed to notice it. Where Mill suspects Hamilton of mere confusion, Stirling accuses him of disingenuousness. Mill demurely declines to press any such charge (cv). He did not even suggest that Reid and Kant made awkward allies in principle. In an earlier article on "Bain's Psychology" he had indeed yoked Reid and Kant together as members of the *a priori* school of psychological analysis. But he went on to point out that the question of the connection between our faculties and the nature of the external reality was an issue of ontology rather than psychology; and here Reid was "decidedly of opinion that Matter—not the set of phenomena so called, but the actual Thing, of which these are effects and manifestations—is cognizable by us as a reality in the universe."[37] This comment suggests that Mill thought of Hamilton as discussing metaphysics in a wide sense—both "the science of being" and psychology; Reid, Kant, and Hamilton were allies in so far as they belonged to the same camp in psychology, but they made an ill-assorted trio in matters of ontology. Here Kant and Reid belonged to different camps and no one could tell where Hamilton stood. Mansel's reply to Mill was to insist that everything in Reid, and everything in Hamilton which expressed an allegiance to Reid, should be as it were put in Kantian brackets. We might perceive things themselves, but the "thing itself" which we perceive is not the "thing-in-itself," but only the phenomenally objective thing. The thing known in perception was the appearance to us of a noumenon of which nothing whatever could be known.[38]

There is something to be said for Mansel's claims. Reid at times writes as if knowledge is doubly relative: in the knower, it is a state of an ego of which we only know the states, though convinced that it exists as a continuing substance; and, in the known, what we know is states of things external to us, though again we are irresistibly convinced of their continued substantial existence. But we cannot safely go far along this path. Reid did not like to talk of substances, and certainly did not wish to introduce them as mysterious substrates; to the extent that Mansel rescues Hamilton by claiming that

---

[37]"Bain's Psychology" (1859), in *Essays on Philosophy and the Classics*, *Collected Works*, XI (Toronto: University of Toronto Press, 1978), 341, 343.
[38]Mansel, *The Philosophy of the Conditioned* (London: Strachan, 1866), 81ff.

external things are known "relatively" as phenomena related to imperceptible noumena, he goes against the evident thrust of Reid's views. The further one presses Hamilton's attachment to Kant beyond his avowed enthusiasm for the destructive attack on positive metaphysics, the harder it is to get any textual backing for the case. It is doubtless true that a sophisticated Kantian would have been untroubled by Mill's attack, but it is quite implausible to suggest that that is what Sir William Hamilton was.

At all events, Mill's approach to Hamilton is initially entirely negative. Mill does not put forward any view of his own on the relativity of knowledge. The reason is a good one so far as it goes. Mill's distinction between the *a priori* and *a posteriori* schools of psychology is one which only partially overlaps his main theme. For in the *Examination*, just as in the *Logic*, Mill's hostility is directed against those who attempt to infer the nature of the world from the contents and capacities of our minds. In principle, there is no reason why there should be any overlap between *a priorism* in psychology and the view that mental capacities and incapacities reflect real possibilities and impossibilities in the world. *A priorism*, as Mill describes it, is a psychological approach which refers our most important beliefs about the world, and our moral principles, too, to instincts or to innate capacities or dispositions. The sense in which these are *a priori* is not very easy to characterize, although the fact that many of the instinctive beliefs described by the *a priori* psychologists of Mill's account coincide with the judgments described by Kant as *synthetic a priori* suggests most of the appropriate connotations. Thus the perception that objects occupy a space described by Euclidean geometry embodies the instinctive judgment that bodies *must* occupy space, and the necessity ascribed to the truths of geometry reflects the instinctive judgment that, for instance, two straight lines *cannot* enclose a space, and so on. Such judgments, says Mill, purport to be *a priori* in the sense that they have to be presumed true before experience is possible, or at any rate characterizable. Whether they are held to be *temporally* prior to experience is, he recognizes, not essential: there is no need to deny that children have to learn arithmetic in order to deny that its truths reflect the teachings of experience. Mill sees that it is quite arguable that the capacity to recognize necessities of thought is one which matures in the child, and requires experience to set it to work. Indeed, at times, he seems to suggest that the dispute between *a priori* and *a posteriori* psychologists is an empirical dispute in which there need not be only two opposing sides. For if the issue is one of how much of an adult's understanding of the world we can account for as the result of individual learning, there will be a continuum between psychologists who stress the extent to which such an understanding is as it were preprogrammed into the human organism and those who stress how much of it can be accounted for by trial-and-error learning from the organism's environment. In like manner, with reference to the area of moral and prudential reasoning, there would be a similar continuum between those who see us as relatively plastic and malleable organisms and those who claim to see some moral and prudential attachments more or less genetically built in.

Now, in so far as the argument proceeds in these terms, it will still follow a pattern which is visible in Mill's own approach. That is, the environmentalist must attempt to show some way in which the capacity, whose acquisition he is trying to explain, could have been built up through experience; the innatist will respond by showing that there are features of such a capacity which are simply omitted or more subtly misrepresented by such an account. The question of how much of what we perceive of the world is to be credited to the programme by which the percipient organism organizes its physical interaction with the world, and how much is to be set down to learning, is then an empirical question, or rather a whole series of empirical questions. This was the point at which Mill and Herbert Spencer came close to agreement. Spencer's long discussion of the nature of intuitive knowledge in the *Fortnightly Review* is a protest against being assigned to the rationalist camp by Mill, in which Spencer's central point is that when we refer our sensations to external objects as their causes this is, as it were, a hypothesis proffered by the organism, a hypothesis which we cannot consciously shake, and one on which we cannot help acting. Nonetheless, it is only a hypothesis; it is, however, one which seems to have been programmed into us by evolution, and one whose reliability is most readily accounted for by the theory that the external world is, indeed, much as we perceive it is.[39] The doctrine is not one which would perturb Mill; he ascribed something very like it to Reid.[40]

This assertion, however, does imply that Mill's own interest in the relativity of knowledge as a central issue in epistemology rather than psychology, would necessarily be slight. That the organic constitution of human beings sets limits to what they could hope to know about the world was an uninteresting empirical truth; interesting truths about the ways in which we were prone to illusions in some areas, or about the ways in which we estimated the size, shape, movement, or whatever of external bodies, would emerge piecemeal. Mill never quite propounded a version of the verification principle, and therefore never went to the lengths of suggesting that what one might call transcendental relativism or transcendental idealism was simply meaningless, because its truth or falsity could make no observational difference. But he came very close.

[39]Herbert Spencer, "Mill *versus* Hamilton—The Test of Truth," *Fortnightly Review*, I (15 July, 1865), 548.
[40]"Bain's Psychology," *CW*, XI, 343–4.

He came particularly close when he turned from Hamilton's views on the positive relativity of knowledge to Hamilton's negative case, as set out in his critique of Cousin. In his attack on Cousin, Hamilton had denied that we can ever attain to positive knowledge of "the Infinite" and "the Absolute"; Mill dismantles Hamilton's various arguments to this effect, distinguishing Kantian arguments to show that we can know nothing of noumena from arguments against the possibility of an "infinite being." They are, he points out, directed at very different targets. That our knowledge is phenomenal, not noumenal, "is true of the finite as well as of the infinite, of the imperfect as well as of the completed or absolute" (58–9). The "Unconditioned," in so far as it is to be identified with the noumenal, is certainly not an object of knowledge for us. But "the Absolute" and "the Infinite" are in considerably worse shape than the merely noumenal. These, though Hamilton never meant to go so far, are shown up as a tissue of contradictory attributes: "he has established, more thoroughly perhaps than he intended, the futility of all speculation respecting those meaningless abstractions 'The Infinite' and 'The Absolute,' notions contradictory in themselves, and to which no corresponding realities do or can exist" (58). To Mansel's reply that Hamilton had not tried to argue that they were meaningless abstractions, Mill had a ready retort:

I never pretended that he did; the gist of my complaint against him is, that he did not perceive them to be unmeaning. "Hamilton," says Mr Mansel, "maintains that the terms absolute and infinite are perfectly intelligible as abstractions, as much so as relative and finite." *Quis dubitavit?* It is not the terms absolute and infinite that are unmeaning; it is "The Infinite" and "The Absolute." Infinite and Absolute are real attributes, abstracted from concrete objects of thought, if not of experience, which are at least believed to possess those attributes. "The Infinite" and "The Absolute" are illegitimate abstractions of what never were, nor could without self-contradiction be supposed to be, attributes of any concrete. (58n.)

Mill's harassment of Hamilton on the Absolute and the Infinite has few lessons of great moment. It is interesting that Mill does not adopt, as he might have done, Hobbes's method of dealing with the question of infinity. Where Hobbes had said that "infinite" characterizes not the attribute itself, but our incapacity to set a limit to whatever attribute is in question, Mill treats it as an attribute, that of being greater than any completed attribute of the appropriate sort—a line of infinite length is thus longer than any completed line. Some attributes could be characterized as absolutely present, but not infinitely so, others as infinitely but not absolutely present. The purity of water has an absolute limit, viz., when all impurities are absent, but there is no sense to be given to the notion of infinitely pure water. Concerning this issue, Mill changed his mind on minor points from one edition to another. He began by claiming that power could be infinite, but knowledge only absolute, because absolute knowledge meant knowing everything there is to be known; but under pressure from Mansel and other critics, he agreed that a being of infinite power would know everything he could think or create, so that his knowledge would be infinite also (37–8). But he is casual about such concessions, quite rightly seeing them as having little bearing on the main question, whether there is any sense at all to be attached to such notions as "the Absolute."

It is surprising that Mill does not press his opponents harder on the meaninglessness of propositions about beings with infinite attributes and the rest. Mansel in particular, but Hamilton also, was very vulnerable to the charge that in showing God or the Unconditioned to be beyond our conceiving, they had also shown them to be beyond our believing. Both Hamilton and Mansel were utterly committed to the principle that what was not a possible object of knowledge was nevertheless a proper object of belief. Mansel stated his position with characteristic lucidity in the Preface to his Bampton Lectures:

"the terms *conceive, conception*, &c., as they are employed in the following Lectures, always imply an apprehension of the *manner* in which certain attributes can coexist with each other, so as to form a whole or complex notion. . . . Thus when it is said that the nature of God as an absolute and infinite being is inconceivable, it is not meant that the terms *absolute* and *infinite* have no meaning—as mere terms they are as intelligible as the opposite terms *relative* and *finite*—but that we cannot apprehend *how* the attributes of absoluteness and infinity coexist with the personal attributes of God, though we may believe *that*, in some manner unknown to us, they do coexist. In like manner, we cannot *conceive how* a purely spiritual being sees and hears without the bodily organs of sight and hearing; yet we may *believe that* He does so in some manner. Belief is possible in the mere fact (τὸ ὅτι). Conception must include the manner (τὸ πῶς).[41]

The obvious question invited is, *what* is the mere fact believed in? If we cannot form any conception of the state of affairs which is said to be the object of our belief, it is not clear that we can be said to know what we believe at all. Mill's attack on the discussion of "the Infinite" and "the Absolute" concentrates, as we have just seen, on the claim that they cannot be talked about because they are literal self-contradictions; Mansel does not quite go to the length of saying that self-contradictory propositions might be true, though we cannot imagine how, and Mill does not press on him the obvious dilemma that he must either say *that*, or admit that the terms he is using no longer bear their usual meaning, and perhaps bear no clear meaning at all.

What Mill does argue against Hamilton is that no sooner has Hamilton

[41]*Limits of Religious Thought*, 5th ed. (London: Murray, 1867), xi n–xii n. (Not in the 4th ed.)

routed those of his opponents who believe that we have direct knowledge of
the unconditioned, or perhaps an indirect and implicit knowledge only,
than he joins forces with them by letting what they describe as "knowledge"
back into his system under the label of "belief." If one were looking for the
weak points in Mill's account of Hamilton, this brief attack would surely be
one place to seek them in. In essence, Mill's complaint is that whatever
Hamilton had maintained about the relativity of knowledge, and whatever
scepticism he had evinced about the Unconditioned, everything would
have been

reduced to naught, or to a mere verbal controversy, by his admission of a second
kind of intellectual conviction called Belief; which is anterior to knowledge, is the
foundation of it, and is not subject to its limitations; and through the medium of
which we may have, and are justified in having, a full assurance of all the things
which he has pronounced unknowable to us; and this not exclusively by revelation,
that is, on the supposed testimony of a Being whom we have ground for trusting as
veracious, but by our natural faculties (60).

Mill's outrage is intelligible enough. If one supposes that philosophical first
principles are supposed to furnish a set of premises from which we can
deduce the general reliability of our knowledge, then some such method as
that of Descartes is the obvious one to pursue, and it would seem that first
principles must be better known than anything that hangs upon them. At
least it would seem scandalous to any Cartesian to suppose that we merely
believed in our own existence and yet *knew* that bodies could not inter-
penetrate or that the sun would rise again in the morning. Yet it is doubtful
whether this is how Mill ought to have understood Hamilton. Spencer, who
tackled the issue more sympathetically, suggested a more plausible interpretation, and one which does more justice than Mill's to the difference
between a Cartesian and a Kantian view of first principles. Mill, who treats
the difference between belief and knowledge very much as twentieth-
century empiricism was to do—that is, regarding knowledge as justified
true belief (65n)—cannot allow for a difference in the ways of treating
particular knowledge claims and claims about the whole of our knowledge.
But Spencer does just that. When we claim to know something, we assume
that we can set our belief against external evidence; but we cannot peel off
the whole of our knowledge of the world from the hidden world of which it
is knowledge and claim that we now know that it is knowledge.[42] All we can
do is *believe* that it really is knowledge. More than one twentieth-century
philosopher of science has similarly claimed that we can only make sense of
the sciences' claim to supply us with knowledge of the world if we *believe* in
an occult, underlying, objective order in the world, which is beyond experience but accounts for its possibility.

[42]Spencer, "Mill *versus* Hamilton," 548.

It is only when Mill comes to sum up the successes and failures of the philosophy of the conditioned that he supplies the reader with what is most required—an explanation of what Mill himself understands by inconceivability, and how he explains it, in opposition to the intuitionists and innatists. The explanation occupies a considerable space, but it is worth noticing two main points. The first is Mill's claim that the majority of cases of inconceivability can be explained by our experience of inseparable associations between attributes, and the other his claim that most of the things that Hamilton claims to be inconceivable are not difficult, let alone impossible, to conceive. What is most likely to scandalize twentieth-century readers is the way Mill treats it as an empirical psychological law that we cannot conjoin contradictory attributes, and therefore cannot conceive things with contradictory attributes. The source of the scandal is obvious: we are inclined to hold that it is a matter of logic that a thing cannot have inconsistent attributes, not because of any property of things or our minds, but because a proposition is logically equivalent to the negation of its negation, and to ascribe a property and its contradictory to an object is simply to say nothing. The assertion negates and is negated by the denial of it. The law of non-contradiction, on this view, cannot be interpreted psychologically, without putting the cart before the horse: that a man cannot be both alive and not alive is not the consequence of our *de facto* inability to put the ideas of life and death together.

Mill, however, suggests something like a gradation, from flat contradiction through decreasingly well-attested repugnances of attributes:

We cannot represent anything to ourselves as at once being something, and not being it; as at once having, and not having, a given attribute. The following are other examples. We cannot represent to ourselves time or space as having an end. We cannot represent to ourselves two and two as making five; nor two straight lines as enclosing a space. We cannot represent to ourselves a round square; nor a body all black, and at the same time all white. (69–70.)

But he goes on to make something nearer a sharp break between flat contradiction and everything else:

A distinction may be made, which, I think, will be found pertinent to the question. That the same thing should at once be and not be—that identically the same statement should be both true and false—is not only inconceivable to us, but we cannot imagine that it could be made conceivable. We cannot attach sufficient meaning to the proposition, to be able to represent to ourselves the supposition of a different experience on this matter. We cannot therefore even entertain the question, whether the incompatibility is in the original structure of our minds, or is only put there by our experience. The case is otherwise in all the other examples of inconceivability. (70.)

These, Mill begins by saying, are only the result of inseparable association; but he rather confusingly qualifies this by suggesting that even there the inconceivability somehow involves the contradictoriness of what is said to be inconceivable: "all inconceivabilities may be reduced to inseparable association, combined with the original inconceivability of a direct contradiction" (70). The point he is making is, evidently, the following. We cannot conceive of a state of affairs characterized as A and not-A, because the conception corresponding to A is just the negative of the conception of not-A. In other cases, there is no direct contradiction; it is A and B we are asked to conceive jointly, and if we are unable to do so it is because *in our experience* B is always associated with not-A. Hence the attempt to conceive A and B turns out to be a special case of trying to conceive A and not-A, and the real point at issue between Mill and the opposition is the nature of our certainty that in these proposed instances B really does imply not-A. Mill thinks it is an empirical conviction, implanted by experience, reflecting the way the world actually *is*, but telling us nothing about how it *has* to be. The opposition have no common doctrine; the Kantian members of it think that the conviction reflects how the world *has* to be, but only in the sense that since "the world" is a phenomenal product of our minds working upon unknown and unknowable data it must obey the laws of our own minds; Catholic transcendentalists like W. G. Ward claimed to be objectivists and realists on this issue, where the Kantians were subjectivists and phenomenalists; they held that real inconceivabilities in our minds reflect the necessity of a certain rational structure to the universe, a structure that is not a matter of choice even for Omnipotence itself. So, in attacking Mill's attempt to explain the truths of mathematics in experiential terms, Ward says:

I have never even once experienced the equality of 2+9 to 3+8, and yet am convinced that not even Omnipotence could overthrow that equality. I have most habitually experienced the warmth-giving property of fire, and yet see no reason for doubting that Omnipotence (if it exist) can at any time suspend or remove that property.[43]

Mill himself makes something like a concession to the Kantian mode of analysis, though it is a physiological rather than a psychological version of transcendental idealism that he perhaps offers. In the body of the text he claims that "a round square" is in principle no more inconceivable than a heavy square or a hard square; to suppose that one might exist is no more than to suppose that we might simultaneously have those sensations which we call seeing something round and those which we call seeing something square:

we should probably be as well able to conceive a round square as a hard square, or a heavy square, if it were not that, in our uniform experience, at the instant when

[43]Ward, "Necessary Truth," 298–9.

a thing begins to be round it ceases to be square, so that the beginning of the one impression is inseparably associated with the departure or cessation of the other (70).

But in a later footnote he drew back:

It has been remarked to me by a correspondent, that a round square differs from a hard square or a heavy square in this respect, that the two sensations or sets of sensations supposed to be joined in the first-named combination are affections of the same nerves, and therefore, being different affections, are mutually incompatible by our organic constitution, and could not be made compatible by any change in the arrangements of external nature. This is probably true, and may be the physical reason why when a thing begins to be perceived as round it ceases to be perceived as square; but it is not the less true that this mere fact suffices, under the laws of association, to account for the inconceivability of the combination. I am willing, however, to admit, as suggested by my correspondent, that "if the imagination employs the organism in its representations," which it probably does, "what is originally unperceivable in consequence of organic laws" may also be "originally unimaginable." (70n–1n.)

The note nicely illustrates the difficulty of seeing quite what Mill's case was. Even here he seems determined to appeal to the laws of association, and yet the case he is partially conceding is that there are structural constraints on what things *can* be perceived and therefore come to be associated. Evidently the one thing he is determined not to concede is that the laws of the Macrocosm can be inferred from the laws of the Microcosm; but as he says, he is here at one with Hamilton and Mansel.

Yet it is this view which Mill mostly writes to defend, and perhaps in a form which does set him apart from Hamilton and Mansel. For Mill plainly treats the question of what we can and cannot conceive as a flatly factual one, and so, in turn, he treats the laws of number or the findings of geometry as flatly factual too. Indeed, he goes so far as to claim that even with our present mental and physical constitution we could envisage alternative geometries and different arithmetical laws. "That the reverse of the most familiar principles of arithmetic and geometry might have been made conceivable, even to our present mental faculties, if those faculties had coexisted with a totally different constitution of external nature, is," says Mill, "ingeniously shown in the concluding paper of a recent volume, anonymous, but of known authorship, 'Essays, by a Barrister' [i.e., Fitzjames Stephen]" (71n), and he quotes the paper at length. The gist of it is that we can perfectly well imagine a world in which $2+2=5$; for all we need imagine is a world in which "whenever two pairs of things are either placed in proximity or are contemplated together, a fifth thing is immediately created and brought within the contemplation of the mind engaged in putting two and two together" (71n). Mill does not suggest, what is surely rather plausible, that such a statement of the case is self-destructive, in that it presupposes that what we should say under such conditions is not that $2+2=5$, but, as he does say, that associating pairs creates a fifth object. The supposition, of course, is much more complicated in any case than Mill allows. As Frege later argued, things are only countable under a common concept—a cow and a sheep are not a pair of cows nor a pair of sheep, but they are a pair of animals, mammals, familiar English objects, and so on. Are we to suppose that they spontaneously generate a fifth something or other when conceptualized one way but not another? Can we stop the process by thinking of four things, not as two pairs but as a trio and an individual? Are addition and subtraction supposed to cease to be isomorphic, so that $5-2=3$, even though $2+2=5$? Nor is it clear what the notion of contemplating pairs is going to embrace. If I read a word of six letters, do I read a word of three pairs of letters, and if so, is it not a word of at least seven letters? Or will it stay one word of only six letters so long as I read it as one word only—in which case how will anyone ever *learn* to read? There is, no doubt, *something* contingent about the fact that our system of geometry and arithmetic apply in the world, but it is hardly so flatly contingent as this account suggests.

Mill is much more persuasive when he sets out to deny Hamilton's claims about the limitations from which our thinking necessarily suffers. Mill distinguishes three kinds of inconceivability, which, he says, Hamilton habitually confuses. The first is what we have been examining until now, the supposed impossibility of *picturing* the states of affairs at stake, either directly or indirectly as the result of its making contradictory demands on the imagination. The second is the apparent incredibility of what is perfectly visualizable. Mill's example is the existence of the Antipodes; we could model a globe in clay and recognize that there need be no absolute "up" or "down," but still fail to see how people could remain on the surface of the globe at what we were sure to think of as its underside (74–5). Finally, there is a sense in which an event or state of affairs is inconceivable if it is impossible to see what might explain it: "The inconceivable in this third sense is simply the inexplicable." Mill says, and quite rightly, that it merely invites confusion to employ "inconceivable" to cover mere inexplicability:

This use of the word inconceivable, being a complete perversion of it from its established meanings, I decline to recognise. If all the general truths which we are most certain of are to be called inconceivable, the word no longer serves any purpose. Inconceivable is not to be confounded with unprovable, or unanalysable. A truth which is not inconceivable in either of the received meanings of the term—a truth which is completely apprehended, and without difficulty believed, I cannot consent to call inconceivable merely because we cannot account for it, or deduce it from a higher truth. (76.)

Oddly enough, it was Mansel who got into the most serious muddle here, and for no very obvious reason. He denied that Hamilton had ever used the term "inconceivable" to cover more than the unimaginable, and yet, as we have seen already, employed the term himself in Mill's third sense. We believe *that* the will is free, but we cannot explain *how* it is, and so, on Mansel's view, we have here a believable inconceivability.[44] Had he stuck simply to saying that we can conceive *that* something is the case where we cannot conceive *how* it is, there would be no problem—what is imaginable and credible is the bare fact, what is unimaginable is a mechanism which might account for it. The connection, as Mill is quick to see, between the narrower, proper senses of inconceivable, and the wider, improper sense, is that the offer of a hypothetical mechanism to account for a phenomenon makes it so much the easier both to visualize it and to believe in its existence. None of this, of course, is to deny that Mansel is quite right to suggest that the mind does indeed boggle at the task of *explaining* how the physical interaction of brain and world results in perceptions which are themselves not in any obvious sense physical phenomena at all; all it shows is that there is no point in muddying the waters by suggesting that the *facts* are inconceivable when what one means is that they are in certain respects inexplicable.

Having cleared up these terminological difficulties, Mill then embarks on the question of whether, as Hamilton claims, the philosophy of the conditioned shows that there are propositions about the world which are inconceivable and yet true. The examples Mill has in mind, as we have seen, are such propositions as that space is finite, or, conversely, that space is infinite. The language of conceivability causes a few more difficulties, even after Mill's sanitizing operations, for between Mill and Mansel there remains a difference of opinion on the question of what it is to have a conception of any state of affairs. Mansel seems to require that there should be some kind of one-to-one relationship between the elements in our conception and that of which it is the conception. Mill does not entirely repudiate this view; it will serve as a criterion for having an *adequate*—or perhaps one had better say, a complete—conception of the phenomenon that one should be able to enumerate the elements in one's conception and match them to the components of the thing conceived. But, says Mill, in one of his most felicitous moves, it is impossible to have a wholly adequate conception of anything whatever, since everything and anything can be envisaged in an infinite number of ways. The obsession with the infinite and absolute in Hamilton and Mansel is ill-defended by Mansel's arguments about adequacy, since, says Mill, there is no suggestion that a number like 695,788 is inconceivable, and yet it is pretty clear that we do not enumerate its components when we think of it (84).

What, then, is it for us to conceive of space as infinite, or conversely, as

[44]Mansel, *Limits of Religious Thought*, 5th ed., xvi, 95ff. (Not in the 4th ed.)

finite? On Mill's view, we can conceive of an infinite space by simply conceiving of what we call space and believing that it is of greater extent than any bounded space.

We realize it as space. We realize it as greater than any given space. We even realize it as endless, in an intelligible manner, that is, we clearly represent to ourselves that however much of space has been already explored, and however much more of it we may imagine ourselves to traverse, we are no nearer to the end of it than we were at first. . . . (85.)

The same confidence applies to conceiving of space as finite. Mill supposes that all we need to imagine is that at some point or other an impression of a wholly novel kind would announce to us that we were indeed at the end of space. The extent to which neither Mill nor Hamilton, nor Mansel for that matter, takes the full measure of Kant is somewhat surprising. There is no suggestion that drawing the boundaries of space is conceptual nonsense because boundaries are something one draws *in* space, so that if space is finite it must be finite but unbounded. There is no attempt to explore further what could lead us to recognize an experience as, say, the experience of reaching the end of time or the end of space.

For, as we have seen, Mill does not do more than skirt round the suggestion that "infinite" may have something odd about it, if it is treated as an ordinary first-order predicate, or that "Space" may be the name of an object to which it is only dubiously proper to apply a predicate like "finite." Mill does not extend the notion of "meaninglessness" beyond its most literal applications. He thinks that it *is* impossible to conceive what is meant by a literally meaningless utterance, or one to which *we* can attach no meaning, but that this is not a philosophically interesting sort of inconceivability:

If any one says to me, Humpty Dumpty is an Abracadabra, I neither knowing what is meant by an Abracadabra, nor what is meant by Humpty Dumpty, I may, if I have confidence in my informant, believe that he means something, and that the something which he means is probably true: but I do not believe the very thing which he means, since I am entirely ignorant what it is. Propositions of this kind, the unmeaningness of which lies in the subject or predicate, are not those generally described as inconceivable. (78–9.)

For Mill, then, in so far as the states of affairs described by Hamilton as inconceivable are picked out by intelligible propositions, it becomes a question of fact, even if one which there is no hope of deciding, which branch of the antinomies proposed by Hamiton is true. In that case, what of the philosophy of the conditioned? The answer, says Mill, is that there is in it a good deal less than meets the eye. Hamilton's claim that "Thought is only of the conditioned," and that the "Conditioned is the mean between two extremes—two inconditionates, exclusive of each other, *neither of which can be conceived as possible*, but of which, on the principles of contradiction and excluded middle, *one must be admitted as necessary*,"[45] turns out to be nothing better than noise. It "must be placed in that numerous class of metaphysical doctrines, which have a magnificent sound, but are empty of the smallest substance" (88).

V. GOD AND PROFESSOR MANSEL

WITH HAMILTON THUS ROUTED, Mill turns to meet Mansel's application of the philosophy of the conditioned to religious thought. Neither Mill's attack nor Mansel's response stands out as a model of dispassionate and impersonal inquiry. Mill all but accuses the clergy of being under a professional obligation to talk nonsense (104), and Mansel replies in kind.[46] Mill opens his assault by paying Mansel a backhanded compliment: "Clearness and explicitness of statement being in the number of Mr. Mansel's merits, it is easier to perceive the flaws in his arguments than in those of his master, because he often leaves us less in doubt what he means by his words" (91). In fact, it is not always quite clear where Mansel does and where he does not rest on arguments borrowed from Hamilton; against Mill he tended to argue by complaining of Mill's defective appreciation of the history of philosophy, a procedure which has the defect of turning the interesting question of where Mill and Mansel disagreed over the possible extent of a human knowledge of God's nature into a much less interesting question, about the extent of Mill's acquaintance with traditional natural theology. Mansel was probably right in his conjecture that in some sense Mill thought traditional metaphysics was pointless and nonsensical, but he was far too annoyed to tackle the question that he had really set for himself—namely, if traditional natural theology and traditional metaphysics were as essentially flawed as *The Limits of Religious Thought* maintained, was Mill not right? Why was not agnosticism the proper resting place?

Still, Mill hardly encouraged Mansel to adopt a conciliatory attitude. After a rapid summary of Mansel's argument that we cannot form an adequate conception of God—since God as Absolute and Infinite is inconceivable by us—he comes to Mansel's conclusion that we can only fall back on revelation. That the God thus revealed can or cannot have any particular characteristics, Mansel says it is not for reason to declare; the credibility of a revelation is a matter of historical probabilities, "and no argument grounded on the incredibility of the doctrine, as involving an intellectual

---

[45]*Discussions*, 14.
[46]*Philosophy of the Conditioned*, 170–1.

absurdity, or on its moral badness as unworthy of a good or wise being, ought to have any weight, since of these things we are incompetent to judge" (90). It is not, says Mill, a new doctrine, but "it is simply the most morally pernicious doctrine now current . . ." (90).

Readers who have begun to weary of the hunting of the Absolute will probably take it on trust that in so far as "the Absolute" means the unrelated-to-anything-in-our-experience it is no great achievement to show that we have no knowledge of the Absolute. But Mill presses Mansel rather harder than this, for he at last challenges him to make good on the claim that we are able and indeed obliged on the strength of revelation to believe in this unknowable entity. Mansel, says Mill, succeeds in showing that "the Absolute" and "the Infinite" as defined by himself are simply self-contradictory; but, on Mill's view, this entails their being also unbeliev-able. "Believing God to be infinite and absolute must be believing some-thing, and it must be possible to say what" (98). Mansel's argument to the effect that "the Absolute" and "the Infinite" are involved in self-contradiction is altogether too devastating for his own good, for Mansel certainly does not want to say that the divine nature is really and inherently contradictory. Mansel, indeed, went out of his way to deny any such suggestion; *credo quia impossibile* he thought unworthy of any sane man.[47] His reply to Mill, abusive though it is, shows how little he wished to get himself into such depths, for when Mill taunts him with not being able to say *what* the object of his belief is, he falls back on propositions which Mill readily admits to be intelligible, such as the proposition that God made the world, though we cannot tell how He did it. The explanation of the trouble is simple, though rather strange. Mansel thought it an aid to Christian belief to show that the sceptic could not attack its doctrines on rational grounds; but the way in which he rescued them from the sceptic was by making them too elusive to disbelieve. Inevitably the price he paid was making them too elusive to be believed either.

The single thing in the *Examination* that most heartened his allies and most outraged his opponents was Mill's assault on what he took to be the immorality of Mansel's doctrine of the unknowability of the moral attri-butes of God. To Mill the issue was simple enough. When the clergy talked of God's power they generally meant what we would mean by talking of human power, for instance the divine ability to throw us into the inferno; only on God's moral attributes did they equivocate and suggest that God's goodness was not as mortal goodness.

Is it unfair to surmise that this is because those who speak in the name of God, have need of the human conception of his power, since an idea which can overawe and

---

[47]*Limits of Religious Thought*, 4th ed., vii.

enforce obedience must address itself to real feelings; but are content that his goodness should be conceived only as something inconceivable, because they are so often required to teach doctrines respecting him which conflict irreconcilably with all goodness that we can conceive? (104.)

Whether it is or not, Mill's case is that Mansel cannot hope to argue that God's moral attributes are unlike their human analogues without thereby sacrificing the right to expect us to worship Him. There is, as any reader of Mansel's Bampton Lectures can see, an awkwardness in Mansel's case, analogous to the awkwardness of his epistemology. The case he presents is the familiar one: the Christian who believes in the infinite power and goodness of God is confronted with a world in which the just suffer and the wicked flourish. The austere Mansel does not argue in the Kantian manner that we are thereby licensed to expect a reconciliation of virtue and happiness in the life hereafter. What he does instead is suggest that the inscrutability of God extends to the inscrutable goodness He exhibits. It is not clear that Mansel intends to show that God's *goodness* is not ours; mostly, he argues that how God is working out an overall plan for His universe, a plan which is good in the same sense as a human plan would be good, simply remains unknowable. The goodness of God's agents particularly exercises Mansel: what would be cruelty or injustice if done otherwise than in obedience to God's commands is, we must hope, not cruelty or injustice after all. But, once again, it is less a matter of the imperfect analogy between human and divine attributes (which is the object of Mill's complaint) than of the imperfection of our knowledge of the Almighty's programme, for the sake of which these orders were given. In this light one can understand why Mansel's reply to Mill takes the form of a rather querulous complaint that surely Mill cannot deny that a son may recognize the goodness of his father's actions without wholly understanding them—and Mill does not deny it.

Mill, however, surely gets the best of the dispute, with his famous outburst, for all that Mansel tries to dismiss it as "an extraordinary outburst of rhetoric."[48]

If, instead of the "glad tidings" that there exists a Being in whom all the excellences which the highest human mind can conceive, exist in a degree inconceivable to us, I am informed that the world is ruled by a being whose attributes are infinite, but what they are we cannot learn, nor what are the principles of his government, except that "the highest human morality which we are capable of conceiving" does not sanction them; convince me of it, and I will bear my fate as I may. But when I am told that I must believe this, and at the same time call this being by the names which express and affirm the highest human morality, I say in plain terms that I will not. Whatever power such a being may have over me, there is one thing which he shall not do: he

[48]*Philosophy of the Conditioned*, 167.

shall not compel me to worship him. I will call no being good, who is not what I mean when I apply that epithet to my fellow-creatures; and if such a being can sentence me to hell for not so calling him, to hell I will go. (103.)

VI. OTHER MAJOR ISSUES

AS ONE MIGHT GUESS from the title of Mansel's *The Philosophy of the Conditioned*, it was that doctrine which Mansel, like Mill, saw as Hamilton's most distinctive contribution to philosophy (109). The rest of this Introduction will take its cue from the combatants, and confine itself to the piecemeal treatment of some major issues. The most interesting of these would seem to be the following: Mill's phenomenalist analysis of matter and mind; his demolition of Hamilton's account of causation, which is perhaps a major curiosity rather than a major issue; his account of conception, judgment, and inference, and his assessment of Hamilton's contribution to logic; and, finally, his analysis of the freedom of the will.

MATTER AND MIND

Mill's account of matter and mind begins with what amounts to a hostile review of Hamilton's own hostile review of Thomas Brown's *Lectures on the Philosophy of the Mind*. (Hamilton's article appeared in the *Edinburgh Review* in October, 1830, and was reprinted in his *Discussions*.) Hamilton declared that it was a striking proof of the low state of intellectual life in Britain that Brown's *Lectures* had not hitherto received their just deserts:

The radical *inconsistencies* which they involve, in every branch of their subject, remain undeveloped; their unacknowledged *appropriations* are still lauded as original; their endless *mistakes*, in the history of philosophy, stand yet uncorrected; and their frequent *misrepresentations* of other philosophers continue to mislead. In particular, nothing has more convinced us of the general neglect, in this country, of psychological science, than that Brown's ignorant attack on *Reid*, and, through Reid, confessedly on *Stewart*, has not long since been repelled;—except, indeed, the general belief that it was triumphant.[49]

Hamilton claimed that Brown played fast and loose not only with the testimony of consciousness, a vice to which all philosophers are liable to succumb, but with the testimony of Reid. Brown was what Hamilton called a *cosmothetic idealist*, and Hamilton was at pains to insist that between the testimony of consciousness—which is all on behalf of "Natural Realism" or "Natural Dualism"—and the inferences of idealism there is a great opposition. Reid, on Hamilton's view, was a realist and dualist, where Brown falsely makes him out to be an idealist of the same kind as himself.

[49]*Discussions*, 44.

Mill devotes a chapter to showing not merely that Reid wavered in his convictions on the question, but that when he was plainly committed to any view, that view was cosmothetic idealism. Moreover, very few of Hamilton's arguments against Brown hold water, and when Hamilton adduces, to attack Brown, general principles, such as the impossibility of representative perception, the result, on Mill's account, is to leave Brown untouched and most of Hamilton's own argument in ruins (164). Mill distinguishes, with Hamilton, three views about perception which have been held by those he lumps together as cosmothetic idealists: the first is the view that what is really perceived is not a state of the perceiver's mind, but something else, whether a motion in the brain as in Hobbes or an Idea in the mind as in Berkeley; the second is the view that what is perceived *is* a state of mind, but that *it* and the perceiving of it are distinguishable. These two doctrines, says Mill, really are doctrines of mediate or representative perception, as Hamilton says they are. There is a something which is the direct object of perception and which represents the external object. The third view, however, and the view which Brown held, is not a theory of *representative* perception at all, for there is no *tertium quid*, no object of direct perception from which the existence of some other object is inferred. The object of perception here is "a state of mind identical with the act by which we are said to perceive it" (155). There is here no very clear distinction between a certain sort of phenomenalism on the one hand and outright realism on the other, indeed—a point which Mill does not make, but which some current versions of a "sense data" theory of perception do.[50]

Brown's account of the perception of external objects is invulnerable to the objection that there is no way of knowing whether the object of perception resembles, or truly or faithfully represents, the external object itself. For Brown does not claim that it bears any such relationship to anything external. The relation is causal, not pictorial. In effect, to perceive something in the outside world just is to be in a certain sensory state and to conclude non-inferentially that the cause of this state lies in something external to oneself. And this, says Mill happily, is the only rational interpretation to be placed on the views of Reid as well. Indeed,

if Brown's theory is not a theory of mediate perception, it loses all that essentially distinguishes it from Sir W. Hamilton's own doctrine. For Brown, also, thinks that we have, on the occasion of certain sensations, an instantaneous and irresistible conviction of an outward object. And if this conviction is immediate, and necessitated by the constitution of our nature, in what does it differ from our author's direct consciousness? Consciousness, immediate knowledge, and intuitive knowledge, are, Sir W. Hamilton tells us, convertible expressions; and if it be granted that whenever our senses are affected by a material object, we immediately and intui-

[50]See Jonathan Bennett, *Locke, Berkeley, Hume* (Oxford: Clarendon Press, 1971), Chap. vi.

tively recognise that object as existing and distinct from us, it requires a great deal of ingenuity to make out any substantial difference between this immediate intuition of an external world, and Sir W. Hamilton's direct perception of it. (156–7.)

Brown, on Mill's account, gets the better of Hamilton by consistently denying that some properties of things are known as they really are in the (unknowable) object and some not; Brown genuinely held the doctrine of the relativity of knowledge in an unconfused form (167). In this Brown was on the opposite side to both Reid and Hamilton, but it was an issue on which not even Hamilton was willing to suggest that Brown was unaware of the differences between his own views and those of Reid. Brown's theory of perception explains *all* our knowledge of the attributes of matter in terms of the sensory promptings of an external cause, while Reid's, like Hamilton's, allows us "a direct intuition of the Primary Qualities of bodies" (176). Mill, of course, thinks that Brown's view is the only one consistent with his premises; certainly, as Mill argues both earlier and later in the *Examination*, Hamilton can hardly hope to keep his half-way house. Either he must be a thoroughgoing vulgar realist and agree that what we see just are things, endowed with the attributes we see them to have, the plain man's view; or else, if he is to allow himself such corrections of consciousness as are required when he says, for instance, that no two people see the same object, or indeed that each of us sees two "suns," say, because we receive an image through each eye, and in so saying departs very widely from what any plain man believes, then he must adopt a much more wholesale subjectivism.

Mill's own account of what we believe when we believe in the existence of the outside world is the best known part of the *Examination*. It is hard to know whether to be more surprised by the confidence with which he puts it forward or by the contrast between that confidence and the diffidence, so reminiscent of Hume, with which he confesses that it will not yield a plausible analysis of mind. Mill's account of matter seeks to analyze it in terms of possible sensations. In effect, the requirements of something's being a material thing, distinct from our sensations of it, are the following: it must be public in the sense that it can be perceived by many different people, whereas each of them alone can have his actual sensations; it must be "perdurable," that is, it must exist unperceived, and must outlast the fleeting experiences of it which those who perceive it may have; and it must retain the same properties even if these make it "look different" in different circumstances.

We mean, that there is concerned in our perceptions something which exists when we are not thinking of it; which existed before we had ever thought of it, and would exist if we were annihilated; and further, that there exist things which we never saw, touched, or otherwise perceived, and things which never have been perceived by man. This idea of something which is distinguished from our fleeting impressions by what, in Kantian language, is called Perdurability; something which is fixed and the same, while our impressions vary; something which exists whether we are aware of it or not, and which is always square (or of some other given figure) whether it appears to us square or round—constitutes altogether our idea of external substance. Whoever can assign an origin to this complex conception, has accounted for what we mean by the belief in matter. (178–9.)

The question is, of course, whether an appeal to "possible sensations" can account for all this. Perhaps the first thing that should be said is that Mill is oddly reticent about employing the fact that human beings are *embodied* consciousnesses in any of the argument; later, he employs the sensations of muscular effort and resistance as part of the primitive data which he suggests the mind works on in arriving at a conception of space. But it is on the face of it odd to begin arguing about the belief in an *external* world without raising any question about what external can mean unless "external to me," and how it can mean that, unless we are spatially located from the beginning—and how, if we are so located, it can make any sense to begin to construct a world whose existence we seem to have to assume in order to talk about the constructive task in the first place. Mill can, of course, retort that he is *not* talking about spatial externality yet. What he is talking about initially is permanence; it is a second part of the case to show that a permanent object in sensation has to be construed—or is naturally to be construed—as a spatially external object. That is, so long as we do not insist on publicity, and do not have too many qualms about whether something could be *round* or *square* except in a spatially extended world, we could perhaps break up the belief in a material world into a belief in something permanent which holds together the objects of sense and into a second belief that it is located in space as well as in time. If we think of the percipient as a non-spatial ego in which subjective experiences inhere and which has a history as the history of one such being, we might think of the non-ego as the objective correlate of the percipient self. It is not at all clear that Mill had any such possibility in mind, and it is quite clear that we shall not get very much out of Mill's account by pressing it; nonetheless, to the extent that Mill takes over the terminology of Hamilton, in which we are said to be conscious of an Ego and a non-Ego, the question whether the non-Ego is an external—that is spatially external—world is evidently an open one. The first step establishes a non-Ego as a deliverance of consciousness, if we side with Hamilton, and as an inference if we side with Mill; only subsequent steps can establish its nature.

Mill at any rate is eager to show that so long as the mind is credited with a capacity to form expectations, we can see how the mind would move from having had experiences in certain circumstances in the past, to believing in possible experiences realized by similar conditions in the future. These, Mill says, are not *bare* possibilities but conditional certainties—by which he merely means to insist that he does not suggest that, in the every-day sense, it is only "possible" that when we look at a chair we shall have the appropriate sensations. He means that we shall quite certainly have the appropriate sensations, but, of course, only in the appropriate conditions. The mind, then, faces the fact that its experiences occur in various deter-minate ways; it constructs the hypothesis that this orderliness will be found in all sorts of other areas, and finds it confirmed. The content of the hypothesis is that the world contains permanent possibilities of sensation, and the world turns out to do so. Mill is eager not to turn the Permanent Possibilities themselves into mental constructions; in a footnote replying to a critic who had complained that Mill had offered "no proofs that objects *are* external to us," he says that he had never attempted any such proof:

I am accounting for our conceiving, or representing to ourselves, the Permanent Possibilities as real objects external to us. I do not believe that the real externality to us of anything, except other minds, is capable of proof. But the Permanent Pos-sibilities are external to us in the only sense we need care about; they are not constructed by the mind itself, but merely recognised by it; in Kantian language, they are *given* to us, and to other beings in common with us. (187n.)

It is their givenness which explains the sense in which they are objective rather than subjective; whether this makes them external in a sense which would satisfy the plain man as well as the philosopher remains to be seen.

That there is an external world is a sort of hypothesis, then. It is formed entirely unconsciously, of course, but the awkwardness is not its genesis but its meaning. Mill seems unworried by this, and given the remark quoted immediately above, it is easy to see why. He could share Brown's view of what the belief in an external world amounted to—namely belief in an underlying cause of our sensory experience—since his interest lay not in disputing the adequacy of the analysis, but in accounting for the fact thus analyzed without invoking anything like an original conviction of the exis-tence of an external world. Not for nothing did Mill call his account the psychological theory of the belief in an external world; he thought that Hamilton, Reid, and for that matter Brown, too, had erred by adopting the "introspective" method of analysis, by which he meant that they were too ready to infer from the present existence of a belief in their own minds that it was part of the mind's native constitution. The psychological theory was in principle no more than a genetic hypothesis, a hypothesis about how the belief could have grown up. As such, it seems to be a rather difficult one to bring to empirical test, although such a test seems appropriate for it; the difficulties are too obvious to be worth dwelling on, but they make one wonder why Mill did not make more of the question whether there was any way of averting them. Would he have regarded infantile efforts at focussing on remote objects as evidence one way or the other? Would a new-born baby's recoil from what looks like a sheer drop be evidence about how original a sense of spatial location might be? In the absence of more discussion in Mill's work, speculation is fruitless.

Whether Mill's analysis of matter would satisfy the plain man's notions about matter is a question to which he does devote some attention. He has two rather different stances. The first is that the belief in matter goes beyond the belief in the permanent possibility of sensation: we move from believing that we shall have certain sensations under certain conditions to believing that the whole series of possible sensations has an underlying cause. Now, on this view, we are at any rate inclined to ask whether this belief in an underlying cause actually means anything—since it makes no observational difference whether or not there is such a cause, there is some difficulty in knowing what difference is made by its affirmation or denial. Believers in parsimony, Occam's Razor, or other austerities of thought will perhaps incline to reject it on the grounds that we should believe as little as we must to account for the facts; Mill thinks that Hamilton's "Law of Parsimony" should cause him an analogous embarrassment, but makes nothing of it in this context—he is concerned to reduce the number of our primary intuitions, rather than to purge the plain man's ontology. This being his aim, he is quite content to argue that

Whatever relation we find to exist between any one of our sensations and something different from *it*, that same relation we have no difficulty in conceiving to exist between the sum of all our sensations and something different from *them*. . . . This familiarity with the idea of something different from *each* thing we know, makes it natural and easy to form the notion of something different from *all* things that we know, collectively as well as individually. It is true we can form no conception of what such a thing can be; our notion of it is merely negative; but the idea of a substance, apart from its relation to the impressions which we conceive it as making on our senses, *is* a merely negative one. There is thus no psychological obstacle to our forming the notion of a something which is neither a sensation nor a possibility of sensation, even if our consciousness does not testify to it; and nothing is more likely than that the Permanent Possibilities of sensation, to which our consciousness does testify, should be confounded in our minds with this imaginary conception. All experience attests the strength of the tendency to mistake mental abstractions, even negative ones, for substantive realities. (185.)

On the whole, this argument suggests that the generality of mankind hold *mistaken* views about matter, though its intention may only be to suggest that they hold unverifiable views. But Mill also suggests that he and the plain man may not be at odds.

Matter, then, may be defined, a Permanent Possibility of Sensation. If I am asked, whether I believe in matter, I ask whether the questioner accepts this definition of it.

If he does, I believe in matter: and so do all Berkeleians. In any other sense than this, I do not. But I affirm with confidence, that this conception of Matter includes the whole meaning attached to it by the common world, apart from philosophical, and sometimes from theological, theories. The reliance of mankind on the real existence of visible and tangible objects, means reliance on the reality and permanence of Possibilities of visual and tactual sensations, when no such sensations are actually experienced. (183.)

This view, in contrast to the first one, suggests that the plain man *qua* plain man believes in Permanent Possibilities only; the belief in an unknowable underlying substance is either imposed on him by philosophers, or adopted by the plain man only *qua* amateur philosopher.

The argument between phenomenalists and their opponents has, of course, continued unabated ever since. It is not only the plain man who feels uneasily that Mill's "permanent possibilities of sensation" moves awkwardly between an account of matter which stresses that it is permanently and objectively available to be sensed, and one which dissolves that objective existence into the fact that minds are permanently available to sense—but not necessarily to sense anything other than their own contents. It is at the very best difficult to feel that a possible, but non-actual sensation is more solid, more material, more firmly part of the furniture of the world than an actual sensation is.

Before turning to Mill's attempt to provide a phenomenalist account of personal identity, therefore, we should look to Mill's expansion of his analysis of matter in the shape of his account of our knowledge of its primary qualities. Mill's analysis is devoted to several different tasks, of which the most important is to show that the "psychological theory" can deal with the generation of the idea of Extension, which

has long been considered as one of the principal stumbling blocks of the Psychological Theory. Reid and Stewart were willing to let the whole question of the intuitive character of our knowledge of Matter, depend on the inability of psychologists to assign any origin to the idea of Extension, or analyse it into any combination of sensations and reminiscences of sensation. Sir W. Hamilton follows their example in laying great stress on this point. (216.)

But Mill also wants to explain two other things, firstly, the difference between what we treat as subjective feelings as distinct from what we treat as perceptions of something in the object and, secondly, why we group the objective properties of bodies together as their primary qualities. These did not cause much controversy among Mill's critics, but the attempts at generating the idea of extension along the lines laid down in Bain's treatise on psychology did. The fundamental complaint was always the same, that all attempts to explain where we might have acquired the concept of extension presuppose that we have it already. As Mill says in the footnote in which he replies to them:

A host of critics, headed by Dr. McCosh, Mr. Mahaffy, and the writer in *Blackwood*, have directed their shafts against this chapter. . . . The principal objection is the same which was made to the two preceding chapters [on the Psychological Theory of the belief in an external world, and its application to mind]: that the explanation given of Extension presupposes Extension: that the notion itself is surreptitiously introduced, to account for its own origin. (240.)

The distinction between sensations referred mostly to the subject of perception and those referred mostly to the object, Mill explains fairly casually. That we *can* refer the experience to an outer object is the major difference between sensation and other mental phenomena; so, the pleasure of a man eating a good meal *can* be said to inhere in the meal, but is more readily ascribed to the man than the meal, because pleasure and pain are part of a class of "sensations which are highly interesting to us on their own account, and on which we willingly dwell, or which by their intensity compel us to concentrate our attention on them." The result is that in our consciousness of them "the reference to their Object does not play so conspicuous and predominant a part . . ." (212). Mill does not appeal to the way in which the pleasure and, to a lesser extent, the pain caused by a given object varies from one person to another as a reason for distinguishing the pleasure and pain from what causes them; nor does he suggest that there is anything problematic in treating secondary qualities like colour in the same way as pleasure and pain. The distinction he is interested in is really that which his opponents see as a distinction between the essence of matter, and all else. If we can imagine a thing losing its colour without ceasing to exist, and losing its capacity to give pain or pleasure without ceasing to exist, then colour and pleasure lie on the side of the secondary qualities; if we cannot imagine an object losing its extension or impenetrability without ceasing to exist, then these are its primary qualities. That we in fact agree in thinking of resistance, extension, and figure as the primary qualities of matter, indeed think of matter as consisting of these attributes "together with miscellaneous powers of exciting other sensations" (214), Mill readily admits. That we group these together he explains by the fact that sensations of smell, taste, and hearing do not cohere directly, but "through the connexion which they all have, by laws of coexistence or of causation, with the sensations which are referable to the sense of touch and to the muscles; those which answer to the terms Resistance, Extension, and Figure. These, therefore, become the leading and conspicuous elements. . . ." (213.)

So the question eventually comes to that of whether the associationist psychology can explain our conception of things as being spatially extended, with the implications that this property suggests, that they must have boundaries or figure, if we are to tell one thing from another, and that they must be less than wholly interpenetrable. Resistance, or relative impenetrability, Mill explains as an inference from the experience of obstructed muscular movement when this is combined with appropriate sensations of touch. The combination assures us that the impediment to movement is not internal paralysis or something similar. Figure, Mill deals with rather casually as the conjoined information of sight and touch; he invokes a good deal of not very persuasive psychological evidence to suggest that a blind man either has a different conception of figure from that of a sighted man or no conception at all, and even toys with the less than obviously coherent claim that a blind man might think the external world was composed entirely of one object. But it is evidently the analysis of extension that is crucial to his case. He makes it at second hand by way of an extended quotation from Bain. The gist of the case is simple enough. We have certain sensations connected with the contraction of our voluntary muscles, and these are different according to the extent of such contraction, so that we can discriminate half, wholly, or very partially contracted muscles; these are associated with the sweep of a limb or other bodily movement. Now it would obviously be putting the cart before the horse if Mill and Bain were to employ the idea of a limb sweeping a certain amount of *space* in explaining the origins of our idea of space. Most of Mill's critics, as we have seen, said that this was just what they had done. Whether the charge can be rebutted is very difficult to decide. In a sense, Mill is between the devil and the deep blue sea. Any notion of the sweep of a limb which is distinctively *non*-spatial looks inadequate to generate a conception of space at all, while any notion adequate to the generation of a concept of space seems to get there by starting with some notion of space already. If we make the sweep of a limb purely temporal—that is, if we say that the non-spatial notion is simply one of the length of time it takes for sensations to succeed each other—we escape the charge of paralogism, but we do not get very close to the usual idea of space. Mill does not make this admission; on his analysis, the blind man's conception of space *is* temporal not spatial, and even the sighted majority have a conception which is basically temporal:

a person blind from birth must necessarily perceive the parts of extension—the parts of a line, of a surface, or of a solid—in conscious succession. He perceives them by passing his hand along them, if small, or by walking over them if great. The parts of extension which it is possible for him to perceive simultaneously, are only very small parts, almost the minima of extension. Hence, if the Psychological theory of the idea of extension is true, the blind metaphysician would feel very little of the difficulty which seeing metaphysicians feel, in admitting that the idea of Space is, at bottom, one of time—and that the notion of extension or distance, is that of a motion of the muscles continued for a longer or a shorter duration. (222–3.)

The temptation remains to say what is shown here is only that a man who has our conception of space can measure distances by the time it takes to cover them; it does nothing to suggest that time alone can convey that conception of space to one who does not have it. Just as Mill's analysis of the external world provides us with "possibilities of sensation" external to our actual sensations only in the same way that the number six is external to the series of numbers from one to four, so here he seems to offer us extension in one dimension when we want it in another.

The point at which Mill himself admitted to defeat was in the analysis of mind rather than matter. The general line that he saw himself obliged to pursue was what we should expect; if matter was a permanent possibility of being sensed, the "Ego" should be amenable to analysis as the permanent possibility of having sensations. Mill's first concern is to show that there is nothing in such a phenomenalism to justify charges of atheism or all-embracing scepticism. If the mind is a series of mental states, there is no bar to immortality in that: a series can go on forever just as readily as a substance can. No doubt metaphysicians have been eager to argue that we *must* be immortal, on the grounds that the soul, being a substance, is indestructible, but such arguments, says Mill, are so feeble that philosophers have increasingly given them up. The existence of God is equally untouched: "Supposing me to believe that the Divine Mind is simply the series of the Divine thoughts and feelings prolonged through eternity, that would be, at any rate, believing God's existence to be as real as my own" (192). And the existence of other minds is as well vouched for on phenomenalist as on substantialist premises. We know in our own cases that between bodily effects and their bodily causes there intervene mental events—sensations, motives, and so on—and we infer inductively that the same thing is true in other cases; we see bodies like our own and believe on excellent evidence that there are minds associated with them. "I conclude that other human beings have feelings like me, because, first, they have bodies like me, which I know, in my own case, to be the antecedent condition of feeling; and because, secondly, they exhibit the acts, and other outward signs, which in my own case I know by experience to be caused by feelings" (191). Mill thus concludes that Reid's accusation, that the phenomenalist ends as a solipsist, fails.

But this is not to say that the phenomenalist position is freed of all difficulty. The pressure in favour of phenomenalism is the same in the case of mind as in the case of matter; we have no knowledge of mind as it is in itself, only of its phenomena. Just like Hume, Mill holds that what we perceive are the mind's modifications, such as thoughts, sensations, desires, and aversions. What we have in the way of evidence is a stream of experience; is the mind or the self more than such a stream, therefore? Mill answers that it seems that it must be more. The reason lies in the nature of memory and expectation. In themselves memories and expectations are simply part of the stream of consciousness, but their oddity is that they essentially involve *beliefs*, and beliefs of an awkward kind. When we expect a future experience, we expect something to happen to *us*, and when we remember a past experience, we remember that something happened to *us*.

Nor can the phænomena involved in these two states of consciousness be adequately expressed, without saying that the belief they include is, that I myself formerly had, or that I myself, and no other, shall hereafter have, the sensations remembered or expected. The fact believed is, that the sensations did actually form, or will hereafter form, part of the self-same series of states, or thread of consciousness, of which the remembrance or expectation of those sensations is the part now present. If, therefore, we speak of the Mind as a series of feelings, we are obliged to complete the statement by calling it a series of feelings which is aware of itself as past and future; and we are reduced to the alternative of believing that the Mind, or Ego, is something different from any series of feelings, or possibilities of them, or of accepting the paradox, that something which *ex hypothesi* is but a series of feelings, can be aware of itself as a series. (194.)

In essence, Mill's problem is that if matter is a hypothesis that a mind formulates to account for the regularity of its experience, a unitary self must be presupposed to do the hypothesizing, and a unitary self that, furthermore, can view *its* experience as something regular enough to need explaining by such a hypothesis. But if my construction of my experienced world depends on a prior identification of the data of experience as my sensations and so on, there seems no hope of accounting for *me* in the same terms—for, out of what would *I* construct *me*? Mill insists in a long footnote that he merely intends to leave open the question of what the mind's nature really is, neither, as some of his critics have alleged, adopting the "psychological theory" in spite of the objections, nor accepting the common view of the mind as a substance (204n–7n). Indeed, says Mill in the main text,

The truth is, that we are here face to face with that final inexplicability, at which, as Sir W. Hamilton observes, we inevitably arrive when we reach ultimate facts; and in general, one mode of stating it only appears more incomprehensible than another, because the whole of human language is accommodated to the one, and is so incongruous with the other, that it cannot be expressed in any terms which do not deny its truth (194).

This abstemiousness about putting forward any explanation of the inexplicable did not save Mill from Bradley. In his *Ethical Studies* Bradley did his best to kill off the psychological theory with a famous joke: "Mr. Bain collects that the mind is a collection. Has he ever thought who collects Mr. Bain?"[51] and went on to say of Mill that when he had "the same fact

---

[51]Francis Herbert Bradley, *Ethical Studies* (Oxford: Clarendon Press, 1924), 39n.

before him, which gave the lie to his whole psychological theory, he could not ignore it, he could not recognize it, he would not call it a fiction; so he put it aside as a 'final inexplicability,' and thought, I suppose, that by covering it with a phrase he got rid of its existence."[52] This judgment is transparently unjust, but there is something extremely unsatisfactory about Mill's agnosticism all the same.

One cannot do the subject justice here, but we may at any rate agree that Mill could have done more. He could, for example, have explored the idea that the self can be a serial self, without needing a non-serial percipient self to give it unity, or that it is a logical construction which does not require a constructor; he could have pressed the "error theory" implicit in what he says about the way ordinary language favours one view of personal identity, and attempted to pull apart the implications of the language from the bare facts of the world. The fact remains that he did not.

CAUSATION

Although there are grounds for treating Mill's attack on Hamilton's account of causation in conjunction with discussion of free-will—namely, that Mill discusses the "volitional" theory of causation while he is attacking Hamilton, and in the process commits himself to the view that we have no direct power over our own volitions (298–9)—there is more to be said for tackling it briefly and on its own. For on causation Mill adds nothing to his own account in the *Logic*, whereas on the subject of the freedom of the will he supplements what he says in the *Logic*, and in addition fills out the theory of punishment and the conception of justice that we find in *Utilitarianism* and *On Liberty*. His attack on Hamilton's theory of causation is brief and dismissive. The issue was what we might expect: Hamilton appealed to the innate structure of the mind, and Mill thought the appeal quite illicit. On this topic Hamilton's case was an odd one. For he did not appeal to a positive intuition of the connectedness of events, nor to anything like Kant's synthetic *a priori* principle of the rule-governed succession of events. Rather, he appealed to an *in*capacity of the mind. The incapacity in question was the mind's inability to conceive of what he called an "absolute commencement." This incapacity, as Mill says, is on Hamilton's account not entirely reliable as a guide to how things are, for acts of the free will are cases of just such an absolute commencement. It does seem at first, however, the sort of thing on which one *might* found a view of causation. That is, we cannot regard any event as an uncaused happening, because we cannot conceive of any such thing; we must, therefore, look for

[52]*Ibid.*, 40n.

the cause of it. The difficulty lies in Hamilton's explanation of the nature of the incapacity. Hamilton does not make any claim for its fundamental status. He explains it is a case of the general incapacity to imagine that there could be an increase or decrease in the quantum of existence in the world. This is, of course, a sort of relative of the principles of the conservation of energy or the conservation of matter; so read, Hamilton might be saying that the aim of causal explanation is to show how a fixed quantity of matter undergoes changes of form. The reason why he put the problem in this odd way was very probably his scholastic enthusiasm for the Aristotelian four causes, but Mill was surely right to say that the only one of the Aristotelian causes which corresponded to the modern conception of cause was the efficient cause. Hamilton went on to claim that the effect is the very same thing as the cause, presumably meaning only that effects must be made out of the same fixed quantum of matter. This was to ignore the efficient cause in favour of the material, and, in thus deciding to leave out of account the changeable element in causation, Hamilton simply left out causation. "Suppose the effect to be St. Paul's: in assigning its causes, the will of the government, the mind of the architect, and the labour of the builders, are all cast out, for they are all transitory, and only the stones and mortar remain" (292). In any case, says Mill, it is plainly absurd to suppose that the law of the conservation of matter is an original endowment of the mind; until they are taught otherwise, men believe that when water evaporates, it is annihilated, and do not think that when wood is reduced to ashes, the missing wood must be somewhere in some shape or other, even if only as smoke. It therefore looks as if Hamilton's interpretation of our incapacity to conceive an absolute commencement is suicidally ill-adapted to provide a theory of causation. Had he employed the principle in its most natural sense, as referring to the inconceivability of an uncaused *event*, it might have been bald, though it would have been addressed to the right topic; however, to employ it, not as a principle about the effects of events upon each other, but as a principle about the unchangeable quantity of existence in the world, made it simply irrelevant to the topic in hand.

LOGIC

Mill declines to provide a positive account of causation, on the entirely proper grounds that he has done more than enough in that line in the *Logic*. Instead he turns to Hamilton's views on logic. Anyone who wearies of Mill's hounding of Hamilton through the questions of how we form concepts, what it is to judge something to be the case, and so on, will wish that Mill had declined the chase on the grounds that here, too, he had done enough in the first two books of the *Logic*. The question, what is a concept, resolves itself for Mill into the familiar question whether there are any abstract ideas; he offers a thumbnail sketch of the three possible views on universals, declares that Realism is dead beyond hope of revival, and proceeds to set out the rival attractions of Nominalism and Conceptualism. The view of the nominalists was that "there is nothing general except names. A name, they said, is general, if it is applied in the same acceptation to a plurality of things; but every one of the things is individual" (302), and this is the view of the mediaeval nominalists' successors such as Berkeley. The conceptualists, of whom Locke is representative, agree that "External objects indeed are all individual" but maintain nonetheless that "to every general name corresponds a General Notion, or Conception, called by Locke and others an Abstract Idea. General Names are the names of these Abstract Ideas." (302.) Mill complains of Hamilton that he will not settle for one or other of these positions, but seems to swing between agreeing with Berkeley that we simply cannot form ideas of, for example, a triangle which is neither isosceles nor scalene nor equilateral—in which case he would be a nominalist—and a manner of talking about "Abstract General Notions" which is only consistent with conceptualism. Mill himself settles for nominalism, by explaining that we may have abstractions without having any abstract ideas.

General concepts, therefore, we have, properly speaking, none; we have only complex ideas of objects in the concrete: but we are able to attend exclusively to certain parts of the concrete idea: and by that exclusive attention, we enable those parts to determine exclusively the course of our thoughts as subsequently called up by association; and are in a condition to carry on a train of meditation or reasoning relating to those parts only, exactly as if we were able to conceive them separately from the rest (310).

Attention is fixed by naming the *respect* in which we are to attend to whatever it is. Mill insists that words are therefore only signs, and there can be such things as natural signs; anything which will direct the attention in the appropriate way will form the basis of classification and conceptualization. "We may be tolerably certain that the things capable of satisfying hunger form a perfectly distinct class in the mind of any of the more intelligent animals; quite as much so as if they were able to use or understand the word food" (315).

Mill's eventual aim is to vindicate against Hamilton the doctrine that there can be a logic of truth as well as a logic of consistency. In the process he sets out to criticize Hamilton's account of what is involved in judgment and reasoning. The two basic complaints that Mill levels against Hamilton are that his account of judgment appears to make all true propositions analytic, and that his account of reasoning makes it impossible to see how one can ever *find out* something by reasoning. Here again we are in a much-trodden field, and one where there has since Mill's day been a continuous effort to disengage questions of logical implication from questions about the novelty to any particular reasoner of the conclusion he reaches by deductive inference. In the matter of judgment, Mill had an interest in insisting on the importance of *belief*, and thus of the idea of truth. In editing his father's *Analysis of the Phenomena of the Human Mind*, he had remarked on the imperfections of the associationist analysis of belief in terms of the association of two ideas.[53] To believe that the grass is green and to deny that the grass is green, we need to have the same propositional content in mind; it is the judgment we make of its being true to fact or false to fact that is different. In so far as associating ideas is supposed to be mentally analogous to depicting a state of affairs, it leaves out what is distinctive about judging that something is or is not the case; for a picture to become an assertion or a denial it needs to have something else added to it, namely the judgment that it is or is not how things are.

Mill takes up the theme against Hamilton with additions. Hamilton had rashly suggested that judgment was a process of seeing whether one concept was part of another, though he also claimed that in judgment we looked to see if two concepts were capable of coexistence or were mutually repugnant. But this argument he glossed in such a way as to suggest at any rate that such an inspection yielded what we should normally think of as a synthetic judgment. We put together such concepts as *water*, *rusting*, and *iron*, and if they are congruent, reach the judgment that "water rusts iron." Mill comments pretty sharply on this fearful muddle. It confuses judgments about the compatibility of our concepts with judgments about the coexistence of attributes in the world, and in any event does not make the necessary move from contemplating a state of affairs as possible to asserting that it is actualized.

The discussion is complicated to some degree by the psychological overtones of any discussion of concepts. Hamilton at times seems to be wanting to say that an established truth *is* analytic, in that our concepts embody everything we associate with that of which they are the concept; so, only new truths would be synthetic, and they would make us revise our concepts in such a way that what had been synthetic now became analytic. This cannot be said to be an attractive doctrine in general, nor can Hamilton be said to have showed much sign of really wishing to articulate it; it would mean that a statement such as "all men are mortal" would be speaker-relative both in meaning and in epistemological status. For somebody whose concept "man" included "mortal" it would be analytic, and for somebody whose concept did not, it would be synthetic. Even then, in

[53]James Mill, *Analysis*, I, 402n–4n.

Hamilton's account, we are not much further forward, for if concepts are *congruent* when propositions are possibly true, and if they are related *as part to whole* when they are necessarily true, how are they related when something is said to be true only contingently? As Mill complains, the necessary reference to a belief about the world seems to have been omitted.

Take, for instance, Sir W. Hamilton's own example of a judgment, "Water rusts iron:" and let us suppose this truth to be new to us. Is it not like a mockery to say with our author, that we know this truth by comparing "the *thoughts*, water, iron, and rusting?" Ought he not to have said the *facts*, water, iron, and rusting? and even then, is comparing the proper name for the mental operation? We do not examine whether three thoughts agree, but whether three outward facts coexist. If we lived till doomsday we should never find the proposition that water rusts iron in our concepts, if we had not first found it in the outward phænomena. (332.)

Mill's chapter on reasoning is concerned with the problem which had haunted the *Logic*, that is, how can reasoning give us new knowledge? Mill requires a theory of reasoning which accounts for the way in which we can, by bringing judgments to bear on each other, learn what we could not know by inspecting them separately. The conventional complaint against Mill to the effect that he habitually confuses psychological and logical questions really does seem warranted here, for most of his objections to Hamilton boil down to the claim that if we move from "all men are mortal" via "Socrates is a man" to "Socrates is mortal" by seeing that a concept comprehended under a concept is comprehended under any concept that comprehends that second concept, then it is impossible to see how we could *move* from premises to conclusion. Did we once have the greater concept clear in our mind, subsequently forget part of it, and then recall it (343–5)? Mill produces what he takes to be a conclusive refutation of the "conceptualist" view that reasoning is eliciting the implications of concepts, when he offers geometrical reasoning as a plain case of achieving new knowledge of things rather than merely of concepts by a process of reasoning alone.

Here are two properties of circles. One is, that a circle is bounded by a line, every point of which is equally distant from a certain point within the circle. This attribute is connoted by the name, and is, on both theories [that is, Nominalism and Conceptualism], a part of the concept. Another property of the circle is, that the length of its circumference is to that of its diameter in the approximate ratio of 3.14159 to 1. This attribute was discovered, and is now known, as a result of reasoning. Now, is there any sense, consistent with the meaning of the terms, in which it can be said that this recondite property formed part of the concept circle, before it had been discovered by mathematicians? Even in Sir W. Hamilton's meaning of concept, it is in nobody's but a mathematician's concept even now: and if we concede that mathematicians are to determine the normal concept of a circle for mankind at large, mathematicians themselves did not find the ratio of the diameter to the circumference in the concept, but put it there; and could not have done so until the long train of difficult reasoning which culminated in the discovery was complete. (346–7.)

This discussion, of course, ties in with Mill's account of geometry in the *Logic*, with its insistence that geometry was not about definitions but about the things picked out by the definitions.[54]

Mill goes on to criticize Hamilton's account of logic in terms which the preceding discussion would lead us to expect. Hamilton intended, so far as one can see, to describe logic as a purely formal science, and to explain the domain of what we should now call philosophical logic as that of the analysis of the mental operations necessary for valid thinking and inference—concept formation, definition, and so on. But this is notoriously an area in which the absence of an adequate notation hindered all efforts at distinguishing clearly between formal and material considerations. Mill, moreover, was an unabashed primitivist in such matters. He complained in the *Examination* that Hamilton's attempt to explicate the law of non-contradiction by such formulae as "A=not-A=0" or "A−A=0" was merely a "misapplication and perversion of algebraical symbols" (376), and his letters reveal that he had no inkling of the importance of the work of Boole.[55] In the absence of an adequate notation, it is difficult to develop a coherent account of what is meant by restricting the notion of logic to formal considerations. Mill is wholly successful in showing that Hamilton made a fearful chaos of it. What everyone since has found less convincing is Mill's positive account of a logic which should be wider than the logic of consistency. It is not that his fundamental position is incoherent, though it is loosely stated.

If any general theory of the sufficiency of Evidence and the legitimacy of Generalization be possible, this must be Logic κατ'ἐξοχήν, and anything else called by the name can only be ancillary to it. For the Logic called Formal only aims at removing one of the obstacles to the attainment of truth, by preventing such mistakes as render our thoughts inconsistent with themselves or with one another: and it is of no importance whether we think consistently or not, if we think wrongly. It is only as a means to material truth, that the formal, or to speak more clearly, the conditional, validity of an operation of thought is of any value; and even that value is only negative: we have not made the smallest positive advance towards right thinking, by merely keeping ourselves consistent in what is, perhaps, systematic error. (369–70.)

Here, evidently, Mill divides general logic into what one might call the realm of inductive support on the one hand, and the realm of deductive

---

[54]J. S. Mill, *A System of Logic, Ratiocinative and Inductive, Collected Works*, Vols. VII and VIII (Toronto: University of Toronto Press, 1973), VII, 224–7 (II, v, i).

[55]Mill to John Elliot Cairnes (5/12/71), in Francis E. Mineka and Dwight N. Lindley, eds., *The Later Letters, Collected Works*, Vols. XIV–XVII (Toronto: University of Toronto Press, 1972), XVII, 1862–3.

implication on the other. The general principle that deductive arguments are conclusive because there is no way to affirm their premises and deny their conclusions without self-contradiction is one which Mill seems to adopt for himself. The so-called principle of non-contradiction, says Mill, "is the principle of all Reasoning, so far as reasoning can be regarded apart from objective truth or falsehood. For, abstractedly from that considera- tion, the only meaning of validity in reasoning is that it neither involves a contradiction, nor infers anything the denial of which would not contradict the premises." (378.) Yet Mill does not want to draw such a sharp line between inductive and deductive arguments as either his opponents at the time or his successors now would do. The suggestion, even in the quotation immediately above, is that where objective truth or falsehood *is* in ques- tion, there is a sense of "validity" other than that employed in deductive reasoning. And that in turn suggests another heretical doctrine, that Mill thinks of the relation between premises and conclusions as relations of evidential support; some evidential support is so good that when we see plainly what we are saying we see that we should contradict ourselves by simultaneously asserting the premises and denying the conclusion. But instead of concluding that induction and deduction are wholly different operations, Mill inclines to the view that there is no real inference in deductive arguments.

The twentieth-century reader's unease at all this must be a good deal increased by two passages which betoken the same unwillingness to give any weight at all to the formal/material distinction. Mill seems at first to see that there is something odd about the so-called law of identity which, he agrees, lies at the basis of all reasoning, though it is not clear what it is that he dislikes. At one point he suggests that the law of identity amounts to saying that a statement true in one form of words remains true in another form of words bearing the same meaning. To elucidate the law, says Mill, we need very much more than a statement like "A is identical with A." We need, indeed,

a long list of such principles as these: When one thing is before another, the other is after. When one thing is after another, the other is before. When one thing is along with another, the other is along with the first. When one thing is like, or unlike, another, the other is like (or unlike) the first: in short, as many fundamental principles as there are kinds of relation. For we have need of all these changes of expression in our processes of thought and reasoning. (374.)

If the law of identity is fundamental in reasoning, it must be a general licence "to assert the same meaning in any words which will, consistently with their signification, express it" (374). This suggests that Mill does not think that identity is a property of things, but wishes to gloss it in terms of the equivalence of propositions. But he ends by admitting to some uncertainty whether the fundamental laws of logic are really necessities of thought or merely habits which we have acquired by seeing that these laws apply to all phenomena. That they do apply to phenomena, Mill certainly says here. Speaking of the laws of identity, contradiction, and excluded middle, he says,

I readily admit that these three general propositions are universally true of all phænomena. I also admit that if there are any inherent necessities of thought, these are such. I express myself in this qualified manner, because whoever is aware how artificial, modifiable, the creatures of circumstances, and alterable by circumstances, most of the supposed necessities of thought are (though real necessities to a given person at a given time), will hesitate to affirm of any such necessities that they are an original part of our mental constitution. Whether the three so-called Fundamental Laws are laws of our thoughts by the native structure of the mind, or merely because we perceive them to be universally true of observed phænomena, I will not positively decide: but they are laws of our thoughts now, and invincibly so. They may/or may not be capable of alteration by experience, but the conditions of our existence deny to us the experience which would be required to alter them. (380–1.)

Mill's last encounter with Hamilton on the logical front concerns two doctrines on which Hamilton very much prided himself. These are the claim that we can and should distinguish between syllogisms taken in "extension" and taken in "comprehension," and the doctrine of the quantification of the predicate. Mill is very fierce against the first, but mostly because he thinks Hamilton failed to see that the extension of a class is no clue to the meaning of a class name. Thus the meaning of "table" is explained by the attributes in virtue of which tables are such; anyone who knows what they are knows what "table" means and what a table is. The number of things which happen to be tables is neither here nor there; to know that they *are* tables requires that we know the attributes of tables already, and once we know that, we know all there is to be known about the meaning of the word "table." Whether this view entails that there is no light to be cast on the syllogism by treating it in terms of the calculus of classes is debatable. Mill follows Hamilton into a fog of visual imagery. According to Hamilton, says Mill, we should think of "all oxen ruminate" as meaning "If all creatures that ruminate were collected in a vast plain, and I were required to search the world and point out all oxen, they would all be found among the crowd on that plain, and none anywhere else. Moreover, this would have been the case in all past time, and will at any future, while the present order of nature lasts." (387.) Mill's objection is not that this is not implicit in the proposition, but that such a claim is not what is present to the mind. What is present to the mind is that two attributes are conjoined.

Hamilton is now best remembered for his doctrine of the quantification of the predicate. This is not to say that he is kindly remembered for it; it is little more than a curiosity of the history of logic, and Hamilton's own version of it has been described as presented with "quite fantastic incompetence."[56] The most that anyone now tries to do is rescue Hamilton from such charges. It is, however, hard to see quite what Hamilton was trying to add to the traditional theory of the syllogism, the more so because his later elucidations of the doctrine, produced in the heat of controversy with De Morgan, not only diminish the claims of the doctrine in respect of the number of new forms of proposition added to the traditional square of opposition, but, as De Morgan pointed out, render invalid syllogisms he had earlier claimed as valid. Mill does not tackle Hamilton on these technical issues. Rather, he challenges him on his claim that the quantification of the predicate is a principle of mental hygiene. Hamilton appeals to "the self-evident truth,—That we can only rationally deal with what we already understand, determines the simple logical postulate,—*To state explicitly what is thought implicitly*."[57] The postulate is a fairly ludicrous piece of advice; conversation would be impossible if we said *everything* we thought.

The true place of the doctrine of the quantified predicate lies in the theory of the syllogism, and particularly in the area of Aristotle's claims about the permissible and impermissible forms of proposition. Hamilton's claim that we can quantify the predicate makes good sense in the case of affirmative propositions like "all x is y" or "some x is y," where we can give clear meaning to "all x is some y" and "all x is all y," and again to "some x is all y" and "some x is some y." Even here there is trouble lurking, since "all x is all y" may be interpreted either as "every x is every y"—which is true if there is only one x, only one y and x is y—or as a class-proposition to the effect that everything in x is in y and vice versa. Hamilton plainly wanted to read it as a class proposition, and only so could it give the required meaning to what he called "parti-partial negatives" like "some x is not some y," where he wanted to admit as possible propositions even "some A is not some A" as in "*Some animal* (say, rational) *is not some animal* (say, irrational)."[58] Then when pressed by his critics, he added the doctrine that *some* meant, not *some at least*, but *some only*, and this move collapsed the particular affirmative and particular negative propositions of the traditional square of opposition into each other, so destroying the claim that with the quantified predicate we achieve eight distinct forms of proposition, which can be put into four pairs of contradictories in the usual way.

The whole subject of how to interpret the quantification of the predicate in the case of negative propositions is bedevilled by the awkwardness of the verbal formulae involved, and it is no wonder that Hamilton and De Morgan argued at cross-purposes for the better part of twenty years.

[56]Arthur Norman Prior, *Formal Logic* (Oxford: Clarendon Press, 1955), 148.
[57]*Discussions*, 646.
[58]*Ibid.*, 163.

However sympathetic to the quantification of the predicate one may feel, it seems clear that most of what Hamilton hoped to achieve is much more readily achieved by resorting to Euler circles. With the aid of these and the predicate calculus it is possible to spell out several versions of what is implied by Hamilton's claims. No point which can readily be related to Hamilton's thought is served by so doing, and, because syllogistic logic is of interest to most modern logicians for what it suggests about the capacity of mediaeval logicians to anticipate twentieth-century controversies, rather than for more directly instructive reasons, Hamilton's muddles, late in the day, are unexciting stuff. One can say on Hamilton's behalf that the theory of the quantification of the predicate opens up an interesting area of logic, which remained largely inaccessible until a more adequate notation was developed. The later history of the subject runs through De Morgan's speculations about the "numerically definite" syllogism and on to twentieth-century work on "the logic of plurality." But to all this Mill had no contribution to offer, and Hamilton rather a small one.

On the issues as he saw them Mill's demolition of Hamilton's claims for the doctrine is brief, lucid, and complete. He objects to Hamilton's rewriting of some as " some only"; although Hamilton may be right that there is a *sous entendu* of conversation to the effect that if I have seen, and know that I have seen, all your children, I should not remark merely that I had seen some of them, this fact is no reason to clutter up the theory of the syllogism (400–1). "Some A is B" is a single judgment, says Mill, and the predicate calculus would no doubt be thought to be on his side in formalizing it as $\exists x(Ax \ \& \ Bx)$, but "some only of A is B" is a compound judgment, and here, too, the modern formula would give Mill comfort, for it would be $\exists x(Ax \ \& \ Bx) \ \& \ \exists x(Ax \ \& \ -Bx)$. The same doubling up is required also when we attempt to quantify the predicate in the case of universal affirmatives. So, says Mill, Hamilton is *not* asking us to make explicit what is already implicit, since what he says is implicit (that is, in our minds already) is nothing of the sort. The Hamiltonian rewritings merely substitute two judgments for one. Mill adds a footnote to explain that we individuate judgments by way of seeing what *quaesitum* we answer, and he quotes one of Hamilton's own authorities to the effect that the "cause why the quantitative note is not usually joined with the predicate, is that there would thus be two quaesita at once; to wit, whether the predicate were affirmed of the subject, and whether it were denied of everything beside" (400n–1n). Mill's conclusion is what one would expect:

The general result of these considerations is, that the utility of the new forms is by no means such as to compensate for the great additional complication which they introduce into the syllogistic theory; a complication which would make it at the same time difficult to learn or remember, and intolerably tiresome both in the learning and in the using. . . . The new forms have thus no practical advantage which can countervail the objection of their entire psychological irrelevancy; and the invention and acquisition of them have little value, except as one among many other feats of mental gymnastic, by which students of the science may exercise and invigorate their faculties. (403.)

Given that Hamilton's claims had been for the psychological and theoretical merits of the doctrine, it is hard to blame Mill for not going out of his way to find a more plausible and persuasive version of the doctrine to criticize.

FREEDOM OF THE WILL

The last issue on which we shall see how Mill takes Hamilton to task is that of the freedom of the will. As we should imagine, the Philosophy of the Conditioned found the questions of how the will determined action, and how the will was itself moved (if not determined) to act, the occasion for a riot of declared nescience. Mansel, whose commitment to the unanswerability of ultimate questions was stronger than Hamilton's, placed the question whether and in what way the will was free on the list of topics where philosophy proceeded by denying the intelligibility of the claims of reductionists, materialists, and necessitarians, rather than by defending an articulated account of the nature of the will and its free operation. But it was, if anything was, the central issue on which he proposed to stand and fight. For Mansel, the two opposing armies were those of the philosophy of Personality on the one side and those of Necessity on the other, and, although he did not do anything to defend this view of the nature of the battlefield or his own place in the ranks of the personalists in *The Philosophy of the Conditioned*, the opposition itself appears plainly enough almost throughout his Bampton Lectures.[59] Mill attacks some of the *obiter dicta* in Mansel's *Prolegomena Logica*, but in criticism he sticks pretty closely to Hamilton. However, for most readers, Mill's positive views provide the interest of the chapter, for Mill commits himself to a number of views on punishment, the nature of justice, and the analysis of responsibility which outraged his critics at the time, and which still are live philosophical positions.

Mill says, rather plausibly, that Hamilton's account of the freedom of the will is central to the whole Philosophy of the Conditioned. Hamilton brings the supposed incapacity of the human mind to conceive an "absolute commencement" into head-on conflict with our apparently intuitive conviction that we are free agents, whose acts of will are indeed absolute commencements. Hamilton's Philosophy of the Conditioned, moreover, denied the teachings of common sense on the freedom of the will. Where

[59]See Mansel, *Limits of Religious Thought*, 4th ed., 56ff.

Reid had come close to Dr. Johnson's famous assertion that "we *know* our will is free, and *there's* an end on't,"[60] Hamilton thought we *knew* nothing of the sort. Even Reid had agreed that people act from motives; a motive must in some fashion determine the action—even if the motive was not a direct cause of action, it was surely one of the co-operating causes which determined the will, and the will in turn was the direct cause of the action (444). Mill gratefully acknowledges Hamilton's assistance in repudiating Reid's common-sense position, though he does so in a somewhat barbed fashion: "Sir W. Hamilton having thus, as is often the case (and it is one of the best things he does), saved his opponents the trouble of answering his friends, his doctrine is left resting exclusively on the supports which he has himself provided for it" (445). But the freedom of the will is central to Hamilton's metaphysics in more than providing a paradigm of the conditioned nature of thought, and in more than providing a point at which Hamilton's distinctive views emerged clearly by contrast with those of Reid. For Hamilton's theology rested on human freedom. In effect, he held that the existence of a non-natural origin of action was the chief ground for supposing that there was a personal Creator, rather than, say, a material First Cause or a Platonic Form, at the origin of the universe. It is not just that the human personality provides, and has to provide, the model in terms of which we imagine God to ourselves—this was the burden of Mansel's case—it is that unless human agency is somehow outside the ordinary natural course of events, there is no reason why the universe should not be thought of as having a wholly natural origin.

Mill does not so much argue against this view, though he does do so, as complain about the wickedness of resorting to such arguments at all:

the practice of bribing the pupil to accept a metaphysical dogma, by the promise or threat that it affords the only valid argument for a foregone conclusion—however transcendently important that conclusion may be thought to be—is not only repugnant to all the rules of philosophizing, but a grave offence against the morality of philosophic enquiry (438–9).

The only thing about Mill's attack on Hamilton's theology that is of much philosophical interest is negative. Mill does not suggest that a (really or only apparently) contracausal freedom of agency could have appeared in the world by purely natural processes. He insists instead that Hamilton's argument for the existence of God is a poor one compared with his own favoured argument, that from design (439).[61] And he argues against Hamilton that a necessitarian or determinist could believe in God as a First

[60]James Boswell, *Life of Johnson*, ed. George Birkbeck Hill and L. F. Powell, 6 vols. (Oxford: Clarendon Press, 1934–50), II, 82.

[61]See, e.g., "Theism," in *Essays on Ethics, Religion, and Society, Collected Works*, X (Toronto: University of Toronto Press, 1969), 446–52, 456.

Cause with no more difficulty over the First Cause's own origins than the libertarian had. But he does not suggest anything like the kind of theory of emergent properties which might explain the way in which a sufficient degree of, say, neurological complexity and brain capacity causes a change of kind in the determination of action without introducing supernatural causes. The fact has a certain historical interest in showing how little Mill had absorbed of the evolutionary theory which would so naturally have provided him with just such an explanation.

All this, however, is almost by the way. For Mill's aim is to present the positive case for necessitarianism or—since he rejected the idea of any "*must* in the case, any necessity, other than the unconditional universality of the fact" (446)—what he preferred to call determinism. The determinist holds no more complicated a belief than that human actions are not exempt from the causality in terms of which we explain all other phenomena. He hold that "volitions do, in point of fact, follow determinate moral antecedents with the same uniformity, and (when we have sufficient knowledge of the circumstances) with the same certainty, as physical effects follow their physical causes" (446). Mill encourages us to test the belief against evidence, both individual and social, and assures the reader that it is confirmed by the predictability of people's behaviour. Mill, like empiricists before and after him, assumes rather readily that all prediction rests upon knowledge of physical causes. There is no such thing as real unpredictability, no genuine indeterminacy in the facts; all there is is the residual ignorance of the observer. "The cases in which volitions seem too uncertain to admit of being confidently predicted, are those in which our knowledge of the influences antecedently in operation is so incomplete, that with equally imperfect data there would be the same uncertainty in the predictions of the astronomer and the chemist" (446). Such uncertainties do not induce the scientist to abandon his belief in the universal reign of causality, and they ought not to induce anything of the sort in human affairs: "we must reject equally in both cases the hypothesis of spontaneousness . . ." (446).

Hamilton had expressed uncertainty about the revelations of consciousness on the subject of free will. Mill thinks that this is proper, because the only *unchallengeable* deliverances of consciousness are those where there really is no room for error—whatever I now feel, I really do now feel, and cannot think I do not. But freedom is not a matter of current feeling; it is a hypothesis, namely, the hypothesis that I could have done something other than what I actually did do. As a counterfactual, its content is *ex hypothesi* not present to consciousness; so consciousness simply cannot tell us that we are free. Although Mill half credits Hamilton with this realization, he argues that Hamilton sometimes lapses into saying we intuit our own freedom—inconceivable though it is on his own account to do so—and argues that, more interestingly, Hamilton holds that what we intuit is not our *freedom* but rather *our moral responsibility*, in which freedom of the will is implicit. This introduction of the concept of responsibility gives Mill the opportunity to leave Hamilton's case on one side, and to return to the argument with the Owenites which dominates the discussion of freedom and necessity in Book Six of the *Logic*. Mill wishes to distinguish his own, determinist doctrine from two species of Fatalism. The first is pure or Asiatic fatalism, which "holds that our actions do not depend upon our desires. Whatever our wishes may be, a superior power, or an abstract destiny, will overrule them, and compel us to act, not as we desire, but in the manner predestined." (465.) The second doctrine is that of Owenite fatalism, or "Modified Fatalism":

our actions are determined by our will, our will by our desires, and our desires by the joint influence of the motives presented to us and of our individual character; but that, our character having been made for us and not by us, we are not responsible for it, nor for the actions it leads to, and should in vain attempt to alter them (465).

The doctrine Mill held against both varieties of fatalism was not fatalist, merely determinist: that

not only our conduct, but our character, is in part amenable to our will; that we can, by employing the proper means, improve our character; and that if our character is such that while it remains what it is, it necessitates us to do wrong, it will be just to apply motives which will necessitate us to strive for its improvement, and so emancipate ourselves from the other necessity (466).

The Owenites had argued from their position of modified fatalism that it was unjust to punish people, or, which was in their eyes, though not in everyone's, the same thing, that punishment was ineffective as a means of social control and therefore amounted to gratuitous cruelty. The reason why their views on punishment mattered to Mill in the *Examination* was perhaps rather different from the reason why they mattered when he was writing the *Logic*. In his youth, Mill had obviously been very vulnerable to the accusation that his character had been made for him, and not by him, and that he was an artefact of James Mill's designing. The argument in the *Logic* is directed almost entirely to showing that we can improve our characters, that we are not the helpless slaves of antecedent circumstances, and can choose to become something other than we have so far been brought up to be. The discussion in the *Examination* is less passionate. It takes off from the fact that, on Mill's analysis, the idea of responsibility is wholly bound up with the idea of punishment. To show that there is an analysis of responsibility consistent with determinism is, in effect, to show that there is such a thing as just punishment in a determinist world.

Mill accepts that it is unjust to punish people for what they cannot help, or when they could not have acted otherwise than they did. But his analysis of what we mean when we say that a person could have acted otherwise rephrases the statement, in the classical empiricist mould, as a claim that the person would have acted otherwise if he or she had so chosen. That all else could have remained unchanged, and that the person in question should have acted differently, is what Mill denies. When Mansel says that we know that we could have acted differently, even if *everything* else had been the same, Mill agrees, "though the antecedent phænomena remain the same: but not if my judgment of the antecedent phænomena remains the same. If my conduct changes, either the external inducements or my estimate of them must have changed." (448n.) We cannot act against our strongest motive, so freedom must consist in being able to act according to it. Mill goes on to claim that this kind of freedom is entirely consistent with determinism—as it evidently is—and that it is entirely consistent with holding ourselves and others responsible for their actions. Mill begins by insisting that "Responsibility means punishment" (454). He distinguishes at once between two different ways in which we may be said to be liable to punishment.

When we are said to have the feeling of being morally responsible for our actions, the idea of being punished for them is uppermost in the speaker's mind. But the feeling of liability to punishment is of two kinds. It may mean, expectation that if we act in a certain manner, punishment will actually be inflicted upon us, by our fellow creatures or by a Supreme Power. Or it may only mean, knowing that we shall deserve that infliction. (454.)

Mill sees that it is the idea of deserving punishment which needs explaining. Expecting to suffer is very obviously consistent with a complete absence of free will.

Mill, in essence, provides a naturalistic theory of punishment. If a society has some sense of right and wrong, then those who cultivate anti-social dispositions, and threaten the security and well-being of everyone else, will naturally be thought to be behaving wrongly, and will be objects of fear and dislike to everyone else. They will therefore be left out of the distribution of common benefits and will have whatever measures of self-defence others think necessary employed against them. The wrongdoer

is certain to be made accountable, at least to his fellow creatures, through the normal action of their natural sentiments. And it is well worth consideration, whether the practical expectation of being thus called to account, has not a great deal to do with the internal feeling of being accountable; a feeling, assuredly, which is seldom found existing in any strength in the absence of that practical expectation. (455.)

Now it is noticeable here that Mill introduces a consideration which haunts the subsequent discussion of punishment much as, with its contractual overtones, it haunts Mill's account of justice in *Utilitarianism* and much as it haunts *On Liberty*. This is the suggestion that society is founded on some sort of implicit agreement about the reciprocity of good and evil; we get security against the attacks of others in return for our forbearance, and we are punished when we break this agreement. Being practically held to account is a way of having the reciprocal nature of social agreement brought home to us. People who never enter into egalitarian relations cease to have notions like "fair play" in their moral lexicon. The importance of some such conception of justice as fairness is not much developed any-where in Mill's work, though it emerges in Mill's interpretation of what utility requires. Here it emerges in what he says about the retributive element in punishment, and in a rather Kantian interpretation of the con-nection between punishment and the good of the criminal himself.

The main aim of Mill's account, however, is to show how punishment is not shown to be unjust on determinist interpretations of it. After arguing, rather neatly, that even if we believed that the "criminal" class consisted of creatures who had no control at all over their noxious behaviour we should endeavour to control them by measures very like what we now call punishment, he confronts head on the opponent who says that all this is beside the point. The root of the difficulty is a question of justice: "On the theory of Necessity (we are told) a man cannot help acting as he does; and it cannot be just that he should be punished for what he cannot help" (458). Mill's first response to this is at least odd, at worst catastrophic. He says that the claim that the criminal could not help it needs qualification; if he is of vicious temperament, the criminal cannot help committing the crime, but if "the impression is strong in his mind that a heavy punishment will follow, he can, and in most cases does, help it" (458). On this view the threat of punishment is a countervailing motive, which so to speak pushes the criminal in the opposite direction to that in which his criminal character pushes him. Mill's critics all saw that there was something very wrong here, but nobody seems to have pointed out that, on Mill's analysis, anyone who commits a crime can always make precisely the claim that Mill is trying to rebut. If he cannot help doing wrong when he is not threatened, the proper conclusion to draw is that when he is threatened and still offends, those who have threatened him have not done so effectively. If he could not help it, *un*threatened, how can he help it, inadequately threatened?

Mill's great concern to show that we are responsible for our characters may be thought to indicate some awareness of the trouble he had caused himself. The criminal who explains to the court that it is unfortunate that he has such a bad character, but that once he had it, it overwhelmed all the threats the law was prepared to utter, could be told that he had no more business going around with a bad character than he would have had going around with a loaded revolver. The retort, however, will not do much to save Mill's case. Anyone who is faced with that argument can simply respond by saying that without a sufficient motive to improve his character he *could not* improve it; given the initial badness of his character, it was no use looking to any internal motive for change; and as for the absence of an external motive, how could he be blamed for that? Mill, indeed, does not linger on the question of the agent's motives. He turns rather to the question of what makes punishment just. In explaining this, he gives hostages both to fortune and to Kant. Punishment has two proper goals, the good of the criminal and the defence of the just rights of others. If punishment is not inflicted to protect the just rights of others, it is mere aggression on the individual punished. But, many of Mill's readers might wonder, how can he argue that a proper purpose of punishment is to do the offender good? Is not *On Liberty* devoted to denouncing precisely such a claim? And when Mill says: "To punish him for his own good, provided the inflictor has any proper title to constitute himself a judge, is no more unjust than to administer medicine" (458)—is this not in flat contradiction to his attacking Whewell for suggesting that the law on quarantine was for the sufferer's own good?[62] Mill responds to this charge in a long footnote. He seems to see only part of the point, for he begins by saying that of course we punish children for their own good, and we may treat "adult communities which are still in the infantine stage of development" in the same way; but he seems to draw back a little over adult offenders. "And did I say, or did any one ever say, that when, for the protection of society, we punish those who have done injury to society, the reformation of the offenders is not one of the ends to be aimed at, in the kind and mode, at least, of the punishment?" (459n.) There is here, perhaps, a suggestion to the effect that Mill accepts Kant's view that nobody can be punished *simply* to do him good, but that once he forfeits his right to immunity from all punishment, we may properly consider how to reform him when we consider what punishment to inflict.

The same awkwardness emerges when Mill talks of the legitimate defence of our just rights as a ground of punishment. Looked at from society's point of view, it is just to punish offenders who transgress the rights of others, "as it is just to put a wild beast to death (without unnecessary suffering) for the same object" (460). To say this seems precisely to ignore the whole question of the distinction between punishment applied to free moral agents and mere measures of social control applied to non-human

[62]J. S. Mill, *On Liberty*, in *Essays on Politics and Society, Collected Works*, Vols. XVIII and XIX (Toronto: University of Toronto Press, 1977), XVIII, 223; and "Whewell's Moral Philosophy," *CW*, X, 197–8.

creatures. But then Mill moves on to the question of whether the criminal can complain of being treated unjustly, and says that the crucial element in holding ourselves responsible for our actions lies in our recognizing that other people have *rights*. Doing so is, in essence, placing ourselves at their point of view, and if we do so we shall see that there is no injustice in their defending themselves against any disposition on our part to infringe those rights. Once again, the importance of equality emerges in the observation that we shall more readily recognize the justice of their defending their rights by punishing offences against them, the more often we have ourselves stood up for our own rights in this way. Something much nearer an appeal to fairness than to simple utility is evidently at stake.

Thereafter, Mill's account is very like Hume's or, indeed, one may say, like most empiricist accounts. *Mere* retribution is of no value, and would amount to gratuitous cruelty; something like retribution is warranted, as a way of satisfying the natural hostility and outrage which criminal acts arouse in us, but such a justification is instrumental, a case of means-ends argument, and not an appeal with arithmetical overtones to fitness or to an eternal justice. The means-ends arguments for punishment reinforce the determinists' case, for it would evidently be both silly and cruel to inflict punishment where it could not modify behaviour, or to threaten it where it could not do so in prospect. Mill appeals to the same considerations to explain why we should punish only the guilty. If we are aiming to deter people from committing crimes, there is no point in punishing those who have not committed crimes, since there is then no basis for an association of ideas between the crime on the one hand and the punishment on the other.

It goes without saying that Mill raises all sorts of issues that have not been tackled here. The general implausibility of his analysis of responsibility has been argued at length in various other places, and almost every point he makes about motivation, about the justification of punishment, and about the compatibility of freedom and determinism has been the subject of exhaustive, but still quite unexhausted controversy for the past hundred years. A review of these arguments is not necessary here. Two negative points will suffice. It is worthy of notice that Mill does not seem to see that his opponents are groping, even if only dimly, towards the crucial point that what we call punishment is very far from being a means of social control of an obviously utilitarian kind. Why, for example, do we not endeavour to remodel the characters of those who have not yet offended, but who are likely to? Why do we not set penalties for offences for maximum deterrence at minimum cost? So effective would capital punishment be if threatened for parking offences that it is doubtful if more than one or two persons a year would be executed in the whole United States, yet the idea seems absurd. Mill has nothing to say about this issue, perhaps because he takes for granted constraints on the utilitarian calculus which are of rather doubtfully utilitarian origin. Secondly, it is worth noticing that the two places where the *Examination* is at its most interesting and least persuasive are where Mill discusses personal identity and where he analyzes individual responsibility. The reason is easy enough to point to, and extremely hard to explicate. In essence, Mill's epistemology requires us to treat our own selves and our own behaviour as if they are external objects and the behaviour of external objects. We can, of course, treat other persons in this "external" or third-person fashion; we can treat some parts of our past in this way, and, up to a point, our own distant futures. The wholesale assimilation of the first-person and third-person view of the world looks much more problematic. If it *is* essentially an incoherent project, we should expect the incoherence to appear just where it does in the *Examination*, that is, when our view of our own identity is being assimilated to our view of the identity of other persons and objects, and when our control over our own activity is being assimilated to the control we may exercise over things and over other persons. If readers of the *Examination* are unlikely to find it quite such an exemplary work of empiricist self-criticism as Hume's *Treatise of Human Nature*, it will, at least in these respects, stand the comparison.

Textual Introduction

JOHN M. ROBSON

I. BACKGROUND

AN EXAMINATION OF SIR WILLIAM HAMILTON'S PHILOSOPHY is in several respects exceptional among Mill's works. Although he devoted several major essays (such as "Bentham" and "Coleridge"), and one book (*Auguste Comte and Positivism*—originally a pair of essays) to individuals, only here did he subject an author's texts to a searching and detailed analysis, sustained by an admitted polemical intent. Only part of the work is devoted to an exposition of Mill's own views, and a few passages at most could be said to provide the kind of synthesis so typical of his other major writings. The kinds of revisions revealed by collation of the editions are also unusual in two related respects: a much higher proportion than in his other works is devoted to answering critics; and far more of the changes are in the form of added footnotes than is usual for him. Another difference is that the response to the book was immediate and strong: it elicited more reviews and critical replies in a short period of time than his *Principles of Political Economy*, *System of Logic*, and even *On Liberty*. Published in 1865, the first edition (of 1000 copies) sold out so quickly that a second edition was prepared within a couple of months, and a third edition, which was published two years after the first, would have appeared sooner had Mill not wished to answer his critics fully and at leisure. A fourth edition, the last in his lifetime, appeared in 1872 only five years after the third, and the work continued in demand for about twenty years.[1]

As will be shown below, the evidently controversial nature of the argu-

[1]The work is identified in Mill's bibliography as "An Examination of Sir W. Hamilton's Philosophy, and of the Principal Philosophical Questions discussed in his writings. 8vo Volume, first published in 1865." (MacMinn, 96.) In his library, Somerville College, Oxford, is a copy of the first edition, without corrections or changes, and for the most part unopened, and a copy of the two-volume American edition, New York: Holt, 1873.

Fifth and sixth London editions appeared in 1878 and 1889 (the latter also Longmans, New York) while American editions appeared in 1866, 1868 (both Spencer of Boston), 1873, and 1884 (both Holt of New York). A French translation was published in 1869 (Paris), though, surprisingly, there seems to have been no German translation until 1908 (it was not included in the twelve-volume *Gesammelte Werke* edited by Theodor Gomperz).

ment explains much of the demand for the *Examination*; to some extent, however, Mill himself became more widely known at this time. His election campaign of 1865, though it came after both the first and second editions, must have increased the sales to troubled opponents as well as supporters. Also, the extraordinary interest in his other writings in these years added to, as well as reflected, his new prominence.[2]

The content and form of the argument is best seen against at least a brief outline of Mill's interest in and acquaintance with Hamilton's writings— they did not meet one another or, evidently, correspond. Sir William Hamilton (1788–1856), like Mill, was widely known long before any writings appeared under his name; indeed, unlike Mill, he began publishing significant articles anonymously only in his early forties. Described in 1814 to De Quincey by John Wilson as a "monster of erudition,"[3] and remembered as a student at Oxford for his unexampled knowledge of obscure commentators on the Classics, he was elected Professor of Civil History at Edinburgh in 1821, but can hardly have become famous in that capacity, as the emolument soon ceased and he stopped lecturing. In 1829 appeared the first of his fifteen articles in the *Edinburgh Review*, his review of Cousin; one can probably assume that the tribal telegraph began to send the message that Hamilton was "coming out," and Mill in London may soon have known; the Cousin review, coincidentally, appeared in the same number (Vol. L, October, 1829) as the third of Macaulay's attacks on James Mill and Utilitarianism, and so it is almost certain that the younger Mill saw it, even if he did not know who had written it. In any case, the earliest extant reference comes in a letter from Mill to Carlyle of 2 August, 1833, in which he mistakenly assumes that Sir William Hamilton is the "strangest old schoolman (in a new body only forty years old)" to whom Carlyle had talked in the preceding winter. Mill's assumption may have been founded on knowledge that Hamilton was the author of the erudite (but undoubtedly not to Mill persuasive) "Recent Publications on Logical Science" in the *Edinburgh* for April, 1833. Carlyle corrected Mill, saying that he had meant "a *ganz ausgestorbener Mann*," considerably inferior to Hamilton, whom he also had met.[4] It seems very likely that in the next year, after moving to London, Carlyle is referring to the proposed *London Review* and to Mill when he writes to Hamilton to say that there is talk of founding "a new

----

[2]In 1865, in addition to the two editions of the *Examination*, Mill published the periodical and first book editions of *Auguste Comte and Positivism*, the third edition of *Considerations on Representative Government*, the sixth editions of both the *Logic* and the *Principles*, and People's Editions of the *Principles*, *On Liberty*, and *Representative Government*.

[3]See David Masson, ed., *The Collected Writings of Thomas De Quincey*, 14 vols. (Edinburgh: Black, 1889–90), V, 308.

[4]See Francis E. Mineka, ed., *The Earlier Letters of John Stuart Mill, Collected Works*, Vols. XII and XIII (Toronto: University of Toronto Press, 1963), XII, 173 (2/8/33) (henceforth referred to as *EL*, *CW*, with volume and page numbers); and, for Carlyle, Alexander Carlyle,

periodical, gn another than the bibliopolic principle, with intent to show Liberalism under a better than its present rather sooty and ginshop aspect," and that having been asked whether Hamilton might write for it, had "answered, Possible." Hamilton, a strong Whig, writing later to Sarah Austin, indicates cautious interest in such a connection, but says his help could at best be occasional: ". . . I am too much occupied with matters apart from all popular interest, and have in the 'Edinburgh Review' an outlet more than sufficient for any superfluous energy with which I may be distressed."[5] In the event, Hamilton did not contribute to the *London Review* (or the *London and Westminster*), but one may assume that Mill was aware of him from this time on, and would know of his widely discussed election to the Chair of Logic and Metaphysics at Edinburgh in 1836. Mill, however, makes no direct allusion to Hamilton until 1842, when, having virtually finished his *Logic*, he speculates that, if John Austin does not review it for the *Edinburgh*, it is likely that Hamilton will, in a manner "hostile, but intelligent."[6] Still Hamilton had not published a book, but in 1846, ten years later than he had anticipated, his edition of Thomas Reid's *Works* appeared, packed with his own footnotes and supplementary dissertations (the latter oddly and confusingly incomplete, as we shall see). Though he had suffered a severe stroke in 1844, he continued to lecture, and in 1852 published a collection of his review articles, *Discussions on Philosophy and Literature, Education and University Reform*. Mill, who owned the second edition (1853), obviously read it soon after its publication, for he added references to it in the fourth edition of his *Logic* (1856, the year of Hamilton's death). In 1859 Mansel's two-volume edition of Hamilton's *Lectures on Metaphysics* appeared, followed in 1860 by the companion two-volume *Lectures on Logic*.[7]

II. THE WRITING OF THE *EXAMINATION*

AT THIS POINT, one may cite Mill's account in his *Autobiography* of his reasons for turning to Hamilton's philosophy as a subject. (This account, it should be noted, was written in 1869–70, that is, in the years between the

---

ed., *Letters of Thomas Carlyle to John Stuart Mill, John Sterling, and Robert Browning* (London: Unwin, 1923), 61 (18/7/33), and 78 (28/10/33). Mill may also have known that Captain Thomas Hamilton, author of *Man and Manners in America* (1833), was Sir William's brother. (Mill reviewed a review of Captain Hamilton's book in his "State of Society in America," in *Essays on Politics and Society, Collected Works*, Vols. XVIII and XIX [Toronto: University of Toronto Press, 1977], XVIII, 91–115.)

[5]See John Veitch, *Memoir of Sir William Hamilton, Bart.* (Edinburgh: Blackwood, 1869), 128 (letter of 8/7/34), and 175 (letter of 26/11/34).

[6]*EL, CW*, XIII, 528 (to Austin, 7/7/42). In fact, no review appeared.

[7]The order and form of publication of Hamilton's works, and the order in which Mill read them, led to some confusion, as will be seen below.

third and fourth editions of his *Examination*.) He was at that time seeking a subject, feeling, apparently, that he had completed, at least for the time being, all he was able to do of the writing programme he and Harriet had agreed on in the 1850s.[8] In particular, *Considerations on Representative Government* (first and second editions) and *Utilitarianism* (in its periodical form) had appeared in 1861, and *The Subjection of Women*, presumably in almost its final form, had been put aside in readiness for a more propitious occasion for publication. He wrote in Avignon in January, 1862, "The Contest in America," and, after a seven-month trip to Greece and Turkey, in September (one must assume) composed, back in Avignon, a review of Cairnes's *The Slave Power*.[9]

In the *Autobiography*, after mentioning the latter article, he says that the *Examination* was his "chief product" during the "next two years." He had, however, begun serious study and consideration of Hamilton a year earlier, when he read Hamilton's *Lectures* (which he erroneously dates as 1860 and 1861) "towards the end of the latter year, with a half formed intention of giving an account of them in a Review";[10] in fact, he wrote to Alexander Bain in November, 1861, saying that he intended to "take up Sir William Hamilton," and try to make an article on him for the *Westminster Review*.[11] However, he soon decided (actually, within about a month)[12] that to do so "would be idle," for "justice could not be done to the subject in less than a volume." But should he write such a work? On reflection, he thought he should. As he indicates, up to this time he "had not neglected" the *Discussions in Philosophy*,[13] though he had postponed study of the "Notes to Reid" because of "their unfinished state. . . ." Actually, it was not the "Notes" (Hamilton's erudite and lengthy footnotes to passages in his edition of Reid), but the "Supplementary Dissertations" added at the end of the volume that were incomplete.

The story is a very peculiar and confusing one: for reasons that are inadequately given by Mansel in the sixth edition or by Veitch in the *Memoir of Sir William Hamilton*, the first edition, prepared by Hamilton

[8]See the account in the Textual Introduction, *Essays on Ethics, Religion, and Society, Collected Works*, X (Toronto: University of Toronto Press, 1969), cxxii ff.

[9]*Autobiography*, ed. Jack Stillinger (Boston: Houghton Mifflin, 1969), 160–1. The former article was published in *Fraser's* in February, 1862; the latter in the *Westminster* in October, 1862.

[10]*Ibid.*, 161.

[11]Bain, *John Stuart Mill* (London: Longmans, 1882), 118 (cf. Francis E. Mineka and Dwight N. Lindley, eds., *The Later Letters, Collected Works*, Vols. XIV–XVII [Toronto: University of Toronto Press, 1972], XV, 746; subsequently referred to as *LL, CW*, with volume and page numbers). Bain adds that Mill "chose the *Westminster* when he wanted free room for his elbow."

[12]See Bain, *ibid.*, letter of December, 1861 (*LL, CW*, XV, 752): ". . . I have given up the idea of doing it in anything less than a volume."

[13]Presumably Mill is using the short title, and not implying that he had ignored the rest of *Discussions on Philosophy and Literature, Education and University Reform*.

himself, breaks off (as Mill indicates, 3 below) in the middle of a sentence in Note D*** of the "Dissertations," on 914; stereotyped editions appeared in the same form until 1863 (seven years after Hamilton's death), when a sixth (also stereotyped) edition, prepared by Mansel, had a completion (after an insertion in square brackets) of Note D***, and further material.[14] Though intriguing as a bibliographic puzzle, this curiosity would not be worth dwelling on here, had not Mill contributed to the difficulty by mentioning (33n), in a passage added in his fourth edition (1872), that his attention had been drawn to a section (Note N, itself "unfortunately left unfinished") in "the posthumous continuation" of the "Dissertations," and so suggesting, in conjunction with his earlier remark that the work was incomplete, that he had not seen the sixth (expanded) edition of Reid's *Works* until he was preparing his own fourth edition. And Mill added in 1872 another note (255n) quoting from the additional material, again hinting that he had just come across it. However, Mill in fact was aware of the sixth edition when he wrote the *Examination*, for he quotes from the added material in his first edition (1865), mentioning that the passage comes from "one of the fragments recently [i.e., in 1863] published by his editors, in continuation of the Dissertations on Reid" (117). And, referring to Note D***, he says in the first edition, "this Dissertation . . . originally broke off abruptly, but the conclusion . . . has recently been supplied from the author's papers . . ." (251n). Indeed, the first reference in the *Examination* includes the observation that the "Dissertations" leave off, "scarcely half finished," in mid-sentence; to make this judgment, he must have had the other "half" before his eyes.

In any case, it would seem likely that Mill did not carefully study Hamilton's edition of Reid until after his reading of the *Lectures* in late 1861. That reading was to him disappointing, for the *Discussions*, containing Hamilton's "vigorous polemic against the later Transcendentalists, and his strenuous assertion of some important principles, especially the Relativity of human knowledge," had attracted Mill's sympathy and admiration, much as he realized the difference between himself and Hamilton concerning the bases of mental philosophy.[15] "His Lectures," says Mill,

and the Dissertations on Reid dispelled this illusion: and even the Discussions, read by the light which these threw on them, lost much of their value. I found that the

---

[14]The matter is called by Mansel "Supplementary Part, to complete Former Editions," and includes a "Postscript" (989–90), dated 23 August, 1862, explaining (inadequately) the additions; these consist of the remainder of D***, and E-U (there is no J), U*, V-Y (all on 915–88), and "Addenda" (989*–91*).

Another confusion in Mill's mind, excusable only by the actual dates of publication of Hamilton's writings, may be seen in the variants at 163, when Mill in the first edition had Hamilton quoting, in his paper on Brown (1830), from his *Lectures*, which he did not begin to deliver until 1836. But the *Discussions* (including the paper on Brown) were published in 1852, and Mill may not have noticed when Hamilton began his lecturing.

[15]*Autobiography*, 161.

points of apparent agreement between his opinions and mine were more verbal than real; that the important philosophical principles which I had thought he recognised, were so explained away by him as to mean little or nothing, or were continually lost sight of, and doctrines entirely inconsistent with them were taught in nearly every part of his philosophical writings. My estimation of him was therefore so far altered, that instead of regarding him as occupying a kind of intermediate position between the two rival philosophies, holding some of the principles of both, and supplying to both powerful weapons of attack and defence, I now looked upon him as one of the pillars, and in this country from his high philosophical reputation the chief pillar, of that one of the two which seemed to me to be erroneous.[16]

Mill goes on, in a passage of intensity and force, to explain why Hamilton, a man of "imposing character" and "great personal merits and mental endowments," came to embody for him his most resolute enemies, the Intuitionists (he makes special reference to Mansel, paraphrasing his attack in the *Examination* on the immorality of Mansel's view of God), and so to justify "a thorough examination of all [Hamilton's] most important doctrines, and an estimate of his general claims to eminence as a philosopher." Or, in stronger language: "there ought to be a hand-to-hand fight between [the school of Intuition and the school of Experience and Association], . . . controversial as well as expository writings were needed, and . . . the time was come when such controversy would be useful."[17] As he had said to Bain in December, 1861, after having "studied all Sir W. Hamilton's works pretty thoroughly": "The great recommendation of this project is, that it will enable me to supply what was prudently left deficient in the *Logic*, and to do the kind of service which I am capable of to rational psychology, namely, to its Polemik."[18] Much the same attitude was conveyed to George Grote on 10 January, 1862:

My meditations on Sir W. Hamilton's work have shaped themselves into an intention that an examination of his philosophy considered as representative of the best form of Germanism, shall be the subject of the next book I write: for it cannot be done in anything less than a book, without assuming points which it is of great importance to prove. I have tolerably settled in my own mind what I have got to say on most of the principal points.[19]

Presumably he put aside Hamilton during the long trip to Greece referred to above, but with characteristic energy and thoroughness he was back at the task before the end of the year, mentioning in December to Theodor Gomperz his interest in Gomperz's work on the principle of contradiction,

---

[16]*Ibid.*, 161–2.

[17]*Ibid.*, 163.

[18]Bain, *John Stuart Mill*, 118 (*LL*, *CW*, XV, 752). Mill added to the sixth edition (1865) of his *Logic* eleven footnoted references to the *Examination* (cf. the Textual Introduction, *A System of Logic*, *Collected Works*, Vols. VII and VIII [Toronto: University of Toronto Press, 1973], VII, lxxxv and n.).

[19]*LL, CW*, XV, 763. The letter continues: "But I do not feel properly equipped for such a piece of work until I have read your account of Plato, in which I expect to find much new and

for he had "commenced writing something to which a full understanding of that subject is indispensable," and he had not yet thoroughly mastered it.[20] Bain says (without specific dates) that Mill, who was regularly corresponding with him at the time, "read all Hamilton's writings three times over; and all the books that he thought in any way related to the subjects treated of."[21] These included, by early 1863, Mansel's *Limits of Religious Thought* (a "detestable, . . . absolutely loathsome book") and (re-read) Ferrier's *Institutes*.[22] The year of 1863 was not busy by Mill's standards, his only major article being "Austin on Jurisprudence" in the October *Edinburgh*, and the only edition being the first book version of *Utilitarianism*. He spent April and May in Avignon, and then spent the next months in London (with a few days botanizing); he was busy enough socially in those months to express relief to Gomperz on 5 July that his life was "about to relapse into its usual wholesome tranquillity," adding: ". . . I have been enabled to have a few days work at my book on Hamilton with which I now mean to persevere steadily."[23] Returning to Avignon in early September, he was able to tell John Chapman on 5 October that, having finished his review of Austin, he was "at present chiefly writing on metaphysics."[24] To Bain he said on 22 November that he had finished the

valuable thought on the great problems of metaphysics." Though he saw Grote's *Plato* in manuscript, it was not in fact published until 1865, too late to be of use for the *Examination*.

Grote, replying to the letter and refusing Mill's invitation that he join Helen Taylor and himself on a trip to Greece (which its historian never visited), added: "Your intimation of what you had been doing about Sir W. Hamilton's works was still more interesting [than a passage in Lucian mentioned by Mill], as it holds out to me the hope that you may one of these days revert to those higher speculative and logical subjects with which he busies himself." (Harriet Grote, *The Personal Life of George Grote* [London: Murray, 1873], 257.) When the *Examination* appeared, Grote wrote to say: "it has completely answered my expectations, and that is saying as much of it as I *can* say. It is full of valuable expansions of the doctrines more briefly adumbrated in your Logic, and of contributions to the most obscure and recondite expositions of Psychological Science. . . .

"I am certainly very glad that poor Sir W. H. did not live to read such a crushing refutation. It is really so terrible, that I shall be almost pleased if either Mansel or T. S. Baynes are able, on any particular points, to weaken the force of it, and make something of a defence." (*Ibid.*, 275, letter of June, 1865.)

On 20 November, 1865, while writing his review of the *Examination*, Grote praised in particular Mill's treatment of Matter as a Permanent Possibility of Sensation, and his vindication of the derivation of belief in coexistent parts of extension from successive conscious phenomena of motion; here also he notes his pleasure at being able to record his homage to James Mill. (Yale University Library; partly printed in *ibid.*, 278.) Grote's interest in Hamilton continued: not only did he review the *Examination* in the *Westminster*, saying some complimentary things about Hamilton, but also sent Bain a paper on "what Sir William Hamilton says in reference to Aristotle's views of common sense," used by Bain in his *Mental and Moral Science* (1868). (*Ibid.*, 290, letter to Bain of October, 1867.)

[20]*LL, CW*, XV, 809 (14/12/62). The "something" is undoubtedly what became part of Chapter xxi below.

[21]*John Stuart Mill*, 119. Cf. n.30 below.

[22]*LL, CW*, XV, 817 (7/1/63) and 836–7 (13/2/63), both to Bain.

[23]*Ibid.*, 866.

[24]*Ibid.*, 889.

book, "as far as regards the first writing," and would not start rewriting until he had seen Bain's more "matured form" of the analysis of primary qualities (i.e., in the second edition of his *The Senses and the Intellect*).[25] And again, on 4 December, he reports to Henry Fawcett: ". . . I have had little time to think on any scientific subject except Metaphysics, on which I am making good progress in the work I am about."[26]

It is probably to the work of this period that Mill and Bain refer as occasioning Mill's decreased respect for Hamilton after the careful study of his writings. Mill says: "As I advanced in my task, the damage to Sir W. Hamilton's reputation became greater than I at first expected, through the almost incredible multitude of inconsistencies which shewed themselves on comparing different passages with one another."[27] Bain's version is similar: "His picture of Hamilton grew darker as he went on; chiefly from the increasing sense of his inconsistencies. He often wished that Hamilton were alive to answer for himself."[28] This coincidence is not surprising, of course, for Bain had the *Autobiography* by him, as well as Mill's letter of 22 November, 1863, in which the tone is even sharper:

I was not prepared for the degree in which this complete acquaintance lowers my estimate of the man & of his speculations. I did not expect to find them a mass of contradictions. There is scarcely a point of importance on which he does not hold conflicting theories, or profess doctrines which suppose one theory while he himself holds another. I think the book will make it very difficult to hold him up as an authority on philosophy hereafter. It almost goes against me to write so complete a demolition of a brother-philosopher after he is dead, not having done it while he was alive—& the more when I consider what a furious retort I sh[d] infallibly have brought upon myself, if he had lived to make it.[29]

In fact this letter gives us the best picture of Mill's progress. Enclosing a table of contents (now lost), he says that on all these heads he has "written chapters which are not unfit to print even now," though he is, on the basis of "a third consecutive reading of Hamilton's philosophical writings from beginning to end," making "notes for additions & improvements" on the "blank pages" (i.e., the versos) of the manuscript. And he continued with

[25]*Ibid.*, 900. For the use made of Bain, see 216–19, 226–7, and 231–6 below.
[26]*Ibid.*, 907.
[27]*Autobiography*, 163.
[28]*John Stuart Mill*, 119. See also Mill's response (124n) to the defence by the "Inquirer" of inconsistencies in Hamilton. It is at the least ironical that Mill himself has been so much assailed for inconsistencies; of course, no one escapes hanging, if not on this charge, then on its opposite, purblind single-mindedness. And some critics wish Mill were alive to answer other of his critics.
[29]*LL, CW*, XV, 901–2. Mill was undoubtedly right in his concluding conjecture (and cf. the regret he expresses in his "Introductory Remarks," 2–3 below); Veitch comments, understating the case, that Hamilton "was fond of controversial writings, and enjoyed the learned railings of the Scioppian style" (46).

his reading, asking Bain for information about Immanuel von Fichte, Vogt, and Moleschott (none of whom, incidentally, was demonstrably to influence his views).[30]

The next year, 1864, also saw little publication by Mill, with no major essays or new works, only the second edition of *Utilitarianism* and the third of *On Liberty* appearing (both with the most trivial of revisions), and it may reasonably be argued that most of his working time in the first half of the year was given to rewriting the *Examination*, both in Avignon and London.[31] Writing to Bain on 18 March, 1864, to thank him for the second edition of his *The Senses and the Intellect*, Mill says that the "remaining portion" of the *Examination* will—presumably as a result of Bain's work—"now be plain sailing." And, after discussing related matters at length, he concludes by saying that he hopes to have "at least some chapters of the Hamilton in a state to shew" to Bain in June.[32] He notified Gomperz in June that, after hard work, the book was "well advanced towards completion,"[33] and he was able to let Bain read "the finished MS. of a large part of the book," on which Bain made "a variety of minor suggestions," and Mill "completed the work for the press the same autumn."[34] Though we do not know when he approached Longman, by late October he told Augustus De Morgan that he anticipated publication in the spring of 1865,[35] and his attention had turned to his articles on Comte, which were finished in February, and appeared in the *Westminster* for April and July, 1865.

The *Examination* was published in an edition of 1000 copies on 13

[30]*LL, CW*, XV, 901–2. Such insights as we have into Mill's habits of composition, being rare, are worth citing. See, for example, Mill's letter to Bain of 7/1/63, where he mentions going "deliberately through the whole writings of Hamilton, writing down in the form of notes, the substance of what I as yet find to say on each point. This will make it comparatively easy to write the book when I have finished the preparatory work." (*LL, CW*, XV, 816.) See also a footnote added in 1867, where Mill (presumably ironically) thanks Mansel for reminding him of two passages he would "not have failed to quote" in the first edition, if he "had kept references to them" (22n). What he sometimes did (as did his father) was to list page numbers in the backs of books, presumably to return to them later to make notes; there are surviving only a very few (and none of them here relevant) of what must have been voluminous copied quotations. There is no evidence that (here unlike his father) he kept a Commonplace Book containing quotable passages.

[31]He returned to London in mid-February, went back to Avignon in April, travelled back to London in June, stayed there until early September, and then passed the rest of 1864 and most of January, 1865, in Avignon.

[32]*LL, CW*, XV, 926, 929.

[33]*Ibid.*, 945 (26/6/64).

[34]*John Stuart Mill*, 120. Cf. Mill to Gomperz: "My book on Hamilton is now finished, with the exception of a final revision which I shall give it a few months hence before sending it to press" (*LL, CW*, XV, 954; 22/8/64).

[35]*LL, CW*, XV, 963 (28/10/64). He here is looking forward to De Morgan's paper on Infinity, because, as he says, the topic is touched on in the *Examination* (where De Morgan's paper is not mentioned).

April,[36] and by the end of the month had sold four hundred copies;[37] a second edition also of 1000 copies was called for, revised, printed, and published by 24 July.[38] As the surviving correspondence and the printed record demonstrate, Mill soon was engaged in replying to friend and foe, and the debate, private and public, continued for some years. He wrote, during its later phase:

It was my business however to shew things exactly as they were, and I did not flinch from it. I endeavoured always to treat the philosopher whom I criticized with the most scrupulous fairness; and I knew that he had abundance of disciples and admirers to correct me if I ever unintentionally did him injustice. Many of them accordingly have answered me, more or less elaborately; and they have pointed out oversights and misunderstandings, though few in number, and mostly very unimportant in substance. Such of those as had (to my knowledge) been pointed out before the publication of the latest edition (at present the third) have been corrected there, and the remainder of the criticisms have been, as far as seemed necessary, replied to.[39]

The year 1865 having been extremely busy for Mill, 1866 was even more demanding, as his parliamentary duties, which for him meant constant mental as well as physical presence, speeches, and heavy responsibilities outside the House in connection with the Jamaica Committee and the Hyde Park riots, occupied a great deal of his time. In that year also his "Grote's Plato," a short book in itself, appeared, as did the slightly revised second edition of *Auguste Comte and Positivism*. But he found time to read and consider the responses to the *Examination*, and to report on them to Grote[40] and to Bain, the latter of whom says that Mill, after the close of the session in August, and a subsequent tour of the Alps and Pyrenees, settled down in Avignon to write his Rectorial Address for St. Andrews, and "to answer the attacks on Hamilton for the third edition; both which feats he accomplished before the opening of the session of 1867"[41] in February. Mill

[36]Longman Chronological Register, 1860–77, f. 56, in the Longman Archive, University of Reading. On 11 March, he told Herbert Spencer he would soon offer him a copy of the work which (he vainly hoped) would contain "little or nothing to qualify the expression of the very high value I attach to your philosophical labours" (*LL, CW*, XVI, 1011).

[37]*LL, CW*, XVI, 1041 (to Longman, 30/4/65).

[38]Longman Chronological Register, 1860–77, f. 60. (Longman Impression Book 15, f. 158, gives August, but the Division Book for the period, also in the Longman Archive, confirms the July dating.) See also *LL, CW*, XVI, 1090–1 (to Spencer, 12/8/65), which concerns the note dealing with Spencer's repudiation of part of Mill's account of his views, the note being appended to the second edition of the *Examination* (Mill saw Spencer's review too late for other treatment), and then placed where it belongs in the third edition (see 143 below).

[39]*Autobiography*, 163–4. Not all of Hamilton's students, it may be noted, were unequivocally opposed to Mill's views, for Fraser and Masson, as Mill indicates in his Preface, were not in agreement with most of the Edinburgh alumni.

[40]See *LL, CW*, XVI, 1223 (25/12/66), which refers to Mill's desire to identify Grote as the author of the *Westminster* article on the *Examination*, and also to Bolton's *Inquisitio Philosophica*. And cf. *ibid*., 1068 (18/6/65).

[41]*John Stuart Mill*, 124.

was aware of the need for a third edition in April of 1866,[42] but (with Longman's concurrence) decided not to rush the rewriting,[43] and had "got through fully three fourths of the revision" by the end of the year.[44] Though the edition (again of 1000 copies) was not published until May,[45] it seems likely that, as Bain says, he had finished the revision before his return to London for the session, because early in February he told W. G. Ward, towards whom he always showed more than courtesy, that he would not be able in the revision to take account of Ward's "Science, Prayer, Free Will, and Miracles," even if he immediately saw proof of it.[46]

The volume continued to sell, though more slowly: as Longman Division Books show, by June, 231 copies were disposed of, and in the next twelve months, till June, 1868, another 232. In the following twelve-month periods 162, 161, 141, and 148 were sold, so that by June, 1872 (what with some wastage and copies otherwise distributed), there were only twenty-seven copies left.

Further replies and discussions appeared in these years, and the French translation by Cazelles, published in 1869, brought forth notices in France. Mill proceeded with the substantial task of replying to critics, presumably reading and pondering the responses as they appeared. When he turned his hand to the actual revision we do not know, it being likely that, as usual, he waited until it was evident that a new edition was needed, which, as the account books suggest, was probably during 1871, there being only 176 copies on Longman's hands by June of that year. In any case, he wrote to Cairnes in April of 1872 to say that, as well as rereading and (to our regret) culling old letters, he had been "correcting proofs for new editions" of the *Logic* (the eighth, which appeared in July) and the *Examination* (the fourth, our copy-text, which appeared in October).[47]

III. THE REVISIONS

COMMENTING ON MILL'S REPLIES in the third edition "to the host of critics" who had assailed the *Examination*, Bain says, with justice: "The additional scope given to the author's polemical ability greatly enhanced the interest

[42]*LL, CW*, XVI, 1161 (to Longman, 28/4/66); only 150 copies were then still in hand (Longman to Mill, 25/4/66; British Library of Political and Economic Science, Mill-Taylor Collection, I, #96, f. 226). By June the stock was down to 117 copies (Division Book).

[43]Longman to Mill (30/4/66), Mill-Taylor Collection, I, #95, ff. 223–4.

[44]*LL, CW*, XVI, 1223 (to Grote, 25/12/66).

[45]On 26 May he promised to send J. E. Cairnes a copy on publication (*ibid.*, 1271), but Longman Chronological Register, f. 79, gives 16 May as the date of publication, and is supported in the May dating by the Division Book.

[46]*Ibid.*, 1238 (9/2/67), and 1239 (11/2/67).

[47]*Ibid.*, XVII, 1879 (6/4/72), and Longman Impression Book 18, f. 238.

of the book."[48] Indeed the temper, the tone, and to a significant extent the focus of the work were altered by the revisions in the third and fourth editions. As is so often the case, Mill's own comments in his Preface to the third edition (and those added there in the fourth) give no clear guidance to his rewriting and imply that much less took place than is the actual case. In 1867 he wrote:

Where criticism or reconsideration has convinced me that anything in the book was erroneous, or that any improvement was required in the mode of stating and setting forth the truth, I have made the requisite alterations. When the case seemed to require that I should call the reader's attention to the change, I have done so; but I have not made this an invariable rule. Mere answers to objectors I have generally relegated to notes. . . . A slight modification in a sentence, or even in a phrase, which a person unacquainted with the former editions might read without observing it, and of which, even if he observed it, he would most likely not perceive the purpose, has sometimes effaced many pages of hostile criticism. (cvi.)

And in the fourth edition he calls attention only to the two corrections deriving from Veitch and a reply to Ward (see the discussion below).

The changes were very considerable indeed. Using the crudest of measures, the number of pages,[49] to give a sense of the amount of change, one finds that the first and second editions are of the same length, 560 pages of text.[50] The third, however, has 633 pages (an additional 73, or 13 per cent), and the fourth has 650 (a further 17 pages, or 3 per cent). This measure even on its own terms seriously underestimates the amount of addition, for much of the new material—far more than in any other of Mill's heavily revised works—is in footnotes, set in very small type with minimal leading.[51]

Substantive variants. As the account just given would indicate, the second edition was very little revised. Of the total of almost five hundred substantive variants in all editions, fewer than forty occurred in the second edition, almost all of them being very minor revisions of wording in the text. The great bulk of the changes, some 345, or just over 70 per cent, were

[48]*John Stuart Mill*, 128.

[49]The format and type sizes remained constant through the editions, which were all printed by the same firm, Savill and Edwards (Savill, Edwards and Co. for the third and fourth editions). The principals in the firm of Longmans were, as might be expected, playing managerial chairs during these years: the first edition (1865) was published by Longman, Green, Longman, Roberts, and Green; the second edition (a few months later in 1865), by Longmans, Green, and Co.; the third—and, surprisingly, the fourth—(1867 and 1872) by Longmans, Green, Reader, and Dyer.

[50]Actually, the note concerning Spencer, mentioned above, appears on page 561 of the second editon, but became, as Mill intended, an incorporated footnote in subsequent editions.

[51]The count is also misleading because each of the editions was totally reset and, even though the type sizes were maintained, the proportions of text and footnotes were in some cases altered, resulting, with some changes to and from long and short pages, in different amounts of blank space at the ends of chapters. And, of course, with the additions, those blank spaces varied in size from edition to edition.

made in the third edition, and of these nearly one-third were added footnotes or parts of footnotes. The fourth edition accounts for the remaining one hundred odd variants, with an even larger proportion (about two-fifths) being either added footnotes or parts of footnotes (the latter being here more significant than in the third edition, as Mill responded to criticisms of replies he had added in notes in 1867).

For purposes of comparison as well as analysis, one may classify the variants into four groups: (1) major alterations, involving changes of opinion, the introduction of new information, and responses to criticism; (2) changes resulting from the passage of time; (3) qualifications and clarifications of a minor kind, generally involving semantic shifts; and (4) minor changes in syntax, changes entailed by other changes, italicization, terminal punctuation, and merely referential footnotes. In Mill's other works one finds, as would be expected, a great preponderance of changes of the third and fourth kinds; in the *Examination*, however, there are as many of the first kind as of the fourth (just over 180 in each case), comparatively fewer of the third kind (120), so typical of Mill elsewhere, and only a handful (8) of the second kind. What may appear strange about this pattern disappears on closer inspection: the vast majority of the type (1) changes (two-thirds of which occur in notes) are responses to critics of a kind rare even in the *Logic* and the *Principles*. The paucity of type (2) changes of a simple sort is explained by the relatively short time (seven years) from the first edition to the last in Mill's lifetime, and by the nature of the text, which is such as virtually to preclude comments that would be affected by the passage of a few years. As to the slightly smaller percentage of type (3) changes, it may be noted that while such changes are found in virtually everything republished by Mill, the greatest volume of them occurs in editions revised in the early 1850s.

The distribution of the changes within the work is informative, but before turning to such questions it is worth citing a few examples to illustrate in general the sort of revision that Mill engaged in, and to call attention to some features that might otherwise not be strongly evident. As indicated above, most of what have been counted as type (1) changes are in response to criticism. As an illustration of those occurring in footnotes, one may cite 32n–3n, added in the third edition like most of the other notes not found in the first edition, where Mill quotes Alexander Fraser in support of his position, as against Mansel and the anonymous reviewer in the *North American Review*, and goes on to differ from Fraser's interpretation of Hamilton. The note includes (32^{t-t}) a variant arising from a type (3) revision (a qualification) in the fourth edition, and concludes with a lengthy passage added in the fourth edition, arising from the continuation of Hamilton's "Dissertations on Reid" having been called to Mill's attention (a matter discussed at lxxiii above). This note is typical of others in its length, in its dealing with more than one critic (and issue), and in its containing elements from both the third and fourth editions.

Of the major changes that occur in the text rather than the notes, several may be cited to illustrate different motivations and results. Very few passages were deleted; one of the longest instances (as usual, deriving from the third edition) occurs at 19^e—but in fact the deletion is only seemingly made, for, in revised form, most of the text is used in the long addition, 20^{g-g22}, which shows Mill responding to the criticisms of John Cunningham and Mansel. (An actual deletion of considerable length will be seen at 189^f.) Another long addition in the text, exceptional in its length, but again typical in dealing with more than one critic (four in this case) and deriving from the third edition, will be seen at 24^{m-m32}. An interesting example of a more temperate or cautious judgment is seen at 82^n, where (discussing Hamilton's views of antinomies) Mill originally commented: "I think he has failed to make out either point", but in the third edition deleted the sentence. Actually this change is related to others occurring later in the chapter (see 88n and 87^{c-c}), where the justification will be found. (The footnote on 81 is one of the few where Mill mentions what he had said "in the first edition"; actually in these cases—which are not full retractions—the matter appeared in both the first and second editions.)

Most of these examples, as mentioned above, relate to criticism, though seldom does Mill admit to actual mistakes in fact or judgment (in the last example, he refers merely, 88n, to "an over-statement"); there are a few places, however, where he makes—not in a full spirit of repentance—revisions. His controversy with John Veitch, Hamilton's biographer, to which further reference will be made below, led to Mill's admission in the Preface to the fourth edition (cvii–cviii below) that he had made two "errors" which, though they did not "affect anything of importance in the criticism" of Hamilton's interpretation of Aristotle, needed correction. These may be seen in Mill's last chapter, at 503^{k-k} and 503n, in the first of which Mill silently added "by the editors," in response to Veitch's complaint that Hamilton was not guilty of mistaking the meaning of an Aristotelian term, his editors having searched out a passage to bear out his text. The second of these changes is almost parallel, except that here Mill mentions Veitch and the accusation, and goes on to say that the editors "would have done more wisely by making no reference, than one which so totally fails to support the inference drawn from it" (503n).[52] Another interesting correction will be seen at 143n and $^{p-p}$: Mill, as always, had assumed that in mentioning Herbert Spencer he would give no offence; Spencer, as always,

---

[52]See also xci–xcii below.

took offence; and Mill, as always, hastened to apologize—without giving very much away.

Another kind of variant included in type (1) reflects Mill's work on his other writings. Most evident here are additions bearing a relation to his "Bailey on Berkeley's Theory of Vision" and "Berkeley's Life and Writings."[53] The former appeared in *Dissertations and Discussions*, Vol. II, which Mill revised for its second edition (March, 1867), just before completing his revision of the *Examination* for its third edition (May, 1867). It is therefore reasonable to assume that the adding in the third edition of 178[a-a] was the result of his having just looked carefully over this article, especially if one compares 178[a-a] with pages 249–50 and 255 of the article.[54] Similarly, the later article, "Berkeley's Life and Writings" (published in November, 1871), was fresh in Mill's mind when he revised the *Examination* for its fourth edition (1872), and surely one may assume that his reading for that article is reflected in the additions in 1872 seen at 163[g-g] and 230[s-s] (with the second, cf. "Berkeley's Life and Writings," 456–7). A variant connected in subject matter with these is of a slightly different sort: in the third edition a reference was added 236[z-z] to Thomas Nunneley's *On the Organs of Vision*, published in 1858, which (given that date) Mill could have mentioned (it would have been apposite) in revising "Bailey on Berkeley" (see, e.g., 263–5 of that article) in 1867, but did not. Nunneley is mentioned, however, in the passage (454–7) of "Berkeley's Life and Writings" that treats of the same issue.

A regrettably frequent source of confusion for readers wishing to identify or check Mill's references may be illustrated by 85n, added in the third edition, and modified in three places in the fourth. The note begins: "Mr. Mansel replies (p. 134) . . ."[55]—but Mill does not here say to which of Mansel's works he refers (he quotes from four in the *Examination*). Admittedly, if readers knew that the note had been added in 1867 they would have been likely to guess that Mill was citing *The Philosophy of the Conditioned*, which appeared in 1866 as a reply to the *Examination*. Even if that guess had been correctly made, however, the reader would hardly suspect that the final two sentences of the note were added in 1872 (see 85[v-v]), and the reference therein ("Mr. Mansel says we do . . .") is to Mansel's reply to Mill's third edition in his "Supplementary Remarks," in the *Contemporary Review* for September, 1867. (Compare the long foot-

---

[53]These essays are in *Essays on Philosophy and the Classics, Collected Works*, XI (Toronto: University of Toronto Press, 1978), 245–69, and 449–71.

[54]One may also infer that this double consideration kept the matter in Mill's mind when one looks at "Berkeley's Life and Writings," 455 and n.

[55]Here one sees another example of a softened tone: in the first edition the sentence began: "Mr. Mansel, entirely missing the point of this argument . . ." (see 85[t], and cf. [u-u]).

note, 76n–7n, where Mill in the fourth edition, without notice, sandwiches between two passages of the third edition three sentences, including a quotation, referring simply to Mansel's "rejoinder"—i.e., again the essay in the *Contemporary Review*.) Similar problems must have beset careful readers when Mill does not indicate that he is referring to two of McCosh's works at, for example, 75n, where there is a footnote compounded of 1867 and 1872 passages, in which, again, neither title is given.

Actually Mill was aware (how could he not have been?) of the desirability of indicating that certain passages had been added subsequent to the first publication. He wrote to Augustus De Morgan in 1865: "I have sometimes thought I ought to have some mark for alterations and additions. But one could scarcely give distinctive marks to all the successive strata of new matter, and a mere note of distinction from the edition immediately previous would not answer the [purposes of] those readers who only possess a still earlier one."[56] In the third edition of the *Examination* he in fact made a much less than half-hearted attempt, and, alas, a misleading one, to indicate added footnote material. Of the more than one hundred footnotes or parts of footnotes that were added to the third edition, some ten are parts of notes, and of these four appeared in 1867 between square brackets.[57] And in 1872, of some twenty parts added to notes, five were placed between square brackets.[58] Unfortunately, not only is the device used sporadically for parts of notes and not at all for full notes and the text, but also it is unexplained and confusing (there is no distinction, for example, in the fourth edition between additions made in 1867 and those made in 1872). Even assuming that Mill intended to indicate only additions within footnotes that he considered important (and here one would want to challenge his judgment), examination reveals problems. For example, in the footnote that appears below on 71–4, the paragraph on 72n, running "Hardly . . . spare." and that on 74n, running "The 'Geometry of Visibles' . . . truths." were added in 1867 as the contiguous concluding paragraphs to a note found in the first and second editions; Mill placed square brackets around them. However, in 1872 he added six paragraphs between those two, placed square brackets around those added in 1872, and deleted those around the two added in 1867. So the indication of the earlier addition (an indication he evidently thought important in 1867) is lost, even to anyone trying to understand the device, and such a person would also, at least *prima facie*,

---

[56]*LL, CW*, XVI, 1108 (25/10/65). The method (described below) of recording variants in this edition meets Mill's criteria, but one dare not infer that he would therefore approve of it.

[57]In this edition the passages appear at 45n, 72n–4n, 216n–17n, 463n, where they are signalled (as are all variants) by superscript letters keyed to variant notes on the page. Much as one would have liked to adopt Mill's method, it is, as the account above will hint, and any attempt to apply it will show, woefully inadequate.

[58]See 72n–4n, 74n, 93n–4n, 107n, 421n.

assume that the unbracketed portions of the note all date from the same edition. Another confusing instance is that at 93n–4n, where the square brackets were added in 1872 to a passage introduced in 1867 without brackets; uniquely, the brackets here evidently signal the rewriting that occurred for the fourth edition.[59]

Some of the type (1) changes, it will be noted, entail other changes, which have been counted as type (4). An example is to be found at 154^{c-c}, where in 1872 an addition to the footnote of a needed explanation of Mill's judgment that a particular element in Kant's reasoning is "strangely sophistical" resulted in the deletion of that characterization from the text (154^b).[60] Similarly, the footnote added in 1867 to 266 (a response to Mahaffy's argument), entailed (as Mill therein explains) the addition of "persistent" to the text (266^{i-i}).[61] It need hardly be mentioned that many additions and revisions, especially the longer ones, brought with them referential footnotes, which similarly have been counted as type (4) variants (see, e.g., 24n, which results from 24^{m-m32}).

Before leaving the type (1) variants, one may mention a few of a minor kind. One of these shows Mill as sharing the frailties of most people: on 386, in an illustrative logical example, he (carelessly?) said, "A dolphin is a fish"; sometime before the third edition the error was caught, and "herring" swam into the dolphin's place. And finally, the added reference in 1867 to Whately's *Logic* at 410^{a-a} may indicate that he had again looked at that work so important in his mental history—or, of course, someone such as Alexander Bain (then working on his own *Logic*) may have mentioned the appositeness of the citation.

Type (2) changes, that is, those resulting from the passage of time, being rare in the *Examination*, may be dealt with briefly. One obvious type, reflecting a changed status (or a change in Mill's knowledge of status) may be seen at 92^{d-d}, where "Mr. Calderwood" becomes "Dr. Calderwood" in 1867, and at 164^{k-k} and 165^{l-l}, where Ward's doctorate is similarly recognized in 1872.[62] The reasons for other changes of this type are less easy to

---

[59]This passage is even more confusing, for Mill adds a mention (without title or page) to Mansel's "rejoinder," while retaining the original reference (with title and page), which appears to apply to the (unsignalled) new citation.

[60]It could be argued that the added part of the note is a type (3) change; as will be evident, the categorization is more useful than certain.

[61]The change in the text would be treated as type (3) (a qualification) were it not for the explanation in the note.

[62]Calderwood was given a LL.D. by Glasgow in 1865 (subsequent to Mill's first edition). The case of Ward is somewhat more puzzling, for the honorary degree of Doctor of Philosophy had been conferred on him by Pope Pius IX in 1854, long before the first edition of the *Examination*. How or when Mill became aware of the dignity is not known (he addressed Ward in letters simply as "Dear Sir"), and we are forced to fall back on R. H. Hutton's amusing animadversions on the matter: " 'Ideal' Ward was his Oxford nickname; 'Squire Ward' was his

establish: at 116^f a reference to his father changes in 1867 from "Mr. Mill" to simply "Mill";[63] and in 1872 at 216^f, "Professor Bain, of Aberdeen," loses his institutional identification.[64] It is also puzzling to see that Mill added an apposite reference (217^{h-h}) to his *Auguste Comte and Positivism* (published in 1865) in 1872, rather than in 1867.[65] The added reference in 1872 to Cazelles's writings at 250^{a-a} is easier to explain—at least until one tries (in our case almost in vain) to identify exactly which published (rather than proposed) works Mill intends. An example of the interesting kind of type (2) change found frequently in the *Logic* is seen at 422^{d-d}, where Mill mentions, in 1867, that there had been "developments of the doctrine of the Unity of Force" since Hamilton's death.

Moving to type (3) changes, those involving qualifications, we may begin with one very typical of Mill's revisions: at 280^{g-g}, in the second edition, he added the words "appear to" in the passage asserting that Pasteur's "important experiments . . . appear to have finally exploded the ancient hypothesis of Equivocal Generation. . . ."[66] Other examples of his continuous search for the precisely correct way of expressing uncertainty are quite common: see, for example, 8$^{e-e, f-f, g-g}$, where in 1867 "we should know" becomes "we might know", and "since the new impressions would doubtless be linked with the old" becomes "if the new impressions were linked with the old". For further illustration of Mill's habit of mind, see 183^{k-k} ("unintentional" added before "sanction" in 1867), 188^{c-c} ("an even" substituted in 1872 for "a much" before "more unqualified manner", in what may be called a combined precept and example as Mill tries to avoid the imputed sin), 213^{b-b} ("(as I believe, with nearly all philosophers)" modified

title in the Isle of Wight, where he had estates; 'Dr. Ward' was the description by which he was best known to the Catholic theologians; while his friends knew him simply as Mr. Ward." Later, Hutton says of the Metaphysical Society (founded in 1869), "There, indeed, he was 'Dr.' Ward . . ." (quoted in Wilfrid Ward, *William George Ward and the Catholic Revival* [London and New York: Macmillan, 1893], 375 and 378). But Mill refused to join the Metaphysical Society, and one cannot suggest that he ceased to regard Ward as a friend.

[63]Changes of the contrary kind occur in other of Mill's works, for example in the *Logic* (*CW*, VIII, 649^{e-e}) where "Mr. Mill" became "Mr. James Mill" in 1868, presumably to make what had become a necessary distinction; were it not for these changes elsewhere, one might assume that the revision in the *Examination* was simply a third edition correction of the erroneously maintained courtesy (a Freudian slip?) to the living in the first edition.

[64]Perhaps it was no longer needed, because Bain—though still at Aberdeen—had gained, in Mill's view, national (at least) celebrity.

[65]The addition is to part of a note added in 1867, which could just as easily at that date have concluded with the reference. The 1867 change is in one of those additions marked off by square brackets in a footnote; here again the diligent reader of the fourth edition will be confused, for the brackets were retained in 1872, with the further addition placed inside them.

[66]It is just possible—illustrating the problems of a nearly impressionistic classification—that we have here a type (2) change: was there some discussion (unknown to us) of the reliability of Pasteur's work that came to Mill's attention in the brief period between the first and second editions?

to "as I believe (with the great majority of philosophers)"), and 237^a (the removal of "fully" in 1867, in a change whose significance becomes apparent when one reads 237n–8n, also added in 1867). The example at 397^{f-f} is interesting in that it shows a reversion to an earlier reading of a single word which might be taken (on that ground as well as on the ground of sense) as a typographical error (and is so questioned in the variant note), but which could represent a hesitancy over a legitimate choice of words ("subject" was altered to "object" in the second edition, with "subject" being restored in the third).

A type (3) change of a significant kind, representing a search after more precise expression of a concept, may be seen at 220^{i-i}, where Mill says (in 1865) of Brown and others who held the psychological theory: "Their argument is not, as Sir W. Hamilton fancied, a fallacious confusion between two meanings of the word length, but an identification of them as one", and (in 1867), substituting a semi-colon for the last comma, replaces the last clause with: "they maintain the one to be the product of the other."[67] Compare, as a type, 141^{m-m}, where the original wording, "the time at which memory commences", was altered (in the fourth edition) to the more accurate, "the time to which memory goes back". Another slight example of the kind found in larger number in works more often revised by Mill is seen in the double change at 178^{c-c}: here Mill originally wrote, "there is in our perceptions"; in the second edition he altered the wording to "there is involved in our perceptions"; and he settled, in the third, for "there is concerned in our perceptions".

One final illustration of type (3) changes points again to Mill's frequent tempering of judgments in what, at this stage in the controversy and in his career, cannot be seen as mere caution. At 480^{d-d} he first published his opinion of a blunder in this form: "If Sir W. Hamilton could think so, his ignorance of the subject must have been greater than can be imputed to any educated mind, not to speak of a philosopher." In 1867, rewriting of the first part of the sentence produced a still stern, but less particular and insulting condemnation: "to think so would require an ignorance of the subject greater than can be imputed to any educated mind, not to speak of a philosopher."

There is no need to dwell on the type (4) variants, which on the whole reflect the sort of revision in which anyone engages who tries to make syntax more transparent and emphasis more obvious. A few, however, may be cited, just to suggest the effect of such fine tuning, and to show that some are not entirely trivial. At 175^{s-s} the change (one of the rare second-

---

[67]This is seen as a type (3) rather than a type (1) variant because it does not evidently indicate either a change of judgment or new information; it will be evident, of course, that a very indistinct line divides the two classes.

edition variants) from "nothing different in it from his own" to "nothing in it different from his own" clearly makes the sentence easier to read. Throughout the volume Mill habitually uses the first-person singular, and seems to have been more careful than many of his "cotemporaries" in saving the first-person plural for editorial (as well as normal) usage: it is therefore slightly surprising to find "we" at 136^{i-i}, but not at all surprising to see that "I" replaced it in 1867. Simple removal of unnecessary emphasis is seen at 6^{a-a} and 7^{d-d}, where italics were removed from "outside" and "something" in 1867. One variant of moot significance—it could even be considered a type (1)—is found at 458^{r-r}, where "On the theory of Necessity (we are told) man cannot help acting as he does" is modified by the perhaps trivial and perhaps important insertion of "a" before "man".[68]

A major problem for editors (though not for most more fortunate folk) lies in deciding which changes in a text should be seen as minor variants and which as printer's errors.[69] Some examples where the latter choice was made are 119.31 and 35,[70] 348.11,[71] 382.14,[72] 478.21[73] and 483.19.[74] Examples of the former choice, that is, where the evidence and/or sense suggest that a variant reading is useful (even when, in some cases, a typographical error is almost certain), are 42^{q-q}, 306^{a-a},[75] 289^{b-b}, and 382^{f-f}.[76] It is virtu-

---

[68]Since Mill is reporting others' views, the change is *prima facie* less significant than the variant in the People's Edition of *On Liberty* where the shift from species to individual has a much more marked effect on the sense. See *Essays on Politics and Society, CW*, XVIII, 224.37, and XIX, 657.

[69]An explanation of the decisions made here will be found in the headnote to Appendix B.

[70]Mill's square brackets indicating (though he does not explain that they do so) tampering with Hamilton's text were placed correctly in the first and second editions: i.e., the text read as it is here printed, "*that* I [believe]" and "conscious of [the". In the third edition the reading (retained in the fourth) was "that [I believe]" and "conscious [of the ".

[71]In the first and second editions (the reading here accepted), Archbishop Whately is noted to have said that Logic is both a Science and an Art "in an intelligible sense." In the third and fourth editions, in what at first glance is acceptable, the sentence ends, "is an intelligible sense."

[72]The reading in the first three editions (the final colon introduces a quotation from Hamilton) is: "Sir W. Hamilton, therefore, needs another kind of argument to establish the doctrine that the Laws of Identity, Contradiction, and Excluded Middle, are laws of all existence: and here we have it:" but in the fourth edition "leave" replaces "have" in the last clause. Here again at first glance the final reading is plausible (partly because of the uncertain reference of "it," which, if taken to refer to "doctrine," would make the final reading more intelligible, but which, if—as seems right—taken to refer to "argument" makes the original reading more likely), but is rejected in our text.

[73]Only slightly less plausible than the previous two examples is the mistaken substitution here in 1867 of "qualities" for "quantities."

[74]The omission or misplacing of quotation marks in the passage from Hamilton concerning Descartes makes it extremely difficult to determine who is being quoted; the difficulty becomes an impossibility because of Hamilton's errors in translation and ascription, until his sources are consulted.

[75]The reason for listing these as variants is consideration for the reader, hypothesized by Mill in a passage quoted above, who may own an early edition that he wishes to compare, and

ally certain that the printer misread Mill's hand in places, but in general it seems wisest to adopt the conservative principle of retaining what appears in the printed text, except where there is strong evidence; some such cases of caution are revealed if one looks at the collation of Mill's quotations with their sources, as at 203n.5 and 8, where the compositor read (and we print) "any," where O'Hanlon, whom Mill is quoting, has "my." A pair of typographical errors deserve mention because they signal the existence of two states of Gathering K in the fourth edition: in the correct state, at 103.35 the reading is "But if what I am told", and at 104.19, "Is it unfair . . .?"; in the incorrect state (probably the second, resulting from the forme being pied), the readings are "But if what am I told", and "It is unfair . . .?" (There are other, non-substantive, indications of resetting in the gathering.)

Accidental variants. The pattern of changes in punctuation does not match that of the substantives, for the largest number (over 190) occurs in the second edition, the great bulk being, as expected, the deletion of a comma or a pair of commas (72 cases, the most numerous kind of change overall) or the addition of a comma or a pair of commas (34 cases). Considering only types of change where there are at least ten instances, one finds in the second edition twenty-six places where a semi-colon was substituted for a colon, and nineteen places where the reverse change occurs. In fourteen instances Mill reduced an initial capital letter to lower case.

In the third edition there are about 170 changes in punctuation and initial capitalization, markedly fewer in relation to the accidental and substantive changes in the second and fourth editions, when judged by the pattern in Mill's other works. The reason may be that none of his other heavily revised writings received their most thorough reworking this late in his life, or without his wife's assistance, and that, with so much of the substantive revision consisting of added footnotes, Mill scrutinized the text less carefully—or it may be that, by his judgment at least, the second edition was quite well punctuated—or, indeed, the explanation may lie, at least in the main, in the habits and predilections of the compositors of this and other of Mill's works. In any case, the third edition reveals again as the most

---

might be surprised by the differences in these two places. In the first, "unnecessarily" appears rather than the correct "necessarily"; in the second, five lines (in the original setting) were omitted (both corrections were made in 1867).

[76] The first of these is the change, in the second edition, from "coals" to "coal" in the clause "the water, and the wood or coal, were not destroyed." Mill may have carelessly used the plural form (in British usage, indicating individual bits of coal), or, of course, the compositor may have misread his hand (cf. the next footnote) or simply made an error. The second, which occurs within a quotation, looks like a conscious change by Mill, in the second edition, in an attempt (unsuccessful by grammatical standards) to improve Hamilton's sense by changing "what does this imply?" to "what does it imply?"

frequent changes the addition (52 instances) or deletion (51 instances) of individual or paired commas; next most frequent are the lowering of initial capitals (19 instances), though here initial letters are raised eleven times; and in ten instances a semi-colon replaces a colon. In seven instances of various kinds the changes have been judged to be typographical errors.

The fourth edition reveals some 150 changes of these kinds, the most interesting fact about them being that forty are of the sort we have considered as typographical errors (and so in these cases we have in our text adopted the reading of the third edition). Of the total, the addition (27 instances, four read as typographical errors) and deletion (62 instances, 19 read as typographical errors) of individual or paired commas again predominate; continuing the general pattern of lightening punctuation, in fifteen cases (three seen as typographical errors) semi-colons replace colons; in raw scores, raising and lowering of initial letters tie with ten instances each, but nine of the latter, as against two of the former, appear to be typographical errors.[77]

The spelling changes provide, as is usual in Mill's texts, more opportunity for speculation than grounds for judgment, especially in the absence of manuscripts and proof. The most common alterations are from "s" to "z" (and the reverse) in verbals, and of initial "i" to "e" (and the reverse). Of the first of these, the treatment of "cognize" (and its cognates) will illustrate Mill's (or someone else's) indecision: in the third edition, in one instance "s" becomes "z", while in another "z" becomes "s"; in the fourth edition, in three cases "s" becomes "z", while in two the reverse change occurs; in two passages added to the text, one in the third and one in the fourth edition, the former uses the "z" form (which is retained in the fourth edition), while the latter uses the "s" form. Changes from "e" to "i" (and the reverse) include six cases (four in the second edition, two in the third) where "enquiry" (or one of its cognates) becomes "inquiry", two (one in the second edition, one in the fourth) where cognates of "inclose" become "enclose", and the alteration in the third edition (one instance each) of "intangle" and "indorse" to "entangle" and "endorse". As to the vexing question of final single or double "l", in four cases (on the same page) in the second edition "recall" became "recal", and the same change is found twice in the third edition and once in the fourth—but also in the fourth the four "recal"s of the second edition reverted to the "recall" of the first. (The one use of "foretel" persists through all editions, and "dispel", added in the third edition in one place, remains in the fourth.) There seems no clear guidance as to whether or not Mill preferred a hyphen after the prefix "co", except in "coexist" and its cognates, where the clearly dominant form is without the hyphen; also it

[77]It may be noted that overall only seven changes reverse changes in earlier editions.

seems doubtful to assume that he came to prefer "phenomenon" to "phænomenon", because, although the former is adopted once in each of the third and fourth editions where a change occurs, as well as in more than ten passages added in those editions, the latter form persists. All in all, it seems wise to conclude that many, though not all, of the changes reflect the preferences of compositors rather than of Mill.

Mill's references and sources. As the Bibliographic Index (Appendix D) reveals, there are direct or indirect references to about 190 works in the *Examination*, and over 80 references to persons not specifically as authors. Of the cited works, nearly 60 per cent are quoted, the bulk of the quotations coming, of course, from the writings of Hamilton. There are references to, and quotations from many of, twenty-two books or reviews prompted at least in part by Mill's attack on Hamilton, and Mill refers to five of his own writings (usually because they were mentioned by his critics). One interesting finding is that of the works Mill cites when controverting Hamilton's view of contrariety, having, he says, "only looked up the authorities nearest to hand" (412–13), the London Library has copies of eight which he had known from youth.[78]

For the most part his treatment of his sources is fair, and transcriptions reasonably accurate, but of course his judgments were polemical, and much resented by members of the other "school" of philosophy. A good deal of the argument is carried on, as is common in the genre, by quotation and counter-quotation, so the proportion of quoted matter is much higher here than in Mill's other major works.[79] Mill made a genuine attempt to answer his critics, but he was as little sympathetic to some of them as they were to him, and so it is misleading to estimate either the strengths or the weaknesses of his opponents (or even his allies) by his citations in the *Examination*. A few specific instances may be mentioned, partly at least for their curiosity.

The changes Mill made in the fourth edition as a result of Veitch's criticisms have already been touched upon, but the matter merits a few further words, for Mill chose to ignore most of what Veitch had to say. The justification is in a letter to Bain:

Mr Veitch sent me a copy of the Life of Hamilton. His replies to my strictures are so

---

[78] The editions of the works on logic which Mill cites by Aldrich, Bartholinus, Brerewood, Du Hamel, Fell, Keckermann, Smith, and Wallis, at present in the London Library, were very probably given by Mill to the Library with other of his father's books. The last two are autographed "J. Mill" on the title page. Of the others, Ammonius, Burgersdijck, Du Trieu, and Sanderson are (or were) in his library, Somerville College.

[79] In many of his review essays, however, quotation bulks very large indeed, because the great periodicals saw, as one of their functions, making reviewed works known by their contents to their subscribers; in the *Examination* Mill's intention was to expose rather than reveal.

very weak (Mansel & water, with an infusion of vinegar) that I shall hardly [feel] any need of giving them the distinction of a special notice; except that I am bound to admit that the passage of Aristotle which H. seemed to have misunderstood, was not indicated by any reference of his own, but of the editors. That is quite sufficient for my purpose; since Mansel at least has learning, & that passage of Aristotle was I suppose, the nearest he could find to bearing out what Hamilton said. But after all H. must have known what A. meant by ἐνέργεια. I agree with you as to the general impression which the book gives of Hamilton. Only as it shews advantageously a side of his character which I had no knowledge of, that of his private affections, the general result rather raised him in my eyes.[80]

Veitch (who was using the first and third editions of the *Examination*, with page references to the third) attacked Mill for alleging that Hamilton's philosophic positions were conditioned by his unreasoned acceptance of the doctrine of free will, and that he bribed his pupils to accept metaphysical dogmas "by the promise or threat" that they afford the only valid support for "foregone" conclusions.[81] These remarks Mill ignored, as he also passed by Veitch's admission that Mill was in the main right in suggesting that Hamilton lacked (in Veitch's phrasing) "the historical imagination as exercised in philosophy," though Mill notices Veitch's claim that Mill was completely wrong in imputing to Hamilton a weakness in perceiving (Mill's words) "the mutual relations of philosophical doctrines."[82] This latter question is gone into more thoroughly by Veitch in his appended Note C, where he examines and attempts to refute Mill's expositions of Hamilton on Hume, Leibniz, and Aristotle (to only part of the last of which did Mill respond, in the changes alluded to above).[83] The "vinegar" of Veitch's attack is most evident in his Note A, concerning Hamilton on Cousin's view of the Infinite and Absolute, where, in language stronger than Mill's about Hamilton, Veitch refers to Mill's "gross, even ludicrous, misrepresentation of Hamilton's doctrines," and says, in a classical example of the rhetorical device of *occupatio*, that there is no need for further rebuttal than that found in Mansel's "admirably clear, acute, and powerful exposure of Mr Mill's misconceptions" in his *Philosophy of the Conditioned*.[84] Given Veitch's special acquaintance with Hamilton's *Lectures* (he was one of Hamilton's students),[85] it is interesting to find him assailing Mill for treating them as of equal value with Hamilton's "deliberate writing";[86] it is even more interesting to find Veitch nonetheless using the

---

[80]*LL, CW*, XVII, 1613 (7/6/69).

[81]Veitch, *Memoir*, 196n–7n, quoting *Examination*, 492–3 and 438–9.

[82]Veitch, 381–3, quoting *Examination*, 499.

[83]Veitch, 429–48, referring to *Examination*, 498n-9n, 499–500 and 501–21, and 503.

[84]Veitch, 404 and 404n (the whole discussion occupies 404–20).

[85]He and Calderwood (who was second on Hamilton's prize list in 1847) were classmates in Hamilton's logic class of 1850.

[86] Veitch, 379 and 435. Mill also compares the *Lectures* to Hamilton's "later speculations" (372); in objecting to Mill's use of the *Lectures*, Veitch bears out this comparison, pointing out

Lectures in an attempt to refute Mill on a substantive issue,[87] and then showing no hesitation in bestowing fulsome praise on them in other contexts, and going so far as to devote his Note B to citing the high opinions of the *Lectures* expressed in the United States.[88]

The emotional disadvantages of engaging in this kind of controversy are illustrated by the rather unusual reaction of Patrick Proctor Alexander to Mill's ignoring his riposte to Mill's response to his attack. Alexander, in what Mill accurately characterized as a "rollicking style" (460n), assaulted the *Examination* in *Mill and Carlyle. An examination of Mr. John Stuart Mill's doctrine of causation in relation to moral freedom. With an occasional discourse on Sauerteig, by Smelfungus* (Edinburgh: Nimmo, 1866)—the title itself giving clear enough indication that Alexander inclined to the Carlylian side of the conjunction. In the third edition Mill responded at some length (see the citations in the Bibliographic Index), but not very much to the satisfaction of Alexander, who replied with *Moral Causation; or, Notes on Mr. Mill's notes to the chapter on "freedom" in the third edition of his "Examination of Sir W. Hamilton's Philosophy"* (Edinburgh: Nimmo, 1868), the rollicking introduction to which reveals (7) that others had called his style "disgustingly flippant." "The success of this work," Alexander later commented, "was, sooth to say, not much; I am not aware that any one ever bought or read it; and the notices of it in the press were few, slight, and for the most part, I rather think, contemptuous." He had, however, sent a copy to Mill, and anticipated a reply in Mill's fourth edition—but no such reply was there! Alexander therefore prepared a second edition of his *Moral Causation* ("revised and extended"), which he planned to issue so that Mill could reply in a fifth edition. But again frustrated, in this case by Mill's death, Alexander issued his second edition (Edinburgh and London: Blackwood, 1875), in the Preface to which (as

---

that they were prior to "nearly all" the footnotes and all the "Dissertations on Reid"—indeed to everything but the early *Edinburgh* articles in the *Discussions* (209–10).

[87] Veitch, 446.

[88] *Ibid.*, 421–8. Since Mill chose not to notice so much, it may be mentioned that Veitch chose not to mention one instance of Mill's expressing a judgment that Veitch would have appeared to accept. In discussing Hamilton's odd and unoriginal treatment of mathematics, Mill mentions that Hamilton is much inferior to Dugald Stewart on the matter, and that the "cloud of witnesses" Hamilton summons makes us no wiser (470). Veitch does not quote Mill, but includes the following passage from a letter to Hamilton from Napier about Hamilton's article on its first appearance: "One criticism [of the article, by various people], I confess, I was not quite prepared for—viz., that the argument is injured by the 'cloud of witnesses,' which, it is said, has been huddled together without discrimination, and without any rational view of the value of authorities. Lord Brougham, in a letter I received yesterday among others, makes this remark, and adds, that he is sorry the writer, whom he praises for ability and learning, should have adopted a tone in regard to mathematics so different from that of the cautious and philosophical D. Stewart." (174; 1/2/36.) Lest it be thought that Brougham and Napier are quoting Mill thirty years in advance, it should be noted that Hamilton himself refers in his article to the "cloud of witnesses"—and, indeed, they are all quoting St. Paul (Hebrews, 12:1).

well as the remark about the success of the first edition quoted above) he includes a complaint against Mill's having said in his fourth edition that only Mansel and McCosh had published rejoinders to the replies in the third.[89] In this context it should be noted that Mill objects (cvii) to McCosh's assumption that criticisms unrefuted are triumphant; he calls attention to the fact that the subject of the work is the philosophy of Hamilton, not McCosh contra Mill.[90]

Since anyone who has attempted to follow the intricacies of these controversies with sympathy and understanding may well have felt a heaviness of spirit, I may be forgiven the mention of one other curiosity. The perceptiveness of the rather taciturn John Grote (younger brother of George) might well lead one to anticipate valuable comments on the *Examination* in his *Exploratio Philosophica*.[91] But all one finds is the following example of scholarly eccentricity, which does not permit of condensation:

> Since the following pages have been in course of printing, I have become aware of a book which Mr Mill is publishing, or has published, on the subject of his philosophical differences with Sir William Hamilton. I speak in this doubtful manner only because I have purposely avoided learning further. Perhaps this will be understood. To have waited, and referred to what Mr Mill may thus say, would have involved a wider controversy. If criticism of Mr Mill had been in any degree my main purpose, I should have been bound to do this: but, as I have said, I have only used Mr Mill's published views (and so for the other books I have noticed) to compare my own with: I have said as little as may be of approving and disapproving, and spoken only of agreement and disagreement: let us suppose Mr Mill, as he has written hitherto, to be A, a character in rather a lengthened philosophical discussion, and if the actual Mr Mill has changed his views, or, which is exceedingly likely, I have misunderstood him, then let it not be supposed that it is Mr Mill that I am discussing with at all. For myself, I am curious to see, when these pages are published, what Mr Mill may have said on any subject of which I may have spoken, and I think that such involuntary controversy may possibly not be the worst form of it. And after all, since what I have said about Mr Mill and Sir William Hamilton in conjunction is not much, it is possible that what Mr Mill says of the philosophy of the latter may not refer to it, and may concern some other subject, as, for instance, the Philosophy of the Unconditioned. ("Introduction," xxx.)

Effects of the revisions. The fourth edition—or, more truthfully, the third, where most of the changes appeared—of the *Examination* is, in tone

---

[89]*Moral Causation*, 2nd ed., iv. Alexander's works may be recommended to connoisseurs of what—were it not for Sir William Hamilton—might be thought of as the Edinburgh style.

[90]It may be noted that McCosh calls forth some of Mill's most acerb remarks, among them this: "I must add, that the chapter of Dr M'Cosh from which I am now quoting, that headed 'The Logical Notion,' contains much sound philosophy, and little with which I disagree except the persistent illusion which the author keeps up throughout the chapter that I do disagree with him" (317n). Hamilton does not escape this kind of comment, of course: see, e.g., "Sir W. Hamilton . . . thus, as is often the case (and it is one of the best things he does), saved his opponents the trouble of answering his friends . . ." (445).

[91]Cambridge: Deighton, Bell; London: Bell and Daldy, 1865.

as well as length, a markedly different work from the first edition, even though virtually nothing was removed. It is, I believe, both unnecessary and unwise to comment extensively on the different ways in which the two versions affect a reader, but a few comments may assist an understanding of the controversial circumstances. Alan Ryan comments in his Introduction on the two kinds of material in the *Examination*: on the one hand, and most extensively, an exposition and criticism of Hamilton's (and to a lesser extent, Mansel's) views; on the other, an exposition and defence of Mill's (usually) countering views. While the two cannot be exactly isolated, for Mill almost necessarily interweaves his views with his criticism of Hamilton, Chapters xi, xii, and xiii are devoted to Mill's account of his own psychological theory, which is compared not in these chapters, but in the surrounding ones, to the views of Hamilton and his school. Also Chapter xxvi, on the Freedom of the Will, contains a good deal of exposition and defence of Mill's view. One may consider as well the chapters where Mansel receives most attention, especially vii, "The Philosophy of the Conditioned, as Applied by Mr. Mansel to the Limits of Religious Thought," and xiv, which deals with Mansel's as well as Hamilton's treatment of Associationism, as being specially related to Mill's views.[92]

So, in the crudest terms, of the twenty-eight chapters (which vary widely in length), six may be considered as most relevant to a consideration of Mill's direct presentation of his ideas, and all but one of these appear in the first half (measured in chapters) of the work. In fact, measured in pages, in the first two editions these fourteen chapters occupy 270 of the total 560 pages, or 46 per cent. In the third edition these fourteen chapters come to 326 of 633 pages, or 51.5 per cent, and in the fourth to 340 of 650, or 52.3 per cent, not in themselves very startling increases, except that they account for 70 additional pages, leaving only 20 for the chapters of the latter half. When one looks at the five chapters in the first half specially relevant to Mill's views, the point is more clearly made: 42 of the 70 pages added to the first fourteen chapters (33 pages in 1867, 9 in 1872) appear there.[93] (And of the 20 added in the latter half, 11 appear in Chapter xxvi.) Furthermore, two other chapters in the first half, devoted in the first edition to critical examinations of Hamilton's views on the relativity of human knowledge (Chapter iii) and the Philosophy of the Conditioned (Chapter vi), were greatly expanded for the third edition, and further enlarged for the fourth, to accommodate some of Mill's strongest statements of his views counter-

[92]Mansel, of course, is dealt with frequently in other places, most extensively in the first quarter of the work, but also in Chapters xvi and xvii. It may be noted also that xiv, on Association, was particularly enlarged in 1872, perhaps because Mill had edited his father's *Analysis* in the preceding years.

[93]It should be mentioned that the majority of these additions come in the appended notes to xi and xii (combined), xiii, and xiv.

ing those of Hamilton's defenders. In these two chapters (both, it will be noted, again in the first half of the work) a further 26 pages appeared by the fourth edition, and so, adding these to those already accounted for, 68 pages of the 70 added in the first half between the first and fourth editions appear in chapters having to do particularly with Mill's own views and his arguments against the major metaphysical positions of Hamilton and the application of those views by Mansel. (And Chapter xxvi, which is related to these same matters, accounts for slightly more than half of the additions to the second half.) One should also recall the point made above, that a majority of the additions come in footnotes that consist of Mill's defence or counter-attack against critics who most frequently are assailing Mill's views rather than supporting Hamilton's.

Without going into even more painful games of numbers, one may, I believe, accept certain conclusions about the overall rhetorical and tonal effects of the revisions, and make at least suggestions concerning what seemed important to Mill about his vocal readers' reactions. In the first version, less than half the work was given over to the exposition of Hamilton's and Mill's countering views on metaphysics and psychology; the larger part dealt mainly with other aspects of Hamilton's thought (see Mill's explanation of the divisions on 301; cf. 109, 417, 430, 470), most particularly with his logical speculations. By and large, almost no one took up the challenge—the challenge is certainly there, for the polemic is very strong in the latter half—to defend Hamilton on logic, or mathematics, or any other special topic, and so the latter half of the work finally remained (with the exception of Chapter xxvi) much as it had been in the first edition. (The interesting comments in the concluding chapter on Hamilton's personal qualities do little to affect the tone.) But many a critic seized metaphysical and theological cudgels to belabour Mill—not even here, in general, to defend the corpus of Hamilton—and Mill, not without some selection of ground where response would be, in his view, most telling, took the field of their choice, that is, the areas covered in the first half of the work. There is nothing odd in these reactions, of course, but they do suggest that it was not Sir William Hamilton who attracted the critics' attention, but the battle between the two philosophies, and the way it was being waged by the active combatant, Mill. Surely it may, at the least, be surmised that here lies the explanation for what has appeared odd to many, Mill's choice of Hamilton as a subject for what is, after all, his third longest work, and one on which he bestowed much labour. He was looking for a fight, and Hamilton (as he discovered during his careful study) provided both issue and occasion. Organizing the work as he did—and exception can be taken to the details of his *dispositio*[94]—he called attention to what he considered most important,

---

[94]Mill's consummate expository skill, his level tone, and the speed with which he enters into topics all disguise what are sometimes rather weak transitions in the *Examination*. Much

and (perhaps) most provoking. The event proved him right, for not only did the argument centre on the issues between intuitionism and empiricism, but it was a clamorous one, more immediately intense than that aroused by any of his other works. The *Examination*, whatever the modern view, passed its own test.

IV. THE PRESENT TEXT

AS THROUGHOUT the *Collected Works*, the copy-text is that of the final edition in Mill's lifetime, in this case, the fourth, 1872. It has been collated with the three previous editions, and the few manuscript fragments reproduced in Appendix A. Substantive textual changes among the editions are recorded, substantive here meaning all changes except spelling, initial capitalization, word division, punctuation, demonstrable typographical errors, alterations in the form and style of references, and such printing-house concerns as type size.

Our goals are (a) an accurate text as little interrupted by editorial apparatus as is consistent with (b) the immediate reconstruction of earlier versions without separate instructions for each variant, and (c) the minimum number of levels of type on the page. This minimum number is three: the text of the fourth edition; in slightly smaller type, Mill's own footnotes and referential footnotes added (in square brackets) by the editor; and in still smaller type, footnotes giving the variant readings. In the

---

detail would be here inappropriate, but one may note briefly that, while Mill moves generally from metaphysics to logic (thereby, as a glance at his footnotes will show, following Hamilton's *Lectures*), with the final five chapters dealing with special topics, the flow is not always smooth. The first six chapters, constituting the main assault on Hamilton's metaphysics, hold together well enough, but Chapter vii, on Mansel (whose ideas admittedly are involved from iii–vi), is interpolated. There is no lead from it to viii, and the opening of viii (which suggests Mill's uneasiness over the arrangement) refers back to the matter of ii ff. and vi, and hints at what will come later. From viii through x we have exposition and criticism of some of Hamilton's psychological views; x is paired with xi, which gives Mill's views, the empirical position being continued through xiii, by which time one is quite far from Hamilton, to whom (and to Mansel) the argument returns in xiv. No persuasive transitions occur between xiv and xv, xv and xvi (in xvi it would have been appropriate to refer back to viii, where this discussion is promised), or xvi and xvii. Logic is the unifying thread from xvii through xxiii, and the little structuring help Mill gives is adequate. There is an acknowledged leap from xxiii to xxiv, as Mill indicates his move from matters purely psychological and logical to questions relating to the Philosophia Prima (or better, Ultima), but these are all dealt with in the one chapter, one must suppose, for xxv reveals a clear signpost, though it is one that suggests the path behind has been meandering: we are now done with the main part of Hamilton's psychology, that on Cognitive Faculties, leaving Feelings and Conative Faculties. But Hamilton, Mill says, barely treats of these, and the following discussion in xxv is solely on pleasure and pain. Only a weak transition to xxvi, on the freedom of the will, occurs, and xxvii, on Hamilton's view of mathematics, is justified solely on the ground that the examination would be incomplete without it. The concluding chapter does its work well, giving—as is typical of Mill—a little ground, only to seize it back again.

text itself, the usual indicators (*, †, etc.) call attention to Mill's footnotes; editorial notes of reference are signalled by the same indicators (in separate sequence) enclosed in square brackets. Small italic superscript letters, in alphabetical sequence (beginning anew in each chapter) call attention to variant readings (and, in the seven cases where manuscript fragments occur, to their existence). These variants are of three kinds: addition of a word or words, substitution of a word or words, deletion of a word or words. The illustrative examples below are chosen for their ease of presentation and reference, not for their significance.

Addition of a word or words: see 83^{p-p}. In the text, the word "invariably" appears as "^{p}invariably^p"; the variant note reads "$^{p-p}+67,72$". Here the plus sign indicates that the word was added; the following numbers indicate the editions in which the added word appears. The editions are indicated by the last two numbers of their publication dates, with superscript numerals to distinguish between the first and second editions, both of which appeared in 1865: that is, 65^1=first edition (1865), 65^2=second edition (1865), 67=third edition (1867), and 72=fourth edition (1872), the copy-text. The only exception is that one change of "a" to "an" (before "useful" at 471.11) and three changes of "an" to "a" (before "hyperphysical" at 190.9, and twice before "hypothetical" at 410.12 and 16) are not recorded. If a variant occurs within a quotation, and the earlier version (i.e., that in the variant note) is the reading of the source from which Mill is quoting, the word "Source" precedes the edition indicators in the variant note (see 382^{f-f}). (If the reading in the text, as opposed to that in the variant note, is the same as that of the source, no such indication is necessary.) If the quoted text varies from the source, but does not vary among editions, there is no variant note (the variant reading is given, however, in Appendix D, the Bibliographic Appendix: see, e.g., the entry for 242n.3 under Abbott's *Sight and Touch*, 521, where the "then" in Abbott does not appear in any of Mill's editions).

Placing the example (83^{p-p}) in context, then, the interpretation is that in the first and second editions the reading is "as it is interpreted"; in the third edition (1867) this was altered to "as it is invariably interpreted", and the reading of the third edition was retained (as is clear in the text) in the fourth edition (1872), the copy-text.

When the addition is a long one, the second enclosing superscript may appear several pages after the first one; to make reference easier, the superscript notation in the footnote (which appears on the same page as the first superscript) will give the page number where the variant concludes (see, e.g., 63^{g-g65}).

Substitution of a word or words: see 63^{f-f}. In the text the words "one of the chief sources" appears as "^{f}one of the chief sources^f"; the variant note reads "$^{f-f}65^1,65^2$ the chief source". Here the reading following the edition indicators is that for which "one of the chief sources" was substituted; again putting the variant in context, the interpretation is that in the first and second editions (65^1 and 65^2) the reading was "and be the chief source of the reputation"; in the third edition this was altered to "and be one of the chief sources of the reputation", and this reading was retained (again as is clear in the text) in the fourth edition.

Deletion of a word or words: see 75^g. In the text, a *single* superscript ^{g} appears *centred* between "but" and "could"; the variant note reads "$^g 65^1, 65^2$ it". Here the word following the edition indicators was deleted; again putting the variant in context, the interpretation is that the reading in the first and second editions was "but it could not realize"; the word "it" was deleted in the third edition, and the reading of the third was continued in the fourth edition.

Passages changed more than once. Here two methods are used. In the cases, rare in the *Examination* though common in Mill's other lengthy works (which went through many editions over an extended period of time), when a few words were altered and then altered again, the method followed is that illustrated at 38^{k-k}. Here the text reads "^{j}uncaused, and is therefore most naturally identified with the^j"; the variant note reads "$^{j-j} 65^1, 65^2$ a]   67   the". The interpretation is, that in the first and second editions the reading, in context, was "In this signification it is synonymous with a First Cause." In the third edition the sentence ending was altered to "with the First Cause"; and in the fourth edition (as is evident in the text) to "with uncaused, and is therefore most naturally identified with the First Cause."

The other method is used for changes within lengthy passages added subsequent to the first edition. Most of these, in the *Examination*, occur within added footnotes (discussed below), but examples in the text will be found at 26^{n-n} to $^{q-q}$, where within a long addition ($^{m-m}$, which runs from 24 to 32) there are, all within one sentence, later changes indicated. Passage $^{m-m}$ was added in the third edition, but the wording, in that sentence, was altered in the fourth edition. For example, in 1867 it began: "Indeed, the very fact that Sir W. Hamilton thinks it possible for philosophers to discriminate . . ."; in 1872 the wording became: "Indeed, the discrimination which Sir W. Hamilton thinks it possible for philosophy to make. . . ." In these cases, within the superscript letters indicating an added passage, there will be other superscript sets indicating other changes; the variants are listed separately, and in the order of their appearance in the text.

Variants in Mill's footnotes. By far the most common type is the note added in full (the great majority of them in 1867), as, for example, at 21n, where the first note begins: "[67] This is essentially . . ."; the editorially inserted "[67]" indicates that the note was added in the third edition, and was retained (as is evident) in the fourth. Many of these are simply referential, deriving from variants in the text proper, but their addition is always separately signalled in this way.

Changes within notes are treated in the same manner as changes in the text: see, e.g., 29^{s-s}, where a passage was added in 1872; 29^{r-r}, where a substitution was made, again in 1872; and 34^a, where a clause was deleted, once more in 1872.

Prefaces. No preface appeared in the first or second edition. That to the third edition was reprinted (still entitled "Preface to the Third Edition") in the fourth, with a substantial addition. Mill not having indicated that this matter was added in the fourth edition, we have treated it as a variant in the usual way.

Other textual liberties. The following changes are all silently made in the text, except as specifically indicated. Textual emendations, including typographical errors, are listed in Appendix B below, with a note explaining their choice and treatment.[95] (Typographical errors found only in one or more of the first three editions are not listed.) Long quotations have been set in smaller type; the quotation marks found in such quotations at each line in the left margin of the original editions have been removed. (It may be noted, as will be seen in Appendix B, that in several instances these quotation marks led to typographical errors when the text was reset.) Within these quotations, Mill sometimes used quotation marks and round brackets to signal interpolations; we have deleted the quotation marks and substituted square brackets. As mentioned above, the square brackets that Mill occasionally used to indicate matter added in footnotes have been replaced by variant indicators. Mill's placing of footnote indicators was rather eccentric in this work; we have, wherever it was possible without causing confusion, moved them to the ends of quoted passages. Infrequently the result is that two of his notes have been combined. Also, more infrequently, where Mill gave a single reference for a very lengthy quotation from which he had omitted a considerable passage, we have split his one reference into two. Indications of ellipsis in quotations have been standardized to three dots plus, when required, terminal punctuation. A few trivial alterations in printing style have been made, such as the removal of dashes when combined with other punctuation in introducing quotations and references. The running heads have been altered to suit this edition. When necessary, Mill's references to sources have been amplified and

---

[95]One special departure from the normal practice deserves mention. At 399n.20 "All A is B" is corrected to "All A is all B" even though the four editions have the former reading. The justification for this emendation is that the sense is lost without it, and that elsewhere in the passage, as well as in the authors referred to, the latter reading is always found in analogous contexts.

corrected (the corrections are listed in Appendix C below), with all added information being placed in square brackets, as are all editorial references. These last are also signalled by indicators in square brackets, as mentioned above.

V. APPENDICES

Appendix A gives the readings (with explanatory and variant notes) of the few manuscript fragments that survive.

Appendix B lists the textual emendations with the original readings. The headnote gives the general justification; individual items there entered give, when necessary, the special justifications.

Appendix C gives the original and emended readings of Mill's references that have been silently corrected in his footnotes.

Appendix D, the Bibliographic Appendix, lists all persons and works referred to or quoted in the *Examination*, except mythical persons and those simply used as place-holders in logical examples. Substantive variants between Mill's quotations and his sources are entered, both to correct misquotations and to provide contexts for partial quotations. Because this appendix includes all references to persons and books, it is in effect an index to names and titles, which are therefore omitted from the Index proper.

The *Index* has been prepared by Dr. Bruce L. Kinzer.

ACKNOWLEDGEMENTS

FOR PERMISSION to publish manuscript material, we are indebted to the Columbia University Library, the Houghton Library of Harvard University, to the Yale University Library, and to the National Provincial Bank (literary executors and residual legatees of Mary Taylor, Mill's step-grand-daughter). Our deep gratitude is once again cheerfully offered to the staffs of the British Library, the Somerville College Library, the University of London Library, the University of Reading Library (and especially its Archivist, Mr. J. A. Edwards), the British Library of Political and Economic Science, the London Library, the University of Toronto Library, the library of the Pontifical Institute of Mediæval Studies, the libraries of Knox, Regis, St. Michael's, Trinity, and Wycliffe Colleges, Toronto, and never least, the Victoria University Library. To the members of the Editorial Committee, especially Jean Houston and R. F. McRae, to the copy-editor, Rosemary Shipton, and the editorial, production, and printing staff of the University of Toronto Press, my never failing, though not always expressed, thanks for unstinting co-operation. Among others to whom credit is due, and no discredit should accrue, are Father J. L. Dewan, Mr. Charles P. Finlayson of the Edinburgh University Library, Professor Daniel De Montmollin, Professor Joseph Hamburger, Professor Hugh R. MacCallum, Professors E. Jane and Michael Millgate, Professor Emeritus J. R. O'Donnell, the Reverend J. Owens, Mr. H. Russell of the Belfast Public Libraries, Professor C. A. Silber, Professor F. E. Sparshott, Professor Jack Stillinger, and Professor J. R. Vanstone. In a very real sense the editing of the volume is the work of my colleagues on the Mill project, where good spirits, co-operation, and industry have made the time seem short and be pleasant: Marion Filipiuk, Bruce Kinzer, Martin Kreiswirth, Judith LeGoff, and Rea Wilmshurst. Lady Hamilton, among her other duties, sat up through the nights till the northern dawn transcribing the lecture notes which Sir William was writing for the next afternoon; that my wife did not do the like for me (nor I for her) might suggest a number of conclusions, but I believe that her generous aid to this volume would not have been forthcoming had she (or I) done so.

Preface to the Third Edition[*]

IN FORMER WRITINGS I have perhaps seemed to go in search of objectors, whom I might have disregarded, but who enabled me to bring out my opinions into greater clearness and relief. My present condition is far different; for a host of writers, whose mode of philosophic thought was either directly or indirectly implicated in the criticisms made by this volume on Sir W. Hamilton, have taken up arms against it, and fought as *pro aris et focis*. Among these are included, not solely friends or followers of Sir W. Hamilton, who were under some obligation to say whatever could fairly be said in his defence, but many who stand almost as widely apart from him as I do, though mostly on the reverse side. To leave these attacks unanswered, would be to desert the principles which as a speculative thinker I have maintained all my life, and which the progress of my thoughts has constantly strengthened. The criticisms which have come under my notice (omitting the daily and weekly journals) are the following; there may be others:

Mr. Mansel: *The Philosophy of the Conditioned; comprising some remarks on Sir William Hamilton's Philosophy, and on Mr. J. S. Mill's Examination of that Philosophy.* (First published in Nos. 1 and 2 of the *Contemporary Review*.)[†]

The Battle of the Two Philosophies; by an Inquirer.[‡]

Dr. M'Cosh: *An Examination of Mr. J. S. Mill's Philosophy, being a Defence of Fundamental Truth.*[§]

Dr. Calderwood: "The Sensational Philosophy—Mr. J. S. Mill and Dr. M'Cosh;" in the *British and Foreign Evangelical Review* for April 1866.[¶]

[*This preface, in expanded form (see cvi–cviii below), also appears in the 4th ed. There is no preface in the 1st or 2nd ed.]

[†Henry Longueville Mansel, *The Philosophy of the Conditioned* (London and New York: Strahan, 1866); reprinted from *Contemporary Review*, I (Jan., Feb., 1866), 31–49, 185–219.]

[‡[Lucy March Phillipps,] *The Battle of the Two Philosophies* (London: Longmans, Green, 1866).]

[§James McCosh, *An Examination of Mr. J. S. Mill's Philosophy* (London: Macmillan, 1866).]

[¶Henry Calderwood, "The Sensational Philosophy—Mr. J. S. Mill and Dr. McCosh," *British and Foreign Evangelical Review*, XV (April, 1866), 396–412.]

Dr. Henry B. Smith: "Mill *v.* Hamilton," in the *American Presbyterian and Theological Review* for January 1866.[*]

Mr. H. F. O'Hanlon: *A Criticism of John Stuart Mill's Pure Idealism; and an Attempt to show that, if logically carried out, it is Pure Nihilism.*[†]

Review of this work in *Blackwood's Magazine* for January 1866.[‡]

(The two last mentioned are confined to the doctrine of Permanent Possibilities of Sensation.)

Mr. J. P. Mahaffy, in the Introduction to his translation of Professor Kuno Fischer's account of Kant's *Kritik.* (Confined to the doctrine of Permanent Possibilities, and the subject of Necessary Truths.)[§]

Mr. Patrick Proctor Alexander: "An Examination of Mr. John Stuart Mill's Doctrine of Causation in Relation to Moral Freedom;" forming the greater part of a volume entitled *Mill and Carlyle.*[¶]

Reviews of this work in the *Dublin Review* for October 1865 (with the signature R.E.G.), and in the *Edinburgh Review* for July 1866.[||]

And, earlier than all these, the able and interesting volume of my friend Professor Masson, entitled *Recent British Philosophy: a Review, with Criticisms; including some comments on Mr. Mill's Answer to Sir William Hamilton.*[**]

All these, in regard to such of the main questions as they severally discuss, are unqualifiedly hostile: though some of the writers are, in a personal point of view, most courteous, and even over-complimentary; and the last eminently friendly as well as flattering.

The following are only partially adverse:

Review of the present work in the *North British Review* for September 1865, attributed to Professor Fraser, and bearing the strongest internal marks of that origin.[††] This able thinker, though he considers me to have often misunderstood Sir W. Hamilton, is, on the substantive philosophic

[*Henry Boynton Smith, "Mill's Examination of Hamilton's Philosophy," *American Presbyterian and Theological Review*, IV (Jan., 1866), 126–62.]

[†Hugh Francis O'Hanlon, *A Criticism of John Stuart Mill's Pure Idealism* (Oxford and London: Parker, 1866).]

[‡William Henry Smith, "J. S. Mill on Our Belief in the External World," *Blackwood's Magazine*, XCIX (Jan., 1866), 20–45.]

[§John Pentland Mahaffy, intro. and trans., Kuno Fischer, *A Commentary on Kant's Critick of Pure Reason* (London: Longmans, Green, 1866).]

[¶Edinburgh: Nimmo, 1866.]

[||Robert Ephrem Guy, "Calderwood and Mill upon Hamilton," *Dublin Review*, n.s. V (Oct., 1865), 474–504; John Cunningham, "Mill's *Examination of Sir William Hamilton's Philosophy*," *Edinburgh Review*, CXXIV (July, 1866), 120–50.]

[**David Masson, *Recent British Philosophy* (London and Cambridge: Macmillan, 1865).]

[††Alexander Campbell Fraser, "Mr. Mill's *Examination of Sir W. Hamilton's Philosophy*," *North British Review*, XLIII (Sept., 1865), 1–58.]

doctrines principally concerned, a most valuable ally; to whom I might almost have left the defence of our common opinions.

Mr. Herbert Spencer: "Mill *v.* Hamilton—The Test of Truth;" in the *Fortnightly Review* for July 15, 1865.[*]

Review of the present work in the *North American Review* for July 1866.[†]

The only important criticism, in all essentials favourable, to which I am able to refer, is that in the *Westminster Review* for January 1866, by an illustrious historian and philosopher, who, of all men now living, is the one by whom I should most wish that any writing of mine, on a subject in speculative philosophy, should be approved.[‡] There have also been published since the first edition of the present work, two remarkable books, which, if they do not give me direct support, effect a powerful diversion in my favour. One is Mr. Bolton's *Inquisitio Philosophica; an Examination of the Principles of Kant and Hamilton;*[§] which, along with much other valuable matter, contains a vigorous assault upon my most conspicuous assailant, Mr. Mansel.[¶] The other is Mr. Stirling's *Sir William Hamilton, being the Philosophy of Perception; an Analysis:*[||] an able and most severe criticism on Sir W. Hamilton's inconsistencies, and on his general character as a philosopher, taken from a different point of view from mine, and expressed with far greater asperity than I should myself think justifiable; legitimated, no doubt, to the writer's mind by "a certain vein of disingenuousness"[**] which he finds in Sir W. Hamilton, but which I have not found, and shall not believe until I see it proved.

I must have been quite incapable of profiting by criticism, if I had learnt nothing from assailants so numerous, all of more or less, and some of very considerable, ability. They have detected not a few inadvertences of expression, as well as some of thought: and partly by their help, partly without it, I have discovered others. They have not shaken any statement or opinion of real moment; but I am sincerely indebted to them, both for the errors they have corrected, and for compelling me to strengthen my defences. The point in which it was to be expected that they would oftenest

[*"Mill *versus* Hamilton," *Fortnightly Review*, I (15 July, 1865), 531–50.]

[†Anon., "Mill on Hamilton," *North American Review*, CIII (July, 1866), 250–60.]

[‡George Grote, "John Stuart Mill on the Philosophy of Sir William Hamilton," *Westminster Review*, n.s. XXIX (Jan., 1866), 1–39.]

[§M. P. W. Bolton, *Inquisitio Philosophica* (London: Chapman and Hall, 1866).]

[¶In Chap. vi, pp. 180–97; the assault is on Mansel's *The Philosophy of the Conditioned.*]

[||James Hutchison Stirling, *Sir William Hamilton* (London: Longmans, Green, 1865).]

[**Stirling, p. vii.]

prevail, was in showing me to have erroneously interpreted Sir W. Hamilton. The difficulty to any thinker is so great, in these high regions of speculation, of placing himself completely at the point of view of a different philosophy, and even of thoroughly understanding its language, that it would be very presumptuous in me to imagine that I had always overcome that difficulty; and that too with the warning before me, of the absolute failure of able and accomplished minds on the other side in philosophy, to accomplish this in regard to the modes of thinking with which I am most familiar. I have been surprised, therefore, to find in how few instances, and those how little important, the defenders of Sir W. Hamilton have been able to show that I have misunderstood or incorrectly stated his opinions or arguments. I cannot doubt that more such mistakes remain to be pointed out: and I regret that the greater part of the volume has not yet, in its relation to Sir W. Hamilton, had the benefit of a sufficiently minute scrutiny. Had the unsparing criticism of Mr. Mansel on the first few chapters been continued to the remainder, he would doubtless have pointed out real mistakes; he might perhaps have thrown light on some of the topics from his own thoughts; and I should at least have had to thank him for additional confidence in the statements and opinions which had passed unharmed through the ordeal of his attacks.

Where criticism or reconsideration has convinced me that anything in the book was erroneous, or that any improvement was required in the mode of stating and setting forth the truth, I have made the requisite alterations. When the case seemed to require that I should call the reader's attention to the change, I have done so; but I have not made this an invariable rule. Mere answers to objectors I have generally relegated to notes. With so many volumes to deal with, I could not take express notice of every criticism which they contained. When any of my critics finds that he, or some of his objections, are not individually referred to, let him be assured that it is from no disrespect, but either because I consider them to have been answered by the reply made to some one else, or because their best confutation is to remand the objector to the work itself, or because the edge of the objection has been turned by some, perhaps quite unapparent, correction of the text. A slight modification in a sentence, or even in a phrase, which a person acquainted with the former editions might read without observing it, and of which, even if he observed it, he would most likely not perceive the purpose, has sometimes effaced many pages of hostile criticism.

*   *   *   *   *

[a]Of the assailants to whom I replied, two only have published a rejoinder; Dean Mansel, in the *Contemporary Review* for September 1867, and Dr.

M'Cosh, in the *British and Foreign Evangelical Review* for April 1868.[*] Neither of them appears to me to have added much of value to what he had previously advanced; and so far as concerns Dean Mansel, his regretted death has put a final termination to the controversy between us. I am not, however, thereby exempted from taking notice, however briefly, of such points in his rejoinder as appear to require it. Dr. M'Cosh seems to think it a great triumph of his assaults upon me, that many of them were not noticed in my replies to critics. It is a little unreasonable in Dr. M'Cosh to suppose that in a work, the subject of which is the philosophy of Sir William Hamilton, I was bound to fight a pitched battle with Dr. M'Cosh on the whole line. His book was an attack directed against the whole of my philosophical opinions. I answered such parts of it as had reference to the present work, when they seemed to require an answer, and not to have received it sufficiently in what I had already written. And I have done the same, in the present edition, with his rejoinder.

Besides several unpublished criticisms which I owe to the kindness of correspondents, and which have helped me to correct or otherwise improve some of the details of the work; two more attacks have been made upon it subsequently to the third edition. Professor Veitch, in the Appendices to his interesting *Memoir of Sir W. Hamilton*, has commented sharply on what I have said respecting Sir W. Hamilton's mode of understanding the Relativity of human knowledge, and respecting his failure to apprehend correctly the general character of Hume and Leibnitz as philosophers, as well as some particular passages of Aristotle.[†] On the first subject, that of Relativity, I find so much difficulty in reducing Professor Veitch's statement to distinct propositions, and, so far as I understand his meaning, it differs so little, and that little not to its advantage, from what I have already commented on in answering Mr. Mansel, that I do not think it necessary to burthen this volume with an express reply to him. With regard to Hume and Leibnitz I am content that they who have a competent knowledge of those philosophers should form their own opinion. As regards Sir W. Hamilton's interpretation of Aristotle, Professor Veitch has convicted me of a mistake in treating a citation made by his editors as if it had been made by himself, and of an overstatement of one of Sir W. Hamilton's opinions which I only noticed incidentally.[‡] These errors I have corrected, in their places,[§] and

---

[*Mansel, "Supplementary Remarks on Mr. Mill's Criticism of Sir William Hamilton," *Contemporary Review*, VI (Sept., 1867), 18–31; McCosh, "Mill's Reply to his Critics," *British and Foreign Evangelical Review*, XVII (April, 1868), 332–62.]

[†John Veitch, *Memoir of Sir William Hamilton* (Edinburgh: Blackwood, 1869), App., Note C, pp. 429–48.]

[‡*Ibid.*, p. 447.]

[§See below, pp. 503^{k-k} and 503n.]

it will be found that they do not affect anything of importance in the criticism there made upon Sir W. Hamilton.

Professor Veitch* considers it unfair that I should press against Sir W. Hamilton anything contained in his *Lectures*,[*] these having been hastily written under pressure from time, and not being the most matured expression of some of his opinions. But though thus written, it is admitted that they continued to be delivered by Sir W. Hamilton as long as he performed the duties of Professor; which would not have been the case if he had no longer considered them as a fair representation of his philosophy. A complete representation I never pretended that they were; a correct representation I am bound to think them; for it cannot be believed that he would have gone on delivering to his pupils matter which he judged to be inconsistent with the subsequent developments of his philosophy.

The other thinker who has taken the field against my psychological opinions is Dr. Ward, who, in the *Dublin Review* for October 1871,[†] has made an able attack on the views I have expressed in this and other writings on the subject of what is called Necessary Truth. Some of Dr. Ward's observations are more particularly directed against a portion of my *System of Logic*,[‡] and the fittest place for their discussion is in connexion with that treatise. But the greater part of his article principally regards the chapter of the present work which relates to Inseparable Association, and a reply to it will be found in a note which I have added at the end of that chapter.[*][§]

Memoir, pp. 212–13.
[*Lectures on Metaphysics and Logic, ed. Henry Longueville Mansel and John Veitch, 4 vols. (Edinburgh and London: Blackwood, 1859–60).]
[†William George Ward, "Mr. Mill's Denial of Necessary Truth," *Dublin Review*, n.s. XVII (Oct., 1871), 285–318.]
[‡See *Collected Works*, Vols. VII and VIII (Toronto: University of Toronto Press, 1973), Vol. VIII, pp. 575–7 (a response to Ward's article added in the 8th ed., 1872, to Bk. II, Chap. v, §5).]
[§See the note to Chap. xiv, pp. 267–71 below.]

CHAPTER I

Introductory Remarks

AMONG THE PHILOSOPHICAL WRITERS of the present century in these islands, no one occupies a higher position than Sir William Hamilton. He alone, of our metaphysicians of this and the preceding generation, has acquired, merely as such, an European celebrity: while, in our own country, he has not only had power to produce a revival of interest in a study which had ceased to be popular, but has made himself, in some sense, the founder of a school of thought. The school, indeed, is not essentially new; for its fundamental doctrines are those of the philosophy which has everywhere been in the ascendant since the setting in of the reaction against Locke and Hume, which dates from Reid among ourselves and from Kant for the rest of Europe. But that general scheme of philosophy is split into many divisions, and the Hamiltonian form of it is distinguished by as marked peculiarities as belong to any other of its acknowledged varieties. From the later German and French developments of the common doctrine, it is separated by differences great in reality, and still greater in appearance; while it stands superior to the earlier Scottish and English forms by the whole difference of level which has been gained to philosophy through the powerful negative criticism of Kant. It thus unites to the *prestige* of independent originality, the recommendation of a general harmony with the prevailing tone of thought. These advantages, combined with an intellect highly trained and in many respects highly fitted for the subject, and a knowledge probably never equalled in extent and accuracy of whatever had been previously thought and written in his department, have caused Sir William Hamilton to be justly recognised as, in the province of abstract speculation, one of the important figures of the age.

The acknowledged position of Sir W. Hamilton at the head, so far as regards this country, of the school of philosophy to which he belongs, has principally determined me to connect with his name and writings the speculations and criticisms contained in the present work. The justification of the work itself lies in the importance of the questions, to the discussion of which it is a contribution. England is often reproached by Continental thinkers, with indifference to the higher philosophy. But England did not always deserve this reproach, and is already showing, by no doubtful symptoms, that she will not deserve it much longer. Her thinkers are again beginning to see, what they had only temporarily forgotten, that a true Psychology is the indispensable scientific basis of Morals, of Politics, of the science and art of Education; that the difficulties of Metaphysics lie at the root of all science; that those difficulties can only be quieted by being resolved, and that until they are resolved, positively ^{a}whenever^a possible, but at any rate negatively, we are never assured that any human knowledge, even physical, stands on solid foundations.

My subject, therefore, is ^{b}less^b Sir W. Hamilton, ^{c}than^c the questions which Sir W. Hamilton discussed. It is, however, impossible to write on those questions in our own country and in our own time, without incessant reference, express or tacit, to his treatment of them. On all the subjects on which he touched, he is either one of the most powerful allies of what I deem a sound philosophy, or (more frequently) by far its most formidable antagonist; both because he came the latest, and wrote with a full knowledge of the flaws which had been detected in his predecessors, and because he was one of the ablest, the most ^{d}far-sighted^d, and the most candid. Whenever any opinion which he deliberately expressed, is contended against, his form of the opinion, and his arguments for it, are those which especially require to be faced and carefully appreciated: and it being thus impossible that any fit discussion of his topics should not involve an estimate of his doctrines, it seems worth while that the estimate should be rendered as complete as practicable, by being extended to all the subjects on which he has made, or on which he is believed to have made, any important contribution to thought.

In thus attempting to anticipate, as far as is yet possible, the judgment of posterity on Sir W. Hamilton's labours, I sincerely lament that on the many points on which I am at issue with him, I have the unfair advantage possessed by one whose opponent is no longer in a condition to reply. Personally I might have had small cause to congratulate myself on the reply which I might have received, for though a strictly honourable, he was a most unsparing controversialist, and whoever assailed even the most unimportant of his opinions, might look for hard blows in return. But it would have been worth far more, even to myself, than any polemical success, to have known with certainty in what manner he would have met the objections raised in the present volume. I feel keenly, with Plato, how much more is to be learnt by discussing with a man, who can question and

$^{a-a}$65^1, 65^2 if
$^{b-b}$65^1, 65^2 not
$^{c-c}$65^1, 65^2 but
$^{d-d}$65^1, 65^2 clear-sighted

answer, than with a book, which cannot.[*] But it was not possible to take a general review of Sir W. Hamilton's doctrines while they were only known to the world in the fragmentary state in which they were published during his life. His *Lectures*, the fullest and the only consecutive exposition *e*(as far as it goes)*e* of his philosophy, are a posthumous publication; while the latest and most matured expression of many of his opinions, the "Dissertations on Reid,"[†] left off, scarcely half finished, in the middle of a sentence; and so long as he lived, his readers were still hoping for the remainder. The *Lectures*, it is true, have added less than might have been expected to the knowledge we already possessed of the author's doctrines; but it is something to know that we have now all that is to be had; and though we should have been glad to have his opinions on more subjects, we could scarcely have known more thoroughly than we are now at last enabled to do, what his thoughts were on the points to which he attached the greatest importance, and which are most identified with his name and fame.

[*See, e.g., Plato, *Phædrus*, in *Euthyphro, Apology, Crito, Phædo, Phædrus* (Greek and English), trans. H. N. Fowler (London: Heinemann; Cambridge, Mass.: Harvard University Press, 1917), pp. 564–70 (275^d–277^a).]

[†Appended to Reid's *Works*, ed. Hamilton (Edinburgh: Maclachlan and Stewart, 1846), pp. 741–914.]

e-e+72

CHAPTER II

The Relativity of Human Knowledge

THE DOCTRINE which is thought to belong in the most especial manner to Sir W. Hamilton, and which was the ground of his opposition to the transcendentalism of the later French and German metaphysicians, is that which he and others have called the Relativity of Human Knowledge. It is the subject of the most generally known, and most impressive, of all his writings,[*] the one which first revealed to the English metaphysical reader that a new power had arisen in philosophy; and, together with its developments, it composes the "Philosophy of the Conditioned," which he opposed to the German and French philosophies of the Absolute, and which is regarded by most of his admirers as the greatest of his titles to a permanent place in the history of metaphysical thought.

But the "relativity of human knowledge," like most other phrases into which the words relative or relation enter, is vague, and admits of a great variety of meanings. In one of its senses, it stands for a proposition respecting the nature and limits of our knowledge, in my judgment true, fundamental, and full of important consequences in philosophy. From this amplitude of meaning its significance shades down through a number of gradations, successively more thin and unsubstantial, till it fades into a truism leading to no consequences, and hardly worth enunciating in words. When, therefore, a philosopher lays great stress upon the relativity of our knowledge, it is necessary to cross-examine his writings, and compel them to disclose in which of its many degrees of meaning he understands the phrase.

There is one of its acceptations, which, for the purpose now in view, may be put aside, though in itself defensible, and though, when thus employed, it expresses a real and important law of our mental nature. This is, that we only know anything, by knowing it as distinguished from something else; that all consciousness is of difference; that two objects are the smallest number required to constitute consciousness; that a thing is only seen to be what it is, by contrast with what it is not. The employment of the proposi-

[*Discussions on Philosophy and Literature, Education and University Reform, 2nd ed. (London: Longman, Brown, Green, and Longmans; Edinburgh: Maclachlan and Stewart, 1853).]

tion, that all human knowledge is relative, to express this meaning, is sanctioned by high authorities,* and I have no fault to find with that use of the phrase. But we are not concerned with it in the present case; for it is not in this sense, that the expression is ordinarily or intentionally used by Sir W. Hamilton; though he fully recognises the truth which, when thus used, it serves to express. In general, when he says that all our knowledge is relative, the relation he has in view is not between the thing known and other objects compared with it, but between the thing known and the mind knowing.

All language recognises a distinction between myself—the Ego—and a world, either material, or spiritual, or both, external to me, but of which I can, in some mode and measure, take cognizance. The most fundamental questions in philosophy are those which seek to determine what we are able to know of these external objects, and by what evidence we know it.

In examining the different opinions which are or may be entertained on this subject, it will simplify the exposition very much, if we at first limit ourselves to the case of physical, or what are commonly called material objects. These objects are of course known to us through the senses. By those channels and no otherwise do we learn whatever we do learn concerning them. Without the senses we should not know nor suspect that such things existed. We know no more of what they are, than the senses tell us, nor does nature afford us any means of knowing more. Thus much, in the obvious meaning of the terms, is denied by no one, though there are thinkers who prefer to express the meaning in other language.

There are, however, conflicting opinions as to *what it is* that the senses tell us concerning objects. About one part of the information they give, there is no dispute. They tell us our sensations. The objects excite, or awaken in us, certain states of feeling. A part, at least, of what we know of the objects, is the feelings to which they give rise. What we term the properties of an object, are the powers it exerts of producing sensations in our consciousness. Take any familiar object, such as an orange. It is yellow; that is, it affects us, through our sense of sight, with a particular sensation of colour. It is soft; in other words it produces a sensation, through our muscular feelings, of resistance overcome by a slight effort. It is sweet; for it causes a peculiar kind of pleasurable sensation through our organ of taste. It is of a globular figure, somewhat flattened at the ends: we affirm this on account of sensations that it causes in us, respecting which it is still in dispute among psychologists whether they originally came to us solely through touch and the muscles, or also through the organ of sight.

*In particular by Mr. Bain, who habitually uses the phrase "relativity of knowledge" in this sense. [Cf., e.g., *The Senses and the Intellect*, 2nd ed. (London: Longman, Green, Longman, Roberts, and Green, 1864), pp. 9–10.]

When it is cut open, we discover a certain arrangement of parts, distinguishable as being, in certain respects, unlike one another; but of their unlikeness we have no measure or proof except that they give us different sensations. The rind, the pulp, the juice, differ from one another in colour, in taste, in smell, in degree of consistency (that is, of resistance to pressure) all of which are differences in our feelings. The parts are, moreover, ªoutsideª one another, occupying different portions of space: and even this distinction, it is maintained (though the doctrine is vehemently protested against by some) may be resolved into a difference in our sensations. When thus analysed, it is affirmed that all the attributes which we ascribe to objects, consist in their having the power of exciting one or another variety of sensation in our minds; that to us the properties of an object have this and no other meaning; that an object is to us nothing else than that which affects our senses in a certain manner; that we are incapable of attaching to the word object, any other meaning; that even an imaginary object is but a conception, such as we are able to form, of something which would affect our senses in some new way; so that our knowledge of objects, and even our fancies about objects, consist of nothing but the sensations which they excite, or which we imagine them exciting, in ourselves.

This is the doctrine of the Relativity of Knowledge to the knowing mind, in the simplest, purest, and, as I think, the most proper acceptation of the words. There are, however, two forms of this doctrine, which differ materially from one another.

According to one of the forms, the sensations which, in common parlance, we are said to receive from objects, are not only all that we can possibly know of the objects, but are all that we have any ground for believing to exist. What we term an object is but a complex conception made up by the laws of association, out of the ideas of various sensations which we are accustomed to receive simultaneously. There is nothing real in the process but these sensations. They do not, indeed, accompany or succeed one another at random; they are held together by a law, that is, they occur in fixed groups, and a fixed order of succession: but we have no evidence of anything which, not being itself a sensation, is a substratum or hidden cause of sensations. The idea of such a substratum is a purely mental creation, to which we have no reason to think that there is any corresponding reality exterior to our minds. Those who hold this opinion are said to doubt or deny the existence of matter. They are sometimes called by the name Idealists, sometimes by that of Sceptics, according to the other opinions which they hold. They include the followers of Berkeley and those of Hume. Among recent thinkers, the acute and accomplished

ª⁻ª65¹, 65² *outside*

Professor Ferrier, though by a circuitous path, and expressing himself in a very different phraseology, seems to have arrived at essentially the same point of view. These philosophers maintain the Relativity of our knowledge in the most extreme form in which the doctrine can be understood, since they contend, not merely that all we can possibly know of anything is the manner in which it affects the human faculties, but that there is nothing else to be known; that affections of human or of some other minds are all that we can know to exist.

This, however, is far from being the shape in which the doctrine of the Relativity of our knowledge is usually held. To most of those who hold it, the difference between the Ego and the Non-Ego is not one of language only, nor a formal distinction between two aspects of the same reality, but denotes two realities, each *b*having a separate existence*b*, and neither dependent on the other. In the phraseology borrowed from the Schoolmen by the German Transcendentalists, they regard the Noumenon as in itself a different thing from the Phænomenon, and equally real; many of them would say, much more real, being the permanent Reality, of which the other is but the passing manifestation. They believe that there is a real universe of "Things in Themselves," and that whenever there is an impression on our senses, there is a "Thing in itself," which is behind the phænomenon, and is the cause of it. But as to what this Thing *is* "in itself," we, having no *c*organs*c* except our senses for communicating with it, can only know what our senses tell us; and as they tell us nothing but the impression which the thing makes upon *us*, we do not know what it is *in itself* at all. We suppose (at least these philosophers suppose) that it must be *d*something*d* "in itself," but all that we know it to be is merely relative to us, consisting in the power of affecting us in certain ways, or, as it is technically called, of producing Phænomena. External things exist, and have an inmost nature, but their inmost nature is inaccessible to our faculties. We know it not, and can assert nothing of it with a meaning. Of the ultimate Realities, as such, we know the existence, and nothing more. But the impressions which these Realities make on us—the sensations they excite, the similitudes, groupings, and successions of those sensations, or, to sum up all this in a common though improper expression, the *representations* generated in our minds by the action of the Things themselves—these we may know, and these are all that we can know respecting them. In some future state of existence it is conceivable that we may know more, and more may be known by intelligences superior to us. Yet even this can only be true in the same sense in which a person with the use of his eyes knows more than is

*b-b*65[1], 65[2]   self-existent
*c-c*65[1], 65[2]   organ
*d-d*65[1], 65[2]   *something*

known to one born blind, or in which we should know more than we do if we were endowed with two or three additional senses. We should have more sensations; phænomena would exist to us of which we have at present no conception; and we *might* know better than we now do, many of those which are within our present experience; for *if* the new impressions *were* linked with the old, as the old are with one another, by uniformities of succession and coexistence, we should now have new marks indicating to us known phænomena in cases in which we should otherwise have been unaware of them. But all this additional knowledge would be, like that which we now possess, merely phænomenal. We should not, any more than at present, know things as they are in themselves, but merely an increased number of relations between them and us. And in the only meaning which we are able to attach to the term, all knowledge, by however exalted an Intelligence, can only be relative to the knowing Mind. If Things have an inmost nature, apart not only from the impressions which they produce, but from all those which they are fitted to produce, on any sentient being, this inmost nature is unknowable, inscrutable, and inconceivable, not to us merely, but to every other creature. To say that even the Creator could know it, is to use language which to us has no meaning, because we have no faculties by which to apprehend that there is any such thing for him to know.

It is in this form that the doctrine of the Relativity of Knowledge is held by the greater number of those who profess to hold it, attaching any definite idea to the term. These again are divided into several distinct schools of thinkers, by some of whom the doctrine is held with a modification of considerable importance.

Agreeing in the opinion that what we know of Noumena, or Things in themselves, is but their bare existence, all our other knowledge of Things being but a knowledge of something in ourselves which derives its origin from them; there is a class of thinkers who hold that our mere sensations, and an outward cause which produces them, do not compose the whole of this relative knowledge. The Attributes which we ascribe to outward things, or such at least as are inseparable from them in thought, contain, it is affirmed, other elements, over and above sensations *plus* an unknowable cause. These additional elements are still only relative, for they are not in the objects themselves, nor have we evidence of anything in the objects that answers to them. They are added by the mind itself, and belong, not to the Things, but to our perceptions and conceptions of them. Such properties as the objects can be conceived divested of, such as sweetness or

---

*e-e*65[1], 65[2]   should
*f-f*65[1], 65[2]   since
*g-g*65[1], 65[2]   would doubtless be

sourness, hardness or softness, hotness or coldness, whiteness, redness, or blackness—these, it is sometimes admitted, exist in our sensations only. But the attributes of filling space, and occupying a portion of time, are not properties of our sensations in their crude state, neither, again, are they properties of the objects, nor is there in the objects any prototype of them. They result from the nature and structure of the Mind itself: which is so constituted that it cannot take any impressions from objects except in those particular modes. We see a thing in a place, not because the Noumenon, the Thing in itself, is in any place, but because it is the law of our perceptive faculty that we must see as in some place, whatever we see at all. Place is not a property of the Thing, but a mode in which the mind is compelled to represent it. Time and Space are only modes of our perceptions, not modes of existence, and higher Intelligences are possibly not bound by them. Things, in themselves, are neither in time nor in space, though we cannot represent them to ourselves except under that twofold condition. Again, when we predicate of a thing that it is one or many, a whole or a part of a whole, a Substance possessing Accidents, or an Accident inhering in a Substance—when we think of it as producing Effects, or as produced by a Cause, (I omit other attributes not necessary to be here enumerated,) we are ascribing to it properties which do not exist in the Thing itself, but with which it is clothed by the laws of our conceptive faculty—properties not of the Things, but of our mode of conceiving them. We are compelled by our nature to construe things to ourselves under these forms, but they are not forms of the Things. The attributes exist only in relation to us, and as inherent laws of the human faculties; but differ from Succession and Duration in being laws of our intellectual, not our sensitive faculty; technically termed Categories of the Understanding. This is the doctrine of the Relativity of our knowledge as held by Kant, who has been followed in it by many subsequent thinkers, German, English, and French.

By the side of this there is another philosophy, older in date, which, though temporarily eclipsed and often contemptuously treated by it, is, according to present appearances, likely to survive it. Taking the same view with Kant of the unknowableness of Things in themselves, and also agreeing with him that we mentally invest the objects of our perceptions with attributes which do not all point, like whiteness and sweetness, to specific sensations, but are in some cases constructed by the mind's own laws; this philosophy, however, does not think it necessary to ascribe to the mind certain innate forms, in which the objects are (as it were) moulded into these appearances, but holds that Place, Extension, Substance, Cause, and the rest, are conceptions put together out of ideas of sensation by the known laws of association. This, the doctrine of Hartley, of James Mill, of Professor Bain, and other eminent thinkers, and which is compatible with either the acceptance or the rejection of the Berkeleian theory, is the extreme form of one mode of the doctrine of Relativity, as Kant's is of another. Both schemes accept the doctrine in its widest sense—the entire inaccessibility to our faculties of any other knowledge of Things than that of the impressions which they produce in our mental consciousness.

Between these there are many intermediate systems, according as different thinkers have assigned more or less to the original furniture of the mind on the one hand, or to the associations generated by experience on the other. Brown, for example, regards our notion of Space or Extension as a product of association, while many of our intellectual ideas are regarded by him as ultimate and undecomposable facts. But he accepts, in its full extent, the doctrine of the Relativity of our knowledge, being of opinion that though we are assured of the objective existence of a world external to the mind, our knowledge of that world is absolutely limited to the modes in which we are affected by it. The same doctrine is very impressively taught by one of the acutest metaphysicians of recent times, Mr. Herbert Spencer, who, in his *First Principles*, insists with equal force upon the certainty of the existence of Things in Themselves, and upon their absolute and eternal relegation to the region of the Unknowable.* This is also, apparently, the doctrine of Auguste Comte: though while maintaining with great emphasis the unknowableness of Noumena by our faculties, his aversion to metaphysics prevented him from giving any definite opinion as to their real existence, which, however, his language always by implication assumes.[*]

It is obvious that what has been said respecting the unknowableness of Things "in themselves," forms no obstacle to our ascribing attributes or properties to them, provided these are always conceived as relative to us. If a thing produces effects of which our sight, hearing, or touch can take cognizance, it follows, and indeed is but the same statement in other words, that the thing has *power* to produce those effects. These various powers are its properties, and of such, an indefinite multitude is open to our knowledge. But this knowledge is merely phænomenal. The object is known to us only in one special relation, namely, as that which produces, or is capable of producing, certain impressions on our senses; and all that we really know is these impressions. This negative meaning is all that should be understood by the assertion, that we cannot know the Thing in itself; that we cannot know its inmost nature or essence. The inmost nature or essence of a Thing is apt to be regarded as something unknown, which, if we knew it, would

*[67] [(London: Williams and Norgate), 1862. See, for possible illustration, Pt. I, Chap. iii (esp. concerning the Self), pp. 65–6, and Pt. II, Chap. i, pp. 127ff.] See, however, below, a note near the end of Chap. ix [pp. 143n–4n below].

[*See, e.g., Auguste Comte, *Cours de philosophie positive*, 6 vols. (Paris: Bachelier, 1830–42), Vol. I, pp. 4, 8; Vol. IV, p. 529.]

explain and account for all the phænomena which the thing exhibits to us. But this unknown something is a supposition without evidence. We have no ground for supposing that there is anything which if known to us would afford to our intellect this satisfaction; would sum up, as it were, the knowable attributes of the object in a single sentence. Moreover, if there were such a central property, it would not answer to the idea of an "inmost nature;" for if knowable by any intelligence, it must, like other properties, be relative to the intelligence which knows it, that is, it must [h]solely[h] consist in [i]producing in that intelligence some specifically definite state of consciousness[i]; for this is the only idea we have of knowing; the only sense in which the verb "to know" means anything.

It would, no doubt, be absurd to assume that our words exhaust the possibilities of Being. There may be innumerable modes of it which are inaccessible to our faculties, and which consequently we are unable to name. But we ought not to speak of these modes of Being by any of the names we possess. These are all inapplicable, because they all stand for known modes of Being. We might invent new names for [j]such[j] unknown modes; but the new names would have no more meaning than the x, y, z, of Algebra. The only name we can give them which really expresses an attribute, is the word Unknowable.

The doctrine of the Relativity of our knowledge, in the sense which has now been explained, is one of great weight and significance, which impresses a character on the whole mode of philosophical thinking of whoever receives it, and is the key-stone of one of the only two possible systems of Metaphysics and Psychology. But the doctrine is capable of being, and is, understood in at least two other senses. In one of them, instead of a definite and important tenet, it means something quite insignificant, which no one ever did or could call in question. Suppose a philosopher to maintain that certain properties of objects are in the Thing, and not in our senses; in the thing itself, not as whiteness may be said to be in the thing (namely, that there is in the thing a power whereby it produces in us the sensation of white), but in quite another manner; and are known to us not indirectly, as the inferred causes of our sensations, but by direct perception of them in the outward object. Suppose the same philosopher nevertheless to affirm strenuously that all our knowledge is merely phænomenal, and relative to ourselves; that we do not and cannot know anything of outward objects, except relatively to our own faculties. I think our first feeling respecting a thinker who professed both these doctrines, would be to wonder what he could possibly mean by the latter of them. It would seem

[h-h]+72
[i-i]65[1], 65[2], 67   impressing that intelligence in some specific way
[j-j]65[1], 65[2]   the

that he must mean one of two trivialities; either that we can only know what we have the power of knowing, or else that all our knowledge is relative to us inasmuch as it is we that know it.

There is another mode of understanding the doctrine of Relativity, intermediate between these insignificant truisms and the substantial doctrine previously expounded. The position taken may be, that perception of Things as they are in themselves is not entirely denied to us, but is so mixed and *confounded* with impressions derived from their action on us, as to give a relative character to the whole aggregate. Our absolute knowledge may be vitiated and disguised by the presence of a relative element. Our faculty (it may be said) of perceiving things as they are in themselves, though real, has its own laws, its own conditions, and necessary mode of operation: our cognitions consequently depend, not solely on the nature of the things to be known, but also on that of the knowing faculty, as our sight depends not solely upon the object seen, but upon that together with the structure of the eye. If the eye were not achromatic, we should see all visible objects with colours derived from the organ, as well as with those truly emanating from the object. Supposing, therefore, that Things in themselves are the natural and proper object of our knowing faculty, and that this faculty carries to the mind a report of what is in the Thing itself, apart from its effects on us, there would still be a portion of uncertainty in these reports, inasmuch as we could not be sure that the eye of our mind is achromatic, and that the message it brings from the Noumenon does not arrive tinged and falsified, in an unknown degree, through an influence arising from the necessary conditions of the mind's action. We may, in short, be looking at Things in themselves, but through imperfect glasses: what we see may be the very Thing, but the colours and forms which the glass conveys to us may be partly an optical illusion. This is a possible opinion: and one who, holding this opinion, should speak of the Relativity of our knowledge, would not use the term wholly without meaning. But he could not, consistently, assert that *all* our knowledge is relative; since his opinion would be that we have a capacity of Absolute knowledge, but that we are liable to mistake relative knowledge for it.

In which, if in any, of these various meanings, was the doctrine of Relativity held by Sir W. Hamilton? To this question, a more puzzling one than might have been expected, we shall endeavour in the succeeding chapter to find an answer.

[k-k]65[1], 65[2]   confused

The Doctrine of the Relativity of Human Knowledge, as Held by Sir William Hamilton

IT IS HARDLY POSSIBLE to affirm more strongly or more explicitly than Sir W. Hamilton has done, that Things in themselves are to us altogether unknowable, and that all we can know of anything is its relation to us, composed of, and limited to, the Phænomena which it exhibits to our organs. Let me cite a passage from one of the Appendices to the *Discussions*.

Our whole knowledge of mind and of matter is relative, conditioned—relatively conditioned. Of things absolutely or in themselves, be they external, be they internal, we know nothing, or know them only as incognisable; and become aware of their incomprehensible existence, only as this is indirectly and accidentally revealed to us, through certain qualities related to our faculties of knowledge, and which qualities, again, we cannot think as unconditioned, irrelative, existent in and of themselves. All that we know is therefore phænomenal,—phænomenal of the unknown. . . . Nor is this denied; for it has been commonly confessed, that, as substances, we know not what is Matter, and are ignorant of what is Mind.*

This passage might be matched by many others, equally emphatic, and in appearance equally decisive; several of which I shall have occasion to quote. Yet in the sense which the author's phrases seem to convey—in the only *ªimportantª* meaning capable of being attached to them—the doctrine they assert was certainly not held by Sir W. Hamilton. He by no means admits that we know nothing of objects except their existence, and the impressions produced by them upon the human mind. He affirms this in regard to what have been called by metaphysicians the Secondary Qualities of Matter, but denies it of the Primary.

On this point his declarations are very explicit. One of the most elaborate of his "Dissertations on Reid" is devoted to expounding the distinction. The "Dissertation" begins thus:

The developed doctrine of Real Presentationism, the basis of Natural Realism [the doctrine of the author himself] asserts the consciousness or immediate percep-

---

*Discussions on Philosophy, [App. I(B),] pp. 643–4.

ª⁻ª65¹, 65² substantial

tion of certain essential attributes of Matter objectively existing; while it admits that other properties of body are unknown in themselves, and only inferred as causes to account for certain subjective affections of which we are cognizant in ourselves. This discrimination, which to other systems is contingent, superficial, extraneous, but to Natural Realism necessary, radical, intrinsic, coincides with what since the time of Locke has been generally known as the distinction of the Qualities of Matter or Body, using these terms as convertible, into Primary and Secondary.*

Further on, he states, in additional development of so-called Natural Realism,

that we have not merely a notion, a conception, an imagination, a subjective representation—of Extension, for example—called up or suggested in some incomprehensible manner to the mind, on occasion of an extended object being presented to the sense; but that in the perception of such an object we really have, as by nature we believe we have, an immediate knowledge of that external object *as extended*.[†]

If we are not percipient of any extended reality, we are not percipient of body as existing; for body exists, and can only be known immediately and in itself, *as extended*. The material world, on this supposition, sinks into something unknown and problematical; and its existence, if not denied, can, at least, be only precariously affirmed, as the occult cause, or incomprehensible occasion, of certain subjective affections we experience in the form either of a sensation of the secondary quality or of a perception of the primary.[‡]

Not only, in Sir W. Hamilton's opinion, do we know, by direct consciousness or perception, certain properties of Things as they exist in the Things themselves, but we may also know those properties as in the Things, by demonstration *à priori*. "The notion of body being given, every primary quality is to be evolved out of that notion, as necessarily involved in it, independently altogether of any experience of sense."[§] "The Primary Qualities may be deduced *à priori*, the bare notion of matter being given; they being, in fact, only evolutions of the conditions which that notion necessarily implies."[¶] He goes so far as to say, that our belief of the Primary Qualities is, not merely necessary as involved in a fact of which we have a direct perception, but necessary in itself, by our mental constitution. He speaks of "that absolute or insuperable resistance which we are compelled, independently of experience, to think that every part of matter would oppose to any attempt to deprive it of its space, by compressing it into an inextended."[||]

The following is still more specific. "The Primary" Qualities "are apprehended as they are in bodies; the Secondary, as they are in us: the

*"Dissertations" appended to Sir W. Hamilton's Edition of Reid's *Works*, [Note D,] p. 825.
[†]*Ibid*., p. 842.   [§]*Ibid*., p. 844n.   [||]*Ibid*., p. 848.
[‡]*Ibid*.   [¶]*Ibid*., p. 846.

Secundo-primary" (a third class created by himself, comprising the mechanical as distinguished from the geometrical properties of Body)

as they are in bodies and as they are in us. . . . We know the Primary qualities immediately as objects of perception; the Secundo-primary both immediately as objects of perception and mediately as causes of sensation; the Secondary only mediately as causes of sensation. In other words: The Primary are known immediately in themselves; the Secundo-primary, both immediately in themselves and mediately in their effects on us; the Secondary, only mediately in their effects on us. . . . We are conscious, as objects, in the Primary Qualities, of the modes of a not-self; in the Secondary, of the modes of self; in the Secundo-primary, of the modes of self and of a not-self at once.*

There is nothing wonderful in Sir W. Hamilton's entertaining these opinions; they are held by perhaps a majority of metaphysicians. But it is surprising that, entertaining them, he should have believed himself, and been believed by others, to maintain the Relativity of all our knowledge. What he deems to be relative, in any sense of the term that is not insignificant, is only our knowledge of the Secondary Qualities of objects. Extension and the other Primary Qualities he positively asserts that we have an immediate intuition of, "as they are in bodies"—"as modes of a not-self;" in express contradistinction to being known merely as causes of certain impressions on our senses or on our minds. As there cannot have been, in his own thoughts, a flat contradiction between what he would have admitted to be the two cardinal doctrines of his philosophy, the only question that can arise is, which of the two is to be taken in a non-natural sense. Is it the doctrine that we know certain properties as they are in the Things? Were we to judge from a foot-note to the same Dissertation, we might suppose so. He there observes—"In saying that a thing is known in itself, I do not mean that this object is known in its absolute existence, that is, out of relation to us. This is impossible: for our knowledge is only of the relative. To know a thing in itself or immediately, is an expression I use merely in contrast to the knowledge of a thing in a representation, or mediately:"† in other words, he merely means that we perceive objects directly, and not through the *species sensibiles* of Lucretius,[*] the Ideas of *b*Locke*b*, or the Mental Modifications of Brown.[†] Let us suppose this

---

Ibid., pp. 857–8. †P. 866n.

[*The attribution is mistaken. The notion originates with Aristotle; see *On the Soul*, in *On the Soul, Parva Naturalia, on Breath* (Greek and English), trans. W. S. Hett (London: Heinemann; Cambridge, Mass.: Harvard University Press, 1935), pp. 136, 180 (II, xii, 424ª19; III, viii, 432ª4). See also p. 155 below.]

[†See e.g., *Lectures on the Philosophy of Mind*, 19th ed., 4 vols. (Edinburgh: Black; London: Longman, 1851), Vol. II, p. 83. Brown does not use the term very often, but Hamilton uses it in his *Discussions* to distinguish Brown's theory from Reid's.]

*b–b*65¹, 65², 67 Berkeley

granted, and that the knowledge we have of objects is gained by direct perception. Still, the question has to be answered whether the knowledge so acquired is of the objects as they are in themselves, or only as they are relatively to us. Now what, according to Sir W. Hamilton, *is* this knowledge? Is it a knowledge of the Thing, merely in its effects on us, or is it a knowledge of somewhat in the Thing, ulterior to any effect on us? He asserts in the plainest terms that it is the latter. Then it is not a knowledge wholly relative to us. If what we perceive in the Thing is something of which we are only aware as existing, and as causing impressions on us, our knowledge of the Thing is only relative. But if what we perceive and cognise is not merely a cause of our subjective impressions, but a Thing possessing, in its own nature and essence, a long list of properties, Extension, Impenetrability, Number, Magnitude, Figure, Mobility, Position, all perceived as "essential attributes" of the Thing as "objectively existing"— all as "Modes of a Not-Self" and by no means as an occult cause or causes of any Modes of Self—(and that such is the case Sir W. Hamilton asserts in every form of language, leaving no stone unturned to make us apprehend the breadth of the distinction) then I am willing to believe that in affirming this knowledge to be entirely relative to Self, such a thinker as Sir W. Hamilton had a meaning, but I have no small difficulty in discovering what it is.

The place where we should expect to find this difficulty cleared up, is the formal exposition of the Relativity of Human Knowledge, in the first volume of the *Lectures*. He declares his intention of

now stating and explaining the great axiom that all human knowledge, consequently that all human philosophy, is only of the relative or phænomenal. In this proposition, the term *relative* is opposed to the term *absolute*; and therefore, in saying that we know only the relative, I virtually assert that we know nothing absolute,— nothing existing absolutely, that is, in and for itself, and without relation to us and our faculties. I shall illustrate this by its application. Our knowledge is either of matter or of mind. Now, what is matter? What do we know of matter? Matter, or body, is to us the name either of something known, or of something unknown. In so far as matter is a name for something known, it means that which appears to us under the forms of extension, solidity, divisibility, figure, motion, roughness, smoothness, colour, heat, cold, &c.; in short, it is a common name for a certain series, or aggregate, or complement, of appearances or phænomena manifested in coexistence.

But as these phænomena appear only in conjunction, we are compelled by the constitution of our nature to think them conjoined in and by something; and as they are phænomena, we cannot think them the phænomena of nothing, but must regard them as the properties or qualities of something that is extended, solid, figured, &c. But this something, absolutely and in itself, *i.e.* considered apart from its phænomena—is to us as zero. It is only in its qualities, only in its effects, in its relative or phænomenal existence, that it is cognizable or conceivable; and it is only by a law of thought which compels us to think something absolute and unknown, as the basis or condition of the relative and known, that this something obtains a kind of incomprehensible reality to us. Now, that which manifests its qualities—in other words, that in which the appearing causes inhere, that to which they belong,—is called their *subject*, or *substance*, or *substratum*. To this subject of the phænomena of extension, solidity, &c., the term *matter* or *material substance* is commonly given; and therefore, as contradistinguished from these qualities, it is the name of something unknown and inconceivable.

The same is true in regard to the term *mind*. In so far as mind is the common name for the states of knowing, willing, feeling, desiring, &c., of which I am conscious, it is only the name for a certain series of connected phænomena or qualities, and, consequently, expresses only what is known. But in so far as it denotes that subject or substance in which the phænomena of knowing, willing, &c., inhere—something behind or under these phænomena,—it expresses what, in itself or in its absolute existence, is unknown.

Thus, mind and matter, as known or knowable, are only two different series of phænomena or qualities; mind and matter, as unknown and unknowable, are the two substances, in which these two different series of phænomena or qualities are supposed to inhere. *c*The existence of an unknown substance is only an inference*c* we are compelled to make from the existence of known phænomena; and the distinction of two substances is only inferred from the seeming incompatibility of the two series of phænomena to coinhere in one.

Our whole knowledge of mind and matter is thus, as we have said, only relative; of existence, absolutely and in itself, we know nothing: and we may say of man what Virgil said of Æneas, contemplating in the prophetic sculpture of his shield the future glories of Rome—
> "Rerumque ignarus, imagine gaudet."*

Here is an exposition of the nature and limits of our knowledge, which would have satisfied Hartley, Brown, and even Comte. It cannot be more explicitly laid down, that Matter, as known to us, is but the incomprehensible and incognisable basis or substratum of a bundle of sensible qualities, appearances, phænomena; that we know it "only in its effects;" that its very existence is "only an inference we are compelled to make" from those sensible appearances *d*. On the subject of Mind, again, could it have been more explicitly affirmed, that all we know of Mind is its successive states "of knowing, willing, feeling, desiring, &c.," and that Mind, considered as "something behind or under these phænomena," is to us unknowable?

Subsequently he says, that not only all the knowledge we have of anything, but all which we could have if we were a thousandfold better endowed than we are, would still be only knowledge of the mode in which the thing would affect us. Had we as many senses (the illustration is his

---

Lectures, Vol. I, pp. 136–8. [Virgil, *Aeneid*, in *Works*, trans. H. Rushton Fairclough, 2 vols. (London: Heinemann; New York: Putnam's Sons, 1916), Vol. II, p. 110 (VIII, 730).]

*c-c*65[1], 65[2] [*in italics*]

*d*65[1], 65[2] : a doctrine, by the way, which, under the name of Cosmothetic Idealism, is elsewhere the object of some of his most cutting attacks

own) as the inhabitants of Sirius, in the *Micromegas* of Voltaire;[*] were there, as there may well be, a thousand modes of real existence as definitely distinguished from one another as are those which manifest themselves to our present senses, and "had we, for each of these thousand modes, a separate organ competent to make it known to us,—still would our whole knowledge be, as it is at present, only of the relative. Of existence, absolutely and in itself, we should then be as ignorant as we are now. We should still apprehend existence only in certain special modes—only in certain relations to our faculties of knowledge."*

Nothing can be truer or more clearly stated than all this: but the clearer it is, the more irreconcileable does it appear with our author's doctrine of the direct cognoscibility of the Primary Qualities. If it be true that Extension, Figure, and the other qualities enumerated, are known "immediately in themselves," and not, like Secondary qualities, "in their effects on us;" if the former are "apprehended as they are in bodies," and not, like the Secondary, "as they are in us;" if it is these last exclusively that are "unknown in themselves, and only inferred as causes to account for certain subjective affections in ourselves:" while, of the former, we are immediately conscious as "attributes of matter objectively existing;" and if it is not to be endured that matter should "sink into something unknown and problematical," whose existence "can be only precariously affirmed as the occult cause or incomprehensible occasion of certain subjective affections we experience in the form either of a sensation of the secondary quality or of a perception of the primary" (being precisely what Sir W. Hamilton, in the preceding quotations, appeared to say that it is); if these things be so, our faculties, as far as the Primary Qualities are concerned, do cognise and know Matter as it is in itself, and not merely as an unknowable and incomprehensible substratum; they do cognise and know it as it exists absolutely, and not merely in relation to us; it is known to us directly, and not as a mere "inference" from Phænomena.

Will it be said that the attributes of extension, figure, number, magnitude, and the rest, though known as in the Things themselves, are yet known only relatively to us, because it is by our faculties that we know them, and because appropriate faculties are the necessary condition of knowledge? If so, the "great axiom" of Relativity is reduced to this, that we can know Things as they are in themselves, but can know no more of them than our faculties are competent to inform us of. If such be the meaning of Relativity, our author might well maintain that it is a truth "harmoniously re-echoed by every philosopher of every school;" nor need he have added

[*See *Micromégas*, in *Œuvres complètes*, 66 vols. (Paris: Renouard, 1817–25), Vol. XXXIX, pp. 141–67.]
Lectures, Vol. I, p. 153.

"with the exception of a few late Absolute theorizers in Germany;"* for certainly neither Schelling nor Hegel claims for us any other knowledge than such as our faculties are, in their opinion, competent to give.

Is it possible, that by knowledge of qualities "as they are in Bodies," no more was meant than knowing that the Body must have qualities whereby it produces the affection of which we are conscious in ourselves? But this is the very knowledge which our author predicates of Secondary Qualities, as contradistinguished from the Primary. Secondary he frankly acknowledges to be occult qualities: we really, in his opinion, have no knowledge, and no conception, what that is in an object, by virtue of which it has its specific smell or taste. But Primary qualities, according to him, we know all about: there is nothing occult or mysterious to us in these; we perceive and conceive them as they are in themselves, and as they are in the body they belong to. They are manifested to us, not, like the Secondary qualities, only in their effects, in the sensations they excite in us, but in their own nature and essence.

Perhaps it may be surmised, that in calling knowledge of this sort by the epithet Relative, Sir W. Hamilton meant that though we know those qualities as they are in themselves, we only discover them through their relation to certain effects in us; that in order that there may be Perception there must also be Sensation; and we thus know the Primary Qualities, in their effects on us and also in themselves. But neither will this explanation serve. This theory of Primary Qualities does not clash with the Secondary, but it runs against the Secundo-primary. It is this third class, which, as he told us, are known "both immediately in themselves and mediately in their effects on us." The Primary are only known "immediately in themselves." He has thus with his own hands deliberately extruded from our knowledge of the Primary qualities the element of relativity to us:—except, to be sure, in the acceptation in which knowing is itself a relation, inasmuch as it implies a knower; whereby instead of the doctrine that Things in themselves are not possible objects of knowledge, we obtain the "great axiom" that they cannot be known unless there is somebody to know them. *e*

Discussions, Appendix [I(B)], p. 644.

*e*65[1], 65[2] [*paragraph*] Perhaps it may be suspected (and some phrases in the longest of our extracts might countenance the idea) that in calling our knowledge relative, Sir W. Hamilton was not thinking of the knowledge of qualities, but of Substances, of Matter and Mind; and meant that qualities might be cognised absolutely, but that Substances being only known through their qualities, the knowledge of Substances can only be regarded as relative. But this interpretation of his doctrine is again inadmissible. For the relativity of which he is continually speaking is relativity *to us*, while the relativity which this theory ascribes to Substances is relativity to their attributes; and if the attributes are known otherwise than relatively to us, so must the substances be. Besides, we have seen him asserting the necessary relativity of our knowledge of Attributes, no less positively than of Substances. Speaking of Things in themselves, we found him saying that we "become aware of their incomprehensible existence

Can any light be derived from the statement that we do not know any qualities of things except those which are in connexion with our faculties, or, as our author expresses it (surely by a very strained use of language), which are "analogous to our faculties?"* If, by "our faculties," is to be understood our knowing faculty, this proposition is but the trivial one already noticed, that we can know only what we can know. And this is what the author actually seems to mean; for in a sentence immediately following, he paraphrases the expression "analogous to our faculties," by the phrase that we must "possess faculties accommodated to their apprehension."† To be able to see, we must have a faculty accommodated to seeing. Is this what we are intended to understand by the "great axiom?" ƒ But if "our faculties" does not here mean our knowing faculty, it must mean our sensitive faculties; and the statement is, that, to be known by us, a quality must be "analogous" (meaning, I suppose, related) to our senses. But what is meant by being related to our senses? That it must be fitted to give us sensations. We thus return as before to an identical proposition.

ᵍ There is still another possible supposition; that, in calling our knowledge relative in contradistinction to absolute, Sir W. Hamilton was not thinking of our knowledge of qualities, but of substances—of Matter and Mind; and meant that qualities might be cognised absolutely, or as they are in themselves, but that, since substances are only known through their qualities, the knowledge of substances is not knowledge of them as they are in themselves, but is merely relative. According to this interpretation, the relativity which Sir W. Hamilton ascribes to our knowledge of substances is relativity not to us, but to their attributes: we "become aware of their incomprehensible existence only as this is revealed to us through certain qualities." And when he adds, "which qualities, again, we cannot think as unconditioned, irrelative, existent in and of themselves,"[*] thus predicating relativity of attributes also (considered as known or conceived by us), he means relativity to a substance. We can only know a substance through its qualities, but also, we can only know qualities as inhering in a substance. Substance and attribute are correlative, and can only be thought together: the knowledge of each, therefore, is relative to the other; but need not be,

---

*Lectures, Vol. I, pp. 141, 153.
†Ibid., p. 153.
[*Discussions, App. I(B), pp. 643–4; cf. p. 13 above.]

only as this is revealed to us through certain qualities . . . which qualities, again, we cannot think as unconditioned, irrelative, existent in and of themselves." [Discussions, App. I(B), pp. 643–4.] There is no reservation here in favour of the Primary Qualities. Whatever, in his theory, was meant by relativity of knowledge, he intended it of qualities as much as of substances, of Primary Qualities as much as of Secondary. [cf. 20ᵍ⁻ᵍ²² below]
ƒ65¹, 65² [paragraph]
ᵍ⁻ᵍ²²+67, 72

and indeed is not, relative to us. For we know attributes as they are in themselves, and our knowledge of them is only relative inasmuch as attributes have only a relative existence. It is relative knowledge in a sense not contradictory to absolute. It is an absolute knowledge, though of things which only exist in a necessary relation to another thing called a substance.*

I am not disposed to deny that this interpretation of Sir W. Hamilton's doctrine is, to a certain point, correct. He did draw a distinction between our manner of knowing attributes and our manner of knowing substances; and did regard certain attributes (the primary qualities) as objects of direct and immediate knowledge; which, in his opinion, substances are not, but are merely assumed or inferred from phænomena, by a law of our nature which compels us to think phænomena as attributes of something beyond themselves. I do not doubt that when he said that our knowledge of attributes is relative, the necessity of thinking every attribute as an attribute of a substance was present to his mind, and formed a part of his meaning. *h*There is, however, abundant evidence that the relativity which Sir W. Hamilton ascribed to our knowledge of attributes was not merely relativity to their substances, but also relativity to us. He affirms of attributes as positively as of substances, that all our knowledge of them is relative to us. The passages already quoted apply as much to attributes as to substances. "In saying that we know only the relative, I virtually assert that we know *nothing* absolute—nothing existing absolutely, that is, in and for itself, and *without relation to us and our faculties*."† "In saying that a thing is known in itself, I do not mean that this object is known in its absolute existence, that is, *out of relation to us*. This is impossible, for *our knowledge is only of the relative*."‡ In the following passages he is speaking solely of attributes. "By the expression *what they are in themselves*, in reference to the primary qualities, and of *relative notion* in reference to the secondary, Reid cannot mean that the former are known to us absolutely and in themselves, that is, out of relation to our cognitive faculties; for he elsewhere admits that all our knowledge is relative."§ "We can know, we can conceive, only what is relative. Our knowledge of qualities or phænomena is necessarily relative; for these exist only as they exist in

---

*[67] This is essentially the interpretation put on Sir W. Hamilton's meaning by the ingenious reviewer [John Cunningham] of the present work in the *Edinburgh Review* [CXXIV (July, 1866), 146–9].

†[67] *Lectures*, Vol. I, p. 137.

‡[67] "Dissertations on Reid," [Note D,] p. 866n.

§[67] Foot-note to Reid, [*Works*, ed. Hamilton (Edinburgh: Maclachlan and Stewart, 1846,] p. 313n.

h-h[*manuscript fragment exists; see* Appendix A *below*]

relation to our faculties."* The distinction, therefore, which Sir W. Hamilton recognises between our knowledge of substances and that of attributes, though authentically a part of his philosophy, is quite irrelevant here.[h] He affirms without reservation, that certain attributes (extension, figure, &c.) are known to us as they really exist out of ourselves; and also that all our knowledge of them is relative to us. And these two assertions are only reconcileable, if relativity to us is understood in the altogether trivial sense, that we know them only so far as our faculties permit.[†g]

The conclusion I cannot help drawing from this collation of passages is, that Sir W. Hamilton either never held, or when he wrote the "Dissertations" had ceased to hold [i](for his theory respecting knowledge of the Primary Qualities does not occur in the *Lectures*)[i] the doctrine for which he has been so often praised and nearly as often attacked—the Relativity of Human Knowledge. He certainly did sincerely believe that he held it. But he repudiated it in every sense which makes it other than a barren truism. In the only meaning in which he really maintained it, there is nothing to maintain. It is an identical proposition, and nothing more.

And to this, or something next to this, he [j] reduces it in [k]the first portion of[k] the summary with which he concludes its exposition. "From what has been said," he observes, "you will be able, I hope, to understand what is meant by the proposition, that all our knowledge is only relative. It is relative, 1st. Because existence is not cognisable absolutely in itself, but only in special modes; 2nd. Because these modes can be known only if they stand in a certain relation to our faculties." Whoever can find anything more in these two statements, than that we do not know all about a Thing, but only as much about it as we are capable of knowing, is more ingenious or more fortunate than myself.

He adds, however, to these reasons why our knowledge is only relative, a third reason. "3rd. Because the modes, thus relative to our faculties, are assented to, and known by, the mind only under modifications determined by those faculties themselves."[‡] Of this addition to the theory we took

*[67] *Ibid.*, pp. 322n–3n. I am indebted to Mr. Mansel (*Philosophy of the Conditioned*, p. 79) for reminding me of the last two passages. I should not have failed to quote them in the first edition, if I had kept references to them.

†[67] I may add that even the Edinburgh Reviewer's supposition [see Cunningham, p. 148] does not save either the relativity of human knowledge *to us*, or its relativity in the sense in which relative is opposed to absolute, as doctrines of Sir W. Hamilton: for by the Reviewer's interpretation our knowledge of attributes would be relative only to their substances; absolute in their cognition by us.

‡*Lectures*, Vol. I, p. 148.

[i–i]+67, 72
[j]65[1], 65[2]   openly
[k–k]+67, 72

notice near the conclusion of the preceding chapter.[*] It shall have the advantage of a fuller explanation in Sir W. Hamilton's words.

In the perception of an external object, the mind does not know it in immediate relation to itself, but mediately, in relation to the material organs of sense. If, therefore, we were to throw these organs out of consideration, and did not take into account what they contribute to, and how they modify, our knowledge of that object, it is evident that our conclusion in regard to the nature of external perception would be erroneous. Again, an object of perception may not even stand in immediate relation to the organ of sense, but may make its impression on that organ through an intervening medium. Now, if this medium be thrown out of account, and if it be not considered that the real external object is the sum of all that externally contributes to affect the sense, we shall, in like manner, run into error. For example, I see a book—I see that book through an external medium (what that medium is, we do not now inquire) and I see it through my organ of sight, the eye. Now, as the full object presented to the mind (observe that I say the mind) in perception, is an object compounded of the external object emitting or reflecting light, i.e., modifying the external medium—of this external medium—and of the living organ of sense, in their mutual relation, let us suppose, in the example I have taken, that the full or adequate object perceived is equal to twelve, and that this amount is made up of three several parts; of four, contributed by the book,—of four, contributed by all that intervenes between the book and the organ,—and of four, contributed by the living organ itself. I use this illustration to show that the phænomenon of the external object is not presented immediately to the mind, but is known by it only as modified through certain intermediate agencies; and to show, that sense itself may be a source of error, if we do not analyze and distinguish what elements, in an act of perception, belong to the outward reality, what to the outward medium, and what to the action of sense itself. But this source of error is not limited to our perceptions; and we are liable to be deceived, not merely by not distinguishing in an act of knowledge what is contributed by sense, but by not distinguishing what is contributed by the mind itself. This is the most difficult and important function of philosophy; and the greater number of its higher problems arise in the attempt to determine the shares to which the knowing subject, and the object known, may pretend in the total act of cognition. For according as we attribute a larger or a smaller proportion to each, we either run into the extremes of Idealism and Materialism, or maintain an equilibrium between the two.*

The proposition, that our cognitions of objects are only in part dependent on the objects themselves, and in part on elements superadded by our organs or by our minds, is not identical, nor primâ facie absurd. It cannot, however, warrant the assertion that all our knowledge, but only that the part so added, is relative. If our author had gone as far as Kant, and had said that all *the primary qualities which we think we perceive in bodies, are* put in by the mind itself, he would have really held, in one of its forms, the doctrine of the Relativity of our knowledge. But what he does say, far from

[*See p. 12 above.]
*Lectures, Vol. I, pp. 146–8.

*-*65[1], 65[2], 67   which constitutes knowledge is

implying that the whole of our knowledge is relative, distinctly imports that all of it which is real and authentic is the reverse. If any part of what we fancy that we perceive in the objects themselves, originates in the perceiving organs or in the cognising mind, thus much is purely relative; but since, by supposition, it does not all so originate, the part that does not, is as much absolute as if it were not liable to be mixed up with these delusive subjective impressions. The admixture of the relative element not only does not take away the absolute character of the remainder, but does not even (if our author is right) prevent us from recognising it. The confusion, according to him, is not inextricable. It is for us to "analyze and distinguish what elements" in an "act of knowledge" are contributed by the object, and what by our organs, or by the mind. We may neglect to do this, and as far as the mind's share is concerned, can only do it by the help of philosophy; but it is a task to which in his opinion philosophy is equal. By thus stripping off such of the elements in our apparent cognitions of Things as are but cognitions of something in us, and consequently relative, we may succeed in uncovering the pure nucleus, the direct intuitions of Things in themselves; as we correct the observed positions of the heavenly bodies by allowing for the error due to the refracting influence of the atmospheric medium, an influence which does not alter the facts, but only our perception of them.

^{m}This last doctrine, however,—that the mind's own constitution contributes along with the outward object, to make up what is called our knowledge of the object,—is what Mr. Mansel maintains Sir W. Hamilton to have meant by the assertion that our whole knowledge of the object is relative. And this is the foundation of all that Mr. Mansel presents as a refutation of the present chapter.

If it be true (to use Mr. Mansel's words) that, in the constitution of our knowledge, the mind "reacts on the objects affecting it, so as to produce a result different from that which would be produced, were it merely a passive recipient,"* this modifying action of the mind must consist, as is affirmed by Kant and by all others who profess the doctrine, in making us ascribe to the object, and apprehend as in the object, properties which are not really in the object, but are merely lent to it by the constitution of our mental nature. Now, if the attributes which we perceive, or think we perceive, in objects, are partly given by the mind, but not wholly, being also partly given by the nature of the object itself (which is admitted to be Sir W. Hamilton's opinion); this joint agency of the object and of the mind's own laws in generating what we call our knowledge of the object, may be conceived in two ways.

*[67] Mansel, [*Philosophy of the Conditioned,*] p. 64.

$^{m-m32}$+67, 72

First: The two factors may be jointly operative in every part of the effect. Every attribute with which we perceive the thing as invested, may be a joint product of the thing itself and of the modifying action of the mind. If this be the case, we do not really know any property as it is in the object: we have no reason to think that the object as we apprehend it, and as we figure to ourselves that we perceive and know it, agrees in any respect with the object that exists without us; but only that it depends upon that outward object, as one of its joint causes. Such was the opinion of Kant; and whoever is of this opinion, holds, in one of its forms, as I have expressly admitted, the genuine doctrine of the Relativity of our knowledge. For all must agree with Mr. Mansel when he says, that an object of thought, into which the mind puts a positive element of its own, thereby making it different from what it otherwise would be, *is* that which it is, only relatively to the mind. This seems to be Mr. Mansel's own mode of representing to himself the combined action of the mind and the object in perception. For he compares it to the action of an acid and an alkali in forming a neutral salt;* and to a chemical fusion together of two elements, in contradistinction to a mere mechanical juxtaposition.† If we had never seen, and could not get at, the acid or the alkali except as united in the salt, Mr. Mansel could not think that our knowledge of the salt gave us any knowledge of the acid or the alkali themselves.

But, secondly: There is another mode in which the co-operation of the object and the mind's own properties in producing our cognition of the object, may be conceived as taking place. Instead of their being joint agents in producing our cognitions of all the attributes with which we mentally clothe the object, some of the attributes as cognised by us may come from the object only, and some from the mind only, or from both. Now it is not open to a holder of this second opinion, as it is to one of the first, to affirm that all the attributes are only known relatively to us. Such of them, indeed, as are made to be that which they are by what the mind puts into them, are, on this theory, only known relatively to the mind: they have even no existence except relatively to the mind. But those into which no positive element is introduced by the mind's laws (I say no positive element, because a mere negative limitation by the mind's capacities is nothing to the purpose), these, as their cognition contains nothing but what is presented in the external object, must be held to be known not relatively, but absolutely. The doubt how much of what we apprehend in them is due to our own constitution, and how much to the external world, has no place here: they are, by supposition, wholly perceptions of something in the external world.

*[67] *Ibid.*, p. 71.
†[67] *Ibid.*, p. 75.

Now, this second view of the joint action of the mind and the outward thing, as the two factors in our cognition of the thing, is Sir W. Hamilton's. The passages in which he characterizes our knowledge of the Primary Qualities place this beyond question. He affirms clearly and consistently that extension, figure, and the other Primary Qualities are known by us "as they are in bodies," and not "as they are in us;" that they are known as "essential attributes of matter objectively existing;" as "modes of a not-self," not even combined, as in the Secundo-primary, with any "modes of self;"[*] so that no element originating in our subjective constitution interferes with the purity of the apperception. In this respect the physical phenomena which Mr. Mansel calls in as illustrations afford no parallel. No one would say that the acid in a neutral salt is perceived and known by us in the salt as what it is as an acid. Indeed, the ⁿdiscrimination whichⁿ Sir W. Hamilton thinks it possible for philosophy to ºmake,º between that in our knowledge which the object contributes and that which the mind contributes, ᵖalmost requires as its condition that some attributes should beᵖ wholly contributed by the one and some by the other: for if every attribute was the joint product of both, ᑫit is difficult to see what means the case could affordᑫ of making the discrimination, any more than of discriminating between the acid and the alkali in Mr. Mansel's salt. The question, how much of the salt is due to the acid and how much to the alkali, is not merely unresolvable, but intrinsically absurd.*

[*"Dissertations on Reid," Note D, pp. 825 and 857–8; quoted more extensively above, p. 15.]

*[72] Sir W. Hamilton has the appearance of disclaiming the opinion here attributed to him, and professing the alternative opinion that every attribute is a joint product of the object and the mind, in the following foot-note to Reid:

"The distinctions of perception and sensation, and of primary and secondary qualities, may be reduced to one higher principle. Knowledge is partly objective, partly subjective; both these elements are essential to every cognition, but in every cognition they are always in the inverse ratio of each other. Now, in perception and the primary qualities, the objective element preponderates; whereas the subjective element preponderates in sensation and the secondary qualities. See Notes D and D*." (Pp. 313n–14n.)

But a reference to the Notes in question will shew, that in admitting a subjective element in the Primary Qualities, he only meant that a subjective element *accompanies* our apprehension of them; that whenever we perceive the primary qualities we are conscious of a sensation also. "Sensation proper," he says, "is the *conditio sine qua non* of a Perception proper of the Primary qualities." And again, "Every Perception proper has a Sensation proper as its condition." "The fact of Sensation proper and the fact of Perception proper imply each other:" they always co-exist,

ⁿ⁻ⁿ67   very fact that
º⁻º67   discriminate
ᵖ⁻ᵖ67   shows that he regarded some attributes as
ᑫ⁻ᑫ67   there would be no means

Mr. Mansel's mode of reconciling Sir W. Hamilton's emphatic declaration, that we know the Primary Qualities as they are in objects, with his assertion of the entire incognoscibility of Things in themselves, is by saying that "objects" are not identical with "things in themselves."* "Objective existence," he says,

does not mean existence *per se*; and a phenomenon does not mean a mere mode of mind. Objective existence is existence as an object, in perception, and therefore in relation; and a phenomenon may be material, as well as mental. The thing *per se* may be only the unknown cause of what we directly know; but what we directly know is something more than our own sensations. In other words, the phenomenal effect is material as well as the cause, and is, indeed, that from which our primary conceptions of matter are derived.†

Now, this is a possible opinion; it was really the opinion of Kant. That philosopher did recognise a direct object of our perceptions, different from the thing itself, and intermediate between it and the perceiving mind. And it was open to Kant to do so; because he held what Sir W. Hamilton calls a representative theory of perception. He maintained that the object of our perception, and of our knowledge, is a representation in our own minds. In his philosophy, both object and subject are accommodated within the mind itself—the object within the subject. The mind has no perception of the external thing, nor comes into any contact with it in the act of perception.‡ Was this Sir W. Hamilton's opinion? On the contrary, if there be a doctrine of his philosophy which he has laboured at beyond any other, against, as he

---

though "in the degree or intensity of their existence they are always found in an inverse ratio to one another" ("Dissertations," [Note D*,] p. 880). This co-existence does not prevent the two from being entirely distinct. "The apprehensions of the Primary" qualities "are perceptions, not sensations; of the Secondary, sensations, not perceptions; of the Secundo-primary, perceptions and sensations together" ([*ibid.*, Note D,] p. 858). Perceptions, the apprehensions of the Primary qualities, are themselves wholly objective.

*[67] Mansel, [*Philosophy of the Conditioned*,] p. 79n.

†[67] *Ibid.*, pp. 82–3.

‡[67] Such, at least, is the doctrine of Kant in the first edition of the *Kritik*, though, in the so-called Refutation of Idealism introduced into the second, he is sometimes supposed to have intended to explain it away [see *Kritik der Reinen Vernunft*, Vol. II of *Sämmtliche Werke*, ed. Karl Rosenkranz and Friedrich Schubert, 14 vols. in 12 (Leipzig: Voss, 1838–40), pp. 31–238 (1st ed.), and 772–5 (the Refutation in the 2nd ed.).]; but Mr. Mahaffy (Intro., Pt. IV [pp. xxxviii–liii], and notes to Appendix C) seems to have explained away the explanation [cf. George Gordon Byron, "Dedication ii," *Don Juan*, in *Works*, ed. Thomas Moore, 17 vols. (London: Murray, 1832–33), Vol. XV, p. 101]; and Mr. Stirling, who holds "the second edition of the *Kritik of Pure Reason* to supersede the first," (p. 30n,) still credits Kant with this doctrine, interpreting in a sense consistent with it, the externality which Kant ascribes to objects in space. Kant's external and internal were both internal to the mind. Nothing but the noumenon was external to it.

affirms, nearly all philosophers, it is, that the thing we perceive is the real thing which exists outside us, and that the perceiving mind is in direct contact with it, without any intermediate link whatever. We never hear from Sir W. Hamilton of three elements in our cognition of the outward world, but of two only, the mind, and the real object; which he sometimes calls the external object, sometimes Body, sometimes Matter, sometimes a Non-ego. Yet, according to Mr. Mansel, he must have believed that this object, which he so strenuously contended to be the very thing itself, is not the very thing *in* itself, but that behind it there is another Thing in itself, the unknown cause of it. I can discover no trace in Sir W. Hamilton's writings of any such entity. The outward things which he believed to exist, he believed that we perceive and know: not, indeed, "absolutely or in themselves," because only in such of their attributes as we have senses to reveal to us; but yet as they really are. He did not believe in, or recognise, a Thing *per se*, itself unknowable, but engendering another material object called a phænomenon, which is knowable. The only distinction he recognised between a phænomenon and a Thing *per se*, was that between attributes and a substance. But he believed the primary attributes to be known by us as they exist in the substance, and not in some intermediate object.*

*[67] If any doubt could remain that Mr. Mansel defends Sir W. Hamilton by ascribing to him an opinion he never held, the following passage would dispel it. "If, indeed," says Mr. Mansel "Hamilton had said with Locke, that the primary qualities are in the bodies themselves, whether we perceive them or no, he would have laid himself open to Mr. Mill's criticism. But he expressly rejects this statement, and contrasts it with the more cautious language of Descartes, 'ut sunt, vel saltem esse possunt.'" ([*Philosophy of the Conditioned*,] pp. 83–4. [The Locke reference is to the *Essay Concerning Human Understanding*, in *Works*, New ed., 10 vols. (London: Tegg, *et al.*, 1823), Vol. I, p. 126 (Bk. II, Chap. viii, §23); the Descartes quotation is from René Descartes, *Principia Philosophiæ*, 4th ed. (Amsterdam: Elzevir, 1664), p. 18 (I, lxx).]) Sir W. Hamilton may never have said, *totidem verbis*, that the Primary Qualities are in the bodies even when we do not perceive them: but can any one who has read his writings doubt that this was his opinion? The passage which Mr. Mansel refers to as "rejecting" it runs as follows: "On the doctrine of both philosophers" (Locke and Descartes) "we know nothing of material existence in itself: we know it only as represented, or in idea. When Locke, therefore, is asked, how he became aware that the known idea truly represents the unknown reality, he can make no answer. On the first principles of his philosophy, he is wholly and necessarily ignorant whether the idea does or does not represent to his mind the attributes of matter, as they exist in nature. His assertion is, therefore, confessedly without a warrant; it transcends, ex hypothesi, the sphere of possible knowledge. Descartes is more cautious. He only says, that our ideas of the qualities in question represent those qualities as they are, or as they may exist; 'ut sunt, vel saltem esse possunt.' The Cosmothetic Idealist can only assert to them a problematical reality." ("Dissertations on Reid," [Note D,] p. 839.)

Mr. Mansel actually thinks this an adoption of Descartes' opinion; and does not see that Sir W. Hamilton merely pronounces Descartes to be right and Locke wrong

The mark by which Mr. Mansel distinguishes between the object and the Thing in itself, is that the object is in space and time, but the Thing out of space and time; space and time having merely a subjective existence, in us, not in external nature. This is Kantism, but it is not Hamiltonism. I do not believe that the expression "out of space and time" is to be found once in all Sir W. Hamilton's writings. It belongs to the Kantian, not to the Hamiltonian philosophy. Sir W. Hamilton does indeed hold with Kant, and on

---

from their own point of view, that of Cosmothetic Idealism. As Cosmothetic Idealists, they have, he says, no evidence that the qualities we perceive are in the object itself, and are as we perceive them. Not admitting that we directly perceive the qualities in the object, they cannot do more than assert problematically that the qualities are in the object; and this Descartes saw, and Locke, more inconsistently, did not see. But what they as Cosmothetic Idealists could not affirm, Sir W. Hamilton, as a Natural Realist, could; because, as a Natural Realist, he held that we directly perceive the qualities in the object. Mr. Mansel mistakes one of the thousand statements by Sir W. Hamilton of his difference with the Cosmothetic Idealists, for an adhesion to them. ʳ(Mr. Mansel, in his rejoinder, admits and withdraws this error ["Supplementary Remarks," p. 20n].)ʳ Sir W. Hamilton, as Professor Fraser observes, believed that "the solid and extended percepts which our sensations reveal to us, exist, whether we are conscious or not." (["Mr. Mill's *Examination*,"] p. 22.) He believed that bodies exist whether we perceive them or not, and that they always carry their "essential attributes," the Primary Qualities, with them: if, therefore, he had thought that the Primary Qualities only exist while we perceive them, he must have thought so of the bodies likewise, and must have believed that we create the bodies in the act of perceiving them; which Kant, who deemed the body we perceive to be really in the mind, did believe; but if Sir W. Hamilton did, his whole philosophy of perception is without a meaning.

In the essay in his *Discussions*, headed "Philosophy of Perception," Sir W. Hamilton speaks of the knowledge of external objects claimed by a Natural Realist, *ipsissimis verbis*, as knowledge of "things in themselves." (*Discussions*, p. 57, in the statement of the opinion of Hypothetical Realists.)

For a critical examination of the doctrine ascribed to Sir W. Hamilton by Mr. Mansel, that of an external object cognizable by us, and an uncognizable Noumenon besides, I may refer to Mr. Bolton's able work, [*Inquisitio Philosophica*,] pp. 218ff.

ˢMr. Mansel, in his rejoinder, though he does not give up the theory of the tertium quid, does not further insist on it; but attempts to shew that when Sir W. Hamilton speaks of knowing the Primary qualities as they are in themselves, and as they are in the body, he means knowing them in immediate relation to the mind, in contradistinction to knowing them mediately through a mental representation, or merely inferring them as the hypothetical cause of a mental state. ["Supplementary Remarks," pp. 20–1.] I admit, and have already admitted, that Sir W. Hamilton did mean this, and did say that he meant it. But the "immediate relation to the mind" which Sir W. Hamilton thus distinguished from the different modes of mediate relation, is no other than that between perceiver and perceived: and to say that all

---

ʳ⁻ʳ67   As a specimen of misunderstanding of a philosopher's opinions by his commentator and defender, this, it must be acknowledged, stands high.
ˢ⁻ˢ+72

Kant's shewing, that space and time are *à priori* forms of the mind, but he believes that they are also external realities, known empirically.* And it is worth notice, that he grounds the outward reality of Space, not on his favourite evidence, that of our Natural Beliefs, but on the specific reason, that (Extension being only another name for Space), if Space was not an outward thing cognizable *à posteriori*, we could not, as he affirms that we do, cognize Extension as an external reality. He must therefore have thought, not that Space is a mere form in which our perceptions of objects are clothed by the laws of our perceiving faculty, but that we perceive real things in real space.†

Mr. Mansel is not the only one of my critics who has interpreted Sir W. Hamilton's doctrine of our direct knowledge of outward objects, as if those outward objects were a *tertium quid*, between the mind and the real outward, or if the expression may be permitted, the outer outward object. For, irreconcilable as this supposition is with the evidence of his writings, it is the only one which can be thought of to give a substantial meaning to his doctrine of Relativity, consistent with the external reality of the Primary Qualities. Professor Masson consequently had already taken refuge in the same interpretation as Mr. Mansel; but propounded it in the modest form of

---

our knowledge is relative, meaning only *this* relation, is but to say, that we know of external things only what we perceive of them, and that in order that we may know an object of sense it must be presented to our senses. The knowledge, when we do get it, according to Sir W. Hamilton, is not (in the case of Primary qualities) knowledge of an impression made on our own sensitive faculty, which would be really relative knowledge; it is knowledge of the Thing as it exists in itself, independently of our perceptions. It is this which, as I have pointed out, reduces the pretended Relativity to a name.

It is a great confirmation of the unmeaningness of the Relativity Doctrine in Sir W. Hamilton's hands, that those who have most studied his philosophy, Dean Mansel and Professor Veitch, are reduced to such straits in the attempt to find a meaning for it, and do not always find the same meaning.[s]

*[67] See *Lectures*, Vol. II, pp. 113–14; *Discussions*, p. 16; "Dissertations on Reid," [Note D*,] p. 882; and, in further illustration, foot-note to Reid, p. 126n; passages strangely overlooked by Mr. Mansel ([*Philosophy of the Conditioned*,] p. 138).

†[67] When Sir W. Hamilton says ("Dissertations on Reid," [Note D,] p. 841) that although Space is a native, necessary, *à priori* form of imagination, we yet have an immediate perception of a really objective extended world, Mr. Mansel imagines that Sir W. Hamilton is maintaining at once the subjectivity of Space, and the objectivity of bodies as occupying space. But Sir W. Hamilton himself declares unequivocally that these two opinions contradict one another, unless reconciled by the supposition that Space is objective and external to us as well as subjective: not, therefore, properly a form of our mind, but an outward reality which has a form of our mind corresponding to it. See the whole of the passages referred to in the last note.

an hypothesis, not a dogmatical assertion. The North American Reviewer in like manner says:

An existence non-ego may be immediately cognizable consistently with the doctrine of the relativity of knowledge, provided this non-ego be phenomenal, that is, necessarily dependent on some other incognizable existence among the real causes of things. . . . If the meaning of the word phenomenon which we have attributed to Hamilton be a valid one, his philosophy escapes from this criticism by affirming that the primary qualities of matter, that is, the having extension, figure, &c., though not cognized as the effects of matter on us, are yet modes of existence implying an unknown substance, and are hence phenomenal in Hamilton's meaning of the word.*

This explanation might pass, if Sir W. Hamilton's assertion of the relativity of our knowledge to our mind were all contained in the word phænomenal, and could be explained away by supposing that word to mean relativity not to us, but to an unknown cause. But I need not requote his declaration that our knowledge of Qualities is all relative to us, nor his assertion that nevertheless certain qualities are in the object, and are perceived and known in the object, and that the object perceived and known is no other than the real Thing itself. Nowhere in his works do I find any recognition of another real Thing, which is not the Thing perceived by us through its attributes. He does not tell us of a Body perceived, and an unperceived Substance in the background: the Body is the Substance. He does indeed say that the Substance is only an inference from the Attributes; but he also says that certain attributes are perceived as in the real external Thing; and he never drops the smallest hint of any real external thing *in* which the attributes can be, except the Substance itself, which he expressly defines as "that which manifests its qualities," that in which the "phænomena or qualities are supposed to inhere."[*]

Professor Fraser, in the (in many respects) profound Essay of which he has done this work the honour of making it the occasion, vindicates at once the consistency of Sir W. Hamilton, and the substantial significance of his doctrine of Relativity, by ascribing to him, in opposition to his incessant declarations, Mr. Fraser's own far clearer views of the subject. Mr. Fraser, like myself, believes the Primary Qualities to have no more existence out of our own or other minds, than the Secondary Qualities have, or than our pains and pleasures have; and he asks, "Where does he" (Sir W. Hamilton) "say that we have an absolute knowledge of the primary qualities of matter, in any other sense than that in which he says that we have a like knowledge of a feeling of pain or pleasure in our minds while it is being felt, or of an act

*[67] [Anon., "Mill on Hamilton," *North American Review*, CIII (July, 1866),] 252–3.
[*Lectures, Vol. I, pp. 137, 138.]

of consciousness while it is being acted?"* To this "where," I answer, in every place where he says that we know the Primary Qualities not as they are in us, but as they are in the Body. That is asserting an absolute knowledge of them, as distinguished from relativity to us: and he would not have made a similar assertion of our pains and pleasures, or of our acts of internal consciousness. Again, asks Mr. Fraser, "How does the assertion that we are percipient directly, and not through a medium, of phenomena of solidity and extension, contradict the principle that all our knowledge is relative, when the assertion that we are percipient, directly and not through a medium, of the phenomena of sensation or emotion or intelligence does not?"† Because the phænomena of sensation or emotion or intelligence are admitted to be perceived or felt as facts that have no reality out of us, and the facts being only relative to us, the knowledge of the facts partakes of the same relativity: but the phænomena of solidity and extension are alleged by Sir W. Hamilton to be perceived as facts whose reality is out of our minds, and in the material object: which is indeed knowing them relatively to the outward object, but is the diametrical opposite of knowing them relatively to us.‡m

*[67] Fraser, ["Mr. Mill's *Examination*,"] p. 16.
†[67] *Ibid*., p. 15.
‡[67] Mr. Fraser affirms (p. 20) with me, and contrary to Mr. Mansel and the North American Reviewer [see pp. 252–6], that in Sir W. Hamilton's opinion "there is nothing *behind* the proper objects of sense-consciousness, these being the very things or realities themselves which we call material, external, extended, solid." Instead of recognizing three elements, a Noumenal real thing, a Phænomenal real thing, and the perceiving mind, the middle one of the three being that which the mind cognizes, Mr. Fraser sees that Sir W. Hamilton recognised but one real Thing, the very Thing which we perceive; unknown to us in its essence, but perceived and known through its attributes; and by means of those attributes, actually brought into what Sir W. Hamilton calls our consciousness. This Mr. Fraser regards [*ibid*.] as "a distinct and important contribution by Sir W. Hamilton to the theory of matter previously common in this country," because bringing matter into our conscious-ness is part of the way towards making it (what Mr. Fraser believes it to be) wholly a phænomenon of mind. But Sir W. Hamilton did not intend his doctrine to lead to this; he admits Matter into our consciousness because, contrary to the general opinion of philosophers, he thinks (see below, Chap. viii) that we can be conscious of what is outside our mind. Sir W. Hamilton, in short, was not a Berkeleian, as Mr. Fraser is, and as that philosopher almost admits (p. 26) that the interpretation which he would like to put on Sir W. Hamilton's doctrine would make Sir W. Hamilton.
Mr. Fraser seems to me, throughout his defence of Sir W. Hamilton, to have yielded to the natural tendency of a consistent thinker when standing up for an inconsistent one, to interpret ambiguous utterances ʳwhichʳ face two ways, as if they looked only one way; though the part of their author's philosophy towards

ʳ⁻ʳ67 intended to

It has ^{v}now^v been shown, by accumulated proof, that Sir W. Hamilton did not hold any opinion in virtue of which it could rationally be asserted that all human knowledge is relative; but did hold, as one of the main elements of his philosophical creed, the opposite doctrine, of the cognoscibility of external Things, in certain of their aspects, as they are in themselves, absolutely.

But if this be true, what becomes of his dispute with Cousin, and with Cousin's German predecessors and teachers? That celebrated controversy surely meant something. Where there was so much smoke there must have been some fire. Some difference of opinion must really have existed between Sir W. Hamilton and his antagonists.

Assuredly there was a difference, and one of great importance from the point of view of either disputant; not unimportant in the view of those who dissent from them both. In the succeeding chapter I shall endeavour to point out what the difference was.

———

which those expressions face on their other side, is thereby set at nought and abolished.

^{u}Since the publication of the third edition of this work, my attention has been drawn to a passage (unfortunately left unfinished) in the posthumous continuation of Sir W. Hamilton's "Dissertations on Reid," which strikingly confirms the opinion I have expressed, that the relativity of human knowledge, as understood by him, is a mere identical proposition.

"That all knowledge consists in a certain relation of the object known to the subject knowing, is self-evident. What is the nature of this relation, and what are its conditions, is not, and never can be, known to us; because we know only the qualities of our own faculties of knowledge, as relations to their objects, and we only know the qualities of their objects, as relations to our minds. All qualities both of mind and of matter are therefore only known to us as relations; we know nothing in itself. We know not the cause of this relation, we know nothing of its conditions, the fact is all. *The relation is the relation of knowledge.* We know nothing consequently of the kind of the relation; we have no consciousness and no possible knowledge whether the relation of knowledge has any analogy to the relations of similarity, contrariety, identity, difference—we have no consciousness that it is like any other, or any modification of any other: these are all relations of a different kind between object and object; this between subject and object: we can institute no point of comparison." (Reid, [Note N,] p. 965.)

That is to say, we know nothing except in relation to us, but that relation is simply the relation of being known by us, and this is the only relation cognizable by us which exists between the knower and the known. Our knowledge is relative, but only in the sense that knowing is itself a relation. Would Cousin, or Hegel, or Schelling, have had the slightest objection to admit that our knowledge even of the Absolute is relative, in the sense that it is we that know it?^{u}

$^{u-u}$+72
$^{v-v}$65^1, 65^2 thus

CHAPTER IV

In What Respect Sir William Hamilton
Really Differs from the Philosophers
of the Absolute

THE QUESTION REALLY AT ISSUE in Sir W. Hamilton's celebrated and striking review of Cousin's philosophy,[*] is this: Have we, or have we not, an immediate intuition of God. The name of God is veiled under two extremely abstract phrases, "The Infinite" and "The Absolute," perhaps from a reverential feeling: such, at least, is the reason given by Sir W. Hamilton's disciple, Mr. Mansel,* for preferring the more vague expressions. But it is one of the most unquestionable of all logical maxims, that the meaning of the abstract must be sought for in the concrete, and not conversely; and we shall see, both in the case of Sir W. Hamilton and of Mr. Mansel, that the process cannot be reversed with impunity.[†]

[*"On the Philosophy of the Unconditioned," in *Discussions*, pp. 1–38, a review of Victor Cousin, *Cours de philosophie: Introduction à l'histoire de la philosophie* (Paris: Pichon and Didier, 1828); subsequent references are to the edition in Mill's library (Brussels: Hauman, 1836).]

*Bampton Lectures. *The Limits of Religious Thought.* 4th ed. [London: Murray, 1859], p. 42.

†[67] Mr. Mansel denies the correctness of the representations made in this paragraph ([*Philosophy of the Conditioned*,] pp. 90–6); and at least seems to assert, that the question between M. Cousin and Sir W. Hamilton did not relate to the possibility of knowing *the* Infinite Being, but to a "pseudo-concept of the Infinite," [p. 93,] which Sir W. Hamilton believed to be not a proper predicate of God, but a representation of a non-entity. And Mr. Mansel affirms (p. 92) that to substitute the name of God in the place of the Infinite and the Absolute, is exactly to reverse Sir W. Hamilton's argument. We have here a direct issue of fact, of which every one is a judge who will take the trouble to read Sir W. Hamilton's Essay. I maintain that [a] what M. Cousin affirms and Sir W. Hamilton denies, is the cognoscibility not of an Infinite and Absolute which is not God, but of the Infinite and Absolute which is God. [See below pp. 35–6.] I might refer to almost any page of the Essay; I will only quote the application which Sir W. Hamilton himself makes of his own doctrine. "True, therefore, are the declarations of a pious philosophy: 'A God under-

[a]67 there is not a shadow of ground for this statement of Mr. Mansel; and that

I proceed to state, chiefly in the words of Sir W. Hamilton, the opinions of the two parties to the controversy. Both undertake to decide what are the facts which (in their own phraseology) are given in Consciousness; or, as others say, of which we have intuitive knowledge. According to Cousin, there are, in every act of consciousness, three elements; three things of which we are intuitively aware. There is a finite element; an element of plurality, compounded of a Self or Ego, and something different from Self, or Non-ego. There is also an infinite element; a consciousness of something infinite. "At the same instant when we are conscious of these [finite] existences, plural, relative, and contingent, we are conscious likewise of a

---

stood would be no God at all.' 'To think that God is, as we can think him to be, is blasphemy.' The Divinity, in a certain sense, is revealed; in a certain sense, is concealed: he is at once known and unknown. But the last and highest consecration of all true religion, must be an altar Ἀγνώστῳ Θεῷ—'To the unknown and unknowable God.' " (*Discussions*, p. 15n. [For the quotation, see Acts, 17:23.]) When this is what the author of the Essay presents as its practical result, it is too much to tell us that the Essay is not concerned about God but about a "Pseudo-Infinite," and that we are not entitled, when we find in it an assertion about the Infinite, to hold the author to the assertion as applicable to God. We shall next be told that Mr. Mansel himself, in his Bampton Lectures, is not treating the question of our knowledge of God. It is very true that the only Infinite about which either Sir W. Hamilton or Mr. Mansel proves anything, is a Pseudo-Infinite; but they are not in the least aware of this; they fancy that this Pseudo-Infinite is the real Infinite, and that in proving it to be unknowable by us, they prove the same thing of God.

The reader who desires further elucidation of this point, may consult the sixth chapter of Mr. Bolton's *Inquisitio Philosophica*. That acute thinker also points out [see, e.g., pp. 190–4] various inconsistencies and other logical errors in Mr. Mansel's work, with which I am not here concerned, my object in answering him not being recrimination, but to maintain my original assertions against his denial.

[b]Mr. Mansel, in his rejoinder, quotes from his Bampton Lectures [*Limits of Religious Thought*] some passages in which he says, and others in which he implies, that "our human conception of the Infinite is not the true one," and that "the infinite of philosophy is not the true Infinite:" and thinks it very unfair that, with these passages before me, I should accuse him of mistaking a pseudo-infinite for the real Infinite. ["Supplementary Remarks," p. 23, where Mansel gives the references in his *Limits of Religious Thought* for the passages he cites.] But the mistake from which he clears himself is not that which I charged him with. I maintained, that the abstraction "The Infinite," in whatever manner understood, as distinguished from some particular attribute possessed in an infinite degree, has no existence, and is a pseudo-infinite. [See pp. 94ff. below.] Mr. Mansel, on the contrary, affirmed throughout, and affirms in the very passages which he quotes, that "The Infinite" has a real existence, and is God: though when we attempt to conceive what it is, we only reach a mass of contradictions, which is a pseudo-infinite. Mr. Mansel did not suppose *his* pseudo-infinite to be the true Infinite; but my assertion, which stands unrefuted, is, that his "true Infinite" is a pseudo-infinite; and that in proving it to be unknowable by us, he mistakenly fancied that he had proved this of God.[b]

[b–b]+72

superior unity in which they are contained, and by which they are explained; a unity absolute as they are conditioned, substantive as they are phænomenal, and an infinite cause as they are finite causes. This unity is God."* The first two elements being the Finite and God, the third element is the relation between the Finite and God, which is that of cause and effect. These three things are immediately given in every act of consciousness, and are, therefore, apprehended as real existences by direct intuition.

Of these alleged elements of Consciousness, Sir W. Hamilton only admits the first; the Finite element, compounded of Self and a Not-self, "limiting and conditioning one another."[*] He denies that God is given in immediate consciousness—is apprehended by direct intuition. It is in no such way as this that God, according to him, is known to us: and as an Infinite and Absolute Being he is not, and cannot be, known to us at all; for we have no faculties capable of apprehending the Infinite or the Absolute. The second of M. Cousin's elements being thus excluded, the third (the Relation between the first and second) falls with it; and Consciousness remains limited to the finite element, compounded of an Ego and a Non-ego.

In this contest it is almost superfluous for me to say, that I am entirely with Sir W. Hamilton. The doctrine, that we have an immediate or intuitive knowledge of God, I consider to be bad metaphysics, involving a false conception of the nature and limits of the human faculties, and grounded on a superficial and erroneous psychology. Whatever relates to God I hold [c] to be matter of inference; I would add, of inference à posteriori. And in so far as Sir W. Hamilton has contributed, which he has done very materially, towards discrediting the opposite doctrine, he has rendered, in my estimation, a [d]valuable[d] service to philosophy. But though I assent to his conclusion, his arguments seem to me very far from inexpugnable: a sufficient answer, I conceive, might without difficulty be given to [e]most[e] of them, though I do not say that it was always competent to M. Cousin to give it. And the arguments, in the present case, are of as much importance as the conclusion: not only because they are quite as essential a part of Sir W. Hamilton's philosophy, but because they afford the premises from which some of his followers, if not himself, have drawn inferences which I venture to think extremely mischievous. While, therefore, I sincerely applaud the scope and purpose of this celebrated piece of philosophical criticism, I think it important to sift with some minuteness the reasonings it employs, and the general mode of thought which it exemplifies.

*Discussions, p. 9. [Mill's square brackets.]
[*Ibid.]

[c]65[1], 65[2]   with Sir W. Hamilton
[d-d]65[1], 65[2]   good
[e-e]65[1], 65[2]   all

The question is, as already remarked, whether we have a direct intuition of "the Infinite" and "the Absolute:" M. Cousin maintaining that we have—Sir W. Hamilton that we have not; that the Infinite and the Absolute are inconceivable to us, and, by consequence, unknowable.

It is proper to explain to any reader not familiar with these controversies, the meaning of the terms. Infinite requires no explanation. It is universally understood to signify that, to the magnitude of which there is no limit. If we speak of infinite duration, or infinite space, we are supposed to mean duration which never ceases, and extension which nowhere comes to an end. Absolute is much more obscure, being a word of several meanings; but, in the sense in which it stands related to Infinite, it means (conformably to its etymology) that which is finished or completed. There are some things of which the utmost ideal amount is a limited quantity, though a quantity never actually reached. In this sense, the relation between the Absolute and the Infinite is (as Bentham would have said) a tolerably close one, namely a relation of contrariety. For example, to assert an absolute minimum of matter, is to deny its infinite divisibility. Again, we may speak of absolutely, but not of infinitely, pure water. The purity of water is not a fact of which, whatever degree we suppose attained, there remains a greater beyond. It has an absolute limit: it is capable of being finished or complete, in thought, if not in reality. The extraneous substances existing in any vessel of water cannot be of more than finite amount, and if we suppose them all withdrawn, the purity of the water cannot, even in idea, admit of further increase.

*f*The idea of Absolute, in this sense of the term, being thus contrasted with that of Infinite, they cannot, both of them, be truly predicated of God; or, if truly, not in respect of the same attributes. But the word Absolute, without losing the signification of perfect or complete, may drop that of limited. It may continue to mean the *whole* of that to which it is applied; but without requiring that this whole should be finite. Granted (for instance) a being of infinite power, that Being's knowledge, if supposed perfect, must be infinite; and may therefore, in an admissible sense of the term, be said to

---

*f-f*65[1], 65[2]   Though the idea of Absolute is thus contrasted with that of Infinite, the one is equally fitted with the other to be predicated of God; but not in respect of the same attributes. There is no incorrectness of speech in the phrase Infinite Power: because the notion it expresses is that of a Being who has the power of doing all things which we know, or can conceive, and more. But in speaking of knowledge, Absolute is the proper word, and not Infinite. The highest degree of knowledge that can be spoken of with a meaning, only amounts to knowing all that there is to be known: when that point is reached, knowledge has attained its utmost limit. So of goodness, or justice: they cannot be more than perfect. There are not infinite degrees of right. The will is either entirely right, or wrong in different degrees: downwards there are as many gradations as we choose to distinguish, but upwards there is an ideal limit. Goodness (unlike time or space) can be imagined complete—such that there can be no greater goodness beyond it.

Such is the signification of the term Absolute, when coupled and contrasted with Infinite. But the word has other meanings

be both absolute and infinite.* In this acceptation there is no inconsistency or incongruity in predicating both these words of God.

The word Absolute, however, has other meanings, which have nothing to do with perfection or completeness[f], though often mixed and confounded with [h]it[h]; the more readily as they are all [i]habitually predicated of the Deity[i]. By Absolute is often meant the opposite of Relative; and this is rather many meanings than one; for Relative also is a term used very indefinitely, and wherever it is employed, the word Absolute always accompanies it as its negative. In another of its senses, Absolute means that which is independent of anything else: which exists, and is what it is, by its own nature, and not because of any other thing. In this [j]fourth sense as in the third[j], Absolute stands for the negation of a relation; not now of Relation in general, but of the specific relation expressed by the term Effect. In this signification it is synonymous with [k]uncaused, and is therefore most naturally identified with the[k] First Cause. The meaning of a First

*[67] In the first edition of this work it was maintained, that though Power admits of being regarded as Infinite, Knowledge does not; because "the highest degree of knowledge that can be spoken of with a meaning, only amounts to knowing all that there is to be known." [See 37[f-f] above.] But Mr. Mansel [*Philosophy of the Conditioned*, p. 105] and the "Inquirer" (author of *The Battle of the Two Philosophies* [see pp. 24–6]) have justly remarked, that on the supposition of an Infinite Being, "all that there is to be known" includes all which a Being of infinite power can think or create; consequently, the power being infinite, the knowledge, if supposed complete, must be infinite too. In regard to the moral attributes, it was said in the first edition, that Absolute is the proper word for them, and not Infinite, since those attributes "cannot be more than perfect. There are not infinite degrees of right. The will is either entirely right, or wrong in different degrees." [See 37[f-f] above.] In this I did not properly distinguish between moral rightness or justice [g]as predicated of acts or mental states, and the same regarded as attributes of a person. Conformity to the standard of right has a positive limit, which can only be reached, not surpassed; but persons, though all exactly conforming to the standard, may differ in the strength of their adherence to it: influences (temptations for example) might detach one of them from it, which would have no effect upon another. There are thus, consistently with complete observance of the rule of right, innumerable gradations of the attribute considered as in a person. But, on the other hand, there is an extreme limit to these gradations—the idea of a Person whom no influences or causes, either in or out of himself, can deflect in the minutest degree from the law of right. This I apprehend to be a conception of absolute, not of infinite, righteousness. The doctrine, therefore, of the first edition, that an Infinite Being may have attributes which are absolute, but not infinite, still appears to me maintainable. But as it is immaterial to my argument, and was only the illustration nearest at hand of the meaning of the terms, I withdraw it from the discussion.[g]

[g-g][*manuscript fragment exists; see* Appendix A *below*]
[h-h]65[1], 65[2]   this
[i-i]65[1], 65[2]   liable to be predicated of God
[j-j]65[1], 65[2]   third sense as in the second
[k-k]65[1], 65[2]   a] 67 the

Cause is, that all other things exist, and are what they are, by reason of it and of its properties, but that it is not itself made to exist, nor to be what it is, by anything else. It does not depend, for its existence or attributes, on other things: there is nothing upon the existence of which its own is conditional: it exists absolutely. [l]

[m]In which of these meanings is the term used in the polemic with M. Cousin? M. Cousin makes no distinction at all between the Infinite and the Absolute. Sir W. Hamilton distinguishes them as two species of a higher genus, the Unconditioned; and[m] defines the Infinite as "the unconditionally unlimited," the Absolute as "the unconditionally limited."* Here is a new word introduced, the word "unconditionally;" of which we look in vain for any direct explanation, [n]but which needs it as much as either of the words which it is employed to explain. In the Essay itself, this is the only attempt made to define the Absolute: but in the reprint Sir W. Hamilton appends the following note:

"The term Absolute is of a twofold (if not threefold) ambiguity, corresponding to the double (or treble) signification of the word in Latin." The third application he, with reason, dismisses, as here irrelevant. The other two are as follows:

"1. *Absolutum* means what is *freed* or *loosed*: in which sense the Absolute will be what is aloof from relation, comparison, limitation, condition, dependence, &c., and thus is tantamount to τὸ ἀπόλυτον of the lower

Discussions, p. 13.

[l]65[1], 65[2] [*footnote:*] *Sir W. Hamilton (*Discussions*, p. 14n) distinguishes and defines the first two of these meanings: Absolute in the sense of "finished, perfected, completed," and Absolute as opposed to Relative. The third meaning he does not expressly notice, but seems to confuse it with the second. The meaning, however, with which it is really allied, and to which it may in a certain sense be reduced, is the first: as will be seen hereafter.

[m-m]65[1], 65[2] Sir W. Hamilton (after Kant) unites the Infinite and the Absolute under a larger abstraction, the Unconditioned, regarding it as a genus of which they are the two species.[†] [*footnote:*] [†]See the same note. [*text:*] Having often occasion to speak of the two in conjunction, he is entitled to a form of abridged expression: let us hope he takes due care that it shall be nothing more. But when the Absolute and the Infinite are thus spoken of as two species of the Unconditioned, it is necessary to know in which of the senses just discriminated the word Absolute is to be understood. Sir W. Hamilton professes that it is in the first sense; that of finished, perfected, completed. He adds that this is the only sense in which, for himself, he uses the term.[‡] [*footnote:*] [‡]Note, ut supra. [*text:*] If we should find, then, that he does not strictly keep to this resolution, we may conclude that the falling off is not intentional.

In accordance with his professions he

[n-n41]65[1], 65[2] and which is far from conveying so distinct a meaning, as, considering its great importance in Sir W. Hamilton's philosophy, it ought. Indeed, throughout his writings, he uses the word Condition, and its derivatives, Conditioned and Unconditioned, as if it was impossible to understand them in more than one meaning, and as if nobody could require to be told what that meaning is: though in English metaphysics two of the three phrases, until he introduced them, were new, and though there are no expressions in all philosophy which require definition and illustration more.* [*the footnote, without any change in its wording, was moved in 67 to 55 below*]

Greeks.[*] In this meaning the Absolute is not opposed to the Infinite." This is an amplification of my third meaning.

"2. *Absolutum* means *finished, perfected, completed*; in which sense the Absolute will be what is out of relation, &c. as finished, perfect, complete, total, and thus corresponds to τὸ ὅλον and τὸ τέλειον of Aristotle.[†] In this acceptation—and it is that in which for myself I exclusively use it,—the Absolute is diametrically opposed to, is contradictory of, the Infinite."* This second meaning of Sir W. Hamilton, which I, in the first edition, by a blameable inadvertence, confounded with my own first meaning,† must be reckoned as a fifth, compounded of the first and third—of the idea of finished or completed, and the idea of being out of relation. How to make an intelligible meaning out of the two combined, is the question. One can, with some difficulty, find a meaning in being "aloof from relation, comparison, limitation, condition, dependence;" but what is meant by being all this "as finished, perfect, complete, total?" Does it mean, being *both* out of relation and also complete? and must the Absolute in Sir W. Hamilton's second sense be also Absolute in his first, and be out of all relation whatever? or does the particle "*as*" signify that it is out of relation only in respect of its completeness, which (I suppose) means that it does not depend for its completeness on anything but itself? Mr. Mansel's comment, which otherwise does not help us much, decides for the latter. "Out of relation as completed" means (he says)‡ "self-existent in its completeness, and not implying the existence of anything else."§ Without further attempt to clear

[*See, e.g., Sextus Empiricus, *Against the Logicians*, II, in *Sextus Empiricus* (Greek and English), trans. R. G. Bury, 4 vols. (London: Heinemann; New York: Putnam's Sons, 1933–49), Vol. II, p. 380 (273), and Plotinus, *Operum philosophicorum omnium* (Basil: Lecythus, 1580), Ennead VI, §§18 and 22, pp. 582–3 and 586–7.]

[†See Aristotle, *The Metaphysics* (Greek and English), trans. Hugh Tredennick, 2 vols. (London: Heinemann; New York: Putnam's Sons, 1923), Vol. I, p. 280 (V, xxvi, 1023^{b}27ff.), p. 266 (V, xv, 1021^{b}13ff.).]

*[67] *Discussions*, p. 14n.

†[67] And, in consequence, erroneously charged Sir W. Hamilton with having, in one of his arguments against Cousin, departed from his own meaning of the term. I have freed the text from everything which depended on this error, the only serious misrepresentation of Sir W. Hamilton which has been established against me. [See, e.g., pp. 39^l and 39^{m-m} above, and 52–3^{e-e} and 91^{b-b} below, apparently in response to Mansel, *Philosophy of the Conditioned*, pp. 103ff.]

‡[67] Mansel, [*Philosophy of the Conditioned*,] p. 104.

§[67] But the assimilation with τὸ ὅλον and τὸ τέλειον again throws us out; for τὸ ὅλον, with all Greek thinkers, meant either the completed aggregate of all that exists, or an abstract entity which they conceived as the Principle of Wholeness—in virtue of which, and by participation in which, that universal aggregate and all other wholes *are* wholes. Either of these would be an additional meaning for the word Absolute, different from all which have yet been mentioned.

up the obscurity, let it suffice that Sir W. Hamilton's Absolute, though not synonymous with a "finished, perfected, completed," but limited, whole, includes that idea, and is therefore incompatible with Infinite.*[n]

Having premised these verbal explanations, I proceed to state, as far as possible in Sir W. Hamilton's own words, the heads of his argumentation to prove that the °Absolute and Infinite are° unknowable. His first summary statement of the doctrine is as follows:

The unconditionally unlimited, or the Infinite, the unconditionally limited, or the Absolute, cannot positively be construed to the mind: they can be conceived only by a thinking away from, or abstraction of, those very conditions under which thought itself is realized; consequently, the notion of the Unconditioned is only negative; negative of the conceivable itself. For example: On the one hand, we can positively conceive neither an absolute whole, that is, a whole so great that we cannot also conceive it as a relative part of a still greater whole; nor an absolute part, that is, a part so small that we cannot also conceive it as a relative whole divisible into smaller parts. On the other hand, we cannot positively represent, or realize, or construe to the mind (as here Understanding and Imagination coincide) an infinite whole, for this could only be done by the infinite synthesis in thought of finite wholes, which would itself require an infinite time for its accomplishment; nor, for the same reason, can we follow out in thought an infinite divisibility of parts. The result is the same, whether we apply the process to limitation in space, in time, or in degree. The unconditional negation, and the unconditional affirmation of limitation; in other words, the Infinite and the Absolute properly so called, are thus equally inconceivable to us.[†]

This argument, that the Infinite and the Absolute are unknowable by us because the only conceptions we are able to form of them are negative, is stated still more emphatically a few pages later.

Kant has clearly shown, that the Idea of the Unconditioned can have no objective reality,—that it conveys no knowledge,—and that it involves the most insoluble contradictions. But he ought to have shown that the Unconditioned had no objective application, because it had, in fact, no subjective affirmation; that it afforded no real knowledge, because it contained nothing even conceivable; and that it is self-contradictory, because it is not a notion, either simple or positive, but only *a fasciculus of negations*—negations of the Conditioned in its opposite extremes, and bound together merely by the aid of language, and their common character of incomprehensibility.[‡]

*[67] I demur, however, to Sir W. Hamilton's assertion, that for himself he exclusively uses the term in this meaning. In the whole of the discussion respecting the relativity of our knowledge, Absolute, with Sir W. Hamilton, is simply the opposite of relative, and contains no implication of "finished, perfected, completed." Moreover, in this very Essay, when arguing against M. Cousin, who uses Absolute in a sense compatible with Infinite, Sir W. Hamilton continually falls into M. Cousin's sense.

[†]*Discussions*, p. 13.
[‡]*Ibid.*, p. 17.

°-°65[1], 65[2]   Unconditioned is

Let us note, then, as the first and most fundamental of Sir W. Hamilton's arguments, that our ideas of the Infinite and the Absolute are *purely negative, and the Unconditioned which combines the two, "a* fasciculus of negations." I reserve consideration of the validity of this and every other part of the argumentation, until we have the whole before us. He proceeds:

As the conditionally limited (which we may briefly call the Conditioned) is thus the only possible object of knowledge and of positive thought,—thought *necessarily* supposes condition. *To think* is *to condition*; and conditional limitation is the fundamental law of the possibility of thought. For, as the greyhound cannot outstrip his shadow, nor (by a more appropriate simile) the eagle outsoar the atmosphere in which he floats, and by which alone he is supported; so the mind cannot transcend that sphere of limitation, within and through which exclusively the possibility of thought is realized. Thought is only of the conditioned; because, as we have said, to think is simply to condition. The *Absolute* is conceived merely by a negation of conceivability; and all that we know, is known as—

"Won from the cold and formless *Infinite*."[*]

How, indeed, it could ever be doubted that thought is only of the conditioned, may well be deemed a matter of the profoundest admiration. Thought cannot transcend consciousness; consciousness is only possible under the antithesis of a subject and object of thought known only in correlation, and mutually limiting each other; while, independently of this, all that we know either of subject or object, either of mind or matter, is only a knowledge in each of the particular, of the plural, of the different, of the modified, of the phænomenal. We admit that the consequence of this doctrine is—that philosophy, if viewed as more than a science of the conditioned, is impossible. Departing from the particular, we admit that we can never, in our highest generalizations, rise above the Finite; that our knowledge, whether of mind or matter, can be nothing more than a knowledge of the relative manifestations of an existence which in itself it is our highest wisdom to recognise as beyond the reach of philosophy. This is what, in the language of St. Austin, *Cognoscendo ignoratur, et ignoratione cognoscitur*.*

The dictum that "to think is to condition" *(the meaning of which will be examined hereafter)* may be noted as our author's second argument. And here ends the positive part of his argumentation. There remains his refutation of opponents. After an examination of Schelling's opinion, into which I need not follow him, he grapples with M. Cousin, against whom he undertakes to show, that "his argument to prove the correality of his three Ideas proves directly the reverse;" "that the conditions under which alone he allows intelligence to be possible, necessarily exclude the possibility of a knowledge, not to say a conception, of the Absolute;" and "that the Abso-

[*John Milton, *Paradise Lost*, in *The Poetical Works of Mr. John Milton* (London: Tonson, 1695), p. 62 (III, 12).]

Discussions, pp. 14–15. [The quotation is mistakenly attributed to St. Augustine by Hamilton.]

p-p65[1], 65[2], 67 "only a
q-q65[1], 65[2] unnecessarily [*printer's error; Source agrees with* 67, 72]
r-r65[1], 65[2] , whatever be meant by it,

lute, as defined by him, is only a relative and a conditioned."* Of this argument in three parts, if we pass over (or, as our author would say, discount) as much as is only *ad hominem*, what is of general application is as follows:

First: M. Cousin and our author are agreed that there can be no knowledge except "where there exists a plurality of terms;"[*] there are at least a perceived and a perceiver, a knower and a known. But this necessity of "difference and plurality" as a condition of knowledge, is inconsistent with the meaning of the Absolute, which

as absolutely universal, is absolutely one. Absolute unity is convertible with the absolute negation of plurality and difference. . . . The condition of the Absolute as existing, and under which it must be known, and the condition of intelligence, as capable of knowing, are incompatible. For, if we suppose the Absolute cognisable: it must be identified either—1°, with the subject knowing: or, 2°, with the object known: or, 3°, with the indifference of both. The first hypothesis, and the second, are contradictory of the Absolute. For in these the Absolute is supposed to be known, either as contradistinguished from the knowing subject, or as contradistinguished from the object known: in other words, the Absolute is asserted to be known as absolute unity, *i.e.*, as the negation of all plurality, while the very act by which it is known, affirms plurality as the condition of its own possibility. The third hypothesis, on the other hand, is contradictory of the plurality of intelligence; for if the subject and the object of consciousness be known as one, a plurality of terms is not the necessary condition of intelligence. The alternative is therefore necessary: either the Absolute cannot be known or conceived at all; or our author is wrong in subjecting thought to the conditions of plurality and difference.†

Secondly: In order to make the Absolute knowable by us, M. Cousin, says the author, is obliged to present it in the light of an absolute cause: now causation is a relation; therefore M. Cousin's Absolute is but a relative. Moreover, "what exists merely as a cause, exists merely for the sake of something else—is not final in itself, but simply a mean towards an end. . . . Abstractly considered, the effect is therefore superior to the cause." Hence an absolute cause "is dependent on the effect for its perfection;" and, indeed,

even for its reality. For to what extent a thing exists necessarily as a cause, to that extent it is not all-sufficient to itself; since to that extent it is dependent on the effect, as on the condition through which it realizes its existence; and what exists abso-

---

Ibid., p. 25.
[*Ibid.*, p. 30, translating Cousin, *Cours de philosophie: Introduction*, Leçon v, p. 129.]
†*Ibid.*, p. 33.

*⁻*65¹, 65² Under the first head; that the Unconditioned is not a possible object of thought, because it includes both the Infinite and the Absolute, and these are exclusive of one another.†
[*footnote:*]†*Ibid.*, p. 28ff. [*text:*] [*paragraph:*] Under the second;
*⁻*65¹, 65² We now arrive at the third head.

lutely as a cause, exists therefore in absolute dependence on the effect for the reality of its existence. An absolute cause, in truth, only exists in its effects: it never *is*, it always *becomes*: for it is an existence *in potentia*, and not an existence *in actu*, except through and by its effects. The Absolute is thus, at best, something merely inchoative and imperfect.*

Let me ask, *en passant*, ᵛwhy M. Cousin is under an obligation to thinkᵛ that if the Absolute, or, to speak plainly, if God, is only known to us in the character of a cause, he must therefore "exist merely as a cause," and be merely "a mean towards an end?" It is surely possible to maintain that the Deity is known to us only as he who feeds the ravens, without supposing that the Divine Intelligence exists solely in order that the ravens may be fed.†

In reviewing the series of arguments adduced by Sir W. Hamilton for the incognoscibility and inconceivability of the Absolute, the first remark that

---

*Ibid., p. 35. ᵘIn the first edition three points of our author's argument were discussed, instead of two only: but I now perceive that the remaining argument is *ad hominem* merely, and has reference to M. Cousin's confusion of the Absolute with the Infinite.ᵘ

†[Cf. Job, 38:41, for the concluding image.] A passage follows, which being only directed against a special doctrine of M. Cousin, (that God is determined to create by the necessity of his own nature—that an absolute creative force cannot but pass into creative activity [see *Cours de philosophie: Introduction*, Leçon v, pp. 139–40])—I should have left unmentioned, were it not worth notice as a specimen of the kind of arguments which Sir W. Hamilton can sometimes use. On M. Cousin's hypothesis, says our author, "One of two alternatives must be admitted. God, as necessarily determined to pass from absolute essence to relative manifestation, is determined to pass either from the better to the worse, or from the worse to the better. A third possibility, that both states are equal, as contradictory in itself and as contradicted by our author, it is not necessary to consider. The *first* supposition must be rejected. The necessity in this case determines God to pass from the better to the worse, that is, operates to his partial annihilation. The power which compels this must be external and hostile, for nothing operates willingly to its own deterioration; and as superior to the pretended God, is either itself the real deity, if an intelligent and free cause, or a negation of all deity, if a blind force or fate. The *second* is equally inadmissible: that God, passing into the universe, passes from a state of comparative imperfection into a state of comparative perfection. The divine nature is identical with the *most perfect nature*, and is also identical with the first cause. If the first cause be not identical with the most perfect nature, there is no God, for the two essential conditions of his existence are not in combination. Now, on the present supposition, the most perfect nature is the derived; nay, the universe, the creation, the γινόμενον, is, in relation to its cause, the actual, the ὄντως ὄν. [See, e.g., Plato, *Sophist*, in *Theætetus, Sophist* (Greek and English), trans. H. N. Fowler (London: Heinemann; Cambridge, Mass.: Harvard University Press, 1921), p. 370 (245ᵈ3), p. 378 (247ᵈ7–ᵉ4).] It would also be the divine, but that divinity

ᵘ⁻ᵘ+67, 72
ᵛ⁻ᵛ65¹, 65²   where is the necessity for supposing

occurs is, that most of them lose their application by simply substituting for the metaphysical abstraction "The Absolute," the more intelligible concrete expression "Something Absolute." If the first phrase has any meaning, it must be capable of being expressed in terms of the other. When we are told of an "Absolute" in the abstract, or of an Absolute Being, even though called God, we are entitled, and if we would know what we are talking about, are bound to ask, absolute in *what*? Do you mean, for example, absolute in goodness, or absolute in knowledge? or do you, perchance, mean absolute in ignorance, or absolute in wickedness? for any

---

supposes also the notion of cause, while the universe, *ex hypothesi*, is only an effect." (P. 36.)

This curious subtlety, that creation must be either passing from the better to the worse or from the worse to the better (which, if true, would prove that God cannot have created anything unless from all eternity) can be likened to nothing but the Eleatic argument that motion is impossible, because if a body moves it must either move where it is or where it is not; an argument, by the way, for which Sir W. Hamilton often expresses high respect; and of which he has here produced a very successful imitation. If it were worth while expending serious argument upon such a curiosity of dialectics, one might say it assumes that whatever is now worse must always have been worse, and that whatever is now better must always have been better. For, on the opposite supposition, perfect wisdom would have begun to will the new state at the precise moment when it began to be better than the old. We may add that our author's argument, though never so irrefragable, in no way avails him against M. Cousin; for (as he has himself said, only a sentence before) on M. Cousin's theory the universe can never have had a beginning, and God, therefore, never was in the dilemma supposed.

*w*On this Mr. Mansel remarks, "Hamilton is not speaking of states of things, but of states of the Divine nature, as creative or not creative: and Mr. Mill's argument, to refute Hamilton, must suppose a time when the new nature of God begins to be better than the old." (*[Philosophy of the Conditioned,]* p. 107n.) This is not a happy specimen of Mr. Mansel's powers of confutation. If God made the universe at the precise moment when it was wisest and best to do so—and if the universe was made by a perfectly wise and good being, this must have been the case—who besides Mr. Mansel, or, according to him, Sir W. Hamilton, would assert that God, in doing so, acquired a new nature? or passed out of one state into another state of his own nature? Did he not simply remain in the state of perfect wisdom and goodness in which he was before?

Mr. Mansel makes the odd assertion [*ibid.*], that this argument of Sir W. Hamilton is taken from Plato. There is very little in common between it and the passage in the *Republic* in which Socrates, to disprove the fabulous metamorphoses of the gods into the forms of men, animals, or inanimate things, argues that no being would voluntarily change itself from better to worse. I cannot be mistaken in the passage of Plato which Mr. Mansel has in view, for he had himself cited a part of it, with the same intention, in the notes to his Bampton Lectures (*[Limits of Religious Thought,]* p. 209).*w* [See Plato, *Republic* (Greek and English), trans. Paul Shorey, 2 vols. (London: Heinemann; Cambridge, Mass.: Harvard University Press, 1946), Vol. I, pp. 190–2 (II, 381^{b-c}).]

w-w+67, 72

one of these is as much an Absolute as any other. And when you talk of something in the abstract which is called the Absolute, does it mean one, or more than one, of these? or does it, peradventure, mean all of them? When (descending to a less lofty height of abstraction) we speak of The Horse, we mean to include every object of which the name horse can be predicated. Or, to take our examples from the same region of thought to which the controversy belongs—when The True or The Beautiful are spoken of, the phrase is meant to include all things whatever that are true, or all things whatever that are beautiful.* If this rule is good for other abstractions, it is good for the Absolute. The word is devoid of meaning unless in reference to predicates of some sort. What is absolute must be absolutely something; absolutely this or absolutely that. The Absolute, then, ought to be a genus comprehending whatever is absolutely anything—whatever possesses any predicate in finished completeness. If we are told therefore that there is some one Being who is, or which is, The Absolute—not something absolute, but the Absolute itself,—the proposition can be understood in no other sense than that the supposed Being possesses in absolute completeness *all* predicates; is absolutely good, and absolutely bad; absolutely wise, and absolutely stupid; and so forth.† The conception of such a being, I will not say of such a God, is worse than a "fasciculus of negations;" it is a fasciculus of contradictions: and our author might have spared himself the

---

*[67] Mr. Mansel considers this sentence a curious specimen of my reading in philosophy, and informs me that "Plato expressly distinguishes between 'the beautiful' and 'things that are beautiful' as the One in contrast to the Many—the Real in contrast to the Apparent." ([*Philosophy of the Conditioned*,] pp. 108–9 [referring to *Republic*, pp. 516–18 (V, 476ᵃ⁻ᵉ)].) Mr. Mansel will doubtless be glad to hear that I already possessed the very elementary knowledge of Plato which he seeks to impart to me; indeed (if it were of any consequence) I have elsewhere given an account of this theory of Plato, and made the excuses which may justly be made for such a doctrine in Plato's time. [See "Grote's Plato," in *Essays on Philosophy and the Classics, Collected Works*, Vol. XI (Toronto: University of Toronto Press, 1978), pp. 421ff.] But to recognize it as a theory which it is necessary to take into consideration now, is to follow the example of the later German transcendentalists in putting philosophy back to its very *incunabula*.

†[67] The "Inquirer" objects, that merely negative predicates should be excluded from the account; and that many of those here mentioned are merely negative: absolute littleness being but the negation of greatness; weakness, of strength; folly, of wisdom; evil, of good (p. 22). But (without meddling with the very disputable position, that all bad qualities are merely deficiency of good ones) the question is, not whether the qualities which the "Inquirer" enumerates are negative, but whether they are capable of being predicated as absolute. If they are, the general or abstract Absolute logically includes them. And, surely, negations are still more susceptible of being absolute than positive qualities. The "Inquirer" will hardly deny that "absolutely none" is as correct an employment of the word absolute as "absolutely all." With regard to Infinite, the same writer says, "To talk of infinite

trouble of proving a thing to be unknowable, which cannot be spoken of but in words implying the impossibility of its existence. To insist on such a truism is not superfluous, for there have been philosophers who saw that this must be the meaning of "The Absolute," and yet accepted it as a reality. "What kind of an Absolute Being is that," asked Hegel, "which does not contain in itself all that is actual, even evil included?"* Undoubtedly: and it is therefore necessary to admit, either that there is no Absolute Being, or that the law, that contradictory propositions cannot both be true, does not apply to the Absolute. Hegel chose the latter side of the alternative; and by this, among other things, has fairly earned the honour which will probably be awarded to him by posterity, of having logically extinguished transcendental metaphysics by a series of *reductiones ad absurdissimum.*

What I have said of the Absolute is true, *mutatis mutandis*, of the Infinite. This also is a phrase of no meaning, except in reference to some particular predicate; it must mean the infinite in something—as in size, in duration, or in power. These are intelligible conceptions. But an abstract Infinite, a Being not merely infinite in one or in several attributes, but which is "The Infinite" itself, must be not only infinite in greatness, but also in littleness; its duration is not only infinitely long, but infinitely short; it is not only infinitely awful, but infinitely contemptible; it is the same mass of contradictions as its companion the Absolute. There is no need to prove that neither of them is knowable, since, if the universal law of Belief is of objective validity, neither of them exists.

It is these unmeaning abstractions, however, these muddles of self-contradiction, which alone our author has proved, against Cousin and others, to be unknowable. He has shown, without difficulty, that we cannot know The Infinite or The Absolute. He has not shown that we cannot know a concrete reality as infinite or as absolute. Applied to this latter thesis, his reasoning breaks down.

We have seen his principal argument, the one on which he substantially relies. It is, that the Infinite and the Absolute are unknowable because inconceivable, and inconceivable because the only notions we can have of them are purely negative. If he is right in his antecedent, the consequent

---

littleness—infinite non-extension or non-duration—is to talk of infinite nothing. Which is indeed to talk, we must not say infinite, but absolute nonsense." [*Ibid.*] It is hardly fair to refer a pupil of Sir W. Hamilton to mathematics; but the "Inquirer" might have learnt from Sir W. Hamilton himself that it is not nonsense to talk of infinitely small quantities.

*Quoted by Mr. Mansel, *The Limits of Religious Thought*, p. 30 [translated by Mansel from Georg Wilhelm Friedrich Hegel, *Vorlesungen über die Geschichte der Philosophie*, ed. Carl Ludwig Michelet, in *Werke*, 20 vols. (Berlin: Duncker and Humblot, 1834–54), Vol. XV, p. 275].

follows. A conception made up of negations is a conception of Nothing. It is not a conception at all.

But *is* a conception, by the fact of its being a conception of something infinite, reduced to a negation? This is quite true of the senseless abstraction "The Infinite." That indeed is purely negative, being formed by excluding from the concrete conceptions classed under it, all their positive elements. But in place of "the Infinite," put the idea of Something infinite, and the argument collapses at once. "Something infinite" is a conception which, like most of our complex ideas, contains a negative element, but which contains positive elements also. Infinite space, for instance: is there nothing positive in that? The negative part of this conception is the absence of bounds. The positive are, the idea of space, and of space greater than any finite space. So of infinite duration: so far as it signifies "without end" it is only known or conceived negatively; but in so far as it means time, and time longer than any given time, the conception is positive. The existence of a negative element in a conception does not make the conception itself negative, and a non-entity. It would surprise most people to be told that "the life eternal" is a purely negative conception; that immortality is inconceivable. Those who hope for it for themselves have a very positive conception of what they hope for. True, we cannot have an *adequate* conception of space or duration as infinite; but between a conception which though inadequate is real, and correct as far as it goes, and the impossibility of any conception, there is a wide difference. Sir W. Hamilton does not admit this difference. He thinks the distinction without meaning. "To say that the infinite can be thought, but only inadequately thought, is a contradiction *in adjecto*; it is the same as saying that the infinite can be known, but only known as finite."* I answer, that to know it as greater than anything finite is not to know it as finite. The conception of Infinite as that which is greater than any given quantity, is a conception we all possess, sufficient for all human purposes, and as genuine and good a positive conception as one need wish to have. It is not adequate; our conception of a reality never is. But it is positive; and the assertion that there is nothing positive in the idea of infinity can only be maintained by leaving out and ignoring, as Sir W. Hamilton invariably does, the very element which constitutes the idea. Considering how many recondite laws of physical nature, afterwards verified by experience, have been arrived at by trains of mathematical reasoning grounded on what, if Sir W. Hamilton's doctrine be correct, is a non-existent conception, one would be obliged to suppose that conjuring is a highly successful mode of the investigation of nature. If, indeed, we trifle by setting up an imaginary Infinite which is infinite in

*Lectures, Vol. II, p. 375.

nothing in particular, our notion of it is truly nothing, and a "fasciculus of negations." But this is a good example of the bewildering effect of putting nonsensical abstractions in the place of concrete realities. Would Sir W. Hamilton have said that the idea of God is but a *negation, or a fasciculus of negations?* As having nothing greater than himself, he is indeed conceived negatively. But as himself greater than all other real or imaginable existences, the conception of him is positive.

Put Absolute instead of Infinite, and we come to the same result. "The Absolute," as already shown, is a heap of contradictions, but "absolute" in reference to any given attribute, signifies the possession of that attribute in finished perfection and completeness. A Being absolute in knowledge, for example, is one who knows, in the literal meaning of the term, everything. Who will pretend that this conception is negative, or unmeaning to us? We cannot, indeed, form an adequate conception of a being as knowing everything, since to do this we must have a conception, or mental representation, of all that he knows. But neither have we an adequate conception of any person's finite knowledge. I have no adequate conception of a shoemaker's knowledge, since I do not know how to make shoes: but my conception of a shoemaker and of his knowledge is a real conception; it is not a fasciculus of negations. If I talk of an Absolute Being (in the sense in which we are now employing the term) I use words without meaning; but if I talk of a Being who is absolute in wisdom and goodness, that is, who knows everything, and at all times intends what is best for every sentient creature, I understand perfectly what I mean: and however much the fact may transcend my conception, the shortcoming can only consist in my being ignorant of the details of which the reality is composed: as I have a positive, and may have a correct conception of the empire of China, though I know not the aspect of any of the places, nor the physiognomy of any of the human beings, comprehended therein.

It appears, then, that the leading argument of Sir W. Hamilton to prove the inconceivability and consequent unknowability of the Unconditioned, namely, that our conception of it is merely negative, holds good only of an abstract Unconditioned which cannot possibly exist, and not of a concrete Being, supposed infinite and absolute in certain definite attributes.* Let us now see if there be any greater value in his other arguments.

*[67] The answer of Mr. Mansel and the "Inquirer" [pp. 20–6] to the preceding argument, is, that it confounds the infinite with the indefinite. They could not have understood the argument worse if they had never read it. Indefinite, in its ordinary acceptation, is that which has a limit, but a limit either variable in itself, or unknown to us. Infinite is that which has no limit. In what Mr. Mansel calls the metaphysical

*-*65¹, 65², 67   "fasciculus of negations?"

The first of them is, [z] that all knowledge is of things plural and different; that a thing is only known to us by being known as different from something else; from ourselves as knowing it, and also from other known things which

---

use of the word indefinite, he affirms it to mean "indefinitely increasable." ([*Philosophy of the Conditioned*,] p. 114.) Elsewhere he says "An indefinite time is that which is capable of perpetual addition: an infinite time is one so great as to admit of no addition." ([*Ibid.*,] p. 50n.) I now ask, which of these is the correct expression for that which is greater than everything finite. Is this a property which can be affirmed of anything which has an undetermined limit? or of anything which is indefinitely increasable? or of anything which is capable of perpetual addition? Is a merely indefinite time greater than every finite time? Is a merely indefinite space greater than every finite space? Is a merely indefinite power greater than every finite power? The property of being greater than everything finite belongs, and can belong, only to what is in the strictest sense of the term, both popular and philosophical, Infinite.

[v]Mr. Mansel, in his rejoinder, defends himself by saying that Descartes and Cudworth agree with him in giving the name indefinite to what I (and as he acknowledges, the mathematicians) understand by infinite. ["Supplementary Remarks," pp. 24–5.] I cannot affirm that Descartes and Cudworth have nowhere done this; but they certainly have not done it in the passages which Mr. Mansel quoted, either in his first reply [*Philosophy of the Conditioned*, pp. 112–13,] or in this. All that either Descartes or Cudworth says in those passages is that the indefiniteness, to our minds, of the possible extension of the physical universe, is not tantamount to, nor a proof of, its infinity; as of course it is not. [In the *Philosophy of the Conditioned*, Mansel refers to René Descartes, *Principia Philosophia*, pp. 6–7 (I, xxvi–xxvii) and 27–8 (II, xxi), and a letter of Descartes to Henry More, in *Lettres de Mr Descartes*, ed. Claude Clerselier, 3 vols. (Paris: Angot, 1657–67), Vol. I, pp. 360–1; and to Ralph Cudworth, *The True Intellectual System of the Universe*, trans. John Harrison, 3 vols. (London: Tegg, 1845), Vol. III, p. 131. In his "Supplementary Remarks," Mansel adds a reference to Leibniz, but does not cite any further passages from Descartes or Cudworth.]

Mr. Mansel adds that even supposing me to be in the right, it would only follow, not that Sir W. Hamilton is wrong, but that he and I do not mean the same thing by the same term. Whoever has read the present note must, however, be aware, that I maintain my position to be true even in what Mr. Mansel affirms to be Sir W. Hamilton's meaning of the term.[v]

[v-v]+72
[z]65[1], 65[2]   that the Unconditioned is inconceivable, because it includes both the Infinite and the Absolute, and these are contradictory of one another. This is not an argument against the possibility of knowing the Infinite and the Absolute, but against jumbling the two together under one name. If the Infinite and the Absolute are each cognisable separately, of what importance is it that the two conceptions are incompatible? If they are so, the fault is in lumping up incompatible conceptions into an incomprehensible and impossible compound. The argument is only tenable as against the knowability and the possible existence of something which is at once "The Infinite" and "The Absolute," abstractions which do contradict one another, but not more flagrantly than each of them contradicts itself. When, instead of abstractions, we speak of Things which are infinite and absolute in respect of given attributes, there is no incompatibility. There is nothing contradictory in the notion of a Being infinite in some attributes and absolute in others, according to the different nature of the attributes.

The next argument is,

are not it. Here we have at length something which the mind can rest on as a fundamental truth. It is one of the profound psychological observations which the world owes to Hobbes;[*] it is fully recognised both by M. Cousin and by Sir W. Hamilton; and it has, more recently, been admirably illustrated and applied by Mr. Bain and by Mr. Herbert Spencer. That to know a thing is to distinguish it from other things, is, as I formerly remarked, one of the truths which the very ambiguous expression "the relativity of human knowledge" has been employed to denote [a] . With this doctrine I have no quarrel. But Sir W. Hamilton proceeds to argue that the Absolute, being "absolutely One," cannot be known under the conditions of plurality and difference, and as these are the acknowledged conditions of all our knowledge, cannot, therefore, be known at all. There is here, as it seems to me, a strange confusion of ideas. Sir W. Hamilton seems to mean that, being absolutely One, it cannot be known as plural. But the proposition that plurality is a condition of knowledge, does not mean that the thing known must be known as itself plural. It means, that a thing is only known, by being known as distinguished from something else. The plurality required is not within the thing itself, but is made up between itself and other things. Again, even if we concede that a thing cannot be known at all unless known as plural, does it follow that it cannot be known as plural because it is also One? [b]Are the One and the Many, then,[b] incompatible things, instead of different aspects of the same thing? Sir W. Hamilton surely does not mean by Absolute Unity, an indivisible Unit; the minimum, instead of the maximum of Being. He must mean, as M. Cousin certainly means, an absolute Whole; the Whole which comprehends all things. If this be so, does not this Whole not only admit of, but necessitate, the supposition of parts? Is not an Unity which comprehends everything, *ex vi termini* known as a plurality, and the most plural of all pluralities, plural in an unsurpassable degree? If there is any meaning in the words, must not Absolute Unity be Absolute [c]Totality, which is the highest degree of Plurality[c]? There is no escape from the alternative: [d]the Absolute[d] either means a single atom or monad, or it means Plurality in the extreme degree.

Though it is hardly needful, we will try this argument by the test we

[*Mill would appear to be referring to the ideas expounded by Thomas Hobbes in "Physics, or the Phenomena of Nature," Part IV of *Elements of Philosophy: The First Section, Concerning Body*, in *The English Works*, ed. William Molesworth, 11 vols. (London: Bohn, 1839–45), Vol. I, pp. 393–6 (Chap. xxv, §§5–6).]

[a]65[1], 65[2] : and in the case of Sir W. Hamilton the shadow of this other Relativity always floats over his discussion of the doctrine of Relativity in its more special sense, and at times (as in the paper "Conditions of the Thinkable" forming an Appendix [I(A), pp. 601–33] to the *Discussions*) entirely obscures it
[b–b]65[1], 65[2] Since when have the One and the Many been
[c–c]65[1], 65[2] Plurality likewise
[d–d]65[1], 65[2] "The Absolute"] 67 The Absolute

applied to a previous one; by substituting the concrete, God, for the abstract Absolute. Would Sir W. Hamilton have said that God is not cognizable under the condition of Plurality—is not known as distinguished from ourselves, and from the objects in nature? Call any positive Thing by a name which expresses only its negative predicates, and you may easily prove it under that name to be incognizable and a non-entity. Give it back its full name (if Mr. Mansel's reverential feelings will permit), its positive attributes reappear, and you find, to your surprise, that what *is* a reality can be known as one.*

The next argument is chiefly directed against the doctrine of M. Cousin, that we know the Absolute as Absolute Cause.[*] This doctrine, says Sir W. Hamilton, destroys itself. The idea of a Cause is irreconcilable with the Absolute, for a Cause is relative, and implies an Effect: this Absolute, therefore, is not an Absolute at all. *ef*This would be unanswerable, if by the

*[67] Mr. Mansel, as I have mentioned [see p. 34n above], vehemently objects to testing what Sir W. Hamilton says of the Infinite by its applicability to God, affirming that the Infinite which Sir W. Hamilton is speaking of, namely the Infinite as we conceive it, is a "pseudo-infinite." [*Philosophy of the Conditioned*, p. 93.] This is a curious inversion of the parts of Sir W. Hamilton and of his critic. It is I who assert that Sir W. Hamilton's Infinite is a pseudo-infinite; it is he who maintains that it is the real. At least he substitutes this pseudo-infinite which is really inconceivable, for an intelligible infinite, a concrete Deity, and proving the inconceivability of the one, thinks he has sufficiently proved the inconceivability of the other. It was his business, it is what he professes, to prove that God, considered as Infinite, is inconceivable by us. Instead of this, he proves the inconceivability of an Infinite which is not and cannot be God, and which does not and cannot exist, and leaves it to Mr. Mansel to discover (after others have pointed it out) that this is a pseudo-infinite.

Mr. Mansel is still more indignant that I should try what Sir W. Hamilton says of the Absolute, by the test of applicability to God, and says that this is actually inverting Sir W. Hamilton's meaning, since his definition of the Absolute, "the unconditionally limited," is contradictory to the nature of God. [Hamilton, *Discussions*, p. 13; Mansel, *Philosophy of the Conditioned*, p. 106.] But Sir W. Hamilton is here arguing with M. Cousin, who does not mean by Absolute the limited, but the complete, and who does predicate it of God. As Mr. Bolton truly remarks "In discussing the doctrines of Schelling and Cousin, Hamilton uses the word Absolute in conformity with their usage, according to which the Infinite and the Absolute are not opposed, or contraries, as in Hamilton's own terminology." (P. 159n.) Nor for this does he deserve any blame; for if the Absolute which he affirms to be unknowable, because it cannot be known under the conditions of Plurality, is Absolute only in his own sense of the term, and not in M. Cousin's, he has not refuted M. Cousin.

[*See *Discussions*, p. 33, directed against Cousin, *Cours de philosophie: Introduction*, Leçon v, pp. 149–50.]

*e–e*65[1], 65[2]   Here, surely, is one of the most unexpected slips in logic ever made by an experienced logician. At the beginning of the discussion we noted three meanings of the word Absolute. Two of them Sir W. Hamilton himself discriminated with precision. Of these, we thought that the one concerned in the present discussion was that of "finished, perfected,

Absolute we were obliged to understand something which is not only "out of" all relation, but incapable of ever passing into relation. But is this what any one can possibly mean by the Absolute, who identifies it with the Creator? Granting that the Absolute implies an existence in itself, standing in no relation to anything: the only Absolute with which we are concerned, or in which anybody believes, must not only be capable of entering into relation with things, but must be capable of entering into any relation whatever, except that of dependence, with anything. May it not be known in some, at least, of those relations, and particularly in the relation of a Cause? And if it is a "finished, perfected, completed"[*] Cause, *i.e.* the most a cause that it is possible to be—the cause of everything except itself— then, if known as such, it is known as an Absolute Cause.[e] Has Sir W. Hamilton shown that an Absolute Cause, thus understood, is inconceivable, or unknowable? No: all he shows is, that, though [g]capable of being known, it[gf] is known relatively to something else, namely, to its effects; and that such knowledge of God is not of God in himself, but of God in relation to his works. The truth is, M. Cousin's doctrine is too legitimate a product of the metaphysics common to them both, to be capable of being refuted by Sir W. Hamilton. For this knowledge of God in and by his effects, according to M. Cousin, *is* knowing him as he is in himself: because the creative power whereby he causes, is in himself, is inseparable from him, and belongs to his essence.[†] And as far as I can see, the principles common to the two philosophers are as good a warrant to M. Cousin for saying this, as to Sir W. Hamilton for maintaining that extension and figure are [h]"essential attributes"[h] of matter, and perceived as such by intuition.

I have now examined, with one exception, every argument (which is not merely *ad hominem*) advanced by Sir W. Hamilton to prove against M. Cousin the unknowableness of the Unconditioned. The argument which I have reserved, is the emphatic and oracular one, that the Unconditioned must be unthinkable, because "to think is to condition."[‡] I have kept this

[*Discussions, p. 14n; cf. p. 39[l] above.]
[†See *Cours de philosophie: Introduction*, Leçon v, pp. 140–1.]
[‡Discussions, p. 14; cf. p. 42 above.]

completed." Sir W. Hamilton said so; and added, that it is the meaning which, for himself, he exclusively employs: and, up to this time, he has really kept to it. But now, suddenly and without notice, that meaning is dropped, and another substituted, that in which absolute is the reverse of relative. We are told, as a sufficient refutation of M. Cousin's doctrine, that his Absolute, since it is defined as a Cause, is only a Relative. But if Absolute means finished, perfected, completed, may there not be a finished, perfected, and completed Cause? *i.e.* the most a Cause that it is possible to be—the cause of everything except itself?

[f-f][*manuscript fragment exists; see* Appendix A *below*]

[g-g]65[1], 65[2]   absolute in the only sense relevant to the question, it is not absolute in another and a totally different sense; since what is known as a cause,

[h-h]65[1], 65[2]   of the essence

for the last, because it will occupy us the longest time: for we must begin by finding the meaning of the proposition; which cannot be done very briefly, so little help is afforded us by the author.

According to the best notion I can form of the meaning of "condition," either as a term of philosophy or of common life, it means that on which something else is contingent, or (more definitely) which being given, something else exists, or takes place. I promise to do something *on condition* that you do something else: that is, if you do this, I will do that; if not, I will do as I please. A Conditional Proposition, in logic, is an assertion in this form: "If so and so, then so and so." The conditions of a phænomenon are the various antecedent circumstances which, when they exist simultaneously, are followed by its occurrence. As all these antecedent circumstances must coexist, each of them in relation to the others is a *conditio sine quâ non*; *i.e.* without it the phænomenon will not follow from the remaining conditions, though it perhaps may from some set of conditions totally different.

If this be the meaning of Condition, the Unconditioned should mean, that which does not depend for its existence or its qualities on any antecedent; in other words, it should be synonymous with ᶦUncausedᶦ. This, however, cannot be the meaning intended by Sir W. Hamilton: for, in a passage already quoted from his argument against Cousin, he speaks of the effect as a condition of its cause. The condition, therefore, as he understands it, needs not be an antecedent, and may be a subsequent fact to that which it conditions.

He appears, indeed, in his writings generally, to reckon as a condition of a thing, anything necessarily implied by it: and uses the word Conditioned almost interchangeably with Relative. For relatives are always in pairs: a term of relation implies the existence of two things, the one which it is affirmed of, and another: parent implies child, greater implies less, like implies another like, and *vice versâ*. Relation is an abstract name for all concrete facts which concern more than one object. Wherever, therefore, a relation is affirmed, or anything is spoken of under a relative name, the existence of the correlative may be called a condition of the relation, as well as of the truth of the assertion. When, accordingly, Sir W. Hamilton calls an effect a condition of its cause, he speaks intelligibly, and the received use of the term affords him a certain amount of justification for thus speaking.

But, if the Conditioned means the Relative, the Unconditioned must mean its opposite; and in this acceptation, the Unconditioned would mean all Noumena; Things in themselves, considered without reference to the effects they produce in us, which are called their phænomenal agencies or

ᶦ⁻ᶦ65¹, 65², 67   the First Cause

properties. Sir W. Hamilton does, very frequently, seem to use the term in this sense. In denying all knowledge of the Unconditioned, he often seems to be denying any other than phænomenal knowledge of Matter or of Mind. Not only, however, he does not consistently adhere to this meaning, but it directly conflicts with the only approach he ever makes to a definition or an explanation of the term. We have seen him declaring that the Unconditioned is the genus of which the Infinite and the Absolute are the two species. But Things in themselves are not all of them infinite and absolute. Matter and Mind, as such, are neither the one nor the other. It is evident that Sir W. Hamilton had never decided what extent he intended giving to the term Unconditioned. Sometimes he gives it one degree of amplitude, sometimes another. Between the meanings in which he uses it there is undoubtedly a link of connexion; but this only makes the matter still worse than if there were none. The phrase has that most dangerous kind of ambiguity, in which the meanings, though essentially different, are so nearly allied that the thinker unconsciously interchanges them one with another.*

[j] The probability is that when our author asserts that "to think is to

*In page 8 of the *Discussions*, speaking of the one of M. Cousin's three elements of Consciousness which that author "variously expresses by the terms *unity, identity, substance, absolute cause, the infinite, pure thought*, &c.," Sir W. Hamilton says, "we will briefly call it the Unconditioned." What M. Cousin "denominates *plurality, difference, phænomenon, relative cause, the finite, determined thought*, &c.," Sir W. Hamilton says, "we would style the Conditioned." [See, e.g., Cousin, *Cours de philosophie: Introduction*, Leçon iv, pp. 108ff., and Leçon v, pp. 122–4.] This, I think, is as near as he ever comes to an explanation of what he means by these words. It is obviously no explanation at all. It tells us what (in logical language) the terms denote, but not what they connote. An enumeration of the things called by a name is not a definition. If the name, for instance, were "dog," it would be no definition to say that what are variously denominated spaniels, mastiffs, and so forth, "we would style" dogs. The thing wanted is to know what attributes common to all these the word signifies,—what is affirmed of a thing by calling it a dog. [For the placing of this footnote in 65^1, 65^2, see 39–41^{n-n} above.]

[j]65^1, 65^2 But now, will either of these two meanings of Condition—the condition which means a correlative, or the conditions the aggregate of which composes the cause,—will either of them give a meaning to the proposition, "To think is to condition?" The second we may at once exclude. Our author cannot possibly mean that to think an object is to assign to it a cause. But he may, perhaps, mean that to think it is to give it a correlative. For this is true, and true in more senses than one. Whoever thinks an object, gives it at least one correlative, by giving it a thinker; and as many more as there are objects from which he distinguishes it. But is this any argument against those who say that the Absolute is thinkable? Did any of them ever suggest the possibility of thinking it without a thinker? Or did any of them profess to think it in any other manner than by distinguishing it from other things? If to do this is to condition, those who say that we can think the Absolute, say that we can condition it: and if the word Unconditioned is employed to make an apparent hindrance to our doing so, it is employed to beg the question.

condition," he uses the word Condition in neither of these senses, but in a third meaning, equally familiar to him, and recurring constantly in such phrases as "the conditions of our thinking faculty," "conditions of thought," and the like. He means by Conditions something similar to Kant's Forms of Sense and Categories of Understanding; a meaning more correctly expressed by another of his phrases, "Necessary Laws of Thought." He is applying to the mind the scholastic maxim, "Quicquid recipitur, recipitur ad modum recipientis." He means that our perceptive and conceptive faculties have their own laws, which not only determine what we are capable of perceiving and conceiving, but put into our perceptions and conceptions elements not derived from the thing perceived or conceived, but from the mind itself: That, therefore, we cannot at once infer that whatever we find in our perception or conception of an object, has necessarily a prototype in the object itself: and that we must, in each instance, determine this question by philosophic investigation. According to this doctrine, which no fault can be found with our author for maintaining, though often for not carrying it far enough—the "conditions of thought" would mean the attributes with which, it is supposed, the mind cannot help investing every object of thought—the elements which, derived from its own structure, cannot but enter into every conception it is able to form; even if there should be nothing corresponding in the object which is the prototype of the conception: though our author, in most cases, (therein differing from Kant) believes that there is this correspondence.

We have here an intelligible meaning for the doctrine that to think is to condition ^{k}; and as Mr. Mansel, in his reply, guarantees this as the true meaning of Sir W. Hamilton,[*] I will accept it as being so. If, then (which I do not here discuss), the philosophical doctrine be true, which was held partially by Sir W. Hamilton, and in a more thorough-going manner by Kant, viz. that, in the act of thought, the mind, by an à priori necessity, invests the object of thought with attributes which are not in itself, but are created by the mind's own laws; and if we consent to call these necessities

[*Philosophy of the Conditioned, pp. 66–7.]

$^{k-k57}65^1$, 65^2 : but the doctrine is of as little use for our author's purpose in this interpretation as in the two preceding. What he aims at proving against Cousin is, that the Absolute is unthinkable. His argument for this (if I have interpreted him right) is, that we can only think anything, in conformity to the laws of our thinking faculty. But his opponents never alleged the contrary. Even Schelling was not so gratuitously absurd as to deny that the Absolute must be known according to the capacities of that which knows it—though he was forced to invent a special capacity for the purpose. And M. Cousin holds that the Absolute is known by the same faculties by which we know other things. They both maintained, not that the Absolute could be thought, apart from the conditions of our thinking faculty, but that those conditions are compatible with thinking the Absolute: and the only answer that could be made to them would be to disprove this: which the author has been trying to do; by what inconclusive arguments, I have already endeavoured to show.

of thought the conditions of thought; then evidently to think is to condition, and to think the Unconditioned would be to think the unthinkable. But the Unconditioned, in this application of the term, is not identical with the Infinite plus the Absolute. The Infinite and the Absolute are not necessarily, in this sense, unconditioned. The words infinite and absolute, as I have already said, have no meaning save as expressing some concrete reality or supposed reality, possessing infinitely or absolutely attributes of some sort, which attributes, as finite and limited, we are able to think. In thinking these attributes, we are not able to divest ourselves of our mental conditions, but we can think the attributes as surpassing the conditions. "To condition," and "to think under conditions," are ambiguous phrases. An Infinite Being may be thought, and is thought, *with reference* to the conditions, but not as limited by them. The most familiar examples of the alleged necessary conditions of thought, are Time and Space: we cannot, it is affirmed, think anything, except in time and space. Now, an Infinite Being is not thought as *in* time and space, if this means as occupying a portion of time or a portion of space. But (substituting for Time the word Duration, to get rid of the theological antithesis of Time and Eternity) we do actually conceive God *in reference* to Duration and Extension, namely, as occupying *'*the whole of both; and these being conceived as infinite, to conceive a Being as occupying the whole of them is to conceive that Being as infinite. If thinking God as eternal and omnipresent is thinking him in Space and Time, we do think God in Space and Time: if thinking him as eternal and omnipresent is not thinking him in Space and Time, we are capable of thinking something out of Space and Time. Mr. Mansel may make his choice between the two opinions. I have already shown that the ideas of infinite space and time are real and positive conceptions:[*] that of a Being who is in all Space and in all Time is no less so. To think anything, must of course be to condition it by attributes which are themselves thinkable; but not necessarily to condition it by a limited quantum of those attributes: on the contrary, we may think it under a degree of them greater than all limited degrees, and this is to think it as infinite.*kl

[*See pp. 48ff. above.]

*[67] "To be conceived as unconditioned," says Mr. Mansel, "God must be conceived as exempt from action in time: to be conceived as a person, if his personality resembles ours, he must be conceived as acting in time." ([*Philosophy of the Conditioned*,] pp. 17–18.) Exempt from action in time, as much as you please; in other words, not necessitated to it, nor restricted by its conditions; but did any one ever conceive the Deity as *not* acting in time? Nay, even if he is not conceived as a person, but only as the first principle of the universe, "one absolutely first principle on which everything else depends," [p. 7,] a belief which is held by Mr. Mansel along with the Christian doctrine of the Divine Personality (pp. 7–18); even

l–l[manuscript fragment exists; see Appendix A *below*]

If we now ask ourselves, as the result of this long discussion, what Sir W. Hamilton can be considered as having accomplished in this celebrated Essay, our answer must be: That he has established, more thoroughly perhaps than he intended, the futility of all speculation respecting those meaningless abstractions "The Infinite" and "The Absolute," notions contradictory in themselves, and to which no corresponding realities do or can exist.* ^{m} Respecting the unknowableness, not of "the Infinite," or "the Absolute," but of concrete persons or things possessing infinitely or absolutely certain specific attributes, I cannot think that our author has proved anything; nor do I think it possible to prove them any otherwise unknowable, than that they can only be known in their relations to us, and not as Noumena, or Things in themselves. This, however, is true of the finite as well as of the infinite, of the imperfect as well as of the completed or

---

so, the first principle of everything which takes place in Time, must, from the very meaning of the words, not only be conceived as acting in Time, but must really act in Time, and in all Time. Action in Time does not belong to the Deity as a Person, but quite as much to the Deity as the first principle of all things, which is what Mr. Mansel means by the Unconditioned.

*[67] On this Mr.Mansel's remark is that Sir W. Hamilton did not assert these to be unmeaning abstractions. ([*Ibid.*,] pp. 110–11.) I never pretended that he did; the gist of my complaint against him is, that he did not perceive them to be unmeaning. "Hamilton," says Mr. Mansel, "maintains that the terms absolute and infinite are perfectly intelligible as abstractions, as much so as relative and finite." [*Ibid.*, p. 110.] *Quis dubitavit?* It is not the terms absolute and infinite that are unmeaning; it is "The Infinite" and "The Absolute." Infinite and Absolute are real attributes, abstracted from concrete objects of thought, if not of experience, which are at least believed to possess those attributes. "The Infinite" and "The Absolute" are illegitimate abstractions of what never were, nor could without self-contradiction be supposed to be, attributes of any concrete. I regret to differ, on this point, from my distinguished reviewer [George Grote] in the *Westminster Review*, who considers these to be intelligible abstractions, though of a higher reach of abstraction than the preceding (p. 14). The distinction is seized by one of my American critics, Dr. H. B. Smith, who regards it as the difference between talking "about the Infinite and Absolute as entities," and considering them "simply as modes or predicates of real existences." (["Mill's Examination,"] p. 134.) That there are persons "in Laputa or the Empire" (as Sir W. Hamilton phrases it [*Discussions*, p. 21]) who do talk about them as entities, up to any pitch of wild nonsense, I am quite aware; and against these Sir W. Hamilton's Essay, as the protest, though the insufficient protest, of a rival Transcendentalist, has its value.

^{m}65^1, 65^2 His own favourite abstraction "The Unconditioned," considered as the sum of these two, necessarily shares the same fate. If, indeed, it be applied conformably to either of the received meanings of the word condition—if it be understood either as denoting a First Cause, or as a name for all Noumena—it has in each case a signification which can be understood and reasoned about. But as a phrase afflicted with incurable ambiguity, and habitually used by its introducer in several meanings, with no apparent consciousness of their not being the same, it seems to me a very infelicitous creation, and a useless and hurtful intruder into the language of philosophy. [*paragraph*]

absolute. Our author has merely proved the uncognoscibility of a being which is *nothing but* infinite, or *nothing but* absolute: and since nobody supposes that there is such a being, but only beings which are something positive carried to the infinite, or to the absolute, to have established this point cannot be regarded as any great achievement. He has not even refuted M. Cousin; whose doctrine of an intuitive cognition of the Deity,[*] like every other doctrine relating to intuition, can only be disproved by showing it to be a mistaken interpretation of facts; which, again, as we shall see hereafter, can only be done by pointing out in what other way the seeming perceptions may have originated, which are erroneously supposed to be intuitive.

[*See *Cours de philosophie: Introduction*, Leçon v, *passim*.]

CHAPTER V

What is Rejected as Knowledge by Sir William Hamilton, Brought Back Under the Name of Belief

WE HAVE FOUND Sir W. Hamilton maintaining with great earnestness, and taking as the basis of his philosophy, an opinion respecting the limitation of human knowledge, which, if he did not mean so much by it as the language in which he often clothed it seemed to imply, meant at least this, that the Absolute, the Infinite, the Unconditioned, are necessarily unknowable by us. I have discussed this opinion as a serious philosophical dogma, expressing a definite view of the relation between the universe and human apprehension, and fitted to guide us in distinguishing the questions which it is of any avail to ask, from those which are altogether closed to our investigations.

But had the doctrine, in the mind of Sir W. Hamilton, meant ten times more than it did—had he upheld the relativity of human knowledge in the fullest, instead of the scantiest meaning of which the words are susceptible—the question would still have been reduced to naught, or to a mere verbal controversy, by his admission of a second *kind* of intellectual conviction called Belief; which is anterior to knowledge, is the foundation of it, and is not subject to its limitations; and through the medium of which we may have, and are justified in having, a full assurance of all the things which he has pronounced unknowable to us; and this not exclusively by revelation, that is, on the supposed testimony of a Being whom we have ground for trusting as veracious, but by our natural faculties.

From some philosophers, this distinction would have the appearance of a mere fetch—one of those transparent evasions which have sometimes been resorted to by the assailants of received opinions, that they might have an opportunity of ruining the rational foundations of a doctrine without exposing themselves to odium by its direct denial: as the writers against Christianity in the eighteenth century, after declaring some doctrine to be contradictory to reason, and exhibiting it in the absurdest possible light, were

*-*65[1], 65[2] source

wont to add that this was not of the smallest consequence, religion being an affair of faith, not of reason. But Sir W. Hamilton evidently meant what he says; he was expressing a serious conviction, and one of the tenets of his philosophy: he really recognised *under the name of* Belief a substantive source, I was going to say, of knowledge; I may at all events say of trustworthy evidence. This appears in the following passages:

> The sphere of our belief is much more extensive than the sphere of our knowledge, and therefore, when I deny that the Infinite can by us be *known*, I am far from denying that by us it is, must, and ought to be, *believed*. This I have indeed anxiously evinced, both by reasoning and authority.*

> St. Austin accurately says, "We know, what rests upon *reason*; but believe, what rests upon *authority*." But reason itself must rest at last upon authority; for the original data of reason do not rest on reason, but are necessarily accepted by reason on the authority of what is beyond itself. These data are, therefore, in rigid propriety, Beliefs or Trusts. Thus it is that in the last resort we must perforce philosophically admit, that belief is the primary condition of reason, and not reason the ultimate ground of belief. We are compelled to surrender the proud *Intellige ut credas* of Abelard, to content ourselves with the humble *Crede ut intelligas* of Anselm.†

And in another part of the same Dissertation, (he is arguing that we do not believe, but know, the external world)—

> If asked, indeed, how we know that we know it? how we know that what we apprehend in sensible perception is, as consciousness assures us, an object, external, extended, and numerically different from the conscious subject? how we know that this object is not a mere mode of mind, illusively presented to us as a mere mode of matter; then indeed we must reply that we do not in propriety *know* that what we are compelled to perceive as not-self is not a perception of self, and that we can only on reflection *believe* such to be the case, in reliance on the original necessity of so believing, imposed on us by our nature.‡

It thus appears that, in Sir W. Hamilton's opinion, Belief is a *conviction of higher authority* than Knowledge; Belief is ultimate, knowledge only derivative; Knowledge itself finally rests on Belief; natural beliefs are the

---

*Letter to Mr. Calderwood, in Appendix [iii], to *Lectures*, Vol. II, pp. 530–1.

†"Dissertations on Reid," [Note A,] p. 760. [For St. Augustine, see *De Utilitate credendi ad Honoratum liber unus*, in *Opera Omnia*, Vols. XXXII–XLVII of Jacques Paul Migné, ed., *Patrologiæ cursus completus, Series latina* (Paris: Migné, 1841–49), Vol. XLII, col. 83 (Cap. xi). The attribution of "Intellige ut credas" to Peter Abelard is mistaken. For St. Anselm, see *Proslogion seu Alloquium de Dei Existentia*, in *Opera Omnia*, Vols. CLVIII–CLIX of *ibid.* (1853–54), Vol. CLVIII, col. 227 (Cap. i).]

‡[Note A,] p. 750.

ᵇ⁻ᵇ65¹, 65²   in
ᶜ⁻ᶜ65¹, 65²   higher source of evidence

sole warrant for all our knowledge. Knowledge, therefore, is an inferior ground of assurance to natural Belief; and as we have beliefs which tell us that we know, and without which we could not be assured of the truth of our knowledge, so we have, and are warranted in having, beliefs beyond our knowledge; beliefs respecting the Unconditioned—respecting that which is in itself unknowable.

I am not now considering what it is that, in our author's opinion, we are bound to believe concerning the unknowable. What here concerns us is, the nullity to which this doctrine reduces the position to which our author seemed to cling so firmly—viz., that our knowledge is relative to ourselves, and that we can have no knowledge of the infinite and absolute. In telling us that it is impossible to the human faculties to know anything about Things in themselves, we naturally suppose he intends to warn us off the ground—to bid us understand that this subject of enquiry is closed to us, and exhort us to turn our attention elsewhere. It appears that nothing of the kind was intended: we are to understand, on the contrary, that we may have the best grounded and most complete assurance of the things which were declared unknowable—an assurance not only equal or greater in degree, but the same in nature, as we have for the truth of our knowledge: and that the matter ^{d}in^d dispute was only whether this assurance or conviction shall be called knowledge, or by another name. If this be all, I must say I think it not of the smallest consequence. If no more than this be intended by the "great axiom"[*] and the elaborate argument against Cousin, a great deal of trouble has been taken to very little purpose; and the subject would have been better left where Reid left it, who did not trouble himself with nice distinctions between belief and knowledge, but was content to consider us as knowing that which, by the constitution of our nature, we are forced, with entire conviction, to believe. According to Sir W. Hamilton, we believe premises, but know the conclusions from them. The ultimate facts of consciousness are "given less in the form of cognitions than of beliefs:" "Consciousness in its last analysis, in other words our primary experience, is a faith."* But if we know the theorems of Euclid, and do not know the definitions and axioms on which they rest, the word knowledge, thus singularly applied, must be taken in a merely technical sense. ^{e}To say that we believe the premises, but know the conclusion, would be understood by every one as meaning that we had other independent evidence of the conclusion. If we only know it through the premises, the same name ought

[*Lectures, Vol. I, p. 136; cf. p. 16 above.]
*Discussions, p. 86.

$^{d-d}$65^1, 65^2 of
$^{e-e}$+67, 72

in reason to be given to our assurance of both. *e In common language, when Belief and Knowledge are distinguished, Knowledge is understood to mean complete conviction, Belief a conviction somewhat short of complete; or else we are said to believe when the evidence is probable (as that of testimony), but to know, when it is intuitive, or demonstrative from intuitive premises: we believe, for example, that there is a Continent of America, but know that we are alive, that two and two make four, and that the sum of any two sides of a triangle is greater than the third side. This is a distinction of practical value: but in Sir W. Hamilton's use of the term, it is the intuitive convictions that are the Beliefs, and those which are dependent and contingent upon them, compose our knowledge. Whether a particular portion of our convictions, which are not more certain, but if anything less certain, than the remainder, and according to our author rest on the same ultimate basis, shall in opposition to the common usage of mankind, receive exclusively the appellation of knowledge, is at the most a question of terminology, and can only be made to appear philosophically important by confounding difference of name with difference of fact. That anything capable of being said on such a subject should pass for a fundamental principle of philosophy, and be ƒone of the chief sourcesƒ of the reputation of a metaphysical system, is but an example how the mere forms of logic and metaphysics can blind mankind to the total absence of their substance.

ᵍIt must not be supposed, from anything which has been here said, that I wish to abolish the distinction between Knowledge and Belief (meaning True Belief) or maintain that it is necessarily a distinction without a difference. Those terms are employed to denote more than one real difference, and neither of them can conveniently be dispensed with in philosophy.† What concerns us in the present chapter is not the rationale of the distinction between knowledge and belief, but whether that distinction

*[67] Accordingly Sir W. Hamilton himself, in one of the "Dissertations on Reid," says that "the principles of our knowledge must be themselves knowledge." ([Note A,] p. 763.) And there are few who will not approve this use of language, and condemn the other.

†[67] There is much dispute among philosophers as to the difference between Knowledge and Belief; and the strife is not likely to terminate, until they perceive that the real question is, not what the distinction is, but what it shall be; what one among several differences already known and recognised, the words shall be employed to denote. "The word belief," says Dr. M'Cosh, in this more discerning than the generality, "is unfortunately a very vague one, and may stand for a number of very different mental affections. When I am speaking of first or intuitive princi-

ƒ-ƒ65¹, 65²   the chief source
ᵍ-ᵍ65 +67, 72

is relevant to the question between Sir W. Hamilton and M. Cousin about the Infinite and the Absolute; and whether Sir W. Hamilton is warranted in giving back under the name of Belief, the assurance or conviction respecting these objects which he refuses under the name of knowledge. My position is, that the Infinite and Absolute which Sir W. Hamilton has been proving to be unknowable, being made up of contradictions, are as incapable of being believed as of being known; that the only attitude in reference to them, of any intellect which apprehends the meaning of language, is that of disbelief. On the other hand, there are Infinites and Absolutes which, not being self-contradictory, admit of being believed, namely, concrete realities supposed to be infinite or absolute in respect of certain attributes: but Sir W. Hamilton, as I maintain, has done nothing towards proving that

---

ples, I use the term to signify our conviction of the existence of an object not now present, and thus I distinguish primitive faith from primitive knowledge, in which the object is present." (*Examination*, pp. 36–7.) This distinction agrees well with usage in the cases to which Dr. M'Cosh applies it: we know that which we perceive by the senses, and believe that which we only remember: we know that we ourselves, and (while we look at them) our house and garden, exist, and believe the existence of the Czar of Russia and the island of Ceylon. Every definition of Belief, as distinguished from Knowledge, must include these cases, because in them the conviction which receives the name of Belief falls short of the complete assurance implied in the word knowledge: our memory may deceive us; the Czar or the island may have been swallowed up by an earthquake. But if we attempt to carry out Dr. M'Cosh's distinction through the entire region of thought, the whole of what we call our scientific knowledge, except the primary facts or intuitions on which it is grounded, has to pass into the category of Belief; for the objects with which it is conversant are seldom present.

Mr. Mansel might be supposed to be adopting Dr. M'Cosh's distinction, when he says, "We believe that the true distinction between knowledge and belief may ultimately be referred to the presence or absence of the corresponding intuition." ([*Philosophy of the Conditioned*,] p. 126n.) But his criterion of the distinction, and, according to him, Sir W. Hamilton's also, is the following: we believe that a thing is, but do not know even *that* it is, unless we can conceive how, or in what manner, it is. "When I say that I believe in the existence of a spiritual being who can see without eyes, I cannot conceive the *manner* in which seeing co-exists with the absence of the bodily organ of sight" (*ibid.*). "We cannot conceive the manner in which the unconditioned and the personal are united in the Divine Nature; yet we may believe that, in some manner unknown to us, they are so united. To conceive the union of two attributes in one object of thought, I must be able to conceive them as united in some particular manner: when this cannot be done, I may nevertheless believe *that* the union is possible, though I am unable to conceive *how* it is possible." [*Ibid.*, pp. 18–19.] This may be more briefly expressed by saying that we can believe what is inconceivable, but can know only what is conceivable; and undoubtedly both these contrasted propositions are maintained by Sir W. Hamilton. But to regard them as a clue to the distinction in his mind between knowledge and belief, would be to misunderstand his opinions: for the convictions which he

such concrete realities cannot be known, in the way in which we know other things, namely, in their relations to us. When, therefore, he affirms that though the Infinite cannot by us be known, "by us it is, must, and ought to be believed,"[*] I answer, that the Infinite which, as he has so laboriously proved, cannot be known, neither is, must, nor ought to be believed; not because it cannot be known, but because there exists no such thing for us to know; unless, with Hegel, we hold that the Absolute is not subject to the Law of Contradiction, but is at once a real existence and the synthesis of contradictories. And, on the other hand, the Infinite and Absolute which are really capable of being believed, are also, for anything Sir W. Hamilton has shown to the contrary, capable of being, in certain of their aspects, known.[g]

---

most emphatically characterized as beliefs, in contradistinction to knowledge, are what he calls our natural and necessary beliefs, "the original data of reason," ["Dissertations on Reid," Note A, p. 760,] which, far from being inconceivable, are usually tested by being themselves conceivable while their negations are not. If knowledge were distinguished from belief by our being aware of the manner as well as the fact, we could not believe and know the same fact; our knowledge could not rest, as he says it does, on a belief that it is itself true.

But indeed, this notion of Sir W. Hamilton that we have two convictions on the same point, one guaranteeing the other—our knowledge of a truth, and a belief in the truth of that knowledge—seems to me a piece of false philosophy, resembling the doctrine he elsewhere rejects, that we have both a feeling and a consciousness of the feeling. We do not know a truth and believe it besides; the belief *is* the knowledge. Belief, altogether, is a genus which includes knowledge: according to the usage of language we believe whatever we assent to; but some of our beliefs are knowledge, others are only belief. The first requisite which, by universal admission, a belief must possess, to constitute it knowledge, is that it be true. The second is, that it be well grounded; for what we believe by accident, or on evidence not sufficient, we are not said to know. The grounds must, moreover, be sufficient for the very highest degree of assurance; for we do not consider ourselves to know, as long as we think there is any possibility (I mean any appreciable possibility) of our being mistaken. But when a belief is true, is held with the strongest conviction we ever have, and held on grounds sufficient to justify that strongest conviction, most people would think it worthy of the name of knowledge, whether it be grounded on our personal investigations, or on the appropriate testimony, and whether we know only the fact itself, or the manner of the fact. And I am inclined to think that the purposes of philosophy, as well as those of common life, are best answered by making this the line of demarcation.

[*Lectures, Vol. II, App. iii, p. 531; cf. p. 61 above.]

CHAPTER VI

The Philosophy of the Conditioned

THE "PHILOSOPHY OF THE CONDITIONED," in its wider sense, includes all the doctrines that we have been discussing. In its narrower, it consists, I think, mainly of a single proposition, which Sir W. Hamilton often reiterates, and insists upon as a fundamental law of human intellect. Though suggested by Kant's Antinomies of Speculative Reason, in the form which it bears in Sir W. Hamilton's writings it belongs, I believe, originally to himself. No doctrine which he has anywhere laid down is more characteristic of his mode of thought, and none is more strongly associated with his fame.

For the better understanding of this theory, it is necessary to premise some explanations respecting another doctrine, which is also his, but not peculiar to him. He protests, frequently and with emphasis, against the notion that whatever is inconceivable must be false. "There is no ground," he says, "for inferring a certain fact to be impossible, merely from our inability to conceive its possibility."* I regard this opinion as perfectly just. It is one of the psychological truths, highly important, and by no means generally recognised, which frequently meet us in his writings, and which give them, in my eyes, most of their philosophical value. I am obliged to add, that though he often furnishes a powerful statement and vindication of such truths, he seldom or never consistently adheres to them. Too often what he has affirmed in generals is taken back in details, and arguments of his own are found to rest on philosophical commonplaces which he has himself repudiated and refuted. I am afraid that the present is one of these cases, and that Sir W. Hamilton will sometimes be found contending that a thing cannot possibly be true because we cannot conceive it: but at all events he disclaims any such inference, and broadly lays down, that things not only may be, but are, of which it is impossible for us to conceive even the possibility.

Before showing how this proposition is developed into the "Philosophy of the Conditioned," let us make the ground safe before us, by bestowing a

*Discussions, [App. I (A),] p. 624.

brief consideration upon the proposition itself, its meaning, and the foundations on which it rests.

We cannot conclude anything to be impossible, because its possibility is inconceivable to us; for two reasons. First; what seems to us inconceivable, and, so far as we are personally concerned, may really be so, usually owes its inconceivability only to a strong association. When, in a prolonged experience, we have often had a particular sensation or mental impression, and never without a certain other sensation or impression immediately accompanying it, there grows up so firm an adhesion between our ideas of the two, that we are unable to think of the former without thinking the latter in close combination with it. And unless other parts of our experience afford us some analogy to aid in disentangling the two ideas, our incapacity of imagining the one fact without the other grows, or is prone to grow, into a belief that the one cannot exist without the other. This is the law of Inseparable Association, an element of our nature of which few have realized to themselves the full power. It was for the first time largely applied to the explanation of the more complicated mental phænomena by Mr. James Mill;[*] and is, in an especial manner, the key to the phænomenon of inconceivability. As that phænomenon only exists because our powers of conception are determined by our limited experience, Inconceivables are incessantly becoming Conceivables as our experience becomes enlarged. There is no need to go farther for an example than the case of Antipodes. This physical fact was, to the early speculators, inconceivable: not, of course, the fact of persons in that position; this the mind could easily represent to itself; but the possibility that, being in that position, and not being nailed on, nor having any glutinous substance attached to their feet, they could help falling off. Here was an inseparable, though, as it proved to be, not an indissoluble association, which while it continued made a real fact what is called inconceivable; and because inconceivable, it was unhesitatingly believed to be impossible. Inconceivabilities of similar character have, at many periods, obstructed the reception of new scientific truths: the Newtonian system had to contend against several of them; and we are not warranted in assigning a different origin and character to those which still subsist, because the experience that would be capable of removing them has not occurred. If anything which is now inconceivable by us were shown to us as a fact, we should soon find ourselves able to conceive it. We should even be in danger of going over to the opposite error, and believing that the negation of it is inconceivable. There are many cases in the history

[*Analysis of the Phenomena of the Human Mind, 2 vols. (London: Baldwin and Cradock, 1829).]

of science (I have dilated on some of them in another work)[*] where something which had once been inconceivable, and which people had with great difficulty learnt to conceive, becoming itself fixed in the bonds of an inseparable association, scientific men came to think that it alone was conceivable, and that the conflicting hypothesis which all mankind had believed, and which a vast majority were probably believing still, was inconceivable. In Dr. Whewell's writings on the Inductive Sciences, this transition of thought is not only exemplified but defended.[†] Inconceivability is thus a purely subjective thing, arising from the mental antecedents of the individual mind, or from those of the human mind generally at a particular period, and cannot give us any insight into the possibilities of Nature.

But, secondly, *even assuming* that inconceivability is not solely the consequence of limited experience, but that some incapacities of conceiving are inherent in the mind, and inseparable from it; this would not entitle us to infer, that what we are thus incapable of conceiving cannot exist. Such an inference would only be warrantable, if we could know *à priori* that we must have been created capable of conceiving whatever is capable of existing: that the universe of thought and that of reality, the Microcosm and the Macrocosm (as they once were called) must have been framed in complete correspondence with one another. That this is really the case has been laid down expressly in some systems of philosophy, by implication in more, and is the foundation (among others) of the systems of Schelling and Hegel: but an assumption more destitute of evidence could scarcely be made, nor can one easily imagine any evidence that could prove it, unless it were revealed from above.

What is inconceivable, then, cannot therefore be inferred to be false. But let us vary the terms of the proposition, and express it thus: what is inconceivable, is not therefore incredible. We have now a statement, which may mean either exactly the same as the other, or more. It may mean only that our inability to conceive a thing, does not entitle us to deny its possibility, nor its existence. Or it may mean that a thing's being inconceivable to us is no reason against our believing, and legitimately believing, that it actually is. This is a very different proposition from the preceding. Sir W.

[*See *Logic*, Bk. II, Chap. v, §6, and Bk. V, Chap. iii, §3, in *Collected Works*, Vol. VII, pp. 238ff.; Vol. VIII, pp. 752ff.]

[†See William Whewell, *History of the Inductive Sciences*, 3rd ed., 3 vols. (London: Parker, 1857); *History of Scientific Ideas*, 3rd ed., 2 vols. (London: Parker, 1858); *Novum Organon Renovatum*, 3rd ed. (London: Parker, 1858); and *On the Philosophy of Discovery* (London: Parker, 1860).]

*a-a*65[1], 65[2]   were it granted

Hamilton, as we have said, goes this length. It is now necessary to enter more minutely than at first seemed needful, into the meaning of "inconceivable;" which, like almost all the metaphysical terms we are forced to make use of, is weighed down with ambiguities.

Reid pointed out and discriminated two meanings of the verb "to conceive,"* giving rise to two different meanings of inconceivable. But Sir W. Hamilton uses "to conceive" in three meanings, and has accordingly three meanings for Inconceivable; though he does not give the smallest hint to his readers, nor seems ever to suspect, that the three are not one and the same.

The first meaning of Inconceivable is, that of which the mind cannot form to itself any representation; either (as in the case of Noumena) because no attributes are given, out of which a representation could be framed, or because the attributes given are incompatible with one another—are such as the mind cannot put together in a single image. Of this last case numerous instances present themselves to the most cursory glance. The fundamental one is that of a simple contradiction. We cannot represent anything to ourselves as at once being something, and not being it; as at once having, and not having, a given attribute. The following are other examples. We cannot represent to ourselves time or space as having an end. We cannot represent to ourselves two and two as making five; nor two straight lines as

*"To conceive, to imagine, to apprehend, when taken in the proper sense, signify an act of the mind which implies no belief or judgment at all. It is an act of the mind by which nothing is affirmed or denied, and which, therefore, can neither be true nor false. But there is another and a very different meaning of these words, so common and so well authorized in language that it cannot be avoided; and on that account we ought to be the more on our guard, that we be not misled by the ambiguity. . . . When we would express our opinion modestly, instead of saying, 'This is my opinion,' or 'This is my judgment,' which has the air of dogmaticalness, we say, 'I conceive it to be thus—I imagine, or apprehend it to be thus;' which is understood as a modest declaration of our judgment. In like manner, when anything is said which we take to be impossible, we say, 'We cannot conceive it:' meaning that we cannot believe it. Thus we see that the words *conceive*, *imagine*, *apprehend*, have two meanings, and are used to express two operations of the mind, which ought never to be confounded. Sometimes they express simple apprehension, which implies no judgment at all; sometimes they express judgment or opinion. . . . When they are used to express simple apprehension they are followed by a noun in the accusative case, which signifies the object conceived; but when they are used to express opinion or judgment, they are commonly followed by a verb in the infinitive mood. 'I conceive an Egyptian pyramid.' This implies no judgment. 'I conceive the Egyptian pyramids to be the most ancient monuments of human art.' This implies judgment. When they are used in the last sense, the thing conceived must be a proposition, because judgment cannot be expressed but by a proposition." (Reid, [*Essays*] *on the Intellectual Powers* [*of Man*], p. 223 of Sir W. Hamilton's edition [Edinburgh: Maclachlan and Stewart, 1846], to which edition all my references will be made.)

enclosing a space. We cannot represent to ourselves a round square; [b]nor[b] a body all black, and at the same time all white.

These things are literally inconceivable to us, our minds and our experience being what they are. Whether they would be inconceivable if our minds were the same but our experience different, is open to discussion. A distinction may be made, which, I think, will be found pertinent to the question. That the same thing should at once be and not be—that identically the same statement should be both true and false—is not only inconceivable to us, but we cannot [c]imagine[c] that it could be made conceivable. We cannot attach sufficient meaning to the proposition, to be able to represent to ourselves the supposition of a different experience on this matter. We cannot therefore even entertain the question, whether the incompatibility is in the original structure of our minds, or is only put there by our experience. The case is otherwise in all the other examples of inconceivability. Our incapacity of conceiving the same thing as A and not A, may be primordial; but our inability to conceive A without B, is because A, by experience or teaching, has become inseparably associated with B: and our inability to conceive A with C, is, because, by experience or teaching, A has become inseparably associated with some mental representation which includes the negation of C. Thus all inconceivabilities may be reduced to inseparable association, combined with the original inconceivability of a direct contradiction. All the cases which I have cited as instances of inconceivability, and which are the strongest I could have chosen, may be resolved in this manner. We cannot conceive a round square, not merely because no such object has ever presented itself in our experience, for that would not be enough. Neither, for anything we know, are the two ideas in themselves incompatible. To conceive a round square, or to conceive a body all black and yet all white, would only be to conceive two different sensations as produced in us simultaneously by the same object; a conception familiar to our experience; and we should probably be as well able to conceive a round square as a hard square, or a heavy square, if it were not that, in our uniform experience, at the instant when a thing begins to be round it ceases to be square, so that the beginning of the one impression is inseparably associated with the departure or cessation of the other.* Thus our inability to form a conception always arises from our being compelled

*[72] It has been remarked to me by a correspondent, that a round square differs from a hard square or a heavy square in this respect, that the two sensations or sets of sensations supposed to be joined in the first-named combination are affections of the same nerves, and therefore, being different affections, are mutually incompatible by our organic constitution, and could not be made compatible by any change in

[b]-[b]65[1], 65[2], 67   or
[c]-[c]65[1], 65[2]   conceive

to form another contradictory to it. We cannot conceive time or space as having an end, because the idea of any portion whatever of time or space is inseparably associated with the idea of a time or space beyond it. We cannot conceive two and two as five, because an inseparable association compels us to conceive it as four; and it cannot be conceived as both, because four and five, like round and square, are so related in our experience, that each is associated with the cessation, or removal, of the other. We cannot conceive two straight lines as enclosing a space, because enclosing a space means approaching and meeting a second time; and the mental image of two straight lines which have once met is inseparably associated with the representation of them as diverging. Thus it is not wholly without ground that the notion of a round square, and the assertion that two and two make five, or that two straight lines can enclose a space, are said, in common and even in scientific parlance, to involve a contradiction. The statement is not logically correct, for contradiction is only between a positive representation and its negative. But the impossibility of uniting contradictory conceptions in the same representation, is the real ground of the inconceivability in these cases. And we should probably have no difficulty in putting together the two ideas supposed to be incompatible, if our experience had not first inseparably associated one of them with the contradictory of the other.*

---

the arrangements of external nature. This is probably true, and may be the physical reason why when a thing begins to be perceived as round it ceases to be perceived as square; but it is not the less true that this mere fact suffices, under the laws of association, to account for the inconceivability of the combination. I am willing, however, to admit, as suggested by my correspondent, that "if the imagination employs the organism in its representations," which it probably does, "what is originally unperceivable in consequence of organic laws" may also be "originally unimaginable."

*That the reverse of the most familiar principles of arithmetic and geometry might have been made conceivable, even to our present mental faculties, if those faculties had coexisted with a totally different constitution of external nature, is ingeniously shown in the concluding paper of a recent volume, anonymous, but of known authorship, *Essays, by a Barrister*.

"Consider this case. There is a world in which, whenever two pairs of things are either placed in proximity or are contemplated together, a fifth thing is immediately created and brought within the contemplation of the mind engaged in putting two and two together. This is surely neither inconceivable, for we can readily conceive the result by thinking of common puzzle tricks, nor can it be said to be beyond the power of Omnipotence. Yet in such a world surely two and two would make five. That is, the result to the mind of contemplating two two's would be to count five. This shows that it is not inconceivable that two and two might make five: but, on the other hand, it is perfectly easy to see why in this world we are absolutely certain that two and two make four. There is probably not an instant of our lives in which we are not experiencing the fact. We see it whenever we count four books, four tables or

Thus far, of the first kind of Inconceivability; the first and most proper meaning in which the word is used. But there is another meaning, in which things are often said to be inconceivable which the mind is under no

chairs, four men in the street, or the four corners of a paving stone, and we feel more sure of it than of the rising of the sun to-morrow, because our experience upon the subject is so much wider and applies to such an infinitely greater number of cases. Nor is it true that every one who has once been brought to see it, is equally sure of it. A boy who has just learnt the multiplication table is pretty sure that twice two are four, but is often extremely doubtful whether seven times nine are sixty-three. If his teacher told him that twice two made five, his certainty would be greatly impaired.

It would also be possible to put a case of a world in which two straight lines should be universally supposed to include a space. Imagine a man who had never had any experience of straight lines through the medium of any sense whatever, suddenly placed upon a railway stretching out on a perfectly straight line to an indefinite distance in each direction. He would see the rails, which would be the first straight lines he had ever seen, apparently meeting, or at least tending to meet at each horizon; and he would thus infer, in the absence of all other experience, that they actually did enclose a space, when produced far enough. Experience alone could undeceive him. A world in which every object was round, with the single exception of a straight inaccessible railway, would be a world in which every one would believe that two straight lines enclosed a space. In such a world, therefore, the impossibility of conceiving that two straight lines can enclose a space would not exist." [James Fitzjames Stephen, "Mr. Mansel's Metaphysics," in *Essays by a Barrister* (London: Smith, Elder, 1862), pp. 333–4.]

In the "Geometry of Visibles" which forms part of Reid's *Inquiry into the Human Mind*, it is contended that if we had the sense of sight, but not that of touch, it would appear to us that "every right line being produced will at last return into itself," and that "any two right lines being produced will meet in two points." [In *Works*, ed. Hamilton,] Chap. vi, §9 (p. 148.) The author adds, that persons thus constituted would firmly believe "that two or more bodies may exist in the same place." For this they would "have the testimony of sense," and could "no more doubt of it than they can doubt whether they have any perception at all, since they would often see two bodies meet and coincide in the same place, and separate again, without having undergone any change in their sensible qualities by this penetration." (*Ibid.*, p. 151.)

[d]Hardly any part of the present volume has been so maltreated, by so great a number of critics, as the illustrations here quoted from an able and highly instructed cotemporary thinker; which, as they were neither designed by their author nor cited by me as anything more than illustrations, I do not deem it necessary to take up space by defending. When a selection must be made, one is obliged to consider what one can best spare.

[e]Some of my correspondents, looking upon the illustrations by "A Barrister" as (what they are not) an essential part of my argument, think me bound either to defend them or to give them up. As they are, in my opinion, perfectly defensible, I am ready, thus challenged, to stand up for them. And I select, among the attacks made on them, that of Dr. M'Cosh (*Examination of Mr. J. S. Mill's Philosophy*, pp. 209–11), as one of the fairest, and including what is most worthy of notice in the others. Of the first illustration, Dr. M'Cosh says:

"Were we placed in a world in which two pairs of things were always followed by

[d–d]74+67, 72
[e–e]+72

incapacity of representing to itself in an image. It is often said, that we are unable to conceive *as possible* that which, in itself, we are perfectly well able to conceive: we are able, it is admitted, to conceive it as an imaginary

---

a fifth thing, we might be disposed to believe that the pairs caused the fifth thing, or that there was some prearranged disposition of things producing them together; but we could not be made to judge that $2 + 2 = 5$, or that the fifth thing is not a different thing from the two and the two. On the other supposition put, of the two pairs always suggesting a fifth, we should explain their recurrence by some law of association, but we would not confound the 5 with the $2 + 2$, or think that the two pairs could make five." [P. 210.]

This passage is a correct description of what would happen if the presentation of the fifth thing were posterior, by a perceptible interval, to the juxtaposition of the two pairs, so that we should have time to judge that the two and two make four previously to perceiving the fifth. But the supposition is that the production of the fifth is so instantaneous in the very act of seeing, that we never should see the four things by themselves as four: the fifth thing would be inseparably involved in the act of perception by which we should ascertain the sum of the two pairs. I confess it seems to me that in this case we should have an apparent intuition of two and two making five.

To the second illustration, Dr. M'Cosh replies: "I allow that this person as he looked one way, would see a figure presented to the eye of two straight lines approaching nearer each other; and that as he looked the other way he would see a like figure. But I deny that in combining the two views he would ever decide that the four lines seen, the two seen first and the two seen second, make only two straight lines. In uniting the two perceptions in thought, he would certainly place a bend or a turn somewhere, possibly at the spot from which he took the two views. He would continue to do so till he realized that the lines seen on either side did not in fact approach nearer each other. Or, to state the whole phenomenon with more scientific accuracy: Intuitively, and to a person who had not acquired the knowledge of distance by experience, the two views would appear to be each of two lines approaching nearer each other; but without his being at all cognisant of the relation of the two views, or of one part of the lines being further removed from him than another. As experience told him that the lines receded from him on each side, he would contrive some means of combining his observations, probably in the way above indicated; but he never could make two straight lines enclose a space." [Pp. 210–11.]

Now it seems to me that the supposed percipient *could* not account for his apparent perceptions in the manner indicated; he *could* not believe that there was a turn or a bend anywhere. "At the spot from which he took the two views" he would have the evidence of his senses that there was no bend. Looking along the interval between the lines, he would again have the evidence of sense that they were not deflected either way, but maintained an uniform direction. Until therefore, experience of the laws of perspective had corrected his judgment, he would have the apparent evidence of his senses that two straight lines met in two points. This appearance, until shown by further experience to be an illusion, would probably decide his belief: and any doubts that might be raised by a contemplation of straight lines which were nearer to him, would be silenced by the supposition that two straight lines will inclose a space if only they are produced far enough.

Dr. M'Cosh may himself be cited as a witness to the intrinsic possibility of conceiving combinations which I should have thought were universally regarded as

object, but unable to conceive it realized. This extends the term inconceivable to every combination of facts which to the mind simply contemplating it, appears incredible.* It was in this sense that Antipodes were inconceivable. They could be figured in imagination; they could even be painted, or

---

inconceivable. When distinguishing between the two meanings of inconceivable (in pp. 235–6 of his book) he says: "We cannot be made to decide or believe that Cleopatra's Needle should be in Paris and Egypt at the same time; yet with some difficulty we can simultaneously image it in both places." Now when we consider that in order really to image the *same* Needle (and not two Needles exactly similar) in two places at once we must actually imagine the two places, Paris and Alexandria, superposed upon one another and occupying the same portion of space, it seems to me that this conception is quite as impossible to us as the reverse of a geometrical axiom; and is, indeed, of much the same character.[e]

The "Geometry of Visibles" has been noticed only by Dr. M'Cosh (pp. 211–13), who rejects it, as founded on the erroneous doctrine (as he considers it) that we cannot perceive by sight the third dimension of space. I regard this, on the contrary, as not only a true doctrine, but one from which Dr. M'Cosh's own opinion does not materially differ: and if it be true, it is impossible to resist Reid's conclusion [see *Inquiry*, pp. 149–50], that to beings possessing only the sense of sight, the paradoxes here quoted, and several others, would be truths of intuition—self-evident truths.[d]

[f]Dr. Ward, in the *Dublin Review*, contests this doctrine ["Mr. Mill's Denial of Necessary Truth," pp. 304–5]; and an argument against it has been sent to me by the intelligent and instructed correspondent already once referred to. For a reply I might refer them to the chapter on the Geometry of Visibles, in Reid's work; but I will point out, in few words, where I think they are in error. They contend that Reid's Idomenians would not possess the notion which we attach to the term straight line, but would call by that name what they would really image to themselves as a circular arc. But Reid's position (and he assigns good reasons for it) is the reverse of this; that what we, who have the sense of touch, perceive as a circular arc with ourselves in the centre, Idomenians could only perceive as a straight line; and that, consequently, all the appearances which Reid enumerates would be by them apprehended, and, as they would think, perceived, as phenomena of straight lines.

Dr. M'Cosh also returns to the charge, but holds a different doctrine from my other two critics, being of opinion that the Idomenians would really have the notion of a straight line. [See "Mill's Reply," p. 356.] For the consequences of this I refer him back to Reid. He adds, that as touch alone can reveal to us impenetrability, the Idomenians could argue nothing as to bodies *penetrating* one another. [See *Inquiry*, pp. 150–2.] But, they could have the conception of the only penetration Reid contended for, namely, of bodies meeting and coinciding in the same place, and separating again without alteration. And for this they would have the evidence of sense. The fact is literally true of the visual images, which to them would be the whole bodies; and as they could form no notion of one thing passing behind another, their only impression would be of penetration.[f]

*[72] I do not mean, which is *really* incredible, as Mr. Mansel, in his rejoinder, supposes I do, and consequently charges me with imputing to Sir W. Hamilton that in the Law of the Conditioned he maintains that of two *incredible* alternatives one must be *believed*. ["Supplementary Remarks," p. 27.]

[f-f]+72

modelled in clay. The mind could put the parts of the conception together, but *g* could not realize the combination as one which could exist in nature. The cause of the inability was the powerful tendency, generated by experience, to *expect* falling off, when a body, not of adhesive quality, was in contact only with the under side of another body. The association was not so powerful as to disable the mind from conceiving the body as holding on; doubtless because other facts of our experience afforded models on which such a conception could be framed. But though not disabled from conceiving the combination, the mind was disabled from believing it. The difference between belief and conception, and between the conditions of belief and those of simple conception, are psychological questions into which I do not enter. It is sufficient that inability to believe can coexist with ability to conceive, and that a mental association between two facts which is not intense enough to make their separation unimaginable, may yet create, and, if there are no counter associations, always does create, more or less of difficulty in believing that the two can exist apart: a difficulty often amounting to a local or temporary impossibility.

This is the second meaning of Inconceivability; which by Reid is carefully distinguished from the first,[*] but his editor Sir W. Hamilton employs the word in both senses indiscriminately.* How he came to miss the distinction is tolerably obvious to any one who is familiar with his writings, and especially with his theory of Judgment; but needs not be pointed out here. It is more remarkable that he gives *i*to*i* the term a third sense,

---

[*See *On the Intellectual Powers*, pp. 375–9.]

*[67] It is curious that Dr. M'Cosh, with this volume before him, and occupied in criticizing it, did not find out until his book was passing through the press, and then only from the sixth edition of my *System of Logic*, that I was aware of the difference between these two meanings of "to conceive." (M'Cosh, [*Examination*,] p. 241n. [See *System of Logic*, Bk. II, Chap. vii, §3, in *Collected Works*, Vol. VII, p. 269.]) He consequently thought it necessary to tell me, what I had myself stated in the text, that Antipodes were inconceivable only in the second sense. [McCosh, *Examination*, pp. 240–1.]

*h*Dr. M'Cosh continually charges me with confounding the two meanings, and arguing from one of them to the other. [See "Mill's Reply," pp. 357–8.] But he must be well aware that intuitional philosophers in general (I do not say that Dr. M'Cosh) assign as the sufficient, and conclusive proof of inconceivability in the one sense, inconceivability in the other. They argue that a proposition must be true, and ought to be believed—on the ground that we cannot conceive its opposite, meaning that we cannot frame a mental representation of it. It is therefore quite pertinent to show (when it can be done) that this inability to join the ideas together is not inherent in our constitution, but is accounted for by the conditions of our experience; for to shew this, is to destroy the argument principally relied on as a proof that the judgment is a necessary one.*h*

*g*65[1], 65[2]   it
h-h+72
i-i+67, 72

answering to a third signification of the verb "to conceive." To conceive any thing, has with him not only its two ordinary meanings—to represent the thing as an image, and to be able to realize it as possible—but an additional one, which he denotes by various phrases. One of his common expressions for it is, "to construe to the mind in thought." This, he often says, can only be done "through a higher notion." "We think, we conceive, we comprehend a thing only as we think it as within or under something else."* So that a fact, or a supposition, is conceivable or comprehensible by us (conceive and comprehend being with him in this case synonymous) only by being reduced to some more general fact, as a particular case under it. Again, "to conceive the possibility" of a thing, is defined "conceiving it as the consequent of a certain reason."† The inconceivable, in this third sense, is simply the inexplicable. Accordingly all first truths are, according to Sir W. Hamilton, inconceivable. "The primary data of consciousness, as themselves the conditions under which all else is comprehended, are necessarily themselves incomprehensible . . . that is . . . we are unable to conceive through a higher notion how that is possible, which the deliverance avouches actually to be."‡ And we shall find him arguing things to be inconceivable, merely on the ground that we have no higher notion under which to class them. This use of the word inconceivable, being a complete perversion of it from its established meanings, I decline to recognise. If all the general truths which we are most certain of are to be called inconceivable, the word no longer serves any purpose. Inconceivable is not to be confounded with unprovable, or unanalysable. A truth which is not inconceivable in either of the received meanings of the term—a truth which is completely apprehended, and without difficulty believed, I cannot consent to call inconceivable merely because we cannot account for it, or deduce it from a higher truth.§

*Lectures, Vol. III, p. 102.
†Ibid., p. 100.
‡"Dissertations on Reid," [Note A,] p. 745.
§[67] Mr. Mansel refuses to admit ([Philosophy of the Conditioned,] pp. 131ff.) that Sir W. Hamilton confounds these different senses of the word Conception, and asserts that he always adheres to the meaning indicated by him in a foot-note to Reid (p. 377n), and answering to the first meaning of inconceivable, namely, unimaginable. Of the second meaning Mr. Mansel says, "When Hamilton speaks of being 'unable to conceive as possible,' he does not mean, as Mr. Mill supposes, physically possible under the law of gravitation or some other law of matter, but mentally possible as a representation or image; and thus the supposed second sense is identical with the first." (P. 132n.) According to this interpretation, when Sir W. Hamilton says of anything that it cannot be conceived as possible, he does not mean possible in fact, but possible to thought, in other words, that it cannot be conceived as conceivable. I, however, do Sir W. Hamilton the justice of believing, that when he added the words "as possible" to the word conceive, he intended to add something to the idea. Accordingly he uses the phrases "to understand as possible," "to

These being Sir W. Hamilton's three kinds of inconceivability; is the inconceivability of a proposition in any of these senses, consistent with believing it to be true? The third kind *is avowedly compatible not only with belief, but with our strongest and most natural beliefs*. An inconceiv-

comprehend as possible," as equivalents for "to conceive as possible." [See, e.g., *Discussions*, p. 15; *Lectures*, Vol. III, p. 101.] I believe that by "possible" he meant, as people usually do, possible in fact. And I have the authority of Mr. Mansel himself for so thinking. Mr. Mansel, in another place expresses what was probably the real meaning of Sir W. Hamilton, and laments that Sir W. Hamilton did not state it distinctly. "To conceive a thing as possible," says Mr. Mansel, "we must conceive the manner in which it is possible; but we may believe in the fact without being able to conceive the manner."([*Philosophy of the Conditioned*,] p. 36n.) *This makes no sense if understood as Mr. Mansel, in his rejoinder, says that it ought to be— "mentally possible as a notion, not physically possible as a fact." ["Supplementary Remarks," p. 27.] There is no *manner* of being possible as a mere notion: the elements of the notion can be put together in the mind, or they cannot. A *manner* of being possible can only refer to possibility as a fact.* When people say that they cannot conceive *how* a thing is possible, they always mean, that but for evidence to the contrary, they should have supposed it impossible. And this I always find to be the case when Sir W. Hamilton uses the phrase. I know not of any *manner* of a possibility that would enable us to conceive the thing "*as* possible" unless it removed some obstacle to believing that the thing *is* possible. Such, for instance, would be the case, if we have found or imagined something which is capable of causing the thing; or some means or mechanism by which it could be brought about (the desideratum in Mr. Mansel's illustration of a being who sees without eyes [*Philosophy of the Conditioned*, p. 126n]); or if we have had an actual intuition of the thing as existing: which, when sufficiently familiar, makes it no longer seem to require any ground of possibility beyond the fact itself. In short, the *how* of its existence, which enables us to conceive it as possible, must be a how which affords at least a semblance of explanation of Mr. Mansel's *that*. This is distinctly recognised by Sir W. Hamilton in one of the passages I have quoted, in which "to conceive the possibility" of a thing is defined "conceiving it as the consequent of a certain reason." By conceiving a thing as possible, he meant apprehending some fact, or imagining some hypothesis, which would explain its possibility; which would be, in the Leibnitzian sense, its Sufficient Reason. For, an explanation, even hypothetical, of a thing which previously seemed to admit of none, removes a difficulty in believing it. *We have a natural tendency to disbelieve anything which, while it has never been presented in our experience, also contradicts our habitual associations: but the suggestion to our mind of some possible conditions which would be a Sufficient Reason for its existence, takes away its incredibility, and enables us to "conceive it as possible." This view of Sir W. Hamilton's meaning explains, though it does not justify, his using the term in its third signification; which Mr. Mansel also endeavours to reduce to the first ([*ibid*.,] p. 132n), but which may be better identified with the second: for of First Truths also it is impossible to assign any Sufficient Reason.*

*ʲ⁻ʲ67 This is reducible to my second meaning of inconceivable, that which is synonymous with incredible.

ᵏ⁻ᵏ[manuscript fragment exists; see Appendix A *below.]

*ˡ⁻ˡ65¹, 65² we may disregard, not only as inadmissible, but as avowedly compatible with belief

able of the second kind can not only be believed, but believed with full understanding. In this case we are perfectly able to represent to ourselves mentally what is said to be inconceivable; only, from an association in our mind, it does not look credible: but, this association being the result of experience or of teaching, contrary experience or teaching is able to dissolve it; and even before this has been done—while the thing still feels incredible, the intellect may, on sufficient evidence, accept it as true. An inconceivable of the first kind, inconceivable in the proper sense of the term—that which the mind is actually unable to put together in a representation—may nevertheless be believed, if we attach any meaning to it, but cannot be said to be believed with understanding. We cannot believe it on direct evidence, i.e. through its being presented in our experience, for if it were so presented it would immediately cease to be inconceivable. We may believe it because its falsity would be inconsistent with something which we otherwise know to be true. Or we may believe it because it is affirmed by some one wiser than ourselves, who, we suppose, may have had the experience which has not reached us, and to whom it may thus have become conceivable. But the belief is without understanding, for we form no mental picture of what we believe. We do not so much believe the fact, as believe that we should believe it if we could have the needful presentation in our experience; and that some other being has, or may have, had that presentation. Our inability to conceive it, is no argument whatever for its being false, and no hindrance to our believing it, to the above-mentioned extent.

But though facts, which we cannot join together in an image, may be united in the universe, and though we may have sufficient ground for believing that they are so united in point of fact, it is impossible to believe a proposition which conveys to us no meaning at all. If any one says to me, Humpty Dumpty is an Abracadabra, I neither knowing what is meant by an Abracadabra, nor what is meant by Humpty Dumpty, I may, if I have confidence in my informant, believe that he means something, and that the something which he means is probably true: but I do not believe the very thing which he means, since I am entirely ignorant what it is. Propositions of this kind, the unmeaningness of which lies in the subject or predicate, are not those generally described as inconceivable. The unmeaning propositions spoken of under that name, are usually those which involve contradictions. That the same thing is and is not—that it did and did not rain at the same time and place, that a man is both alive and not alive, are forms of words which carry no signification to my mind. As Sir W. Hamilton truly says,* one half of the statement simply sublates or takes away the meaning which the other half has laid down. The unmeaningness here resides in the

*Lectures, Vol. III, p. 99.

copula. The word *is* has no meaning, except as exclusive of *is not*. The case is more hopeless than that of Humpty Dumpty, for no explanation by the speaker of what the words mean can make the assertion intelligible. Whatever may be meant by a man, and whatever may be meant by alive, the statement that a man can be alive and not alive is equally without meaning to me. I cannot make out anything which the speaker intends me to believe. The sentence affirms nothing of which my mind can take hold. Sir W. Hamilton, indeed, maintains the contrary. He says, "When we conceive the proposition that A is not A, we clearly comprehend the separate meaning on the terms *A* and *not A*, and also the import of the assertion of their identity."* We comprehend the separate meaning of the terms, but as to the meaning of the assertion, I think we only comprehend what the same form of words would mean in another case. The very import of the form of words is inconsistent with its meaning anything when applied to terms of this particular kind. Let any one who doubts this, attempt to define what is meant by applying a predicate to a subject, when the predicate and the subject are the negation of one another. To make sense of the assertion, some new meaning must be attached to *is* or *is not*, and if this be done the proposition is no longer the one presented for our assent. Here, therefore, is one kind of inconceivable proposition which nothing whatever can make credible to us. Not being able to attach any meaning to the proposition, we are equally incompetent to assert that it is, or that it is not, possible in itself. But we have not the power of believing it; and there the matter must rest.

We are now prepared to enter on the peculiar doctrine of Sir W. Hamilton, called the Philosophy of the Conditioned. Not content with maintaining that things which from the natural and fundamental laws of the human mind are for ever inconceivable to us, may, for aught we know, be true, he goes farther, and says, we know that many such things are true. "Things there are which may, nay *must*, be true, of which the understanding is wholly unable to construe to itself the possibility."† Of what nature these things are, is declared in many parts of his writings, in the form of a general law. It is thus stated in the review of Cousin:

The Conditioned is the mean between the two extremes—two unconditionates, exclusive of each other, neither of which can be conceived as possible, but of which, on the principles of contradiction and excluded middle, one must be admitted as necessary. . . . The mind is not represented as conceiving two propositions subversive of each other as equally possible; but only, as unable to understand as possible, either of the extremes; one of which, however, on the ground of their mutual repugnance, it is compelled to recognise as true.‡

In the "Dissertations on Reid" he enunciates, in still more general terms,

Ibid., p. 113.
†*Discussions*, [App. I (A),] p. 624.
‡*Ibid.*, p. 15.

as "the Law of the Conditioned: That all positive thought lies between two extremes, neither of which we can conceive as possible, and yet as mutual contradictories, the one or the other we must recognise as necessary." And it is (he says) "from this impotence of intellect" that "we are unable to think aught as absolute. Even absolute relativity is unthinkable."*

The doctrine is more fully expanded in the Lectures on Logic, from which I shall quote at greater length.

All that we can positively think . . . lies between two opposite poles of thought, which, as exclusive of each other, cannot, on the principles of Identity and Contradiction, both be true, but of which, on the principle of Excluded Middle, one or the other must. Let us take, for example, any of the general objects of our knowledge. Let us take body, or rather, since body as extended is included under extension, let us take extension itself, or space. Now extension alone will exhibit to us two pairs of contradictory inconceivables,† that is, in all, four incomprehensibles, but of which, though all are equally unthinkable . . . we are compelled, by the law of Excluded Middle, to admit some two as true and necessary.

Extension may be viewed either as a whole or as a part; and in each aspect it affords us two incogitable contradictions. 1st. Taking it as a whole: space, it is evident, must either be limited, that is, have an end, and circumference; or unlimited, that is, have no end, no circumference. These are contradictory suppositions; both, therefore, cannot, but one must, be true. Now let us try positively to comprehend, positively to conceive,‡ the possibility of either of these two mutually exclusive alternatives. Can we represent, or realize in thought, extension as absolutely limited? in other words, can we mentally hedge round the whole of space, conceive§ it absolutely bounded, that is, so that beyond its boundary there is no outlying, no surrounding space? This is impossible. Whatever compass of space we may enclose by any limitation of thought, we shall find that we have no difficulty in transcending these limits. Nay, we shall find that we cannot but transcend them; for we are unable to think any extent of space except as within a still ulterior space, of which, let us think till the powers of thinking fail, we can never reach the circumference. It is thus impossible for us to think space as a totality, that is, as absolutely bounded, but all-containing. We may, therefore, lay down this first extreme as inconceivable.¶ We cannot think space as limited.

Let us now consider its contradictory: can we comprehend the possibility of infinite or unlimited space? To suppose this is a direct contradiction in terms; it is to comprehend the incomprehensible. We think, we conceive,‖ we comprehend a thing, only as we think it as within or under something else; but to do this of the infinite is to think the infinite as finite, which is contradictory and absurd.

*"Dissertations on Reid," [Note D***,] p. 911.

†To save words in the text, I shall simply indicate in foot-notes the places at which the author passes from one of the three meanings of the word Inconceivable to another. In this place he is using it in the first or second meaning, probably in the first.

‡First ᵐand second senses confused togetherᵐ.

§First sense.

¶First sense.

‖Third sense.

ᵐ⁻ᵐ65¹, 65²   sense

Now here it may be asked, how have we then the word *infinite*? How have we the notion which this word expresses? The answer to this question is contained in the distinction of positive and negative thought. We have a positive concept of a thing when we think it by the qualities of which it is the complement. But as the attribution of qualities is an affirmation, as affirmation and negation are relatives, and as relatives are known only in and through each other, we cannot, therefore, have a consciousness of the affirmation of any quality, without having at the same time the correlative consciousness of its negation. Now, the one consciousness is a positive, the other consciousness is a negative notion. But, in point of fact, a negative notion is only the negation of a notion; we think only by the attribution of certain qualities, and the negation of these qualities and of this attribution is simply, in so far, a denial of our thinking at all. As affirmation always suggests negation, every positive notion must likewise suggest a negative notion: and as language is the reflex of thought, the positive and negative notions are expressed by positive and negative names. Thus it is with the infinite. The finite is the only object of real or positive thought; it is that alone which we think by the attribution of determinate characters; the infinite, on the contrary, is conceived only by the thinking away of every character by which the finite was conceived: in other words, we conceive it only as inconceivable.* . . .

It is manifest that we can no more realize the thought or conception of infinite, unbounded, or unlimited space, than we can realize the conception of a finite or absolutely bounded space.† But these two inconceivables are reciprocal contradictories: we are unable to comprehend‡ the possibility of either, while, however, on the principle of Excluded Middle, one or other must be admitted. . . .

It is needless to show that the same result is given by the experiment made on extension considered as a part, as divisible. Here if we attempt to divide extension in thought, we shall neither, on the one hand, succeed in conceiving the possibility§ of an absolute minimum of space, that is, a minimum *ex hypothesi* extended, but which cannot be conceived as divisible into parts,¶ nor, on the other, of carrying on this division to infinity. But as these are contradictory opposites,‖

one or the other of them must be true.

In other passages our author applies the same order of considerations to Time, saying that we can neither conceive an absolute commencement, nor an infinite regress; an absolute termination, nor a duration infinitely prolonged; though either the one or the other must be true. And again, of the Will: we cannot, he says, conceive the Will to be Free, because this would be to conceive an event uncaused, or, in other words, an absolute commencement: neither can we conceive the Will not to be Free, because this would be supposing an infinite regress from effect to cause. The will, however, must be either free or not free; and in this case, he thinks we have

---

*Third sense, gliding back into the first.
†Here the return to the first sense is completed.
‡*n*Second sense*n*.
§Second sense.
¶First sense.
‖*Lectures*, Vol. III, pp. 100–4.

*n-n*65[1], 65[2]   Here the second sense makes its appearance

independent grounds for deciding one way, namely, that it is free, because if it were not, we could not be accountable for our actions, which our consciousness assures us that we are.[*]

This, then, is the Philosophy of the Conditioned: into the value of which it now remains to enquire.

In the case of each of the Antinomies which the author presents, he undertakes to establish two things: that neither of the rival hypotheses can be conceived by us as possible, and that we are nevertheless certain that one or the other of them is true. °

To begin with his first position, that we can neither conceive an end to space, nor space without end.

That we are unable to conceive an end to space I fully acknowledge. To account for this there needs no inherent incapacity. We are disabled from forming this conception, by known psychological laws. We have never perceived any object, or any portion of space, which had not other space beyond it. And we have been perceiving objects and portions of space from the moment of birth. How then could the idea of an object, or of a portion of space, escape becoming inseparably associated with the idea of additional space beyond? Every instant of our lives helps to rivet this association, and we never have had a single experience tending to disjoin it. The association, under the present constitution of our existence, is indissoluble. But we have no ground for believing that it is so from the original structure of our minds. We can suppose that in some other state of existence we might be transported to the end of space, when, being apprised of what had happened by some impression of a kind utterly unknown to us now, we should at the same instant become capable of conceiving the fact, and learn that it was true. After some experience of the new impression, the fact of an end to space would seem as natural to us as the revelations of sight to a person born blind, after he has been long enough couched to have become familiar with them. But as this cannot happen in our present state of existence, the experience which would render the association dissoluble is never obtained; and an end to space remains inconceivable.

One half, then, of our author's first proposition, must be conceded. But the other half? Is it true that we are incapable of conceiving infinite space? I have already shown strong reasons for dissenting from this assertion: and those which our author, in this and other places, assigns in its support, seem to me quite untenable.

He says, "we think, we conceive, we comprehend, a thing, only as we think it as within or under something else. But to do this of the infinite is to

[*See *ibid.*, Vol. II, pp. 404–13.]

°65¹, 65²   I think he has failed to make out either point. [*Cf.* 87–8^(c–c) *and* 88n *below*.]

think the infinite as finite, which is contradictory and absurd." When we come to Sir W. Hamilton's account of the Laws of Thought, we shall have some remarks to make on the phrase "to think one thing within or under another;" a favourite expression with the Transcendental school, one of whose characteristics ^{p} is, that they are always using the prepositions in a metaphorical sense. But granting that to think a thing is to think it under something else, we must understand this statement as it is ^{q}invariably^q interpreted by those who employ it. According to them, we think a thing when we make any affirmation respecting it, and we think it under the notion which we affirm of it. Whenever we judge, we think the subject under the predicate. Consequently when we say "God is good," we think God under the notion "good." Is this, in our author's opinion, to think the infinite as finite, and hence "contradictory and absurd?"

If this doctrine hold, it follows that we cannot predicate anything of a subject which we regard as being in any of its attributes, infinite. We are unable, without falling into a contradiction, to assert anything not only of God, but of Time, and of Space. Considered as a *reductio ad absurdum*, this is sufficient. But we may go deeper into the matter, and deny the statement that to think anything "under" the notion expressed by a general term is to think it as finite. None of our general predicates are, in the proper sense of the term, finite; they are all, at least potentially, infinite. "Good" is not a name for the things or persons possessing that attribute which exist now, or at any other given moment, and which are only a finite aggregate. It is a name for all those which ever did, or ever will, or even in hypothesis or fiction can, possess the attribute. This is not a limited number. It is the very nature and constituent character of a *general* notion that its extension (as Sir W. Hamilton would say) is ^{r}without limit^r.

But he might perhaps say, that though its extension, consisting of the possible individuals included in it, ^{s}may^s be infinite, its *comprehension*, the set of attributes contained in it (or as I prefer to say, connoted by its name) is a limited quantity. Undoubtedly it is. But see what follows. If, because the comprehension of a general notion is finite, anything infinite cannot without contradiction be thought under it, the consequence is, that a being possessing in an infinite degree a given attribute, cannot be thought under that very attribute. Infinite goodness cannot be thought as goodness, because that would be to think it as finite. Surely there must be some great confusion of ideas in the premises, when this comes out as the conclusion.

Our author goes on to repeat the argument used in his reply to Cousin,

^{p}65^1, 65^2 it
$^{q-q}$+67, 72
$^{r-r}$65^1, 65^2 infinite
$^{s-s}$+67, 72

that Infinite Space is inconceivable, because all the conception we are able to form of it is negative, and a negative conception is the same as no conception. "The infinite is conceived only by the thinking away of every character by which the finite was conceived." To this assertion I oppose my former reply. Instead of thinking away every character of the finite, we think away only the idea of an end, or a boundary. Sir W. Hamilton's proposition is true of "The Infinite," the meaningless abstraction; but it is not true of Infinite Space. In trying to form a conception of that, we do not think away its positive characters. We leave to it the character of Spacc; all that belongs to it as space; its three dimensions, with all their geometrical properties. We leave to it also a character which belongs to it as Infinite, that of being greater than any 'finite' space. If an object which has these well-marked positive attributes is unthinkable, because it has a negative attribute as well, the number of thinkable objects must be remarkably small. Nearly all our positive conceptions which are at all complex, include negative attributes. I do not mean merely the negatives which are implied in affirmatives, as in saying that snow is white we imply that it is not black; but independent negative attributes superadded to these, and which are so real that they are often the essential characters, or differentiæ, of classes. Our conception of dumb, is of something which *cannot* speak; of the brutes, as of creatures which *have not* reason; of the mineral kingdom, as the part of Nature which *has not* organization and life; of immortal, as that which *never* dies. Are all these examples of the Inconceivable? So false is it that to think a thing under a negation is to think it as unthinkable.

In other passages, Sir W. Hamilton argues that we cannot conceive infinite space, because we should require infinite time to do it in. It would of course require infinite time to carry our thoughts in succession over every part of infinite space. But on how many of our finite conceptions do we think it necessary to perform such an operation? Let us try the doctrine upon a complex whole, short of infinite; such as the number 695,788. Sir W. Hamilton would not, I suppose, have maintained that this number is inconceivable. How long did he think it would take to go over every separate unit of this whole, so as to obtain a perfect knowledge of that exact sum, as different from all other sums, either greater or less? Would he have said that we could have no conception of the sum until this process had been gone through? We could not, indeed, have an *adequate* conception. Accordingly we never have an adequate conception of any real thing. But we have a *real* conception of an object if we conceive it by any of its attributes that are sufficient to distinguish it from all other things. We have a conception of any large number, when we have conceived it by some one of its modes of composition, such as that indicated by the position of its digits. We seldom

ᵗ⁻'65¹, 65²   other

get nearer than this to an adequate conception of any large number. But for all intellectual purposes, this limited conception is sufficient: for it not only enables us to avoid confounding the number, in our calculations, with any other numerical whole—even with those so nearly equal to it that no difference between them would be perceptible by sight or touch, unless the units were drawn up in a manner expressly adapted for displaying it—but we can also, by means of this attribute of the number, ascertain and add to our conception as many more of its properties as we please. If, then, we can obtain a real conception of a finite whole without going through all its component parts, why deny us a real conception of an infinite whole because to go through them all is impossible? Not to mention that even in the case of the finite number, though the units composing it are limited, yet, Number being infinite, the possible modes of deriving any given number from other numbers are numerically infinite; and as all these are necessary parts of an adequate conception of any number, to render our conception even of this finite whole perfectly adequate would also require an infinite time.*

But though our conception of infinite space can never be adequate, since we can never exhaust its parts, the conception, as far as it goes, is a real conception. We ^{x} realize in imagination the various attributes composing it. We realize it as space. We realize it as greater than any given space. We even realize it as endless, in an intelligible manner, that is, we clearly represent to ourselves that however much of space has been already explored, and however much more of it we may imagine ourselves to traverse, we are no nearer to the end of it than we were at first ^{y}; since^y, however often we repeat the process of imagining distance extending in any direction from us, that process is always susceptible of being carried further. This conception is both real and perfectly definite. ^{z}A merely negative notion may correspond to any number of the most heterogeneous positive things, but this notion corresponds to one thing only.^{z} We possess

---

*[67] Mr. Mansel ^{u} replies that our system of numeration enables us to "exhaust any finite number, by dealing with its items in large masses," but that no such process can "exhaust the infinite." ([*Philosophy of the Conditioned*,] p. 134.) ^{v}My argument is^v that we need not exhaust the infinite to be enabled to conceive it; since, in point of fact, we *do* not exhaust the finite numbers which it is admitted that we can and do conceive. ^{w}Mr. Mansel says we do ["Supplementary Remarks," p. 27]; which reduces the question to a difference in the meaning of the word exhaust. In the only sense that is of importance to the argument, we do not mentally exhaust any large number, since we do not acquire an adequate idea of it.^{w}

^{u}67 , entirely missing the point of this argument,
$^{v-v}$67 If Mr. Mansel had considered a little, he would have seen my argument to be
$^{w-w}$+72
^{x}65^1, 65^2 completely
$^{y-y}$65^1, 65^2 time [*printer's error?*]
$^{z-z}$65^1, 65^2 It is not vague and indeterminate, as a merely negative notion is.

it as completely as we possess any of our clearest conceptions, and can avail ourselves of it as well for ulterior mental operations. As regards the Extent of Space, therefore, Sir W. Hamilton *has not* made out his point: one of the two contradictory hypotheses is not inconceivable.

The same thing may be said, equally decidedly, respecting the Divisibility of Space. According to our author, a minimum of divisibility, and a divisibility without limit, are both inconceivable. I venture to think, on the contrary, that both are conceivable. Divisibility, of course, does not here mean physical separability of parts, but their mere existence; and the question is, can we conceive a portion of extension so small as not to be composed of parts, and can we, on the other hand, conceive parts consisting of smaller parts, and these of still smaller, without end? As to the latter, smallness without limit is as positive a conception as greatness without limit. We have the idea of a portion of space, and to this we add that of being smaller than any given portion. The other side of the alternative is still more evidently conceivable. It is not denied that there is a portion of extension which to the naked eye appears an indivisible point; it has been called by philosophers the *minimum visibile*. This minimum we can indefinitely magnify by means of optical instruments, making visible the still smaller parts which compose it. In each successive experiment there is still a *minimum visibile*, anything less than which, cannot be discerned with that instrument, but can with one of a higher power. Suppose, now, that as we increase the magnifying *powers* of our instruments, and before we have reached the limit of possible increase, we arrive at a stage at which that which seemed the smallest visible space under a given microscope, does not appear larger under one which, by its mechanical construction, is adapted to magnify more—but still remains apparently indivisible. I say, that if this happened, we should believe in a minimum of extension; *and as we should be unable to conceive, that is, to represent to ourselves in an image, anything smaller, any further divisibility would be as inconceivable to us as it would be unbelievable*.

There would be no difficulty in applying a similar line of argument to the case of Time, or to any other of the Antinomies, (there is a long list of them,* to some of which I shall have to return for another purpose,) but it would needlessly encumber our pages. In no one case mentioned by Sir W. Hamilton do I believe that he could substantiate his assertion, that "the Conditioned," by which he means every object of human knowledge, lies

---

*See the catalogue at length, in the Appendix [iii] to the second volume of the *Lectures*, pp. 527–9.

a-a65[1], 65[2]   does not seem to have
b-b65[1], 65[2]   power
c-c65[1], 65[2]   or, if some *à priori* metaphysical prejudice prevented us from believing it, we should at least be enabled to conceive it

between two "inconditionate" hypotheses, both of them inconceivable. Let me add, that even granting the inconceivability of the two opposite hypotheses, I cannot see that any distinct meaning is conveyed by the statement that the Conditioned is "the mean" between them, or that "all positive thought," "all that we can positively think," "lies between" these two "extremes," these "two opposite poles of thought." The extremes are, Space in the aggregate considered as having a limit, Space in the aggregate considered as having no limit. Neither of these, says Sir W. Hamilton, can we think. But what we can positively think (according to him) is not Space in the aggregate at all; it is some limited Space, and this we think as square, as circular, as triangular, or as elliptical. Are triangular and elliptical a mean between infinite and finite? They are, by the very meaning of the words, modes of the finite. So that it would be more like the truth to say that we think the pretended mean under one of the extremes; and if infinite and finite are "two opposite poles of thought," then in this polar opposition, unlike voltaic polarity, all the matter is accumulated at one pole. But this counter-statement would be no more tenable than Sir W. Hamilton's; for in reality, the thought which he affirms to be a medium between two extreme statements, has no correlation with those statements at all. It does not relate to the same object. The two counter-hypotheses are suppositions respecting Space at large, Space as a collective whole. The "conditioned" thinking, said to be the mean between them, relates to parts of Space, and classes of such parts: circles and triangles, or planetary and stellar distances. The alternative of opposite inconceivabilities never presents itself in regard to them; they are all finite, and are conceived and known as such. What the notion of extremes and a mean can signify, when applied to propositions in which different predicates are affirmed of different subjects, passes my comprehension: but it served to give greater apparent profundity to the "Fundamental Doctrine," in the eyes not of disciples (for Sir W. Hamilton was wholly incapable of quackery) but of the teacher himself.

[d]If these arguments are valid, the "Law of the Conditioned" rests on no rational foundation. The proposition that the Conditioned lies between two hypotheses concerning the Unconditioned, neither of which hypotheses

[d-d]65[1], 65[2]   We have now to examine the second half of the "Law of the Conditioned," namely, that although the pair of contradictory hypotheses in each Antinomy are both of them inconceivable, one or the other of them must be true.

I should not, of course, dream of denying this, when the propositions are taken in a phænomenal sense; when the subjects and predicates of them are interpreted relatively to us. The Will, for example, is wholly a phænomenon; it has no meaning unless relatively to us; and I of course admit that it must be either free or caused. Space and Time, in their phænomenal character, or as they present themselves to our perceptive faculties, are necessarily either bounded or boundless, infinitely or only finitely divisible. The law of Excluded Middle, as well as that of Contradiction, is common to all phænomena. But it is a doctrine of our author that these laws are true, and cannot but be known to be true, of Noumena likewise. It is not merely

we can conceive as possible,[d] must be placed in that numerous class of metaphysical doctrines, which have a magnificent sound, but are empty of the smallest substance.*

*[67] In the first edition, besides denying the inconceivability of the pairs of contradictory hypotheses in Sir W. Hamilton's Antinomies, I also contested the assertion that one or other of them must be true; arguing, that the law of Excluded Middle, though true of all phænomena, and therefore of Space and Time in their phænomenal character, is not a law of Things. "The law of Excluded Middle is, that whatever predicate we suppose, either that or its negative must be true of any given subject: and this I do not admit when the subject is a Noumenon; inasmuch as every possible predicate, even negative, except the single one of Non-entity, involves, as a part of itself, something positive, which part is only known to us by phænomenal experience, and may have only a phænomenal existence." This, being an over-statement, and, when reduced to its proper bounds, not necessarily conflicting with anything said by Sir W. Hamilton on the present subject, I abandon. But I retain a portion of my remarks, illustrative of the abusive application of which the Principle of Excluded Middle is susceptible. "The universe, for example, must, it is affirmed, be either infinite or finite: but what do these words mean? That it must be either of infinite or finite magnitude. Magnitudes certainly must be either infinite or finite, but before affirming the same thing of the Noumenon Universe, it has to be established that the universe as it is in itself is capable of the attribute magnitude. How do we know that magnitude is not exclusively a property of our sensations—of the states of subjective consciousness which objects produce in us? Or if this supposition displeases, how do we know that magnitude is not, as Kant considered it [e]to be[e], a form of our minds, an attribute with which the laws of thought invest every conception that we can form, but to which there may be nothing analogous in the Noumenon, the Thing in itself? The like may be said of Duration, whether infinite or finite, and of Divisibility, whether stopping at a minimum or prolonged without limit. Either the one proposition or the other must of course be true of duration and of matter as they are perceived by us—as they present themselves to our faculties; but duration itself is held by Kant to have no real existence out of our minds; and as for matter, not knowing what it is in itself, we know not whether, as affirmed of matter in itself, the word divisible has any meaning. Believing divisibility to be an acquired notion, made up of the elements of our sensational experience, I do not admit that the Noumenon Matter must be either infinitely or finitely divisible." [Cf. 87[d-d] above.]

Space as cognisable by our senses, but Space as it is in itself, which he affirms must be either of unlimited or of limited extent. Now, not to speak at present of the Principle of Contradiction, I demur to that of Excluded Middle as applicable to Things in themselves. . . . [Here appear, in immediate succession, the two passages JSM quotes from himself in the footnote above.] As already observed, the only contradictory alternative of which the negative side contains nothing positive is that between Entity and Non-entity, Existing and Non-existing; and so far as regards that distinction, I admit the law of Excluded Middle as applicable to Noumena; they must either exist or not exist. But this is all the applicability I can allow to it.

If the preceding arguments are valid, the "Law of the Conditioned" breaks down in both its parts. It is not proved that the Conditioned lies between two hypotheses concerning the Unconditioned, neither of which hypotheses we can conceive as possible. And it is not proved, that, as regards the Unconditioned, one or the other of these hypotheses must be true. Both propositions

[e-e]+67, 72

The Philosophy of the Conditioned, as Applied by Mr. Mansel to the Limits of Religious Thought

MR. MANSEL may be affirmed, by a fair application of the term, to be, in metaphysics, a pupil of Sir W. Hamilton. I do not mean that he agrees with him in all his opinions; for he avowedly dissents from the peculiar Hamiltonian theory of Cause: still less that he has learnt nothing from any other teacher, or from his own independent speculations. On the contrary, he has shown considerable power of original thought, both of a good and of what seems to me *a*not a good*a* quality. But he is the admiring editor of Sir W. Hamilton's *Lectures*; he invariably speaks of him with a deference which he pays to no other philosopher; he expressly accepts, in language identical with Sir W. Hamilton's own, the doctrines regarded as specially characteristic of the Hamiltonian philosophy, and may with reason be considered as a representative of the same general mode of thought. Mr. Mansel has bestowed especial cultivation upon a province but slightly touched by his master—the application of the Philosophy of the Conditioned to the theological department of thought; the deduction of such of its corollaries and consequences as directly concern religion.

The premises from which Mr. Mansel reasons are those of Sir W. Hamilton. He maintains the necessary relativity of all our knowledge. He holds that the Absolute and the Infinite, or, to use a more significant expression, an Absolute and an Infinite Being, are inconceivable by us; and that when we strive to conceive what is thus inaccessible to our faculties, we fall into self-contradiction. That we are, nevertheless, warranted in believing, and bound to believe, the real existence of an absolute and infinite being, and that this being is God. God, therefore, is inconceivable and unknowable by us, and cannot even be thought of without self-contradiction; that is (for Mr. Mansel is careful thus to qualify the assertion), thought of *as* Absolute, and *as* Infinite. Through this inherent impos-

*a-a*65¹, 65²   a bad

sibility of our conceiving or knowing God's essential attributes, we are disqualified from judging what is or is not consistent with them. If, then, a religion is presented to us, containing any particular doctrine respecting the Deity, our belief or rejection of the doctrine ought to depend exclusively upon the evidences which can be produced for the divine origin of the religion; and no argument grounded on the incredibility of the doctrine, as involving an intellectual absurdity, or on its moral badness as unworthy of a good or wise being, ought to have any weight, since of these things we are incompetent to judge. This, at least, is the drift of Mr. Mansel's argument; but I am bound to admit that he affirms the conclusion with a certain limitation; for he acknowledges, that the moral character of the doctrines of a religion ought to count for something among the reasons for accepting or rejecting, as of divine origin, the religion as a whole. That it ought also to count for something in the interpretation of the religion when accepted, he neglects to say; but we must in fairness suppose that he would admit it. These concessions, however, to the moral feelings of mankind, are made at the expense of Mr. Mansel's logic. If his theory is correct, he has no right to make either of them.

There is nothing new in this line of argument as applied to theology. That we cannot understand God; that his ways are not our ways; that we cannot scrutinize or judge his counsels—propositions which, in a reasonable sense of the terms, could not be denied by any Theist—have often before been tendered as reasons why we may assert any absurdities and any moral monstrosities concerning God, and miscall them Goodness and Wisdom. The novelty is in presenting this conclusion as a corollary from the most advanced doctrines of modern philosophy—from the true theory of the powers and limitations of the human mind, on religious and on all other subjects.

My opinion of this doctrine, in whatever way presented, is, that it is simply the most morally pernicious doctrine now current; and that the question it involves is, beyond all others which now engage speculative minds, the decisive one between moral good and evil for the Christian world. It is a momentous matter, therefore, to consider whether we are obliged to adopt it. Without holding Mr. Mansel accountable for the moral consequences of the doctrine, further than he himself accepts them, I think it supremely important to examine whether the doctrine itself is really the verdict of a sound metaphysic; and essential to a true estimation of Sir W. Hamilton's philosophy to enquire, whether the conclusion thus drawn from his principal doctrine, is justly affiliated on it. I think it will appear that the conclusion not only does not follow from a true theory of the human faculties, but is not even correctly drawn from the premises from which Mr. Mansel infers it.

We must have the premises distinctly before us as conceived by Mr. Mansel, since we have hitherto seen them only as taught by Sir W. Hamilton. Clearness and explicitness of statement being in the number of Mr. Mansel's merits, it is easier to perceive the flaws in his arguments than in those of his master, because he often leaves us less in doubt what he means by his words.

To have "such a knowledge of the Divine Nature" as would enable human reason to judge of theology, would be, according to Mr. Mansel, "to conceive the Deity as he is." This would be to "conceive him as First Cause, as Absolute, and as Infinite."* The First Cause Mr. Mansel defines in the usual manner. About the meaning of Infinite there is no difficulty. But when we come to the Absolute we are on more slippery ground. Mr. Mansel, however, tells us his meaning plainly. By the Absolute, he does not mean what Sir W. Hamilton *b*professes always to mean by it, something which includes the idea of completed or finished. He adopts the other meaning, which Sir W. Hamilton mentions, but disclaims—*b* the opposite of Relative. "By the Absolute is meant that which exists in and by itself, having no necessary relation to any other Being."[*]

This explanation by Mr. Mansel of Absolute in the sense in which it is opposed to Relative, is more definite in its terms than that which Sir W. Hamilton gives when attempting the same thing. For Sir W. Hamilton recognises (as already remarked) this second meaning of Absolute, and this is the account he gives of it: "*Absolutum* means what is freed or loosed; in which sense the Absolute will be what is aloof from relation, comparison, limitation, condition, dependence, &c., and thus is tantamount to τὸ ἀπόλυτον of the lower Greeks."† May it not be surmised that the vagueness in which the master here leaves the conception, was for the purpose of avoiding difficulties upon which the pupil, in his desire of greater precision, has unwarily run? Mr. Mansel certainly gains nothing by the more definite character of his language. The *c*words, "having no necessary relation to any other Being,"*c* admit of two constructions. The words, in their natural sense, only mean, *capable of existing out of relation to anything else*. The

---

Limits of Religious Thought, 4th edition, pp. 29–30.
[*Ibid.*, p. 30.]
†*Discussions*, p. 14n. [Cf. pp. 39–40 above.]

*b-b*65¹, 65² means in the greater part of his argument against Cousin, that which is completed or finished. He means what Sir W. Hamilton means only once (as we have already seen)

*c-c*65¹, 65² first words of his definition, "that which exists in and by itself," would serve for the description of a Noumenon: but Mr. Mansel's Absolute is only meant to denote one Being, identified with God, and God is not the only Noumenon. This, however, I will not dwell upon. But the remaining words, "having no necessary relation to any other Being," bring him into a much greater difficulty. For they argument requires that they should mean, *incapable of existing in relation with anything else*. Mr. Mansel cannot intend the latter. He cannot mean that the Absolute is incapable of entering into relation with any other being; for he would not affirm this of God; on the contrary, he is continually speaking of God's relations to the world and to us. Moreover, he accepts, from *d*Dr.*d* Calderwood, an interpretation inconsistent with this.* This, however, is the meaning necessary to support his case. For what is his first argument? That God cannot be known by us as Cause, as Absolute, and as Infinite, because these attributes are, to our conception, incompatible with one another. And why incompatible? Because "a Cause cannot, as such, be absolute; the Absolute cannot, as such, be a cause. The cause, as such, exists only in relation to its effect: the cause is a cause of the effect; the effect is an effect of the cause. On the other hand, the conception of the Absolute involves a possible existence out of all relation."† But in what manner is a possible existence out of all relation, incompatible with the notion of a cause? Have not causes a possible existence apart from their effects? Would the sun (for example) not exist if there were no earth or planets for it to illuminate? Mr. Mansel seems to think that what is capable of existing out of relation, cannot possibly be conceived or known in relation. But this is not so. Anything which is capable of existing in relation, is capable of being conceived or known in relation. If the Absolute Being cannot be conceived as Cause, it must be that he cannot exist as Cause; he must be incapable of causing. If he can be in any relation whatever to any finite thing, he is conceivable and knowable in that relation, if no otherwise. Freed from this confusion of ideas, Mr. Mansel's argument resolves itself into this—The same Being cannot be thought by us both as Cause and as Absolute, because a Cause *as such* is not Absolute, and Absolute as such is not a Cause; which is exactly as if he had said that Newton cannot be thought by us both as an Englishman and as a mathematician, because an Englishman, as such, is not a mathematician, nor a mathematician, as such, an Englishman.‡

Limits of Religious Thought, p. 200. [See Henry Calderwood, *The Philosophy of the Infinite* (Edinburgh: Constable; London: Hamilton and Adams, 1854), pp. 18–38.]

†*Limits of Religious Thought*, p. 31.

‡[67] Mr. Mansel, in his reply accuses me of mutilating his argument. ([*Philosophy of the Conditioned*,] p. 151.) I therefore add the remainder of it. "We attempt to escape from this apparent contradiction by introducing the idea of succession in time. The Absolute exists first by itself, and afterwards becomes a Cause. But here we are checked by the third conception, that of the Infinite. How can the Infinite become that which it was not from the first? If Causation is a possible mode of existence, that which exists without causing is not infinite; that

*d–d*65¹, 65²   Mr.

Again, Mr. Mansel argues, that, "supposing the Absolute to become a cause," since *ex vi termini* it is not necessitated to do so, it must be a voluntary agent, and therefore conscious; for "volition is only possible in a conscious being."* But consciousness, again, is only conceivable as a relation; and any relation conflicts with the notion of the Absolute, since relatives are mutually dependent on one another. Here it comes out distinctly as a premise in the reasoning, that to be in a relation at all, even if only a relation to itself, the relation of being "conscious of itself," is inconsistent with being the Absolute.†

which becomes a cause has passed beyond its former limits." (*Limits of Religious Thought*, pp. 31–2.)

This alleged inconsistency of thought in supposing the Infinite to *become* a cause, because to do so would be to become something which it was not from the first, applies, like nearly all the rest of Mr. Mansel's argumentation, only to the self-contradictory fiction, "The Infinite," which is supposed either infinite without reference to any attributes, or infinite in all possible attributes. Substitute for this the notion of a Being infinite in given attributes, and the incompatibility disappears. Surely the most familiar form of the notion of an infinite being, is that of a Being infinite in power. Power is not only compatible with, but actually means, capability of causing. Can we be told that a Being infinite in its capability of causing, cannot to our conceptions, consistently with its infinity, actually cause anything, but the power, because infinite, must remain dormant through eternity? or, as the opposite alternative, that this Being must be conceived as having exercised from all eternity the whole of its infinite power of causing, because any later exercise of that power would be *passing* into causation? Either hypothesis Mr. Mansel affirms (*Limits of Religious Thought*, p. 204) to be inconceivable of an Infinite Being. But if an Infinite Being means a Being of infinite wisdom and goodness as well as power, the conception of that infinite power as only partly exercised is so far from being a contradiction, that it is not even a paradox.

Limits of Religious Thought, p. 32.

†[67] How does Mr. Mansel reconcile this argument with the definition of the Absolute which he himself accepts from Dr. Calderwood [*The Philosophy of the Infinite*, pp. 18–38]? "The Absolute is that which is free from all *necessary* relation, that is, which is free from every relation as a condition of existence; but it may exist in relation, provided that relation be not a necessary condition of its existence, that is, provided the relation may be removed without affecting its existence." (Mansel, *Limits of Religious Thought*, p. 200.) A better definition of an Absolute Being could scarcely be devised; and that Mr. Mansel should borrow it, and then deny the latter half of it, proves him to be greatly inferior to Dr. Calderwood in the important accomplishment of understanding his own meaning. For before it can be maintained that to be a conscious being contradicts the notion of the Absolute, because consciousness is a relation, the power just admitted in the Absolute of existing in relation provided it is not bound to any relation, must be either denied or forgotten.

*e*Mr. Mansel, in his rejoinder ["Supplementary Remarks," p. 28n], says that he did not mean to admit the second half of Dr. Calderwood's definition; and he holds to the doctrine*e* "The absolute, as such, *f* must be out of all relation" (not merely

*e–e*67   In Mr. Mansel's reply, the denial or forgetfulness still continues.
*f*67   " he says, "

Mr. Mansel, therefore, must alter his definition of the Absolute if he would maintain his argument. He must either fall back on the happy ambiguity of Sir W. Hamilton's definition, "what is aloof from relation," which does not decide whether the meaning is merely that it can exist out of relation, or that it is incapable of existing in it; or he must take courage, and affirm that an Absolute Being is incapable of all relation. But as he will certainly refuse to predicate this of God, the consequence follows, that God is not an Absolute Being.

The whole of Mr. Mansel's argument for the inconceivability of the Infinite and of the Absolute is one long *ignoratio elenchi*. It has been pointed out in a former chapter that the words Absolute and Infinite have no real meaning, unless we understand by them that which is absolute or infinite in some given attribute; as space is called infinite, meaning that it is infinite in extension; and as God is termed infinite in the sense of possessing infinite power, and absolute in the sense of absolute goodness, or knowledge.[*] It has also been shown that Sir W. Hamilton's arguments for the unknowableness of the Unconditioned, do not prove that we cannot know an object which is absolute or infinite in some specific attribute, but only that we cannot know an abstraction called "The Absolute" or "The Infinite," which is supposed to have all attributes at once. The same remark is applicable to Mr. Mansel,* with only this difference, that he, with the laudable ambition I have already noticed of stating everything explicitly,

---

capable of existing out of relation) "and consequently cannot be conceived in the relation of plurality." (*Philosophy of the Conditioned*, p. 117.)

[*See pp. 47ff. above]

*[67] Mr. Mansel protests against this passage, as attributing to him the use of the word "Absolute" in the sense attached to it by Sir W. Hamilton, which includes perfection, though he had expressly stated that he used the term in a different sense. "When Mr. Mill charges Mr. Mansel with undertaking to prove the impossibility of conceiving a Being *absolutely* just or *absolutely* wise (*i.e.* as he supposes, *perfectly* just or wise) he actually forgets that he has just been criticising Mr. Mansel's definition of the Absolute, as something having a possible existence out of relation." (*[Philosophy of the Conditioned*,] pp. 153–4.) And he asks what I can mean by goodness or knowledge "out of all relation." If I have, in this passage, exchanged Mr. Mansel's definition of the Absolute for Sir W. Hamilton's, by including in it the notion of "finished, perfected, completed," [*Discussions*, p. 14n,] Mr. Mansel had set me the example. As long as he kept to his own definition, I did the same: I only followed him when he himself imported the idea of perfection from the other meaning of the term, and reasoned from it as one of the characteristics of the Absolute. Does the reader doubt this? He shall see. We cannot, says Mr. Mansel, reconcile the idea of the Absolute with that of a Cause, because "if the condition of causal activity is a higher state than that of quiescence, the Absolute, whether acting voluntarily or involuntarily, has passed from a condition of comparative imperfection to one of comparative perfection, and therefore was not originally

draws this important distinction himself, and says, of his own motion, that the Absolute he means is the abstraction. He says, that the Absolute *and Infinite* can be "nothing less than the sum of all reality," the complex of all positive predicates, even those which are exclusive of one another: and expressly identifies it with Hegel's Absolute Being, which contains in itself "all that is actual, even evil included."* "That which is conceived as absolute and infinite," says Mr. Mansel, "must be conceived as containing within itself the sum not only of all actual, but of all possible modes of being."† One may well agree with Mr. Mansel that this farrago of contradictory attributes cannot be conceived: but what shall we say of his equally positive averment that it must be believed? If this be what the Absolute is, what does he mean by saying that we must believe God to be the Absolute?

The remainder of Mr. Mansel's argumentation is suitable to this commencement. The Absolute, as conceived, that is, as he defines it, cannot be "a whole composed of parts," or "a substance consisting of attributes," or

a conscious subject in antithesis to an object. For if there is in the absolute any principle of unity, distinct from the mere accumulation of parts or attributes, this principle alone is the true absolute. If, on the other hand, there is no such principle, then there is no absolute at all, but only a plurality of relatives. The almost unanimous voice of philosophy, in pronouncing that the absolute is both one and simple, must be accepted as the voice of reason also, so far as reason has any voice in the matter. But this absolute unity, as indifferent and containing no attributes,

---

perfect. If the state of activity is an inferior state to that of quiescence, the Absolute, in becoming a cause, has lost *its original perfection*." (*Limits of Religious Thought*, pp. 34–5. The italics are my own.) Again "While it is impossible to represent in thought any object except as finite, it is equally impossible to represent any finite object, or any aggregate of finite objects, as *exhausting the universe of being*. Thus the hypothesis which would annihilate the Infinite is itself shattered to pieces against the rock of the Absolute." (*Ibid.*, p. 38.) In spite, therefore, of his own definition, Mr. Mansel thinks it part of the notion of the Absolute that it is the Perfect, and that it exhausts the universe of being, *i.e.*, is the completed whole of existence.

It thus appears that if I am chargeable with anything, it is with having neglected to point out one confusion of ideas the more in Mr. Mansel, and, this time, a confusion between two ideas which he had expressly discriminated. But even if I had really committed the blunder he imputes to me, it would not have affected the question between us: for he always (and, as I think, rightly) assumes that the Being whose conceivability by us is the subject of discussion, has to be conceived *both* as absolute and as infinite (the Infinito-Absolute of Sir W. Hamilton); and if he had escaped untouched from my criticism of Sir W. Hamilton in respect of the Absolute, he would still have been inextricably involved in it as regards the Infinite.

Limits of Religious Thought, p. 30.
†*Ibid.*, p. 31.

⁻+67, 72

can neither be distinguished from the multiplicity of finite beings by any characteristic feature, nor be identified with them in their multiplicity.*

It will be noticed that the Absolute, which was just before defined as having all attributes, is here declared to have none: but this, Mr. Mansel would say, is merely one of the contradictions inherent in the attempt to conceive what is inconceivable.

Thus we are landed in an inextricable dilemma. The Absolute cannot be conceived as conscious, neither can it be conceived as unconscious: it cannot be conceived as complex, neither can it be conceived as simple: it cannot be conceived by difference, neither can it be conceived by the absence of difference: it cannot be identified with the universe, neither can it be distinguished from it.[*]

Is this chimerical abstraction the Absolute Being whom anybody need be concerned about, either as knowable or as unknowable? Is the inconceivableness of this impossible fiction any argument against the possibility of conceiving God, who is neither supposed to have no attributes nor to have all attributes, but to have good attributes? Is it any hindrance to our being able to conceive a Being absolutely just, for example, or absolutely wise? Yet it is of this that Mr. Mansel undertook to prove the impossibility.

Again, of the Infinite: according to Mr. Mansel, being "that than which a greater is inconceivable," it "consequently can receive no additional attribute or mode of existence which it had not from all eternity." It must therefore be the same complex of all possible predicates which the Absolute is, and all of them infinite in degree. It "cannot be regarded as consisting of a limited number of attributes, each unlimited in its kind. It cannot be conceived, for example, after the analogy of a line, infinite in length, but not in breadth; or of a surface, infinite in two dimensions of space, but bounded in the third; or of an intelligent being, possessing some one or more modes of consciousness in an infinite degree, but devoid of others."[†] This Infinite, which is infinite in all attributes, and not solely in those which it would be thought decent to predicate of God, cannot, as Mr. Mansel very truly says, be conceived. For

the Infinite, if it is to be conceived at all, must be conceived as potentially everything and actually nothing; for if there is anything general which it cannot become, it is thereby limited; and if there is anything in particular which it actually is, it is thereby excluded from being any other thing. But again, it must also be conceived as actually everything and potentially nothing; for an unrealized potentiality is likewise a limitation. If the infinite can be that which it is not, it is by that very possibility marked out as incomplete, and capable of a higher perfection. If it is actually everything, it possesses no characteristic feature by which it can be distinguished from anything else, and discerned as an object of consciousness.[‡]

*Ibid., p. 33.   †Ibid., p. 30.
[*Ibid.]   ‡Ibid., p. 48.

Here certainly is an Infinite whose infinity does not seem to be of much use to it. But can a writer be serious who bids us conjure up a conception of something which possesses infinitely all conflicting attributes, and because we cannot do this without contradiction, would have us believe that there is a contradiction in the idea of infinite goodness, or infinite wisdom? Instead of "the Infinite," substitute "an infinitely good Being," and Mr. Mansel's argument reads thus: If there is anything which an infinitely good Being cannot become—if he cannot become bad—that is a limitation, and the goodness cannot be infinite. If there is anything which an infinitely good Being actually is (namely good), he is excluded from being any other thing, as from being wise or powerful. I hardly think that Sir W. Hamilton would patronize this logic, learnt though it be in his school.*

It cannot be necessary to follow up Mr. Mansel's metaphysical dissertation any farther. It is all, as I have said, the same *ignoratio elenchi*. I have been able to find only one short passage in which he attempts to show that we are unable to represent in thought a particular attribute carried to the infinite. For the sake of fairness, I cite it in a note.† All the argument that I

*[67] By the time Mr. Mansel gets to this place, he grows tired of giving relevant answers, and thinks that any verbal repartee will suffice. To the first half of my statement, his answer is this: "Is becoming bad a higher perfection?" ([*Philosophy of the Conditioned*,] p. 158.) I reply, that Mr. Mansel seems to think so; inasmuch as he says "If the infinite can be that which it is not, it is by that very possibility marked out as incomplete, and capable of a higher perfection." [*Ibid*., p. 155.] If the infinite is God, and, as such, good, to become bad would be to become what it is not, and consequently, according to Mr. Mansel, to attain a higher perfection. To the second half he replies by identifying the manner in which the Infinite, by being anything in particular, is excluded from being any other thing, with the manner in which a thing, by being a horse, is excluded from being a dog. Let me remind him that a horse and a dog are substances, and that we are talking about attributes. A substance cannot become another substance, but it may put on any number of additional attributes. Does not the whole of the discussion turn upon attributes? Does the question, what the Infinite can or cannot be or become, mean anything but what attributes it can have or acquire? As a Substance the Infinite is the Infinite, and cannot become anything else. Does it follow from this that by possessing one attribute, it is excluded from possessing any other? Or is it possible that Mr. Mansel means, that the "Infinite, if it is to be conceived at all," must be conceived as capable of changing its substance, and becoming a finite dog, thereby excluding itself from being a horse? That would indeed be a stretch beyond anything I have charged him with.

†"A thing—an object—an attribute—a person—or any other term signifying one out of many possible objects of consciousness, is by that very relation necessarily declared to be finite. An infinite thing, or object, or attribute, or person, is therefore in the same moment declared to be both finite and infinite. . . . And on the other hand, if all human attributes are conceived under the conditions of difference, and relation, and time, and personality, we cannot represent in thought any such attribute magnified to infinity; for this again is to conceive it as finite and infinite at the same time. We can conceive such attributes, at the utmost, only *indefinitely*;

can discover in it, I conceive that I have already answered, as stated much better by Sir W. Hamilton.

Mr. Mansel thinks it necessary to declare that the contradictions are not in "the nature of the Absolute" or Infinite "in itself, but only" in "our own conception of that nature."* He did not mean to say that the Divine Nature is itself contradictory. But he says "We are compelled by the constitution of our minds, to believe in the existence of an Absolute and Infinite Being."† Such being the case, I ask, is the Being, whom we must believe to be infinite and absolute, infinite and absolute in the meaning which those terms bear in Mr. Mansel's *definition* of them? If not, he is bound to tell us in what other meaning. Believing God to be infinite and absolute must be believing something, and it must be possible to say what. If Mr. Mansel means that we must believe the reality of an Infinite and Absolute Being in some other sense than that in which he has proved such a Being to be inconceivable, his point is not made out, since he undertook to prove the inconceivability of the very Being in whose reality we are required to believe. But the truth is that the Infinite and Absolute which he says we must believe in, are the very Infinite and Absolute of his definitions. The Infinite is that which is opposed to the Finite; the Absolute, that which is opposed to the Relative. He has therefore either proved nothing, or vastly more than he intended. For the contradictions which he asserts to be involved in the notions, do not follow from an imperfect mode of apprehending the Infinite and Absolute, but lie in the definitions of them; in the meaning of the *phrases* themselves. The contradictions are in the very object which we are called upon to believe. If, therefore, Mr. Mansel would escape from the conclusion that an Infinite and Absolute Being is intrinsically impossible, it must be by affirming, with Hegel, that the law of Contradiction does not apply to the Absolute; that, respecting the Absolute, contradictory propositions may both be true.‡

Let us now pass from Mr. Mansel's metaphysical argumentation on an

---

that is to say, we may withdraw our thoughts, for the moment, from the fact of their being limited; but we cannot conceive them as *infinite*; that is to say, we cannot positively think of the absence of the limit; for, the instant we attempt to do so, the antagonist elements of the conception exclude one another, and annihilate the whole." (*Limits of Religious Thought*, p. 60.)

Ibid., p. 39.
†*Ibid.*, p. 45.
‡[67] Mr. Mansel's summary of his reply on this portion of the case is as follows: "The reader may now, perhaps, understand the reason of an assertion which Mr. Mill regards as supremely absurd, namely, that we must believe in the existence of an absolute and infinite Being, though unable to conceive the nature of such a Being. To believe in such a Being is simply to believe that God made the world: to declare the nature of such a Being inconceivable, is simply to say that we do not know how

*h-h*65¹, 65²   definitions
*i-i*65¹, 65²   words

irrelevant issue, to ^{j}a^j much more important subject ^{k}, that^k of his practical conclusion, namely, that we cannot know the divine attributes in such a manner, as can entitle us to reject any statement respecting the Deity on the ground of its being inconsistent with his character. Let us examine whether

the world was made. If we believe that God made the world, we must believe that there was a time when the world was not, and when God alone existed, out of relation to any other being. But the mode of that sole existence we are unable to conceive, nor in what manner the first act took place by which the absolute and self-existent gave existence to the relative and dependent." ([*Philosophy of the Conditioned*,] pp. 161–2.)

I know not how Mr. Mansel discovers that I regard as supremely absurd the notion that we may believe, and may have good grounds for believing, things which are inconceivable to us. As he most truly says, there is no one with whose mode of thinking such an opinion would more flagrantly conflict. But I venture to think that one may deem it possible to have a real and positive, though inadequate, conception of an infinite Being, without supposing oneself to know how God made the world. Mr. Mansel resumes "Where is the incongruity of saying, I believe that a being exists possessing certain attributes, though I am unable in my present state of knowledge to conceive the manner of that existence?" ([*Ibid.*,] p. 163.) Assuredly, nowhere: provided that you do not invest the object of your belief with contradictory attributes; for my admission of the believability of what is inconceivable, stops at the self-contradictory: consequently I do not admit the believability of such an Absolute and Infinite as Mr. Mansel has been mystifying us with. The sum of what I am maintaining against him is, that the Absolute and Infinite which are believable, and the Absolute and Infinite which are inconceivable, are different things: That the Absolute and Infinite of which, as he has shown, the conception annihilates itself by the contradictions it involves, is that which possesses absolutely and infinitely all attributes, and that this is as unbelievable as it is inconceivable: That the Absolute and Infinite which is believable is that which possesses absolutely and infinitely some given attributes, which in their finite degrees are known to us, and is therefore conceivable; and involves no contradiction, unless we include among the attributes some that contradict one another, in which case it is indeed inconceivable, but also unbelievable.

When Mr. Mansel maintains ([*ibid.*,] pp. 14–18, and 142) that being infinite is, to our conceptive faculty, inconsistent with being a Person, I answer, that it is being "The Infinite" which is so. When he insists (if he does insist) that the Creator must, in some manner inconceivable to us, *be* this non-entity; when he identifies the Creator with something which we must believe to be "the sole existence, having no plurality beyond itself," and "simple, having no plurality within itself," ([*ibid.*,] p. 100,) thus literally annihilating all plurality in the universe; when he says "we believe that" God's "own nature is simple and uniform, admitting of no distinction between various attributes, nor between any attribute and its subject," but yet conceivable by us "only by means of various attributes, distinct from the subject and from each other," ([*ibid.*,] p. 28,) *i.e.* conceived by us as he is not; it appears to me that in thus following the old theologians in the mystical metaphysics which is always at the service of mystical theology, he encumbers Theism and Christianity with (to say the least) very unnecessary difficulties.

$^{j-j}$65^1, 65^2 the
$^{k-k}$+67, 72

this assertion is a legitimate corollary from the relativity of human knowledge, either as it really is, or as it is understood to be by Sir W. Hamilton and by Mr. Mansel.

The fundamental property of our knowledge of God, Mr. Mansel says, is that we do not and cannot know him as he is in himself: certain persons, therefore, whom he calls Rationalists, he condemns as unphilosophical, when they reject any statement as inconsistent with the character of God.[*] This is a valid answer, as far as words go, to some of the later Transcendentalists—to those who think that we have an intuition of the Divine Nature; though even as to them it would not be difficult to show that the answer is but skin-deep. But those "Rationalists" who hold, with Mr. Mansel himself, the relativity of human knowledge, are not touched by his reasoning. We cannot know God as he is in himself (they reply); granted: and what then? Can we know man as he is in himself, or matter as it is in itself? We do not claim any other knowledge of God than such as we have of man or of matter. Because I do not know my fellow-men, nor any of the powers of nature, as they are in themselves, am I therefore not at liberty to disbelieve anything I hear respecting them as being inconsistent with their character? I know something of Man and Nature, not as they are in themselves, but as they are relatively to us; and it is as relative to us, and not as he is in himself, that I suppose myself to know anything of God. The attributes which I ascribe to him, as goodness, knowledge, power, are all relative. They are attributes (says the rationalist) which my experience enables me to conceive, and which I consider as proved, not absolutely, by an intuition of God, but phænomenally, by his action on the creation, as known through my senses and my rational faculty. These relative attributes, each of them in an infinite degree, are all I pretend to predicate of God. When I reject a doctrine as inconsistent with God's nature, it is not as being inconsistent with what God is in himself, but with what he is as manifested to us. If my knowledge of him is only phænomenal, the assertions which I reject are phænomenal too. If those assertions are inconsistent with my relative knowledge of him, it is no answer to say that all my knowledge of him is relative. That is no more a reason against disbelieving an alleged fact as unworthy of God, than against disbelieving another alleged fact as unworthy of Turgot, or of Washington, whom also I do not know as Noumena, but only as Phænomena.

There is but one way for Mr. Mansel out of this difficulty, and he adopts it. He must maintain, not merely that an Absolute Being is unknowable in himself, but that the Relative attributes of an Absolute Being are unknowable likewise. He must say that we do not know what Wisdom, Justice,

[*See *Limits of Religious Thought*, Lecture iii, pp. 45–66, esp. 55–6.]

Benevolence, Mercy, are, as they exist in God. Accordingly he does say so. The following are his direct utterances on the subject: as an implied doctrine, it pervades his whole argument.

It is a fact which experience forces upon us, and which it is useless, were it possible, to disguise, that the representation of God after the model of the highest human morality which we are capable of conceiving, is not sufficient to account for all the phenomena exhibited by the course of his natural Providence. The infliction of physical suffering, the permission of moral evil, the adversity of the good, the prosperity of the wicked, the crimes of the guilty involving the misery of the innocent, the tardy appearance and partial distribution of moral and religious knowledge in the world—these are facts which no doubt are reconcilable, we know not how, with the Infinite Goodness of God, but which certainly are not to be explained on the supposition that its sole and sufficient type is to be found in the finite goodness of man.*

In other words, it is necessary to suppose that the infinite goodness ascribed to God is not the goodness which we know and love in our fellow-creatures, distinguished only as infinite in degree, but is different in kind, and another quality altogether. When we call the one finite goodness and the other infinite goodness, we do not mean what the words assert, but something else: we intentionally apply the same name to things which we regard as different.

Accordingly Mr. Mansel combats, as a heresy of his opponents, the opinion that infinite goodness differs only in degree from finite goodness. The notion "that the attributes of God differ from those of man in degree only, not in kind, and hence that certain mental and moral qualities of which we are immediately conscious in ourselves, furnish at the same time a true and adequate image of the infinite perfections of God," (the word *adequate* must have slipped in by inadvertence, since otherwise it would be an inexcusable misrepresentation) he identifies with "the vulgar Rationalism which regards the reason of man, in its ordinary and normal operation, as the supreme criterion of religious truth."† And in characterizing the mode of arguing of this vulgar Rationalism, he declares its principles to be, that "all the excellences of which we are conscious in the creature, must necessarily exist in the same manner, though in a higher degree, in the Creator. God is indeed more wise, more just, more merciful, than man; but for that very reason, his wisdom and justice and mercy must contain nothing that is incompatible with the corresponding attributes in their human character."‡ It is against this doctrine that Mr. Mansel feels called on to make an emphatic protest.

Ibid., Preface to the fourth edition, p. xiii.
†*Ibid.*, p. 26.
‡*Ibid.*, p. 28.

Here, then, I take my stand on the acknowledged principle of logic and of morality, that when we mean different things we have no right to call them by the same name, and to apply to them the same predicates, moral and intellectual. Language has no meaning for the words Just, Merciful, Benevolent, save that in which we predicate them of our fellow-creatures; and unless that is what we intend to express by them, we have no business to employ the words. If in affirming them of God we do not mean to affirm these very qualities, differing only as greater in degree, we are neither philosophically nor morally entitled to affirm them at all. If it be said that the qualities are the same, but that we cannot conceive them as they are when raised to the infinite, I grant that we cannot adequately conceive them in one of their elements, their infinity. But we can conceive them in their other elements, which are the very same in the infinite as in the finite development. Anything carried to the infinite must have all the properties of the same thing as finite, except those which depend upon the finiteness. Among the many who have said that we cannot conceive infinite space, did any one ever suppose that it is *not* space? that it does not possess all the properties by which space is characterized? Infinite Space cannot be cubical or spherical, because these are modes of being bounded: but does any one imagine that in ranging through it we might arrive at some region which was not extended; of which one part was not outside another; where, though no Body intervened, motion was impossible; or where the sum of two sides of a triangle was less than the third side? The parallel assertion may be made respecting infinite goodness. What belongs to it *either as Infinite or as Absolute* I do not pretend to know; but I know that infinite goodness must be goodness, and that what is not consistent with goodness, is not consistent with infinite goodness. If in ascribing goodness to God I do not mean what I mean by goodness; if I do not mean the goodness of which I have some knowledge, but an incomprehensible attribute of an incomprehensible substance, which for aught I know may be a totally different quality from that which I love and venerate—and even must, if Mr. Mansel is to be believed,[*] be in some important particulars opposed to this—what do I mean by calling it goodness? and what reason have I for venerating it? If I know nothing about what the attribute is, I cannot tell that it is a proper object of veneration. To say that God's goodness may be different in kind from man's goodness, what is it but saying, with a slight change of phraseology, that God may possibly not be good? To assert in words what we do not think in meaning, is as suitable a definition as can be given of a moral falsehood. Besides, suppose that certain unknown attributes are

[*See *ibid*., Preface to the 4th ed., pp. xiii–xvi.]

$^{l-l}$65^1, 65^2 as Infinite (or more properly as Absolute)

ascribed to the Deity in a religion the external evidences of which are so conclusive to my mind, as effectually to convince me that it comes from God. Unless I believe God to possess the same moral attributes which I find, in however inferior a degree, in a good man, what ground of assurance have I of God's veracity? All trust in a Revelation presupposes a conviction that God's attributes are the same, in all but degree, with the best human attributes.

If, instead of the "glad tidings" that there exists a Being in whom all the excellences which the highest human mind can conceive, exist in a degree inconceivable to us, I am informed that the world is ruled by a being whose attributes are infinite, but what they are we cannot learn, nor what are the principles of his government, except that "the highest human morality which we are capable of conceiving"[*] does not sanction them; convince me of it, and I will bear my fate as I may. But when I am told that I must believe this, and at the same time call this being by the names which express and affirm the highest human morality, I say in plain terms that I will not. Whatever power such a being may have over me, there is one thing which he shall not do: he shall not compel me to worship him. I will call no being good, who is not what I mean when I apply that epithet to my fellow-creatures;* and if such a being can sentence me to hell for not so calling him, to hell I will go.[†]

Neither is this to set up my own limited intellect as a criterion of divine or of any other wisdom. If a person is wiser and better than myself, not in some unknown and unknowable meaning of the terms, but in their known human acceptation, I am ready to believe that what this person thinks may be true, and that what he does may be right, when, but for the opinion I have of him, I should think otherwise. But this is because I believe that he and I have at bottom the same standard of truth and rule of right, and that he probably understands better than I the facts of the particular case. If I thought it not improbable that his notion of right might be my notion of wrong, I should not defer to his judgment. In like manner, one who sincerely believes in an absolutely good ruler of the world, is not warranted in disbelieving any act ascribed to him, merely because the very small part of its circumstances which we can possibly know does not sufficiently justify it. But if what I am told respecting him is of a kind which no facts that

[**Ibid*., p. xiii.]

*[72] Mr. Mansel, in his rejoinder, says that this means that I will call no being good "the phenomena of whose action in any way differ from those of a good man." ["Supplementary Remarks," p. 30.] This is a misconstruction; he should have said "no being, the principle or rule of whose action is different from that by which a good man endeavours to regulate his actions."

[†Cf. Samuel Johnson, *London, A Poem*, in *Works*, 14 vols. (London: Buckland, Rivington, *et al.*, 1787–88), Vol. XI, p. 324 (l. 116).]

can be supposed added to my knowledge could make me perceive to be right; if his alleged ways of dealing with the world are such as no imaginable hypothesis respecting things known to him and unknown to me, could make consistent with the goodness and wisdom which I mean when I use the terms, but are in direct contradiction to their signification; then, if the law of contradiction is a law of human thought, I cannot both believe these things, and believe that God is a good and wise being. If I call any being wise or good, not meaning the only qualities which the words import, I am speaking insincerely; I am flattering him by epithets which I fancy that he likes to hear, in the hope of winning him over to my own objects. For it is worthy of remark that the doubt whether words applied to God have their human signification, is only felt when the words relate to his moral attributes; it is never heard of in regard to his power. We are never told that God's omnipotence must not be supposed to mean an infinite degree of the power we know in man and nature, and that perhaps it does not mean that he is able to kill us, or consign us to eternal flames. The Divine Power is always interpreted in a completely human signification, but the Divine Goodness and Justice must be understood to be such only in an unintelligible sense. Is it unfair to surmise that this is because those who speak in the name of God, have need of the human conception of his power, since an idea which can overawe and enforce obedience must address itself to real feelings; but are content that his goodness should be conceived only as something inconceivable, because they are so often required to teach doctrines respecting him which conflict irreconcilably with all goodness that we can conceive?*

*[67] I quote in Mr. Mansel's words nearly the whole of his answer to the preceding remarks.

"Mr. Mansel asserts, as many others have asserted before him, that the relation between the communicable attributes of God and the corresponding attributes of man is one not of identity but of analogy; that is to say, that the Divine attributes have the same relation to the Divine nature that the human attributes have to human nature. Thus, for example, there is a Divine justice and there is a human justice; but God is just as the Creator and Governor of the world, having unlimited authority over all his creatures, and unlimited jurisdiction over all their acts; and man is just in certain special relations, as having authority over some persons and some acts only, so far as is required for the needs of human society. So, again, there is a Divine mercy and there is a human mercy; but God is merciful in such a manner as is fitting compatibly with the righteous government of the universe; and man is merciful in a certain limited range, the exercise of the attribute being guided by considerations affecting the welfare of society or of individuals. Or to take a more general case: Man has in himself a rule of right and wrong implying subjection to the authority of a superior (for conscience has authority only as reflecting the law of God); while God has in himself a rule of right and wrong, implying no higher authority, and determined absolutely by his own nature. The case is the same when we look at

I am anxious to say once more, that Mr. Mansel's conclusions do not go the whole length of his arguments, and that he disavows the doctrine that God's justice and goodness are *wholly* different from what human beings understand by the terms. He would, and does, admit that the qualities as conceived by us bear *some likeness* to the justice and goodness which

---

moral attributes not externally in their active manifestations, but internally, in their psychological constitution. If we do not attribute to God the same complex mental constitution of reason, passion, and will, the same relation to motives and induce-ments, the same deliberation and choice of alternatives, the same temporal succes-sion of facts in consciousness, which we ascribe to man,—it will follow that those psychological relations between reason, will, and desire, which are implied in the conception of human action, cannot represent the Divine excellences in them-selves, but can only illustrate them by analogies from finite things. And if man is liable to error in judging of the conduct of his fellow-men, in proportion as he is unable to place himself in their position, or to realize to himself their modes of thought and principles of action—if the child, for instance, is liable to error in judging the actions of the man, or the savage of the civilised man—surely there is far more room for error in men's judgment of the ways of God, in proportion as the difference between God and man is greater than the difference between a man and a child. . . . We will simply ask, whether Mr. Mill really supposes the word *good* to lose all community of meaning when it is applied, as it certainly is, to different persons among our fellow creatures with express reference to their different duties and different qualifications for performing them? The duties of a father are not the same as those of a son; is the word therefore wholly equivocal when we speak of one person as a good father, and another as a good son? Nay, when we speak generally of a man as good, has not the epithet a tacit reference to human nature and human duties? and yet is there no community of meaning when the same epithet is applied to other creatures? Ἡ ἀρετὴ πρὸς τὸ ἔργον τὸ οἰκεῖον [Aristotle, *The Nichoma-chean Ethics* (Greek and English), trans. H. Rackham (London: Heinemann; New York: Putnam's Sons, 1926), p. 326 (VI, i, 1139ª18)],—the goodness of any being whatever has relation to the nature and office of that being. We may therefore test Mr. Mill's declamation by a parallel case. A wise and experienced father addresses a young and inexperienced son: "My son," he says, "there may be some of my actions which do not seem to you to be wise or good, or such as you would do in my place. Remember, however, that your duties are different from mine; that your knowledge of my duties is very imperfect; and that there may be things which you cannot now see to be wise and good, but which you may hereafter discover to be so." "Father," says the son, "your principles of action are not the same as mine; the highest morality which I can conceive at present does not sanction them; and as for believing that you are good in anything of which I do not plainly see the goodness"—we will not repeat Mr. Mill's alternative; we will only ask whether it is not just possible that there may be as much difference between man and God as there is between a child and his father?" ([*Philosophy of the Conditioned*,] pp. 164–70.)

There is a mode of controversy which I do not remember to have seen in any enumeration of Fallacies, but which will some day find a place there, under some such name as the Inversion of Parts. It consists in indignantly vindicating as against your adversary the very principle which he is asserting against yourself. Would not

belong to God, since man was made in God's image. But such a semi-concession, which no Christian could avoid making, since without it the whole Christian scheme would be subverted, cannot save him; he is not relieved by it from any difficulties, while it destroys the whole fabric of his argument. The Divine goodness, which is said to be a different thing from human goodness, but of which the human conception of goodness is some imperfect reflexion or resemblance, does it agree with what men call

---

any reader of the above passage suppose that it is Mr. Mansel who is contending against me for the "community of meaning" of the word good, to whatever being it is applied; instead of me against him? It is I who say that as goodness in a good father is the very same quality with goodness in a good son, so goodness in a good God must be, in all but degree, the same quality as goodness in a good man, or we are not entitled to call it goodness. It is Mr. Mansel who denies this, affirming that there is more than a difference of degree. And unless he is to be understood as surrendering this point by the illustrations he now employs, his defence is no defence at all; for it confounds a difference in the outward circumstances in which a moral quality has to be exercised, with a difference in the quality itself. In his imaginary dialogue between a son and a father, does the son really think the father's conduct inconsistent with such goodness as, under the father's teaching, he has realized in himself, or learnt to recognise in others? Does he not think that it is the same goodness, but acting under a knowledge of facts, and an appreciation of means, such as he does not himself possess? Does the son think that the father's conduct is not justifiable by the same moral law which he prescribes to the son, and that in order to justify the father it is necessary to suppose him actuated by another *kind* of morality, not the same, but merely having the same relation to the father's nature that the other goodness has to the son's nature? If the son has implicit confidence in the father, he will not answer, in the words put into his mouth by Mr. Mansel, "your principles of action are not the same as mine." He will say, "your principles of action I well know: they are those which you have taught to me—those by which, in my best moments, I endeavour, though with inferior strength, to guide my conduct. You are incapable of acting on any others. Knowing your principles, and not knowing what conduct, in your different position, the principles require, but being convinced that you do know, I am certain that you act on those principles." All the allowance for human ignorance which can be demanded on similar grounds in judging of what is ascribed to God, I have amply granted.

On the latter part of the paragraph in the text, Mr. Mansel makes some further remarks. To the statement that "the doubt whether words applied to God have their human signification, is only felt when the words relate to his moral attributes—it is never heard of in regard to his power," Mr. Mansel makes answer, "We meet Mr. Mill's confident assertion with a direct denial, and take the opportunity of informing him that the conception of infinite Power has suggested the same difficulties, and has been discussed by philosophers and theologians in the same manner, as those of infinite Wisdom and infinite Goodness. Has Mr Mill never heard of such questions as, Whether Omnipotence can reverse the past?—Whether God can do that which he does not will to do?—Whether God's perfect foreknowledge is compatible with his own perfect liberty?—Whether God could have made a better world than the existing one?" ([*Ibid.*,] p. 172.) In return for the information thus liberally bestowed, I humbly reply, that I have "heard of such questions:" but I see in them (with the

goodness in the *essence* of the quality—in what *constitutes* it goodness? If it does, the "Rationalists" are right; it is not illicit to reason from the one to the other. If not, the divine attribute, whatever else it may be, is not goodness, and ought not to be called by the name. Unless there be some human conception which agrees with it, no human name can properly be applied to it; it is simply the unknown attribute of a thing unknown; it has no existence in relation to us, we can affirm nothing of it, and owe it no worship. Such is the inevitable alternative.*

To conclude: Mr. Mansel has not made out any connexion between his philosophical premises and his theological conclusion. The relativity of human knowledge, the uncognoscibility of the Absolute, and the contradic-

---

exception of the second, which relates to the meaning of Power, not of Infinite power) only enquiries, mostly frivolous, how much *more* power God has than man. There is no difference in the conception of the power itself, which is in both cases the same, namely, the conformity of the event to the volition. The divine omnipotence is always supposed to mean an infinite degree of this, and not of anything else. But infinite goodness, according to Mr. Mansel, means not an infinite degree, but a different kind, not admitting of any common definition with human goodness.

*m*Mr. Mansel's answer to this is a curious one. He says that "if power, as predicated of man, means the conformity of the event to the volition, man assuredly can do no more than he actually wills to do; for there can be no conformity except where there is a volition and an event." ["Supplementary Remarks," p. 30n.] We may know that the event would conform to our volition although it has not actually taken place. Most people, I believe, if they said that they had the power of throwing themselves into a well, would mean that *if* they willed so to throw themselves, the effect would follow. And if it were asked whether there are any limits to God's power, the question would mean, Is there anything which if willed by him, nevertheless would not take place. What else can be meant when we speak of a living being as having power, I cannot divine.*m*

The concluding sentence Mr. Mansel censures as attributing discreditable motives to opponents. Had it not been for this proof, I should have thought it unnecessary to say, that no imputation was intended on the sincerity either of classes or of individuals. But the effect of men's necessities of position on their opinions as well as on their conduct, is far too widely reaching and influential an element in human affairs, to be *always* passed over in silence for fear of offending personal susceptibilities.

*[67] Mr. Mansel says, "The question really at issue is not whether the Rationalist argument is licit or illicit, but whether, in its lawful use, it is to be regarded as infallible or fallible." ([*Philosophy of the Conditioned*,] p. 175.) If this were all, there would be nothing for him and the Rationalists to quarrel about; for who ever asserted, of any human reasoning, that it is infallible? Neither, I believe, would any "Rationalist" dissent from Mr. Mansel's view of the "lawful use" of the argument, which he declares throughout his Eighth Lecture [*Limits of Religious Thought*, pp. 152–75] to be only admissible (as one argument among others) on the question of the authenticity of a Revelation. No Rationalists, I should suppose, believe that what

m-m +72

tions which follow the attempt to conceive a Being with all or without any attributes, are no obstacles to our having the same kind of knowledge of God which we have of other things, namely not as they exist absolutely, but relatively. The proposition, that we cannot conceive the moral attributes of God in such a manner as to be able to affirm of any doctrine or assertion that it is inconsistent with them, has no foundation in the laws of the human mind: while, if admitted, it would not prove that we should ascribe to God attributes bearing the same name as human qualities, but not to be understood in the same sense; it would prove that we ought not to ascribe any moral attributes to God at all, inasmuch as no moral attributes known or conceivable by us are true of him, and we are condemned to absolute ignorance of him as a moral being.

---

they reject as inconsistent with the Divine Goodness was really revealed by God. They do not both admit it to be revealed and believe it to be false. They believe that it is either a mistaken interpretation, or found its way by human means into documents which they may nevertheless consider as the records of a Revelation. They concede, therefore, to Mr. Mansel (and unless the hypothesis were admitted of a God who is not good, they cannot help conceding) that the moral objections to a religious doctrine are only valid ^{n}against its truth^n if they are strong enough to outweigh whatever external evidences there may be of its having been divinely revealed. But when the question is, *how much* weight is to be allowed to moral objections, the difference will be radical between those who think that the Divine Goodness is the same thing with human goodness carried to the infinite, and Mr. Mansel, who thinks that it is a different quality, only having some analogy to the human. Indeed it is hard to see how any one, who holds the latter opinion, can give more than a nominal weight to any such argument against a religious doctrine. For, if things may be right according to divine goodness which would be wrong according to even an infinite degree of the human, and if all that is known is that there is some analogy between the two, while no one pretends to have any knowledge how far the analogy reaches, and it may be presumed to be as distant as the remainder of the Divine Nature is from the human, it is impossible to assign any determinate weight to an argument grounded on contradiction of such an analogy. It becomes a mere dialectical *locus communis*: an argument to be taken up and laid down as suits convenience, and which different men will hold valid in different cases, according to their fancies or prepossessions.

$^{n-n}$+72

CHAPTER VIII

Of Consciousness, as Understood by Sir William Hamilton

IN THE DISCUSSION of the Relativity of human knowledge and the Philosophy of the Conditioned, we have brought under consideration those of Sir W. Hamilton's metaphysical doctrines which have the greatest share in giving to his philosophy the colour of individuality which it possesses, and the most important of those which can be regarded as belonging specially to himself. On a certain number of minor points, and on one of primary importance, Causation, we shall again have to examine opinions of his which are original. But on most of the subjects which remain to be discussed, at least in the psychological department (as distinguished from the logical), Sir W. Hamilton is merely an eminent representative of one of the two great schools of metaphysical thought; that which derives its popular appellation from Scotland, and of which the founder and most celebrated champion was a philosopher whom, on the whole, Sir W. Hamilton seems to prefer to any other, Dr. Reid. For the future, therefore, we shall be concerned less with Sir W. Hamilton's philosophy as such, than with the general mode of thought to which it belongs. We shall be engaged in criticizing doctrines common to him with many other thinkers; but in doing so we shall take his writings as text-books, and deal with the opinions chiefly in the form in which he presented them. No other course would be so fair to the opinions themselves: not only because they have not, within the last half century, had so able a teacher, and never one so well acquainted with the teachings of others, but also because he had the great advantage of coming last. All theories, at their commencement, bear the burthen of mistakes and inadvertences not inherent in the theories themselves, but either personal to their authors, or arising from the imperfect state of philosophical thought at the time of their origin. At a later period, the errors which accidentally adhered to the theory are stript off, the most obvious objections to it are perceived, and more or less successfully met, and it is rendered, at least apparently, consistent with such admitted truths as it at first seemed to contradict. One of the unfairest, though commonest tricks of controversy, is that of directing the attack exclusively against the first crude form of a doctrine.* Whoever should judge Locke's philosophy as it is in Locke, Berkeley's philosophy as it is in Berkeley, or Reid's as it is in Reid, would often condemn them on the ground of incidental misapprehensions, which form no essential part of their doctrine, and from which its later adherents and expositors are free. Sir W. Hamilton's is the latest form of the Reidian theory; and by no other of its supporters has that theory been so well guarded, or expressed in such discriminating terms, and with such studious precision. Though there are a few points on which the earlier philosopher seems to me nearer the truth, on the whole it is impossible to pass from Reid to Sir W. Hamilton, or from Sir W. Hamilton back to Reid, and not be struck with the immense progress which their common philosophy has made in the interval between them.

All theories of the human mind profess to be interpretations of Consciousness: the conclusions of all of them are supposed to rest on that ultimate evidence, either immediately or remotely. What Consciousness directly reveals, together with what can be legitimately inferred from its revelations, composes, by universal admission, all that we know of the mind, or indeed of any other thing. When we know what any philosopher considers to be revealed in Consciousness, we have the key to the entire character of his metaphysical system.

There are some peculiarities requiring notice, in Sir W. Hamilton's mode of conceiving and defining Consciousness. The words of his definition do not, of themselves, indicate those peculiarities. Consciousness, he says, is "the recognition by the mind or ego of its own acts or affections;" and in this, as he truly observes, "all philosophers are agreed."† But all philosophers have not, by any means, meant the same thing by it. Most of them (including Reid and Stewart) have meant, as the words naturally mean, Self-consciousness. They have held, that we can be conscious only of some state of our own mind. The mind's "own acts or affections" are in the mind itself, and not external to it: accordingly we have, in their opinion, the direct evidence of consciousness, only for the internal world. An external world is but an inference, which, according to most philosophers, is justified, or even, by our mental constitution, compelled: according to others, not justified.

Nothing, however, can be farther from Sir W. Hamilton's mind than he declares this opinion to be. Though consciousness, according to him, is a recognition of the mind's own acts and affections, we are nevertheless conscious of things outside the mind. Some of the mind's acts are perceptions of outward objects; and we are, of course, conscious of those acts:

*This, for example, is the secret of most of the apparent triumphs which are so frequently gained over the population theory of Malthus, and the political economy of Ricardo.

†*Lectures*, Vol. I, pp. 193 and 201.

now, to be conscious of a perception, necessarily implies being conscious of the thing perceived.

It is palpably impossible that we can be conscious of an act, without being conscious of the object to which that act is relative. This, however, is what Dr. Reid and Mr. Stewart maintain. They maintain that I can know *that* I know, without knowing *what* I know—or that I can know the knowledge without knowing what the knowledge is about: for example, that I am conscious of perceiving a book, without being conscious of the book perceived,—that I am conscious of remembering its contents without being conscious of these contents remembered—and so forth.*

An act of knowledge existing and being what it is only by relation to its object, it is manifest that the act can be known only through the object to which it is correlative; and Reid's supposition that an operation can be known in consciousness to the exclusion of its object, is impossible. For example, I see the inkstand. How can I be conscious that my present modification exists,—that it is a perception and not another mental state,—that it is a perception of sight, to the exclusion of every other sense,—and finally, that it is a perception of the inkstand, and of the inkstand only,—unless my own consciousness comprehend within its sphere the object, which at once determines the existence of the act, qualifies its kind, and distinguishes its individuality? Annihilate the inkstand, you annihilate the perception; annihilate the consciousness of the object, you annihilate the consciousness of the operation. It undoubtedly sounds strange to say, I am conscious of the inkstand, instead of saying, I am conscious of the perception of the inkstand. This I admit, but the admission can avail nothing to Dr. Reid, for the apparent incongruity of the expression arises only from the prevalence of that doctrine of perception in the schools of philosophy, which it is his principal merit to have so vigorously assailed.†

This is Sir W. Hamilton's first difference, on the subject of Consciousness, from his predecessor, Reid. In being conscious of those of our mental operations which regard external objects, we are, according to Sir W. Hamilton, conscious of the objects. Consciousness, therefore, is not solely of the ego and its modifications, but also of the non-ego.

This first difference is not the only one. Consciousness, according to Sir W. Hamilton, may be of things external to self, but it can only be of things actually present. In the first place, they must be present in time. We are not conscious of the past. Thus far Sir W. Hamilton agrees with Reid, who holds that memory is of the past, consciousness only of the present. Reid, however, is of opinion that memory is an "immediate knowledge of the past,"[*] exactly as consciousness is an immediate knowledge of the present. Sir W. Hamilton contends that this opinion of Reid is "not only false," but "involves a contradiction in terms." Memory is an act, and an act "exists only in the *now*:"‡ it can therefore be cognizant only of what now is. In the case of memory, what now is, is not the thing remembered, but a

Ibid., p. 212.
†*Ibid.*, pp. 228–9.
[*On the Intellectual Powers*, p. 339.]
‡*Lectures*, Vol. I, pp. 218–19.

present representation of it in the mind, which representation is the sole object of consciousness. We are aware of the past, not immediately, but mediately, through the representation.

An act of memory, is merely a present state of mind, which we are conscious of, not as absolute, but as relative to, and representing, another state of mind, and accompanied with the belief that the state of mind, as now represented, has actually been. . . . All that is immediately known in the act of memory, is the present mental modification; that is, the representation and concomitant belief. . . . So far is memory from being an immediate knowledge of the past, that it is at best only a mediate knowledge of the past; while in philosophical propriety, it is not a knowledge of the past at all, but a knowledge of the present, and a belief of the past. . . . We may doubt, we may deny that the representation and belief are true. We may assert that they represent what never was, and that all beyond their present mental existence is a delusion:[*]

but it is impossible for us to doubt or deny that of which we have immediate knowledge.

Again, that of which we are conscious must not only be present in time, it must also, if external to our minds, be present in place. It must be in direct contact with our bodily organs. We do not immediately perceive a distant object.

To say, for example, that we perceive by sight the sun or moon, is a false or an elliptical expression. We perceive nothing but certain modifications of light, in immediate relation to our organ of vision; and so far from Dr. Reid being philosophically correct when he says that "when ten men look at the sun or moon, they all see the same individual object," the truth is that each of these persons sees a different object, because each person sees a different complement of rays, in relation to his individual organ:*

to which, in another place, he adds, that each individual sees two different objects, with his right and with his left eye.

It is not by perception, but by a process of reasoning, that we connect the objects of sense with existences beyond the sphere of immediate knowledge. It is enough that perception affords us the knowledge of the non-ego at the point of sense. To arrogate to it the power of immediately informing us of external things which are only the causes of the object we immediately perceive, is either positively erroneous, or a confusion of language arising from an inadequate discrimination of the phænomena.[†]

[*Ibid., pp. 219–21.]
*Ibid., Vol. II, p. 153. [Reid, On the Intellectual Powers, p. 284.]
†[Ibid., pp. 153–4 (i.e., "another place" is the sentence immediately following the passage previously quoted).] And elsewhere: "It is self-evident that if a thing is to be an object immediately known, it must be known as it exists. Now, a body must exist in some definite part of space, in a certain place; it cannot, therefore, be immediately known as existing, except it be known in its place. But this supposes the mind to be immediately present to it in space." (Foot-note to Reid, p. 302n.)

I do not guarantee the conclusiveness of this reasoning; but it has been an error of philosophers in all times to flank their good arguments with bad ones.

There can, I think, be no doubt that these remarks on knowledge of the past and perception of the distant, are correct, and a great improvement upon Reid.

It appears, then, that the true definition of Consciousness in Sir W. Hamilton's use of the term, would be Immediate Knowledge. And he expressly says, "*Consciousness* and *immediate knowledge* are thus terms universally convertible: and if there be an immediate knowledge of things external, there is consequently the Consciousness of an outer world."* Immediate knowledge, again, he treats as universally convertible with Intuitive knowledge:† and the terms are really equivalent. We know intuitively, what we know by its own evidence—by direct apprehension of the fact, and not through the medium of a previous knowledge of something from which we infer it. Regarded in this light, our author's difference with Reid as to our being conscious of outward objects, would appear, on his own showing, to be chiefly a dispute about words: for Reid also says that we have an immediate and intuitive knowledge of things without, ᵃand (if Sir W. Hamilton understands him rightly) that it is immediate and intuitive in the same meaning and mode, as that claimed for us by Sir W. Hamiltonᵃ. Sir W. Hamilton stretches the word Consciousness so as to include this knowledge, while Reid, with greater regard for the origin and etymology of the word, restricts it to the cases in which the mind is "conscia *sibi*."[*] Sir W. Hamilton has a right to his own use of the term; but care must be taken that it do not serve as a means of knowingly or unknowingly begging any question. One of the most disputed questions in psychology is exactly this—Have we, or not, an immediate intuition of material objects? and this question must not be prejudged by affirming that those objects are in our consciousness. On the contrary, it is only allowable to say that they are in our consciousness, after it ᵇhadᵇ been already proved that we cognise them intuitively.

It is a little startling, after so much has been said of the limitation of Consciousness to immediate knowledge, to find Sir W. Hamilton, in the "Dissertations on Reid," maintaining that "consciousness comprehends every cognitive act; in other words, whatever we are not conscious of, that we do not know."‡ If consciousness comprehends all our knowledge, but yet is limited to immediate knowledge, it follows that all our knowledge must be immediate, and that we have, therefore, no knowledge of the past or of the absent. Sir W. Hamilton might have cleared up this difficulty by

---

Discussions, p. 51.
†*Lectures*, Vol. I, p. 221n; and Vol. IV, p. 73.
[*See *On the Intellectual Powers*, pp. 258–60.]
‡"Dissertations on Reid," [Note B,] p. 810.

ᵃ⁻ᵃ65¹, 65²   though he does not call it a consciousness
ᵇ⁻ᵇ65¹, 65²   has

saying, as he had already done, that our mediate cognitions—those of the past and the absent—though he never hesitates to call them knowledge, are in strict propriety Belief. We could then have understood his meaning. But the explanation he actually gives is quite different. It is, that "all our mediate cognitions are contained in our immediate."[*] This is a manifest attempt to justify himself in calling them, not belief, but knowledge, like our immediate cognitions. But what is the meaning of "contained?" If it means that our mediate cognitions are *part* of our immediate, then they are themselves immediate, and we have no mediate cognitions. Sir W. Hamilton has told us, that in the case of a remembered fact, what we immediately cognise is but a present mental representation of it, "accompanied with the belief that the state of mind, as now represented, has actually been."[†] Having said this, he also says that the past fact, which does not now exist, is "contained"[‡] in the representation and in the belief which do exist. But if it is contained in them, it must have a present existence too, and is not a past fact. Perhaps, however, by the word "contained," all that is meant is, that it is implied in them; that it is a necessary or legitimate inference from them. But if it is only this, it remains absent in time; and what is absent in time, our author has said, is not a possible object of consciousness. If, therefore, a past fact is an object of knowledge, we *can* know what we are not conscious of; consciousness does not comprehend all our cognitions. To state the same thing in another manner; a remembered fact is either a part of our consciousness, or it is not. If it is, Sir W. Hamilton is wrong when he says that we are not conscious of the past. If not, he is wrong, either in saying that we can know the past, or in saying that what we are not conscious of, we do not know.

This inconsistency, which emerges only in the "Dissertations," I shall not further dwell upon: it is chiefly important as showing that the most complicated and elaborate version of Sir W. Hamilton's speculations is not always the freest from objection. The doctrine of his *Lectures* is, that a part of our knowledge—the knowledge of the past, the future, and the distant—is mediate and representative, but that such mediate knowledge is not Consciousness; consciousness and immediate knowledge being coextensive.

From our author's different deliverances as above quoted, it appears that he gives two definitions of Consciousness. In the one, it is synonymous with direct, immediate, or intuitive knowledge; and we are conscious not only of ourselves but of outward objects, since, in our author's opinion, we know these intuitively. According to the other definition, consciousness is

[**Ibid.*]
[†*Lectures*, Vol. I, p. 219.]
[‡*Ibid.*, p. 218.]

the mind's recognition of its own acts and affections. It is not at once obvious how these two definitions can be reconciled: for Sir W. Hamilton would have been the last person to say that the outward object is identical with the mental act or affection. He must have meant that consciousness is the mind's recognition of its own acts and affections together with all that is therein implied, or as he would say, contained. But this involves him in a new inconsistency: for how can he then refuse the name of consciousness to our mediate knowledge—to our knowledge or belief (for instance) of the past? The past reality is certainly *implied* in the present recollection of which we are conscious: and our author has said that all our mediate knowledge is contained in our immediate, *as he has elsewhere said that* knowledge of the outward object is contained in our knowledge of the perception. If, then, we are conscious of the outward object, why not of the past sensation or impression?

From the definition of Consciousness as "the recognition by the mind or Ego of its own acts or affections,"[*] our author might be supposed to think (as has been actually thought by many philosophers) that consciousness is not the fact itself of knowing or feeling, but a subsequent operation by which we become aware of that fact. This however is not his opinion. By "the mind's recognition of its acts and affections" he does not mean anything different from the acts and affections themselves. He denies that we have one faculty by which we know or feel, and another by which we know that we know, and by which we know that we feel. These are not, according to him, different facts, but the same fact seen under another point of view. And he takes this occasion for making a remark, of wide application in philosophy, which it would be of signal service to all students of metaphysics to keep constantly in mind; that difference of names often does not signify difference of things, but only difference in the particular *aspect* under which a thing is considered.[†] On the real identity between our various mental states and our consciousness of them, he seems to be of the opinion which was maintained before him by Brown, and which is stated by Mr. James Mill, with his usual clearness and force, in the following passage:

Having a sensation, and having a feeling, are not two things. The thing is one, the names only are two. I am pricked by a pin. The sensation is one; but I may call it sensation, or a feeling, or a pain, as I please. Now, when, having the sensation, I say I feel the sensation, I only use a tautological expression; the sensation is not one thing, the feeling another; the sensation is the feeling. When instead of the word

[*_Ibid._, p. 193.]
[†See _ibid._, pp. 193–5.]

c–c65¹   *implied*
d–d65¹, 65²   just as
e–e65¹, 65²   relation

feeling, I use the word conscious, I do exactly the same thing—I merely use a tautological expression. To say I feel a sensation, is merely to say that I feel a feeling; which is an impropriety of speech. And to say I am conscious of a feeling, is merely to say that I feel it. To have a feeling is to be conscious; and to be conscious is to have a feeling. To be conscious of the prick of the pin, is merely to have the sensation. And though I have these various modes of naming my sensation, by saying, I feel the prick of a pin, I feel the pain of a prick, I have the sensation of a prick, I have the feeling of a prick, I am conscious of the feeling; the thing named in all these various ways is one and the same.

The same explanation will easily be seen to apply to ideas. Though at present I have not the sensation, called the prick of a pin, I have a distinct idea of it. The having an idea, and the not having it, are distinguished by the existence or non-existence of a certain feeling. To have an idea, and the feeling of that idea, are not two things; they are one and the same thing. To feel an idea, and to be conscious of that feeling, are not two things; the feeling and the consciousness are but two names for the same thing. In the very word feeling, all that is implied in the word Consciousness is involved.

Those philosophers, therefore, who have spoken of Consciousness as a feeling distinct from all other feelings, committed a mistake, and one, the evil consequences of which have been most important; for, by combining a chimerical ingredient with the elements of thought, they involved their enquiries in confusion and mystery from the very commencement.

It is easy to see what is the nature of the terms Conscious and Consciousness, and what is the marking function which they are destined to perform. It was of great importance, for the purpose of naming, that we should not only have names to distinguish the different classes of our feelings, but also a name applicable equally to all those classes. This purpose is answered by the concrete term, Conscious, and the abstract of it, Consciousness. Thus, if we are in any way sentient; that is, have any of the feelings whatsoever of a living creature; the word Conscious is applicable to the feeler, and Consciousness to the feeling: that is to say, the words are Generical marks, under which all the names of the subordinate classes of the feelings of a sentient creature are included. When I smell a rose, I am conscious; when I have the idea of a fire, I am conscious; when I remember, I am conscious; when I reason, and when I believe, I am conscious; but believing and being conscious of belief, are not two things, they are the same thing: though this same thing I can name at one time without the aid of the generical mark, while at another time it suits me to employ the generical mark.*

Sir W. Hamilton's doctrine is exactly this, except that he expresses the latter part of it in less perspicuous phraseology, saying that consciousness is "the fundamental form, the generic condition" of all the modes of our mental activity;† "in fact, the general condition of their existence."‡ But, while holding the same theory with Brown and ƒ Mill, he completes it by the addition that though our mental states and our consciousness of them are

---

*James Mill, *Analysis of the Phenomena of the Human Mind*, Vol. I, pp. 170–2.
†*Discussions*, p. 48.
‡*Lectures*, Vol. I, p. 193.
ƒ65¹, 65² Mr.

only the same fact, they are the same fact regarded in different relations. Considered in themselves, as acts and feelings, or considered in relation to the external object with which they are concerned, we do not call them consciousness. It is when these mental modifications are referred to a subject or ego, and looked at in relation to Self, that consciousness is the term used: consciousness being "the self-affirmation that certain modifications are known by me, and that these modifications are mine." In this self-affirmation, however, no additional fact is introduced. It "is not to be viewed as anything different from" the "modifications themselves."* There is but one mental phænomenon, the act of feeling: but as this implies an acting or feeling Self, we give it a name which connotes its relation to the Self, and that name is Consciousness. Thus, "consciousness and knowledge"—and I think he would have added feeling (the mind's "affections") as well as knowledge—

are not distinguished by different words as different things, but only as the same thing considered in different aspects. The verbal distinction is taken for the sake of brevity and precision, and its convenience warrants its establishment. . . . Though each term of a relation necessarily supposes the other, nevertheless one of these terms may be to us the more interesting, and we may consider that term as the principal, and view the other only as subordinate and correlative. Now, this is the case in the present instance. In an act of knowledge, my attention may be principally attracted either to the object known, or to myself, as the subject knowing; and in the latter case, although no new element be added to the act, the condition involved in it,—*I know that I know*, becomes the primary and permanent matter of consideration. And when, as in the philosophy of mind, the act of knowledge comes to be specially considered in relation to the knowing subject, it is, at last, in the progress of the science, found convenient, if not absolutely necessary, to possess a scientific word in which this point of view should be permanently and distinctively embodied.†

If any doubt could have existed, after this passage, of Sir W. Hamilton's opinion on the question, it would have been removed by one of the fragments recently published by his editors, in continuation of the "Dissertations on Reid." I extract the words:

Consciousness is not to be regarded as aught different from the mental modes or movements themselves. It is not to be viewed as an illuminated place within which objects coming are presented to, and passing beyond are withdrawn from, observation; nor is it to be considered even as an observer—the mental modes as phænomena observed. Consciousness is just the movements themselves, rising above a certain degree of intensity. . . . It is only a comprehensive word for those mental movements which rise at once above a certain degree of intension.‡

*Ibid.
†Ibid., pp. 194–5.
‡Supplement to Reid [i.e., "Dissertations on Reid," Note H], p. 932. The qualification here first introduced, of "rising above a certain degree of intensity," has

We now pass to a question which is of no little importance to the character of Sir W. Hamilton's system of philosophy. We found, not long ago, that he makes between Knowledge and Belief a broad distinction, on which he lays great stress, and which plays a conspicuous part both in his own speculations and in those of some of his followers. Let us now look at this distinction in the light thrown upon it by those doctrines of Sir W. Hamilton which are the subject of the present chapter.

Though Sir W. Hamilton allows a mediate, or representative, knowledge of the past and the absent, he has told us that "in philosophical propriety" it ought not to be called knowledge, but belief. We do not, properly speaking, know a past event, but believe it, by reason of the present recollection which we immediately know. We do not, properly speaking, perceive or

---

reference to a doctrine of our author to be fully considered hereafter, that of latent mental states. It makes no abatement from the doctrine that consciousness of a feeling *is* the feeling; for mental states which are not intense enough to rise into consciousness, are, according to the same theory, not intense enough to be felt: and if felt, the feeling, and the consciousness of the feeling, are one and the same.

It was not without some difficulty, and after considerable study, that I was able to satisfy myself that Sir W. Hamilton held the sound and rational theory with which I have credited him in the text. For he often states and defends his doctrine in a manner which might lead one to think, that in saying that to know, and to know that we know, are but one fact, he does not mean one fact, but two facts which are inseparable. This misapprehension of his meaning is favoured by *the* repeated use of (what we seldom meet with in his writings) a false illustration; that of the sides and angles of a triangle. "The sides suppose the angles—the angles suppose the sides,—and, in fact, the sides and angles are in themselves, in reality, one and indivisible." (*Lectures*, Vol. I, p. 194.) "The sides and angles of a triangle (or trilateral) as mutually correlative—as together making up the same simple figure—and as, without destruction of that figure, actually inseparable from it, and from each other, are *really* one; but inasmuch as they have peculiar relations, which may, in thought, be considered severally and for themselves, they are *logically* twofold." ("Dissertations on Reid," [Note B,] p. 806n.) According to this, the sides are in reality the angles looked at in a particular point of view; and the angles the same thing as the sides, regarded in a particular relation to something else. When this was the illustration selected of the identity between Consciousness and Knowledge, it was natural to suppose that the writer regarded these two as no otherwise one than the sides and angles of a triangle are. But a closer examination has satisfied me that Sir W. Hamilton was only wrong respecting sides and angles, and not respecting Consciousness and Knowledge. On the former subject he has against him not only the reason of the case, but his own authority; for he says, when discoursing on another subject: "It is not more reasonable to identify sense with judgment, because the former cannot exist without an act of the latter, *than it would be to identify the sides and angles of a mathematical figure, because sides and angles cannot exist apart from each other*." (Foot-note to Reid, p. 590n.) [A draft of the latter part of this note exists in manuscript; see Appendix A below.]

*g–g*65¹, 65², 67   his

know the sun, but we perceive and know an image in contact with our organs, and believe the existence of the sun through "a process of reasoning,"[*] which connects the image that we directly perceive, with something else as its cause. Again, though we cannot know an Infinite or an Absolute Being, we may and ought to believe in the reality of such a Being. But in all these cases the belief itself, the conviction we feel of the existence of the sun, and of the reality of the past event, and which according to Sir W. Hamilton we ought to feel of the existence of *a Being who is* the Infinite and the Absolute—this belief is a fact present in time and in place—a phænomenon of our own mind; of this we are conscious; this we immediately know. Such, it is impossible to doubt, is Sir W. Hamilton's opinion.

Let us now apply to this the general principle emphatically affirmed by him, and forming the basis of his argument against Reid and Stewart on the subject of Consciousness. "It is palpably impossible that we can be conscious of an act, without being conscious of the object to which that act is relative."[†] "The knowledge of an operation necessarily involves the knowledge of its object." "It is impossible to make consciousness conversant about the intellectual operations to the exclusion of their objects,"[‡] and therefore, since we are conscious of our perceptions, we must be conscious of the external objects perceived. Such is Sir W. Hamilton's theory. But perceptions are not the only mental operations we are conscious of, which point to an external object. This is no less true of beliefs. We are conscious of belief in a past event, in the reality of a distant body, and (according to Sir W. Hamilton) in the existence of the Infinite and the Absolute. Consequently, on Sir W. Hamilton's principle, we are conscious of the objects of those beliefs; conscious of the past event, conscious of the distant body, conscious of the Infinite and of the Absolute. To disclaim this conclusion would be to bring down upon himself the language in which he criticized Reid and Stewart; it would be to maintain "that I can know *that* I [believe] without knowing *what* I [believe]—or that I can know the [belief] without knowing what the [belief] is about: for example, that I am conscious of [remembering a past event] without being conscious of [the past event remembered]; that I am conscious of [believing in God], without being conscious of the [God believed in]."[§] If it be true that "an act of knowledge" exists, and is what it is, "only by relation to its object," this must be equally true of an act of belief: and it must be as "manifest" of the one act as

[*Lectures, Vol. II, p. 153.]
[†Ibid., Vol. I, p. 212.]
[‡Ibid., p. 211.]
[§Ibid., p. 212; the square brackets, which are Mill's, contain his substitutions.]
h-h+67, 72

of the other, "that it can be known only through the object to which it is correlative."[*] Therefore past events, distant objects, and the Absolute, inasmuch as they are believed, are as much objects of immediate knowledge as things finite and present: since they are presupposed and implicitly contained in the mental fact of belief, exactly as a present object is implicitly contained in the mental fact of perception. Either, therefore, Sir W. Hamilton was wrong in his doctrine that consciousness of our perceptions implies consciousness of their external object, or if he was right in this, the distinction between Belief and Knowledge collapses: all objects of Belief are objects of Knowledge: Belief and Knowledge are the same thing: and he was wrong in asserting that the Absolute ought to be believed, or wrong in maintaining against Cousin that it is incapable of being known.

Another reasoner might escape from this dilemma by saying that the knowledge of the object of belief, which is implied in knowledge of the belief itself, is not knowledge of the object as existing, but knowledge of it as believed—the mere knowledge *what it is* that we believe. And this is true; but it could not be said by Sir W. Hamilton; for he rejects the same reasonable explanation in the parallel case. He will not allow it to be said that when we have what we call a perception, and refer it to an external object, we are conscious not of the external object as existing, but of ourselves as inferring an external existence. He maintains that the actual outward existence of the object is a deliverance of consciousness, because "it is impossible that we can be conscious of an act without being conscious of the object to which that act is relative."[†] He cannot, then, reject as applied to the act of Belief, a law which, when he has occasion for applying it to the acts of Perception and Knowledge, he affirms to be common to all our mental operations. If we can be conscious of an operation without being conscious of its object, the reality of an external world is not indeed subverted, but there is an end to Sir W. Hamilton's theory of the mode in which it is known, and to his particular mode of proving it.

The difficulty in which Sir W. Hamilton is thus involved seems to have become, though very insufficiently, perceptible to himself. Towards the end of his Lectures on Logic, after saying that "we may be equally certain of what we believe as of what we know," and that, "it has, not without ground, been maintained by many philosophers, both in ancient and modern times, that the certainty of all knowledge is, in its ultimate analysis, resolved into a certainty of belief,"* he adds, "But, on the other hand, the manifestation of this belief necessarily involves knowledge; for we cannot believe without some consciousness or knowledge of the belief, and con-

[*Ibid., p. 228.]   *Ibid., Vol. IV, p. 70.
[†Ibid., p. 212.]

sequently without some consciousness or knowledge of the object of the belief." The remark which this tardy reflexion suggests to him is merely this: "The consideration, however, of the relation of Belief and Knowledge does not properly belong to Logic, except so far as it is necessary to explain the nature of Truth and Error. It is altogether a metaphysical discussion; and one of the most difficult problems of which Metaphysics attempts the solution."* Accordingly, he takes the extremely unphilosophical liberty of leaving it unsolved. But when a thinker is compelled by one part of his philosophy to contradict another part, he cannot leave the conflicting assertions standing, and throw the responsibility of his scrape on the arduousness of the subject. A palpable self-contradiction is not one of the difficulties which can be adjourned, as belonging to a higher department of science. Though it may be a hard matter to find the truth, that is no reason for holding to what is self-convicted of error. If Sir W. Hamilton's theory of consciousness is correct, it does not leave the difference between Belief and Knowledge in a state of obscurity, but abolishes that distinction entirely, and along with it a great part of his own philosophy. If his premises are true, we not only cannot believe what we do not know, but we cannot believe that of which we are not conscious; the distinction between our immediate and our mediate or representative cognitions, and the doctrine of things believable but not knowable, must both succumb; or if these can be saved, it must be by abandoning the proposition, which is at the root of so much of his philosophy, that consciousness of an operation is consciousness of the object of the operation.

But when Sir W. Hamilton began to perceive that if his theory is correct nothing can be believed except in so far as it is known, he did not therefore renounce the attempt to distinguish Belief from Knowledge. In the very same Lecture, he says, "Knowledge and Belief differ not only in degree but in kind. Knowledge is a certainty founded upon insight; Belief is a certainty founded upon feeling. The one is perspicuous and objective; the other is obscure and subjective. Each, however, supposes the other: and an assurance is said to be a knowledge or a belief, according as the one element or the other preponderates."† If Sir W. Hamilton had bestowed any sufficient consideration on the difficulty, he would hardly have consented to pay himself with such mere words. If each of his two certainties supposes the other, it follows that whenever we have a certainty founded upon feeling, we have a parallel certainty founded upon insight. We therefore have always insight when we are certain; and we are never certain except to the extent to which we have insight. It is not a case in which we can talk of one or the other element preponderating. They must be equal and coextensive.

*Ibid., p. 73.   †Ibid., p. 62.

The whole of what we know we must believe; and the whole of what we believe we must know: for we know that we believe it, and the act of belief "can only be known through the object to which it is correlative." Our conviction is not divided, in varying proportions, between knowledge and belief: the two must always keep abreast of one another.

All this follows, whatever may be the meaning of the "insight" which forms the distinction in kind between belief and knowledge. But what is this insight? "The immediate consciousness of an object" (he goes on to say) "is called an *intuition*, an *insight*."* So that if knowledge is distinguished from belief by being grounded on insight, it is distinguished by being grounded on immediate consciousness. But belief also supposes immediate consciousness, since "we cannot believe without some consciousness or knowledge of the belief, and consequently without some consciousness or knowledge of the object of the belief." Not merely without some consciousness, but, if our author's theory is correct, without a consciousness coextensive with the belief. As far as we believe, so far we are conscious of the belief, and so far, therefore, if the theory be true, we are conscious of the thing believed.

But though Sir W. Hamilton cannot extricate himself from this entanglement, having, by the premises he laid down, cut off his own retreat, other thinkers can find a way through it. For, in truth, what can be more absurd than the notion that belief of anything implies knowledge of the thing believed? Were this so, there could be no such thing as false belief. Every day's experience shows that belief of the most peremptory kind— assurance founded on the most intense "feeling," is compatible with total ignorance of the thing which is the object of belief; though of course not with ignorance of the belief itself. And this absurdity is a full refutation of the theory which leads to it—that consciousness of an operation involves consciousness of that about which the operation is conversant. The theory does not *seem* so absurd when affirmed of knowledge as of belief, because, (the term knowledge being only applied in common parlance to what is regarded as true, while belief may confessedly be false,) to say that if we are conscious of our knowledge, we must be conscious of that which we know, is not so manifestly ridiculous, as it is to affirm that if we are conscious of a mistaken belief, we must be conscious of a non-existent fact. Yet the one proposition must be equally true with the other, if consciousness of an act involves consciousness of the object of the act. It is over the ruins of this false theory that we must force our way out of the labyrinth in which Sir W. Hamilton has imprisoned us. It may be true, or it may not, that an external world is an object of immediate knowledge. But assuredly we cannot conclude that we have an immediate knowledge of external things, because

Ibid., p. 73.

we have an immediate knowledge of our cognitions of them; whether those cognitions are to be termed belief, with Reid, or knowledge, with Sir W. Hamilton.*

*[i]Mr. Mansel gets over this criticism on Sir W. Hamilton very easily. "Hamilton," he says, "maintains that we cannot be conscious of a mental operation without being conscious of its object. On this Mr. Mill retorts, that if, as Hamilton admits, we are conscious of a belief in the Infinite and the Absolute, we must be conscious of the Infinite and the Absolute themselves; and such consciousness is knowledge. The fallacy of this retort is transparent. The immediate object of Belief is a *proposition* which I hold to be true, not a *thing* apprehended in an act of conception. I believe in an Infinite God; *i.e.*, I believe *that* God is infinite. I believe that the attributes which I ascribe to God exist in him in an infinite degree. Now, to believe this proposition I must, of course, be conscious of its meaning; but I am not therefore conscious of the Infinite God as an object of conception; for this would require further an apprehension of the manner in which these infinite attributes coexist so as to form one object." ([*Philosophy of the Conditioned*,] p. 129n.)

A very simple explanation, if only it be a true one. Sir W. Hamilton had no need to feel embarrassed in applying his doctrine, that the knowledge of an operation involves the knowledge of its object, to the operation called Belief; for the object of Belief is but a proposition, and knowledge of the proposition is the only knowledge required. Strange, that when this explanation stood so obvious, Sir W. Hamilton should have missed it—should not only have felt that there was a difficulty, but remanded it to the abstruser Metaphysics, as part of "one of the most difficult problems of which Metaphysics attempts the solution." [*Lectures*, Vol. IV, p. 73.] Sir W. Hamilton was often confused and inconsistent, but rarely, if ever, on subjects which he had studied, superficial. He would have brushed away Mr. Mansel's distinction with the decisive stroke with which he so often levels a fallacy. The object of Belief is a proposition; but is not the object of Knowledge propositions? Is not all knowledge a series of judgments; and is not a judgment expressed in words, a proposition? It is true that knowledge is of things; but we know things only by their attributes: our knowledge of a thing is made up of our knowledge of a certain number of its attributes, every one of which may be expressed in a proposition. When we are said to know a Thing, the meaning is either that we know it as possessing some attribute, or that we know it and its attributes together as existing. So when we do not know the Thing, but have a belief respecting it, the belief is either that it possesses some attribute, or is a belief of its existence, which is called believing *in* it. When the question is one of attributes, the object of belief is a

[i-i]65[1], 65[2]   In many parts of Sir W. Hamilton's writings, it seems as if the distinction which he draws between knowledge and belief was meant to correspond to the difference between what we can explain by reference to something else, and those ultimate facts and principles which cannot be referred to anything higher. He often speaks of knowledge as resting ultimately on belief, and of ultimate principles as not known, but believed by a necessity of our nature. The distinction is real, but the employment of the words knowledge and belief to express it, is arbitrary and incongruous. To say that we believe the premises, but know the conclusion, would be understood by every one as meaning that we had other independent evidence of the conclusion. If we only know it through the premises, the same name ought in reason to be given to our assurance of both. Accordingly Sir W. Hamilton himself says, in one of the "Dissertations on Reid" ([Note A,] p. 763), that "the principles of our knowledge must be themselves knowledge." And there are few who will not approve this use of language, and condemn the other.

proposition, but so is the object of knowledge. When the question is one of existence, the object of knowledge is a Thing, but so is the object of belief.

The "Inquirer" (pp. 31–3), unlike Mr. Mansel, thinks that this is "a very intricate point;" that there is a real metaphysical difficulty, and that Sir W. Hamilton was aware of it; that he perceived two facts, both true, which he could not reconcile with one another, and that he died without having had time to find the reconciliation. On this I remark, first, that the difficulty is not in reconciling two facts, but two of Sir W. Hamilton's opinions, and that the only solution would be to give up one of them. Secondly, that, whatever the solution might be, he had nearly the whole of his philosophical life to find it in; for the inconsistent opinions are two of the cardinal doctrines of his philosophy. The "Inquirer" thinks that we ought to look indulgently on inconsistencies, as being mere incidents of growth; as indeed they are in a learner, who, independently of his ignorance of Things, is not yet fully master of his own thoughts: but a teacher is supposed to be full grown. While admitting (p. 7) that I have proved against Sir W. Hamilton "continual inconsistencies and discrepancies," the "Inquirer" maintains that all sound philosophy, while incomplete, must be liable to the objection of inconsistency. I confess I cannot see the necessity that our thoughts should be contradictory because our knowledge is incomplete; that because there is much that we do not know, we should not have sufficiently considered what we do know, to avoid holding in conjunction opinions which conflict with one another. The "Inquirer" probably confounds two different things: the belief in contradictories, and the recognition of positive truths which merely limit one another, but to what extent or at what points we cannot yet determine.[i]

CHAPTER IX

Of the Interpretation of Consciousness

ACCORDING TO ALL PHILOSOPHERS, the evidence of Consciousness, if only we can obtain it pure, is conclusive. This is an obvious, but by no means a mere identical proposition. If consciousness be defined as intuitive knowledge, it is indeed an identical proposition to say, that if we intuitively know anything, we do know it, and are sure of it. But the meaning lies in the implied assertion, that we do know some things immediately, or intuitively. That we must do so is evident, if we know anything; for what we know mediately, depends for its evidence on our previous knowledge of something else: unless, therefore, we knew something immediately, we could not know anything mediately, and consequently could not know anything at all. That imaginary being, a complete Sceptic, might be supposed to answer, that perhaps we do not know anything at all. I shall not reply to this problematical antagonist in the usual manner, by telling him that if he does not know anything, I do. I put to him the simplest case conceivable of immediate knowledge, and ask, if we ever feel anything? If so, then, at the moment of feeling, do we know that we feel? Or if he will not call this knowledge, will he deny that when we have a feeling, we have at least some sort of assurance, or conviction, of having it? This assurance or conviction is what other people mean by knowledge. If he dislikes the word, I am willing in discussing with him to employ some other. By whatever name this assurance is called, it is the test to which we bring all our other convictions. He may say it is not certain; but such as it may be, it is our model of certainty. We consider all our other assurances and convictions as more or less certain, according as they approach the standard of this. I have a conviction that there are icebergs in the Arctic seas. I have not had the evidence of my senses for it: I never saw an iceberg. Neither do I intuitively believe it by a law of my mind. My conviction is mediate, grounded on testimony, and on inferences from physical laws. When I say I am convinced of it, I mean that the evidence is equal to that of my senses. I am as certain of the fact as if I had seen it. And, on a more complete analysis, when I say I am convinced of it, what I am convinced of is that if I were in the Arctic seas I should see it. We mean by knowledge, and by certainty, an assurance similar and equal to that afforded by our senses: if the evidence in any other case can be brought up to this, we desire no more. If a person is not satisfied with this evidence, it is no concern of anybody but himself, nor, practically, of himself, since it is admitted that this evidence is what we must, and may with full confidence, act upon. Absolute scepticism, if there be such a thing, may be dismissed from discussion, as raising an irrelevant issue, for in denying all knowledge it denies none. The dogmatist may be quite satisfied if the doctrine he maintains can be attacked by no arguments but those which apply to the evidence of the senses. If his evidence is equal to that, he needs no more; nay, it is philosophically maintainable that by the laws of psychology we can conceive no more, and that this is the certainty which we call perfect.

The verdict, then, of consciousness, or, in other words, our immediate and intuitive conviction, is admitted, on all hands, to be a decision without appeal. The next question is, *to what* does consciousness bear witness? And here, at the outset, a distinction manifests itself, which is laid down by Sir W. Hamilton, and stated, in a very lucid manner, in the first volume of his *Lectures*. I give it in his own words.

A fact of consciousness is that whose existence is given and guaranteed by an original and necessary belief. But there is an important distinction to be here made, which has not only been overlooked by all philosophers, but has led some of the most distinguished into no inconsiderable errors.

The facts of consciousness are to be considered in two points of view; either as evidencing their own ideal or phænomenal existence, or as evidencing the objective existence of something else beyond them. A belief in the former is not identical with a belief in the latter. The one cannot, the other may possibly, be refused. In the case of a common witness, we cannot doubt the fact of his personal reality, nor the fact of his testimony as emitted,—but we can always doubt the truth of that which his testimony avers. So it is with consciousness. We cannot possibly refuse the fact of its evidence as given, but we may hesitate to admit that beyond itself of which it assures us. I shall explain by taking an example. In the act of External Perception, consciousness gives as a conjunct fact, the existence of Me or Self as perceiving, and the existence of something different from Me or Self as perceived. Now the reality of this, as a subjective datum—as an ideal phænomenon—it is absolutely impossible to doubt without doubting the existence of consciousness, for consciousness is itself this fact; and to doubt the existence of consciousness is absolutely impossible; for as such a doubt could not exist except in and through consciousness, it would, consequently, annihilate itself. We should doubt that we doubted. As contained—as given—in an act of consciousness, the contrast of mind knowing and matter known cannot be denied.

But the whole phænomenon as given in consciousness may be admitted, and yet its inference disputed. It may be said, consciousness gives the mental subject as perceiving an external object, contradistinguished from it as perceived: all this we do not, and cannot, deny. But consciousness is only a phænomenon;—the contrast between the subject and object may be only apparent, not real; the object given as an external reality, may only be a mental representation which the mind is, by an unknown law, determined unconsciously to produce, and to mistake for something different from itself. All this may be said and believed, without self-contradiction,—nay, all this has, by the immense majority of modern philosophers, been actually said and believed.

In like manner, in an act of Memory, consciousness connects a present existence with a past. I cannot deny the actual phænomenon, because my denial would be suicidal, but I can without self-contradiction assert that consciousness may be a false witness in regard to any former existence; and I may maintain, if I please, that the memory of the past, in consciousness, is nothing but a phænomenon, which has no reality beyond the present. There are many other facts of consciousness which we cannot but admit as ideal phænomena, but may discredit as guaranteeing aught beyond their phænomenal existence itself. The legality of this doubt I do not at present consider, but only its possibility; all that I have now in view being to show that we must not confound, as has been done, the double import of the facts, and the two degrees of evidence for their reality. This mistake has, among others, been made by Mr. Stewart. . . .

With all the respect to which the opinion of so distinguished a philosopher as Mr. Stewart is justly entitled, I must be permitted to say, that I cannot but regard his assertion that the present existence of the phænomena of consciousness and the reality of that to which these phænomena bear witness, rest on a foundation equally solid—as wholly untenable. The second fact, the fact testified to, may be worthy of all credit—as I agree with Mr. Stewart in thinking that it is; but still it does not rest on a foundation equally solid as the fact of the testimony itself. Mr. Stewart confesses that of the former no doubt had ever been suggested by the boldest sceptic; and the latter, in so far as it assures us of our having an immediate knowledge on the external world,—which is the case alleged by Mr. Stewart,—has been doubted, nay denied, not merely by sceptics, but by modern philosophers almost to a man. This historical circumstance, therefore, of itself, would create a strong presumption, that the two facts must stand on very different foundations; and this presumption is confirmed when we investigate what these foundations themselves are.

The one fact,—the fact of the testimony, is an act of consciousness itself; it cannot, therefore, be invalidated without self-contradiction. For, as we have frequently observed, to doubt of the reality of that of which we are conscious is impossible: for as we can only doubt through consciousness, to doubt of consciousness is to doubt of consciousness by consciousness. If, on the one hand, we affirm the reality of the doubt, we thereby explicitly affirm the reality of consciousness, and contradict our doubt; if, on the other hand, we deny the reality of consciousness, we implicitly deny the reality of our denial itself. Thus, in the act of perception, consciousness gives, as a conjunct fact, an ego or mind, and a non-ego or matter, known together, and contradistinguished from each other. Now, as a present phænomenon, this double fact cannot possibly be denied. I cannot, therefore, refuse the fact, that, in perception, I am conscious of a phænomenon which I am compelled to regard as the attribute of something different from my mind or self. This I must perforce admit, or run into self-contradiction. But admitting this, may I not still, without self-contradiction, maintain that what I am compelled to view as the phænomenon of something different from me is nevertheless (unknown to me) only a modification of my mind? In this I admit the fact of the testimony of consciousness as given, but deny the truth of its report. Whether this denial of the truth of consciousness as a witness is or is not legitimate, we are not, at this moment, to consider: all I have in view at present is, as I said, to show that we must distinguish in consciousness two kinds of facts,—the fact of consciousness testify-ing, and the fact of which consciousness testifies; and that we must not, as Mr. Stewart has done, hold that we can as little doubt of the fact of the existence of an external world, as of the fact that consciousness gives in mutual contrast, the phænomenon of self in contrast to the phænomenon of not-self.*

He adds, that since no doubt has been, or can be, entertained of the facts given in the act of consciousness itself, "it is only the authority of these facts as evidence of something beyond themselves,—that is, only the second class of facts,—which become matter of discussion; it is not the reality of consciousness that we have to prove, but its veracity."[*]

By the conception and clear exposition of this distinction, Sir W. Hamil-ton has contributed materially to make the issues involved in the great question in hand, more intelligible; and the passage is a considerable item for the appreciation both of his philosophy and of his philosophical powers. It is one of the proofs that, whatever be the positive value of his achieve-ments in metaphysics, he had a greater capacity for the subject than many metaphysicians of high reputation, and particularly than his two distin-guished predecessors in the same school of thought, Reid and Stewart.

There are, however, some points in this long extract which are open to criticism. The distinction it draws, is, in the main, beyond question, just. Among the facts which Sir W. Hamilton considers as revelations of con-sciousness, there is one kind which, as he truly says, no one does or can doubt, another kind which they can and do. The facts which cannot be doubted are those to which the word consciousness is by most philosophers confined: the facts of internal consciousness; "the mind's own acts and affections."[†] What we feel, we cannot doubt that we feel. It is impossible to us to feel, and to think that perhaps we feel not, or to feel not, and think that perhaps we feel. What admits of being doubted, is the revelation which consciousness is supposed to make (and which our author considers as itself consciousness) of an external reality. But according to him, though we may doubt this external reality, we are compelled to admit that con-sciousness testifies to it. We may disbelieve our consciousness; but we cannot doubt what its testimony is. This assertion cannot be granted in the same unqualified manner as the others. It is true that I cannot doubt my present impression: I cannot doubt that when I perceive colour or weight, I perceive them as in an object. Neither can I doubt that when I look at two fields, I perceive which of them is the farthest off. The majority of philosophers, however, would not say that perception of distance by the

*Lectures, Vol. I, pp. 271–5. [The references to Stewart are to Philosophical Essays (Edinburgh: Creech and Constable, 1810), pp. 3–11.]
[*Ibid., p. 276.]
[†Ibid., p. 193.]

eye is testified by consciousness; because although we really do so perceive distance, they believe it to be an acquired perception. It is at least possible to think that the reference of our sensible impressions to an external object is, in like manner, acquired; and if so, though a fact of our consciousness in its present artificial state, it would have no claim to the title of a fact of consciousness generally, ᵃor to the unlimited credence given to what is originally consciousnessᵃ. This point of psychology we shall have to discuss farther on.

Another remark needs to be made. All the world admits with our author, that it is impossible to doubt a fact of internal consciousness. To feel, and not to know that we feel, is an impossibility. But Sir W. Hamilton is not satisfied to let this truth rest on its own evidence. He wants a demonstration of it. As if it were not sufficiently proved by consciousness itself, he attempts to prove it by a *reductio ad absurdum*. No one, he says, can doubt consciousness, because, doubt being itself consciousness, to doubt consciousness would be to doubt that we doubt. He sets so high a value on this argument, that he is continually recurring to it in his writings; it actually amounts to a feature of his philosophy.* Yet it seems to me no better than a fallacy. It treats doubt as something positive, like certainty, forgetting that doubt is uncertainty. Doubt is not a state of consciousness, but the negation of a state of consciousness. Being nothing positive, but simply the absence of a belief, it seems to be the one intellectual fact which may be true without self-affirmation of its truth; without our either believing or disbelieving that we doubt. If doubt is anything other than merely negative, it means an insufficient assurance; a disposition to believe, with an inability to believe confidently. But there are degrees of insufficiency; and if we suppose, for argument's sake, that it is possible to doubt consciousness, it may be possible to doubt different facts of consciousness in different degrees. The general uncertainty of consciousness might be the one fact that appeared least uncertain. The saying of Socrates, that the only thing he knew was

---

*It is rather more speciously put in a foot-note on Reid: "To doubt that we are conscious of this or that, is impossible. For the doubt must at least postulate itself; but the doubt is only a datum of consciousness: therefore in postulating its own reality, it admits the truth of consciousness, and consequently annihilates itself." (P. 231n.) In another foot-note he says, "In doubting the fact of his consciousness, the sceptic must at least affirm the fact of his doubt; but to affirm a doubt is to affirm the consciousness of it; the doubt would, therefore, be self-contradictory—*i.e.*, annihilate itself." (P. 442n.) And again: "As doubt is itself only a manifestation of consciousness, it is impossible to doubt that what consciousness manifests, it does manifest, without in thus doubting, doubting that we actually doubt; that is, without the doubt contradicting and therefore annihilating itself." ("Dissertations on Reid," [Note A,] p. 744.)

ᵃ⁻ᵃ65¹, 65², 67   not having been in consciousness from the beginning

that he knew nothing, expresses a conceivable and not inconsistent state of mind.[*] The only thing he felt perfectly sure of may have been that he was sure of nothing else. Omitting Socrates (who was no sceptic as to the reality of knowledge, but only as to its having yet been attained) and endeavouring to conceive the hazy state of mind of a person who doubts the evidence of his senses, it is quite possible to suppose him doubting even whether he doubts. Most people, I should think, must have found themselves in something like this predicament as to particular facts, of which their assurance is all but perfect; they are not quite certain that they are uncertain.*

But though our author's proof of the position is as untenable as it is superfluous, all agree with him in the position itself, that a real fact of consciousness cannot be doubted or denied. Let us now, therefore, return to his distinction between the facts "given in the act of consciousness,"[†] and those "to the reality of which it only bears evidence."[‡] These last, or, in other words, "the *veracity* of consciousness," Sir W. Hamilton thinks it

[*See, e.g., Plato, *Apology*, in *Euthyphro, Apology, Crito, Phædo, Phædrus* (Greek and English), trans. H. N. Fowler (London: Heinemann; Cambridge, Mass.: Harvard University Press, 1917), p. 82 (21ᵈ).]

*In another passage of our author, the same argument reappears in different words, and for a different purpose. He is speaking of the Criterion of Truth. This criterion, he says, "is the necessity determined by the laws which govern our faculties of knowledge, and the consciousness of this necessity is certainty. That the necessity of a cognition, that is, the impossibility of thinking it other than as it is presented—that this necessity, as founded on the laws of thought, is the criterion of truth, is shown by the circumstance that where such necessity is found, all doubt in regard to the correspondence of the cognitive thought and its object must vanish; for to doubt whether what we necessarily think in a certain manner, actually exists as we conceive it, is nothing less than an endeavour to think the necessary as the not necessary or the impossible, which is contradictory." (*Lectures*, Vol. IV, p. 69.)

It is very curious to find Sir W. Hamilton maintaining that our necessities of thought are proof of corresponding realities of existence—that things must actually *be* so and so because it is impossible for us to think them as being otherwise; forgetful of the whole "Philosophy of the Conditioned," and the principle so often asserted by him, that things may, nay, must be true, of which it is impossible for us to conceive even the possibility. But we are here only concerned with his argument, and in that he forgets that to doubt is not a positive but a negative fact. It simply means, not to have any knowledge or assured belief on the subject. Now, how can it be asserted that this negative state of mind is "an endeavour to think" anything? And (even if it were) an endeavour to think a contradiction is not a contradiction. An endeavour to think what cannot be thought, far from being impossible, is the test by which we ascertain its unthinkability. The failure of the endeavour in the case supposed, would not prove that what we were endeavouring to think was unreal, but only that it was unthinkable; which was already assumed in the hypothesis: and our author has carried us round a long circuit, to return to the point from which we set out.

[†*Lectures*, Vol. I, p. 275.]
[‡*Ibid.*, p. 277.]

possible to doubt or deny; he even says, that such facts, more or fewer in number, have been doubted or denied by nearly the whole body of modern philosophers. But this is a statement of the point in issue between Sir W. Hamilton and modern philosophers, the correctness of which, I will venture to affirm that very few if any of them would admit. He represents "nearly the whole body of modern philosophers"[*] as in the peculiar and paradoxical position, of believing that consciousness declares to them and to all mankind the truth of certain facts, and then of disbelieving those facts. That great majority of philosophers of whom Sir W. Hamilton speaks, would, I apprehend, altogether deny this statement. They never dreamed of disputing the veracity of consciousness. They denied what Sir W. Hamilton thinks *it* impossible to deny; the fact of its testimony. They thought it did not testify to the facts to which he thinks it testifies. Had they thought as he does respecting the testimony, they would have thought as he does respecting the facts. As it is, many of them maintained that consciousness gives no testimony to anything beyond itself; that whatever knowledge we possess, or whatever belief we find in ourselves, of anything but the feelings and operations of our own minds, has been acquired subsequently to the first beginnings of our intellectual life, and was not witnessed to by consciousness when it received its first impressions. Others, again, did believe in a testimony of consciousness, but not in the testimony ascribed to it by Sir W. Hamilton. Facts, to which in his opinion it testifies, some of them did not believe at all, others did not believe them to be known intuitively; nay, many of them both believed the facts, and believed that they were known intuitively, and if they differed from Sir W. Hamilton, differed in the merest shadow of a shade; yet it is with these last, as we shall see, that he has his greatest quarrel. In his contest, therefore, with (as he says) the majority of philosophers, Sir W. Hamilton addresses his arguments to the wrong point. He thinks it needless to prove that the testimony to which he appeals, is really given by Consciousness, for that he regards as undenied and undeniable: but he is incessantly proving to us that we ought to believe our consciousness, a thing which few, if any, of his opponents denied.* It is true his appeal is always to the same argument, but that he is never tired of reiterating. It is stated the most systematically in the first Dissertation on Reid, that "on the Philosophy of Common Sense." After

[*Cf. *ibid.*, p. 272.]

*[67] The philosophers who have most insisted on the necessity of a test for consciousness, have always found that test in consciousness itself. Hear Mr. Stirling, the latest of them, who in this respect represents them all: "It is the function of consciousness, though itself infallible, inviolable, and veracious as nothing else is or can be, to test and try and question consciousness to the uttermost" (p. 58).

b-b+72

saying that there are certain primary elements of cognition, manifesting themselves to us as facts of which consciousness assures us, he continues,

How, it is asked, do these primary propositions—these cognitions at first hand— these fundamental facts, feelings, beliefs, certify us of their own veracity? To this the only possible answer is, that as elements of our mental constitution—as the essential conditions of our knowledge, they *must* by us be accepted as true. To suppose their falsehood, is to suppose that we are created capable of intelligence, in order to be made the victims of delusion; that God is a deceiver, and the root of our nature a lie:*

that man is "organized for the attainment, and actuated by the love of truth, only to become the dupe and victim of a perfidious creator."† It appears, therefore, that the testimony of consciousness must be believed, because to disbelieve it, would be to impute mendacity and perfidy to the Creator.

But there is a preliminary difficulty to be here resolved, which may be stated without irreverence. If the proof of the trustworthiness of consciousness is the veracity of the Creator, on what does the Creator's veracity itself rest? Is it not on the evidence of consciousness? The divine veracity can only be known in two ways, 1st, by intuition, or 2ndly, through evidence. If it is known by intuition, it is itself a fact of consciousness, and to have ground for believing it, we must assume that consciousness is trustworthy. Those who say that we have a direct intuition of God, are only saying in other words that consciousness testifies to him. If we hold, on the contrary, with our author, that God is not known by intuition, but proved by evidence, that evidence must rest, in the last resort, on consciousness. All proofs of religion, natural or revealed, must be derived either from the testimony of the senses, or from internal feelings of the mind, or from reasonings of which one or other of these sources supplied the premises. Religion, thus itself resting on the evidence of consciousness, cannot be invoked to prove that consciousness ought to be believed. We must already trust our consciousness, before we can have any evidence of the truth of religion.

I know not whether it is from an obscure sense of this objection to his argument, that Sir W. Hamilton adopts what, in every other point of view, is a very extraordinary limitation of it. After representing the veracity of the Creator as staked on the truth of the testimony of Consciousness, he is content to claim this argument as not amounting to proof, but only to a primâ facie presumption. "Such a supposition" as that of a perfidious creator, "if gratuitous, is manifestly illegitimate." "The data of our original consciousness must, it is evident, *in the first instance*" (the italics are the

*"Dissertations on Reid," [Note A,] p. 743.
†*Ibid.*, p. 745.

author's), "be presumed true. It is only if proved false," which ^{c}it^c can only be by showing them to be inconsistent with one another, "that their authority can, *in consequence of that proof*, be, in the second instance, disallowed."[*] "Neganti incumbit probatio. Nature is not gratuitously to be assumed to work, not only in vain, but in counteraction of herself; our faculty of knowledge is not, without a ground, to be supposed an instrument of illusion."* It is making a very humble claim for the veracity of the Creator, that it should be held valid merely as a presumption, in the absence of contrary evidence; that the Divine Being, like a prisoner at the bar, should be presumed innocent until proved guilty. Far, however, from intending this remark in any invidious sense against Sir W. Hamilton, I regard it as one of his titles to honour, that he has not been afraid, as many men would have been, to subject a proposition surrounded by reverence to the same logical treatment as any other statement, and has not felt himself obliged, as a philosopher, to consider it from the first as final. My complaint ^{d}could only be^d, that his logic is not sufficiently consistent ^{e}; and that the^e divine veracity is entitled either to more or to less weight than he accords to it. He is bound by the laws of correct reasoning to prove his premise without the aid of the conclusion which he means to draw from it. If he can do this—if the divine veracity is certified by stronger evidence than the testimony of consciousness, it may be appealed to, not merely as a presumption, but as a proof. If not, it is entitled to no place in the discussion, even as a presumption. There is no intermediate position for it, good enough for the one purpose, but not good enough for the other. It would be a new view of the fallacy of *petitio principii* to contend that a conclusion is no *proof* of the premises from which it is deduced, but is primâ facie evidence of them.

Our author, however, cannot be convicted of *petitio principii*. Though he has not stated, I think he has enabled us to see, in what manner he avoided it. True, he has deduced the trustworthiness of consciousness from the veracity of the Deity; and the veracity of the Deity can only be known from the evidence of consciousness. But he may fall back upon the distinction between facts given in consciousness itself, and facts "to the reality of which it only bears evidence."[†] It is for the trustworthiness of these last, that he assigns as presumptive evidence (which the absence of counter-evidence raises into proof) the divine veracity. That veracity itself, he may

[*Ibid., p. 743.]
*Ibid., p. 745.
[†Lectures, Vol. I, p. 275.]

$^{c-c}$+67, 72
$^{d-d}$65^1, 65^2 is
$^{e-e}$65^1, 65^2 The

say, is proved by consciousness, but to prove it requires only the other class of facts of consciousness, those given in the act of consciousness itself. There are thus two steps in the argument. "The phænomena of consciousness considered merely in themselves," with reference to which "scepticism is confessedly impossible,"* suffice (we must suppose him to think) for proving the divine veracity; and that veracity, being proved, is in its turn a reason for trusting the testimony which consciousness pronounces to facts without and beyond itself.

Unless, therefore, Sir W. Hamilton was guilty of a paralogism, by adducing religion in proof of what is necessary to the proof of religion, his opinion must have been that our knowledge of God rests upon the affirmation which Consciousness makes of itself, and not of anything beyond itself; that the divine existence and attributes may be proved without assuming that consciousness testifies to anything but our own feelings and mental operations. If this be so, we have Sir W. Hamilton's authority for affirming, that even the most extreme form of philosophical scepticism, the Nihilism (as our author calls it)[*] of Hume, which denies the objective existence of both Matter and Mind, does not touch the evidences of Natural Religion. And it really does not touch any evidences but such as religion can well spare. But what a mass of religious prejudice has been directed against this philosophical doctrine, on the strength of what we have now Sir W. Hamilton's authority for treating as a mere misapprehension.[†]

But something more is necessary to render the divine veracity available in support of the testimony of consciousness, against those, if such there be, who admit the fact of the testimony, but hesitate to admit its truth. The divine veracity can only be implicated in the truth of anything, by proving that the Divine Being intended it to be believed. As it is not pretended that he has made any revelation in the matter, his intention can only be inferred from the *result*: and our author draws the inference from his having made it an original and indestructible part of our nature that our consciousness should declare to us certain facts. Now this is what the philosophers who disbelieve the facts, would not, any of them, admit. Many indeed have

*"Dissertations on Reid," [Note A,] p. 745.

[*See, e.g., *Lectures*, Vol. I, p. 294.]

[†]Accordingly Sir W. Hamilton says elsewhere: "Religious disbelief and philosophical scepticism are not merely not the same, but have no natural connexion." I regret that this statement is followed by a declaration that the former "must ever be a matter" not merely "of regret," but of "reprobation." This imputation of moral blame to an opinion sincerely entertained and honestly arrived at, is a blot which one would willingly not have found in a thinker of so much ability, and in general of so high a moral tone. (*Lectures*, Vol. I, App. i, p. 394.)

*-*65¹, 65²   fact

admitted that we have a *natural tendency* to believe something which they considered to be an illusion: but it cannot be affirmed that God intended us to do whatever we have a natural tendency to. On every theory of the divine government, it is carried on, intellectually as well as morally, not by the mere indulgence of our natural tendencies, but by the regulation and control of them. One philosopher, Hume, has said that the tendency in question seems to be an "instinct," and has called a psychological doctrine, which he regarded as groundless, an "universal and primary opinion of all men." But he never dreamed of saying that we are compelled by our nature to believe it; on the contrary, he says that this illusive opinion "is soon destroyed by the slightest philosophy."[*] Of all eminent thinkers, the one who comes nearest to our author's description of those who reject the testimony of consciousness, is Kant. That philosopher did maintain that there is an illusion inherent in our constitution; that we cannot help conceiving as belonging to Things themselves, attributes with which they are only clothed by the laws of our sensitive and intellectual faculties.[†] But he *g*drew a marked distinction between an illusion and a delusion. He*g* did not believe in a mystification practised on us by the Supreme Being, nor would he have admitted that God intended us permanently to mistake the conditions of our mental conceptions for properties of the things themselves. If God has provided us with the means of correcting an error, it is probable that he does not intend us to be misled by it: and in matters speculative as well as practical, it surely is more religious to see the purposes of God in the dictates of our deliberate reason, than in those of a "blind and powerful instinct of nature."[‡]

As regards almost all, however, if not all philosophers, it may truly be said, that the questions which have divided them have never turned on the veracity of consciousness. Consciousness, in the sense usually attached to it by philosophers,—consciousness of the mind's own feelings and operations, cannot, as our author truly says, be disbelieved. The inward fact, the feeling in our own minds, was never doubted, since to do so would be to doubt that we feel what we feel. What our author calls the *testimony* of consciousness to something beyond itself, may be, and is, denied; but what is denied, has almost always been that consciousness gives the testimony; not that, if given, it must be believed.

At first sight it might seem as if there could not possibly be any doubt

[*David Hume, "Of the Academical or Sceptical Philosophy," Section xii of *An Inquiry Concerning Human Understanding*, in *Essays and Treatises on Several Subjects*, 2 vols. (Edinburgh: Cadell, 1793), Vol. II, p. 169.]

[† See *Kritik der Reinen Vernunft*, pp. 238–50.]

[‡Hume, "Of the Academical or Sceptical Philosophy," p. 169.]

g–g +67, 72

whether our consciousness does or does not affirm any given thing. Nor can there, if consciousness means, as it usually does, self-consciousness. If consciousness tells me that I have a certain thought or sensation, I assuredly have that thought or sensation. But if consciousness, as with Sir W. Hamilton, means a power which can tell me things that are not phænomena of my own mind, there is immediately the broadest divergence of opinion as to what are the things *to* which consciousness testifies. There is nothing which people do not think and say that they know by consciousness, provided they do not remember any time when they did not know or believe it, and are not aware in what manner they came by the belief. For Consciousness, in this extended sense, is, as *I* have so often observed, but another word for Intuitive Knowledge: and whatever other things we may know in that manner, we certainly do not know by intuition what knowledge is intuitive. It is a subject on which both the vulgar and the ablest thinkers are constantly making mistakes. No one is better aware of this than Sir W. Hamilton. I transcribe a few of the many passages in which he has acknowledged it. "Errors" may arise by attributing to "intelligence as necessary and original data, what are only contingent generalizations from experience, and consequently, make no part of its complement of native truths."* And again: "Many philosophers have attempted to establish on the principles of common sense propositions which are not original data of consciousness; while the original data of consciousness, from which their propositions were derived, and to which they owed their whole necessity and truth—these data the same philosophers were (strange to say) not disposed to admit."† It fares still worse with the philosophers chargeable with this error, when Sir W. Hamilton comes into personal controversy with them. M. Cousin's mode of proceeding, for example, he characterizes thus: "Assertion is substituted for proof; facts of consciousness are alleged, which consciousness never knew; and paradoxes that baffle argument, are promulgated as intuitive truths, above the necessity of confirmation."‡ M. Cousin's particular misinterpretation of consciousness was, as we saw, that of supposing that each of its acts testifies to three things, of which three

Lectures, Vol. IV, p. 137. There are writers of reputation in the present day, who maintain in unqualified terms, that we know by intuition the impossibility of miracles. "La négation du miracle," says M. [Auguste] Nefftzer ["*La Vie de Jésus* par M. Ernest Renan,"] (*Revue Germanique* [*et Française*, XXVIII] for September 1863, p. 183), "n'est pas subordonnée à l'expérience; elle est une nécessité logique et un fait de certitude interne; elle doit être le premier article du *credo* de tout historien et de tout penseur."

†"Dissertations on Reid," [Note A,] p. 749.

‡*Discussions*, p. 25.

h–h+67, 72
*i–i*65¹, 65² we

Sir W. Hamilton thinks that it testifies only to one. Besides the finite element, consisting of a Self and a Not-self, M. Cousin believes that there are directly revealed in Consciousness an Infinite (God) and a relation between this Infinite and the Finite.[*] But it is not only M. Cousin who, in our author's opinion, mistakes the testimony of consciousness. He brings the same charge against a thinker with whom he agrees much oftener than with M. Cousin; against Reid. That philosopher, as we have seen, is of opinion, contrary to Sir W. Hamilton, that we have an immediate knowledge of things past. This is to be conscious of them in Sir W. Hamilton's sense of the word, though not in Reid's. Finally, Sir W. Hamilton imputes a similar error, no longer to any particular metaphysician, but to the world at large. He says that we do not see the sun, but only a luminous image, in immediate contiguity to the eye, and that no two persons see the same sun, but every person a different one. Now it is assuredly the universal belief of mankind that all of them see the same sun, and that this is the very sun which rises and sets, and which is 95 (or according to more recent researches 92) millions of miles distant from the earth. Nor can any of the appeals of Reid and Sir W. Hamilton from the sophistries of metaphysicians to Common Sense and the universal sentiment of mankind, be more emphatic than that to which Sir W. Hamilton here lays himself open from Reid and from the non-metaphysical world.*

[*Cf. pp. 34–7 above.]
*Reid himself places the "natural belief" which Sir W. Hamilton rejects, on exactly the level of those which he most strenuously maintains, saying in a passage which our author himself quotes, "The vulgar are firmly persuaded that the very identical objects which they perceive continue to exist when they do not perceive them: and are no less firmly persuaded that when ten men look at the sun or the moon, they all see the same individual object." (On the Intellectual Powers, p. 284.) And Reid avows that he agrees with the vulgar in both opinions. But Sir W. Hamilton, while he upholds the former of these as one to deny which would be to declare our nature a lie, thinks that nothing can be more absurd than the latter of them. "Nothing," he says, "can be conceived more ridiculous than the opinion of philosophers in regard to this. For example, it has been curiously held (and Reid is no exception) that in looking at the sun, moon, or any other object of sight, we are, on the one doctrine, actually conscious of these distant objects, or, on the other, that these distant objects are those really represented in the mind. Nothing can be more absurd: we perceive, through no sense, aught external but what is in immediate relation and in immediate contact with its organ. . . . Through the eye we perceive nothing but the rays of light in relation to, and in contact with, the retina." (Lectures, Vol. II, pp. 129–30.)
The basis of the whole Ideal System, which it is thought to be the great merit of Reid to have exploded, was a natural prejudice, supposed to be intuitively evident, namely, that that which knows, must be of a similar nature [j]to[j] that which is known

j–j651, 652 with

We see, therefore, that it is not enough to say that something is testified by Consciousness, and refer all dissentients to Consciousness to prove it. Substitute for Consciousness the equivalent phrase (in our author's acceptation at least) Intuitive Knowledge, and it is seen that this is not a thing which can be proved by mere introspection of ourselves. Introspection can show us a present belief or conviction, attended with a greater or a less difficulty in accommodating the thoughts to a different view of the subject: but that this belief, or conviction, or knowledge, if we call it so, is intuitive, no mere introspection can ever show; unless we are at liberty to assume that every mental process which is now as unhesitating and as rapid as intuition, was intuitive at its outset. Reid, in his commencements at least, often expressed himself as if he believed this to be the case: Sir W. Hamilton, wiser than Reid, knew better. With him (at least in his better moments) the question, what is and is not revealed by Consciousness, is a question for philosophers. "The first problem of philosophy" is "to seek out, purify, and establish, by intellectual analysis and criticism, the elementary feelings or beliefs, in which are given the elementary truths of which all are in possession:" this problem, he admits, is "of no easy accomplishment;" and the "argument from common sense" is thus

manifestly dependent on philosophy as an art, as an acquired dexterity, and cannot, notwithstanding the errors which they have so frequently committed, be taken out of the hands of the philosophers. Common Sense is like Common Law. Each may be laid down as the general rule of decision; but in the one case it must be left to the

---

by it. "This principle," says our author, "has, perhaps, exerted a more extensive influence on speculation than any other. . . . It would be easy to show that the belief, explicit or implicit, that what knows and what is immediately known must be of an analogous nature, lies at the root of almost every theory of cognition, from the very earliest to the very latest speculations. . . . And yet it has not been proved, and is incapable of proof,—nay, is contradicted by the evidence of consciousness itself." (Foot-note to Reid, p. 300n.)

But though Sir W. Hamilton manifests himself thus thoroughly aware how wide the differences of opinion may be and are respecting our intuitive perceptions, I by no means intend to deny that he on certain occasions affirms the contrary. In the fourth volume of the *Lectures* (p. 95), he says, "I have here limited the possibility of error to Probable Reasoning, for in Intuition and Demonstration, there is but little possibility of important error." After a certain amount of reading of Sir W. Hamilton, one is used to these contradictions. What he here asserts to be so nearly impossible, that no account needs to be taken of it in a classification of Error, he is continually fighting against in detail, and imputing to nearly all philosophers. And when he says that the "revelation" of consciousness is "naturally clear," (*ibid.*, Vol. I, p. 266,) and only mistaken by philosophers because they resort to it solely for confirmation of their own opinions, he *k*merely transports*k* into psychology the dogmatism of theologians.

*k-k*65¹, 65²   is merely transporting

jurist, in the other to the philosopher, to ascertain what are the contents of the rule; and though in both instances the common man may be cited as a witness for the custom or the fact, in neither can he be allowed to officiate as advocate or as judge.*

So far, good. But now, it being conceded that the question, what do we know intuitively, or, in Sir W. Hamilton's phraseology, what does our consciousness testify, is not, as might be supposed, a matter of simple self-examination, but of science, it has still to be determined in what manner science should set about it. And here emerges the distinction between two different methods of studying the problems of metaphysics, forming the radical difference between the two great schools into which metaphysicians are fundamentally divided. One of these I shall call, for distinction, the introspective method; the other, the psychological.

The elaborate and acute criticism on the philosophy of Locke, which is perhaps the most striking portion of M. Cousin's *Lectures on the History of Philosophy*, sets out with a remark which sums up the characteristics of the two great schools of mental philosophy, by a summary description of their methods. M. Cousin observes, that Locke went wrong from the beginning, by placing before himself, as the question to be first resolved, the *origin* of our ideas.[*] This was commencing at the wrong end. The proper course would have been to begin by determining what the ideas now are; to ascertain what it is that consciousness actually tells us, postponing till afterwards the attempt to frame a theory concerning the origin of any of the mental phænomena.

I accept the question as M. Cousin states it, and I contend, that no attempt to determine what are the direct revelations of consciousness, can be successful, or entitled to any regard, unless preceded by what M. Cousin says ought only to follow it, an inquiry into the origin of our acquired ideas. For we have it not in our power to ascertain, by any direct process, what Consciousness told us at the time when its revelations were in their pristine purity. It only offers itself to our inspection as it exists now, when those original revelations are overlaid and buried under a mountainous heap of acquired notions and perceptions.

It seems to M. Cousin that if we examine, with care and minuteness, our present states of consciousness, distinguishing and defining every ingredient which we find to enter into them—every element that we seem to recognise as real, and cannot, by merely concentrating our attention upon it, analyse into anything simpler—we reach the ultimate and primary truths, which are the sources of all our knowledge, and which cannot be

*"Dissertations on Reid," [Note A,] p. 752.
[*See Victor Cousin, *Cours de philosophie. Histoire de la philosophie du dix-huitième siècle*, 2 vols. (Brussels: Hauman, 1836), Vol. II, pp. 114 ff. (17e leçon).]

denied or doubted without denying or doubting the evidence of consciousness itself, that is, the only evidence which there is for anything. I maintain this to be a misapprehension of the conditions imposed on inquirers by the difficulties of psychological investigation. To begin the inquiry at the point where M. Cousin takes it up, is in fact to beg the question. For he must be aware, if not of the fact, at least of the belief of his opponents, that the laws of the mind—the laws of association according to one class of thinkers, the Categories of the Understanding according to another—are capable of creating, out of those data of consciousness which are uncontested, purely mental conceptions, which become so identified in thought with all our states of consciousness, that we seem, and cannot but seem, to receive them by direct intuition; and, for example, the belief in Matter, in the opinion of some of these thinkers, is, or at least may be, thus produced. Idealists, and Sceptics, contend that the belief in Matter is not an original fact of consciousness, as our sensations are, and is therefore wanting in the requisite which, in M. Cousin's and Sir W. Hamilton's opinion, gives to our subjective convictions objective authority. Now, be these persons right or wrong, they cannot be refuted in the mode in which M. Cousin and Sir W. Hamilton attempt to do so—by appealing to Consciousness itself. For we have no means of interrogating consciousness in the only circumstances in which it is possible for it to give a trustworthy answer. Could we try the experiment of the first consciousness in any infant—its first reception of the impressions which we call external; whatever was present in that first consciousness would be the genuine testimony of Consciousness, and would be as much entitled to credit, indeed there would be as little possibility of discrediting it, as our sensations themselves. But we have no means of now ascertaining, by direct evidence, whether we were conscious of outward and extended objects when we first opened our eyes to the light. That a belief or knowledge of such objects is in our consciousness now, whenever we use our eyes or our muscles, is no reason for concluding that it was there from the beginning, until we have settled the question whether it could possibly have been brought in since. If any mode can be pointed out in which within the compass of possibility it might have been brought in, the hypothesis must be examined and disproved before we are entitled to conclude that the conviction is an original deliverance of consciousness. The proof that any of the alleged Universal Beliefs, or Principles of Common Sense, are affirmations of consciousness, supposes two things; that the beliefs exist, and that *there are no means by which they could* have been acquired. The first is in most cases undisputed, but the second is a subject of inquiry which often taxes the utmost resources of psychology.

*−*65[1], 65[2]   they cannot possibly

Locke was therefore right in believing that "the origin of our ideas" is the main stress of the problem of mental science, and the subject which must be first considered in forming the theory of the Mind.[*] Being unable to examine the actual contents of our consciousness until our earliest, which are necessarily our most firmly knit associations, those which are most intimately interwoven with the original data of consciousness, are fully formed, we cannot study the original elements of mind in the facts of our present consciousness. Those original elements can only come to light as residual phænomena, by a previous study of the modes of generation of the mental facts which are confessedly not original; a study sufficiently thorough to enable us to apply its results to the convictions, beliefs, or supposed intuitions which seem to be original, and to determine whether some of them may not have been generated in the same modes, so early as to have become inseparable from our consciousness before the time ^{m}to which memory goes back^m. This mode of ascertaining the original elements of mind I call ^{n}, for want of a better word,^{n} the psychological, as distinguished from the simply introspective mode. It is the known and approved method of physical science, adapted to the necessities of psychology. *

It might be supposed from incidental expressions of Sir W. Hamilton, that he was alive to the need of a methodical scientific investigation, to determine what portion of our "natural beliefs" are really original, and what are inferences, or acquired impressions, mistakenly deemed intuitive. To the declarations already quoted to this effect, the following may be added. Speaking of Descartes' plan, of commencing philosophy by a reconsidera-

[*See *Essay Concerning Human Understanding*, *Works*, Vol. I, pp. 82–98 (Bk. II, Chap. i).]

*[67] The "Inquirer" thinks he refutes the preceding paragraph when he says that Consciousness may not have given its full revelation in the infant, and that it would be "contrary to all analogy" to suppose "that consciousness alone, of all our natural properties, needs no development, no education." (P. 52.) If this supposed improvement of consciousness by exercise be admitted, it goes even harder with the Introspective Method than I had maintained. I pointed out an experiment not realizable, but conceivable, which by ascertaining the contents of consciousness antecedently to any acquired experience, would authenticate as the original data of consciousness whatever that experiment revealed. But if consciousness does not tell its tale at once, but requires time and practice to tell it, and does not get it completed until there has been time for impressions originating in experience to be formed, then there is no period at which the Introspective Method, applied to the case, would yield a conclusive result: the natural and acquired testimonies of consciousness are inseparably blended at every stage, and to separate them by mere self-observation, and show that any particular item belongs to the one and not to the other, involves a double impossibility, instead of the single one I contended for.

$^{m-m}65^1$, 65^2, 67   at which memory commences
$^{n-n}$+67, 72

tion of all our fundamental opinions,[*] he says, "There are among our prejudices, or pretended cognitions, a great many hasty conclusions, the investigation of which requires much profound thought, skill, and acquired knowledge. . . . To commence philosophy by such a review, it is necessary for a man to be a philosopher before he can attempt to become one."* And he elsewhere bestows high praise upon Aristotle for not falling "into the error of many modern philosophers, in confounding the natural and necessary with the habitual and acquired connexions of thought," nor attempting "to evolve the conditions under which we think from the tendencies generated by thinking;"† a praise which cannot be bestowed on our author himself. But, notwithstanding the ample concession which he appeared to make when he admitted that the problem was one of extreme difficulty, essentially scientific, and ought to be reserved for philosophers, I regret to say that he as completely sets at naught the only possible method of solving it, as M. Cousin himself. He even expresses his contempt for that method. Speaking of Extension, he says, "It is truly an idle problem to attempt imagining the steps by which we may be supposed to have acquired the notion of Extension, when, in fact, we are unable to imagine to ourselves the possibility of that notion not being always in our possession."‡ That things which we "are unable to imagine to ourselves the possibility of," may be, and many of them must be, true, was a doctrine which we thought we had learnt from the author of the Philosophy of the Conditioned. That we cannot imagine a time at which we had no knowledge of Extension, is no evidence that there has not been such a time. There are mental laws, recognised by Sir W. Hamilton himself, which would inevitably cause such a state of things to become inconceivable to us, even if it once existed. There are artificial inconceivabilities equal in strength to any natural. Indeed it is questionable if there are any natural inconceivabilities, or if anything is inconceivable to us for any other reason than because Nature does not afford the combinations in experience which are necessary to make it conceivable.

I do not think that there can be found, in all Sir W. Hamilton's writings, a single instance in which, before registering a belief as a part of our consciousness from the beginning, he thinks it necessary to ascertain that it °cannot° have grown up subsequently. He demands, indeed, "that no fact be assumed as a fact of consciousness but what is ultimate and simple." But

[*See Descartes, *Dissertatio de Methodo*, in *Opera Philosophica*, 4th ed. (Amsterdam: Elzevir, 1664), pp. 6 ff. (II).]

Lectures, Vol. IV, p. 92.
†"Dissertations on Reid," [Note D**,] p. 894n.
‡*Ibid.*, [Note D*,] p. 882.

°-°65¹, 65²   could not

to pronounce it ultimate, the only condition he requires is that we be not able to "reduce it to a generalization from experience." This condition is realized by its possessing the "character of necessity." "It must be impossible not to think it. In fact, by its necessity alone can we recognise it as an original datum of intelligence, and distinguish it from any mere result of generalization and custom."* In this Sir W. Hamilton is at one with the whole of his own section of the philosophical world; with Reid, with Stewart, with Cousin, with Whewell, *p*and we may add, with Kant*p*.† The test by which they all decide a belief to be a part of our primitive consciousness—an original intuition of the mind—is the necessity of thinking it. Their proof that we must always, from the beginning, have had the belief, is the impossibility of getting rid of it now. This argument, applied to any of the disputed questions of philosophy, is doubly illegitimate: neither the major nor the minor premise is admissible. For, in the first place, the very fact that the *q*questions are*q* disputed, disproves the alleged impossibility. Those against *r*whose dissent*r* it is needful to defend the belief which

Lectures, Vol. I, pp. 268–70.

†[67] In the first edition I added, "and even with Mr. Herbert Spencer:" but that powerful thinker, in his paper in the *Fortnightly Review*, disclaims the doctrine. [See "Mill *versus* Hamilton," *Fortnightly Review*, I (15 July, 1865), 536–9.] As I now understand Mr. Spencer, he maintains that the impossibility of getting rid of a belief is a proof of its truth, and also of its being a primary, or ultimate, truth, but not of its being intuitive, since even our primary forms of thought are, in Mr. Spencer's opinion, products of experience, either our own, or inherited by us from ancestors by the laws of the development of organization. I had confounded the two ideas, of a primary truth and an intuitive truth, which had never, as far as I know, been distinguished by any one except Mr. Spencer; and had, therefore, identified his theory with the ordinary doctrine of the intuitive philosophy; which I now see to be a misconception, though I think both theories open to refutation by the same arguments, and the difference between them not material to the test of truth, though highly important to psychology. [Cf. *p-p* below.]

I perceive also that I was mistaken, when, in an early chapter of this work (Chap.

*p-p*65¹, 65²   we may add, with Kant, and even with Mr. Herbert Spencer   [*at the end of the text in* 65² (*cf.* 504*m*) *the following note (partly reproduced in* 143n *above) appears:*] Addendum./Note to p. 150./After this page had passed through the press, there appeared in the fifth number of the *Fortnightly Review*, a paper by Mr. Herbert Spencer, discussing several of the philosophical questions which divide me from that powerful thinker, and especially the question whether inconceivability is a test of truth. As I have no special controversy with Mr. Spencer in the present work, some other occasion would be more suitable for an examination of his arguments; but since he expresses surprise at my having classed him with Sir W. Hamilton and others, as one of those whose test for deciding a belief to be an original intuition of the mind, is the necessity of thinking it, I deem it right that the same volume in which his opinion has been erroneously stated, should contain the correction. As I . . . *as* 72 . . . I had, in truth, confounded . . . *as* 72 . . . with that of the intuitive school, which . . . *as* 72 . . . refutation by substantially the same arguments.

*q-q*65¹, 65²   question is

*r-r*65¹, 65²   whom

is affirmed to be necessary, are unmistakeable examples that it is not necessary. It may be a necessary belief to those who think it so; they may personally be quite incapable of not holding it. But even if this incapability extended to all mankind, it might be merely the effect of a strong associa-

---

ii [p. 10]) I classed Mr. Spencer among the philosophers who hold, in its widest sense, the doctrine of the Relativity of human knowledge: for the external things which, he contends, we cannot help believing to be connected with all our sensations, are not, according to him, entirely uncognizable by us. [See *ibid.*, pp. 546–8.] On the contrary, he believes that "the more or less coherent relations among" one's "states of consciousness, are generated by experience of the more or less constant relations in something beyond his consciousness:" *i.e.*, that for every proposition which we can truly assert about the similitudes, successions, and coexistences of our states of consciousness, there is a corresponding similitude, succession, or coexistence really obtaining among Noumena beyond our consciousness, and even that we can have "experience" of the same. (*Ibid.*, p. 548.) This prodigious amount of knowledge respecting the "Unknowable" is only consistent with the doctrine of Relativity if we understand that doctrine in the very limited sense in which Sir W. Hamilton holds it. This abates nothing from the value of the psychological analyses due to Mr. Spencer, whose services to philosophy as an applier and defender of the "experience hypothesis" are beyond all price.

Mr. Spencer, in the same paper, adheres to his doctrine that the test of truth in the last resort is the inconceivability of its negation, and maintains that doctrine with his usual argumentative power. In one part of his argument, he seems to put a sense upon it which would leave little, if any, difference between his opinion and my own. He seems to say that the proposition, Things equal to the same thing are equal to one another, is known to be true by the inconceivability of its negation, in the same manner in which it might be said that two unequal lines placed side by side are known to be unequal by the inconceivability of their being equal, *i.e.*, "I find it impossible, while contemplating the lines, to get rid of the consciousness" of their inequality. (*Ibid.*, p. 539.) If the inconceivableness of the negative only means that I cannot resist the evidence of my senses for the affirmative, I have no objection to admit this as the test of any truth, even a geometrical axiom. I believe that my knowledge of the axiom is of exactly the same kind as my knowledge of the inequality of the two lines: I know it because I see it; and as I cannot have this positive intuition together with its negative, this may be called, if any one pleases, the inconceivability of the negative. But I do not therefore rest the belief that things equal to the same thing are equal to one another on an *à priori* incapacity of my mind to conceive them unequal. I believe that I am only unable to conceive them unequal because I have always seen them to be equal, and am renewing that experience at almost every instant of my life.

Mr. Spencer asks, If an axiom of mathematics is said to be known "only by induction from personal experiences," "on what warrant are personal experiences asserted? The testimony of experience is given only through memory," and the "trustworthiness of memory" is open to more doubt than the "immediate consciousness" of the mathematical truth. (*Ibid.*, p. 549.) Instead, however, of immediate consciousness, let us call it immediate observation, which is a mode of consciousness, and the "personal experiences" which it yields become the most certain evidence which it is possible to have: not depending upon memory, but upon

tion; like the impossibility of believing Antipodes; and it cannot be shown that even where the impossibility is, for the time, real, it might not, as in that case, be overcome. The history of science teems with inconceivabilities which have been conquered, and supposed necessary truths which have first ceased to be thought necessary, then to be thought true, and have finally come to be deemed impossible.* These philosophers,

---

direct perception, which can be repeated at any moment; corroborated, however, by a vast mass of memories, both of our own and of other people, which by their number, ubiquity, and variety operate as a complete insurance against the possible error of memory in any single instance.

*[67] Mr. Mahaffy, after distinguishing, as I have done, between the two kinds of so-called inconceivables [see pp. 69ff. above], the Unimaginable and the simply Incredible, says, "There seems to be a definite distinction between them, not of degree, but of kind. We may safely defy Mr. Mill to point out a case where an unimaginable (inconceivable) was proved true, or even possible. And the reason is plain. The latter depends upon the form of the thinking or intuiting faculty; the former, merely upon empirical association." (Pp. viii–ix.) In Mr. Mahaffy's philosophical system the distinction passes for one of kind, but he must surely see that it admits of being construed as a difference only of degree. If an empirical association between two ideas, not so strong as to be altogether irresistible, makes it difficult to image in our own minds the corresponding facts as disjoined, it is but rational to believe that a stronger empirical association, produced by still more incessant repetition, will convert that difficulty into a conditional impossibility; an inability only to be overcome by contrary experience, which experience the conditions of our terrestrial existence may not permit. And if, as I have before observed, "a mental association between two facts, which is not intense enough to make their separation unimaginable, may yet create, and if there are no counter-associations, always does create, more or less of difficulty in believing that the two can exist apart; a difficulty often amounting to a local or temporary impossibility;" [p. 75 above] an association which is so intense as to make the separation unimaginable, may surely create an impossibility of belief, not local or temporary, but as durable as the experience which gave rise to the association.

Mr. Spencer, who is almost willing to rest the claims of inconceivability as a test of truth on its expressing "the net result of our experience up to the present time," has given an excellent exposition of this point. ["Mill *versus* Hamilton," p. 536.] He sees clearly that the difference between the two kinds of inconceivable is only one of degree—the degree of strength of the cohesion between the two ideas. The proposition "the ice was hot" he justly classes as not unimaginable, but merely unbelievable; the unbelievableness, however, arising from a difficulty, though not amounting to an impossibility, of combining the two ideas in a representation. "The elements of the proposition cannot be put together in thought without great resistance. Between those other states of consciousness which the word ice connotes, and the state of consciousness named cold, there is an extremely strong cohesion—a cohesion measured by the resistance to be overcome in thinking of the ice as hot." (*Ibid.*, p. 543.) The merely unbelievable is thus distinguished from Mr. Mahaffy's unimaginable, not by a generic difference, but by a minor degree of unimaginability. And the seeming incredibility is strictly proportioned to the degree of difficulty in combining the two thoughts in one representation.

therefore, and among them Sir W. Hamilton, mistake altogether the true conditions of psychological investigation, when, instead of proving a belief to be an original fact of consciousness by showing that it *cannot, by any known means,* have been acquired, they conclude that it was not acquired, for the reason, often false, and never sufficiently substantiated, that our consciousness cannot get rid of it now.

Since, then, Sir W. Hamilton not only neglects, but repudiates, the only scientific mode of ascertaining our original beliefs, what does he mean by

---

With regard to Mr. Mahaffy's assertion, that nothing unimaginable has ever been "proved true, or even possible;" the point would have been more effectually maintained if he could have said "nothing which *seemed* unimaginable;" for whatever has been "proved true" or even "possible" has thereby become imaginable. People had much difficulty, and most people have some difficulty still, in representing to themselves sunrise as a motion not of the sun but of the earth; but no one has called this notion of sunrise either inconceivable or unimaginable after knowing it to be the true notion. Let us first, then, state the question correctly: Has anything which *seemed* unimaginable been proved true, or possible? It is hardly practicable to give such an answer to this question as will silence the retort, that what was called unimaginable was really no more than incredible; for since unimaginableness, as I have said, exists in numerous degrees, graduating from a slight difficulty to at least a temporary impossibility, there is no definite line of demarcation between the absolutely unimaginable (if there be such a thing) and the totally incredible, nor even between what is unimaginable by a given person, and what is merely incredible to him. Most of the questions which lie on that border land are still disputed. For example: is a creation *a nihilo*, or Matter capable of thinking, unimaginable, or only incredible? Both the one and the other are habitually ranked among the most unimaginable of all things. Yet the one is firmly believed by all Materialists, and the other by all Christians. Every Materialist, therefore, and every Christian, may be called as a witness that things which are unimaginable are not only possible but true. To take another instance—an event without a cause. Is that unimaginable, or only incredible? All who regard the category of Cause and Effect as a necessity of thought, including Sir W. Hamilton, and Mr. Mahaffy himself [pp. iii–xvi], maintain it to be unimaginable. Yet most of these believe it to be both possible and true in the case of human freewill. Not only therefore what to one man seems unimaginable, another believes to be true, but the same man believes to be true what to himself seems unimaginable: witness the whole Philosophy of the Conditioned.

Dr. M'Cosh thinks that antipodes were unbelievable, not in consequence of an association, but because "the alleged fact seemed contrary to a law of nature established by observation. A gathered experience seemed to show that there was an absolute up and down, and that heavy bodies tended downwards." ([*Examination*,] p. 240.) Of course it was the apparent experience that generated the association. But if there had been no more in the matter than an intellectual conviction, the conviction would have given way as soon as any one made the remark that the experience was confined to a region in which the direction of *down* coincided with direction towards the earth. It is because our intellectual convictions generate temporarily inseparable associations, that they give way so slowly before evidence.

*–*65[1], 65[2]   could not

treating the question as one of science, and in what manner does he apply science to it? Theoretically, he claims for science an exclusive jurisdiction over the whole domain, but practically he gives it nothing to do except to settle the relations of the supposed intuitive beliefs among themselves. It is the province of science, he thinks, to resolve some of these beliefs into others. He prescribes, as ʻaʻ rule of judgment, what he calls "the Law of Parcimony." No greater number of ultimate beliefs are to be postulated than is strictly indispensable. Where one such belief can be looked upon as a particular case of another—the belief in Matter, for instance, of the cognition of a Non-ego—the more special of the two necessities of thought merges in the more general one. This identification of two necessities of thought, and subsumption of one of them under the other, he is not wrong in regarding as a function of science. He affords an example of it, when, in a manner which we shall hereafter characterize, he denies to Causation the character, which philosophers of his school have commonly assigned to it, of an ultimate belief, and attempts to identify it with another and more general law of thought. This limited function is the only one which, it seems to me, is reserved for science in Sir W. Hamilton's mode of studying the primary facts of consciousness. In the mode he practises of ascertaining them to be facts of consciousness, there is nothing for science to do. For, to call them so because in his opinion he himself, and those who agree with him, cannot get rid of the belief in them, does not seem exactly a scientific process.* It is, however, characteristic of what I have called the introspec-

*[67] The "Inquirer" thinks that Sir W. Hamilton demanded, as evidence that a supposed fact of consciousness is not acquired, but original, not only that it should not be reducible to a generalization from experience, but that it should lie "at the root of all experience;" which the "Inquirer" understands to mean "that no experience is possible unless this belief, this mode of thought, is already present with us." (P. 54.) If Sir W. Hamilton meant this, he took no pains to show that he meant it. The authority quoted is a passing expression: "Whenever in an analysis of the intellectual phenomenon, we arrive at an element which we cannot reduce to a generalization from experience, *but which lies at the root of all experience*, and which we cannot, therefore, resolve into any higher principle, this we properly call a fact of consciousness." (*Lectures*, Vol. I, p. 270.) The idea of the words in italics is no further developed; it is omitted from the definition in the next page, "A fact of consciousness is thus, that whose existence is given and guaranteed by an original and necessary belief" (unless the idea is supposed to be implied in the word "original"); and Sir W. Hamilton never, as far as I am aware, recurs to it in his attempts to prove the originality of a belief. This is the more remarkable, because Kant makes a continual and obtrusive use of this criterion; we are always hearing from him that this or that mental element cannot be the product of experience, because its pre-existence is required to render experience possible; which goes far to show that Sir W. Hamilton's abstinence was intentional, and grounded on a sense

ʻ–ʻ65¹   the

tive, in contradistinction to the psychological, method of metaphysical inquiry. The difference between these methods will now be exemplified by showing them at work on a particular question, the most fundamental one in philosophy, the distinction between the Ego and the Non-ego.

We shall first examine what Sir W. Hamilton has done by his method, and shall afterwards attempt to exemplify the use which can be made of the other.

---

of the extreme difficulty of proving, in any of the disputed cases, what Kant so confidently affirms. It is not unusual with Sir W. Hamilton to adopt, from other philosophers, single expressions of which the full meaning forms no part of his own mode of thought.

CHAPTER X

Sir William Hamilton's View of the Different Theories Respecting the Belief in an External World

SIR W. HAMILTON brings a very serious charge against the great majority of philosophers. He accuses them of playing fast and loose with the testimony of consciousness; rejecting it when it is inconvenient, but appealing to it as conclusive when they have need of it to establish any of their opinions. "No philosopher has ever openly thrown off allegiance to the authority of consciousness."* No one denies "that as all philosophy is evolved from consciousness, so, on the truth of consciousness, the possibility of all philosophy is dependent."† But if any testimony of consciousness be supposed false,

the truth of no other fact of consciousness can be maintained. The legal brocard, *Falsus in uno, falsus in omnibus*, is a rule not more applicable to other witnesses than to consciousness. Thus every system of philosophy which implies the negation of any fact of consciousness is not only necessarily unable, without self-contradiction, to establish its own truth by any appeal to consciousness; it is also unable, without self-contradiction, to appeal to consciousness against the falsehood of any other system. If the absolute and universal veracity of consciousness be once surrendered, every system is equally true, or rather all are equally false; philosophy is impossible, for it has now no instrument by which truth can be discovered, no standard by which it can be tried; the root of our nature is a lie. But though it is thus manifestly the common interest of every scheme of philosophy to preserve intact the integrity of consciousness, almost every scheme of philosophy is only another mode in which this integrity has been violated. If, therefore, I am able to prove the fact of this various violation, and to show that the facts of consciousness have never, or hardly ever, been fairly evolved, it will follow, as I said, that no reproach can be justly addressed to consciousness as an ill-informed, or vacillating, or perfidious witness, but to those only who were too proud or too negligent to accept its testimony, to employ its materials, and obey its laws.‡

That nearly all philosophers have merited this imputation, our author

---

Lectures, Vol. I, p. 277.
†*Ibid.*, p. 285.
‡*Ibid.*, pp. 283–4.

endeavours to show by a classified enumeration of the various theories which they have maintained respecting the perception of material objects. No instance can be better suited for trying the dispute. The question of an external world is the great battle-ground of metaphysics, not so much from its importance in itself, as because while it relates to the most familiar of all our mental acts, it forcibly illustrates the characteristic differences between the two metaphysical methods.

"We are immediately conscious in perception," says Sir W. Hamilton,

of an ego and a non-ego, known together, and known in contrast to each other. This is the fact of the Duality of Consciousness. It is clear and manifest. When I concentrate my attention in the simplest act of perception, I return from my observation with the most irresistible conviction of two facts, or rather two branches of the same fact; that I am, and that something different from me exists. In this act I am conscious of myself as the perceiving subject, and of an external reality as the object perceived; and I am conscious of both existences in the same indivisible moment of intuition. The knowledge of the subject does not precede, nor follow, the knowledge of the object; neither determines, neither is determined by the other. Such is the fact of perception revealed in consciousness, and as it determines mankind in general in their almost equal assurance of the reality of an external world, as of the existence of our own minds.[*]

We may, therefore, lay it down as an undisputed truth, that consciousness gives, as an ultimate fact, a primitive duality; a knowledge of the ego in relation and contrast to the non-ego; and a knowledge of the non-ego in relation and contrast to the ego. The ego and non-ego are thus given in an original synthesis, as conjoined in the unity of knowledge, and in an original antithesis, as opposed in the contrariety of existence. In other words, we are conscious of them in an indivisible act of knowledge together and at once, but we are conscious of them as, in themselves, different and exclusive of each other.

Again, consciousness not only gives us a duality, but it gives its elements in equal counterpoise and independence. The ego and non-ego—mind and matter—are not only given together, but in absolute co-equality. The one does not precede, the other does not follow; and in their mutual relation, each is equally dependent, equally independent. Such is the fact as given in and by consciousness.

Or rather (he should have said) such is the answer we receive, when we examine and interrogate our *present* consciousness. To assert more than this, merely on this evidence, is to beg the question instead of solving it.

Philosophers have not, however, been content to accept the fact in its integrity, but have been pleased to accept it only under such qualifications as it suited their systems to devise. In truth, there are just as many different philosophical systems originating in this fact, as it admits of various possible modifications. An enumeration of these modifications, accordingly, affords an enumeration of philosophical theories.

In the first place, there is the grand division of philosophers into those who do,

[*Ibid., p. 288.]

and those who do not, accept the fact in its integrity. Of modern philosophers, almost all are comprehended under the latter category, while of the former, if we do not remount to the schoolmen and the ancients, I am only aware of a single philosopher before Reid,[*] who did not reject, at least in part, the fact as consciousness affords it.

As it is always expedient to possess a precise name for a precise distinction, I would be inclined to denominate those who implicitly acquiesce in the primitive duality as given in consciousness, the Natural Realists, or Natural Dualists, and their doctrine, Natural Realism or Natural Dualism.

This is, of course, the author's own doctrine.

In the second place, the philosophers who do not accept the fact, and the whole fact, may be divided and subdivided into various classes by various principles of distribution.

The first subdivision will be taken from the total, or partial, rejection of the import of the fact. I have previously shown that to deny any fact of consciousness as an actual phænomenon is utterly impossible.

(But it is very far from impossible to believe that something which we now confound with consciousness, may have been altogether foreign to consciousness *when this was unmingled with acquired impressions*.)

But though necessarily admitted as a present phænomenon, the import of this phænomenon—all beyond our actual consciousness of its existence—may be denied. We are able, without self-contradiction, to suppose, and consequently to assert, that all to which the phænomenon of which we are conscious refers, is a deception; [say rather, an unwarranted inference;] that for example, the past, to which an act of memory refers, is only an illusion involved in our consciousness of the present,—that the unknown subject to which every phænomenon of which we are conscious involves a reference, has no reality beyond this reference itself,—in short, that all our knowledge of mind or matter is only a consciousness of various bundles of baseless appearances. This doctrine, as refusing a substantial reality to the phænomenal existence of which we are conscious, is called Nihilism; and consequently, philosophers, as they affirm or deny the authority of consciousness in guaranteeing a substratum or substance to the manifestation of the ego and non-ego, are divided into Realists or Substantialists, and into Nihilists or Non-Substantialists. Of positive or dogmatic Nihilism there is no example in modern philosophy. . . . But as a sceptical conclusion from the premises of previous philosophers, we have an illustrious example of Nihilism in Hume; and the celebrated Fichte admits that the speculative principles of his own idealism would, unless corrected by his practical, terminate in this result.*

The Realists, or Substantialists, those who do believe in a substratum, but reject the testimony of consciousness to an *immediate* cognizance of an

[*Peter Poiret, according to Hamilton's editors.]

Lectures, Vol. I, pp. 292–4. [See Johann Gottlieb Fichte, *Die Bestimmung des Menschen*, in *Sämmtliche Werke*, ed. J. H. Fichte, 8 vols. (Berlin: Verlag von Veit, 1845), Vol. II, p. 245.]

*a-a*65[1], 65[2], 67   in its primitive state

Ego and a Non-ego, our author divides into two classes, according as they admit the real existence of two substrata, or only of one. These last, whom he denominates Unitarians or Monists, either acknowledge the ego alone, or the non-ego alone, or regard the two as identical. Those who admit the ego alone, looking upon the non-ego as a product evolved from it (*i.e.* as something purely mental) are the Idealists. Those who admit the non-ego alone, and regard the ego as evolved from it (*i.e.* as purely material) are the Materialists. The third class acknowledge the equipoise of the two, but deny their antithesis, maintaining "that mind and matter are only phænomenal modifications of the same common substance. This is the doctrine of Absolute Identity, a doctrine of which the most illustrious representatives among recent philosophers are Schelling, Hegel, and Cousin."*

There remain those who admit the coequal reality of the Ego and the Non-ego, of mind and matter, and also their distinctness from one another, but deny that they are known immediately. These are Dualists, but

are distinguished from the Natural Dualists of whom we formerly spoke, in this—that the latter establish the existence of the two worlds of mind and matter on the immediate knowledge we possess of both series of phænomena—a knowledge of which consciousness assures us; whereas the former, surrendering the veracity of consciousness to our immediate knowledge of material phænomena, and consequently, our immediate knowledge of the existence of matter, still endeavour, by various hypotheses and reasonings, to maintain the existence of an unknown external world. As we denominate those who maintain a Dualism as involved in the fact of consciousness, Natural Dualists; so we may style those dualists who deny the evidence of consciousness to our immediate knowledge of aught beyond the sphere of mind, Hypothetical Dualists, or Cosmothetic Idealists.

To the class of Cosmothetic Idealists, the great majority of modern philosophers are to be referred. Denying an immediate or intuitive knowledge of the external reality, whose existence they maintain, they, of course, hold a doctrine of mediate or representative perception; and, according to the various modifications of that doctrine, they are again subdivided into those who view, in the immediate object of perception, a representative entity present to the mind, but not a mere mental modification, and into those who hold that the immediate object is only a representative modification of the mind itself. It is not always easy to determine to which of these classes some philosophers belong. To the former, or class holding the cruder hypothesis of representation, certainly belong the followers of Democritus and Epicurus, those Aristotelians who held the vulgar doctrine of species (Aristotle himself was probably a natural dualist), and in recent times, among many others, Malebranche, Berkeley, Clarke, Newton, Abraham Tucker, &c. To these is also, but problematically, to be referred, Locke. To the second, or class holding the finer hypothesis of representation, belong, without any doubt, many of the Platonists, Leibnitz, Arnauld, Crousaz, Condillac, Kant, &c., and to this class is also probably to be referred Descartes.[†]

In our own country the best known and typical specimen of this mode of

Lectures, Vol. I, p. 296.
†*Ibid.*, pp. 295–6.

thinking, is Brown; and it is upon him that our author discharges most of the shafts which this class of thinkers, as being the least distant from him of all his opponents, copiously receive from him.*

With regard to the various opinions thus enumerated, I shall first make a remark of general application, and shall then advert particularly to the objects of Sir W. Hamilton's more especial animadversion, the Cosmo-thetic Idealists.

Concerning all these classes of thinkers, except the Natural Realists, Sir W. Hamilton's statement is, that they deny some part of the testimony of consciousness, and by so doing invalidate the appeals which they neverthe-less make to consciousness, as a voucher for their own doctrines. If he had said that they all run counter, in some particular, to the general sentiment of mankind—that they all deny some common opinion, some natural belief (meaning by natural, not one which rests on a necessity of our nature, but merely one which, in common with innumerable varieties of false opinion, mankind have a strong tendency to adopt); had he said only this, no one could have contested its truth; but it would not have been a *reductio ad absurdum* of his opponents. For all philosophers, Sir W. Hamilton as much as the rest, deny some common opinions, which others might call natural beliefs, but which those who deny them consider, and have a right to consider, as natural prejudices; held, nevertheless, by the generality of

*In one of the "Dissertations on Reid" (Note C) Sir W. Hamilton gives a much more elaborate, and more minutely discriminated enumeration and classification of the opinions which have been or might be held respecting our knowledge of mind and of matter. But the one which I have quoted from the *Lectures* is more easily followed, and sufficient for all the purposes for which I have occasion to advert to it. I shall only cite from the later exposition a single passage which exhibits in a strong light the sentiments of our author towards philosophers of the school of Brown.

"Natural Realism and Absolute Idealism are the only systems worthy of a philosopher; for, as they alone have any foundation in consciousness, so they alone have any consistency in themselves. . . . Both build upon the same fundamental fact, that the extended object immediately perceived is identical with the extended object actually existing;—for the truth of this fact, both can appeal to the common sense of mankind; and to the common sense of mankind Berkeley did appeal not less confidently, and perhaps more logically than Reid. . . . The scheme of Hypothetical Realism or Cosmothetic Idealism, which supposes that behind the non-existent world perceived, lurks a correspondent but unknown world existing, is not only repugnant to our natural beliefs, but in manifold contradiction with itself. The scheme of Natural Realism may be ultimately difficult—for, like all other truths, it ends in the inconceivable; but Hypothetical Realism—in its origin—in its development—in its result, although the favourite scheme of philosophers, is philosophically absurd." (P. 817n.)

Sir W. Hamilton may in general be depended on for giving a perfectly fair statement of the opinions of adversaries; but in this case his almost passionate contempt for the later forms of Cosmothetic Idealism has misled him. No Cos-mothetic Idealist would accept as a fair statement of his opinion, the monstrous proposition that a "non-existent world" is "perceived."

mankind in the persuasion of their being self-evident, or, in other words, intuitive, and deliverances of consciousness. Some of the points on which Sir W. Hamilton is at issue with natural beliefs, relate to the very subject in hand—the perception of external things. We have found him maintaining that we do not see the sun, but an image of it, and that no two persons see the same sun; in contradiction to as clear a case as could be given of natural belief. And we shall find him affirming, in opposition to an equally strong natural belief, that we immediately perceive extension only in our own organs, and not in the objects we see or touch. Beliefs, therefore, which seem among the most natural that can be entertained, are sometimes, in his opinion, delusive; and he has told us that to discriminate which these are, is not within the competence of everybody, but only of philosophers. He would say, of course, that the beliefs which he rejects were not in our consciousness originally. And nearly all his opponents say the same thing of those which *they* reject. Those, indeed, who, like Kant, believe that there are elements present, even at the first moment of internal consciousness, which do not exist in the object, but are derived from the mind's own laws, are fairly open to Sir W. Hamilton's criticism. It is not my business to justify, in point of consistency, any more than of conclusiveness, the *b* reasoning, by which Kant, after getting rid of the outward reality of all the attributes of Body, persuades himself that he demonstrates the externality of Body itself.* But, as regards all existing schools of thought not descended from Kant, Sir W. Hamilton's accusation is without ground.

There is something more to be said respecting the mixed multitude of metaphysicians whom our author groups together under the title of Cosmothetic Idealists, and whose mode of thought he judges more harshly than that of any other school. He represents them as holding the doctrine that we perceive external objects, not by an immediate, but by a mediate or representative perception. And he recognises three divisions of them, according to three different forms in which this hypothesis may be entertained.† The supposed representative object may be regarded, first, as not a

---

*In the *Lehrsatz* of the 21st Supplement to the *Kritik der Reinen Vernunft* [p. 773]; the Lemma at p. 184 of Mr. Haywood's Translation. [*Critick of Pure Reason*, trans. Francis Haywood, 2nd ed. (London: Pickering, 1848).] See also, in Haywood, the note at pp. xxxviii–xl of the Second Preface; being Supplement II ["Vorrede zur zweiten Auflage,"] in Rosenkranz and Schubert's edition of the collected works, Vol. II, pp. 684–6. *c*This reasoning of Kant, to my mind, strangely sophistical, nevertheless does not place the externality of Bodies out of the mind. It is "externality in Space," and Space, in his philosophy, does not exist out of the mind.*c*

†*Discussions*, p. 57.

*b*65[1], 65[2], 67   strangely sophistical
c-c+72

state of mind, but something else; either external to the mind, like the *species sensibiles* of some of the ancients, and the "motions of the brain" of some of the early moderns;[*] or in the mind, like the Ideas of Berkeley. Secondly, it may be regarded as a state of mind, but a state different from the mind's act in perceiving or being conscious of it: of this kind, perhaps, are the Ideas of Locke. Or, thirdly, as a state of mind identical with the act by which we are said to perceive it. This last is the form in which, as Sir W. Hamilton truly says, the doctrine was held by Brown.*

Now, the first two of these three opinions may fairly be called what our author calls them—theories of mediate or representative perception. The object which, in these theories, the mind is supposed directly to perceive, is a tertium quid, which by the one theory is, and by the other is not, a state or modification of mind, but in both is distinct equally from the act of perception, and from the external object: and the mind is cognizant of the external object vicariously, through this third thing, of which alone it has immediate cognizance—of which alone, therefore, it is, in Sir W. Hamilton's sense of the word, conscious. Against both these theories Reid, Stewart, and our author, are completely triumphant, and I am in no way interested in pressing for a rehearing of the cause.

But the third opinion, which is Brown's, cannot with any justness of thought or propriety of language be called a theory of mediate or representative perception. Had Sir W. Hamilton taken half the pains to understand Brown which he took to understand far inferior thinkers, he never would have described Brown's doctrine in terms so inappropriate.

Representative knowledge is always understood by our author to be knowledge of a thing by means of an image of it; by means of something which is *like* the thing itself. "Representative knowledge," he says, "is only deserving of the name of knowledge in so far as it is conformable with the intuitions which it represents."[†] The representation must stand in a relation to what it represents, like that of a picture to its original: as the representation in memory of a past impression of sense, does to that past impression; as a representation in imagination does to a supposed possible presentation of sense; and as the Ideas of the earlier Cosmothetic Idealists were supposed to do to the outward objects of which they were the image or impress. But the Mental Modifications of Brown and those who think with him, are not supposed to bear any resemblance to the objects which excite them.[†] These objects are supposed to be unknown to us, except as the causes of the mental modifications. The only relation between the two is

[*Ibid.*, p. 72. See p. 15 above. For Descartes, see *Principia Philosophia*, p. 188 (IV, clxxxix).]

Ibid., p. 58. [See Brown, *Lectures*, Vol. II, pp. 22–90.]

†"Dissertations on Reid," [Note B,] p. 811.

[†See Brown, *Lectures*, Vol. II, pp. 32–62.]

that of cause and effect. Brown, being free from the vulgar error [d] that a cause must be like its effect, and admitting no knowledge of the cause (beyond its bare existence) except the effect itself, naturally found nothing in it which it was possible to compare with the effect, or in virtue of which any resemblance could be affirmed to exist between the two. In another place, Sir W. Hamilton makes an ostensible distinction between the fact of *resembling*, and that of *truly representing*, the objects; but defines the last expression to mean, affording us "such a knowledge of their nature as we should have were an immediate intuition of the reality in itself competent to man."* No one who is at all acquainted with Brown's opinions will pretend him to have maintained that we have anything of this sort. He did not believe that the mental modification afforded us any knowledge whatever of the nature of the external object. There is no need to quote passages in proof of this; it is a fact patent to whoever reads his *Lectures*.[*] It is the more strange that Sir W. Hamilton should have failed to recognise this opinion of Brown, because it is exactly the opinion which he himself holds respecting our knowledge of objects in respect of their Secondary Qualities. These, he says, are "in their own nature occult and inconceivable," and are known only in their effects on us, that is, by the mental modifications which they produce.[†]

Further, Brown's is not only not a theory of *representative* perception, but it is not even a theory of *mediate* perception. He assumes no tertium quid, no object of thought intermediate between the mind and the outward object. He recognises only the perceptive act; which with him means, and is always declared to mean, the mind itself perceiving. It will hardly be pretended that the mind itself is the "representative object" interposed by him between itself and the outward thing which is acting upon it; and if it is not, there certainly is no other. But if Brown's theory is not a theory of mediate perception, it loses all that essentially distinguishes it from Sir W. Hamilton's own doctrine. For Brown, also, thinks that we have, on the occasion of certain sensations, an instantaneous and irresistible conviction of an outward object. And if this conviction is immediate, and necessitated by the constitution of our nature, in what does it differ from our author's direct consciousness? Consciousness, immediate knowledge, and intuitive knowledge, are, Sir W. Hamilton tells us, convertible expressions; and if it be granted that whenever our senses are affected by a material object, we immediately and intuitively recognise that object as existing and distinct

*"Dissertations on Reid," [Note D,] p. 842.

[*See Brown, *Lectures*, Vol. II, pp. 22–90.]

†"Dissertations on Reid," [Note D,] p. 846: and the fuller explanation at pp. 854 and 857.

[d]65[1], 65[2]   of supposing

from us, it requires a great deal of ingenuity to make out any substantial difference between this immediate intuition of an external world, and Sir W. Hamilton's direct perception of it.

The distinction which our author makes, resolves itself, as explained by him, into the difference of which he has said so much, but of which he seemed to have so confused an idea, between Belief and Knowledge. In Brown's opinion,[*] and I will add, in Reid's, the mental modification which we experience from the presence of an object, raises in us an irresistible *belief* that the object exists. No, says Sir W. Hamilton: it is not a belief, but a *knowledge*: we have indeed a belief, and our knowledge is certified by the belief; but this belief of ours regarding the object is a belief that we *know* it.

In perception, consciousness gives, as an ultimate fact, *a belief of the knowledge of the existence of something different from self*. As ultimate, this belief cannot be reduced to a higher principle; neither can it be truly analysed into a double element. We only believe that this something *exists*, because we believe that we *know* (are conscious of) this something as existing; the belief of the existence is necessarily involved in the belief of the knowledge of the existence. Both are original, or neither. Does consciousness deceive us in the latter, it necessarily deludes us in the former; and if the former, *though* a fact of consciousness, is false, the latter, *because* a fact of consciousness, is not true. The beliefs contained in the two propositions,

    1°. I believe that a material world exists;

    2°. I believe that I immediately know a material world existing (in other words, I believe that the external reality itself is the object of which I am conscious in perception),

though distinguished by philosophers, are thus virtually identical. The belief of an external world was too powerful, not to compel an acquiescence in its truth. But the philosophers yielded to nature, only in so far as to coincide in the dominant result. They falsely discriminated the belief in the existence, from the belief in the knowledge. With a few exceptions, they held fast by the truth of the first; but they concurred, with singular unanimity, in abjuring the second.*

Accordingly, Brown is rebuked because, while rejecting our natural belief that we *know* the external object, he yet accepts our natural belief that it *exists* as a sufficient warrant for its existence. But what real distinction is there between Brown's intuitive belief of the existence of the object, and Sir W. Hamilton's intuitive knowledge of it? Just three pages previous, Sir W. Hamilton had said, "Our knowledge rests ultimately on certain facts of consciousness, which as primitive, and consequently incomprehensible, are given less in the form of cognitions than of beliefs."[†] The consciousness of an external world is, on his own showing, primitive and incomprehensible; it therefore is less a cognition than a belief. But if we do not so much

[*See, e.g., *Lectures*, Vol. I, pp. 430–1; Vol. II, pp. 11, 85–90.]
Discussions, p. 89.
†*Ibid.*, p. 86.

know as believe an external world, what is meant by saying that we believe that we know it? Either we do not know, but only believe it, and if so, Brown and the other philosophers assailed were right; or knowledge and belief, in the case of ultimate facts, are identical, and then, believing that we know is only believing that we believe, which according to our author's and to all rational principles, is but another word for simple believing.

It would not be fair, however, to hold our author to his own confused use of the terms Belief and Knowledge. He never succeeds in making anything like an intelligible distinction between these two notions considered generally, but in particular cases we may be able to find something which he is attempting to express by them. In the present case his meaning seems to be, that Brown's Belief in an external object, though instantaneous and irresistible, was supposed to be *suggested* to the mind by its own sensation; *e*which suggestion Brown regarded as a case of a more general law,[*] whereby every fact suggests the intuitive belief of a cause or antecedent with which it is invariably connected:*e* while Sir W. Hamilton's Knowledge of the object is supposed to arise along with the sensation, and to be co-ordinate with it. And this is what Sir W. Hamilton means by calling Brown's a mediate, his own an immediate cognition of the object: the real difference being that, on Sir W. Hamilton's theory, the cognition of the ego or *f*of*f* its modification, and that of the non-ego, are simultaneous, while on Brown's the one immediately precedes the other. Our author expresses this meaning, though much less clearly, when he declares Brown's theory to be "that in perception, the external reality is not the immediate object of consciousness, but that the ego is only determined in some unknown manner to represent the non-ego, which representation, though only a modification of mind or self, we are compelled by an illusion of our nature, to mistake for a modification of matter, or non-self."* This being our author's conception of the doctrine which he has to refute, let us see in what manner he proceeds to refute it.

"You will remark," he says,

that Brown (and Brown only speaks the language of all the philosophers who do not allow the mind a consciousness of aught beyond its own states,) misstates the phænomenon when he asserts that, in perception, there is a reference from the internal to the external, from the known to the unknown. That this is not the fact, our observation of the phænomenon will at once convince you. In an act of perception, I am conscious of something as self and of something as not self: this is the simple fact. The philosophers, on the contrary, who will not accept this fact,

[*See Brown, *Lectures*, Vol. II, pp. 22–63.]
Lectures, Vol. II, p. 86.

e-e+67, 72
f-f+67, 72

misstate it. They say that we are conscious of nothing but a certain modification of mind; but this modification involves a reference to,—in other words, a representation of,—something external as its object. Now this is untrue. We are conscious of no reference, of no representation: we believe that the object of which we are conscious is the object which exists.

To this argument (of the worth of which something has been said already) I shall return presently. But he subjoins a second.

Nor could there possibly be such reference or representation; for reference or representation supposes a knowledge already possessed of the object referred to or represented; but perception is the faculty by which our first knowledge is acquired, and therefore cannot suppose a previous knowledge as its condition."*

And further on:

Mark the vice of the procedure. We can only, 1°, assert the existence of an external world inasmuch as we know it to exist; and we can only, 2°, assert that one thing is representative of another, inasmuch as the thing represented is known, independently of the representation. But how does the hypothesis of a representative perception proceed? It actually converts the fact into an hypothesis: actually converts the hypothesis into a fact. On this theory, we do not know the existence of an external world, except on the supposition that that which we do know, truly represents it as existing. The hypothetical realist cannot, therefore, establish the fact of the external world, except upon the fact of its representation. This is manifest. We have, therefore, next to ask him, how he knows the fact, that the external world is actually represented. A representation supposes something represented, and the representation of the external world supposes the existence of that world. Now the hypothetical realist, when asked how he proves the reality of the outer world, which, *ex hypothesi*, he does not know, can only say that he infers its existence from the fact of its representation. But the fact of the representation of an external world supposes the existence of that world; therefore he is again at the point from which he started. He has been arguing in a circle.†

Let me first remark that this reasoning assumes the whole point in dispute; it presupposes that the supposition which it is brought to disprove is impossible. The theory of the third form of Cosmothetic Idealism is, that though we are conscious only of the sensations which an object gives us, we are determined by a necessity of our nature, which some call an instinct, others an intuition, others a fundamental law of belief, to ascribe these sensations to something external, as their substratum, or as their cause. There is surely nothing *à priori* impossible in this supposition. The supposed instinct or intuition seems to be of the same family with many other Laws of Thought, or Natural Beliefs, which our author not only admits without scruple, but enjoins obedience to, under the usual sanction, that otherwise our intelligence must be a lie. In the present case, however, he,

*Ibid._, p. 106.
†*Ibid._, pp. 138–9.

without the smallest warrant, excludes this from the list of possible hypotheses. He says that we cannot infer a reality from a mental representation, unless we already know the reality independently of the mental representation. Now he could hardly help being aware that this is the very matter in dispute. Those who hold the opinion he argues against, do not admit the premise upon which he argues. They say that we may be, and are, necessitated to infer a cause, of which we know nothing whatever except its effect. And why not? Sir W. Hamilton thinks us entitled to infer a substance from attributes, though he allows that we know nothing of the substance except its attributes.

But this is not the worst, and there are few specimens of our author in which his deficiencies as a philosopher stand out in a stronger light. As Burke in politics, so Sir W. Hamilton in metaphysics, was too often a polemic rather than a connected thinker: the generalizations of both, often extremely valuable, seem less the matured convictions of a scientific mind, than weapons snatched up for the service of a particular quarrel. If Sir W. Hamilton can only seize upon something which will strike a hard blow at an opponent, he seldom troubles himself how much of his own edifice may be knocked down by the shock. Had he examined the argument he here uses, sufficiently to determine whether he could stand by it as a deliberate opinion, he would have perceived that it committed him to the doctrine that there is no such thing as representative knowledge. But it is one of Sir W. Hamilton's most positive tenets that there *is* representative knowledge, and that Memory, among other things, is an example of it. Let us turn back to his discussion of that subject, and see what he, at that time, considered representative knowledge to be.

Every act, and consequently every act of knowledge, exists only as it now exists; and as it exists only in the Now, it can be cognizant only of a now-existent object. But the object known in memory is, *ex hypothesi*, past; consequently, we are reduced to the dilemma, either of refusing a past object to be known in memory at all, or of admitting it to be only mediately known, in and through a present object. That the latter alternative is the true one, it will require a very few explanatory words to convince you. What are the contents of an act of memory? An act of memory is merely *a present state of mind which we are conscious of not as absolute, but as relative to, and representing, another state of mind, and accompanied with the belief that the state of mind, as now represented, has actually been*. I remember an event I saw—the landing of George IV at Leith. This remembrance is only *a consciousness of certain imaginations, involving the conviction that these imaginations now represent ideally what I formerly really experienced*. All that is immediately known in the act of memory, is the present mental modification, that is, the representation and concomitant belief. Beyond this mental modification we know nothing; and this mental modification is not only known to consciousness, but only exists in and by consciousness. *Of any past object, real or ideal, the mind knows and can know nothing*, for, *ex hypothesi*, no such object now exists; or if it be said to know such an object, it can only be said to know it mediately, *as represented in the present mental modification*. Properly speaking, however, we know only the actual and present, and all real knowledge is an immediate knowledge. What is said to be mediately known, is, in truth, not known to be, but only believed to be: for its existence is *only an inference resting on the belief, that the mental modification truly represents what is in itself beyond the sphere of knowledge*.*

Had Sir W. Hamilton totally forgotten all this, when a few lectures afterwards, having then in front of him a set of antagonists who needed the theory here laid down, he repudiated it—denying altogether the possibility of the mental state so truly and clearly expressed in this passage, and affirming that we cannot possibly recognise a mental modification to be representative of something else, unless we have a present knowledge of that something else, otherwise obtained?[*] With merely the alteration of putting instead of a past state of mind, a present external object, the Cosmothetic Idealists might borrow his language down to the minutest detail. They, too, believe that the mental modification is a present state of mind, which we are conscious of, not as absolute, but as relative to, and representing, "an external object, and accompanied with the belief that the object as now represented, actually" is: that we know something (viz. matter) only "as represented in the present mental modification," and that "its existence is only an inference, resting on the belief that the mental modification truly represents what is in itself beyond the sphere of knowledge." They do not, strictly speaking, require quite so much as this: for the word "represents," especially with "truly" joined to it, suggests the idea of a resemblance, such as does, in reality, exist between the picture of a fact in memory, and the present impression to which it corresponds; but the Cosmothetic Idealists only maintain that the mental modification arises from *something*, and that the reality of this unknown something is testified by a natural belief. That they apply to one case the same theory which our author applies to another, does not, of course, prove them to be right; but it proves the suicidal character (to use one of his favourite expressions)[†] of our author's argument, when he scouts the supposition of an instinctive inference from a known effect to an unknown cause, as an hypothesis which can in no possible case be legitimate; forgetful that its legitimacy is required by his own psychology, one of the leading doctrines of which is entirely grounded on it.

It is not only in treating of Memory, that Sir W. Hamilton requires a process of thought precisely similar to that which, when employed by opponents, he declares to be radically illegitimate. I have already men-

Ibid., Vol. I, pp. 219–20.
[*See *ibid.*, pp. 295ff.]
[†See, e.g., *Discussions*, p. 64.]

tioned[*] that in his opinion our perceptions of sight are not perceptions of the outward object, but of its image, a "modification of light in immediate relation to our organ of vision," and that no two persons see the same sun; propositions in direct conflict with the "natural beliefs" to which he so often refers, and to which Reid, not without reason, appeals in this instance;[†] for assuredly people in general are as firmly convinced that what they see is the real sun, as that what they touch is the real table. Let us hear Sir W. Hamilton once more on this subject.

It is not by perception, but by a process of reasoning, that we connect the objects of sense with existences beyond the sphere of immediate knowledge. It is enough that perception affords us the knowledge of the non-ego at the point of sense. To arrogate to it the power of immediately informing us of external things, *which are only the causes of the object we immediately perceive*, is either positively errone-ous, or a confusion of language arising from an inadequate discrimination of the phænomenon.*

Here is a case in which we know something to be a representation, though, in our author's opinion, that which it represents not only is not, at the present time, known to us, but never was, and never will be so. The Cosmothetic Idealists desire only the same liberty which Sir W. Hamilton here exercises, of concluding from a phænomenon directly known, to something unknown which is the cause of the phænomenon. They postu-late the possibility that what our author holds to be true of the non-ego at a distance, may be true of the non-ego at the point of sense, namely, that it is not known immediately, but as a necessary inference from what is known. To shut the door upon this supposition as inherently inadmissible, and make an exactly similar one ourselves as often as our system requires it, does not befit a philosopher, or a critic of philosophers.†

[*See pp. 112ff. above.]
[†See, e.g., *On the Intellectual Powers*, pp. 284–5.]
*Lectures, Vol. II, pp. 153–4.
†Some of the inconsistencies here pointed out in Sir W. Hamilton's speculations respecting Perception have been noticed, and ably discussed, by Mr. Bailey, in the fourth letter of the Second Series of his *Letters on the Philosophy of the Human Mind*. [(London: Longman, Brown, Green, Longmans, and Roberts, 1858), pp. 46–64.]
    In treating of Modified Logic, Sir W. Hamilton justifies, after his own manner, the assumption made alike by himself and by the Cosmothetic Idealists; and the grounds of justification are as available to them as to him. "Real truth is the correspondence of our thoughts with the existences which constitute their objects. But here a difficulty arises: how can we know that there is, that there can be, such a correspondence? All that we know of the objects is through the presentations of our faculties; but whether these present the objects as they are in themselves, we can never ascertain, for to do this it would be requisite to go out of ourselves,—out of our faculties,—to obtain a knowledge of the objects by other faculties, and thus to

In the controversy with Brown, which forms the second paper in the *Discussions*,[*] and much of which *h*is reproduced verbatim in*h* our author's *Lectures*,[†] the argument which I have now examined does not *i*appear.*i* In the room of it, we have the following argument. If Brown is right, "the mind either *knows* the reality of what it represents, or it does not." The first supposition is dismissed for the absurdities it involves, and because it is inconsistent with Brown's doctrine. But if the mind does not know the reality of what it represents, the "alternative remains, that the mind is *blindly* determined to *represent*, and *truly* to represent, the reality which it does not know." And if so, the mind "either blindly determines itself" or "is blindly determined" by a supernatural power. The latter supposition he rejects because it involves a standing miracle; the former as "utterly irra-

---

compare our old presentations with our new." The very difficulty which we have seen him throwing in the teeth of the Cosmothetic Idealists. "But all this, even were the supposition possible, would be incompetent to afford us the certainty required. For were it possible to leave our old, and to obtain a new, set of faculties, by which to test the old, still the veracity of these new faculties would be equally obnoxious to doubt as the veracity of the old. For what guarantee could we obtain for the credibility in the one case, which we do not already possess in the other? The new faculties could only assert their own truth; but this is done by the old; and it is impossible to imagine any presentations of the non-ego by any finite intelligence to which a doubt might not be raised, whether these presentations were not merely subjective modifications of the conscious ego itself." It is a very laudable practice in philosophizing to state the difficulties strongly. But when the difficulty is one which in any case has to be surmounted, we should allow others to surmount it in the same mode which we adopt for ourselves. This mode, in the present case, is our author's usual one: "All that could be said in answer to such a doubt is that if such were true, our whole nature is a lie:" in other words, our nature prompts us to believe that the modification of the conscious ego points to, and results from, a non-ego with corresponding properties. (*Lectures*, Vol. IV, pp. 67–8.) The Cosmothetic Idealists do but say the same thing: and they have as good a right to say it as our author.

*g*In saying that the Cosmothetic Idealists can make out as good a case for their opinion as Sir W. Hamilton for his, I do not say that their case is good against Berkeley, who held that the non-ego we are compelled to postulate as the cause of our sensations is not matter, but a mind. Minds, Berkeley would say, we know to exist, in ourselves by consciousness, in other beings by evidence. Matter we do not know to exist, for all the indications of it are otherwise explicable: we ought not, therefore, to assume its existence until it is shown that our sensations cannot be caused by a Mind. Sir W. Hamilton escapes from this argument by his doctrine, that Matter with its Primary and Secundo-primary qualities is directly and immediately perceived.*g*

[*"Philosophy of Perception," *Discussions*, pp. 39–99.]

[†See *Lectures*, Vol. I, pp. 278–83.]

g–g+72

*h–h*65¹, 65²   was transcribed from

*i–i*65¹, 65²   reappear. Sir W. Hamilton perhaps had meanwhile become aware of its inconsistency with his own principles.

tional, inasmuch as it would explain an effect, by a cause wholly inadequate to its production. On this alternative, knowledge is supposed to be the effect of ignorance,—intelligence of stupidity—life of death."* All this artillery is directed against the simple supposition that by a law of our nature, a modification of our own minds may assure us of the existence of an unknown cause. The author's persistent ignorance of Brown's opinion is *j* surprising. Brown knows nothing of the mental modification as *truly representing* the unknown reality; he claims no knowledge as arising out of ignorance, no intelligence growing out of stupidity. He claims only an instinctive belief implanted by nature; and the menacing alternative, that the mind must either determine itself to this belief, or be determined to it by a special interference of Providence, could be applied with exactly as much justice to the earth's motion. But though Sir W. Hamilton's weapon falls harmless upon Brown, it recoils with terrible effect upon his own theories of representative cognition. A remembrance, for example, does represent, and truly represent, the past fact remembered: and we do, through that representation, mediately know the past fact, which in any other sense of the word, according to our author, we do not know. Although therefore the conclusion "that the mind is blindly determined to represent, and truly to represent, the reality which it does not know," is not obligatory upon Brown, it is upon Sir W. Hamilton. On his own showing he has to choose between the absurdity that the mind "blindly determines itself," and the perpetual miracle of its being determined by divine interference. This is one of the weakest exhibitions of Sir W. Hamilton that I have met with in his writings. For the difficulty by which he thought to overwhelm Brown, and which does not touch Brown, but falls back upon himself, is no difficulty at all, but the merest moonshine. The transcendent absurdity, as he considers it, that the mind should be blindly determined to represent, and truly to represent, the reality which "it does not know," instead of an absurdity, is the exact expression of a fact. It is a literal description of what takes place in an act of memory. As often as we recollect a past event, and on the faith of that recollection, believe or know that the event really happened, the mind, by its constitution, is "blindly determined to represent, and truly to represent" a fact which, except as witnessed by that representation, "it does not know."†

Discussions, p. 67.

†Our belief in the veracity of Memory is evidently ultimate: no reason can be given for it which does not presuppose the belief, and assume it to be well grounded. This point is forcibly urged in the Philosophical Introduction to *k*Dr.*k* Ward's able work, *On Nature and Grace*: a book the readers of which are likely to be limited by

*j*65[1], 65[2]   truly
*k–k*65[1], 65[2], 67   Mr.

It may generally, I think, be observed of Sir W. Hamilton, that his most *recherché* arguments are his weakest: they certainly are so in the present case. It would have been wiser in him to have been contented with his first and simpler argument, that Brown's doctrine conflicts with consciousness,

---

its being addressed specially to Catholics, but showing a capacity in the writer which might otherwise have made him one of the most effective chàmpions of the Intuitive school. [See William George Ward, *On Nature and Grace* (London: Burns and Lambert, 1860), esp. Chap. i, §1, pp. 5–6, and 25–9.] Though I do not believe morality to be intuitive in *Dr.* Ward's sense, I think his book of great practical worth, by the strenuous manner in which it maintains morality to have another foundation than the arbitrary decree of God, and shows, by great weight of evidence, that this is the orthodox doctrine of the Roman Catholic Church.

*Dr. Ward, returning to this subject in the *Dublin Review*, says that in declaring our belief in the veracity of Memory to be ultimate, I am admitting "an exception" to the doctrine of what he calls the Phenomenist school, and "an exception which no phenomenist had made before." The necessity of making this exception, he deems a powerful argument against the doctrine itself. "If ever there were a paradoxical position" mine, according to him, "is one on the surface. It is most intelligible to say that there are no trustworthy intuitions; and it is most intelligible to say that there are many such; but on the surface it is the *ne plus ultra* of paradox, to say that there is *just one* such, and no more." ("Mr. Mill's Denial of Necessary Truth," pp. 309–10.)

First, on what account is it more improbable that there should be "just one" source of intuitive knowledge besides present consciousness, making two in all, than that there should be three, four, or any other number. To me it seems that there is no antecedent presumption in the case, but a mere question of evidence. Dr. Ward, with good reason, challenges me to explain "where the distinction lies between acts of memory and other alleged intuitions" which I do not admit as such. The distinction is, that as all the explanations of mental phenomena presuppose Memory, Memory itself cannot admit of being explained. Whenever this is shown to be true of any other part of our knowledge, I shall admit that part to be intuitive. Dr. Ward thinks that there are various other intuitions "more favourably circumstanced for the establishment of their trustworthiness" than Memory itself, and he gives as an example our conviction of the wickedness of certain acts. [*Ibid.*, p. 310.] My reason for rejecting this as a case of intuition is, that the conviction can be explained without presupposing, as part of the explanation, the very fact itself; which the belief in Memory cannot.

Dr. Ward has been too hasty in saying that no phenomenist ever before made this "exception." I doubt if he could point out any phenomenist who has not made it, either expressly or by implication. All who have attempted the explanation of the human mind by sensation have postulated the knowledge of past sensations as well as of present; some of them have expressly said so. Take Hume, for instance, the most extreme of Phenomenists: he always excepts Memory from the sources of knowledge of which he attempts to find an explanation. In his "Sceptical Doubts," he says "It may be a subject worthy curiosity, to inquire what is the nature of that evidence which assures us of any real existence and matter of fact, beyond the

$^{l-l}65^1$, 65^2, 67   Mr.
$^{m-m}$+72

inasmuch as "we are conscious of no reference, of no representation:"[*] or, to speak more clearly, we are not aware that the existence of an external reality is suggested to us by our sensations. We seem to become aware of both at once.

The fact is as alleged, but it proves nothing, being consistent with Brown's doctrine. Whether the belief in a non-ego arose in our first act of perception, simultaneously with the sensation, or not until suggested by the sensation, we have, as I before remarked, no means of directly ascertaining.[†] As far as depends on direct evidence, the subject is inscrutable. But this we may know, that even if the suggestion theory were true, the belief suggested would by the laws of association become so intimately blended with the sensation suggesting it, that long before we were able to reflect on our mental operations, we should have become entirely incapable of thinking of the two things as other than simultaneous. An appeal to consciousness avails nothing, when, even though the doctrine opposed were true, the appeal might equally, and with the same plausibility, be made. The facts are

---

present testimony of our senses, *or the records of our memory*." And again, "all reasonings concerning matter of fact seem to be founded in the relation of Cause and Effect. By means of that relation alone can we go beyond the evidence of our *memory* and senses." ["Sceptical Doubts concerning the Operations of the Understanding," Section iv of *An Inquiry Concerning Human Understanding*, in *Essays and Treatises*, Vol. II, p. 39.] And in his "Sceptical Solution of these Doubts," where he is attempting to explain Belief by the laws of Association, he asserts that belief "where it reaches beyond the *memory* and senses" is amenable to his theory. [Section v in *ibid.*, p. 68.] It would be easy to quote equally decisive passages from other Phenomenists. How, indeed, could any one make Experience the source of all our knowledge without postulating the belief in Memory as the fundamental fact? What is Experience but Memory?

For myself, I do admit other sources of knowledge than sensation and the memory of sensation, though not than consciousness and the memory of consciousness. I have distinctly declared that the elementary *relations* of our sensations to one another, viz. their resemblances, and their successions and coexistences, are subjects of direct apprehension. And I have avowedly left the question undecided whether our perception of ourselves—of our own personality—is not a case of the same kind. It is curious that while Dr. Ward ["Mill's Denial," pp. 309–10] thinks I am bound to explain why I acknowledge only one case of intuition, Dr. M'Cosh charges me with postulating as great a number of first principles as are demanded by either the Scotch or the German metaphysicians, and has devoted a whole chapter of his book to an enumeration of them; including several which, as he might have known, I regard as truths indeed, but not as ultimate principles. [See McCosh, *Examination*, Chap. iii, pp. 50–69.] I do not know what extreme of supposed psychological analysis Dr. M'Cosh thought it incumbent on me to profess. In my estimation, the doctrine of "all or none" is no more a necessity in philosophy than in politics.[m]

[*Lectures, Vol. II, p. 106.]
[†See pp. 139ff. above.]

alike consistent with both opinions, and, for aught that appears, Brown's is as likely to be true as Sir W. Hamilton's. The difference between them, as already observed, is extremely small, and I will add, supremely unimportant. If the reality of matter is certified to us by an irresistible belief, it matters little whether we reach the belief by two steps, or by only one.

The really important difference of opinion on the subject of Perception, between Brown and Sir W. Hamilton, is far other than this. It is, that Sir W. Hamilton believes us to have a direct intuition not solely of the reality of matter, but also of its primary qualities, Extension, Solidity, Figure, &c., which, according to him, we know as in the material object, and not as modifications of ourselves: while Brown believed that matter is suggested to us only as an unknown something, all whose attributes, as known or conceived by us, are resolvable into affections of our senses. In Brown's opinion we are cognizant of a non-ego in the perceptive act, only in the indefinite form of something external; all else we are able to know of it is only that it produces certain affections in us: which is also our author's opinion as regards the Secondary Qualities. The difference therefore, between Brown and Sir W. Hamilton, is not of the kind which Sir W. Hamilton considers it to be, but consists mainly in this, that Brown really held what Sir W. Hamilton held only verbally, the doctrine of the Relativity of [n] our knowledge. I shall attempt, further on, to show that on the point on which they really differed, Brown was right, and Sir W. Hamilton totally wrong.*

The considerations which have now been adduced are subversive of a great mass of triumphant animadversion by our author on the ignorance

*There is also a difference between Brown and Sir W. Hamilton in the particular category of intuitive knowledge to which they referred the cognition of the existence of matter. Brown deemed it a case of the belief in causation, which again he regarded as a case of our intuitive belief in the constancy of the order of nature. "I do not," he says, "conceive that it is by any peculiar intuition we are led to believe in the existence of things without. I consider this belief as the effect of that more general intuition, by which we consider a new consequent, in any series of accustomed events, as the sign of a new antecedent, and of that equally general principle of association, by which feelings that have frequently co-existed, flow together and constitute afterwards one complex whole." (*Lectures*, Vol. II, p. 11; Lecture xxiv.) That is, he thought that when an infant finds the motions of his muscles, which have been accustomed to take place unimpeded, suddenly stopped by what he will afterwards learn to call the resistance of an external object, the infant intuitively (though perhaps not instantaneously) believes that this unexpected phænomenon, the stoppage of a series of sensations, is conjoined with, or as we now say, caused by, the presence of some new antecedent: [o] which, not being the infant himself, nor a state of his sensations, we may call an outward object.

[n]65^1, 65^2, 67   all
[o]65^1, 65^2 something

and carelessness of Brown, and some milder criticism on Reid. Sir W. Hamilton thinks it astonishing that neither of these philosophers should have recognised Natural Realism, and the third form of Cosmothetic Idealism, as two different modes of thought. Reid, whom he makes a great point of claiming as a Natural Realist, was, he says, quite unaware of the possibility of the other opinion, and did not guard against it by his language, leaving it, therefore, open to dispute whether, instead of being a Natural Realist, he was not, like Brown, a Cosmothetic Idealist of the third class; while Brown, on the other hand, never conceived Natural Realism, nor thought it possible that Reid held any other than his own opinion, as he invariably affirms him to have done.[*] I apprehend that both philosophers are entirely clear of the blame thus imputed to them. Reid never imagined Brown's doctrine, nor Brown Reid's, as anything different from his own, because in truth they were not different. If the distinction between a Natural Realist and a Cosmothetic Idealist of the third class, be that the latter believes the existence of the external object to be inferred from, or suggested by, our sensations, while the former holds it to be neither the one nor the other, but to be apprehended in consciousness simultaneously and co-ordinately with the sensations, Reid was as much a Cosmothetic Idealist as Brown *p* . The question does not concern philosophy, but the history of philosophy, which is Sir W. Hamilton's strongest point, and was not at all a strong point with either Brown or Reid; but the matter of fact is worth the few pages necessary for clearing it up, because Sir W. Hamilton's vast and accurate learning goes near to obtaining for his statements, on any such matter, implicit confidence, and it is therefore important to show that even where he is strongest, he is sometimes wrong.

In the severe criticism on Brown from which I have quoted, and which, though in some respects unjust, in others I cannot deny to be well merited, some of the strongest expressions have reference to the gross misunderstanding of Reid, of which Brown is alleged to have been guilty in not perceiving him to have been a Natural Realist. "We proceed," says our author,

to consider the greatest of all Brown's errors, in itself and in its consequences, his misconception of the cardinal position of Reid's philosophy, in supposing that philosopher as a *hypothetical* realist, to hold with himself the third form of the *representative* hypothesis, and not, as a *natural* realist, the doctrine of an *intuitive* Perception.*

Brown's transmutation of Reid from a *natural* to a *hypothetical* realist, as a misconception of the grand and distinctive tenet of a school by one even of its

---

[*See Lecture xxiii, *Lectures*, Vol. II, pp. 63–85; "Dissertations on Reid," Note C, pp. 819–24; cf. Brown, *Lectures*, Vol. II, pp. 22–42.]
Discussions, p. 58.

*p*65[1], 65[2]   , and in the very same manner

disciples, is without a parallel in the whole history of philosophy; and this portentous error is prolific; *chimæra chimæram parit*. Were the evidence of the mistake less unambiguous, we should be disposed rather to question our own perspicacity than to tax so subtle an intellect with so gross a blunder.*

And he did, in time, feel some misgiving as to his "own perspicacity." When, in preparing an edition of Reid, he was obliged to look more closely into that author's statements, we find a remarkable lowering of the high tone of these sentences; and he felt obliged, in revising the paper for the *Discussions*, to write "This is too strong," after a passage in which he had said that "Brown's interpretation of the fundamental tenet of Reid's philosophy is not a simple misconception, but an absolute reversal of its real and even *unambiguous* import."[†] Well would it have been for Brown's reputation if all Sir W. Hamilton's attempts to bring home blunders to him, had been as little successful as this.

In the work in which Reid first brought his opinions before the world, the *Inquiry into the Human Mind*, his language is so unequivocally that of a Cosmothetic Idealist, that it admits of no mistake. It is almost more unambiguous than that of Brown himself. The external object is always said to be perceived through the medium of "natural signs:" these signs being our sensations, interpreted by a natural instinct. Our sensations, he says, belong to that

class of natural signs which . . . though we never before had any notion or conception of the thing signified, do suggest it, or conjure it up, as it were, by a natural kind of magic, and at once give us a conception and create a belief of it.[‡]

I take it for granted that the notion of hardness, and the belief of it, is first got by means of that particular sensation which, as far back as we can remember, does invariably suggest it, and that, if we had never had such a feeling, we should never have had our notion of hardness.[§]

Again,

when a coloured body is presented, there is a certain apparition to the eye, or to the mind, which we have called *the appearance of colour*. Mr. Locke calls it *an idea*, and, indeed, it may be called so with the greatest propriety. This idea can have no existence but when it is perceived. It is a kind of thought, and can only be the act of a percipient or thinking being. By the constitution of our nature, we are led to conceive this idea as a sign of something external, and are impatient till we learn its meaning.[¶]

*Ibid., pp. 56–7.
[†]*Ibid.*, p. 60.
[‡]*Inquiry into the Human Mind, Works* (Hamilton's ed.), p. 122.
[§]*Ibid.*
[¶]*Ibid.*, p. 137.

I must be excused if I am studious to prove, by an accumulation of citations, that these are not passing expressions of Reid, but the deliberate doctrine of his treatise.

I think it appears from what hath been said, that there are natural suggestions; particularly, that sensation suggests the notion of present existence, and the belief that what we perceive or feel does now exist. . . . And, in like manner, certain sensations of touch, by the constitution of our nature, suggest to us extension, solidity, and motion.*

By an original principle of our constitution, a certain sensation of touch both suggests to the mind the conception of hardness, and creates the belief of it: or, in other words, this sensation is a natural sign of hardness.[†]

The word *gold* has no similitude to the substance signified by it; nor is it in its own nature more fit to signify this than any other substance; yet, by habit and custom, it suggests this and no other. In like manner, a sensation of touch suggests hardness, although it hath neither similitude to hardness, nor, as far as we can perceive, any necessary connexion with it. The difference betwixt these two signs lies only in this—that, in the first, the suggestion is the effect of habit and custom; in the second, it is not the effect of habit, but of the original constitution of our minds.[‡]

Extension, therefore, seems to be a quality *suggested* to us [the italics are Reid's] by the very same sensations which suggest the other qualities above mentioned. When I grasp a ball in my hand, I perceive it at once hard, figured, and extended. The feeling is very simple, and hath not the least resemblance to any quality of body. Yet it suggests to us three primary qualities perfectly distinct from one another, as well as from the sensation which indicates them. When I move my hand along the table, the feeling is so simple that I find it difficult to distinguish it into things of different natures, yet it immediately suggests hardness, smoothness, extension, and motion—things of very different natures, and all of them as distinctly understood as the feeling which suggests them.[§]

The feelings of touch, which suggest primary qualities, have no names, nor are they ever reflected upon. They pass through the mind instantaneously, and serve only to introduce the notion and belief of external things, which by our constitution, are connected with them. They are natural signs, and the mind immediately passes to the thing signified, without making the least reflection upon the sign, or observing that there was any such thing.[¶]

This passage, with many others of like import, Sir W. Hamilton might usefully have meditated on, before he laid so much stress on the testimony of consciousness that the apprehension is *not* through the medium of a sign.

Ibid., p. 111.
[†]*Ibid*., p. 121.
[‡]*Ibid*.
[§]*Ibid*., pp. 123–4. [The words in square brackets are Mill's.]
[¶]*Ibid*., p. 124.

Let a man press his hand against the table—he feels it hard. But what is the meaning of this? The meaning undoubtedly is, that he hath a certain feeling of touch, from which he concludes, without any reasoning or comparing ideas, that there is something external really existing, whose parts stick so firmly together, that they cannot be displaced without considerable force. There is here a feeling, and a conclusion drawn from it, or some way suggested by it. . . . The hardness of the table is the conclusion, the feeling is the medium by which we are led to that conclusion.*

How a sensation should instantly make us conceive and believe the existence of an external thing altogether unlike to it, I do not pretend to know; and when I say that the one suggests the other, I mean not to explain the manner of their connexion, but to express a fact, which every one may be conscious of, namely, that by a law of our nature, such a conception and belief constantly and immediately follow the sensation.†

There are three ways in which the mind passes from the appearance of a natural sign to the conception and belief of the thing signified—by original principles of our constitution, by custom, and by reasoning. Our original perceptions are got in the first of these ways. . . . In the first of these ways, Nature, by means of the sensations of touch, informs us of the hardness and softness of bodies; of their extension, figure, and motion; and of that space in which they move and are placed.‡

In the testimony of Nature given by the senses, as well as in human testimony given by language, things are signified to us by signs: and in one as well as the other, the mind, either by original principles or by custom, passes from the sign to the conception and belief of the things signified. . . . The signs in original perceptions are sensations, of which Nature hath given us a great variety, suited to the variety of the things signified by them. Nature hath established a real connexion between the signs and the things signified, and Nature hath also taught us the interpretation of the signs—so that, previous to experience, the sign suggests the thing signified, and creates the belief of it.§

It is by one particular principle of our constitution that certain features express anger; and by another particular principle, that certain features express benevolence. It is, in like manner, by one particular principle of our constitution that a certain sensation signifies hardness in the body which I handle; and it is by another particular principle that a certain sensation signifies motion in that body.¶

I doubt if it would be possible to extract from Brown himself an equal number of passages ᵠ expressing as clearly and positively, and in terms as irreconcilable with any other opinion, the doctrine which our author terms the third form of Cosmothetic Idealism; in the exact shape, too, in which

*Ibid._, p. 125.
†_Ibid._, p. 131.
‡_Ibid._, p. 188.
§_Ibid._, pp. 194–5.
¶_Ibid._, p. 195.

ᵠ65¹, 65², 67   (and I might have cited many more)

Brown held it, unencumbered by the gratuitous addition which Sir W. Hamilton fastens on him, that the sign must "truly represent" the thing signified,—a notion which Reid takes good care that he shall not be supposed to entertain, since he repeatedly declares that there is no resemblance between them. That Reid, at least when he wrote the *Inquiry*, was a Cosmothetic Idealist; that up to that time it had never occurred to him that the ˹convictions˺ of the existence and qualities of external objects could be regarded as anything but suggestions by, and conclusions from, our sensations—is too obvious to be questioned by any one who has the text fresh in his recollection. Accordingly Sir W. Hamilton acknowledges as much in his edition of Reid, both in the foot-notes and in the appended "Dissertations." After restating his own doctrine, that our natural beliefs assure us of outward objects, only by assuring us that we are immediately conscious of them, he adds, "Reid himself seems to have become obscurely aware of this condition: and though he never retracted his doctrine concerning the mere *suggestion* of extension, we find in his *Essays on the Intellectual Powers* assertions in regard to the immediate perception of external things, which would tend to show that his later views were more in unison with the necessary convictions of mankind."* And in another place he says of the doctrine maintained by Reid "in his earlier work," that it is one which "if he did not formally retract in his later writings, he did not continue to profess."† It is hard that Brown should be charged with blundering to a degree which is "portentous" and "without a parallel in the whole history of philosophy," for attributing to Reid an opinion which Sir W. Hamilton confesses that Reid maintained in one of his only two important writings, and did not retract in the other. But Sir W. Hamilton is still more wrong than he confesses. He is in a mistake when he says that Reid, though he did not retract the opinion, did not continue to profess it. For some reason, not apparent, he did cease to employ the word Suggestion. But he continued to use terms equivalent to it.

Every different perception is conjoined with a sensation that is proper to it. *The one is the sign*, the other thing signified.‡

I touch the table gently with my hand, and I feel it to be smooth, hard, and cold. These are qualities of the table perceived by touch: but I *perceive them by means* of a sensation which indicates them.§

Observing that the agreeable sensation is raised when the rose is near, and ceases when it is removed, I am led by my nature to *conclude* some quality to be in the rose,

*Foot-note to Reid, p. 129n.
†"Dissertations on Reid," [Note C,] p. 821.
‡*Essays on the Intellectual Powers, Works*, p. 312.
§*Ibid.*, p. 311.

˹–˺65¹, 65²   conviction

which is the cause of this sensation. This quality in the rose is the object perceived; and that act of my mind by which I have the conviction and belief of this quality, is what in this case I call perception.*

Of this passage even Sir W. Hamilton honestly says in a foot-note, that it "appears to be an explicit disavowal of the doctrine of an intuitive or immediate perception."[*] Again:

When a primary quality is perceived, *the sensation immediately leads our thought to the quality signified by it*, and is itself forgot. . . . The sensations belonging to primary qualities . . . carry the thought to the external object, and immediately disappear and are forgot. *Nature intended them only as signs*; and when they have served that purpose they vanish.[†]

Nature has connected our perception of external objects with certain sensations. *If the sensation is produced, the corresponding perception follows*, even when there is no object, and in that case is apt to deceive us.[‡]

In perception, whether original or acquired, there is something which may be called *the sign*, and something which is signified to us, or *brought to our knowledge by that sign*. In original perception, *the signs are the various sensations* which are produced by the impressions made upon our organs. *The things signified, are the objects perceived* in consequence of those sensations, by the original constitution of our nature. Thus, when I grasp an ivory ball in my hand, I have a certain sensation of touch. Although this sensation be in the mind, and have no similitude to anything material; yet, by the laws of my constitution, *it is immediately followed* by the conception and belief, that there is in my hand a hard smooth body of a spherical figure, and about an inch and a half in diameter. This belief is grounded neither upon reasoning, nor upon experience; it is the immediate effect of my constitution, and this I call original perception.[§]

All these are as unequivocal, and the last passage as full and precise a statement of Cosmothetic Idealism, as any in the *Inquiry*. In the "Dissertations" appended to Reid,[¶] Sir W. Hamilton, who never fails in candour, acknowledges in the fullest manner the inferences which may be drawn from passages like these, but thinks that they are balanced by others which "seem to harmonize exclusively with the conditions of natural presentationism,"[‖] and on the whole is "decidedly of opinion that, as the great end—the governing principle of Reid's doctrine was to reconcile philosophy with the necessary convictions of mankind, he intended a doctrine of natural, consequently a doctrine of presentative, realism; and that he would have at once surrendered, as erroneous, every statement

Ibid., p. 310.
[*Foot-note to Reid, p. 310n.]
†*Essays on the Intellectual Powers, Works*, p. 315.
‡*Ibid.*, p. 320.
§*Ibid.*, p. 332.
¶"Dissertations on Reid," [Note C,] pp. 819–24, and [Note D*,] pp. 882–5.
‖*Ibid.*, [Note D*,] p. 882.

which was found at variance with such a doctrine."* But it is clear that the doctrine of perception through natural signs did not, in Reid's opinion, contradict "the necessary convictions of mankind;" being brought into harmony with them by his doctrine, that the signs, after they have served their purpose, are "forgot," which, as he conclusively shows in many places, it was both natural and inevitable that they should be. The passages which Sir W. Hamilton cites as inconsistent with any doctrine but Natural Realism,[*] are those in which Reid affirms that we perceive objects *immediately*, and that the external things which really exist are the very ones which we perceive. But Reid evidently did not think these expressions inconsistent with the doctrine that the notion and belief of external objects are irresistibly suggested through natural signs. Having this notion and belief irresistibly suggested, is what he means by perceiving the external object. He says so in more than one of the passages I have just quoted: and neither in his chapter on Perception, nor anywhere else, does he speak of perception as implying anything more. In that chapter he says, "If we attend to that act of our mind which we call the perception of an external object of sense, we shall find in it these three things: First, some conception or notion of the object perceived; Secondly, a strong and irresistible conviction and belief of its present existence; and, Thirdly, that this conviction and belief are immediate, and not the effect of reasoning."† We see in this as in a hundred other places, what Reid meant when he said that our perception of outward objects is immediate. He did not mean that it is not a conviction suggested by something else, but only that the conviction is not the effect of reasoning. "This conviction is not only irresistible, but it is immediate; that is, it is not by a train of reasoning and argumentation that we come to be convinced of the existence of what we perceive."‡ As Nature has given us the signs, so it is by an original law of our nature that we are enabled to interpret them. When Reid means anything but this in contending for an immediate perception of objects, he merely means to deny that it takes place through an image in the brain or in the mind, as maintained by Cosmothetic Idealists of the first or the second class.

The only plausible argument produced by Sir W. Hamilton in proof of Reid's Natural Realism, and against his having held, as Brown thought,[†] Brown's own opinion, is, that when in the speculations of Arnauld he had before him exactly the same opinion, he failed to recognise it.§ But on a

*Ibid., [Note C,] p. 820.
[*See, e.g., *Lectures*, Vol. II, pp. 80–4.]
†*Essays on the Intellectual Powers*, Essay II, Chap. v, p. 258.
‡Same Essay, p. 259.
[†See Brown, *Lectures*, Vol. II, p. 80.]
§Same Essay, [i.e., Reid, Essay II,] Chap. xiii [pp. 295–8]. For Sir W. Hamilton's remarks, see *Lectures*, Vol. II, pp. 50–3; *Discussions*, pp. 75–7; and "Dissertations on Reid," [Note C,] p. 823.

careful examination of Reid's criticism on Arnauld, it will be seen, that as long as Reid had to do with Arnauld's direct statement of his opinion, he found nothing *in it different* from his own; but was puzzled, and thought that Arnauld attempted to unite inconsistent opinions, because, after throwing over the "ideal theory," and saying that the only real ideas are our perceptions, he maintained that it is still true, in a sense, that we do not perceive things directly, but through our ideas. What! asks Reid, do we perceive things through our perceptions? But if we merely put the word sensations instead of perceptions, the doctrine is exactly that of Reid in the *Inquiry*—that we perceive things through our sensations. Most probably Arnauld meant this, but was not so understood by Reid. If he meant anything else, his opinion was not the same as Reid's, and we need no explanation of Reid's not recognising it.[*]

One of the collateral indications that Reid's opinion agreed with Brown's, and not with Sir W. Hamilton's, is that in treating this question he seldom or never uses the word Knowledge, but only Belief. On Sir W. Hamilton's doctrine, the distinction between these two terms, however vaguely and mistily conceived by him, is indispensable. The total absence of any recognition of it in Reid, shows that of the two opinions, if there was one which he had never conceived the possibility of, it was not Brown's, as Sir W. Hamilton supposes, but Sir W. Hamilton's. In our author's mind this indication ought to have decided the question: for in the case of another philosopher he, on precisely the same evidence, brings in a verdict of Cosmothetic Idealism. Krug's system, he says, as first promulgated, "was, like Kant's, a mere Cosmothetic Idealism; for while he allowed a *knowledge* of the internal world, he only allowed a *belief* of the external."*

It is true, Reid did not believe in what our author terms "representative perception," if by this be meant perception through an image in the mind, supposed, like the picture of a fact in memory, to be *like* its original. But neither (as I have repeatedly observed) did Brown. What Brown held was exactly the doctrine of Reid in the passages that I have extracted. He thought that certain sensations, irresistibly, and by a law of our nature, suggest, without any process of reasoning, and without the intervention of any *tertium quid*, the notion of something external, and an invincible belief in its real existence. If representative perception be this, both Reid and Brown believed in it: if anything else, Brown believed *in* it no more than Reid. Not only was Reid a Cosmothetic Idealist of Brown's exact type, but

[*See Antoine Arnauld, *Des vrayes et des fausses idées, contre ce qu'enseigne l'auteur de la Recherche de la vérité* (Cologne: Schouten, 1683), pp. 34–58 (Chaps. v and vi).]

*"Dissertations on Reid," [Note A,] p. 797.

*−*65[1]   different in it
−+65[2], 67, 72

in stating his own doctrine, he has furnished, as far as I am aware, the clearest and best statement extant of their common opinion. They differed, indeed, as to our having, in this or in any other manner, an intuitive perception of any of the *attributes* of objects; Reid, like Sir W. Hamilton, affirming, while Brown denied, that we have a direct intuition of the Primary Qualities of bodies. But Brown did not deny, nor would Sir W. Hamilton accuse him of denying, the wide difference between his opinion and Reid's on this latter point.

Before closing this chapter, I will notice the curious fact, that after insisting with so much emphasis upon the recognition of an Ego and a Non-ego as an element in all consciousness, Sir W. Hamilton is obliged to admit that the distinction is in certain cases a mistake, and that our consciousness sometimes recognises a Non-ego where there is only an Ego. It is a doctrine of his, repeated in many parts of his works, that in our *internal* consciousness there is no non-ego. Even the remembrance of a past fact, or the mental image of an absent object, is not a thing separable or distinguishable from the mind's act in remembering, but is another name for that act itself. Now it is certain, that in thinking of an absent or an imaginary object, we naturally imagine ourselves to be thinking of an objective something, distinguishable from the thinking act. Sir W. Hamilton, being obliged to acknowledge this, resolves the difficulty in the very manner for which he so often rebukes other thinkers—by representing this apparent testimony of consciousness as a kind of illusion. "The object," he says, "is in this case given as really identical with the conscious ego, but still consciousness distinguishes it, as an accident, from the ego, as the subject of that accident: it projects, as it were, this subjective phænomenon from itself,—views it at a distance,—in a word, objectifies it."* But if, in one half of the domain of consciousness—the internal half—it is in the power of consciousness to "project" out of itself what is merely one of its own acts, and regard it as external and a non-ego, why are those accused of declaring consciousness a lie, who think that this may possibly be the case with the other half of its domain also, and that the non-ego altogether may be but a mode in which the mind represents to itself the possible modifications of the ego? How the truth stands in respect to this matter I will endeavour, in the following chapter, to investigate. For the present, I content myself with asking, why the same liberty in the interpretation of Consciousness, which Sir W. Hamilton's own doctrine cannot dispense with, should be held to be an insurmountable objection to the "counter-doctrine."

Lectures, Vol. II, p. 432.

ᵘ⁻ᵘ65¹   counter-doctrine?

CHAPTER XI

The Psychological Theory of the Belief in an External World

WE HAVE SEEN Sir W. Hamilton at work on the question of the reality of Matter, by the introspective method, and, as it seems, with little result. Let us now approach the same subject by the psychological. I proceed, therefore, to state the case of those who hold that the belief in an external world is not intuitive, but an acquired product.

This theory postulates the following psychological truths, all of which are proved by experience, and are not contested, though their force is seldom adequately felt, by Sir W. Hamilton and the other thinkers of the introspective school.

It postulates, first, that the human mind is capable of Expectation. In other words, that after having had actual sensations, we are capable of forming the conception of Possible sensations; sensations which we are not feeling at the present moment, but which we might feel, and should feel if certain conditions were present, the nature of which conditions we have, in many cases, learnt by experience.

It postulates, secondly, the laws of the Association of Ideas. So far as we are here concerned, these laws are the following: 1st. Similar phænomena tend to be thought of together. 2nd. Phænomena which have either been experienced or conceived in close contiguity to one another, tend to be thought of together. The contiguity is of two kinds; simultaneity, and immediate succession. Facts which have been experienced or thought of simultaneously, recall the thought of one another. Of facts which have been experienced or thought of in immediate succession, the antecedent, or the thought of it, recalls the thought of the consequent, but not conversely. 3rd. Associations produced by contiguity become more certain and rapid by repetition. When two phænomena have been very often experienced in conjunction, and have not, in any single instance, occurred separately either in experience or in thought, there is produced between them what has been called Inseparable, or less correctly, Indissoluble Association: by which is not meant that the association must inevitably last to the end of life—that no subsequent experience or process of thought can possibly avail to dissolve it; but only that as long as no such experience or process of thought has taken place, the association is irresistible; it is impossible for us to think the one thing disjoined from the other. 4th. When an association has acquired this character of inseparability—when the bond between the two ideas has been thus firmly riveted, not only does the idea called up by association become, in our consciousness, inseparable from the idea which suggested it, but the facts or phænomena answering to those ideas come at last to seem inseparable in existence: things which we are unable to conceive apart, appear incapable of existing apart; and the belief we have in their coexistence, though really a product of experience, seems intuitive. Innumerable examples might be given of this law. One of the most familiar, as well as the most striking, is that of our acquired perceptions of sight. Even those who, with Mr. Bailey, consider the perception of distance by the eye as not acquired, but intuitive, admit that there are many perceptions of sight which, though instantaneous and unhesitating, are not intuitive.[*] What we see is a very minute fragment of what we think we see. We see artificially that one thing is hard, another soft. We see artificially that one thing is hot, another cold. We see artificially that what we see is a book, or a stone, each of these being not merely an inference, but a heap of inferences, from the signs which we see, to things not visible. [a]We see, and cannot help seeing, what we have learnt to infer, even when we know that the inference is erroneous, and that the apparent perception is deceptive. We cannot help seeing the moon larger when near the horizon, though we know that she is of precisely her usual size. We cannot help seeing a mountain as nearer to us and of less height, when we see it through a more than ordinarily transparent atmosphere.[a]

Setting out from these premises, the Psychological Theory maintains, that there are associations naturally and even necessarily generated by the order of our sensations and of our reminiscences of sensation, which, supposing no intuition of an external world to have existed in consciousness, would inevitably generate the belief, and would cause it to be regarded as an intuition.

What is it we mean [b], or what is it which leads us to say, that the objects we perceive are[b] external to us, and not a part of our own thoughts? We mean, that there [c]is concerned[c] in our perceptions something which exists when we are not thinking of it; which existed before we had ever thought of

[*See Samuel Bailey, *A Review of Berkeley's Theory of Vision* (London: Ridgway, 1842), pp. 105–17; cf. *Letters on the Philosophy of the Human Mind*, 2nd ser., pp. 46–50.]

[a]–[a]+67, 72
[b]–[b]65[1], 65[2]   when we say that the object we perceive is
[c]–[c]65[1]   is]   65[2]   is involved

it, and would exist if we were annihilated; and further, that there exist things which we never saw, touched, or otherwise perceived, and things which never have been perceived by man. This idea of something which is distinguished from our fleeting impressions by what, in Kantian language, is called Perdurability; something which is fixed and the same, while our impressions vary; something which exists whether we are aware of it or not, and which is always square (or of some other given figure) whether it appears to us square or round—constitutes altogether our idea of external substance. Whoever can assign an origin to this complex conception, has accounted for what we mean by the belief in matter. Now all this, according to the Psychological Theory, is but the form impressed by the known laws of association, upon the conception or notion, obtained by experience, of Contingent Sensations; by which are meant, sensations that are not in our present consciousness, and ^{d}individually^d never were in our consciousness at all, but which in virtue of the laws to which we have learnt by experience that our sensations are subject, we know that we should have felt under given supposable circumstances, and under these same circumstances, might still feel.

I see a piece of white paper on a table. I go into another room ^{e}. If the phænomenon always followed me, or if, when it did not follow me, I believed it to disappear è rerum naturâ, I should not believe it to be an external object. I should consider it as a phantom—a mere affection of my senses: I should not believe that there had been any Body there. But,^{c} though I have ceased to see it, I am persuaded that the paper is still there. I no longer have the sensations which it gave me; but I believe that when I again place myself in the circumstances in which I had those sensations, that is, when I go again into the room, I shall again have them; and further, that there has been no intervening moment at which this would not have been the case. Owing to this ^{f}property^f of my mind, my conception of the world at any given instant consists, in only a small proportion, of present sensations. Of these I may at the time have none at all, and they are in any case a most insignificant portion of the whole which I apprehend. The conception I form of the world existing at any moment, comprises, along with the sensations I am feeling, a countless variety of possibilities of sensation: namely, the whole of those which past observation tells me that I could, under any supposable circumstances, experience at this moment, together with an indefinite and illimitable multitude of others which though I do not know that I could, yet it is possible that I might, experience in circumstances not known to me. These various possibilities are the impor-

$^{d-d}$65^1, 65^2 perhaps
$^{e-e}$65^1, 65^2 , and
$^{f-f}$65^1, 65^2 law

tant thing to me in the world. My present sensations are generally of little importance, and are moreover fugitive: the possibilities, on the contrary, are permanent, which is the character that mainly distinguishes our idea of Substance or Matter from our notion of sensation. These possibilities, which are conditional certainties, need a special name to distinguish them from mere vague possibilities, which experience gives no warrant for reckoning upon. Now, as soon as a distinguishing name is given, though it be only to the same thing regarded in a different aspect, one of the most familiar experiences of our mental nature teaches us, that the different name comes to be considered as the name of a different thing.

There is another important peculiarity of these certified or guaranteed possibilities of sensation; namely, that they have reference, not to single sensations, but to sensations joined together in groups. When we think of anything as a material substance, or body, we either have had, or we think that on some given supposition we should have, not some *one* sensation, but a great and even an indefinite number and variety of sensations, generally belonging to different senses, but so linked together, that the presence of one announces the possible presence at the very same instant of any or all of the rest. In our mind, therefore, not only is this particular Possibility of sensation invested with the quality of permanence when we are not actually feeling any of the sensations at all; but when we are feeling some of them, the remaining sensations of the group are conceived by us in the form of Present Possibilities, which might be realized at the very moment. And as this happens in turn to all of them, the group as a whole presents itself to the mind as permanent, in contrast not solely with the temporariness of my bodily presence, but also with the temporary character of each of the sensations composing the group; in other words, as a kind of permanent substratum, under a set of passing experiences or manifestations: which is another leading character of our idea of substance or matter, as distinguished from sensation.

Let us now take into consideration another of the general characters of our experience, namely, that in addition to fixed groups, we also recognise a fixed Order in our sensations; an Order of succession, which, when ascertained by observation, gives rise to the ideas of Cause and Effect, according to what I hold to be the true theory of that relation, and is ^{g}on any theory^g the source of all our knowledge ^{h}what^h causes produce what effects. Now, of what nature is this fixed order among our sensations? It is a constancy of antecedence and sequence. But the constant antecedence and sequence do not generally exist between one actual sensation and another. Very few such sequences are presented to us by experience. In almost all

$^{g-g}65^1, 65^2$ in any case
$^{h-h}65^1$ *what*

the constant sequences which occur in Nature, the antecedence and consequence do not obtain between sensations, but between the groups we have
been speaking about, of which a very small portion is actual sensation, the
greater part being permanent possibilities of sensation, evidenced to us by a
small and variable number of sensations actually present. Hence, our ideas
of causation, power, activity, do not become connected in thought with our
sensations as *actual* at all, save in the few physiological cases where these
figure by themselves as the antecedents in some uniform sequence. Those
ideas become connected, not with sensations, but with groups of possibilities of sensation. The sensations conceived do not, to our habitual
thoughts, present themselves as sensations actually experienced, inasmuch as not only any one or any number of them may be supposed absent,
but none of them need be present. We find that the modifications which are
taking place more or less regularly in our possibilities of sensation, are
mostly quite independent of our consciousness, and of our presence or
absence. Whether we are asleep or awake the fire goes out, and puts an end
to one particular possibility of warmth and light. Whether we are present or
absent the corn ripens, and brings a new possibility of food. Hence we
speedily learn to think of Nature as made up solely of these groups of
possibilities, and the active force in Nature as manifested in the modification of some of these by others. The sensations, though the original foundation of the whole, come to be looked upon as a sort of accident depending
on us, and the possibilities as much more real than the actual sensations,
nay, as the very realities of which these are only the representations,
appearances, or effects. When this state of mind has been arrived at, then,
and from that time forward, we are never conscious of a present sensation
without instantaneously referring it to some one of the groups of possibilities into which a sensation of that particular description enters; and if
we do not yet know to what group to refer it, we at least feel an irresistible
conviction that it must belong to some group or other; *i.e.* that its presence
proves the existence, here and now, of a great number and variety of
possibilities of sensation, without which it would not have been. The whole
set of sensations as possible, form a permanent background to any one or
more of them that are, at a given moment, actual; and the possibilities are
conceived as standing to the actual sensations in the relation of a cause to
its effects, or of canvas to the figures painted on it, or of a root to the trunk,
leaves, and flowers, or of a substratum to that which is spread over it, or, in
transcendental language, of Matter to Form.

When this point has been reached, the Permanent Possibilities in question have assumed such unlikeness of aspect, and such difference of ᶦappa-

---

ᶦ⁻ᶦ65¹, 65²   position relatively

rent relation[i] to us, from any sensations, that it would be contrary to all we know of the constitution of human nature that they should not be conceived as, and believed to be, at least as different from sensations as sensations are from one another. Their groundwork in sensation is forgotten, and they are supposed to be something intrinsically distinct from it. We can withdraw ourselves from any of our (external) sensations, or we can be withdrawn from them by some other agency. But though the sensations cease, the possibilities remain in existence; they are independent of our will, our presence, and everything which belongs to us. We find, too, that they belong as much to other human or sentient beings as to ourselves. We find other people grounding their expectations and conduct upon the same permanent possibilities on which we ground ours. But we do not find them experiencing the same actual sensations. Other people do not have our sensations exactly when and as we have them: but they have our pos-sibilities of sensation; whatever indicates a present possibility of sensations to ourselves, indicates a present possibility of similar sensations to them, except so far as their organs of sensation may vary from the type of ours. This puts the final seal to our conception of the groups of possibilities as the fundamental reality in Nature. The permanent possibilities are common to us and to our fellow-creatures; the actual sensations are not. That which other people become aware of when, and on the same grounds, as I do, seems more real to me than that which they do not know of unless I tell them. The world of Possible Sensations succeeding one another according to laws, is as much in other beings as it is in me; it has therefore an existence outside me; it is an External World.

If this explanation of the origin and growth of the idea of Matter, or External Nature, contains nothing at variance with natural laws, it is at least an admissible supposition, that the element of Non-ego which Sir W. Hamilton regards as an original datum of consciousness, and which we certainly do find in [j]what we now call our[j] consciousness, may not be one of its primitive elements—may not have existed at all in its first manifesta-tions. But if this supposition be admissible, it ought, on Sir W. Hamilton's principles, to be received as true. The first of the laws laid down by him for the interpretation of Consciousness, the law (as he terms it) of Parcimony, forbids to suppose an original principle of our nature in order to account for phænomena which admit of possible explanation from known causes. If the supposed ingredient of consciousness be one which might grow up (though we cannot prove that it did grow up) through later experience; and if, when it had so grown up, it would, by known laws of our nature, appear as completely intuitive as our sensations themselves; we are bound, accord-ing to Sir W. Hamilton's and all sound philosophy, to assign to it that origin.

Where there is a known cause adequate to account for a phænomenon, there is no justification for ascribing it to an unknown one. And what evidence does Consciousness furnish of the intuitiveness of an impression, except instantaneousness, apparent simplicity, and unconsciousness on our part of how the impression came into our minds? These features can only prove the impression to be intuitive, on the hypothesis that there are no means of accounting for them otherwise. If they not only might, but naturally would, exist, even on the supposition that it is not intuitive, we must accept the conclusion to which we are led by the Psychological Method, and which the Introspective Method furnishes absolutely nothing to contradict.

Matter, then, may be defined, a Permanent Possibility of Sensation. If I am asked, whether I believe in matter, I ask whether the questioner accepts this definition of it. If he does, I believe in matter: and so do all Berkeleians. In any other sense than this, I do not. But I affirm with confidence, that this conception of Matter includes the whole meaning attached to it by the common world, apart from philosophical, and sometimes from theological, theories. The reliance of mankind on the real existence of visible and tangible objects, means reliance on the reality and permanence of Possibilities of visual and tactual sensations, when no such sensations are actually experienced. We are warranted in believing that this is the meaning of Matter in the minds of many of its most esteemed metaphysical champions, though they themselves would not admit as much: for example, of Reid, Stewart, and Brown. For these three philosophers alleged that all mankind, including Berkeley and Hume, really believed in Matter, inasmuch as unless they did, they would not have turned aside to save themselves from running against a post. Now all which this manœuvre really proved is, that they believed in Permanent Possibilities of Sensation. We have therefore the *k*unintentional*k* sanction of these three eminent defenders of the existence of matter, for affirming, that to believe in Permanent Possibilities of Sensation *l*is*l* believing in Matter. It is hardly necessary, after such authorities, to mention Dr. Johnson,[*] or any one else who resorts to the *argumentum baculinum* of knocking a stick against the ground. Sir W. Hamilton, a far subtler thinker than any of these, never reasons in this manner. He never supposes that a disbeliever in what he means by Matter, ought in consistency to act in any different mode from those who believe in it. He knew that the belief on which all the practical consequences depend, is the belief in Permanent Possibilities of Sensation,

[*See James Boswell, *Life of Johnson*, 2nd ed., 3 vols. (London: Dilly, 1793), Vol. I, p. 436.]

k-k+67, 72
*l-l*65¹ *is*

and that if nobody believed in a material universe in any other sense, life would go on exactly as it now does. He, however, did believe in more than this, but, I think, only because it had never occurred to him that mere Possibilities of Sensation could, to our artificialized consciousness, present the character of objectivity which, as we have now shown, they not only can, but unless the known laws of the human mind were suspended, must necessarily, present.

Perhaps it may be objected, that the very possibility of framing such a notion of Matter as Sir W. Hamilton's—the capacity in the human mind of imagining an external world which is anything more than what the Psychological Theory makes it—amounts to a disproof of the theory. If (it may be said) we had no revelation in consciousness, of a world which is not in some way or other identified with sensation, we should be unable to have the notion of such a world. If the only ideas we had of external objects were ideas of our sensations, supplemented by an acquired notion of permanent possibilites of sensation, we must (it is thought) be incapable of conceiving, and therefore still more incapable of fancying that we perceive, things which are not sensations at all. It being evident however that some philosophers believe this, and it being maintainable that the mass of mankind do so, the existence of a perdurable basis of sensations, distinct from sensations themselves, is proved, it might be said, by the possibility of believing it.

Let me first restate what I apprehend the belief to be. We believe that we perceive a something closely related to all our sensations, but different from those which we are feeling at any particular minute; and distinguished from sensations altogether, by being permanent and always the same, while these are fugitive, variable, and alternately displace one another. But these attributes of the object of perception are properties belonging to all the possibilities of sensation which experience guarantees. The belief in such permanent possibilities seems to me to include all that is essential or characteristic in the belief in substance. I believe that Calcutta exists, though I do not perceive it, and that it would still exist if every percipient inhabitant were suddenly to leave the place, or be struck dead. But when I analyse the belief, all I find in it is, that were these events to take place, the Permanent Possibility of Sensation which I call Calcutta would still remain; that if I were suddenly transported to the banks of the Hoogly, I should still have the sensations which, if now present, would lead me to affirm that Calcutta exists here and now. We may infer, therefore, that both philosophers and the world at large, when they think of matter, conceive it really as a Permanent Possibility of Sensation. But the majority of philosophers fancy that it is something more; and the world at large, though they have really, as I conceive, nothing in their minds but a Permanent Possibility of Sensation, would, if asked the question, undoubtedly agree with the philosophers: and though this is sufficiently explained by the tendency of the human mind to infer difference of things from difference of names, I acknowledge the obligation of showing how it can be possible to believe in an existence transcending all possibilities of sensation, unless on the hypothesis that such an existence actually is, and that we actually perceive it.

The explanation, however, is not difficult. It is an admitted fact, that we are capable of all conceptions which can be formed by generalizing from the observed laws of our sensations. Whatever relation we find to exist between any one of our sensations and something different from *it*, that same relation we have no difficulty in conceiving to exist between the sum of all our sensations and something different from *them*. The differences which our consciousness recognises between one sensation and another, give us the general notion of difference, and inseparably associate with every sensation we have, the feeling of its being different from other things: and when once this association has been formed, we can no longer conceive anything, without being able, and even being compelled, to form also the conception of something different from it. This familiarity with the idea of something different from *each* thing we know, makes it natural and easy to form the notion of something different from *all* things that we know, collectively as well as individually. It is true we can form no conception of what such a thing can be; our notion of it is merely negative; but the idea of ^{m}a substance, apart from its relation to the impressions which we conceive it as making^m on our senses, *is* a merely negative one. There is thus no psychological obstacle to our forming the notion of a something which is neither a sensation nor a possibility of sensation, even if our consciousness does not testify to it; and nothing is more likely than that the Permanent Possibilities of sensation, to which our consciousness does testify, should be confounded in our minds with this imaginary conception. All experience attests the strength of the tendency to mistake mental abstractions, even negative ones, for substantive realities; and the Permanent Possibilities of sensation which experience guarantees, are so extremely unlike in many of their properties to actual sensations, that since we are capable of imagining something which transcends sensation, there is a great natural probability that we should suppose these to be it.

But this natural probability is converted into certainty, when we take into consideration that universal law of our experience which is termed the law of Causation, and which makes us ^{n}mentally connect with the beginning of everything, some^n antecedent condition, or Cause. The case of Causation is one of the most marked of all the cases in which we extend to the sum total of our consciousness, a notion derived from its parts. It is a striking

---

$^{m-m}65^1, 65^2$ substance, apart from the impressions it makes
$^{n-n}65^1, 65^2$ unable to conceive the beginning of anything without an

example of our power to conceive, and our tendency to believe, that a relation which subsists between every individual item of our experience and some other item, subsists also between our experience as a whole, and something not within the sphere of experience. By this extension to the sum of all our experiences, of the internal relations obtaining between its several parts, we are led to consider sensation itself—the aggregate whole of our sensations—as deriving its origin from antecedent existences transcending sensation. That we should do this, is a consequence of the particular character of the uniform sequences, which experience discloses to us among our sensations. As already remarked, the constant antecedent of a sensation is seldom another sensation, or set of sensations, actually felt. It is much oftener the existence of a group of possibilities, not necessarily including any actual sensations, except such as are required to show that the possibilities are really present. Nor are actual sensations indispensable even for this purpose; for the presence of the object (which is nothing more than the immediate presence of the possibilities) may be made known to us by the very sensation which we refer to it as its effect. Thus, the real antecedent of an effect—the only antecedent which, being invariable and unconditional, we consider to be the cause—may be, not any sensation really felt, but solely the presence, at that or the immediately preceding moment, of a group of possibilities of sensation. Hence it is not with sensations as actually experienced, but with their Permanent Possibilities, that the idea of Cause comes to be identified: and we, by one and the same process, acquire the habit of regarding Sensation in general, like all our individual sensations, as an Effect, and also that of conceiving as the causes of most of our individual sensations, not other sensations, but general possibilities of sensation. If all these considerations put together do not completely explain and account for our conceiving these Possibilities as a class of independent and substantive entities, I know not what psychological analysis can be conclusive.

It may perhaps be said, that the preceding theory gives, indeed, some account of the idea of Permanent Existence which forms part of our conception of matter, but gives no explanation of our believing these permanent objects to be external, or out of ourselves. I apprehend, on the contrary, that the very idea of anything out of ourselves is derived solely from the knowledge experience gives us of the Permanent Possibilities. Our sensations we carry with us wherever we go, and they never exist where we are not; but when we change our place we do not carry away with us the Permanent Possibilities of Sensation: they remain until we return, or arise and cease under conditions with which our presence has in general nothing to do. And more than all—they are, and will be after we have ceased to feel, Permanent Possibilities of sensation to other beings than ourselves. Thus our actual sensations and the permanent possibilities of sensation, stand out in obtrusive contrast to one another: and when the idea of Cause has been acquired, and extended by generalization from the parts of our experience to its aggregate whole, nothing can be more natural than that the Permanent Possibilities should be classed by us as existences generically distinct from our sensations, but of which our sensations are the effect.*

The same theory which accounts for our ascribing to an aggregate of possibilities of sensation, a permanent existence which our sensations themselves do not possess, and consequently a greater reality than belongs to our sensations, also explains our attributing greater objectivity to the Primary Qualities of bodies than to the Secondary. For the sensations which correspond to what are called the Primary Qualities (as soon at least as we come to apprehend them by two senses, the eye as well as the touch) are always present when any part of the group is so. But colours, tastes, smells, and the like, being, in comparison, fugacious, are not, in the same degree, conceived as being always there, even when nobody is present to perceive them. The sensations answering to the Secondary Qualities are only occasional, those to the Primary, constant. The Secondary, moreover, vary with different persons, and with the temporary sensibility of our organs; the Primary, when perceived at all, are, as far as we know, the same to all persons and at all times.

*[67] My able American critic, Dr. H. B. Smith, contends through several pages (pp. 152–7) that these facts afford no proofs that objects *are* external to us. I never pretended that they do. I am accounting for our conceiving, or representing to ourselves, the Permanent Possibilities as real objects external to us. I do not believe that the real externality to us of anything, except other minds, is capable of proof. But the Permanent Possibilities are external to us in the only sense we need care about; they are not constructed by the mind itself, but merely recognised by it; in Kantian language, they are *given* to us, and to other beings in common with us. "Men cannot act, cannot live," says Professor Fraser, "without assuming an external world, in some conception of the term external. It is the business of the philosopher to explain what that conception ought to be. For ourselves we can conceive only—(1) An externality to our present and transient experience in *our own* possible experience past and future, and (2) An externality to our own conscious experience, in the contemporaneous, as well as in the past or future experience of *other minds*." (["Mr. Mill's *Examination*,"] p. 26.) The view I take of externality, in the sense in which I acknowledge it as real, could not be more accurately expressed than in Professor Fraser's words. Dr. Smith's criticisms continually go wide of the mark because he has somehow imagined that I am defending, instead of attacking, the belief in Matter as an entity *per se*. As when he says (pp. 157–8) that my reasoning assumes, contrary to my own opinion, "an *à priori* necessity and validity of the law of cause and effect, or invariable antecedence and consequence." This might fairly have been said if I were defending the belief in the supposed hidden cause of our sensations: but I am only accounting for it; and to do so I assume only the tendency, but not the legitimacy of the tendency, to extend all the laws of our own experience to a sphere beyond our experience.

CHAPTER XII

The Psychological Theory of the Belief in Matter, How Far Applicable to Mind

IF THE DEDUCTIONS in the preceding chapter are correctly drawn from known and admitted laws of the human mind, the doctrine which forms the basis of Sir W. Hamilton's system of psychology, that Mind and Matter, an ego and a non-ego, are original data of consciousness, is deprived of its foundation. Although these two elements, an Ego and a Non-ego, are in *(what we call)* our consciousness now, and are, or seem to be, inseparable from it, there is no reason for believing that the latter of them, the non-ego, was in consciousness from the beginning; since, even if it was not, we can perceive a way in which it not only might, but must have grown up. We can see that, supposing it absent in the first instance, it would inevitably be present now, not as a deliverance of consciousness in Sir W. Hamilton's sense, for to call it so is to beg the question; but as an instantaneous and irresistible suggestion and inference, which has become by long repetition undistinguishable from a direct intuition. I now propose to carry the inquiry a step farther, and to examine whether the Ego, as a deliverance of consciousness, stands on *b* firmer ground than the Non-ego; whether, at the first moment of our experience, we already have in our consciousness the conception of Self as a permanent existence; or whether it is formed subsequently, and admits of a similar analysis to that which we have found that the notion of Not-self is susceptible of.

It is evident, in the first place, that our knowledge of mind, like that of matter, is entirely relative; Sir W. Hamilton indeed affirms this of mind, in *an even* more unqualified manner than he believes it of matter, making no *distinction between Primary and Secondary* Qualities.

In so far as mind is the common name for the states of knowing, willing, feeling, desiring, &c., of which I am conscious, it is only the name for a certain series of connected phænomena or qualities, and consequently expresses only what is

a−a +72
b 65¹, 65² any
c−c 65¹, 65², 67 a much
d−d 65¹, 65², 67 reservation of any Primary

known. But in so far as it denotes that subject or substance in which the phænomena of knowing, willing, &c., inhere—something behind or under these phænomena—it expresses what, in itself, or in its absolute existence, is unknown.*

We have no conception of Mind itself, as distinguished from its conscious manifestations. We neither know nor can imagine it, except as represented by the succession of manifold feelings which metaphysicians call by the name of States or Modifications of Mind. It is nevertheless true that our notion of Mind, as well as of Matter, is the notion of a permanent something, contrasted with the perpetual flux of the sensations and other feelings or mental states which we refer to it; a something which we figure as remaining the same, while the particular feelings through which it reveals its existence, change. This attribute of Permanence, supposing that there were nothing else to be considered, would admit of the same explanation when predicated of Mind, as of Matter. The belief I entertain that my mind exists when it is not feeling, nor thinking, nor conscious of its own existence, resolves itself into the belief of a Permanent Possibility of these states. If I think of myself as in dreamless sleep, or in the sleep of death, and believe that I, or in other words my mind, is or will be existing through these states, though not in conscious feeling, the most scrupulous examination of my belief will not detect in it any fact actually believed, except that my capability of feeling is not, in that interval, permanently destroyed, and is suspended only because it does not meet with the combination of ^{e}conditions^e which would call it into action: the moment it did meet with that combination it would revive, and remains, therefore, a Permanent Possibility. Thus far, there seems no hindrance to our regarding Mind as nothing but the series of our sensations (to which must now be added our internal feelings), as they actually occur, with the addition of infinite possibilities of feeling requiring for their actual realization conditions which may or may not take place, but which as possibilities are always in existence, and many of them present. ^{f}

Lectures, Vol. I, p. 138.

$^{e-e}$65[1], 65[2]   outward circumstances

^{f}65[1], 65[2]   [*paragraph*] The Permanent Possibility of feeling, which forms my notion of Myself, is distinguished, by important differences, from the Permanent Possibilities of sensation which form my notion of what I call external objects. In the first place, each of these last represents a small and perfectly definite part of the series which, in its entireness, forms my conscious existence—a single group of possible sensations, which experience tells me I might expect to have under certain conditions; as distinguished from mere vague and indefinite possibilities, which are considered such only because they are not known to be impossibilities. My notion of Myself, on the contrary, includes all possibilities of sensation, definite or indefinite, certified by experience or not, which I may imagine inserted in the series of my actual and conscious states. In the second place, the Permanent Possibilities which I call outward objects, are possibilities of sensation only, while the series which I call Myself includes, along with and as called up by these, thoughts, emotions, and volitions, and

In order to the further understanding of the bearings of this theory of the Ego, it is advisable to consider it in its relation to three questions, which may very naturally be asked with reference to it, and which often have been asked, and sometimes answered very erroneously. If the theory is correct, and my Mind is but a series of feelings, or, as it has been called, a thread of consciousness, however supplemented by believed Possibilities of consciousness which are not, though they might be, realized; if this is all that Mind, or Myself, amounts to, what evidence have I (it is asked) of the existence of my fellow-creatures? What evidence of a hyperphysical world, or, in one word, of God? and, lastly, what evidence of immortality?

Dr. Reid unhesitatingly answers, None.[*] If the doctrine is true, I am alone in the universe.

I hold this to be one of Reid's most palpable mistakes. Whatever evidence to each of the three points there is on the ordinary theory, exactly that same evidence is there on this.

In the first place, as to my fellow-creatures. Reid seems to have imagined that if I myself am only a series of feelings, the proposition that I have any fellow-creatures, or that there are any Selves except mine, is but words without a meaning. But this is a misapprehension. All that I am compelled to admit if I receive this theory, is that other people's Selves also are but series of feelings, like my own. Though my Mind, as I am capable of conceiving it, be nothing but the succession of my feelings, and though Mind itself may be merely a possibility of feelings, there is nothing in that doctrine to prevent my conceiving, and believing, that there are other successions of feelings besides those of which I am conscious, and that these are as real as my own. The belief is completely consistent with the metaphysical theory. Let us now see whether the theory takes away the grounds of it.

What are those grounds? By what evidence do I know, or by what considerations am I led to believe, that there exist other sentient creatures; that the walking and speaking figures which I see and hear, have sensations and thoughts, or in other words, possess Minds? The most strenuous Intuitionist does not include this among the things that I know by direct intuition. I conclude it from certain things, which my experience of my own

[*See, e.g., *On the Intellectual Powers*, pp. 426–34.]

Permanent Possibilities of such. Besides that these states of mind are, to our consciousness, generically distinct from the sensations of our outward senses, they are further distinguished from them by not occurring in groups, consisting of separate elements which coexist, or may be made to coexist, with one another. Lastly (and this difference is the most important of all) the Possibilities of Sensation which are called outward objects, are possibilities of it to other beings as well as to me: but the particular series of feelings which constitutes my own life, is confined to myself: no other sentient being shares it with me.

states of feeling proves to me to be marks of it. These marks are of two kinds, antecedent and subsequent; the previous conditions requisite for feeling, and the effects or consequences of it. I conclude that other human beings have feelings like me, because, first, they have bodies like me, which I know, in my own case, to be the antecedent condition of feelings; and because, secondly, they exhibit the acts, and other outward signs, which in my own case I know by experience to be caused by feelings. I am conscious in myself of a series of facts connected by an uniform sequence, of which the beginning is modifications of my body, the middle is feelings, the end is outward demeanour. In the case of other human beings I have the evidence of my senses for the first and last links of the series, but not for the intermediate link. I find, however, that the sequence between the first and last is as regular and constant in those other cases as it is in mine. In my own case I know that the first link produces the last through the intermediate link, and could not produce it without. Experience, therefore, obliges me to conclude that there must be an intermediate link; which must either be the same in others as in myself, or a different one: I must either believe them to be alive, or to be automatons: and by believing them to be alive, that is, by supposing the link to be of the same nature as in the case of which I have experience, and which is in all other respects similar, I bring other human beings, as phænomena, under the same generalizations which I know by experience to be the true theory of my own existence. And in doing so I conform to the legitimate rules of experimental enquiry. The process is exactly parallel to that by which Newton proved that the force which keeps the planets in their orbits is identical with that by which an apple falls to the ground. It was not incumbent on Newton to prove the impossibility of its being any other force; he was thought to have made out his point when he had simply shown, that no other force need be supposed. We know the existence of other beings by generalization from the knowledge of our own: the generalization merely postulates that what experience shows to be a mark of the existence of something within the sphere of our consciousness, may be concluded to be a mark of the same thing beyond that sphere.

This logical process loses none of its legitimacy on the supposition that neither Mind nor Matter is anything but a permanent possibility of feeling. Whatever sensation I have, I at once refer it to one of the permanent groups of possibilities of sensation which I call material objects. But among these groups I find there is one (my own body) which is not only composed, like the rest, of a mixed multitude of sensations and possibilities of sensation, but is also connected, in a peculiar manner, with all my sensations. Not only is this special group always present as an antecedent condition of every sensation I have, but the other groups are only enabled to convert their respective possibilities of sensation into actual sensations, by means of some previous change in that particular one. I look about me, and though there is only one group (or body) which is connected with all my sensations in this peculiar manner, I observe that there is a great multitude of other bodies, closely resembling in their sensible properties (in the sensations composing them as groups) this particular one, but whose modifications do not call up, as those of my own body do, a world of sensations in my consciousness. Since they do not do so in my consciousness, I infer that they do it out of my consciousness, and that to each of them belongs a world of consciousness of its own, to which it stands in the same relation in which what I call my own body stands to mine. And having made this generalization, I find that all other facts within my reach *accord* with it. Each of these bodies exhibits to my senses a set of phænomena (composed of acts and other manifestations) such as I know, in my own case, to be effects of consciousness, and such as might be looked for if each of the bodies has really in connexion with it a world of consciousness. All this is as good and genuine an inductive process on the theory we are discussing, as it is on the common theory. Any objection to it in the one case would be an equal objection in the other. I have stated the postulate required by the one theory: the common theory is in need of the same. If I could not, from my personal knowledge of one succession of feelings, infer the existence of other successions of feelings, when manifested by the same outward signs, I could just as little, from my personal knowledge of a single spiritual substance, infer by generalization, when I find the same outward indications, the existence of other spiritual substances.

As the theory leaves the evidence of the existence of my fellow-creatures exactly as it was before, so does it also with that of the existence of God. Supposing me to believe that the Divine Mind is simply the series of the Divine thoughts and feelings prolonged through eternity, that would be, at any rate, believing God's existence to be as real as my own. And as for evidence, the argument of Paley's *Natural Theology*, or, for that matter, of his *Evidences of Christianity*, would stand exactly where it does.[*] The Design argument is drawn from the analogy of human experience. From the relation which human works bear to human thoughts and feelings, it infers a corresponding relation between works, more or less similar but super-human, and superhuman thoughts and feelings. If it proves these, nobody but a metaphysician needs care whether or not it proves a mysterious

_____

[*William Paley, *Natural Theology: or, Evidences of the existence and attributes of the Deity* (London: Faulder, 1802); *A View of the Evidences of Christianity*, 3 vols. (London: Faulder, 1794).]

*–*65[1]   agree

substratum for them. Again, the arguments for Revelation undertake to prove by testimony, that within the sphere of human experience works were done requiring a greater than human power, and words said requiring a greater than human wisdom. These positions, and the evidences of them, neither lose nor gain anything by our supposing that the wisdom only means wise thoughts and volitions, and that the power means thoughts and volitions followed by imposing phænomena.

As to immortality, it is precisely as easy to conceive that a succession of feelings, a thread of consciousness, may be prolonged to eternity, as that a spiritual substance for ever continues to exist: and any evidence which would prove the one, will prove the other. Metaphysical theologians may lose the *à priori* argument by which they have sometimes flattered themselves with having proved that a spiritual substance, by the essential constitution of its nature, *cannot* perish. But they had better drop this argument in any case. To do them justice, they seldom insist on it now.

The notion that metaphysical Scepticism, even at the utmost length to which it ever has been, or is capable of being, carried, has for its logical consequence atheism, is grounded on an entire misapprehension of the Sceptical argument, and has no *locus standi* except for persons who think that whatever accustoms people to a rigid scrutiny of evidence is unfavourable to religious belief. This is the opinion, doubtless, of those who do not believe in any religion, and seemingly of a great number who do: but it is not the opinion of Sir W. Hamilton, who says that "religious disbelief and philosophical scepticism are not merely not the same, but have no natural connexion;"* and who, as we have seen, makes use of the veracity of the Deity as his principal argument for trusting the testimony of consciousness to the substantiality of Matter and of Mind, which would have been a gross *petitio principii* if he had thought that our assurance of the divine attributes required that the objective existence of Matter and Mind should be first recognised.

The theory, therefore, which resolves Mind into a series of feelings, with a background of possibilities of feeling, can effectually withstand the most invidious of the arguments directed against it. But, groundless as are the extrinsic objections, the theory has intrinsic difficulties which we have not yet set forth, and which it seems to me beyond the power of metaphysical analysis to remove. Besides present feelings, and possibilities of present feeling, there is another class of phænomena to be included in an enumeration of the elements making up our conception of Mind. The thread of consciousness which composes the mind's phænomenal life, consists not

Lectures, Vol. I, p. 394.

only of present sensations, but likewise, in part, of memories and expectations. Now what are these? In themselves, they are present feelings, states of present consciousness, and in that respect not distinguished from sensations. They all, moreover, resemble some given sensations or feelings, of which we have previously had experience. But they are attended with the peculiarity, that each of them involves a belief in more than its own present existence. A sensation involves only this: but a remembrance of sensation, even if not referred to any particular date, involves the suggestion and belief that a sensation, of which it is a copy or representation, actually existed in the past: and an expectation involves the belief, more or less positive, that a sensation or other feeling to which it directly refers, will exist in the future. Nor can the phænomena involved in these two states of consciousness be adequately expressed, without saying that the belief they include is, that I myself formerly had, or that I myself, and no other, shall hereafter have, the sensations remembered or expected. The fact believed is, that the sensations did actually form, or will hereafter form, part of the self-same series of states, or thread of consciousness, of which the remembrance or expectation of those sensations is the part now present. If, therefore, we speak of the Mind as a series of feelings, we are obliged to complete the statement by calling it a series of feelings which is aware of itself as past and future; and we are reduced to the alternative of believing that the Mind, or Ego, is something different from any series of feelings, or possibilities of them, or of accepting the paradox, that something which *ex hypothesi* is but a series of feelings, can be aware of itself as a series.

The truth is, that we are here face to face with that final inexplicability, at which, as Sir W. Hamilton observes, we inevitably arrive when we reach ultimate facts; and in general, one mode of stating it only appears more incomprehensible than another, because the whole of human language is accommodated to the one, and is so incongruous with the other, that it cannot be expressed in any terms which do not deny its truth. The real stumbling block is perhaps not in any theory of the fact, but in the fact itself. The true incomprehensibility perhaps is, that something which has ceased, or is not yet in existence, can still be, in a manner, present: that a series of feelings, the infinitely greater part of which is past or future, can be gathered up, as it were, into a single present conception, accompanied by a belief of reality. I think, by far the wisest thing we can do, is to accept the inexplicable fact, without any theory of how it takes place; and when we are obliged to speak of it in terms which assume a theory, to use them with a reservation as to their meaning.

I have stated the difficulties attending the attempt to frame a theory of Mind, or the Ego, similar to what I have called the Psychological Theory of

Matter, or the Non-ego. No such difficulties attend the theory in its application to Matter; and I leave it, as set forth, to pass for whatever it is worth as an antagonist doctrine to that of Sir W. Hamilton and the Scottish School, respecting the non-ego as a deliverance of consciousness.*

*Mr. Mansel, in his *Prolegomena Logica*, shows a perception of the difference here pointed out between the character of the Psychological explanation of the belief in Matter, and that of the belief in Mind; and he resolves the question by drawing a distinction between the two Noumena, not often drawn by philosophers posterior to Berkeley. He considers the Ego to be a direct presentation of consciousness, while with regard to the Non-ego he is not far from adopting the Berkeleian theory. The whole of his remarks on the subject are well worth reading. See *Prolegomena Logica* [*: An inquiry into the psychological character of logical processes* (Oxford: Graham, 1851)], pp. 123–35.

This attempt to bring out into distinctness the mode in which the notions of Matter and Mind, considered as Substances, may have been generated in us by the mere order of our sensations, has naturally received from those whose metaphysical opinions were already made up, a much greater amount of opposition than of assent. I think I have observed, however, that the repugnance shown to it by writers has been in tolerably correct proportion to the evidence they give of deficiency in that indispensable aptitude of a metaphysician, facility in placing himself at the point of view of a theory different from his own: and that those who have ever (if the expression may be pardoned) thought themselves into the Berkeleian or any other Idealistic scheme of philosophy, however little favourable towards other parts of the present volume, have either let this part of it alone, or expressed more or less approbation of it. Those who are completely satisfied with the popular every-day notion of Matter, or whose metaphysics have been adopted from any of the Realistic thinkers who undertake to legitimate that common notion, are usually content with going round the counter-theory on the outside, and seldom place themselves sufficiently at the centre of it to perceive what a person ought to think or do, who occupies that position. They no longer, indeed, commit so gross a blunder as that which, not very long ago, even Reid, Stewart, and Brown rushed blindly into—that of charging a Berkeleian with inconsistency if he did not walk into the water or into the fire. Acquaintance with the German metaphysicians, and (it is but just to add) the teachings of Sir W. Hamilton, have had that much of beneficial result. But if such thinkers as these three could pass judgment on Berkeley's doctrine while showing by such conclusive proof that they had never understood its very alphabet—that, however much consideration they may have given to the mere arguments of Berkeley, they had not begun to realize his doctrine in their own minds—to look at the sensible universe as he saw it, and see what consequences would follow; it is not wonderful that those who have got on a few steps further than this, have still much to do, before they are able to accommodate their conceptive faculties to the conditions of what I have called the Psychological Theory, and follow that theory correctly into the ramification of its applications.

In principle, I must admit that my opponents, as a body, have referred the Psychological Theory to the right test. They have aimed at showing that its attempt to account for the belief in Matter (I say Matter only, because I do not profess to have adequately accounted for the belief in Mind) implies or requires that the belief should already exist, as a condition of its own

ʰ⁻ʰ²⁰⁸+67, 72

production. The objection, if true, is conclusive; but they are not very particular about the proof of its truth. They, one and all, think their case made out, if I employ, in any part of the exposition, the language of common life—a language constructed on the basis of the notions into the origin of which I am inquiring. If I say, that after we have seen a piece of paper on a table, our belief that it is still there during our absence means a belief that if we went again into the room we should see it, they cry out, Here is belief in Matter already assumed; the idea of going into a room implies belief in matter. If, as a proof that modifications may take place in our possibilities of sensation while the sensations are not in actual consciousness, I say that whether we are asleep or awake the fire goes out, I am told that I am assuming a knowledge of ourselves as a substance, and of the difference between being asleep and awake. They forget that to go into a room, to be asleep or awake, are expressions which have a meaning in the Psychological Theory as well as in theirs; that every assertion that can be made about the external world, which means anything on the Realistic theory, has a parallel meaning on the Psychological. Going into a room, on the Psychological theory, is a mere series of sensations felt, and possibilities of sensation inferred,* but distinguishable from every other combination of sensations and possibilities, and which, with others like to itself, forms as vast and variegated a picture of the universe as can be had on the other theory; indeed, as I maintain, the very same picture. The Psychological theory requires that we should have a conception of this series of actual and contingent sensations, as distinct from any other; but it does not require that we should have referred these sensations to a substance ulterior to all sensation or possibility of sensation. To suppose so, is to commit the same kind of misapprehension, though in a less extreme degree, which Reid, Stewart, and Brown committed.

When, in attempting an intelligible discussion of an abstruse metaphysical question, I have occasion to speak of any combination of physical facts, I must speak of it by the only names there are for it. I must employ language, every word of which expresses, not things as we perceive them, or as we may have conceived them originally, but things as we conceive them now. I was addressing readers, all of whom had the acquired notion of Matter, and nearly all of them the belief in it: and it was my business to show, to these believers in Matter, a possible mode in which the notion and belief of it might have been acquired, even if Matter, in the metaphysical meaning of the term, did not exist. In endeavouring to point out to them, by what facts the notion might have been generated, it was competent to me to

---

*[67] This particular series includes volitions in addition to sensations; but the difference is of no consequence; and the theory would stand if we suppose ourselves carried into the room instead of walking into it.

state those facts in the language which was not only the most intelligible, but, to the minds I was addressing, the truest. The real paralogism would have been, if I had said anything implying, not the existence of Matter, but that the belief in it or the notion of it was part of the facts by which I was maintaining that this belief and notion may have been generated. But in no single instance have any adversaries whom I am aware of, been able to show this: and if they fairly placed themselves at the point of view of the Psychological explanation, they would see that I could not, in any circumstances whatever, have been reduced to this necessity: because there is, as I have said, for every statement which can be made concerning material phænomena in terms of the Realistic theory, an equivalent meaning in terms of Sensation and Possibilities of Sensation alone, and a meaning which would justify all the same processes of thought.[*] In fact, almost all philosophers who have narrowly examined the subject, have decided that Substance need only be postulated as a support for phænomena, or as a bond of connexion to hold a group or series of otherwise unconnected phænomena together: let us only, then, think away the support, and suppose the phænomena to remain, and to be held together in the same groups and series by some other agency, or without any agency but an internal law, and every consequence follows without Substance, for the sake of which Substance was assumed. The Hindoos thought that the earth required to be supported by an elephant; but the earth turned out quite capable of supporting itself, and "hanging self-balanced" on its own "centre."[†] Descartes thought that a material medium filling the whole space between the earth and the sun, was required to enable them to act on one another;[‡] but it has been found sufficient to suppose an immaterial law of attraction, and the medium and its vortices dropped off as superfluities.

To dispel some of the haze which seems still to hang about the data assumed by the Psychological theory of the belief in Matter, it will be well that, as I have stated what laws and capacities, in one word what conditions, that theory postulates in the mind itself, I should also state what conditions it postulates in Nature; in that which, to use the Kantian phraseology, is given to the mind, as distinguished from the mind's own constitution.

First, then, it postulates Sensations; and a certain Order among sensations. And the Order postulated, is of more kinds than one.

In the first place, there is the mere fact of succession. Sensations exist before and after one another. This is as much a primordial fact as sensation itself; it is a feature always present in sensation, and we have the strongest

[*See, e.g., pp. 182–3 and 192 above.]
[†Milton, *Paradise Lost*, in *Works*, p. 186 (VII, 242).]
[‡See Descartes, *Principia Philosophiæ*, pp. 48ff. (III, xxvff.)]

ground that can ever be had for regarding it as ultimate, because every genesis we assign to any other fact of perception or thought, includes it as a condition. I shall be told, that this is postulating the reality of Time: and it is so, if by Time be understood an indefinite succession of successions, unequal in rapidity. But an entity called Time, and regarded as not a succession of successions, but as something *in* which the successions take place, I do not and need not postulate.* Neither do I decide whether this inseparable attribute of our sensations is annexed to them by the laws of mind, or given in the sensations themselves; nor whether, at this great height of abstraction, the distinction does not disappear. Let me say also, that I have never pretended to account by association for the idea of Time. It is the seeming infinity of Time, as of Space, which, after Mr. James Mill,[*] I have tendered that explanation of: and that of this it is the true and sufficient one, is to me obvious.

Sensations are not only successive, they are also simultaneous: it often happens that several of them are felt, apparently at the same instant. This attribute of sensations is not so evidently primordial as their succession. There are philosophers who think that the sensations deemed simultaneous are very rapidly successive, their distinction from other cases of succession being that they may succeed one another in any order. I do not agree in this opinion; but, even supposing it correct, we should equally have to postulate the distinction. We should have to assume that plurality of sensations exists in two modes, one consciously successive, the other felt as simultaneous, and that the mind is able to distinguish between the one sort and the other.

Besides this twofold order inherent in sensations, of being either successive or simultaneous, there is an order within that order: they are successive or simultaneous in constant combinations. The same antecedent sensation is followed by the same consequent sensation; the same sensation is accompanied by the same set of simultaneous sensations. I use these expressions for shortness, for the uniformity of order is not quite so simple as this. The consequent sensation is not always *actually* felt after the

---

*[67] This objective conception of Time, as *holding* the successions instead of *being* them, is probably suggested by our being able to measure time, and number its parts. But what we call measuring Time is only comparing successions, and measuring the length or rapidity of one series of successions by that of another. Rapidity of succession, indeed, is a phrase which derives all its meaning from such a comparison. I say that the words of a person to whom I am listening succeed one another more rapidly than the tickings of a clock, because, after I have heard a word and a ticking simultaneously, a second word occurs before a second ticking. The only ultimate facts or primitive elements in Time are Before and After; which (the knowledge of opposites being one) involve the notion of Neither before nor after, *i.e.* simultaneous.

[*See *Analysis*, Vol. II, pp. 100–19 (Chap. xiv, §5).]

antecedent, nor are all the synchronous sensations actually felt whenever one of them is felt. But the one which is felt gives us assurance, grounded on experience, that each of the others, if not felt, is feelable, *i.e.*, will be felt if the other facts be present which are the known antecedent conditions of such a sensation as it is. For example, I have the sensations of colour and of a visible disk, which are parts of our present conception of a cast-iron ball. I infer that there are, now or presently to be had by me, simultaneously with those visual sensations, another feeling, called the sensation of hardness. But I do not have this last sensation inevitably and at once. Why? Because (as I also know by experience) no sensation of hardness is ever felt unless preceded by a condition, the same in all cases, but itself sensational, the sensations of muscular exertion and pressure. The visual sensation is synchronous, not necessarily with the actual sensation of hardness, but with a present possibility of that sensation. When we feel the one, we are not always feeling the other, but we know that it is to be felt on the ordinary terms: we know that so soon as the muscular sensations take place which are the observed preliminary to *every* sensation of hardness, that particular sensation of hardness will certainly be had, simultaneously with the visual sensation. This is what is meant by saying that a Body is a group of simultaneous possibilities of sensation, not of simultaneous sensations. It rarely happens that the sensations which enter into the group can all be experienced at once; because many of them are never had without a long series of antecedent sensations, including volitions, which may be incompatible with the sensations and volitions necessary for having others. The sensations which we receive when we study the internal structure of a closed body, are not to be obtained without having previously the complex series of sensations and volitions concerned in the operation of opening it. The sensations we receive from the complicated process by which food nourishes us, must be long waited for after our first sight of the food, and many of them are not even then to be had without our being led up to them through a long series of muscular and other sensations. But the very first sensations we have, that are sufficient to identify the group, guarantee to us the possibility or potentiality of all the others. The potentiality becomes actuality on the occurrence of certain known conditions *sine quâ non* of each, which are conditions not of having that particular sensation at a given moment, but of having any sensation of that kind; conditions which, when analysed, are themselves also merely sensational. Any one who had thrown his mind, by an act of imagination, into the Psychological theory, would see at a glance all these applications and developments of it, even if he did not follow them out into detail. But men will not, and mostly cannot, throw their minds into any theory with which they are not familiar; and the bearings and consequences of the Psychological theory will have to be developed and minutely expounded innumerable times, before it will be seen as it is, and have whatever chance it deserves of being accepted as true.

I have postulated, first, Sensations; secondly, succession and simultaneousness of sensations; thirdly, an uniform order in their succession and simultaneousness, such that they are united in groups, the component sensations of which are in such a relation to one another, that when we experience one, we are authorized to expect all the rest, conditionally on certain antecedent sensations called organic, belonging to the *kind* of each. This is all we need postulate with regard to the groups, considered in themselves, or considered in relation to the perceiving Subject. Let us examine whether it is necessary to postulate anything additional respecting the groups considered in relation to one another.

In Dr. M'Cosh's opinion, the Psychological theory overlooks this part of the subject.* In quoting the analysis of our conception of Matter into Resistance, Extension, and Figure, together with miscellaneous powers of exciting other sensations, he observes, "There is a palpable omission here, for it omits those powers by which one body operates upon another; thus the sun has a power to make wax white, and fire to make lead fluid."[*] If Dr. M'Cosh had entered even a very little way into the mode of thought which he is combating, he must have seen that after mentioning the attribute of exciting sensations, it could not be necessary to add that of making something else excite sensations. If Body altogether is only conceived as a power of exciting sensations, the action of one body upon another is simply the modification by one such power, of the sensations excited by another; or, to use a different expression, the joint action of two powers of exciting sensations. It is easy for any one competent to such enquiries who will make the attempt, to understand how one group of Possibilities of Sensation can be conceived as destroying or modifying another such group.

Let there be granted a synchronous group, connected by the contingent simultaneousness already described, which renders each of the component sensations a mark of the possibility of having all the others; while each, independently of the others, has conditions *sine quâ non* of its own, also sensational, but of the kind which, in common language, we call organic, and refer to an internal sense. Let us suppose that these organic conditions,

---

*[67] M'Cosh, [*Examination,*] p. 118. The same observation applies to another of my critics, the writer in *Blackwood's Magazine*, who says "The qualities by which they [Things] act upon each other, cannot be resolved into any receptivity or subjectivity of mine." ([W. H. Smith, "J. S. Mill on Our Belief in the External World,"] p. 28.)

[*McCosh, *ibid.*; the concluding clauses derive from Locke, *Essay Concerning Human Understanding, Works*, Vol. I, p. 236 (Bk. II, Chap. xxi, §1).]

instead of existing for one or more sensations of the group and not for the rest, do not at present exist for any of them. The whole of the possibilities of sensation which form the group, and which mutually testify to each other's presence, are now dormant: but they are ready to start into actuality at any moment, when the conditions *sine quâ non* which belong to them separately are realized: and whenever any of them thus starts up, it informs us (so far as our experience happens to have reached) what others are ready to do so in the same manner. This dormancy of all the possibilities, while, as real possibilities guaranteeing one another, they continue to exist, constitutes, on the Psychological theory, the fact which is at the bottom of the assertion that the body is in existence when we are not perceiving it. This fact is all that we need postulate to account for our conceiving the groups of Possibilities of Sensation as permanent and independent of us; for our projecting them into objectivity; and for our conceiving them as perhaps capable of being Possibilities of Sensation to other beings in like manner as to ourselves, as soon as we have conceived the idea of other sentient beings than ourselves. And since we do actually recognise other sentient beings as existing, and receive impressions from them which entirely accord with this hypothesis, we accept the hypothesis as a truth, and believe that the Permanent Possibilities of Sensation really are common to ourselves and other beings.

Having thus arrived at the conception of an absent group of Possibilities, there is surely no more difficulty in conceiving the annihilation or alteration of the Possibilities while absent, than of the sensations themselves when present. The log which I saw on the fire an hour ago, has been consumed and has disappeared when I look again; the Possibilities of Sensation which I called by that name, are possibilities no longer. The ice which I placed in front of the fire at the same time, is now water; such Possibilities of Sensation as form part of the groups called ice and not of the groups called water, have ceased and given place to others. All this is intelligible without supposing the wood, the ice, or the water, to be anything underneath or beyond Permanent Possibilities of Sensation. Why, then, when I ascribe the disappearance of the wood, and the conversion of the ice into water, to the presence of the fire, must I suppose the fire to be something underneath a Possibility of Sensation? My experience informs me that those other Possibilities of Sensation do not vanish or change in the manner mentioned, unless another Possibility of Sensation known by the name of fire, has existed immediately before, and continued to exist simultaneously with the change. Changes in the Permanent Possibilities I find to have always for their antecedent conditions, other Permanent Possibilities, and to be connected with them by an order or law, as uniform as that which connects the elements of each group with one another; indeed by a still stricter order, for the laws of succession, those of Cause and Effect, are laws of more rigid precision than those of simultaneousness. But the facts, between which the observed uniformities of succession exist, are facts of sense; that is, either actual sensations, or possibilities of sensation inferred from the actual. Thus the whole variety of the facts of nature as we know it, is given in the mere existence of our sensations, and in the laws or order of their occurrence.*

I have now given an exposition of the Psychological Theory, and of the mode in which it accounts for what is supposed to be our natural conviction of the existence of Matter, from the objective point of view, as I had previously done from the subjective; and I think it will be found that the exposition does not presuppose anything which I have not expressly postulated, and that I have not postulated any of the facts or notions which I undertake to explain. It may be said that I postulate an Ego—the sentient Subject of the sensations. I have stated what subjective, as well as what objective data I postulate. Expectation being one of these, in so far as reference to an Ego is implied in Expectation I do postulate an Ego. But I am entitled to do so, for up to this stage it is not Self, but Body, that I have been endeavouring to trace to its origin as an acquired notion.†

*[67] Mr. O'Hanlon, in his little pamphlet puts his difficulty on this subject in the following terms: "Your permanent possibilities of sensation are, so long as they are not felt, nothing actual. Yet you speak of change taking place in them, and that independently of our consciousness and of our presence or absence. . . . If the fire, apart from any consciousness, be some positive condition or conditions of warmth and light, if the corn be some positive condition or conditions of food, my thesis is made out, and your Pure Idealism falls to the ground. If, on the other hand, the fire be nothing positive apart from any consciousness, then, since it is nothing at all when so apart, you can have no right to speak of modifications taking place in it whether we are asleep or awake, present or absent." ([A Criticism of John Stuart Mill's Pure Idealism,] pp. 12 and 14.)

I give great credit to my young antagonist, not only for the neatness of his dilemma, but for having gone so directly to the point at which is the real stress of the dispute. But I think he will perceive, from what I have said in the text, in what manner one may have a right to speak of modifications as taking place in a possibility. [See, e.g., p. 181 above.] And I think he will be able to see that the condition of a phænomenon needs not necessarily be anything positive, in his sense of the word, or objective; it may be anything, positive or negative, actuality or possibility, without which the phænomenon would not have occurred, and which may therefore be justly inferred from its occurrence.

†[67] Mr. O'Hanlon says: "Conceding the entire truth of the position, that there are associations naturally and even necessarily generated by the order of our sensations, and of our reminiscences of sensation, which, supposing no intuition of an external world to have existed in consciousness, would inevitably generate the belief, and would cause it to be regarded as an intuition;—conceding, I say, for argument's sake, the entire truth of this position, it may still be true that though we have no intuition of the external world, the inference that such a world exists is a

I now pass to this very subject, the Ego, and to the objections which have been made against the manner in which it is treated in the preceding chapter.

Having shown that in order to account for the belief in Matter, or, in other words, in a non-ego supposed to be presented in or along with sensation, it is not necessary to suppose anything but sensations and possibilities of sensation connected in groups; it was natural and necessary to enquire whether the Ego, supposed to be presented in or along with all consciousness whatever, is also an acquired notion, explicable in the same manner. I therefore stated this phænomenal theory of the Ego; freed it from the prejudice which attaches to it on the score of consequences to which it does not lead, the non-existence, first, of our fellow-creatures, and secondly, of God;* but showed that it has intrinsic difficulties, which no

---

legitimate one." (P. 14.) Undoubtedly it may. Malebranche, for instance, according to whose system Matter is not perceived, nor in any way cognised, nor capable of being cognised, by our minds, all the things that we see or feel existing only as ideas in the Divine Mind, nevertheless fully believed in the reality of this superfluous wheel in the mechanism of the universe, which merely revolves while the machinery does its work independently of it—because he thought that God himself had asserted its existence in the Scriptures: and whoever agrees with Malebranche in his premises is likely to agree with him in his conclusion. [See Nicolas de Malebranche, *Recherche de la vérité*, Vol. II of *Œuvres*, ed. Jules Simon, 2 vols. (Paris: Charpentier, 1842), pp. 253ff. (Bk. III, Pt. 2, Chap. vi).] But with most people, whether philosophers or common men, the evidence on which Matter is believed to exist independently of our minds, is either that we perceive it by our senses, or that the notion and belief of it come to us by an original law of our nature. If it be shown that there is no ground for either of these opinions—that all we are conscious of may be accounted for without supposing that we perceive Matter by our senses, and that the notion and belief in Matter may have come to us by the laws of our constitution without being a revelation of any objective reality, the main evidences of Matter are at an end; and though I am perfectly willing to listen to any other evidence, Malebranche's argument is, I must confess, quite as conclusive as any that I expect to find.

*[67] Some of my critics have impugned the arguments of the preceding chapter on this particular point. They have said (Mr. O'Hanlon [p. 10] is the one who has said it with the greatest compactness and force) that persons, equally with inanimate things, may be conceived as mere states of my own consciousness; that the same processes of thought which, according to the Psychological theory, can generate the belief in Matter even if it does not exist, must be equally competent to engender the belief of the existence of other Minds: and that the principles of the theory require us, under the law of Parcimony, to conclude that if the belief may have been, it has been, thus generated: consequently the theory takes away all evidence of the existence of other minds, or of other threads of consciousness than our own.

It would undoubtedly do so, if the only evidence of the existence of other threads of consciousness was a natural belief, as a natural belief is the only evidence which

one has been able to remove; since certain of the attributes comprised in our notion of the Ego, and which are at the very foundation of it, namely Memory and Expectation, have no equivalent in Matter, and cannot be reduced to any elements similar to those into which Matter is resolved by the Psychological theory. Having stated these facts, as inexplicable by the Psychological theory, I left them to stand as facts, without any theory whatever: not adopting the Permanent Possibility hypothesis as a sufficient theory of Self in spite of the objections to it, as some of my critics have

---

rational persons now acknowledge of the existence of Matter. But there is other evidence, which does not exist in the case of Matter, and which is as conclusive, as the other is inconclusive. The nature of this has been stated, with sufficient fulness of development, in the preceding chapter, and Mr. O'Hanlon has rightly understood it to be a simple extension of "the principles of inductive evidence, which experience shows hold good of my states of consciousness, to a sphere without my consciousness." But he objects: "The doing so postulates two things: (a) That there is a sphere beyond my consciousness; the very thing to be proved. (b) That the laws which obtain in my consciousness, also obtain in the sphere beyond it." (Pp. 7–8.)

To this I reply, that it does not postulate these two things, but, to the extent required by the present question, proves them. There is nothing in the nature of the inductive principle that confines it within the limits of my own consciousness, when it exceptionally happens that an inference surpassing the limits of my consciousness can conform to inductive conditions.

I am aware, by experience, of a group of Permanent Possibilities of Sensation which I call my body, and which my experience shows to be an universal condition of every part of my thread of consciousness. I am also aware of a great number of other groups, resembling the one that I call my body, but which have no connexion, such as that has, with the remainder of my thread of consciousness. This disposes me to draw an inductive inference, that those other groups are connected with other threads of consciousness, as mine is with my own. If the evidence stopped here, the inference would be but an hypothesis; reaching only to the inferior degree of inductive evidence called Analogy. The evidence, however, does not stop here; for,—having made the supposition that real feelings, though not experienced by myself, lie behind those phænomena of my own consciousness which, from their resemblance to my body, I call other human bodies,—I find that my subsequent consciousness presents those very sensations, of speech heard, of movements and other outward demeanour seen, and so forth, which, being the effects or consequents of actual feelings in my own case, I should expect to follow upon those other hypothetical feelings if they really exist: and thus the hypothesis is verified. It is thus proved inductively that there is a sphere beyond my consciousness: i.e., that there are other consciousnesses beyond it; for there exists no parallel evidence in regard to Matter. And it is proved inductively, that so far as respects those other consciousnesses, linked to as many groups of Permanent Possibilities of Sensation similar to my own body, the laws which obtain in my consciousness also obtain in the sphere beyond it; that those other threads of consciousness are beings similar to myself.

The legitimacy of this process is open to no objections, either real or imaginary, but such as may equally be made against inductive inferences within the sphere of

imagined, and have wasted no small amount of argument and sarcasm in exposing the untenability of such a position: neither, on the other hand, did I, as others have supposed, accept the common theory of Mind, as a so-called Substance. Since the state in which I profess to leave the question has been so ill understood, it is incumbent on me to explain myself more fully.

Since the fact which alone necessitates the belief in an Ego, the one fact which the Psychological theory cannot explain, is the fact of Memory (for

---

our own actual or possible consciousness. Facts of which I never *have* had consciousness are as much unknown facts, as much apart from my actual experience, as facts of which I cannot have consciousness. When I conclude, from facts that I immediately perceive, to the existence of other facts such as *might* come into my actual consciousness (which the feelings of other people never can) but which never *did* come into it, and of which I have no evidence but an induction from experience; how do I know that I am concluding rightly—that the inference is warranted, from an actual consciousness to a contingent possibility of consciousness which has never become actual? Surely because this conclusion from experience is verified by further experience; because those other experiences which I ought to have if my inference was correct, really present themselves. This verification, which is the source of all my reliance on induction, justifies the same reliance wherever it is found. The alien threads of consciousness of which I presume the existence from the analogy of my own body, manifest the truth of the presumption by visual and tactual effects within my own consciousness, resembling those which follow from sensations, thoughts, or emotions felt by myself. The reality beyond the sphere of my consciousness rests on the twofold evidence, of its antecedents, and its consequents. It is an inference upwards from the manifestations, and downwards from the antecedent conditions; and whichever of these inferences is first drawn, the other is its verification.

I venture to hope that these considerations may remove Mr. O'Hanlon's difficulty. But whatever the difficulty may be, it is not peculiar to the Psychological theory, but has equally to be encountered on every other. For no one supposes that other people's feelings or states of consciousness are a matter of direct intuition to us, or of Natural Belief. We do not directly perceive other minds: their reality is not known to us immediately, but by means of evidence. And there is no evidence by which it can be proved to me that there is a conscious being within each of the human bodies that I see, without a process of induction involving the very same assumptions which are required by the Psychological Theory.

I will delay the reader a few moments more while I reply to a minor difficulty of Mr. O'Hanlon. He urges, that the Psychological theory inserts an alien consciousness between two consciousnesses of my own, as the effect of one of them and the cause of the other. "A boy cuts his finger and screams. The knife, the blood, and the boy's body are only (in Mr. Mill's view) actual and possible groups of my sensations, and the scream is an actual sensation. I infer, continuing to accept Mr. Mill's theory, that between the scream and the other sensations, namely between two sets of states of my own consciousness, a foreign consciousness had the feeling I call pain, and also that the sensations of cutting its finger, the same sensations, belong as much to it as to me, combined with certain additions, and in a very peculiar manner. Yet if I was not by, the boy, the knife, the blood, the scream, would only exist

Expectation I hold to be, both psychologically and logically, a consequence of Memory), I see no reason to think that there is any cognizance of an Ego until Memory commences. There seems no ground for believing, with Sir W. Hamilton and Mr. Mansel, that the Ego is an original presentation of consciousness; that the mere impression on our senses involves, or carries with it, any consciousness of a Self, any more than I believe it to do of a Not-self. Our very notion of a Self takes its commencement *(there is every reason to suppose)* from the representation of a sensation in memory, when awakened by the only thing there is to awaken it before any associations have been formed, namely, the occurrence of a subsequent sensation similar to the former one. The fact of recognising a sensation, of being reminded of it, and, as we say, remembering that it has been felt before, is the simplest and most elementary fact of memory: and the inexplicable tie, or law, the organic union (as Professor Masson calls it)[*] which connects the present consciousness with the past one, of which it reminds me, is as near as I think we can get to a positive conception of Self. That there is something real in this tie, real as the sensations themselves, and not a mere product of the laws of thought without any fact corresponding to it, I hold to be indubitable. The precise nature of the process by which we cognise it, is open to much dispute. Whether we are directly conscious of it in the act of remembrance, as we are of succession in the fact of having successive sensations, or whether, according to the opinion of Kant, we are not conscious of a Self at all, but are compelled to assume it as a necessary condition of Memory,* I do not undertake to decide. But this original

---

potentially." (Pp. 8–9.) Whatever seeming absurdity, and real confusion, exists here, are only attributable to the fact, that Mr. O'Hanlon, notwithstanding his acuteness, has not yet sufficiently thought himself into the theory he denies. On the same evidence on which I recognise foreign threads of consciousness, I believe that the Permanent Possibilities of Sensation are common to them and to me; but not the actual sensations. The evidence proves to me, that although the knife, the blood, and the boy's body would, if I were absent, be mere potentialities of sensation relatively to me, the similar potentialities which I infer to exist in him have been realized as actual sensations; and it is as conditions of the sensations in him, and not of sensations in me, that they form a part of the series of causes and effects which take place out of my consciousness. The chain of causation is the following: 1. A modification in a set of Permanent Possibilities of Sensation common to the boy and me. 2. A sensation of pain in the boy, not felt by me. 3. The scream, which is a sensation in me.

[*Recent British Philosophy, p. 335.]

*[67] Mr. Mahaffy thinks that the question may be decided in favour of Kant on the evidence of consciousness itself. "Are you," he asks, "conscious of being presented with yourself as a substance? or are you only conscious that in every act

*i–i*67   , there . . . suppose,

element, which has no community of nature with any of the things answering to our names, and to which we cannot give any name but its own peculiar one without implying some false or ungrounded theory, is the Ego, or Self. As such, I ascribe a reality to the Ego—to my own Mind—different from that real existence as a Permanent Possibility, which is the only reality I acknowledge in Matter: and by fair experiential inference from that one Ego, I ascribe the same reality to other Egoes, or Minds.

Having thus, as I hope, more clearly defined my position in regard to the reality of the Ego, considered as a question of Ontology, I return to my first starting point, the Relativity of human knowledge, and affirm (being here in entire accordance with Sir W. Hamilton) that whatever be the nature of the real existence we are compelled to acknowledge in Mind, the Mind is only known to itself phænomenally, as the series of its feelings of consciousnesses. We are forced to apprehend every part of the series as linked with the other parts by something in common, which is not the feelings themselves, any more than the succession of the feelings is the feelings themselves: and as that which is the same in the first as in the second, in the second as in the third, in the third as in the fourth, and so on, must be the same in the first and in the fiftieth, this common element is a permanent element. But beyond this, we can affirm nothing of it except the states of consciousness themselves. The feelings or consciousnesses which belong or have belonged to it, and its possibilities of having more, are the only facts there are to be asserted of Self—the only positive attributes, except permanence, which we can ascribe to it. In consequence of this, I occasionally use the words "mind" and "thread of consciousness" interchangeably, and treat Mind as existing, and Mind as known to itself, as convertible: but this is only for brevity, and the explanations which I have now given must always be taken as implied.[h]*

of thought you must presuppose a permanent self, and always refer it to self, while still that self you cannot grasp, and it remains a hidden basis upon which you erect the structure of your thoughts? Which of these opinions will most men adopt? After all, Kant's view is the simpler, and the more consistent with the ordinary language." (P. lvi.)

*[72] Dr. M'Cosh has renewed his attack upon the doctrine of Permanent Possibilities. ["Mill's Reply to his Critics," pp. 340–7; the earlier attack is in McCosh's *Examination*, pp. 112–21.] But I cannot find in his later remarks, so far as they are to the purpose, much more than a repetition of his earlier. On some minor points he does present some novelties. He is severe upon me for hesitating to decide whether the attribute of succession as between our sensations is given in the sensations themselves, or annexed to them by a law of the mind. The first supposition he characterizes as a mere verbal generalization like those which I have laid to the charge of Condillac [see Mill's "Coleridge," in *Essays on Ethics, Religion, and Society, Collected Works*, Vol. X (Toronto: University of Toronto Press, 1969),

p. 129]; forgetting the opinion held by some acute metaphysicians, and which is no mere verbal generalization, that to have sensations in succession is only the same thing as having more sensations than one. The other supposition, that the attribute of succession is annexed to our sensations by a law of the mind, he says is giving to the mind the "power of generating in the course of its exercise a totally new idea," an opinion, he says, utterly inconsistent with my "empirical theory;" he does not say with what theory. ["Mill's Reply," p. 343.] In any scheme of human knowledge that I am able to form, the resemblances and the successions and coexistences of our sensations are real facts, and objects of direct apprehension. Whether we are said to apprehend them by our senses or by our minds (which is the real meaning of the alternative I have left open) affects no theory of mine, and is to me a matter of indifference.

The most curious part of Dr. M'Cosh's reply is that he thinks, according to my "theory" there is no difference between sensations and thoughts. According to him, if I am right, the facts of external nature being only possibilities of sensation, ought to succeed one another according to "mental laws, say the laws of association." The reader will scarcely believe that I am not misrepresenting Dr. M'Cosh; but I refer him to the article, pp. 345 and 346.

Dr. M'Cosh still maintains that the action of bodies on one another cannot be accounted for on the hypothesis of Immateriality, takes credit for having, on this point, detected me in an oversight, and seems to consider the answer I was "obliged" to give him as an afterthought of my own. [*Ibid.*, pp. 346–8.] This only proves that Dr. M'Cosh has forgotten, if he ever knew, the very elements of the Berkeleian controversy. Whoever knows anything of that, has got far beyond the stage of thought at which Dr. M'Cosh remains. Berkeley would indeed have been easily answered if his doctrine could give no account of the greater part of all the phænomena of physical nature.

CHAPTER XIII

The Psychological Theory of the Primary Qualities of Matter

FOR THE REASONS which have been set forth, I conceive Sir W. Hamilton to be wrong in his statement that a Self and a Not-self are immediately apprehended in our primitive consciousness. We have, in all probability, no notion of Not-self, until after considerable experience of the recurrence of sensations according to fixed laws, and in groups.* *"Nor is it* credible that the first sensation which we experience awakens in us any notion of an Ego or Self. To refer it to an Ego is to consider it as part of a series of states of consciousness, some portion of which is already past. The identification of a present state with a remembered state cognised as past, is what, to my thinking, constitutes the cognition that it is I who feel it. "I" means he who saw, touched, or felt something yesterday or the day before. No single sensation can suggest personal identity: this requires a series of sensations, thought of as forming a line of succession, and summed up in thought into a Unity.

But (however this may be) throughout the whole of our sensitive life except its first beginnings, we unquestionably refer our sensations to a *me* and a not-me. As soon as I have formed, on the one hand, the notion of Permanent Possibilities of Sensation, and on the other, of that continued series of feelings which I call my life, both these notions are, by an irresistible association, recalled by every sensation I have. They represent two things, with both of which the sensation of the moment, be it what it may, stands in relation, and I cannot be conscious of the sensation without being conscious of it as related to these two things. They have accordingly

---

*[67] In the first edition I said: "But without the notion of not-self, we cannot have that of self, which is contrasted with it." [See *a-a* below.] In saying this I overlooked the fact, that my own sensations and other feelings, as distinguished from what I call Myself, are a sufficient Not-self to make the Self apprehensible. The contrast necessary to all cognition is sufficiently provided for by the antithesis between the Ego and particular modifications of the Ego.

*a-a*65¹, 65² But without the notion of not-self, we cannot have that of self which is contrasted with it: and independently of this, it is not

received relative names, expressive of the double relation in question. The thread of consciousness which I apprehend the sensation as a part of, is the *subject* of the sensation. The group of Permanent Possibilities of Sensation to which I refer it, and which is partially realized and actualized in it, is the *object* of the sensation. The sensation itself ought to have a correlative name; or rather, ought to have two such names, one denoting the sensation as opposed to its Subject, the other denoting it as opposed to its Object. But it is a remarkable fact, that this necessity has not been felt, and that the need of a correlative name to every relative one has been considered to be satisfied by the terms Object and Subject themselves; the object and the subject not being attended to in the relation which they respectively bear to the sensation, but being regarded as directly correlated with one another. It is true that they are related to one another, but only through the sensation: their relation to each other consists in the peculiar and different relation in which they severally stand to the sensation. We have no conception of either Subject or Object, either Mind or Matter, except as something to which we refer our sensations, and whatever other feelings we are conscious of. The very existence of them both, so far as cognisable by us, consists only in the relation they respectively bear to our states of feeling. Their relation to each other is only the relation between those two relations. The immediate correlatives are not the pair, Object, Subject, but the two pairs, Object, Sensation objectively considered; Subject, Sensation subjectively considered. The reason why this is overlooked, might easily be shown, and would furnish a good illustration of that important part of the Laws of Association which may be termed the Laws of Obliviscence.

I have next to speak of a psychological fact, also a consequence of the Laws of Association, and without a full appreciation of which, the idea of Matter can only be understood in its original groundwork, but not in the superstructure which the laws of our actual experience have raised upon it. There are certain of our sensations which we are accustomed principally to consider subjectively, and others which we are principally accustomed to consider objectively. In the case of the first, the relation in which we most frequently, most habitually, and therefore most easily consider them, is their relation to the series of feelings of which they form a part, and which, consolidated by thought into a single conception, is termed the Subject. In the case of the second, the relation in which we by preference contemplate them is their relation to some group, or some kind of group, of Permanent Possibilities of Sensation, the present existence of which is certified to us by the sensation we are at the moment feeling—and which is termed the Object. The difference between these two classes of our sensations, answers to the distinction made by the majority of philosophers between the Primary and the Secondary Qualities of Matter.

We can, of course, think of all or any of our sensations in relation to their Objects, that is, to the permanent groups of possibilities of sensation to which we mentally refer them. This is the main distinction between our sensations, and what we regard as our purely mental feelings. These we do not refer to any groups of Permanent Possibilities; and in regard to them the distinction of Subject and Object is merely nominal. These feelings have no Objects, except by metaphor. There is nothing but the feeling and its Subject. Metaphysicians are obliged to call the feeling itself the object. Our sensations, on the contrary, have all of them objects; they all are capable of being classed under some group of Permanent Possibilities, and being referred to the presence of that particular set of possibilities as the antecedent condition or cause of their own existence. There are, however, some of our sensations, in our consciousness of which the reference to their Object does not play so conspicuous and predominant a part as in others. This is particularly the case with sensations which are highly interesting to us on their own account, and on which we willingly dwell, or which by their intensity compel us to concentrate our attention on them. These are, of course, our pleasures and pains. In the case of these, our attention is naturally given in a greater degree to the sensations themselves, and only in a less degree to that whose existence they are marks of. And of the two conceptions to which they stand in relation, the one to which we have most tendency to refer them is the Subject; because our pleasures and pains are of no more importance as marks than any of our other sensations, but are of very much more importance than any others as parts of the thread of consciousness which constitutes our sentient life. Many indeed of our internal bodily pains we should hardly refer to an Object at all, were it not for the knowledge, late and slowly acquired, that they are always connected with a local organic disturbance, of which we have no present consciousness, and which is therefore a mere Possibility of Sensation. Those of our sensations, on the contrary, which are almost indifferent in themselves, our attention does not dwell on; our consciousness of them is too momentary to be distinct, and we pass on from them to the Permanent Possibilities of Sensation which they are the signs of, and which alone are important to us. We hardly notice the relation between these sensations and the subjective chain of consciousness of which they form so extremely insignificant a part: the sensation is hardly anything to us but the link which draws into our consciousness a group of Permanent Possibilities; this group is the only thing distinctly present to our thoughts. The unimpressive organic sensation merges in the mere mental suggestion, and we seem to cognise directly that which we think of only by association, and know only by inference. Sensation is in a manner blotted out, and Perception seems to be installed in its place. This truth is expressed, though not with sufficient distinctness, in a favourite doctrine of Sir W. Hamilton, that in the operations of our senses Sensation is greatest when Perception is least, and least when it is greatest; or, as he, by a very inaccurate use of mathematical language, expresses it, Sensation and Perception are in the inverse ratio of one another.

With regard to those sensations which, without being absolutely indifferent, are not, in any absorbing degree, painful or pleasurable, we habitually think of them only as connected with, or proceeding from, Objects. And I am disposed to believe, contrary to the opinion of many philosophers, that any of our senses, or at all events any combination of more than one sense, would have been sufficient to give us some idea of Matter. If we had only the senses of smell, taste, and hearing, but had the sensations according to fixed laws of coexistence so that whenever we had any one of them it marked to us a present possibility of having all the others, I am inclined to think that we should have formed the notion of groups of possibilities of sensation, and should have referred every particular sensation to one of these groups, which, in relation to all the sensations so referred to it, would have become an Object, and would have been invested in our thoughts with the permanency and externality which belong to Matter. But though we might, in this supposed case, have had an idea of Matter, that idea would necessarily have been of a very different complexion from what we now have. For, as we are actually constituted, our sensations of smell, taste, and hearing, and *as I believe (with the great majority of* philosophers) those of sight also, are not grouped together directly, but through the connexion which they all have, by laws of coexistence or of causation, with the sensations which are referable to the sense of touch and to the muscles; those which answer to the terms Resistance, Extension, and Figure. These, therefore, become the leading and conspicuous elements in all the groups: where these are, the group is: every other member of the group presents itself to our thoughts, less as what it is in itself, than as a mark of these. As the entire group stands in the relation of Object to any one of the component sensations which is realized at a given moment, so do these special parts of the group become, in a manner, Object, in relation not only to actual sensations, but to all the remaining Possibilities of Sensation which the group includes. The Permanent Possibilities of sensations of touch and of the muscles, form a group within the group—a sort of inner nucleus, conceived as more fundamental than the rest, on which all the other possibilities of sensation included in the group seem to depend; these being regarded, in one point of view, as effects, of which that nucleus is the cause, in another as attributes, of which it is the substratum or substance.

*-*65¹, 65²   (as I believe, with nearly all

In this manner our conception of Matter comes ultimately to consist of Resistance, Extension, and Figure, together with miscellaneous powers of exciting other sensations. These three attributes become its essential constituents, and where these are not found, we hesitate to apply the name.

Of these properties, which are consequently termed the Primary Qualities of Matter, the most fundamental is Resistance: as is proved by numerous scientific controversies. When the question arises whether something which affects our senses in a peculiar way, as for instance whether Heat, or Light, or Electricity, is or is not Matter, what seems always to be meant is, does it offer any, however trifling, resistance to motion? If it were shown that it did, this would at once terminate all doubt. That Resistance is only another name for a sensation of our muscular frame, combined with one of touch, has been pointed out by many philosophers, and can scarcely any longer be questioned. When we contract the muscles of our arm, either by an exertion of will, or by an involuntary discharge of our spontaneous nervous activity, the contraction is accompanied by a state of sensation, which is different according as the locomotion consequent on the muscular contraction continues freely, or meets with an impediment. In the former case, the sensation is that of motion through empty space. After having had (let us suppose) this experience several times repeated, we suddenly have a different experience: the series of sensations accompanying the motion of our arm is brought, without intention or expectation on our part, to an abrupt close. This interruption would not, of itself, necessarily suggest the belief in an external obstacle. The hindrance might be in our organs; it might arise from paralysis, or simple loss of power through fatigue. But in either of these cases, the muscles would not have been contracted, and we should not have had the sensation which accompanies their contraction. We may have had the will to exert our muscular force, but the exertion has not taken place.* If it does take place, and is accompanied by the usual muscular sensation, but the ᶜdistinctive feeling which I have called the

*Sir W. Hamilton thinks that we are conscious of resistance through a "mental effort or nisus to move," distinct both from the original will to move, and from the muscular sensation: "for we are," he says, "conscious of it, though, by a narcosis or stupor of the sensitive nerves we lose all feeling of the movement of the limb; though by a paralysis of the motive nerves no movement of the limb follows the mental effort to move; though by an abnormal stimulus of the muscular fibres, a contraction in them is caused even in opposition to our will." ("Dissertations on Reid," [Note D,] pp. 864n–5n.) If all this is true—though by what experiments it has been substantiated we are not told—it does not by any means show that there is a mental *nisus* not physical, but merely removes the seat of the *nisus* from the nerves to the brain.

ᶜ⁻ᶜ65¹, 65²   expected sensation of locomotion

sensation of motion in empty space[c] does not follow, we have what is called the feeling of Resistance, or in other words, of muscular [d]action[d] impeded; and that feeling is the fundamental element in the notion of Matter which results from our common experience. But simultaneously with this feeling of Resistance, we have also feelings of touch; sensations of which the organs are not the nerves diffused through our muscles, but those which form a network under the skin; the sensations which are produced by passive contact with bodies, without muscular action. As these skin sensations of simple contact invariably accompany the muscular sensation of resistance—for we must touch the object before we can feel it resisting our pressure—there is early formed an inseparable association between them. Whenever we feel resistance we have first felt contact [e]. Whenever[e] we feel contact, we know that were we to exercise muscular action, we should feel more or less resistance. In this manner is formed the first fundamental group of Permanent Possibilities of Sensation; and as we in time recognise that all our other sensations are connected in point of fact with Permanent Possibilities of resistance—that in coexistence with them we should always, by sufficient search, encounter something which would give us the feeling of contact combined with the muscular sensation of resistance; our idea of Matter, as a Resisting Cause of miscellaneous sensations, is now constituted.

Let us observe, in passing, the elementary example here afforded of the Law of Inseparable Association, and the efficacy of that law to construct what, after it has been constructed, is undistinguishable, by any direct interrogation of consciousness, from an intuition. The sensation produced by the simple contact of an object with the skin, without any pressure—or even with pressure, but without any muscular reaction against it—is no more likely than a sensation of warmth or cold would be, to be spontaneously referred to any cause external to ourselves. But when the constant coexistence, in experience, of this sensation of contact with that of Resistance to our muscular effort whenever such effort is made, has erected the former sensation into a mark or sign of a Permanent Possibility of the latter; from that time forward, no sooner do we have the skin sensation which we call a sensation of contact, than we cognise, or, as we call it, perceive, something external, corresponding to the idea we now form of Matter as a *resisting* object. Our sensations of touch have become *representative* of the sensations of resistance with which they habitually coexist: just as philosophers have shown that the sensations of different shades of colour given by our sense of sight, and the muscular sensations accompanying the

[d-d]65[1], 65[2]   motion
[e-e]65[1], 65[2]   ; whenever

various movements of the eye, become representative of those sensations of touch and of the muscles of locomotion, which are the only real meaning of what we term the distance of a body from us.*

The next of the primary qualities of Body is Extension; which has long been considered as one of the principal stumbling blocks of the Psychological Theory. Reid and Stewart were willing to let the whole question of the intuitive character of our knowledge of Matter, depend on the inability of psychologists to assign any origin to the idea of Extension, or analyse it into any combination of sensations and reminiscences of sensation. Sir W. Hamilton follows their example in laying great stress on this point.

The answer of the opposite school I will present in its latest and most improved form, as given by Professor Bain, *f* in the First Part of his great work on the Mind.†

*Sir W. Hamilton draws a distinction between two kinds of resistance, or rather, between two senses of the word: the one, that which I have mentioned, and which is a sensation of our muscular frame; the other, the property of Matter which the old writers called Impenetrability, being that by which, however capable of being compressed into a smaller space, it refuses to part with all its extension, and be extruded from space altogether. [See "Dissertations," Note D, pp. 849, 851–2.] But these two kinds of resistance are merely two modes of regarding and naming the same state of consciousness; for if the body could be pressed entirely out of space, the only way in which we should discover that it had vanished would be by the sudden cessation of all sensations of resistance. It is always the muscular sensation which constitutes the presence, and its negation the absence, of body, in any given portion of space.

†*The Senses and the Intellect* [London: Parker, 1855], pp. 113–17. My first extract is from the original edition; for in the one recently published (and enriched by many valuable improvements) the exposition I now quote is given more summarily, and in a manner otherwise less suited for my purpose. [2nd ed. (London: Longman, Green, Longman, Roberts, and Green, 1864), pp. 111–15.]

*g*Dr. M'Cosh, without any warrant, speaks of Mr. Bain as having "elaborated into a minute system the general statements scattered throughout Mr. Mill's *Logic*" ([*Examination*,] p. 121); and in another passage refers to him and to Mr. Herbert Spencer (Mr. Herbert Spencer!) as merely following out an investigation indicated by me. (*Ibid*., pp. 123–4.) Coleridge reminded one of his critics, that there are such things in the world as springs, and that the water a man draws does not necessarily come from a hole made in another man's cistern. ["Preface to Christabel," in *Christabel; Kubla Khan, a Vision; The Pains of Sleep* (London: Murray, 1816), p. vi.] Mr. Bain did not stand in need of any predecessor except our common precursors, and has taught much more to me, on these subjects, than there is any reasonable probability that I can have taught to him. Dr. M'Cosh falls into a corresponding mistake concerning myself, when he ascribes my regarding it "as impossible for the mind to rise to first or final causes, or to know the nature of things," to "the influence" of M. Comte. (*Examination*, pp. 7–8.) The larger half of

*f*65¹, 65², 67   of Aberdeen,
g-g+67, 72

Mr. Bain recognises two principal kinds or modes of discriminative sensibility in the muscular sense: the one corresponding to the degree of intensity of the muscular effort—the amount of energy put forth; the other corresponding to the duration—the longer or shorter continuance of the same effort. The first makes us acquainted with degrees of resistance: which we estimate by the intensity of the muscular energy required to overcome it. To the second we owe, in Mr. Bain's opinion, our idea of Extension.

When a muscle begins to contract, or a limb to bend, we have a distinct sense of how far the contraction and the bending are carried; there is something in the special sensibility that makes one mode of feeling for half-contraction, another mode for three-fourths, and another for total contraction. Our feeling of moving organs, or of contracting muscles, has been already affirmed to be different from our feeling of dead tension—something more intense, keen, and exciting; and I am now led to assert, from my best observations and by inference from acknowledged facts, that the extent of range of a movement, the degree of shortening of a muscle, is a matter of discriminative sensibility. I believe it to be much less pronounced, less exact, than the sense of resistance above described, but to be not the less real and demonstrable.

If we suppose a weight raised, by the flexing of the arm, first four inches, and then eight inches, it is obvious that the mere amount of exertion or expended power will be greater, and the sensibility increased in proportion. In this view, the sense of range would simply be the sense of a greater or less continuance of the same effort, that effort being expended in movement. We can have no difficulty in believing that there should be a discriminating sensibility in this case; it seems very natural that we should be differently affected by an action continued four or five times longer than another. If this be admitted, as true to observation, and as inevitably arising from the existence of any discrimination whatsoever of degrees of expended power, everything is granted that is contended for at present. It is not meant to affirm that at each degree of shortening of a muscle, or each intermediate attitude of a limb, there is an impression made on the centres that can be distinguished from the impression

---

my *System of Logic*, including all its fundamental doctrines, was written before I had even seen the *Cours de Philosophie Positive*. That work was indebted to M. Comte for many valuable thoughts, but a short list would exhaust the chapters, and even the pages, which contain them. [See the Textual Introduction to *System of Logic*, *Collected Works*, Vol. VII, pp. lxxviii, lxxxii–lxxxiii, and xc–xci.] As for the general doctrine which Dr. M'Cosh's words so imperfectly express—that our knowledge is only of the coexistences and sequences, or the similitudes, of phænomena; I was familiar with it before I was out of boyhood from the teachings of my father, who had learnt it where M. Comte learnt it—from the methods of physical science, and the writings of their philosophical predecessors. Ever since the days of Hume, that doctrine has been the general property of the philosophic world. From the time of Brown it has entered even into popular philosophy.[g] [h]I have given a brief history of it in *Auguste Comte and Positivism*.[h] [See *Collected Works*, Vol. X, pp. 265–9.]

[h-h]+72

of every other position or degree of shortening; it is enough to require that the range or amount of movement gone over should be a matter of distinct perception, through the sensibility to the amount of force expended *in time*, the degree of effort being the same. The sensibility now in question differs from the former (from sensibility to the intensity of effort) chiefly in making the degree turn upon *duration*, and not upon the amount expended each instant; and it seems to me impossible to deny that force increased or diminished simply as regards continuance, is as much a subject of discriminative sensibility as force increased or diminished in the intensity of the sustained effort. . . .

If the sense of degrees of range be thus admitted as a genuine muscular determination, its functions in outward perception are very important. The attributes of extension and space fall under its scope. In the first place, it gives the feeling of *linear extension*, inasmuch as this is measured by the sweep of a limb, or other organ moved by muscles. The difference between six inches and eighteen inches is expressed to us by the different degrees of contraction of some one group of muscles; those, for example, that flex the arm, or, in walking, those that flex or extend the lower limb. The inward impression corresponding to the outward fact of six inches in length, is an impression arising from the continued shortening of a muscle, a true muscular sensibility. It is the impression of a muscular effort having a certain continuance; a greater length produces a greater continuance (or a more rapid movement) and in consequence an increased feeling of expended power.

The discrimination of length in any one direction includes *extension* in any direction. Whether it be length, breadth, or height, the perception has precisely the same character. Hence superficial and solid dimensions, the size or magnitude of a solid object, come to be felt in a similar manner. . . .

It will be obvious that what is called *situation* or Locality must come under the same head, as these are measured by distance taken along with direction; direction being itself estimated by distance, both in common observation and in mathematical theory. In like manner, *form* or *shape* is ascertained through the same primitive sensibility to extension or range.

By the muscular sensibility thus associated with prolonged contraction we can therefore compare different degrees of the attribute of space, in other words, difference of length, surface, situation, and form. When comparing two different lengths we can feel which is the greater, just as in comparing two different weights or resistances. We can also, as in the case of weight, acquire some absolute standard of comparison, through the permanency of impressions sufficiently often repeated. We can engrain the feeling of contraction of the muscles of the lower limb due to a pace of thirty inches, and can say that some one given pace is less or more than this amount. According to the delicacy of the muscular tissue we can, by shorter or longer practice, acquire distinct impressions for every standard dimension, and can decide at once whether a given length is four inches or four and a half, nine or ten, twenty or twenty-one. This sensibility to size, enabling us to dispense with the use of measures of length, is an acquirement suited to many mechanical operations. In drawing, painting, and engraving, and in the plastic arts, the en-grained discrimination of the most delicate differences is an indispensable qualification.

The third attribute of muscular discrimination is the *velocity* or speed of the movement. It is difficult to separate this from the foregoing. In the feeling of range, velocity answers the same purpose as continuance; both imply an enhancement of effort, or of expended power, different in its nature from the increase of dead effort in one fixed situation. We must learn to feel that a slow motion for a long time is the same as a quicker motion with less duration; which we can easily do by seeing that they both produce the same effect in exhausting the full range of a limb. If we experiment upon the different ways of accomplishing a total sweep of the arm, we shall find that the slow movements long continued are equal to quick motions of short continuance, and we are thus able by either course to acquire to ourselves a measure of range and lineal extension. . . .

We would thus trace the perception of the mathematical and mechanical properties of matter to the muscular sensibility alone. We admit that this perception is by no means very accurate if we exclude the special senses, but we are bound to show at the outset that these senses are not essential to the perception, as we shall afterwards show that it is to the muscular apparatus associated with the senses that their more exalted sensibility must be also ascribed. The space moved through by the foot in pacing may be appreciated solely through the muscles of the limb, as well as by the movements of the touching hand or the seeing eye. Whence we may accede to the assertion sometimes made, that the properties of space might be conceived, or felt, in the absence of an external world, or of any other matter than that composing the body of the percipient being; for the body's own movements in empty space would suffice to make the very same impressions on the mind as the movements excited by outward objects. A perception of length, or height, or speed, is the mental impression, or state of consciousness, accompanying some mode of muscular movement, and this movement may be generated from within as well as from without; in both cases the state of consciousness is exactly the same.

A theory of Extension somewhat similar, though less clearly unfolded, was advanced by Brown,[*] and as it stands in his statement, fell under the criticism of Sir W. Hamilton; who gives it, as he thinks, a short and crushing refutation, as follows:

As far as I can find his meaning in his cloud of words, he argues thus:—The notion of Time or succession being supposed, that of *longitudinal* extension is given in the succession of feelings which accompanies the gradual contraction of a muscle; the notion of this succession constitutes, *ipso facto*, the notion of a certain length; and the notion of this length (he quietly takes for granted) is the notion of longitudinal extension sought. The paralogism here is transparent. Length is an ambiguous term; and it is length in space, extensive length, and not length in time, protensive length, whose notion it is the problem to evolve. To convert, therefore, the notion of a certain kind of length (and that certain kind being also confessedly only length in time) into the notion of a length in space, is at best an idle begging of the question— Is it not? Then I would ask, whether the series of feelings of which we are aware in the gradual contraction of a muscle, involves the consciousness of being a succession in length, (1) in time alone? or (2) in space alone? or (3) in time and space together? These three cases will be allowed to be exhaustive. If the first be affirmed; if the succession appear in consciousness a succession in time exclusively, then nothing has been accomplished; for the notion of extension or space is in no way contained in the notion of duration or time. Again, if the second or third is affirmed;

[*See *Lectures*, Vol. I, pp. 524–48, and Vol. II, pp. 1–22.]

if the series appear to consciousness a succession in length, either in space alone, or in space and time together, then is the notion it behoved to generate employed to generate itself.*

The dilemma looks formidable, but one of its horns is blunt; for the very assertion of Brown, and of all who hold the Psychological theory, is that the notion of length in space, not being in our consciousness originally, is constructed by the mind's laws out of the notion of length in time. Their argument is not, as Sir W. Hamilton fancied, a fallacious confusion between two different meanings of the word length [1]; they maintain the one to be a product of the other[i]. Sir W. Hamilton did not fully understand the argument. He saw that a *succession* of feelings, such as that which Brown spoke of, could not possibly give us the idea of *simultaneous* existence. But he was mistaken in supposing that Brown's argument implied this absurdity. The notion of simultaneity must be supposed to have been already acquired; as it necessarily would be at the very earliest period, from the familiar fact that we often have sensations simultaneously. What Brown had to show was, that the idea of the particular mode of simultaneous existence called Extension, might arise, not certainly out of a mere succession of muscular sensations, but out of that added to the knowledge already possessed that sensations of touch may be simultaneous. Suppose two small bodies, A and B, sufficiently near together to admit of their being touched simultaneously, one with the right hand, the other with the left. Here are two tactual sensations which are simultaneous, just as a sensation of colour and one of odour might be; and this makes us cognise the two objects of touch as both existing at once. The question then is, what have we in our minds, when we represent to ourselves the relation between these two objects already known to be simultaneous, in the form of Extension, or intervening Space—a relation which we do not suppose to exist between the colour and the odour. Now those who agree with Brown, say that whatever the notion of Extension may be, we *acquire* it by passing our hand or some other organ of touch, in a longitudinal direction from A to B: that this process, as far as we are conscious of it, consists of a series of varied muscular sensations, differing according to the amount of muscular effort, and, the effort being given, differing in length of time. When we say that there is a space between A and B, we mean that some amount of these muscular sensations must intervene; and when we say that the space is greater or less, we mean that the series of sensations (amount of muscular effort being given) is longer or shorter. If another object, C, is farther off in the same line, we judge its distance to be greater, because to reach it, the

*"Dissertations on Reid," [Note D,] p. 869n.

[i-i]⁶⁵¹, 65²   , but an identification of them as one

series of muscular sensations must be further prolonged, or else there must be the increase of effort which corresponds to augmented velocity. Now this, which is ^{j}not denied to be^j the mode in which we become ^{k}aware^k of extension, ^{l}by any other sense than sight,^{l} is considered by the psychologists in question to *be* extension. The idea of Extended Body they consider to be that of a variety of resisting points, existing simultaneously, but which can be perceived by the same tactile organ only successively, at the end of a series of muscular sensations which constitutes their ^{m}distance^m; and are said to be at different distances from one another because the series of intervening muscular sensations is longer in some cases than in others.*

The theory may be recapitulated as follows. The sensation of muscular motion unimpeded constitutes our notion of empty space, and the sensation of muscular motion impeded constitutes that of filled space. Space is Room—room for movement; which its German name, *Raum*, distinctly confirms. We have a sensation which accompanies the free movement of our organs, say for instance of our arm. This sensation is variously modified by the direction, and by the amount of the movement. We have different states of muscular sensation corresponding to the movements of the arm upward, downward, to right, to left, or in any radius whatever of a sphere of which the joint, that the arm revolves round, forms the centre.

*It is not pretended that all this was clearly seen by Brown. It is impossible to defend the theory as Brown stated it. He seems to have thought that the essence of extension consisted in divisibility into parts. "A succession of feelings" (he says) "when remembered by the mind which looks back upon them, was found to involve, necessarily, the notion of *divisibility into separate parts*, and therefore of *length, which is only another name for continued divisibility*." (Lecture xxiv, Vol. II, p. 3 of the 19th edition, 1851.) He thought that he had explained all that needed explanation in the idea of space, when he had shown how the notion of continued divisibility got into it. This appears when he says, "It would not be easy for any one to define matter more simply, than as that which has parts, and that which resists our efforts to grasp it; and in our analysis of the feelings of infancy, we have been able to discover how both these notions may have arisen in the mind." [*Ibid.*, p. 7.] But if divisibility into parts constitutes all our notion of extension, every sensation we have must be identified with extension, for they are all divisible into parts (parts in succession, which Brown thinks sufficient) when they are prolonged beyond the shortest instant of duration which our consciousness recognises. It is probable that Brown did not mean this, but thought that all he had to account for in the conception of space, was its divisibility, because he tacitly assumed that all the rest of the notion was already given in the fact of muscular movement. And this, properly understood, is maintainable; but Brown cannot here be acquitted of a charge to which he is often liable, that of leaving an important philosophical question only half thought out.

$^{j-j}65^1$, 65^2, 67   unquestionably
$^{k-k}65^1$ *aware*
$^{l-l}$+72
$^{m-m}65^1$ *distance*

We have also different states of muscular sensation according as the arm is moved *more*; whether this consists in its being moved with greater velocity, or with the same velocity during a longer time: and the equivalence of these two is speedily learnt, by ["finding that a greater effort conducts the hand in a shorter time from the same point to the same point; from the tactual impression A to the tactual impression B"]. These different kinds and qualities of muscular sensation, experienced in getting from one point to another (that is, obtaining in succession two sensations of touch and resistance, the objects of which are regarded as simultaneous) are all we mean by saying that the points are separated by spaces, that they are at different distances, and in different directions. An intervening series of muscular sensations before the one object can be reached from the other, is the only peculiarity which (according to this theory) distinguishes simultaneity in space, from the simultaneity which may exist between a taste and a colour, or a taste and a smell: and we have no reason for believing that Space or Extension in itself, is anything different from that which we recognise it by. It appears to me that this doctrine is sound, and that the muscular sensations in question are the sources of all the notion of Extension which we should ever obtain from the tactual and muscular senses without the assistance of the eye.

But the participation of the eye in generating our actual notion of Extension, very much alters its character, and is, I think, the main cause of the difficulty felt in believing that Extension derives its meaning to us from a phænomenon which is not synchronous but successive. The fact is, that the conception we now have of Extension or Space is an eye picture, and comprehends a great number of parts of Extension at once, or in a succession so rapid that our consciousness confounds it with simultaneity. How, then (it is naturally asked) can this vast collection of consciousnesses which are sensibly simultaneous, be generated by the mind out of its consciousness of a succession—the succession of muscular feelings? An experiment may be conceived, which would throw great light on this subject, but which unfortunately is more easily imagined than obtained. There have been persons born blind who were mathematicians, and I believe even naturalists; and it is not impossible that one day a person born blind may be a metaphysician. The first who is so, will be able to enlighten us on this point. For he will be an *experimentum crucis*[*] on the mode in which extension is conceived and known, independently of the eye. Not having the assistance of that organ, a person blind from birth must necessarily

[*For the term (usually, but mistakenly, attributed to Bacon), see Robert Hooke, *Micrographia* (London, 1665), p. 54.]

[n–n]65[1], 65[2]   experience

perceive the parts of extension—the parts of a line, of a surface, or of a solid—in conscious succession. He perceives them by passing his hand along them, if small, or by walking over them if great. The parts of extension which it is possible for him to perceive simultaneously, are only very small parts, almost the minima of extension. Hence, if the Psychological theory of the idea of extension is true, the blind metaphysician would feel very little of the difficulty which seeing metaphysicians feel, in admitting that the idea of Space is, at bottom, one of time—and that the notion of extension or distance, is that of a motion of the muscles continued for a longer or a shorter duration. If this analysis of extension appeared as paradoxical to the metaphysician born blind, as it does to Sir W. Hamilton, this would be a strong argument against the Psychological theory. But if, on the contrary, it did not at all startle him, that theory would be very strikingly corroborated.

We have no experiment directly in point. But we have one which is the very next thing to it. We have not the perceptions and feelings of a metaphysician blind from birth, told and interpreted by himself. But we have those of an ordinary person blind from birth, told and interpreted for him by a metaphysician. And the English reader is indebted for them to Sir W. Hamilton. Platner, "a man no less celebrated as an acute philosopher than as a learned physician and an elegant scholar,"[*] endeavoured to ascertain by observation what notion of extension was possessed by a person born blind, and made known the result in words which Sir W. Hamilton has rendered into his clear English.

In regard to the visionless representation of space or extension, the attentive observation of a person born blind, which I formerly instituted in the year 1785, and again, in relation to the point in question, have continued for three whole weeks— this observation, I say, has convinced me, that the sense of touch, by itself, is altogether incompetent to afford us the representation of extension and space, and is not even cognisant of local exteriority; in a word, that a man deprived of sight has absolutely no perception of an outer world, beyond the existence of something effective, different from his own feeling of passivity, and in general only of the numerical diversity—shall I say of impressions, or of things? In fact, to those born blind, *time serves instead of space*. Vicinity and distance means in their mouths nothing more than the shorter or longer time, the smaller or greater number of feelings, which they find necessary to attain from some one feeling to another. That a person blind from birth employs the language of vision—that may occasion considerable error; and did, indeed, at the commencement of my observations, lead me wrong; but, in point of fact, he knows nothing of things as existing out of each other; and (this in particular I have very clearly remarked) if objects, and the parts of his body touched by them, did not make different *kinds* of impression on his nerves of sensation, he would take everything external for one and the same. In his own body, he absolutely did not discriminate head and foot at all by their distance,

[**Lectures*, Vol. II, p. 173.]

but merely by the difference of the feelings (and his perception of such differences was incredibly fine) which he experienced from the one and from the other, and moreover through time. In like manner, in external bodies, he distinguished their figure, merely by the varieties of impressed feelings; inasmuch, for example, as the cube, by its angles, affected his feeling differently from the sphere. *

The highly instructive representation here given by Platner, of this person's state of mind, is exactly that which we have just read in Mr. Bain, and which that philosopher holds to be the primitive conception of extension by all of us, before the wonderful power of sight and its associations, in abridging the mental processes, has come into play. The conclusion which, as we have seen, Platner draws from the case, is that we obtain the idea of extension solely from sight; and even Sir W. Hamilton is staggered in his belief of the contrary. But Platner, though unintentionally, puts a false colour on the matter when he says that his patient had no perception of extension. He used the terms expressive of it with such propriety and discrimination, that Platner, by his own account, did not at first suspect him of not meaning by those terms all that is meant by persons who can see. He therefore meant something; he had impressions which the words expressed to his mind; he had conceptions of extension, after his own manner. But his idea of degrees of extension was but the idea of a greater or smaller number of sensations experienced in succession "to attain from some one feeling to another;" that is, it was exactly what, according to Brown's and Mr. Bain's theory, it ought to have been. And, the sense of touch and of the muscles not being aided by sight, the sensations continued to be conceived by him only as successive: his mental representation of them remained a conception of a series, not of a coexistent group. Though he must have had experience of simultaneity, for no being who has a plurality of senses can be without it, he does not seem to have thoroughly realized the conception of the parts of space as simultaneous. Since what was thus wanting to him, is the principal feature of the conception as it is in us, he seemed to Platner to have no notion of extension. But Platner, fortunately, being a man who could both observe, and express his observations precisely, has been able to convey to our minds the conception which his patient really had of extension; and we find that it was the same as our own, with the exception of the element which, if the Psychological theory be true, was certain to be added to it by the sense of sight. For, when this sense is awakened, and its sensations of colour have become *representative* of the tactual and muscular sensations with which they are coexistent, the fact that we can receive a vast number of sensations of colour at the same instant (or what appears such to our consciousness) puts us in the same position as if we had been

Lectures, Vol. II, pp. 174–5. [Hamilton is translating from Ernst Platner, *Philosophische Aphorismen*, 2 vols. (Leipzig: Schwicktschen Verlag, 1793, 1800), Vol. I, pp. 440–1.]

able to receive that number of tactual and muscular sensations in a single instant. The ideas of all the successive tactual and muscular feelings which accompany the passage of the hand over the whole of the coloured surface, are made to flash on the mind at once: and impressions which were successive in sensation become coexistent in thought. From that time we do with perfect facility, and are even compelled to do, what Platner's patient never completely succeeded in doing, namely, to think all the parts of extension as coexisting, and to believe that we perceive them as such. And if the laws of inseparable association, which are already admitted as the basis of other acquired perceptions of sight, are considered in their application to this case, it is certain that this apparent perception of successive elements as simultaneous °would° be generated and would supply all that there is in our idea of extension, more than there was in that of Platner's patient.*

*[67] Mr. Mahaffy thinks (pp. xx–xxi) that Platner omitted to ascertain whether his patient was capable of recognising simultaneity; and is of opinion that he could not do so, or that if he could, it must have been owing to his education among people possessed of sight. "The question remains: can we postulate a sense of such simultaneity originally, before any space or extension is given? I am disposed to agree with Brown, that, although we can afterwards analyse them, all simultaneous feelings form originally one mental state; which of course excludes simultaneity until the analysis obtained by the aid of space and extension give us the elements separately. Hence, until at least one body was given as extended, we should not obtain the notion." Brown may very possibly be right [see *Lectures*, Vol. I, pp. 294–305], but it does not follow that the analysis necessary to our distinguishing different sensations in one mass of simultaneous feeling, can only take place by means of space and extension. If the simultaneous sensations differ in kind, as a sound, for instance, and a smell, all that is necessary to our being able to distinguish them when together is that we should at some other time have experienced them separate. We should then know the compound, and also the elements: and since these are not chemically fused into a product bearing no resemblance to its factors, but retain when combined their identity with what they are in their separate state, our knowledge of them separately would enable us to recognise them in the compound; in other words, to feel two sensations as simultaneous.

Dr. M'Cosh says that the experience of other observers (and particularly Mr. Kinghan, Principal of the Institution for the Blind at Belfast) as well as experiments by Dr. M'Cosh himself on young children born blind, do not confirm Platner's statement, but prove that those born blind have "a very clear notion of figure and distance, ᵖgot directly from the sense of touch." ([*Examination*,] p. 143n.) This is just what might have been expected, for I am far from agreeing with Platner that the notions of figure and distance come originally from sight. The sense of sight is not necessary to give the perception of simultaneity; but, giving a prodigious number of simultaneous sensations in one glance, it greatly quickens all processes dependent on observation of the fact of simultaneousness. A person born blind can acquire, by a more gradual process, all that there is in our notion of Space except the visible picture: but he will be much longer before he realizes it completely, and in the case of Platner's patient that point does not seem to have been reached.ᵖ

°-°65¹ *would*
ᵖ-ᵖ[*manuscript fragment exists; see* Appendix A *below*]

I shall quote, in continuation, part of the exposition by Mr. Bain, of the machinery by which our consciousness of Extension becomes an appendage of our sensations of Sight. It is a striking example of the commanding influence of that sense; which, though it has no greater variety of original impressions than our other special senses, yet owing to the two properties, of being able to receive a great number of its impressions at once, and to receive them from all distances, takes the lead altogether from the sense of touch: and is not only the organ by which we read countless possibilities of tactual and muscular sensations which can never, to us, become realities, but substitutes itself for our touch and our muscles even where we can use them—causes their actual use as avenues to knowledge, to become, in many cases, obsolete,—the sensations themselves to be little heeded and very indistinctly remembered,—and communicates its own prerogative of simultaneousness to impressions and conceptions originating in other senses, which it could never have given, but only suggests, through visible marks associated with them by experience.

"The distinctive impressibility of the eye," says Mr. Bain,

is for Colour. This is the effect specific to it as a sense. But the feeling of Colour by itself, implies no knowledge of any outward object, as a cause or a thing wherein the colour inheres. It is simply a mental effect or influence, a feeling or conscious state, which we should be able to distinguish from other conscious states, as for example, a smell or a sound. We should also be able to mark the difference between it and others of the same kind, more or less vivid, more or less enduring, more or less voluminous. So we should distinguish the qualitative differences between one colour and another. Pleasure or pain, with discrimination of intensity and of duration, would attach to the mere sensation of colour. Knowledge or belief in an external or material coloured body, there would be none.

But when we add the active or muscular sensibility of the eye, we obtain new products. The sweep of the eye over the coloured field gives a feeling of a definite amount of *action*, an exercise of internal power, which is something totally different from the passive feeling of light. This action has many various modes, all of the same quality, but all distinctively felt and recognised by us. Thus the movements may be in any direction—horizontal, vertical, or slanting; and every one of these movements is felt as different from every other. In addition to these, we have the movements of adjustment of the eye, brought on by differences in the remoteness of objects. We have distinctive feelings belonging to these different adjustments, just as we have towards the different movements across the field of view. If the eyes are adjusted, first to clear vision for an object six inches from the eye, and afterwards change their adjustment to suit an object six feet distant, we are distinctly conscious of the change, and of the degree or amount of it; we know that the change is greater than in extending the adjustment to a three-feet object, while it is less than we should have to go through for a twenty-feet object. Thus in the alterations of the eyes for near and far, we have a distinctive consciousness of amount or degree, no less than in the movements for right and left, up and down. Feelings with the character of activity are thus incorporated with the sensibility to colour; the luminous impression is associated with exertion on our part, and is no longer a purely passive state. We find that the light changes as our activity changes, we recognise in it a certain connexion with our movements; and association springs up between the passive feeling and the active energy of the visible ["visual"] organ, or rather of the body generally; for the changes of view are owing to movements of the head and trunk, as well as to the sweep of the eye within its own orbit. . . .

When, along with a forward movement, we behold a steadily varying change of appearance in the objects before us, we associate the change with the locomotive effort, and after many repetitions, we firmly connect the one with the other. We then know what is implied in a certain feeling in the eye, a certain adjustment of the lenses and a certain inclination of the axes, of all of which we are conscious; we know that these things are connected with the further experience of a definite locomotive energy needing to be expended, in order to alter this consciousness to some other consciousness. Apart from this association, the eye-feeling might be recognised as differing from other eye-feelings, but there could be no other perception in the case. Experience connects these differences of ocular adjustment with the various exertions of the body at large, and the one can then imply and reveal the others. The feeling that we have when the eyes are parallel and vision distinct, is associated with a great and prolonged effort of walking, in other words, with a long distance. An inclination of the eyes of two degrees, is associated with two paces to bring us up to the nearest limit of vision, or with a stretch of some other kind, measured in the last resort by pacing, or by passing the hand along the object. The change from an inclination of 30° to an inclination of 10°, is associated with a given sweep of the arm, carrying the hand forward over eight inches and a half.*

These slight changes in the action of the muscles that move the eye, habitually effected in a time too short for computation, are the means by which our visual impressions from the whole of that portion of the universe which is visible from the position where we stand, may be concentrated within an interval of time so small that we are scarcely conscious of any interval; and they are, in my apprehension, the generating cause of all that we have in our notion of extension over and above what Platner's patient had in his. He had to conceive two or any number of bodies (or resisting objects) with a long train of sensations of muscular contraction filling up the interval between them: while we, on the contrary, think of them as rushing upon our sight, many of them at the same instant, all of them at what is scarcely distinguishable from the same instant; and this visual imagery effaces from our minds any distinct consciousness of the series of muscular sensations of which it has become representative. The simultaneous visual sensations are to us *symbols* of tactual and muscular ones which were slowly successive.

This symbolic relation being far briefer, is habitually thought of in place of that it symbolizes: and by the continued use of such symbols, and the union of them into more complex ones, are generated our ideas of visible extension—ideas which, like

The Senses and the Intellect, pp. 370–4. I now quote from the second edition (1864). The corresponding passage in the first edition begins at p. 363. [Mill's square brackets.]

those of the algebraist working out an equation, are wholly unlike the ideas symbolized; and which yet, like his, occupy the mind to the entire exclusion of the ideas
symbolized.

This last extract is from Mr. Herbert Spencer,* whose *Principles of
Psychology*, in spite of some doctrines which he holds in common with the
intuitive school, are on the whole one of the finest examples we possess of
the Psychological Method in its full power. His treatment of this subject,
and Mr. Bain's, are at once corroborative and supplementary of one
another: and to them I must refer the reader who desires an ampler elucidation of the general question. The remainder of this chapter will be devoted
to the examination of some peculiarities in Sir W. Hamilton's treatment of
it.

Sir W. Hamilton relies mainly upon one argument to prove that Vision,
without the aid of Touch, gives an immediate knowledge of Extension:
which argument had been anticipated in a passage which he quotes from
D'Alembert.† The following is his own statement of it.

It can easily be shown that the perception of colour involves the perception of
extension. It is admitted that we have by sight a perception of colours, consequently
a perception of the difference of colours. But a perception of the distinction of
colours necessarily involves the perception of a discriminating line; for if one colour
be laid beside or upon another, we only distinguish them as different by perceiving
that they limit each other, which limitation necessarily affords a breadthless
line,—a line of demarcation. One colour laid upon another, in fact, gives a line
returning upon itself, that is, a figure. But a line and a figure are modifications of
extension. The perception of extension, therefore, is necessarily given in the
perception of colours.‡

And farther on:

All parties are, of course, at one in regard to the fact that we see colour. Those who
hold that we see extension, admit that we see it only as coloured; and those who
deny us any vision of extension, make colour the exclusive object of sight. In regard
to this first position, all are, therefore, agreed. Nor are they less harmonious in
reference to the second;—that the power of perceiving colour involves the power of
perceiving the differences of colours. By sight we, therefore, perceive colour, and
discriminate one colour, that is, one coloured body,—one sensation of colour, from
another. This is admitted. A third position will also be denied by none, that the
colours discriminated in vision, are, or may be, placed side by side in immediate
juxtaposition; or, one may limit another by being superinduced partially over it. A
fourth position is equally indisputable; that the contrasted colours, thus bounding

Principles of Psychology [London: Longman, Brown, Green, and Longmans,
1855], p. 224.
    †*Lectures*, Vol. II, p. 172. [See Jean le Rond d'Alembert, *Mélanges de littérature,
d'histoire, et de philosophie*, new ed., 5 vols. (Amsterdam: Chatelain, 1759–67), p.
110.]
    ‡*Ibid.*, p. 165.

each other, will form by their meeting a visible line, and that, if the superinduced colour be surrounded by the other, this line will return upon itself, and thus constitute the outline of a visible figure. These four positions command a peremptory assent; they are all self-evident. But their admission at once explodes the paradox under discussion [—that extension cannot be cognised by sight alone]. And thus: A line is extension in one dimension,—length; a figure is extension in two,—length and breadth. Therefore, the vision of a line is a vision of extension in length; the vision of a figure, the vision of extension in length and breadth.*

I must acknowledge that I cannot make the answer to this argument as thorough and conclusive as I could wish; for we have not the power of making an experiment, the completing converse of Platner's. There is no example of a person born with the sense of sight, but without those of touch and the muscles: and nothing less than this would enable us to define precisely the extent and limits of the conceptions which sight is capable of giving, *q*independently*q* of association with impressions of another sense. There are, however, considerations well adapted to moderate the extreme confidence which Sir W. Hamilton places in this argument. First, it must be observed that when the eye, at present, takes cognizance of *r*a*r* visible figure, it does not cognise it by means of colour alone, but by all those motions and modifications of the muscles connected with the eye, which have so great a share in giving us our acquired perceptions of sight. To determine what can be cognised by sight alone, we must suppose an eye incapable of these changes; which can neither have the curvature of its lenses modified nor the direction of its axis changed by any mode of muscular action; which cannot, therefore, travel along the boundary line that separates two colours, but must remain fixed with a steady gaze on a definite spot. If we once allow the eye to follow the direction of a line or the periphery of a figure, we have no longer merely sight, but important muscular sensations superadded. Now there is nothing more certain than that an eye with its axis immovably fixed in one direction, gives a full and clear vision of but a small portion of space, that to which the axis directly points, and only a faint and indistinct one of the other points surrounding it. When we are able to see any considerable portion of a surface so as to form a distinct idea of it, we do so by passing the eye over and about it, changing slightly the direction of the axis many times in a second. When the eye is pointed directly to one spot, the faint perceptions we have of others are barely sufficient to serve as indications for directing the axis of the eye to each of them in turn, when withdrawn from the first. Physiologists have explained this by the fact, that the centre of the retina is furnished with a

Ibid., pp. 167–8. [The words in square brackets are Mill's.]

*q–q*65¹   independent
r–r+67, 72

prodigiously greater number of nervous papillæ, much finer and more delicate individually, and crowded closer together, than any other part. Whatever be its explanation, the fact itself is indubitable; and seems to warrant the conclusion that if the axis of the eye were immovable, and we were without the muscular sensations which accompany and guide its movement, the impression we should have of a boundary between two colours would be so vague and indistinct as to be merely rudimentary.

A rudimentary conception must be allowed, for it is evident that even without moving the eye we are capable of having two sensations of colour at once, and that the boundary which separates the colours must give some specific affection of sight, otherwise we should have no discriminative impressions capable of afterwards becoming, by association, representative of the cognitions of lines and figures which we owe to the tactual and the muscular sense. But to confer on these discriminative impressions the name which denotes our matured and perfected cognition of Extension, or even to assume that they have in their nature anything in common with it, seems to be going beyond the evidence. [s]Berkeley acknowledged a very considerable amount of perception by the eye alone, of something which it was possible to call by the name of extension; and that which is so perceived has, since his time, been known to philosophers as Visible Extension, in contradistinction to Tangible.[*] But Berkeley maintained that Visible Extension not only is not the same thing as Tangible Extension, but has not the smallest likeness to it, and that a person born with only one of the two senses, and afterwards acquiring the other, would, until there had been time to learn their mutual relation by experience, never suspect that there was any connexion between them.[†] In point of fact, those who are born blind and afterwards acquire sight, know by the information of others that the eye pictures and the tactual sensations come from the same objects: yet even with that help it is always a work of time and difficulty to connect the one with the other.[s] Sir W. Hamilton appears to think that extension as revealed by the eye, is identical with the extension which we know by touch, except that it is only in two dimensions. "It is not," he says, "all kind of extension and form that is attributed to sight. It is not figured extension in all the three dimensions, but only extension as involved in plane figures; that is, only length and breadth."[*] But to have the notion of extension even in length and breadth as we have it, is to have it in such a manner that we might know certain muscular facts without having tried: as,

[*See George Berkeley, *An Essay towards a New Theory of Vision*, in *Works*, 3 vols. (London: Priestley, 1820), Vol. I, pp. 261ff. (§§lii ff.).]

[†*Ibid.*, p. 277 (§lxxix).]

Lectures, Vol. II, p. 160.

[s-s]+72

for instance, that if we placed our finger on the spot corresponding to one end of a line, or boundary of a surface, we should have to go through a muscular motion before we could place it on the other. Is there the smallest reason to suppose that on the evidence of sight alone, we could arrive at this conclusion in anticipation of the sense of touch? I cannot admit that we could have what is meant by a perception of superficial space, unless we conceived it as something which the hand could be moved across; and, whatever may be the retinal impression conveyed by the line which bounds two colours, I see no ground for thinking that by the eye alone we could acquire the conception of what we now mean when we say that one of the colours is outside the other.* On this point I may again quote Mr. Bain.

I do not see how one sensation can be felt as out of another, without already supposing that we have a feeling of space. If I see two distinct objects before me, as

*[67] The following case, however, which I quote from Dr. M'Cosh, if correctly reported, would require a considerable modification of the preceding doctrine. "The best reported case" of a person born blind, but who acquired eyesight by means of a surgical operation, "is that of Dr. [Joann Christoph August] Franz of Leipsig ([“Memoir of the Case of a Gentleman born blind,”] *Philosophical Transactions of the Royal Society of London*, [CXXXI,] 1841 [59–68]). The youth had been born blind, and was seventeen years of age when the experiment was wrought which gave him the use of one eye. When the eye was sufficiently restored to bear the light, a sheet of paper on which two strong black lines had been drawn, the one horizontal, the other vertical, was placed before him at the distance of about three feet. He was now allowed to open the eye, and after attentive examination he called the lines by their right ʹdenominations,ʺ that is, according to Dr. M'Cosh, horizontal and vertical.ʹ "ʹThe outline in black of a square, six inches in diameter, within which a circle had been drawn, and within the latter a triangle, was, after careful examination, recognised and correctly described by him.ʹ ʹAt the distance of three feet, and on a level with the eye, a solid cube and a sphere, each of four inches diameter, was placed before him.ʹ ʹAfter attentively examining these bodies, he said he saw a quadrangular and a circular figure, and after some consideration he pronounced the one a square and the other a disc. His eye being then closed, the cube was taken away and a disc of equal size substituted and placed next to the sphere. On again opening his eye he observed no difference in these objects, but regarded them both as discs. The solid cube was now placed in a somewhat oblique position before the eye, and close beside it a figure cut out of pasteboard, representing a plane outline prospect of the cube when in this position. Both objects he took to be something like flat quadrates. [qy. quadrilaterals?] A pyramid placed before him with one of its sides towards his eye he saw as a plain [plane?] triangle. This object was now turned a little, so as to present two of its sides to view, but rather more of one side than of the other: after considering and examining it for a long time, he said that this was a very extraordinary figure; it was neither a triangle, nor a quadrangle, nor a circle; he had no idea of it, and could not describe it; in fact, said he, I must give it up. On the conclusion of these experiments, I asked him to describe the sensations the objects had produced, whereupon he said, that im-

ʳ⁻ʳ67 denominations"—what?

two candle flames, I apprehend them as different objects, and as distant from one another by an interval of space; but this apprehension presupposes an independent experience and knowledge of lineal extension. There is no evidence to show that, at the first sight of these objects, and before any association is formed between visible appearances and other movements, I should be able to apprehend in the double appearance a difference of place. I feel a distinctness of impression, undoubtedly, partly optical and partly muscular, but in order that this distinctness may mean to

---

mediately on opening his eye he had discovered a difference in the two objects, the cube and the sphere, placed before him, and perceived that they were not drawings; but that he had not been able to form from them the idea of a square and a disc, until he perceived a sensation of what he saw in the points of his fingers, as if he really touched the object. [A very significant fact, both psychologically and physiologically.] When I gave the three bodies (the sphere, cube, and pyramid) into his hand, he was much surprised he had not recognised them as such by sight, as he was well acquainted with mathematical figures by his touch." ([McCosh, *Examination*,] pp. 163–5 [quoting Franz, pp. 64–5]. [Mill's square brackets.])

The case as stated looks like an experimental proof, that not only something which admits of being called extension, but an extension which is promptly identified with that already known by touch, "though in two dimensions only," may be perceived by sight at the very first use of the eyes, before the muscular action necessary for directing the eye has been learnt by practice. There is one suspicious circumstance in the recital—the youth's instantaneous perception that the cube and the sphere were not drawings; for how could one who had never before had any sensation of sight, "distinguish without help a drawing from its object"? Cheselden's patient was for a long time deceived by pictures, and asked which was the lying sense, feeling or seeing. [See William Cheselden, "An Account of some Observations," *Philosophical Transactions of the Royal Society of London*, XXXV (1728), 449.] We ought, moreover, to have been expressly told whether, previous to the operation, the blindness was absolutely complete; which in many of the cases cited by Mr. Samuel Bailey it was not, and, according to Cheselden, in cases of congenital cataract it seldom is so. [*Ibid.*, p. 447.] If no material circumstance is omitted in the report of Dr. Franz's case, the doctrine in the text will require a certain amount of correction. What is there called a rudimentary conception of figure by the eye, must be more than rudimentary; it must be, in its way, considerably developed; and it must be such that "after attentive examination" it could be recognised as corresponding with the circles and quadrangles already known by touch. On this last point the report does not agree with other recorded cases. In a recent case, for example, recorded by Mr. Nunneley (I quote at second hand from Professor Fraser in the *North British Review*) the boy could indeed, after couching, "at once perceive a difference in the shapes of objects," could see that the cube and the sphere "were not of the same visible figure," but could not tell which was which: "it was not till they had been many times placed in his hands, that he learnt to distinguish by sight the one which he had just had in his hands from the other placed beside it. He gradually became more correct in his judgments, but it was only after several days that he could tell by the eye alone which was the sphere and which the cube; when asked, he always, before answering, wished to take both in his hands. Even when

$^{u-u}+72$
$^{v-v}67$ know what a drawing is

me a difference of position in space, it must reveal the additional fact, that a certain movement of my arm would carry my hand from the one flame to the other; or that some other movement of mine would change by a definite amount the appearance I now see. If no information is conveyed respecting the possibility of movements of the body generally, no idea of space is given, for we never consider that we have a notion of space, unless we distinctly recognise this possibility. But how a vision to

———

this was allowed, when immediately afterwards the objects were placed before the eyes, he was not certain of the figure." [A. C. Fraser, "Berkeley's Theory of Vision," *North British Review*, XLI (Aug., 1864), 215, who is quoting Thomas Nunneley, *On the Organs of Vision* (London: Churchill, 1838), p. 32.]

If Dr. Franz's case is fairly reported, his patient was probably of more than ordinary natural quickness of observation, and identified the figures not by resemblance proper, but by analogy, or resemblance of relations. Though beholding for the first time a visual square and circle, he was no doubt aware through the persons who surrounded him, that the objects shown to his sight were objects which could be touched—which he already knew by touch. During the "careful examination" and "consideration" which preceded his recognition of them, he was probably employed in asking himself to what, in his experience of tangible objects, these visible objects bore the greatest affinity. Now, he was "well acquainted with mathematical figures by touch," and had therefore acquired a complete idea of a closed figure, and of the boundary which incloses it—the outline separating object from not-object. A relation similar to that between a tangible figure and its boundary, exists between the visual periphery and the mass of colour it incloses. This mere analogy might be sufficient to direct his choice, when a visual object had at any rate to be identified with a tangible. The grand difficulty was in discovering that any visual object was the same with any tangible: but, this difficulty once surmounted by the information of others, a small circumstance might give him a hint for pairing the one class of objects with the other. In his familiarity, by touch and the muscles, with (let us say) a triangular outline, he had become aware of sudden and sharp bends in it, and knew that there were three of these in the tangible periphery. There was the same number of peculiar points in the visual outline, which might not spontaneously have reminded him of the bends he knew by touch, but, if a choice had to be made, were more analogous to them than anything in a circular outline. Being required therefore to give to this object the name of something tangible, he was naturally led to calling it a triangle. It is by no means evident that if left entirely to himself, he would have found out, except by gradual experience, that the phænomenon analogous to extension, which he perceived by sight, was the extension which he already knew by touch. I may add, that since we have from sight distinctive sensations answering to the various figures, it is no more than natural that these sensations, however unlike the tactual sensations which they represent, should have relations among themselves, resembling the mutual relations of those. *w*The same explanation may probably serve for the lad's ability to distinguish by sight a vertical line from a horizontal. He was probably told that one of them was horizontal and the other vertical, and was only asked which was which; and without further information we cannot tell what small circumstance may have determined him to guess the one rather than the other.*w* To sum up my view of Dr. Franz's case, it does not prove that we perceive extension by sight, but only that we have

w-w+72

the eye can reveal beforehand what would be the experience of the hand or the other moving members, I am unable to understand.*

Sir W. Hamilton does not limit the perception of Extension to sight and touch, either separately or combined with one another. "The opinions," he says,

so generally prevalent, that through touch, or touch and muscular feeling, or touch

discriminative sensations of sight, corresponding to all the diversities of superficial extension: but, if rightly reported, it greatly widens the range of those discriminative sensations, and almost shows that by sight alone we might rise to the height of Reid's Geometry of Visibles [see Reid's *Inquiry*, pp. 147–52].

**The Senses and the Intellect*, 2nd ed., pp. 376–7; 1st ed., p. 369. To this passage, Mr. Bain has appended, in his second edition the following instructive note:

"In following a wide ranging movement, or in expatiating over a large prospect, we must move the eyes or the head; and probably every one would allow that, in such a case, feelings of movement make a part of our sensation and our subsequent idea. The notion of a mountain evidently contains feelings of visual movement. But when we look at a circle, say, one tenth of an inch in diameter, the eye can take in the whole of it without movement, and we might suppose that the sensation is, in that case, purely optical, there being no apparent necessity for introducing the muscular consciousness. A characteristic optical impression is produced; we should be able to discriminate between the small circle and a square, or an oval, or between it and a somewhat larger or somewhat smaller circle, from the mere optical difference of the effect on the retina. Why then may we not say, that, through the luminous tracing alone, we have the feeling of visible form?

By making an extreme supposition of this nature, it is possible to remove the case from a direct experimental test. We may still, however, see very strong grounds for maintaining the presence of a muscular element even in this instance. In the first place, our notions of form are manifestly obtained by working on the large scale, or by the survey of objects of such magnitude as to demand the sweep of the eye, in order to comprehend them. We lay the foundations of our knowledge of visible outline in circumstances where the eye must be active, and must mix its own activity with the retinal feelings. The idea of a circle is first gained by moving the eye round some circular object of considerable size. Having done this, we transfer the fact of motion to smaller circles, although they would not of themselves demand an extensive ocular sweep. So that when we look at a little round body, we are already pre-occupied with the double nature of visible form, and are not in a position to say how we should regard it, if that were our first experience of a circle.

But, in the second place, the essential *import* of visible form is something not attainable without the experience of moving the eye. If we looked at a little round spot, we should know an optical difference between it and a triangular spot, and we should recognise it as identical with another round spot; but that is merely retinal knowledge, or optical discrimination. That would not be to recognise form, because by form we never mean so little as a mere change of colour. We mean by a round form something that would take a given sweep of the eye to comprehend it; and unless we identify the small spot with the circles previously seen, we do not perceive it to be a circle. It may remain in our mind as a purely optical meaning; but we can never cross the chasm that separates an optical meaning from an effect combining light and movement, in any other way than by bringing in an experience of movement." (Pp. 377n–8n.)

and sight, or touch, muscular feeling, and sight,—that through these senses, exclusively, we are percipient of extension, &c., I do not admit. On the contrary, I hold that all sensations whatsoever of which we are conscious as one out of another, *eo ipso* afford us the condition of immediately and necessarily apprehending extension; for in the consciousness itself of such reciprocal outness is actually involved a perception of difference of place in space, and, consequently, of the extended.*

It may safely be admitted that whenever we are conscious of two sensations as "one out of another," in the sense of locality, we have a perception of space; for the two expressions are equivalent. But to have a consciousness of difference between two sensations which are felt simultaneously, is not to feel them as "one out of another" in this sense; and the very question to be decided is, whether any of our senses, apart from feelings of muscular motion, gives us the notion of "one out of another" in the sense necessary to support the idea of Extension.

Sir W. Hamilton thinks that whenever two different nervous filaments are simultaneously affected at their extremities, the sensations received through them are felt as one out of the other. It is extremely probable that the affection of two distinct nervous filaments is the condition of the discriminative sensibility which furnishes us with sensations capable of becoming representative of objects one out of the other. But that is a different thing from giving us the perception directly. Undoubtedly we recognise difference of place in the objects which affect our senses, whenever we are aware that those objects affect different parts of our organism. But when we are aware of this, we already have the notion of Place. We must be aware of the different parts of our body as one out of another, before we can use this knowledge as a means of cognising a similar fact in regard to other material objects. This Sir W. Hamilton admits; and what, therefore, he is bound to prove is, that the very first time we received an impression of touch, or of any other sense, affecting more than one nervous filament, we were conscious of being affected in a plurality of places. This he does not even attempt to do; and direct proof is palpably unattainable. As a matter of indirect evidence, we may oppose to this theory Mr. Bain's, according to which, apart from association, we should not have any impression of *this* kind, and should in general be conscious only of a greater mass or "volume"[*] of sensation when we were affected in two places, than when only in one; like the more massive sensation of heat which we feel when our bodies are immersed in a warm bath, compared with that which we feel when heat of the same, or even of greater intensity, is applied only to our hands or feet. Mr. Bain's doctrine, being as consistent

*"Dissertations on Reid," [Note D,] p. 861n.

[*See Bain, *The Senses and the Intellect*, 1st ed., p. 178; see also McCosh, *Examination*, p. 153, where Bain's view is discussed.]

*-*65¹   the

with the admitted facts of the case as Sir W. Hamilton's, has a good claim, on his own law of Parcimony, to be preferred to it. But, besides, there are recorded facts which agree with Mr. Bain's theory, and are quite irreconcilable with Sir W. Hamilton's; and to find such we need not travel beyond Sir W. Hamilton's own pages.

One of them is the very case we have already had before us, that recorded by Platner. The facts of this case are quite inconsistent with the opinion, that we have a direct perception of extension when an object touches us in more than one place, including the extremities of more than one nervous filament. Platner expressly says that his patient, when an object touched a considerable part of the surface of his body, but without exciting more than one *kind* of sensation, was conscious of no local difference—no "outness" of one part of the sensation in relation to another part—but only (we may presume) of a greater *quantity* of sensation; as Mr. Bain would call it, a greater *ʸ*volume*ʸ*. As Platner expresses it, "if objects and the parts of his body touched by them, did not make different kinds of impression on his nerves of sensation, he would take everything external for one and the same. In his own body, he absolutely did not discriminate head and foot at all by their distance, but merely by the difference of the feelings."[*] Such an experiment, reported by a competent observer, is of itself almost enough to overthrow Sir W. Hamilton's theory.

In like manner, the patient in Cheselden's celebrated case, after his second eye was couched, described himself as seeing objects twice as large with both eyes as with one only;[†] that is, he had a double quantity, or double volume of sensation, which suggested to his mind the idea of a double size.*

[*See pp. 223–4 above.]
[†Cheselden, p. 450.]
*I may here observe that Sir W. Hamilton (and the same mistake has been made by Mr. Bailey [*A Review of Berkeley's Theory of Vision*, pp. 166–83]) considers Cheselden's case as evidence that the "perception of externality," as distinguished from that of distance from the eye, is given by sight as well as by touch, because the young man said that objects at first seemed "to touch his eyes, as what he felt did his skin." [Cheselden, p. 448.] He seems to think that, on the other theory, the boy should have been metaphysician enough to recognise in the perception "a mere affection of the organ," or at least should have perceived the objects "as if in his eyes." (Foot-note to Reid, p. 177n.) But he was not accustomed to conceive tangible objects as if in his fingers. He conceived them as touching his fingers: and he simply transferred the experience of touch to the newly-acquired sense. All his notions of perception were associated with direct contact; and as he did not perceive any of the objects of sight to be at a distance from the organ by which he perceived them, he concluded that they must be in contact with it.
*ᶻ*Mr. Nunneley's case, on this point, agrees with Cheselden's. The boy "said

*ᵛ–ᵛ*65¹ *volume*
ᶻ–ᶻ+67, 72

Another case, for the knowledge of which I am also indebted to Sir W. Hamilton—who knew it through an abstract given by M. Maine de Biran[*] of the original report "by M. Rey Régis, a medical observer, in his *Histoire naturelle de l'âme*"[†]—is as incompatible with Sir W. Hamilton's theory as Platner's case. It is the case of a patient who lost the power of movement in one-half of his body, apparently from temporary paralysis of the motory nerves, while the functions of the sensory nerves seemed unimpaired. This patient, it was found, had lost the power of localizing his sensations.

Experiments, various and repeated, were made to ascertain with accuracy, whether the loss of motive faculty had occasioned any alteration in the capacity of feeling; and it was found that the patient, though as acutely alive as ever to the sense of pain, felt, when this was secretly inflicted, as by compression of his hand under the bedclothes, a sensation of suffering or uneasiness, by which, when the pressure became strong, he was compelled lustily to cry out; but a sensation merely general, he being altogether unable to localize the feeling, or to say whence the pain proceeded. . . . The patient, as he gradually recovered the use of his limbs, gradually also recovered the power of localizing his sensations.*

It would be premature to establish a scientific inference upon a single experiment: but if confirmed by repetition, this is an experimentum crucis.[‡] So far as one experiment can avail, it [a] proves, that sensation without motion does not give the perception of difference of place in our bodily organs (not to speak of outward objects), and that this perception is even now entirely an inference, dependent on the muscular feelings.[†]

---

everything touched his eyes, and walked carefully about with his hands held up before him, to prevent things hurting his eyes by touching them."[z]

[*See Marie François Pierre Gonthier Maine de Biran, *Nouvelles Considérations sur les rapports du physique et du moral de l'homme*, ed. Victor Cousin (Paris: Ladrange, 1834), pp. 96–7.]

[†Rey Régis was a pseudonym for Cazillac; the reference is to his *Histoire naturelle et raisonnée de l'âme*, 2 vols. (London [Lyons], 1789), Vol. I, p. 27.]

*"Dissertations on Reid," [Note D,] p. 875n.

[‡See pp. 222–3 above.]

†[67] Dr. M'Cosh says: "This case is valueless, as evidently the functions of the nervous apparatus were deranged." ([*Examination*,] p. 151n.) I am far from pretending that this single experiment is conclusive; but I can as little admit that it ought to count for nothing. The functions of the motor nerves were deranged; but no derangement appears to have been remarked in those of the nerves of sensation; unless, by a *petitio principii*, the incapacity of localizing the sensations is considered to prove it. We cannot indeed prove that those nerves were not also in a morbid state: but pathological cases, which are admitted to be the nearest equivalents in physiology to experiments in inorganic science, would lose all their scientific value if it could be assumed without evidence that the disease extended to other functions than those in which it was observed. Even if a physical derangement were proved, one not unimportant point would have been ascertained by the experiment—that a morbid affection may take away the power of localizing sensations,

[a]65[1], 65[2]   fully

It gives a very favourable idea of Sir W. Hamilton's sincerity and devotion to truth, that he should have drawn from their obscurity, and made generally known, two cases which make such havoc with his own opinions as this and Platner's; for though he did not believe the cases to be really inconsistent with his theory, he can hardly have been entirely unaware that they could be used against it.

The only other point in Sir W. Hamilton's doctrines respecting the Primary Qualities which it is of importance to notice, is one, I believe, peculiar to himself, and certainly not common to him with any of his eminent predecessors in the same school of thought. It is the doctrine, that those qualities are not perceived—are not directly and immediately cognized—in things external to our bodies, but only in our bodies themselves. "A Perception," he says,

of the Primary Qualities does not, originally, and in itself, reveal to us the existence, and qualitative existence, of aught beyond the organism, apprehended by us as extended, figured, divided, &c. The primary qualities of things external to our organism we do not perceive, *i.e.* immediately know. For these we only learn to *infer*, from the affections which we come to find that they determine in our organs;—affections which, yielding us a perception of organic extension, we at length discover, by observation and induction, to imply a corresponding extension in the extra-organic agents.

Neither, according to him, do we perceive, or immediately know, "extension in its true and absolute magnitude;" our perceptions giving different impressions of magnitude from the same object, when placed in contact with different parts of our body.

As perceived extension is only the recognition of one organic affection in its outness from another; as a minimum of extension is thus, to perception, the smallest extent of organism in which sensations can be discriminated as plural; and as in one part of the organism this smallest extent is perhaps some million, certainly some myriad, times smaller than in others; it follows that, to perception, the same real extension will appear, in this place of the body, some million or myriad times greater than in that. Nor does this difference subsist only as between sense and sense; for in the same sense, and even in that sense which has very commonly been held exclusively to afford a knowledge of absolute extension, I mean Touch proper, the minimum, at one part of the body, is some fifty times greater than it is at another.*

Thus, according to Sir W. Hamilton, all our cognitions of extension and figure in anything except our own body, and of the real amount of extension even in that, are not perceptions, or states of direct consciousness, but

---

without taking away the sensations. Localization, therefore, does not depend on the same conditions with the sensations themselves, still less is it inseparably involved in them.

"Dissertations on Reid," [Note D,] pp. 881–2.

"inferences," and even inferences "by observation and induction" from our experience. Now, we know how contemptuous he is of Brown, and other "Cosmothetic Idealists," for maintaining that the existence of extension or extended objects otherwise than as an affection of our own minds, is not a direct perception but an inference. We know how he reproaches this opinion with being subversive of our Natural Beliefs; how often he repeats that the testimony of consciousness must be accepted entire, or not accepted at all; how earnestly and in how many places he maintains

that we have not merely a notion, a conception, an imagination, a subjective representation of Extension, for example, called up or suggested in some incomprehensible manner to the mind, on the occasion of an extended object being presented to the sense; but that in the perception of such an object we have, *as by nature we believe we have*, an immediate knowledge or consciousness of that external object *as extended*. In a word, that in sensitive perception, the extension as known, and the extension as existing, are convertible; known because existing, and existing, since known.*

All this, it appears, is only true of the extension of our own bodies. The extension of any other body is not known immediately or by perception, but as an inference from the former. I ask any one, whether this opinion does not contradict our "natural beliefs" as much as any opinion of the Cosmothetic Idealists can do; whether to the natural, or non-metaphysical man, it is not as great a paradox to affirm that we do not perceive extension in anything external to our bodies, as that we do not perceive extension in anything external to our minds; and whether, if the natural man can be brought to assent to the former, he will find any additional strangeness or apparent absurdity in the latter. This is only one of the many instances in which the philosopher who so vehemently accuses other thinkers of affirming the absolute authority of Consciousness when it is on their own side, and rejecting it when it is not, lays himself open to a similar charge. The truth is, it is a charge from which no psychologist, not Reid himself, is exempt. No person of competent understanding has ever applied himself to the study of the human mind, and not discovered that some of the common opinions of mankind respecting their mental consciousness are false, and that some notions, apparently intuitive, are really acquired. Every psychologist draws the line where he thinks it can be drawn most truly. Of course it is possible that Sir W. Hamilton has drawn it in the right place, and Brown in the wrong. Sir W. Hamilton would say that the common opinions which he contests are not Natural Beliefs, though mistaken for such. And Brown thinks exactly the same of those which are repugnant to his own doctrine. Neither of *b*them*b* can justify himself but by pointing out a mode

Ibid., [Note D,] p. 842.

*b-b*65¹ these

in which the apparent perceptions, supposed to be original, may have been acquired; and neither can charge the other with anything worse than having made a mistake in this extremely delicate process of psychological analysis. Neither of them has a right to give to a mistake in such a matter, the name of a rejection of the testimony of consciousness, and attempt to bring down the other by an argument which is of no possible value except *ad invidiam*, and which in its invidious sense is applicable to them both, and to all psychologists deserving the name.

ᶜNOTE TO THE PRECEDING CHAPTER

A host of critics, headed by Dr. M'Cosh, Mr. Mahaffy, and the writer in *Blackwood* [W. H. Smith], have directed their shafts against this chapter; but Professor Fraser, himself a host, is on my side. [See "Berkeley's Theory of Vision," pp. 202, 218n.] The essential point in the controversy being the analysis of Extension, I shall confine my notice to the arguments bearing upon that point.

The principal objection is the same which was made to the two preceding chapters: that the explanation given of Extension presupposes Extension: that the notion itself is surreptitiously introduced, to account for its own origin. The case of the objectors is most compactly stated by Mr. Mahaffy, in the following extract:

The briefest way of criticizing the long passage [quoted from Mr. Bain] will be to enumerate its fallacies in general heads. (α) A knowledge of our organism as extended must not be begged, when we are going to explain extension; hence, such expressions as the "range of a limb" or "sweep of a limb," must either be carefully confined to the mere succession of feelings in moving it, or they beg the question: and indeed, as suggesting extension in the very statement, they should be avoided when we are describing the phenomena from which extension is to be derived. (β) Any mention or postulating of *direction* cannot be for a moment allowed; for what possible meaning can direction have except in space? In particular, lineal (by which I suppose Mr. Bain principally means rectilinear) direction would be only given with great difficulty by the moving of limbs, and we should be brought back to the old Greek notion of circular motion being the most natural. This difficulty, as well as a host of others, are urged with great acuteness by Mr. Abbott. ([Thomas Kingsmill Abbott,] *Sight and Touch* [(London: Longman, Green, Longman, Roberts, and Green, 1864)], Chap. v [pp. 60ff.].) More especially he states, from E. H. Weber, that touch cannot give us the idea of a right line at all, and consequently not the slightest idea of direction. [Abbott, p. 70, referring to Ernst Heinrich Weber, "Der Tastsinn und das Gemeingefühl," in Rudolph Wagner, *Handwörterbuch der Physiologie*, 4 vols. (Braunschweig: Bieweg, 1842–53), Vol. III, pp. 481–588.] (γ) No such notion as velocity or rapidity can be admitted, far less such a notion as the comparison of quicker and slower motions. In fact, the idea of motion requires as its logical antecedent both space and time, and is not identical with pure succession. Suppose we had nothing but the series of our thoughts to analyse, we could never get beyond the idea of a series, nor could we ever by any chance get the notion of acceleration or retardation in it. For what is quicker or slower? Nothing but more space traversed in less time, and *vice versâ*. Motion cannot be apprehended without something fixed, which is only given us by relations of space, as Kant has well shown. The *motion* of our thoughts, then, is in the first place, only an analogical expression; and secondly, could never have been felt without something in space whereby not only to measure the increased or diminished velocity of our thinking, but even to learn that there is any velocity at all in the matter. The evidence of dreaming seems to corroborate this view. Why is it, that, the intuitions of velocity afforded us by space being removed, the current of thoughts is found by itself completely incompetent to suggest or estimate speed at all? (δ) What we necessarily use to *measure* extension must not for that reason have originally *suggested* it. And yet all that the association school ever attempt to prove is only this: that all the measures of extension can be traced to series of muscular feelings in time. The knowledge of extension is one thing, and primitive; the measure of extension is another, and empirical; and we should not accept Mr. Bain's confusion of them together (perhaps identification of them), without some further proof than his bare statement.

Upon all these assumptions, however, the theory of Mr. Bain is based, and the intelligent reader will find them scattered over the very surface of the argument. I would call particular attention to the passage . . . "We must learn to feel that a slow motion for a long time is the same as a quicker motion with less duration, which we can easily do by seeing that they both produce the same effect in exhausting the full range of the limb." Surely it is clear that without space we could never get the idea of motion, which involves space as much as time—in fact, a series in time only changes, it does not move; and even granting we had the idea, we could never discriminate whether that motion was quicker or slower, except the notion of something permanent in space, and motion in space, were given. The same *petitio principii* is made by Mr. Mill.*

This orderly and succinct mode of setting forth the objection is a great convenience for answering it. I shall take Mr. Mahaffy's points in his own order.

(α) The phraseology employed to express the data common to both parties must, at least in the commencement, be that which common language affords; since no other would enable the reader to understand, without a laborious process, on a subject already so difficult, what are the facts meant. But the phraseology, of course, must not be so used as to assume anything which either the theory itself, or the theory opposed to it, does not admit. As Mr. Mahaffy observes, "such expressions as the range of a limb, or the sweep of a limb," must "be carefully confined to the mere succession of feelings in moving it." And if the reader turns back to the first

*[67] Mahaffy, pp. xviii–xx. [The first square brackets are Mill's. Mahaffy quotes from Bain, *The Senses and the Intellect*, 1st ed., pp. 113–17 (the same passage Mill quotes, pp. 216–19 above).]

of the quoted passages, he will find that Mr. Bain has been most industrious in directing attention to the feelings involved in the motion of a limb, as the point to be attended to, in contradistinction to the motion itself, and in showing that his expressions are to be understood of the former, and not of the latter.

(β) Direction, Mr. Mahaffy maintains, must not be mentioned or referred to in the analysis of extension, because direction means space, and space must not be called in to account for itself. It would have been nearer the truth if, instead of saying that direction means space, he had said that space means direction. Space is the aggregate of directions, as Time is of successions. To postulate direction, therefore, is to postulate, not space, but the element which the notion of space is made of. Mr. Bain, however, does not postulate direction. He postulates the distinctive sensations which, from the first, accompany the motions of a limb in what we, with our acquired perceptions, call variety of directions. There are such distinctive sensations, otherwise we should not even now know, when our eyes are shut, in what direction our arm is moving. According to Mr. Bain, the difference in the sensations depends on the difference in the muscles exerted. "All directions that call forth the play of the same muscles, are similar directions as respects the body: different muscles mean different directions."* These sensations, shading, as they do, gradually into one another, without abruptness or break, are well fitted to give rise to the feeling of continuity, which unites all our different notions of different directions into one notion of space.†

*[67] *The Senses and the Intellect*, p. 203 (2nd ed.).

†[67] With regard to Mr. Abbott's difficulties, the following is a specimen of them: "Let us suppose a blind man trying to get the notion of distance from the motion of his hand. He finds a certain sweep of the hand brings it into contact with a desk; the distance of which, therefore, is represented by that effort. But it requires a greater effort to reach the eyes or the nose; and distance being = locomotive effort, it is demonstrated that the nose extends beyond the desk. The top of the head must be conceived as more remote, and the back farthest of all." [*Sight and Touch*, p. 70.] Mr. Abbott seems to suppose that a blind man's permanent impression of the distance of objects from him, will be derived from his very first experiment; and denies him the common privilege belonging to all experience, of correcting and completing itself. If the nose is really nearer to his hand than the desk, will he not soon find a way of reaching the nearer object with less locomotive effort than the more distant? If it be said, that this can only be done by bending his arm, and that flexure of the arm is attended with more sense of effort than protension of it, the answer is that even if this were true, the effort is of a different kind; and the blind man would speedily distinguish between the two, and would learn that objects reached by his bended arm are nearer to his body, by all the other tests of proximity, than those which can only be reached with the arm extended. Dr. M'Cosh falls into a fallacy of the same kind ([*Examination*,] p. 135.)

Mr. Abbott's book, a repetition of the attack made by Mr. Bailey on Berkeley's

(γ) Velocity or rapidity, comparison of quicker and slower motions, must not, Mr. Mahaffy says, be postulated, because quicker or slower have no meaning but with reference to the greater or smaller space traversed in a given time. It is true that the two motions derive their name from space; but are the motions themselves therefore undistinguishable? A saw and a hatchet are so called on account of the different kind of work they do; but can we not also distinguish the two objects when we see them? Again I say, what is postulated is not the space traversed, but the greater or less energy of the muscular sensation. It only remains to be explained how we learn that a more energetic sensation lasting a shorter time, is equivalent to a less energy continued for a longer time. Mr. Bain thinks we learn this by their both producing the same effect in "exhausting the full range of the limb;" by which he means, attaining the extreme limit of the sensation which accompanies protension—the point beyond which no further addition to it can be made. Where is the *petitio principii* here? I think that the solution is an admissible one—that we may fairly be supposed to take the entire series of the sensations which accompany the stretching out of the limb, as a unit of measurement, divisible into an ascending scale of degrees, which may be passed through in a shorter or a longer time, but the sum of which is always equal to itself. I have myself pointed out another road by which we might arrive at the same equivalence. We have two simultaneous sensations of touch with our two hands. We then move the right hand until it joins the left, and touches the same object. It need not be supposed that we yet know them as our hands, or the object as a body, or know of our right hand as moving through space. But the two simultaneous sensations of touch, either of which we may prolong or repeat at pleasure, have given us the notion of a permanent element in touch, and of two such permanent elements as coexisting. We have now had the two sensations of touch with a single hand, but separated by a series of the sensations accompanying muscular movement: and we find that to get from one of the tactual sensations to the other requires a shorter time, in proportion to the energy of the intervening muscular sensations. In this mental process time is postulated, but not space: and it is contended that the shorter time, or its equivalent, the greater energy, required to get from one object of touch to another already recognised as simultaneous, is the measure, in the last resort, of their distance in space. The eye then comes in, and with its greater powers of simultaneous sensation, it gathers up, by its acquired perceptions, a host of such measurements in one apparent intuition.

Theory of Vision, has sufficient ability to require an answer by itself, had not this been effectually done by Professor Fraser in an elaborate and able paper ["Berkeley's Theory of Vision"] in the *North British Review* for August, 1864, which I trust will eventually be reprinted in a more permanent form.

(δ) "What we necessarily use to measure extension" need not, as Mr. Mahaffy justly observes, have originally suggested it: but if all the facts of consciousness involved in what we call extension can be accounted for on the supposition that the measure is the thing itself, no other evidence needs be required.* The apparent testimony of consciousness to a difference between them, is perfectly explicable by the totally altered aspect which, as I have shown in the text, our cognizance of Extension puts on when the sense of sight has assumed the lead of it. When a larger collection of carefully observed facts respecting persons blind from birth, shall have been subjected to an acuter and more discriminating analysis, the additional insight which we may hope to obtain into the psychology of such persons, will probably dissipate the remains of obscurity which still hang over some of the details of the subject.

Dr. M'Cosh [*Examination*, pp. 101–72,] and the writer in *Blackwood* are constructive thinkers as well as critics, and endeavour to prove, in a direct manner, that the notion of extension is not acquired through our muscular sensations. The evidence on which they chiefly insist is that, antecedently to experience, we localize our sensations at different points of our body: according to Dr. M'Cosh, at the extremities of the nerve-fibres; every sensation being, by nature, felt at the point where the nerve terminates. The writer in *Blackwood* says, "We do not commence our sentient life with sensations felt nowhere—we certainly have no memory of pains that were not felt somewhere—in that arena, in fact, which we come to call our body." The absence of remembrance of what took place soon after birth being, as I have so often observed, no proof that it did not happen, the proof offered is,

that no ingenuity whatever will get our pains into our bodies, or give us knowledge of these bodies, unless we commence with the admission that certain pains and pleasures of a physical order are, as soon as they attain to any distinctness, felt in different parts of a certain arena, thus localizing each other. . . . Many writers describe this localization as an acquired perception. Now, no one doubts for a moment that the accurate localization of our sensations is acquired by experience; but that experience, we maintain, would not be possible were there not some vague localization given us at once, by simultaneous sensations felt in different parts of our system. How else do we get our first idea of space or position?[†]

---

*[67] The writer in *Blackwood* thinks it absurd that the measure should "measure itself" ([Smith,] p. 32)—that muscular sensation, as a measure of distance, should be employed in measuring muscular sensation. But are not quantities usually measured by quantities of the same kind? A foot rule measures length by its own length. A bushel measures solid contents by its own contents. The tickings of a clock measure other successions by their own succession. A weight measures other weights by itself.

[†][67] *Ibid.*, pp. 26–7.

To this last question I have already endeavoured to give an answer.* With regard to the localization, so far as it regards our external sensations, I see no difficulty in believing that it takes place altogether by the process to which, as the writer admits, we are indebted for our power of "accurate localization." I am bit by an animal, or my skin is irritated at some point, and I am at first unable, as occasionally happens even now, to fix the exact place of the sensation. I move my hand along the surface until I find the place where the friction of the hand relieves the irritation, or where its contact increases the smart. I am now expressing these facts in the ordinary language of mankind, but I have sufficiently explained the sense which that language bears in my own doctrine. The view I have taken of the manner in which we obtain our cognition of place, does not rest on any previous localization, even vague, of our sensations. Nor does the localizing of a sensation, say in one of our limbs, amount to anything but attributing to the sensation an uniform and close conjunction, either synchronous or by immediate succession, with the group of sensations of various kinds which constitute my perception of the limb. In general we probably first discover that the sensation is connected with the limb, by perceiving that the exciting cause of the sensation is connected with it. Mr. Bain states the matter as follows:

I can associate one pain with the sight of my finger, another pain with the sight of my toe, and a third with the position of my arm that determines the crown of my head. An infant at the outset knows not where to look for the cause of an irritation when anything touches it; by and by the child observes a coincidence between a feeling and a pressure operating on some one part; whence a feeling in the hand is associated with the sight of the hand, and so for other members.—When the feeling is more internal, as in the interior of the trunk, we have greater difficulty in tracing the precise seat, often we are quite at a loss on the point. In this case we have to trust to some indications that come to the surface, or to the effect of superficial pressure on the deep parts. By getting a blow on the ribs we come to connect feelings in the chest with the place in our map of the body: we can thus make experiments on the deep-seated organs and learn the meaning of their indications. But the more inaccessible the parts, the more uncertainty is there in assigning the locality of their sensations.†

*[67] If distance and direction are explicable in the way I have pointed out, place and position follow by obvious consequence. If once it be admitted that impressions of touch can be cognised as at once simultaneous and separated by a series of muscular feelings, i.e. at once distant and simultaneous, and that this amounts to cognising them as in space; the position of these impressions among one another, which constitutes their place, will easily result from the different quantities of muscular sensation required for passing from one to the other, combined with the distinctive qualities of the muscular sensation dependent on what we call difference in the direction of the motion.

†[67] *The Senses and the Intellect*, 2nd ed., pp. 397–8.

There are some difficulties, not yet completely resolved, respecting the localization of our internal pains, for the solution of which we need more careful and intelligent observation of infants. But I think enough is known to show that the localization of our sensations is not the starting point of our knowledge of place and position, but follows it. It is true that (as Dr. M'Cosh observes) "if a child is wounded in the arm, it will not hold out its foot."* But, before it has given evidence of having "any acquired perceptions," will it hold out its arm either? On the theory that the localization is an acquired perception, it should do neither the one nor the other.†

Dr. M'Cosh has another argument to prove that we have an original power of localizing our sensations, and, strange to say, it is the very one which is usually thought to be the strongest proof that the power is acquired: viz., the persistence of the association which makes us refer sensations to a limb, after the limb has been cut off. "Müller," says Dr. M'Cosh, "has collected a number of such cases," of which one will be a sufficient sample: "a student named Schmidts, from Aix, had his arm amputated above the elbow thirteen years ago; he has never ceased to have sensations as if in the fingers."‡ It is a singular oversight in Dr. M'Cosh to adduce these facts as proof that we localize the sensation at the extremities of the nerves. He forgets that after the arm was cut off, the extremity of the nerve was in the stump, and that it is there, and not in the fingers, that, if his theory were true, the sensation ought to have been felt. The reference of it to the limb which was gone could only be a case of irresistible association. It does not directly negative the existence of an instinctive localization; but it proves that, if there be any such, an acquired association can overpower it. So in respect to the following fact, also quoted from Müller: "When, in the restoration of a nose, a flap of skin is turned down from the forehead and made to unite with the stump of the nose, the new nose thus formed has, as long as the isthmus of skin by which it maintains its original connexions remains undivided, the same sensations as if it were still on the forehead; in other words, when the nose is touched, the patient feels the impression in

---

*[67] M'Cosh, [*Examination*,] p. 150.

†[67] Dr. M'Cosh says (same page) "It is hard to believe that the instantaneous voluntary drawing back of a limb when wounded, and the shrinking of the frame when boiling liquid is poured down the throat, can proceed from an application of an observed law as to the seat of sensations." The obvious solution of this difficulty is, that both the drawing back and the shrinking, when they take place in an extremely young infant, are purely automatic; a reflex action, produced, without the intervention of the will, by the irritation of the motor nerves: a solution quite conformable to physiology.

‡[67] *Ibid.*, p. 148. [McCosh is quoting Johannes Peter Müller, *Elements of Physiology*, trans. William Baly (London: Taylor and Walton, 1837), p. 695n.]

the forehead."* But the nerve that conveys the impression no longer terminates in the forehead; it terminates in the new nose; and according to Dr.
M'Cosh's theory the sensation should be felt there, exactly as it is after the
"isthmus of skin" has been divided, the old nervous connexion cut off, and
a new one gradually formed. Dr. M'Cosh's facts well nigh destroy his own
theory; but they are such as, on the association theory, would certainly
happen. The last, especially, is of great value to that theory, because it is
one of the strongest instances which show that there is a distinctive "Quale"
(as one of Dr. M'Cosh's German authorities calls it)[*] belonging to the sensation conveyed by each one of the nerves, which hinders it from being confounded with the sensation conveyed by any other nerve, and enables it to
form associations special to itself with the part of the body it serves, which,
as we see, persist even after it has been taken away to serve another part.

*d*Dr. M'Cosh, in his reply, denies that his facts conflict with his theory,
for his theory is, that we intuitively localize our sensations, not where the
nerves really terminate, but where they "normally" terminate; that is, not
where the termination is, but where it ought to be. ["Mill's Reply," p. 350.]
In other words, we, naturally and intuitively, feel our sensations in a place
which, in the case of an amputated limb, is not only outside our body, but
may be at a distance of one or two feet from it: and this seat of sensation in
the space outside our bodies follows us wherever we go. This is what Dr.
M'Cosh would rather believe, than that the reference of the feeling to such
a place is an illusion produced by association. In support of his opinion he
refers to a case mentioned by Professor Valentin (along with three others of
a similar character) in which a girl whose left hand was congenitally
imperfect, said she had the internal sensation of a palm of the hand and five
fingers (which she did not possess) as perfectly in her left hand as in her
right.[†] But what does this prove, except that she had the same sensations
in the nerves of her left hand as in those of her right, which of course,
therefore, carried the same association. Dr. M'Cosh should show a case in
which sensations were referred to non-existent fingers when there were no
real fingers to suggest the notion.

*[67] *Ibid.*, p. 149. [Quoted from Müller, p. 697.]

[*McCosh, *Examination*, pp. 167–8, translating from Wilhelm Wundt, *Beiträge
zur Theorie der Sinneswahrnehmung* (Leipzig and Heidelberg: Winter'sche Verlagshandlung, 1862), p. 60.]

[†See Gabriel Gustav Valentin, "Ueber die subjectiven Gefühle von Personen,
welche mit mangelhaften Extremitäten geboren sind," *Repertorium für Anatomie
und Physiologie*, I (1836–37), 328–37, esp. 330; McCosh ("Mill's Reply," pp. 351–2)
takes the reference from an addition by William Baly to Müller's text, p. 696.]

*d–d*249+72

According to Dr. M'Cosh, the reference of sensations to a lost limb contradicts not his but the association theory; since the lapse of years after the loss of the limb would be sufficient to destroy the old association. [*Ibid.*, p. 351.] And this, in the great majority of cases, it probably does. But it is a frequent experience that a sensation exactly like one we have formerly felt, and like nothing else, revives even after many years a long forgotten remembrance. Again, Dr. M'Cosh says that in the case of the new nose, the affection, according to the association theory, "should have been felt in the forehead, not till the isthmus was cut, but till the old association was gone; and this," according to me, "might not have been for twenty years." [*Ibid.*] This overlooks an important feature in the case. When not only the old nervous connexion has been cut off, but a new one formed, between the new nose and the nervous trunk which connected the old nose with the brain, the sensations become identical with those which were referred to the old nose when it existed; and the reference of them to the nose is thus supported by as old and strong an association as the previous reference of them to the forehead: with the difference that while every day helps to dissolve the one association, every day strengthens and rivets the other.

The only further case referred to by Dr. M'Cosh, is one mentioned by Schopenhauer on the authority of Frorieps; that of "Eva Lauk, an Esthonian girl, fourteen years old, born without arms or legs, but who, according to her mother, had developed herself intellectually quite as rapidly as her brothers and sisters, and without the use of limbs had reached a correct judgment concerning the magnitude and distance of visible objects, quite as quickly as they."* This, unfortunately, is all the information which Schopenhauer gives on this interesting case. In Dr. M'Cosh's judgment, it entirely disproves the opinion "that a sweep of the arm or leg, considered merely as a group of sensations without extension," could give the idea of extension. [*Ibid.*, p. 352.] He means, probably, that it proves that the idea can be acquired without any use of arms or legs. But we do not know of what nature the girl's idea of extension was. What we are told is, that she had notions of magnitude and distance, which she applied to objects with the same correctness as other people. But her notion of distance may have been only such as could be formed by the time expended in being carried to the spot; and her notion of magnitude may have been acquired when objects were in contact with her body—perhaps still by means of muscular

---

*[72] [McCosh, "Mill's Reply," pp. 352–3, who takes the passage from Arthur Schopenhauer,] *Die Welt als Wille und Vorstellung* [2 vols. (Leipzig; Brockhaus)], ed. 1844, Vol. II, p. 40. [Schopenhauer takes the case from A. Heuck, "Bemerkungen über ein vierzehnjähriges Mädchen ohne Extremitäten," *Neue Notizen aus dem Gebiete der Natur- und Heilkunde* (ed. Ludwig Friedrich von Froriep and Robert Froriep), VII (July, 1838), cols. 1–5.]

feelings of pressure and motion. Above all, it must be remembered that the girl was surrounded by people possessing legs and arms, and had their aid in associating the discriminating sensations of sight with the facts, of touch and of the muscles, to which they correspond. Such assistance is a great help even to children who have the ordinary complement of legs and arms; they all must acquire the association much more quickly through the help given them by the acts and words of other people. It may be confidently assumed that Eva Lauk had this help, probably in more than usual measure, and did not find out wholly by herself that a greater mass of visual sensation indicated a greater mass of tactual sensation answering to it.[d]

I believe I have noticed every plausible objection to Mr. Bain's and my own analysis of Extension, which has a sufficiently individual character to require an answer by itself. The subject is in need of further study before all its obscure corners will be completely lighted up; but this it can hardly fail to receive, now that highly competent thinkers are engaged in extending our knowledge of the Mind by the application of the Psychological Method, grounded on the Laws of Association.[c]

CHAPTER XIV

How Sir William Hamilton
and Mr. Mansel Dispose of the Law
of Inseparable Association

IT HAS BEEN OBVIOUS in the preceding discussions, and is known to all who have studied the best masters of what I have called the Psychological, in opposition to the merely Introspective method of metaphysical enquiry, that the principal instrument employed by them for unlocking the deeper mysteries of mental science, is the Law of Inseparable Association. This law, which it would seem specially incumbent on the Intuitive school of metaphysicians to take into serious consideration, because it is the basis of the rival theory which they have to encounter at every point, and which it is necessary for them to refute first, as the condition of establishing their own, is not so much rejected as ignored by them. Reid and Stewart, who had met with it only in Hartley, thought it needless to take the trouble of understanding it. The best informed German and French philosophers are barely aware, if even aware, of its existence.* And in this country and age, in which it has been employed by thinkers of the highest order as the most potent of all instruments of psychological analysis, the opposite school usually dismiss it with a few sentences, so smoothly gliding over the surface of the subject, as to prove that they have never, even for an instant, brought the powers of their minds into real and effective contact with it.

Sir W. Hamilton has written a rather elaborate Dissertation on the Laws

*As lately as the year 1864 has been published the first work (I believe) in the French language, which recognises the Association Psychology in its modern developments: an able and instructive *Etude sur l'Association des Idées* [Paris: Durand, 1864], by M. P. M. Mervoyer. ªSince then, the excellent introductory discourses prefixed by M. Cazelles to his translations from the English psychologists [see, e.g., "Introduction du traducteur," in Herbert Spencer, *Les premiers principes*, 3rd ed. (Paris: Germer Baillière, 1883), pp. i–lxxx], and the remarkable work of M. Taine, *De l'Intelligence* [2 vols., Paris: Hachette, 1870], have, it is to be hoped, permanently naturalized the Association Psychology among French thinkers and students.ª

$a-a$+72

of Association; and the more elementary of them had engaged a considerable share of his attention.* But he nowhere shows that he had the smallest
suspicion of this, the least familiar and most imperfectly understood of
these laws. I find in all his writings only two or three passages in which he
touches, even cursorily, on this mode of explaining mental phænomena.
The first and longest of these occurs in the treatment, not of any of the
greater problems of mental philosophy, but of a very minor question;
whether, in the perception of outward objects, our cognition of wholes
precedes that of their component parts, or the *contrary.* More fully;

*In this Dissertation [D***], which originally broke off abruptly, but the conclusion of which has recently been supplied from the author's papers, he attempts to
simplify the theory of Association; reducing Association by Resemblance, not
indeed to Association by Contiguity, but to that combined with an elementary law,
for the first time expressly laid down by Sir W. Hamilton, though implied in all
Association and in all Memory: viz., that a present sensation or thought suggests
the remembrance of what he calls *the same* sensation or thought (meaning one
exactly similar) experienced at a former time. This leaves Resemblance of simple
sensations as a distinct principle of association, the foundation of all the rest, while
it resolves resemblance of complex phenomena into that simple principle combined
with the law of Contiguity.

By virtue of this speculation, Sir W. Hamilton thinks it possible to reduce
Association to a single law: "Those thoughts suggest each other, which had previously constituted parts of the same entire or total act of cognition." (*Lectures*, Vol.
II, p. 238, and the corresponding passages of the Dissertation [see, e.g., p. 912].)
This appears to me, I confess, far from a happy effort of generalization; for there is
no possibility of bringing under it the elementary case of suggestion, which our
author has the merit of being the first to put into scientific language. The sweet taste
of to-day, and the similar sweet taste of a week ago which it reminds me of, have not
"previously constituted parts of the same act of cognition;" unless we take literally
the expression by which they are spoken of as the *same* taste, though they are no
more the same taste than two men are the same man if they happen to be exactly
alike. It is a further objection, that the attempted simplification, even if otherwise
correct, would merely unite two clear notions into one obscure one; for the notion
of feelings which suggest one another because they resemble, or because they have
been experienced together, is universally intelligible, while that of forming parts of
the same act of cognition involves all the metaphysical difficulties which surround
the ideas of Unity, Totality, and Parts.

After thus, as he fancies, reducing all the phænomena of Association to a single
law, Sir W. Hamilton asks, how is this law itself explained? and justly observes that
it may be an ultimate law, and that ultimate laws are necessarily unexplainable. But
he nevertheless quotes, with some approbation, an attempt by a German writer, H.
Schmid, to explain it by an *à priori* theory of the human mind, which may be
recommended to notice as a choice specimen of a school of German metaphysicians
who have remained several centuries behind the progress of philosophical enquiry,
having never yet felt the influence of the Baconian reform. See *Lectures*, Vol. II,
pp. 240–3 [and Heinrich Schmid, *Versuch einer Metaphysik der inneren Natur*
(Leipzig: Brockhaus, 1834), pp. 242–4].

*b–b*65¹, 65²   contrary?

"whether, in Perception, do we first obtain a general knowledge of the complex wholes presented to us by sense, and then, by analysis and limited attention, obtain a special knowledge of their several parts; or do we not first obtain a particular knowledge of the smallest parts to which sense is competent, and then, by synthesis, collect them into greater and greater wholes?"* Sir W. Hamilton declares for the first theory, and quotes as supporters of the second, Stewart and James Mill; to the latter of whom, more than to any other thinker, mankind are indebted for recalling the attention of philosophers to the law of Inseparable Association, and pointing out the important applications of which it is susceptible. Through the conflict with Mr. Mill on the very subordinate question which he is discussing, Sir W. Hamilton is led to quote a part of that philosopher's exposition of Inseparable Association; and it is a sign how little he was aware of the importance of the subject, that a theory of so wide a scope and such large consequences should receive the only recognition he ever gives it in a bye corner of his work, incidentally to one of the smallest questions therein discussed. I shall extract the very passages which he quotes from Mr. Mill, because, in a small space, they state and illustrate very happily the two most characteristic properties of our closest associations: that the suggestions they produce are, for the time, irresistible; and that the suggested ideas (at least when the association is of the synchronous kind as distinguished from the successive) become so blended together, that the compound result appears, to our consciousness, simple.

"Where two or more ideas," says Mr. Mill,

have been often repeated together, and the association has become very strong, they sometimes spring up in such close combination as not to be distinguishable. Some cases of sensation are analogous. For example, when a wheel, on the seven parts of which the seven prismatic colours are respectively painted, is made to revolve rapidly, it appears not of seven colours, but of one uniform colour, white. By the rapidity of the succession, the several sensations cease to be distinguishable; they run, as it were, together, and a new sensation, compounded of all the seven, but apparently a single one, is the result. Ideas, also, which have been so often conjoined, that whenever one exists in the mind, the others immediately exist along with it, seem to run into one another, to coalesce, as it were, and out of many to form one idea; which idea, however in reality complex, appears to be no less simple than any one of those of which it is compounded. . . .

It is to this great law of association that we trace the formation of our ideas of what we call external objects; that is, the ideas of a certain number of sensations received together so frequently that they coalesce, as it were, and are spoken of under the idea of unity. Hence what we call the idea of a tree, the idea of a stone, the idea of a horse, the idea of a man.

In using the names, tree, horse, man, the names of what I call objects, I am referring, and can be referring, only to my own sensations; in fact, therefore, only

*Lectures, Vol. II, p. 144.

naming a certain number of sensations, regarded as in a particular state of combination; that is, of concomitance. Particular sensations of sight, of touch, of the muscles, are the sensations, to the ideas of which, colour, extension, roughness, hardness, smoothness, taste, smell, so coalescing as to appear one idea, I give the name idea of a tree.

To this case of high association, this blending together of many ideas, in so close a combination that they appear not many ideas, but one idea, we owe, as I shall afterwards more fully explain, the power of classification, and all the advantages of language. It is obviously, therefore, of the greatest moment, that this important phænomenon should be well understood.

Some ideas are by frequency and strength of association so closely combined that they cannot be separated. If one exists, the other exists along with it, in spite of whatever effort we may make to disjoin them.

For example; it is not in our power to think of colour, without thinking of extension; or of solidity, without figure. We have seen colour constantly in combination with extension, spread, as it were, upon a surface. We have never seen it except in this connexion. Colour and extension have been invariably conjoined. The idea of colour, therefore, uniformly comes into the mind, bringing that of extension along with it; and so close is the association, that it is not in our power to dissolve it. We cannot, if we will, think of colour, but in combination with extension. The one idea calls up the other, and retains it, so long as the other is retained.

This great law of our nature is illustrated in a manner equally striking by the connexion between the ideas of solidity and figure. We never have the sensations from which the idea of solidity is derived, but in conjunction with the sensations whence the idea of figure is derived. If we handle anything solid it is always either round, square, or of some other form. The ideas correspond with the sensations. If the idea of solidity rises, that of figure rises along with it. The idea of figure which rises is, of course, more obscure than that of extension; because, figures being innumerable, the general idea is exceedingly complex, and hence, of necessity, obscure. But such as it is, the idea of figure is always present when that of solidity is present; nor can we, by any effort, think of the one without thinking of the other at the same time.*

Other illustrations follow, concluding with these words: "The following of one idea after another idea, or after a sensation, so certainly that we cannot prevent the combination, nor avoid having the *consequent* feeling as often as we have the *antecedent*, is a law of association, the operation of which we shall afterwards find to be extensive, and bearing a principal part in some of the most important phænomena of the human mind."† And the promise of this sentence is amply redeemed in the sequel ᶜofᶜ the treatise.

The only remark which this highly philosophical exposition suggests to Sir W. Hamilton, is a disparaging reflection on Mr. Mill's philosophy in general. He says that Mr. Mill, in his "ingenious" treatise, "has pushed the

---

Analysis of the Phenomena of the Human Mind, Vol. I, pp. 68–73. [Quoted by Hamilton, *Lectures*, Vol. II, pp. 146–9.]

†*Ibid.*, p. 75. [Not quoted by Hamilton.]

ᶜ⁻ᶜ65¹, 65² to

principle of Association to an extreme which refutes its own exaggeration,—analysing not only our belief in the relation of effect and cause into
that principle, but even the primary logical laws," so that it is no wonder he
should "account for our knowledge of complex wholes in perception, by the
same universal principle."[*] Having, on the strength of this previous
verdict of exaggeration, dispensed with enquiring how much the law of
Inseparable Association can really accomplish, he makes no use of its most
obvious applications, even while transcribing them into his own pages. One
of the psychological facts stated in the passage quoted, the impossibility, to
us, of separating the idea of extension and that of colour, is a truth strongly
insisted on by Sir W. Hamilton himself. In the very next Lecture but one to
that from which I have been quoting, he strenuously maintains, that we can
neither conceive colour without extension, nor extension without colour.
Even the born blind, he thinks, have the sensation of darkness, that is, of
black colour, and mentally clothe all extended objects with it.* Except the
last position, which has no evidence and no probability,[†] the doctrine is
undoubtedly true, and the fact is so obviously a case of the law of association, that even Stewart, little partial as he was to that mode of explaining
mental phænomena, does not dream of attributing it to anything else. "In
consequence," says Stewart, "of our always perceiving extension at the
same time at which the sensation of colour is excited in the mind, we find it
impossible to think of that sensation without conceiving extension along
with it." He gives this as one of the instances "of very intimate associations
formed between two ideas which have no necessary connexion with one
another."[†] A mental analysis by way of association which was sufficiently
obvious to recommend itself to Stewart, will scarcely be charged with
"pushing the principle to an extreme." In fact, if an association can ever

[*Lectures, Vol. II, p. 146.]
*Ibid., pp. 168–72.
†According to the doctrine of all advanced psychologists, to which Sir W.
Hamilton gives an express adhesion, it is impossible to have a consciousness of
darkness without having had a consciousness of light. Besides, it is a notorious
optical fact that a completely black object occupying the whole sphere of vision is
invisible; it reflects no light. Blackness, therefore, (the complete blackness of
absolute darkness,) is not a sensation, but the total absence of sensation; it is, in
fact, nothing at all; and to say that a person born blind cannot imagine extension
without clothing it with nothing at all, is to assert something not very intelligible. In
the case of a person who has *become* blind, it might have a meaning; for blackness
to him, like darkness to us, does not stand for mere inability to see, but for the usual
effort to see, not followed by the usual consequence.

[†Dugald Stewart, *Elements of the Philosophy of the Human Mind*, 3 vols., Vol.
I (London: Strahan and Cadell; Edinburgh: Creech, 1792), p. 341; quoted by
Hamilton, *Lectures*, Vol. II, pp. 161–2.]

become inseparable by dint of repetition, how could the association be-tween colour and extension fail of being so? The two facts never exist but in immediate conjunction, and the experience of that conjunction is repeated at every moment of life which is not spent in darkness. Yet after transcrib-ing this explanation both from Stewart and from Mill, Sir W. Hamilton remains as insensible to it as if it had never been given; and without a word of refutation, composedly registers the inseparableness of the two ideas as an ultimate mental fact proving them both to be original perceptions of the same organ, the eye. Sir W. Hamilton's authority can have little weight against the doctrine which accounts for the more complex parts of our mental constitution by the laws of association, when it is so evident that he rejected that doctrine not because he had examined it and found it wanting, but without examining it; having taken for granted that it did not deserve examination.*

*[72] In one of the unfinished dissertations left among his papers, and intended for his edition of Reid (in which it now stands as Note E) Sir W. Hamilton did attempt to disprove the doctrine that our incapacity to conceive colour without extension is an effect of association. His arguments (pp. 919, 920), are first, that of D'Alembert (discussed in a former chapter), that when two colours meet we must be conscious of the line which separates them; and the junction, therefore, of two colours cannot be conceived apart from extension. But suppose that we are only perceiving a single colour, which occupies the whole field of vision: our invariably seeing this as extended cannot be explained by something which only happens when we see two colours; unless the impression received from the two adheres to the one by associa-tion. Sir W. Hamilton, therefore, is reduced to say that the field of vision "has a right and a left, an upper and an under side, and may be divided into halves, quarters, &c., indefinitely," an argument which begs the question, since it assumes that the homogeneously coloured field is already perceived as composed of parts, that is, as extended.

Sir W. Hamilton's other argument is that "we cannot be conscious of a colour without being conscious of that colour in contrast to, and therefore out of, another colour,—without, therefore, being conscious of the extended." This seems an assumption without grounds. If a single colour occupies the whole field of vision, it can surely be recognised as colour. The contrast, which is essential to conscious-ness, needs not be between one colour and another; it may be between colour and the absence of sensation, or between colour and a sensation of some other sense. I am supposing the sensation of colour to be intermittent; for if it were constant, I admit that it would cease to be felt at all.

The converse incapacity to conceive extension without colour, Sir W. Hamilton deals with very summarily (p. 917), by saying that there is no object of vision, either actual or conceivable, which is not coloured. This is the very explanation given by the Association theory. All objects of vision are coloured, counting black as a colour, which, when it stands in contrast with positive colours, we may legitimately do; by the laws of Association, therefore, what is always seen as coloured is always conceived as coloured. In combating, as he thinks, the Association theory, Sir W. Hamilton is obliged to have recourse to it.

How imperfect was his acquaintance with the secondary laws, the *axiomata media*[*] of association, is plainly seen in his argument against Stewart and Mill on the comparatively insignificant question with which he started. The thesis he is asserting is, that "in place of ascending upwards, from the minimum of perception to its maxima, we descend from masses to details."

"If the opposite doctrine" (says Sir W. Hamilton)

were correct, what would it involve? It would involve as a primary inference, that, as we know the whole through the parts, we should know the parts better than the whole. Thus, for example, it is supposed that we know the face of a friend, through the multitude of perceptions which we have of the different points of which it is made up; in other words, that we should know the whole countenance less vividly than we know the forehead and eyes, the nose and mouth, &c., and that we should know each of these more feebly than we know the various ultimate points, in fact, unconscious minima of perception, which go to constitute them. According to the doctrine in question, we perceive only one of these ultimate points at the same instant, the others by memory incessantly renewed. Now let us take the face out of perception into memory altogether. Let us close our eyes, and let us represent in imagination the countenance of our friend. This we can do with the utmost vivacity; or, if we see a picture of it, we can determine with a consciousness of the most perfect accuracy, that the portrait is like or unlike. It cannot, therefore, be denied that we have the fullest knowledge of the face as a whole, that we are familiar with its expression, with the general result of its parts. On the hypothesis, then, of Stewart and Mill, how accurate should be our knowledge of these parts themselves. But make the experiment. You will find, that unless you have analysed,—unless you have descended from a conspectus of the whole face to a detailed examination of its parts,—with the most vivid impression of the constituted whole, you are almost totally ignorant of the constituent parts. You may probably be unable to say what is the colour of the eyes, and if you attempt to delineate the mouth or nose, you will inevitably fail. Or look at the portrait. You may find it unlike, but unless, as I said, you have analysed the countenance, unless you have looked at it with the analytic scrutiny of a painter's eye, you will assuredly be unable to say in what respect the artist has failed,—you will be unable to specify what constituent he has altered, though you are fully conscious of the fact and effect of the alteration. What we have shown from this example may equally be done from any other—a house, a tree, a landscape, a concert of music, &c.*

[*See Francis Bacon, *Novum Organum*, in *Works*, ed. James Spedding, Robert Leslie Ellis, and Douglas Denon Heath, 14 vols. (London: Longman, *et al.*, 1857–74), Vol. I, p. 205 (Bk. I, Aph. 104).]

Lectures, Vol. II, pp. 149–50. Those who are acquainted with Mr. Bailey's attempt to disprove Berkeley's Theory of Vision, will be reminded by this passage of an exactly similar argument employed by that able thinker and writer, to prove the intuitive character of what philosophers almost unanimously consider as the acquired perceptions of sight. [See Bailey, *A Review of Berkeley's Theory of Vision*, pp. 105–17.] I have given the same answer to Mr. Bailey on another occasion, which I give to Sir W. Hamilton here. [See Mill, "Bailey on Berkeley's Theory of Vision," in *Essays on Philosophy and the Classics*, *Collected Works*, Vol. XI, pp. 257 ff.]

I have already made mention of a very important part of the Laws of Association, which may be termed the Laws of Obliviscence.[*] If Sir W. Hamilton had sufficiently attended to those laws, he never could have maintained, that if we knew the parts before the whole, we must continue to know the parts better than the whole. It is one of the principal Laws of Obliviscence, that when a number of ideas suggest one another by association with such certainty and rapidity as to coalesce together in a group, all those members of the group which remain long without being specially attended to, have a tendency to drop out of consciousness. Our consciousness of them becomes more and more faint and evanescent, until no effort of attention can recall it into distinctness, or at last recall it at all. Any one who observes his own mental operations will find this fact exemplified in every day of his life. Now the law of attention is admitted to be, that we attend only to that which, either on its own or on some other account, interests us. In consequence, what interests us only momentarily we only attend to momentarily; and do not go on attending to it, when that, for the sake of which alone it interested us, has been attained. Sir W. Hamilton would have found these several laws clearly set forth, and abundantly exemplified, in the work of Mr. Mill which he had before him. It is there shown how large a proportion of all our states of feeling pass off without having been attended to, and in many cases so habitually that we become finally incapable of attending to them. This subject was also extremely well understood by Reid, who, little as he had reflected on the principle of Association, was much better acquainted with the laws of Obliviscence than his more recent followers, and has excellently illustrated and exemplified some of them.* Among those which he has illustrated the most successfully, one is, that the very great number of our states of feeling which, being themselves neither painful nor pleasurable, are important to us only as signs of something else, and which by repetition have come to do their work as signs with a rapidity which to our feelings is instantaneous, cease altogether to be attended to; and through that inattention our consciousness of them either ceases altogether, or becomes so fleeting and indistinct as to leave no revivable trace in the memory. This happens, even when the impressions which serve the purpose of signs are not mere ideas, or reminiscences, of sensation, but actual sensations. After reading a chapter of a book, when we lay down the volume do we remember to have been individually conscious of the printed letters and syllables which have passed before us? Could we recall, by any effort of mind, the visible aspect presented by them, unless some unusual circumstance has fixed our atten-

[*See p. 211 above.]

*See his *Inquiry into the Human Mind*, Chap. v, §§ 2 and 8; Chap. vi, §§ 2, 3, 4, 7, 8, 19; *Intellectual Powers*, Essay II, Chaps. xvi and xvii.

tion upon it during the perusal? Yet each of these letters and syllables must have been present to us as a sensation for at least a passing moment, or the sense could not have been conveyed to us. But the sense being the only thing in which we are interested—or, in exceptional cases, the sense and a few of the words or sentences—we retain no impression of the separate letters and syllables. This instance is the more instructive, inasmuch as, the whole process taking place within our means of observation, we know that our knowledge began with the parts, and not with the whole. We know that we perceived and distinguished letters and syllables before we learnt to understand words and sentences; and the perceptions could not, at that time, have passed unattended to; on the contrary, the effort of attention of which those letters and syllables must have been the object, was probably, while it lasted, equal in intensity to any which we have been called upon to exercise in after life. Were Sir W. Hamilton's argument valid, one of two things would follow. Either we have even now, when we read in a book, a more vivid consciousness of the letters and syllables than of the words and sentences, [d](and by parity of reason a more vivid consciousness of the words and sentences than of the general purport of the discourse):[d] or else, we could read sentences off hand at first, and only by subsequent analysis discovered the letters and syllables. If ever there was a *reductio ad absurdum*, this is one.

The facts on which Sir W. Hamilton's argument rests, are obviously accounted for by the laws which he ignores. In our perceptions of objects, it is generally the wholes, and the wholes alone, that interest us. In his example, that of a friend's countenance, it is (special motives apart) only the friend himself that we are interested about; we care about the features only as signs that it is our friend whom we see, and not another person. Unless therefore the face commands our attention by its beauty or strangeness, or unless we stamp the features on our memory by acts of attention directed upon them separately, they pass before us, and do their work as signs, with so little consciousness that no distinct trace may be left in the memory. We forget the details even of objects which we see every day, if we have no motive for attending to the parts as distinguished from the wholes, and have cultivated no habit of doing so. That this is consistent with having known the parts earlier than the wholes, is proved not only by the case of reading, but by that of playing on a musical instrument, and a hundred other familiar instances; by everything, in fact, which we learn to do. When the wholes alone are interesting to us, we soon forget our knowledge of the component parts, unless we purposely keep it alive by conscious comparison and analysis.

[d–d]65[1], 65[2], 67   and a more . . . discourse;

This is not the only fallacy in Sir W. Hamilton's argument. Considered as a reply to Mr. Mill's explanation of the origin of our ideas of objects, it entirely misses the mark. If the argument and examples had proved their point, which it has been seen that they do not, they would have proved that we perceive and know, to some extent or other, the object as a whole, before knowing its *integrant* parts. But it is not of integrant parts that Mr. Mill was speaking; and he might have admitted all that Sir W. Hamilton contends for, without surrendering his own opinion. The question does not relate to parts in extension. It does not concern Mr. Mill's theory whether we know, or do not know, a man as such, before we distinguish, in thought or in perception, his head from his feet. What Mr. Mill said was, that our idea of an object, whether it be of the man, or of his head, or of his feet, is compounded by association from our ideas of the colour, the shape, the resistance, &c., which belong to those objects.[*] These are what philosophers have called the metaphysical parts, not the integrant parts, of the total impression. Now I have never heard of any philosopher who maintained that *these* parts were not known until after the objects which they characterize; that we perceive the body first, and its colour, shape, form, &c., only afterwards. Our senses, which on all theories are at least the avenues through which our knowledge of bodies comes to us, are not adapted by nature to let in the perception of the whole object at once. They only open to let pass single attributes at a time. And this is as much Sir W. Hamilton's opinion as any one's else, except where he is sustaining an argument which makes him blind to it.

As is often the case with our author, the conclusion he is maintaining is worth more than his argument to prove it, and though not the whole truth, has truth in it. That we perceive the whole before the parts will not stand examination as a general law, but is very often true as a particular fact: our first impression is often that of a confused mass, of which all the parts seem blended, and our subsequent progress consists in elaborating this into distinctness. It was well to point out this fact: but if our author had paid more attention to its limits, he might have been able to give us a complete theory of it, instead of leaving it, as he has done, an empirical observation, which waits for some one to raise it into a scientific law.

The same want of comprehension of the power of an inseparable association, which was shown by Sir W. Hamilton in the case of Colour and Extension, is exhibited in the only other case in which he adduces any argument to prove that an idea was not produced by association. The case is that of causality, and the argument is the ordinary one of metaphysicians of his school. "The *necessity* of so thinking cannot be derived from a

[*See *Analysis*, Vol. I, pp. 40–82 (Chaps. ii–iii).]

custom of so thinking. The force of custom, influential as it may be, is still always limited to the customary; and the customary never reaches, never even approaches to the necessary."* *e*If this were so, not only could an inseparable association generate no necessity of belief, but there could be no such thing as inseparable association; no entirely irresistible conjunction between two mental states.*e* The paviour *f*, however,*f* who cannot use his rammer without the accustomed cry, the orator who had so often while speaking twirled a string in his hand that he became unable to speak when he accidentally dropped it, are, it seems to me, examples of a "customary" which did approach to, and even reach, the "necessary." "Association may explain a strong and special, but it can never explain a universal and absolutely irresistible belief."[*] Not when the conjunction of facts which engenders the association, is itself universal and irresistible? "What I cannot but think, must be *à priori*, or original to thought: it cannot be engendered by experience upon custom."† As if experience, that is to say, association, were not perpetually engendering both inabilities to think, and inabilities not to think. "We can think away each and every part of the knowledge we have derived from experience."‡ Associations derived from experience are doubtless separable by a sufficient amount of contrary experience; but, in the cases we are considering, no contrary experience is to be had. On the theory that the belief in causality results from association, "when association is recent, the causal judgment should be weak, and rise only gradually to full force, as custom becomes inveterate."§ And how do we know that it does not? The whole process of acquiring our belief in causation takes place at an age of which we have no remembrance, and which precludes the possibility of testing the matter by experiment: and all theories agree that our first type of causation is our own power of moving our limbs; which is as complete as it can be, and has formed as strong associations as it is capable of forming, long before the child can observe or communicate its mental operations.

It is strange that almost all the opponents of the Association psychology should found their main or sole argument in refutation of it upon the feeling of necessity; for if there be any one feeling in our nature which the laws of association are obviously equal to producing, one would say it is that. Necessary, according to Kant's definition,[†] and there is none better, is

---

*Discussions, Appendix I[A] on Causality, p. 615.
[**Ibid.*]
†*Lectures*, Vol. II, p. 191.
‡*Ibid.*, Vol. IV, p. 74.
§*Discussions*, [App. I(A),] p. 615.
[†See *Kritik der Reinen Vernunft*, p. 462.]

e–e+72
f–f+72

that of which the negation is impossible. If we find it impossible, by any trial, to separate two ideas, we have all the feeling of necessity which the mind is capable of. Those, therefore, who deny that association can generate a necessity of thought, must be willing to affirm that two ideas are never so knit together by association as to be practically inseparable. But to affirm this is to contradict the most familiar experience of life. Many persons who have been frightened in childhood can never be alone in the dark without irrepressible terrors. Many a person is unable to revisit a particular place, or to think of a particular event, without recalling acute feelings of grief or reminiscences of suffering. If the facts which created these strong associations in individual minds, had been common to all mankind from their earliest infancy, and had, when the associations were fully formed, been forgotten, we should have had a Necessity of Thought—one of the necessities which are supposed to prove an objective law, and an *à priori* mental connexion between ideas.* Now, in all the supposed natural beliefs and necessary conceptions which the principle of Inseparable Association is employed to explain, the generating causes of the association did begin nearly at the beginning of life, and are common either to all, or to a very large portion of mankind.†

*[72] Dr. Ward (["Mr. Mill's Denial of Necessary Truth,"] p. 291) takes exception to these instances, as exemplifying not a necessity of thought but a necessity of feeling—which has never been affirmed to prove an objective law, or an *à priori* connexion between ideas. I answer that what I sought to prove by the instances, was that two ideas may be "so knit together by association as to be practically inseparable." And I added, not that a necessity of feeling proves a necessity of thought, but that under certain conditions it would generate one. If the person in whose mind a given spot is associated with terrors, had entirely forgotten the fact by which it came to be so; and if the rest of mankind, or even only a great number of them, felt the same terror on coming to the same place, and were equally unable to account for it; there would certainly grow up a conviction that the place had a natural quality of terribleness, which would probably fix itself in the belief that the place was under a curse, or was the abode of some invisible object of terror. Feelings common to many persons, which are at once irresistible and unaccountable, almost always pass into equivalent judgments and beliefs. Indeed, this is the precise way in which the fact of our sensations is translated into belief in an external world; and we should, in the case supposed, seem to have the same evidence of the terrific quality, which we have of any of the qualities of objects.

†[67] I find it necessary here to correct a misunderstanding to which I never should have suspected myself to be liable. Dr. M'Cosh employs nearly the whole of his ninth chapter (Judgment or Comparison) in protesting against the doctrine, that an inseparable association necessarily produces belief; and concludes with a solemn appeal to the young to raise themselves above the influence of mere association, and learn "that it is our duty to found our beliefs on a previous judgment" and "to base our beliefs on an inspection of realities and actualities." (*[Examination,*] pp. 214–15.) In all of which, aimed as it is at myself, Dr. M'Cosh is preaching not only to a person already converted, but to an actual missionary of the same doctrine. I have certainly called attention [see pp. 75 and 145n above] to the

The beggarly account now exhibited, is, I believe, all that Sir W. Hamilton has anywhere written against the Association psychology. But it is not all that has been said against that psychology from Sir W. Hamilton's point of view. In this as in various other cases, to supply what Sir W. Hamilton has omitted, recourse may advantageously be had to Mr. Mansel.

Mr. Mansel, though in some sense a pupil of Sir W. Hamilton, is a pupil who may be usefully consulted even after his master. Besides that he now and then sees things which his master did not see, he very often fights a better battle against adversaries. Moreover, as I before remarked,[*] he has a decided taste for clear statements and definite issues; and this is no small advantage when the object is, not victory, but to understand the subject.

Mr. Mansel joins a distinct issue with the Association psychology, and brings the question to the proper test. "It has been already observed," he says, in his *Prolegomena Logica*,

that whatever truths we are compelled to admit as everywhere and at all times necessary, must have their origin, not without, in the laws of the sensible world, but within, in the constitution of the mind itself. Sundry attempts have, indeed, been made to derive them from sensible experience and constant association of ideas; but this explanation is refuted by a criterion decisive of the fate of all hypotheses: it does not account for the phænomena. It does not account for the fact that *other associations, as frequent and as uniform, are incapable of producing a higher conviction than that of a relative and physical necessity only.**

This is coming to the point, and evinces a correct apprehension of the conditions of scientific proof. If other associations, as close and as habitual as those existing in the cases in question, do not produce a similar feeling of necessity of thought, the sufficiency of the alleged cause is disproved, and the theory must fall. Mr. Mansel is within the true conditions of the Psychological Method.

---

important psychological truth, not unrecognised by Dr. M'Cosh, that a strong mental association between two facts, even short of inseparability, has a great tendency to make us believe in a connexion between the facts themselves; but I thought that if there ever had been a writer who was assiduous in warning people against this tendency (to which, in my *Logic* [*Collected Works*, Vol. VIII, pp. 750ff. (Bk. V, Chap. iii, §3)], I have given a conspicuous place in the enumeration of Fallacies) and exhorting them to ground their beliefs exclusively on the evidence, that writer was myself. Dr. M'Cosh's work is unimpeachable in point of candour and fairness; but this instance shows how little he is to be relied on for correctly apprehending the maxims and tendencies of a philosophy different from his own.

*g*Dr. M'Cosh, in his reply, interprets the phraseology of this Note as if I had accused him of "preaching" in some disparaging sense. ["Mill's Reply," p. 356.] I was merely alluding to the almost proverbial expression, "prêcher un converti," which I thought that Dr. M'Cosh would have understood. [Cf. I Corinthians, 1:21.]*g*

[*See p. 91 above.]

Prolegomena Logica, beginning of Chap. iv, pp. 90–1.

g–g+72

But ^{h}what are^h these cases of uniform and intimate association, which do not give rise to a feeling of mental necessity? The following is Mr. Mansel's first example of them:

I may imagine the sun rising and setting as now for a hundred years, and afterwards remaining continually fixed in the meridian. Yet my experiences of the alternations of day and night have been at least as invariable as of the geometrical properties of bodies. I can imagine the same stone sinking ninety-nine times in the water, and floating the hundredth, but my experience invariably repeats the former phænomenon only.*

The alternation of day and night is invariable in our experience; but is the phænomenon day so closely linked in our experience with the phænomenon night, that we never perceive the one, without, at the same or the immediately succeeding moment, perceiving the other? That is a condition present in the inseparable associations which generate necessities of thought. Uniformities of sequence in which the phænomena succeed one another only at a certain interval, do not give rise to inseparable associations.† There are also mental conditions, as well as physical, which are required to create such an association. Let us take Mr. Mansel's other instance, a stone sinking in the water.[*] We have never seen it float, yet we have no difficulty in conceiving it floating. But, in the first place, we have not been seeing stones sinking in water from the first dawn of consciousness, and in nearly every subsequent moment of our lives, as we have been seeing two and two making four, intersecting straight lines diverging instead of enclosing a space, causes followed by effects and effects preceded by causes. But there is a still more radical distinction than this. No frequency of conjunction between two phænomena will create an inseparable association, if counter-associations are being created all the while. If we sometimes saw stones floating as well as sinking, however often we might have seen them sink, nobody supposes that we should have formed an inseparable association between them and sinking. We have not seen a stone float, but we are in the constant habit of seeing either stones or other

*Ibid., pp. 96–7.

†[67] Mr. Mahaffy has misunderstood the meaning of this statement, which is certainly too incautiously expressed. (P. xxiv.) The phænomena which must have been simultaneous or immediately successive to create an inseparable association, need not have been actual perceptions: an association, and even an inseparable association, may be created between two ideas, if they have been habitually present together, or in immediate succession, merely in thought. This truth is so universally recognised by writers on Association, that it did not seem to require statement. But the succession which generates an inseparable association, must, either in fact or in thought, be an immediate succession; or rather, one without any conscious or perceptible interval.

[*Prolegomena Logica, p. 97.]

$^{h-h}$65^1 what are

things which have the same tendency to sink, remaining in a position which they would otherwise quit, being maintained in it by an unseen force. The sinking of a stone is but a case of gravitation, and we are abundantly accustomed to see the force of gravity counteracted. Every fact of that nature which we ever saw or heard of, is *pro tanto* an obstacle to the formation of the inseparable association which would make a violation of the law of gravity inconceivable to us. Resemblance is a principle of association, as well as contiguity: and however contradictory a supposition may be to our experience *in hâc materiâ*, if our experience *in aliâ materiâ* furnishes us with types even distantly resembling what the supposed phænomenon would be if realized, the associations thus formed will generally prevent the specific association from becoming so intense and irresistible, as to disable our imaginative faculty from embodying the supposition in a form moulded on one or other of those types.*

*[67] In an able manuscript critique on "the Experience Hypothesis" which has been communicated to me, the familiar truth that fire burns is given as an example of an uniform sequence which does not generate a necessity of thought. No one (the writer observes) will say that we have a more frequent perception of the fact that parallel lines do not inclose a space, than we have of the fact that fire burns: yet we can without difficulty imagine human beings remaining unburnt in a fiery furnace; nay, we may even believe it, if we admit the supposition either of magic or of a miracle. No doubt: but this is fully explained by the counter-associations. Though we have never seen a human being in the fire unburnt, being in the fire is not inseparably associated with destruction, for we have seen abundance of other objects, immersed in intense fire, yet resisting its action. The conception of a man in the same position, is within the limits of the power characteristic of imagination, of varying (only slightly in this instance) our mental combinations of the elements given by experience. The writer asks, why then cannot imagination produce all combinations? The only ones it cannot produce are precisely those which are prevented by associations really irresistible, associations that have never been counteracted by counter-associations, and by the operation of which, elements with which certain combinations in imagination would be incompatible, are forced into our mental representations.

The same writer says, we believe by a necessity of thought that a tangent touches a circle at one point only, yet this necessary belief, far from being the result of uniform experience, is contradicted by uniform experience, since the tangents and circles of experience touch one another at more than one point—coalesce in an appreciable portion of their extent. I answer, that the circle in our imagination is copied from those only, among the circles of our experience, in which sense can detect no variation from the definition of a circle, *i.e.* whose radii are not perceptibly unequal. Now, if the radii are, to our perception, equal, a line which is to our perception straight, will touch the circle in what is to our perception a single point. And there are many such circles, not perhaps in nature, but certainly in the products of mechanical art. The belief therefore does not conflict, but accords, with an uniform experience. And even on the contrary supposition—even if there were no circles in experience but such as are appreciably different from the geometrical

Again, says Mr. Mansel, "experience has uniformly presented to me a horse's body in conjunction with a horse's head, and a man's head with a man's body; just as experience has uniformly presented to me space inclosed within a pair of curved lines and not within a pair of straight lines:" yet I have no difficulty in imagining a centaur, but cannot imagine a space inclosed by two straight lines.

Why do I, in the former case, consider the results of my experience as contingent only and transgressible, confined to the actual phænomena of a limited field, and possessing no value beyond it; while in the latter I am compelled to regard them as necessary and universal? Why can I give in imagination to a quadruped body what experience assures me is possessed by bipeds only? And why can I not, in like manner, invest straight lines with an attribute which experience has uniformly presented in curves?*

I answer:—Because our experience furnishes us with a thousand models on which to frame the conception of a centaur, and with none on which to frame that of two straight lines inclosing a space. Nature, as known in our experience, is uniform in its laws, but extremely varied in its combinations. The combination of a horse's body with a human head has nothing, *primâ facie*, to make any wide distinction between it and any of the numberless varieties which we find in animated nature. To a common, even if not to a scientific mind, it is within the limits of the variations in our experience. Every similar variation which we have seen or heard of, is a help towards conceiving this particular one; and tends to form an association, not of fixity but of variability, which frustrates the formation of an inseparable association between a human head and a human body exclusively. We know of so many different heads, united to so many different bodies, that we have little difficulty in imagining any head in combination with any body. Nay, the mere mobility of objects in space is a fact so universal in our experience, that we easily conceive any object whatever occupying the place of any other; we imagine without difficulty a horse with his head removed, and a human head put in its place. But what model does our experience afford on which to frame, or what elements from which to construct, the conception of two straight lines inclosing a space? There are no counter-associations in that case, and consequently the primary association, being founded on an experience beginning from birth, and never for many minutes intermitted in our waking hours, easily becomes insepar-

ideal, our senses would no less inform us that in the degree in which a visible circle and straight line approximate to the definitions, the extent of their contact with one another approximates to a point: which, by the principles of Induction, makes the ultimate truth as much a truth of experience, as if it were directly cognised by the senses.

Prolegomena Logica, pp. 99–100.

able. Had but experience afforded a case of ⁱpersistentⁱ illusion, in which two straight lines after intersecting had appeared again to approach, the counter-association formed might have been sufficient to render such a supposition imaginable, and defeat the supposed necessity of thought. In the case of parallel lines, the laws of perspective do present such an illusion: they do, to the eye, appear to meet in both directions, and consequently to inclose a space: and by supposing that we had no access to the evidence which proves that they do not really meet, an ingenious thinker, whom I formerly quoted, was able to give the idea of a constitution of nature in which all mankind might have believed that two straight lines could inclose a space.[*] That we are unable to believe or imagine it in our present circumstances, needs no other explanation than the laws of association afford: for the case unites all the elements of the closest, intensest, and most inseparable association, with the greatest freedom from conflicting counter-associations which can be found within the conditions of human life.*

In all the instances of phænomena invariably conjoined which fail to create necessities of thought, I am satisfied it would be found that the case is wanting in some of the conditions required by the Association psychology, as essential to the formation of an association really inseparable. It is the more to be wondered at that Mr. Mansel should not have perceived the easy answer which could be given to his argument, since he himself comes very near to giving the same explanation of many impossibilities of thought, which is given by the Association theory. "We can only," he says, "conceive in thought what we have experienced in presentation;"† and no other

[*Stephen; see above, p. 72n.]

*[67] Mr. Mahaffy says that I need not have gone beyond our present world for illusions which, according to my doctrine, ought to have made it possible to conceive something that is contradictory to a mathematical axiom: and proceeds to mention illusions the illusory character of which is at once seen, from the immediate accessibility of the evidence which disproves them; double vision, and the apparent crookedness of a stick in the water. As a protection against future irrelevances of this kind, I have inserted in the text the word "persistent" before "illusion." [See ⁱ⁻ⁱ above.] Mr. Mahaffy argues as if the illusions in our experience never got corrected by contrary experience, but would permanently deceive us unless overridden by an à priori conviction. "Every child," he says, "who looks down a long street, sees two parallel right lines converging, and we very rarely proceed to verify or question the result. . . . Most assuredly no child has verified for himself that the very long parallel lines which he has met, and sees to be equidistant, as far as he can easily judge, and which he sees do not change their direction suddenly—that these parallel lines do not meet." (Pp. xxvii–xxviii.) Does a child, then, never walk down a street? or does Mr. Mahaffy think it necessary to the child's enlightenment that he should walk down every street?

†Prolegomena Logica, p. 112n.

ⁱ⁻ⁱ+67, 72

reason is necessary for our being unable to conceive a thing, than that we have never experienced it. He even holds that the stock example of a necessity of thought, the belief in the uniformity of the course of nature, can be accounted for by experience, without any objective necessity at all. "We cannot conceive," he says, "a course of nature without uniform succession, as we cannot conceive a being who sees without eyes or hears without ears; because we cannot, under existing circumstances, experience the necessary intuition. But such things may nevertheless exist; and under other circumstances, they might become objects of possible conception, the laws of the process of conception remaining unaltered."* I am aware that when Mr. Mansel uses the words Presentation and Intuition, he does not mean exclusively presentation by the senses. Nevertheless, if he had only written the preceding passage, no one would have suspected that he could have required any other cause for our inability to conceive a bilineal figure, than the impossibility of our perceiving one. It is sufficient, in his opinion, to constitute any propositions necessary, that "while our constitution *and circumstances* remain as they are, we cannot but think them."† It is superabundantly manifest that many propositions which all admit to be grounded only on experience, are necessary under this definition. Mr. Mansel even asserts a more complete dependence of our possibilities of thought upon our opportunities of experience than there appears to me to be ground for: since he affirms that "we can only conceive in thought what we have experienced in presentation," while in reality it is sufficient that we should have experienced in presentation things bearing some similarity to it.

ʲNOTE TO THE PRECEDING CHAPTER

Dr. Ward, one of the ablest living defenders of the intuitional metaphysics, has, in the *Dublin Review* for October 1871, made a vigorous attack upon the doctrines of this chapter. His arguments in part coincide (though with a difference in the illustrations) with those already noticed, of Mr. Mansel: several of them, however, are distinct: and as I believe that in answering them, I am answering the best that is likely to be said by any future champion, I will take up Dr. Ward's points one by one.

Dr. Ward thus expresses the test of necessary truth:

If in any case I know by my very conception of some ens, that a certain attribute, not included in that conception, is truly predicable of that ens, such predication is a

Ibid., pp. 149–50.
†*Ibid.*, p. 150.

ʲ⁻ʲ²⁷¹+72

self-evidently necessary proposition. Take, for instance, the axiom that all trilateral figures are triangular. If, by my very conception of a trilateral figure, I know its triangularity . . . then I know infallibly that a trilateral non-triangular figure is an intrinsically repugnant chimera; that in no possible region of existence could such a figure be found; that not even an Omnipotent Being could form one.

Consequently "the triangularity of all trilateral figures is cognizable as a self-evidently necessary truth;" not grounded on, nor deriving its evidence from, experience.[*]

It is not denied, nor deniable, that there are properties of things which we know to be true (as Dr. Ward expresses it) by our "very conception" of the thing. But this is no argument against our knowing them solely by experience, for (as is truly and aptly said by Professor Bain in his *Logic*) these are cases in which in the very process of forming the conception, we have experience of the fact.[†] It is not likely that Dr. Ward has returned to the notion (so long abandoned and even forgotten by intuitionists) of ideas literally innate, and thinks that we bring with us into the world the conception of a trilateral figure ready made. He doubtless believes that it is at least suggested by observation of objects. Now, the fact of three sides and that of three angles are so intimately linked together in external nature, that it is impossible for the conception of a three-sided figure to get into the mind without carrying into the mind with it the conception of three angles. Therefore, when we have once got the conception of a trilateral, we have no need of further experience to prove triangularity. The conception itself, which represents all our previous experience, suffices. And if the Association theory be true, it must follow from it, that whenever any property of external things is in the relation to the things which is required for the formation of an inseparable association, that property will get into the conception, and be believed without further proof. Dr. Ward will say that triangularity is not included in the conception of a trilateral. But this is only true in the sense that triangularity is not in the connotation of the name. Many attributes not included in the definition are included in the conception. Dr. Ward cannot but see that on the experience hypothesis, this not only may, but must be the case.*

[*"Mr. Mill's Denial of Necessary Truth," pp. 288–9.]

[†Cf. Alexander Bain, *Logic*, 2 pts. (London: Longmans, Green, Reader, and Dyer, 1870), Pt. II, pp. 168–70.]

*[72] The belief, however, when grounded on the conception without a fresh appeal to experience—when got at, as Dr. Ward expresses it [p. 299], not by observation of external nature, but of our own mind—is only justified exactly so far as we are entitled to assume that the conception in our mind represents the facts of outward experience. Only if space itself is everywhere what we conceive it to be, can our conclusions from the conception be everywhere objectively true. The truths of geometry are valid wherever the constitution of space agrees with what it is within our means of observation. That space cannot anywhere be differently

Dr. Ward goes on to deny that uniformity of experience can produce the belief that the truth thus uniformly experienced is necessary. If it could, he says, the fact itself of the uniformity of nature—the fact that phænomena succeed each other according to uniform laws—resting on a broader basis of experience than any particular law of nature, has all the conditions for being regarded as a necessary truth, and must produce "a practical necessity of fancying that in every possible region of existence phænomena succeed each other by uniform laws;"* now, we are under no such necessity, as I myself have strenuously maintained.[*] But my answer to Mr. Mansel's instances is applicable to this of Dr. Ward's. Is it seriously that he compares our experience of the uniformity of nature, in point of obviousness and familiarity, with our experience of the straightness of straight lines? The uniformity is, in the first stages of our experience, an actual paradox; first appearances are against it; they seem to show that some events do indeed succeed each other with an approach, though only an approach, to uniformity, but that a far greater number have no fixed order whatever. How can it be maintained that we have, at that early period of our observations, such experience of this universal truth, as to incorporate it in our conception of every object in nature, and create an irresistible association of uniformity of sequence with all possible events? As we gradually learn the correct *interpretation* of our experience, and become aware that uniformity of sequence *is* an universal truth, a powerful, though even then, not an irresistible association, does grow up; accordingly the law that whatever begins to exist has a cause, is classed by most of the intuitional philosophers as a necessary truth, though (strange to say) a necessary truth with an exception.

But Dr. Ward contends (Dr. M'Cosh had already said the same thing)† that there is a fallacy of ambiguity in the phrase "necessity of thought." He charges me with using the phrase "in two senses fundamentally different. A necessity of thought may, no doubt, be most intelligibly understood to mean a law of nature whereby under certain circumstances I *necessarily think* this, that, and the other judgment. But it may also be understood to mean a law of nature whereby I *think as necessary* this, that, and the other judgment." He agrees with me

that from a necessity of thought in the *former* sense, no legitimate argument whatever can be deduced for a necessity of objective truth. Supposing I felt

---

constituted, or that almighty power could not make a different constitution of it, we know not. This may serve as an answer to some other remarks of Dr. Ward (pp. 301–3), to which it would tax the reader's patience too much to give a fuller reply.

*[72] [Ward,] p. 290.

[*See pp. 261n–2n above, and the section of Mill's *Logic* there cited.]

†[72] [McCosh,] *Examination of Mr. J. S. Mill's Philosophy*, pp. 43–4.

unusually cold a few moments ago, it is a necessity of thought that I should now *remember* the circumstance. Yet that past experience was no necessary truth. It is a necessity of thought again that I expect the sun to rise to-morrow: and many similar instances could be adduced. The only necessity of thought which proves the self-evident necessity of objective truth, is the necessity of thinking that such truth is self-evidently necessary.*

Not denying the validity of this distinction, I maintain that it does not affect the argument; because the one necessity is always proved by the other. The evidence always given, and the only evidence which I believe can be given, that we must think anything as necessary, is that we necessarily think it. This, under various names, a Fundamental Law of Belief, the Inconceivability of the Opposite, and so on, is the staple of the Intuitionist argument. Surely, if I disprove the necessity of thinking the thing at all, I disprove that it must be thought as necessary. What other proof can be given of the necessity of a truth, I confess myself ignorant. The consensus of mankind will not do, since that is disproved by being disputed; and Dr. Ward's argument, that a truth must be independent of experience if it can be deduced from the conception, has been met by showing that it is deduced from the conception only after experience has put it there.

Dr. Ward says that "mere constant and uniform experience cannot possibly account for the mind's conviction of self-evident necessity." Nor do I pretend that it does. The experience must not only be constant and uniform, but the juxtaposition of the facts in experience must be immediate and close, as well as early, familiar, and so free from even the semblance of an exception that no counter association can possibly arise. Dr. Ward gives two contrasted examples: "I have never even once experienced the equality of $2 + 9$ to $3 + 8$, and yet am convinced that not even Omnipotence could overthrow that equality. I have most habitually experienced the warmth-giving property of fire, and yet see no reason for doubting that Omnipotence can at any time suspend or remove that property. That which I have *never* experienced I regard as *necessary*; that which I have habitually and unexceptionably experienced I regard as *contingent*."[†]

To the first example I answer, that if the equality of $2 + 9$ and $3 + 8$ does not come to us in the first instance by direct experience (though fully ratified by it), neither does it come by direct intuition. It is gained by a succession of steps, each resting on actual trial. True, it may be but a mental trial; as by merely fancying myself "holding two pebbles in one hand and nine in the other, and then transferring one pebble from the larger to the smaller group."[*] But the mere imagination of this transfer would not, and

*[72] [Ward,] p. 292.
†[72] *Ibid.*, pp. 298–9.
[*Ibid.*, p. 298.]

ought not to carry conviction to me, if I had not previously observed that change of place makes no difference in the number of objects. All reasoning from conceptions is open to, and finally rests upon, an appeal to the sensations. With respect to the warmth-giving property of fire, the instance is not happily chosen; for warmth is so much the *differentia* of fire, the principal connotation of the word, that what was believed not to warm would certainly not be called fire. But (disregarding this) Dr. Ward's illustration may be met in the same manner in which I have met the similar illustrations of Mr. Mansel. Fire, it is true, will always, under certain needful conditions, give warmth; but the sight of fire is very often unattended with any sensation of warmth. It is not concomitance of the outward facts that creates the association, but concomitance of the sensible impressions. The visible presence of fire and the sensation of warmth are not in that invariable conjunction and immediate juxtaposition, which might disable us from conceiving the one without the other, and might therefore lead us to suppose their conjunction to be a necessary truth.

Dr. Ward's criticisms on the view I take of the Law of Causation belong not to the present work, but to my *System of Logic*. One more of his objections, however, may be noticed here. He says, that while I account for the "power of ascertaining axioms by mere mental experience" from "one of the characteristic properties of geometrical forms," viz., that they can be painted in the imagination with a distinctness equal to reality, I entirely leave out of account arithmetical and algebraic axioms, though these, equally with geometrical, can be arrived at by merely mental experimentation.* I do not leave them out of account, but have assigned, in my *Logic*, another and equally conclusive reason why they can be studied in our conceptions alone, namely, that arithmetical and algebraic truths being true not of any particular kind of things, but of all things whatever, any mental conceptions whatever will adequately represent them.[j][*]

*[72] *Ibid.*, p. 302. [The reference to Mill's *Logic* is to Bk. II, Chap. v, §5, *Collected Works*, Vol. VII, p. 234.]

[*See *System of Logic*, Bk. II, Chap. vi, §2, *Collected Works*, Vol. VII, pp. 255–6.]

CHAPTER XV

Sir William Hamilton's Doctrine of
Unconscious Mental Modifications

THE LAWS OF OBLIVISCENCE noticed in the preceding chapter, are closely connected with a question raised by Sir W. Hamilton, and discussed at some length in his *Lectures*: Whether there are unconscious states of mind: or, as he expresses it in the eighteenth Lecture, "Whether the mind exerts energies, and is the subject of modifications, of neither of which it is conscious." Our author pronounces decidedly for the affirmative, in opposition to most English philosophers, by whom, he says, "the supposition of an unconscious action or passion of the mind, has been treated as something either unintelligible or absurd;"* and in opposition, no less, to *a*at least one expression*a* of opinion by our author himself.† *b* This is one of the numerous inconsistencies in Sir W. Hamilton's professed opinions, which a close examination and comparison of his speculations brings to light, and which show how far he was in reality from being the systematic thinker which, on a first impression of his writings, he seems to be. In one point of view, these self-contradictions are fully as much an honour as a discredit to him; since they frequently arise from his having acutely seized some important psychological truth, greatly in advance of his general mode of thought, and not having brought the remainder of his philosophy up to it. Instead of having reasoned out a consistent scheme of thought, of which every part fits in with the other parts, he seems to have explored the deeper regions of the mind only at the points which had some direct connexion with the conclusions he had adopted on a few special questions of

Lectures, Vol. I, p. 338.

†[72] "Every act of mind is an act of consciousness" (*ibid.*, Vol. II, p. 277). Another statement to the same effect which I erroneously quoted in former editions (*ibid.*, p. 73) does not belong to Sir W. Hamilton. [See 272*b* below.]

*a-a*65¹, 65², 67   isolated expressions

*b*65¹, 65², 67   The following is one: "Every act of mind is an act of consciousness."† [*footnote:*] †*Ibid.*, Vol. II, p. 277. [*text:*] Here is another:‡ [*footnote:*] ‡*Ibid.*, p. 73. [*text:*] "We must say of all our states of mind, whatever they may be, that it" (a state of mind) "can be nothing else than it is felt to be. Its very essence consists in being felt; and when it is not felt, it is not."

philosophy: and from his different explorations he occasionally, as in the present case, brought back different results. But, in the place where he treats directly of this particular question, he decides unequivocally for the existence of latent mental modifications. The subject is in itself not unimportant, and his treatment of it will serve as an example by which to estimate his powers of thought in the province of pure psychology.

Sir W. Hamilton recognises three different kinds, or, as he calls them, degrees, of mental latency. Two of these will be seen, on examination, to be entirely irrelevant.

The first kind of latency, is that which belongs to all the parts of our knowledge which we are not thinking of at the very moment. "I know a science, or language, not merely while I make a temporary use of it, but inasmuch as I can apply it when and how I will. Thus the infinitely greater part of our spiritual treasures lies always beyond the sphere of consciousness, hid in the obscure recesses of the mind."* But this stored-up knowledge, I submit, is not an "unconscious action or passion of the mind." It is not a mental state, but a capability of being put into a mental state. When I am not thinking of a thing, it is not present to my mind at all. It may become present when something happens to recall it; but it is not latently present now; no more than any physical thing which I may have hoarded up. I may have a stock of food with which to nourish myself hereafter; but my body is not in a state of latent nourishment by the food which is in store. I have the power to walk across the room, though I am sitting in my chair; but we should hardly call this power a latent act of walking. What required to be shown was, not that I may possess knowledge without recalling it, but that it can be recalled to my mind, I remaining unconscious of it all the time.†

*Ibid., Vol. I, p. 339.

†Sir W. Hamilton deliberately rejects this obvious distinction, and in his Lecture on Memory (Lect. xxx) maintains that all the knowledge we possess, whether we are thinking of it or not, is at all times present to us, though unconsciously. "This is certainly," (he says) "an hypothesis, because whatever is out of consciousness can only be assumed; but it is an hypothesis which we are not only warranted, but necessitated by the phænomena, to establish." (Ibid., Vol. II, p. 209.) This confident assertion is supported only by a passage from an author of whom the reader has already heard something, H. Schmid (Versuch einer Metaphysik); by whom, however, the conclusion is not elicited from "the phænomena," but drawn, à priori, from the assertion that the act of knowledge is "an energy of the self-active powers of a subject one and indivisible; consequently a part of the ego must be detached or annihilated if a cognition once existent be again extinguished." [Ibid., pp. 211–12.] This palpable begging of the whole point in dispute (which Schmid makes no scruple of propping up by half-a-dozen other arbitrary assumptions) of course makes it necessary to explain how anything can be forgotten; which Schmid resolves by declaring that nothing ever is; it merely passes into latency. Of all this, not a shadow of evidence is exhibited; anything being set down as fact, which can be

The second degree of latency exists when the mind contains systems of knowledge, or certain habits of action, which it is wholly unconscious of possessing in its ordinary state, but which are revealed to consciousness in certain extraordinary exaltations of its powers. The evidence on this point shows that the mind frequently contains whole systems of knowledge, which, though in our normal state they have faded into absolute oblivion, may, in certain abnormal states, as madness, febrile delirium, somnambulism, catalepsy, &c., flash out into luminous consciousness, and even throw into the shade of unconsciousness those other systems by which they had, for a long period, been eclipsed and even extinguished.

He then cites from various authors some of the curious recorded cases "in which the extinct memory of whole languages was suddenly restored, and, what is even still more remarkable, in which the faculty was exhibited of actually repeating, in known or unknown tongues, passages which were never within the grasp of conscious memory in the normal state."* These, however, are not cases of latent states of mind, but of a very different thing—of latent memory. It is not the mental impressions that are latent, but the power of reproducing them. Every one admits, without any apparatus of proof, that we may have powers and susceptibilities of which we are not conscious; but these are capabilities of being affected, not actual affections. I have the susceptibility of being poisoned by prussic acid, but this susceptibility is not a present phænomenon, constantly taking place in my body without my perceiving it. The capability of being poisoned is not a present modification of my body; nor is the capability I perhaps have of recollecting, should I become delirious, something which I have forgotten while sane, a present modification of my mind. These are future contingent

---

educed from the idea of the Ego evolved by Schmid out of the depths of his moral consciousness. His style of philosophizing may be judged from the following specimen: "Every mental activity belongs to the one vital activity of mind in general; it is, therefore, indivisibly bound up with it, and can neither be torn from, nor abolished in it." [*Ibid.*, p. 213.] Therefore he has only to call every impression in memory a "mental activity" to prove that when we have once had it, we can never more get rid of it. If he had but happened to call it a mental *act*, it would have been all over with his argument; for there may surely be passing acts of one permanent activity. Schmid further argues, from the same premises, that feelings, volitions, and desires, are retained in the mind without the medium of memory, that is, we retain the states themselves, not the notions or remembrances of them: from which it follows, that I am at this moment desiring and willing to rise from my bed yesterday morning, and every previous morning since I began to have a will. Schmid has an easy answer to all attempts at explaining mental phænomena by physiological hypotheses, viz., that "Mind, howbeit conditioned by bodily relations, still ever preserves its self-activity and independence." [*Ibid.*, p. 218.] As if to determine whether it does so or not, was not the very point in dispute between him and the physiological hypotheses. These reasonings are quite worthy of Schmid; but it is extremely unworthy of Sir W. Hamilton to accept and endorse them.

*_Ibid._, Vol. I, pp. 339–40.

states, not present actual ones. The real question is, can I undergo a present actual mental modification without being aware of it?

We come, therefore, to the third case, which is the only one really in point, and enquire, whether there are, in our ordinary mental life, "mental modifications, *i.e.* mental activities and passivities, of which we are unconscious, but which manifest their existence by effects of which we are conscious?" Sir W. Hamilton decides that there are: and even "that what we are conscious of is constructed out of what we are not conscious of;" that "the sphere of our conscious modifications is only a small circle in the centre of a far wider sphere of action and passion, of which we are only conscious through its effects."*

His first example is taken from the perception of external objects. The facts which he adduces are these. 1st. Every *minimum visibile* is composed of still smaller parts, which are not separately capable of being objects of vision; "they are, severally and apart, to consciousness as zero." Yet every one of these parts "must by itself have produced in us a certain modification, real though unperceived,"† since the effect of the whole can only be the sum of the separate effects of the parts. 2nd. "When we look at a distant forest, we perceive a certain expanse of green. Of this, as an affection of our organism, we are clearly and distinctly conscious. Now, the expanse of which we are conscious is evidently made up of parts of which we are not conscious. No leaf, perhaps no tree, may be separately visible. But the greenness of the forest is made up of the greenness of the leaves; that is, the total impression of which we are conscious, is made up of an infinitude of small impressions of which we are not conscious." 3rd. Our sense of hearing tells the same tale. There is a *minimum audibile*; the faintest sound capable of being heard. This sound, however, must be made up of parts, each of which must affect us in some manner, otherwise the whole which they compose could not affect us. When we hear the distant murmur of the sea,

this murmur is a sum made up of parts, and the sum would be as zero if the parts did not count as something. . . . If the noise of each wave made no impression on our sense, the noise of the sea, as the result of these impressions, could not be realized. But the noise of each several wave, at the distance we suppose, is inaudible; we must, however, admit that they produce a certain modification beyond consciousness, on the percipient subject; for this is necessarily involved in the reality of their result.‡

It is a curious question how Sir W. Hamilton failed to perceive that an unauthorized assumption has slipped into his argument. Because the

Ibid., pp. 347, 348, 349.
†*Ibid.*, p. 350.
‡*Ibid.*, p. 351.

minimum visibile consists of parts (as we know through the microscope), and because the minimum visibile produces an impression on our sense of sight, he jumps to the conclusion that each one of the parts does so too. But it is a supposition consistent with what we know of nature, that a certain *quantity* of the cause may be a necessary condition to the production of *any* of the effect. The minimum visibile would on that supposition *be* this certain quantity; and the two halves into which we can conceive it divided, though each contributing its half to the formation of that which produces vision, would not each separately produce half of the vision, the concurrence of both being necessary to produce any vision whatever. And so of the distant murmur of the sea: the agency which produces it is made up of the rolling of many different waves, each of which, if sufficiently near, would affect us with a perceptible sound; but at the distance at which they are, it may require the rolling of many waves to excite an amount of vibration in the air sufficient, when enfeebled by extension, to produce any effect whatever on our auditory nerves, and, through them, on our mind. The supposition that each wave affects the mind separately because their aggregate affects it, is therefore, to say the least, an unproved hypothesis.

The counter-hypothesis, that in order to the production of any quantity whatever of the effect, there is needed a certain minimum quantity of the cause, it is the more extraordinary that Sir W. Hamilton should have overlooked, since he has not only himself adopted a similar supposition in some other cases,* but it is a necessary part of his theory in this very case. He will not admit as possible, that less than a certain quantity of the external agent, produces no mental modification; but he himself supposes that less than a certain quantity of mental modification produces no consciousness. Yet if his *à priori* argument is valid for the one sequence, it is valid for the other. If the effect of a whole must be the sum of similar effects produced by all its parts, and if every state of consciousness is the effect of a modification of mind which is made up of an infinitude of small parts, the state of consciousness also must be made up of an infinitude of small states of consciousness, produced by these infinitely small mental modifications respectively. We are not at liberty to adopt the one theory for the first link in the double succession, and the other theory for the other link. Having shown no reason why either theory should be preferred, our author would have acted more philosophically in not deciding between them. But to

---

*"In the internal perception of a series of mental operations, a certain time, a certain duration, is necessary for the smallest section of continuous energy to which consciousness is competent. Some minimum of time must be admitted as the condition of consciousness." (*Ibid.*, p. 369.) And again: "It cannot certainly be said, that the minimum of sensation infers the maximum of perception; for perception always supposes a certain quantum of sensation." (*Ibid.*, Vol. II, p. 102.)

accommodate half the fact to one theory and half to the other, without assigning any reason for the difference, is to exceed all rational license of scientific hypothesis.

After these examples from Perception, our author passes to cases of Association: and as he here states some important mental phænomena well and clearly, I shall quote him at some length.

It sometimes happens, that we find one thought rising immediately after another in consciousness, but whose consecution we can reduce to no law of association. Now in these cases we can generally discover by an attentive observation, that these two thoughts, though not themselves associated, are each associated with certain other thoughts; so that the whole consecution would have been regular, had these intermediate thoughts come into consciousness, between the two which are not immediately associated. Suppose, for instance, that A, B, C, are three thoughts,—that A and C cannot immediately suggest each other, but that each is associated with B, so that A will naturally suggest B, and B naturally suggest C. Now it may happen, that we are conscious of A, and immediately thereafter of C. How is the anomaly to be explained? It can only be explained on the principle of latent modifications. A suggests C, not immediately, but through B; but as B, like the half of the *minimum visibile* or *minimum audibile*, does not rise into consciousness, we are apt to consider it as non-existent. You are probably aware of the following fact in mechanics. If a number of billiard balls be placed in a straight row and touching each other, and if a ball be made to strike, in the line of the row, the ball at one end of the series, what will happen? The motion of the impinging ball is not divided among the whole row; this, which we might *à priori* have expected, does not happen, but the impetus is transmitted through the intermediate balls which remain each in its place, to the ball at the opposite end of the series, and this ball alone is impelled on. Something like this seems often to occur in the train of thought. One idea mediately suggests another into consciousness,—the suggestion passing through one or more ideas which do not themselves rise into consciousness. The awakening and awakened ideas here correspond to the ball striking and the ball struck off; while the intermediate ideas of which we are unconscious, but which carry on the suggestion, resemble the intermediate balls which remain moveless, but communicate the impulse. An instance of this occurs to me with which I was recently struck. Thinking of Ben Lomond, this thought was immediately followed by the thought of the Prussian system of education. Now conceivable connexion between these two ideas in themselves, there was none. A little reflection, however, explained the anomaly. On my last visit to the mountain, I had met upon its summit a German gentleman, and though I had no consciousness of the intermediate and unawakened links between Ben Lomond and the Prussian schools, they were undoubtedly these,—the German,—Germany,—Prussia,—and, these media being admitted, the connexion between the extremes was manifest.*

Though our author says that the facts here described can only be explained on the supposition that the intervening ideas never came into consciousness at all, he is aware that another explanation is conceivable, namely that they were momentarily in consciousness, but were forgotten,

Ibid., Vol. I, pp. 352–3.

agreeably to the law of Obliviscence already spoken of: which, in fact, is the explanation given by Stewart. The same two explanations may be given of his final example, drawn from a class of phænomena also governed by laws of association, "our acquired dexterities and habits."* When we learn any manual operation, suppose that of playing on the pianoforte, the operation is at first a series of conscious volitions, followed by movements of the fingers: but when, by sufficient repetition, a certain facility has been acquired, the motions take place without our being able to recognise afterwards that we have been conscious of the volitions which preceded them. In this case, we may either hold with Sir W. Hamilton, that the volitions (to which ᶜmustᶜ be added the feelings of muscular contraction, and of the contact of our fingers with the keys) are not, in the practised performer, present to consciousness at all; or, with Stewart, that he is conscious of them, but for so brief an interval, that he has no remembrance of them afterwards.[*] The motions, in this case, are said by Hartley to have become secondarily automatic,[†] which our author supposes to be a third opinion, but ᵈthe difference, if difference it was, between this and Stewart's theory, is not material to the present enquiryᵈ.

Let us now consider the reasons given by Sir W. Hamilton for preferring his explanation to Stewart's. The first and principal of them is, that to suppose a state of consciousness which is not remembered, "violates the whole analogy of consciousness." "Consciousness supposes memory; and we are only conscious as we are able to connect and contrast one instance of our intellectual existence with another."† "Of consciousness, however faint, there must be some memory, however short. But this is at variance with the phænomenon, for the ideas A and C may precede and follow each other without any perceptible interval, and without any the feeblest memory of B."‡

Here again I am obliged, not without wonder, to point out the inconclusive character of the argument. When Sir W. Hamilton says that consciousness implies memory, he means, as his words show, that we are only conscious by means of change; by discriminating the present state from a

---

*Ibid., p. 355.

[*See Stewart, *Elements of the Philosophy of the Human Mind*, Vol. I, pp. 103–31.]

[†See David Hartley, *Observations on Man, his Frame, his Duty, and his Expectations*, 2 pts. (Bath: Leake and Frederick; London: Hitch and Austen, 1749), Vol. I, pp. 108–9.]

†*Lectures*, Vol. I, p. 354.

‡*Ibid.*, p. 355.

ᶜ⁻ᶜ65¹, 65²   may

ᵈ⁻ᵈ65¹, 65², 67   it is not certain that Hartley meant anything at variance with Stewart's theory

state immediately preceding. Granting this, as with proper explanations I do, all it proves is, that any conscious state of mind must be remembered long enough to be compared with the mental state immediately following it. The state of mind, therefore, which he supposes to have been latent, must, if it passed into consciousness, have been remembered until one other mental modification had supervened; which there is assuredly not a particle of evidence that it was not: for our having totally forgotten it a minute after, is no evidence, but a common consequence of the laws of Obliviscence. It is perhaps true that all consciousness must be followed by a memory, but I see no reason why an evanescent state of consciousness must be followed, if by any, by a more than evanescent memory. "It is a law of mind," our author says further on, "that the intensity of the present consciousness determines the vivacity of the future memory. Vivid consciousness, long memory; faint consciousness, short memory."* Well, then: in the case supposed, the intensity of consciousness is at ^{e}a^e minimum, therefore on his own showing the duration of memory should be so too. If the consciousness itself is too fleeting to fix the attention, so, à fortiori, must the remembrance of it. In reality, the remembrance is often evanescent when the consciousness is by no means so, but is so distinct and prolonged as to be in no danger whatever of being supposed latent. Take the case of a player on the pianoforte while still a learner, and before the succession of volitions has attained the rapidity which practice ultimately gives it. In this stage of progress there is, beyond all doubt, a conscious volition, anterior to the playing of each particular note. Yet has the player, when the piece is finished, the smallest remembrance of each of these volitions, as a separate fact? In like manner, have we, when we have finished reading a volume, the smallest memory of our successive volitions to turn the pages? On the contrary, we only know that we must have turned them, because, without doing so, we could not have read to the end. Yet these volitions were not latent: every time we turned over a leaf, we must have formed a conscious purpose of turning; but, the purpose having been instantly fulfilled, the attention was arrested in the process for too short a time to leave a more than momentary remembrance of it. The sensations of sight, touch, and the muscles, felt in turning the leaves, were as vivid at the moment as any of our ordinary sensible impressions which are only important to us as means to an end. But because they had no pleasurable or painful interest in themselves; because the interest they had as means passed away in the same instant by the attainment of the end; and because there was nothing to associate the act of reading with these particular sensations, rather

*Ibid., p. 368–9.

$^{e-e}$65^1 the

than with other similar sensations formerly experienced; their trace in the memory was only momentary, unless something unusual and remarkable connected with the particular leaves turned over, detained them in remembrance.

If sensations which are evidently in consciousness may leave so brief a memory that they are not felt to leave any memory *whatever*, what wonder that the same should happen when the sensations are of so fugitive a character, that it can be debated whether they were in consciousness at all? However true it may be that there must be some memory wherever there is consciousness, what argument is this against a theory which supposes a low degree of consciousness, attended by just the degree of memory which properly belongs to it?

Imagine an argument in physics, corresponding to this in metaphysics. Some of my readers are probably acquainted with the important experiments of M. Pasteur, which *appear to* have finally exploded the ancient hypothesis of Equivocal Generation, by showing that even the smallest microscopic animalcules are not produced in a medium from which their still more microscopic germs have been effectually excluded. What should we think of any one who deemed it a refutation of M. Pasteur, that the germs are not discernible by the naked eye? who maintained that invisible animalcules must proceed, if from germs at all, from visible germs? This reasoning would be an exact parallel to that of Sir W. Hamilton.

The only other argument of our author against Stewart's doctrine, is confined to the phænomenon of acquired habits, in which case, he says, the supposition of real but forgotten consciousness "would constrain our assent to the most monstrous conclusions:" since, in reading aloud, if the matter be uninteresting, we may be carrying on a train of thought (even of "serious meditation") on a totally different subject, and this, too, "without distraction or fatigue:" which, he says, would be impossible, if we were separately conscious of, or (as he rather gratuitously alters the idea), separately attentive to, "each least movement in either process."* Sir W. Hamilton here loses sight of a part of his own philosophy, which deserves his forgetfulness the less as it is a very valuable part. In one of the most important psychological discussions in his *Lectures*,[†] he forcibly maintains that we are capable of carrying on several distinct series of states of consciousness at once; and goes so far as to contend not only that our consciousness, but what is more than consciousness, our "*concentrated consciousness, or attention*,"[*] is capable of being divided among as many

Ibid., p. 360.
†*Ibid.*, pp. 238–54.
[*Ibid.*, p. 360.]

*-*65[1], 65[2]   at all
g-g+65[2], 67, 72

as six simultaneous impressions.* Returning to the same subject in another place, he quotes from a modern French philosopher, Cardaillac (in a work entitled *Etudes Elémentaires de Philosophie*),[*] an excellent and conclusive passage, showing the great multitude of states more or less conscious, which often coexist in the mind, and help to determine the subsequent trains of thought or feeling; and illustrating the causes that determine which of these shall in any particular case predominate over the rest.† Our consciousness, therefore, according to Sir W. Hamilton, ought not to have much difficulty in finding room for the two simultaneous series of states which he quarrels with Stewart's hypothesis for requiring: and we are not bound, under the penalty of "monstrous conclusions," to consider one of these series as latent. Sir W. Hamilton indeed says truly, that "the greater the number of objects to which our consciousness is simultaneously extended, the smaller is the intensity with which it is able to consider each;"‡ but the intensity of consciousness necessary for reading aloud with correctness in a language familiar to us, not being very considerable, a great part of our power of attention is disposable for "the train of serious meditation"[†] which is supposed to be passing through our minds at the same time. For all this, I would not advise any person (unless one with the peculiar gift ascribed to Julius Cæsar)[‡] to stake anything on the substantial value of a train of thought carried on by him while reading aloud a book on another subject. Such thoughts, I imagine, are always the better for being revised when the mind has nothing else to do than to consider them.

It is strange, but characteristic, that Sir W. Hamilton cannot be depended on for remembering, in one part of his speculations, the best things which he has said in another; not even the truths into which he has thrown so

*Ibid., p. 254.

[*Jean-Jacques Séverin de Cardaillac, *Etudes élémentaires de philosophie*, 2 vols. (Paris: Firmin-Didot, 1830), Vol. II, pp. 137–8.]

†*Lectures*, Vol. II, pp. 250–8. From this long exposition I shall only extract a single passage, but I recommend the whole of it to the attentive consideration of readers.

"Thus, if we appreciate correctly the phænomena of Reproduction or Reminiscence, we shall recognise, as an incontestable fact, that our thoughts suggest each other not one by one successively, as the order to which language is astricted might lead us to infer; but that the complement of circumstances under which we at every moment exist, awakens simultaneously a great number of thoughts; these it calls into the presence of the mind, either to place them at our disposal, if we find it requisite to employ them, or to make them co-operate in our deliberations, by giving them, according to our nature and our habits, an influence, more or less active, on our judgments and consequent acts." (P. 258.)

‡Ibid., Vol. I, p. 237.

[†*Ibid.*, p. 360.]

[‡See Plutarch, *Life of Cæsar*, in *Lives* (Greek and English), trans. Bernadotte Perrin, 11 vols. (London: Heinemann; New York: Putnam's Sons, 1919), Vol. VII, p. 484 (XVII, §4).]

much of the powers of his mind, as to have made them, in an especial manner, his own.

Notwithstanding the failure of Sir W. Hamilton to adduce a single valid reason for preferring his hypothesis to that of Stewart, it does not follow that he is not, at least in certain cases, in the right. The difference between the two opinions being beyond the reach of experiment, and both being equally consistent with the facts which present themselves spontaneously, it is not easy to obtain sure grounds for deciding between them. The essential part of the phænomenon is, that we have, or once had, many sensations, and that many ideas do, or once did, enter into our trains of thought, which sensations and ideas we afterwards, in the words of James Mill, are "under an acquired incapacity of attending to:"* and that when our incapacity of attending to them has become complete, it is, to our subsequent consciousness, exactly as if we did not have them at all: we are incapable, by any self-examination, of being aware of them. We know that these lost sensations and ideas, for lost they appear to be, leave traces of having existed; they continue to be operative in introducing other ideas by association. Either, therefore, they have been consciously present long enough to call up associations, but not long enough to be remembered a few moments later; or they have been, as Sir W. Hamilton supposes, unconsciously present; or they have not been present at all, but something instead of them, capable of producing the same effects. I am myself inclined to agree with Sir W. Hamilton, and to admit his unconscious mental modifications, in the only shape in which I can attach any very distinct meaning to them, namely, unconscious modifications of the nerves. There are much stronger facts in support of this hypothesis than those to which Sir W. Hamilton appeals—facts which it is far more difficult to reconcile with the doctrine that the sensations are felt, but felt too momentarily to leave a recognisable impression in memory. In the case, for instance, of a soldier who receives a wound in battle, but in the excitement of the moment is not aware of the fact, it is difficult not to believe that if the wound had been accompanied by the usual sensation, so vivid a feeling would have forced itself to be attended to and remembered. The supposition which seems most probable is, that the nerves of the particular part were affected as they would have been by the same cause in any other circumstances, but that, the nervous centres being intensely occupied with other impressions, the affection of the local nerves did not reach them, and no sensation was excited. In like manner, if we admit (what physiology is rendering more and more probable) that our mental feelings, as well as our sensations, have for their physical antecedents particular states of the nerves; it may well be

*Analysis of the Phenomena of the Human Mind, Vol. I, p. 33.

believed that the apparently suppressed links in a chain of association, those which Sir W. Hamilton considers as latent, really are so; that they are not, even momentarily, felt; the chain of causation being continued only physically, by one organic state of the nerves succeeding another so rapidly that the state of mental consciousness appropriate to each is not produced. We have only to suppose, either that a nervous modification of too short duration does not produce any sensation or mental feeling at all, or that the rapid succession of different nervous modifications makes the feelings produced by them interfere with each other, and become confounded in one mass. The former of these suppositions is extremely probable, while of the truth of the latter we have positive proof. An example of it is the experiment which Sir W. Hamilton quoted from Mr. Mill, and which had been noticed before either of them by Hartley.[*] It is known that the seven prismatic colours, combined in certain proportions, produce the white light of the solar ray. Now, if the seven colours are painted on spaces bearing the same proportion to one another as in the solar spectrum, and the coloured surface so produced is passed rapidly before the eyes, as by the turning of a wheel, the whole is seen as white. The physiological explanation of this phænomenon may be deduced from another common experiment. If a lighted torch, or a bar heated to luminousness, is waved rapidly before the eye, the appearance produced is that of a ribbon of light; which is universally understood to prove that the visual sensation persists for a certain short time after its cause has ceased. Now, if this happens with a single colour, it will happen with a series of colours: and if the wheel on which the prismatic colours have been painted, is turned with the same rapidity with which the torch was waved, each of the seven sensations of colour will last long enough to be contemporaneous with all the others, and they will naturally produce by their combination the same colour as if they had, from the beginning, been excited simultaneously. If anything similar to this obtains in our consciousness generally (and that it obtains in many cases of consciousness there can be no doubt) it will follow that whenever the organic modifications of our nervous fibres succeed one another at an interval shorter than the duration of the sensations or other feelings corresponding to them, those sensations or feelings will, so to speak, overlap one another, and becoming simultaneous instead of successive, will blend into a state of feeling, probably as unlike the elements out of which it is engendered, as the colour white is unlike the prismatic colours. And this may be the source of many of those states of internal or mental feeling which we cannot distinctly refer to a prototype in experience, our experi-

[*Hamilton, *Lectures*, Vol. II, pp. 147–9; James Mill, *Analysis*, Vol. I, p. 68; Hartley, *Observations on Man*, Vol. I, p. 9.]

ence only supplying the elements from which, by this kind of mental chemistry, they are composed. The elementary feelings may then be said to be latently present, or to be present but not in consciousness. The truth, however, is that the feelings themselves are not present, consciously or latently, but that the nervous modifications which are their usual antecedents have been present, while the consequents have been frustrated, and another consequent has been produced instead.*

*[67] These considerations may serve as an answer to Dr. M'Cosh, when he maintains, with many other of the intuitive philosophers, that association cannot generate a mental state specifically distinct from the elements out of which it is composed; which amounts to a denial of the possibility of mental chemistry. [*Examination*, pp. 182–4.] I had thought that such an experiment as that of the wheel with the seven colours, in which seven sensations, following one another very rapidly, become, or at least generate, one sensation, and that one totally different from any of the seven, sufficiently proved the possibility of what Dr. M'Cosh denies; but he writes as if he had never heard of that experiment. "I can discover," he says, "no evidence that two sensations succeeding one another will ever be anything else than two sensations." (*Ibid.*, p. 185.) The analogous facts in the case of ideas cannot be appealed to, for they are the very matter disputed; but there is abundance of similar instances in sensation. Dropping succession of colours, let Dr. M'Cosh look at an ordinary wheel revolving with the rapidity which is often seen in machinery, and he will have a sensation which is not one of rotatory motion at all, but a dizzy spectrum apparently stationary, with the exception of a slight degree of tremulous movement.

ʰDr. M'Cosh, in his reply, says he was perfectly aware of the experiments of the luminous ring and the wheel with the seven colours. He does not seem to have known of the other fact which I mentioned, that a wheel may be in such rapid rotation as to seem stationary; for he offers instead of it "a wheel in rapid motion appearing stationary when made visible by instantaneous electric light," of which he gives the true explanation that, seeing the wheel only for the instant, we do not really see it move. ["Mill's Reply," p. 354.] The wheel in my example is rotating in broad daylight.

But these examples of mental chemistry, being taken from sensation, are (says Dr. M'Cosh) merely organic. He requires me to produce examples from purely mental affections. And how do we know that our mental affections are not also organic, having for their immediate antecedents states of the nerves and brain? This is not only possible, but the progress of science has rendered it almost certain, even to those who are far from being Materialists in the ordinary sense of the term. There are, however, abundant proofs that association can generate new mental affections. Let us take, as one of the obvious examples, the love of money. Does any one think that money has intrinsically, by its own nature, any more value to us than the first shining pebbles we pick up, except for the things it will purchase? Yet its association with these things not only makes it desired for itself, but creates in many minds a passionate love of it, far surpassing the desire they feel for any of the uses to which it can be put. Not only the love of money, but the love of acquisition, of possession, of accumulation, is a feeling created by association. What is desired for itself is the use and enjoyment of individual objects: the possession of a store of them is at first

ʰ⁻ʰ+72

desired as a means to that; but after it has been long pursued as a means, it becomes itself an end—the object of the passion of appropriation, or property, a passion *sui generis*, and (as life has hitherto been carried on) one of the principal moving powers in human affairs. These, Dr. M'Cosh may say, are feelings, and what I want is intellectual states; I desiderate examples of "the power of association to generate new ideas, and to produce belief." [*Ibid.*, p. 353.] As an example, then, of new ideas, take the idea of infinity. Infinity is not a fact of intuition, nor of consciousness. We do not perceive space (for example) to be infinite. But every object we see or touch, and every portion of space that we cognise, is cognised along with something beyond it. We hence become incapable of conceiving any object or space without something beyond; that is, we conceive space as infinite. And along with this new idea a belief is generated; for it has been, and is, the general belief of mankind, without any other evidence of it, that space is actually infinite. As a further example of a belief generated by association, take the acquired perceptions of sight. On the lowest estimate of these which is made by any psychologist, we spontaneously believe that we see much which we only infer: the ideas of the inferred facts are so blended by the power of association with the sensations which suggest them, that the ideas are confounded with sensations, and believed to be direct perceptions of sight.[h]

CHAPTER XVI

Sir William Hamilton's Theory of Causation

SIR W. HAMILTON commences his treatment of the question of Causation, by warning the reader against "some philosophers who, instead of accommodating their solutions to the problem, have accommodated the problem to their solutions."[*] It might almost have been supposed that this expression had been invented to be applied to Sir W. Hamilton himself. He has defined the problem in a manner in which it *had* been defined by no one else, for no visible reason but to adapt it to a solution which no one else had thought of.*

"When we are aware," he says,

of something which begins to exist, we are, by the necessity of our intelligence, constrained to believe that it has a Cause. But what does this expression, that it has a cause, signify? If we analyse our thought, we shall find that it simply means, that as we cannot conceive any new existence to commence, therefore, all that now is seen to arise under a new appearance, had previously an existence under a prior form. We are utterly unable to realize in thought, the possibility of the complement of existence being either increased or diminished. We are unable, on the one hand, to conceive nothing becoming something, or, on the other, something becoming nothing. When God is said to create out of nothing, we construe this to thought by supposing that he evolves existence out of himself; we view the Creator as the cause of the universe. "Ex nihilo nihil, in nihilum nil posse reverti,"[†] expresses, in its purest form, the whole intellectual phænomenon of causality.

There is thus conceived an absolute tautology between the effect and its causes. We think the causes to contain all that is contained in the effect, the effect to contain nothing which was not contained in the causes. Take as example: A neutral salt is an effect of the conjunction of an acid and alkali. Here we do not, and here we cannot, conceive that, in effect, any new existence has been added, nor can we conceive

[*_Lectures_, Vol. II, p. 376.]

*When I say no one else, I ought perhaps to except Krug, from whom in another place our author quotes a sentence, containing at least the germ of his own theory. (_Ibid._, Vol. IV, p. 135. [See Wilhelm Traugott Krug, _Logik_, 2nd ed. (Königsberg: Unzer, 1819), §148.])

[†Persius, _Satires_, in _Juvenal and Persius_ (Latin and English), trans. G. G. Ramsay (London: Heinemann; New York: Putnam's Sons, 1920), p. 352 (III, 84).]

*-*65[1]   has

that any has been taken away. Put another example: Gunpowder is the effect of a mixture of sulphur, charcoal, and nitre, and those three substances are again the effect,—result, of simpler constituents, either known or conceived to exist. Now, in all this series of compositions, we cannot conceive that aught begins to exist. The gunpowder, the last compound, we are compelled to think, contains precisely the same quantum of existence that its ultimate elements contained prior to their combination. Well, we explode the powder. Can we conceive that existence has been diminished by the annihilation of a single element previously in being, or increased by the addition of a single element which was not heretofore in nature? "Omnia mutantur; nihil interit,"[*] is what we think—what we must think. This then is the mental phænomenon of causality,—that we necessarily deny in thought that the object which appears to begin to be, really so begins; and that we necessarily identify its present with its past existence.*

This being Sir W. Hamilton's idea of what Causality means, he thinks it unnecessary to suppose, with most of the philosophers of the intuitive school, a special principle of our nature to account for our believing that every phænomenon must have a cause. The belief is accounted for, "not from a power, but from an impotence of mind,"† namely, from the Law of the Conditioned; or in other words, from the incapacity of the human mind to conceive the Absolute. We are unable to conceive and construe to ourselves an absolute commencement. Whatever we think, we cannot help thinking as existing; and whatever we think as existing, we are compelled to think as having existed through all past, and as destined to exist through all future, time. It does not at all follow that this is really the fact, for there are many things inconceivable to us, which not only may, but must, be true. Accordingly it may be true that there is an absolute commencement; it may not be true that every phænomenon has a cause. Human volitions in particular may come into existence uncaused, and, in Sir W. Hamilton's opinion, they do so. But to us a beginning and an end of existence are both inconceivable.

We are unable to construe in thought, that there can be an atom absolutely added to, or an atom absolutely taken away from, existence in general. Make the experiment. Form to yourselves a notion of the universe; now, can you conceive that the quantity of existence, of which the universe is the sum, is either amplified or diminished? You can conceive the creation of the world as lightly as you can conceive the creation of an atom. But what is creation? It is not the springing of nothing into something. Far from it: it is conceived, and is by us conceivable, merely as the evolution of a new form of existence, by the fiat of the Deity. Let us suppose the very crisis of creation. *Can we realize it to ourselves, in thought, that the moment after the universe came into manifested being, there was a larger complement of existence in the universe and its Author together, than there was the*

[*Ovid, *Metamorphoses* (Latin and English), trans. Frank Justus Miller, 2 vols. (London: Heinemann; New York: Putnam's Sons, 1916), Vol. II, p. 376 (XV, 165).]
   Lectures, Vol. II, pp. 377–8.
   †*Ibid.*, p. 397.

moment before, in the Deity himself alone? This we cannot imagine. What I have now said of our conceptions of creation, holds true of our conceptions of annihilation. We can conceive no real annihilation—no absolute sinking of something into nothing. But, as creation is cogitable by us only as an exertion of divine power, so annihilation is only to be conceived by us as a withdrawal of the divine support. All that there is now actually of existence in the universe, we conceive as having virtually existed, prior to creation, in the Creator; and in imagining the universe to be annihilated by its Author, we can only imagine this as the retractation of an outward energy into power.*

Had this extraordinary view of Causation proceeded from a thinker of less ability and authority than Sir W. Hamilton, I think there are few readers, who, on reaching the sentence which I have marked by italics, would not have set down the entire speculation as a *mauvaise plaisanterie*.

But since any opinion, however strange, of Sir W. Hamilton, must be believed to be serious, and no serious opinion of such a man ought to be dismissed unexamined, I shall proceed to enquire, whether the problem of which he propounds this solution, *is* the problem of Causation, and whether the solution is a true one. To take the last question first; is it a fact that we cannot conceive a beginning of existence? Is it true that whenever we conceive a thing as existing, we are incapable of conceiving a time when it did not exist, or a time when it will exist no longer?

If, by incapacity to conceive an absolute commencement, were only meant that we cannot imagine a time when nothing existed; and if our incapacity of conceiving annihilation, only means that we cannot represent to ourselves an universe devoid of existence; I do not deny it. Whatever else we may suppose removed, there always remains the conception of empty space: and Sir W. Hamilton is probably right in his opinion, that we cannot imagine even empty space without clothing it mentally with some sort of colour or figure. Whoever admits the possibility of Inseparable Association, can scarcely avoid thinking that these are cases of it; and that we are unable to imagine any object but as occupying space, or to imagine it removed without leaving that space either vacant, or filled by something else. But we can conceive both a beginning and an end to all physical existence. As a mere hypothesis, the notion that matter cannot be annihilated arose early; but as a settled belief, it is the tardy result of scientific enquiry. All that is necessary for imagining matter annihilated is presented in our daily experience. We see apparent annihilation whenever water dries up, or fuel is consumed without a visible residuum. The fact could not offer itself to our immediate perceptions in a more palpable shape, if the annihilation were real. Having an exact type on which to frame the conception of matter annihilated, the vulgar of all countries easily and perfectly conceive

Ibid., pp. 405–6.

it. Those to whom, if to anybody, it is inconceivable, are philosophers and men of science, who having formed their familiar conception of the universe on the opposite theory, have acquired an inseparable association of their own, which they cannot overcome. To them the vapour which has succeeded to the water dried up by the sun, the gases which replace the fuel transformed by combustion, have become irrevocably a part of their conception of the entire phænomenon. But the ignorant, who never heard of these things, are not in the least incommoded by the want of them; and if they were not told the contrary, would live and die without suspecting that the water, and the wood or *b*coal*b*, were not destroyed.

All this is not denied by Sir W. Hamilton; but his answer to it is, that if the universe were to perish it would still remain capable of existing, which, it seems, amounts to the same thing. We conceive it as having "virtually existed before it was created," and as virtually existing after it is destroyed. We cannot conceive that there was, at the moment after creation, "a larger complement of existence in the universe and its Author together, than there was the moment before in the Deity himself alone." Creation is to us merely the conversion of power into outward existence; annihilation only "the retractation of an outward energy into power." So that potential existence is exactly the same thing as actual existence; the difference is formal only. Not only is power a real entity, but the power to create an universe *is* the universe: all created things are but a part of its substance, and can be reabsorbed into it. And this is presented to us, not as a recondite ontological theory, forced upon philosophers as an escape from an otherwise insuperable difficulty, but as a statement of what we all think, and cannot but think, from the very constitution of our thinking faculty. Is this the fact? Does any one, except Sir W. Hamilton, think that in computing the sum total of existence, worlds which God might have created but did not, count for exactly as much as they would if he had really created them? There is a corollary from this doctrine which also deserves attention. If the sum of potential and actual existence is always the same, then with every increase of actual existence, there must be a diminution of power: for if there was once the power without the universe, and is now the same quantity of power and also the universe, what our author nautically terms the "complement of existence"[*] has been increased: which is contrary to the theory. By every exercise, therefore, of creative power, God is less powerful: he has less power now, by a whole universe, than before his power of creating the universe had been transmuted into act; and were he to "retract" the actual existence into potential, he would be more powerful than he now

[*Lectures, Vol. II, p. 377; cf. p. 286 above.]

*b-b*65[1]   coals

is, by that exact amount. Is this what all mankind think, and are under an original necessity of thinking? Is this the mode in which, by the "law of the Conditioned,"[*] every one of us is absolutely necessitated to construe the idea of Creation? Sir W. Hamilton says it is.

By a desperate attempt to put an intelligible meaning into the theory, somebody may interpret it to mean that before the universe existed in fact, it existed as a thought in the Divine Mind; and that the idea of an universe, complete in all its details, is equivalent in the "complement of existence" to an actual universe. This is not, perhaps, incapable of being maintained; but it affords no escape from the difficulty. For, this idea in the Divine Mind— is the Divine Mind now denuded of it? Has the Deity *forgotten* the universe, from the time when the divine conception was reduced into act? If not, there are now *both* the universe and the idea of the universe; that is, a double "complement of existence" instead of a single.*

But were it ever so true that we are incapable of conceiving a commencement of anything, and are necessitated to believe that whatever now exists must have existed in the same or another shape through all past time:—that Sir W. Hamilton should imagine *this* to be the law of Cause and Effect, must be accounted one of the most singular hallucinations to be found in the writings of any eminent thinker. According to Sir W. Hamilton, when we say that everything must have a cause, we mean that nothing begins to exist, but everything has always existed. I ask any one, either philosopher or common man, whether he does not mean the exact reverse; whether it is not because things do begin to exist, that a cause must be supposed for their existence. The very words in which the axiom of Causation is commonly stated, and which our author, in the first words of his exposition, adopts, are, that everything which *begins to exist* must have a cause. Is it possible that this axiom can be grounded on the fact that we

[*See, e.g., *ibid.*, p. 404.]
  *The curious notion that potential existence is tantamount to actual reappears in the Appendix to the *Discussions*. "The creation *a Nihilo* means only, that the universe, when created, was not merely put into form, an original chaos, or complement of brute matter, having preceded a plastic energy of intelligence; but that the universe was called into actuality from potential existence by the Divine fiat. The Divine fiat therefore was the proximate cause of the creation; and the Deity, containing the cause, contained, potentially, the effect." ([App. I(A),] p. 620n.)
  It is so frequent in our author's writings to find doctrines of a very decided character laid down in one page, and implicitly or even directly denied in another, that so strange a doctrine as the one in question could not be expected to escape that fate. Accordingly, in [App. II(B)] p. 703 of the same volume, "the Potential" is defined to be, "what is not at this, but may be at another time." If so, the universe, when it only existed potentially, *was not*: and did not count as part of the "complement" of present existence.

never suppose anything to begin to exist? Does not he who takes away a beginning of existence, take away all causation, and all need of a cause? Sir W. Hamilton entirely mistakes what it is, which causation is called in to explain. The Matter composing the universe, whatever philosophical theory we hold concerning it, we know by experience to be constant in quantity; never beginning or ending, only changing its ᶜformsᶜ. But its forms have a beginning and ending: and it is its forms, or rather its changes of form—the end of one form and beginning of another—which alone we seek a cause for, and believe to have a cause. It is *events*, that is to say, *changes*, not substances, that are subject to the law of Causation. The question for the psychologist is not why we believe that a substance, but why we believe that a change in the form of a substance, must have a cause. Sir W. Hamilton, in a tardy defence of his theory against objections,* is forced, in a sort of way, to admit this, and virtually to acknowledge that all which we really consider as caused, we consider as beginning to exist. Nothing is caused but events: and it will hardly be said that we conceive an event as having never had a beginning, but been in existence as an event just as much before it happened as when it did happen. An event then being the only thing which suggests the belief or the idea of having or requiring a cause, Sir W. Hamilton may be charged with the scientific blunder which he imputes, far less justly, to Brown: he "professes to explain the phænomcnon of causality, but previously to explanation, evacuates the phænomenon of all that desiderates explanation."†

Sir W. Hamilton was familiar with the teaching of the Aristotelian schools concerning the four Causes—or rather the four meanings of the word Cause, for synonymy and homonymy were, in their classifications, very often confounded: 1, Materia. 2, Forma. 3, Efficiens. 4, Finis: Efficiens being the only one of these which answers either to the common, or to the modern philosophical notion of Cause. Sir W. Hamilton confounds Materia with Efficiens; or rather ignores Efficiens altogether, and imagines that when the rest of the world are speaking of Efficiens, they mean Materia. It is the very thing which they pre-eminently do not mean. Sir W. Hamilton may choose to call nothing Existence except the permanent element in phænomena; but it is the changeable element, and no other, which is referred to a cause, or which could ever have given the notion of causation.

Sir W. Hamilton says that the total cause—that the "concurring or co-efficient causes, in fact, constitute the effect."‡ And again, "an effect" is

Lectures, Vol. II, Appendix [iv] on Causation, p. 538.
†*Ibid.*, Vol. II, p. 384.
‡*Ibid.*, Vol. I, p. 59.

ᶜ⁻ᶜ65¹, 65² form

"nothing more than the sum or complement of all the partial causes, the concurrence of which constitutes its existence."* "An effect is nothing but the actual union of its constituent entities;" "causes always continue actually to exist in their effects."† Because the original matter continues to exist in the matter transformed, the Efficiens which transformed it continues to exist in the fact of the change! Of course he takes as his example a case in which the material is the prominent thing, that of a salt, compounded of an acid and an alkali.

Considering the salt as an effect, what are the concurrent causes,—the co-efficients,—which constitute it what it is? There are, first, the acid, with its affinity to the alkali; secondly, the alkali, with its affinity to the acid; and thirdly, the translating force (perhaps the human hand) which made their affinities available, by bringing the two bodies within the sphere of mutual attraction. Each of these three concurrents must be considered as a partial cause; for abstract any one, and the effect is not produced.‡

Strange that even this first degree of analysis should not have opened his eyes to the fact, that the moment he admits into *causa efficiens* anything more than *materia*, his theory is at an end. For he will indeed find in the salt, two of his three "co-efficients," the acid and the alkali, with their *ᵈ*affinity*ᵈ*; but where will he find in it "the translating force, perhaps the human hand?" This essential "concause" does not embarrass him at all; it costs him nothing to make away with it altogether. "This last," he says, "as a transitory condition and not always the same, we shall throw out of account."§ If we throw out of account all that is transitory, we have no difficulty in proving that all that is left is permanent. But the transitory conditions are as much a part of the cause as the permanent conditions. Our author has just before said that he takes the term causes "as synonymous for all without which the effect would not be;" and if the effect is "the sum or complement" of all the causes, the transitory as well as the permanent elements must be found in it. To exclude all the transitory part of the cause, is to exclude the whole cause, except the materials. Suppose the effect to be St. Paul's: in assigning its causes, the will of the government, the mind of the architect, and the labour of the builders, are all cast out, for they are all transitory, and only the stones and mortar remain.¶

Ibid., p. 97.
†*Ibid.*, Vol. II, p. 540.
‡*Ibid.*, Vol. I, p. 59.
§*Ibid.*, p. 97.
¶On the same shoal is stranded an argument appended to the same discussion, which our author seems to think of considerable value in the establishment of a First Cause. The progress from cause to effect, he says, is from the simpler to the more

ᵈ⁻ᵈ65¹, 65² affinities

It will have been remarked, that in propounding this theory of the belief in Causation, Sir W. Hamilton gives up Causation as a necessary law of the universe; maintaining that a fact is not to be supposed impossible to Nature because we are impotent to conceive it, and indeed regarding the free acts of an intelligent being as an exception to the universality of the law of Cause and Effect. But while in one place he pays this homage to his own principles, in another he entirely takes leave of them, and glides back into the beaten path of the school of thought which, erecting human capacities of conception into the measure of the universe, maintains that causes must be, because we are incapable of conceiving phænomena without them. After describing the process of ascending from cause to cause, quite gratuitously, as a progress towards unity, Sir W. Hamilton says,

Philosophy thus, as the knowledge of effects in their causes, necessarily tends, not towards a plurality of ultimate or first causes, but towards one alone. This first cause, the Creator, it can indeed never reach, as an object of immediate knowledge; but, as the convergence towards unity in the ascending series is manifest in so far as that series is within our view [here he confounds convergence from many to few with convergence towards one] *and as it is even impossible for the mind to suppose the convergence not continuous and complete*, it follows, unless all analogy be rejected—unless our intelligence be declared a lie, that we must, philosophically, believe in that ultimate or primary unity which, in our present existence, we are not destined in itself to apprehend.*

A deliverance more radically at variance with the author's own canons, could scarcely have been made. For, first, one of the principal of them is, that our inability to conceive a thing as possible, is no argument whatever against its being true. In the second place, the alleged impossibility of

---

complex. "The lower we descend in the series of causes, the more complex will be the product; the higher we ascend, it will be the more simple." To prove this, he appeals to his example, the composition of a salt. (*Ibid.*, pp. 59–60.) Now, the salt is indeed more complex than either of its chemical ingredients, the acid and the alkali; but need it be, or is it, more complex than the remaining "co-efficient," the human hand, or whatever power, natural or artificial, brings the acid and alkali together? The event which causes, may be in any degree whatever a more complex fact, than the event which is caused by it.

*e*Professor Bain (*Logic*, Pt. II, p. 36) considers Sir W. Hamilton's theory of Causation to be an anticipation of the scientific doctrine of the Conservation of Force. There is, doubtless, some analogy between them, but they seem to me radically different. Force is the principle of Change, and is, therefore, really the leading ingredient in causation: but the conservation in Sir W. Hamilton's theory is conservation of the element which has nothing to do with change. It is only equivalent to the old established fact of the unchangeableness in the quantity of Matter, in other words, of Resistance.*e*

Lectures, Vol. I, p. 60. [The words in square brackets are Mill's.]

e-e+72

conceiving any of the phænomena of the universe to be uncaused, applies equally, on his own showing, to the First Cause itself. For, though he here talks only of one inconceivability, we are, if his theory be correct, under the pressure of two counter-inconceivabilities—being equally unable to conceive an uncaused beginning, or an infinite regress from effect to cause: it is equally inconceivable to us that there should, as that there should not, be a First Cause. In this difficulty, by what right does he (I mean merely as a philosopher, and on his own principles) select one of the rival inconceivabilities as the real interpreter of Nature, in preference to the other? And, having selected it, why apply it up to a certain point, and there stop? Why must all the phænomena of experience be referred to a single Cause, because we cannot conceive anything uncaused, and that single Cause be proclaimed uncaused, notwithstanding the same impossibility? An argument by Sir W. Hamilton would not be complete unless it wound up with his tiresome final appeal, "unless our intelligence be declared a lie." It is time to understand, once for all, what this means. Does it mean that if our intelligence cannot conceive one thing apart from another, the one thing cannot exist without the other? If yes, what becomes of the Philosophy of the Conditioned? If no, what becomes of the present argument?*

Sir W. Hamilton makes a far better figure when arguing against other theories of Causation, than when maintaining his own. He is usually acute in finding the weak points in other people's philosophies; and he brings this talent into play, effectively enough, on the present subject. He is not, indeed, at all successful in combating the doctrine (substantially that of Hume and Brown) that it is experience which proves the fact of causation,

*[72] It has been suggested to me by a correspondent to whom I have more than once adverted, as an explanation of Sir W. Hamilton's conflicting language respecting conceivability as a test of truth, that he probably distinguished between what may be termed unilateral and bilateral inconceivableness. I state the distinction in the words of my able correspondent. "Bilateral inconceivableness is no test of truth, for the obvious reason that it applies equally to two contradictory propositions. But Hamilton thought unilateral inconceivableness—an inconceivableness limited to one side of a question only—a proof of a positive deliverance of consciousness on the other side. Hamilton therefore frequently employs the principle that what is unilaterally inconceivable must be false, while he invariably denies that bilateral inconceivableness is any test of falsehood."

Sir W. Hamilton may have had some such distinction in his mind, though if he had, it would not have been going out of his way to have stated it, instead of constantly enunciating the doctrine that things inconceivable to us may be true, in language which recognises no difference between the two cases. But the distinction, if he made it, is of no service to him. If it is possible for anything to be true which is inconceivable to us, the inconceivability of a supposition cannot be a deliverance of consciousness against it. On the contrary, the fact that both sides of an alternative which has no third side may be inconceivable, is a *reductio ad absurdum* of the opinion that inconceivability is an evidence of falsehood.

and association which generates the idea: for against this he only has to say, that experience and association cannot account for necessity. Now, as to real necessity, we do not know that it exists in the case. Sir W. Hamilton himself is of opinion that it does not, and that there are phænomena (the volitions of rational intelligences) which do not depend on causes. And as for the *feeling* of necessity, or what is termed a necessity of thought, it is (as I have already observed),[*] of all mental phænomena positively the one which an inseparable association is the most evidently competent to generate. I cannot, therefore, attribute any value to Sir W. Hamilton's discussion of this point; but in his refutation of some of the theories of causation which have originated in his own hemisphere of the intellectual world, he is very felicitous. Take, for example, the doctrine of Wolf and the Leibnitzians (though not of Leibnitz), which "attempts to establish the principle of Causality upon the principle of Contradiction."[†] "Listen," says our author,

to the pretended demonstration:—Whatever is produced without a cause, is produced by nothing; in other words, has nothing for its cause. But nothing can no more be a cause than it can be something. The same intuition which makes us aware, that nothing is not something, shows us that everything must have a real cause of its existence.—To this it is sufficient to say, that the existence of causes being the point in question, the existence of causes must not be taken for granted, in the very reasoning which attempts to prove their reality. In excluding causes, we exclude all causes; and consequently we exclude Nothing, considered as a cause; it is not, therefore, allowable, contrary to that exclusion, to suppose Nothing as a cause, and then from the absurdity of that supposition to infer the absurdity of the exclusion itself. If everything must have a cause, it follows that, upon the exclusion of other causes, we must accept of Nothing as a cause. But it is the very point at issue, whether everything must have a cause or not; and therefore it violates the first principles of reasoning to take this quæsitum itself as granted. This opinion, [adds our author,] is now universally abandoned.*

But there is another theory of Causation which is not abandoned, but has formed for some time past the stronghold of the Intuitive school. This is, that we acquire both our notion of Causation, and our belief in it, from an internal consciousness of power exerted by ourselves, in our voluntary actions: that is, in the motions of our bodies, for our will has no other direct action on the outward world. This relation of the act of will to the bodily movement, it is maintained, is "not a simple relation of succession. The will is not for us a pure act without efficiency; it is a productive energy; so that in volition there is given to us the notion of cause; and this notion we subsequently transport,—project out from our internal activities, into the changes of the external world."

[*See p. 261 above.]
[†*Lectures*, Vol. II, p. 396.]
*Ibid., p. 397.

To this doctrine Sir W. Hamilton gives the following conclusive answer.

This reasoning, in so far as regards the mere empirical fact of our consciousness of causality, in the relation of our will as moving and of our limbs as moved, is refuted by the consideration, that between the overt fact of corporeal movement of which we are cognisant, and the internal act of mental determination of which we are also cognisant, there intervenes a numerous series of intermediate agencies of which we have no knowledge; and consequently, that we can have no consciousness of any causal connexion between the extreme links of this chain,—the volition to move and the limb moving, as this hypothesis asserts. No one is immediately conscious, for example, of moving his arm through his volition. Previously to this ultimate movement, muscles, nerves, a multitude of solid and fluid parts must be set in motion by the will, but of this motion we know, from consciousness, actually nothing. A person struck with paralysis is conscious of no inability in his limb, to fulfil the determination of his will; and it is only after having willed, and finding that his limbs do not obey his volition, that he learns by this experience, that the external movement does not follow the internal act. But as the paralytic learns after the volition that his limbs do not obey his mind; so it is only after the volition that the man in health learns that his limbs do obey the mandates of his will.*

With this reasoning, borrowed as our author admits from Hume, I entirely agree; and I wonder that it did not prove to Sir W. Hamilton how little the objection to a doctrine, that it is opposed to our natural beliefs, deserves the exaggerated value he sets upon it; for if there is a natural belief belonging to us, I should suppose it to be, that we are directly conscious of ability to move our limbs. It is, nevertheless, our author's opinion that the belief is groundless, and that we learn even a fact so closely connected with us, in the way in which any bystander learns it; by outward observation.†

*Ibid., pp. 391–2. The same argument is restated in the "Dissertations on Reid" with some additional development. "Volition to move a limb, and the actual moving of it, are the first and last in a series of more than two successive events, and cannot, therefore, stand to each other, immediately, in the relation of cause and effect. They may, however, stand to each other in the relation of cause and effect, mediately. But then, if they can be known in consciousness as thus mediately related, it is a necessary condition of such knowledge, that the intervening series of causes and effects, through which the final movement of the limb is supposed to be mediately dependent on the primary volition to move, should be known to consciousness immediately under that relation. But this intermediate, this connecting series is confessedly unknown to consciousness at all, far less as a series of causes and effects. It follows therefore à fortiori, that the dependency of the last on the first of these events, as of an effect upon its cause, must be to consciousness unknown. In other words: having no consciousness that the volition to move is the efficacious force (power) by which even the event immediately consequent on it (say the transmission of the nervous influence from brain to muscle) is produced, such event being, in fact, itself to consciousness occult; multo minus can we have a consciousness of that volition being the efficacious force by which the ultimate movement of the limb is mediately determined." ([Note D,] pp. 866n–7n.)

†Sir W. Hamilton adds, as a further objection to the theory, that it does not account for that, in our notion of causation, which is the sole ground for rejecting

Mr. Mansel, who agrees with Sir W. Hamilton in so many of his opinions, separates from him here, and adopts a modified form of the Volitional Theory. He acknowledges the validity of Hume's and Sir W. Hamilton's argument, and does not derive the idea of Power or Causation from mind acting upon body—from my will producing my bodily motions—but from myself producing my will. "In every act of volition, I am fully conscious that it is in my power to form the resolution or to abstain; and this constitutes the presentative consciousness of free will and of power."* And the sole notion we have of causation in the outward universe, as anything more than invariable antecedence and consequence, "is that of a relation between two objects, similar to that which exists between ourselves and our volitions."† Thus interpreted, continues Mr. Mansel, it is

an interesting illustration of the universal tendency of men to identify, as far as may be, other agents with themselves, even when the identification tends to the destruction of all clear thinking:—furnishing a psychological explanation of a form of speech which has prevailed and will continue to prevail among all people in all times, but not properly to be called a *necessary truth*, nor capable of any scientific application; inasmuch as, in any such application, it may be true or false, without our being able to determine which, as the object of which it treats never comes within the reach of our faculties. What is meant by *power* in a fire to melt wax? How and when is it exerted, and in what manner does it come under our cognizance? Supposing such power to be suspended by an act of Omnipotence, the Supreme Being at the same time producing the succession of phænomena by the immediate interposition of his own will,—could we in any way detect the change? Or suppose the course of nature to be governed by a pre-established harmony, which ordained that at a certain moment fire and wax should be in the neighbourhood of each other, that, at the same moment, fire by itself should burn, and wax by its own laws should melt, neither affecting the other,—would not all the perceptible phænomena be precisely the same as at present? These suppositions may be extravagant, though they are supported by some of the most eminent names in philosophy; but the mere possibility of making them shows that the rival hypothesis is not a necessary truth; the various principles being opposed, only like the vortices of Descartes and the gravitation of Newton, as more or less plausible methods of accounting for the same physical phænomena.‡

Mr. Mansel recognises the possibility that in some other portion of the universe, phænomena may succeed one another at random, without laws of causation, or by laws which are continually changing. We cannot, he says,

---

the Experience theory of it: its "quality of necessity and universality." [*Lectures*, Vol. II, p. 392.] And this is true: the philosophers who combat the Experience theory of causation by the Volitional one, deprive themselves of a very bad, but still the best argument on their side of the question.

Prolegomena Logica, p. 139.

†*Ibid*., p. 140.

‡*Ibid*., pp. 142–3. [For Descartes, see *Principia Philosophiæ*, pp. 51, 61 ff. (III, xxx, lxv ff.).]

*f*conceive*f* this state of things, but we can *g*suppose*g* it; and this very inability to conceive a phænomenon as taking place without a cause—in other words, this subjective necessity of the law of cause and effect—results, in his opinion, merely from the conditions of our experience. If we were asked, why a physical change must have a cause,

we should probably reply—Because matter cannot change of itself. But why cannot we think of matter as changing itself? Because *power*, and the *origination of change*, or self-determination, have never been given to us, save in one form, that of the actions of the conscious self. What I am to conceive as taking place, I must conceive as taking place in the only manner of taking place in which it has ever been presented to me. [Here Mr. Mansel exaggerates one of the consequences of the law of Inseparable Association, through his having reached the consequence only empirically, and not analysed it by *h*means of*h* the law.] This reduces the law of Causality, in one sense indeed to an empirical principle, but to an empirical principle of a very peculiar character; one namely, in which it is psychologically impossible that experience should testify in more than one way. Such principles, however empirical in their origin, are co-extensive in their application with the whole domain of thought.*

And further on,

To call the Principle of Causality as thus explained a Law of Thought, would be incorrect. We cannot think the contrary, not because the laws of thought forbid us, but because the material for thought is wanting. Thought is subject to two different modes of restriction: firstly, from its own laws, by which it is restricted as to its form; and secondly, from the laws of intuition, by which it is restricted as to its matter. The restriction, in the present instance, is of the latter kind. We cannot conceive a course of nature without uniform succession, as we cannot conceive a being who sees without eyes or hears without ears; because we cannot, under existing circumstances, experience the necessary intuition. But such things may, notwithstanding, exist; and under other circumstances, they might become objects of possible conception, the laws of the process of conception remaining unaltered.†

In this exposition, which, I do not hesitate to say, contains more sound philosophy than is to be found on the same subject in all Sir W. Hamilton's writings, I must, nevertheless, take exception to the main doctrine—that the type on which we frame our notion of Power or Causation in general, is the power, not of our volitions over matter, but of our Self over our volitions. In common with one half of the psychological world, I am wholly ignorant of my possessing any such power. I can indeed influence my own volitions, but only as other people can influence my volitions, by the employment of appropriate means. Direct power over my volitions I am

Ibid., p. 148. [The words in square brackets are Mill's.]
†*Ibid.*, pp. 149–50.

*f-f*65¹   *conceive*
*g-g*65¹   *suppose*
h-h+65², 67, 72

conscious of none. However possible it may be that I possess this power without knowing it, a fact of consciousness contestable and contested cannot well be the source and prototype of an idea common to all mankind. I agree, however, with Mr. Mansel[*] in the opinion which he shares with Comte, James Mill, and many others who see nothing in causation but invariable antecedence; that we naturally, and unavoidably, form our first conception of all the agencies in the universe from the analogy of human volitions. The obvious reason is, that nearly everything which is interesting to us, comes, in our earliest infancy, either from our own voluntary motions, or (a consideration too much neglected) from the voluntary motions of others; and, among the few sequences of phænomena which at that time fall within the scope of our perceptions, scarcely any others afford us the spectacle of an apparently absolute commencement; of one thing setting others in motion without being in motion itself—or originating changes in other things, while not itself undergoing any visible change. But as I do not believe, any more than Sir W. Hamilton or Mr. Mansel, that the state of mind called volition carries with it a prophetic anticipation, which can inform us prior to experience that volition will be followed by an effect; I conceive that, no more in this than in any other case of causation, have we evidence of anything more than what experience informs us of: and it informs us of nothing except immediate, invariable, and unconditional sequence.

It is allowed on all hands that part, at least, of our idea of power, is the expectation we feel, that when the cause exists, we shall perceive the effect; but Hume himself admits that in the common notion of power there is an additional element, an animal *nisus*, as he calls it,[†] which would be more properly termed a conception of effort. That this idea of effort enters into our notion of Power, is to my mind one of the strongest proofs that this notion is not derived from the relation of ourselves to our volitions, but from that of our volitions to our actions. The idea of Effort is essentially a notion derived from the action of our muscles, or from that combined with affections of our brain and nerves. Every one of our muscular movements has to contend against resistance, either that of an outward object, or the mere friction and weight of the moving organ; every voluntary motion is consequently attended by the muscular sensation of resistance, and if sufficiently prolonged, by the additional muscular sensation of fatigue. Effort, considered as an accompaniment of action upon the outward world, means nothing, to us, but those muscular sensations. Since we experience

[*See *ibid.*, pp. 149–53.]

[†See "Of the Idea of Necessary Connection," Section vii of *An Inquiry Concerning Human Understanding*, in *Essays and Treatises*, Vol. II, p. 82, and Note C, pp. 601–2.]

them whenever we voluntarily move an object, we by a mere act of natural generalization, the unconscious result of association, on beholding the same object moved by the wind or by any other agent, conceive the wind as overcoming the same obstacle, and figure it to ourselves as putting forth the same effort. Children and savages sincerely mistake it for a conscious effort. We outgrow that belief; but it is not conformable to the mode of action of the human intellect that it should pass *uno saltu*, from a complete assimilation of the two phænomena, to conceiving them as totally different. The "natural tendency of men" so justly characterized by Mr. Mansel, "to identify, as far as may be, other agents with themselves,"[*] does not admit itself baffled and give up the attempt after the first failure. The consequents being the same, when the mind is no longer able to suppose an exact parity in the antecedents, it still thinks that there must be something in common between them: and when obliged to admit that there is volition in one case, and a mere unconscious object in the other, it interposes between the antecedent and the consequent an abstract entity, to express what is supposed common to the animate and the inanimate agency—through which they both work, and in the absence of which nothing would be effected. This purely subjective notion, the product of generalization and abstraction acting on the real feeling of muscular or nervous effort, is Power. And this, I conceive, is the psychological rationale of Comte's great historical generalization, that the metaphysical conception (as he terms it) of the universe succeeds by a natural law to the Fetish conception, and becomes the agent by which the Fetish theory is transformed into Polytheism, this into Monotheism, and Monotheism itself is frittered away into energies and attributes of Nature, and other subordinate abstractions.[†]

Thus much respecting Causation as a conception of the mind. The law of Cause and Effect in its objective aspect, as the fundamental principle in the order of the universe, the basis of most of our knowledge, and the guide of all our action, has been so fully treated in its numerous bearings in my *System of Logic*, that it is needless for me to speak further of it here.[‡]

[**Prolegomena Logica*, p. 142.]
[†See, e.g., Auguste Comte, *Cours de philosophie positive*, Vol. V, pp. 85–7, 383–6, 432n–3n.]
[‡See *System of Logic*, Bk. III, Chap. v, in *Collected Works*, Vol. VII, pp. 323ff.]

CHAPTER XVII

The Doctrine of Concepts, or General Notions

WE NOW ARRIVE at the questions which form the transition from Psychology to Logic—from the analysis and laws of the mental operations, to the theory of the ascertainment of objective truth: the natural link between the two being the theory of the particular mental operations whereby truth is ascertained or authenticated. According to the common classification, from which Sir W. Hamilton does not deviate, these operations are three: Conception, or the formation of General Notions; Judgment; and Reasoning. We begin with the first.

On this subject two questions present themselves: first, whether there are such things as General Notions, and secondly, what they are. If there are General Notions, they must be the notions which are expressed by general terms; and concerning general terms, all who have the most elementary knowledge of the history of metaphysics are aware that there are, or once were, three different opinions.

The first is that of the Realists, who maintained that General Names are the names of General Things. Besides individual things, they recognised another kind of Things, not individual, which they technically called Second Substances, or Universals *a parte rei*. Over and above all individual men and women, there was an entity called Man—Man in general, which inhered in the individual men and women, and communicated to them its essence. These Universal Substances they considered to be a much more dignified kind of beings than individual substances, and the only ones the cognizance of which deserved the names of Science and Knowledge. Individual existences were fleeting and perishable, but the beings called Genera and Species were immortal and unchangeable.

This, the most prevalent philosophical doctrine of the middle ages, is now universally abandoned, but remains a fact of great significance in the history of philosophy; being one of the most striking examples of the tendency of the human mind to infer difference of things from difference of names,—to suppose that every different class of names implied a corresponding class of real entities to be denoted by them. Having two such different names as "man" and "Socrates," these inquirers thought it quite out of the question that man should only be a name for Socrates, and others like him, regarded in a particular light. Man, being a name common to many, must be the name of a substance common to many, and in mystic union with the individual substances, Socrates and the rest.

In the later middle ages there grew up a rival school of metaphysicians, termed Nominalists, who repudiating Universal Substances, held that there is nothing general except names. A name, they said, is general, if it is applied in the same acceptation to a plurality of things; but every one of the things is individual. The dispute between these two sects of philosophers was very bitter, and assumed the character of a religious quarrel: authority, too, interfered in it, and as usual on the wrong side. The Realist theory was represented as the orthodox doctrine, and belief in it was imposed as a religious duty. It could not, however, permanently resist philosophical criticism, and it perished. But it did not leave Nominalism in possession of the field. A third doctrine arose, which endeavoured to steer between the two. According to this, which is known by the name of Conceptualism, generality is not an attribute solely of names, but also of thoughts. External objects indeed are all individual, but to every general name corresponds a General Notion, or Conception, called by Locke[*] and others an Abstract Idea. General Names are the names of these Abstract Ideas.

Realism being no longer extant, nor likely to be revived, the contest at present is between Nominalism and Conceptualism; each of which counts illustrious names among its modern adherents. Sir W. Hamilton professes allegiance to both, affirming "that the opposing parties are really at one."* But his general mode of thought, and habitual phraseology, are purely Conceptualist. This is already apparent in the passage I shall first quote, which contains his statement of the fact to be explained. It is preceded by a remark on Abstraction which is perfectly just, and throws great light on the processes of human thought. Abstraction, he says, is simply the concentration of our attention on a particular object, or a particular quality of an object, and diversion of it from everything else. There may be abstraction, therefore, without generalization. "The notion of the figure of the desk before me is an abstract idea,—an idea that makes part of the total notion of that body, and on which I have concentrated my attention, in order to consider it exclusively. This idea is abstract, but it is at the same time individual; it represents the figure of this particular desk, and not the figure of any other body."[†]

[*See *Essay Concerning Human Understanding, Works*, Vol. II, pp. 138–9 (Bk. II, Chap. xxxii, §§6–8).]

Lectures, Vol. II, p. 296; and foot-note to Reid, p. 412n.

[†]*Lectures*, Vol. II, pp. 287–8.

There are, therefore, "individual abstract notions;" but there are also "Abstract General Notions." These are formed

when, comparing a number of objects, we seize on their resemblances; when we concentrate our attention on these points of similarity, thus abstracting the mind from a consideration of their differences; and when we give a name to our notion of that circumstance in which they all agree. The general notion is thus one which makes us know a quality, property, power, notion, relation; in short, any point of view under which we recognise a plurality of objects as a unity. It makes us aware of a quality, a point of view, common to many things. It is a notion of resemblance; hence the reason why general names or terms, the signs of general notions, have been called *terms of resemblance (termini similitudinis)*. In this process of generalization, we do not stop short at a first generalization. By a first generalization we have obtained a number of classes of resembling individuals. But these classes we can compare together, observe their similarities, abstract from their differences, and bestow on their common circumstance a common name. On these second classes we can again perform the same operation, and thus ascending the scale of general notions, throwing out of view always a greater number of differences, and seizing always on fewer similarities in the formation of our classes, we arrive at length at the limit of our ascent in the notion of *being* or *existence*. Thus placed on the summit of the scale of classes, we descend by a process the reverse of that by which we have ascended; we divide and subdivide the classes, by introducing always more and more characters, and laying always fewer differences aside; the notions become more and more composite, until we at length arrive at the individual.

I may here notice that there is a twofold quantity to be considered in notions. It is evident that, in proportion as the class is high, it will, in the first place, contain under it a greater number of classes, and in the second, will include the smallest complement of attributes. Thus *being* or *existence* contains under it every class; and yet when we say that a thing exists, we say the very least of it that is possible. On the other hand, an individual, though it contain nothing but itself, involves the largest amount of predication. For example, when I say—this is Richard, I not only affirm of the subject every class from existence down to man, but likewise a number of circumstances proper to Richard as an individual. Now, the former of these quantities, the external, is called the Extension of a notion; the latter, the internal quantity, is called its Comprehension or Intension. . . . The internal and external quantities are in the inverse ratio of each other. The greater the extension, the less the comprehension; the greater the comprehension, the less the extension.*

As a popular account of Classification, for learners, to be followed by a more scientific exposition, this fully answers its purpose; but it is expressed in the common language of Conceptualists, and we should naturally conclude from it that the author was a Conceptualist. He however asserts the doctrine of the Nominalists, that there are no general notions, and that the notion suggested by a general name is always singular or individual, to be "not only true but self-evident." And he quotes as "irrefragable"† the

Ibid., pp. 288–90.
†*Ibid.*, pp. 297–8.

argument of Berkeley, directed against the very possibility of Abstract Ideas. The passage from Berkeley is in the Introduction to his *Principles of Human Knowledge*, and is as follows:

It is agreed, on all hands, that the qualities or modes of things, do never really exist each of them apart by itself, and separated from all others, but are mixed, as it were, and blended together, several in the same object. But, we are told, the mind, being able to consider each quality singly, or abstracted from those other qualities with which it is united, does by that means frame to itself abstract ideas. For example, there is perceived by sight an object extended, coloured, and moved; this mixed or compound idea the mind resolving into its simple constituent parts, and viewing each by itself, exclusive of the rest, does frame the abstract ideas of extension, colour, and motion. Not that it is possible for colour or motion to exist without extension; but only that the mind can frame to itself by *abstraction* the idea of colour exclusive of extension, and of motion exclusive of both colour and extension.

Again, the mind having observed that in the particular extensions perceived by sense, there is something common and alike in all, and some other things peculiar, as this or that figure or magnitude, which distinguish them one from another; it considers apart or singles out by itself that which is common, making thereof a most abstract idea of extension, which is neither line, surface, nor solid, nor has any figure or magnitude, but is an idea entirely prescinded from all these. So, likewise, the mind, by leaving out of the particular colours perceived by sense, that which distinguishes them one from another, and retaining that only which is common to all, makes an idea of colour in abstract, which is neither red, nor blue, nor white, nor any other determinate colour. And, in like manner, by considering motion abstractedly not only from the body moved, but likewise from the figure it describes, and all particular directions and velocities, the abstract idea of motion is framed; which equally corresponds to all particular motions whatever that may be perceived by sense.

Whether others have this wonderful faculty of abstracting their ideas, they best can tell: for myself I find, indeed, I have a faculty of imagining, or representing to myself the ideas of those particular things I have perceived, and of variously compounding and dividing them. I can imagine a man with two heads, or the upper part of a man joined to the body of a horse. I can consider the hand, the eye, the nose, each by itself abstracted or separated from the rest of the body. But then whatever hand or eye I imagine, it must have some particular shape and colour. Likewise the idea of man that I frame to myself, must be either of a white, or a black, or a tawny, a straight, or a crooked, a tall, or a low, or a middle-sized man. I cannot by any effort of thought conceive the abstract idea above described. And it is equally impossible for me to form the abstract idea of motion distinct from the body moving, and which is neither swift nor slow, curvilinear nor rectilinear; and the like may be said of all other abstract general ideas whatsoever. To be plain, I am myself able to abstract in one sense, as when I consider some particular parts or qualities separated from others, with which though they are united in some object, yet it is possible they may really exist without them. But I deny that I can abstract one from another, or conceive separately, those qualities which it is impossible should exist so separated; or that I can frame a general notion by abstracting from particulars in the manner aforesaid. Which two last are the proper acceptations of *abstraction*.

And there are grounds to think most men will acknowledge themselves to be in my case.*

It is evident, indeed, that the existence of Abstract Ideas—the conception of the class-qualities by themselves, and not as embodied in an individual—is effectually precluded by the law of Inseparable Association.

In what manner Sir W. Hamilton manages to combine two theories, which in words are, and in substance have always been believed to be, directly contradictory of one another, we learn only from his Lectures on Logic. The hearers of those on Metaphysics, unless the Professor supplied oral elucidations which do not appear in the text, must have been considerably puzzled by finding the task of reconciling the two doctrines thrown entirely on themselves. In the Lectures on Logic, however, an attempt is made to perform it for them. It is there stated, that the General Notion, which Sir W. Hamilton terms a Concept, and which is the notion we form of some "point of similarity"[*] between individual objects,

is not cognizable in itself, that is, it affords no absolute or irrespective object of Knowledge, but can only be realized in consciousness by applying it as a term of relation, to one or more of the objects, which agree in the point or points of resemblance which it expresses. . . . The moment we attempt to represent to ourselves any of these concepts, any of these abstract generalities, as absolute objects, by themselves, and out of relation to any concrete or individual realities, their relative nature at once reappears; for we find it altogether impossible to represent any of the qualities expressed by a concept, except as attached to some individual and determinate object, and their whole generality consists in this, that though we must realize them in thought under some singular of the class, we may do it under any. Thus, for example, we cannot actually represent the bundle of attributes contained in the concept *man* as an absolute object by itself, and apart from all that reduces it from a general cognition to an individual representation. We cannot figure in imagination any object adequate to the general notion or term *man*; for the man to be here imagined must be neither tall nor short, neither fat nor lean, neither black nor white, neither man nor woman, neither young nor old, but all and yet none of these at once. The relativity of our concepts is thus shown in the contradiction and absurdity of the opposite hypothesis.[†]

This is sound doctrine, but it is pure Nominalism; as the passage first quoted from our author was pure Conceptualism. It is very necessary that I should quote the additional elucidations given in the succeeding Lecture. A Concept or (General) Notion, he there says, is in this distinguished from a "Presentation of Perception, or Representation of Phantasy," that

*Ibid., pp. 298–300. [Hamilton is quoting from Berkeley, *A Treatise Concerning the Principles of Human Knowledge*, Introduction, §§vii, viii, x, in *Works*, Vol. I, pp. 5–8.]

[*Lectures, Vol. III, p. 125.]

†Ibid., pp. 128–9.

our knowledge through either of the latter is a direct, immediate, irrespective, determinate, individual, and adequate cognition; that is, a singular or individual object is known in itself, by itself, through all its attributes, and without reference to aught but itself. A concept, on the contrary, is an indirect, mediate, indeterminate, and partial cognition of any one of a number of objects, but not an actual representation either of them all, or of the whole attributes of any one object. . . . *

Formed by comparison, [concepts] express only a relation. They cannot, therefore, be held up as an absolute object to consciousness—they cannot be represented as universals, in imagination. They can only be thought of in relation to some one of the individual objects they classify, and when viewed in relation to it, they can be represented in imagination; but then, as actually represented, they no longer constitute general attributions, they fall back into mere special determinations of the individual object in which they are represented. Thus it is, that the generality or universality of concepts is potential, not actual. They are only generals, inasmuch as they may be applied to any of the various objects they contain; but while they cannot be actually elicited into consciousness, except in application to some one or other of these, so they cannot be so applied without losing, *pro tanto*, their universality. Take, for example, the concept *horse*. In so far as by *horse* we merely think of the word, that is, of the combination formed by the letters *h, o, r, s, e,*—this is not a concept at all, as it is a mere representation of certain individual objects. This I only state and eliminate, in order that no possible ambiguity should be allowed to lurk. By *horse*, then, meaning not merely a representation of the word, but a concept relative to certain objects classed under it,—the concept *horse*, I say, cannot, if it remain a concept, that is, a universal attribution, be represented in imagination; but, except it be represented in imagination, it cannot be applied to any object, and, except it be so applied, it cannot be realized in thought at all. You may try to escape the horns of the dilemma, but you cannot. You cannot realize in thought an absolute or irrespective concept, corresponding in universality to the application of the word; for the supposition of this involves numerous contradictions. An existent horse is not a relation, but an extended object possessed of a determinate figure, colour, size, &c.; *horse*, in general, cannot, therefore, be represented, except by an image of something extended, and of a determinate figure, colour, size, &c. Here now emerges the contradiction. If, on the one hand, you do not represent something extended and of a determinate figure, colour, and size, *ª*you have no representation of any horse. There is, therefore, in this alternative, nothing which can be called the actual concept or image of a horse at all. If, on the other hand, you do represent something extended, and of a determinate figure, colour, and size,*ª* then you have, indeed, the image of an individual horse, but not a universal concept coadequate with *horse* in general. For how is it possible to have an actual representation of a figure, which is not a determinate figure? but if of a determinate figure, it must be that of some one of the many different figures under which horses appear; but then, if it be only of one of these, it cannot be the general concept of the others, which it does not represent. In like manner, how is it possible to have the actual representation of a thing coloured, which is not the representation of a determinate colour, that is, either white, or black, or grey, or brown, &c.? but if it be any one of these, it can only represent a horse of this or that particular colour,

Ibid., p. 131.

ª-ª+Source, 67, 72   [*printer's error in* 65[1], 65[2]]

and cannot be the general concept of horses of every colour. The same result is given by the other attributes; and what I originally stated is thus manifest—that concepts have only a potential, not an actual, universality, that is, they are only universal, inasmuch as they may be applied to any of a certain class of objects, but as actually applied, they are no longer general attributions, but only special attributes.*

But if, as our author says, concepts are "incapable of being realized in thought at all," except as representations of individual objects, how are they, even potentially, universal? Being mere mental creations, they *are* nothing except what they can be thought as being; and they cannot be thought as being universal, but only as being part of the thought of an individual object, though the individual object needs not always be the same. This is not a potential universality, though it is an universal potentiality. If, then, the Nominalists are thus completely right, how can it be that the Conceptualists are not wrong?

Our author thinks that the apparent difference between them is a mere case of verbal ambiguity; arising from the "employment of the same terms to express the representations of Imagination, and the notions or concepts of the Understanding." "A relation," he says,

cannot be represented in imagination. The two terms,—the two relative objects, can be severally imaged in the sensible phantasy, but not the relation itself. This is the object of the Comparative Faculty, or of Intelligence Proper. To objects so different as the images of sense and the unpicturable notions of intelligence, different names ought to be given.†

In Germany the question of nominalism and conceptualism has not been agitated, and why? Simply because the German language supplies terms by which concepts (or notions of thought proper) have been contradistinguished from the presentations and representations of the subsidiary faculties.‡

We are therefore to understand that although Imagination cannot figure to itself anything general or universal, Thought Proper, or the Comparative Faculty, or the Understanding, can. But I do not believe that Berkeley, whose argument our author declares "irrefragable," or any other of the great Nominalist thinkers whom he enumerates, would have accepted this distinction. They would, I apprehend, have denied that the attributes included in the so-called General Notion can be ᵇthoughtᵇ separately, any more than they can be imaged separately. But why do I talk of Berkeley? Sir W. Hamilton has himself negatived the distinction in the very passage

*Ibid., pp. 134–6.
†Ibid., Vol. II, p. 312.
‡Ibid., Vol. III, p. 136. The words he means are Begriff and Anschauung. See foot-note to Reid, p. 412n.

ᵇ⁻ᵇ65¹ thought

just quoted, when he says, "the concept *horse* cannot, if it remain a concept, that is, a universal attribution, be represented in imagination; but, *except it be represented in imagination*, it cannot be applied to any object, and except it be so applied, *it cannot be realized in thought*." The simple question is, Can the attributes of horse as a class be objects of thought, except as part of a representation of some individual horse? If the Concept cannot exist in the mind except enveloped in the miscellaneous attributes of an individual—which is the truth, and fully recognised as such in the passages quoted from Sir W. Hamilton,—then it can no more be thought separately by the intellect than depicted separately in the imagination.

This notion of a Concept as something which can be thought, but "cannot in itself be depicted to sense or imagination,"* is supported, as we saw, by calling it a relation. "As the result of a comparison," a concept "necessarily expresses a relation:"† and "a relation cannot be represented in imagination."[*] If a concept is a relation, what relation is it, and between what? "As the result of a comparison," it must be a relation of resemblance among the things compared. I might observe that a concept, which is defined by our author himself "a bundle of attributes,"[†] does not signify the mere fact of resemblance between objects; it signifies our mental representation of that in which they resemble; of the "common circumstance"[‡] which Sir W. Hamilton spoke of in his exposition of Classification. The attributes are not the relation, they are the *fundamentum relationis*. This objection, however, I can afford to wave. However inappropriate the expression, let us admit that a concept is a relation. But if a relation cannot be represented in imagination, our author has just said that "the two terms, the two relative objects,"[§] can. The relation, according to him, though it cannot be imagined, can be thought. But can a relation be thought without thinking the related objects between which it exists? Assuredly, no: and this impossibility can the less be denied by Sir W. Hamilton, as it is the basis on which he founds his theory of Consciousness—of the direct apprehension of the Ego and the Non-ego. Consequently, when we think a relation, we must think it as existing between some particular objects which we think along with it: and a Concept, even if it be the apprehending of a relation, can only be thought as individual, not as general.

*Mansel, *Prolegomena Logica*, p. 15. What a mere play upon words the distinction is, is shown by Mr. Mansel's saying, a few pages later, "In every complete act of conception, the attributes forming the concept are contemplated as coexisting in a possible object of intuition." (P. 29.) So that they *are* "depicted to imagination;" only they are not depicted separately.

†*Lectures*, Vol. III, p. 128.

[*Ibid., Vol. II, p. 312.]

[†Ibid., Vol. III, p. 129.]

[‡Ibid., Vol. II, p. 298.]

[§Ibid., p. 312.]

The true theory of Concepts needs not, I think, be sought farther off than in our author's own account of their origin. "In the formation," he says,

of a concept or notion, the process may be analysed into four momenta. In the first place, we must have a plurality of objects presented or represented by the subsidiary faculties. These faculties must furnish the rude material for elaboration. In the second place, the objects thus applied are, by an act of the Understanding, compared together, and their several qualities judged to be similar or dissimilar. In the third place, an act of volition, called Attention, concentrates consciousness on the qualities thus recognised as similar; and that concentration, by attention, on them, involves an abstraction of consciousness from those which have been recognised and thrown aside as dissimilar; for the power of consciousness is limited, and it is clear or vivid precisely in proportion to the simplicity or oneness of the object. Attention and Abstraction are the two poles of the same act of thought: they are like the opposite scales in a balance, the one must go up as the other goes down. In the fourth place, the qualities, which by comparison are judged similar, and by attention are constituted into an exclusive object of thought,—these are already, by this process, identified in consciousness; for they are only judged similar, inasmuch as they produce in us indiscernible effects. Their synthesis in consciousness may, however, for precision's sake, be stated as a fourth step in the process. But it must be remembered, that at least the three latter steps are not, in reality, distinct and independent acts, but are only so distinguished and stated, in order to enable us to comprehend and speak about the indivisible operation in the different aspects in which we may consider it.*

Let me remark, in passing, the fresh ᶜrecognitionᶜ in the last sentence, of an important principle, already several times adverted to, in the theory of Naming.

The formation, therefore, of a Concept, does not consist in separating the attributes which are said to compose it, from all other attributes of the same object, and enabling us to conceive those attributes, disjoined from any others. We neither conceive them, nor think them, nor cognise them in any way, as a thing apart, but solely as forming, in combination with numerous other attributes, the idea of an individual object. But, though thinking them only as part of a larger agglomeration, we have the power of fixing our attention on them, to the neglect of the other attributes with which we think them combined. While the concentration of attention actually lasts, if it is sufficiently intense, we may be temporarily unconscious of any of the other attributes, and may really, for a brief interval, have nothing present to our mind but the attributes constituent of the concept. In general, however, the attention is not so completely exclusive as this; it leaves room in consciousness for other elements of the concrete idea: though of these the consciousness is faint, in proportion to the energy of the concentrative effort; and the moment the attention relaxes, if the same concrete idea continues to be contemplated, its other constituents

*Ibid., Vol. III, pp. 132–3.

ᶜ⁻ᶜ65¹, 65²   illustration afforded

come out into consciousness. General concepts, therefore, we have, properly speaking, none; we have only complex ideas of objects in the concrete: but we are able to attend exclusively to certain parts of the concrete idea: and by that exclusive attention, we enable those parts to determine exclusively the course of our thoughts as subsequently called up by association; and are in a condition to carry on a train of meditation or reasoning relating to those parts only, exactly as if we were able to conceive them separately from the rest.

What principally enables us to do this is the employment of signs, and particularly the most efficient and familiar kind of signs, viz. Names. This is a point which Sir W. Hamilton puts well and strongly, and there are many reasons for stating it in his own language.

The concept thus formed by an abstraction of the resembling from the non-resembling qualities of objects, would again fall back into the confusion and infinitude from which it has been called out, were it not rendered permanent for consciousness, by being fixed and ratified in a verbal sign. Considered in general, thought and language are reciprocally dependent; each bears all the imperfections and perfections of the other; but without language there could be no knowledge realized of the essential properties of things, and of the connexion of their accidental states.*

The rationale of this is, that when we wish to be able to think of objects in respect of certain of their attributes—to recall no objects but such as are invested with those attributes, and to recall them with our attention directed to those attributes exclusively—we effect this by giving to that combination of attributes, or to the class of objects which possess them, a specific Name. We create an artificial association between those attributes and a certain combination of articulate sounds, which guarantees to us that when we hear the sound, or see the written characters corresponding to it, there will be raised in the mind an idea of some object possessing those attributes, in which idea those attributes alone will be suggested vividly to the mind, our consciousness of the remainder of the concrete idea being faint. As the name has been directly associated only with those attributes, it is as likely, in itself, to recall them in any one concrete combination as in any other. What combination it shall recall in the particular case, depends on recency of experience, accidents of memory, or the influence of other thoughts which have been passing, or are even then passing, through the mind: accordingly, the combination is far from being always the same, and seldom gets itself strongly associated with the name which suggests it; while the association of the name with the attributes that form its conventional signification, is constantly becoming stronger. The association of that particular set of attributes with a given word, is what keeps them

Ibid., p. 137.

together in the mind by a stronger tie than that with which they are associated with the remainder of the concrete image. To express the meaning in Sir W. Hamilton's phraseology, this association gives them an unity* in our consciousness. It is only when this has been accomplished, that we possess what Sir W. Hamilton terms a Concept; and this is the whole of the mental phænomenon involved in the matter. We have a concrete representation, certain of the component elements of which are distinguished by a mark, designating them for special attention; and this attention, in cases of exceptional intensity, excludes all consciousness of the others.

Sir W. Hamilton thinks, however, that we can form, though scarcely preserve, concepts without the aid of signs. "Language," he says, "is the attribution of signs to our cognitions of things. But as a cognition must have been already there, before it could receive a sign; consequently, that knowledge which is denoted by the formation and application of a word, must have preceded the symbol which denotes it." A sign, however, he continues, in one of his happiest specimens of illustration,

is necessary to give stability to our intellectual progress,—to establish each step in our advance as a new starting point for our advance to another beyond. A country may be overrun by an armed host, but it is only conquered by the establishment of fortresses. Words are the fortresses of thought. They enable us to realize our dominion over what we have already overrun in thought; to make every intellectual conquest the basis of operations for others still beyond. Or another illustration: You have all heard of the process of tunnelling—of tunnelling through a sand-bank. In this operation it is impossible to succeed, unless every foot, nay almost every inch in our progress, be secured by an arch of masonry, before we attempt the excavation of another. Now, language is to the mind precisely what the arch is to the tunnel. The power of thinking and the power of excavation are not dependent on the word in the one case, on the mason-work in the other; but without these subsidiaries, neither process could be carried on beyond its rudimentary commencement. Though, therefore, we allow that every movement forward in language must be determined by an antecedent movement forward in thought; still, unless thought be accompanied at each point of its evolution, by a corresponding evolution of

*One of the best and profoundest passages in all Sir W. Hamilton's writings, is that in which he points out (though only incidentally) what are the conditions of our ascribing Unity to any aggregate. "Though it is only by experience we come to attribute an external unity to aught continuously extended, that is, consider it as a system or constituted whole; still, in so far as we do so consider it, *we think the parts as held together by a certain force*, and the whole, therefore, as endowed with a power of resisting their distraction. It is, indeed, only by finding that a material continuity resists distraction, that we view it as more than a fortuitous aggregation of many bodies, that is, as a single body. The material universe, for example, though not *de facto* continuously extended, we consider as one system in so far, but only in so far, as we find all bodies tending together by reciprocal attraction." ("Dissertations on Reid," [Note D,] pp. 852–3.)

language, its further development is arrested. . . . Admitting even that the mind is capable of certain elementary concepts without the fixation and signature of language, still these are but sparks which would twinkle only to expire, and it requires words to give them prominence, and by enabling us to collect and elaborate them into new concepts, to raise out of what would otherwise be only scattered and transitory scintillations, a vivid and enduring light.*

Mr. Mansel, who agrees with Sir W. Hamilton in the essentials of his doctrine of Concepts, goes beyond him on this point, being of opinion that without signs we could not form concepts at all.[*] The objection, that we must have had the concept before we could have given it a name, he meets by the suggestion that names when first used are names only of individual objects, but being extended from one object to another under the law of Association by Resemblance, they become specially associated with the points of Resemblance, and thus generate the Concept. In Mr. Mansel's opinion, no one, "without the aid of symbols," can advance

beyond the individual objects of sense or imagination. In the presence of several individuals of the same species, the eye may observe points of similarity between them; and in this no symbol is needed; but every feature thus observed is the distinct attribute of a distinct individual, and however similar, cannot be regarded as identical. For example: I see lying on the table before me a number of shillings of the same coinage. Examined severally, the image and superscription of each is undistinguishable from that of its fellow; but in viewing them side by side, *space* is a necessary condition of my perception, and the difference of locality is sufficient to make them distinct, though similar individuals. The same is the case with any representative image, whether in a mirror, in a painting, or in the imagination, waking or dreaming. It can only be depicted as occupying a certain place; and thus as an individual, and the representative of an individual. It is true that I cannot say that it represents this particular coin rather than that; and consequently it may be considered as the representative of all, successively but not simultaneously. To find a representative which shall embrace all at once, I must divest it of the condition of occupying space; and this, experience assures us can only be done by means of *symbols*, verbal or other, by which the concept is fixed in the understanding. Such, for example, is a verbal description of the coin in question, which contains a collection of attributes freed from the condition of locality, and hence from all resemblance to an object of sense. If we substitute Time for Space, the same remarks will be equally applicable to the objects of our internal consciousness. Every appetite and desire, every affection and volition, as *presented*, is an individual state of consciousness, distinguished from every other by its relation to a different period of time. States in other respects exactly similar may succeed one another at regular intervals; but the hunger which I feel to-day is an individual feeling as numerically distinct from that which I felt yesterday or that which I shall feel to-morrow, as a shilling lying in my pocket is from a similar shilling lying at the bank. Whereas my *notion* of hunger, or fear, or volition, is a general concept, having no relation to one period of time rather than to another, and, as such, requires, like other concepts, a representative sign. Language, taking the word in its

Lectures, Vol. III, pp. 138–40.
[*See *Prolegomena Logica*, p. 15.]

widest sense, is thus indispensable, not merely to the communication, but to the formation of Thought.*

This is a step in advance of Sir W. Hamilton's doctrine, but is open to the same criticism, namely, that after showing all Concepts to be concrete and individual, it endeavours to make out by an indirect process, a sort of abstract existence for them. According to Mr. Mansel, signs are necessary to concepts, because signs alone can give this abstract existence. Signs are wanted, to emancipate our mental apprehension from the conditions of space and time which are in all our concrete representations. The other miscellaneous attributes which have to be cast out, do not, he seems to think, embarrass the formation of the Concept; but it is hampered by the conditions of space and time, and only by means of a sign can we get rid of these. But *do* we get rid of them by employing signs? To take Mr. Mansel's own instance: When we establish our concept of a shilling by a verbal description of the coin, does the description enable us to conceive a shilling as not occupying any space? When we think of a shilling, either by name or anonymously, is not the circumstance of occupying space called up as an inevitable part of the mental representation? Not, indeed, the circumstance of occupying a *given part* of space; but if that is what Mr. Mansel means, it would follow that we need signs to enable us to form a mental representation even of an individual object, provided it be moveable: for the same object does not always occupy the same part of space. The truth is, that the condition of space cannot be excluded; it is an essential part of the concept of Body, and of every kind of bodies. But any given space, or any given time, is not a part of the concept, any more than any of the slight peculiarities in which one shilling differs from another are part of the concept of a shilling. Some space and time, and some individual peculiarities, are always thought along with the concept, and make up the whole, of which it can only be thought as a part: but these are not directly recalled by the class-name, and the attributes composing the concept are. Mr. Mansel, therefore, has not, I conceive, hit the mark: but in the passages which follow, there is real power of metaphysical discrimination.

Observe what actually takes place in the formation of language and thought among ourselves. To the child learning to speak, words are not the signs of thoughts, but of intuitions:† the words *man* and *horse* do not represent a collection of attributes, but are only the name of the individual now before him. It is not until the name has been successively appropriated to various individuals, that reflection begins to inquire into the common features of the class. Language, therefore, as

Ibid., pp. 15–17.
†By intuitions Mr. Mansel means the Anschauungen of Kant, or what Mr. Mansel himself otherwise calls Presentations of Sense, to which he adds Representations of Imagination [see *Prolegomena Logica*, pp. 9–14].

taught to the infant, is chronologically prior to thought and posterior to sensation. In inquiring how far the same process can account for the invention of language, which now takes place in the learning it, the real question at issue is simply this. Is the act of giving names to *individual objects of sense*, a thing so completely beyond the power of a man created in the full maturity of his faculties, that we must suppose a Divine Instructor performing precisely the same office as is now performed for the infant by his mother or his nurse; teaching him, that is, to associate *this sound* with *this sight*? . . . All concepts are formed by means of signs which have previously been representative of individual objects only. . . . Similarities are noticed earlier than differences: and our first abstractions may be said to be performed for us, as we learn to give the same name to individuals presented to us under slight, and at first unnoticed, circumstances of distinction. The same name is thus applied to different objects, long before we learn to analyse the growing powers of speech and thought, to ask what we mean by each several instance of its application, to correct and fix the signification of words used at first vaguely and obscurely. To point out each successive stage of the process by which signs of intuition become gradually signs of thought, is as impossible as to point out the several moments at which the growing child receives each successive increase of his stature.*

These remarks of Mr. Mansel remove, as it seems to me, the only real argument for the supposition that Concepts, or what are called General Notions, are formed without the aid of signs. But the counter-doctrine must be received with an important reservation. Signs are necessary, but the signs need not be artificial; there are such things as natural signs. The only reality there is in the Concept is, that we are somehow enabled and led, not once or accidentally, but in the common course of our thoughts, to attend specially, and more or less exclusively, to certain parts of the presentation of sense or representation of imagination which we are conscious of. Now, what is there to make us do this? There must be something which, as often as it recurs either to our senses or to our thoughts, *directs* our attention to those particular elements in the perception or in the idea: and whatever performs this office is virtually a sign; but it needs not be a word; the process certainly takes place, to a limited extent, in the inferior animals; and even with human beings who have but a small vocabulary, many processes of thought take place habitually by other symbols than words. It is a doctrine of one of the most fertile thinkers of modern times, Auguste Comte, that besides the logic of signs, there is a logic of images, and a logic of feelings.[*] In many of the familiar processes of thought, and especially in uncultured minds, a visual image serves instead of a word. Our visual sensations—perhaps only because they are almost always present along with the impressions of our other senses—have a facility of becoming associated with them. Hence, the characteristic visual appearance of an

Ibid., pp. 19–20, and 29–31.
[*See *Système de politique positive, ou Traité de sociologie, instituant la religion de l'humanité*, 4 vols. (Paris: Mathias, *et al.*, 1851–54), Vol. I, p. 450.]

object easily gathers round it, by association, the ideas of all other peculiarities which have, in frequent experience, coexisted with that appearance: and, summoning up these with a strength and certainty far surpassing that of the merely casual associations which it may also raise, it concentrates the attention on them. This is an image serving for a sign—the logic of images. The same function may be fulfilled by a feeling. Any strong and highly interesting feeling, connected with one attribute of a group, spontaneously classifies all objects according as they possess or do not possess that attribute. We may be tolerably certain that the things capable of satisfying hunger form a perfectly distinct class in the mind of any of the more intelligent animals; quite as much so as if they were able to use or understand the word food. We here see in a strong light the important truth, that hardly anything universal can be affirmed in psychology except the laws of association. As almost all general propositions which can be laid down respecting Mind, are consequences of these laws, so do these ultimate laws, in varying cases, generate different derivative laws; and are continually raising up exceptions to the empirical generalizations yielded by direct psychical observation, which, so far as true, being mere cases of the wider laws, are always limited by them.

We have now attained a theory of Classification, of Class Notions, and of Class Names, which is clear, free from difficulties, and, in its essential elements, understood and assented to by Sir W. Hamilton. With the exception of a few minor matters, I find no fault in his theory. It is where his theory ends and his practice begins, that I am obliged to diverge from him. His theory is a complete condemnation of his practice. His theory is that of Nominalism; but he affirms, in opposition to every Conceptualist, that Nominalism and Conceptualism are the same, and on this justification expounds all the operations of the intellect in the language, and on the assumptions, of Conceptualism. If a Concept does not exist as a separate or independent object of thought, but is always a mere part of a concrete image, and has nothing that discriminates it from the other parts except a special share of attention, guaranteed to it by special association with a name; what is meant by the paramount place assigned to Concepts in all the intellectual processes? Can it be right to found the whole of Logic, the entire theory of Judgment and Reasoning, upon a thing which has merely a fictitious or constructive existence? Is it correct to say that we think by means of Concepts? Would it not convey both a clearer and a truer meaning, to say that we think by means of ideas of concrete phænomena, such as are presented in experience or represented in imagination, and by means of names, which being in a peculiar manner associated with certain elements of the concrete images, arrest our attention on those elements? Sir W. Hamilton has told us that a concept cannot, as such, be "realized in thought," or "elicited into consciousness."[*] Can it be, that we think and reason by means of that which cannot be thought, of which we cannot become conscious? Of course Sir W. Hamilton did not mean, nor do I, that we cannot think or be conscious of the attributes which are said to compose the concept; but we can only be conscious of them as forming a representation jointly with other attributes which do not enter into the concept. And the difference between the parts of the same representation which are inside and those which are outside what is called the concept, is not that the former are attended to and the latter not, for neither of these is always true. It is, that foreseeing that we shall frequently or occasionally desire to attend only to the former, we have made for ourselves, or have received from our predecessors, a contrivance for being reminded of them, which also serves for fixing our exclusive attention upon them when called to mind. To say, therefore, that we think by means of concepts, is only a circuitous and obscure way of saying that we think by means of general or class names.* [d] To give an intelligible idea of the fact, we always need to translate it out of the former language into the latter. It is possible, no doubt, so to define the terms that both expressions shall mean the same thing. But the less appropriate language has the immense disadvantage, that it cannot be used without tacitly assuming that these mere parts of our complex concrete perceptions and ideas have a separate mental existence, which is admitted not to belong to them. No one, more fully than Sir W. Hamilton, recognises the true theory; but the acknowledgment only serves him as an excuse for

[*_Lectures_, Vol. III, pp. 135, 134; cf. p. 306 above.]
*It is for want of apprehending this view of the matter that Sir W. Hamilton (_Lectures_, Vol. III, pp. 31–2) brings a charge of self-contradiction against Archbishop Whately, because, having in the commencement and throughout his treatise on Logic, represented Reasoning as the object-matter of that science, he, in certain passages, says that Logic is entirely conversant with the use of language. [Cf. Richard Whately, _Elements of Logic_ (London: Mawman, 1828), pp. 1 and 56n.] This is a contradiction only from Sir W. Hamilton's point of view. If Archbishop Whately's had been the same—if he had thought as Sir W. Hamilton did respecting Concepts, considered as the object-matter of Reasoning—he would have been justly liable to the imputation cast upon him. But the Archbishop's two statements are perfectly consistent, if we suppose his opinion to have been, that the formation of Concepts, and the subsequent process of combining them in arguments, are themselves processes of language. This doctrine (which is in fact Mr. Mansel's [see _Prolegomena Logica_, pp. 15–32, 56–69]) Sir W. Hamilton deems too absurd to be imputed to the Archbishop (_Discussions_, p. 138). Yet he fancies himself a Nominalist, and does understand and assent to all the arguments of Nominalism. Unfortunately an intelligent assent to one of two conflicting doctrines is in his case no guarantee against holding, for all practical purposes [e]of thought[e], the other.

[d]65[1], 65[2] [_footnote appears at the end of this paragraph; moved in 67 presumably because another note was added at that place_]
[e-e]+67, 72

delivering himself up unreservedly to all the logical consequences of the false theory. To read the account which he and Mr. Mansel, in common with the great majority of modern logicians, give of our intellectual processes—which they always make to consist essentially of some operation practised upon concepts—no one would ever imagine that concepts were not complete, rounded off, distinct and separate possessions of the mind, habitually dealt with by it quite apart from anything else; and this, in the general opinion of Conceptualists, they are: but according to Sir W. Hamilton and Mr. Mansel, they are secretly, all the while, incapable of being thought except as parts of something else which has always to be dealt with along with them, but which these philosophers, in their expositions, suppress as completely, as if they had forgotten that its necessary presence is part of their theory. For these and other reasons, I *think that the words Concept, General Notion, and other phrases of like import, convenient as they are for the lighter and every-day uses of philosophical discussion, should be abstained from where precision is required*. Above all, I hold that nothing but confusion ever results from introducing the term Concept into Logic, and that instead of the Concept of a class, we should always speak of the signification of a class name.*

The signification of a class name has two aspects, corresponding to the distinction to which Sir W. Hamilton attaches so much importance, between the Extension and the Comprehension of a concept; which is merely a bad expression for the distinction between the two modes of signification of a concrete general name. Most names are still, what according to Mr. Mansel they all were originally, names of objects;[*] and do not cease to be so by becoming class names; but, though names of objects, they become expressive of certain attributes of those objects, and when predicated of an

---

*[67] Dr. M'Cosh says, "I think it desirable to have a phrase to denote, not the 'signification of a class name,' but the thing signified by the class name; and the fittest I can think of is Concept." But the "thing signified" by the class name is the class; the various objects called by the name: and class is a sufficient name for these, nor has the word Concept, to my knowledge, ever been predicated of them, but only of Sir W. Hamilton's "bundles of attributes." ([*Examination,*] pp. 276–7.) *Dr. M'Cosh's use of the word Concept, for the thing conceived, not the conception, is, I believe, peculiar to himself.*

I must add, that the chapter of Dr. M'Cosh from which I am now quoting, that headed "The Logical Notion," contains much sound philosophy, and little with which I disagree except the persistent impression which the author keeps up throughout the chapter that I do disagree with him. [*Ibid.*, Chap. xix, pp. 267–84.]

[*Prolegomena Logica*, pp. 25–32.]

*-*65[1], 65[2] consider it nothing less than a misfortune, that the words Concept, General Notion, or any other phrase to express the supposed mental modification corresponding to a class name, should ever have been invented
-+72

object, they affirm of it those attributes. The name is said, in the language of logicians, to *de*note the objects and *con*note the attributes. *White* denotes chalk and other white substances, and connotes the particular colour which is common to them. *Bird* denotes eagles, sparrows, crows, geese, and so forth, and connotes life, the possession of wings, and the other properties by which we are guided in applying the name. The various objects denoted by the class name are what is meant by the Extension of the concept, while the attributes connoted are its Comprehension. It must be remarked, however, that the Extension is not anything intrinsic to the concept; it is the sum of all the objects, in our concrete images of which, the concept is included: but the Comprehension is the very concept itself, for the concept means nothing but our mental representation of the sum of the attributes composing it.

And here it is important to take notice of a psychological truth, which forms an additional reason for preferring the expression that we think by general names, to that of thinking by concepts. Since the concept only exists as a part of a concrete mental state; if we say that we think by means of it, and not by the whole which it is a part of, it ought at least to be *the* part by which we think. Since that is the only distinction between it and the remainder of the presentation or representation in which it is embedded, at least that distinction should be real: all which enters into the concept ought to be operative in thought. So far is this from being true, that in our processes of thought, seldom more than a part, sometimes a very small part, of what is comprehended in the concept, is attended to, or comes into play. This is forcibly stated, though in Conceptualist phraseology, by Mr. Mansel. "We can," he says,

and in the majority of cases do, employ concepts as instruments of thought, without submitting them to the test of even possible individualization. . . . I cannot *conceive* a triangle which is neither equilateral, nor isosceles, nor scalene; but I can judge and reason about a triangle without at the moment trying to conceive it at all. This is one of the consequences of the representation of concepts by language. *The sign is substituted for the notion signified*; a step which considerably facilitates the performance of complex operations of thought; but in the same proportion endangers the logical accuracy of each successive step, as we do not, in each, stop to verify our signs. Words, as thus employed, resemble algebraical symbols, which, during the process of a long calculation, we combine in various relations to each other, without at the moment thinking of the original signification assigned to each.*

The attempt to stand at once on two incompatible theories, leads to strange freaks of expression. Mr. Mansel describes us as thinking by means of concepts which we are incapable of forming, and do not even attempt to form, but use the signs instead. Yet he will not consent to call this thinking by the signs, but insists that it is the concepts which are even in this case the

Ibid., pp. 31–2.

"instruments of thought." It is surely a very twisted logical position which, when he is so entirely right in what he has to say, compels him to use so strangely contorted a mode of saying it.

The same important psychological fact is excellently illustrated by Sir W. Hamilton in one of the very best chapters of his works, the Tenth Lecture on Logic, in which it is stated as follows:

As a notion or concept is the fictitious whole or unity made up of a plurality of attributes,—a whole, too, often of a very complex multiplicity; and as this multiplicity is only mentally held together, inasmuch as the concept is fixed and ratified in a sign or word; it frequently happens that, in its employment, the word does not suggest the whole amount of thought for which it is the adequate expression, but, on the contrary, we frequently give and take the sign, either with an obscure or indistinct consciousness of its meaning, or even without an actual consciousness of its signification at all.*

The word does not always serve the purpose of fixing our attention on the whole of the attributes which it connotes; some of them may be only recalled to mind faintly, others possibly not at all: a phænomenon *easily*ʰ to be accounted for by the laws of Obliviscence. But the part of the attributes signified which the word does recal, may be all that it is necessary for us to think of, at the time and for the purpose in hand; it may be a sufficient part to set going all the associations by means of which we proceed through that thought to ulterior thoughts. Indeed, it is because part of the attributes have generally sufficed for that purpose, that the habit is acquired of not attending to the remainder. When the attributes not attended to are really of no importance for the end in view, and if attended to would not have altered the results of the mental process, there is no harm done: much of our valid thinking is carried on in this manner, and it is to this that our thinking processes owe, in a great measure, their proverbial rapidity. This kind of thinking was called, by Leibnitz, Symbolical. A passage of one of the early writings of that eminent thinker, in which it is brought to notice with his accustomed clearness, is translated by Sir W. Hamilton, from whom I re-quote it.

For the most part, especially in an analysis of any length, we do not view at once (non simul intuemur) the whole characters or attributes of the thing, but in place of these we employ signs, the explication of which into what they signify we are wont, at the moment of actual thought, to omit, knowing or believing that we have this explication always in our power. Thus, when I think a chiliagon (or polygon of a thousand sides) I do not always consider the various attributes of the side, of the equality, and of the number or thousand, but use these words (whose meaning is obscurely and imperfectly presented to the mind) in lieu of the notions which I have of them, because I remember, that I possess the signification of these words, though

*Lectures, Vol. III, pp. 171–2.

ʰ⁻ʰ65¹, 65², 67   easy

their application and explication I do not at present deem to be necessary:—this mode of thinking, I am used to call *blind* or *symbolical*: we employ it in Algebra and in Arithmetic, but in fact universally. And certainly when the notion is very complex, we cannot think at once all the ingredient notions: but where this is possible,—at least, inasmuch as it is possible,—I call the cognition *intuitive*. Of the primary elements of our notions, there is given no other knowledge than the intuitive: as of our composite notions there is, for the most part, possible only a symbolical.*

Yet the elements which are thus habitually left out, and of which in the case of a composite notion, if Leibnitz is right, some *must* be left out, are really parts of the signification of the name, and if the word Concept has any meaning, are parts of the concept. Leibnitz accordingly knew better than to say, as Mr. Mansel says[*] and Sir W. Hamilton implies, that even in these cases we think by means of the concept. According to him we sometimes think entirely without the concept, generally only by a part of it, which may be the wrong part, or an insufficient part, but which may be, and in all sound thinking is, sufficient. On this point, therefore, a false apprehension of the facts of thought is conveyed by the doctrine which speaks of Concepts as its instrument. Leibnitz would perhaps have said, that the name is the instrument in one of the two kinds of thinking, and the concept in the other. The more reasonable doctrine surely is, that the name is the instrument in both; the difference being, that in one case it does the whole, and in the other only a part, perhaps the minimum, of the work for which it is intended and fitted, that of reminding us of the portions of our concrete mental representations which we expect that we shall have need of attending to.

*Ibid., p. 181. [From Gottfried Wilhelm von Leibniz, *Meditationes de Cognitione, Veritate et Ideis*, in *Opera Philosophica*, ed. Johann Eduard Erdmann (Berlin: Eichler, 1840), pp. 79–80.] It will be remarked that Leibnitz here employs the word Intuitive in a sense entirely different from that which British metaphysicians, and Sir W. Hamilton himself, attach to the word. In Leibnitz's sense, we cognise a thing intuitively in as far as we are conscious of the attributes of the thing itself; symbolically in as far as we merely think of its name, as standing for an aggregate of attributes, without having all, or perhaps any, of those attributes present to our mind. I cannot help being surprised that Sir W. Hamilton should have regarded this distinction of Leibnitz as coinciding with that of Kant and the modern German thinkers between Begriff and Anschauung, in other words, Concept and Presentation. Sir W. Hamilton considers Begriff to be a name for "the symbolical notions of the understanding," in contrast with Anschauung, which means "the intuitive presentations of Sense and representations of Imagination." (*Ibid.*, p. 183.) He is right as to Anschauung, but as for "symbolical notions of the understanding," our thinking is called by Leibnitz symbolical exactly in so far as it takes place without any "notions," any concept or Begriff at all, by virtue of the mere knowledge that there is a Begriff which the word represents, and which we could recal if we wanted it. When thinking is completely symbolical, the meaning of the word is eliminated from thought, and only the word remains: as in Leibnitz's own illustration from algebra.

[*Prolegomena Logica, pp. 44–8.]

In summary; if the doctrine, that we think by concepts, means that a concept is the only thing present to the mind along with the individual object which (to use Sir W. Hamilton's language) we think under the concept, this is not true: since there is always present a concrete idea or image, of which the attributes comprehended in the concept are only, and cannot be conceived as anything but, a part. Again, if it be meant that the concept, though only a part of what is present to the mind, is the part which is operative in the act of thought, neither is this true: for what is operative is, in a great majority of cases, much less than the entire concept, being that portion only which we have retained the habit of distinctly attending to. In neither of these senses, therefore, do we think by means of the concept: and all that is true is, that when we refer any object or set of objects to a class, some at least of the attributes included in the concept are present to the mind; being recalled to consciousness and fixed in attention, through their association with the class-name.

Before leaving this part of the subject, it seems necessary to remark, that Sir W. Hamilton is by no means consistent in the extension which he gives to the signification of the word Concept. In most cases in which he uses it, he makes it synonymous with General Notion, and allows concepts of classes only, not of individuals.* It is thus that he expressly defines the term. "A Concept," he says, "is the cognition or idea of the general character or characters, point or points, in which a plurality of objects coincide."† "Concept," he says again, "is convertible with *general notion*, or more correctly, *notion* simply."‡ He speaks of the extending of the term to our direct knowledge of individuals, as an "abusive employment" of it.§ He also says, "Notions and Concepts are sometimes designated by the style of *general notions,—general conceptions*. This is superfluous, for in propriety of speech, notions and concepts are, in their very nature, general."¶ In certain places, however, he speaks of concepts of individuals. "If I think of Socrates as son of Sophroniscus, as Athenian, as philosopher, as pugnosed, these are only so many characters, limitations, or determinations which I predicate of Socrates, which distinguish him from all other men, and together make up my *notion* or *concept* of him."ǁ And again, "When the Extension of a concept becomes a minimum, that is, when it contains no other notions under it, it is called an individual."** And further on,

It is evident that the more distinctive characters the concept contains, the more minutely it will distinguish and determine, and that if it contain a plenum of distinctive characters, it must contain the distinctive, the determining characters of

---

Lectures, Vol. III, pp. 119, 121, 126, 127, 128, 130, *cum multis aliis*.
†*Ibid.*, p. 122.
‡*Discussions*, p. 283n.
§*Lectures*, Vol. III, p. 121. ǁ*Ibid.*, p. 78.
¶*Ibid.*, p. 126. **Ibid.*, p. 146.

some individual object. How do the two quantities now stand? In regard to the comprehension or depth, it is evident that it is here at its maximum, the concept being a complement of the whole attributes of an individual object, which, by these attributes, it thinks and discriminates from every other. On the contrary, the extension or breadth of the concept is here at its minimum; for, as the extension is great in proportion to the number of objects to which the concept can be applied, and as the object here is only an individual one, it is evident that it could not be less without ceasing to exist at all.*

But, in the sequel of the same exposition, he again seems to surrender this use of the word Concept as an improper one, saying, "If a concept be an individual, that is, only a bundle of individual qualities, it is . . . not a proper abstract concept at all, but only a concrete representation of Imagination."†
And indeed, no other doctrine is consistent with the proposition elsewhere laid down by our author (though founded, as I think, on an error), that the "words Conception, Concept, Notion, should be limited to the thought of what cannot be represented in imagination, as the thought suggested by a general term."‡

Mr. Mansel, on the contrary, justifies the phrase, concept of an individual, maintaining that "the subjects of all logical judgments are concepts."§ "The man," he says,

as an individual existing at some past time, cannot become immediately an object of thought, and hence is not, properly speaking, the subject of any logical proposition. If I say, Cæsar was the conqueror of Pompey, the immediate object of my thought is not Cæsar as an individual existing two thousand years ago, but a concept now present in my mind, comprising certain attributes which I believe to have coexisted in a certain man. I may *historically* know that these attributes existed in one individual only; and hence my concept, virtually universal, is actually singular, from the accident of its being predicable of that individual only. But there is no *logical* objection to the theory that the whole history of mankind may be repeated at recurring intervals, and that the name and actions of Cæsar may be successively found in various individuals at corresponding periods of every cycle.¶

If this be so, one of two things follows. Either, if I met with a person who exactly corresponded to the concept I have formed of Cæsar, I must suppose that this person actually is Cæsar, and lived in the century preceding the birth of Christ; or else, I cannot think of Cæsar as Cæsar, but only as *a* Cæsar; and all those which are mistakenly called proper names are general names, the names of virtual classes, signifying a set of attributes which carry the name with them, wherever they are found. Either theory

*Ibid., p. 148.
†Ibid., p. 152.
‡Foot-note to Reid, p. 360n.
§Prolegomena Logica, p. 63.
¶Ibid., p. 62.

seems to be sufficiently refuted by stating it. Surely the true doctrine is that of Sir W. Hamilton, that what is called my concept of Cæsar is the presentation in imagination of the individual Cæsar as such. Mr. Mansel might have learnt better from Reid, who says "Most words (indeed all general words) are the signs of ideas: but proper names are not; they signify individual things, and not ideas."* And again, soon after:

The same proper name is never applied to several individuals on account of their similitude, because the very intention of a proper name is to distinguish one individual from all others; and hence it is a maxim in grammar that proper names have no plural number. A proper name signifies nothing but the individual whose name it is; and when we apply it to the individual, we neither affirm nor deny anything concerning him.[†]

The whole of Reid's doctrine respecting names and general notions is not only far more clear, but nearer to the true doctrine of the connotation of names, than Sir W. Hamilton's or Mr. Mansel's.[‡]

---

*Essays on the Intellectual Powers, Works, p. 404. By ideas Reid here means (as he fully explains) attributes.

[†]Ibid., p. 412.

[‡]Accordingly, when Sir W. Hamilton contends, in opposition to Reid, that there are definitions which are not nominal but notional, since they have for their object "the more accurate determination of the contents of a notion," (foot-note to Reid, p. 691n,) there is no real difference of meaning between them: the contents of a notion being simply the connotation of a name.

Sir W. Hamilton enters, at some length, into the explanation of what is meant by the clearness, and the distinctness, of Concepts. A concept, according to him, is clear, if we can distinguish it as a whole from other concepts; distinct, if we can discriminate the characters or attributes of which it is the sum (Lectures, Vol. III, p. 158). The last statement is intelligible, but what does the first mean? If we do not know of what characters the concept is composed, seeing that it has no existence but in those characters, how can we know it so as to distinguish it from other concepts? Our author certainly had not a clear conception of what makes a conception clear; and the proof is, that he adopts as part of his text a quotation from Esser's Logic, in which Esser makes the clearness of a concept to depend on our being able to distinguish, not the concept itself, but the objects included under it; on our being able, in short, to apply the class-name correctly. According to Esser, "a concept is said to be clear, when the degree of consciousness by which it is accompanied is sufficient to discriminate" not itself from other concepts, but "what we think in and through it, from what we think in and through other notions:" and "notions absolutely clear" are "notions whose objects" (not as Sir W. Hamilton says, themselves) cannot "possibly be confounded with aught else, whether known or unknown." (Ibid., pp. 160–1. [Cf. Wilhelm Esser, System der Logik, 2nd ed. (Munster: Theissing, 1830), pp. 91–2.]) So that, according to Esser, the clearness of a concept has reference to its Extension, the distinctness to its Comprehension. This is not the only instance in which our author helps out his own expositions by passages from other authors, written from a point of view more or less different from his own.

CHAPTER XVIII

Of Judgment

THOUGH, AS HAS APPEARED in the last chapter, the proposition that we think by concepts is, if not positively untrue, at least an unprecise and misleading expression of the truth, it is not, however, to be concluded that Sir W. Hamilton's view of Logic, being wholly grounded on that proposition, must be destitute of value. Many writers have given good and valuable expositions of the principles and rules of Logic, from the Conceptualist point of view. The doctrines which they have laid down respecting Conception, Judgment, and Reasoning, have been capable of being rendered into equivalent statements respecting Terms, Propositions, and Arguments; these, indeed, were what the writers really had in their thoughts, and there was little amiss except a mode of expression which attempted to be more philosophical than it knew how to be. To say nothing of less illustrious examples, this is true of all the properly logical part of Locke's *Essay*. His admirable Third Book requires hardly any other alteration to bring it up to the scientific level of the present time, than to be corrected by blotting out everywhere the words Abstract Idea, and replacing them by "the connotation of the class-name."[*]

We shall, accordingly, proceed to examine the explanation of Judgment, and of Reasoning, which Sir W. Hamilton has built on the foundation of the doctrine of Concepts.

"To judge," he says, "is to recognise the relation of congruence or of confliction in which two concepts, two individual things, or a concept and an individual, compared together, stand to each other. This recognition, considered as an internal consciousness, is called a Judgment; considered as expressed in language, it is called a Proposition or Predication."*

To be certain of understanding this, we must inquire what is meant by a relation of congruence or of confliction between concepts. To consult Sir W. Hamilton's definitions of words is, as we have seen, not a sure way of ascertaining the sense in which he practically uses them; but it is one of the ways, and we are bound to employ it in the first instance. A few pages

[*Cf. Mill's *System of Logic*, Bk. I, Chap. vi, §3, in *Collected Works*, Vol. VII, p. 115.]

Lectures, Vol. III, pp. 225–6.

before, he has given a sort of definition of these terms. "Concepts, in relation to each other, are said to be either *Congruent* or *Agreeing*, inasmuch as they may be connected in thought; or *Conflictive*, inasmuch as they cannot. The confliction constitutes the *Opposition* of notions." This Opposition is twofold. "1°. *Immediate* or *Contradictory* Opposition, called likewise *Repugnance*; and 2°. *Mediate* or *Contrary* Opposition. The former emerges when one concept abolishes directly, or by simple negation, what another establishes; the latter, when one concept does this not directly, or by simple negation, but through the affirmation of something else."*

Congruent Concepts, therefore, ^adoes^a not mean concepts which coincide, either wholly or in any of their parts, but such as are mutually compatible; capable of being predicated of the same individual; of being combined in the same presentation of sense or representation of imagination. This is more clearly expressed in a passage from Krug, which our author adopts as part of his own exposition.

Identity is not to be confounded with Agreement or Congruence, nor Diversity with Confliction. All identical concepts are, indeed, congruent, but all congruent notions are not identical. Thus *learning* and *virtue*, *beauty* and *riches*, *magnanimity* and *stature*, are congruent notions, inasmuch as, in thinking a thing, they can easily be combined in the notion we form of it, although themselves very different from each other. In like manner, all conflicting notions are diverse or different notions, for unless different, they could not be mutually conflictive; but, on the other hand, all different concepts are not conflictive; but those only whose difference is so great that each involves the negation of the other; as for example, *virtue* and *vice*, *beauty* and *deformity*, *wealth* and *poverty*.†

Thus interpreted, our author's doctrine is, that to judge, is to recognise whether two concepts, two things, or a concept and a thing, are capable of coexisting as parts of the same mental representation. This I will call Sir W. Hamilton's first theory of Judgment; I will venture to add, his best.

But he soon after proceeds to say,

When two or more thoughts are given in consciousness, there is in general an endeavour on our part to discover in them, and to develop, a relation of congruence or of confliction; that is, we endeavour to find out whether these thoughts will or will not coincide—may or may not be blended into one. If they coincide, we judge, we enounce, their congruence or compatibility: if they do not coincide, we judge, we enounce, their confliction or incompatibility. Thus, if we compare the thoughts, *water*, *iron*, and *rusting*, find them congruent, and connect them into a single thought, thus—*water rusts iron*—in that case we form a judgment.

But if two notions be judged congruent, in other words, be conceived as one, this

Ibid., pp. 213–14.
†*Ibid.*, p. 214. [Cf. Krug, *Logik*, pp. 118–20.]

^{a–a}65¹, 65² do

their unity can only be realized in consciousness, inasmuch as one of these notions is viewed as an attribute or determination of the other. For, on the one hand, it is impossible for us to think as one two attributes, that is, two things viewed as determining, and yet neither determining or qualifying the other; nor, on the other hand, two subjects, that is, two things thought as determined, and yet neither of them determined or qualified by the other.*

In this regress from *ignotum* to *ignotius*, the next thing to be ascertained is, what relation between one thought and another is signified by the verb "to determine." Such explanation as our author deemed it necessary to give, may be found a few pages further back. He there stated, that by determining a notion, he means adding on more characters, by each of which "we limit or determine more and more the abstract vagueness or extension of the notion; until at last, if every attribute be annexed, the sum of attributes contained in the notion becomes convertible with the sum of attributes of which some concrete individual or reality is the comple- ment."† Substituting, then, the definition for what it defines, we find our author's opinion to be, that two notions can only be congruent, that is, capable of being blended into one, if we conceive one of them as adding on additional attributes to the other. This is not yet very clear. We must have recourse to his illustration. "For example, we cannot think the two attri- butes *electrical* and *polar* as a single notion, unless we convert the one of these attributes into a subject, to be determined or qualified by the other." Do we ever think the two attributes electrical and polar as a single notion? We think them as distinct parts of the same notion, that is, as attributes which are constantly combined. "But if we do,—if we say, *what is electri- cal is polar*, we at once reduce the duality to unity; *we judge that polar is one of the constituent characters of the notion electrical, or that what is electrical is contained under the class of things, marked out by the common character of polarity.*"‡ The last italics are mine, intended to mark the place where an intelligible meaning first emerges. "We may, therefore, articu- lately define a judgment or proposition to be the product of that act in which we pronounce that of two notions, thought as subject and as predicate, *the one does or does not constitute a part of the other*, either in the quantity of Extension, or in the quantity of Comprehension."§

This is Sir W. Hamilton's second theory of Judgment, enunciated at a distance of exactly three pages from the first, without the smallest suspi- cion on his part that they are not one and the same. Yet they differ by the whole interval which separates *a part of* from *along with*. According to the

*Ibid., pp. 226–7.
†Ibid., p. 194.
‡Ibid., p. 227.
§Ibid., p. 229.

first theory, concepts are recognised as congruent whenever they are not mutually repugnant; when they are capable of being objectively realized along with one another; when the attributes comprehended in both of them can be simultaneously possessed by the same object. According to the second theory, they are only congruent when the one concept is actually a part of the other. The only circumstance in which the two theories resemble is, that both of them are unfolded out of the vague expression "capable of being connected in thought."[*] They are, in fact, two different and conflicting interpretations of that expression. How irreconcilable they are, is apparent when we descend to particulars. Krug's examples, learning and virtue, beauty and riches, &c., are congruent in the first sense, since they are attributes which can be thought as existing together in the same subject. But is the concept learning a part of the concept virtue, the concept beauty a part of the concept riches, or vice versâ? Sir W. Hamilton would scarcely affirm that they are in a relation of part and whole in Comprehension; and such relation as they have in Extension is not a relation between the concepts, but between the aggregates of real things of which they are predicable. One of those aggregates might be part of the other, though it is not; but one of the concepts can never be part of the other. No one can ever find the notion beauty in the notion riches, nor conversely.

Our author having thus gently slid back into the common Conceptualist theory of judgment, that it consists in recognising the identity or non-identity of two notions, adheres to it thenceforward with as much consistency as we need ever expect to find in him. We may consider as his final theory of Judgment, on which his subsequent logical speculations are built, that a judgment is a recognition in thought, a proposition a statement in words, that one notion is or is not a part of another. He makes use of the word notion [b](doubtless)[b] to include the case in which either of the terms of the proposition is singular. The two notions, one of which is recognised as being or not being a part of the other, may be either Concepts, that is, General Notions, or one of them may be a mental representation of an individual object.

The first objection which, I think, must occur to any one, on the contemplation of this definition, is that it omits the main and characteristic element of a judgment and of a proposition. Do we never judge or assert anything but our mere notions of things? Do we not make judgments and assert propositions respecting actual things? A Concept is a mere creation of the mind: it is the mental representation formed within us of a phænomenon; or rather, it is a part of that mental representation, marked off by a sign, for a

[*Cf. *ibid.*, p. 227.]

[b-b]65[1], 65[2] , doubtless,

particular purpose. But when we judge or assert, there is introduced a new element, that of objective reality, and a new mental fact, Belief. Our judgments, and the assertions which express them, do not enunciate our mere mode of mentally conceiving things, but our conviction or persuasion that the facts as conceived actually exist: and a theory of Judgments and Propositions which does not take account of this, cannot be the true theory. In the words of Reid, "I give the name of Judgment to every determination of the mind concerning *what is true* or *what is false*. This, I think, is what logicians, from the days of Aristotle, have called judgment."* And this is the very element which Sir W. Hamilton's definition omits from it.

I am aware that Sir W. Hamilton would have an apparent answer to this. He would, I suppose, reply, that the belief of actual reality, implied in assent to a proposition, is not left out of account, but brought to account in another place. The belief, he would say, is not inherent in the judgment, but in the notions which are the subject and predicate of the judgment; these being either mental representations of real objects, which if represented in the mind at all, must be represented as real, or Concepts formed by a comparison of real objects, which therefore exist in the mind as concepts of realities. Accordingly, when we judge and make assertions respecting objects known to be imaginary, the judgments are accompanied with no belief in any real existence except that of the mental images; what our author calls the "presentations of phantasy."[*] When, indeed, a judgment is formed or an assertion is made respecting something imaginary which is supposed to be real, as for instance concerning a ghost, there is a belief in the real existence of more than the mental image; but this belief is not anything superadded to the comparison of concepts; it already existed in the concepts; a ghost was thought as something having a real existence.

This, at least, is what might be said in behalf of Sir W. Hamilton, though he has not himself said it. But though it ^cescapes from^c the objection ^dagainst^d omitting the element Belief from the definition of Judgment, it does so by an entire inversion of the logical process of definition. The element of Belief, or Reality, may indeed be in the concepts; but it never could have got into the concepts, if it had not first been in the judgments by which the concepts were constructed. If the belief of reality had been absent from those judgments originally, it never could have come round to them through the concepts. Belief is an essential element in a judgment; it may be either present or absent in a concept. Our author, and those who

Essays on the Intellectual Powers, Works, p. 415.
[*Cf. *Lectures*, Vol. III, p. 131.]

^{c–c}65¹, 65²   evades
^{d–d}65¹, 65², 67   to

agree with him, postpone this part of the subject until they are treating of the distinction between True and False Propositions. They then say, that if the relation which is judged to exist between the notions, exists between the corresponding realities, the proposition is true, and if not, false. But if the operation of forming a judgment or a proposition includes anything at all, it includes judging that the judgment or the proposition is true. The recognition of it as true is not only an essential part, but the essential element of it as a judgment; leave that out, and there remains a mere play of thought, in which no judgment is passed. It is impossible to separate the idea of Judgment from the idea of the truth of a judgment; for every judgment consists in judging something to be true. The element Belief, instead of being an accident which can be passed in silence, and admitted only by implication, constitutes the very difference between a judgment and any other intellectual fact, and it is contrary to all the laws of Definition to define Judgment by anything else. The very meaning of a judgment, or a proposition, is something which is capable of being believed or disbelieved; which can be true or false; to which it is possible to say yes or no. And though it cannot be believed until it has been conceived, or (in plain terms) understood, the real object of belief is not the concept, or any relation of the concept, but the fact conceived. That fact need not be an outward fact; it may be a fact of internal or mental experience. But even then the fact is one thing, the concept of it is another, and the judgment is concerning the fact, not the concept. The fact may be purely subjective, as that I dreamed something last night; but the judgment is not the cognition of a relation between the presentation *I* and the concept *having dreamed*, but the cognition of the real memory of a real event.

This first, and insuperable objection, the force of which will be seen more and more the further we proceed, is applicable to the Conceptualist doctrine of Judgment, howsoever expressed, and to Sir W. Hamilton's as one of the modes of expressing that doctrine. There are other objections special to Sir W. Hamilton's form of it.

In what I have called Sir W. Hamilton's first theory of judgment, we found him saying that the comparison, ending in a recognition of congruence or confliction, may be between "individual things"[*] as well as between concepts. But in his second theory, one at least of the terms of comparison must be a concept. For a judgment, according to this theory, is "the product of that act in which we pronounce that of two notions, thought as subject and predicate, the one does or does not constitute a part of the other."[†] Now a concept, that is, a bundle of attributes, may be a part of another concept, and may be a part of our mental image of an individual

[*Ibid., p. 226.]   [†Ibid., p. 229.]

object; but one notion of an individual object cannot be a part of another notion of an individual object. One object may be an integrant part of another, but it cannot be a part in Comprehension or in Extension, as these words are understood of a Concept. St. Paul's is an integrant part of London, but neither an attribute of it, nor an object of which it is predicable.

Since, therefore, a judgment, in Sir W. Hamilton's second theory, is the recognition of the relation of part and whole, either between two concepts, or between a concept and an individual presentation; the theory supposes that the mind furnishes itself with concepts, or general notions, before it begins to judge. Now this is not only evidently false, but the contrary is asserted, in the most decisive terms, by Sir W. Hamilton himself. He affirms, and it is denied by nobody, that every Concept is built up by a succession of judgments. We conceive an object mentally as having such and such an attribute, because we have first judged that it has that attribute in reality. Let us see what our author says on this point in his Lectures on Metaphysics. He says that there is a judgment involved in every mental act.

The fourth condition of consciousness, which may be assumed as very generally acknowledged, is that it involves judgment. A judgment is the mental act by which one thing is affirmed or denied of another. It may to some seem strange that consciousness, the simple and primary act of intelligence, should be a judgment, which philosophers in general [including Sir W. Hamilton in his second theory] have viewed as a compound and derivative operation. This is, however, altogether a mistake. A judgment is, as I shall hereafter show you, a simple act of mind, for every act of mind implies a judgment. Do we perceive or imagine without affirming, in the act, the external or internal existence of the object? Now these fundamental affirmations are the affirmations,—in other words, the judgments,—of consciousness. *

And in a subsequent part of his Course:

You will recollect that, when treating of Consciousness in general, I stated to you that consciousness necessarily involves a judgment; and as every act of mind is an act of consciousness, every act of mind, consequently, involves a judgment. A consciousness is necessarily the consciousness of a determinate something, and we cannot be conscious of anything without virtually affirming its existence, that is, judging it to be. Consciousness is thus primarily a judgment or affirmation of existence. Again, consciousness is not merely the affirmation of naked existence, but the affirmation of a certain qualified or determinate existence. We are conscious that we exist, only in and through our consciousness that we exist in this or that particular state—that we are so and so affected,—so and so active: and we are only conscious of this or that particular state of existence, inasmuch as we discriminate it as different from some other state of existence, of which we have been previously conscious and are now reminiscent; but such a discrimination supposes, in consciousness, the affirmation of the existence of one state of a specific character, and

*Ibid., Vol. I, pp. 204–5. [The words in square brackets are Mill's.]

the negation of another. On this ground it was that I maintained, that consciousness necessarily involves, besides recollection, or rather a certain continuity of representation, also judgment and comparison; and consequently, that, *so far from comparison or judgment being a process always subsequent to the acquisition of knowledge through perception and self-consciousness, it is involved as a condition of the acquisitive process.**

But if judgment is a comparison of two concepts, or of a concept and an individual object, and a recognition that one of them is a part of (or even merely congruent with) the other, it *must* be a process "always subsequent to the acquisition of knowledge," or, in other words, to the formation of Concepts. The theory of Judgment in the third volume of the *Lectures*, belongs to a different mode of thinking altogether from the theory of Consciousness in the first and second; and when Sir W. Hamilton was occupied with either of them, he must have temporarily forgotten the other.

But in the third volume itself the same inconsistency is obtruded on us still more openly. We are there told in plain words,

Both concepts and reasonings may be reduced to judgments: for the act of judging, that is, the act of affirming or denying one thing of another in thought, is that in which the Understanding or Faculty of comparison is essentially expressed. A concept is a judgment: for, on the one hand, *it is nothing but the result of a foregone judgment, or series of judgments fixed and recorded in a word*, a sign, and it is only amplified by the annexation of a new attribute, through a continuance of the same process. On the other hand, as *a concept is thus the synthesis or complexion, and the record, I may add, of one or more prior acts of judgment*, it can, it is evident, be analysed into these again; every concept is, in fact, a judgment or a fasciculus of judgments,—these judgments only not explicitly developed in thought, and not formally expressed in terms.†

That the same philosopher should have written these words, and a little more than a hundred pages after should have defined a judgment as the result of a comparison of concepts, either between themselves, or with individual objects, is, I think, the very crown of the self-contradictions which we have found to be sown so thickly in Sir W. Hamilton's speculations. Coming from a thinker of such ability, it almost makes one despair of one's own intellect and that of mankind, and feel as if the attainment of truth on any of the more complicated subjects of thought were impossible.

It is necessary to renounce one of these theories or the other. Either a concept is not the "synthesis and record of one or more prior acts of judgment," or a judgment is not, at least in all cases, the recognition of a relation of which one or both of the terms are Concepts. The least that could be required of Sir W. Hamilton would be so to modify his doctrine as to admit two kinds of judgment: the one kind, that by which concepts are

**Ibid.*, Vol. II, pp. 277–8.
†*Ibid.*, Vol. III, p. 117.

formed, the other that which succeeds their formation. When concepts have been formed, and we subsequently proceed to analyse them, then, he might say, we form judgments which recognise one concept as a whole, of which another is a part. But the judgments by which we constructed the concepts, and every subsequent judgment by which, to use his own words, we amplify them by the addition of a new attribute, have nothing to do with comparison of concepts: it is the Anschauungen, the intuitions, the presentations of experience, which we in this case compare and judge.*

Take, for instance, Sir W. Hamilton's own example of a judgment, "Water rusts iron:"[*] and let us suppose this truth to be new to us. Is it not like a mockery to say with our author, that we know this truth by comparing "the *thoughts*, water, iron, and rusting"? Ought he not to have said the *facts*, water, iron, and rusting? and even then, is comparing the proper name for the mental operation? We do not examine whether three thoughts agree, but whether three outward facts coexist. If we lived till doomsday we should never find the proposition that water rusts iron in our concepts, if we had not first found it in the outward phænomena. The proposition expresses a sequence, and what we call a causation, not between our concepts, but between the two sensible presentations of moistened iron

*This mode of escape from contradiction is the one which has, in substance, been resorted to by Mr. Mansel. He distinguishes what he terms Psychological from what he denominates Logical judgments. Psychological judgments merely assert that some object of consciousness, either external or internal, is present: they "may be generally stated in the proposition, This is here." These are the only judgments which are implied in, and necessary to, the formation of Concepts: and these judgments, as they assert a matter of present consciousness, are necessarily true. "But the psychological judgment must not be confounded with the logical. The former is the judgment of a relation between the conscious subject and the immediate object of consciousness: the latter is the judgment of a relation which two objects of thought bear to each other. . . . The logical judgment necessarily contains two concepts, and hence must be regarded as logically and chronologically posterior to the conception, which requires one only." (*Prolegomena Logica*, pp. 53–5.)

But the operation by which a concept is built up, supposes much more than a cognition of the present existence of a fact or facts of consciousness, and a judgment in the form, "This is here." It supposes the whole process of comparing facts of consciousness, and recognising, or in other words, judging, in what points they resemble. It implies that the mind, in its "psychological" judgments, does to the Intuitions or Presentations everything which it is supposed to do to the Concepts in the "logical" ones. Consequently the distinction between Mr. Mansel's two kinds of judgments is in their matter only, not in the mental operation, and is therefore, as he would say, extra-logical; to which I will add, insignificant. It will be shown in the text that there is no psychological difference between the two, and that the discrimination of one class of judgments as conversant with Presentations and another with Concepts, and the attribution to the latter class of the name of logical, are founded on a false theory.

[*Lectures, Vol. III, p. 227.]

and rust. When we have already judged this sequence to exist outside us, that is, independently of our intellectual combinations, we know it, and once known, it may find its way into our concepts. But we cannot elicit out of a concept any judgment which we have not first put into it; which we have not consciously assented to, in the act of forming the concept. Whenever, therefore, we form a new judgment—judge a truth new to us—the judgment is not a recognition of a relation between concepts, but of a succession, a coexistence, or a similitude, between facts.

This is the smallest sacrifice on the part of Sir W. Hamilton's theory of Judgment, which would satisfy his theory of Consciousness. But when thus reconciled with a part of his system with which it now conflicts, it would not be the better founded. It might still be chased from point to point, unable to make a stand anywhere. For let us next suppose, that the judgment is not new; that the truth, Water rusts iron, is known to us of old. When we again think of it, and think it as a truth, and assent to it, should we even then give a correct account of what passes in our mind, by calling this act of judgment a comparison of our thoughts—our concepts—our notions—of water, rust, and iron? We do not compare our artificial mental constructions, but consult our direct remembrance of facts. We call to mind that we have seen, or learned from credible testimony, that when iron is long in contact with water, it rusts. The question is not one of notions, but of beliefs; belief of past and expectation of future presentations of sense. Of course it is psychologically true that when I believe, I have a notion of that which I believe; but the ultimate appeal is not to the notion, but to the presentation or intuition. If I am in any doubt, what is the question I ask myself? Is it—Do I think of, or figure to myself, water as rusting iron? or is it—Did I ever perceive, and have other people perceived, that water rusts iron? There are persons, no doubt, whose criterion of judgment is the relation between their own concepts, but these are not the persons whose judgments the world has usually found worth adopting. If the question between Copernicus and Ptolemy had depended on whether we *conceive* the earth moving and the sun at rest, or the sun moving and the earth at rest, I am afraid the victory would have been with Ptolemy.

But, again, even if judging were entirely a notional operation, consisting of the recognition of some relation between concepts, it remains to be proved that the relation is that of Whole and Part. Could it, even then, be said, that every judgment in which I predicate one thing of another, on the faith of previous judgments recorded, as our author says, in the concepts, consists in recognising that one of the concepts includes the other as a part of itself? When I judge that Socrates is mortal, or that all men are mortal, does the judgment consist in being conscious that my concept mortal is part of my representation of Socrates, or of my concept man?

This doctrine ignores the famous distinction, admitted, I suppose, in

some shape or other, by all philosophers, but most familiar to modern
metaphysics in the form in which it is stated by Kant—the distinction
between Analytical and Synthetical judgments. Analytical judgments are
supposed to unfold the contents of a concept; affirming explicitly of a class,
attributes which were already part of the corresponding concept, and may
be brought out into distinct consciousness by mere analysis of it. Synthetical judgments, on the contrary, affirm of a class, attributes which are not
in the concept, and which we therefore do not and cannot judge to be a part
of the concept, but only to be conjoined in fact with the attributes composing the concept. This distinction, though obtruded upon our author by
many of the writers with whom he was familiar, has so little in common with
his mode of thought, that he only slightly refers to it, in a very few passages
of his works: in one of these, however,* he speaks of it as of something very
important, *expresses his preference for the terms Explicative and Ampliative as names for it*, and discusses, not the distinction itself, but its history;
apparently unconscious that his own theory entirely does away with it.
According to that, all judgments are analytical, or, *as he prefers to say*,
explicative. Even giving up so much of his theory as contradicts his own
doctrine on the formation of concepts, the part remaining would compel
him to maintain that all judgments which are not new are analytical, and
that synthetical judgments are limited to truths, or supposed truths, which
we learn for the first time. *

   This discrepancy between our author and almost all philosophers, even
of his own general way of thinking, (including, among the rest, Mr. Mansel), arises from the fact, that he understands by concept something different from what they have usually understood by it. The concept of a class, in
Sir W. Hamilton's acceptation of the term, includes all the attributes which
we have judged, and still judge, to be common to the whole class. It means,
in short, our entire knowledge of the class. But, with philosophers in
general, the concept of the class as such,—my concept of man, for example, as distinguished from my mental representation of an individual
man,—includes, not all the attributes which I ascribe to man, but such of
them only as the classification is grounded on, and as are implied in the
meaning of the name. Man is a living being, or Man is rational, they would
call analytical judgments, because the attributes *of* life and rationality are
of the number of those which are already given in the concept Man: but

   *"Dissertations on Reid," [Note A,] pp. 787n–8n.

   *-e*65¹, 65²   proposes new names for it (Explicative and Ampliative)
   *-f*65¹, 65²   in his own phrase
   *65¹, 65²   And this, I presume, was what he had in his mind when he suggested, as proper
for synthetical judgments, the name of ampliative.
   -h+67, 72

Man is mortal, they would account synthetical, because, familiar as the fact is, it is not already affirmed in the very name Man, but has to be superadded in the predicate.

It is quite lawful for a philosopher (though seldom prudent) to alter the meaning of a word, provided he gives fair notice of his intention; but he is bound, if he does so, to remain consistent with himself in the new meaning, and not to transfer to it propositions which are only true in the old. This condition Sir W. Hamilton does not observe. It often happens that different opinions of his belong to different and inconsistent systems of thought, apparently through his retaining from former writers some doctrine, the grounds of which he has, by another doctrine, subverted. His whole theory of Concepts being infected by an inconsequence of this description, the retention of all the Conceptualist conclusions along with Nominalist premises, it is no wonder if further oversights of the same kind meet us in every part of the details. The following is one of the most palpable. As we just mentioned, the concept of a class in our author's sense, includes all the attributes of the class, so far as the thinker is acquainted with them; the whole of the thinker's knowledge of the class. This is Sir W. Hamilton's own doctrine; but along with it he retains a doctrine belonging to the other meaning of Concept, which I have contrasted with his. "The exposition of the Comprehension of a notion is called its Definition:"* and again "Definition is the analysis of a complex concept into its component parts or attributes."† But a thing is not analysed into its component parts if any of the parts are left out. The two opinions taken together lead, therefore, to the remarkable consequence, that the definition of a class ought to include the whole of what is known of the class. Those who mean by the concept not all known attributes of the class, but such only as are included in the connotation of the name, may be permitted to say of a Definition that it is the analysis of the concept: but to Sir W. Hamilton this was not permissible. To crown the inconsistency, he still presents the stock example, Man is a rational animal, as a good definition, and a typical specimen of what a Definition is;‡ as if the notions animal and rational exhausted the whole of the concept Man, according to his meaning of Concept—the entire sum of the attributes common to the class. It would hardly be believed, prior to a minute examination of his writings, how much vagueness of thought, leading to the unsuspecting admission of opposite doctrines in the same breath, lurks under the specious appearance of philosophical precision which distinguishes him.§

*_Lectures_, Vol. III, p. 143.
†_Ibid._, p. 151.
‡_Ibid._, pp. 143–4.
§In his non-recognition of the difference between Analytical and Synthetical

To return, from Sir W. Hamilton's self-contradictions, to the merits of the question itself; the word Judgment, by universal consent, is coextensive with the word Proposition: a Judgment must be so defined that a Proposition shall be the expression of it in words. Now, if a Judgment expresses a relation between Concepts (which for the purpose of the present discussion I have conceded) the corresponding Proposition represents that same relation by means of names: the names, therefore, must be signs of the concepts, and the concepts must be the meaning of the names. To make this tenable, the Concept must be so construed as to consist of those attributes only which are connoted by the name. Corporeity, life, rationality, and any other attributes of man which are part of the meaning of the word, insomuch that where those attributes were not, we should withhold the name of man—these are part of the concept. But mortality, and all the other human attributes which are the subject of treatises either on the human body or on human nature, are not in the concept, because we do not affirm them of any individual by merely calling him a man; they are so much additional knowledge. The concept Man is not the sum of all the attributes of a man, but only of the essential attributes—of those which constitute him a man; in other words, those on which the class Man is grounded, and which are connoted by the name—what used to be called the essence of Man, that without which Man cannot be, or in other words, would not be what he is called. Without mortality, or without thirty-two teeth, he would still be called a man: we should not say, This is not a man; we should say, This man is not mortal, or has fewer than thirty-two teeth.

Instead, therefore, of saying with Sir W. Hamilton, that the attributes

---

judgments, it is already implied that he never recognises the Connotation of Names; which in itself is enough to vitiate his whole logical system, and is a great point of inferiority in him to the best Conceptualist thinkers, who do recognise it, though in a misleading phraseology. To the same cause may be ascribed the extremely vulgar character of the explanation of some of the leading metaphysical terms, in his eighth Lecture. For example, the distinction between essential and accidental qualities he defines thus—that the essential qualities of a thing are those "which it cannot lose without ceasing to be." [*Ibid.*, Vol. I, p. 150.] This, which is a retrogression from Conceptualism to Realism, does but prove that he simply transcribed his definition from the Realistic Schoolmen. In a later part of his *Lectures* (Vol. IV, p. 11) he, *more suo*, forgets this definition, and replaces it by ᶦone of his ownᶦ; but in this second definition he betrays that he never saw the genuine meaning which lay under the distinction, so badly expressed by the schoolmen in the language of a false system. Sir W. Hamilton, in distinguishing Essential from Unessential properties, means only the difference between attributes of the whole genus, and those confined to some of its species. Sir W. Hamilton's knowledge of the scholastic writings was extraordinary; but many students of them who had not a tithe of that knowledge, have brought back and appropriated much more of the important materials for thought which those writings abundantly contain.

ᶦ⁻ᶦ65¹, 65²   another, drawn from his own thoughts

composing the concept of the predicate are part of those which compose
the concept of the subject, we ought to say, they are either a part, or are
invariably conjoined with them, not in our conception, but in fact. Propositions in which the concept of the predicate is part of the concept of the
subject, or, to express ourselves more philosophically, in which the attributes connoted by the predicate are part of those connoted by the subject,
are a kind of Identical Propositions: they convey no information, but at
most remind us of what, if we understood the word which is the subject of
the proposition, we knew as soon as the word was pronounced. Propositions of this kind are either definitions, or parts of definitions. These
judgments are analytical: they analyse the connotation of the subject-
name, and predicate separately the different attributes which the name
asserts collectively. All other affirmative judgments are synthetical, and
affirm that some attribute or set of attributes is, not a part of those connoted
by the subject-name, but an invariable accompaniment of them.*

*This is perfectly understood by Mr. Mansel, who says, "When I assert that A is
B, I do not mean that the attributes constituting the concept A are identical with
those constituting the concept B, for this is only true in identical judgments; but that
the object in which the one set of attributes is found, is the same as that in which the
other is found. To assert that all philosophers are liable to error is not to assert that
the signification of the term *philosopher* is identical with that of *liable to error*; but
that the attributes comprehended in these two distinct terms are in some manner
united in the same subject." (*Prolegomena Logica*, pp. 58–9.) What Mr. Mansel
here enunciates distinctly, was contained, though less distinctly, in Sir W. Hamilton's first theory of judgment, especially as he illustrated it from Krug. [See
Lectures, Vol. III, pp. 225–48; see Krug, *Logik*, §57.] In adhering to that first
theory, as well as in limiting the concept to the attributes connoted by the name—
for that limitation clearly results from his definition of a Concept (p. 60), in combination with other passages—Mr. Mansel, as it appears to me, is much nearer the truth
than Sir W. Hamilton; and would perhaps be nearer still, if he were not entangled in
the meshes of the Hamiltonian phraseology.
   An example how that phraseology controls him, is his strange assertion that
every concept "must contain a plurality of attributes" as a condition of its conceivability; "for a simple idea, like a *summum genus*, is by itself inconceivable." Inconceivable it truly is, but not in any sense in which conceivability is required of a
concept: only in the sense of not being conceivable separately. "Simple ideas are
never conceived as such, but only as forming parts of a complex object;" in other
words, they are inconceivable in the sense in which, according to Sir W. Hamilton's
doctrine and Mr. Mansel's own, all concepts are inconceivable. (*Prolegomena
Logica*, pp. 184–5.)
   From a similar entanglement, although his account of Definition and Division is
decidedly better than Sir W. Hamilton's, he follows that philosopher in treating the
latter logical operation as a division of the Concept: as if the concept were divided
by dividing the things which it is predicable of (*ibid.*, pp. 191–4).
   ʲDr. M'Cosh thinks that there are judgments (other than those in which the
predicates are proper names) which do not affirm or deny attributes, viz. those in

ʲ⁻ʲ+67, 72

There remains something to be said on another very prominent feature in Sir W. Hamilton's theory of Judgment. Having said, that in every judgment we compare "two notions, thought as subject and predicate," and pronounce that "the one does or does not constitute a part of the other," he adds, "either in the quantity of Extension, or in the quantity of Comprehension."* He developes this distinction as follows:

If the Subject or determined notion be viewed as the containing whole, we have an Intensive or Comprehensive proposition; if the Predicate or determining notion be viewed as the containing whole, we have an Extensive proposition. . . . The relation of subject and predicate is contained within that of whole and part, for we can always view either the determining or the determined notion as the whole which contains the other. The whole, however, which the subject constitutes, and the whole which the predicate constitutes, are different, being severally determined by the opposite quantities of comprehension and of extension; and as subject and predicate necessarily stand to each other in the relation of these inverse quantities, it is manifestly a matter of indifference, in so far as the meaning is concerned, whether we view the subject as the whole of comprehension which contains the predicate, or the predicate as the whole of extension which contains the subject. In point of fact, in single propositions it is rarely apparent which of the two wholes is meant; for the copula *is, est,* &c., equally denotes the one form of the relation or the other. Thus, in the proposition *man is two-legged,*—the copula here is convertible with *comprehends or contains in it,* for the proposition means *man contains in it two-legged,* that is, the subject *man* as an intensive whole or complex notion, comprehends as a part the predicate *two-legged.* Again, in the proposition, *man is a biped,* the copula corresponds to *contained under,* for this proposition is tantamount to *man is contained under biped,*—that is, the predicate *biped,* as an extensive whole or class, contains under it as a part the subject *man.* But in point of fact, neither of the two propositions unambiguously shows whether it is to be viewed as of an intensive or of an extensive purport; nor in a single proposition is this of any moment. All that can be said is that the one form of expression is better accommodated to express the one kind of proposition, the other better accommodated to express the other. It is only when propositions are connected into syllogisms, that it becomes evident whether the subject or the predicate be the whole in or under which the other is contained; and it is only as thus constituting two different—two contrasted, forms of reasoning—forms the most general, as under each of these every other is included,—that the distinction becomes necessary in regard to concepts and propositions.†

which we compare what he terms "mere Abstracts." "We cannot call such attributive; thus, there would be no propriety in saying that 4 is an attribute of 2 + 2." ([*Examination,*] p. 294.) But is not *making* 4, an attribute of 2 + 2? Further on he says, that the predicate in this class of propositions "has no quantity or extension, for it is not a class notion. When we say that $3 \times 3 = 9$, neither subject nor predicate has an indefinite number of objects embraced in it." (*Ibid.*, p. 333.) The objects embraced in 9 are nine apples, nine marbles, nine hours, nine miles, and all the other aggregations of which nine can be predicated. Every numeral is the name of a class, and a most comprehensive class, consisting of things of all imaginable qualities. And the same observation applies to $3 \times 3.^j$

*Lectures, Vol. III, p. 229.

†Ibid., pp. 231–3.

I shall not insist on such of the objections to this passage as have been sufficiently stated; the impropriety, for instance, of saying that the notion Man *contains* the predicate two-legged, when that attribute is evidently not part of the signification of the word; or that the meaning of a proposition is, that an attribute is part of a notion: which, the first time it is observed, it cannot possibly be, and at no time is this the thing asserted by a proposition, unless by those which are avowedly definitions. All these considerations I at present forego: and I will even give our author's theory its necessary correction, by restoring to Propositions the alternative meaning which belongs to them, namely, that a certain attribute is *either* part of a given set of attributes, or invariably coexists with them. Having thus dissociated the doctrine in the quotation from all errors which are incidental and not essential to it, we may state it as follows:—Every proposition is capable of being understood in two meanings, which involve one another, inasmuch as if either of them is true the other is so, but which are nevertheless different; of which only one may be, and commonly is, in the mind; and the words used do not always show which. Thus, All men are bipeds, may either mean, that the objects called men are all of them numbered among the objects called bipeds, which is interpreting the proposition in Extension; or that the attribute of having two feet is one of, or coexists with, the attributes which compose the notion Man: which is interpreting the proposition in Comprehension.

I maintain, that these two supposed meanings of the proposition are not two matters of fact or of thought, reciprocally inferrible from one another, but one and the same fact, written in different ways; that the supposed meaning in Extension is not a meaning at all, until interpreted by the meaning in Comprehension; that all concepts and general names which enter into Propositions, require to be construed in Comprehension, and that their Comprehension is the whole of their meaning.

That the meaning in Extension follows if the meaning in Comprehension is granted, is a point which both sides are agreed in. If the attribute signified by biped is either one of, or always conjoined with, the attributes signified by man, we are entitled to assert that the class Man is included in, is a part of, the class Biped. But my position is, that this second assertion is not a conclusion from, but a mere repetition of, the first. For what is the second assertion, if we leave out of it all reference to the attributes? It can then only mean, that we have ascertained the fact independently of the attributes— that is, that we have examined the aggregate whole "all men," and the still greater aggregate whole "all bipeds," and that all the former were found among the latter. Now, do we assert this? or would it be true? Assuredly no one of us ever represented and contemplated, even with his mind's eye, either of these wholes: still less did we ever compare them as realities, and ascertain that the fact is as stated. Neither could this be done, by anything short of infinite power: for all men and all bipeds, except a comparatively few, have either ceased to exist, or have not yet come into existence. What, then, do we mean by making an assertion concerning all men? The phrase does not mean, all and each of a certain great number of objects, known or represented individually. It means, all and each of an unascertained and indefinite number, mostly not known or represented at all, but which if they came within our opportunities of knowledge, might be recognised by the possession of a certain set of attributes, namely, those forming the connotation of the word ^{k}. "All men," and "the class man," are expressions which point to nothing but attributes; they cannot be interpreted except in comprehension. To say, all men are bipeds, is merely to say, given the attributes of man, that of being a biped will be found along with them; which is the meaning in Comprehension. If the proposition has nothing to do with the concept Man except as to its comprehension, still less has it with the concept Biped. When I say, All men are bipeds, what has my assertion to do with the class biped as to its Extension? Have I any concern with the remainder of the class, after Man is subtracted from it? Am I necessarily aware even whether there is any remainder at all? I am thinking of no such matter, but only of the attribute two-footed, and am intending to predicate that. I am thinking of it as an attribute of man, but of what else it may happen to be an attribute does not concern me. Thus, all propositions into which general names enter, and consequently all reasonings, are in Comprehension only. Propositions and Reasonings may be written in Extension, but they are always understood in Comprehension. The only exception is in the case of propositions which have no meaning in Comprehension, and have nothing to do with Concepts—those of which both the subject and the predicate are proper names; such as, Tully is Cicero, or, St. Peter is not St. Paul. These words connote nothing, and the only meaning they have is the individual whom they *de*note. But where a meaning in Comprehension, or, in other words, in Connotation, is possible, that is always the one intended. And Sir W. Hamilton's distinction (though he lays great stress on it) between Reasoning in Comprehension and Reasoning in Extension, will be found (as we shall see hereafter)[*] to be a mere superfetation on Logic.

It is worth while to add, that even could it be admitted that general propositions have a meaning in Extension capable of being conceived as different from their meaning in Comprehension, Sir W. Hamilton would still be wrong in deeming that the recognition of this meaning depends on, or can possibly result from, a comparison of the Concepts. The Extension

[*See pp. 386ff. below.]

^{k}65^1 Man

of a concept, as I have before remarked, is not, like the Comprehension, intrinsic and essential to the concept; it is an external and wholly accidental relation of the concept, and no contemplation or analysis of the concept itself will tell us anything about it. It is an abstract name for the aggregate of objects possessing the attributes included in the concept: and whether that aggregate is greater or smaller does not depend on any properties of the concept, but on the boundless productive powers of Nature.

CHAPTER XIX

Of Reasoning

IN COMMON with the majority of modern writers on Logic, whose language is generally that of the Conceptualist school, Sir W. Hamilton considers Reasoning, as he considers Judgment, to consist in a comparison of Notions: either of Concepts with one another, or of Concepts with the mental representations of individual objects. Only, in simple Judgment, two notions are compared immediately; in Reasoning, mediately. Reasoning is the comparison of two notions by means of a third. As thus: "Reasoning is an act of mediate Comparison or Judgment; for to reason is to recognise that two notions stand to each other in the relation of a whole and its parts, through a recognition that these notions severally stand in the same relation to a third."* The foundation, therefore, of all Reasoning is "the self-evident principle that a part of the part is a part of the whole."† "Without reasoning we should have been limited to a knowledge of what is given by immediate intuition; we should have been unable to draw any inference from this knowledge, and have been shut out from the discovery of that countless multitude of truths, which, though of high, of paramount importance, are not self-evident."‡ This recognition that we discover a "countless multitude of truths," composing a vast proportion of all our real knowledge, by mere reasoning, will be found to jar considerably with our author's theory of the reasoning process, and with his whole view of the nature and functions of Logic, the science of Reasoning: but this inconsistency is common to him with nearly all the writers on Logic, because, like him, they teach a theory of the science too small and narrow to contain their own facts.

Notwithstanding the great number of philosophers who have considered the definition cited above to be a correct account of Reasoning, the objections to it are so manifest, that until after much meditation on the subject, one can scarcely prevail on oneself to utter them: so impossible does it seem that difficulties so obvious should always be passed over unnoticed, unless they admitted of an easy answer. Reasoning, we are told, is a mode of ascertaining that one notion is a part of another; and the use of reasoning

Lectures, Vol. III, p. 274.
†*Ibid.*, p. 271.
‡*Ibid.*, p. 277.

is to enable us to discover truths which are not self-evident. But how is it possible that a truth, which consists in one notion being part of another, should not be self-evident? The notions, by supposition, are both of them in our mind. To perceive what parts they are composed of, nothing surely can be necessary but to fix our attention on them. We cannot surely concentrate our consciousness on two ideas in our own mind, without knowing with certainty whether one of them as a whole includes the other as a part. If we have the notion biped and the notion man, and know what they are, we must know whether the notion of a biped is part of the notion we form to ourselves of a man. In this case the simply Introspective method is in its place. We cannot need to go beyond our consciousness of the notions themselves.

Moreover, if it were really the case that we can compare two notions and fail to discover whether one of them is a part of the other, it is impossible to understand how we could be enabled to accomplish this by comparing each of them with a third. A, B, and C, are three concepts, of which we are supposed to know that A is a part of B, and B of C, but until we put these two propositions together we do not know that A is a part of C. We have perceived B in C intuitively, by direct comparison: but what is B? By supposition it is, and is perceived to be, A and something more. We have therefore, by direct intuition, perceived that A and something more is a part of C, without perceiving that A is a part of C. Surely there is here a great psychological difficulty to be got over, to which logicians of the Conceptualist school have been surprisingly blind.

Endeavouring, not to understand what they say, for they never face the question, but to imagine what they might say, to relieve this apparent absurdity, two things occur to ᵃthe mindᵃ. It may be said, that when a notion is in our consciousness, but we do not know whether something is or is not a part of it, the reason is that we have forgotten some of its parts. We possess the notion, but are only conscious of part of it, and it does its work in our trains of thought only symbolically. Or, again, it may be said that all the parts of the notion are in our consciousness, but are in our consciousness indistinctly. The meaning of having a distinct notion, according to Sir W. Hamilton, is that we can discriminate the characters or attributes of which it is composed. The admitted fact, therefore, that we can have indistinct notions, may be adduced as proof that we can possess a notion, and not be able to say positively what is included in it. These are the best, or rather the only presentable arguments I am able to invent, in support of the paradox involved in the Conceptualist theory of Reasoning.

It is a great deal easier to refute these arguments than it was to discover

ᵃ⁻ᵃ65¹   one

them. The refutation, like the original difficulty, is two deep. To begin; a notion, part of which has been forgotten, is to that extent a lost notion, and is as if we had never had it. The parts which we can no longer discern in it are not in it, and cannot therefore be proved to be in it, by reasoning, any more than by intuition. We may be able to discover by reasoning that they ought to be there, and may, in consequence, put them there; but that is not recognising them to be there already. As a notion in part forgotten is a partially lost notion, so an indistinct notion is a notion not yet formed, but in process of formation. We have an indistinct notion of a class when we perceive in a general way that certain objects differ from others, but do not as yet perceive in what; or perceive some of the points of difference, but have not yet perceived, or have not yet generalized, the others. In this case our notion is not yet a completed notion, and the parts which we cannot discern in it, are undiscernible because they are not yet there. As in the former case, the result of reasoning may be to put them there; but it certainly does not effect this by proving them to be there already.

But even if these explanations had solved the mystery of our being conscious of a whole and unable to be directly conscious of its part, they would yet fail to make intelligible how, not having this knowledge directly, we are able to acquire it through a third notion. By hypothesis we have forgotten that A is a part of C, until we again become aware of it through the relation of each of them to B. We therefore had not forgotten that A is a part of B, nor that B is a part of C. When we conceived B, we conceived A as a part of it; when we conceived C, we conceived B as a part of it. In the mere fact, therefore, of conceiving C, we were conscious of B in it, and consciousness of A is a necessary part of that consciousness of B, and yet our consciousness of C did not enable us to find in it our consciousness of A, though it was really there, and though they both were distinctly present. If any one can believe this, no contradiction and no impossibility in any theory of Consciousness need stagger him. Let us now substitute for the hypothesis of forgetfulness, the hypothesis of indistinctness. We had a notion of C, which was so indistinct that we could not discriminate A from the other parts of the notion. But it was not too indistinct to enable us to discriminate B, otherwise the reasoning would break down as well as the intuition. The notion of B, again, indistinct as it may have been in other respects, must have been such that we could with assurance discriminate A as contained in it. Here then returns the same absurdity: A is distinctly present in B, which is distinctly present in C, therefore A, if there be any force in reasoning, is distinctly present in C; yet A cannot be discriminated or perceived in the consciousness in which it is distinctly present: so that, before our reasoning commenced, we were at once distinctly conscious of

A, and entirely unconscious of it. There is no such thing as a reduction to absurdity if this is not one.

The reason why a judgment which is not intuitively evident, can be arrived at through the medium of premises, is that judgments which are not intuitively evident do not consist in recognising that one notion is part of another. When that is the case, the conclusion is as well known to us *ab initio* as the premises; which is really the case in analytical judgments. When reasoning really leads to the "countless multitudes of truths" not self-evident, which our author speaks of—that is, when the judgments are synthetical—we learn, not that A is part of C, because A is part of B and B of C, but that A is conjoined with C, because A is conjoined with B, and B with C. The principle of the reasoning is not, a part of the part is a part of the whole, but, a mark of the mark is a mark of the thing marked, *Nota notæ est nota rei ipsius.*[*] It means, that two things which constantly coexist with the same third thing, constantly coexist with one another; the things meant not being our concepts, but the facts of experience on which our concepts ought to be grounded.

This theory of reasoning is free from the objections which are fatal to the Conceptualist theory. We cannot discover that A is a part of C through its being a part of B, since if it really is so, the one truth must be as much a matter of direct consciousness as the other. But we can discover that A is conjoined with C through its being conjoined with B; since our knowledge that it is conjoined with B, may have been obtained by a series of observations in which C was not perceptible. C, we must remember, stands for an attribute, that is, not an actual presentation of sense, but a power of producing such presentations: and that a power may have been present without being apparent, is in the common course of things, implying nothing more than that the conditions necessary to determine it into act were not all present. This power or potentiality, C, may in like manner have been ascertained to be conjoined with B, by another set of observations, in which it was A's turn to be dormant, or perhaps to be active, but not attended to. By combining the two sets of observations, we are enabled to discover what was not contained in either of them, namely, a constancy of conjunction between C and A, such that one of them comes to be a mark of the other: though, in neither of the two sets of observations, nor in any others, may C and A have been actually observed together; or, if observed, not with the frequency, or under the experimental conditions, which would

[*This idea derives from Aristotle: see *The Categories*, in *The Categories, On Interpretation, Prior Analytics* (Greek and English), trans. Harold P. Cooke and Hugh Tredennick (London: Heinemann; Cambridge, Mass.: Harvard University Press, 1938), p. 16 (1^b 9–12).]

warrant us in generalizing the fact. This is the process by which we do, in reality, acquire the greater part of our knowledge; all of it (as our author says) which is not "given by immediate intuition."[*] But no part of this process is at all like the operation of recognising parts and a whole; or of recognising any relation whatever between Concepts; which have nothing to do with the matter, more than is implied in the fact, that we cannot reason about things without conceiving them, or representing them to the mind.

The theory which supposes Judgment and Reasoning to be the comparison of concepts, is obliged to make the term concept stand for, not the thinker's or reasoner's own notion of a thing, but a sort of normal notion, which is understood as being owned by everybody, though everybody does not always use it; and it is this tacit substitution of a concept floating in the air for the very concept I have in my own mind, which makes it possible to fancy that we can, by reasoning, find out something to be in a concept, which we are not able to discover in it by consciousness, because, in truth, *that* concept is not in [b]our[b] consciousness. But a concept of a thing, which is not that whereby I conceive it, is to me as much an external fact, as a presentation of the senses can be: it is another person's concept, not mine. It may be the conventional concept of the world at large—that which it has been tacitly agreed to associate with the class; in other words, it may be the connotation of the class-name; and if so, it may very possibly contain elements which I cannot directly recognise in it, but may have to learn from external evidence: but this is because I do not know the signification of the word, the attributes which determine its application—and what I have to do is to learn them: when I have done this, I shall have no difficulty in directly recognising as a part of them, anything which really is so. But with regard to all attributes not included in the signification of the name, not only I do not find them in the concept, but they do not even become part of it after I have learnt them by experience; unless we understand by the concept, not, with philosophers in general, only the essence of the class, but with Sir W. Hamilton, all its known attributes. Even in Sir W. Hamilton's sense, they are not found in the concept, but added to it; and not until we have already assented to them as objective facts—subsequently, therefore, to the reasoning by which they were ascertained.

Take such a case as this. Here are two properties of circles. One is, that a circle is bounded by a line, every point of which is equally distant from a certain point within the circle. This attribute is connoted by the name, and is, on both theories, a part of the concept. Another property of the circle is, that the length of its circumference is to that of its diameter in the approxi-

[*Lectures, Vol. III, p. 277.]

[b]-[b]+67, 72

mate ratio of 3·14159 to 1. This attribute was discovered, and is now known, as a result of reasoning. Now, is there any sense, consistent with the meaning of the terms, in which it can be said that this recondite property formed part of the concept circle, before it had been discovered by mathematicians? Even in Sir W. Hamilton's meaning of concept, it is in nobody's but a mathematician's concept even now: and if we concede that mathematicians are to determine the normal concept of a circle for mankind at large, mathematicians themselves did not find the ratio of the diameter to the circumference in the concept, but put it there; and could not have done so until the long train of difficult reasoning which culminated in the discovery was complete.

It is impossible, therefore, rationally to hold both the opinions professed simultaneously by Sir W. Hamilton—that Reasoning is the comparison of two notions through the medium of a third, and that Reasoning is a source from which we derive new truths. And the truth of the latter proposition being indisputable, it is the former which must give way. The theory of Reasoning which attempts to unite them both, has the same defect which we have shown to vitiate the corresponding theory of Judgment: it makes the process consist in eliciting something out of a concept which never was in the concept, and if it ever finds its way there, does so after the process, and as a consequence of its having taken place.

CHAPTER XX

On Sir William Hamilton's Conception of Logic as a Science. Is Logic the Science of the Laws, or Forms, of Thought?

HAVING DISCUSSED the nature of the three psychological processes which, together, constitute the operations of the Intellect, and having considered Sir W. Hamilton's theory of each, we are in a condition to examine the general view which he takes of the Science or Art, whose purpose it is to direct our intellectual operations into their proper course, and to protect them against error.

Sir W. Hamilton defines Logic "the Science of the Laws of Thought as Thought."* He proceeds to justify each of the component parts of this definition. And first, is Logic a Science?

Archbishop Whately says that it is both a Science and an Art.[*] He says this in an intelligible sense. He means that Logic both determines what is, and prescribes what should be. It investigates the nature of the process which takes place in Reasoning, and lays down rules to enable that process to be conducted as it ought. For this distinction, Sir W. Hamilton is very severe on Archbishop Whately. In the Archbishop's sense of the words, he says, it never has been, and never could have been, disputed that Logic is both a Science and an Art. But

the discrimination of art and science is wrong. Dr. Whately considers science to be any knowledge viewed absolutely, and not in relation to practice,—a signification in which every art would, in its doctrinal part, be a science; and he defines art to be the application of knowledge to practice, in which sense Ethics, Politics, and all practical sciences, would be arts. The distinction of arts and sciences is thus wrong. But . . . were the distinction correct it would be of no value, for it would distinguish nothing, since art and science would mark out no real difference between the various branches of knowledge, but only different points of view under which the same branch might be contemplated by us,—each being in different relations at once a science and an art. In fact, Dr. Whately confuses the distinction of science theoretical and science practical with the distinction of science and art.†

*Lectures, Vol. III, p. 4.
[*Elements of Logic, p. 1.]
†Lectures, Vol. III, p. 11; see also Discussions, pp. 133–4.

But if the difference between science and art is not the same as that between knowledge theoretical and practical, we are entitled to ask, what is it? If Archbishop Whately has placed the distinction where it is not, does his rather peremptory critic and censor tell us where it is? He declines the problem. "I am well aware that it would be no easy matter to give a general definition of science as contradistinguished from art, and of art as contradistinguished from science; but if the words themselves cannot validly be discriminated, it would be absurd to attempt to discriminate anything by them."[*] In the only other part of his *Lectures* where the distinction between Art and Science is touched on,* he says that the "apparently vague and capricious manner in which the terms art and science are applied," is not "the result of some accidental and forgotten usage," but is founded on a "rational principle which we are able to trace."[†] But when the reader is expecting a statement of this rational principle, Sir W. Hamilton puts him off with a merely historical explanation. Without stating what the usage actually is, he derives it from a distinction drawn by Aristotle between "a habit productive," and "a habit practical," which he admits to be "not perhaps beyond the reach of criticism:" which he does not undertake to "vindicate," and which he confesses to have been lost sight of by the moderns ever since they ceased to think "mechanical" arts "beneath their notice,"[‡] all these being called arts without any reference to Aristotle's supposed criterion.† So that Sir W. Hamilton cannot claim even accord-

[*_Lectures_, Vol. III, pp. 11–12.]
*_Ibid._, Vol. I, pp. 115–19.
[†_Ibid._, p. 116.]
[‡_Ibid._, pp. 118–19.]
†I give the Aristotelian distinction in Sir W. Hamilton's words. "In the Aristotelic philosophy the terms πρᾶξις and πρακτικός, that is, *practice* and *practical*,—were employed both in a generic or looser, and in a special or stricter signification. In its generic meaning, πρᾶξις, *practice*, was opposed to theory or speculation, and it comprehended under it, practice in its special meaning, and another co-ordinate term to which practice, in this its stricter signification, was opposed. This term was ποίησις, which we may inadequately translate by *production*. The distinction of πρακτικός and ποιητικός consisted in this: the former denoted that action which terminated in action,—the latter, that action which resulted in some permanent product. For example, dancing and music are practical, as leaving no work after their performance: whereas painting and statuary are productive, as leaving some product over and above their energy. Now Aristotle, in formally defining art, defines it as a habit productive, and not as a habit practical, ἕξις ποιητικὴ μετὰ λογου [see *Nichomachean Ethics*, pp. 334–5 (VI, iv, 1140ᵃ21–2)]; and though he has not always himself adhered strictly to this limitation, his definition was adopted by his followers, and the term in its application to the practical sciences (the term practical being here used in its genuine meaning), came to be exclusively confined to those whose end did not result in mere action or energy. Accordingly as Ethics, Politics, &c., proposed happiness as their end, and as happiness was an energy, or at least the concomitant of energy, these sciences terminated in action, and were

ance with usage for the distinction which he seems, but does not distinctly profess, to patronize. Yet the principal fault he finds with Archbishop Whately's distinction, is that it does not agree with usage. According to it, he says, "ethics, politics, religion, and all other practical sciences would be arts:"* and he speaks of the "incongruity we feel in talking of the art of Ethics, the art of Religion, &c., though these are eminently practical sciences."†

Religion may *be here* placed out of the question, for if there be incongruity with common feelings in calling Religion an art, there is quite as much in calling it a science, and especially a practical science, as if the theoretical doctrines of religion were no part of religion. If religion is either a science or an art, it must be both, and it is commonly understood to consist preeminently in things different from either, namely, a state of the feelings, and a disposition of the will. As for Ethics and Politics, the one and the other are, like Logic, both sciences and arts. Ethics, so far as it consists of the theory of the moral sentiments, and the investigation of those conditions of human well-being, disclosed by experience, which the practical part of Ethics has for its object to secure, is, in all senses of the word, a science. The rules or precepts of morals are an art. If there is any reluctance felt to speak of an art of morals, it is not because people prefer calling morals a science, but because most people are unwilling to look upon it as scientific at all, but prefer to regard it as a matter of instinct, *or of religious belief,* or as depending solely on the state of the will and the affections. In the case of Politics there is not, even to the vulgarest apprehension, any incongruity in the use of the word art: on the contrary, "the art of government" is the vernacular expression, and "science of government" a sort of speculative refinement. Philosophic writers on politics have generally preferred to call their subject a science, in order to indicate that it is a fit subject for speculative thinkers, the word art being apt to suggest to modern ears (it did not to the ancients) something which is the proper business only of practitioners. In reality Politics includes both a science and an art. The Science of Politics treats of the laws of political phænomena; it is the

---

consequently *practical*, not *productive*. On the other hand, Logic, Rhetoric, &c., did not terminate in a mere—an evanescent action, but in a permanent—an enduring product. For the end of Logic was the production of a reasoning, the end of Rhetoric the production of an oration, and so forth." (*Lectures*, Vol. I, pp. 117–18.) The English language expresses the same distinction by the two verbs, *to do* and *to make*.

Discussions, p. 134.
†*Lectures*, Vol. I, p. 116.

*-*65¹   here be
-+67, 72

science of human nature under social conditions. The Art of Politics consists (or would consist if it existed) of rules, founded on the science, for the right guidance and government of the affairs of society.

But, says Sir W. Hamilton, if the difference between Science and Art were merely that between affirmations and precepts, the distinction would be of no value, since it would "mark out no real difference between the various branches of knowledge, but only different points of view under which the same branch might be contemplated by us,—each being in different relations at once a science and an art." Was it from Sir W. Hamilton we should have expected to hear that a distinction is of no value, because it does not mark a difference between two things, but a difference in the *c*points*c* of view in which we may regard the same thing? How often has he told us, of many of the most important distinctions in philosophy, that they are precisely of this character! The remark, moreover, in the particular case, is so extremely superficial, that, coming from an author of whom it was by no means the habit to look only at the surface of things, it is one of the strongest of the many proofs which appear in his works, how little thought he had bestowed upon the sciences or arts, beyond his own speciality. The reason why systems of precepts require to be distinguished from systems of truths, is, that an entirely different classification is required for the purposes of theoretical knowledge, and for those of its practical application. Take the art of navigation, for example: where is the single science corresponding to this art, or which could with any propriety be included under the same name with it? Navigation is an art dependent on nearly the whole circle of the physical sciences: on astronomy, for the marks by which it determines the ship's place on the ocean; on optics, for the construction and use of its instruments; on abstract mechanics, to understand and regulate the ship's movements; on pneumatics, for the laws of winds; on hydrostatics, for the tides and currents, and the waves as influenced by *d*winds*d*; on meteorology, for the weather; on electricity, for thunderstorms; on magnetism, for the use of the compass; on physical geography, and so on nearly to the end of the list. Not only has each one of all these sciences furnished its contingent towards the rules composing the one art of navigation, but many single rules could only have been framed by the union of considerations drawn from several different sciences. For the purposes of the art, the rules by themselves are sufficient, wherever it has been found practicable to make them sufficiently precise. But if the learner, not content with knowing and practising the rules, wishes to understand their reasons, and so possess science as well as art, he finds no one science corresponding in its object-matter with the art; he must extract from many

*c-c*65[1]   point
*d-d*65[1]   wind

sciences those truths of each which have been turned to practical account for the furtherance of navigation. All this is obvious to any one (not to say a person of Sir W. Hamilton's sagacity), who has sufficiently reflected on the sciences and arts, to be aware of the relation between them. Archbishop Whately's distinction, therefore, in no way merits the contemptuous treatment which it receives in the *Lectures*, and still more in the *Discussions*.[*] It is eminently practical, it conforms to the natural and logical order of thought, and accords better with the ends and even with the custom of language, than any other mode in which Arts can be distinguished from Sciences. Sir W. Hamilton, though he condemns it, has not ventured to set up any competing distinction in its place, but (as we have seen) almost intimates that no satisfactory one can be found.

Next after the question whether Logic is a science, comes the consideration of its object-matter as a science, namely, "the Laws of Thought as Thought."[†] "The consideration of this head," says our author, "divides itself into three questions—1. What is Thought? 2. What is Thought as Thought? 3. What are the Laws of Thought as Thought?"* These three questions are successively discussed.

To the question, "What is Thought?" Sir W. Hamilton answers—It is not the direct perception of an object, nor its representation in memory or imagination, nor its mere suggestion by association, but is a product of intelligence. Intelligence acts only by comparison.

All thought is a comparison, a recognition of similarity or difference, a conjunction or disjunction, in other words a synthesis or analysis of its objects. In Conception, that is, in the formation of Concepts (or general notions) it compares, disjoins or conjoins, attributes; in an act of Judgment, it compares, disjoins or conjoins, concepts; in Reasoning, it compares, disjoins or conjoins, judgments. In each step of this process there is one essential element; to think, to compare, to conjoin or disjoin, it is necessary to recognise one thing *through* or *under* another, and therefore, in defining Thought proper, we may either define it as an act of Comparison, or as a recognition of one notion as *in* or *under* another. It is in performing this act of thinking a thing under a general notion, that we are said to understand or comprehend it. For example: An object is presented, say a book: this object determines an impression, and I am even conscious of the impression, but without recognising to myself what the thing is; in that case, there is only a perception, and not properly a thought. But suppose I do recognise it for what it is, in other words, compare it with and *reduce it under* a certain concept, class, or complement of attributes, which I call *book*; in that case, there is more than a perception,—there is a thought.†

Further on, he again defines an act of thought as "the recognition of a

[*See *Lectures*, Vol. III, pp. 11–12; *Discussions*, pp. 130–4.]
[†See *Lectures*, Vol. III, p. 4.]
Ibid., p. 12.
†*Ibid*., pp. 13–14.

thing as coming *under* a concept; in other words, the marking an object by an attribute or attributes previously known as common to sundry objects, and to which we have accordingly given a general name."* And subsequently, as "the comprehension of a thing under a general notion or attribute;"† and again, "the cognition of any mental object by another in which it is considered as included; in other words, thought is *the knowledge of things under conceptions*."‡ And again, "Thought is the Knowledge of a thing *through* a concept or general notion, or of one notion *through* another."§

From these different expressions we may infer, that the author confines the name Thought to cases where there is a judgment; and, it would seem, a judgment affirming more than mere existence. We think an object, or make anything an object of thought, when we are able to predicate something of it; to affirm that it is something in particular; that it is a certain sort of thing; that it belongs to a class—has something which is (or may be) common to it with a number of other things; that it has, in short, a certain attribute, or attributes. This is intelligible, and unobjectionable: but our author's technical expressions, instead of facilitating the understanding of it, tend, on the contrary, very much to confuse it. Like the transcendental metaphysicians generally, Sir W. Hamilton, when he attempts to state the nature of a mental phænomenon with peculiar precision, does it by a peculiarly unprecise employment of the common prepositions. What light is thrown upon the simple process of referring objects to a class, by calling it the recognition of one thing through, or in, or under, another? What distinct signification is conveyed by the phrases, "thinking a thing under a general notion," "reducing it under a concept," "knowing things under, or through, conceptions?" To find the meaning of the explanation we have to resort to the thing explained. The only passage in which the author speaks distinctly, is that in which he paraphrases these expressions by the following: "the marking an object by an attribute or attributes previously known as common to sundry objects, and to which we have accordingly given a general name." To think of an object, then, is to mark it by an attribute or set of attributes, which has received a name, or (what is much more essential) which gives a name to the object. It gives to the object the concrete name, to which its own abstract name, if it has an abstract name, corresponds: but it is not indispensable that the attribute should have received a name, provided it gives one to the object possessing it. An animal is called a bull, in sign of its possessing certain attributes, but there does not exist an abstract word

*Ibid., p. 15.
†Ibid., p. 21.
‡Ibid., p. 40.
§Ibid., p. 43.

bullness. Having, then, in Sir W. Hamilton's language, thought the object, by marking it with a name derived from an attribute, it is perhaps an allowable, though an obscure, expression, to say that we know the thing through the attribute, or through the notion of the attribute: but what is meant by saying that we know it, or think it *under* the attribute? We know it and think it, simply as possessing the attribute. The other phrase, while seeming to mean more, means less. Again, when we are asserted to "know one notion through another;" when, for example, we think, or judge, that men, meaning all men, are mortal; is this to know the notion Man through the notion Mortal? The knowledge we really have, is that the objects Men have the attribute mortality; in other words, that the outward facts by which we distinguish men, exist along with subjection to the outward fact, death. If there is a recommendation I would inculcate on every one who commences the study of metaphysics, it is, to be always sure what he means by his particles. A large portion of all that perplexes and confuses metaphysical thought, comes from a vague use of those small words.

After this definition of Thought, our author proceeds to explain what he means by Thought as Thought. He means, "that Logic is conversant with the form of thought, to the exclusion of the matter."* We have here arrived at one of the cardinal points in Sir W. Hamilton's philosophy of Logic. However he may vary on other doctrines, to this he is constant, that the province of Logic is the form, not the matter, of thought. It is a pity that the only terms he can find to denote the distinction, are a pair of the obscurest and most confusing expressions in the whole range of metaphysics. Still more unfortunate *e*it is*e*, that, thinking it necessary to employ such terms, he has never, in unambiguous language, explained their meaning. When Archbishop Whately, in somewhat similar phraseology, tells us that Logic has to do with the form of the reasoning process, but not with its matter, we know what he means.[*] It is, that Logic is not concerned with the actual truth either of the conclusion or of the premises, but considers only whether the one follows from the other; whether the conclusion must be true if the premises are true. Sir W. Hamilton is not content to mean only this. He means much more; but if we wish to know what, the only information he here gives us is a quotation from a German philosopher, Esser.

We are able, by abstraction, to distinguish from each other,—1°. The object thought of; and 2°. The kind and manner of thinking it. Let us, employing the old established technical expressions, call the first of these the *matter*, the second the *form*, of the thought. For example, when I think that the book before me is a folio, the matter of the thought is book and folio, the form of it is a judgment.[†]

Ibid., p. 15.
[*See, e.g., *Elements of Logic*, pp. 13–14.]
[†*Lectures*, Vol. III, p. 15; cf. Esser, *Logik*, p. 4.]

*e–e*65[1], 65[2]   is it

Thus far Esser. The Form, therefore, of Thought, with which alone Logic is conversant, is not the object thought of, but "the kind and manner of thinking it." It is not necessary to show that this explanation is insufficient. But to find any other, we must have recourse, not to Sir W. Hamilton, but to Mr. Mansel. One of the chapters of Mr. Mansel's *Prolegomena Logica* is entitled "On the Matter and Form of Thought." It commences as follows:

The distinction between Matter and Form in common language relatively to works of Art, will serve to illustrate the character of the corresponding distinction in Thought. The term Matter is usually applied to whatever is given to the artist, and consequently, as given, does not come within the province of the art itself to supply. The Form is that which is given in and through the proper operation of the art. In Sculpture, for example, the Matter is the marble in its rough state as given to the sculptor; the Form is that which the sculptor in the exercise of his art communicates to it.

Let me here ask, had the block of marble no form at all when it came out of the quarry?

The distinction between Matter and Form in any mental operation is analogous to this. The former includes all that is given *to*, the latter all that is given *by*, the operation. In the division of notions, for example, whether performed by an act of pure thinking or not, the generic notion is that given to be divided; the addition of the difference in the act of division constitutes the species. And accordingly, Genus is frequently designated by logicians the *material*, Difference the *formal*, part of the Species. [An illustration which, whatever else it may do, does not illustrate.] So likewise in any operation of pure thinking, the Matter will include all that is given to and out of the thought; the Form is what is conveyed in and by the thinking act itself.*

This is a fair account of the meaning of Matter and Form in the Kantian philosophy, and the philosophies which descend genealogically from the Kantian. But this meaning must always be taken with, and interpreted by, the characteristic doctrine of the Kantian metaphysics, that the mind does not perceive, but itself creates, all the most general attributes which, by a natural illusion, we ascribe to outward things; which attributes, consequently, are called, by that philosophy, Forms. Extension and Duration, for example, it calls forms of our sensitive faculty; Substance, Causality, Quantity, forms of our Understanding, which is our faculty of thought. These, however, are not what Sir W. Hamilton and Mr. Mansel[*] mean, when they say that Logic is the science of the *forms* of thought. They do not mean that it is the science of Substance, Causality, and Quantity. The truth is, that as soon as the word Form is stretched beyond its proper signification of bodily figure, it becomes entirely vague: every thinker uses

*_____
Prolegomena Logica, pp. 226–7. [The words in square brackets are Mill's.]
[*Ibid.*, p. 233.]

*–*65¹   form [*printer's error?*]

it in a sense of his own. The only bond connecting its various meanings, is the negative one of opposition to Matter. Whenever anything is called Form, there is something which, relatively to it, is regarded as Matter: and whenever anything is called Matter, there is something capable of being superinduced upon it, which when superinduced will be styled its Form. How completely the notion of Form accompanies that of Matter as its relative opposite, we have an illustrious example in Aristotle, when he defines the Soul as the Form of the Body;[*] so, at least, Sir W. Hamilton *g*, very freely,*g* translates ἐντελέχεια.* It would be quite warranted by the practice of metaphysicians, to call any compound the form of its component elements; water, for instance, the form of hydrogen and oxygen. And since there is nothing that may not be regarded as matter relatively to something which can be constructed out of it, and which is form relatively to it, but matter relatively to some other thing, we have form within form, like a nest of boxes. Kant actually calls the conclusion of a syllogism the form of it, the premises being its matter: so that in every train of reasoning, the successive conclusions pass over one by one from Form to Matter.[†] Without going this length, Sir W. Hamilton,† after Krug, considers the propositions and terms as the matter of the syllogism, and the mode in which they are connected as its form. Yet propositions and terms (*i.e.* concepts) are classed by him as Forms of Thought. Thus it is impossible to draw any line between the Matter of Thought and its Form, or to convey any distinct conception of the province of a science by saying that it is conversant with the one and not with the other. We may, however, in a general way, understand Sir W. Hamilton to mean, that Logic is not concerned with the actual contents of our knowledge—with the particular objects, or truths, which we know—but only with our mode of knowing them: with what the mind does when it knows, or thinks, irrespectively of the particular things which it thinks about: with the theory of the act or fact of thinking, so far as that fact is the same in all our thought, or can be reduced to universal principles.

[*See Aristotle, *On the Soul*, pp. 66–70 (II, i, 412^{a-b}).]

*See Reid, [*Inquiry*,] p. 202, and Sir W. Hamilton's foot-note [pp. 202n–3n]. A still odder example is given by Reid in his *Essays on the Active Powers*. "In the scholastic ages, an action good in itself was said to be *materially* good, and an action done with a right intention was called *formally* good. This last way of expressing the distinction is still familiar among theologians." (*Works*, [ed. Hamilton,] pp. 649–50.)

[†See Kant, *Logik*, in *Prolegomena zu einer jeden Künftigen Metaphysik, die als Wissenschaft wird Auftreten Können und Logik*, in *Werke*, Vol. III, p. 306.]

†*Lectures*, Vol. III, pp. 287–8. [See Krug, *Logik*, §85.] So also Mr. Mansel, *Prolegomena Logica*, p. 235.

g-g+67, 72

But the fact of thinking is a psychological phænomenon; and Logic is a different thing from Psychology. It is for the purpose of marking this difference that Sir W. Hamilton adds a third point to his definition of Logic, calling it the science not simply of Thought as Thought, but of the Laws of Thought as Thought. For Psychology also treats of thought, considered merely as thought; and professes to give an acount of Thought as a mental operation. In what, then, consists the difference between the two? I cannot venture to state it in any but our author's own words.

The phænomena of the formal, or subjective phases of thought, are of two kinds. They are either such as are contingent, that is, such as may or may not appear; or they are such as are necessary, that is, such as cannot but appear. These two classes of phænomena are, however, only manifested in conjunction; they are not discriminated in the actual operations of thought; and it requires a speculative analysis to separate them into their several classes. In so far as these phænomena are considered merely as phænomena, that is, in so far as philosophy is merely observant of them as manifestations in general, they belong to the science of Empirical or Historical Psychology. But when philosophy, by a reflective abstraction, analyses the necessary from the contingent forms of thought, there results a science, which is distinguished from all others by taking for its object-matter the former of these classes; and this science is Logic. Logic, therefore, is at last fully and finally defined as the science of the necessary forms of thought.*

If language has any meaning, this passage must be understood to say, that the "laws" or "forms" which are the province of Logic, are certain "phænomena" of thought, distinguished from its other phænomena by being necessarily present in it,—"such as cannot but appear,"—while the remaining phænomena "may or may not appear." If this be meant, we are landed in a strange conclusion. There is a science, Psychology, which is the science of all mental phænomena, and among others, of the phænomena of Thought, and yet another science, Logic, is required to teach us its *necessary* phænomena. There is a portion of the properties of Thought which are expressly excluded from the science which treats of Thought, to be reserved as the matter of another science, and these are precisely its Necessary *h*qualities*h*. Those which are merely contingent, "such as may or may not appear"—the properties which are not common to all thought, or do not belong to it at all times—these, it seems to be said, Psychology knows something about: but the Necessary properties, "such as cannot but appear"—the properties which all thoughts possess, which thought must possess, without the possession of which it would not be thought—these Psychology knows not of, and it is the office of a different science to investigate them. We may next expect to be told, that the science of dynamics knows nothing of the laws of motion, the composition of forces,

Lectures, Vol. III, p. 24.

*h-h*65[1], 65[2], 67   properties

the theory of continuous and accelerating force, the doctrines of Momentum and Vis Viva, &c.; it only knows of wind power and water power, steam power and animal power, and the accidents by flood and field which accompany them and disturb their operation.

This, however, supposes that our author means what he expressly says. It assumes that by the "Laws of Thought," and the "Necessary Forms of Thought," he means the modes in which, and the conditions subject to which, by the constitution of our nature, we cannot but think. But when we turn over a few pages, to the placc where he is preparing to treat of those laws or necessary forms one by one, it appears that this is an entire mistake. Laws now no longer mean necessities of nature; they are laws in a totally different sense; they mean precepts: and the "necessary forms of thought" are not attributes which it must, but only which it ought to possess.

When I speak of laws, and of their absolute necessity in relation to thought, you must not suppose that these laws and that necessity are the same in the world of mind as in the world of matter. For free intelligences, a law is an ideal necessity given in the form of a precept, which we ought to follow, but which we may also violate if we please; whereas, for the existences which constitute the universe of nature, a law is only another name for those causes which operate blindly and universally in producing certain inevitable results. By *law of thought*, or by *logical necessity*, we do not, therefore, mean a physical law, such as the law of gravitation, but a general precept which we are able certainly to violate, but which if we do not obey, our whole process of thinking is suicidal, or absolutely null. These laws are, consequently, the primary conditions of the possibility of valid thought; and . . . the whole of Pure Logic is only an articulate development of the various modes in which they are applied.*

Lectures, Vol. III, pp. 78–9. It might have been supposed that the double meaning of the word law, though in the last century it could blind even a Montesquieu, had been sufficiently written about since that time, to be understood by minds of far less calibre than Sir W. Hamilton's: yet in this passage he does not recognise it, but seems rather to think that the difference between a law in the scientific, and a law in the legislative or ethical sense, does not turn on an ambiguity of the word, but on the difference between "the world of mind" and "the world of matter:" a "free intelligence" knowing only precepts, which it has power to disobey, and not being ruled, like the physical world, by laws from which it cannot escape. Yet Sir W. Hamilton is the same philosopher who is for ever telling us of necessities of thought which are absolutely irresistible to us—from which we can by no mental effort emancipate ourselves; and upon this alleged fact the larger half of his philosophy is grounded. When we find all this forgotten, we almost fancy that we have opened a volume of some other writer by mistake. Treating of the same question in another place, our author remembers his own philosophy much better. In the Lecture in which he divides mental science into the "Phænomenology of Mind" and its "Nomology," the former a classification and analysis of our mental faculties, the latter an investigation of their "laws," the word Laws always stands for "necessary and universal facts," "the Laws by which our faculties are governed," not precepts by which they ought to be governed: and of these necessary

So that, after all, the real theory of Thought—the laws, in the scientific sense of the term, of Thought as Thought—do not belong to Logic, but to Psychology: and it is only the *validity* of thought which Logic takes cognisance of. It is not with Thought as Thought, but only as Valid thought, that Logic is concerned. There is nothing to prevent us from thinking contrary to the laws of Logic: only, if we do, we shall not think rightly, or well, or conformably to the ends of thinking, but falsely, or inconsistently, or confusedly. This doctrine is at complete variance with the saying of our author in his controversy with Whately, that Logic is, and never could have been doubted to be, in Whately's sense of the terms, both a Science and an Art. For the present definition reduces it to the narrowest conception of an Art—that of a mere system of rules. It leaves Science to Psychology, and represents Logic as merely offering to thinkers a collection of precepts, which they are enjoined to observe, not in order that they may think, but that they may think correctly, or validly.

It appears to me, however, that our author, though inconsistent with himself, is much nearer the mark in this mode of regarding Logic than in the previous one. I conceive it to be true that Logic is not the theory of Thought as Thought, but of valid Thought; not of thinking, but of correct thinking. It is not a Science distinct from, and coordinate with, Psychology. So far as it is a science at all, it is a part, or branch, of Psychology; differing from it, on the one hand as a part differs from the whole, and on the other, as an Art differs from a Science. Its theoretic grounds are wholly borrowed from Psychology, and include as much of that science as is required to justify the rules of the art. Logic has no need to know more of the Science of Thinking, than the difference between good thinking and bad. A consequence of this is, that the Necessary Laws of Thought, those which our author in his first doctrine reserved especially to Logic, are precisely those with which Logic has least to do, and which belong the most exclusively to Psychology. What is common to all thought, whether good or bad, and inseparable from it, is irrelevant to Logic, unless by the light it may indirectly throw on something besides itself. The properties of Thought which concern Logic, are some of its contingent properties; those, namely, on the presence of which depends good thinking, as distinguished from bad.

I therefore accept our author's second view of the province of Logic, which makes it a collection of precepts or rules for thinking, grounded on a

---

and universal facts it is expressly said that the Laws of Thought, with which Logic is concerned, are a part. They are classed with "the Laws of Memory," "the Laws of Association," "the laws which govern our capacities of enjoyment," all of which are correctly described as necessary facts, and not as precepts. (*Ibid.*, Vol. I, pp. 121ff.) The whole of this is thrown to the winds when the time comes for taking up Logic as a separate science.

scientific investigation of the requisites of valid thought. It is this doctrine which governs his treatment of the details of Logic, and it is by this that we must interpret the assertion that Logic has for its only subject the Form of Thought. By the Form of Thought we must understand Thinking itself; the whole work of the Intellect. The Matter of Thought is the sensations, perceptions, or other presentations (intuitions, as Mr. Mansel calls them),[*] in which the intellect has no share; which are supplied to it, independently of any action of its own. What the mind adds to these, or puts into them, is Forms of Thought. Logic, therefore, is concerned only with Forms, since, being rules for thinking, it can have no authority but over that which depends on thought. Logic and Thinking are coextensive; it is the art of Thinking, of all Thinking, and of nothing but Thinking. And since every distinguishable variety of thinking act is called a Form of Thought, the Forms of Thought compose the whole province of Logic; though it would be hardly possible to invent a worse phrase for expressing so simple a fact.

But what *are* the Forms of Thought? Kant, as already observed, gives to that expression a very wide extent. He holds that every ⁱfundamentalⁱ attribute which we ascribe to external objects is a Form of Thought, being created, not simply discerned, by our thinking faculty.[†] Neither Sir W. Hamilton nor Mr. Mansel goes this length; and at all events they do not consider the theory of the various attributes of bodies to be a part of Logic. It was incumbent on them, therefore, to state clearly what are the Forms of Thought with which Logic is concerned, and for which it supplies precepts. This question is never put, in an express form, by Sir W. Hamilton: but the answer which he rather leaves to be picked up than directly presents, may be gathered from his classification of our intellectual operations. These he reduces to three, Conception, Judgment, and Reasoning. He must have recognised, therefore, that number of general Forms of Thought. The Forms of Thought are Conception, Judgment, and Reasoning: Logic is the Science of the Laws (meaning the rules) of these three operations. If, however, we rigorously hold our author to this short list, we shall perpetually mistake his meaning: for (as already observed) the mode in which the word Form is used, allows of form within form to an unlimited extent. Every concept, judgment, or reasoning, after having received its form from the mind, may again be contemplated as the Matter of some further mental act; and the product of that further act (according to Kant),[‡] or the relation of the product to the matter (according to Sir W. Hamilton and Mr.

[*See *Prolegomena Logica*, pp. 9–10.]
[†*Kritik der Reinen Vernunft*, pp. 745–7.]
[‡*Ibid.*]

ⁱ⁻ⁱ+72

Mansel), is again a Form of Thought; as we find, to our confusion, when we proceed further, and the more profusely, the further we proceed. We have, first, however, to consider a proposition of Sir W. Hamilton, which qualifies his definition of the province of Logic. He says:

"Logic considers Thought, not as the operation of thinking, but as its product; it does not treat of Conception, Judgment, and Reasoning, but of Concepts, Judgments, and Reasonings."*

Let me begin by saying that I give my entire adhesion to this distinction, and propose to reform the definition of Logic accordingly. It does not, as we now see, relate to the Laws of Thought as Thought, but to those of the Products of Thought. Instead of the Laws of Conception, Judgment, and Reasoning, we must speak of the Laws of Concepts, Judgments, and Reasonings. This would be mere nonsense in the scientific sense of the word law: for a product, as such, can have no laws but those of the operation which produces it. But understanding by laws, as it seems we are intended to do, Precepts, Logic becomes the science of the precepts for the formation of concepts, judgments, and reasonings: or rather (a science of precepts being an improper expression) the science of the conditions on which right concepts, judgments, and reasonings depend. Thus, Logic is the Art of Thinking, which means of correct thinking, and the Science of the Conditions of correct thinking. This seems to me a sufficiently accurate definition of it. But, in attempting a deeper metaphysical analysis of the distinction he has just drawn, our author raises fresh difficulties. He says:

The form of thought may be viewed on two sides, or in two relations. It holds, as has been said, a relation both to its subject and to its object, and it may accordingly be viewed either in the one of these relations or in the other. In so far as the form of thought is considered in reference to the thinking mind,—to the mind by which it is exerted,—it is considered as an act, or operation, or energy; and in this relation it belongs to Phænomenal Psychology. Whereas, in so far as this form is considered in reference to what thought is about, it is considered as the product of such an act, and in this relation it belongs to Logic. Thus Phænomenal Psychology treats of thought proper as conception, judgment, reasoning: Logic, or the Nomology of the Understanding, treats of thought proper as a concept, as a judgment, as a reasoning.†

Just when the puzzled reader fancied that he had at last arrived at something clear, comes an explanation which throws all back into darkness. The learner who had been wandering in the mazes of "Thought as Thought," laws which are not laws, and "Forms of Thought" in which Form stands for something which he never before heard of in connexion with that word, at last descried what seemed to be firm ground: he was told that Conception, Judgment, and Reasoning are acts of the mind, that Concepts,

*Lectures, Vol. III, p. 73.
†Ibid., pp. 73–4.

Judgments, and Reasonings are products of those acts, and that Psychology is conversant with the former and Logic with the latter. And now it turns out that the products *are* the acts. The two series of things are one and the same series. They are both of them only "Thought proper." The product is another word for the act itself, considered in one of its aspects— "in reference to what thought is about." It is curious that this should occur only a few pages after Whately has been rebuked for reducing a distinction to inutility, by making it coincide with a difference not between things, but between the aspects in which the same thing is regarded.

Sir W. Hamilton therefore is of opinion that the thinking act, though verbally, is not psychologically different from the thought itself. He does not hold, with Berkeley, that an Idea is a concrete object distinct from the mind, and contained in it, like furniture in a house; nor with Locke (if that was Locke's opinion), that it is a modification of the mind, but a modification distinct from the mind's act in cognising it; but with Brown, that a sensation is only myself feeling, and a thought only myself thinking. Concepts, Judgments, and Reasonings, are only acts of conceiving, judging, and reasoning; acts of thought, considered not in their relation to the thinking mind, but to their object, to "what thought is about."* But what *is* thought about? Not about Concepts, for all our thoughts are not about the thinking act. It must be about the objective presentation, the Anschauung, or Intuition, which the Concept represents, or from which it has been abstracted. According, therefore, to the doctrine here distinctly laid down by Sir W. Hamilton, there are but two things present in any of our intellectual operations; on one hand, the mind itself thinking (that is, conceiving, judging, or reasoning), and, on the other, a mental presentation or representation of the phænomenal Reality which it conceives, or concerning which it judges or reasons. I can understand that the thinking act, or in other words, the mind in a thinking state, may be contemplated in its relation to the Reality thought of, and may receive a name which connotes

---

*Sir W. Hamilton holds a corresponding theory in regard to the identity of an imagination with the imagining act. "A representation considered as an object is logically, not really, different from a representation considered as an act. Here object and act are merely the same indivisible mode of mind viewed in two different relations. Considered by reference to a mediate object represented, it is a representative object: considered by reference to the mind representing and contemplating the representation, it is a representative act. A representative object being viewed as posterior in the order of nature, but not of time, to the representative act, is viewed as a *product*; and the representative act being viewed as prior in the order of nature, though not of time, to the representative object, is viewed as a producing process." ("Dissertations on Reid," [Note B,] p. 809.) Sir W. Hamilton has not explained how, in the order of nature, or in any other order, a thing can be prior, or posterior, or prior and posterior, to itself.

that Reality; but how does this entitle us to call it a *product* of thought? How can the act of thought, or the mind thinking, be looked upon, even hypothetically, as a product of thinking? How can Concepts, Judgments, and Reasonings be regarded as products of thought, ʲifʲ they are the thought itself? Can they be both the act and something resulting from the act? Are they results and products of themselves?

I conceive that there is a way out of this difficulty; a sense in which the two assertions can be reconciled, though it has not been pointed out by Sir W. Hamilton, and is hardly compatible with some of his opinions. There is a difference between what can properly be called Acts of the mind, and the other mental phænomena which may be termed its passive States. And I know but one way of conceiving the distinction, in which it can possibly be upheld, namely, by considering as Acts only those mental phænomena which are results of Volition. Now, the first formation of a Concept, and generally (though not always) any fresh operation of judgment or reasoning, requires a mental effort, a concentration of consciousness upon certain definite objects, which concentration depends on the will, and is called Attention. When this takes place, the mind is properly said to be active. But after frequent repetition of this act of will, the associations to which it has given rise are sufficiently riveted to do their work spontaneously; the effort of attention, after becoming less and less, is finally null, and the operation, originally voluntary, becomes, in Hartley's language, secondarily automatic.[*] When this transition has been completed, what remains of the mental phænomenon has lost the character of an Act, and become numbered among passive States. It is now either a mere mental representation of an object, differing from those copied directly from sense, only in having certain of its parts artificially made intense and prominent; or it is a *fasciculus* of representations of imagination, held together by the tie of an association artificially produced. When the mental phænomenon has assumed this passive character, it comes to be termed a Concept, or, more familiarly and vaguely, an Idea, and to be felt as if it were, not the mind modified, but something in the mind: and in this ultimate phasis of its existence we may properly consider it, not as an act, but as the product of a previous act; since it now takes place without any conscious activity, and becomes a subject on which fresh activity may be exercised, by an act of voluntary attention concentrating consciousness on it, or on some particular part of it. This explanation, which I leave for the consideration of philosophers, would not have suited Sir W. Hamilton, since it would have required him to limit the extent which he habitually gave to the expression

[*See *Observations on Man*, Vol. I, p. 104.]

ʲ⁻ʲ65¹, 65² when

"mental act." [k] Every phænomenon of mind, down to the mere reception of a sensation, he regards as an act: therein differing from Kant, and annihilating the need and use of the word, the sole function of which is to distinguish what the mind originates, from what something else originates in the mind.

To return to the definition of Logic, as the science of the Forms of Thought, considered in relation, not to the thinking act itself, but, so far as they are distinguishable from it, to the products of thought. The products of thought are Concepts, Judgments, and Reasonings, and the Forms of Thought are Conception, Judgment, and Reasoning. Logic is the science of those Forms, so far as concerns the rules for the right formation of the products: or, as our author elsewhere phrases it, the science of the "formal conditions" of valid thinking.[*] These modes of expression have a rare power of darkening the subject, but I am endeavouring to give them an intelligible interpretation, by means of that which they profess to explain. If, then, all thinking consists in adding, to given matter, a Form derived from the mind itself, what shall we say of the division, on which so much stress is laid, of Thinking itself into two kinds, Formal and Material Thinking, the first of which alone belongs to Logic, or at all events to pure Logic? Mr. Mansel has written a volume for the express purpose of showing that Logic is only concerned with Formal Thinking; and Sir W. Hamilton's division of Logic into Pure and Modified, agrees with Mr. Mansel's distinction.[†] Yet, according to the definition we have just considered, all thinking whatever is Formal Thinking: since all thinking is either conceiving, judging, or reasoning, and these are the Forms of Thought. If Logic investigates the conditions requisite for the right formation of concepts, of judgments, and of reasonings, it investigates all the conditions of right thought, for there are no other kinds of thought than these; and if it does all this, what is left for the so-called Material Thinking which Logic is said not to be concerned with?

The answer to this question affords an additional specimen of the incurable confusion, in which the processes of thought are involved by the unhappy misapplication to them of the metaphorical word Form. Though Concepts, Judgments, and Reasonings, are said to be the forms of thought, and the only forms which thought takes, or rather gives; the metaphysicians who deal in Forms are in the habit of using phrases which signify that Concepts, Judgments, and Reasonings, though themselves Forms, have also, in themselves, a formal part and a material. Different concepts,

[*See, e.g., *Lectures*, Vol. III, pp. 64, 79.]
[†See *Prolegomena Logica*, pp. 227–9, 237–40.]

[k]65[1], 65[2], 67   It has been said, not without reason, of Condillac and others, that their psychological explanations treat our mental nature as entirely passive, ignoring its active side. The contrary error may with equal reason be imputed to Sir W. Hamilton, that of ignoring the passive side.

judgments, and reasonings, have different matter, according to what it is that the conception, the judgment, or the reasoning, is about: and as whatever part of anything is not its Matter, is always styled its Form, whatever is common to all Concepts, or whatever belongs to them irrespectively of all differences in their matter, is said to be their Form; and so of Judgments and of Reasonings. Thus, the difference between an affirmative and a negative judgment is a difference of form, because a judgment may be either affirmative or negative whatever be the matter to which it relates. The difference between a categorical and an hypothetical syllogism is a difference of form, because it neither depends on, nor is it at all affected by, any differences in the matter. Logic, according to Mr. Mansel[*]—pure Logic, according to Sir W. Hamilton—is conversant only with the Forms of Concepts, Judgments, and Reasonings, not with their Matter. Not only is it concerned exclusively with the Forms of thought, but exclusively with the Forms of those Forms. And here I fairly renounce any further attempt to deduce Sir W. Hamilton's or Mr. Mansel's *conception* of Logic from their definitions of it. I collect it from the general evidence of their treatises, and I proceed to show why I consider it to be wrong.

Logic, Sir W. Hamilton has told us, lays down the laws or precepts indispensable to Valid Thought; the conditions to which thought is bound to conform, under the penalty of being invalid, ineffectual, not accomplishing its end. And what is, peculiarly and emphatically, the end of Thinking? Surely it is the attainment of Truth. Surely, if not the sole, at all events the first and most essential constituent of valid thought, is that its results should be true. Concepts, Judgments, and Reasonings, should agree with the reality of things, meaning by things the Phænomena or sensible presentations, to which those mental products have reference. A concept, to be rightly framed, must be a concept of something real, and must agree with the real fact which it endeavours to represent, that is, the collection of attributes composing the concept must really exist in the objects marked by the class-name, and in no others. A judgment, to be rightly framed, must be a true judgment, that is, the objects judged of must really possess the attributes predicated of them. A reasoning, to be rightly framed, must conduct to a true conclusion, since the only purpose of reasoning is to make known to us truths which we cannot learn by direct intuition. Even those who take the most limited view of Logic, allow that the conclusion must be true conditionally—provided that the premises are true. The most important, then, and at bottom the only important quality of a thought being its truth, the laws or precepts provided for the guidance of thought must surely have for their principal purpose that the products of thinking shall be true.

[*See, e.g., *ibid.*, pp. 240–5.]

*⁻*65¹, 65² conceptions

Yet with this, according to Mr. Mansel, Logic has no concern;[*] and Sir W. Hamilton reserves it for a sort of appendix to the science, under the title of Modified Logic. Questions of truth and falsity, according to both writers, regard only Material Thinking, while Formal Thinking is the province of Logic. The only precepts for thinking with which Logic concerns itself, are those which have some other purpose than the conformity of our thoughts to the fact. Yet every possible precept for thought, if it be an honest one, must have this for at least its ultimate object. What, then, is excluded from Logic, and what is left in it, by the doctrine that it is only concerned with Formal Thinking? What is excluded is the whole of the evidences of the validity of thought. What is included is part of the evidences of its invalidity.

In no case can thinking be valid unless the concepts, judgments, and conclusions resulting from it are conformable to fact. And in no case can we satisfy ourselves that they are so, by looking merely at the relations of one part of the train of thought to another. We must ascend to the original sources, the presentations of experience, and examine the train of thought in its relation to these. But we can sometimes discover, without ascending to the sources, that the process of thought is *not* valid; having been so conducted that it cannot possibly avail for obtaining concepts, judgments, or conclusions in accordance with fact. This, for example, is the case, if we have allowed ourselves to travel from premises to a conclusion through an ambiguous term. The process then gives no ground at all for believing the conclusion to be true: it is perhaps true, but we have no more reason to believe so than we had before. Or again, the concept, the judgment, or the reasoning may involve a contradiction, and so cannot possibly correspond to any real state of facts. It is with this part of the subject only, in the opinion of these philosophers, that Logic concerns itself. According to Mr. Mansel, Logic "accepts, as logically valid, all such concepts, judgments, and reasonings, as do not, directly or indirectly, imply contradictions; pronouncing them thus far to be legitimate as thoughts, that they do not in ultimate analysis destroy themselves . . . leaving to this or that branch of material science to determine how far the same products of thought are guaranteed by the testimony of this or that special experience."* Mr. Mansel has not here conceived his own view of the subject with his usual precision. He narrows the field of Logic more than he intends. That to which he confines the name of Logic, accepts as valid all concepts and judgments that do not imply contradictions, but by no means all reasonings. It rejects these not only when self-contradictory, but when simply inconclusive. It condemns a reasoning not only if it draws a conclusion inconsis-

[*See *ibid.*, pp. 237–40, 265–8.]
Ibid., p. 265.

tent with the premises, but if it draws one which the premises do not warrant; not only if the conclusion must, but if it may, be false though the premises be true. For the notion of true and false *will* force its way even into Formal Logic, whatever pains Sir W. Hamilton and Mr. Mansel give themselves to make the notions of consistent and inconsistent, or of thinkable and unthinkable, do duty instead of it. The ideas of truth and falsity cannot be eliminated from reasoning. We may abstract from actual truth, but the validity of reasoning is always a question of conditional truth—whether one proposition must be true if others are true, or whether one proposition can be true if others are true. When Judgments or Reasonings are in question, "the conditions of the thinkable" are simply the conditions of the believable.

What Mr. Mansel and Sir W. Hamilton really mean, is to segregate from the remainder of the theory of the investigation of truth, as much of it as does not require any reference to the original sufficiency of the groundwork of facts, or the correctness of their interpretation, and call this exclusively Logic, or Pure Logic. They assume that concepts have been formed and judgments made somehow; and if there is nothing within the four corners of the concept or the judgment which proves it absurd, that is, no self-contradiction, they do not question it further. Whether it is grounded on fact or on mere supposition, and if on fact, whether the fact is represented correctly, they do not ask; but think only of the conditions necessary for preventing errors from getting into the process of thought, which were not in the notions or the premises from whence it started. The theory of these conditions (of which the doctrine of the Syllogism is the principal part) Mr. Mansel calls Logic, and Sir W. Hamilton Pure Logic. The expression "Formal Logic," which is sometimes applied to it, is perhaps as distinctive and as little misleading as any other, and is that which, for want of a better, I am content to use. That this part of Logic should be distinguished and named, and made an object of consideration separately from the rest, is perfectly natural. What I protest against, is the doctrine of Sir W. Hamilton, Mr. Mansel, and many other thinkers, that this part is the whole; that there is no other Logic, or Pure Logic, at all; that whatever is more than this, belongs not to a general science and art of Thinking, but (in the words of Mr. Mansel) to this or that material science.[*]

This doctrine assumes, that with the exception of the rules of Formal, that is, of Syllogistic Logic, no other rules can be framed which are applicable to thought generally, abstractedly from particular matter: That a general theory is possible respecting the relations which the parts of a process of thought should bear to one another, but not respecting the

[*Ibid.]

proper relations of all thought to its matter: That the problem which Bacon set before himself, and led the way towards resolving, is an impossible one: That there is not, and cannot be, any general Theory of Evidence: That when we have taken care that our notions and propositions concerning Things shall be consistent with themselves and with one another, and have drawn no inferences from them but such the falsity of which would be inconsistent with assertions already made, we have done all that a philosophy of Thought can do—and the agreement and disagreement of our beliefs with the laws of the thing itself, is in each case a special question, belonging to the science of that thing in particular: That the study of nature, the search for objective truth, does not admit of any rules, nor its attainment, of any general test. For if there are such rules, if there is such a test, and the consideration of it does not belong to Logic, to what science or study does it belong? There is no other science, which, irrespectively of particular matter, professes to direct the intellect in the application of its powers to any matter on which knowledge is possible. These philosophers must therefore think that there can be no such rules, or that if there are, they can only be of the vaguest possible description. Sir W. Hamilton says as much.

If we abstract from the specialities of particular objects and sciences, and consider only the rules which ought to govern our procedure in reference to the object-matter of the sciences in general,—and this is all that a universal Logic can propose,—these rules are few in number, and their applications simple and evident. A Material or Objective Logic, except in special subordination to the circumstances of particular sciences, is therefore of very narrow limits, and all that it can tell us is soon told.*

It is very true that all Sir W. Hamilton can tell us of it is soon told. Nothing can be more meagre, trite, and indefinite than the little which he finds to say respecting what he calls Modified Logic. And no wonder, when we consider the following extraordinary deliverance, which I quote from the conclusion of his Thirtieth Lecture on Logic. Speaking of Physical Science generally, Sir W. Hamilton thus expresses himself:

In this department of Knowledge there is chiefly demanded a patient habit of attention to details, in order to detect phænomena; and, these discovered, their generalization is usually so easy that there is little exercise afforded to the higher energies of Judgment and Reasoning. It was Bacon's boast that Induction, as applied to nature, would equalize all talents, level the aristocracy of genius, accomplish marvels by co-operation and method, and leave little to be done by the force of individual intellects. This boast has been fulfilled; Science has, by the Inductive Process, been brought down to minds, who previously would have been incompetent for its cultivation, and physical knowledge now usefully occupies many who would otherwise have been without any rational pursuit.†

Lectures, Vol. IV, App. i, p. 232.
†*Ibid.*, p. 138. [See Bacon, *Novum Organum*, in *Works*, Vol. I, pp. 189 and 205 (Bk. I, Aphs. 82 and 105). Cf. *De Augmentis Scientiarum*, in *ibid.*, p. 620 (Bk. V, Chap. ii).]

Sir W. Hamilton had good reason for confining his own logical speculations to a minor and subordinate department of the Science and Art of Thinking, when he was so destitute as this passage proves, of the preliminary knowledge required for making any proficiency in the other and higher branch. Every one who has obtained any knowledge of the physical sciences from really scientific study, knows that the questions of evidence presented, and the powers of abstraction required, in the speculations on which their greater generalizations depend, are such as to task the very highest capacities of the human intellect: and a thinker, however able, who is too little acquainted with the processes actually followed in the investigation of objective truth, to be aware of this fact, is entitled to no authority when he denies the possibility of a Philosophy of Evidence and of the Investigation of Nature; inasmuch as his own ᵐacquirementsᵐ do not furnish him with the means of judging whether it is possible or not.*

If any general theory of the sufficiency of Evidence and the legitimacy of Generalization be possible, this must be Logic κατ' ἐξοχήν, and anything else called by the name can only be ancillary to it. For the Logic called

---

*Accordingly all that Sir W. Hamilton has to say concerning the requisites of a legitimate Induction, is that there must be no instances to the contrary, and that the number of observed instances must be "competent." (*Lectures*, Vol. IV, pp. 168–9.) If this were all that "a Material or Objective Logic" could "tell us," Sir W. Hamilton's treatment of it would be quite justified. The point of view of a complete Induction, namely one in which the nature of the instances is such, that no other result than the one arrived at is consistent with the universal Law of Causation, had never risen above Sir W. Hamilton's horizon. The same low reach of thought, not for want of power, but of the necessary knowledge, shows itself in every part of the little he says concerning the investigation of Nature. For example, he implicitly follows the mistake of Kant in affirming an intrinsic difference between the inferences of Induction and those of Analogy. [Cf. Kant, *Logik*, in *Werke*, Vol. III, pp. 320–1.] Induction, he says, infers that "if a number of objects of the same class possess in common a certain attribute, . . . this attribute is possessed by all the objects of that class;" while Analogy infers that "if . . . two or more things agree in several internal and essential characters . . . they agree, likewise, in all other essential characters, that is, they are constituents of the same class." (*Lectures*, Vol. IV, pp. 165–6.) A little more familiarity with the subject would have shown him that the two kinds of argument are homogeneous, and differ only in degree of evidence. The type of them both is, the inference that things which agree with one another in certain respects, agree in certain other respects. Any argument from known points of agreement to unknown, is an inference of analogy: and induction is no more. Induction concludes that if a number of As have the attribute B, all things which agree with them in being As agree with them also in having the attribute B. The only peculiarity of Induction, as compared with other cases of analogy, is, that the known points of agreement from which further agreement is inferred, have been summed up in a single word and made the foundation of a class. For further explanations, see my *System of Logic*, Bk. III, Chap. xx. [In *Collected Works*, Vol. VII, pp. 554ff.]

ᵐ⁻ᵐ65¹   requirements [*printer's error?*]

Formal only aims at removing one of the obstacles to the attainment of truth, by preventing such mistakes as render our thoughts inconsistent with themselves or with one another: and it is of no importance whether we think consistently or not, if we think wrongly. It is only as a means to material truth, that the formal, or to speak more clearly, the conditional, validity of an operation of thought is of any value; and even that value is only negative: we have not made the smallest positive advance towards right thinking, by merely keeping ourselves consistent in what is, perhaps, systematic error. This by no means implies that Formal Logic, even in its narrowest sense, is not of very great, though purely negative, value. On the contrary, I sub-scribe heartily to all that is said of its importance by Sir W. Hamilton and Mr. Mansel. It is good to have our path clearly marked out, and a parapet put up at all the dangerous points, whether the path leads us to the place we desire to reach, or to another place altogether. But to call this alone Logic, or this alone Pure Logic, as if all the rest of the Philosophy of Thought and Evidence were merely an adaptation of this to something else, is to ignore the end to which all rules laid down for our thinking operations are meant to be subservient. The purpose of them all, is to enable us to decide whether anything, and what, is proved true. Formal Logic conduces indirectly to this end, by enabling us to perceive, either that the process which has been performed is one which could not possibly prove anything, or that it is one which will prove something to be true, unless the premises happen to be false. This indirect aid is of the greatest importance; but it is important because the end, the ascertainment of truth, is important; and it is impor-tant only as complementary to a still more fundamental part of the opera-tion, in which Formal Logic affords no help.

I do not deny the scientific convenience of considering this limited portion of Logic apart from the rest—the doctrine of the Syllogism, for instance, apart from the theory of Induction; and of teaching it in an earlier stage of intellectual education. It can be taught earlier, since it does not, like the inductive logic, presuppose a practical acquaintance with the processes of scientific investigation; and the greatest service to be derived from it, that of keeping the mind clear, can be best rendered before a habit of confused thinking has been acquired. Not only, however, is it indispens-able that the larger Logic, which embraces all the general conditions of the ascertainment of truth, should be studied in addition to the smaller Logic, which only concerns itself with the conditions of consistency; but the smaller Logic ought to be, at least finally, studied as part of the greater—as a portion of the means to the same end; and its relation to the other parts—to the other means—should be distinctly displayed. If thought be anything more than a sportive exercise of the mind, its purpose is to enable us to know what can be known respecting the facts of the universe: its judgments and conclusions express, or are intended to express, some of those facts: and the connexion which Formal Logic, by its analysis of the reasoning process, points out between one proposition and another, exists only because there is a connexion between one objective truth and another, which makes it possible for us to know objective truths which have never been observed, in virtue of others which have. This possibility is an eternal mystery and stumbling-block to Formal Logic. The bare idea that any new truth can be brought out of a Concept—that analysis can ever find in it anything which synthesis has not first put in—is absurd on the face of it: yet this is all the explanation that Formal Logic, as viewed by Sir W. Hamilton, is able to give of the phænomenon; and Mr. Mansel expressly limits the province of Logic to analytic judgments—to such as are merely identical. But what the Logic of mere consistency cannot do, the Logic of the ascertainment of truth, the Philosophy of Evidence in its larger acceptation, can. It can explain the function of the Ratiocinative process as an instrument of the human intellect in the discovery of truth, and can place it in its true correlation with the other instruments. It is therefore alone competent to furnish a philosophical theory of Reasoning. Such partial account as can be given of the process by looking at it solely by itself, however useful and even necessary to accurate thought, does not dispense with, but points out in a more emphatic manner the need of, the more comprehensive Logic of which it should form a part, and which alone can give a meaning or a reason of existence to the Logic styled Formal, or to the reasoning process itself.

CHAPTER XXI

The Fundamental Laws of Thought
According to Sir William Hamilton

HAVING MARKED OUT, as the sole province of Logic, the "Laws of Thought," Sir W. Hamilton naturally proceeds to specify what these are. The "Fundamental Laws of Thought," of which all other laws that can be laid down for thought are but particular applications, are, according to our author, three in number: the Law of Identity; the Law of Contradiction; and the Law of Excluded Middle. In his *Lectures* he recognised a fourth, "the Law of Reason and Consequent," which seems to be compounded of the Law of Causation, and the Leibnitzian "Principle of Sufficient Reason."[*] But as, in his later speculations, he no longer considered this as an ultimate law, it needs not be further spoken of.

These three laws he otherwise denominates "The Conditions of the Thinkable:"* from which it might have been supposed that he regarded them as Laws of Thought in the scientific sense of the word law; conditions to which thought *cannot but* conform, and apart from which it is impossible. One would have said, à priori, that he could not mean anything but this: since otherwise the expression "Conditions of the Thinkable" is perverted from its meaning. Nevertheless, this is not what he means, at least in this place. It is on this very occasion that he disclaims, as applicable to laws of thought, the scientific meaning of the term, and declares them to be (like the laws made by Parliament) general precepts; not necessities of the thinking act, but instructions for right thinking. Yet it would not have been claiming too much for these three laws, to have regarded them as laws in the more peremptory sense; as actual necessities of thought. Our author could hardly have meant that we are able to disbelieve that a thing is itself, or to

[*See, e.g., Leibniz, *Essais de théodicée sur la bonté de Dieu, la liberté de l'homme, et l'origine du mal* (Amsterdam: Troyel, 1710), pp. 114–15, 156–7 (I, §§7, 44).]

Lectures, Vol. III, p. 79. In the Appendix to the *Lectures* he calls them the Laws of the Thinkable; and the laws of Conception, Judgment, and Reasoning he distinguishes from them under the name of "the laws of Thinking in a strict sense." (*Ibid.*, Vol. IV, App. iv, pp. 244–5.)

believe that a thing is, and at the same time that it is not. He not only, like other people, constantly assumes this to be an impossibility, but makes that impossibility the ground of some of his leading philosophical doctrines; as when he says that it is impossible for us to doubt the actual facts of consciousness "because the doubt implies a contradiction."* It is true that a person may, in one sense, believe contradictory propositions, that is, he may believe the affirmative at some times and the negative at others, alternately forgetting the two beliefs. It is also true that he may yield a passive assent to two forms of words, which, had he been fully conscious of their meaning, he would have known to be, either wholly or in part, an affirmation and a denial of the same fact. But when once he is made to see that there is a contradiction, it is totally impossible for him to believe it.

Now, to compel people to see a contradiction where a contradiction is, constitutes the entire office of Logic in the limited sense in which Sir W. Hamilton conceives it: and he is quite right in regarding the whole of Logic, in that narrow sense, as resting on the three laws specified by him. To call them the fundamental laws of Thought is a *a* misnomer; but they are the laws of Consistency. All inconsistency is a violation of some one of these laws; an unconscious violation, for knowingly to violate them is impossible.

Something remains to be said respecting the three Laws considered singly, as well as respecting our author's mode of regarding them.

The Law or Principle of Identity (*Principium Identitatis*) is no other than the time-honoured axiom, "Whatever is, is," or, in another phraseology, "A thing is the same as itself:" the proposition which Locke, in his chapter on Maxims, treated with so much disrespect.[*] Sir W. Hamilton, probably finding it difficult to establish the "principle of all logical affirmation" on such a basis as this, presents the axiom[†] in a modified shape, as an assertion of the identity between a whole and its parts; or rather between a whole Concept, and its parts in Comprehension—the attributes which compose it; for Logic, as conceived by him, has nothing to do with any wholes but Concepts, abstracting altogether (as he asserts) from the reality of the things conceived.[‡]

*Foot-note to Reid, p. 713n, and in many other places.

[*See *Essay Concerning Human Understanding*, *Works*, Vol. III, pp. 23–5 (Bk. IV, Chap. vii, §4).]

†*Lectures*, Vol. III, pp. 79–80.

‡We here see our author by implication admitting that a Concept has no parts except its parts in Comprehension; what he elsewhere calls its parts in Extension being in no sense parts of the Concept, but parts of something else, namely, of the aggregate of concrete objects to which the Concept corresponds. Had Sir W.

*a*65[1], 65[2]   mere

Although our author still so far defers to the old version of the Principle of Identity, as to say that it is "expressed in the formula *A is A*, or *A* = *A*,"[*] I must admit that while paying this tribute of respect to our ancient friend, he has taken a very substantial and useful liberty with him, and has made him mean much more than he ever meant before. The only fault that can be found (but that is a serious one) is, that if we accept this view of the maxim, we shall require many "principles of logical affirmation" instead of one. For if we are to make a separate principle for every mode in which we have occasion to re-affirm the same thing in different words, we need a large number of them. If we require a special principle to entitle us, when we have affirmed a set of attributes jointly, to affirm over again the same attributes severally, we require also a long list of such principles as these: When one thing is before another, the other is after. When one thing is after another, the other is before. When one thing is along with another, the other is along with the first. When one thing is like, or unlike, another, the other is like (or unlike) the first: in short, as many fundamental principles as there are kinds of relation. For we have need of all these changes of expression in our processes of thought and reasoning. What is at the bottom of them all is, that Logic (to borrow a phrase from our author)[†] postulates to be allowed to assert the same meaning in any words which will, consistently with their signification, express it. The use and meaning of a Fundamental Law of Thought is, that it asserts in general terms the right to do something, which the mind needs to do in cases as they arise. It is in this sense that the Dictum de Omni et Nullo is called the fundamental law of the Syllogism. But, for this purpose, it is necessary that the Law or Postulate should be stated in so comprehensive and universal a manner as to cover every case in which the act authorized by it requires to be done. Looked at in this light, the Principle of Identity ought to have been expressed thus: Whatever is true in one form of words, is true in every other form of words which conveys the same meaning. Thus worded, it fulfils the requirements of a First Principle of Thought; for it is the widest possible expression of an act of thought which is always legitimate, and continually has to be done.*

Hamilton adhered to this rational doctrine, he must have given up his Judgments in Extension: instead of which he not only retains them, but considers them as also founded on the Principle of Identity: though he has expressly limited that principle in a manner inconsistent with founding any judgments on it save Judgments in Comprehension. This contradiction was worth pointing out, but is not worth insisting on, since it may be rectified by extending the scope of the First Law to the identity of *any* whole with its parts, instead of limiting it to the identity of a Concept with its parts in Comprehension only.

[*Lectures, Vol. III, pp. 79–80.]

[†See *ibid*., p. 114.]

*[67] This principle provides for the whole of what Kant terms Conclusions of Understanding [Kritik der Reinen Vernunft, pp. 245–7], and Dr. M'Cosh Implied or

Understood in this sense, the Principle of Identity absorbs into itself a Postulate of Logic on which Sir W. Hamilton lays great stress, and which he did good service in making prominent, though we shall hereafter find that he sometimes misapplies it. He expresses it as follows: "The only Postulate of Logic which requires an articulate enouncement is the demand, that before dealing with a judgment or reasoning expressed in language, the import of its terms should be fully understood; in other words, Logic postulates to be allowed to state explicitly in language, all that is implicitly contained in the thought."* There cannot be a more just demand: but let us carefully note the terms in which our author enunciates it, that he may be held to them afterwards. Everything may be stated explicitly in language, which is "implicitly contained in the thought," that is (according to his own interpretation) in the "import of the terms" used. In other words, we have a right to *express* explicitly, what has already been asserted in terms which really mean, though they do not explicitly declare it. Observe, what has been already asserted; not what can be *inferred* from something that has been asserted. One proposition may imply another, but unless the implication is in the very meaning of the terms, it avails nothing. It may be impossible that the one proposition should be true without the other being true also, and yet Logic cannot "postulate" to be allowed to affirm this last; she must be required to prove it. Interpreted in this, its true sense, Sir W. Hamilton's postulate is legitimate, but is only a particular case of the Principle of Identity in its most generalized shape. It is a case of postulating to be allowed to express a given meaning in another form of words.

As already mentioned, Sir W. Hamilton represents the Principle of Identity to be "the principle of all logical affirmation." This I can by no means admit, whether the Principle in question is taken in Sir W. Hamilton's narrower, or in my own wider sense. The reaffirmation in new language of what has already been asserted—or (descending to particulars and adopting our author's phraseology) the thinking of a Concept through an attribute which is a part of itself—can, as I formerly observed, be admitted as a correct account of the nature of affirmation, only in the case of Analytical Judgments. In a Synthetical Judgment, the attribute predicated is thought not as part of, but as existing in a common subject along with, the group of attributes composing the Concept: and of this operation of thought it is plain that no principle of Identity can give any account, since

---

Transposed Judgments. ([*Examination*,] p. 296.) They are not conclusions, nor fresh acts of judgment, but the original judgment, expressed in other words.

Lectures, Vol. III, p. 114.

b–b65[1]   assert

there is a new element introduced, which is not identical with any part of what pre-existed in thought. This is clearly seen by Mr. Mansel, who expressly limits the dominion of the Law of Identity to analytical judgments;* and, with perfect consistency, regards these as the only judgments with which Logic, as such, is concerned. If, then, the Law of Identity is to be upheld as the principle "of all logical affirmation," we must understand that logical affirmation does not mean all affirmation, but only affirmations which communicate no fact, and merely assert that what is called by a name, is what the name declares it to be.

If our author had stated the Law of Identity to be the principle not of "logical affirmation," but of affirmative Reasoning, he would have said something far more plausible, and which had been maintained by many of his predecessors. The truth is, however, that as far as that law is a principle of reasoning at all, it is as much a principle of negative, as of affirmative reasoning. In proving a negative, as much as in proving an affirmative, we require the liberty of exchanging a proposition for any other that is æquipollent with it, and of predicating separately of any subject, all attributes which have been predicated of it jointly. These liberties the mind rightfully claims in all its intellectual operations. The Principle of Identity is not the peculiar groundwork of any special kind of thinking, but an indispensable postulate in all thinking.

The second of the "Fundamental Laws" is the Law or Principle of Contradiction (*Principium Contradictionis*); that two assertions, one of which denies what the other affirms, cannot be thought together. Most people would have said, cannot be believed together; but our author resolutely refuses to recognise belief as any element in the scientific analysis of a proposition. "This law," he says, "is the principle of all logical negation and distinction,"[†] and "is logically expressed in the formula, What is contradictory is unthinkable." To this he subjoins, as an equivalent mathematical formula, "$A = $ not $A = 0$, or $A - A = 0$:"[‡] a misapplication and perversion of algebraical symbols, not to be omitted among other evidences how little familiar he was with mathematical modes of thought.

Concerning the name of this law, Sir W. Hamilton observes that "as it enjoins the absence of contradiction as the indispensable condition of thought, it ought to be called, not the Law of Contradiction, but the Law of Non-Contradiction, or of *non-repugnantia*."[§] It seems that no extent and accuracy of knowledge concerning the opinions of predecessors, can preserve a thinker from giving an erroneous interpretation of their meaning by

Prolegomena Logica, pp. 196–7.
[†]*Lectures*, Vol. III, p. 82.
[‡]*Ibid*., p. 81.
[§]*Ibid*., p. 82.

antedating a confusion of ideas which exists in his own mind. The Law of Contradiction does not "enjoin the absence of contradiction;" it is not an injunction at all. If those who wrote before Sir W. Hamilton of the Law or Principle of Contradiction, had meant by those terms what he did, namely, a rule or precept, it would have been, no doubt, absurd in them to have given the name Law of Contradiction, to a Precept of Non-Contradiction. But I venture to assert that when they spoke of the Law of Contradiction (which most of them, I believe, never did, but called it the Principle) they were no more dreaming of enjoining anything, than when they spoke of the Law or Principle of Identity they intended to enjoin identity. They used those terms in their proper scientific, and not, as Sir W. Hamilton does, in their moral or legislative sense. By the Law of Identity they meant one of the properties of identity, namely, that a proposition which is identical must be true. And by the Law of Contradiction they meant one of the properties of contradiction, namely, that what is contradictory cannot be true. We should express their meaning better if instead of the word Law, we used the expressions, Doctrine of Identity, and Doctrine of Contradiction. This is what they had in their minds, and even expressed by their words; for the word Principle, with them, meant a particular kind of Doctrine, namely, one which is the groundwork, and justifying authority, of a whole class of operations of the mind. If the word Law is to be retained, Principium Contradictionis would be better translated, not Law of Contradiction but Law of Contradictory Propositions; were it not for the consideration, that the principle of Excluded Middle is also a law of contradictory propositions.

The Law of Contradiction, according to Sir W. Hamilton, is the "principle of all logical negation."* I do not see how it can be the principle of any negation except the denial that a thing is the contradictory of itself. That a sight is not a taste is a negation, and it must be a very narrow use of the term which refuses it the title of a logical negation. But there is no contradiction between a sight and a taste. That blue is not green, involves no logical contradiction. We could believe that a green thing may be blue, as easily as we believe that a round thing may be blue, if experience did not teach us the incompatibility of the former attributes, and the compatibility of the latter. The negative judgment, that a man is not a horse, may indeed be said to be grounded on the Principle of Contradiction, inasmuch as the opposite assertion, that a man is a horse, is in certain of its parts contradictory, though in others only false. The word man ^{c}may be^c understood as signifying (in precise logical language, connoting) among ^{d}the^d other properties,

*Ibid.

$^{c-c}$65^1, 65^2, 67   is
$^{d-d}$+72

that of having exactly two legs—the word horse, that of having four; and in respect of this particular part of the meaning of the terms, the subject and the predicate are contradictory, the one affirming and the other denying the extra number of legs. But suppose the subject and predicate of the judgment to be names of classes constituted by positive attributes without negative, as mathematician and moralist, or merchant and philosopher. An affirmation uniting them may then be false, but cannot possibly be self-contradictory. The Law of Contradiction cannot be the ground on which it is asserted that a mathematician is not a moralist, for the two Concepts are only different, not contradictory, nor even repugnant.

Others have said, that the Law or Doctrine of Contradiction is the principle of Negative Reasoning. But the obvious truth is, that it is the principle of all Reasoning, so far as reasoning can be regarded apart from objective truth or falsehood. For, abstractedly from that consideration, the only meaning of validity in reasoning is that it neither involves a contradiction, nor infers anything the denial of which would not contradict the premises. Valid reasoning, from the point of view of merely Formal Logic, is a negative conception; it means, reasoning which is not self-destructive; which cannot be discovered to be worthless from its own data. It would be absurd to suppose that the validity of the reasoning process itself, either affirmative or negative, could be proved from the Doctrine of Contradiction; for though a given syllogism may be proved valid by showing that the falsity of the conclusion, combined with the truth of one premise, would contradict the truth of the other, this can only be done by another syllogism, so that the validity of Reasoning would be taken for granted in the attempt to prove it. The Law of Contradiction is a principle of reasoning in the same sense, and in the same sense only, as the Law of Identity is. It is the generalization of a mental act which is of continual occurrence, and which cannot be dispensed with in reasoning. As we require the liberty of substituting for a given assertion, the same assertion in different words, so we require the liberty of substituting, for any assertion, the denial of its contradictory. The affirmation of the one and the denial of the other are logical equivalents, which it is allowable and indispensable to make use of as mutually convertible.

The third "Fundamental Law" is the law or principle of Excluded Middle (*principium Exclusi Medii vel Tertii*), of which the purport is, that, of two directly contradictory propositions, one or the other must be true. I am now expressing the axiom in my own language, for the tortuous phraseology* by which our author *escapes from* recognising the ideas of truth and falsity, having already been sufficiently exemplified, may here be disregarded.

Ibid., p. 83.

e–e65[1], 65[2]   evades

This axiom is the other half of the doctrine of Contradictory Propositions. By the law of Contradiction, contradictory propositions cannot both be true; by the law of Excluded Middle, they cannot both be false. Or, to state the meaning in other language, by the law of Contradiction a proposition cannot be both true and false; by the law of Excluded Middle it must be either true or false—there is no third possibility.

Sir W. Hamilton says that this law is "the principle of disjunctive judgments."* By disjunctive judgments, logicians have always meant, judgments in this form: Either this is true or that is true. The law of Excluded Middle cannot be the principle of any disjunctive judgment but those in which the subject of both the members is the same, and one of the predicates a simple negation of the other: as, A is either B or not B. That indeed rests on the principle of Excluded Middle, or rather, is the very formula of that principle. It is here to be remarked that Sir W. Hamilton, after Krug, but by a very unaccountable departure from the common usage of logicians, confines the name of Disjunctive Judgments to those in which all the alternative propositions have the same subject: "D is either B, or C, or A."† This is not only an arbitrary change in the meaning of words, but renders the classification of propositions incomplete, leaving two kinds of disjunctive propositions (Either B, C, or D, is A, and Either A is B or C is D) unrecognised and without a name. But even in our author's restricted sense of the word Disjunctive, I cannot see how the Law of Excluded Middle can be said to be the principle of *all* disjunctive judgments. The judgment that A is either B or not B, is warranted and its truth certified by the Law of Excluded Middle: but the judgment that A is either B or C, both B and C being positive, requires some other voucher than the law that one or other of two contradictories must be true. Thus, "X is either a man or a brute," is not a judgment grounded on the principle of Excluded Middle, since brute is not a bare negation of man, but includes the positive attribute of being an animal, which X may possibly not be.

It might be said, with more plausibility, that the Law of Excluded Middle is the principle of Disjunctive Reasoning. Thus, in the last example, "X is either a man or a brute" may be a conclusion from two premises, that X is an animal, and that every animal is either a man or a brute: the latter of which is a disjunctive judgment grounded on the Law of Excluded Middle. But it is not the fact that all disjunctive conclusions are inferred from premises of this nature. Having been told that A has lost a son, I conclude that either B, C, or D (A having no other sons) is dead: what kind of reasoning is this? Disjunctive, surely: it has a disjunctive premise, and leads to a disjunctive conclusion. But the disjunctive premise (Every son of A is either B, C, or

*Ibid., p. 84.
†Ibid., p. 239. [Cf. Krug, *Logic*, §57.]

D) does not rest on the Law of Excluded Middle, or on any necessity of thought; it rests on my knowledge of the individual fact.

The third Law, however, like the two others, is one of the principles of all reasonings, being the generalization of a process which is liable to be required in all of them. As the Doctrine of Contradiction authorizes us to substitute for the assertion of either of two contradictory propositions, the denial of the other, so the doctrine of Excluded Middle empowers us to substitute for the denial of either of two contradictory propositions, the assertion of the other. Thus all the three principles which our author terms the Fundamental Laws of Thought, are universal postulates of Reasoning; and as such, are entitled to the conspicuous position which our author assigns to them in Logic: though it is evident that they ought not to be placed at the very beginning of the subject, but at the earliest, in its Second Part, the theory of Judgments, or Propositions: since they essentially involve the ideas of Truth and Falsity, which are attributes only of judgments, not of names, or concepts.

It is another question altogether, what we ought to think of these three principles, considered not as general expressions of legitimate intellectual processes, but as themselves speculative truths. Sir W. Hamilton considers them to be such in a very universal sense indeed, since he thinks we are bound to regard them as true beyond the sphere of either real or imaginable phænomenal experience—to be true of Things in Themselves—of Noumena. "Whatever," he says,

violates the laws, whether of Identity, of Contradiction, or of Excluded Middle, we feel to be absolutely impossible, not only in thought, but in existence. Thus we cannot attribute even to Omnipotence the power of making a thing different from itself, of making a thing at once to be and not to be, of making a thing neither to be nor not to be. These three laws thus determine to us the sphere of possibility and of impossibility: and this not merely in thought but in reality, not only logically but metaphysically.*

And in another place: "If the true character of objective validity be universality, the laws of Logic are really of that character, for those laws constrain us, by their own authority, to regard them as the universal laws not only of human thought, but of universal reason."† A few pages before, our author took pains to impress upon us that we were not to regard these laws as necessities of thought, but as general precepts "which we are able to violate:"[*] but they now appear to be necessities of thought and something more.

I readily admit that these three general propositions are universally true

*Ibid., p. 98.
†Ibid., Vol. IV, p. 65.
[*Ibid., p. 79.]

of all phænomena. I also admit that if there are any inherent necessities of thought, these are such. I express myself in this qualified manner, because whoever is aware how artificial, modifiable, the creatures of circumstances, and alterable by circumstances, most of the supposed necessities of thought are (though real necessities to a given person at a given time), will hesitate to affirm of any such necessities that they are an original part of our mental constitution. Whether the three so-called Fundamental Laws are laws of our thoughts by the native structure of the mind, or merely because we perceive them to be universally true of observed phænomena, I will not positively decide: but they are laws of our thoughts now, and invincibly so. They may or may not be capable of alteration by experience, but the conditions of our existence deny to us the experience which would be required to alter them. Any assertion, therefore, which conflicts with one of these laws—any proposition, for instance, which asserts a contradiction, though it were on a subject wholly removed from the sphere of our experience, is to us unbelievable. The belief in such a proposition is, in the present constitution of nature, impossible as a mental fact.*

But Sir W. Hamilton goes beyond this: he thinks that the obstacle to belief does not lie solely in an incapacity of our believing faculty, but in objective incapacities of existence; that the "Fundamental Laws of Thought" are laws of Existence too, and may be known to be true not only of Phænomena but also of Noumena. Of this, however, as of all else relating to Noumena, the verdict of philosophy, I apprehend, must be that we are entirely ignorant. The distinction itself is but an idle one; for since Noumena, if they exist, are wholly unknowable by us, except phænomenally, through their effects on us; and since all attributes which exist for us, even in our fancy, are but phænomena, there is nothing for us either to affirm or deny of a Noumenon except phænomenal attributes: existence

*[67] "When remembering a certain thing as in a certain place, the place and the thing are mentally represented together; while to think of the non-existence of the thing in that place, implies a consciousness in which the place is represented but not the thing. Similarly, if instead of thinking of an object as colourless, we think of it as having colour, the change consists in the addition to the concept of an element that was before absent from it—the object cannot be thought of first as red and then as not red, without one component of the thought being totally expelled from the mind by another. The law of the Excluded Middle, then, is simply a generalization of the universal experience that some mental states are directly destructive of other states. It formulates a certain absolutely constant law, that the appearance of any positive mode of consciousness cannot occur without excluding a correlative negative mode: and that the negative mode cannot occur without excluding the correlative positive mode: the antithesis of positive and negative being, indeed, merely an expression of this experience. Hence it follows that if consciousness is not in one of the two modes, it must be in the other." (Mr. Herbert Spencer, ["Mill versus Hamilton,"] in Fortnightly Review for July 15, 1865 [p. 533].)

itself, as we conceive it, being merely the power of producing phænomena. Now in respect to phænomenal attributes, no one denies the three "Fundamental Laws" to be universally true. Since then they are laws of all Phænomena, and since Existence has to us no meaning but one which has relation to Phænomena, we are quite safe in looking upon them as laws of Existence. This is sufficient for those who hold the doctrine of the Relativity of human knowledge. But Sir W. Hamilton, as has been seen, does not hold that doctrine, though he holds a verbal truism which he chooses to call by the same name. His opinion is that we do know something more than phænomena: that we know the Primary Qualities of Bodies as existing in the Noumena, in the things themselves, and not as mere powers of affecting us. Sir W. Hamilton, therefore, needs another kind of argument to establish the doctrine that the Laws of Identity, Contradiction, and Excluded Middle, are laws of all existence: and here we have it:

> To deny the universal application of the three laws, is, in fact, to subvert the reality of thought; and as this subversion is itself an act of thought, it in fact annihilates itself. When, for example, I say that A is, and then say that A is not, by the second assertion I sublate or take away what, by the first assertion, I posited or laid down; thought, in the one case, undoing by negation what, in the other, it had by affirmation done.

This proves only that a contradiction is unthinkable, not that it is impossible in point of fact. But what follows goes more directly to the mark.

> But when it is asserted that A existing and A non-existing are at once true, what does ᶠitᶠ imply? It implies that negation and affirmation correspond to nothing out of the mind,—that there is no agreement, no disagreement between thought and its objects; and this is tantamount to saying that truth and falsehood are merely empty sounds. For if we only think by affirmation and negation, and if these are only as they are exclusive of each other, it follows, that unless existence and non-existence be opposed objectively in the same manner as affirmation and negation are opposed subjectively, all our thought is a mere illusion. Thus it is that those who would assert the possibility of contradictions being at once true, in fact annihilate the possibility of truth itself, and the whole significance of thought.*

Of this favourite style of argument with our author we have already had many specimens, and have said so much about them, that we can afford to be brief in the present instance. Assuming it to be true that "to deny the universal application of the three laws" as laws of existence "is to subvert the reality of thought:" is anything added to the force of this consideration by saying that "this subversion is itself an act of thought?" If the reality of thought *can* be subverted, is there any peculiar enormity in doing it by means of thought itself? In what other way can we imagine it to be done?

Lectures, Vol. III, pp. 99–100.

ᶠ⁻ᶠSource, 65¹   this

And if it were true that thought is an invalid process, what better proof of this could be given than that we could, by thinking, arrive at the conclusion that our thoughts are not to be trusted? Sir W. Hamilton always seems to suppose that the imaginary sceptic, who doubts the validity of thought altogether, is obliged to claim a greater validity for his subversive thoughts than he allows to the thoughts they subvert. But it is enough for him to claim the same validity, so that all opinions are thrown into equal uncertainty.* Sir W. Hamilton, of all men, ought to know this, for when he is himself on the sceptical side of any question, as when speaking of the Absolute, or anything else which he deems inaccessible to the human faculties, this is the very line of argument he employs. He proves the invalidity, as regards those subjects, of the thinking process, by showing that it lands us in contradictions.†

But it is entirely inadmissible that to suppose that a law of thought need not necessarily be a law of existence, invalidates the thinking process. If, indeed, there were any law necessitating us to think a relation between *phænomena* which does not in fact exist between the phænomena, then certainly the thinking process would be proved invalid, because we should be compelled by it to think true something which would really be false. But

---

*The principal extant interpreter of the ancient Scepticism, Sextus Empiricus, expressly defines as its essence and scope, τὸ παντὶ λόγῳ λόγον ἴσον ἀντικεῖσθαι. (*Pyrrh. Hypot.*) [Sextus Empiricus, *Outlines of Pyrrhonism*, in *Sextus Empiricus*, Vol. I, p. 8 (Chap. vi).] It is, indeed, impossible to conceive Scepticism otherwise. Anything more would not be Scepticism, but Negative Dogmatism.

†"If I," says our author, "have done anything meritorious in philosophy, it is in the attempt to explain the phænomena of these contradictions, in showing that they arise only when intelligence transcends the limits to which its legitimate exercise is restricted." (*Lectures*, Vol. I, App. i, p. 402.) "In generating its antinomies, Kant's Reason transcended its limits, violated its laws. . . . Reason is only self-contradictory when driven beyond its legitimate bounds." (*Ibid.*, Vol. II, App. iv, p. 543.) "It is only when transcending that sphere, when founding on its illegitimate as on its legitimate exercise, that it affords a contradictory result. . . . The dogmatic assertion of necessity—of Fatalism, and the dogmatic assertion of Liberty, are the counter and equally inconceivable conclusions from reliance on the illegitimate and one-sided." (*Ibid.*, Vol. I, App. i, p. 403.) To the same effect Mr. Mansel, throughout his *Limits of Religious Thought*.

In one of the Appendices to the Lectures on Metaphysics (Vol. II, App. iii, pp. 527–9), Sir W. Hamilton makes out a long list of contradictions or antinomies (of which we shall have something to say hereafter) involved, as he thinks, in the attempt to conceive the Infinite, and which he considers as evidence that the notion is beyond the reach of the human faculties. Yet he will not allow that the fact of leading to contradictions, which he habitually urges as an argument against the validity of some thought, would be admissible as an argument against Thought in general, if it could be brought home to it. At least he will not allow it in this place: for in his theory of the veracity of Consciousness he does (*ibid.*, Vol. I, p. 277).

if the mind is incapable of thinking anything respecting Noumena except the Phænomena which it considers as proceeding from them, and to which it can appeal to test its thoughts; and if we are under no necessity of thinking these otherwise than in conformity to what they really are; we may refuse to believe that our generalizations from the Phænomenal attributes of Noumena can be applied to Noumena in any other aspect, without in the least invalidating the operation of thought in regard to anything to which thought is applicable. We may say to Sir W. Hamilton what he says himself in another case: "I only say that thought is limited; but, within its limits, I do not deny, I do not subvert, its truth."* As he elsewhere observes, translating from Esser, truth consists "solely in the correspondence of our thoughts with their objects."† If the only real objects of thought, even when we are nominally speaking of Noumena, are Phænomena, our thoughts are true when they are made to correspond with Phænomena: and, the possibility of this being denied by no one, the thinking process is valid whether our laws of thought are laws of absolute existence or not.

*Ibid., Vol. III, p. 100.
†Ibid., p. 107 [cf. Esser, Logik, pp. 65–6]; see also Vol. IV, p. 61.

CHAPTER XXII

Of Sir William Hamilton's Supposed Improvements in Formal Logic

OF ALL Sir W. Hamilton's philosophical achievements, there is none, except perhaps his "Philosophy of the Conditioned," on account of which so much merit has been claimed for him, as the additions and corrections which he is supposed to have contributed to the doctrine of the Syllogism. These may be summed up in two principal theories, with their numerous corollaries and applications; the recognition of two kinds of Syllogism, Syllogisms in Extension and Syllogisms in Comprehension; and the doctrine of the Quantification of the Predicate. To the former of these, Sir W. Hamilton ascribed great importance. According to him, all previous logicians, "with the doubtful exception of Aristotle," "have altogether overlooked the reasoning in Comprehension"—"have marvellously overlooked one, and that the simplest and most natural of these descriptions of reasoning,—the reasoning in the quantity of comprehension:" and he claims, in directing attention to it, to have "relieved a radical defect and vital inconsistency in the present logical system."* For the other theory, that of the Quantification of the Predicate, still loftier claims are advanced both by himself and by others. Mr. Baynes, with an enthusiasm natural and not ungraceful in a pupil, concludes his Essay on the subject (which still remains the clearest exposition of his master's doctrine) with the following words:

We cannot, however, close without expressing the true joy we feel (though, were the feeling less strong, we might shrink from the intrusion), that in our own country, and in our time, this discovery has been made. We rejoice to know that one has at length arisen, able to recognise and complete the plan of the mighty builder, Aristotle,—to lay the top-stone on that fabric, the foundations of which were laid more than two thousand years ago, by the master-hand of the Stagirite, which, after the labours of many generations of workmen, who have from time to time built up one part here and taken down another there—remains substantially as he left it; but which, when finished, shall be seen to be an edifice of wondrous beauty, harmony, and completeness.[†]

Lectures, Vol. III, pp. 297, 304, 378; Vol. IV, App. v, p. 250.

[†]*An Essay on the New Analytic of Logical Forms, being that which gained the prize proposed by Sir William Hamilton in the year 1846 for the best exposition of*

Previous to discussing these additions to the Syllogistic Theory, it is necessary to revert to a doctrine which has been briefly stated in a former chapter,[*] but did not then receive all the elucidation it requires, and which has a most important bearing on both of Sir W. Hamilton's supposed discoveries. This is, that all Judgments (except where both the terms are proper names) are really judgments in Comprehension; though it is customary, and the natural tendency of the mind, to express most of them in terms of Extension. In other words, we never really predicate anything but attributes, though, in the usage of language, we commonly predicate them by means of words which are names of concrete objects.

When, for example, I say, The sky is blue; my meaning, and my whole meaning, is that the sky has that particular colour. I am not thinking of the class blue, as regards extension, at all. I am not caring, nor necessarily knowing, what blue things there are, or if there is any blue thing except the sky. I am thinking only of the sensation of blue, and am judging that the sky produces this sensation in my sensitive faculty; or (to express the meaning in technical language) that the quality answering to the sensation of blue, or the power of exciting the sensation of blue, is an attribute of the sky. When again I say, All oxen ruminate, I have nothing to do with the predicate, considered in extension. I may know, or be ignorant, that there are other ruminating animals besides oxen. Whether I do or do not know it, it does not, unless by mere accident, pass through my mind. In judging that oxen ruminate, I do not, unless accidentally, think under the notion ruminate (to borrow Sir W. Hamilton's phraseology) any other notion than that of an ox. The Comprehension of the predicate—the attribute or set of attributes signified by it—are all that I have in my mind; and the relation of this attribute or these attributes to the subject, is the entire matter of the judgment.

In one of the examples above given, the predicate is an adjective, and in the other a verb, which, in a logical point of view, is classed with adjectives: but its being a noun substantive makes no difference. For reasons easily shown, a substantive is more strongly associated with the ideas of the concrete objects denoted by it, than an adjective or a verb is. But when we predicate a substantive—when we say, Philip is a man, or, A ᵃherringᵃ is a fish—do the words man and fish signify anything to us but the bundles of attributes connoted by them? Do the propositions mean anything except

---

the new Doctrine propounded in his Lectures. With an Historical Appendix. By Thomas Spencer Baynes, Translator of the Port Royal Logic (p. 80). [See also Antoine Arnauld and Pierre Nicole, *The Port-Royal Logic*, trans. Baynes, 3rd ed. (Edinburgh: Sutherland, Knox, 1854).]

[*See pp. 339–41 above.]

ᵃ⁻ᵃ65¹, 65²   dolphin

that Philip has the human attributes, and a *herring* the piscine ones? Assuredly not. Any notion of a multitude of other men, among whom Philip is ranked, or a variety of fishes besides *herrings*, is foreign to the proposition. The proposition does not decide whether there is this additional quantity or no. It affirms the attributes of its own particular subject, and of no other.

Passing now from the predicate to the subject, we shall find that the subject also, if a general term or notion, is always construed in Comprehension, that is, by the attributes which constitute it, and has no other meaning in thought. When I judge that all oxen ruminate, what do I mean by all oxen? I have no image in my mind of all oxen. I do not, nor ever shall, know all of them, and I am not thinking even of all those I do know. "All oxen," in my thoughts, does not mean particular animals—it means the objects, whatever they may be, that have the attributes by which oxen are recognised, and which compose the notion of an ox. Wherever these attributes shall be found, there, as I judge, the attribute of ruminating will be found also: that is the entire purport of the judgment. Its meaning is a meaning in attributes, and nothing else. It supposes subjects, but merely as all attributes suppose them.

But there is another mode of interpreting the same proposition, by considering it as *a* part of the statement of a classification and mental co-ordination of the objects which exist in nature. The proposition is then looked upon as an assertion respecting given objects; affirming what other individual objects they are classed among by the general scheme of human language. Thus interpreted, the proposition "all oxen ruminate" may be read as follows: If all creatures that ruminate were collected in a vast plain, and I were required to search the world and point out all oxen, they would all be found among the crowd on that plain, and none anywhere else. Moreover, this would have been the case in all past time, and will at any future, while the present order of nature lasts. This is the proposition "All oxen ruminate" interpreted in Extension. Will any one say that a process of thought like this passes in the mind of whoever makes the affirmation? It is a point of view in which the proposition may be regarded; it is one of the aspects of the fact asserted in the proposition. But it is not the aspect in which the proposition presents it to the mind.

It will, however, very naturally be objected—If the meaning in our mind is that the bovine attributes are always accompanied by the attribute of ruminating, why do we, except for the purposes of abstract logic or metaphysics, never say this, but always say "All oxen ruminate?" The

$b-b65^1, 65^2$ dolphin
$c-c65^1, 65^2$ dolphins
$d-d+65^2, 67, 72$

reason is, that we have no other convenient and compact mode of speaking. Most attributes, and nearly all large "bundles of attributes," have no names of their own. We can only name them by a circumlocution. We are accustomed to speak of attributes not by names given to themselves, but by means of the names which they give to the objects they are attributes of. We do not talk of the phænomena which accompany piscinity; we talk of the phænomena of fishes. We do not frame a definition of piscinity, but a definition of a fish. The definition, however, of a fish is exactly the same which the definition of piscinity would be; it is an enumeration of the same attributes. Language is constructed upon the principle of naming concrete objects first: it does not always name abstractions at all, and when it does, the names are almost always derived from those of concrete objects. The reasons are obvious. Objects—even classes of objects—being conceivable by a much less effort of abstraction than attributes, are in the necessary order of things conceived and named earlier, and remain always more familiar to the mind: attributes, even when they come to be conceived, cannot be conceived in a detached state, but are always (as may be said by an adaptation of the Hamiltonian phraseology) thought through objects of some sort. Consequently all familiar propositions are expressed in the language which denotes objects, and not in that which denotes attributes. Nor is this all. What is primarily important to us in our sensations and impressions, is their permanent groups. In our particular and passing sensations (unless in cases of exceptional intensity) the important thing to us is, not the sensation itself, but to what group it belongs; what concrete object, what Permanent Possibility of Sensation, it indicates the presence of. The mind consequently hurries on from the sensible impressions that proceed from an outward object, to the object itself, and its subsequent thoughts revolve round that. It is on the concrete object indicated, that the expectation of future sensations depends; and the concrete object, consequently, in most cases, exclusively engages our thoughts, and stimulates us to mark it by a name. The name, to answer its purpose, must remind ourselves, and inform others, of the sensations we or they have to expect: that is, it must connote an attribute, or set of attributes. And men did not at first name attributes in any other than this indirect manner. They gave no direct names to attributes, because they did not conceive attributes as having any separate existence. As they began by naming only concrete objects, so the first names by which they expressed even the results of abstraction, were not names of attributes in the abstract, regarded apart from their objects, but names of concrete objects signifying the presence of the attributes. Men talked of blue, or of blue things, before they talked of blueness. Even when they did talk of blueness, it was originally not as the attribute, but as an imaginary cause of the attribute, which cause they figured to themselves as itself a concrete thing, residing in the object.

It thus appears that though all judgments consist in ascribing attributes, the original and natural mode of expressing them was by general names denoting concrete objects, and only connoting attributes; and by the structure of language this remains the only concise mode, and the only one which, addressing itself to familiar associations, conveys the meaning at once, to minds not exercised in metaphysical abstraction. But this does not alter the obvious truth, that concrete objects are only known by attributes, are only distinguished by attributes, and that the concrete names by which we speak of them mean nothing but attributes, or "bundles of attributes." Our representation in thought of a concrete object is but a representation of attributes, and our concept of a class of concrete objects is but a certain portion of those attributes, not, indeed, separately conceived or imaged, but exclusively attended to. There is, therefore, nothing in our mind when we affirm a general proposition, but attributes, and their coexistence or repugnance: and the position is made out, that all judgments, expressed by means of general terms, are judgments in Comprehension, though always, unless for some special purpose, expressed in Extension.

If this be the true doctrine of Judgments, what is meant by saying that there are two sorts of Judgment, one in Extension, the other in Comprehension, and two kinds of reasoning corresponding to these, one of which, that in Comprehension, had been overlooked by all logicians, except possibly Aristotle, up to the time of Sir W. Hamilton? All our ordinary judgments are in Comprehension only, Extension not being thought of. But we may, if we please, make the Extension of our general terms an express object of thought, and this may be called thinking in Extension, though it is rather thinking about Extension. When I judge that all oxen ruminate, I have nothing in my thoughts but the attributes and their coexistence. But when, by reflection, I perceive what the proposition implies, I remark, that other things may ruminate besides oxen; and that the unknown multitude of things which ruminate form a mass, with which the unknown multitude of things having the attributes of oxen is either identical, or is wholly comprised in it. Which of these two is the truth I may not know, and if I did, took no notice of it when I assented to the proposition "all oxen ruminate." But I perceive, on consideration, that one or other of them must be true. Though I had not this in my mind when I affirmed that all oxen ruminate, I can have it now; I can make the concrete objects denoted by each of the two names an object of thought, as a collective though indefinite aggregate; in other words, I can make the Extension of the names (or notions) an object of direct consciousness. When I do this, I perceive that this operation introduces no new fact, but is only a different mode of contemplating the very fact which I had previously expressed by the words "all oxen ruminate." The fact is the same, but the mode of contemplating it is different: the mental operation, the act of thought, is not only a distinct act, but an act of a different kind.

There is thus, in all propositions (save those in which both terms are Proper, that is, in significant, names) a judgment concerning attributes (called by Sir W. Hamilton a judgment in Comprehension), which we make as a matter of course, and a possible judgment in or concerning Extension, which we may make, and which will be true if the former is true. Nevertheless (as has just been shown), the conditions of primitive thought, and subsequent convenience, cause us generally to enunciate our propositions in terms appropriate to the derivative judgment which we seldom make, rather than to the primitive judgment which we always make. And this explains why, though the meaning of all propositions in which general terms are used is in Comprehension, writers on logic always explain the rules of the Syllogism in reference to Extension alone. It is because the framers of the rules did not concern themselves with propositions or reasonings as they exist in thought, but only as they are expressed in language. And in this they were justified. For the syllogism is not the form in which we necessarily reason, but a test of reasoning: a form into which we may translate any reasoning, with the effect of exposing all the points at which any unwarranted inference can have got in. According to this view of the Syllogism—for the justification of which I must refer to the Second Book of my *System of Logic*[*]—the syllogistic theory is only concerned with providing forms suitable to test the validity of inferences; and it was not necessary that the forms in which reasoning was directed to be written, should be those in which it is carried on in thought, so long as they are practically equivalent, that is, so long as the propositions in words are always true or false according as the judgments in thought are so. The propositions in Extension, being, in this sense, exactly equivalent to the judgments in Comprehension, served quite as well to ground forms of ratiocination upon: and as the validity of the forms was more easily and conveniently shown through the concrete conception of comparing classes of objects, than through the abstract one of recognising coexistence of attributes, logicians were perfectly justified in taking the course, which, in any case, the established forms of language would doubtless have forced upon them. They are thus deserving of no blame, though their mode of proceeding has been attended with some practical mischief, by diverting the attention of thinkers from what really constitutes the meaning of Propo-

[*See *Collected Works*, Vol. VII, pp. 196–9 (Bk. II, Chap. iii, §5).]

sitions. It has also been one of the causes of the prejudice so general in the last three centuries, against the syllogistic theory. For a doctrine which defined one of the two great processes of the discovery of truth as consisting in the operation of placing objects in a class and then finding them there, can never, I think, have really satisfied any competent thinker, however he may have acquiesced in it for want of a better. There must always have been a dormant sense of discontent, an obscure feeling that this was a description of the reasoning process by one of its accidents, though an inseparable accident.*

Sir W. Hamilton distinguishes two kinds of Syllogism, Extensive and Comprehensive.

For while every syllogism infers that the part of a part is a part of the whole, it does this either in the quantity of Extension—the Predicate of the two notions compared in the Question and Conclusion being the greatest whole, and the subject the smallest part; or in the counter quantity of Comprehension, the subject of these two notions being the greatest whole, and the Predicate the smallest part.

He acknowledges, however, that both syllogisms are identically the same argument; "every syllogism in the one quantity being convertible into a

---

*[67] Dr. M'Cosh has some partially just observations on this subject. He admits that "in by far the greater number of propositions, the primary and uppermost sense is in Comprehension." ([*Examination*,] p. 292.) He says, however, that in some, "the uppermost thought is in Extension. Thus, when the young student of Natural History is told that the crocodile is a reptile, his idea is of a class, of which he may afterwards learn the marks." (*Ibid.*, p. 293.) And it is true that when the known purpose of the statement is to declare what place the object occupies in a classification, a fact of classification is the real meaning of the proposition. This is emphatically the exception which proves the rule. Dr. M'Cosh adds, "the mind in its discursive operations tends to go on from Comprehension to Extension." [*Ibid.*] This I admit; but the thought in Comprehension comes first: the thought in Extension rests on the thought in Comprehension, and follows it; but is so closely linked with it that it can hardly help following. The circumstance, however, that the proposition is familiarly expressed in concrete language, does not prove it to be thought in Extension. The practice of so expressing it must, no doubt, as Dr. M'Cosh says, "proceed from some law of thought as applied to things;" but the law of thought it proceeds from is merely the obvious one, that concrete language, requiring for its formation a lower degree of abstraction, was earliest formed, took possession of the field, and is still the most familiar. [*Ibid.*] When Dr. M'Cosh goes on to say that although "so far as propositions are concerned, spontaneous thought is chiefly in Comprehension," the case is "different in regard to reasoning, the uppermost thought in which is always in Extension," (*ibid.*, p. 303,) I cannot agree with him. If the meaning, in consciousness, of the premises when separate, is in Comprehension, it is not natural that the derivative and subordinate meaning in Extension should leap to the front as soon as the premises are brought together. But if, instead of "in reasoning," Dr. M'Cosh had said "in the artificial formula of Reasoning called Syllogism," I think he would have been right.

syllogism absolutely equivalent in the other quantity."* And what is the difference in form and language between the two syllogisms? According to our author it is merely a difference in the order of the premises. The following,

> "Every morally responsible agent is a free agent;
> Man is a morally responsible agent;
> Therefore man is a free agent,"†

is, according to him, a syllogism in Extension. Transpose the premises, and write it thus,

> "Man is a responsible agent;
> But a responsible agent is a free agent;
> Therefore, man is a free agent,"‡

and we have, according to him, a syllogism in Comprehension. Far, however, from constituting two kinds of reasoning, this does not even supply us with two different forms of it. He himself says elsewhere, that "the transposition of the propositions of a syllogism affords no modifications of form yielding more than a superficial character."§ And even this superficial difference he with his own hands abolishes, saying, that any syllogism whatever "can be perspicuously expressed not only by the normal, but by any of the five consecutions of its propositions which deviate from the regular order," and that "a syllogism in Comprehension is equally susceptible of a transposition of its propositions as a syllogism in Extension."¶ So that the slight distinction of form which he seemed at first to contend for, does not exist; a Syllogism in Comprehension, and the corresponding Syllogism in Extension, are word for word the same. Instead of "every syllogism in the one quantity" being "convertible into a syllogism absolutely equivalent in the other quantity," every syllogism is already a syllogism in both quantities.‖

The distinction, therefore, is not between two kinds, or even between two forms, of syllogism, but between two modes of construing the meaning of the same syllogism. And what are these two modes? Sir W. Hamilton says, that they are distinguished by a difference in the meaning of the copula.

Lectures, Vol. III, pp. 286–7.
†*Ibid.*, p. 270.
‡*Ibid.*, p. 273.
§*Ibid.*, p. 399.
¶*Ibid.*, pp. 397–8.
‖It is curious to observe with what facility Sir W. Hamilton drives two conflicting opinions together in a team. The passages quoted in the text are destructive of any notion of a different order of the premises in a Syllogism of Extension and in one of Comprehension. Yet this notion maintains full possession of our author's mind. We have found him accusing all logical writers of overlooking Reasoning in Com-

In the one process, that, to wit, in extension, the copula *is*, means *is contained under*, whereas in the other, it means *comprehends in*. Thus, the proposition *God is merciful*, viewed as in the one quantity, signifies *God is contained under merciful*, that is, the notion *God* is contained under the notion *merciful*; viewed as in the other, means, *God comprehends merciful*, that is, the notion God *comprehends in it* the notion *merciful*.*

I cannot admit this to be a true analysis of the meaning of the proposition, either in Extension or in Comprehension. The statement that God is merciful I construe as an affirmation not concerning the notion God, but the Being God. Interpreted in Comprehension I hold it to mean, that this Being has the attribute signified by the word merciful, or, in our author's language, comprehended in the concept. Interpreted in Extension I render it thus: The Being, God, is either the only being, or one of the beings, forming the class merciful, or, in other words, possessing the attribute mercifulness. Thus stated, who can doubt which of the two is the original and natural judgment, and which is a derivative and artificial mode of restating it? The difference between them is slight, but real, and consists in this, that the second construction introduces the idea of other possible merciful beings, an idea not suggested by the first construction. This suggestion gives rise to the idea of a *class* merciful, and of God as a member of that class: notions which are not present to the mind at all when it simply assents to the proposition that God is merciful. To make a distinction between Reasoning in Extension and in Comprehension, when the same syllogism serves for both, could only be admissible if we employed the same words having sometimes in our mind the meaning in Extension, sometimes that in Comprehension: but in reality all reasoning is thought solely in Comprehension, except when we, for a technical purpose, perform a second act of thought upon the Extension—which in general we do not, and have no need to, consider.

Nor is this the only objection to Sir W. Hamilton's doctrine. There is another, less obvious, but equally fatal. The statement in Comprehension is, that A has the attributes comprehended in B. The statement in Exten-

---

prehension; but he thinks that they exceptionally recognised it in the case of the Sorites, and that in that case, by a contrary error, they "altogether overlooked the possibility of a Reasoning in Extension," solely because, in the Sorites, they inverted the usual order of the premises. (*Ibid.*, pp. 379 and ff.) On a similar foundation stands his charge against the Fourth Figure, of being "a monster undeserving of toleration," [*ibid.*, p. 424,] because instead of keeping to one of the two quantities, Extension and Comprehension, it reasons (he says) across from one of them to the other. This is merely because the Fourth Figure, while it draws the same conclusion which might have been drawn in the First, reverses the order of the premises. (*Ibid.*, pp. 425–8.)

Ibid., p. 274.

sion is, that A belongs to the class of things which have the attributes comprehended in B. These statements are either, as I affirm them to be, one and the same assertion in slightly different words, or they are different assertions. If they are the same assertion, there is but one judgment, which is both in Extension and in Comprehension, and but one kind of reasoning, which is in both. But supposing them, for the sake of argument, to be two different assertions, the judgment respecting Extension is a corollary from that in Comprehension, expressing an artificial point of view in which we may regard the natural judgment. Now, on this supposition, that the judgment respecting Extension is not the same, but an additional judgment, it is, like all other judgments, a judgment in Comprehension. "A is part of class B" must be interpreted thus: The phænomenon A possesses, or the concept A comprehends, the attribute of being included in the class B. So that, while every judgment in Comprehension warrants, by way of immediate inference, a corresponding judgment respecting Extension, this very judgment respecting Extension is itself but a particular kind of judgment in Comprehension. Even, therefore, on the untenable doctrine that there are two different judgments in the case, the distinction between judgments in Extension and judgments in Comprehension is not sustainable; and the supposed addition to the theory of the Syllogism is a mere excrescence and incumbrance on it.

How great the incumbrance is, all are able to judge, who follow our author through the details of the syllogistic logic. He not only finds it necessary to expound and demonstrate every one of the doctrines twice over, as adapted to Extension and to Comprehension, but struggles to express all the fundamental principles in a manner combining both points of view; and is thereby compelled either to state those principles in terms too wide and abstract for easy apprehension, in order that what is laid down respecting wholes and their parts may be applicable to both kinds of wholes (in Extension and in Comprehension), or else to embarrass the learner with the necessity of carrying on two trains of thought at once, in the attempt to apprehend a single principle. I need not dwell on the additional error, of considering the relation of whole and parts as the foundation of the Syllogism in both aspects. To the point of view of Extension that relation is applicable. In every affirmative proposition, if true, the object or class of objects denoted by the subject is a part (when it is not the whole) of the class of objects denoted by the predicate. But no similar relation exists between the two "bundles of attributes" comprehended in the subject and in the predicate, except in the case of Analytical Judgments, that is, of merely verbal propositions. In Synthetical Judgments, that is, in all propositions which convey information about anything except the meaning of words, the relation between the two sets of attributes is not a relation of Whole and Part, but a relation of Coexistence.

I now pass to the doctrine of the Quantification of the Predicate; examining it by the light of the same principles which we have applied to the distinction between the supposed two kinds of Reasoning.

It will be desirable to state in Sir W. Hamilton's own words, as first published in 1846, the claims he prefers in behalf of this doctrine, and the important consequences to which he considers it to lead.

The self-evident truth,—That we can only rationally deal with what we already understand, determines the simple logical postulate,—*To state explicitly what is thought implicitly*. From the consistent application of this postulate, on which Logic ever insists, but which Logicians have never fairly obeyed, it follows:—that, logically, we ought to take into account the *quantity*, always understood in thought, but usually, and for manifest reasons, elided in its expression, not only of the *subject*, but also of the *predicate* of a judgment. This being done, and the necessity of doing it will be proved against Aristotle and his repeaters, we obtain, *inter alia*, the ensuing results:

1°. That the *preindesignate terms* of a proposition, whether subject or predicate, are never, on that account, thought as *indefinite* (or indeterminate) in quantity. The only indefinite, is *particular*, as opposed to *definite*, quantity; and this last, as it is either of an extensive *maximum* undivided, or of an extensive *minimum* indivisible, constitutes quantity *universal* (general) and quantity *singular* (individual). In fact, *definite* and *indefinite* are the only quantities of which we ought to hear in Logic; for it is only as indefinite that particular, it is only as definite that individual and general, quantities have any (and the same) logical avail.

2°. The revocation of the *two terms of a Proposition* to their *true relation*; a proposition being always an *equation* of its subject and its predicate.

3°. The consequent reduction of the *Conversion of Propositions* from three species to *one*—that of Simple Conversion.

4°. The reduction of all the *General Laws of Categorical Syllogisms* to a *Single Canon*.

5°. The evolution from that *one canon* of all the species and varieties of Syllogism.

6°. The *abrogation* of all the *Special Laws of Syllogism*.

7°. A demonstration of the *exclusive possibility of Three Syllogistic Figures*; and (on new grounds) the scientific and final *abolition of the Fourth*.

8°. A manifestation that *Figure* is an *unessential variation* in syllogistic form; and the consequent *absurdity of Reducing* the syllogisms of the other figures to the first.

9°. An enouncement of *one Organic Principle* for *each Figure*.

10°. A determination of the true *number* of the legitimate *Moods*, with

11°. Their *amplification* in number (*thirty-six*);

12°. Their numerical *equality* under all the figures; and

13°. Their *relative equivalence*, or virtual identity, throughout every schematic difference.

14°. That in the *second* and *third* figures, the extremes holding both the same relation to the middle term, there *is not*, as in the first, *an opposition and subordina-*

tion between a term major and a term minor mutually containing and contained, in the counter wholes of Extension and Comprehension.

15°. Consequently, in the *second* and *third* figures, there is *no determinate major and minor premise*, and there are *two indifferent conclusions*; whereas, in the *first*, the *premises* are *determinate*, and there is a *single proximate conclusion*.

16°. That the *third*, as the figure in which *Comprehension* is predominant, is more appropriate to *Induction*.

17°. That the *second*, as the figure in which *Extension* is predominant, is more appropriate to *Deduction*.

18°. That the *first*, as the figure in which *Comprehension* and *Extension* are in equilibrium, is common to *Induction* and *Deduction* indifferently.*

The doctrine which leads to all these consequences, or rather, which necessitates all these changes of expression (for they are no more), is that the Predicate is always quantified in thought; that we always think it either as signifying the whole, or as signifying only a part, of the objects included in its Extension. "In reality and in thought, every quantity is necessarily either all, or some, or none."† The proposition, All A is B, must mean, in thought, either All A is all B, or All A is some B. When I judge that all oxen ruminate, it must not only be true, but I must mean, either that All ox is all ruminating, or that All ox is some ruminating. Logic, therefore, postulates to express in words what is already in the thoughts, and to write all *ᵉ* propositions in one or other of these forms: which makes it necessary that all the rules for reasoning should be altered, at least in expression, and grounded on the relation of exact equality between the terms.

But if, as I have endeavoured to show, the predicate B is present in thought only in respect of its Comprehension; if it be an error to suppose that it is thought of as an aggregate of objects at all; still less is it thought of as an aggregate with a determinate quantity, as some or all. I repeat the appeal which I have already made to every reader's consciousness: Does he, when he judges that all oxen ruminate, advert even in the minutest degree to the question, whether there is anything else which ruminates? Is this consideration at all in his thoughts, any more than any other consideration foreign to the immediate subject? One person may know that there are other ruminating animals, another may think that there are none, a third may be without any opinion on the subject: but if they all know what is

Discussions, App. II [A], pp. 650–1.

†*Ibid.*, App. II [B], p. 691n. But the whole meaning of this assertion, as available for our author's purpose, is destroyed by the statement which he is presently obliged to make, that "the Indesignate is thought, either precisely, as whole or as part, *or vaguely, as the one or the other, unknown which, but the worse always presumed.*" [*Ibid.*] The concession, though fatal to himself, is short of the truth; for the Indesignate is not necessarily thought either as a whole, or as part, or as "unknown which:" it is often not thought in any relation of quantity at all.

ᵉ65¹   other

meant by ruminating, they all, when they judge that every ox ruminates, mean exactly the same thing. The mental process they go through, as far as that one judgment is concerned, is precisely identical; though some of them may go on further, and add other judgments to it.*

The fact, that the proposition "Every A is B" only means Every A is *some* B, far from being always present in thought, is not at first seized without some difficulty by the tyro in logic. It requires a certain effort of thought to perceive that when we say, All As are Bs, we only identify A with a *h*portion*h* of the class B. When the learner is first told that the proposition All As are Bs can only be converted in the form "Some Bs are As," I apprehend that this strikes him as a new idea; and that the truth of the statement is not quite obvious to him, until verified by a particular example in which he already knows that the simple converse would be false, such as, All men are animals, therefore all animals are men. So far is it from being true that the proposition, All As are Bs, is spontaneously quantified in thought as All A is some B.

*Not only we do not (unless exceptionally for some special purpose) quantify the predicate in thought, but we do not even quantify the subject, in the sense which Sir W. Hamilton's theory requires. Even in an universal proposition, we do not think of the *f*subject*f* as an aggregate whole, but as its several parts: we do not judge that all A is B, but that all As are Bs, which is a different thing. That what is true of the whole must be true of any part, only holds good when the whole means the parts themselves, and not when it means the aggregate of them. All A, is a very different notion from Each A. What is true of A only as a whole, forms no element of a judgment concerning its parts—even concerning all its parts. Sir W. Hamilton thinks that the relation of quantity in extension which the class A bears to the class B, is always present in my thoughts when I predicate B of A. This relation of quantity, however, does not belong to individual As, but specifically and solely to A as a whole, and as a whole I am not thinking of it. When I am predicating B of all As severally, I am not adverting to any property or relation which belongs to A as their aggregate. Accordingly we do not say, all ox ruminates, but all oxen ruminate. The distinction is of little importance when A is only coextensive with part of B; for if A altogether is but a part, still more must this be true of any particular A, and it is indifferent whether we say all A is some B, or each of the As is some B. But it is quite another matter when the assertion is that all A is all B. This, if true at all, is true *only* of A considered as a whole; and expresses a relation between the two classes as totals, not between either of them and its parts. Now, to affirm that when we judge every A to be a B, we always, and necessarily, recognise in thought a fact which is not true of every, or even of any A, but only of the aggregate composed of all As, seems to me as baseless a fancy as ever implanted itself in the intellect of an eminent thinker. *g*It is, in short (as observed by one of my correspondents), a conclusive reason against the assimilation of a judgment to an equation, that in equations the terms are used collectively, and in judgments mostly distributively.*g*

*f-f*65[2]   object [*printer's error?*]
g-g+72
*h-h*65[1]   part

The pretension, therefore, of the doctrine of a Quantified Predicate, to be a more correct representation and analysis of the reasoning process than the common doctrine of the syllogism, I hold to be psychologically false. And this is fatal to the doctrine, if we admit Sir W. Hamilton's theory that Logic is the science of the laws according to which we *must* think in order that our thought may be valid. But according to the very different view I myself take of Formal Logic, this doctrine might still be a valuable addition to it: since, in my view, the Syllogistic theory altogether is not an analysis of the reasoning process, but only furnishes a test of the validity of reasonings, by supplying forms of expression into which all reasonings may be translated if valid, and which, if they are invalid, will detect the hidden flaw. In this point of view it might well be, that a form which always exhibited the quantity of the predicate might be an improvement on the common form. And I am not disposed to deny that for occasional use, and for purposes of illustration, it is so. The exposition of the theory of the syllogism is made clearer, by pointing out that All As are B only implies that All A is some B, while No As are B excludes A from the whole of B. This, in fact, is taught to all who learn logic in the common way, by what is called the doctrine of Suppositio; or (in the many books which leave this doctrine out) by the theory of Conversion, and the syllogistic rules against Undistributed Middle, and against proceeding à *non distributo ad distributum*. There is no harm, and some little good, in giving to these essential doctrines the more explicit expression demanded for them by Sir W. Hamilton. But to obtain any advantage from it, we must be content with quantifying such propositions as, in their unquantified form, are really asserted and used. To foist in any others, overlays and confuses, instead of illuminating, the theory. "All A is some B" is admissible, because it is the quantification really implied in All As are B; but "All A is all B" is inadmissible, because it is not the equivalent of any single proposition capable of being asserted in an unquantified form. As all reasoning, except in the process of teaching Logic, will always be carried on in the forms which men use in real life; and as the only purpose of providing other forms, is to supply a test for those which are really used; it is essential that the forms provided should be forms into which the propositions expressed in common language can be translated—that every proposition in logical form, should be the exact equivalent of some proposition in the common form. Now, there is no proposition capable of being expressed in the ordinary form, which is equivalent to the proposition, All A is all B. That form of expression combines the import of two propositions in common language, expressive of two separate judgments, All As are Bs, and All Bs are As.

If this had not been denied, I should have deemed it too obvious to require either proof or illustration. But Sir W. Hamilton does deny it, and therefore some enforcement of it is indispensable. When we make an assertion in the cramped and unnatural form, All man is all rational, can anything seem more evident than that to cover the whole ground occupied by this statement, two judgments are required; namely, first, that every man has the attribute reason; and secondly, that nothing which is not man has that attribute, or (which is the same thing) that every rational creature has the attributes of man? How is it possible to make only one judgment, out of an assertion divisible into two parts, one of which may be unknown and the other known, one unthought of and the other thought of, one false and the other true?*

Unless Sir W. Hamilton was prepared to maintain that whenever the universal converse of an universal affirmative proposition would be true, we cannot know the one without knowing the other, it is in vain for him to contend that a form which asserts both of them at once is only one proposition. If in judging that "All equilateral triangles are equiangular," we judge that all equilateral triangles are all equiangular, in what condition of judgment is the mind of the tyro to whom it has just been proved that all equilateral triangles are equiangular, but who does not yet know the proof of the converse proposition that all equiangular triangles are equilateral? If "All equilateral triangles are all equiangular" is only one judgment, what is the proposition that all equilateral triangles are equiangular? Is it half a judgment?†

*The only answer I can imagine to this is, that having the two concepts Man and Rational, and being engaged in actually comparing them with each other, we *must* perceive and judge whether the one is merely a part of the other, or a whole coinciding with it. But this answer it is not competent to Sir W. Hamilton, or any other Conceptualist, to make. An adversary of Sir W. Hamilton might make it. I have myself said, and have offered as a *reductio ad absurdum* of his analysis of Reasoning, that if we have two concepts and compare them, we cannot but perceive any relation of whole and part which exists between them. [See pp. 342ff. above.] Sir W. Hamilton however is precluded from making this reply; for all Reasoning, even to the longest process in Mathematics, consists, according to him, in discovering this relation of whole and part by circuitous means, when direct comparison does not disclose it. From his point of view, therefore, the argument is not tenable; and from mine it has no pertinence, since I do not admit that Reasoning is a comparison of Concepts at all.

†Sir W. Hamilton goes the length of asserting that to a person who knows all trilateral figures to be triangular, the proposition "all triangles are trilateral" must, if expressed as understood, be written "All triangles are all trilateral:" as if every proposition which I affirm respecting a subject, must include all I know about it. (Appendix [v(f)] to *Lectures*, Vol. IV, pp. 292 and ff.)

That the proposition All A is all B is not a single judgment, but compounded of two, has already been urged against Sir W. Hamilton by Mr. De Morgan, and we are in possession of Sir W. Hamilton's answer (*Discussions*, Appendix II, pp. 687–8). Unhappily Mr. De Morgan (by an oversight not usual with that able thinker) gave

This is not the only case in which Sir W. Hamilton insists upon wrapping up two different assertions in one form of words, and demands that they shall be considered one assertion. He strenuously contends that the form "Some A is B," or (in its quantified form) "Some A is some B," ought in logical propriety to be used and understood in the sense of "some and *some*

Sir W. Hamilton an apparent triumph, by mistaking the two judgments which the pretended single proposition is composed of. He appears to have said, that the proposition "All Xs are all Ys," is compounded of the propositions "All Xs are some Ys," and "Some Xs are all Ys." [See Augustus De Morgan, "On the Symbols of Logic," *Proceedings of the Cambridge Philosophical Society*, I (25 Feb., 1850), 92.] Sir W. Hamilton replies, that these two propositions are (in his own peculiar language) incompossible, inasmuch as we cannot think X both as some Y, that is, a part of Y, and as the whole. The argument is little better than a quibble, because other people do not (though Sir W. Hamilton does) mean by some, *some only*; they mean *some at least*; and if the first of Mr. De Morgan's two propositions identifies X with only some of Y, the second superadds the remainder. But in reality the two judgments which go to the composition of "All A is all B," are not judgments with quantified predicates at all. They are, All A is B, and All B is A. The one ascribes the attributes of B to every A, the other the attributes of A to every B. Judgments more distinct and independent of one another do not exist.

According to Sir W. Hamilton "ordinary language quantifies the Predicate as often as this determination becomes of the smallest import." And he cites such instances as "Virtue is the *only* nobility;" "Of animals man alone is rational," and the like. (*Lectures*, Vol. IV, App. [v], pp. 259–61.) The truth is, that ordinary language quantifies the predicate in the rare cases in which it is quantified in thought, and in no others. And even then the quantified proposition is an abbreviated expression of two judgments. The German logician Scheibler, to whom our author refers in a foot-note (*ibid.*, p. 261), could have set him right here. [Christoph Scheibler, *Opera philosophica*, 2 vols. (Frankfurt: Wustii, 1665).]

[i]"Sir W. Hamilton," says Mr. Grote, "insists on stating explicitly, not merely all that is thought implicitly, but a great deal more; adding to it something else, which may, indeed, be thought conjointly, but which more frequently is not thought at all. He requires us to pack two distinct judgments into one and the same proposition: he interpolates the meaning of the Propositio Conversa *simpliciter* into the form of the Propositio Convertenda (when an universal affirmative) and then claims it as a great advantage, that the proposition thus interpolated admits of being converted *simpliciter*, and not merely *per accidens*. . . . If a man is prepared to give us information on one Quæsitum, why should he be constrained to use a mode of speech which forces on his attention at the same time a second and distinct Quæsitum, so that he must either give us information about the two at once, or confess himself ignorant respecting the second?" (["John Stuart Mill on the Philosophy of Sir William Hamilton,"] pp. 31–2.) Mr. Grote goes on to cite from Sir W. Hamilton's own collection of authorities, an excellent passage from a Jewish philosopher of the fourteenth century, Levi Ben Gerson, which exactly confutes Sir W. Hamilton's doctrine. "The cause why the quantitative note is not usually joined with the predicate, is that there would thus be two quæsita at once; to wit, whether the predicate were affirmed of the subject, and whether it were denied of everything

[i–i]+67, 72

only."* No shadow of justification is shown for thus deviating from the practice of all writers on logic, and of all who think and speak with any approach to precision, and adopting into logic a mere *sous-entendu* of common conversation in its most unprecise form. If I say to any one, "I saw some of your children to-day," he might be justified in inferring that I did not see them all, not because the words mean it, but because, if I had seen them all, it is most likely that I should have said so: though even this cannot be presumed unless it is presupposed that I must have known whether the children I saw were all or not. But to carry this colloquial mode of interpreting a statement into Logic, is something novel. If Some A is B is to be understood of some *only*, it is a double judgment, compounded of the propositions, Some As are Bs, and Some As are not Bs. If quantified in our author's manner, the propositions would run thus: Some A is some B, and Some (other) A is not any B. If two statements, one of which affirms and the other denies a different predicate of a different subject, are not two distinct judgments, it is impossible to say what are so. One of the great uses of discipline in Formal Logic, is to make us aware when something which claims to be a single proposition, really consists of several, which, not being necessarily involved one in another, require to be separated, and considered each by itself, before we admit the compound assertion. This separation may be called, with reason, stating explicitly in words what is implicitly in thought. But it is a new postulate of Logic to state *im*plicitly in words what is *ex*plicitly in thought, and I do not think that Logic is at all enriched by the acquisition.

With these compound propositions falls the whole pretension of the quantified mode of expression to yield legitimate inferences which are not recognised by the old Logic. Whatever can be proved from "All A is all B," can be proved in the old form from one or both of its elements, All As are Bs, and All Bs are As. Whatever can be proved from "Some, and only some, A is some (or all) B," can be proved in the old form from its elements,

---

beside. For when we say, All Man is all Rational, we judge that all man is rational, and judge likewise that rational is denied of everything but man. But these are, in reality, two different quæsita; and therefore it has become usual to state them, not in one, but in two several propositions. And this is self-evident, seeing that a quæsitum in itself, asks only—Does or does not this inhere in that? and not, Does or does not this inhere in that, and at the same time inhere in nothing else."[i] [Quoted by Grote, p. 32n, from Hamilton, *Lectures*, Vol. IV, App. v(g), pp. 310–11.]

Propositions in Extension have absolutely no meaning but what they derive from Comprehension. The Logic of the quantified predicate takes the Comprehension out of them, and leaves them a *caput mortuum*.

*See, among many other places, *Discussions*, Appendix II[B], pp. 690n–1n, where he says, "Every quantity is necessarily either *all*, or *none*, or *some*; of these, the third is formally *exclusive* of the other two."

Some As are Bs, Some As are not Bs, and (in the case last mentioned) All Bs are As. If we choose to alter the forms of all our propositions, the forms of our syllogisms naturally require alterations too; and there may be a greater number of forms in which quantified conclusions can be drawn from quantified premises, than in which unquantified conclusions can be drawn from unquantified premises. But there is not a single instance, nor is it possible in the nature of things that there should be an instance, in which a conclusion that is provable from quantified premises, could not be proved from the same premises unquantified, if we set forth all those which are really involved. If there could be such an instance, the quantified Syllogism would be a real addition to the theory of Logic: if not, not.

As I have already once remarked, it does not follow, because the quantified Syllogism is not a true expression of what is in thought, that ʲthe occasionalʲ writing the predicate with a quantification may not be a real help to the *art* of Logic. Though not a correct analysis of the reasoning process, it may, in some cases, enable us more readily to see whether the conclusion really follows from the premises. But without rejecting it as an available help for this purpose, I must observe that its use in this capacity appears to me extremely limited; for two reasons. First; the problem is, to test the validity of a reasoning as expressed in the language in which men ordinarily reason. We do this by taking the propositions as they are, and measuring the extent of the assertions made in the two premises and in the conclusion respectively, so as to ascertain whether the former are broad enough to cover and include the latter. This it requires some practice to do, but the task is not avoided by quantifying the predicate; on the contrary, it must have been actually performed before the predicate can be correctly quantified; so that by quantifying it in expression, no trouble is saved. My second reason is, that after the predicate has been quantified, it is often equally or more difficult to follow the consecution of the thought through the symbols, than as expressed in ordinary language. Take one of the common cases of invalid inference, a syllogism in the first figure with the major premise particular, such as this:

> Some Ms are Ps
> All Ss are Ms
> Therefore all Ss are Ps;

the inference fails, because the Ms which are identified with Ss may not be the same Ms which are Ps, but other Ms. Let us now quantify the predicates thus:

> Some Ms are some Ps
> All Ss are some Ms
> Therefore all Ss are some Ps;

ʲ⁻ʲ+67, 72

is the invalidity of the inference at all clearer? Does it require less exertion of thought to perceive that "some Ms" may not mean the same *some* in both premises, than it did to recognise the equivalent truth as to M in the minor, and "some M" in the major premise? On the contrary, the quantified form is the more plausibly misleading of the two, since the middle term, though really ambiguous, is, in that form, verbally the same, which in the unquantified form it is not.

The general result of these considerations is, that the utility of the new forms is by no means such as to compensate for the great additional complication which they introduce into the syllogistic theory; a complication which would make it at the same time difficult to learn or remember, and intolerably tiresome both in the learning and in the using. The sole purpose of any syllogistic forms is to afford an available test for the process of drawing inferences in the common language of life from premises in the same common language; and the ordinary forms of Syllogism effect this purpose completely. The new forms do not, in any appreciable degree, facilitate the process, while they are chargeable, in a far greater degree than the common forms, with diverting the mind from the true meaning of propositions (the ascription of attributes to objects considered severally), and concentrating it upon the highly artificial, and generally unimportant, consideration of the relation of extent between classes of objects, considered not severally, but as collective wholes. The new forms have thus no practical advantage which can countervail the objection of their entire psychological irrelevancy; and the invention and acquisition of them have little value, except as one among many other feats of mental gymnastic, by which students of the science may exercise and invigorate their faculties. They should, in short, be dealt with as Sir W. Hamilton deals with Mr. De Morgan's forms of "numerically definite" Syllogism, viz. "taken into account by Logic as authentic forms, but then relegated as of little use in practice, and cumbering the science with a superfluous mass of moods."*

Lectures, Vol. IV, App. [vi], p. 355. [See De Morgan, *Formal Logic* (London: Taylor and Walton, 1847), p. 142.]

CHAPTER XXIII

Of Some Minor Peculiarities of Doctrine in Sir William Hamilton's View of Formal Logic

THE TWO THEORIES EXAMINED in the preceding chapter are the only important novelties which Sir W. Hamilton has introduced into the Science or Art of Logic. But he has here and there departed from the common doctrine of logicians on subordinate points. Some of these deviations deserve notice from their connexion with some principal part of our author's doctrine, others chiefly as throwing light on the character of his mind. The one to which I shall first advert is of the former class.

I. Almost all writers on the Syllogistic Logic have directed attention to the fact, that though we cannot, while observing the forms of Logic, draw a false conclusion from true premises, we may draw a true one from false premises: in other words, the falsity of the premises does not prove the falsity of the conclusion; nor does the truth of the conclusion prove the truth of the premises. The warning is needed; for it is by no means unusual to mistake a refutation of the reasons from which a doctrine has been deduced for a disproof of the doctrine itself; and there is no error of thought more common than the acceptance of premises because they lead to a conclusion already assented to as true. Not only is this caution useful, but it is relevant to Logic, even in the restricted point of view of Formal Logic. When it is affirmed that Formal Logic has nothing to do with Material Truth, all that ought to be meant, is that in Logic we are not to consider whether the conclusion supposed to be proved is true in fact. But we are to consider whether it is true conditionally, true if the premises are true: that question is the specific business of Formal Logic: if Formal Logic does not teach us that, there is nothing for it to teach. The theorem, that in a valid Syllogism the falsity of the premises does not prove the falsity of the conclusion, is as germane to Logic as that the truth of the premises proves the truth of the conclusion. We have therefore reason to be surprised at finding Sir W. Hamilton delivering himself as follows:

Logic does not warrant the truth of its premises, except in so far as these may be the formal conclusions of anterior reasonings; it only warrants (on the hypothesis that the premises are truly assumed) the truth of the inference. In this view the conclusion may, as a separate proposition, be true; but if this truth be not a necessary consequence from the premises, it is a false conclusion, that is, in fact, no conclusion at all. Now on this point there is a doctrine prevalent among logicians, which is not only erroneous, but if admitted, is subversive of the distinction of Logic as a purely formal science. The doctrine in question is in its result this,—that if the conclusion of a syllogism be true, the premises may be either true or false, but that if the conclusion be false, one or both of its premises must be false: in other words, that it is possible to infer true from false, but not false from true. As an example of this I have given the following syllogism:

> Aristotle is a Roman;
> A Roman is a European;
> Therefore, Aristotle is a European.

The inference, in so far as expressed, is true; but I would remark, that the whole inference which the premises necessitate, and which the conclusion, therefore, virtually contains, is not true,—is false. For the premises of the preceding syllogism gave not only the conclusion, *Aristotle is a European*, but also the conclusion, *Aristotle is not a Greek*; for it not merely follows from the premises, that Aristotle is conceived under the universal notion of which the concept *Roman* forms a particular sphere, but likewise that he is conceived as excluded from all the other particular spheres which are contained under that universal notion. The consideration of the truth of the premise, *Aristotle is a Roman*, is, however, more properly to be regarded as extralogical; but if so, then the consideration of the conclusion, *Aristotle is a European*, on any other view than as a mere formal inference from certain hypothetical antecedents, is likewise extralogical. Logic is only concerned with the formal truth,—the technical validity,—of its syllogisms, and anything beyond the legitimacy of the consequence it draws from certain hypothetical antecedents, it does not profess to vindicate. Logical truth and falsehood are thus contained in the correctness and incorrectness of logical inference; and it was, therefore, with no impropriety that we made a true or correct, and a false or incorrect, syllogism convertible expressions.*

The statement that a true proposition may be correctly inferred from false premises, or in other words, that a true opinion may be supported by false reasons, is one of which we could hardly have expected to find the truth disputed, whatever might be said of the connexion of Logic with it. So unlooked-for a paradox required to be defended by the strongest arguments: who, then, would expect such shabby, not arguments, but hints of arguments, as the author presents us with? He stops short in the middle of the first, as if afraid that it would break down if relied upon, and hurries to the second, which is still more incapable of bearing weight. "The consideration of the conclusion, *Aristotle is a European*, on any other view than as a mere formal inference from certain hypothetical antecedents, is extralogical." Nobody proposes to consider it as anything but a formal inference from certain hypothetical antecedents. The gist of the whole question is

Lectures, Vol. III, pp. 450–1.

that it is such an inference, and consequently that a proposition really true, may be a formal inference from premises wholly or partially false: in other words, the falsity of the conclusion does not follow from the falsity of the premises. It is as much the business of the theory of "formal inference" to show what conclusions are not formally legitimate, as what are. It is not the business of Formal Logic to determine what is actualiy true, but it is, to tell what does or does not follow from what. In the first unfinished part of his argument, Sir W. Hamilton makes a faint attempt to show that the conclusion, Aristotle is a European, is not true. He admits it to be true as far as expressed, but says that it virtually contains something which is false, namely, that Aristotle is not a Greek. By what analysis can he find this in the proposition, Aristotle is a European? He does not pretend that it is in the proposition considered in itself, but only in the proposition as inferred from "Aristotle is a Roman." But it is a strange doctrine that a proposition is true or false not according to what it asserts, but according to the mode in which the belief of it has been arrived at. It is a very irrational mode of speaking to say that a proposition, besides its obvious meaning, contains a meaning which the words do not convey, which in the mouths of other people it does not bear, but which is so essential a part of it as by its falsity to make the proposition false which otherwise would be true. Suppose that the register of a man's birth having been destroyed, some one to whom the date is of importance, proves it by a false entry in the parish books: would that make the man not to have been born on the day he was born on? But let us concede this point, however unreasonable, and admit that the proposition Aristotle is a European, when inferred from the premise that he is a Roman, includes that premise as part of its own meaning. Does it therefore contain an implication that he is not a Greek? Suppose that I have never heard of Greeks; or that, having heard of them, I suppose a Greek to be a kind of Roman, or a Roman a kind of Greek. Will this ignorance or misapprehension on my part, prevent me from concluding, that if a Roman is a European and Aristotle a Roman, Aristotle must be a European; or will it make the inference illegitimate, or the conclusion false? One sentence in our quotation from Sir W. Hamilton is a singular illustration of the length he will go to support a favourite thesis. "The premises," he says, "of the syllogism gave not only the conclusion, Aristotle is a European, but also the conclusion, Aristotle is not a Greek." Let us try:

> Aristotle is a Roman;
> A Roman is a European;
> Therefore, Aristotle is not a Greek.

This is Formal Logic. This is the philosopher who is so rigidly bent upon excluding from Logic all consideration of what is true or false *vi materiæ*.

What shadow of connexion is there, unless it be *vi materiæ*, between this conclusion, and those premises? Nothing can explain this aberration in a thinker of Sir W. Hamilton's acuteness, except his dogged determination in no shape to recognise belief as an element of judgment, or truth as in any way concerned in Pure Logic.

Sir W. Hamilton has a salvo for all this, though it is one which would not occur to everybody. According to him there are two kinds of truth, or rather the word truth has two meanings, so that it is possible for a proposition to be true although it is false. There is Formal Truth, and Real Truth.* Real Truth is "the harmony between a thought and its matter."[*] Formal Truth is of two kinds, Logical, and Mathematical. Logical Truth is "the harmony or agreement of our thoughts with themselves as thoughts, in other words the correspondence of thought with the universal laws of thinking."[†] And Mathematical Truth is some other harmony of thought, in which truth of fact is equally dispensed with. In another place, he says that if the consequent is correctly "evolved out of" the antecedent, the conclusion out of the premises, this is "Logical or Formal or Subjective truth: and an inference may be subjectively or formally true, which is objectively or really false."† To support his denial of the common doctrine, he has to alter the meaning of words, and make false in the new meaning what cannot be denied to be true in the old. But I object *in toto* to such an abuse of terms as affirming a false proposition to be true, because it is in such a relation to another false proposition, that if that false proposition had been true it would have been true likewise. There is no fitness in the word truth, to express this mere relation of consecution between false propositions. No qualification by adjectives, whether "logical," or "formal," or "subjective," will make this assertion anything but a solecism in language, claiming to be the correction of a philosophical doctrine.

The whole theory of the difference between Formal and Real Truth is treated as it deserves, in a passage from one of Sir W. Hamilton's favourite authorities, Esser, which he quotes, and, strange to say, quotes with approbation.

One party of philosophers, [says Esser,] defining truth in general, the absolute harmony of our thoughts and cognitions,—divide truth into a formal or logical, and into a material or metaphysical, according as that harmony is in consonance with the laws of formal thought, or over and above, with the laws of real knowledge. The criterion of formal truth they place in the principles of Contradiction and of Sufficient Reason, enouncing that what is non-contradictory and consequent is formally true. This criterion, which is positive and immediate of formal truth

*Ibid., Vol. IV, pp. 64–8.
[*Ibid., p. 66.]
[†Ibid., p. 65.]
†Ibid., Vol. II, p. 343.

(inasmuch as what is non-contradictory and consequent can always be thought as possible), they style a negative and mediate criterion of material truth: as what is self-contradictory and logically inconsequent is in reality impossible; at the same time, what is not self-contradictory and not logically inconsequent, is not, however, to be regarded as having an actual existence. But here the foundation is treacherous: the notion of truth is false. When we speak of truth, we are not satisfied with knowing that a thought harmonizes with a certain system of thoughts and cognitions; but, over and above, we require to be assured that what we think is real, and is as we think it to be. Are we satisfied on this point, we then regard our thoughts as true; whereas if we are not satisfied of this, we deem them false, how well soever they may quadrate with any theory or system. It is not, therefore, in any absolute harmony of mere thought, that truth consists, but solely in the correspondence of our thoughts with their objects. The distinction of formal and material truth is thus not only unsound in itself, but opposed to the notion of truth universally held, and embodied in all languages. But if this distinction be inept, the title of Logic, as a positive standard of truth, must be denied; it can only be a negative criterion, being conversant with thoughts and not with things, with the possibility and not with the actuality of existence.*

After all the experience we have had of the facility with which Sir W. Hamilton forgets in one part of his speculations what he has thought in another, it remains scarcely credible that he endorses, in his third volume, this emphatic protest against the distinction which he draws, and the opinion which he maintains, in his second and fourth. "Two opposite doctrines," he says, "have sprung up, which, on opposite sides, have overlooked the true relations of Logic;"† and one of these is the doctrine (the "inaccuracy" our author styles it)[*] which Esser, in this passage, protests against. And he thereupon quotes Esser's condemnation[†] of his (Sir W. Hamilton's) own doctrine. Truly, if arguments *ad hominem* were sufficient, a controversialist who undertakes to refute Sir W. Hamilton would have an easy task.

II. I have already noticed one unacknowledged departure by our author from the usage of Logicians as regards the sense of the word Disjunctive; confining Disjunctive judgments to those in which all the alternative propositions have the same subject: A is either B, or C, or D. This limitation excludes two other forms of the assertion of an alternative: that in which the propositions have different subjects but the same predicate, "Either A, or B, or C, is D;" and that in which they have different subjects and different predicates, "Either A is B, or C is D." The former is exemplified in such judgments as these, Either Brown or Smith did this act; Either John or Thomas is dead. The latter in such as these: Either the witness has told a falsehood, or the prisoner has committed a murder; Either Macbeth has

*Ibid., Vol. III, pp. 106–7. [Cf. Esser, *Logik*, pp. 65–6.]
†Ibid., p. 106.
[*Ibid., p. 107.]
[†I.e., in the passage quoted above.]

killed all Macduff's children, or Macduff has children who were not there present.[*] While arbitrarily excluding both these kinds of assertion from the class and denomination in which they had always been placed, our author does not assign to them any other; so that the effect is not a mere innovation in language, but a hiatus in his logical system; these two kinds of judgment having no place, name, or recognition in it. I have now to point out a second deviation from the received doctrine of logicians in connexion with the same subject. In respect to the class of judgments to which he restricts the name of Disjunctive, those in which two or more predicates are disjunctively affirmed of the same subject, he takes for granted through the whole of his exposition,* that when we say, A is either B or C, we imply that it cannot be both: that we may as legitimately argue, A is either B or C, but it is B, therefore it is not C, as we may argue, A is either B or C, but it is not B, therefore it is C. This is what enables him to affirm, as he does, that the principle of Disjunctive Judgments is the Law of Excluded Middle. The predicates are supposed to be either explicitly or implicitly contradictory, so that one or other of them must be true of the subject, but both of them cannot. I conceive this to be both an incompleteness in his theory, and a positive error in fact. An incompleteness, because we may judge, and legitimately judge, that a thing is either this or that, though aware that it may possibly be both. Sir W. Hamilton is so severe on the ordinary Logic for omitting, as he thinks, some valid forms of thought, that it was peculiarly incumbent on him not to commit a similar oversight in his own exposition of the science. But Sir W. Hamilton does not merely leave unrecognised those disjunctive judgments in which the alternative predicates are mutually compatible; he assumes that the disjunctive form of assertion denies their compatibility, which it assuredly does not. If we assert that a man who has acted in some particular way, must be either a knave or a fool, we by no means assert, or intend to assert, that he cannot be both. Very important consequences may sometimes be drawn from our knowledge that one or other of two perfectly compatible suppositions must be true. Suppose such an argument as this. To make an entirely unselfish use of despotic power a man must be either a saint or a philosopher; but saints and philosophers are rare; therefore those are rare, who make an entirely unselfish use of despotic power. The conclusion follows from the premises, and is of great practical importance. But does the disjunctive premise necessarily imply, or must it be construed as supposing, that the same person cannot be both a saint and a philosopher? Such a construction would be ridiculous.†

[*See William Shakespeare, *Macbeth*, IV, iii, 211–19.]
Lectures, Vol. III, pp. 326ff.
†Mr. Mansel does not fall into this mistake (*Prolegomena Logica*, p. 221).

There is a great quantity of intricate and obscure speculation, in our author's *Lectures* and their Appendices, relating to Disjunctive and Hypothetical Propositions. But, much as he had thought on the subject, the simple idea never seems to have occurred to him *(though he might have found it in Archbishop Whately's *Logic*)*, that every Disjunctive judgment is compounded of two or more Hypothetical ones. "Either A is B, or C is D," means, If A is not B, C is D; and if C is not D, A is B.[*] This is obvious enough to most people; but if Sir W. Hamilton had thought of it, he probably would have denied it: its admission would not have been in keeping with the disposition he shows in so many places, to consider as one judgment all that it is possible to assert in one formula. Again, though he takes much pains to determine what is the real import of a Hypothetical Judgment, the thought never occurs to him that it is a judgment concerning judgments. If A is B, C is D, means, The judgment C is D follows as a consequence from the judgment A is B. Not seeing this, Sir W. Hamilton tacitly adopts the assertion of Krug, that the conversion of a hypothetical syllogism into a categorical "is not always possible."*

III. The next of Sir W. Hamilton's minor innovations in Logic has reference to the Sorites. It is scarcely necessary to say, that a Sorites is an argument in the form, A is B, B is C, C is D, D is E, therefore A is E: an abridged expression for a series of Syllogisms, but not requiring to be decomposed into them in order to make its conclusiveness visible. Sir W. Hamilton accuses all writers on Logic of having overlooked the possibility of a Sorites in the second or third Figure.[†] By this he does not mean, one in which the ultimate syllogism, which sums up the argument, is in the second or third figure, for this all logicians have admitted. For example, to the Sorites given above, there might be added the proposition, No F is E; in which case, the ultimate syllogism would be, A is E, but no F is E, therefore A is not an F: a syllogism in the second figure. Or there might be added, at the opposite end of the series, A is G; when the ultimate syllogism would be in the third figure; A is E, but A is G, therefore some G is an E. These are real Sorites, real chain arguments, and they conclude in the second and third figures: we may call them, if we please, Sorites in the second and in the third figure, the truth being that they are Sorites in which one of the steps is in the second or third figure, all the others being in the first. And every one who understands the laws of the second and third figures (or even the general laws of the Syllogism) can see that no more than one step in either of

[*See Whately, *Elements of Logic*, pp. 107–9, 112–13.]
Lectures, Vol. III, p. 342. [See Krug, *Logik*, p. 258.]
†*Ibid.*, Vol. IV, App. ix, p. 395.

a–a+67, 72

them is admissible in a Sorites, and that it must either be the first or the last. About this, however, Logicians have always been agreed. These are not the kinds of Sorites which Sir W. Hamilton contends for. By a Sorites in the second or third figure, he means one in which all the steps are in the second, or all in the third, figure (a thing impossible in a real Sorites) and in which, accordingly, instead of a succession of middle terms establishing a connexion between the two extremes, there is but one middle term altogether. His paradigm in the second figure would be, No B is A, No C is A, No D is A, No E is A, All F is A, therefore no B, or C, or D, or E, is F. In the third figure, it would be, A is B, A is C, A is D, A is E, A is F, therefore some B, and C, and D, and E, are F. One would have thought that anybody who had the smallest notion of the meaning of a Sorites, must have seen that either of these is not a Sorites at all. It is not a chain argument. It does not ascend to a conclusion by a series of steps, each introducing a new premise. It does not deduce one conclusion from a succession of premises, all necessary to its establishment. It draws as many different conclusions as there are syllogisms, each conclusion depending only on the two premises of one syllogism. That no B is F, follows from No B is A, and All F is A; not from those premises combined with No C is A, No D is A, No E is A. That some B is F, follows from A is B and A is F; and would be proved, though all the other premises of the pretended Sorites were rejected. If Sir W. Hamilton had found in any other writer such a misuse of logical language as he is here guilty of, he would have roundly accused him of total ignorance of logical writers. Since it cannot be imputed to any such cause in himself, I can only ascribe it to the passion which appears to have seized him, in the later years of his life, for finding more and more new discoveries to be made in Syllogistic Logic. If he had transported his ardour for originality into the other departments of the science, in which there was so great an unexhausted field for discovery, he might have enlarged the bounds of philosophy to a much greater extent, than I am afraid he will now be found to have done.

IV. I next turn to a singular misapplication of logical language, in which Sir W. Hamilton departs from all good authorities, and misses one of the most important distinctions drawn by the Aristotelian logic. I refer to his use of the word Contrary. He confounds contrariety with simple incompatibility. "Opposition of Notions," he says,

is twofold: 1°. *Immediate* or *Contradictory Opposition*, called likewise *Repugnance* (τὸ ἀντιφατικῶς ἀντικεῖσθαι, ἀντίφασις, *oppositio immediata* sive *contradictoria, repugnantia*); and 2°. *Mediate* or *Contrary Opposition* (τὸ ἐναντίως ἀντικεῖσθαι, ἐναντιότης, *oppositio media* vel *contraria*). The former emerges, when one concept abolishes (*tollit*) directly or by simple negation, what another establishes, *ponit*; the latter, when one concept does this not directly or by simple negation, but through the affirmation of something else.*

The exemplification and illustration of this is not of our author's devising, but is a citation from Krug, who had preceded him in the error.

To speak now of the distinction of Contradictory and Contrary Opposition, or of Contradiction and Contrariety; of these the former, Contradiction, is exemplified in the opposites,—*yellow*, *not yellow*; *walking*, *not walking*. Here each notion is directly, immediately, and absolutely, repugnant to the other,—they are reciprocal negatives. This opposition is, therefore, properly called that of *Contradiction* or of *Repugnance*; and the opposing notions themselves are *contradictory* or *repugnant* notions, in a single word, *contradictories*. The latter, or Contrary Opposition, is exemplified in the opposites, *yellow*, *blue*, *red*, &c., *walking*, *standing*, *lying*, &c.[†]

It can hardly have been imagined by Krug or Sir W. Hamilton, that this is the meaning of Contrariety in common discourse, or that any one ever speaks of yellow or blue as the contrary of red, or even as the opposite of it. The very phrase, "*the* contrary," testifies that a thing cannot have more contraries than one. Black is regarded as the contrary of white, but no other contrariety is recognised among colours at all. Sir W. Hamilton, versed as he was in the literature of logic, can hardly have fancied that the world of logicians, any more than the common world, was on his side. In the language of logicians, as in that of life, a thing has only one contrary—its extreme opposite; the thing farthest removed from it in the same class. Black is the contrary of white, but neither of them is the contrary of red. Infinitely great is the contrary of infinitely small, but is not the contrary of finite. It is the more strange that Krug and Sir W. Hamilton should have misunderstood or rejected this, as the definition they ignore is the foundation of the distinction between Contradictory and Contrary Propositions, in the famous Parallelogram of Opposition. The contrary proposition to All A is B, is No A is B, its extreme opposite; the assertion most widely differing from it that can be made; denying, not it merely, but [b]every part of it[b]. Its contradictory is merely, Some A is not B. Sir W. Hamilton could not have imagined the distinction between these negative propositions to be, that the one denies by simple negation, the other through the affirmation of something else.

That the teachers of the Syllogistic Logic have taken this view, and not Sir W. Hamilton's, of the meaning of Contrariety, might be shown by any number of quotations. I have only looked up the authorities nearest at

---

Lectures, Vol. III, pp. 213–14. [See Aristotle, *On Interpretation*, in *The Categories, On Interpretation, Prior Analytics*, pp. 124–8 (17^b), and *Metaphysics*, pp. 24–8 (1055^a–1056^b).]

[†]*Lectures*, Vol. III, pp. 214–15. [See Krug, *Logik*, pp. 118–20.]

[b–b]65^1, 65^2 a great deal more

hand. I begin with Aristotle: Τὰ γὰρ πλεῖστον ἀλλήλων διεστηκότα τῶν ἐν τῷ αὐτῷ γένει, ἐναντία ὁρίζονται.*

Aristotle again: Τὰ γὰρ ἐναντία τῶν πλεῖστον διαφερόντων περὶ τὸ αὐτό.[†]

Aristotle ἐν τῷ δεκάτῳ τῆς θεολογικῆς πραγματείας, as cited by Ammonius Hermiæ: Ἐπεὶ δὲ διαφέρειν ἐνδέχεται ἀλλήλων τὰ διαφέροντα πλεῖον καὶ ἔλαττον, ἔστι τις, καὶ μεγίστη διαφορά, καὶ ταύτην λέγω ἐναντίωσιν.[*]

Ammonius himself thereon: Ἡ τῶν ἐναντίων διαφορὰ μεγίστη τῶν ἄλλων, καὶ οὐδὲν ἔχουσα ἐξωτέρω αὐτῆς δυνάμενον πεσεῖν.[‡]

My next extract shall be from a well-known treatise, which Sir W. Hamilton particularly recommended to his pupils: Burgersdyk's *Institutiones Logicæ*.

Oppositorum species sunt quinque: Disparata, contraria, relative opposita, privative opposita, et contradictoria.

Disparata sunt, quorum unum pluribus opponitur, eodem modo. Sic homo et equus, album et cæruleum, sunt disparata: quia homo non equo solum, sed etiam cani, leoni, cæterisque bestiarum speciebus, et album, non solum cæruleo, sed etiam rubro, viridi, cæterisque coloribus mediis, opponitur *eodem modo*, hoc est, eodem oppositorum genere. . . .

Contraria sunt duo absolute, quæ sub eodem genere plurimum distant.[§]

This passage informs us, not only that what Sir W. Hamilton terms Contraries were not so called by the Aristotelian logicians, but also what they were called. They were called Disparates: a term employed by Sir W. Hamilton, but in a totally different meaning.[¶]

The next is from one of the ablest, and, though in a comparatively small compass, one of the completest in essentials, of all the expositions I have seen of Logic from the purely Aristotelian point of view: *Manuductio ad Logicam*, by the Père Du Trieu, of Douai.

Contraria sunt, quæ posita sub eodem genere maxime a se invicem distant, eidem subjecto susceptivo vicissim insunt, a quo se mutuo expellunt, nisi alterum insit a natura; ut, *album*, et *nigrum*.

In hac definitione continentur quatuor conditiones, sive leges contrariorum.

Prima, ut sint sub eodem genere. . . .

Categoriæ, Cap. vi [6ª17–18; in *The Categories, On Interpretation, Prior Analytics*, p. 44].

†Περὶ Ἑρμηνείας, Cap. xiv [23ᵇ23–4; *On Interpretation*, p. 174].

[*Metaphysics*, Vol. II, p. 20 (X, iii, 1055ª4–6).]

‡[Ammonius Hermiæ,] *Ammonii Hermiæ in Aristotelis de Interpretatione Librum Commentarius*, ed. Aldi [i.e., Venice: Aldus, 1546], pp. 175–6.

§[Franco Burgersdijck, *Institutionum logicarum libri duo* (Cambridge: Field, 1660), pp. 94–5,] Lib. I, Cap. 22; Theorema i.

¶*Lectures*, Vol. III, p. 224.

Secunda conditio contrariorum est ut sub illo eodem genere maxime distent, id est *precise* repugnent. . . . Hinc excluduntur disparata.*

The next is from Saunderson's *Logicæ Artis Compendium*, one of the best-known elementary treatises on Logic by British authors.

Oppositio Contraria est inter terminos contrarios. Sunt autem ea contraria quæ posita sub eodem genere maxime inter se distant, et vim habent expellendi se vicissim ex eodem subjecto susceptibili.[†]

Crackanthorp:

Contraria sunt Opposita quorum unum alteri sic opponitur ut nulli alteri aut æque aut magis opponatur. Sic Albedo Nigredini, Homini Brutum, Rationale Irrationali contrarium est. Nam nihil est quod æque Albedini opponitur atque Nigredo, et sic in reliquis.

On the other hand,

Disparata sunt Opposita quorum unum uni sic opponitur, ut alteri vel æque vel magis opponatur. Sic Liberalitas et Avaritia disparata sunt. Nam Avaritia magis opponitur Prodigalitati quam Liberalitati. Sic Albedo et Rubedo disparata sunt, quia Albedo æque opponitur Viriditati atque Rubedini, et magis Nigredini quam ambobus. Nam plus inter se semper distant extrema, quam vel media inter se, vel medium ab alterutro extremo.[‡]

Brerewood:

Contraria a Dialecticis ita definiri solent: Sunt Opposita quæ sub eodem genere posita maxime a se invicem distant, et eodem subjecto susceptibili vicissim insunt, a quo se mutuo expellunt, nisi alterum insit a natura. . . . Sed quoniam hæc definitio (quamvis sit præcipue in Dialecticorum scholis authoritans) laborat et tædio, et summa difficultate, placet ex Aristotele faciliorem adducere, et breviorem: *Contraria sunt quæ sub eodem genere posita, maxime distant.*[§]

Samuel Smith:

Contraria sunt quæ sub eodem genere posita, maxime a se invicem distant, et eidem susceptibili vicissim insunt, a quo se mutuo expellunt, nisi alterum eorum insit a natura. Ad Contraria igitur tria requiruntur: primo ut sint sub eodem genere, scilicet Qualitatis: nam solarum qualitatum est contrarietas; secundo, ut maxime a se invicem distent in natural positiva, id est, ut ambo extrema sint positiva.[¶]

*[(London: printed McMillan, 1826), Tractatus Primus,] Pars Tertia, Cap. iii, Art. 1 [p. 74].

[†][Robert Sanderson, *Logicæ Artis Compendium*, 2nd ed. (Oxford: Lichfield and Short, 1618), p. 52,] Pars Prima, Cap. xv [§4].

[‡][Richard Crakanthorp,] *Logicæ* [(London: Teage, 1622), Lib. II,] Cap. xx [p. 206].

[§][Edward Brerewood,] *Tractatus Quidam Logici de Prædicabilibus et Prædicamentis*. [Oxford: Turner, 1628.] Tractatus Decimus, "de Post-Prædicamentis," §§8 and 9. [Pp. 404–5. (The concluding sentence, which appears in modified form in all the other Latin texts quoted, is a translation of the passage of Aristotle's *Categories* cited above [VI, 6ª17–18]).]

[¶]*Aditus ad Logicam* [7th ed.] (Oxford [: Hall], 1656), Lib. I, Cap. xiv [p. 56].

Wallis:

Contraria definiri solent, quæ sub eodem genere maxime distant. Ut calidum et frigidum, album et nigrum: quæ contrariæ qualitatis dici solent.*

Even Aldrich, right for once, may be added to the list of Oxford authorities.

Contraria sub eodem genere maxime distant. Non maxime distant *omnium*; magis enim distant quæ nec idem genus summum habent, magis Contradictoria: sed maxime eorum quæ in genere conveniunt.[†]

Keckermann does not employ this, but another definition of Contraries; not, however, Sir W. Hamilton's: and all his examples of Contraries are taken from Extreme Opposites.[‡]

Casparus Bartholinus:

Contraria sunt, quæ sub eodem genere maxime distant, eidemque subjecto susceptibili a quo se mutuo expellunt, vicissim insunt, nisi alterum insit a natura.[§]

Du Hamel:

Oppositio contraria est inter duo extrema positiva, quæ sub eodem genere posita maxime distant, et ab eodem subjecto sese expellunt.[¶]

Grammatica Rationis, sive Institutiones Logicæ:

Contraria adversa sunt accidentia, posita sub eodem genere, quæ maxime distant, et se mutuo pellunt ab eodem subjecto in quo vicissim insunt.[‖]

Familiar as Sir W. Hamilton was with the whole series of writers on Logic, he cannot have overlooked, and can hardly have forgotten, such passages as these. I have not had the fortune to meet with a single passage, from a single Aristotelian writer, [c]which[c] can be cited in his support. I presume, therefore, that he intentionally made (or adopted from Krug) a change in the meaning of a scientific term, the inverse of that which it is the proper office and common tendency of science to make. Instead of giving a

---

*[John Wallis,] *Institutio Logicæ* [3rd ed. (Oxford: West, Crosley, Clements, and Peisley, 1702), p. 63], Lib. I, Cap. xvi.

[†][Henry Aldrich,] *Artis Logicæ Compendium* [Oxford: Sheldonian Theatre, 1704], "Quæstionum Logicarum Determinatio," quæst. 19 [p. 118].

[‡][Bartholomæus Keckermannus,] *Systema Logicæ* [(Geneva: de la Rouière, 1611); see pp. 278ff. (Lib. I, Sectio Posterior, Cap. vi).]

[§]*Enchiridion Logicum* [*ex Aristotele*, 3rd ed.], (Leipzig [: Cober], 1618), Lib. I, Cap. xxiii [p. 186].

[¶][Jean Baptiste Du Hamel,] *Philosophia vetus et nova ad usum scholæ accommodata*, 5th ed. (Amsterdam [: Gallet], 1700), [Vol. I,] pp. 197–8.

[‖][John Fell, *Grammatica Rationis*,] (Oxford [: Sheldonian Theatre], 1673) [p. 111].

[c-c]65[1], 65[2]   who

more determinate signification to a name vaguely used, by binding it down to express a precise specific distinction, he laid hold of a name which already denoted a definite species, and applied it to the entire genus, which stood in no need of a name; leaving the particular species unnamed. But if he knowingly took this very unscientific liberty with a scientific term, diverting it from both its scientific and its popular meaning,—leaving the scientific vocabulary, never too rich, with one expression the fewer, and an important scientific distinction without a name,—he at least should not have done so without informing the reader. He should not have led the unsuspecting learner to believe that this was the received use of the term. Remark, too, that he embezzles not only the English word, but its Greek and Latin equivalents, exactly as if he agreed with the writers of the Greek and Latin treatises, and was only explaining their meaning.

V. One of the charges brought by Sir W. Hamilton against the common mode of stating the doctrine of the Syllogism, is that it does not obviate the objection often made to the syllogism of being a *petitio principii*, grounded on the admitted truth, that it can assert nothing in the conclusion which has not already been asserted in the premises. This objection, our author says, "stands hitherto unrefuted, if not unrefutable."* But he entertains the odd idea, that it can be got rid of by merely writing the propositions in a different order, putting the conclusion first. One might almost imagine that a little irony had been intended here. Putting the conclusion first, certainly makes it impossible any longer to say that the syllogism asserts in the conclusion what has *already* been asserted in the premises; and if any one is of opinion that the logical relation between premises and a conclusion depends on the order in which they are pronounced, such an objector, I must allow, is from this time silenced. But our author can have meditated very little on the meaning of the objection of *petitio principii* against the Syllogism, when he thought that such a device as this would remove it. The difficulty, which that objection expresses, lies in a region far below the depth to which such logic reaches; and he was quite right in regarding the objection as unrefuted. Nor is its refutation, I conceive, possible, on any theory but that which considers the Syllogism not as a process of Inference, but as the mere interpretation of the record of a previous process; the major premise as simply a formula for making particular inferences; and the conclusions of ratiocination as not inferences from the formula, but inferences drawn according to the formula. This theory, and the grounds of it, having been very fully stated in another work, need not be further noticed here.[*]

Lectures, Vol. IV, App. x, p. 401, and Appendix [II(A)] to *Discussions*, p. 652n.

[*See *System of Logic*, Bk. II, Chap. iii, §4, in *Collected Works*, Vol. VII, p. 193.]

CHAPTER XXIV

Of Some Natural Prejudices Countenanced by Sir William Hamilton, and Some Fallacies Which He Considers Insoluble

WE HAVE CONCLUDED our review of Sir W. Hamilton as a teacher of Logic; but there remain to be noticed a few points, not strictly belonging either to Logic or to Psychology, but rather to what is inappropriately termed the Philosophia Prima. It would be more properly called *ultima*, since it consists of the widest generalizations respecting the laws of Existence and Activity; generalizations which by an unfortunate, though at first inevitable mistake, men fancied that they could reach *uno saltu*, and therefore placed them at the beginning of science, though, if they were ever legitimate, they could only be so as its tardy and final result. Every physical science, up to the time of Bacon, consisted mainly of such first principles as these: The ways of Nature are perfect: Nature abhors a vacuum: *Natura non habet saltum*: Nothing can come out of nothing: Like can only be produced by like: Things always move towards their own place: Things can only be moved by something which is itself moving; and so forth. And the Baconian revolution was far indeed from expelling such doctrines from philosophy. On the contrary, the Cartesian movement, which went on for a full century simultaneously with the Baconian, threw up many more of these imaginary axioms concerning things in general, which took a deep root in Continental philosophy, found their way into English, and are by no means, even now, discredited as they deserve to be. Most of these were fully believed by the philosophers who maintained them, to be intuitively evident truths— revelations of Nature in the depths of human consciousness, and recognisable by the light of reason alone: while all the time they were merely bad generalizations of the vulgarest outward experience; rough interpretations of the appearances most familiar to sense, and which therefore had grown into the strongest associations in thought; never tested by the conditions of legitimate induction, not only because those conditions were still unknown, but because these wretched first attempts at generalization were deemed to have a higher than inductive origin, and were erected into general laws from which the order of the universe might be deduced, and to which every scientific theory for the explanation of phenomena must be required to conform. It is a material point in the estimation of a philosopher and of his doctrines, whether he has taken his side for or against this mode of philosophizing; whether he has countenanced any of these spurious axioms by his adhesion. Sir W. Hamilton cannot be acquitted of having done so, in more than one instance.

In treating of the problem of Causality, Sir W. Hamilton had occasion to argue, that we ought not to postulate a special mental law in order to explain the belief that everything must have a cause, since that belief is sufficiently accounted for by the "Law of the Conditioned," which makes it impossible for us to conceive an absolute commencement of anything.[*] I do not mean to return to the discussion of this theory of Causality; but let us ask ourselves why we are interdicted from assuming a special law, in order to account for that which is already sufficiently accounted for by a general one. The real ground of the prohibition is what our author terms the Law of Parcimony; a principle identical with the famous maxim of the Nominalists, known as Occam's Razor—*Entia non sunt multiplicanda præter neces-sitatem*;[†] understanding by Entia, not merely substances but also Powers. Sir W. Hamilton, instead of resting it on this logical injunction, grounds it on an ontological theory. His reason is, "Nature never works by more and more complex instruments than are necessary."* He cites, with approbation, the maxims of Aristotle, "that God and Nature never operate without effect (οὐδὲν μάτην, οὐδὲν ἐλλειπῶς, ποιοῦσι); they never operate super-fluously (μηδὲν περίεργον—περιττῶς—ἀργῶς); but always through one rather than through a plurality of means (καθ' ἕν, μᾶλλον ἢ κατὰ πολλὰ):"† thus borrowing a general theory of the very kind which Bacon exploded, to support a rule which can stand perfectly well without it. Have *we* authority to declare that there is anything which God and Nature never do? Do we know all Nature's combinations? Were we called into counsel in fixing its limits? By what canons of induction has this theory ever been tried? By

[*See *Lectures*, Vol. II, pp. 376ff.]

[†This formulation is mistakenly attributed to William of Ockham; it appears to have originated with John Ponce, in an annotation to Duns Scotus, *Opera omnia*, ed. Luke Wadding, John Ponce, *et al.*, 12 vols. (Lyons: Durand, 1639), Vol. VII, p. 723.]

*Appendix [I(A)] to *Discussions*, p. 622.

†*Ibid.*, p. 629. [For the Greek passages, cf. Aristotle, *On the Heavens* (Greek and English), trans. W. K. C. Guthrie (London: Heinemann; Cambridge, Mass.: Harvard University Press, 1939), p. 30 (I, iv, 271^{a}34–5); *Parts of Animals*, in *Parts of Animals, Movement of Animals, Progression of Animals* (Greek and English), trans. A. L. Peck (London: Heinemann; Cambridge, Mass.: Harvard University Press, 1937), p. 396 (IV, xi, 691^{b}4); *On the Heavens*, pp. 206–8 (II, xii, 292^{a}22–^{b}25).]

what observations has it been verified? We know well that Nature, in many of its operations, works by means which are of a complexity so extreme, as to be an almost insuperable obstacle to our investigations. On what evidence do we presume to say that this complexity was necessary, and that the effect could not have been produced in a simpler manner? If we look into the meaning of words, of what kind is the necessity which is supposed to be binding on God and Nature—the pressure they are unable to escape from? Is there any necessity in Nature which Nature did not make? or if not, what did? What is this power superior to Nature and its author, and to which Nature is compelled to adapt itself?

There is one supposition under which this doctrine has an intelligible meaning—the hypothesis of the Two Principles. If the universe was moulded into its present form by a Being who did not make it wholly, and who was impeded by an obstacle which he could only partially overcome—whether that obstacle was a rival intelligence, or, as Plato thought, an inherent incapacity in Matter;[*] it is on that supposition admissible, that the Demiourgos may have always worked by the simplest possible means; the simplest, namely, which were permitted by the opposition of the conflicting Power, or the intractableness of the material. This is, in fact, the doctrine of Leibnitz's *Théodicée*; his famous theory that a world, made by God, must be the best of all possible worlds, that is, the best world which could be made under the conditions by which, as it would appear, Providence was restricted.[†] This doctrine, commonly called Optimism, is really Manicheism, or, to call it by [a]its[a] more proper name, Sabæism. The word "possible" assumes the existence of hindrances insurmountable by the divine power, and Leibnitz was only wrong in calling a power limited by obstacles by the name Omnipotence: for it is almost too obvious to be worth stating, that real Omnipotence could have effected its ends totally without means, or could have made any means sufficient. This Sabæan theory is the only one by which the assertion, that Nature always works by the simplest means, can be made consistent with known fact. Even so, it remains wholly unproved; and, were it proved, would be but a speculative truth of Theology, incapable of affording any practical guidance. We could never be justified in rejecting an hypothesis for being too complicated; it being beyond our power to set limits to the complication of the means that might possibly be necessary, to evade the obstacles which Ahriman or Matter may have perversely thrown in the Creator's way.

[*See *Timæus*, in *Timæus, Critias, Cleitophon, Menexenus, Epistles* (Greek and English), trans. R. G. Bury (London: Heinemann; New York: Putnam's Sons, 1929), pp. 108ff. (47[c]ff.).]

[†See *Théodicée*, pp. 115ff. (§§8ff.).]

[a]–[a]65[1], 65[2]   a

The "Law of Parcimony" needs no such support; it rests on no assumption respecting the ways or proceedings of Nature. It is a purely logical precept; a case of the broad practical principle, not to believe anything of which there is no evidence. When we have no direct knowledge of the matter of fact, and no reason for believing it except that it would account for another matter of fact, all reason for admitting it is at an end when the fact requiring explanation can be explained from known causes. The assumption of a superfluous cause, is a belief without evidence; as if we were to suppose that a man who was killed by falling over a precipice, must have taken poison as well. The same principle which forbids the assumption of a superfluous fact, forbids that of a superfluous law. When Newton had shown that the same theorem would express the conditions of the planetary motions and the conditions of the fall of bodies to the earth, it would have been illogical to recognise two distinct laws of nature, one for heavenly and the other for earthly attraction; since both these laws, when stripped of the circumstances ascertained to be irrelevant to the effect, would have had to be expressed in the very same words. The reduction of each of the two generalizations to the expression of only those circumstances which influence the result, reduces both of them to the same proposition; and to decline to do so, would be to make an assumption of difference between the cases, for which none of the observations afforded the smallest ground. The rule of Parcimony, therefore, whether applied to facts or to theories, implies no theory concerning the propensities or proceedings of Nature. If Nature's ways and inclinations were the reverse of what they are supposed to be, it would have been as illegitimate as it is now, to assume a fact of Nature without any evidence for it, or to consider the same property as two different properties, because found in two different kinds of objects.

In another place, Sir W. Hamilton says that the Law of Parcimony, which he terms "the most important maxim in regulation of philosophical procedure when it is necessary to resort to an hypothesis," has "never, perhaps, been adequately expressed;" and he proposes the following expression for it: "Neither *more* nor *more onerous* causes are to be assumed, than are necessary to account for the phænomena."* This conception of some causes as "more onerous" to the general scheme of things than others, is a distinction greatly requiring what our author says it has never yet had—to be "articulately expressed." He does not, however, articulate it in general terms, but only in its application to the particular question of Causality. From this we may collect,—1st. That a "positive power" is a more onerous hypothesis than a "negative impotence." 2nd. That a special hypothesis, which serves to explain only one phænomenon, is more oner-

*Appendix [I(A)] to *Discussions*, p. 628n.

ous than a general one which will explain many. 3rd. That the explanation of an effect by a cause of which the very existence is hypothetical, is more onerous than its hypothetical explanation by a cause otherwise known to exist. The last two of these three canons are but particular cases of the general rule, that we should not assume an hypothetical cause of a phænomenon which admits of being accounted for by a cause of which there is other evidence.* The remaining canon, that we should prefer the hypothesis of an incapacity to that of a power, is, I apprehend, only valid when its infringement would be a violation of one of the other two rules.

The time-honoured, but gratuitous, assumption, respecting Nature, on which I have now commented, is not the only generality of the pre-Baconian type which Sir W. Hamilton has countenanced. He gives his sanction to the old doctrine that "a thing can act only where it is." The dictum appears in this direct form in one of the very latest of his writings, the notes for an intended memoir of Professor Dugald Stewart.[†] He has so much faith in it as to make it the foundation of two of his favourite theories. One is, that

the thing perceived, and the percipient organ, must meet in place, must be contiguous. The consequence of this doctrine is a complete simplification of the theory of perception, and a return to the most ancient speculation on the point. All sensible cognition is, in a certain acceptation, reduced to Touch, and this is the very conclusion maintained by the venerable authority of Democritus. According to this doctrine, it is erroneous to affirm that we are percipient of distant objects.[‡]

Conformably to this, we have seen him not only maintaining, in opposition to Reid,[[*]] that we do not see the sun—that we see only an image of it in our eye—but also, that we directly perceive Extension, whether by sight or touch, only in our own bodily organs: thus preferring the à priori axiom, that a thing can only act where it is, to the authority of those "natural beliefs" which he, in other cases, so strenuously asserts against impugners,

---

*This is what Newton meant by a *vera causa*, in his celebrated maxim, "Causas rerum naturalium non plures admitti debere quam quæ *et veræ sint*, et earum phænomenis explicandis sufficiant." [Isaac Newton, *Philosophiæ Naturalis Principia Mathematica*, in *Opera*, ed. Samuel Horsley, 5 vols. (London: Nichols, 1779–85), Vol. III, p. 2.] It is singular that Sir W. Hamilton does not seem to have understood, that by *veræ causæ* Newton meant agencies the existence of which was otherwise authenticated: for he says, "In their plain meaning, the words et *veræ sint* are redundant; or what follows is redundant, and the whole rule a barren truism." (Foot-note to Reid, p. 236n.)[b]But in the Appendix [I(A)] to the *Discussions* (p. 631) Sir W. Hamilton puts the right interpretation on Newton's maxim.[b]

[†]*Lectures*, Vol. II, App. i, p. 522.

[‡]*Ibid.*

[*See Reid, *Inquiry*, pp. 182–6.]

[b-b]+72

and so often affirms that we ought either to accept as a whole, or never appeal to at all.

The other theory which our author maintains on the authority of the same dictum, is that the mind acts directly throughout the whole body, and not through the brain only.

There is no good ground to suppose that the mind is situate solely in the brain, or exclusively in any part of the body. On the contrary, the supposition that it is really present wherever we are conscious that it acts,—in a word, the Peripatetic aphorism, The soul is all in the whole, and all in every part,—is more philosophical, and consequently, more probable than any other opinion. . . . Even if we admit that the nervous system is the part to which it is proximately united, still the nervous system is itself universally ramified throughout the body; and we have no more right to deny that the mind feels at the finger-points, as consciousness assures us, than to assert that it thinks exclusively in the brain.*

Sir W. Hamilton should at least have shown how this hypothesis can be reconciled with the fact, that a slight pressure on the nerve at a place intermediate between the finger and the brain, takes away the mind's power of feeling in the finger, while at any point above the ligature the feeling is the same as before. *cIf he object that the mode in which the pressure impedes sensation need not be by interrupting the communication between the finger and the brain, but may be by disturbing the functions of the nerve itself, we may ask, why is this disturbance confined to the part of the nerve which is below the point of pressure, while above that point the functions remain unimpaired? Many other objections might be brought against Sir W. Hamilton's theory, if my object were to discuss the physiological question; but my object is only*c* to show the amount of evidence which Sir W. Hamilton will disregard, rather than admit that one thing can act directly upon another without immediate contact.† What he would have thought of the application of his doctrine to the solar system, he has not told us *d*(the recent developments of the doctrine of the Unity of Force being posterior to his time)*d*: but it commits him to the opinion, that gravitation acts through an intervening medium, which he must postulate, first as existing, and secondly, as possessed of inscrutable properties; in palpable repugnance to his own Law of Parcimony, and to all the canons grounded thereon. Descartes postulated his vortices in obedience to the same axiom.[*]

*Lectures, Vol. II, pp. 127–8.
†In the Lectures, I mean: for, in the "Dissertations on Reid" the doctrine, that we feel in the toe, and not in a sensorium commune, is at least so far retracted, that the possibility of the opposite theory is explicitly acknowledged. ([Note D,] p. 861n.)
[*See pp. 198, 375 above.]

c–c65¹, 65²   I shall not here enquire how much is positively proved by this experiment, or with what hypotheses it is inconsistent: my object is
d–d+67, 72

What, however, is the worth of this doctrine, that things can only act upon one another by direct contact? Mr. Carlyle says, "a thing can only act where it is; with all my heart; only where is it?"[*] In one sense of the word, a thing *is* wherever its action is: its power is there, though not its corporeal presence. But to say that a thing can only act where its power is, would be the idlest of mere identical propositions. And where is the warrant for asserting that a thing cannot act when it is not locally contiguous to the thing it acts upon? Shall we be told that such action is inconceivable? Even if it was, this, according to Sir W. Hamilton's philosophy, is no evidence of impossibility. But that it is conceivable, is shown by every fairy tale, as well as by every religion. Then, again, what is the meaning of contiguity? According to the best physical knowledge we possess, things are never actually contiguous: what we term contact between particles, only means that they are in the degree of proximity at which their mutual repulsions are in equilibrium with their attractions. If so, instead of never, things always act on one another at some, though it may be a very small distance. The belief that a thing can only act where it is, is a common case of inseparable, though not ultimately indissoluble, association. It is an unconscious generalization, of the roughest possible description, from the most familiar cases of the mutual action of bodies, superficially considered. The temporary difficulty found in apprehending any action of body upon body unlike what people were accustomed to, created a Natural Prejudice, which was long a serious impediment to the reception of the Newtonian theory: but it was hoped that the final triumph of that theory had extinguished it; that all educated persons were now aware that action at a distance is intrinsically quite as credible as action in contact, and that there is no reason, apart from specific experience, to regard the one as in any respect less probable than the other. That Sir W. Hamilton should be an instance to the contrary, is an example of the obstinate vitality of these *idola tribûs*,[†] and shows that we are never safe against the rejuvenescence of the most superannuated error, if in throwing it off we have not reformed the bad habit of thought, the wrong and unscientific tendency of the intellect, from which the error took its rise.*

[*Thomas Carlyle, *Sartor Resartus*, 2nd ed. (Boston: Munroe, 1837), p. 59 (I, viii).]

[†See Bacon, *Novum Organum*, in *Works*, Vol. I, pp. 163 and 169 (Bk. I, Aphs. 41 and 52).]

*In the course of his speculations our author comes across a fact which is positively irreconcileable with his axiom; the fact of repulsion. This brings him to a dead stand. He knows not whether to advance or recede. Repulsion, he says, "remains, as apparently an *actio in distans*, even when forced upon us as a fact, still inconceivable as a possibility." He is soon afterwards obliged to confess that the same is true of attraction: "As attraction and repulsion seem equally *actiones in distans*, it is not more difficult to realize to ourselves the action of the one, than the

Though but remotely connected with the preceding considerations, yet as belonging in common with them to the subject of Fallacies, I will notice in this place the curious partiality which our author shows to a particular group of sophisms, the Eleatic arguments for the impossibility of motion. He *deemed* these arguments, though leading to a false conclusion, to be irrefutable; as Brown thought concerning Berkeley's argument against the existence of matter—that as a mere play of reasoning it was unanswerable, while it was impossible for the human mind to admit the conclusion;[*] forgetting that if this were so it would be a *reductio ad absurdum* of the reasoning faculty. There is no philosopher to whom, I imagine, Sir W. Hamilton would have less liked to be assimilated, than Brown; and he would probably have defended himself against the imputation, by saying that the Eleatic arguments do not prove motion to be impossible, but only to be inconceivable by us. Yet if a fact which we see and feel every minute of our lives, is not conceivable by us, what is? Our author does not enter at any length into the question, but expresses his opinion on several occasions incidentally. "It is," he says, "on the inability of the mind to conceive either the ultimate indivisibility, or the endless divisibility of space and time, that the arguments of the Eleatic Zeno against the possibility of motion are founded; arguments which at least show, that motion, however certain as a fact, cannot be conceived possible, as it involves a contradiction."* We have been told in very emphatic terms by Sir W. Hamilton, that the Law of Contradiction is binding not on our conceptions merely, but on Things.[†] If, then, motion involves a contradiction, how is it possible? and if it is possible, and a fact, as we know it to be, how can it involve a contradiction? The appearance of contradiction must necessarily be fallacious, even were we unable to point out the fallacy. Our author, apparently, has attempted to resolve it, and failed. He calls the argument "an exposition of the contradictions involved in our notion of motion," and says that its "fallacy has not yet been detected."† And, again, "The Eleatic Zeno's demonstration of the

---

action of the other." ("Dissertations on Reid," [Note D,] p. 852.) Action from *a* distance being "a fact," though inconceivable, this fact would seem to require of him the retractation of his axiom: yet he does not retract it. I need hardly remark that attraction and repulsion are not inconceivable; except indeed in another of the numerous senses of that equivocal word; that in which it is used when our author tells us that all ultimate facts are inconceivable, meaning only that they are inexplicable.

[*See Brown, *Lectures*, Vol. II, p. 19.]
Lectures, Vol. II, p. 373. To the same effect, Vol. IV, p. 71.
[†See *ibid.*, Vol. III, p. 81.]
†Foot-note to Reid, p. 102n.

e–e+67, 72
*f–f*65[1], 65[2]   believed

impossibility of motion is not more insoluble than could be framed a proof that the Present has no reality: for however certain we may be of both, we can positively think neither."* It must, one would suppose, be a great difficulty, which could appear insoluble to Sir W. Hamilton. The "demonstration," at all events, cannot yet have been refuted, and superhuman ingenuity must be needed to refute it. Yet the fallacy in it has been pointed out again and again; and the contradictions which Sir W. Hamilton regards it as an exposure of, do not exist.

Zeno's reasonings against motion, as handed down by Aristotle,[*] consist of four arguments, which are stated and criticised with considerable prolixity by Bayle.[†] Several of these are substantially the same argument in different forms, and if we examine the two most plausible of them it will suffice. The first is the ingenious fallacy of Achilles and the Tortoise. If Achilles starts a thousand yards behind the tortoise, and runs a hundred times as fast; still, while Achilles runs those thousand yards, the tortoise will have got on ten; while Achilles runs those ten, the tortoise will have run a tenth of a yard; and as this process may be continued to infinity, Achilles will never overtake the tortoise. In our author's opinion, this argument is logically correct, and evolves a contradiction in our idea of motion. But it is neither logically correct, nor evolves a contradiction in anything. It assumes, of course, the infinite divisibility of space. But we have no need to entangle ourselves in the metaphysical discussion whether this assumption is warrantable. Let it be granted or not, the argument always remains *fallacious. The fallacy lies in the assertion that "this process may be continued to infinity." Infinity is here ambiguous. The conclusion drawn is that the process may be continued for an *infinite duration* of time. But the premise is only true in the sense, that it may be continued for an *infinite number of divisions* of time. The argument confounds infinity and infinite divisibility. It* assumes that to pass through an infinitely divisible space, requires an infinite time. But the infinite divisibility of space means the infinite divisibility of *finite* space: and it is only infinite space which cannot be passed over in less than infinite time. What the argument proves is, that to pass over the infinitely divisible space, requires an infinitely divisible time: but an infinitely divisible time may itself be finite; the smallest finite time is infinitely divisible; the argument, therefore, is consistent with the

*Appendix [I(A)] to *Discussions*, p. 606.

[*See Aristotle, *The Physics* (Greek and English), trans. Philip H. Wickstead and Francis M. Cornford, 2 vols. (London: Heinemann; Cambridge, Mass.: Harvard University Press, 1963), Vol. II, pp. 176–90 (VI, Chap. ix, 239^b–240^b).]

[†See Pierre Bayle, *Dictionnaire historique et critique*, 2 vols. (Rotterdam: Reinier Leers, 1697), *s.v.* Zenon d'Elée, Vol. II, pp. 1267–9.]

*–*65^1, 65^2 a fallacy. For it

tortoise's being overtaken in the smallest finite time. It is a sophism of the type Ignoratio Elenchi, or, as Archbishop Whately terms it, Irrelevant Conclusion;[*] an argument which proves a different proposition from that which it pretends to prove, the difference of meaning being disguised by *h*an ambiguity*h* of language.

The other plausible form of Zeno's argument is at first sight more favourable to Sir W. Hamilton's theory, being a real attempt to prove that the fact of motion involves impossible conditions. The usual mode of stating it is this. If a body moves, it must move either in the place where it is, or in the place where it is not: but either of these is impossible: therefore it cannot move. First of all, this argument, even if we were unable to refute it, does not exhibit any contradiction in our "notion" of motion. We do not conceive a body as moving either in the place where it is, or in the place where it is not, but from the former to the latter: in other words, we conceive the body as in the one place and in the other at successive instants. Where is the "contradiction" between being in one place at this moment, and in another at the next? As for the fallacy itself, it is strange that when everybody sees the answer to it, a practised logician should have any difficulty in putting that answer into logical forms. It is not necessary that motion should be *in* a place. *i*A body*i* must be in a place; but motion is not*j*a body*j*—it is a change: and that a change of place should be either in the old place or in the new, is a real contradiction in terms. To put the thing in another way; Place may be understood in two senses: it may either be a divisible, or an indivisible part of space. If it be a divisible part, as a room, or a street, it is true that in that sense, every motion is in a place, that is, within a limited portion of space: but in this meaning of the term the dilemma breaks down, for the body really moves in the place where it is; the room, the field, or the house. If, on the contrary, we are to understand by Place an indivisible minimum of space, the proposition that motion must be in a place is evidently false; for motion cannot be *in* that which has no parts; it can only be *to* or *from* it.

A parallel sophism might easily be invented, turning upon Time instead of Space. It might be said that sunset is impossible, since if it be possible, it must take place either while the sun is still up, or after it is down. The answer is obvious: it is just the change from one to the other which is sunset. And so it is the change from one position in space to another which is motion. The parallelism between the two cases was evidently seen by Sir W. Hamilton, and the sophism was too hard for him in both: and this is what he must have meant by saying that we cannot "positively think" the

[*See *Elements of Logic*, p. 187.]

*h–h*65[1], 65[2]   similarity
*i–i*65[1], 65[2]   An object
*j–j*65[1], 65[2]   an object

Present. That he should have missed the solution of the fallacy is strange enough: but, as a matter of fact, the assertion that we have no positive perception, on the one hand of Motion, on the other, of present time, deserves notice as one of the most curious deliverances of so earnest an asserter of "our natural beliefs."

These paralogisms are only part of a long list of puzzles concerning infinity, which, though by no means hard to clear up, appear to our author insoluble. I append in a note the entire list.* Many of them are resolved by

*"Contradictions proving the Psychological Theory of the Conditioned.

1. Finite cannot comprehend, contain, the Infinite.—Yet an inch or minute, say, are finites, and are divisible *ad infinitum*, that is, their terminated division incogitable.

2. Infinite cannot be terminated or begun.—Yet eternity *ab ante* ends *now*; and eternity *a post* begins *now*. So apply to Space.

3. There cannot be two infinite maxima.—Yet eternity *ab ante* and *a post* are two infinite maxima of time.

4. Infinite maximum if cut in two, the halves cannot be each infinite, for nothing can be greater than infinite, and thus they could not be parts; nor finite, for thus two finite halves would make an infinite whole.

5. What contains infinite quantities (extensions, protensions, intensions) cannot be passed through,—come to an end. An inch, a minute, a degree contains these; *ergo*, &c. Take a minute. This contains an infinitude of protended quantities, which must follow one after another; but an infinite series of successive protensions can, *ex termino*, never be ended; *ergo*, &c.

6. An infinite maximum cannot but be all-inclusive. Time *ab ante* and *a post* infinite and exclusive of each other; *ergo*, &c.

7. An infinite number of quantities must make up either an infinite or a finite whole. I. The former.—But an inch, a minute, a degree, contain each an infinite number of quantities; therefore an inch, a minute, a degree, are each infinite wholes; which is absurd. II. The latter.—An infinite number of quantities would thus make up a finite quantity, which is equally absurd.

8. If we take a finite quantity (as an inch, a minute, a degree), it would appear equally that there are, and that there are not, an equal number of quantities between these and a greatest, and between these and a least.

9. An absolutely quickest motion is that which passes from one point to another in space in a minimum of time. But a quickest motion from one point to another, say a mile distance, and from one to another, say a million million of miles, is thought the same; which is absurd.

10. A wheel turned with quickest motion; if a spoke be prolonged, it will, therefore, be moved by a motion quicker than the quickest. The same may be shown using the rim and the nave.

11. Contradictory are Boscovich Points, which occupy space, and are unextended. Dynamism, therefore, inconceivable. *E contra*,

12. Atomism also inconceivable; for this supposes atoms,—minima extended but indivisible.

13. A quantity, say a foot, has an infinity of parts. Any part of this quantity, say an inch, has also an infinity. But one infinity is not larger than another. Therefore an inch is equal to a foot.

the observations already made, their difficulty being merely that of separating the two ideas of Infinite and Infinitely Divisible. To our author's thinking, infinite divisibility and the Finite contradict one another. But even allowing (which, as was seen in a former chapter, I do not) that infinite divisibility is inconceivable, it does not therefore involve a contradiction. The remaining puzzles mostly result from inability to conceive that one infinity can be greater or less than another: a conception familiar to all mathematicians. Our author refuses to consider that a space or a time which is infinite in one direction and bounded in another, is necessarily less than a space or a time which is infinite in every direction. The space between two parallels, or between two diverging lines or surfaces, extends to infinity, but it is necessarily less than entire space, being a part of it. Not only is one infinity greater than another, but one infinity may be infinitely greater than another. Mathematicians habitually assume this, and reason from it; and the ^{k}result^k always coming out true, the assumption is justified. But mathematicians, I must admit, seldom know exactly what they are about when they do this. As the results always prove right, they know empirically that the process cannot be wrong—that the premises must be true in a sense; but in what sense, it is beyond the ingenuity of most of them to understand. The doctrine long remained a part of that mathematical mysticism, so mercilessly shown up by Berkeley in his *Analyst*, and *Defence of Freethinking in Mathematics*.[*] To clear it up required a philosophical mathematician—one who should be both a mathematician and a metaphysician: and it found one. To complete Sir W. Hamilton's discomfiture, this philosophic mathematician is his old antagonist Mr. De Morgan, whom he described as too much of a mathematician to be anything of a philosopher.* Mr. De Morgan, however, has proved himself, as far as this subject is concerned, a far better metaphysician than Sir W. Hamilton. He has let the light of reason into all the logical obscurities and paradoxes of the infinitesimal calculus. By merely following out, more thoroughly than had been done before, the rational conception of infinitesimal division, as

---

14. If two divaricating lines are produced *ad infinitum* from a point where they form an acute angle, like a pyramid, the base will be infinite, and, at the same time, not infinite; 1°. Because terminated by two points; and, 2°. Because shorter than the sides; 3°. Base could not be drawn, because sides infinitely long.

15. An atom, as existent, must be able to be turned round. But if turned round, it must have a right and left hand, &c., and these its signs [sides?] must change their place: therefore, be extended." (*Lectures*, Vol. II, App. iii, pp. 527–9.) [Mill's square brackets.]

[*In *Works*, Vol. II, pp. 401–5, and Vol. III, pp. 1–62, respectively.]

*Appendix [II(B)] to *Discussions*, p. 707.

$^{k-k}$65^1, 65^2, 67   results

synonymous with division into as many and as small parts as we choose, *without any limit,* Mr. De Morgan, in his *Algebra*,[*] has fully explained and justified the conception of successive orders of differentials, each of them infinitely less than the differential of the preceding, and infinitely greater than that of the succeeding order. Whoever is acquainted with this masterly specimen of analysis, will find his way through Sir W. Hamilton's series of riddles respecting Infinity, without ever being at a loss for their solution. I shall therefore trouble the reader no further with them in this place.

[*Augustus De Morgan, *The Elements of Algebra* (London: Taylor, 1835).]

-+67, 72

CHAPTER XXV

Sir William Hamilton's Theory of Pleasure and Pain

I HAVE NOW CONCLUDED my remarks on the principal department of Sir W. Hamilton's psychology, that which relates to the Cognitive Faculties. The remaining two of the three portions into which he divides the subject, are the Feelings, and what he terms the Conative Faculties, meaning those which tend to Action. On the Conative Faculties, however, he barely touches, in the concluding part of his last lecture; and of the Feelings he does not treat at any length. What he propounds on the subject, chiefly consists of a general theory of Pleasure and Pain. Not a theory of what they are in themselves, for he is not so much the dupe of words as to suppose that they are anything but what we feel them to be. The speculation with which he has presented us, does not relate to their essence, but to the causes they depend on; "the general conditions which determine the existence of Pleasure and Pain . . . the fundamental law by which these phænomena are governed in all their manifestations."*

The inquiry is scientifically legitimate, and of great interest; but we must not be very confident that it is a practicable one, or can lead to any positive result. It is quite possible that in seeking for the law of pleasure and pain, like Bacon in seeking for the laws of the sensible properties of bodies, we may be looking for unity of cause, where there is a plurality, perhaps a multitude, of different causes. Such attempts, however, even if unsuccessful, are far from being entirely useless. They often lead to a more careful study of the phænomenon in some of its aspects, and to the discovery of relations between them, not previously understood, which though not adequate to the formation of an universal theory of the phænomenon, afford a clearer insight into some of its forms and varieties. This merit must be allowed to Sir W. Hamilton's theory, in common with several others which preceded it on the same subject. But, regarded as a theorem of the universal conditions which are present whenever pleasure (or pain) is present, and absent whenever it is absent, the doctrine will hardly bear

*Lectures, Vol. II, p. 434.

investigation. The simplest and most familiar cases are exactly those which obstinately refuse to be reduced within it.

I shall, as usual, state Sir W. Hamilton's theory in his own words, though in the present case it is a questionable advantage, the terms being so general and abstract that they are scarcely capable of being understood, apart from the illustrations. "Pleasure," he says, "is a reflex of the spontaneous and unimpeded exertion of a power, of whose energy we are conscious. Pain, a reflex of the overstrained or repressed exertion of such a power."* By a "reflex" he has shortly before said that he means merely a "concomitant;"† but I think it will appear that he means at least an effect. At all events, these are what he regards as the ultimate conditions of pleasure and pain; the most general expression of the circumstances in which they occur.

This theory was of course suggested by the pleasures and pains of intellectual or physical exertion, or, as it is otherwise termed, exercise. These are the phænomena which principally afford to it such foundation of fact, and such plausibility in speculation, as it possesses. As we all know, moderate exertion, either of body or mind, is pleasurable; a greater amount is painful, except when set in motion by an impulse which renders it, in our author's meaning of the word, "spontaneous:" and a felt impediment to any kind of active exertion, when there is an impulse towards it, is painful. It at first appears as if Sir W. Hamilton had overlooked the pains and pleasures in which the mind and body are passive, as in most of the organic, and a large proportion of the emotional pleasures and pains. He claims, however, to include all these in his formula. The "powers" and "energies" whose free action he holds to be the condition of pleasure, and their impeded or overstrained action, of pain, include our passive susceptibilities as well as our active energies. Accordingly he suggests a correction of his own language, saying that "occupation" or "exercise" would perhaps be fitter expressions than "energy."‡

The term *energy*, which is equivalent to *act*, *activity*, or *operation*, is here used to comprehend also all the mixed states of action and passion of which we are conscious; for, inasmuch as we are conscious of any modification of mind, there is necessarily more than a mere passivity of the subject; consciousness itself implying at least a reaction. [What has become of his doctrine that to be conscious of a feeling is only another phrase for having the feeling?] Be this, however, as it may, the nouns *energy*, *act*, *activity*, *operation*, with the correspondent verbs, are to be understood to denote, indifferently and in general, all the processes of our higher and our lower life of which we are conscious.§

Understanding the theory in this enlarged sense, let us test it by applica-

*Ibid., p. 440.
†Ibid., p. 436.
‡Ibid., pp. 435n, and 466.
§Ibid., p. 435. [The words in square brackets are Mill's.]

tion to one of the simplest of our organic feelings, the pleasure of a sweet taste. This pleasure, according to the theory, arises from the free exercise, without either restraint or excess, of one of our powers or capacities: what capacity shall we call it? That of tasting sweetness? This will not do; for if the capacity of having the sensation of sweet is called into play in any degree, great or small, the effect is a sweet taste, which is a pleasure. Besides, instead of a sweet taste, let us suppose an acrid taste. In this taste the capacity exercised is that of tasting acridity. But the result of the exercise of this capacity, neither repressed nor overstrained, which therefore, according to the theory, should be a pleasure, is an acrid taste, which is a pain. It must, therefore, be meant that the capacity which when freely exercised causes pleasure, and when repressed or overstrained, pain, is some more general capacity than that of sweet or acrid taste—say the power of taste in the abstract: that the power of taste, the organic action of the gustatory nerves, by its spontaneous exercise, yields pleasure, and by its repression, or its strained exercise, produces pain. The theory thus entirely turns upon what is meant by spontaneous; as is shown still more clearly by our author's comments. "It has been stated," he observes in a recapitulation of his doctrine,

that a feeling of pleasure is experienced, when any power is consciously exercised in a suitable manner; that is, when we are neither, on the one hand, conscious of any restraint upon the energy which it is disposed spontaneously to put forth, nor, on the other, conscious of any effort in it to put forth an amount of energy greater either in degree or in continuance, than what it is disposed freely to exert. In other words, we feel positive pleasure, in proportion as our powers are exercised, but not over-exercised; we feel positive pain, in proportion as they are compelled either not to operate, or to operate too much. All pleasure, thus, arises from the free play of our faculties and capacities; all pain from their compulsory repression or compulsory activity.*

All, therefore, depends upon what is meant by "free" or "spontaneous," and what by "compulsory," activity. The difference cannot be that which the words suggest, the presence or absence of will. It cannot be meant, that pleasure accompanies the process when wholly involuntary, and that pain begins when a voluntary element enters into the exercise of the sensitive faculty. There is nothing voluntary in the agonies of the rack, or of an excruciating bodily disease: while, in the case of a pleasure, the exercise of will, in the only mode in which it can be exercised on a feeling, namely, by voluntarily attending to it, instead of converting it from a pleasure into a pain, often greatly heightens the pleasure. This doctrine, therefore, would be absurd, nor is Sir W. Hamilton chargeable with it. What he means by

Ibid., p. 477.

"spontaneous" as applied to the exercise of our capacities of feeling, we gather from the following passage, and others similar to it.

Every power, all conditions being supplied, and all impediments being removed, tends, of its proper nature and without effort, to put forth a certain determinate maximum, intensive and protensive, of free energy. This determinate maximum of free energy, it, therefore, exerts spontaneously: if a less amount than this be actually put forth, a certain quantity of tendency has been forcibly repressed: whereas, if a greater than this has been actually exerted, a certain amount of nisus has been forcibly stimulated in the power. The term *spontaneously*, therefore, provides that the exertion of the power has not been constrained beyond the proper limit,—the natural maximum, to which, if left to itself, it freely springs.—Again, in regard to the term *unimpeded*,—this stipulates that the conditions requisite to allow this spring have been supplied, and that all impediments to it have been removed. This postulates, of course, the presence of an object.*

The spontaneous and unimpeded exercise of a capacity means, therefore, it would appear, the exercise which takes place when "all conditions" are "supplied," and "all impediments removed." Let us apply this to a particular case. I taste, at different instants, two different objects; an orange, and rhubarb. In both cases, all conditions are supplied; the object is present and in contact with my organs; and in both cases, all impediments are removed to the unstrained and natural action of the object upon my gustatory organs. Yet the result is in one case a pleasure, in the other a sensation of nauseousness. On Sir W. Hamilton's theory, it ought, in both cases, to have been pleasure: for in neither does anything interfere with the free action of my sense of taste.

Sir W. Hamilton can scarcely have overlooked this objection, and the answer which he may be supposed to make, is that in the case of the rhubarb, the object itself was of a nature to disturb the gustative faculty, and exact from it a greater degree of action (or less, for I would not undertake to say which) than is exacted by the orange. But where is the proof of this? and what, even, does the assertion mean? A greater degree of what action? Of the action of tasting? If so, a pain should differ from a pleasure only by being more (or perhaps less) intense. Is the action that is meant, some occult process in the organ? But what ground is there for affirming that there is more action of any kind, on the part of the organ or the sense of taste, in a disagreeable savour than in an agreeable one? It is perhaps true that more than a certain quantity of action is always painful: every sensation intensified beyond a certain degree may become a pain. But the converse proposition, that wherever there is a pain there is an excess of action (or a deficiency, for we are offered that alternative), I know of no reason for believing. Moreover, if admitted, it would seem to involve

Ibid., p. 441.

the consequence, that in every case of pain, a less or a greater degree of the cause which produces it is pleasurable [a], which is certainly not true, however true it may be that in many cases of organic pleasure (especially tastes and smells) a less or a greater quantity of the substance which produces the pleasure is either insipid or positively disagreeable[a].

Our author is more than half aware that his theory [b]breaks down when applied to pleasures or pains that are heterogeneous to one another[b]; for he says, "When it is required of us to explain particularly and in detail, why the rose, for example, produces this sensation of smell, assafœtida that other, and so forth, and to say in what peculiar action does the perfect or pleasurable, and the imperfect or painful, activity of an organ consist, we must at once profess our ignorance." He lays the responsibility of the failure, not upon his theory, but upon the general inexplicability of ultimate facts. "But it is the same with all our attempts at explaining any of the ultimate phænomena of creation. In general, we may account for much; in detail, we can rarely account for anything: for we soon remount to facts which lie beyond our powers of analysis and observation."*

This appears to me a great misconception, on our author's part, of what may rightfully be demanded from a theorist. He is not entitled to frame a theory from one class of phænomena, extend it to another class which it does not fit, and excuse himself by saying that if we cannot make it fit, it is because ultimate facts are inexplicable. Newton did not proceed in this manner with the theory of gravitation. He made it an absolute condition of adopting the theory, that it should fit; and when, owing to incorrect data, he could not make it fit perfectly, he abandoned the speculation for many years. If the smell of a rose and the smell of assafœtida are ultimate facts, be it so: but in that case, it is useless setting up a theory to explain them. If we do propound a theory, we are bound to prove all it asserts: and this, in the present case, is, that in smelling a rose the organ is in "perfect" activity, but when smelling assafœtida, in "imperfect," which is either greater or less than perfect. It is not philosophical to assert this, and fall back upon the incomprehensibility of the subject as a dispensation from proving it. What is a hindrance to proving a theory, ought to be a hindrance to affirming it.

What meaning, in fact, can be attached to perfect and imperfect activity, as the phrases are here used? Perfection or imperfection is treated as a question of quantity; activity is called perfect when there is exactly the right quantity, imperfect when there is either more or less. But what is the test of right or wrong quantity, except the pleasure or pain attending it? The

*Ibid., pp. 494–5.

[a-a]+72
[b-b]65[1], 65[2], 67   does not fit the passive organic feelings

theory amounts to this, that pleasure or pain is felt, according as the activity is of the amount fitted to produce the one or the other. In this futile mode of explaining the phænomena our author had been preceded by Aristotle, one of the greatest of recorded thinkers, but who must have been more than human if, in the state of knowledge and scientific cultivation in his time, he had avoided slips which hardly any one, even now, is able completely to guard against. Aristotle's theory, which, as understood by our author, differs little from his own, is presented by Sir W. Hamilton in the following words:

When a sense, for example, is in perfect health, and it is presented with a suitable object of the most perfect kind, there is elicited the most perfect energy, which, at every instant of its continuance, is accompanied with pleasure. The same holds good with the function of Imagination, Thought, &c. Pleasure is the concomitant in every case where powers and objects are in themselves perfect, and between which there subsists a suitable relation.*

The conditions whereon, upon this showing, pleasure depends, are the healthiness of the sense, and the perfection of the object presented to it. This is simply making the fact its own theory. When is a sense in perfect health, and its object perfect? The function of a sense is twofold; as a source of cognition, and of feeling. If the perfection meant be in the function of cognition, the doctrine that pleasure depends on this is manifestly erroneous: according to Sir W. Hamilton, it is even the reverse of the truth, for he holds that the knowledge given by an act of sense, and the feeling accompanying it, are in an inverse proportion to one another. *There remains* the supposition that the perfection, of which Aristotle spoke, was perfection not in respect of cognition but of feeling. It cannot, however, consist in acuteness of feeling, for our acutest feelings are pains. What then constitutes it? Pleasurableness of feeling: and the theory only tells us, that pleasure is the result of a pleasurable state of the sense, and a pleasure-giving quality in the object presented to it. Aristotle and Sir W. Hamilton did not, certainly, state the doctrine to themselves in this manner; but they reduced it to this, by affirming pleasure or pain to depend on the perfect or imperfect action of the sense, when there was no criterion of imperfect or perfect action except that it produced pain or pleasure.

The theory of our author, considered as a *résumé* of the universal conditions of pleasure and pain, being so manifestly inadequate, this is not the place for sifting out the detached fragments of valuable thought which are disseminated through it. Such stray truths may be gleaned from every excursion through the phænomena of human nature by a person of ability.

*Ibid., p. 452. [See Aristotle, *Nichomachean Ethics*, p. 594 (X, iv, 1174ᵇ 27–33).]

ᶜ⁻ᶜ65¹, 65² Remains

What Sir W. Hamilton says of the different classes of mental pleasures and pains, though brief, is very suggestive of thought. To make a proper use of the hints he throws out towards an explanation of the pleasures derived from sublimity and beauty, would require much study, and a wide survey of the subject, as well as of the speculations of other thinkers regarding it. The question has no direct connexion with any other of those discussed in the present volume, and but a slight one with Sir W. Hamilton's merits as a philosopher; since the brevity with which he treats it, gives ground for believing that he had not bestowed on it the amount of thought which would enable his opinion to claim the rank of a philosophic theory.

CHAPTER XXVI

On the Freedom of the Will

THE LAST OF THE THREE CLASSES of mental phænomena, that of Conation, in other words, of Desire and Will, is barely commenced upon in the last pages of Sir W. Hamilton's last lecture:[*] whether it be that in the many years during which he taught the class, he never got beyond this point, or that his teaching in the concluding part of the course was purely oral, and has not been preserved. Nor has he, in any of his writings, treated *ex professo* of this subject; though doubtless he would have done so, had his health permitted him to complete the "Dissertations on Reid." We consequently know little of what his sentiments were on any of the topics comprised in this branch of Psychology, except the *vexata quæstio* of the Freedom of the Will; on which he could not help giving indications, in various parts of his works, both of his opinion and of the reasons on which he grounded it. The doctrine of Free-will was indeed so fundamental with him, that it may be regarded as the central idea of his system—the determining cause of most of his philosophical opinions; and, in a peculiar manner, of the two which are most completely emanations from his own mind, the Law of the Conditioned, and his singular theory of Causation. He breaks ground on the subject at the very opening of his *Lectures*, in his introductory remarks on the utility of the study of Metaphysics. He puts in a claim for metaphysics, grounded on the free-will doctrine, of being the only medium "through which our unassisted reason can ascend to the knowledge of a God." He supports this position by a line of argument which, I think, must be startling to the majority of believers.

"The Deity," he says,

is not an object of immediate contemplation; as existing and in himself, he is beyond our reach; we can know him only mediately through his works, and are only warranted in assuming his existence as a certain kind of cause necessary to account for a certain state of things, of whose reality our faculties are supposed to inform us. The affirmation of a God being thus a regressive inference, from the existence of a special class of effects to the existence of a special character of cause, it is evident, that the whole argument hinges on the fact,—Does a state of things really exist, such as is only possible through the agency of a Divine Cause? For if it can be shown

[*I.e., the last lecture on Metaphysics; see *Lectures*, Vol. II, pp. 517–20.]

that such a state of things does not really exist, then, our inference to the kind of cause requisite to account for it, is necessarily null.

This being understood, I now proceed to show you that the class of phænomena which requires that kind of cause we denominate a Deity, is exclusively given in the phænomena of mind,—that the phænomena of matter, taken by themselves (you will observe the qualification, taken by themselves) so far from warranting any inference to the existence of a God, would, on the contrary, ground even an argument to his negation; that the study of the external world, taken with, and in subordination to, that of the internal, not only loses its atheistic tendency, but, under such subservience, may be rendered conducive to the great conclusion from which, if left to itself, it would dissuade us.*

The reasoning by which he thinks that he establishes this position runs as follows. A God is only an inference from Nature; a cause assumed, as necessary to account for phænomena. Now, fate or necessity, without a God, might account for the phænomena of matter. It is only as man is a free intelligence, that to account for his existence requires the hypothesis of a Creator who is a free intelligence. If our feeling of liberty is an illusion; if our intelligence is only a result of material organization; we are entitled to conclude that in the universe also, the phænomena of intelligence and design are, in the last analysis, the products of brute necessity. Existence in itself being unknown to us, we can only infer its character from the particular order presented to us within the sphere of our experience, which in the case under consideration means observation of our own minds. If, therefore, our intelligence is produced and bounded by a blind fate, the like may be concluded to be true of the Divine Intelligence. If, on the contrary, intelligence in man is a free power, independent of matter, we may legitimately conclude the same thing of the intelligence manifested in the universe. Again, there is properly no God at all unless there is a moral Governor of the world.

Now, it is self-evident, in the first place, that if there be no moral world, there can be no moral governor of such a world; and in the second, that we have, and can have, no ground on which to believe in the reality of a moral world, except in so far as we ourselves are moral agents. . . . But in what does the character of man as a moral agent consist? Man is a moral agent only as he is accountable for his actions,—in other words, as he is the object of praise or blame; and this he is, only inasmuch as he has prescribed to him a rule of duty, and as he is able to act, or not to act, in conformity with its precepts. The possibility of morality thus depends on the possibility of liberty; for if man be not a free agent, he is not the author of his actions, and has, therefore, no responsibility,—no moral personality at all.†

Fully to develop all the just criticisms which might be made on this single thesis, would require a long chapter. In the first place, the practice of

*Lectures, Vol. I, pp. 25–6.
†Ibid., pp. 32–3. See also a passage in the essay on the Study of Mathematics, Discussions, pp. 307–8.

bribing the pupil to accept a metaphysical dogma, by the promise or threat that it affords the only valid argument for a foregone conclusion—however transcendently important that conclusion may be thought to be—is not only repugnant to all the rules of philosophizing, but a grave offence against the morality of philosophic enquiry. The eager attempts of almost every metaphysical writer to create a religious prejudice in favour of the theory he patronizes, are a very serious grievance in philosophy. If I could permit myself, even by way of retort, to follow so bad an example, I might warn the defenders of religion, of the danger of sacrificing, in turn, every one of its evidences to some other. It has been remarked, with truth, that there is not one of the received arguments in support either of natural religion or of revelation, a formal condemnation of which might not be extracted from the writings of sincerely religious thinkers. I am far from imputing this to them as matter of blame: the rejection of what they deem bad arguments in a good cause must always be honourable to them, when led to it by honestly following the promptings of their reason, and not by an egotistic preference for their own special modes of proof. But, looking at the question as one of prudence, it would be wise in them, whatever else they give up, not to part company with the Design argument. For, in the first place, it is the best; and besides, it is by far the most persuasive. It would be difficult to find a stronger argument in favour of Theism, than that the eye must have been made by one who sees, and the ear by one who hears.[*] If, after this, it pleases Sir W. Hamilton or any other person to say that unless we believe in free will, the Being who by hypothesis made the ear and the eye is no God; or that to regard the goodness of God as the result of a necessity, which, from the very meaning of a First Cause, can only be a necessity of his own nature, a love of Good which is part of himself and inseparable from him, is denying him to be a moral being; there is really nothing left for us but, with equal positiveness, to aver the contrary: for the two parties will never be able to agree about the meaning of terms.

This is but one specimen among many of the bad logic which pervades Sir W. Hamilton's attempt to show that Theism depends on the reception of his favourite doctrine. He proceeds, throughout, on the assumption that the falsely called Doctrine of Necessity* is the same thing with Materialism.

[*Cf. Psalms, 94:9.]

*Both Sir W. Hamilton and Mr. Mansel sometimes call it by the fairer name of Determinism. But both of them, when they come to close quarters with the doctrine, in general call it either Necessity, or, less excusably, Fatalism. The truth is, that the assailants of the doctrine cannot do without the associations engendered by the double meaning of the word Necessity, which, in this application, signifies only invariability, but in its common employment, compulsion. Vide *System of Logic*, Bk. VI, Chap. ii [*Collected Works*, Vol. VIII, pp. 836ff.].

He treats those opinions as precisely equivalent.* Yet no two doctrines can be more distinct. Reid, an enemy of both, affirms that Necessity, "far from being a direct inference," "can receive no support from" Materialism.[†] It may be true, nevertheless, that Materialists are always or generally Necessitarians; and it is not denied that many Necessitarians are Materialists: but nearly all the theologians of the Reformation, beginning with Luther, and the entire series of Calvinistic divines represented by Jonathan Edwards, are proofs that the most sincere Spiritualists may consistently hold the doctrine of so-called Necessity. Of such Spiritualists there is an illustrious example in Leibnitz, to say nothing of Condillac[‡] or Brown. They believe man to be a spiritual being, not dependent on Matter, but yet, in respect of his actions as in all other respects, subject to the law of Causation: his volitions not being self-caused, but determined by spiritual antecedents (*e.g.* desires, associations of ideas, &c., all of which are spiritual if the mind is spiritual) in such sort that when the antecedents are the same, the volitions will always be the same. But to confound Necessity with Materialism, though an historical and psychological error, is indispensable to Sir W. Hamilton's argument, which depends for all its plausibility on the picture he draws of a God subject to a "brute necessity" of a purely material character.[*] For if the necessity predicated of human actions is not a material, but a spiritual necessity; if the assertion that the virtuous man is virtuous necessarily, only means that he is so because he dreads a departure from virtue more than he dreads any personal consequence; there is nothing absurd or invidious in taking a similar view of the Deity, and believing that he is necessitated to will what is good, by the love of good and detestation of evil which are in his own nature.

There is also at the root of our author's argument another logical error— that of inferring that whatever is given by observation and analysis as a law of human intelligence, must be supposed to be an absolute law extending to the Divine. He says, truly, that the Divine Intelligence is but an assumption, to account for the phænomena of the universe; and that we can only be warranted in referring the origin of those phænomena to an Intelligence, by

---

*"The atheist who holds *matter or necessity* to be the original principle of all that is." (*Lectures*, Vol. I, pp. 26–7.) "Those who do not allow that mind is matter—who hold that there is in man a principle of action superior to the determinations of a physical necessity, a brute or blind fate." (*Ibid.*, p. 133.) And the entire argument in page 31 of the same volume.

[†]Reid's [*Essays on the Active Powers*,] *Works*, Hamilton's edition, p. 635.

[‡]That Condillac was a Spiritualist, is shown by the chapter on the Soul, which stands as the first chapter of his *Art de Penser*. [See Étienne Bonnot de Condillac, *La Logique, ou les premiers développemens de l'art de penser*, in *Œuvres complètes*, 31 vols. (Paris: Dufart, 1803), Vol. XXX, pp. 5–15 (Part I, Chap. i).]

[*Lectures*, Vol. I, p. 31.]

analogy to the effects of human intellect. But can this analogy be carried up to complete identity in conditions and modes of action between the human and the Divine intelligence? Does Sir W. Hamilton draw this inference in any other case? On the contrary, he holds us bound to believe that the Deity, whether as Will or as Intelligence, is Absolute—unrestricted by any conditions; though, as such, neither knowable nor conceivable by us. And though I do not acknowledge the obligation of believing what can neither be known nor conceived, as little can it be admitted, that the Divine Will cannot be free unless ours is so; any more than that the Divine Intelligence cannot know the truths of geometry by direct intuition, because we are obliged to mount laboriously up to them through the twelve books of Euclid.

So much for Sir W. Hamilton's attempt to prove that one who disbelieves free-will, has no business to believe in a God. Let us now consider his view of the doctrine itself, and of the evidence for it.

His view of the controversy is peculiar, but harmonizes with his Philosophy of the Conditioned, which seems indeed to have been principally suggested to him by the supposed requirements of this question. He is of opinion that Free-will and Necessity are both inconceivable. Free-will, because it supposes volitions to originate without cause;* because it affirms an absolute commencement, which, as we are aware, our author deems it impossible for the human mind to conceive. On the other hand, the mind is equally unable to conceive an infinite regress; a chain of causation going back to all eternity. Both the one and the other theory thus involve difficulties insurmountable by the human faculties. But, as Sir W. Hamilton has so often told us, the inconceivability of a thing by us, is no proof that it is objectively impossible by the laws of the universe; on the contrary, it often happens that both sides of an alternative are alike incomprehensible to us,

---

*[67] Sir W. Hamilton thinks it a fair statement of the Free-will doctrine, that it supposes our volitions to be uncaused. But the "Inquirer" considers this a misstatement, and thinks the real free-will doctrine to be that "I" am the cause. (P. 45.) I prefer the other language, as being more consistent with the use of the word cause in other cases. If we take the word, we must take the acknowledged Law of Causation along with it, viz., that a cause which is the same in every respect, is always followed by the same effects. But on the free-will theory, the *"I"* is the same, and all the other conditions the same, and yet the effect may not only be different, but contrary. For instead of saying that "I" am the cause, the "Inquirer" should at least say, some state or mode of me, which is different when the effect is different: though what state or mode this could be, unless it were a will to will (the notion so justly ridiculed by Hobbes [see "Of Liberty and Necessity," Discourse III of *Tripos*, in *English Works*, ed. Molesworth, Vol. IV, pp. 239–41]), it is difficult to imagine. I persist, therefore, in saying, with Sir W. Hamilton, that, on the free-will doctrine, volitions are emancipated from causation altogether.

a–a67 "*I*"

while from their nature we are certain that the one or the other must be true. Such an alternative, according to Sir W. Hamilton, exists between the conflicting doctrines of Free-will and Necessity. By the law of Excluded Middle, one or other of them must be true; and inconceivability, as common to both, not operating more against one than against the other, does not operate against either. The balance, therefore, must turn in favour of the side for which there is positive evidence. In favour of Free-will we have the distinct testimony of consciousness; perhaps directly, though of this he speaks with some appearance of doubt;* but at all events, indirectly, freedom being implied in the consciousness of moral responsibility. As there is no corresponding evidence in favour of the other theory, the Free-will doctrine must prevail.

How the will can possibly be free must remain to us, under the present limitation of our faculties, wholly incomprehensible. We cannot conceive absolute commencement; we cannot, therefore, conceive a free volition. But as little can we conceive the alternative on which liberty is denied, on which necessity is affirmed. And in favour of our moral nature, the fact that we are free is given us in the consciousness of an uncompromising law of Duty, in the consciousness of our moral accountability; and this fact of liberty cannot be redargued on the ground that it is incomprehensible, for the doctrine of the Conditioned proves, against the necessitarian, that something may, nay must, be true, of which the mind is wholly unable to construe to itself the possibility, whilst it shows that the objection of incomprehensibility applies no less to the doctrine of fatalism than to the doctrine of moral freedom.†

The inconceivability of the Free-will doctrine is maintained by our author, not only on the general ground just stated, of our incapacity to conceive an absolute commencement, but on the further and special ground, that the will is determined by motives. In rewriting the preceding passage for the Appendix to his *Discussions*, he made the following addition to it:

A determination by motives cannot, to our understanding, escape from necessitation. Nay, were we even to admit as true, what we cannot think as possible, still the doctrine of a motiveless volition would be only casualism; and the free acts of an indifferent, are, morally and rationally, as worthless as the pre-ordered passions of a determined will.‡ *How*, therefore, I repeat, moral liberty is possible in man or

*Foot-notes to Reid, pp. 599n, 602n, 624n.
†*Lectures*, Vol. II, pp. 412–13.
‡To the same effect in another passage: "That, though inconceivable, a motiveless volition would, if conceived, be conceived as morally worthless, only shows our impotence more clearly." (Appendix [I(A)] to *Discussions*, pp. 614–15.) And in a foot-note to Reid, "Is the person an *original undetermined* cause of the determination of his will? If he be not, then he is not a *free agent*, and the scheme of Necessity is admitted. If he be, in the first place, it is impossible to *conceive* the possibility of this; and, in the second, if the fact, though inconceivable, be allowed, it is impossible to see how a cause, undetermined by any motive, can be a rational, moral, and accountable cause." (P. 602n.)

God, we are utterly unable speculatively to understand. But . . . the scheme of freedom is not more inconceivable than the scheme of necessity. For whilst fatalism is a recoil from the more obtrusive inconceivability of an *absolute* commencement, on the fact of which commencement the doctrine of liberty proceeds; the fatalist is shown to overlook the equal, but less obtrusive, inconceivability of an *infinite* non-commencement, on the assertion of which non-commencement his own doctrine of necessity must ultimately rest.*

It rests on no such thing, if he believes in a First Cause, which a Necessitarian may. What is more, even if he does not believe in a First Cause, he makes no "assertion of non-commencement;" he only declines to make an assertion of commencement; *b*and, therefore, is not in the position of asserting what is inconceivable: which, however, as Sir W. Hamilton is perpetually declaring, is a position perfectly tenable, and the position he avowedly chooses for himself on this very subject*b*. But to resume the quotation: "As equally unthinkable, the two counter, the two one-sided, schemes are thus theoretically balanced. But, practically, our consciousness of the moral law, which, without a moral liberty in man, would be a mendacious imperative, gives a decisive preponderance to the doctrine of freedom over the doctrine of fate. We are free in act, if we are accountable for our actions."

Sir W. Hamilton is of opinion that both sides are alike unsuccessful in repelling each other's attacks. The arguments against both are, he thinks, to the human faculties, irrefutable.

The champions of the opposite doctrines are at once resistless in assault and impotent in defence. Each is hewn down, and appears to die under the home thrusts of his adversary; but each again recovers life from the very death of his antagonist, and, to borrow a simile, both are like the heroes in Valhalla, ready in a moment to amuse themselves anew in the same bloodless and interminable conflict. The doctrine of Moral Liberty cannot be made conceivable, for we can only conceive the determined and the relative. As already stated, all that can be done is to show, 1°. That, for the *fact* of Liberty, we have immediately or mediately, the evidence of Consciousness; and 2°. That there are among the phænomena of mind, many facts which we *must* admit as actual, but of whose possibility we are wholly unable to form any notion. I may merely observe that the fact of *Motion* can be shown to be impossible, on grounds not less strong than those on which it is attempted to disprove the fact of Liberty.†

These "grounds no less strong" are the mere paralogisms which we examined in a recent chapter,[*] and with regard to which our author

*Appendix [I(A)] to *Discussions*, pp. 624–5.
†Foot-note to Reid, p. 602n.
[*Chap. xxiv, pp. 424ff.]

*b–b*65¹, 65² a distinction of which Sir W. Hamilton, of all men, ought to recognise the importance

showed so surprising a deficiency in the acuteness and subtlety to be expected from the general quality of his mind.

Conformably to these views, Sir W. Hamilton, in his foot-notes on Reid, promptly puts an extinguisher on several of that philosopher's arguments against the doctrine of so-called Necessity. When Reid affirms that Motives are not causes—that they may influence to action, but do not act, Sir W. Hamilton observes: "If Motives influence to action, they must co-operate in producing a certain effect upon the agent; and the determination to act, and to act in a certain manner, is that effect. They are thus, on Reid's own view, in this relation, *causes*, and *efficient* causes. It is of no consequence in the argument whether motives be said to determine a man to act, or to influence (that is, to determine) him to determine himself to act."* This is one of the neatest specimens in our author's writings of a fallacy cut clean through by a single stroke.

Again, when Reid says that acts are often done without any motive, or when there is no motive for preferring the means used, rather than others by which the same end might have been attained, Sir W. Hamilton asks, "Can we conceive any act of which there was not a sufficient cause or concourse of causes why the man performed it and no other? If not, call this cause, or these concauses, the *motive*, and there is no longer a dispute."†

Reid asks, "Is there no such thing as wilfulness, caprice, or obstinacy among mankind?"[*] Sir W. Hamilton, *e contra*: "But are not these all tendencies, and fatal tendencies, to act or not to act? By contradistinguishing such tendencies from motives strictly so called, or rational impulses, we do not advance a single step towards rendering liberty comprehensible."‡

According to Reid, the determination is made by the man, and not by the motive. "But," asks Sir W. Hamilton,

was the *man* determined by no motive to that determination? Was his specific volition to this or to that without a cause? On the supposition that the sum of influences (motives, dispositions, and tendencies) to volition A, is equal to 12, and the sum of influences to counter-volition B equal to 8—can we conceive that the determination of volition A should not be necessary?—We can only conceive the volition B to be determined by supposing that the man *creates* (calls from non-existence into existence) a certain supplement of influences. But this creation as actual, or in itself, is inconceivable, and even to conceive the possibility of this inconceivable act, we must suppose some cause by which the man is determined to exert it. We thus, in *thought*, never escape determination and necessity. It will be observed that I do not consider this inability to the *notion*, any disproof of the *fact* of Free-will.§

---

*Foot-note to Reid, p. 608n. To the same effect see *Discussions*, Appendix [I(A)] on Causality, p. 614.

†Foot-note to Reid, p. 609n.

[*Essays on the Active Powers*, *Works*, p. 610.]

‡Foot-note to Reid, p. 610n.

§*Ibid.*, p. 611n.

Nor is it: but if, as our author so strongly inculcates, "every effort to bring the fact of liberty within the compass of our conceptions only results in the substitution in its place of some more or less disguised form of necessity,"* it is a strong indication that some form of necessity is the opinion naturally suggested by our collective experience of life.[†]

Sir W. Hamilton having thus, as is often the case (and it is one of the best things he does), saved his opponents the trouble of answering his friends, his doctrine is left resting exclusively on the supports which he has himself provided for it. In examining them, let us place ourselves, in the first instance, completely at his point of view, and concede to him the coequal inconceivability of the conflicting hypotheses, an uncaused commencement, and an infinite regress. But this choice of inconceivabilities is not offered to us in the case of volitions only. We are held, as he not only admits but contends, to the same alternative in all cases of causation whatsoever. But we find our way out of the difficulty, in other cases, in quite a different manner. In the case of every other kind of fact, we do not elect the hypothesis that the event took place without a cause: we accept the other supposition, that of a regress, not indeed to infinity, but either generally into the region of the Unknowable, or back to an Universal Cause, regarding which, as we are only concerned with it in [c]respect of attributes bearing[c] relation to what it preceded, and not as itself preceded by anything, we can afford to [d]consider this reference as ultimate[d].

Now, what is the reason, which, in the case of all things within the range of our knowledge except volitions, makes us choose this side of the alternative? Why do we, without scruple, register all of them as depending on causes, by which (to use our author's language) they are determined necessarily, though, in believing this, we, according to Sir W. Hamilton, believe as utter an inconceivability as if we supposed them to take place without a cause? Apparently it is because the causation hypothesis, inconceivable as he may think it, possesses the advantage of having experience on its side. And how or by what evidence does experience testify to it? Not by disclosing any *nexus* between the cause and the effect, any Sufficient Reason in the cause itself why the effect should follow it. No philosopher

---

Lectures, Vol. I, p. 34.

[†]So difficult is it to escape from this fact, that Sir W. Hamilton himself says, "Voluntary conation is a faculty which can only be determined to energy through a pain or pleasure—through an estimate of the relative worth of objects." (*Ibid.*, p. 188.) If I am determined to prefer innocence to the satisfaction of a particular desire, through an estimate of the relative worth of innocence and of the gratification, can this estimate, while unchanged, leave me at liberty to choose the gratification in preference to innocence?

[c–c]+67, 72
[d–d]65[1], 65[2]   make a plain avowal of our ignorance

now makes this supposition, and Sir W. Hamilton positively disclaims it. What experience makes known, is the fact of an invariable sequence between every event and some special combination of antecedent conditions, in such sort that wherever and whenever that union of antecedents exists, the event does not fail to occur. Any *must* in the case, any necessity, other than the unconditional universality of the fact, we know nothing of. Still, this à posteriori "does," though not confirmed by an à priori "must," decides our choice between the two inconceivables, and leads us to the belief that every event within the phænomenal universe, except human volitions, is determined to take place by a cause. Now, the so-called Necessitarians demand the application of the same rule of judgment to our volitions. They maintain that there is the same evidence for it. They affirm, as a truth of experience, that volitions do, in point of fact, follow determinate moral antecedents with the same uniformity, and (when we have sufficient knowledge of the circumstances) with the same certainty, as physical effects follow their physical causes. These moral antecedents are desires, aversions, habits, and dispositions, combined with outward circumstances suited to call those internal incentives into action. All these again are effects of causes, those of them which are mental being consequences of education, and of other moral and physical influences. This is what Necessitarians affirm: and they court every possible mode in which its truth can be verified. They test it by each person's observation of his own volitions. They test it by each person's observation of the voluntary actions of those with whom he comes into contact; and by the power which every one has of foreseeing actions, with a degree of exactness proportioned to his previous experience and knowledge of the agents, and with a certainty often quite equal to that with which we predict the commonest physical events. They test it further, by the statistical results of the observation of human beings acting in numbers sufficient to eliminate the influences which operate only on a few, and which on a large scale neutralize one another, leaving the total result about the same as if the volitions of the whole mass had been affected by such only of the determining causes as were common to them all. In cases of this description the results are as uniform, and may be as accurately foretold, as in any physical enquiries in which the effect depends upon a multiplicity of causes. The cases in which volitions seem too uncertain to admit of being confidently predicted, are those in which our knowledge of the influences antecedently in operation is so incomplete, that with equally imperfect data there would be the same uncertainty in the predictions of the astronomer and the chemist. On these grounds it is contended that our choice between the conflicting inconceivables should be the same in the case of volitions as of all other phænomena; we must reject equally in both cases the hypothesis of spontaneousness, and consider them all as caused. A volition is a moral effect, which follows the corresponding moral causes as certainly and invariably as physical effects follow their physical causes. Whether it *must* do so, I acknowledge myself to be entirely ignorant, be the phænomenon moral or physical; and I condemn, accordingly, the word Necessity as applied to either case. All I know is, that it always *does*.*

This argument from experience Sir W. Hamilton passes unnoticed, but urges, on the opposite side of the question, the argument from Consciousness. We are conscious, he affirms, either of our freedom, or at all events (it is odd that, on his theory, there should be any doubt) of something which implies freedom. If this is true, our internal consciousness tells us *that we have a power, which* the whole outward experience of the human race tells *us that we never use*. This is surely a very unfortunate predicament we are in, and a sore trial to the puzzled metaphysician. Philosophy is far from having so easy a business before her as our author thinks: the arbiter Consciousness is by no means invoked to turn the scale between two equally balanced difficulties; on the contrary, she has to sit in judgment between herself and a complete induction from experience. Consciousness, it will probably be said, is the best evidence; and so it would be, if we were always certain what is Consciousness. But while there are so many varying testimonies respecting this; when Sir W. Hamilton can himself say, "many philosophers have attempted to establish, on the principles of common sense, propositions which are not original data of consciousness, while the original data of consciousness from which these propositions were derived, and to which they owed all their necessity and truth, these same philosophers were (strange to say) not disposed to admit;"† when M. Cousin and nearly all Germany find the Infinite and the Absolute in Consciousness, Sir W. Hamilton thinking them utterly repugnant to it; when philosophers, for many generations, fancied that they had Abstract Ideas—that they could conceive a triangle which was neither equilateral,

---

*[67] The "Inquirer" accuses this argument of "gratuitously assuming that free-will is inconsistent with foreknowledge." (P. 45.) This is a misapprehension. That vexed question is not even approached in the text. All that is maintained is that the possibility *to human intelligence,* of predicting human actions, implies a constancy of observed sequence between the same antecedents and the same consequents, which, in the case of all events except volitions, is deemed to justify the assertion of a law of nature (called in the language of the free-will philosophers Necessity). This constancy of sequence between motives, mental dispositions, and actions, is a strong reason against admitting free-will as a fact; but I have not meddled, and do not intend to meddle, with the metaphysical question whether a contingent event can be foreknown.

†"Dissertations on Reid," [Note A,] p. 749.

$^{e-e}$+72
$^{f-f}$65^1, 65^2 one thing, and
$^{g-g}$65^1, 65^2 another

isosceles, nor scalene,* which Sir W. Hamilton and all other people now consider to be simply absurd; with all these conflicting opinions respecting the things to which Consciousness testifies, what is the perplexed inquirer to think? Does all philosophy end, as in our author's opinion Hume believed it to do, in a persistent contradiction between one of our mental faculties and another?[*] We shall find, there is a solution, which relieves the human mind from this embarrassment: namely, that the question to which experience says yes, and that to which consciousness says no, are different questions.

Let us cross-examine the alleged testimony of consciousness. And, first, it is left in some uncertainty by Sir W. Hamilton whether Consciousness makes only one deliverance on the subject, or two: whether we are conscious only of moral responsibility, in which free-will is implied, or are directly conscious of free-will. In his *Lectures*, Sir W. Hamilton speaks only of the first. In the notes on Reid, which were written subsequently, he seems to affirm both, but the latter of the two in a doubtful and hesitating manner:[†] so difficult, in reality, does he find it to ascertain with certainty what it is that Consciousness certifies. But as there are many who maintain with a confidence far greater than his, that we are directly conscious of free-will,† it is necessary to examine that question.

---

*"Does it not require," says Locke, "some pains and skill to form the general idea of a triangle (which yet is none of the most abstract, comprehensive and difficult?) for it must be neither oblique nor rectangle, neither equilateral, equicrural, nor scalene; but all and none of these at once. In effect, it is something imperfect, that cannot exist; an idea wherein some parts of several different and inconsistent ideas are put together." (*Essay Concerning Human Understanding* [*Works*, Vol. III, pp. 27–8], Bk. IV, Chap. vii, §9.) Yet this union of contradictory elements such a philosopher as Locke was able to fancy that he conceived. I scarcely know a more striking example of the tendency of the human mind to believe that things can exist separately because they can be separately named; a tendency strong enough, in this case, to make a mind like Locke's believe itself to be conscious of that which by the laws of mind cannot be a subject of consciousness to any one.

[*See *Lectures*, Vol. I, App. i(b), p. 395.]

[†See, e.g., Foot-notes to Reid, pp. 599n, and 602n.]

†Mr. Mansel, among others, makes the assertion in the broadest form it is capable of, saying, "In every act of volition, I am fully conscious that I can at this moment act in either of two ways, and that, all the antecedent phænomena being precisely the same, I may determine one way to-day and another way to-morrow." (*Prolegomena Logica*, p. 152.) Yes, though the antecedent phænomena remain the same: but not if my judgment of the antecedent phænomena remains the same. If my conduct changes, either the external inducements or my estimate of them must have changed.

Mr. Mansel (as I have already observed) goes so far as to maintain that our immediate intuition of Power is given us by the ego producing its own volitions, not by its volitions producing bodily movements (pp. 139–40, and 151).

To be conscious of free-will, must mean, to be conscious, before I have decided, that I am able to decide either way. Exception may be taken *in limine* to the use of the word consciousness in such an application. Consciousness tells me what I do or feel. But what I am *able* to do, is not a subject of consciousness. Consciousness is not prophetic; we are conscious of what is, not of what will or can be. We never know that we are able to do a thing, except from having done it, or something equal and similar to it. We should not know that we were capable of action at all, if we had never acted. Having acted, we know, as far as that experience reaches, how we are able to act; and this knowledge, when it has become familiar, is often confounded with, and called by the name of, consciousness. But it does not derive any increase of authority from being misnamed; its truth is not supreme over, but depends on, experience. If our so-called consciousness of what we are able to do is not borne out by experience, it is a delusion. It has no title to credence but as an interpretation of experience, and if it is a false interpretation, it must give way.*

*[67] In answer to the statement that what I am *able* to do is not a subject of consciousness, Mr. Alexander says, "Perhaps it is not; but what I *feel* I am able to do is surely a subject of consciousness. . . . As to 'consciousness is not prophetic, we are conscious of what is, not of what will or can be,' it seems enough to say that if we are conscious of a free force of volition continuously inherent in us, we are conscious of what *is*." (Alexander, *Mill and Carlyle*, pp. 22–3 [quoting Mill, p. 449 above].) If we can be conscious of a force, and can feel an ability, independently of any present or past exercise thereof, the fact has nothing similar or analogous in all the rest of our nature. We are not conscious of a muscular force continuously inherent in us. If we were born with a cataract, we are not conscious, previous to being couched, of our ability to see. We should not feel able to walk if we had never walked, nor to think, if we had never thought. Ability and force are not real entities, which can be felt as present when no effect follows; they are abstract names for the happening of the effect on the occurrence of the needful conditions, or for our expectation of its happening. It is of course possible that this may be all wrong, and that there may be a concrete real thing called ability, of which consciousness discloses to us the positive existence in this one case, though there is no evidence of it in any other. But it is surely, to say the least, much more probable that we mistake for consciousness our habitual affirmation to ourselves of an acquired knowledge or belief. This very common mistake may have escaped the notice of Mr. Alexander, who (p. 23) considers knowledge to be the same thing as direct consciousness! but it is a possibility which it will not do to overlook, when one takes for one's standard the "general consciousness of the race;" especially if, with Mr. Alexander, one restricts "the race" to those who are not philosophers, on the ground that no philosopher "unless he be one of a thousand," can see or feel anything that is inconsistent with his preconceived opinion. (P. 25.) If this be the normal effect of philosophy on the human mind; if, nine hundred and ninety-nine times against one, the effect of cultivating our power of mental discrimination is to pervert it; let us close our books, and accept Hodge as a better authority in metaphysics than Locke or Kant, and, I suppose, in astronomy than Newton. An appeal to consciousness,

But this conviction, whether termed consciousness or only belief, that our will is free—what is it? Of what are we convinced? I am told that whether I decide to do or to abstain, I feel that I could have decided the other way. I ask my consciousness what I do feel, and I find, indeed, that I feel (or am convinced) that I could *h*, and even should,*h* have chosen the other course *i*if I had preferred it, that is, if I had liked it better*i*; but not that I could have chosen one course while I preferred the other. When I say

however, to be of any value, must be to those who have formed a habit of sifting their consciousness, and distinguishing what they perceive or feel from what they infer; to those who can be made to understand that they do not see the sun move: and, to have attained this power of criticising their own consciousness on metaphysical subjects, they must have reflected on those subjects, in a manner and degree which quite entitle any one to the name of a philosopher.

Mr. Alexander denies that the belief that I was free to act can possibly be tested by experience *à posteriori*, since experience only tells me the way in which I did act, and says nothing about my having been able to act otherwise. [Pp. 23–4.] Mr. Alexander's idea of the conditions of proof by experience is not a very enlarged one. Suppose that my experience of myself afforded two undeniable cases, alike in all the mental and physical antecedents, in one of which cases I acted in one way, and in the other in the direct opposite: there would then be proof by experience that I had been able to act either in the one way or in the other. It is by experience of this sort I learn that I can act at all, viz., by finding that an event takes place or not, according as (other circumstances being the same) a volition of mine does or does not take place. But when this power of my volitions over my actions has become a familiar fact, the knowledge of it is so constantly present to my mind as to be popularly called, and habitually confounded with, consciousness. And the supposed power of myself over my volitions, which is termed Free-will, though it cannot be a fact of consciousness, yet if true, or even if believed, would similarly work itself into our inmost knowledge of ourselves, in such a manner as to be mistaken for consciousness.

It would hardly be worth while to notice a pretended inconsistency discovered by Mr. Alexander between what is here said, and my recognition in a former work of a "practical feeling of Free Will"—"a feeling of Moral Freedom which we are conscious of," if Mr. Alexander had not inferred from it that I "was at one time conscious" of what I now, for the convenience of my argument, deny to be a subject of consciousness. [Alexander, p. 22–3, quoting Mill, *A System of Logic*, Bk. VI, Chap. ii, §§1, 3, in *Collected Works*, Vol. VIII, pp. 836, 841.] Mr. Alexander himself quotes the words in which I spoke of this practical feeling of free-will as not one of free-will at all, in a sense implying the theory; and took pains to describe what it really is, expressly declaring our feeling of moral freedom to be a feeling of our being able to modify our own character *if we wish*. When I applied the words feeling and consciousness to this acquired knowledge, I did not use those terms in their strict psychological meaning, there being no necessity for doing so in that place; but, agreeably to popular usage, extended them to (what there is no appropriate scientific name for) the whole of our familiar and intimate knowledge concerning ourselves.

h–h+67, 72
*i–i*65^1, 65^2 *if I had preferred it*

preferred, I of course include with the thing itself, all that accompanies it. I know that I can, because I know that I often do, elect to do one thing, when I should have preferred another in itself, apart from its consequences, or from a moral law which it violates. And this preference for a thing in itself, abstractedly from its accompaniments, is often loosely described as preference for the thing. It is this unprecise mode of speech which makes it not seem absurd to say that I act in opposition to my preference; that I do one thing when I would rather do another; that my conscience prevails over my desires—as if conscience were not itself a desire—the desire to do right. Take any alternative: say to murder or not to murder. I am told, that if I elect to murder, I am conscious that I could have elected to abstain: but am I conscious that I could have abstained if my aversion to the crime, and my dread of its consequences, had been weaker than the temptation? If I elect to abstain: in what sense am I conscious that I could have elected to commit the crime? Only if I had desired to commit it with a desire stronger than my horror of murder; not with one less strong. When we think of ourselves hypothetically as having acted otherwise than we did, we always suppose a difference in the antecedents: we picture ourselves as having known something that we did not know, or not known something that we did know; which is a difference in the external ^{j}inducements^j; or as having desired something, or disliked something, more or less than we did; which is a difference in the internal ^{k}inducements^k.*

^{l}In refutation of this it is said, that in resisting a desire, I am conscious of making an effort; that after I have resisted, I have the remembrance of having made an effort; that "if the temptation was long continued, or if I have been resisting the strong will of another, I am as sensibly exhausted by

*[67] Preferring, as he says, a homely instance, Mr. Alexander supposes that a man puts his finger to his nose, and asks, "Is not he conscious of being able to touch at will either the right side of his nose or the left? Having touched, let us say, the left side, is he not conscious he could have touched the right side had he so willed it, and conscious that he *could* have so willed, chosen, or preferred?" (P. 29.) Mr. Alexander's *naïf* expectation that his opponent's answer will be different because of the futility of the example, reminds one of the *asinus Buridani*. I should, on the supposition which he makes, be aware (I will not say conscious) that I could have touched the right side had I so willed it; and aware that I could, and even should, have so willed, chosen, and preferred, if there had existed a sufficient inducement to make me do so, and not otherwise. If any one's consciousness tells him that he could have done so without an inducement, or in opposition to a stronger inducement, I venture to express my opinion, in words borrowed from Mr. Alexander, that it is not his "veritable consciousness." I will not imitate Mr. Alexander in calling it "a fraudulent substitute palmed upon him" by his philosophical system. [*Ibid.*]

$^{j-j}$65^1, 65^2 motives
$^{k-k}$65^1, 65^2 motives
$^{l-l}$452+67, 72

that effort, as after any physical exertion I ever made:" and it is added, "If my volition is wholly determined by the strongest present desire, it will be decided without any effort. . . . When the greater weight goes down, and the lesser up, no effort is needed on the part of the scales."* It is implied in this argument, that in a battle between contrary impulses, the victory must always be decided in a moment; that the force which is really the strongest, and prevails ultimately, must prevail instantaneously. The fact is not quite thus even in inanimate nature: the hurricane does not level the house or blow down the tree without resistance; even the balance trembles, and the scales oscillate for a short time, when the difference of the weights is not considerable. Far less does victory come without a contest to the strongest of two moral, or even two vital forces, whose nature it is to be never fixed, but always flowing, quantities. In a struggle between passions, there is not a single instant in which there does not pass across the mind some thought, which adds strength to, or takes it from, one or the other of the contending powers. Unless one of them was, from the beginning, out of all proportion stronger than the other, some time must elapse before the balance adjusts itself between forces neither of which is for any two successive instants the same. During that interval the agent is in the peculiar mental and physical state which we call a conflict of feelings: and we all know that a conflict between strong feelings *is*, in an extraordinary degree, exhaustive of the nervous energies.† The consciousness of effort, which we are told of, is this state of conflict. The author I am quoting considers what he calls, I think improperly, an effort, to be only on one side, because he represents to himself the conflict as taking place between me and some foreign power, which I conquer, or by which I am overcome.[*] But it is obvious that "I" am both parties in the contest; the conflict is between me and myself; between (for instance) me desiring a pleasure, and me dreading self-reproach. What causes Me, or, if you please, my Will, to be identified with one side rather than with the other, is that one of the Me's represents a more permanent state of my feelings than the other does. After the temptation has been yielded to, the desiring "I" will come to an end, but the conscience-stricken "I" may endure to the end of life.[l]

I therefore dispute altogether that we are conscious of being able to act in

*[67] [Phillipps,] *The Battle of the Two Philosophies*, pp. 43–4.

†[67] The writer I quote says, "Balancing one motive against another is not willing but judging." [P. 43.] The state of mind I am speaking of is by no means a state of judging. It is an emotional, not an intellectual state, and the judging may be finished before it commences. If there were any indispensable act of judging in this stage, it could only be judging which of the two pains or pleasures was the greatest: and to regard this as the operative force would be conceding the point in favour of Necessitarianism.

[*Ibid., pp. 43–4.]

opposition to the strongest present desire or aversion. The difference between a bad and a good man is not that the latter acts in opposition to his strongest desires; it is that his desire to do right, and his aversion to doing wrong, are strong enough to overcome, and in the case of perfect virtue, to silence, any other desire or aversion which may conflict with them. It is because this state of mind is possible to human nature, that human beings are capable of moral government: and moral education consists in subjecting them to the discipline which has most tendency to bring them into this state. The object of moral education is to educate the will: but the will can only be educated through the desires and aversions; by eradicating or weakening such of them as are likeliest to lead to evil; exalting to the highest pitch the desire of right conduct and the aversion to wrong; cultivating all other desires and aversions of which the ordinary operation is auxiliary to right, while discountenancing so immoderate an indulgence of them, as might render them too powerful to be overcome by the moral sentiment, when they chance to be in opposition to it. The other requisites are, a clear intellectual standard of right and wrong, that moral desire and aversion may act in the proper places, and such general mental habits as shall prevent moral considerations from being forgotten or overlooked, in cases to which they are rightly applicable.

Rejecting, then, the figment of a direct consciousness of the freedom of the will, in other words, our ability to will in opposition to our strongest preference; it remains to consider whether, as affirmed by Sir W. Hamilton, a freedom of this kind is implied in what is called our consciousness of moral responsibility. There must be something very plausible in this opinion, since it is shared even by Necessitarians. Many of these—in particular Mr. Owen and his followers—from a recognition of the fact that volitions are effects of causes, have been led to deny human responsibility. I do not mean that they denied moral distinctions. Few persons have had a stronger sense of right and wrong, or been more devoted to the things they deemed right. What they denied was the rightfulness of inflicting punishment. A man's actions, they said, are the result of his character, and he is not the author of his own character. It is made *for* him, not *by* him. There is no justice in punishing him for what he cannot help. We should try to convince or persuade him that he had better act in a different manner; and should educate all, especially the young, in the habits and dispositions which lead to well-doing: though how this is to be effected without any use whatever of punishment as a means of education, is a question they have failed to resolve. The confusion of ideas, which makes the subjection of human volitions to the law of Causation seem inconsistent with accountability, must thus be very natural to the human mind; but this may be said of a thousand errors, and even of some merely verbal fallacies. In the present case there is more than a verbal fallacy, but verbal fallacies also contribute their part.

What is meant by moral responsibility? Responsibility means punishment. When we are said to have the feeling of being morally responsible for our actions, the idea of being punished for them is uppermost in the speaker's mind. But the feeling of liability to punishment is of two kinds. It may mean, expectation that if we act in a certain manner, punishment will actually be inflicted upon us, by our fellow creatures or by a Supreme Power. Or it may only mean, *m*knowing*m* that we shall deserve that infliction.

The first of these cannot, in any correct meaning of the term, be designated as a consciousness. If we believe that we shall be punished for doing wrong, it is because the belief has been taught to us by our parents and tutors, or by our religion, or is generally held by those who surround us, or because we have ourselves come to the conclusion, by reasoning, or from the experience of life. This is not Consciousness. And, by whatever name it is called, its evidence is not dependent on any theory of the spontaneousness of volition. The punishment of guilt in another world is believed with undoubting conviction by Turkish fatalists, and by professed Christians who are not only Necessitarians, but believe that the majority of mankind were divinely predestined from all eternity to sin and to be punished for sinning. It is not, therefore, the belief that we shall be *made* accountable, which can be deemed to require or presuppose the free-will hypothesis; it is the belief that we ought so to be; that we are justly accountable; that guilt deserves punishment. It is here that *n* issue is joined between the two opinions.

In discussing it, there is no need to postulate any theory respecting the nature or criterion of moral distinctions. It matters not, for this purpose, whether the right and wrong of actions depends on the consequences they tend to produce, or on an inherent quality of the actions themselves. It is indifferent whether we are utilitarians or anti-utilitarians; whether our ethics rest on intuition or on experience. It is sufficient if we believe that there is a difference between right and wrong, and a natural reason for preferring the former; that people in general, unless when they expect personal benefit from a wrong, naturally and usually prefer what they think to be right: whether because we are all dependent for what makes existence tolerable, upon the right conduct of other people, while their wrong conduct is a standing menace to our security, or for some more mystical and transcendental reason. Whatever be the cause, we are entitled to assume

---

*m-m*65[1], 65[2]   being conscious
*n*65[1], 65[2]   the main

the fact: and its consequence is, that whoever cultivates a disposition to wrong, places his mind out of sympathy with the rest of his fellow creatures, and if they are aware of his disposition, becomes a natural object of their active dislike. He not only forfeits the pleasure of their good will, and the benefit of their good offices, except when compassion for the human being is stronger than distaste towards the wrongdoer; but he also renders himself liable to whatever they may think it necessary to do in order to protect themselves against him; which may probably include punishment, as such, and will certainly involve much that is equivalent in its operation on himself. In this way he is certain to be made accountable, at least to his fellow creatures, through the normal action of their natural sentiments. And it is well worth consideration, whether the practical expectation of being thus called to account, has not a great deal to do with the internal feeling of being accountable; a feeling, assuredly, which is seldom found existing in any strength in the absence of that practical expectation. It is not usually found that Oriental despots, who cannot be called to account by anybody, have much consciousness of being morally accountable. And (what is still more significant) in societies in which caste or class distinctions are really strong—a state so strange to us now, that we seldom realize it in its full force—it is a matter of daily experience that persons may show the strongest sense of moral accountability as regards their equals, who can make them accountable, and not the smallest vestige of a similar feeling towards their inferiors who cannot.

°This does not imply that the feeling of accountability, even when proportioned very exactly to the chance of being called to account, is a mere interested calculation, having nothing more in it than an expectation and dread of external punishment. When pain has long been thought of as a consequence of a given fact, the fact becomes wrapt up in associations which make it painful in itself, and cause the mind to shrink from it even when, in the particular case, no painful consequences are apprehended: just as the dislike to spending money, which grows up while money can ill be spared, may be an absorbing passion after the possessor has grown so rich that the expenditure would not really cause him the most trifling inconvenience. On this familiar principle of association it is abundantly certain that even if wrong meant merely what is forbidden, a disinterested detestation of doing wrong would naturally grow up, and might become, in its strength and promptitude, and in the immediateness of its action, without reflection or ulterior purpose, undistinguishable from any of our instincts or natural passions.°

Another fact, which it is of importance to keep in view, is, that the

°-°+67, 72

highest and strongest sense of the worth of goodness, and the odiousness of its opposite, is perfectly compatible with even the most exaggerated form of Fatalism. Suppose that there were two peculiar breeds of human beings,—one of them so constituted from the beginning, that however educated or treated, nothing could prevent them from always feeling and acting so as to be a blessing to all whom they approached; another, of such original perversity of nature that neither education nor punishment could inspire them with a feeling of duty, or prevent them from being active in evil doing. Neither of these races of human beings would have free-will; yet the former would be honoured as demigods, while the latter would be regarded and treated as noxious beasts: not punished perhaps, since punishment would have no effect on them, and it might be thought wrong to indulge the mere instinct of vengeance: but kept carefully at a distance, and killed like other dangerous creatures when there was no other convenient way of being rid of them. We thus see that even under the utmost possible exaggeration of the doctrine of Necessity, the distinction between moral good and evil in conduct would not only subsist, but would stand out in a more marked manner than now, when the good and the wicked, however unlike, are still regarded as of one common nature.

*p*An opponent may say, this is not a distinction between *moral* good and evil; and I am far from intending to beg the question against him. But neither can he be permitted to beg the question, by assuming that the distinction is not moral because it does not imply free-will. The reality of moral distinctions, and the freedom of our volitions, are questions independent of one another. My position is, that a human being who loves, disinterestedly and consistently, his fellow creatures and whatever tends to their good, who hates with a vigorous hatred what causes them evil, and whose actions correspond in character with these feelings, is naturally, necessarily, and reasonably an object to be loved, admired, sympathized with, and in all ways cherished and encouraged by mankind; while a person who has none of these qualities, or so little, that his actions continually jar and conflict with the good of others, and that for purposes of his own he is ready to inflict on them a great amount of evil, is a natural and legitimate object of their fixed aversion, and of conduct conformable thereto: and this whether the will be free or not, and even independently of any theory of the difference between right and wrong; whether right means productive of happiness, and wrong productive of misery, or right and wrong are intrinsic qualities of the actions themselves, provided only we recognise that there is a difference, and that the difference is highly important. What I maintain is, that this is a sufficient distinction between moral good and evil: sufficient for the ends of society and sufficient for the individual conscience:—that

p–p+67, 72

we need no other distinction; that if there be any other distinction, we can dispense with it; and that, supposing acts in themselves good or evil to be as unconditionally determined from the beginning of things as if they were phænomena of dead matter, still, if the determination from the beginning of things has been that they shall take place through my love of good and hatred of evil, I am a proper object of esteem and affection, and if that they shall take place through my love of self and indifference to good, I am a fit object of aversion which may rise to abhorrence. And no competently informed person will deny that, as a matter of fact, those who have held this creed have had as strong a feeling, both emotional and practical, of moral distinctions, as any other people.*ᵖ

*[67] Mr. Alexander draws a woful picture of the pass which mankind would come to, if belief in so-called Necessity became general. All "our current moralities" would come to be regarded "as a form of superstition," all "moral ideas as illusions," by which "it is plain we get rid of them as motives:" consequently the internal sanction of conscience would no longer exist. "The external sanctions remain, but not quite as they were. That important section of them which rests on the *moral* approval or disapproval of our fellow-men has, of course, evaporated:" and "in virtue of a deadly moral indifference," the remaining external sanctions "might come to be much more languidly enforced than as now they are," and the progressive degradation would in a sufficient time "succeed in reproducing the real original gorilla." (Pp. 118–21.) A formidable prospect: but Mr. Alexander must not suppose that other people's feelings, about the matters of highest importance to them, are bound up with a certain speculative dogma, and even a certain form of words, because, it seems, his are. As long as guilt is thoroughly regarded as an evil, it would be quite safe even to hold with Plato, that it is the mental equivalent of bodily disease [see, e.g., *Republic*, p. 418 (IV, 444ᵈ10–ᵉ4)]: people would be none the less anxious to avoid it for themselves, and to cure it in others. Whatever else may be an illusion, it is no illusion that some types of conduct and character are salutary, and others pernicious, to the race and to each of its members; and there is no fear that mankind will not retain the property of their nature by which they prefer what is salutary to what is pernicious, and proclaim and act upon the preference. It is no illusion that human beings are objects of sympathy or of antipathy as they belong to the one type or to the other, and that the sympathies and antipathies excited in us by others react on ourselves. The qualities which each man feels to be odious in others, are odious, without illusion, in himself. The basis of Mr. Alexander's gloomy prophecy thus fails him. I might add, that even if his groundless anticipations came to pass in some other manner, and disinterested love of virtue and hatred of guilt faded away from the earth; though the human race, thus degenerated, would be little worth preserving, it would probably find the means of preserving itself notwithstanding. The external sanctions, instead of being more languidly, would probably be far more rigidly enforced than at present; for more rigorous penalties would be necessary when there was less inward sentiment to aid them: and however destitute of pure virtuous feeling mankind might be, each one of them would be far too well aware of the importance of other people's conduct to his own interest, not to exact those penalties without stint, and without any of the scruples which at present make conscientious men afraid of carrying repression too far.

But these considerations, *however* pertinent to the subject, do not touch the root of the difficulty. The real question is one of justice—the legitimacy of retribution, or punishment. On the theory of Necessity (we are told) *a* man cannot help acting as he does; and it cannot be just that he should be punished for what he cannot help.

Not if the expectation of punishment enables him to help it, and is the only means by which he can be enabled to help it?

To say that he cannot help it, is true or false, according to the qualification with which the assertion is accompanied. Supposing him to be of a vicious disposition, he cannot help doing the criminal act, if he is allowed to believe that he will be able to commit it unpunished. If, on the contrary, the impression is strong in his mind that a heavy punishment will follow, he can, and in most cases does, help it.

The question deemed to be so puzzling is, how punishment can be justified, if men's actions are determined by motives, among which motives punishment is one. A more difficult question would be, how it can be justified if they are not so determined. Punishment proceeds on the assumption that the will is governed by motives. If punishment had no power of acting on the will, it would be illegitimate, however natural might be the inclination to inflict it. Just so far as the will is supposed free, that is, capable of acting *against* motives, punishment is disappointed of its object, and deprived of its justification.

There are two ends which, on the Necessitarian theory, are sufficient to justify punishment: the benefit of the offender himself, and the protection of others. The first justifies it, because to benefit a person cannot be to do him an injury. To punish him for his own good, provided the inflictor has any proper title to constitute himself a judge, is no more unjust than to administer medicine. As far, indeed, as respects the criminal himself, the theory of punishment is, that by counterbalancing the influence of present temptations, or acquired bad habits, it restores the mind to that normal preponderance of the love of right, which *many* moralists and theologians consider to constitute the true definition of our freedom.* In its other

---

*"La liberté, complète, réelle, de l'homme, est la perfection humaine, le but à atteindre." From a paper by M. Albert Réville, ["De la liberté et du progrès à propos des anciens et des modernes,"] in the *Revue Germanique* [*et Française*, XXVII, 21,] for September, 1863, in which the question of free-will is discussed (though only parenthetically) with a good sense and philosophy seldom found in recent writings on that subject.

*t*The "Inquirer" accuses me (pp. 49–51) of throwing aside "a well considered and

*q–q*65[1], 65[2]   though
r–r+67, 72
*s–s*65[1], 65[2]   the best
t–t+67, 72

aspect, punishment is a precaution taken by society in self-defence. To make this just, the only condition required is, that the end which society is attempting to enforce by punishment, should be a just one. Used as a means of aggression by society on the just rights of the individual, punishment is unjust. Used to protect the just rights of others against unjust aggression by

---

deliberate opinion, because it refuses to fit in with a foregone conclusion on another subject," when I affirm that the good of the person punished can ever be one of the ends of punishment; and he quotes, on that subject, my essay on Liberty. I am responsible for the Essay, but not for this absurd perversion of its doctrines. Does it anywhere assert that children ought not to be punished for their own good? that parents, and even the magistrate, when dealing with that class of delinquents, are not entitled to constitute themselves judges of the delinquent's good, and even bound to make it the principal consideration? Did I not expressly leave open, as similar to the case of children, that of adult communities which are still in the infantine stage of development? [See *On Liberty*, in *Collected Works*, Vol. XVIII (Toronto: University of Toronto Press, 1977), p. 224.] And did I say, or did any one ever say, that when, for the protection of society, we punish those who have done injury to society, the reformation of the offenders is not one of the ends to be aimed at, in the kind and mode, at least, of the punishment?

The "Inquirer" adds, "If I deserve punishment, only because my love of right is too weak, and my desire for wrong pleasures is too strong, and therefore punishment will help me to dislike the latter the most, then I equally deserve rewards; 'by counterbalancing the influence of present temptation or bad habits,' rewards 're-store the mind to the normal preponderance of the love of right.' . . . And the more wicked I am, the greater reward I deserve. . . . For children, and for all so far as their own improvement is concerned, rewards for evil-doers must be more moral than punishments, as tending directly to diminish misery, and increase the sum of human happiness." (P. 49.)

Supposing even that the matter of reward were sufficiently plentiful to allow of compensating everybody for every temptation he foregoes, I submit that this plan would scarcely fulfil the other, and still more important end of punishment, the discouragement of future offenders. And even in the case of children, whose own improvement, as long as their education lasts, is the main end to be considered, every one knows, though he may forget it in confuting an adversary, that pain is a stronger thing than pleasure, and punishment vastly more efficacious than reward. Punishment, too, can alone produce the associations which make the conduct that incurs it, ultimately hateful in itself, and which by rendering that which is injurious to society, sincerely distasteful to its individual members, produces the fellowship of feeling which gives them a sense of common interest, and enables them to sympathize and cooperate as creatures of one kin. Thus much to show (if it needs showing) that the preference of punishment to reward as a protection against violations of right, is no inconsistency in the conception of social justice laid down in the text. If the objector now asks—But, supposing this were not so, and that rewarding an offender were as effectual a means of improving his own character and protecting society as punishing him, would it equally commend itself to our feeling of desert? I answer, no. It would conflict with that natural, and even animal, desire of retaliation—of hurting those who have hurt us, either in ourselves or in anything we care for—which, as I have elsewhere maintained, is the root of all that distin-

the offender, it is just. If it is possible to have just rights, *u*(which is the same thing as to have rights at all)*u* it cannot be unjust to defend them. Free-will or no free-will, it is just to punish so far as is necessary for this purpose, *v* as it is just to put a wild beast to death (without unnecessary suffering) for the same object.

---

guishes our feeling of justice from our ordinary sense of expediency. This natural feeling, whether instinctive or acquired, though in itself it has nothing moral in it, yet when moralized by being allied with, and limited by, regard for the general welfare, becomes, in my view of the matter, our moral sentiment of justice. And this sentiment is necessarily offended by rewarding delinquents, and gratified by their punishment. The sentiment is entitled to consideration in a world like ours, in which punishment is really necessary: but granting the absurd supposition of a state of human affairs in which rewarding offenders would really be more expedient than punishing them, there would be no need of this particular moral sentiment, and, like other sentiments the use of which is superseded by changes in the circumstances of mankind, it might, and probably would, die away.

The chapter in which I have discussed this question (*Utilitarianism*, Chap. v [in *Collected Works*, Vol. X, pp. 240ff.]) is quite familiar to Mr. Alexander; who shows himself extremely well acquainted with all parts of it, except those which tell against his own side. Even when he accomplishes (pp. 52 and 59) the great feat of finding in it the two statements, that justice, in the general mind, has a great deal to do with the notion of desert, and that justice is not synonymous with expediency, no one who reads him would suspect that I had explained in the same chapter what, in my view, the notion of desert is, and what there is in our idea of justice besides expediency. Mr. Alexander's perpetual insinuations, and more than insinuations, of bad faith, since he makes a kind of retractation of their grossest meaning in one line of his essay [see p. 72], I pardon, as one of the incidents of his rollicking style; but it is well that he should be aware how easy, if any one were disposed, it would be to retaliate them.

How far Mr. Alexander understands the first elements of the ethical system which he denounces, is shown by one of his arguments, which he is so fond of that he repeats it several times; that if the protection of society is a sufficient reason for hanging any one, it holds good for hanging an innocent person, or a madman (pp. 36, 37, 65, 89). He repeatedly says, that this has just as deterring an effect as hanging a real criminal; being of opinion, apparently, that hanging a person who is not guilty gives people a motive to abstain from being guilty. As to the madman, he asks, "How should the state of mind of the maniac, as unamenable to motive, any way affect the efficacy of our hanging him for murder, as a means to deter others from murder?" (P. 65.) Mr. Alexander really has no claim to be answered, until he has got a step or two beyond this. Perhaps, however, he may be able to see, that all the deterring effect which hanging can produce on men who are amenable to motive, is produced by hanging men who are amenable to motive. Hanging, in addition, those who are not amenable to motive, adds nothing to the deterring effect, and is therefore a gratuitous brutality.*t*

u-u+67, 72
*v*65^1, 65^2 exactly

Now, the primitive consciousness we are said to have, that we are accountable for our actions, and that if we violate the rule of right we shall deserve punishment, I contend is nothing else than our knowledge that punishment will be just: that by such conduct we shall place ourselves in the position in which our fellow creatures, or the Deity, or both, will naturally, and may justly, inflict punishment upon us. By using the word *justly*, I am not assuming, in the explanation, the thing I profess to explain. As before observed, I am entitled to postulate the reality, and the knowledge and feeling, of moral distinctions. These, it is both evident metaphysically and notorious historically, are independent of any theory concerning the will. We are supposed capable of understanding that other people have rights, and all that follows from this. The mind which possesses this idea, if capable of placing itself at the point of view of another person, must recognise it as *w*not unjust*w* that others should protect themselves against any disposition on his part to infringe their rights; and he will do so the more readily, because he also has rights, and his rights continually require the same protection. This, I maintain, is our feeling of accountability, in so far as it can be separated from *x*the associations engendered by*x* the prospect of being actually called to account. No one who understands the power of the principle of association, can doubt its sufficiency to create out of these elements the whole of the feeling of which we are conscious. To rebut this view of the case would require positive evidence; as, for example, if it could be proved that the feeling of accountability precedes, in the order of development, all experience of punishment. No such evidence has been produced, or is producible. Owing to the limited accessibility to observation of the mental processes of infancy, direct proof can as little be produced on the other side: but if there is any validity in Sir W. Hamilton's Law of Parcimony, we ought not to assume any mental phænomenon as an ultimate fact, which can be accounted for by other known properties of our mental nature.

I ask any one who thinks that the justice of punishment is not sufficiently vindicated by its being for the protection of just rights, how he reconciles his sense of justice to the punishment of crimes committed in obedience to a perverted conscience? Ravaillac, and Balthasar Gérard, did not regard themselves as criminals, but as heroic martyrs. If they were justly put to death, the justice of punishment has nothing to do with the state of mind of the offender, further than as this may affect the efficacy of punishment as a means to its end. It is impossible to assert the justice of punishment for crimes of fanaticism, on any other ground than its necessity for the attain-

*w-w*65[1], 65[2]   just
x-x+67, 72

ment of a just end. If that is not a justification, there is no justification. All other imaginary justifications break down in their application to this case.*

If, indeed, punishment is inflicted for any other reason than in order to operate on the will; if its purpose be other than that of improving the culprit himself, or securing the just rights of others against unjust violation, then, I admit, the case is totally altered. If any one thinks that there is justice in the infliction of purposeless suffering; that there is a natural affinity between the two ideas of guilt and punishment, which makes it intrinsically fitting that wherever there has been guilt, pain should be inflicted by way of retribution; I acknowledge that I can find no argument to justify punishment inflicted on this principle. As a legitimate satisfaction to feelings of indignation and resentment which are on the whole salutary and worthy of cultivation, I can in certain cases admit it; but here it is still a means to an end. The merely retributive view of punishment derives no justification from the doctrine I support. But it derives quite as little from the free-will doctrine. Suppose it true that the will of a malefactor, when he committed an offence, was free, or in other words, that he acted badly, not because he was of a bad disposition, but ʸfrom no causeʸ in particular: it is not easy to

*[67] The force of this argument is attested by the straits to which my most persevering assailant, Mr. Alexander, is reduced by it (pp. 63–4). He finds himself obliged to say that, "could we have positive assurance," in the case of such people, "that their outrage of the obligation to respect life was solely an act of self-sacrifice to what they considered a higher and more sacred one, we should be obliged to admit that their doom was not just in the particular instance." This is very well, but we want practice as well as theory. Would you hang them? Mr. Alexander makes a halting half-admission that he would. "A dubious point of justice—dubious, because the true motive of the act must always remain obscure—may here be allowed to be overridden by a plain and potent mandate of expediency." Mr. Alexander therefore would hang men when it is doubtful whether they deserve it; would hang them for what "may really have been an act of sublime virtue." But what is the amount of real dubiousness in cases like these? Of all acts that a man can do, those by which he knowingly sacrifices his life, sometimes with the addition of horrible torments, are the clearest from suspicion of any motives but honest ones. Mr. Alexander talks of Brutus and Charlotte Corday, but I am content with Ravaillac. Is there the smallest reason to doubt that Ravaillac's "outrage of the obligation to respect life" was "an act of self-sacrifice" to what, in his opinion, was "a higher and more sacred one?" What motive had Ravaillac for his abominable action except a supposed duty to God, and did he not deem this his highest and most sacred duty? As for Mr. Alexander's hint [p. 63] that such a man, if not culpable in the act, was "culpable in the perversion of his conscience which led to it," it is the old odious assumption of persecutors, that acts which they cannot show to have been wicked in intention, must have originated in previous wickedness. The act of Ravaillac simply originated in false teaching, coming to him from the same quarter from which had come most of the good teaching which he had received during life. It came from the fountain of goodness, not of wickedness.

ʸ–ʸ65¹, 65²   for no reason

deduce from this the conclusion that it is just to punish him. That his acts were beyond the command of motives might be a good reason for keeping out of his way, or placing him under bodily restraint; but no reason for inflicting pain upon him, when that pain, by supposition, could not operate as a deterring motive.*

While the doctrine I advocate does not support the idea that punishment in mere retaliation is justifiable, it at the same time fully accounts for the general and natural sentiment of its being so. From our earliest childhood, the *idea of doing wrong (that is, of doing what is forbidden, or what is injurious to others) and the idea* of punishment are presented to our mind together, and the intense character of the impressions causes the association between them to attain the highest degree of closeness and intimacy. Is it strange, or unlike the usual processes of the human mind, that in these circumstances we should retain the feeling, and forget the reason on which it is grounded? But why do I speak of forgetting? In most cases the reason has never, in our early education, been presented to the mind. The only ideas presented have been those of wrong and punishment, and an inseparable association has been created between these directly, without the help of any intervening idea. This is quite enough to make the spontaneous feelings of mankind regard punishment and a wrongdoer as naturally fitted

*Several of Sir W. Hamilton's admissions are strong arguments against the alleged self-evident connexion between free-will and accountability. We have found him affirming that a volition not determined by motives "would, if conceived, be conceived as morally worthless;" that "the free acts of an indifferent, are, morally and rationally, as worthless as the preordained passions of a determined will;" and that "it is impossible to see how a cause, undetermined by any motive, can be a rational, moral, and accountable cause." [Appendix I(A) to *Discussions*, pp. 614–15, 624–5, and Foot-note to Reid, p. 602n; cf. pp. 442–3 and 442n above.] If all this be so, there can be no intuitive perception of a necessary connexion between free-will and morality; it would appear, on the contrary, that we are naturally unable to recognise an act as moral, if it is, in the sense of the theory, free.

Mr. Alexander actually thinks that in these passages, Sir W. Hamilton is "asserting the determination of the will by motives;" and cannot believe that he intended "to assert an absolute commencement as the mode under which Freedom, though inconceivable, has yet to be believed:" since this "would have been to rush with his eyes open on the staring contradictory, of a thing at once caused and uncaused." (P. 80.) Yet, presently after, he himself charges Sir W. Hamilton's doctrine with requiring belief in two contrary inconceivables. [Pp. 81n–2n.] In the present case it only requires a belief in one of them, an absolute, or uncaused, commencement. Mr. Alexander does not lay claim to much knowledge of Sir W. Hamilton; and certainly no one who understood what that philosopher, and most others who discuss this question, mean by "to determine," could fail to see that with him the determination of the will by motives means Determinism, or as it is commonly called, Necessity.

z–z+67, 72
*a–a*65^1, 65^2 ideas of doing wrong and

to each other—as a conjunction appropriate in itself, independently of any consequences. Even Sir W. Hamilton recognises as one of the common sources of error, that "the associations of thought are mistaken for the connexions of existence."* If this is true anywhere, it is truest of all in the associations into which emotions enter. A strong feeling, directly excited by an object, is felt (except when contradicted by the feelings of other people) as its own sufficient justification—no more requiring the support of a reason than the fact that ginger is hot in the mouth:[*] and it almost requires a philosopher to recognise the need of a reason for his feelings, unless he has been under the practical necessity of justifying them to persons by whom they are not shared.

That a person holding what is called the Necessitarian doctrine should on that account *feel* that it would be unjust to punish him for his wrong actions, seems to me the veriest of chimeras. Yes, if he really "could not help" acting as he did, that is, if *b*it did not depend on his will*b*; if he was under physical constraint, or *c*even if he was*c* under the action of such a violent motive that no fear of punishment could have any effect; which, if capable of being ascertained, is a just ground of exemption, and is the reason why by the laws of most countries people are not punished for what they were compelled to do by immediate danger of death. But if the criminal was in a state capable of being operated upon by the fear of punishment, no metaphysical objection, I believe, will make him feel his punishment unjust. Neither will he feel that because his act was the consequence of motives, operating upon a certain mental disposition, it was not his own fault. For, first, it was at all events his own defect or infirmity, for which the expectation of punishment is the appropriate cure. And secondly, the word fault, so far from being inapplicable, is the specific name for the kind of defect or infirmity which he has displayed—insufficient love of *d*good*d* and aversion to *e*evil*e*. The weakness of these feelings or their strength is in every one's mind the standard of fault or merit, of degrees of fault and degrees of merit. Whether we are judging of particular actions, or of the character of a person, we are wholly guided by the indications afforded of the energy of these influences. If the desire of right and aversion to wrong have yielded to a small temptation, we judge them to be weak, and our disapprobation is strong. If the temptation to which they have yielded is so great that even strong feelings of virtue might have succumbed to it, our moral reprobation

---

Lectures, Vol. III, p. 47.
[*For the image, see William Shakespeare, *Twelfth Night*, II, iii, 115–16.]

*b-b*65[1], 65[2]   his *will* could not have helped it
c-c+67, 72
*d-d*65[1], 65[2]   right
*e-e*65[1], 65[2]   wrong

is less intense. If, again, the moral desires and aversions have prevailed, but not over a very strong force, we hold that the action was good, but that there was little merit in it; and our estimate of the merit rises, in exact proportion to the greatness of the obstacle which the moral feeling proved strong enough to overcome.

Mr. Mansel* has furnished what he thinks a refutation of the Necessitarian argument, of which it is *f* well to take notice, the more so, perhaps, as it is directed against some remarks on the subject by the present writer in a former work:† remarks which were not intended as an argument for so-called Necessity, but only to place the nature and meaning of that ill-understood doctrine in a truer light. With this purpose in view, it was remarked that "by saying that a man's actions necessarily follow from his character, all that is really meant (for no more is meant in any case whatever of causation) is that he invariably does act in conformity to his character, and that any one who thoroughly knew his character, could certainly predict how he would act in any supposable case. No more than this is contended for by any one but an Asiatic fatalist."[*] "And no more than this," observes Mr. Mansel, "is needed to construct a system of fatalism as rigid as any Asiatic can desire."[†]

Mr. Mansel is mistaken in thinking that the doctrine of the causation of human actions is fatalism at all, or resembles fatalism in any of its moral or intellectual effects. To call it by that name is to break down a fundamental distinction. Real fatalism is of two kinds. Pure, or Asiatic fatalism,—the fatalism of the Œdipus,[‡]—holds that our actions do not depend upon our desires. Whatever our wishes may be, a superior power, or an abstract destiny, will overrule them, and compel us to act, not as we desire, but in the manner predestined. Our love of good and hatred of evil are of no efficacy, and though in themselves they may be virtuous, as far as conduct is concerned it is unavailing to cultivate them. The other kind, Modified Fatalism I will call it, holds that our actions are determined by our will, our will by our desires, and our desires by the joint influence of the motives presented to us and of our individual character; but that, our character having been made for us and not by us, we are not responsible for it, nor for the actions it leads to, and should in vain attempt to alter them. The true

*Prolegomena Logica, Note C at the end [pp. 298–305].

†System of Logic, Bk. VI, Chap. ii. [Collected Works, Vol. VIII, pp. 836ff.]

[*Quoted by Mansel, Prolegomena Logica, pp. 298–9, from Logic, Bk. III, Chap. v, §8 (§7 in the 2nd ed., from which Mansel quotes), Collected Works, Vol. VII, p. 347n.]

[†Prolegomena Logica, p. 299.]

[‡See Sophocles, Œdipus the King, Œdipus at Colonus.]

*f*65¹, 65² as

doctrine of the Causation of human actions maintains, in opposition to both, that not only our conduct, but our character, is in part amenable to our will; that we can, by employing the proper means, improve our character; and that if our character is such that while it remains what it is, it necessitates us to do wrong, it will be just to apply motives which will necessitate us to strive for its improvement, and so emancipate ourselves from the other necessity[g]. In[g] other words, we are under a moral obligation to seek the improvement of our moral character. We shall not indeed do so unless we desire our improvement, and desire it more than we dislike the means which must be employed for the purpose. But does Mr. Mansel, or any other of the free-will philosophers, think that we can will the means if we do not desire the end, or if our desire of the end is weaker than our aversion to the means?*

*[67] This vital truth in moral psychology, that we can improve our character if we will, is a great stumbling block both to the "Inquirer" and to Mr. Alexander. They maintain that this fact makes no difference at all, and that the Causation of human actions is exactly the same thing with Modified Fatalism. That the "Inquirer" cannot see any difference, excites no surprise, since he professes himself unable to understand "how our conduct is amenable to our will if it is wholly caused by our character and circumstances." (P. 46n.) Is not the very doctrine he is contending against, that our character and circumstances cause it *through* our will? Both he and Mr. Alexander protest vehemently, and Mr. Alexander at much length, that the Causation doctrine is as incompatible with Free will as Fatalism is. [See Phillipps, pp. 46–7, and Alexander, pp. 100–18.] As if anybody had denied that. In the very next paragraph, when arguing against Kant, I expressly affirmed it. But, if it is not too much to ask, let them try to put their own opinion in abeyance, and condescend for a few moments to look at the question from mine. Suppose (I have as much right to make the supposition as they have) that a person dislikes some part of his own character, and would be glad to change it. He cannot, as he well knows, change it by a mere act of volition. He must use the means which nature gives to ourselves, as she gave to our parents and teachers, of influencing our character by appropriate circumstances. If he is a Modified Fatalist, he will not use those means, for he will not believe in their efficacy; but will remain passively discontented with himself, or what is worse, will learn to be contented, thinking that his character has been made for him, and that he cannot make it over again, however willing. If, on the contrary, he is a Moral Causationist, he will know that the work is not finally and irrevocably done; that the improvement of his character is still possible by the proper means, the only needful condition being that he should desire, what by the supposition he does desire: consequently if the desire is stronger than the means are disagreeable, he will set about doing that which, if done, will improve his character. I cannot suppose my critics capable of maintaining that such a difference as this, between the two theories, is of no practical importance; and I must, with all courtesy, decline to recognise as entitled to any voice in the question, whoever is not able to seize a distinction so broad and obvious.

Mr. Alexander's curious dictum that a motive is itself an act, can only have a true meaning, or any meaning at all, if understood of this indirect influence of our

[g]–[g]65[1], 65[2]   necessity: in

Mr. Mansel is more rigid in his ideas of what the free-will theory requires, than one of the most eminent of the thinkers who have adopted it. According to Mr. Mansel, the belief that whoever knew perfectly our character and our circumstances could predict our actions, amounts to Asiatic fatalism.[*] According to Kant, in his *Metaphysics of Ethics*, such capability of prediction is quite compatible with the freedom of the will.[†] This seems, at first sight, to be an admission of everything which the rational supporters of the opposite theory could desire. But Kant avoids this consequence, by changing (as lawyers would say) the *venue* of free-will, from our actions generally, to the formation of our character. It is in that, he thinks, we are free, and he is almost willing to admit that while our character is what it is, our actions are necessitated by it. In drawing this distinction, the philosopher of Königsberg saves inconvenient facts at the expense of the consistency of his theory. There cannot be one theory for one kind of voluntary actions, and another theory for the other kinds. When we voluntarily exert ourselves, as it is our duty to do, for the improvement of our character, or when we act in a manner which (either consciously on our part or unconsciously) deteriorates it, these, like all other voluntary acts, presuppose that there was already something in our character, or in that combined with our circumstances, which led us to do so, and accounts for our doing so. The person, therefore, who is supposed able to predict our actions from our character as it now is, would, under the same conditions of perfect knowledge, be equally able to predict what we should do to change our character: and if this be the meaning of necessity, that part of our conduct is as necessary as all the rest. If necessity means more than this abstract possibility of being foreseen; if it means any mysterious compulsion, apart from simple invariability of sequence, I deny it as strenuously as any one *h*in the case of human volitions, but I deny it just as much of all other phænomena*h*. To enforce this distinction was the principal object of the remarks which Mr. Mansel has criticised.[‡] If an unessential distinction from Mr. Mansel's point of view, it is essential from mine, and of supreme importance in a practical aspect.

The free-will metaphysicians have made little endeavour to prove that

---

voluntary acts over our mental dispositions. (Pp. 18–20.) That a person can, by an act of will, either give to himself, or take away from himself, a desire or an aversion, I suppose even Mr. Alexander will hardly affirm: but we can, by a course of self-culture, finally modify, to a greater or less extent, our desires and aversions; which is the doctrine of Moral Causation, as distinguished from Modified Fatalism.

[**Prolegomena Logica*, p. 303.]

[†See *Metaphysik der Sitten*, in *Werke*, Vol. IX, pp. 21–30.]

[‡*Prolegomena Logica*, pp. 299–300.]

h-h+67, 72

we can will in opposition to our strongest desire, but have strenuously maintained that we can will when we have no strongest desire. With this view Dr. Reid formerly, and Mr. Mansel now, have thrown in the teeth of Necessitarians the famous *asinus Buridani*.[*] If, say they, the will were solely determined by motives, the ass, between two bundles of hay, exactly alike, and equally distant from him, would remain undecided until he died of hunger. From Sir W. Hamilton's notes on this chapter of Reid,* I infer that he did not countenance this argument; and it is surprising that writers of talent should have seen anything in it. I wave the objection that if it applies at all, it proves that the ass also has free-will; for perhaps he has. But the ass, it is affirmed, would starve before he decided. Yes, possibly, if he remained all the time in a fixed attitude of deliberation; if he never for an instant ceased to balance one against another the rival attractions, and if they really were so exactly equal that no dwelling on them could detect any difference. But this is not the way in which things take place on our planet. From mere lassitude, if from no other cause, he would intermit the process, and cease thinking of the rival objects at all: until a moment arrived when he would be seeing or thinking of one only, and that fact, combined with the sensation of hunger, would determine him to a decision.

But the argument on which Mr. Mansel lays most stress (it is also one of Reid's)[†] is the following. Necessitarians say that the will is governed by the strongest motive: "but I only know the strength of motives in relation to the will by the test of ultimate prevalence; so that this means no more than that the prevailing motive prevails."[‡] I have heretofore complimented Mr. Mansel on seeing farther, in some things, than his master. In the present instance I am compelled to remark, that he has not seen so far. Sir W. Hamilton was not the man to neglect an argument like this, had there been no flaw in it. The fact is that there are two. First, those who say that the will follows the strongest motive, do not mean the motive which is strongest in relation to the will, or in other words, that the will follows what it does follow. They mean the motive which is strongest in relation to pain and pleasure; since a motive, being a desire or aversion, is proportional to the pleasantness, as conceived by us, of the thing desired, or the painfulness of the thing shunned. And when what was at first a direct impulse towards pleasure, or recoil from pain, has passed into a habit or a fixed purpose, then the strength of the motive means the completeness and promptitude of the association which has been formed between an idea and an outward act.

[*See Reid, *Essays on the Active Powers*, *Works*, p. 609; Mansel, *Prolegomena Logica*, p. 301.]
*Pp. 609n–11n.
[†See *Essays on the Active Powers*, *Works*, pp. 599–636.]
[‡*Prolegomena Logica*, p. 302.]

This is the first answer to Mr. Mansel. The second is, that even supposing there were no test of the strength of motives but their effect on the will, the proposition that the will follows the strongest motive would not, as Mr. Mansel supposes, be identical and unmeaning.[*] We say, without absurdity, that if two weights are placed in opposite scales, the heavier will lift the other up; yet we mean nothing by the heavier, except the weight which will lift up the other. The proposition, nevertheless, is not unmeaning, for it signifies that in many or most cases there *is* a heavier, and that this is always the same one, not one or the other as it may happen. In like manner, even if the strongest motive meant only the motive which prevails, yet if there is a prevailing motive—if, all other antecedents being the same, the motive which prevails to-day will prevail to-morrow and every subsequent day— Sir W. Hamilton was acute enough to see that the free-will theory is not saved. I regret that I cannot, in this instance, credit Mr. Mansel with the same acuteness.

Before leaving the subject, it is worth while to remark, that not only the doctrine of Necessity, but Predestination in its coarsest form—the belief that all our actions are divinely preordained—though, in my view, inconsistent with ascribing any moral attributes whatever to the Deity, yet if combined with the belief that God works according to general laws, which have to be learnt from experience, has no tendency to make us act in any respect otherwise than we should do if we thought our actions really contingent. For if God acts according to general laws, then, whatever he may have preordained, he has preordained that it shall take place through the causes on which experience shows it to be consequent: and if he has predestined that I shall attain my ends, he has predestined that I shall do so by studying and putting in practice the means which lead to their attainment. When the belief in predestination has a paralysing effect on conduct, as is sometimes the case with Mahomedans, it is because they fancy they can infer what God has predestined, without waiting for the result. They think that either by particular signs of some sort, or from the general aspect of things, they can perceive the issue towards which God is working, and having discovered this, naturally deem useless any attempt to defeat it. Because something will certainly happen if nothing is done to prevent it, they think it will certainly happen whatever may be done to prevent it; in a word, they believe in Necessity in the only proper meaning of the term—an issue unalterable by human efforts or desires.

[*Ibid., pp. 302–3.]

CHAPTER XXVII

Sir William Hamilton's Opinions on the Study of Mathematics

NO ACCOUNT of Sir W. Hamilton's philosophy could be complete, which omitted to notice his famous attack on the tendency of mathematical studies:[*] for though there is no direct connexion between this and his metaphysical opinions, it affords the most express evidence we have of those fatal *lacunæ* in the circle of his knowledge, which unfitted him for taking a comprehensive or even an accurate view of the processes of the human mind in the establishment of truth. If there is any pre-requisite which all must see to be indispensable in one who attempts to give laws to human intellect, it is a thorough acquaintance with the modes by which human intellect has proceeded, in the cases where, by universal acknowledgment, grounded on subsequent direct verification, it has succeeded in ascertaining the greatest number of important and recondite truths. This requisite Sir W. Hamilton had not, in any tolerable degree, fulfilled. Even of pure mathematics he apparently knew little but the rudiments. Of mathematics as applied to investigating the laws of physical nature; of the mode in which the properties of number, extension, and figure, are made instrumental to the ascertainment of truths other than arithmetical or geometrical—it is too much to say that he had even a superficial knowledge: there is not a line in his works which shows him to have had any knowledge at all. He had no conception of what the process is. In this he differed greatly and disadvantageously from his immediate predecessor in the same school of metaphysical thought, Professor Dugald Stewart; whose works derive a great part of their value from the foundation of sound and accurate scientific knowledge laid by his mathematical and physical studies, and which his subsequent metaphysical pursuits enabled him, quite successfully to the length of his tether, to clarify and reduce to principles.

If Sir W. Hamilton had contented himself with saying of mathematics, that it is not, of itself alone, a sufficient education of the intellectual

[*"Study of Mathematics—University of Cambridge," *Edinburgh Review*, LXII (Jan., 1836), 409–55; reprinted in *Discussions*, pp. 263–325.]

faculties; that it cultivates the mind only partially; that there are important kinds of intellectual cultivation and discipline which it does not give, and to which, therefore, if pursued to the exclusion of the studies which do give them, it is unfavourable; he would have said something, not new indeed, but true, not of mathematics alone, but of every limited and special employment of the mental faculties; of every study in which the human mind can engage, except the two or three highest, most difficult, and most imperfect, which, requiring all the faculties in their greatest attainable perfection, can never be recommended or thought of as preparatory discipline, but are themselves the chief purpose for which such preparation is required. Sir W. Hamilton, however, has asserted much more than this. He undertakes to show that the study of mathematics is not an useful intellectual discipline at all, except in one comparatively humble particular, which it has in common with some of the most despised pursuits; and that, if prosecuted far, it positively unfits the mind for the useful employment of its faculties on any other object. As might be expected from an attempt to maintain such a thesis by one who, however acute on other matters, had no sufficient knowledge of the subject he was writing about, this celebrated dissertation is one of the weakest parts of his works. He ignores not only the whole of his adversary's case, but the most important part of his own; and has made a far less powerful attack on the tendencies of mathematical studies, than could easily be made by one who understood the subject. He has, in fact, missed the most considerable of the evil effects to the production of which those studies have contributed; and has thrown no light on the intellectual shortcomings of the common run of mathematicians, so signally displayed in their wretched treatment of the generalities of their own science. He finds hardly anything to say to their disadvantage but things so trite and obvious, that the greatest zealot for mathematics could afford to pass them by, insisting only on the inestimable benefits which are to be set against them, and which alone are really to the purpose; for it is no objection to a harrow that it is not a plough, nor to a saw that it is not a chisel.

For instance, are we much the wiser for being once more told, at great length, and with a cloud of witnesses[*] brought to back the assertion, that mathematics, being concerned only with demonstrative evidence, does not teach us, either by theory or practice, to estimate probabilities? Did any mathematician, or eulogist of mathematics, ever pretend that it did? Does the science to which Sir W. Hamilton assigns a place above all others as an intellectual discipline—does Metaphysics enable us to judge of probable evidence? If such a claim has ever been made in its behalf, I am not aware of it; Sir W. Hamilton, certainly, was too well acquainted with the subject to make any such pretension. Metaphysics, like Mathematics, and all the rest

[*See Hebrews, 12:1.]

of the fundamental sciences, demands, not probable, but certain evidence. The province of Probabilities in science is not the abstract, but what M. Comte terms the concrete sciences; those which treat of the combinations actually realized in Nature, as distinguished from the general laws which would equally govern any other combinations of the same elements: zoology and botany, for example, as contrasted with physiology; geology, as opposed to thermology and chemistry.[*] In an abstract science a probability is of no account; it is but a momentary halt on the road to certainty, and a hint for fresh experiments.

Inasmuch as abstract science in general, and mathematics in particular, afford no practice in the estimation of conflicting probabilities, which is the kind of sagacity most required in the conduct of practical affairs, it follows that, when made so exclusive an occupation as to prevent the mind from obtaining enough of this necessary practice in other ways, it does worse than not cultivate the faculty—it prevents it from being acquired, and *pro tanto* unfits the person for the general business of life. It is natural that people who are bad judges of probability, should be, according to their temperament, unduly credulous or unreasonably sceptical; both which charges our author, with great earnestness and a heavy artillery of authorities, drives home against the mathematicians. But he would have made little progress towards proving his case, even by a much more complete catalogue of the intellectual defects of a mathematician who is nothing but a mathematician. A person may be keenly alive to these, and may hate them, as M. Comte did, with a perfect hatred, while upholding mathematical instruction as not only an useful but the indispensable first stage of all scientific education worthy of the name.* Nor can any reasonable view of the subject refuse to recognise, in the very faults which our author imputes to mathematicians, the excesses of a most valuable quality. Let us be assured that for the formation of a well-trained intellect, it is no

[*See Auguste Comte, *Cours de philosophie positive*, Vol. I, pp. 57–9.]

*I do not know that the logical value of mathematics has ever been more finely and discriminatingly appreciated than by M. Comte in his latest work, *Synthèse subjective* ([Paris: Comte et Dalmont, 1856,] p. 98). "Bornée à son vrai domaine, la raison mathématique y peut admirablement remplir l'office universel de la saine logique: induire pour déduire, afin de construire. Renonçant à de vaines prétentions, elle sent que ses meilleurs succès restent toujours incapables de nous faire, partout ailleurs, induire, ou même déduire, et surtout construire. Elle se contente de fournir, dans le domaine le plus favorable, un type de clarté, de précision, et de consistance, dont la contemplation familière peut seule disposer l'esprit à rendre les autres conceptions aussi parfaites que le comporte leur nature. Sa réaction générale, plus négative que positive, doit surtout consister à nous inspirer partout une invincible répugnance pour le vague, l'incohérence, et l'obscurité, que nous pouvons réellement éviter envers des pensées quelconques, si nous y faisons assez d'efforts."

slight recommendation of a study, that it is the means by which the mind is earliest and most easily brought to maintain within itself a standard of complete proof. A mind thus furnished, and not duly instructed on other subjects, may commit the error of expecting in all proof too close an adherence to the type with which it is familiar. That type may and ought to be widened by greater variety of culture; but he who has never acquired it, has no just sense of the difference between what is proved and what is not proved: the first foundation of the scientific habit of mind has not been laid. It has long been a complaint against mathematicians that they are hard to convince: but it is a far greater disqualification both for philosophy, and for the affairs of life, to be too easily convinced; to have too low a standard of proof. The only sound intellects are those which, in the first instance, set their standard of proof high. Practice in concrete affairs soon teaches them to make the necessary abatement: but they retain the consciousness, without which there is no sound practical reasoning, that in accepting inferior evidence because there is none better to be had, they do not by that acceptance raise it to completeness. They remain aware of what is wanting to it.

Besides accustoming the student to demand complete proof, and to know when he has not obtained it, mathematical studies are of immense benefit to his education by habituating him to precision. It is one of the peculiar excellences of mathematical discipline, that the mathematician is never satisfied with an *à peu près*. He requires the *exact* truth. Hardly any of the non-mathematical sciences, except chemistry, has this advantage. One of the commonest modes of loose thought, and sources of error both in opinion and in practice, is to overlook the importance of quantities. Mathematicians and chemists are taught by the whole course of their studies, that the most fundamental differences of quality depend on some very slight difference in proportional quantity; and that from the qualities of the influencing elements, without careful attention to their quantities, false expectations would constantly be formed as to the very nature and essential character of the result produced. If Sir W. Hamilton's mind had undergone this improving discipline, we should not have found him employing the most precise mathematical terms with the laxity which is habitual in his writings. For instance; whenever he means that one of two things diminishes while another increases, he says that they are in the inverse ratio of one another. He affirms this of the Extension and Comprehension of a general notion;* of the number of objects among which our attention is divided, and the intensity with which it is applied to each;† of the knowledge-giving and the sensation-giving properties of an impression of

*See, among other passages, *Lectures*, Vol. III, pp. 146–7.
†*Ibid.*, Vol. I, p. 246.

sense;* and of the intensity and the prolongation of an energy.† That an inverse ratio is the name of a definite relation between quantities, seems never to have occurred to him.

Neither is it a small advantage of mathematical studies, even in their poorest and most meagre form, that they at least habituate the mind to resolve a train of reasoning into steps, and make sure of each step before advancing to another. If the practice of mathematical reasoning gives nothing else, it gives wariness of mind; it accustoms us to demand a sure footing; and though it leaves us no better judges of ultimate premises than it found us (which is no more than may be said of almost all metaphysics) at least it does not suffer us to let in, at any of the joints in the reasoning, any assumption which we have not previously faced in the shape of an axiom, postulate, or definition. This is a merit which it has in common with Formal Logic, and is the chief ground on which some have thought that it could perform the functions and supply the place of that science; an opinion in which I by no means agree.

That mathematics "do not cultivate the power of generalization,"‡ which to our author appears so obvious a truth that he need not give himself the trouble of proving it, will be admitted by no person of competent knowledge, except in a very qualified sense. The generalizations of mathematics, are, no doubt, a different thing from the generalizations of physical science; but in the difficulty of seizing them, and the mental tension they require, they are no contemptible preparation for the most arduous efforts of the scientific mind. Even the fundamental notions of the higher mathematics, from those of the differential calculus upwards, are products of a very high abstraction. Merely to master the idea of centrifugal force, or of the centre of gravity, are efforts of mental analysis surpassed by few in our author's metaphysics. To perceive the mathematical law common to the results of many mathematical operations, even in so simple a case as that of the binomial theorem, involves a vigorous exercise of the same faculty which gave us Kepler's laws, and rose through those laws to the theory of universal gravitation. Every process of what has been called Universal Geometry—that great creation of Descartes and his successors, in which a single train of reasoning solves whole classes of problems at once, and demonstrates properties common to all curves or surfaces, and others common to large groups of them—is a practical lesson in the management of wide generalizations, and abstraction of the points of agreement from those of difference among objects of great and confusing diversity, to which the most purely inductive science cannot furnish many superior. Even so

*Ibid., Vol. II, p. 98.
†Ibid., p. 439.
‡Discussions, p. 282.

elementary an operation as that of abstracting from the particular con-figuration of the triangles or other figures, and the relative situation of the particular lines or points, in the diagram which aids the apprehension of a common geometrical demonstration, is a very useful, and far from being always an easy, exercise of the faculty of generalization so strangely imagined to have no place or part in the processes of mathematics.

Sir W. Hamilton allows no efficacy to mathematical studies in the culti-vation of any valuable intellectual habit, except the single one of continu-ous attention. "Are mathematics then," he asks,

of no value as an instrument of mental culture? Nay, do they exercise only to distort the mind? To this we answer: That their study, if pursued in moderation and efficiently counteracted, may be beneficial in the correction of a certain vice, and in the formation of its corresponding virtue. The vice is the habit of mental distraction; the virtue the habit of continuous attention. This is the single benefit, to which the study of mathematics can justly pretend, in the cultivation of the mind.*

He adds, truly enough, "But mathematics are not the only study which cultivates the attention: neither is the kind and degree of attention which they tend to induce, the kind and degree of attention which our other and higher speculations require and exercise."† So that, according to him, there is no purpose answered by mathematics in general education, but one which would be better fulfilled by something else.

Without stopping to express my amazement at the assertion that the student of mathematics exercises no mental faculty but that of continuous attention, I will avail myself of an admission which Sir W. Hamilton cannot help making, but the full force of which he does not perceive. "We are far," he says, "from meaning hereby to disparage the mathematical genius which *invents* new methods and formulæ, or new and felicitous applications of the old. . . . Unlike their divergent studies, the inventive talents of the mathematician and philosopher in fact approximate."‡ Was, then, Sir W. Hamilton so ill-acquainted with everything deserving the name of mathematical tuition as to suppose that the inventive powers which, in their higher degree, constitute mathematical genius, are not called forth and fostered in the process of teaching mathematics to the merest tyro? What sort of mathematical instruction is it of which solving problems forms no part? We come, within a page afterwards, to the following almost incredible announcement: "Mathematical demonstration is solely occupied in deduc-ing conclusions; probable reasoning, principally concerned in looking out for premises."§ Sir W. Hamilton thinks he can never be severe enough

*Ibid., pp. 313–14.
†Ibid., p. 322.
‡Ibid., p. 290.
§Ibid., p. 291.

upon Cambridge for laying any stress on mathematics as an instrument of mental instruction. Did he ever turn over, I do not say a volume of Cambridge Problems,[*] for these, it may be said, test the knowledge of the pupil rather than his inventive powers, and may be an exercise chiefly of memory: but did he ever see two such volumes as Bland's Algebraical and Geometrical Problems?[†] Did he really imagine that working these was not "looking out for premises?" He seems actually to have thought that learning mathematics meant cramming it; and apparently believed that a mathematical tutor resolves all the equations himself, and merely asks his pupil to follow the solutions. For in every problem which the pupil himself solves, or theorem which he demonstrates, not having previously seen it solved or demonstrated, the same faculties are exercised which, in their higher degrees, produced the greatest discoveries in geometry. Mathematical teaching, therefore, even as now carried on, trains the mind to capacities, which, by our author's admission, are of the closest kin to those of the greatest metaphysician and philosopher. There is some colour of truth for the opposite doctrine in the case of elementary algebra. The resolution of a common equation can be reduced to almost as mechanical a process as the working of a sum in arithmetic. The reduction of the question to an equation, however, is no mechanical operation, but one which, according to the degree of its difficulty, requires nearly every possible grade of ingenuity: not to speak of the new, and in the present state of science insoluble, equations, which start up at every fresh step attempted in the application of mathematics to other branches of knowledge. On all this, Sir W. Hamilton never bestows a thought. It is hardly necessary to point out that any other study, pursued in the manner in which he supposes mathematics to be, would as little exercise any other faculty than that of "continuous attention" as mathematics would. Next to metaphysics, the study he most patronizes is that of languages; of which he has so lofty an opinion, as to say that "to master, for example, the *Minerva* of Sanctius with its commentators, is, I conceive, a far more profitable exercise of mind than to conquer the *Principia* of Newton:"* we may at least say that he was a better judge of the profit that might be derived from it. I, also, rate very

[*See, e.g., *Cambridge Problems, Being a collection of the printed questions proposed to the candidates for the degree of Bachelor of Arts, 1801–1820* (London: Black and Armstrong, 1836).]

[†Miles Bland, *Algebraical Problems* (Cambridge: Nicholson, 1812), and *Geometrical Problems* (Cambridge: Nicholson, 1819).]

Discussions, p. 268n. [The references are to Francisco Sanchez, *Minerva, sive De Causis Latinæ Linguæ Commentarius*, by Caspar Schoppe and Jacobus Perizonius (Franeker: Strickius, 1687), and to Isaac Newton, *Philosophiæ Naturalis Principia Mathematica*, in *Opera*, ed. Samuel Horsley, 5 vols. (London: Nichols, 1779–85), Vols. II–III.]

highly the value, as a discipline to the mind, of the thorough grammatical study of any of the more logically constructed languages: but if the study consisted in learning the *Minerva* of Sanctius, or its commentators either, by rote, I believe the benefit derived would be about the same with that which Sir W. Hamilton considered to result from the exercise of "continuous attention" in mathematics.

It is a characteristic fact, that when the paper "on the Study of Mathematics" originally appeared as an article in the *Edinburgh Review*, no mention was made in it of Mixed or Applied Mathematics: the little which now appears on that subject being a subsequent addition, called forth by Dr. Whewell's reply.[*] Dr. Whewell must have looked down from a considerable height upon an assault on the utility of Mathematics, in which the part of it that, in the opinion of its rational defenders, constitutes three-fourths of its utility, was silently overlooked. When Sir W. Hamilton's attention was called to what he had previously omitted to think of, this is the way in which he disposes of it:

Mathematics can be applied to objects of experience only in so far as these are measurable; that is, in so far as they come, or are supposed to come, under the categories of extension and number. Applied mathematics are, therefore, equally limited and equally unimproving as pure. The sciences, indeed, with which mathematics are thus associated, may afford a more profitable exercise of mind; but this is only in so far as they supply the matter of observation, and of probable reasoning, and therefore *before* this matter is hypothetically subjected to mathematical demonstration or calculus.*

This passage amounts to proof that the writer simply did not know what applied mathematics mean. The words are those of a person who had heard that there was such a thing, but knew absolutely nothing about what it was.

Applied mathematics is not the measurement of extension and number. It is the measurement *by means* of extension and number, of other quantities which extension and number are marks of; and the ascertainment by means of quantities of all sorts, of those qualities of things which quantities are marks of.

For the information of readers who are no better informed than Sir W. Hamilton, and the reminding of those who are, I will illustrate this general statement by bringing it down to particulars; which a person, himself of

[*Hamilton's "On the Study of Mathematics" (a review in the *Edinburgh Review* of William Whewell's *Thoughts on the Study of Mathematics as a Part of a Liberal Education* [Cambridge: Deighton, 1835]) was reprinted in his *Discussions* (pp. 263–325) with Whewell's reply, "To the Editor of the *Edinburgh Review*," LXIII [April, 1836], 270–2, and the editorial note from the *Edinburgh* (*Discussions*, pp. 326–8), and Hamilton's "Notes to the Above Letter" (again from the *Edinburgh*, *ibid.*, 272–5; in *Discussions*, pp. 329–40).]
Discussions, pp. 334–5.

very slender mathematical acquirements, can do, provided he has studied the science as every philosophical student ought to study it, but as Sir W. Hamilton has not done, with especial reference to its Methods.

The first, and typical example of the application of mathematics to the indirect investigation of truth, is within the limits of the pure science itself; the application of algebra to geometry; the introduction of which, far more than any of his metaphysical speculations, has immortalized the name of Descartes, and constitutes the greatest single step ever made in the progress of the exact sciences. Its rationale is simple. It is grounded on the general truth, that the position of every point, the direction of every line, and consequently the shape and magnitude of every enclosed space, may be fixed by the length of perpendiculars thrown down upon two [a]straight lines[a], or (when the third dimension of space is taken into account) upon three [b]plane surfaces[b], meeting one another at right angles in the same point. A consequence, or rather a part, of this general truth, is that curve lines and surfaces may be determined by their *equations*. If from any number of points in a curve line or surface, perpendiculars are drawn to two [c]rectangular axes, or to three rectangular planes[c], there exists between the lengths of these perpendiculars a relation of quantity, which is always the same for the same curve, or surface, and is expressed by an equation in which these variable are combined with certain constant quantities. From this relation, every other property of the curve or surface may always be deduced. In this way, numbers become the means of ascertaining truths not numerical. The periphery of an ellipse is not a number; but a certain numerical relation between straight lines is a mark of an ellipse, being proved to be an inseparable accompaniment of it. The equation which expresses this characteristic mark of any curve, may be handed over to algebraists, to deduce from it, through the properties of numbers, any other numerical relation which depends on it; with the certainty that when the conclusion is translated back again from symbols into words, it will come out a real, and perhaps previously unknown, geometrical property of the curve.

In such an example as this, the application of algebra to geometry appears only in its most elementary form; but its extent is indefinite, and its flights almost beyond the reach of measurement. Its general scheme may be thus stated: In order to resolve any question, either of quality or quantity, concerning a line or space, find something whose magnitude, if known, would give the solution required, and which stands in some known relation to the rectangular co-ordinates (for instance, in the problem of Tangents,

---

[a]-[a] +67, 72
[b]-[b] 65^1, 65^2 , straight lines
[c]-[c] 65^1, 65^2 (or three) rectangular axes

the length of the subtangent). Express this known relation in an equation: if the equation can be resolved, we have solved the geometrical problem. Or if the question be the converse one—not what are the properties of a given line or space, but what line or space is indicated by a given property; find what relation between rectangular co-ordinates that property requires: express it in an equation, and this equation, or some other deducible from it, will be the equation of the curve or surface sought. If it be a known curve or surface, this process will point it out; if not, we shall have obtained the necessary starting point for its study.

This application of one branch of mathematics to another branch, ranks as the first step in Applied Mathematics. The second is the application to Mechanics. The object-matter of Mechanics is the general laws, or theory, of Force in the abstract, that is, of forces, considered independently of their origin. As an extension is not a number, though a numerical fact may be a mark of an extension; so a force is neither a number nor an extension. But a force is only cognisable through its effects, and the effects by which forces are best known are effects in extension. The measure of a force, is the space through which it will carry a body of given magnitude in a given time. Quantities of force are thus ascertained, through marks which are quantities of extension. The other properties of forces are, their direction (a question of extension, which has already been reduced to a numerical relation between co-ordinates), and the nature of the motion which they generate, either singly or in combination; which is a mixed question of direction and of magnitude in extension. All questions of Force, therefore, can be reduced to questions of direction and of magnitude: and as all questions of direction or magnitude are capable of being reduced to equations between numbers, every question which can be raised respecting Force abstractedly from its origin, can be resolved if the corresponding algebraical equation can.

While the laws of Number thus underlie the laws of Extension, and these two underlie the laws of Force, so do the laws of Force underlie all the other laws of the material universe. Nature, as it falls within our ken, is composed of a multitude of forces, of which the origin (at least the immediate origin) is different, and the effects of which on our senses are extremely various. But all these forces agree in producing motions in space; and even those of their effects which are not actual motions, nevertheless travel; are propagated through spaces, in determinate times: they are all, therefore, amenable to, and conform to, the laws of extension and number. Often, indeed, we have no means of measuring these spaces and times; nor, if we could, are the resources of mathematics sufficient to enable us, in cases of great complexity, to arrive at the quantities of things we cannot directly measure, through those which we can. Fortunately, however, we can do this, sufficiently for all practical purposes, in the case of the great cosmic forces, gravitation and light, and to a less but still a considerable extent, heat and electricity. And here the domain of Applied Mathematics, for the present, ends. To it we are indebted, not only for all we know of the laws of these great and universal agencies, considered as connected bodies of truth, but also for the one complete type and model of the investigation of Nature by deductive reasoning; the ascertainment of the special laws of nature by means of the general. I will not offer to the understanding of any one who knows what this operation is, the affront of asking him if it is all performed "before" the matter is "hypothetically subjected to mathematical demonstration or calculus."[*]

In being the great instrument of Deductive investigation, applied mathematics comes to be also the source of our principal inductions, which invariably depend on previous deductions. For where the inaccessibility or unmanageableness of the phænomena precludes the necessary experiments, mathematical deduction often supplies their place, by making us acquainted with points of resemblance which could not have been reached by direct observation. Phænomena apparently very remote from one another, are found, in the mode of their accomplishment, to follow the same or very similar numerical laws; and the mind, grasping up seemingly heterogeneous natural agencies which have the same equation, and classing them together, often lays a ground for the recognition of them as having either a common, or an analogous, origin. What were previously thought to be distinct powers in Nature, are identified with each other, by ascertaining that they produce similar effects according to the same mathematical laws. It was thus that the force which governs the planetary motions was shown to be identical with that by which bodies fall to the ground. Sir W. Hamilton would probably have admitted that the original discovery of this truth required as great a reach of intellect as has ever yet been displayed in abstract speculation. But is no exercise of intellect needed to apprehend the proof? Is it like an experiment in chemistry or an observation in anatomy, which may require mind for its origination, but to recognise which, when once made, requires only eyesight? Is "continuous attention"[†] the only mental capacity required here? [d]To think so would require an ignorance of the subject[d] greater than can be imputed to any educated mind, not to speak of a philosopher.

In the achievements which still remain to be effected in the way of scientific generalization, it is not probable that the direct employment of

[*Discussions, p. 335; cf. p. 477 above.]
[†Ibid., p. 314; cf. p. 475 above.]

[d-d]651, 652   If Sir W. Hamilton could think so, his ignorance of the subject must have been

mathematics will be to any great extent available: the nature of the phænomena precludes such an employment for a long time to come—perhaps for ever. But the process itself—the deductive investigation of Nature; the application of elementary laws, generalized from the more simple cases, to disentangle the phænomena of complex cases—explaining as much of them as can be so explained, and putting in evidence the nature and limits of the irreducible residuum, so as to suggest fresh observations preparatory to recommencing the same process with additional data: *this* is common to all science, moral and metaphysical included; and the greater the difficulty, the more needful is it that the enquirer should come prepared with an exact understanding of the requisites of this mode of investigation, and a mental type of its perfect realization. In the great problems of physical generalization now occupying the higher scientific minds, chemistry seems destined to an important and conspicuous participation, by supplying, as mathematics did in the cosmic phænomena, many of the premises of the deduction, as well as part of the preparatory discipline. But this use of chemistry is as yet only in its dawn; while, as a training in the deductive art, its utmost capacity can never approach to that of mathematics: and in the great enquiries of the moral and social sciences, to which neither of the two is directly applicable, mathematics (I always mean Applied Mathematics) affords the only sufficiently perfect type. Up to this time, I may venture to say that no one ever knew what deduction is, as a means of investigating the laws of nature, who had not learnt it from mathematics; nor can any one hope to understand it thoroughly, who has not, at some time of his life, known enough of mathematics to be familiar with the instrument at work. Had Sir W. Hamilton been so, he would probably have cancelled the two volumes of his Lectures on Logic, and begun again on a different system, in which we should have heard less about Concepts and more about Things, less about Forms of Thought, and more about grounds of Knowledge.

Nor is even this the whole of what the enquirer loses, who knows not scientific Deduction in this its most perfect form. To have an inadequate conception of one of the two instruments by which we acquire our knowledge of nature, and consequently an imperfect comprehension even of the other in its higher forms, is not all. He is almost necessarily without any sufficient conception of human knowledge itself as an organic whole. He can have no clear perception of science as a system of truths flowing out of, and confirming and corroborating, one another; in which one truth sums up a multitude of others, and explains them, special truths being merely general ones modified by specialities of circumstance. He can but imperfectly understand the absorption of concrete truths into abstract, and the additional certainty given to theorems drawn from specific experience, when they can be affiliated as corollaries on general laws of nature—a certainty more entire than any direct observation can give. Neither, therefore, can he perceive how the larger inductions reflect an increase of certainty even upon those narrower ones from which they were themselves generalized, by reconciling superficial inconsistencies, and converting apparent exceptions into real confirmations.* To see these things requires more than a mere mathematician; but the ablest mind which has never gone through a course of mathematics has small chance of ever perceiving them.

In the face of such considerations, it is a very small achievement to fill thirty octavo pages with the ill-natured things which persons of the most miscellaneous character, through a series of ages, have said about mathematicians, from a sneer of the Cynic Diogenes to a sarcasm of Gibbon, or a colloquial platitude of Horace Walpole; without any discrimination as to how many of the persons quoted were entitled to any opinion at all on such a subject; and with such entire disregard of all that gives weight to authority, as to include men who lived and died before algebra was invented, before the conic sections had been defined and studied by the mathematicians of Alexandria, or the first lines of the theory of statics had been traced by the genius of Archimedes; men whose whole mathematical knowledge consisted of a clumsy arithmetic, and the mere elements of geometry.[*] Had there been twenty times as many of these testimonies, what proportion of them would have been of any value? Until quite recently, the professors of the different arts and sciences have made it a considerable part of their occupation to cry down one another's pursuits; and men of the world and *littérateurs* have been, in all ages, ready and eager to join with every set of them against the rest: the man who dares to know what they neither know nor care for, and to value himself on the knowledge, having always and everywhere been regarded as the common enemy. Did Sir W. Hamilton suppose that a person of half his reading

*Ignorance of this important principle of the logic of induction, or want of familiarity with it, continually leads to gross misapplications, even by able writers, of the logic of ratiocination. For instance, we are constantly told that the uniformity of the course of nature cannot be itself an induction, since every inductive reasoning assumes it, and the premise must have been known before the conclusion. Those who argue in this manner can never have directed their attention to the continual process of giving and taking, in respect of certainty, which reciprocally goes on between this great premise and all the narrower truths of experience; the effect of which is, that, though originally a generalization from the more obvious of the narrower truths, it ends by having a fulness of certainty which overflows upon these, and raises the proof of them to a higher level; so that its relation to them is reversed, and instead of an inference from them, it becomes a principle from which any one of them may be *deduced*.

[*See "Study of Mathematics," *passim*.]

*-*65[1], 65[2]   inferred

would have any difficulty in furnishing, at a few hours' notice, an equally long list of amenities on the subject of grammarians or of metaphysicians? When our author does get hold of a witness who has a claim to a hearing, the witness is pressed into the service without any sifting of what he really says; it makes no difference whether he asserts that the study of mathematics does harm, or only that it does not simply suffice for all possible good. One of the authorities on whom most stress is laid is that of Descartes. I extract the important part of the quotation as our author gives it, partly from Descartes himself and partly from Baillet, his biographer. The Italics are Sir W. Hamilton's.

"It was now a long time, [says Baillet,] since he had been convinced of the *small utility* of the *mathematics*, especially when studied on their own account, and not applied to other things. There was nothing, in truth, which appeared to him *more futile* than to occupy ourselves with simple numbers and imaginary figures, as if it were proper to confine ourselves to these *trifles* (bagatelles) without carrying our view beyond. There even seemed to him in this something *worse than useless*. His maxim was, that *such application insensibly disaccustomed us to the use of our reason*, and made us run the danger of losing the path which it traces."[*] The words themselves of Descartes deserve quotation: "Revera nihil *inanius* est, quam circa nudos numeros figurasque imaginarias ita versari, ut velle videamur in talium *nugarum* cognitione conquiescere, atque superficiariis istis demonstrationibus, quæ casu sæpius quam arte inveniuntur, et magis ad oculos et *imaginationem* pertinent, quam ad intellectum, sic incubare, ut quodammodo *ipsa ratione uti desuescamus*; simulque nihil intricatius, quam tali probandi modo, novas difficultates confusis numeris involutas expedire. . . ."[†] Baillet goes on: "In a letter to Mersenne, written in 1630, M. Descartes recalled to him that *he had renounced the study of mathematics for many years: and that he was anxious not to lose any more of his time in the barren operations of geometry and arithmetic, studies which never lead to anything important.*"[‡] Finally, speaking of the general character of the philosopher, Baillet adds:—"In regard to the rest of mathematics" (he had just spoken of astronomy—which Descartes thought, *"though he dreamt in it himself, only a loss of time"*)[§] "in regard to the rest of mathematics, those who know the rank which he held above all mathematicians, ancient and modern, will agree that he was the man in the world best qualified to judge them. We have observed that, after having studied these sciences to the bottom, *he had renounced them as of no use for the conduct of life and solace of mankind.*"*

Whoever reads this passage as if it were all printed in Roman characters,

[*Hamilton's translation of Adrien Baillet, *La Vie de Monsieur Des-Cartes*, 2 vols. (Paris: Horthemels, 1691), Vol. I, pp. 111–13.]

[†René Descartes, *Regulæ ad directionem ingenii* (Amsterdam: Blaev, 1710), p. 12.]

[‡Hamilton's translation of Baillet, Vol. I, p. 225, Hamilton mistakenly attributes the matter to a letter of Descartes to Marin Mersenne of 1630; Baillet is in fact conflating comments from several letters to Mersenne in the 1630s.]

[§Hamilton's mistranslation of *ibid.*, p. 235; Hamilton's parenthesis.]

Discussions, pp. 277–8. [The two parentheses are Hamilton's; the closing passage is Hamilton's translation of Baillet, Vol. II, p. 481.]

and declines to submit his understanding to the italics which Sir W. Hamilton has introduced, will perceive the following three things. First, that Descartes was not speaking of the study of mathematics, but of its exclusive study. His objection is to stopping there, without proceeding to anything ulterior: *conquiescere, incubare*. Secondly, that he was speaking only of pure mathematics, as distinguished from its applications, and under the belief, how prodigiously erroneous we now know, that it did not admit of applications of any importance. Finally, that his disparagement of the pursuit, even as thus limited—his representation of it as "*nugæ*," as "a loss of time," rested mainly on a ground which Sir W. Hamilton gave up, the unimportance of its object-matter. It was a repetition of the objection of Socrates, whom also our author thinks it worth while to cite as an authority on such a question, and who "did not perceive of what utility they [mathematical studies] could be, calculated as they were to consume the life of a man, and to turn him away from many other and important acquirements."* Such an opinion, in the days of Socrates, and from one whose glorious business it was to recal the minds of speculative men to dialectics and morals, reflects no discredit on his great mind. But the objection is one which Sir W. Hamilton, with every thinker of the last two centuries, disclaims. "The question," he expressly says, "does not regard the value of mathematical *science*, considered in itself, or in its objective results, but the utility of mathematical *study*, that is, in its subjective effect, as an exercise of mind."† All that Descartes said against it in this aspect (at least in the passage quoted, which we may suppose to be one of the strongest) is, that by affording other objects of thought, it diverts the mind from the use of *ipsa ratio*, that is, from the study of pure mental abstractions; which Descartes, to the great detriment of his philosophy, regarded as of much superior value to the employment of the thoughts upon objects of sense, "*f*quæ*f* magis ad oculos et imaginationem pertinent."

It was by his example, rather than by his precepts, that Descartes was destined to illustrate the unfavourable side of the intellectual influence of mathematical studies; and he must have been a still more extraordinary man than he was, could he have really understood a kind of mental perversions of which he is himself, in the history of philosophy, the most prominent example. Descartes is the completest type which history presents of the purely mathematical type of mind—that in which the tendencies pro-

---

Ibid., p. 323. [The words in square brackets are Mill's. For the opinion of Socrates, see Xenophon, *Memorabilia*, in *Memorabilia and Œconomicus* (Greek and English), trans. E. C. Marchant (London: Heinemann; New York: Putnam's Sons, 1923), pp. 346–8 (IV, vii, 3–5).]

†*Ibid.*, p. 266.

f-f+67, 72 [*not in* Source]

duced by mathematical cultivation reign unbalanced and supreme. This is visible not only in the abuse of Deduction, which he carried to a greater length than any distinguished thinker known to us, not excepting the schoolmen; but even more so in the character of the premises from which his deductions set out. And here we come upon the one really grave charge which rests on the mathematical spirit, in respect of the influence it exercises on pursuits other than mathematical. It leads men to place their ideal of Science in deriving all knowledge from a small number of axiomatic premises, accepted as self-evident, and taken for immediate intuitions of reason. This is what Descartes attempted to do, and inculcated as the thing to be done: and as he shares with only one other name the honour of having given his impress to the whole character of the modern speculative movement, the consequences of his error have been most calamitous. Nearly everything that is objectionable, along with much of what is admirable, in the character of French thought, whether on metaphysics, ethics, or politics, is directly traceable to the fact that French speculation descends from Descartes instead of from Bacon.* All reflecting persons in England, and many in France, perceive that the chief infirmities of French thinking arise from its geometrical spirit; its determination to evolve its conclusions, even on the most practical subjects, by mere deduction from some single accepted generalization: the generalization, too, being frequently not even a theorem, but a practical rule, supposed to be obtained directly from the fountains of reason: a mode of thinking which erects one-sidedness into a principle, under the misapplied name of logic, and makes the popular political reasoning in France resemble that of a theologian arguing from a text, or a lawyer from a maxim of law. If this be the case even in France, it is still worse in Germany, the whole of whose speculative philosophy is an emanation from Descartes, and to most of whose thinkers the Baconian point of view is still below the horizon. Through Spinoza, who gave to his system the very forms as well as the entire spirit of geometry; through the mathematician Leibnitz, who reigned supreme over the German speculative mind for above a generation; with its spirit temporarily modified by the powerful intellectual individuality of Kant, but flying back after him to its

---

*It is but just to add, that the English mode of thought has suffered in a different, but almost equally injurious manner, by its exclusive following of what it imagined to be the teaching of Bacon, being in reality a slovenly misconception of him, leaving on one side the whole spirit and scope of his speculations. The philosopher who laboured to construct a canon of scientific Induction, by which the observations of mankind, instead of remaining empirical, might be so combined and marshalled as to be made the foundation of safe general theories, little expected that his name would become the stock authority for disclaiming generalization, and enthroning empiricism, under the name of experience, as the only solid foundation of practice.

uncorrected tendencies, the geometrical spirit went on from bad to worse, until in Schelling and Hegel the laws even of physical nature were deduced by ratiocination from subjective deliverances of the mind. The whole of German philosophical speculation has run from the beginning in this wrong groove, and having only recently become aware of the fact, is at present making convulsive efforts to get out of it.* All these mistakes, and this deplorable waste of time and intellectual power by some of the most gifted and cultivated portions of the human race, are effects of the too unqualified predominance of the mental habits and tendencies engendered by elementary mathematics. Applied mathematics in its post-Newtonian development does nothing to strengthen, and very much to correct, these errors, provided the applications are studied in such a manner that the intellect is aware of what it is about, and does not go to sleep over algebraical symbols; a didactic improvement which Dr. Whewell, to his honour be it said, was earnestly and successfully labouring to introduce, thus practically correcting the real defects of mathematics as a branch of general education, at the very time when Sir W. Hamilton, who had not the smallest insight into those defects, selected him for the immediate recipient of an attack on mathematics, which as it only included what Sir W. Hamilton knew of the subject, left out everything which was much worth saying.

It is not solely to Mathematical studies that Sir W. Hamilton professes and shows hostility. Physical investigations generally, apart from their material fruits, he holds but in low estimation. We have seen in a former chapter how singularly unaware he is of the power and exertion of intellect which they often require. Touching their effect on the mind, he makes two serious complaints, which come out at the very commencement of his Lectures on Metaphysics.† The first is, that the study of Physics indisposes persons to believe in Free-will. To this accusation it must plead guilty: physical science undoubtedly has that tendency. But I maintain that this is only because physical science teaches people to judge of evidence. If the free-will doctrine could be proved, there is nothing in the habits of thought engendered by physical science that would indispose any one to yield to the evidence. A person who knows only one physical science, may be unable to feel the force of a kind of proof different from that which is customary in his

---

*The character here drawn of German thought is, I hardly need say, not intended to apply to such a man as Goethe, or to those who received their intellectual impulse from him. In him, indeed, not to speak of his almost universal culture, the intellectual operations were always guided by an intense spirit of observation and experiment, and a constant reference to the exigencies, outward and inward, of practical human life. Such criticism as can justly be made on Goethe as a thinker, rests on entirely different grounds.

†*Lectures*, Vol. I, pp. 35–42.

department; but any one who is generally versed in physical science is accustomed to so many different modes of investigation, that he is well prepared to feel the force of whatever is really proof. Metaphysicians of Sir W. Hamilton's school, who pursue their investigations without regard to the cautions suggested by physical science, are equally catholic and comprehensive in the wrong way; they can mistake for proof anything or everything which is not so, provided it tends to form an association of ideas in their own minds.

The other objection of Sir W. Hamilton to the scientific study of the laws of Matter, is one which we should scarcely have expected from him, namely, that it annihilates Wonder.

"Wonder," says Aristotle, "is the first cause of philosophy;"[*] but in the discovery that all existence is but mechanism, the consummation of science would be an extinction of the very interest from which it originally sprang. "Even the gorgeous majesty of the heavens," says a great religious philosopher,* "the object of a kneeling adoration to an infant world, subdues no more the mind of him who comprehends the one mechanical law by which the planetary systems move, maintain their motion, and even originally form themselves. He no longer wonders at the object, infinite as it always is, but at the human intellect alone which in a Copernicus, Kepler, Gassendi, Newton, and Laplace, was able to transcend the object, by science to terminate the miracle, to reave the heaven of its divinities, and to exorcise the universe. But even this, the only admiration of which our intelligent faculties are now capable, would vanish, were a future Hartley, Darwin, Condillac, or Bonnet, to succeed in displaying to us a mechanical system of the human mind, as comprehensive, intelligible, and satisfactory as the Newtonian mechanism of the heavens."[†]

We may be well assured that no Hartley, Darwin, or Condillac will obtain a hearing, if the "great religious philosopher" can prevent it.

I shall not enter into all the topics suggested by this remarkable argument. I shall not ask whether, after all, it is better to be "subdued" than instructed; or whether human nature would suffer a great loss in losing wonder, if love and admiration remained; for admiration, *pace tantorum virorum*, is a different thing from wonder, and is often at its greatest height when the strangeness, which is a necessary condition of wonder, has died away. But I do wonder at the barrenness of imagination of a man who can see nothing wonderful in the material universe, since Newton, in an evil hour, partially unravelled a limited portion of it. If ignorance is with him a necessary condition of wonder, can he find nothing to wonder at in the

---

[*See *Metaphysics*, Vol. I, p. 12 (I, ii, 982^{b}12ff.).]

*F. H. Jacobi. [See *David Hume über den Glauben, oder Idealismus und Realismus*, in *Werke*, 6 vols. (Leipzig: Fleischer, 1812–25), Vol. II, pp. 54–5.] The entire passage is in *Discussions*, p. 312.

†*Lectures*, Vol. I, p. 37.

origin of the system of which Newton discovered the laws? nothing in the probable former extension of the solar substance beyond the orbit of Neptune? nothing in the starry heavens, which, with a full knowledge of what Newton taught, Kant, in the famous passage which Sir W. Hamilton is so fond of quoting (and quotes in this very lecture),[*] placed on the same level of sublimity with the moral law? If ignorance is the cause of wonder, it is downright impossible that scientific explanation can ever take it away, since all which explanation does, in the final resort, is to refer us back to a prior inexplicable. Were the catastrophe to arrive which is to expel Wonder from the universe—were it conclusively shown that the mental operations are dependent upon organic agency—would wonder be at an end because the fact, at which we should then have to wonder, would be that an arrangement of material particles could produce thought and feeling? Jacobi and Sir W. Hamilton might have put their minds at ease. It is not understanding that destroys wonder, it is familiarity. To a person whose feelings have depth enough to withstand that, no insight which can ever be attained into natural phænomena will make Nature less wonderful. And as for those whose sensibilities are shallow, did Jacobi suppose that *they* wondered one iota the more at the planetary motions, when astronomers imagined them to take place by the complicated evolutions of "cycle on epicycle, orb on orb?"[†] A spectacle which they saw every day, had, we may rely upon it, as little effect in kindling their imaginations then, as now. Hear the opinion of a great poet:* not speaking particularly of wonder, but of the emotions generally which the spectacle of nature excites, and in words which apply to that emotion equally with the rest.

Some are of opinion that the habit of analysing, decomposing, and anatomising, is inevitably unfavourable to the perception of beauty. People are led into this mistake by overlooking the fact that such processes being to a certain extent within the reach of a limited intellect, we are apt to ascribe to them that insensibility of which they are, in truth, the effect, and not the cause. Admiration and love, to which all knowledge truly vital must tend, are felt by men of real genius in proportion as their discoveries in natural philosophy are enlarged; and the beauty, in form, of a plant or an animal, is not made less but more apparent, as a whole, by more accurate insight into its constituent properties and powers.

Hear next one of the most illustrious discoverers in physical science. Instead of regarding understanding as antithetical to wonder, Dr. Faraday

[*Ibid., pp. 39–40; quoting Kant, *Kritik der Praktischen Vernunft*, in *Werke*, Vol. VIII, p. 312.]

[†Milton, *Paradise Lost*, in *Works*, p. 202 (VIII, 84).]

*Wordsworth, in the Biography by his nephew [Christopher Wordsworth, *Memoirs of William Wordsworth*, 2 vols. (London: Moxon, 1851)], Vol. II, p. 159.

complains that people do not wonder sufficiently at the material universe, because they do not sufficiently understand it.

Let us now consider, for a little while, how wonderfully we stand upon this world. Here it is we are born, bred, and live, and yet we view these things with an almost entire absence of wonder to ourselves respecting the way in which all this happens. So small, indeed, is our wonder, that we are never taken by surprise; and I do think that, to a young person of ten, fifteen, or twenty years of age, perhaps the first sight of a cataract or a mountain would occasion him more surprise than he had ever felt concerning the means of his own existence; how he came here; how he lives; by what means he stands upright; and through what means he moves about from place to place. Hence, we come into this world, we live, and depart from it, without our thoughts being called specifically to consider how all this takes place; and were it not for the exertions of some few inquiring minds who have looked into these things, and ascertained the very beautiful laws and conditions by which we *do* live and stand upon the earth, we should hardly be aware that there was anything wonderful in it.*

If any additional authority be desired, the greatest poet of modern Germany was also the keenest scientific naturalist in it.[*]

*[Michael Faraday,] *Lectures on the [Various] Forces of Matter [and on the Chemical History of a Candle* (London: Griffin, Bohn, 1863)], pp. 2–3. The philosophy of this is well given by Mr. Lewes in his valuable work on Aristotle. "Surprise starts from a background of knowledge, or fixed belief. Nothing is surprising to ignorance, because the mind in that state has no preconceptions to be contradicted." ([George Henry Lewes, *Aristotle: A Chapter in the History of Science* (London: Smith, Elder, 1864),] p. 212.)
[*Johann Wolfgang von Goethe.]

CHAPTER XXVIII

Concluding Remarks

IN THE EXAMINATION which I have now concluded of Sir W. Hamilton's philosophical achievements, I have unavoidably laid stress on points of difference from him rather than on those of agreement; the reason being, that I differ from almost everything in his philosophy on which he particularly valued himself, or which is specially his own. His merits, which, though I do not rate them so high, I feel and admire as sincerely as his most enthusiastic disciples, are rather diffused through his speculations generally, than concentrated on any particular point. They chiefly consist in his clear and distinct mode of bringing before the reader many of the fundamental questions of metaphysics; some good specimens of psychological analysis on a small scale; and the many detached logical and psychological truths which he has separately seized, and which are scattered through his writings, mostly applied to resolve some special difficulty and again lost sight of. I can hardly point to anything he has done towards helping the more thorough understanding of the greater mental phænomena, unless it be his theory of Attention (including Abstraction), which seems to me the most perfect we have [a] .* [c] The facts and speculations on Sleep and

---

*Even on this subject he has not been able to avoid some fallacies in reasoning. Thus, in maintaining against Stewart and Brown that we can attend to more than one object at once, he defends this true doctrine by some very bad arguments. He says, that if the mind could "attend to, or be conscious of, only a single object at a time," the conclusion would be involved, "that all comparison and discrimination are impossible." (*Lectures*, Vol. I, p. 252.) This assumes that we cannot compare and discriminate any impressions but those which are exactly simultaneous. May not the condition of discrimination be consciousness not at the same, but at immediately successive instants? May not discrimination depend on *change* of consciousness; the transition from one state to another? This is a tenable opinion; it was actually maintained by the philosophers against whom our author was arguing; and if he thought it erroneous, he should have disproved it. Unless he did, he was not entitled to treat a doctrine shown to involve this consequence, as reduced to absurdity. Another of his proofs of our ability to attend to a plurality of things at once, is our perception of harmony between sounds. He argues that to perceive a relation between two sounds implies a comparison, and that if this comparison is

[a]65^1, 65^2 : but the subject, though a highly important, is a comparatively simple one
[c-c]$+67$, 72

Dreaming, in his Seventeenth Lecture on Metaphysics,[*] have been credited to him as an acquisition to philosophy, and are a good specimen of
inductive enquiry; but their principal merit, both in point of observation
and of thought, is avowedly Jouffroy's.*c

---

not between the sounds themselves, simultaneously attended to, it must be a
comparison of "past sound as retained in memory, with the present as actually
perceived;" which still implies attending to two objects at once (*ibid.*, p. 244). His
opponents however might say, that if there be a comparison, it is not between two
simultaneous impressions, either sensations or memories, but between two successive sounds in the instant of transition. They might add, that the perception of
harmony does not necessarily involve comparison. When a number of sounds in
perfect harmony strike the ear simultaneously, we have but a single impression; we
perceive but one mass of sound. Analysing this into its component parts is an act of
intelligence, not of direct perception, and is performed by fixing our attention first
on the whole, and then on the separate elements, not all at once, but one after
another. *b* These objections to his doctrine our author seems not to have thought of,
because those of Stewart, whom as an opponent he principally had in view, were
different (*ibid.*, Vol. II, p. 145). But they ought to have occurred to him without
prompting, being in complete unison with his doctrine that consciousness of wholes
usually precedes that of their parts; that "instead of commencing with minima,
perception commences with masses." (*Ibid.*, p. 327, and many similar passages.)

Sir W. Hamilton is also inconsistent in affirming that attention is "an act of will or
desire," (*ibid.*, Vol. I, p. 237,) and afterwards that it is in some cases automatic, "a
mere vital and irresistible act." (*Ibid.*, p. 248.) This, however, is only a verbal
inaccuracy. He doubtless meant that attention is generally voluntary, but occasionally automatic.

[*Ibid., pp. 310–37.]

*[67] [See *ibid.*, pp. 324–34, where Hamilton quotes from Théodore Jouffroy,
"Du sommeil," *Mélanges philosophiques*, 2nd ed. (Paris: Ladrange, 1838), pp.
290–302.] I see with regret that what I have said above, or rather perhaps what I
have omitted to say, has given an impression even to friendly critics that I think
considerably less highly of Sir W. Hamilton's intellectual calibre, and of his general
services to mankind, than I do. My business in this work was to estimate not the
man, but the permanent additions made by him to the sum of speculative
philosophy. These I cannot rate very high, but I join sincerely and heartily in the
tribute to his merits, so justly paid by Mr. Grote in the *Westminster Review* (pp.
2–3).

"He kept up the idea of philosophy as a subject to be studied from its own points
of view: a dignity which in earlier times it enjoyed, perhaps to mischievous excess,
but from which in recent times it has far too much receded, especially in England.
He performed the great service of labouring strenuously to piece together the past
traditions of philosophy, to rediscover those which had been allowed to drop into
oblivion, and to make out the genealogy of opinions as far as negligent predecessors
had still left the possibility of doing so. We recognise also in Sir W. Hamilton an
amount of intellectual independence which seldom accompanies such vast erudition. He recites many different opinions, but he judges them all for himself; and,

*b*65[1], 65[2]   The perception of the parts is so far from being distinctly present in our feeling of
the harmony, that in proportion as we consciously realize it we injure the general effect.

With regard to the causes which prevented a thinker of such abundant acuteness, and more than abundant industry, from accomplishing the great things at which he aimed, it would ill become me to speak dogmatically. It would be a very unwarrantable assumption of superiority over a mind like Sir W. Hamilton's, if I attempted to gauge and measure his faculties, or give a complete theory of his successes and failures. The utmost I venture on, is to suggest, as simple possibilities, some of the causes which may have partly contributed to his shortcomings as a philosopher. One of those causes is so common as to be the next thing to universal, but requires all the more to be signalized for its unfortunate consequences: over-anxiety to make safe a foregone conclusion. The whole philosophy of Sir W. Hamil-

————

what is of still greater moment, he constantly gives the reasons for his judgments. To us these reasons are always of more or less value, whether we admit them to be valid or not. . . . To those who dissent from him, as well as to those who agree with him, his reasonings are highly instructive: while the full citations from so many other writers contribute materially not only to elucidate the points directly approached, but also to enlarge our knowledge of philosophy generally."

And in the emphatic words of Professor Masson: "Try him even in respect of the importance of his effects on the national thought. Whether from his learning or by reason of his independent thinkings, was it not he that hurled into the midst of us the very questions of metaphysics, and the very forms of those questions, that have become the academic theses everywhere in this British age for real metaphysical discussion? . . . Let it be said of Sir W. Hamilton that, simply and by whatever means, he did more than any other man to reinstate the worship of Difficulty in the higher mind of Great Britain." ([*Recent British Philosophy*,] pp. 308–9.)

Moreover, as Mr. Grote [p. 2] further observes, "in a subject so abstract, obscure, and generally unpalatable, as Logic and Metaphysics, the difficulty which the teacher finds in inspiring interest is extreme. That Sir W. Hamilton overcame such difficulty with remarkable success is the affirmation of his two editors," and is proved by the profound impression left by the teacher and his teaching on the intellects and feelings of his pupils. The "Inquirer" charges me with ignoring "that which formed the greater part of his work—the living teaching he gave to living men—whereby he has raised up for our age and nation that which we most needed, a school of men who can and do think." (P. 6.) It would be very unworthy to ignore so important an item in his services to mankind. I acknowledge it with a feeling, in which I am surpassed by none, of the inestimable worth of all such services. But if I had been attempting a summary of the benefits which the world owes to Sir W. Hamilton, neither could I have ignored his articles on Education, and especially those on the English Universities, to which it is impossible not to attribute a great influence in shaming those bodies out of their long-continued selfish betrayal of their national trust, and putting the new life into them which they have since manifested and are manifesting, with so much advantage to the spirit of the time and to the national culture.

Even in the character of a speculative thinker, my estimate of Sir W. Hamilton is prodigiously misjudged by those who have made themselves, as they had good right to do, the champions of his philosophic reputation. I cannot sufficiently protest against such assertions as that of Mr. Mansel, to which there are several equivalent

ton seems to have had its character determined by the requirements of the doctrine of Free-will; and to that doctrine he clung, because he had persuaded himself that it afforded the only premises from which human reason could deduce the doctrines of natural religion. I believe that in this persuasion he was thoroughly his own dupe, and that his speculations have weakened the philosophical foundation of religion fully as much as they have confirmed it.

---

^{d}by^d the "Inquirer," [pp. 5–8,] that, if all is true which I have alleged, "Sir W. Hamilton, instead of being a great philosopher, is the veriest blunderer that ever put pen to paper." ([Mansel, *Philosophy of the Conditioned*,] p. 181.) Such exaggerations are intelligible in those by whose own estimate he stands almost at the summit of existing philosophy, and who having climbed, as they think, by his assistance, to the same pinnacle, think an inferior eminence unworthy to be counted for anything at all. But some of the most conspicuous figures in the history of philosophy, distinguished no less by the power of their ^{e}intellect^e than by the greatness of their influence on subsequent thought, have not, at least in my judgment, left behind them even so much of positive addition to philosophic truth as Sir W. Hamilton. Kant, for example, of whose mental powers no one who is not a disciple probably forms a higher estimate than I do, and who holds so essential a place in the development of philosophic thought, that until somebody had done what Kant did, metaphysics according to our present conception of it could not have been constituted—Kant, probably, will be finally judged to have left no noticeable contribution to philosophy which was both new and true, except some of his refutations of predecessors. Kant, it is true, was a more consecutive, and therefore a more consistent thinker than Sir W. Hamilton, and it is chiefly by that quality that he has become one of the turning points in the history of philosophy, which Sir W. Hamilton has no claim to be: but in ability to discern psychological truths uncoloured by a theory, he seems to me inferior to Sir W. Hamilton. Perhaps, though of a very different character of mind, the nearest parallel in philosophic merit to Sir W. Hamilton (apart from erudition, in which he has probably no parallel among philosophers), was Professor Dugald Stewart. Neither of them can be numbered among the great original thinkers who have carried philosophy into one of its indispensable phases, as did Locke, Descartes, Hume, Kant, and with all his shortcomings, even Reid. Neither of them saw into the heart of great psychological questions which had never been fathomed before, like Berkeley, Hartley, Brown, or James Mill. Both of them have thrown considerable light on minor questions: both have gathered, and more or less perfectly assimilated, truths from very opposite quarters: both have committed great oversights, though Sir W. Hamilton, coming last, and having the benefit of the Kantian movement, stood on a considerably higher platform of metaphysical thought. Both had some, though but moderate, powers of analysis; their philosophic style, though extremely unlike, was, in both, excellent: both gave an important stimulus to the national intellect by their extraordinary power as public teachers; and both will be remembered as meritoriously handing on the torch of philosophy, but neither of them, I venture to say, as among those who have much brightened or fed its flame.

$^{d-d}$67 in
$^{e-e}$67 intellects

A second cause which may help to account for his not having effected more in philosophy, is the enormous amount of time and mental vigour which he expended on mere philosophical erudition, leaving, it may be said, only the remains of his mind for the real business of thinking. While he seems to have known, almost by heart, the voluminous Greek commentators on Aristotle, and to have read all that the most obscure schoolman or fifth-rate German transcendentalist had written on the subjects with which he occupied himself; while, not content with a general knowledge of these authors, he could tell with the greatest precision what each of them thought on any given topic, and in what each differed from every other; while expending his time and energy on all this, he had not enough of them left to complete his *Lectures*. Those on Metaphysics, as already remarked, stopped short on the threshold of what was, especially in his own opinion, the most important part of it, and never reached even the threshold of the third and last of the parts into which, in an early lecture, he divided his subject.* Those on Logic he left dependent, for most of the subordinate developments, on extracts strung together from German writers, chiefly Krug and Esser; often not destitute of merit, but generally so vague, as to make all those parts of his exposition in which they predominate, unsatisfactory;† sometimes written from points of view different from Sir W. Hamilton's own, but which he never found time or took the trouble to re-express in adaptation to his own mode of thought.‡ In the whole circle of psychological and logical speculation, it is astonishing how few are the topics into

Lectures, Vol. I, pp. 123–5. This third part is "Ontology, or Metaphysics Proper;" "the science conversant about inferences of unknown being from its known manifestations;" [*ibid*., p. 125,] things not manifested in consciousness, but legitimately inferrible from those which are.

†This is strikingly the case, among many others, with the Lectures on Definition and Division. [*Lectures*, Vol. IV, pp. 1–36 (Lectures xxiv and xxv.)] On those subjects our author lets Krug and Esser think for him. Those authors stand to him instead, not merely of finding a fit expression for his thoughts, but apparently of having any thoughts at all.

‡I have already given an example of this from the *Lectures*, Vol. III, pp. 159–62. His*f* own idea of Clearness as a property of concepts, is that "a concept is said to be clear when the degree of consciousness is such as to enable us to distinguish it" (the concept) "as a whole from others" [*ibid*., p. 158]: but this idea is expounded by a passage from Esser [*ibid*., pp. 160–2], in which it is not the concept, but the objects thought through the concept, which, if sufficiently distinguished from all others, constitute the *ᵍ*concept*ᵍ* a clear one. I confess that Esser has here greatly the advantage over Sir W. Hamilton, who might have usefully corrected his own theory from the borrowed commentary on it.

*f–f*65^1, 65^2 For example, (*Lectures*, Vol. III, pp. 159–62) his
*ᵍ–ᵍ*65^1, 65^2, 67   conception

which he has thrown any of the powers of his own intellect; and on how small a proportion even of these he has pushed his investigations beyond what seemed necessary for the purposes of some particular controversy. In consequence, philosophical doctrines are taken up, and again laid down, with perfect unconsciousness, and his philosophy seems made up of scraps from several conflicting metaphysical systems. The Relativity of human knowledge is made a great deal of in opposition to Schelling and Cousin, but drops out or dwindles into nothing in Sir W. Hamilton's own psychology. The validity of our natural beliefs, and the doctrine that the incogitable is not therefore impossible, are strenuously asserted in this place and disregarded in that, according to the question in hand. On the subject of General Notions he is avowedly a Nominalist, but teaches the whole of Logic as if he had never heard of any doctrine but the Conceptualist; what he presents as a reconcilement of the two being never adverted to afterwards, and serving only as an excuse to himself for accepting the one doctrine and invariably using the language of the other. Arriving at his doctrines almost always under the stimulus of some special dispute, he never knows how far to press them: consequently there is a region of haze round the place where opinions of different origin meet. I formerly quoted from him a felicitous illustration drawn from the mechanical operation of tunnelling; that process affords another, justly applicable to himself. The reader must have heard of that gigantic enterprise of the Italian Government, the tunnel through Mont Cenis. This great work is carried on simultaneously from both ends, in well-grounded confidence (such is now the minute accuracy of engineering operations) that the two parties of workmen will correctly meet in the middle. Were they to disappoint this expectation, and work past one another in the dark, they would afford a likeness of Sir W. Hamilton's mode of tunnelling the human mind.

This failure to think out subjects until they had been thoroughly mastered, or until consistency had been attained between the different views which the author took of them from different points of observation, may, like the unfinished state of the *Lectures*, be with great probability ascribed to the excessive absorption of his time and energies by the study of old writers. That absorption did worse; for it left him with neither leisure nor vigour for what was far more important in every sense, and an entirely indispensable qualification for a master in philosophy—the systematic study of the sciences. Except physiology, on some parts of which his mental powers were really employed, he may be said to have known nothing of any physical science. I do not mean that he was ignorant of familiar facts, or that he may not, in the course of his education, have gone through the curriculum. But it must have been as Gibbon did, who says, in his autobiography, "I was content to receive the passive impressions of my professor's lectures, without any active exercise of my own powers."[*] For any trace the study had left in Sir W. Hamilton's mind, he might as well never have heard of it.*

It is much to be regretted that Sir W. Hamilton did not write the history of philosophy, instead of choosing, as the direct object of his intellectual exertions, philosophy itself. He possessed a knowledge of the materials such as no one, probably, for many generations, will take the trouble of acquiring again; and the erudition of philosophy is emphatically one of the things which it is good that a few should acquire for the benefit of the rest. Independently of the great interest and value attaching to a knowledge of

[*Edward Gibbon, "Memoirs of My Life and Writings," in *Miscellaneous Works*, ed. John Baker Holroyd, Lord Sheffield, 2 vols. (London: Strahan, Cadell and Davies, 1796), Vol. I, p. 66.]

*The signs of Sir W. Hamilton's want of familiarity with the physical sciences meet us in every corner of his works. One, which I have not hitherto found a convenient place for noticing, is the singular view he takes of analysis and synthesis. He imagines that synthesis always presupposes analysis, and that unless grounded on a previous analysis, synthesis can afford no knowledge. "Synthesis without a previous analysis is baseless; for synthesis receives from analysis the elements which it recomposes" (*Lectures*, Vol. I, p. 98). "Synthesis without analysis is a false knowledge, that is, no knowledge at all. . . . A synthesis without a previous analysis is radically and *ab initio* null." (*Ibid.*, 99.) This affirmation is the more surprising, as the example he himself selects to illustrate analysis and synthesis is a case of chemical composition; a neutral salt, compounded of an acid and an alkali. Did he suppose that when a chemist succeeds in forming a salt by synthesis merely, putting together two substances never actually found in combination, he does not make exactly the same addition to chemical science as if he had met with the compound first, and analysed it into its elements afterwards? Did Sir W. Hamilton ever read a memoir by a chemist on a newly-discovered elementary substance? If so, did he not find that the discoverer invariably proceeds to ascertain by synthesis what combinations the new element will form with all other elements for which it has any affinity? Sir W. Hamilton, though he drew his example from physics, forgot all that related to the example, and thought only of psychological investigation, in which it does commonly happen that the compound fact is presented to us first, and we have to begin by analysing it; our synthesis, if practicable at all, taking place afterwards, and serving only to verify the analysis. Therefore, in spite of his own example, Sir W. Hamilton defines synthesis as being always a recomposition and "reconstruction" (*ibid.*, p. 98). Could any one who had the smallest familiarity with physical science have committed this strange oversight?

Another example, to which I shall content myself with referring, is the incapacity of understanding an argument respecting a principle of Mechanics, shown in his controversy with Dr. Whewell respecting the law that the pressure of a lever on the fulcrum, when the weights balance one another, is equal to the sum of the two weights (*Discussions*, pp. 338–9). [See also William Whewell, *An Elementary Treatise on Mechanics*, Vol. I (Cambridge: Deighton; London: Whittaker, 1819), p. 19.]

the historical development of speculation, there is much in the old writers on philosophy, even those of the middle ages, really worth preserving for its scientific value.* But this should be extracted, and rendered into the phraseology of modern thought, by persons as familiar with that as with the ancient, and possessing a command of its language; a combination never yet so perfectly realized as in Sir W. Hamilton. It is waste of time for a mere student of philosophy, to have to learn the familiar use of fifty philosophic phraseologies, all greatly inferior to that of his own time; and if this were required from all thinkers, there would be very little time left for thought. A man who had done it so thoroughly as Sir W. Hamilton, should have made his cotemporaries and successors, once for all, partakers of the benefit; and rendered it unnecessary for any one to do it again, except for verifying and correcting his representations. This, which no one but himself could have done, he has left undone; and has given us, instead, a contribution to mental philosophy which has been more than equalled by many not superior to him in powers, and wholly destitute of erudition. Of all persons, in modern times, entitled to the name of philosophers, the two, probably, whose reading on their own subjects was the scantiest, in proportion to their intellectual capacity, were Dr. Thomas Brown and Archbishop Whately: accordingly they are the only two of whom Sir W. Hamilton, though acknowledging their abilities, habitually speaks with a certain tinge of superciliousness. It cannot be denied that both Dr. Brown and Archbishop Whately would have thought and written better than they did, if they had been better read in the writings of previous thinkers: but I am not afraid that posterity will contradict me when I say, that either of them has done [h] greater service to the world, in the origination and diffusion of important thought, than Sir W. Hamilton with all his learning: because, though indolent readers, they were, both of them, active and fertile thinkers.*

*[67]"We set particular value upon this preservation of the traditions of philosophy, and upon this maintenance of a known perpetual succession among the speculative minds of humanity, with proper comparisons and contrasts. We have found among the names quoted by Sir W. Hamilton, and thanks to his care, several authors hardly at all known to us, and opinions cited from them not less instructive than curious. He deserves the more gratitude, because he departs herein from received usage since Bacon and Descartes. The example set by these great men was admirable, so far as it went to throw off the authority of predecessors; but pernicious so far as it banished those predecessors out of knowledge, like mere magazines of immaturity and error. Throughout the eighteenth century, all study of the earlier modes of philosophizing was, for the most part, neglected. Of such neglect, remarkable instances are pointed out by Sir W. Hamilton." (Mr. Grote, in *Westminster Review*, pp. 3–4.)

*[67] Mr. Grote, agreeing with me as to Brown, demurs to this judgment as regards Archbishop Whately; of which latter comparison Professor Masson, still

[h]65[1], 65[2]   far

It is not that Sir W. Hamilton's erudition is not frequently of real use to him on particular questions of philosophy. It does him one valuable service: it enables him to know all the various opinions which can be held on the questions he discusses, and to conceive and express them clearly, leaving none of them out. This it does, though even this not always; but it does little else, even of what might be expected from erudition when enlightened by philosophy. He knew, with extraordinary accuracy, the ὅτι of every philosopher's doctrine, but gave himself little trouble about the διότι.[*] With one exception, I find no remarks bearing upon that point in any part of his writings.* I imagine he would have been much at a loss if he had been required to draw up a philosophical estimate of the mind of any great thinker. He ᶦrarelyᶦ seems to look at any opinion of a philosopher in connexion with the same philosopher's other opinions. Accordingly, he is

---

more naturally, complains. [See Grote, pp. 37–8; Masson, *Recent British Philosophy*, p. 303.] Our difference, I suspect, is not that I value Sir W. Hamilton less, but Archbishop Whately more. The result of my reading of many of his multifarious writings is a much higher estimation than Mr. Grote's seems to be, both of his originality and of his services to thought. As a metaphysician proper, no one would compare him with Sir W. Hamilton: but I am speaking of him in the more general character of a thinker, and in respect of the number of true and valuable thoughts on many various subjects, metaphysics being one, which he brought into the general stock, and threw into circulation.

Let me add that in speaking of Brown and Whately as active and fertile thinkers, I had no idea that I should be considered as refusing those attributes to Sir W. Hamilton.

[*See Aristotle, *Metaphysics*, Vol. I, p. 6 (I, i, 981ᵃ29); see also Hamilton, *Lectures*, Vol. I, Lecture iii, p. 58.]

*This solitary exception relates to Hume. Respecting the general scope and purpose, the pervading spirit, of Hume's speculations, Sir W. Hamilton does give an opinion, and, I venture to think, a wrong one. He regards Hume's philosophy as scepticism in its legitimate sense. Hume's object, he thinks, was to prove the uncertainty of all knowledge. With this intent he represents him as reasoning from premises "not established by himself," but "accepted only as principles universally conceded in the previous schools of philosophy." These premises Hume showed (according to Sir W. Hamilton) to lead to conclusions which contradicted the evidence of consciousness; thus proving, not that consciousness deceives, but that the premises generally accepted on the authority of philosophers, and leading to these conclusions, must be false. (*Discussions*, pp. 87–8, and elsewhere.)

This is certainly the use which has been made of Hume's arguments, by Reid and many other of his opponents. Admitting their validity as arguments, Reid considered them, not as proving Hume's conclusions, but as a *reductio ad absurdum* of his premises. [See *On the Intellectured Powers*, pp. 484–9.] That Hume however had any foresight of their being put to this use, either for a dogmatical or a purely sceptical purpose, appears to me supremely improbable. If we form our opinion by reading the series of Hume's metaphysical essays straight through, instead of

ᶦ⁻ᶦ65¹, 65², 67   never

weak as to the mutual relations of philosophical doctrines. He seldom knows any of the corollaries from a thinker's opinions, unless the thinker has himself drawn them; and even then he knows them, not as corollaries, but only as opinions. One of the most striking examples he affords of this inability is in the case of Leibnitz; and it is worth while to analyse this instance, because nothing can more conclusively show, how little capable he was of entering into the spirit of a system unlike his own.

If there ever was a thinker whose system of thought could without difficulty be conceived as a connected whole, it was Leibnitz. Hardly any philosopher has taken so much pains to display the filiation of all his main conceptions, in a manner at once satisfactory to his own mind and intelligible to the world. And there is hardly any one in whom the filiation is more complete, these various conceptions being all applications of one common principle. Yet Sir W. Hamilton understands them so ill, as to be able to say, after giving an account of the Pre-established Harmony, that "its author himself probably regarded it more as a specimen of ingenuity than as a

---

judging from a few detached expressions in a single essay (that "on the Academical or Sceptical Philosophy,") I think our judgment will be that Hume sincerely accepted both the premises and the conclusions. It would be difficult, no doubt, to prove this by conclusive evidence, nor would I venture absolutely to affirm it. In the case of the freethinking philosophers of the last century, it is often impossible to be quite certain what their opinions really were; how far the reservations they made, expressed real convictions, or were concessions to supposed necessities of position. Hume, it is certain, made such concessions largely: insincere they can hardly be called, being so evidently intended to be φωνήεντα, at least συνετοῖσι. [Pindar, *Olympian Odes*, in *The Odes of Pindar Including Principal Fragments* (Greek and English), trans. John Sandys (London: Heinemann; Cambridge, Mass.: Harvard University Press, 1937), p. 26 (II, 85).] I have a strong impression that Hume's scepticism, or rather his professed admiration of scepticism, was a disguise of this description, intended rather to avoid offence than to conceal his opinion; that he preferred to be called a sceptic, rather than by a more odious name; and having to promulgate conclusions which he knew would be regarded as contradicting, on one hand the evidence of common sense, on the other the doctrines of religion, did not like to declare them as positive convictions, but thought it more judicious to exhibit them as the results we *might* come to, if we put complete confidence in the trustworthiness of our rational faculty. I have little doubt that he himself did feel this confidence, and wished it to be felt by his readers. There is certainly no trace of a different feeling in his speculations on any of the other important subjects treated in his works: and even on this subject, the general tenor of what he wrote pointing one way, and only single passages the other, it is most reasonable to interpret the latter in the mode which will least contradict the expression of his habitual state of mind in the former.

I cannot but believe, therefore, that Sir W. Hamilton has misunderstood the essential character of Hume's mind: but his hearty admiration and honest vindication of him as a thinker are highly honourable to Sir W. Hamilton, both as a philosopher and as a man.

serious doctrine."* And again: "It is a disputed point whether Leibnitz was serious in his monadology and pre-established harmony."† To say nothing of the injustice done, by this surmise, to the deep sincerity and high philosophic earnestness of that most eminent man; it is obvious to those who study opinions in their relation to the mind entertaining them, that a person, who could thus think concerning the Pre-established Harmony and the Monadology,[*] however correctly he may have seized many particular opinions of Leibnitz, had never taken into his mind a conception of Leibnitz himself as a philosopher. These theories were necessitated by Leibnitz's other opinions. They were the only outlet from the difficulties of the fundamental doctrine of his philosophy, the Principle of Sufficient Reason.[†]

All who know anything of Leibnitz, are aware that he affirmed it to be a principle of the universe, that nothing exists which has not an antecedent ground in reason, and cognisable by reason; a ground which, when known, gives all the properties of the thing by natural and necessary consequence. This Sufficient Reason might be some abstract property of the thing, serving as the pattern on which it was constructed, and being the key to all its other attributes. Such, for example, is the property by which mathematicians define the circle or the triangle, and from which, by mere reasoning, the remaining properties of those figures are deducible. In other cases, the Sufficient Reason of a phænomenon is found in its physical cause. But the mere existence of the cause as an invariable antecedent, does not constitute it the Sufficient Reason of the effect. There must be something in the nature of the cause itself, something capable of being detected in it, which, once known, accounts for its being followed by that particular effect; something which explains the character of the effect, and, had it been known beforehand, would have enabled us to foretel the precise effect that would be produced. To so great a length did Leibnitz carry this doctrine, as to affirm that God (saving actual miracle, which as a highly exceptional fact he was willing to admit)[‡] could not, in the exercise of his ordinary providence, conduct the government of the world except *par la nature des créatures*; through second causes, each containing, in its own properties, wherewithal to furnish a complete explanation of the phænomena to which it gives rise.[§]

Setting out with this *à priori* conception of the order of the universe,

Lectures, Vol. I, p. 304. [See *Théodicée*, pp. 174–6 (§§61, 62).]
†Foot-note to Reid, p. 309n.
[*See Leibniz, *Monadologie*, in *Opera Philosophica*, pp. 705–12.]
[†See p. 372 above.]
[‡See *Théodicée*, pp. 382–3 (II, §§207–8), and pp. 428–30 (III, §§248–9).]
[§*Ibid.*, pp. 347–8 (II, §181).]

Leibnitz found Mind apparently acting upon Matter and Matter upon Mind, and was utterly unable to discover in the nature and attributes of either, any Sufficient Reason for this action. The two substances seemed wholly disparate: there was nothing in them from which action of any kind upon one another could have been presumed to be so much as possible. He saw in this one case, what is true, though he did not see it, in all cases whatever—that there is no *nexus*, no natural link, between agent and patient, between cause and effect, and that all we know or can know of their relation is, that the one always follows the other. But to accept the mere fact as ultimate, without craving for a demonstration, could not enter into Leibnitz's geometrical mind; and was positively forbidden by his Principle of Sufficient Reason. Here was a dilemma! Happily, however, the difficulty of admitting that Mind could act upon Matter, disappeared in the case of an Infinite Mind. In the Omnipotence of the Deity there lay a Sufficient Reason for the possibility of anything which the Deity might be pleased to do. It must be God, therefore, and no subordinate agency, that directly produces the effects on Matter which seem owing to Mind, and the effects on Mind which seem owing to Matter. This being admitted, there were only two possible theories to choose from. Either God, from the beginning, wound up Mind and Matter to go together like two clocks, though without any connexion with one another; and I see an object, not because the object is before my eyes, but because it was prearranged from eternity that the presence of the object and the fact of my seeing should occur at the same instant; or else, at the moment when the object appears, God intervenes, and gives me the perception of sight, exactly as if the object had caused it. The former theory is the Pre-established Harmony; the latter is the doctrine of Occasional Causes, to which, as rather the less grotesque supposition of the two, the Cartesians had been driven by the pressure of the same difficulty. But this hypothesis, as it supposed nothing less than a standing miracle, was wholly inadmissible by Leibnitz. It was inconsistent with the idea which he had formed to himself of the perfections of the Deity. He considered it as assimilating Providence to a bad workman, whose engines will not work unless he himself stands by, and gives them a helping hand; "a watchmaker, who, having constructed a timepiece, would still be obliged himself to turn the hands, to make it mark the hours."* Leibnitz could not find, in the idea of God, any Sufficient Reason why so roundabout a mode of governing the universe should have been chosen by him. He was thus thrown upon the hypothesis of a Pre-established Harmony, as his only refuge; and there can be no doubt that he accepted it, with the full convic-

*Quoted from Leibnitz by Sir W. Hamilton, *Lectures*, Vol. I, p. 303. [See Leibniz, *Troisième Éclaircissement*, in *Opera*, p. 135.]

tion of an intellect accustomed to pursue given premises to their consequences with all the rigour of geometrical demonstration.

The doctrine of Monads was as necessary a corollary from Leibnitz's
first principle as the Pre-established Harmony. Everything, whether physical or spiritual, which has an individual existence, is a compound of
innumerable attributes, between many of which we cannot seize any connexion, but on Leibnitz's theory it was not admissible to suppose that no
connexion exists. There must be something, somewhere, which contains in
its own nature the complete theory and explanation of the combination of
attributes, and is the reason of its being that combination and no other: and
what could this be unless a sort of kernel of the entire Being—the Soul in
the case of a spiritual being, a kind of Essence of the Individual in that of a
merely physical object? The Monads of Leibnitz do not really differ from
the imaginary Essences of the schoolmen, except in not being abstractions,
but objective realities in the completest meaning of the word; which,
indeed, the Substantiæ Secundæ of the Realists already were, only that they
were essences of classes, and were conceived as inhering simultaneously in
numerous individuals, while the Monads of Leibnitz were lively little
beings, the principles of animation and activity, each of them the real agent
or Force at the bottom of one individual. All this may seem poor stuff, and a
melancholy exhibition of a great intellect. But as there is nothing in experience which directly disproves these theories, they are not really more
absurd than many a one which has not so quaint an appearance: and it is the
strength, not the weakness of a systematic intellect, that it does not shrink
from conclusions because they have an absurd look, when they are necessary corollaries from premises which the thinker, and probably most of
those who criticise him, have not ceased to regard as true. Leibnitz was led
to the Monads and the Pre-established Harmony by the same logical
necessity, which made Descartes, far more absurdly, affirm the auto-
matism of animals;[*] and we might as reasonably doubt the seriousness of
the latter opinion, as of the former. The same logical consistency made him
a Necessitarian, and an Optimist; since the doctrine of Sufficient Reason
made God the author of all that happens, consequently of all human
actions; and God's attributes could not be a Sufficient Reason for any world
but the best possible.

Other examples may be given, though none greater than this, of Sir W.
Hamilton's inability to enter into the very mind of another thinker. Is it not,
for instance, a surprising thing, that one who knew Socrates, Plato, and
Aristotle so well, should attribute* to all of them his own opinion that *j*(at

[*See *Dissertatio de Methodo*, pp. 23ff. (V).]
Lectures, Vol. I, pp. 11–12.

j–j+72

least in the case of speculative knowledge)[j] not truth but the search for truth is the important matter, and that the pursuit of it is not for the sake of the attainment, but of the mental activity and energy developed in the search?[*] If there have been three men since speculation began who would have vehemently rejected such a doctrine, they are the three who are here placed at the head of the authorities in its support. Our author arrives at this strange misunderstanding, by giving a meaning to single expressions, derived from his own mode of thought and not from theirs. In Aristotle's case the assertion rests on a mistake of the meaning of the Aristotelian word ἐνέργεια, which did not signify energy, but fact as opposed to possibility, *actus* to *potentia*.[†] One hardly knows what to say to a writer who understands Τέλος οὐ γνῶσις ἀλλὰ πρᾶξις,[*] to mean, "The intellect is perfected not by knowledge but by activity."[‡]

We see, from such instances, how much even Sir W. Hamilton's erudition wanted of what we have a right to expect from erudition in a superior mind—that it should enter into the general spirit of the things it knows, not know them merely in their details. Sir W. Hamilton studied the eminent thinkers of old, only from the outside. He did not throw his own mind into their manner of thought; he did not survey the field of philosophic speculation from their standing point, and see each object as it would be seen with their lights, and with their modes of looking. The opinion of an author stands an isolated fact in Sir W. Hamilton's pages, without foundation in the author's individuality, or connexion with his other doctrines. For want of this elucidation one by another, even the opinions themselves are, as in the case last cited, very liable to be misunderstood. [l]A history of

*[72] "Speculative truth is only pursued and held of value for the sake of intellectual activity" (*ibid.*, p. 10), and again (at p. 13) "speculative truth" is said to be "only valuable as a mean of intellectual activity."

†The very passage quoted from Aristotle [k]by the editors[k] in support of this representation of him, shows that he was using the word in his own and not in Sir W. Hamilton's sense. Τέλος δ' ἡ ἐνέργεια, καὶ τούτου χάριν ἡ δύναμις λαμβάνεται . . . καὶ τὴν θεωρητικὴν (ἔχουσιν) ἵνα θεωρῶσιν· αλλ' οὐ θεωρῶσιν ἵνα θεωρητικὴν ἔχωσιν. [*Ibid.*, p. 12n.] [See *Metaphysics*, Vol. I, p. 458 (IX, viii, 1050ᵃ9–14).]

[*Nichomachean Ethics, p. 8 (I, iii, 1095ᵃ6–7).]

‡[72] [*Ibid.*, p. 12 and n.] Professor Veitch, in the third Appendix to his *Memoir of Sir W. Hamilton* [p. 447], points out that in this last sentence I have done Sir W. Hamilton an injustice. The passage, Τέλος οὐ γνῶσις ἀλλὰ πρᾶξις, was not quoted by himself, but by his editors [see *Lectures*, Vol. I, p. 12n], as the nearest they had found to a justification of the statement that Aristotle held the opinion attributed to him in the text. They would have done more wisely by making no reference, than one which so totally fails to support the inference drawn from it.

[k–k]+72
[l–l]65[1], 65[2] Yet, such [*a manuscript fragment of the 67 version exists; see* Appendix A *below*]

philosophy from his hand, unless proposing to himself a new object had altered his point of view, could not have been final; it would not have been a philosophical history of philosophy; but it would have stood in the same relation to such a work, in which accurate and complete annals stand to political history: it would have been an invaluable protection against the mistakes of subsequent historians, and would have prodigiously abridged their labours. Such, therefore,[l] as his expositions of the opinions of philosophers are, it is greatly to be regretted that we have not more of them; and that his unrivalled knowledge of all the antecedents of Philosophy has enriched the world with nothing but a few selections of passages on topics on which circumstances had led Sir W. Hamilton to write. He is known to have left copious common-place books, without which indeed it would have been hardly possible that such stores of knowledge could be kept within easy reference. Let us hope that they are carefully preserved; that they will, in some form or other, be made accessible to students, and will yet do good service to the future historian of philosophy. Should this hope be fulfilled, future ages will have greater cause than, I think, Sir W. Hamilton's published philosophical speculations will ever give them, to rejoice in the fruits of his labours, and to celebrate his name. [m]

[m]65[2]   ADDENDUM. / NOTE TO p. 150. [*here appears a version of the note that is given above at* p. 143 *(the equivalent of* p. 150 *in* 65[2])]

APPENDICES

Appendix A

Manuscript Fragments

OF THE MASS OF MANUSCRIPT Mill produced in drafting, rewriting, and revising the *Examination*, nothing is known to be extant except the eight fragments printed below, all of which are drafts of revisions for the 3rd ed. Two of them are in the Yale collection, and so presumably derive from the Sotheby's sale of 27 June, 1927; five are in the Houghton Library, Harvard, in the volume of manuscript material bought by George Herbert Palmer from the Avignon bookseller, J. Roumanille; and one is written on a sheet at the end of Mill's final MS of the *Autobiography*, in the Columbia University Library. The five in the Harvard collection, one may reasonably assume, indicate that the relevant revisions were made in Avignon late in 1866; it is quite likely that the two at Yale were simply bundled with papers of more consequence taken back to England by Mary Taylor when she persuaded her aunt, Helen Taylor, to leave the Avignon house in 1905.

In the text above, the placing of these fragments is indicated by superscript letters. Here they are printed with page and line references to the text above, and with variant readings giving the final versions, except for the fifth, which was totally rewritten. Cancellations and interlineations are not indicated.

Fragment 1. Pp. 21.17–22.3 (Yale)

[a]relative *to us*: & this could no longer be contested if the only relativity he meant was not relativity to us but to something else.[a]

[b]But there is[b] abundant evidence that the relativity which [c]he meant to affirm of[c] our knowledge of attributes was not merely relativity to their substances but also relativity to us. [d]Whenever the occasion presents itself he[d] affirms of attributes as positively as of substances, that all our know-

---

[a-a][*this fragmentary sentence, which may be cancelled by a vertical line, does not correspond to anything in the final text*]

[b-b]67   There is, however,

[c-c]67   Sir W. Hamilton ascribed to

[d-d]67   He

ledge of them is relative to us. *e*He asserts this in a passage already quoted.**e* "In saying that a thing is known in itself I do not mean that this object is known in its absolute existence, that is, *out of relation to us*. This is impossible for *our knowledge is only of the relative*." *f*So that, by the relativity of our knowledge he means relativity to us. Again, when speaking expressly of attributes[†]—"by*f* the expression *what they are in themselves*, in reference to the primary qualities, & of *relative notion* in reference to the secondary, Reid cannot mean that the former are known to us absolutely & in themselves, that is, out of relation to our cognitive faculties; for he elsewhere admits that all our knowledge is *g*relative." To the same effect:[‡] "We*g* can know, we can conceive, only what is relative, our knowledge of qualities or phenomena is necessarily relative; for these exist only as they exist in relation to our faculties."[§] The distinction, *h*then, which he draws*h* between our knowledge of substances & that of attributes, though authentically a part of his philosophy, is quite irrelevant here. *i*For he unquestionably thinks, &*i*

Fragment 2. P. 38n.13–27 (Harvard)

as predicated of acts or mental states, & the *a*same as*a* attributes of a person. *b*The *standard* of right is indeed*b* a positive limit, which even ideally can *c*be only*c* reached, not surpassed: but *d*different persons may agree in*d* exactly conforming to the standard, *e*yet*e* differ in the strength of their adherence to it *f*, in so much that influences (temptations for instance)*f* might detach one of them from it, which would have no effect *g*on the other*g*. There are thus, consistently with *h*perfect*h* observance of the rule of

---

*e-e*67   The passages already quoted apply as much to attributes as to substances. "In saying that we know only the relative, I virtually assert that we know *nothing* absolute—nothing existing absolutely, that is, in and for itself, and *without relation to us and our faculties*."[†]

*f-f*67   In the following passages he is speaking solely of attributes. "By

*g-g*67   relative."* "We

*h-h*67   therefore, which Sir W. Hamilton recognises

*i-i*67   He affirms without reservation, that [*presumably there was a further difference in this sentence between the draft and the final version*]

---

*a-a*67   same regarded as
*b-b*67   Conformity to the standard of right has
*c-c*67   only be
*d-d*67   persons, though all
*e-e*67   may
*f-f*67   : influences (temptations for example)
*g-g*67   upon another
*h-h*67   complete

right, innumerable gradations of the attribute, considered as in a *person. This I had overlooked. But*, on the other hand, *the extreme limit of these gradations is the conception* of a Person whom no influences, *no* causes, either in or out of himself, can *make or induce to deviate* from the law of right. This I apprehend, *, is* a conception of Absolute, not of Infinite, righteousness. The doctrine, therefore, of the first edition, that an Infinite Being may have attributes which are Absolute but not *Infinite, appears* to me maintainable. But as it is immaterial to my argument, & was only *brought in as an illustration which lay near* at hand of the meaning of the terms, I withdraw it from *the present discussion*.

Fragment 3. Pp. 52.14–53.15[*] (Harvard)

This *is* unanswerable if by the Absolute we *are* obliged to understand something which is not only "out of" all relation, but *is incapable of ever coming into relation with anything else: but* is this what any one can possibly mean by the *Absolute*, who identifies the Absolute with the Creator? Granting that the Absolute implies an existence *of* itself, standing in no relation to anything; the only Absolute with which we are concerned, or in which anybody believes, must not only be capable of entering into relation with things, but must be capable of entering into any *possible relation* with anything. May it not be known in some at least of those relations, & particularly in the relation of a Cause? And if it is a "finished, perfected, completed" Cause, i.e. the most a Cause that it is possible to be—the cause of everything except itself, then if known as such, it is known as an Absolute Cause. Has Sir W. Hamilton shewn that an Absolute Cause, thus understood, is inconceivable or unknowable? No: all he shews is, that although capable of being known, it

*i-i*67 person. But
*j-j*67 there is an extreme limit to these gradations—the idea
*k-k*67 or
*l-l*67 deflect in the minutest degree
*m-m*67 to be
*n-n*67 infinite, still appears
*o-o*67 the illustration nearest
*p-p*67 the discussion

[* Headed in Mill's hand "p. 50", i.e., of the 2nd ed.]
*a-a*67 would be
*b-b*67 were
*c-c*67 incapable of ever passing into relation. But
*d-d*67 it
*e-e*67 in
*f-f*67 relation whatever, except that of dependence,

Fragment 4. P. 57.19–32 (Harvard)

the whole of both; & these being conceived as Infinite, to conceive a Being as occupying the whole of them is to conceive that Being as infinite. If thinking God as eternal & omnipresent is thinking him in Space & Time, *then we* do think God in space & time. If thinking him as eternal & omnipresent is not thinking him in space & time, *then we can think him* out of Space & Time. *I* have already shewn that the ideas of infinite space & time are real & positive conceptions: that of a Being who is in all *time & space* is no less so. To think anything *must* be to condition it by attributes which are themselves thinkable; but not necessarily to condition it by a limited quantum of those attributes: on the contrary, we may think it under a degree of them greater than all limited degrees, & this is to think it as Infinite.(a)

Fragment 5. P. 77n.33–41 (Columbia)

associations, we have a natural tendency to disbelieve *it,* but the suggestion to our mind of *some set of possible* conditions which would be a Sufficient Reason for its *truth*, takes away its *unbelievability, or in other words* enables us to 'conceive it as possible.' This view of Sir W. Hamilton's meaning *would account for* his using the term in its third signification; which Mr Mansel (p. 132) also *reduces* to the first, but which may be better identified with the second: for of first truths also it is impossible to assign any Sufficient Reason. *That for this reason, however, the truths which are the basis of all our conceptions of things should be nicknamed inconceivable, I hold to be an entirely inadmissible abuse of language.*

a–a67   we
b–b67   we are capable of thinking something
c–c67   Mr. Mansel may make his choice between the two opinions. I
d–d67   Space and in all Time
e–e67   must of course

a–a67   We
b–b67   anything which, while it has never been presented in our experience, also contradicts our habitual associations:
c–c67   some possible
d–d67   existence
e–e67   incredibility, and
f–f67   explains, though it does not justify,
g–g67   endeavours to reduce
h–h67   [*this sentence does not correspond to anything in the final text*]

Fragment 6. P. 118n.32[*] (Harvard)

"is one & indivisible may *logically* (*ratione*) be considered as diverse & plural, & vice versa, what are *really* diverse & plural may *logically* be viewed as one & indivisible. As an example of the former;—the sides & angles of a triangle (or trilateral) as mutually correlative—as together making up the same simple figure—& as, without destruction of that figure, actually inseparable from it, & from each other, are *really* one; but in as much as they have peculiar relations which may, in thought, be considered severally & for themselves, they are *logically* twofold."

Does Sir W. Hamilton mean to say that the sides of a triangle, & its angles, are *really* and *in themselves* one—that there is "identity" between them; & that they only differ as the *same thing* regarded in a different point of view? If so, the words *one*, *same*, & *identity*, must have changed their meaning. I could understand his expressions if they had been used of the figure itself. That, he might justly have said, is identical, is the same in itself, though it may be regarded in two relations or points of view; in relation to its sides, as a trilateral; in relation to its angles, as a triangle. But it might as well be said that a man's head & his feet are the same thing regarded in different points of view, as that the sides & angles of a figure are so.

We shall find, in the sequel, that this particular confusion of ideas is habitual to Sir W. Hamilton: it is quite usual with him to overlook the difference between what is implied by a thing, & what is in the thing itself. The principal novelties which he attempted to introduce into the Science of Logic, originated, as we shall see, in non-observance of this distinction.

The following passage, from the "Discussions", (pp. 47, 48) shews that in calling knowledge & the consciousness of knowledge "really identical" he only meant that they are inseparable. "I can feel without perceiving, I can perceive without imagining, I can imagine without remembering, I can remember without judging (in the emphatic signification), I can judge without willing. One of these acts does not immediately suppose the other. Though modes merely of the same indivisible subject, they are modes in *relation to each other*, really distinct, & admit, therefore, of psychological discrimination. But can I feel without being conscious that I feel? can I remember, without being conscious that I remember? or, can I be conscious, without being conscious that I perceive, or imagine, or reason? . . . . But

[*Headed in Mill's hand "Note (a) continued." In the printed version, Mill quotes part of the passage with which the fragment begins, but then departs totally from the wording of this draft.]

Fragment 7. P. 225n.25–33 (Harvard)

"got directly from the sense of touch". This is *a good answer to Platner's conclusion that those notions are obtained by sight alone: but it does not conflict with Platner's observations, nor with any inference drawn from them by me. It is, on the contrary, exactly what I should expect*. The sense of sight *not being* necessary to give the perception of simultaneity *(though it gives that perception more promptly & on a wider scale) is not necessary to the genesis I have suggested of the idea of extension out of the muscular feelings. Nor do I in the least doubt that a* person born blind can acquire, *though by a much slower* process, all that there is in our notion of Space, except the visible picture: but he will be much longer before he realizes it completely, & in the case of Platner's patient, that point does not seem to have been reached.

Fragment 8. Pp. 503.25–504.7[*] (Yale)

A history of philosophy from his hand, unless proposing to himself a new object had altered his point of view, could not have been final; it would not have been a philosophical history of philosophy; but it would have stood in the same relation to such a work—in which accurate & complete annals stand to political history: it would have *prodigiously abridged the labour of subsequent historians & could have been an invaluable protection against their mistakes*. Such, therefore,

---

*a–a*67   just what might have been expected, for I am far from agreeing with Platner that the notions of figure and distance come originally from sight.
   *b–b*67   is not
   *c–c*67   ; but, giving a prodigious number of simultaneous sensations in one glance, it greatly quickens all processes dependent on observation of the fact of simultaneousness. A
   *d–d*67   by a more gradual

[*Headed in Mill's hand "p. 560", i.e., of the 2nd ed.]
   *a–a*67   been an invaluable protection against the mistakes of subsequent historians, and would have prodigiously abridged their labours

Appendix B

Textual Emendations

THE FOLLOWING LIST includes the corrections and emendations made silently in the text. Accidental typographical errors in the 1st, 2nd, and 3rd editions are not recorded, nor are substantives in those editions, except that those which are probably typographical errors, but have some plausibility, are recorded as variants in the text, with a query as to their status. In the list, after the page and line number of this edition, the first reading is that of the unamended text; this is followed by the corrected reading as it would appear if we followed the style and format of the 4th ed. (i.e., our restyling, for example of quotations, sometimes gives the actual reading in the text a slightly different appearance from that in the list below). The entries conclude, where appropriate, with a justification (in square brackets) for the emendations. The asterisks indicate typographical errors which occurred as a result of the resetting of lines that, in the previous edition, began with the word before which the quotation marks appear (in the original editions all quotations of more than two lines have quotation marks at the beginning of all lines). The four entries between 103 and 112 are included because Gathering K in the 4th ed. exists in two states, one of which contains the erroneous readings.

civ. 7   ).[.)]
Table of Contents, Chap. ix   On the [Of the] [*as in title in text in all eds., and in Table of Contents in* 65^1, 65^2]
Table of Contents, Chap xx   or Forms [, or Forms,] [*as in title in text in all eds.*]
Table of Contents, Chap. xxv   553 [555] [*paging altered in this edition*]
Table of Contents, Chap. xxvi   561 [564] [*paging altered in this edition*]
Table of Contents, Chap. xxvii   591 [607] [*paging altered in this edition*]
Table of Contents, Chap. xxviii   617 [633] [*paging altered in this edition*]
14.18   immediately, [immediately] [*as in* Source, 65^1, 65^2, 67]
16.36   complement [complement,] [*as in* Source, 65^1, 65^2, 67]
17.13   phænomena— [phænomena,—] [*as in* Source, 65^1, 65^2, 67]
18.17   "inferred [inferred]*
31.27   "the phænomena [the "phænomena] [*as in* Source, 67]

43.15　cognizable [cognisable] [*as in* Source, 65^1, 65^2, 67]

44.6　est [best] [*dropped character*]

45.1　[*line space added*] [*as in* 65^1, 65^2]

45n.17　divine [Divine] [*as in* Source, 67; *note added in* 67]

52.12　of a cause [of a Cause] [*as in* 65^1, 65^2, *and elsewhere in sentence*]

55n.4–5　denominates "plurality ["denominates plurality] [*as in* Source, 65^1]

89.　Title CONDITIONED [CONDITIONED,] [*as in* 65^1, 65^2, *and* Table of Contents *of all eds.*]

95.16　a "conscious ["a conscious] [*as in* Source, 65^1, 65^2]

103.35　am I [I am] [*as in* 65^1, 65^2, 67, *and other state of* 72]

104.19　It is [Is it] [*as in* 65^1, 65^2, 67, *and other state of* 72]

111.40　now; [now:] [*as in* 65^1, 65^2, 67, *and other state of* 72]

112.27　organ; [organ:] [*as in* 65^1, 65^2, 67, *and other state of* 72]

116.30　feeling; [feeling:] [*as in* Source, 65^1, 65^2, 67]

117n.2　194,5 [194–5] [*as in* 65^1, 65^2]

119.17　relative. The [relative." "The] [*to indicate that two passages are quoted*]

119.31　[I believe [I [believe] [*as in* 65^1, 65^2, *and to conform to* Source]

119.35　[of the God [of the [God] [*as in* 65^1, 65^2, *and to conform to* Source]

133.6–7　instrumeut [instrument]

138.2　consciousness [Consciousness] [*as in* 65^1, 65^2, *and with same and the following sentences*]

138.22　sense [Sense] [*as in* Source, 65^1, 65^2]

142.15　himself [himself.]

150.20　minds. [minds."] [*as in* 65^1, 65^2, 67; *indicated in this edition by a line space*]

150.22　quality [duality] [*as in* Source, 65^1, 65^2, 67]

151.24　that ["that] [*as in* 65^1, 65^2, 67]*

153n.1　Dissertation C [Note C] [*to conform to usage elsewhere*]

158.8　succ eds [succeeds]

168.6　it [it,] [*as in* 65^1, 65^2, 67]

173.33　decidedly ["decidedly] [*as in* 65^1, 65^2, 67]

173.37　surrendered [surrendered,] [*as in* Source, 65^1, 65^2, 67]

182.10　ourselves [ourselves.]

190.5　mind [Mind] [*as in* 65^1, 65^2, 67, *and elsewhere in same passage*]

205n.8　consciousness, [consciousness;] [*as in* Source, 67; *note added in* 67]

213.19　matter [Matter] [*as in* 65^1, 65^2, *and elsewhere in passage*]

223.5–6　Pyschological [Psychological]

223.12　Pyschological [Psychological]

228.32　conceiving [perceiving] [*as in* Source, 65^1]

237.3　by ["by] [*as in* 65^1, 65^2, 67]

239.11　on the [on] [*as in* Source, 65^1)

252.34　one into [into one] [*as in both* Sources, 65^1]

253.18　into mind [into the mind] [*as in both* Sources, 65^1]

253.34　another, [another idea,] [*as in* Source, 65^1]

253.38　impotant [important]

256.23　results [result] [*as in* Source, 65^1, 65^2]

256.28　constituted [constituent] [*as in* Source, 65^1, 65^2]

272.4　Lecture, [Lecture,* [*footnote:*] *Lectures, i, 338.] [*as in* 65^1, 65^2, 67; *the footnote was erroneously deleted when a revision in* 72 *deleted the other original footnotes on this page*]

273.12　science [science,] [*as in* Source, 65^1, 65^2, 67]

274n.4 be neither [neither be] [*as in* Source, 65[1]]
277.28 immediately [mediately] [*as in* Source, 65[1]]
277.28 consciousness— [consciousness,—] [*as in* Source, 65[1], 65[2], 67]
277.40 Germany, Prussia [Germany,—Prussia] [*as in* Source, 65[1], 65[2], 67]
278.26 ideas of A [ideas A] [*as in* Source, 65[1], 65[2], 67]
281n.9 restricted [astricted] [*as in* Source, 65[1]]
282.40 antecedent [antecedents] [*as in* 65[1], 65[2], 67]
286.25 and an alkali [and alkali] [*as in* Source, 65[1], 65[2], 67]
287.4 compositions [compositions,] [*as in* Source, 65[1], 65[2], 67]
287.6 to the [to their] [*as in* Source, 65[1]]
288.8 retraction [retractation] [*as in* Source, 65[1], 65[2], 67]
288.12 reading [reaching] [*as in* 65[1], 65[2], 67]
289.19 retraction [retractation] [*as in* Source, 65[1], 65[2], 67]
291.22 explanation [explanation,] [*as in* Source, 65[1], 65[2], 67]
294.12 cause [Cause] [*as in* 65[1], 65[2], 67, *and same sentence*]
295.20 this, [this] [*as in* Source, 65[1], 65[2], 67]
295.40 transport— [transport,—] [*as in* Source, 65[1], 65[2], 67]
297.10 is ["is] [*as in* 65[1], 65[2], 67]
298.20 principle [Principle] [*as in* Source, 65[1], 65[2], 67]
304.31 tell; [tell:] [*as in* Source, 65[1], 65[2], 67]
306.7 [*line space added to make references clear*]
306.10 it [it,] [*as in* Source, 65[1], 65[2], 67]
306.14 generals [generals,] [*as in* Source, 65[1], 65[2], 67]
306.25–6 object, and [object, and,] [*as in* Source, 65[1], 65[2], 67]
306.32 extended [extended,] [*as in* Source, 65[1], 65[2], 67]
306.34 extended, [extended] [*as in* Source, 65[1], 65[2], 67]
306.42 then [then,] [*as in* Source, 65[1], 65[2], 67]
307.17 "the employment [the "employment] [*as in* Source, 65[1], 65[2]]*
308n.3 co-existing [coexisting] [*as in* Source, 65[1], 65[2], 67]
309.20 not [not,] [*as in* Source, 65[1], 65[2], 67]
310n.1 iii,137 [iii.137]
318.18 is a part of it [it is a part of] [*as in* 65[1], 65[2]]
319.6 follows:* [follows:†]
319.19 that is [that it is] [*as in* 65[1], 65[2], 67]
322.16–17 "the words [the "words] [*as in* Source, 65[1], 65[2]]*
325.22 manner [manner,] [*as in* Source, 65[1], 65[2], 67]
332.12 ?" ["?] [*the question is JSM's, not* Source's]
333.10 judgment [Judgment] [*as in* 65[1], 65[2], *and elsewhere*]
337n.19 for ["for] [*as in* 65[1], 65[2], 67]
337n.27 Hamilton's. [Hamilton's,]
338.7 subject [Subject] [*as in* Source, 65[1], 65[2], 67]
342.10 those [these] [*as in* Source, 65[1]]
347.13 reasoning [Reasoning] [*as in* 65[1], 65[2], *and elsewhere in same sentence*]
348.11 is [in] [*as in* 65[1], 65[2]]
348n.3 *Ibid* [*Ibid.*]
349n.1 'the ["the]
350n.1 practical, not productive [*practical*, not *productive*] [*as in* Source, 65[1], 65[2], 67]
356.8 soul [Soul] [*as in* 65[1], 65[2], 67, *and to conform to rest of passage*]
368.23 material [Material] [*as in* Source, 65[1], 65[2], 67]

369.16   ἐξοχήν [ἐξοχήν] [*correct in* 65[1], 65[2], 67]
376.19   principle [Principle] [*as in* 65[1], 65[2], *and to conform to rest of passage*]
380.16   Concepts [concepts] [*as in* 65[1], 65[2], 67, *and to conform to rest of passage*]
382.14   leave [have] [*as in* 65[1], 65[2], 67]
382.15   laws [laws,] [*as in* Source, 65[1], 65[2], 67]
384.11   object [objects] [*as in* 65[1], 65[2], *and for sense*]
391n.5   a crocodile [the crocodile] [*as in* Source, 67; *passage added in* 67]
397.5   means every [means Every] [*as in* 65[1], 65[2], 67, *and to conform to rest of passage*]
398.40   all [All] [*for sense*]
399n.12   this [his] [*as in* 65[1], 65[2], 67, *and to match* mine *in same sentence*]
399n.20   is B [is all B] [*for sense*]
400n.7   is [is,] [*as in* 65[1], 65[2], 67]
400n.13   all [All] [*for sense*]
400n.22   Schiebler [Scheibler] [*correctly given in* 65[1]]
401.13   some [Some] [*for sense*]
401.14   some [Some] [*for sense*]
401.29   all [All] [*for sense*]
403.30   words [moods] [*as in* Source]
405.23   *Roman* [*Roman,*] [*as in* Source, 65[1], 65[2], 67]
407.10   the "harmony ["the harmony] [*as in* Source, 65[1], 65[2], 67]
408n.1   Lectures [*Lectures]
410.5   disjunctive [Disjunctive] [*as in* 65[1], 65[2], *and elsewhere in passage*]
411.18   no [No] [*as in* 65[1], 65[2], 67, *and to conform to rest of passage*]
411.38   *immediata,* [*immediata*] [*as in* Source, 65[1], 65[2], 67]
415.18   Logicæ; [Logicæ:] [*as in* 65[1], 65[2], 67, *and for consistency*]
415n.7   Logicæ [*Logicum*]
417.11   vacuum; [vacuum:] [*as in* 65[1], 65[2], *and for consistency*]
423n.7   says [says,] [*reference moved to end of quotation*]
427n.6   now [*now*] [*as in* Source, 65[1], 65[2], 67]
427n.13   these: [these;] [*as in* Source, 65[1], 65[2], 67]
427n.30   same: [same;] [*as in* Source, 65[1], 65[2], 67]
427n.35   *contra.* [*contra,*] [*as in* Source, 65[1], 65[2], 67]
431.34   reaction" (what [reaction." [What] [*for intelligibility and to accommodate altered style*]
432.22   forth, nor [forth, nor,] [*as in* Source, 65[1], 65[2], 67]
438.39   responsibility, [responsibility,—] [*as in* Source, 65[1], 65[2], 67]
440n.2   Lectures i [Lectures, i]
440.16   necessity [Necessity] [*as in* 65[1], 65[2], 67, *and to conform to rest of passage*]
442n.5   Appendix [(Appendix]
443n.2   on [to] [*as* passim]
445.12   egress [regress] [*as in* 65[1], 65[2], 67, *and for sense*]
447.24–5   phliosophers [philosophers]
458n.7   a "well ["a well] [*as in* Source, 67; *passage added in* 67]
468.34   shunned [shunned.]
469.9   happen, [happen.]
478.21   qualities [quantities] [*as in* 65[1], 65[2], *and for sense*]
479.31   Laws [laws] [*as in* 65[1], 65[2], 67, *and elsewhere in sentence*]
483.5   make [makes]
483.11   "It [" 'It] [*as in* Source]

483.11   time, says Baillet, since [time,' says Baillet, 'since] [*JSM adds* says Baillet,]

483.18   traces. [traces.'] [*as in* Source]

483.19   Revera ['Revera] [*as in* Source]

483.25   expedire." . . . [expedire. . . .'] [*to conform to* Source; 65¹, 65², 67 *lack the quotation marks*]

483.29   of ["of] [*as in* 65¹, 65²; *the quotation from Hamilton continues*]

483.36   *mankind."* [mankind.'"] [*as in* Source]

486n.8   35, 42 [35–42] [*as in* 65¹, 65², 67]

487.11   "Wonder, says Aristotle, is . . . philosophy; ["'Wonder,' says Aristotle, 'is . . . philosophy;'] [*as in* Source]

487.15   world,' [world,] [*as in* Source, 65¹, 65²]

487.25   heavens." [heavens.'"] [*as in* Source]

490.10   pyschological [psychological]

491n.20   This [This,] [*as in* 65¹, 65², 67]

503n.7   τῆν [τὴν] [*as in* Source]

503n.7   ἴνα [ἵνα] [*as in* Source, 65¹, 65², 67]

Appendix C

Corrected References

IN THE FOLLOWING LIST the entries take this form: page and line reference in this edition; reading in the copy-text; corrected reading [in square brackets]. The addition of "Vol." or "P." and such changes as "p." to "P." are not noted, if there is no other correction made. In all references to "Footnotes to Reid" we have silently added "n" to JSM's page references. Also, except where a correction is involved, the division or combination of references is not noted. Apart from these exceptions, and the corrections listed below, all other changes are signalled in the text by square brackets.

13n.1   p. 643 [pp. 643–4]
14n.5   844 [844n]
15n.2   866 [866n]
21n.5   866 [866n]
22n.1   p. 320 [pp. 322n–3n]
26n.12   p. 313 [Pp. 313n–14n]
27n.2   Reid, 886 ["Dissertations," p. 880]
27n.8–9   79 [79n]; p. 82 [pp. 82–3]
27n.19   30 [30n]
28n.7   p. 83 [pp. 83–4]
34n.8   90–98 [90–6]
42n.3   p. 13 [pp. 14–15]
43n.4   pp. 32, 33 [p. 33]
44n.1   pp. 34, 35 [p. 35]
45n.19   107 [107n]
50n.4   50 [50n]
52n.24   159 [159n]
61n.9   Pp. 749, 750 [p. 750]
64n.3   p. 36 [pp. 36–7]
64n.19   126 [126n]
64n.24   126 [126n]
74n.2   234, 235 [235–6]
76n.12   132 [132n]
77n.8   36 [36n]
77n.39   132 [132n]
81n.6   100 *et seq.* [100–4]

99n.40   pp. 28, 29 [p. 28]
111n.2   228 [pp. 228–9]
111n.4–112n.1   218–221 [*218–19 †219–21]
118n.20   806 [806n]
123n.13   129 [129n]
132n.1–2   pp. 743–745 [*divided into two*, p. 743, p. 745]
137n.19   p. 129 [pp. 129–30]
141n.6   pp. 52, 53 [P. 52]
142n.4   894 [894n]
149n.1   377 [277]
149n.3   p. 283 [pp. 283–4]
150n.1–151n.2   288–95 [*reference split into two (the first, on p. 150n.1, is to* 288; *and the second, on p. 151n.2 is corrected to* 292–4)]
152n.1   pp. 296–7 [p. 296]
153n.21   817 [817n]
154n.4   p. xxxix [pp. xxxviii—xl]
154n.6   p. 684 [pp. 684–6]
165n.17–18   p. 309 [pp. 309–10]
169n.1   p. 56 [pp. 56–7]
170n.4   p. 123 [pp. 123–4]
205n.9   p. 7 [Pp. 7–8]
214n.8   854, 855 [864n–5n]
220n.1   869 [869n]
224n.1   p. 174 [pp. 174–5]
225n.25   143 [143n]
229n.1   p. 167 [pp. 167–8]
234n.5   p. 376 [pp. 376–7]
234n.5   368 [369]
234n.43   p. 377 [pp. 377n–8n]
235n.1   861 [861n]
237n.8   pp. 874, 875 [p. 875n]
237n.11   151 [151n]
262n.16   p. 90 [pp. 90–1]
266n.16   p. xxvii [Pp. xxvii–xxviii]
266n.19   112 [112n]
267n.1   p. 149 [pp. 149–50]
274n.20   339–346 [339–40]
275n.1–3   347–349 and 349–351 [*references split among three separate notes*]
278n.1   iii [i]
290n.9   620 [620n]
298n.2   p. 149 [pp. 149–50]
302n.3   286 [296]
302n.4   p. 287 [pp. 287–8]
303n.1   287–290 [288–90]
305n.1   p. 298 [pp. 298–300]
306n.1–307n.1   131–137 [131, 134–6] [*reference split between two separate notes*]
317n.6   p. 276 [pp. 276–7]
319n.1   p. 171 [pp. 171–2]
321n.1   121, 127 [121, 126, 127]
321n.3   283 [283n]

321n.5   212 [126]
330n.1   p. 204 [pp. 204–5]
332n.14   53–56 [53–5]
334n.1   787, 788 [787n–8n]
337n.8   p. 58 [pp. 58–9]
358n.1   p. 78 [pp. 78–9]
373n.1   113 [713n]
383n.19   527, 528 [527–9]
393n.4   379–384 [379 and ff.]
396n.2   601 [691n]
400n.19   p. 259 [pp. 259–61]
401n.11   600, 601 [690n–1n]
414n.9   Sect. 5 et 6 [§§8 and 9]
415n.10   p. 197 [pp. 197–8]
416n.2   652 [652n]
420n.1   pp. 628, 631 [p. 628n]
422n.4   861 [861n]
434n.1   p. 495 [pp. 494–5]
438n.1   25 *et seqq.* [25–6]
440n.2   26, 37 [26–7]
449n.6   22 *et seqq.* [22–3]
452n.1   13, 14 [43–4]
466n.7   46 [46n]
491n.20   pp. 247, 248 [p. 248]
497n.13   p. 2 [pp. 3–4]

Appendix D

Bibliographic Index of Persons and Works Cited in the *Examination*, with Variants and Notes

MILL, like most nineteenth-century authors, is cavalier in his approach to sources, seldom identifying them with sufficient care, and frequently quoting them inaccurately. This Appendix is intended to help correct these deficiencies, and to serve as an index of names and titles (which are consequently omitted in the Index proper). The material is arranged in alphabetical order, with an entry for each person or work quoted or referred to in the text.

The entries take the following form:
1. Identification: author, title, etc., in the usual bibliographic form.
2. Notes (if required) giving information about JSM's use of the source, indication if the work is in his library, and any other relevant information.
3. A list of the places where the author or work is quoted, and a separate list of the places where there is reference only. Those works that are reviewed are so noted.
4. A list of substantive variants between JSM's text and his source, in this form: Page and line reference to the present text. Reading in the present text] Reading in the source (page reference in the source).

The list of substantive variants also attempts to place quoted passages in their contexts by giving the beginnings and endings of sentences. Omissions of two sentences or less are given in full; only the length of other omissions is given. Translated material from the French is given in the original. When the style has been altered, the original form is retained in the entries (except that the quotation marks in the left margin of the original, used to signal the continuation of quotations, are omitted).

ABBOTT, THOMAS KINGSMILL. *Sight and Touch: an attempt to disprove the received (or Berkeleian) theory of vision*. London: Longman, Green, Longman, Roberts, and Green, 1864.
NOTE: the reference is in a quotation from Mahaffy. Fraser's article mentioned at 242n was apparently not republished.
QUOTED: 242n
REFERRED TO: 240
242n.3 "Let us suppose] Let us then suppose (70)
242n.5 which, therefore, is] which is therefore (70)
242n.8 farthest] furthest (70)

ABELARD, PETER.
  NOTE: the quotation is in a quotation from Hamilton, who mistakenly attributes the passage
  to Abelard. See St. Augustine.
  QUOTED: 61

ALDRICH, HENRY. *Artis Logicæ Compendium*. Oxford: Sheldonian Theatre, 1704.
  NOTE: JSM's reference is to "Quæstionum Logicarum Determinatio, quæst. 19," which is
  Lib. II, Cap. v, §15 in the 1st ed. (Oxford: Sheldonian Theatre, 1691), but is there
  designated as JSM designates it in the ed. cited (a copy of which is in the London Library,
  and may have been part of JSM's donation of his father's books). The first sentence he
  quotes is the rubric for the section. A copy of the ed. edited by H. L. Mansel (Oxford:
  Graham, 1852) is in JSM's library, Somerville College, inscribed "From the Author" on the
  flyleaf.
  QUOTED: 415
  415.6 "Contraria . . . distant. Non] 19. *Contraria . . . distant.* / §.19. Non (118)

ALEMBERT, JEAN LE ROND D'. *Mélanges de littérature, d'histoire, et de philosophie*. New ed. 5 vols. Amsterdam: Chatelain, 1759–67.
  NOTE: in JSM's library, Somerville College. Both references, which are to the same passage,
  derive from Hamilton.
  REFERRED TO: 228, 255n

ALEXANDER, PATRICK PROCTOR. *Mill and Carlyle. An Examination of Mr. John
  Stuart Mill's Doctrine of Causation in Relation to Moral Freedom. With an
  Occasional Discourse on Sauerteig, by Smelfungus*. Edinburgh: Nimmo, 1866.
  QUOTED: 449n, 450n, 451n, 457n, 460n, 462n, 463n
  REFERRED TO: civ, 449n, 457n, 460n, 463n, 466n, 467n
  449n.3 consciousness. . . . As] consciousness; certain it is at least, it was at one time by Mr
  Mill himself so considered—*vide* "System of Logic," as before quoted—"The practical
  feeling of Free-will common in a greater or less degree to all mankind." [*ellipisis indicates
  4-sentence omission*] As (22–3) [*cf. entry for* 450n.26 *below*]
  449n.23 "general . . . race;"] To the general . . . race, *philosophers with rigour excepted.* (25)
  449n.25 "unless . . . thousand,"] It is not that the philosopher will lie like a thief, in wilful
  misreport of his consciousness; but by the very conditions of the case, unless . . . thousand,
  he is incapable of an accurate observation and candid notation of its contents. (25)
  450n.26 "practical feeling of Free Will"] Perhaps it is not; but what I *feel* I am able to do is
  surely a subject of consciousness; certain it is at least, it was at one time by Mr Mill himself
  so considered—*vide* "System of Logic," as before quoted—"The practical *feeling* of
  Free-will common in a greater or less degree to all mankind." (22) [*cf.* Mill, *A System of
  Logic, CW*, VIII, 836]
  450n.26–7 "a feeling of Moral Freedom which we are conscious of,"] "The *feeling* of moral
  Freedom we are *conscious* of." (22–3) [*cf.* Mill, *A System of Logic, CW*, VIII, 841]
  450n.27–8 "was . . . conscious"] And as Mr Mill himself now interprets this feeling of
  Freedom of which he was . . . conscious, it "must have meant" a being "conscious before he
  had decided that he was *able* to decide either way." (23)
  451n.2 he not] not he (29)
  451n.14–15 "veritable consciousness." . . . " a fraudulent substitute palmed upon him"]
  Should Mr Mill, on the other hand, deny that he is so conscious, we venture to assert with
  some confidence, that his consciousness contradicts that of every man not a Necessitarian
  philosopher; and further, that it is not his veritable consciousness, but a fraudulent
  substitute palmed off upon him by the "system" to which he is wedded. (29)
  457n.2–3 "our current moralities" . . . "as a form of superstition,"] And no man who reasons
  with the least strictness can fail to evolve for himself this result of the doctrine; having done
  which, he can only, on the ground of logic, regard our current Moralities as a form of
  superstition, useful, perhaps—as the Christian religion is admitted still to have its uses by
  many who for themselves will have none of it—but not otherwise entitled to the respect of
  an advanced intelligence. (118)

457n.3–4 "moral ideas as illusions," . . . "it . . . motives:"] Precisely according to the decisiveness with which we recognise moral ideas as *illusions*, it . . . *motives*. (119)

457n.5–7 "The . . . evaporated:"] The . . . evaporated—it has absolutely, so to speak, evaporated in the emancipated world—relatively in the emancipated individual—on the obvious ground of the extinction in him of the special sympathy. (119)

457n.8–9 "in . . . indifference," . . . "might . . . are,"] Also, in the emancipated world, the other remaining "external sanctions" might . . . are, in . . . indifference, which—even in the supposed disappearance of *all* virtue—would be nearly sure to proclaim itself in the virtue of charity. (119) [*JSM has reversed clausal order*]

457n.10–11 "succeed . . . gorilla."] But instantly the *tendency* to so degrade itself would begin to operate in the world, and—give him time—how much we decline to specify—our faith in man is fixed that he would succeed . . . Gorilla, so as even to satisfy the strictest scientific requirements of the Professor Huxley of the period. (120–1)

462n.32 "How should] For how should (65)

462n.3–6 "could . . . assurance," . . . "that . . . one, we should be obliged to admit that their doom was not just in the particular instance."] Of assassins who " regard themselves not as criminals but as heroic martyrs," we may boldly say that could . . . assurance that . . . one, however, on obvious grounds of general expediency, we might acquiesce in the doom awarded them, the Justice of it as *deserved* or *due* to their deed, considered in itself, and as an isolated act, we should very peremptorily deny. *Justifiable* we should call it in general not *just* in the particular instance. (63–4)

462n.12 "may . . . virtue."] Generally, in such cases, while we may doubt if it be morally *just* (deserved) that the particular hero should suffer for what may really have been an act of sublime virtue, his punishment may yet seem *justifiable* to us, on the ground that no society could afford to grow a succession of them. (64)

462n.22 "culpable . . . it."] As to "crimes committed in obedience to a perverted conscience," it seems sufficient to say that we consider them justly (or deservedly) punished *as* so committed; we hold the felon responsible for his crime, if not immediately perhaps, yet mediately as culpable . . . it, in so far as this may fairly be surmised to have emerged under the conditions of sanity. (63)

463n.12–16 "asserting . . . motives;" . . . "to assert an absolute commencement as the mode under . . . though inconceivable, has . . . believed:" . . . "would . . . uncaused."] How, while with emphasis asserting . . . motives, could Hamilton also intend to assert "an absolute commencement" as the *mode* under . . . though "inconceivable, was . . . believed? This would . . . uncaused." (80)

AMMONIUS HERMIÆ. *Ammonii Hermiæ in Aristotelis de Interpretatione Librum Commentarius*. Venice: Aldus, 1546.

NOTE: in JSM's library, Somerville College; Vol. I of the 3-vol. set is inscribed: "This is indeed a liber rarissimus & was bought by me at Norwich upon the sale of M^r. Hobson's books. SP [i.e., Samuel Parr]." The quotation of Aristotle at 413 is from Ammonius, 175.

QUOTED: 413

ANON. "Mill on Hamilton," *North American Review*, CIII (July, 1866), 250–60.

QUOTED: 31

REFERRED TO: cv, 32n

31.3 "An existence] But if Hamilton's more extended use of the word be admissible, then an existence (252)

31.6 things. . . . If the meaning] [*ellipsis indicates 3-sentence omission*] This is the issue of the book; but if the meaning (252–3)

31.6 word phenomenon which] word "phenomenon" which (253)

31.8 figure, &c., though] figure, etc., though (253)

ARCHIMEDES. Referred to: 482

ARISTOTLE.

NOTE: the references at 142, 152, 395 are in quotations from Hamilton; that at 328 is in a

quotation from Reid; one of those at 385 is in a quotation from Hamilton, the other in a quotation from Baynes.
REFERRED TO: cvii, 142, 152, 328, 385, 389, 395, 489n, 494, 502

―――― *Categories*, in *The Categories, On Interpretation, Prior Analytics* (Greek and English). Trans. Harold P. Cooke and Hugh Tredennick. London: Heinemann; Cambridge, Mass.: Harvard University Press, 1938, 12–108.
NOTE: this ed. used for ease of reference. The quotations at 413–16, Latin translations of vi, 6^a17–18, are in quotations from various writers on logic.
QUOTED: 413, 413–16
REFERRED TO: 345

―――― *The Metaphysics* (Greek and English). Trans. Hugh Tredennick. 2 vols. London: Heinemann; New York: Putnam's Sons, 1933.
NOTE: this ed. used for ease of reference. The quotations at 40, 40n are in a quotation from Hamilton; that at 413 is in a quotation from Ammonius Hermiæ; the indirect quotation at 487 is in a quotation from Hamilton; the quotations at 498, 503n derive from Hamilton.
QUOTED: 40, 40n, 411, 413, 487, 498, 503, 503n

―――― *The Nichomachean Ethics* (Greek and English). Trans. H. Rackham. London: Heinemann; New York: Putnam's Sons, 1926.
NOTE: this ed. used for ease of reference. The quotation at 105n is in a quotation from Mansel; that at 349n is in a quotation from Hamilton; those at 503, 503n derive from Hamilton; the references derive from Hamilton.
QUOTED: 105n, 349n, 503, 503n
REFERRED TO: 349, 435

―――― *On the Heavens* (Greek and English). Trans. W. K. C. Guthrie. London: Heinemann; Cambridge, Mass.: Harvard University Press, 1939.
NOTE: this ed. used for ease of reference.
QUOTED: 418

―――― *On Interpretation*, in *The Categories, On Interpretation, Prior Analytics* (Greek and English). Trans. Harold P. Cooke and Hugh Tredennick. London: Heinemann; Cambridge, Mass.: Harvard University Press, 1938, 114–78.
NOTE: this ed. used for ease of reference.
QUOTED: 411–12, 413

―――― *On the Soul*, in *On the Soul, Parva Naturalia, On Breath* (Greek and English). Trans. W. S. Hett. London: Heinemann; Cambridge, Mass.: Harvard University Press, 1935, 8–203.
NOTE: this ed. used for ease of reference. The notion of *species sensibiles*, mistakenly attributed to Lucretius at 15, originated in this work. The reference at 356 derives from Reid and Hamilton.
REFERRED TO: 15, 155, 356

―――― *Parts of Animals*, in *Parts of Animals, Movement of Animals, Progression of Animals* (Greek and English). Trans. A. L. Peck. London: Heinemann; Cambridge, Mass.: Harvard University Press, 1937, 52–430.
NOTE: this ed. used for ease of reference.
QUOTED: 418

―――― *The Physics* (Greek and English). Trans. Philip H. Wickstead and Francis M. Cornford. 2 vols. London: Heinemann; Cambridge, Mass.: Harvard University Press, 1963.
NOTE: this ed. used for ease of reference. The reference derives from Hamilton.
REFERRED TO: 425

ARNAULD, ANTOINE.
NOTE: the reference is in a quotation from Hamilton.
REFERRED TO: 152, 174

—— *Des vrayes et des fausses idées, contre ce qu'enseigne l'auteur de la Recherche de la vérité.* Cologne: Schouten, 1683.
NOTE: the reference derives from Reid.
REFERRED TO: 175

—— and Pierre Nicole. *The Port-Royal Logic.* See Baynes.

BACON, FRANCIS.
NOTE: the reference at 497n is in a quotation from Grote.
REFERRED TO: 368, 417, 418, 430, 485, 485n, 497n

—— *De Augmentis Scientiarum,* in *The Works of Francis Bacon.* Ed. James Spedding, Robert Leslie Ellis and Douglas Denon Heath. 14 vols. London: Longman, *et al.,* 1857–74, I, 415–840.
REFERRED TO: 368

—— *Novum Organum,* in *ibid.,* I, 119–365.
NOTE: the reference at 368 is in a quotation from Hamilton.
QUOTED: 321
REFERRED TO: 368, 423

BAILEY, SAMUEL. *Letters on the Philosophy of the Human Mind.* Second Series. London: Longman, Brown, Green, Longmans, and Roberts, 1858.
NOTE: the references are to Letter IV. The Doctrines of Sir William Hamilton Regarding Perception.
REFERRED TO: 162n, 178

—— *A Review of Berkeley's Theory of Vision, designed to Show the Unsoundness of that Celebrated Speculation.* London: Ridgway, 1842.
REFERRED TO: 178, 236n, 242n–3n, 256n

BAILLET, ADRIEN. *La Vie de Monsieur Des-Cartes.* 2 vols. Paris: Horthemels, 1691.
NOTE: the quotations are in a quotation from Hamilton.
QUOTED: 483

BAIN, ALEXANDER. Referred to: 9, 51, 216n

—— *Logic.* 2 pts. London: Longmans, Green, Reader, and Dyer, 1870.
NOTE: the two pts. are separately paginated. The exact wording suggested by the reference at 268 has not been found, but the doctrine is reflected in the passage cited, as well as elsewhere in the work.
REFERRED TO: 268, 293n

—— *The Senses and the Intellect.* London: Parker, 1855.
NOTE: the reference at 216n is in a quotation from McCosh; the quotation at 241 is in a quotation from Mahaffy. See also 2nd ed. below.
QUOTED: 217–19, 241
REFERRED TO: 216, 216n, 224, 227n, 234n, 235, 236, 240, 249
217.9   "When a muscle] Under this head it may be asserted that when a muscle (113)
217.10   carried; there] carried; that there (113)
218.4–5   former (from . . . effort) chiefly] former chiefly (114)
218.9   effort. . . . [*paragraph*] If] [*ellipsis indicates 1-paragraph omission*] (114)
218.10   If] 26. If (114)
218.10–11   determination] discrimination (114)
218.25–6   manner. . . . [*paragraph*] It] manner. But we shall defer the consideration of this attribute till we come to speak of the senses, more especially Touch and Sight. [*paragraph*] It (115)
218.41   once whether] once as to whether (115)
218.47   The third] 27. The third (116)
219.3   quicker motion with] quicker movement with (116)

219.8   extension. . . . [*paragraph*] We] [*ellipsis indicates 1-paragraph omission*] (116)
219.9   We] 28. We (116)
241.24   quicker motion with] quicker movement with (116)

———— *The Senses and the Intellect.* 2nd ed. London: Longman, Green, Longman, Roberts, and Green, 1864.
NOTE: the exact wording of the reference has not been found, but Bain, in describing the phenomenon, uses "Law of Relativity" and "principle of relativity" in the passage cited (cf. *ibid.*, 5, 325–6, 399ff., and 1st ed. [London: Parker, 1855]). The same wordings occur in Bain's *Mental and Moral Science* (London: Longmans, Green, 1868), 83, 185; in his *The Emotions and the Will*, 2nd ed. (London: Longmans, Green, 1865), 599; and in his *Logic*, I, 3. See also 1st ed. above.
QUOTED: 226–7, 231–4, 234n, 242, 245
REFERRED TO: 5, 216n, 228
226.17–18   eye," . . . "is] eye is (370)
227.3   visible ["visual"] organ] visible organ (371)
227.5   orbit. . . . [*paragraph*] When] [*ellipsis indicates 2-page omission*] (371–4)
227.11   further experience] *further experience* (374)
231.12   "I] The statement here made that all sensations, of which we are conscious as one out of another, afford a condition of apprehending extension, seems to me to imply and take for granted the point in dispute: for I (376)
234n.32   place, the essential] place, as remarked in the text, the essential (377n)
245.26   members.—When] members. [*paragraph*] When (398)
245.28   In this case] In such a case (398)
245.30   By getting a blow on] By a hurt on (398)
245.31   place in our] place on our (398)
245.34   sensations."] sensations; if, in addition, they are not well supplied with distinctive nerves, the difficulty is still greater. (398)

BARTHOLINUS, CASPARUS. *Enchiridion Logicum ex Aristotele.* 3rd ed. Leipzig: Cober, 1618.
NOTE: this ed., which JSM cites, is in the London Library, and may have been one of his father's books given by JSM.
QUOTED: 415
415.14   se mutuo] mutuo se (186)

BAYLE, PIERRE. *Dictionnaire historique et critique.* 2 vols. Rotterdam: Reinier Leers, 1697.
REFERRED TO: 425

BAYNES, THOMAS SPENCER. *An Essay on the New Analytic of Logical Forms, being that which gained the prize proposed by Sir Wm. Hamilton in the year 1846 for the best exposition of the new Doctrine propounded in his Lectures. With an Historical Appendix.* Edinburgh: Sutherland and Knox, 1850.
QUOTED: 385

————, trans. Antoine Arnauld and Pierre Nicole. *The Port-Royal Logic.* 3rd ed. Edinburgh: Sutherland, Knox; London: Simkin, Marshall, 1854.
NOTE: this ed. in JSM's library, Somerville College. The reference derives merely from the title-page of Baynes's *Essay on the New Analytic of Logical Forms.*
REFERRED TO: 386n

BENTHAM, JEREMY. Referred to: 37

BERKELEY, GEORGE.
NOTE: the reference at 153n is in a quotation from Hamilton.
REFERRED TO: 6, 10, 15n, 110, 152, 153n, 155, 163n, 183, 195, 196, 209n, 307, 362, 424, 493n

———— *The Analyst: or, a discourse addressed to an infidel mathematician:*

wherein it is examined whether the object, principles, and inferences, of the modern analysis are more distinctly perceived, or more evidently deduced, than religious mysteries and points of faith, in *The Works of George Berkeley, D. D.* 3 vols. London: Priestley, 1820, II, 401–55.
NOTE: this ed. (now lacking Vol. I) in JSM's library, Somerville College.
REFERRED TO: 428

———— *A Defence of Free-Thinking in Mathematics. In Answer to a Pamphlet of Philalethes Cantabrigiensis, entitled, Geometry no Friend to Infidelity, or a Defence of Sir Isaac Newton and the British Mathematicians. Also, An Appendix concerning Mr. Walton's Vindication of the Principles of Fluxions against the Objections contained in the Analyst. Wherein it is attempted to put this controversy in such a light as that every reader may be able to judge thereof,* in *ibid.,* III, 1–62.
REFERRED TO: 428

———— *An Essay towards a New Theory of Vision,* in *ibid.,* I, 225–316.
REFERRED TO: 230, 242n–3n

———— *A Treatise Concerning the Principles of Human Knowledge, wherein the chief causes of error and difficulty in the sciences, with the grounds of scepticism, atheism, and irreligion, are inquired into,* in *ibid.,* I, 1–106.
NOTE: JSM undoubtedly takes the quotation from Hamilton (who elides the paragraph that JSM does), but makes two errors in transcription that Hamilton does not (see final two entries in the collation below).
QUOTED: 304–5
304.4   "It] VII. It (5)
304.16   Again] VIII. Again (6)
304.28   whatever] whatsoever (6)
304.29–30   sense. [*paragraph*] Whether] sense. [*1-paragraph omission*] X. Whether (6–8)
304.30   abstracting their ideas] [*In Italics*] (8)
304.34   part] parts (8)
304.42   am] own (8)

BIBLE. Referred to: 204n
———— Acts. Quoted: 35
———— I Corinthians.
NOTE: the quotation is indirect.
QUOTED: 262
———— Hebrews.
NOTE: the quotation is indirect.
QUOTED: 471
471.34   a cloud of witnesses] Wherefore seeing we also are compassed about with so great a cloud of witnesses, let us lay aside every weight, and the sin which doth so easily beset *us*, and let us run with patience the race that is set before us. (12:1)
———— Job.
NOTE: the quotation is indirect.
QUOTED: 44
44.13–14   he who feeds the ravens] Who provideth for the raven his food,/When his young ones cry unto God,/And wander for lack of meat. (38:41–3)
———— Psalms.
NOTE: the quotation is indirect.
QUOTED: 439
439.21–2   the eye must have been made by one who sees, and the ear by one who hears.] He that planted the ear, shall he not hear?/He that formed the eye, shall he not see? (94:9)

BLAND, MILES. *Algebraical Problems, producing simple and quadratic equations, with their solutions; designed as an introduction to the higher branches of analytics*. Cambridge: Nicholson, 1812.
REFERRED TO: 476

——— *Geometrical Problems deducible from the first six books of Euclid, arranged and solved. To which is added, an Appendix containing the elements of plane geometry*. Cambridge: Nicholson, 1819.
REFERRED TO: 476

BOLTON, M. P. W. *Inquisitio Philosophica. An Examination of the Principles of Kant and Hamilton*. London: Chapman and Hall, 1866.
QUOTED: 52n
REFERRED TO: vii, 29n, 35n
52n.21–2 "In discussing] It is to be observed that in discussing (159n)
52n.22 Absolute] "Absolute" (159n)

BONNET, CHARLES.
NOTE: the reference is in a quotation from Hamilton.
REFERRED TO: 487

BOSWELL, JAMES. *Life of Johnson*. 2nd ed. 3 vols. London: Dilly, 1793.
NOTE: this ed. in JSM's library, Somerville College.
REFERRED TO: 183

BREREWOOD, EDWARD. *Tractatus Quidam Logici de Prædicabilibus, et Prædicamentis*. 3rd ed. Oxford: Turner, 1637.
NOTE: a copy of this ed. is in the London Library, and may be part of the donation by JSM of his father's books. JSM gives Tractatus Decimus, §§5 and 6, rather than §§8 and 9. (In the 1st ed., *ibid*., 1628, the passage is also in §§8 and 9.)
QUOTED: 414
414.21 "Contraria a Dialecticis] [*paragraph*] Contraria à *Dialecticis* (367)
414.21–3 Sunt Opposita . . . natura.] [*in italics*] (367)
414.22 et eodem] *et eidem* (367)
414.23 natura. . . . Sed] [*ellipsis indicates 1-paragraph omission, and a move from §8 to the beginning of the 1st paragraph of §9*] (367–8)
414.24 præcipue] præcipuæ (368)
414.24 Dialecticorum] *Dialecticorum* (368)
414.24 authoritans] authoritatis (368)
414.25 Aristotele] *Aristotele* (368)
414.25–6 breviorum: *Contraria*] breviorem. [*paragraph*] *Contraria* (368)

BROWN, THOMAS.
NOTE: the references at 168 and 169 are in quotations from Hamilton.
REFERRED TO: 10, 17, 115, 116, 153, 153n, 168, 169, 171, 172, 183, 196, 197, 217n, 239, 291, 294, 362, 440, 490n, 493n, 497, 497n–8n.

——— *Lectures on the Philosophy of Mind*. 19th ed. 4 vols. Edinburgh: Black; London: Longman, 1851.
NOTE: the reference at 225n is in a quotation from Mahaffy; the last reference at 158 is in a quotation from Hamilton.
QUOTED: 167n, 221n
REFERRED TO: 15, 155–9, 163–8, 174–6, 219–21, 224, 225n, 424
167n.4–5 "I do not," . . . "conceive] In the view which I take of the subject, accordingly, I do not conceive (II, 11)
221n.3–4 feelings" . . . "when] feelings, however, when (II, 3)
221n.4 was] we (II, 3)
221n.5 *divisibility . . . parts*] [*not in italics*] (II, 3)
221n.5–6 *length . . . divisibility.*] [*not in italics*] (II, 3)
221n.9 "It would] It certainly, at least, would (II, 7)

221n.10   efforts] effort (II, 7)
221n.12   mind."] mind, and arisen too in circumstances which must lead to the combination of them in one complex notion. (II, 7)

BRUTUS, MARCUS JUNIUS.
NOTE: the reference derives from Alexander.
REFERRED TO: 462n

BURGERSDIJCK, FRANCO. *Institutionum logicarum libri duo*. Cambridge: Field, 1660.
NOTE: in JSM's library, Somerville College. JSM's spelling is Burgersdyk, and he refers to the work as Burgersdicii *Institutiones Logicæ*.
QUOTED: 413
413.14–15   "Oppositorum . . . contradictoria.] [*paragraph*] VI. Oppositorum . . . contradicentia. (94)
413.15–16   contradictoria. [*paragraph*] Disparata] [*1-paragraph omission*] (94)
413.16   Disparata . . . modo.] VIII. [*misprint for* VII.] Disparata . . . modo. (94)
413.16–17   modo. Sic homo & equus, album & cæruleum] modo. [*paragraph*] I. § Sic *homo & equus, album & cæruleum* (94–5)
413.20   oppositorum] oppositionis (95)
413.20–1   genere. . . . [*paragraph*] Contraria] genere. Album & nigrum non sunt disparata, licèt album non solùm nigro, sed etiam mediis coloribus opponatur: aliter enim album nigro opponitur, aliter coloribus mediis. Similitur nec liber & servus disparata sunt, licèt servus non solùm libero, sed etiam domino opponatur, quia non est idem oppositionis genus utrobique: nam dominus & servus sunt relativè opposita; liber & servus, contraria. [*paragraph*] *Contraria* (95)
413.21   Contraria . . . distant.] [*in italics*] (95)
413.21   absolute] *absoluta* (95)

BURIDAN, JEAN.
NOTE: the reference in each case is to the well-known dilemma, Buridan's ass, or *asinus Buridani*. In fact, it is not found in his works, but has traditionally been attributed to him, probably in derision.
REFERRED TO: 451n, 468

BURKE, EDMUND. Referred to: 160

BYRON, GEORGE GORDON. *Don Juan*, in *The Works of Lord Byron*. Ed. Thomas Moore. 17 vols. London: Murray, 1832–33, XV–XVII.
REFERRED TO: 27n

CÆSAR, JULIUS.
NOTE: the reference is to his "peculiar gift"; *s.v.* Plutarch.
REFERRED TO: 281

CALDERWOOD, HENRY. *The Philosophy of the Infinite*. Edinburgh: Constable; London: Hamilton and Adams, 1854.
REFERRED TO: 92, 93n

———— "The Sensational Philosophy—Mr. J. S. Mill and Dr. M'Cosh," *British and Foreign Evangelical Review*, XV (April, 1866), 396–412.
REFERRED TO: ciii

Cambridge Problems: Being a collection of the printed questions proposed to the candidates for the degree of Bachelor of Arts, at the General Examination, from the year 1801 to the year 1820 inclusively. London: Black and Armstrong, 1836.
NOTE: this work is merely illustrative: see also the compilations *Mathematical Problems and Examples . . . 1821–1836* (Cambridge: Grant, 1837), and A. H. Frost, ed., *The Mathematical Questions . . . 1838–49* (Cambridge: Hall, 1849), and volumes for individual years, such as *Cambridge Problems . . . 1843* (Cambridge: Hall, 1843).
REFERRED TO: 476

CARDAILLAC, JEAN-JACQUES SÉVERIN DE. *Etudes élémentaires de philosophie*. 2 vols. Paris: Firmin-Didot, 1830.
NOTE: JSM quotes Hamilton's rendering of the passage from Cardaillac.
QUOTED: 281n

CARLYLE, THOMAS. *Sartor Resartus*. 2nd ed. Boston: Munroe; Philadelphia and Pittsburgh: Kay, 1837.
NOTE: in JSM's library, Somerville College.
QUOTED: 423
423.1–2 "a thing can only act where it is; with . . . only where] Again, *Nothing can act but where it is*: with . . . only WHERE (59; I, viii)

CAZELLES, EMILE HONORÉ. "Introduction du traducteur," in Herbert Spencer, *Les premiers principes*. Trans. E. H. Cazelles. 3rd ed. Paris: Germer Baillière, 1883, i–lxxx.
NOTE: the 1st ed., 1870, was not easily available, but the "Introduction" (to which JSM refers) to the 3rd ed. is dated Sept., 1870. Cazelles also translated (after 1870) Spencer's *Principles of Biology*, and *Principles of Sociology*, Bain's *The Senses and the Intellect*, and Bentham's *The Influence of Natural Religion*; he translated JSM's *Examination* (1869), *Subjection of Women* (1869), *Autobiography* (1874), and *Three Essays on Religion* (1875).
REFERRED TO: 250n

CAZILLAC ["REY RÉGIS"]. *Histoire naturelle et raisonnée de l'âme*. 2 vols. London: n.p., 1789.
NOTE: we have not found Cazillac's forenames. The reference derives from Maine de Biran, who notes that "Régis'" work is little known.
REFERRED TO: 237–8

CHESELDEN, WILLIAM. "An Account of some Observations made by a young Gentleman, who was born blind, or lost his Sight so early, that he had no Remembrance of ever having seen, and was couch'd between 13 and 14 Years of Age," *Philosophical Transactions of the Royal Society of London*, XXXV (1728), 447–50.
NOTE: the quotation at 232n is indirect; that at 236n derives from Hamilton. The passages here cited contain references also to Cheselden's anonymous patient.
QUOTED: 232n, 236n
REFERRED TO: 236
232n.18–19 and asked . . . sense, feeling, or seeing.] We thought he soon knew what Pictures represented, which were shew'd to him, but we found afterwards we were mistaken; for about two Months after he was couch'd, he discovered at once, they represented solid Bodies; when to that Time he consider'd them only as Party-colour'd Planes, or Surfaces diversified with Variety of Paint; but even then he was no less surpriz'd, expecting the Pictures would feel like the Things they represented, and was amaz'd when he found those Parts, which by their Light and Shadow appear'd now round and uneven, felt only flat like the rest; and ask'd . . . Sense, Feeling or Seeing? (449) [*the clause, which JSM has not placed in quotation marks, is, in fact, a direct quotation from Cheselden*]
236n.7–8 "to touch his eyes, as . . . skin."] [*paragraph*] When he first saw, he was so far from making any Judgment about Distances, that he thought all Objects whatever touch'd his Eyes, (as he expressed it) as . . . Skin; and thought no Objects so agreeable as those which were smooth and regular, tho' he could form no Judgment of their Shape, or guess what it was in any Object that was pleasing to him: He knew not the Shape of any Thing, nor any one Thing from another, however different in Shape or Magnitude; but upon being told what Things were, whose Form he before knew from feeling, he would carefully observe, that he might know them again; but having too many Objects to learn at once, he forgot many of them; and (as he said) at first he learn'd to know, and again forgot a thousand Things in a Day. (448)

CLARKE, SAMUEL.
NOTE: the reference is in a quotation from Hamilton.
REFERRED TO: 152

COLERIDGE, SAMUEL TAYLOR. "Preface to Christabel," in *Christabel; Kubla Khan, a Vision; The Pains of Sleep*. London: Murray, 1816.
NOTE: Coleridge refers not to "one of his critics," but "a set of critics."
REFERRED TO: 216n

COMTE, AUGUSTE. Referred to: 17, 216n–17n, 299, 472

———— *Cours de philosophie positive*. 6 vols. Paris: Bachelier, 1830–42.
NOTE: this ed. in JSM's library, Somerville College.
REFERRED TO: 10, 216n–17n, 300, 472

———— *Synthèse subjective*. Paris: Comte and Dalmont, 1856.
NOTE: this ed. in JSM's library, Somerville College.
QUOTED: 472n
472n.9 fournir] former (98)

———— *Système de politique positive, ou Traité de sociologie, instituant la religion de l'humanité*. 4 vols. Paris: Vol. I, Mathias, Carilian-Gœury and Dalmont; Vol. II, Comte, Carilian-Gœury and Dalmont, Mathias and Ladrange; Vols. III and IV, Comte, Carilian-Gœury and Dalmont, 1851–54.
NOTE: this ed. in JSM's library, Somerville College.
REFERRED TO: 314

CONDILLAC, ETIENNE BONNOT DE.
NOTE: the references at 152, and 487 are in quotations from Hamilton.
REFERRED TO: 152, 208n, 364n, 440, 487

———— *La Logique, ou les premiers développemens de l'art de penser*, in *Œuvres complètes*. 31 vols. Paris: Dufart, 1803, XXX.
NOTE: in JSM's library, Somerville College; though JSM's description of Chap. i as "on the Soul" is accurate, the title actually is "Comment la nature donne les premières leçons de l'art de penser."
REFERRED TO: 440n

COPERNICUS, NICOLAS.
NOTE: the reference at 487 is in a quotation from Hamilton.
REFERRED TO: 333, 487

CORDAY, CHARLOTTE.
NOTE: the reference derives from Alexander.
REFERRED TO: 462n

COUSIN, VICTOR. Referred to: 33, 33n, 143, 152, 495

———— *Cours de philosophie. Histoire de la philosophie du dix-huitième siècle*. 2 vols. Brussels: Hauman, 1836.
NOTE: in JSM's library, Somerville College.
REFERRED TO: 139–40, 142

———— *Cours de philosophie: Introduction à l'histoire de la philosophie*. Brussels: Hauman, 1836.
NOTE: this ed. in JSM's library, Somerville College; JSM derives his references from Hamilton's review of the 1st ed. (Paris: Pichon and Didier, 1828) in *Discussions* (originally in the *Edinburgh Review*, L [Oct., 1828], 194–221). The quotations and references all derive from Leçons iv and v. The quotation at 43 is of Hamilton's translation of Cousin's passage; that at 55n is of Hamilton's conflation of passages from Cousin.
QUOTED: 43, 55n
REFERRED TO: 34–7, 34n, 39, 40n, 41n, 43–4, 44n–5n, 47, 51, 52–5, 56n, 59, 62, 64, 79, 83–4, 91n, 120, 136–7, 447

43.8   "where . . . terms;"] La condition de l'intelligence, c'est la différence; et il ne peut y
   avoir acte de connaissance que là où il y a plusieurs termes. (129) [*JSM is quoting from
   Hamilton's translation of Cousin*]

CRAKANTHORP, RICHARD. *Logicæ libri quinque*. London: Teage, 1622.
NOTE: JSM's spelling is Crackanthorp. JSM reverses the order of the two passages.
QUOTED: 414
414.9–10   "Contraria . . . opponatur. Sic] [*paragraph*] *Contraria . . . opponatur*; Sic (206)
414.14–15   "Disparatà sunt . . . opponatur.] [*paragraph*] *Desparata sic dicta disseparata,
   sunt . . . opponatur*. (206)
414.16   quam Liberalitati. Sic] qua liberalitati: Sic (206)

CROUSAZ, JEAN PIERRE DE.
NOTE: the reference is in a quotation from Hamilton.
REFERRED TO: 152

CUDWORTH, RALPH. *The True Intellectual System of the Universe: wherein all the
   reason and philosophy of atheism is confuted, and its impossibility demonstrated*. Trans. John Harrison. 3 vols. London: Tegg, 1845.
NOTE: the reference derives from Mansel.
REFERRED TO: 50n

CUNNINGHAM, JOHN. "Mill's *Examination of Sir William Hamilton's Philosophy*,"
   Edinburgh Review, CXXIV (July, 1866), 120–50.
REFERRED TO: civ, 21n, 22n

DARWIN, ERASMUS.
NOTE: the first reference is in a quotation from Hamilton.
REFERRED TO: 487

DEMOCRITUS.
NOTE: the references are in quotations from Hamilton.
REFERRED TO: 152, 421

DE MORGAN, AUGUSTUS. Referred to: 428
———— *The Elements of Algebra, Preliminary to the Differential Calculus, and Fit
   for the Higher Classes of Schools*. London: Taylor, 1835.
REFERRED TO: 429
———— *Formal Logic: or, The Calculus of Inference, Necessary and Probable*.
   London: Taylor and Walton, 1847.
NOTE: in JSM's library, Somerville College.
QUOTED: 403
403.28   "numerically definite"] A numerically definite proposition is of this kind. (142)
———— "On the Symbols of Logic, the theory of the Syllogism, and in particular of
   the Copula, and the application of the Theory of Probabilities to some questions
   of evidence," *Proceedings of the Cambridge Philosophical Society*, I (Feb.,
   1850), 90–5.
NOTE: the quotation at 400n is indirect.
QUOTED: 400n
REFERRED TO: 399n

DESCARTES, RENÉ.
NOTE: the reference at 152 is in a quotation from Hamilton; those at 483–4 derive from
   Hamilton and Baillet; that at 497n is in a quotation from Grote.
REFERRED TO: 152, 474, 478, 483–5, 493n, 497n

―――― *Dissertatio de Methodo Rectè Utendi Ratione, et Veritatem in Scientiis Investigandi,* in *Opera Philosophica.* 4th ed. Amsterdam: Elzevir, 1664.
NOTE: this ed. (works separately paged) in JSM's library, Somerville College. The reference at 141–2 derives from Hamilton.
REFERRED TO: 141–2, 502

―――― *Lettres de Mr Descartes.* Ed. Claude Clerselier. 3 vols. Paris: Angot, 1657–67.
NOTE: the reference (to a letter to Henry More, of 15 April, 1649) derives from Mansel.
REFERRED TO: 50n

―――― *Principia Philosophiæ,* in *Opera Philosophica.* 4th ed. Amsterdam: Elzevir, 1664.
NOTE: this ed. (works separately paged) in JSM's library, Somerville College. The quotation is in a quotation from Hamilton, cited by Mansel; the reference at 50n derives from Mansel; that at 297 is in a quotation from Mansel.
QUOTED: 28n
REFERRED TO: 29n, 50n, 155, 198, 297, 422
28n.6–7 'ut sunt, vel . . . possunt.'] Cum vero putamus nos percipere colores in objectis, etsi revera nesciamus quidnam sit, quod tunc nomine coloris appellamus, nec ullam similitudinem intelligere possumus, inter colorem quem supponimus esse in objectis, & illum quem experimur esse in sensu; quia tamen hoc ipsum non advertimus, & multa alia sunt, ut magnitudo, figura, numerus, &c. quæ clarè percipimus, non alitera à nobis sentiri vel intelligi, quam ut sunt, aut . . . possunt in objectis; facile in eum errorem delabimur, ut judicemus, id, quod in objectis vocamus colorem, esse quid omnino simile colori quem sentimus, atque ita ut id, quod nullo modo percipimus, à nobis clarè percipi arbitremur. (18)

―――― *Regulae ad directionem ingenii.* Amsterdam: Blaev, 1701.
NOTE: the quotation is in a quotation from Hamilton.
QUOTED: 483
483.19–24 "Revera nihil *inanius . . . nugarum . . . imaginationem ipsa ratione uti desuescamus*] Nam revera nihil inanius . . . nugarum . . . imaginationem . . . ipsa ratione uti desuescamus (12; Reg. IV)

DIOGENES (the Cynic). Referred to: 482

DU HAMEL, JEAN-BAPTISTE. *Philosophia Vetus et Nova ad usum scholæ accommodata.* 5th ed. Amsterdam: Gallet, 1700.
NOTE: a copy of this ed., which JSM cites, is in the London Library, and may have been one of James Mill's books donated by JSM.
QUOTED: 415

DU TRIEU, PHILLIPUS. *Manuductio ad logicam sive dialectica studiosæ juventuti ad logicam præparandæ.* London: printed McMillan, 1826.
NOTE: this reprint, which was formerly in JSM's library, Somerville College (Grote's copy is in the University of London Library), of the 1662 ed. (Oxford: Oxlad and Pocock; also formerly in JSM's library, Somerville College) was made for the group, including JSM, studying at Grote's house in the 1820s (see *Autobiography,* ed. Stillinger, 74).
QUOTED: 413–14
413.34–414.1 genere. . . . [*paragraph*] Secunda] genere: sive illud sit proximum, sicut *albedo* et *nigredo* ponuntur sub *colore*; sive remotum, sicut *injustitia* et *justitia* ponuntur sub diversis generibus proximis, scilicet virtute et vitio, sed illis mediantibus ponuntur sub eodem genere remoto, nempe habitu, et ulterius sub qualitate. Itaque contraria saltem debent esse ejusdem prædicamenti. Per hanc partem excluduntur privantia et contradictoria. [*paragraph*] Secunda (74)
414.2 *precise* repugnent. . . . Hinc] præcise repugnent: quod eodem modo explicandum est quo supra. Hinc (74)

EDWARDS, JONATHAN. Referred to: 440

EPICURUS.
NOTE: the reference is in a quotation from Hamilton.
REFERRED TO: 152

ESSER, WILHELM. *System der Logik*. 2nd ed. 2 vols. Munster: Theissing, 1830.
NOTE: the quotations and references derive from Hamilton's *Lectures*, the editors of which use this ed. of Esser's *Logik*.
QUOTED: 323n, 354, 384, 407–8
REFERRED TO: 355, 494, 494n

EUCLID. *Elements*.
NOTE: as the references are general, no ed. is cited.
REFERRED TO: 62, 441

FARADAY, MICHAEL. *Lectures on the Various Forces of Matter and on the Chemical History of a Candle*. London: Griffin, Bohn, 1863.
QUOTED: 488–9
489.10 into] *into* (3)

FELL, JOHN. *Grammatica Rationis, sive Institutiones Logicæ*. Oxford: Sheldonian Theatre, 1673.
NOTE: a copy of this (the 1st) ed. is in the London Library, and may have been part of the donation by JSM of his father's books.
QUOTED: 415
415.19 "Contraria adversa sunt accidentia, posita] [*paragraph*] *Contraria adversa* sunt *Accidentia* (ut prius definiebantur [p. 52]) posita (121)
415.19 genere] *Genere* (121)

FERRIER, JAMES FREDERICK. Referred to: 7

FICHTE, JOHANN GOTTLIEB. *Die Bestimmung des Menschen*, in *Sämmtliche Werke*. Ed. J. H. Fichte. 8 vols. Berlin: von Velt, 1845, II, 165–319.
NOTE: the reference is in a quotation from Hamilton.
REFERRED TO: 151

FRANZ, JOANN CHRISTOPH AUGUST. "Memoir of the Case of a Gentleman born blind, and successfully operated upon in the 18th year of his age, with Physiological Observations and Experiments," *Philosophical Transactions of the Royal Society of London*, CXXXI (1841), 59–68.
NOTE: the passage here cited contains references to Franz's anonymous patient.
QUOTED: 231n–4n
231n.9–12 a sheet . . . denominations,"] A sheet . . . denominations. (64)
231n.16–17 solid cube and a sphere . . . diameter, was] solid *cube* and a *sphere* . . . diameter, were (65)
231n.18–19 a quadrangular and a circular . . . a square . . . a disc] a *quadrangular* and a *circular* . . . a *square* . . . a *disc* (65)
231n.30–1 it; in fact, said he, I must give it up.] it; "in fact," said he, "I must give it up." (65)
232n.5 object] objects (65)
232n.7–8 surprised he . . . with mathematical] surprised that he . . . with these solid mathematical (65)

FRASER, ALEXANDER CAMPBELL. "Berkeley's Theory of Vision," *North British Review*, XLI (Aug., 1864), 199–230.
QUOTED: 232n–3n
REFERRED TO: 240, 243n
232n.32–3 "at . . . objects,"] After couching, the boy could, in this instance, we are told, at . . . objects. (215)

232n.33–4 "were . . . figure," . . . "it] Though he could not say which was the cube, and which the sphere, he saw that they were . . . figure. It (215)

———— "Mr. Mill's *Examination of Sir W. Hamilton's Philosophy*," *North British Review*, XLIII (Sept., 1865), 1–58.

QUOTED: 29n, 31–2, 32, 32n, 187n

REFERRED TO: civ–cv, 32n–3n

29n.12–13 "the solid . . . extended percepts . . . conscious or] The solid . . . extended *percepts* . . . conscious of them or (22)

31.39 in our minds] in our own minds (16)

32.6 How does] How then does (15)

32n.4–5 "there . . . of sense-consciousness] Except Berkeley, we know no other philosopher in these islands who begins by acknowledging that Matter, whatever it may turn out to be, is at any rate that which we find in our proper conscious experience—that consciousness is not a mere medium for *representing* an extended and solid world which exists behind it,—and that there . . . of *sense*-consciousness (20)

32n.13–14 "a . . . Sir W. . . . country,"] We regard it as a . . . Sir William . . . country. (20)

187n.9–10 "Men cannot . . . live," . . . "without . . . term external.] Man cannot . . . live without . . . term "external." (26)

FRORIEP, LUDWIG FRIEDRICH VON.

NOTE: JSM gives "Frorieps"; see Heuck.

REFERRED TO: 248

FRORIEP, ROBERT.

NOTE: JSM gives "Frorieps"; see Heuck.

REFERRED TO: 248

GASSENDI, PIERRE.

NOTE: the reference is in a quotation from Hamilton.

REFERRED TO: 487

GEORGE IV (of England).

NOTE: the reference is in a quotation from Hamilton.

REFERRED TO: 160

GÉRARD, BALTHASAR. Referred to: 461

GERSON, LEVI BEN.

NOTE: the quotation is taken from Grote (*q.v.* for collation), who takes it from Hamilton.

QUOTED: 400n–1n

GIBBON, EDWARD. Referred to: 482

———— "Memoirs of My Life and Writings," in *Miscellaneous Works*. Ed. John Baker Holroyd, Lord Sheffield. 2 vols. London: Strahan, Cadell and Davies, 1796, I, 1–185.

QUOTED: 495–6

496.1 "I] But as my childish propensity for numbers and calculations was totally extinct, I (I, 65–6)

496.1 impressions] impression (I, 66)

GOETHE, JOHANN WOLFGANG VON. Referred to: 486n, 489

GROTE, GEORGE. "John Stuart Mill on the Philosophy of Sir William Hamilton," *Westminster Review*, n.s. XXIX (Jan., 1866), 1–39.

NOTE: the quotation of Levi Ben Gerson at 400n–1n is taken by JSM from Grote, who takes it from Hamilton.

QUOTED: 400n–1n, 401n, 491n–2n, 492n, 497n

REFERRED TO: cv, 58n, 497n–8n

400n.25 "Sir W. Hamilton," . . . "insists] Sir W. Hamilton, in this proceeding, insists (31)

400n.26   more;] more;* [*footnote omitted] (31)
400n.27   may] may (31)
400n.27   is not] is not (32)
400n.32   accidens. . . . If] accidens. Mr. Mill is, nevertheless, of opinion (pp. 439–443) that
          though "the quantified syllogism is not a true expression of what is in thought, yet writing
          the predicate with a quantification may be sometimes a real help to the Art of Logic." We
          see little advantage in providing a new complicated form, for the purpose of expressing in
          one proposition what naturally throws itself into two, and may easily be expressed in two.
          If (32)
400n.41   quæsita] quæsita (32n)
401n.1   All Man is all Rational] all man is all rational (32n)
401n.1   all man is rational] all man is rational (32n)
401n.2   that rational is denied of everything but man] that rational is denied of everything
          but man (32n)
401n.3   quæsita] quæsita (32n)
401n.4   quæsitum] quæsitum, (32n)
401n.5   only—Does . . . that? and not,] only—Does . . . that? and not (32n)
401n.6   and . . . else."] and . . . else?" (32n)
491n.40   so. We] so. [JSM omits eight sentences] We (2–3)
492n.3   not. . . . To those] not. [ellipsis indicates 4-sentence omission] How far Sir W.
          Hamilton has there furnished good proof of his own doctrines on External Perception, and
          on the Primary Qualities of Matter, we shall not now determine; but to those (3)
492n.4   reasonings are] reasonings on these subjects are (3)
492n.15   "in] Now, in (2)
492n.18   editors,"] editors; and our impression, as readers of his lectures, disposes us to
          credit them. (2–3)

GUY, ROBERT EPHREM ("R.E.G."). "Calderwood and Mill upon Hamilton," *Dublin
    Review*, n.s. V (Oct., 1865), 474–504.
    REFERRED TO: civ

HAMILTON, WILLIAM. *Discussions on Philosophy and Literature, Education and
    University Reform, chiefly from the Edinburgh Review; corrected, vindicated,
    enlarged in notes and appendices.* 2nd ed. London: Longman, Brown, Green
    and Longmans; Edinburgh: Maclachlan and Stewart, 1853.
    NOTE: the reference at 4 is inferential; Hamilton first became widely known through the
    early essays in *Discussions*. The references at 34, 39, 58, 58n are specifically to the first
    essay, "On the Philosophy of the Unconditioned" (which first appeared in the *Edinburgh
    Review* in 1829); those at 51n.5–8, 444n are to App. I (A), "Conditions of the Thinkable
    Systematised"; that at 163 and the quotations at 163 and 168–9 relate to "Philosophy of
    Perception" (which first appeared in the *Edinburgh Review* in 1830); the references at 438n,
    470–2, 482, 487n, 496n and the quotations at 474, 475, 476, 477, 480, 483, 484 are to "On the
    Study of Mathematics" (which first appeared in the *Edinburgh Review* in 1836 and is
    indexed separately); that at 492n is to the third section, "Education," and App. III,
    "Educational."
    QUOTED: 13, 18, 19n–20n, 20, 29n, 34n–5n, 35–6, 36, 39, 39n, 41, 42, 42–3, 43, 43–4, 44, 44n,
    52n, 53, 55n, 58n, 62, 66, 76n–7n, 79, 91, 94, 113, 116, 136, 155, 157, 163, 163–4, 168, 168–9,
    169, 259–60, 260, 290n, 321, 350, 395–6, 396, 396n, 401n, 418, 420, 424, 442–3, 442n, 443,
    463n, 474, 475, 476, 477, 480, 483, 484, 498n
    REFERRED TO: 4, 29n, 34, 39, 39n, 43n, 51n, 58, 58n, 154–5, 161, 163, 174n, 316n, 348n, 352,
    416n, 421n, 428, 438n, 444n, 470–2, 482, 487n, 492n, 496n
    13.14   unknown. . . . Nor] unknown.* [3-sentence footnote omitted] The philosopher
    speculating the worlds of matter and of mind, is thus, in a certain sort, only an ignorant
    admirer. In his contemplation of the universe, the philosopher, indeed, resembles Æneas

contemplating the adumbrations on his shield; as it may equally be said of the sage and of the hero,—/"*Miratur; Rerumque ignarus, Imagine gaudet. [no end quotation marks]*/Nor (App. I, 644)

18.38–19.1   "harmoniously re-echoed by every philosopher of every school;"... "with the exception of a few late Absolute theorizers in Germany;"] With the exception, in fact, of a few late Absolutist theorisers in Germany, this is, perhaps, the truth of all others most harmoniously re-echoed by every philosopher of every school; and, as has so frequently been done, to attribute any merit, or any singularity to its recognition by any individual thinker, more especially in modern times, betrays only the ignorance of the encomiasts. [*JSM has reversed the clausal order*] (App. I, 644)

19n.12–20n.5   "become ... themselves."] [*see* 13.9–13 *in the text above*] (App. I, 643–4)

20.25–7   "become ... qualities." [*see* 13.9–12 *in the text above*] (App. I, 643–4)

29n.23   "things in themselves.] The Hypothetical Realist contends, that he is wholly ignorant of *things in themselves*, and that these are known to him, only through a vicarious phænomenon, of which he is conscious in perception;/"*Rerum*que ignarus, *Imagine* gaudet." (57)

35n.4–5   To ... God] *To ... God* (15n)

35.9   "At] But at (9)

35.9–10   these [finite] existences] these existences (9)

36.10   "limiting and conditioning one another."] In every act of consciousness we distinguish a *Self* or *Ego*, and something different from self, a *Non-ego*; each limited and modified by the other. (9)

39n.3   "finished, perfected, completed,"] [*paragraph*] 2. [Hamilton's second meaning of "Absolute"] *Absolutum* means *finished, perfected, completed*; in which sense the Absolute will be what is out of relation, &c., as finished, perfect, complete, total, and thus corresponds to τὸ ὅλον and τὸ τέλειον of Aristotle. (14n)

39.9–10   "the unconditionally unlimited," ... "the unconditionally limited."] The unconditionally unlimited, or the *Infinite*, the unconditionally limited, or the *Absolute*, cannot positively be construed to the mind; they can be conceived, only by thinking away from, or abstraction of, those very conditions under which thought itself is realised; consequently, the notion of the Unconditioned is only *negative*,—negative of the conceivable itself. (13)

39.16   "The term] [The term (14n)

41.8–12   Infinite ... Absolute ... negative;] *Infinite ... Absolute ... negative*, [*cf. entry for* 39.9–10 *above*] (13)

41.17   coincide)] coincide*) [*footnote omitted*] (13)

41.21–2   space, in time, or in degree] *space, in time*, or in *degree* (13)

41.23   Infinite and the Absolute properly so called, are] *Infinite* and the *Absolute, properly so called*,† are [*footnote omitted*] (13)

41.36   *a fasciculus of negations*] [*not in italics*] (17)

42.6   Conditioned] *Conditioned* (14)

42.15   is known] is only known (14)

42.16   cold] void (14)

42.17   [*paragraph*] How] [*no paragraph*] (14)

42.30   *Cognoscendo ... cognoscitur.*] "*Cognoscendo ... cognoscitur.*" (15)

42.36   "his] In vindicating the truth of this statement, we shall attempt to show:—in the *first* place, that M. Cousin is at fault in all the authorities he quotes in favour of the opinion, that the Absolute, Infinite, Unconditioned, is a primitive notion, cognisable by our intellect; in the *second*, that his (25)

42.37   reverse;" "that] reverse; in the *third*, that (25)

43.2   Absolute;" and "that] Absolute; and in the *fourth*, that (25)

43.8   "where ... plurality of terms;"] "The condition of intelligence," says M. Cousin, "*is difference*; and an active knowledge is only possible where ... *plurality of terms*. (31–2)

43.12   "as] [*paragraph*] Our author [Cousin] admits, and must admit, that the Absolute, as (33)

43.12   one. Absolute] *one*; absolute (33)

43.13   difference. . . . The condition] difference; *the Absolute*, and *the Knowledge of the Absolute*, are therefore *identical*. [*ellipsis indicates 3-sentence omission*] But, on the other hand, it is asserted, that the condition of intelligence, as knowing, is plurality and difference; consequently the condition (33)

43.16–18   first . . . second . . . contradictory of the Absolute] *first . . . second . . . contradictory of the absolute* (33)

43.22   third] *third* (33)

43.23   contradictory . . . intelligence] [*in italics*] (33)

43.26   either] *Either* (33)

43.26   or] *or* (33)

43.31   what] What (35)

43.32–3   end. . . . Abstractly] end; and in the accomplishment of that end, it consummates its own perfection. Abstractly (35)

43.34–6   "is . . . perfection;" . . . "even for its reality] Further, not only is . . . *perfection*,—it is dependent on it even for its *reality* (35)

44.2   which it] which alone it (35)

44.4   in its effects] *in its effects* (35)

44n.11   "One] On this hypothesis, one (36)

44n.13–14   from the better . . . better] [*in italics*] (36)

44n.14   both states are equal] *both states are equal* (36)

44n.15   consider. The] consider. [*paragraph*] The (36)

44n.20–1   fate. The] fate. [*paragraph*] The (36)

44n.24   first cause] *first cause* (36)

44n.27   cause, the actual] cause, the real, the actual (36)

52n.17–18   "the unconditionally limited,"] [*see entry for* 39.9–10 *above*] (13)

53.10   "finished, perfected, completed"] [*see entry for* 39n.3 *and its collation*] (14n)

53.30   "to think is to condition"] [*see* 42.8 *above*] (14)

55n.2   "variously] [*paragraph*] The *first* of these Ideas, elements, or laws, though fundamentally one, our author [Cousin] variously (8)

55n.3–4   &c.," . . . "we will] &c.; (we would (8)

55n.4   Unconditioned."] Unconditioned.) (8)

55n.5   "*plurality*] The *second*, [*see collation for* 55n.2 *above*] he denominates *plurality* (8)

55n.6   &c.," . . . "we would style the Conditioned."] &c.; (we would style it the *Conditioned*.) (8)

58n.22–3   "in Laputa or the Empire"] [*paragraph*] Out of Laputa or the Empire it would be idle to enter into an articulate refutation of a theory, which founds philosophy on the annihilation of consciousness, and on the identification of the unconscious philosopher with God. (21)

62.30   "given . . . cognitions . . . beliefs:"] [*paragraph*] Our knowledge rests ultimately on certain facts of consciousness, which as primitive, and consequently incomprehensible, are given . . . *cognitions . . . beliefs*. (86)

62.31   "Consciousness] But if consciousness (86)

62.31   words our] words, if our (86)

62.31   primary experience] *primary experience* (86)

62.32   is a faith."] be a faith; the reality of our knowledge turns on the veracity of our constitutive beliefs. (86)

66.13   "There] And as the *one* or the other of contradictories must be true, whilst both cannot; it proves, that there (App. I, 624)

66.13–14   ground," . . . "for] ground for (App. I, 624)

66.14–15   our . . . possibility] *our . . . possibility* (App. I, 624)

79.28   "Things] But practically, the *fact*, that we are free, is given to us in the consciousness of an uncompromising law of duty, in the consciousness of our moral accountability; and this fact of liberty cannot be redargued on the ground that it is incomprehensible, for the philosophy of the Conditioned proves, against the necessaritarian, that things (App. I, 624)

79.29   may] *may* (App. I, 624)

79.33   "The] [*paragraph*] The (15)
79.33   between the two] between two (15)
79.33   unconditionates] inconditionates (15)
79.34   neither . . . possible] *neither . . . possible* (15)
79.35–6 one . . . necessary] *one . . . necessary* (15)
79.36   necessary. . . . The] *necessary.* On this opinion, therefore, our faculties are shown to be weak, but not deceitful. The (15)
79.38   the extremes] two extremes (15)
91.23   "*Absolutum*] [*paragraph*] 1. *Absolutum* (14n)
91.23   freed or loosed]*freed* or *loosed* (14n)
94n.14 "finished, perfected, completed,"] [*see 39n.3 and its collation above*] (14n)
113.8   Consciousness . . . world.] *Consciousness . . . world.** [*footnote omitted*] (51)
116.40 "the] But if, on the one hand, consciousness be only realised under specific modes, and cannot therefore exist apart from the several faculties *in cumulo*; and if, on the other, these faculties can all and each only be exerted under the condition of consciousness; consciousness, consequently, is not one of the special modes into which our mental activity may be resolved, but the (48)
116.40 condition"] condition of them all. (48)
157.16 belief of the existence] *belief of the existence* (89)
157.17 belief . . . knowledge . . . existence] *belief . . . knowledge . . . existence* (89)
157.19 is] be (89)
157.22 I . . . exists] *I . . . exists* (89)
157.23 I believe . . . existing] *I believe . . . existing* (89)
157.23–5 I believe . . . perception] *I believe . . . perception* (89)
157.26 identical. The] identical. [*paragraph*] The (89)
157.29 belief in the existence] *belief in the existence* (89)
157.29–30 belief in the knowledge] *belief in the knowledge* (89)
157.30 but they] but, on grounds to which it is not here necessary to advert, they (89)
157.37 "Our] [*paragraph*] Our (86)
157.39 cognitions] *cognitions* (86)
157.39 beliefs] *beliefs* (86)
163.4   "the mind] And here, the mind (67)
163.8   "alternative] The *other* alternative (67)
163.10–11 "either blindly determines itself" or "is blindly determined"] And here the mind either *blindly determines itself*, or is *blindly determined by an extrinsic and intelligent cause.* (67)
163.12 "utterly] The former lemma is the more philosophical, in so far as it assumes nothing hyperphysical; but it is otherwise utterly (67)
168.31–2 "We proceed," . . . "to] [*paragraph*] These being premised, we proceed to (58)
168.34 third] *third* (58)
169.10 "This is too strong," . . . "Brown's . . . is not . . . import.] Brown's . . . is therefore, not . . . import. [This is too strong. See Diss. p. 820.] [*Hamilton's square brackets*] (60)
260.22 "when] On this theory, also, when (App. I, 615)
290n.3 a Nihilo] [*not in italics*] (App. I, 620n)
290n.13–14 "the Potential" . . . "what is . . . time."] [*included as part of Hamilton's scheme of modal predication*] A, / E.) The *Potential*, (τὸ ἐν δυνάμει, potentiale, quod in posse, in potentia, est, &c.,) what *is* . . . *time*, = the not actual. (App. II, 703)
321.23 "Concept," . . . "is] Mr. Stewart has even bestowed on the reproductive imagination the term *Conception*;—happily, we do not think; as both in grammatical propriety, and by the older and correcter usage of philosophers, this term (or rather the product of this operation—*Concept*) is (283n)
321.24 simply."] simply, and in this sense is admirably rendered by the *Begriff* (what is grasped up) of the Germans. (283n)
350.4   "ethics, politics, religion] *Art* he [Whately] defines the application of knowledge to practice; in which signification, *ethics, politics, religion* (134)

350.4–5   practical sciences would be arts:"] *practical sciences*, must be *arts*. (134)

395.9   "The self-evident] In the *second* place, the self-evident (App. II, 650)

395.32–3   species . . . Syllogism] *Species . . . Syllogisms* (App. II, 651)

396.16   "In] Its [the meaning of "some"] *peculiar* indefinitude is a contribution from the contingency of our ignorance, and with our ignorance would disappear; for, (to say nothing of *Individuals* or *Individualised Generals*,) in (App. II, 691n)

396.17   all, or some, or none] *all*, or *none*, or *some* (App. II, 691n)

396n.4   "the Indesignate] The double inadvertence, as I think, of Aristotle, (An. Pr. I. 2.) in recognising the *indesignate* (ἀδιόζιστον) to be at once a quantity and an indefinitude, (for the Indesignate (App. II, 691n)

396n.5–6   *or . . . presumed*] [*not in italics*] (App. II, 691n)

396n.6   *presumed*."] presumed);—this vagueness,—this material, subjective and contingent indefinitude, lay at the root of his [Aristotle's] whole doctrine of Particularity, the indefinitude of which quantity he should have kept purely formal, objective, and necessary, instead of confounding the two indefinitudes together. (App. II, 691n)

401n.12   "Every] Its [the meaning of "some"] *peculiar* indefinitude is a contribution from the contingency of our ignorance, and with our ignorance would disappear; for, (to say nothing of *Individuals* or *Individualised Generals*,) in reality and in thought, every (App. II, 691n) [*cf.* 396.16]

418.21   "Nature] But nature (App. I, 622)

418.22   necessary."] necessary;—μηδὲν περιττῶς; and to excogitate a *particular force*, to perform what can be better explained on the ground of a *general imbecillity*, is contrary to every rule of philosophising. (App. I, 622)

418.23   "that] Not only is it a maxim of his [Aristotle's] philosophy, that (App. I, 629)

418.26   πολλὰ):"] πολλά.) (App. I, 629)

420.29   "the] [*paragraph*] The *Law of Parcimony* (as the rule ought to be distinctively called), the (App. I, 628n)

420.30   when] where (App. I, 628n)

420.30–1   hypothesis," has "never . . . adequately expressed;"] hypothesis, has, though always virtually in force, never . . . adequately enounced. (App. I, 628n)

420.32–3   "Neither *more* nor more *onerous* causes . . . phænomena] It should be thus expressed:—*Neither* MORE, *nor* MORE ONEROUS, *causes . . . phænomena*. (App. I, 628n)

442n.4   conceived, be] conceived possible, be (App. I, 615)

442n.4–5   show our] shews out our (App. I, 615)

443.1   But . . . the] But practically, the *fact*, that we are free, is given to us in the consciousness of an uncompromising law of duty, in the consciousness of our moral accountability; and this fact of liberty cannot be redargued on the ground that it is incomprehensible, for the philosophy of the Conditioned proves, against the necessitarian, that things there are, which *may*, nay *must* be true, of which the understanding is wholly unable to construe to itself the possibility. [*paragraph*] But this philosophy is not only competent to *defend* the fact of our moral liberty, possible though inconceivable, against the assault of the fatalist; it *retorts* against himself the very objection of incomprehensibility by which the fatalist had thought to triumph over the libertarian. It shews, that the (App. I, 624–5)

463n.3–4   "would . . . worthless;"] [*see quotation at* 442n.4 *and its collation*] (App. I, 615)

463n.4–6   "the . . . will;"] [*see* 442.32–4 *above*] (App. I, 624)

474.17   "do] [*paragraph*] That they [mathematics] do (282)

474.17   generalization,"] *generalization* is equally apparent. (282)

475.9–10   "Are mathematics then," . . . "of] [*paragraph*] Are Mathematics then of (313)

475.13   mental distraction] *mental distraction* (314)

475.14   continuous attention] *continuous attention* (314)

475.15   mind."] mind; and it is almost the one only, or at least the one principal, accorded to it by the most intelligent philosophers. (314)

475.16   But] [*paragraph*] But (322)

475.25–6   "We are far," . . . "from] [*paragraph*] We are far from (290)

475.28 old. . . . Unlike] old; but this we assert,—that the most ordinary intellect may, by means of these methods and formulæ, once invented, reproduce and apply, by an effort nearly mechanical, all that the original genius discovered. [*ellipsis indicates 3-sentence omission*] [*paragraph*] Unlike] (290)
475.36 "Mathematical] [*paragraph*] 1.) As to the *difficulties*:—Mathematical (291)
475.36–7 deducing conclusions] *deducing conditions* (291)
475.7–8 looking out for premises] *looking out for premises* (291)
476.30 "to] To (268n)
476.32 Newton:"] Newton. (268n)
477.18 measurable] *mensurable* (334)
480.10–11 "hypothetically . . . calculus."] [*see* 477 *above*] (335)
480.33 "continuous attention"] [*see* 475 *above*] (314)
483.11 "It] [*paragraph*] "It (277)
483.11 time, says Baillet, since] time, since (277)
483.18 traces. The] traces." (Cartesii Regulae ad Directionem Ingenii, Reg. iv. MSS.)—[The (277)
483.19 Revera] "Revera (277)
483.20 talium] taliam (277)
483.25 expedire." . . . Baillet] expedire. Quum vero postea cogitarem, unde ergo fieret, ut primi olim Philosophiæ inventores, neminem Matheseos imperitum ad studium sapientiæ vellent admittere, [a fable, the oldest recorders of which flourished above eight centuries subsequent to Plato,*] [*4-sentence footnote omitted*] tanquam hæc disciplina omnium facillima et maxime necessaria videatur, ad ingenia capessendis aliis majoribus scientiis erudienda et præparanda; plane suspicatus sum, *quamdam eos Mathesim agnovisse, valde diversam a vulgari nostrae ætatis.*"]—Baillet (278)
483.36 mankind."] mankind."† [*footnote omitted*] (278)
484.14 "did] For, though himself [Socrates] not inconversant with these," (which he had studied under the celebrated geometer, Theodorus of Cyrene), "he did (323) [*Hamilton is quoting from Xenophon*]
484.14–15 they" . . . "could] they could (323)
484.17 acquirements."] acquirements."‖ [*footnote*] ‖Xenophontis Memorabilia, 1.iv.c.7, §§3, 5. (323)
484.21 "The] [*paragraph*] Before entering on details, it is proper here, once for all to premise:—In the *first* place, that the (266)
484.21 question," . . . "does] question does (266)
484.22–4 value of mathematical *science*, considered . . . results, but the utility of mathematical *study*, that is, in . . . mind] *value of mathematical* SCIENCE, *considered* . . . *results*, but the *utility of mathematical* STUDY, *that is, in* . . . *mind* (266)
484.24 mind.] *mind*; and in the *second* [place], that the expediency is not disputed, of leaving mathematics, as a co-ordinate, to find their level among the other branches of academical instruction. (266)
498n.20 "not] His [Hume's] reasoning is from their [the foundations of knowledge] subsequent contradiction to their original falsehood; and his premises, not (87)
498n.20 himself," but "accepted] himself, are accepted (87)

—— "Dissertations on Reid," in *The Works of Thomas Reid*. Ed. William Hamilton. Edinburgh: Maclachlan and Stewart; London: Longman, Brown, Green and Longmans, 1846, 742–914.
NOTE: this ed. used for all references and quotations, with the exception of those at 33n, 117, 255n where the 6th ed. (2 vols. [Edinburgh: Maclachlan and Stewart, 1863]), which contains additional material not included in earlier eds. and employed by JSM in these places only, is used. See also Hamilton's "Foot-notes to Reid" below. "Dissertations on Reid" is JSM's title, which we have accepted and used in all cases; in the work, a half-title page gives "Dissertations, Historical, Critical, and Supplementary, by the Editor."
QUOTED: 13–14, 14, 15, 16, 18, 21, 26, 26n–7n, 28n, 33n, 61, 63n, 65n, 76, 80, 113, 114, 117,

118n, 123n, 129n, 132, 132–3, 133, 134, 136, 138–9, 142, 153n, 155, 156, 172, 173–4, 175, 214n, 219–20, 234–5, 237, 238, 239, 255n, 296n, 311n, 362n, 423n–4n, 447

REFERRED TO: 3, 22, 29–30, 30n, 79, 114, 131, 168, 174, 216n, 251n, 334, 422n, 437

13.28–14.1 Realism" . . . "asserts] Realism, asserts (825)

14.11 "that] His philosophy, if that of Natural Realism, founded in the common sense of mankind, made it incumbent on him to shew, that (842)

14.12 example—called up or suggested] example, 'called up or *suggested*,' (842)

14.15 knowledge of] knowledge or consciousness of (842)

14.17 "If] [*no paragraph*] But if (842)

14.20 at least] at best (842)

14.27 "The notion of body being given] Psychologically speaking, an attribute would not be *primary* if it could be thought away from body; and the notion of body being supposed given (844n)

14.29 "The] It is thus apparent that the (846)

14.30 deduced] *deduced* (846)

14.32 implies."] implies: whereas the Secundo-primary and Secondary must be *induced a posteriori*; both being attributes contingently super-added to the naked notion of matter. (846)

14.35 "that] For they [Secundo-primary Qualities] are all only various forms of a relative or superable resistance to displacement, which, we learn by experience, bodies oppose to other bodies, and, among these, to our organism moving through space;—a resistance similar in kind (and therefore clearly conceived) to that (848)

15.1 "The Primary" Qualities "are] 5. The Primary are (857)

15.3–5 Secundo-primary" . . . "as] Secundo-primary, as (857)

15.5 us. . . . We] us. [*ellipsis indicates 3-paragraph omission*] [*paragraph*] 9. Under this head [Considered as in Bodies] we (857)

15.11 us. . . . We] us. [*ellipsis indicates 5½-paragraph omission*] In other words:— We (858)

15.12 self;] self;* [*footnote*:] *How much this differs from the doctrine of Reid, Stewart, &c., who hold that in every sensation there is not only a subjective object of sensation, but also an objective object of perception, see Note D*, §1. (858)

15.13 once."] once.† [*4-paragraph footnote omitted*] (858)

15.29 "In] But in (866n)

15.34 mediately:"] mediately. (866n)

18.13–24 "immediately . . . primary"] [*see passages quoted on 13–15 above*]

21.24 "In] But in (866n)

21.26 out . . . us] [*not in italics*] (866n)

21.26–7 our . . . relative] [*not in italics*] (866n)

26.5–9 "as . . . bodies," . . . "as . . . us;" . . . "essential . . . existing;" . . . "modes . . . not-self," . . . "modes . . . self;"] [*see* 13–15 *above*]

26n.16 proper," . . . "is] proper is (880)

26n.18 condition."] condition; but every Sensation has not a Perception proper as its conditionate—unless, what I think ought to be done, we view the general consciousness of the locality of a sensorial affection as a Perception proper. (880)

26n.18–19 "The fact . . . other:"] But though the fact . . . other, this is all;—for the two cognitions, though coexistent, are not proportionally coexistent. (880)

27n.1–2 "in . . . to one another"] It may accordingly be stated as a general rule—*That, above a certain point, the stronger the Sensation, the weaker the Perception; and the distincter the perception the less obtrusive the sensation*; in other words—*Though Perception proper and Sensation proper exist only as they coexist, in . . . to each other*. (880)

27n.3 "The] [*paragraph*] 16. Using the term strictly, the (858)

27n.4 Primary" qualities "are] Primary are (858)

28n.15 philosophers" (Locke and Descartes) "we] philosophers, we (839)

33n.8 [*paragraph*] "That] [*paragraph*] 1. [first of two principles] That (965) [*Note N breaks off at the end of the passage quoted, before the second principle is discussed*]

33n.15 *The . . . knowledge.*] [*not in italics*] (965)
33n.19 other: these] other. These (965)
33n.21 comparison"] comparison. (965)
61.11 "St.] [*no paragraph*] St (760)
61.11 know] *know* (760)
61.11 but believe] we believe (760)
61.25 a mere mode] a mode (750)
61.29 nature."] nature, / Quæ nisi sit veri, ratio quoque falsa fit omnis. (750)
63n.2 "the] [*paragraph*] IX. The ninth, is that the (763)
63n.2 knowledge.] *Knowledges.* [*footnote:*] *Knowledges*, in common use with Bacon and our English philosophers till after the time of Locke, ought not to be discarded. It is however unnoticed by any English Lexicographer. (763)
65n.2 "the original data of reason,"] But reason itself must rest at last upon authority; for the original data of reason do not rest on reason, but are necessarily accepted by reason on the authority of what is beyond itself. (760)
76.14 "The] For the (745)
76.16 incomprehensible . . . that is . . . we] incomprehensible. [*JSM moves back to the previous sentence*] For it will argue nothing against the trustworthiness of consciousness, that all or any of its deliverances are inexplicable—are incomprehensible; that is, that we (745)
80.1 "the] [*paragraph*] To this head [The Law of Relativity or Integration], I may simply notice, though I cannot now explain, are to be referred those compulsory relatives, imposed upon thought by that great, but as yet undeveloped, law of our intellectual being, which I have elsewhere denominated the (911)
80.1–3 That . . . necessary] *That . . . necessary* (911)
80.3–4 necessary." . . . "from . . . intellect" that "we] *necessary*. From . . . intellect, we (911)
113.32–3 "consciousness . . . act] [*paragraph*] 15.—"*Consciousness . . . act* (810)
114.4–5 "all . . . immediate."] Therefore *all . . . immediate*. (810)
117.34 [*paragraph*] "Consciousness is] [*no paragraph*] Consciousness also is (932)
117.39 intensity. . . . It] [*ellipsis indicates 4-sentence omission*] (932)
117.40 intension."] intension; and as the extensive quantity of such movements is always in the inverse ratio of its intensive, that consciousness will be most perfect which is concentrated within the smallest sphere. (932)
118n.15 "The] As an example of the former [something in itself indivisible, which may be considered by the mind plural];—the (806n)
123n.48–9 "the . . . knowledge."] [*paragraph*] IX. The ninth [condition determining a class of names], is that the . . . *Knowledges.* [*footnote:*] *Knowledges*, in common use with Bacon and our English philosophers till after the time of Locke, ought not to be discarded. It is however unnoticed by any English Lexicographer. (763)
129n.8 "As] For as (744)
132.3 "How] [*paragraph*] Limiting, therefore, our consideration to the question of authority; how (743)
132.9 lie:"] lie. (743)
132.10 "organized] Nature is not gratuitously to be assumed to work, not only in vain, but in counteraction of herself; our faculty of Knowledge is not, without a ground, to be supposed an instrument of illusion; man, unless the melancholy fact be proved, is not to be held organized (745) [*cf. entry for* 133.7 *below*]
132.37 "Such a supposition" . . . "if] But such a supposition, if (743)
132.38 illegitimate." "The] illegitimate. For, on the contrary, the (743)
132.39–133.1 *instance*" . . . "be] *instance*, be (743)
133.1–2 false," . . . "that] false, that (743)
133.4 "neganti . . . probatio.] "Neganti . . . probatio." (745)
133.7 illusion."] [*for the conclusion of the sentence, see entry for* 132.10 *above*]
134.3 "The] [*paragraph*] It is therefore manifest that we may throw wholly out of account /the (745)
134.4–5 themselves," . . . "scepticism is confessedly impossible,"] themselves; seeing that

scepticism in regard to them, under this limitation, is confessedly impossible; and that it is only requisite to consider the argument from Common Sense, as it enables us to vindicate the truth of these phænomena, viewed as attestations of more than their own existence, seeing that they are not, in this respect, placed beyond the possibility of doubt. (745)

136.20   "Many] I should indeed hardly have deemed that it required an articulate statement, were it not that, in point of fact, many (749)

138.15   "The first problem of philosophy" is "to] [*paragraph*] The first problem of Philosophy—and it is one of no easy accomplishment—being thus to (752) [*see next entry*]

138.18–19   possession:" . . . "of no easy accomplishment;" . . . "argument . . . sense" . . . "manifestly] possession; and the argument . . . sense being the allegation of these feelings or beliefs as explicated and ascertained, in proof of the relative truths and their necessary consequences;—this argument is manifestly (752) [*see also entry above*]

138.22   sense] Sense (752) [*treated as printer's error in text*]

142.6   "into] He [Aristotle] did not, it may be observed, fall into (894n)

142.8–9   thought," . . . "to evolve the conditions under] thought. He makes no fruitless attempt to shew the genesis of the former; far less does he attempt to evolve the laws under (894n)

142.10   thinking;"] thinking. (894n)

153n.8–14   Natural Realism . . . themselves. . . . Both build . . . Reid] Both build . . . Reid. . . . Natural Realism . . . themselves (817n) [*JSM has altered the order of Hamilton's sentences*]

153n.16   perceived, lurks] perceived, there lurks (817n)

153n.27   "Representative knowledge," . . . "is] [*paragraph*] In a *third* respect Representative knowledge is *not self-sufficient*; for it is (811)

156.8–10   "such . . . the reality . . . man."] For if we modify the obnoxious language of Descartes and Locke; and, instead of saying that the ideas or notions of the primary qualities *resemble*, merely assert that they *truly represent*, their objects, that is, afford us such . . . the extended reality . . . man,—and this is certainly all that one, probably all that either philosopher, intended,—Reid's doctrine and theirs would be found in perfect unison. (842)

156.18   "in their own nature occult and inconceivable,"] On this ground, the *Primary*, being thought as *essential* to the notion of Body, are distinguished from the *Secundo-primary* and *Secondary*, as *accidental*; while the *Primary* and *Secundo-primary*, being thought as *manifest or conceivable in their own nature*, are distinguished from the *Secondary*, as *in their own nature occult and inconceivable*. (846)

172.20–1   "in . . . work," . . . "if] Reid, therefore, as I have already observed, (p. 129a, note,) may seem to have become doubtful of the tendency of the doctrine advanced in his earlier work; and we ought not, at all events, to hold him rigorously accountable for the consequences of what, if (821)

173.32–3   "seem . . . presentationism,"] For while some of its statements seem . . . presentationism, others, again appear only compatible with those of an egoistical representationism. (882)

173.33   "decidedly] For my own part, I am decidedly (820)

173.35   mankind, he] mankind, that he (820)

175.24   "was] Krug is a Kantian; and as originally promulgated in his 'Entwurf eines neuen Organons,' 1801, (§5), his system was (797)

214n.1–2   "mental . . . move,"] If this volition become transeunt, be carried into effect, it passes into the mental . . . move. (864n)

214n.3   "for we are," . . . "conscious] For we are conscious (864n)

214n.5   of the limb] in the limb (865n)

219.32   *ipso facto*] [*not in italics*] (869n)

219.34   sought. The] sought, (p. 146a.)—The (869n)

219.40   involves] involve (869n)

219.41   in length] or length (869n)

423n.11–424n.1   action . . . action] notion . . . notion (852)
447.21   "many] I should indeed hardly have deemed that it required an articulate statement, were it not that, in point of fact, many (749)
447.23   these] their (749)
447.24   all their] their whole (749)
447.24–5   these same philosophers were (strange to say) not disposed to admit;"] these data the same philosophers were (strange to say!) not disposed to admit. (749)

——— "Foot-notes to Reid," in *The Works of Thomas Reid.* Ed. William Hamilton. Edinburgh: Maclachlan and Stewart; London: Longman, Brown, Green and Longmans, 1846.
NOTE: the references and quotations derive from footnotes provided by Hamilton in this ed. of Reid's *Works.* "Foot-note to Reid" is JSM's usual reference, and we have adopted it throughout, regularizing a few slightly different forms. See also Hamilton's "Dissertations on Reid," above.
QUOTED: 21, 21–2, 26n, 112n, 129n, 138n, 172, 173, 236n, 302, 322, 323n, 373, 421n, 424, 442n, 443, 444, 463n, 500
REFERRED TO: 29–30, 76n, 307n, 356n, 442, 448, 468
21.28   *what they are in themselves,*] "*what they are in themselves,*" (313n)
21.29   *relative notion*] "*relative notion,*" (313n)
21.30–1   absolutely and in themselves] *absolutely and in themselves* (313n)
21.31   out of relation] *out of relation* (313n)
21.33–4   qualities or phænomena] *qualities* or *phænomena* (323n)
21.34–22.1   in relation to our faculties] *in relation to our faculties* (323n)
26n.7–8   objective . . . subjective] *objective . . . subjective* (313n)
26n.9–10   perception . . . primary] *perception . . . primary* (313n)
112n.29   "It] But it (590n)
112n.30–2   *than . . . other*] [*not in italics*] (590n)
129n.5   "In] For, in (442n)
129n.7   consciousness] *consciousness* (442n)
138n.1   principle," . . . "has] principle has (300n)
138n.2–6   other. . . . It . . . speculations. . . . And yet . . . itself.] other; and yet . . . itself. To trace the influence of this assumption would be, in fact, in a certain sort, to write the history of philosophy; for, though this influence has never yet been historically developed, it . . . speculations. [*JSM has moved latter half of first sentence to the end of the quotation*] (300n)
172.16   extension] *extension* (129n)
173.5   "appears] This paragraph appears (310n)
236n.5   "perception of externality"] In the case of Cheselden—that in which the blindness previous to the recovery of sight was most perfect, and, therefore, the most instructive upon record—the patient, though he had little or no perception of distance, *i.e.* of the *degree of externality,* had still a perception of that externality absolutely. (177n)
236n.7–11   "to touch . . . skin." . . . "a . . . organ," . . . "as . . . eyes."] The objects, he said, seemed to "touch his eyes, as what he felt did his skin;" but they did not appear to him as if in his eyes, far less as a mere affection of the organ. (177n) [*JSM has altered the order of the elements of the sentence*]
302.25   "that the opposing parties are really at one."] The opposite parties are substantially at one. (412n)
322.17   "the words Conception, Concept, Notion] The words *Conception, Concept, Notion* (360n)
322.18   in imagination] in the imagination (360n)
323n.6   "the . . . notion,"] By *verbal* definition, is meant the more accurate determination of the signification of a *word*; by *real,* the . . . *notion.* (691n)
373.5   "because . . . contradiction."] Of the former ["the reality of the phænomenon"], scepticism is impossible, because . . . contradiction. (713)

21.23   *nothing*] [*not in italics*] (I, 137)
21.24   *without . . . faculties*] [*not in italics*] (I, 137)
22.19   "From] [*paragraph*] From (I, 148)
22.20   said," . . . "you] said, you (I, 148)
22.22   absolutely in] absolutely and in (I, 148)
22.24   faculties."] faculties; [*sentence continues and is completed with passage quoted at* 22.29–31] (I, 148)
22.30   assented] presented (I, 148)
22.31   those] these (I, 148)
23.3   [*paragraph*] In] [*no paragraph*] In (I, 146)
23.22   itself. I] itself.ᵃ [*footnote omitted*] [*paragraph*] I (I, 147)
31.27–8   "that . . . qualities," . . . "the phænomena . . . inhere."] [*see* 17 *above*] (I, 137, 138)
61.7   [*paragraph*] "The] [*paragraph*] 2°, That the (II, App. iii, 530)
62.23   "great axiom"] [*see* 16 *above*] (I, 136)
65.3–5   "by . . . believed,"] [*see* 61 *above*] (II, App. iii, 531)
76.8   else."] else; but to do this of the infinite is to think the infinite as finite, which is contradictory and absurd. (III, 102)
76.11–12   "to conceive the possibility" . . . "conceiving . . . reason."] When I say that a thing may be, of which I cannot conceive the possibility, (that is, by conceiving . . . reason), I only say that thought is limited; but, within its limits, I do not deny, I do not subvert, its truth. (III, 100)
79.8–9   conceive the proposition that A is not] enounce the proposition, A *is not* (III, 113)
80.8   "All] For if we take a comprehensive view of the phænomena of thought, we shall find that all (III, 100)
80.8   think . . . lies] think, that is, all that is within the jurisdiction of the law of Reason and Consequent, lies (III, 100)
80.10   one] the one (III, 100)
80.15   unthinkable . . . we] unthinkable, and, on the hypothesis in question, all, therefore, equally impossible, we (III, 101)
80.17   Extension may] Extension, then, may (III, 101)
80.18   contradictions] contradictories (III, 101)
80.19   and circumference] a circumference (III, 101)
81.19   inconceivable . . . .] [*ellipsis indicates 6-sentence omission*] (III, 103)
81.20   "It] But to return whence we have been carried, it (III, 103)
81.23   we] if we (III, 103)
81.24–5   admitted. . . . [*paragraph*] It] admitted, the hypothesis is manifestly false, that proposes the subjective or formal law of Reason and Consequent as the criterion of real or objective possibility. [*paragraph*] It (III, 103)
81.30   opposites,"] opposites, they again afford a similar refutation of the hypothesis in question. (III, 104)
82.38–83.1   "we . . . absurd."] [*see* 76, 80 *above*] (III, 102)
110.24   "the recognition . . . its own acts or affections;"] Consciousness is thus, on the one hand, the recognition . . . its acts and affections;—in other words, the self-affirmation, that certain modifications are known by me, and that these modifications are mine. (I, 193)
110.25   "all] In this all (I, 201)
111.3   is palpably] is, therefore, palpably (I, 212)
111.5   *that* I . . . *what* I] that I . . . what I (I, 212)
111.17   my own] my (I, 228)
111.21   It] [*paragraph*] It (I, 228)
111.38–9   "not only false," but "involves . . . terms."] [*paragraph*] I proceed, therefore, to show that Dr. Reid's assertion of memory being an immediate knowledge of the past, is not only false, but that it involves . . . terms.ᵃ [*footnote:*] ᵃCompare *Discussions*, p. 50.—ED. (I, 218)
111.40   "exists only in the *now*;"] Every act, and consequently every act of knowledge, exists only as it now exists; and as it exists only in the *now*, it can be cognisant only of a now-existent object. (I, 219)

112.6–7   been. . . . All] been. I remember an event I saw, —the landing of George IV. at Leith. This remembrance is only a consciousness of certain imaginations, involving the conviction that these imaginations now represent ideally what I formerly really experienced. All (I, 220–1)

112.8   belief. . . . So] [*ellipsis indicates 13-sentence omission*] (I, 220–1)

112.8   far is] far, therefore, is (I, 221)

112.11–12   past. . . . We] past. [*ellipsis indicates that JSM moves back 3 sentences (the last of which he omits)*] But, though in memory we must admit the reality of the representation and belief, as facts of consciousness, we (I, 220–1)

112.14   delusion:"] delusion. (I, 221)

112.27–30   organ:" . . . "It] organ.$^\beta$ [*footnote:*] $^\beta$On this point, see Adam Smith, *Essays on Philosophical Subjects—Ancient Logics and Metaphysics*, p. 153. Cf. *Of the External Senses*, p. 289, (edit. 1800.)—ED. [*text:*] In fact, if we look alternately with each, we have a different object in our right, and a different object in our left, eye. It (II, 153)

112.36   phænomena] phænomenon (II, 154)

114.11–12   "accompanied . . . been."] [*see* 112 *above*] (I, 219)

114.14   "contained"] This [Hamilton's definition of consciousness] being admitted, and professing, as we do, to prove that consciousness is the one generic faculty of knowledge, we, consequently, must maintain that all knowledge is immediate, and only of the actual or present,—in other words, that what is called mediate knowledge, knowledge of the past, knowledge of the absent, knowledge of the non-actual or possible, is either no knowledge at all, or only a knowledge contained in, and evolved out of, an immediate knowledge of what is now existent and actually present to the mind. (I, 217–18)

115.15–16   "the . . . affections,"] [*see* 110 *above*] (I, 193)

116.41   "in . . . existence."] But, on the other hand, consciousness is not to be viewed as anything different from these modifications themselves, but is, in . . . existence, or of their existence within the sphere of intelligence. (I, 193)

117.6   "the] Consciousness is thus, on the one hand, the recognition by the mind or ego of its acts and affections;—in other words, the (I, 193)

117.8–9   "is . . . from" the "modifications themselves."] [*see entry for* 116.41 *above*] (I, 193)

117.12–15   "consciousness and knowledge" . . . "are] Thus, in the present instance, consciousness and knowledge are (I, 194–5)

117.17   establishment. . . . Though] establishment. Knowledge is a relation, and every relation supposes two terms. Thus, in the relation in question, there is, on the one hand, a subject of knowledge,—that is, the knowing mind,—and on the other, there is an object of knowledge,—that is, the thing known; and the knowledge itself is the relation between these two terms. Now though (I, 195)

117.24   permanent] prominent (I, 195)

118n.13   "The] Here the (I, 194)

119.2–3   "a process of reasoning,"] [*see* 112 *above*] (II, 153)

119.15   is palpably] is, therefore, palpably (I, 212)

119.17–18   relative. The knowledge . . . object."] relative. [*JSM moves back a page and a half*] The whole question, therefore, turns upon the proof or disproof of this principle,—for if it can be shown that the knowledge . . . object, it follows that it is impossible to make consciousness conversant about the intellectual operations to the exclusion of their objects. (I, 211)

119.18–19   "It . . . object,"] [*see entry for* 119.17–18 *above*] (I, 211)

119.30–5   "that I can know *that* [I believe] without knowing *what* I [believe]—or that I can know the [belief] without knowing what the [belief] is about: for example, that I am conscious of [remembering a past event] without being conscious of [the past event remembered]; that I am conscious of [believing in God], without being conscious [of the God believed in]."] They [Reid and Stewart] maintain that I can know that I know, without knowing what I know,—or that I can know the knowledge without knowing what the knowledge is about; for example, that I am conscious of perceiving a book without being conscious of the book perceived,—that I am conscious of remembering its contents without being conscious of these contents remembered,—and so forth. (I, 212)

119.35–120.2 "an . . . knowledge" . . . "only . . . object," . . . "manifest" . . . "that . . . correlative."] [*see* 111 *above*] (I, 228)

120.33–4 "we may be . . . know," and that "it] We may, however, be . . . know, and it (IV, 70)

120.35–6 and modern] and in modern (IV, 70)

120.37 belief,"] belief. (IV. 70)

120.37 "But] [*paragraph*] But (IV, 73)

121.3 "The] [*paragraph*] The (IV, 73)

121.4 so] in so (IV, 73)

122.8 "The] Now, the (IV, 73)

122.8 object" . . . "is] object is (IV, 73)

123n.23–4 "one . . . solution."] [*see* 121 *above*] (IV, 73)

126.18 is that] is thus,—that (I, 271)

126.24 them.] them.*ᵃ* [*footnote:*] *ᵃ*See *Reid's Works*, Note A, p. 743, *et seq.*—ED. (I, 271)

127.15 Stewart. . . . [*paragraph*] With] Stewart.*ᵃ* [*ellipsis indicates omission of footnote and 5-sentence quotation from Stewart*] [*paragraph*] With (I, 273)

128.5 not-self."] not-self.*ᵃ* [*footnote referring to Buffier omitted*] (I, 175)

128.7 "it] It (I, 276)

128.10 veracity."] veracity.*ᵃ* [*footnote:*] *ᵃ*See *Reid's Works*, pp. 743–754, *et seq.*—ED. (I, 276)

128.25–6 "the . . . affections." [*see entry for* 110.24 *above*] (I, 193)

130.13–14 "given . . . consciousness" . . . "to . . . evidence."] [*paragraph*] Under this first law [of Parcimony], let it, therefore, be laid down, in the first place, that by a fact of consciousness properly so called, is meant a primary and universal fact of our intellectual being; and, in the second, that such facts are of two kinds,—1°, The facts given . . . consciousness itself; and, 2°, The facts which consciousness does not at once give, but to . . . evidence. (I, 275)

130.15 "the *veracity* of consciousness,"] Philosophy is only a systematic evolution of the contents of consciousness, by the instrumentality of consciousness; it, therefore, necessarily supposes, in both respects, the veracity of consciousness. (I, 276–7)

130n.6–7 "is . . . certainty.] 'The Criterion of truth is . . . certainty.' [*Hamilton is quoting himself*] (IV, 69)

131.6 "nearly . . . philosophers"] [*see* 127 *above*] (I, 272)

133.33–4 "to . . . evidence."] [*see* 130 *above*] (I, 275)

134n.3–6 "Religious disbelief . . . connexion." . . . "must ever be a matter" . . . "of regret," . . . "reprobation."] I would, therefore, earnestly request of you to bear in mind, that religious disbelief . . . connection; and that while the one must ever be a matter of reprobation and regret, the other is in itself deserving of applause. (I, App. i, 394)

136.17 "Errors" . . . "intelligence as] Errors may, however, arise either from overlooking the laws or necessary principles which it does contain; or by attributing to it [intelligence], as (IV, 137)

137n.11 "Nothing," . . . "can] Nothing can (II, 129)

137n.17 organ. . . . Through] organ; and that is true which Democritus of old asserted, that all our senses are only modifications of touch.*ᵃ* [*footnote:*] *ᵃ*See below, vol. ii, lect. xxvii, p. 152.—ED. [*text:*] Through (II, 130)

137n.18 retina."] retina; what we add to this perception must not be taken into account. (II, 130)

138n.11 "I] [*paragraph*] I (IV, 95)

138n.17 "relevation" . . . "naturally clear,"] But admitting all this, I am still bold enough to maintain, that consciousness affords not merely the only revelation, and only criterion of philosophy, but that this revelation is naturally clear,—this criterion, in itself, unerring. (I, 266)

142.1 "There] In the second place, there (IV, 92)

142.4 knowledge. . . . To] knowledge. Now, from both of these considerations, it is evident that to (IV, 92)

142.35 "that] [*paragraph*] The First of these rules ["which afford the exclusive conditions of psychological legitimacy"] is,—That (I, 268)

143.2 "reduce it to a generalization from experience."] Whenever, therefore, in our analysis of the intellectual phænomena, we arrive at an element which we cannot reduce to a generalisation from experience, but which lies at the root of all experience, and which we cannot, therefore, resolve into any higher principle,—this we properly call a fact of consciousness. (I, 270)

143.3 "character of necessity."] [*paragraph*] But, in the second place, this, its character of ultimate priority, supposes its character of necessity. (I, 270)

147n.7–11 "Whenever . . . consciousness."] [*see entry for* 143.2 *above*] (I, 270)

147n.12–14 [*no paragraph*] "A . . . belief"] [*paragraph*] A . . . belief. (I, 271)

149.4–6 "No philosopher . . . consciousness."] [*paragraph*] But, though this be too evident to admit of doubt, and though no philosopher . . . consciousness, we find, nevertheless, that its testimony has been silently overlooked, and systems established upon principles in direct hostility to the primary data of intelligence. (I, 277)

149.6–8 "that . . . dependent."] [*beginning of Lecture XVI*] On the principle, which no one has yet been found bold enough formally to deny, and which, indeed, requires only to be understood to be acknowledged,—viz. that . . . dependent,—it is manifest, at once and without further reasoning, that no philosophical theory can pretend to truth except that single theory which comprehends and develops the fact of consciousness on which it founds, without retrenchment, distortion, or addition. (I, 285)

149.10 "the] [*paragraph*] From these examples, the truth of the position I maintain is manifest,—that a fact of consciousness can only be rejected on the supposition of falsity, and that, the falsity of one fact of consciousness being admitted, the (I, 283)

149.27 and obey] and to obey (I, 284)

150.8 "We] [*no paragraph*] I shall commence with this great fact to which I have already alluded,—that we (I, 288)

150.8–9 perception," . . . "of] perception of (I, 288)

150.18 Such] [*paragraph*] Such (I, 288)

150.20 of our own] of their own (I, 288)

150.20–1 minds." [*paragraph*] We] minds. [*JSM moves ahead 4 pages*] [*no paragraph*] We (I, 288, 292)

150.22 quality] duality [*treated as typographical error in this edition*] (I, 292)

150.33–7 consciousness." . . . [*paragraph*] "Philosophers] consciousness. [*no paragraph*] Philosophers (I, 292)

151.1 integrity.] integrity.ᵅ [*footnote:*] ᵅSee the Author's Suppl. Disser. to *Reid's Works*, Note C.—ED. (I, 293)

151.4 philosopher] philosopherᵝ [*footnote:*] ᵝThis philosopher is doubtless Peter Poiret. John Sergeant is subsequently referred to by Sir W. Hamilton, as holding a similar doctrine in a paradoxical form. See below, vol. ii. pp. 92, 124.—ED (I, 293)

151.6 As] [*no paragraph*] As (I, 293)

151.9–11 Dualism." . . . [*paragraph*] "In] Dualism. [*paragraph*] In (I, 293)

151.14 rejection] rejections (I, 293)

151.15 shown that] shown you, that (I, 293)

151.16–20 impossible." . . . "But] impossible. But (I, 293)

151.24 deception;" . . . "that] deception,—that (I, 293)

151.32 manifestation] manifestations (I, 294)

151.35 philosophy. . . . But] philosophy, for Oken's deduction of the universe from the original nothing,ᵅ [*footnote:*] ᵅSee Oken's *Physiophilosophy*, translated for the Ray Society by Tulk, § 31–43.—ED. [*text:*]—the nothing being equivalent to the Absolute or God, is only the paradoxical foundation of a system of realism; and, in ancient philosophy, we know too little of the book of Gorgias the Sophist, entitled Περὶ τοῦ μὴ ὄντος, ἢ περὶ φύσεως,ᵝ [*footnote:*] ᵝSee Sextus Empiricus, *Adv. Math.* vii. 65.—ED. [*text:*]— *Concerning Nature or the Non-Existent*,—to be able to affirm whether it were maintained by him as a dogmatic and *bona fide* doctrine. But (I, 294)

151.38   result."] result.ᵞ [*footnote:*] ᵞSee a remarkable passage in the *Bestimmung des Menschen*, p. 174, (*Werke*, vol. ii. p. 245), translated by Sir W. Hamilton, *Reid's Works*, p. 129.—ED. (I, 294)

152.9   "that] They [philosophical Unitarians or Monists] reject, however, the evidence of consciousness to their antithesis in existence, and maintain that (I, 296)

152.16   "are] "The Dualists, of whom we are now first speaking, are (I, 295)

152.38   dualist] dualistᵃ [*3-sentence footnote concerning Aristotle's opinion omitted*] (I, 296)

152.43   Descartes."] Descartes.ᵝ [*footnote:*] ᵝSee the Author's *Discussions*, p. 57 *seq.*—ED. (I, 296)

158.24   "that] [*beginning of Lecture XXIV*] IN my last Lecture, having concluded the review of Reid's Historical Account of Opinions on Perception, and of Brown's attack upon that account, I proceeded to the question,—Is Reid's own doctrine of perception a scheme of Natural Realism, that is, did he accept in its integrity the datum of consciousness,—that we are immediately cognitive both of the phænomena of matter and of the phænomena of mind; or did he, like Brown, and the greater number of more recent philosophers, as Brown assumes, hold only the finer form of the representative hypothesis, which supposes that (II, 86)

158.28   non-self."] not-self? (II, 86)

158.31   You will remark," . . . "that] [*no paragraph*] You will remark, likewise, that (II, 106)

158.36   our] an (II, 106)

158.36   the phænomenon] his [Brown's] phænomenon (II, 106)

159.1   are conscious] are there conscious (II, 106)

159.5–8   exists." . . . "Nor] exists. [*no paragraph*] Nor (II, 106)

159.13   "Mark] [*paragraph*] But mark (II, 138)

160.27   Every] [*no paragraph*] Every (I, 219)

160.28   Now] *now* (I, 219)

160.28–9   object. But] object. Memory is an act,—an act of knowledge; it can, therefore, be cognisant only of a now-existent object. But (I, 219)

160.32   true one, it] true, it (I, 219)

160.34–6   *a . . . been*] [*not in italics*] (I, 219)

160.38–9   *a . . . experienced*] [*not in italics*] (I, 219)

160.43–4   *Of . . . nothing*] [*not in italics*] (I, 220)

161.1–2   *as . . . modification*] [*not in italics*] (I, 220)

161.5–6   *only . . . knowledge*] [*not in italics*] (I, 220)

162.12–13   *which . . . perceive*] [*not in italics*] (II, 154)

162n.11   "Real truth is the] [*paragraph*] Real truth is, therefore, the (IV, 67)

163n.1–2   new." . . . "But] new. But (IV, 67)

163n.11–15   itself." . . . "All] itself. All (IV, 68)

163n.16   lie:"] lie,—a supposition which is not, without the strongest evidence, to be admitted; and the argument is as competent against the sceptic in our present condition, as it would be were we endowed with any other conceivable form of Acquisitive and Cognitive Faculties. (IV, 68)

166.1   "we . . . representation:"] [*see* 159 *above*] (II, 106)

176.23–4   "The object," . . . "is in this case given] In the latter case, the object, which may be called the *subject-object*, is given (II, 432)

193.22–4   "religious . . . connexion] [*see entry for* 134n.3–6 *above*] (I, App. i, 394)

223.20–1   "a . . . scholar,"] [*paragraph*] This doctrine [that vision is exclusively responsible for the perception of extension and figure] is maintained among others by Platner,—a . . . scholar. (II, 173)

223.30   exteriority; in] exteriority, (*oertliches Auseinanderseyn*), in (II, 174)

223.34   *time . . . space*] [*not in italics*] (II, 174)

223.36   to another] to some other (II, 174)

223.41   *kinds*] [*not in italics*] (II, 174)

224.1   differences] difference (II, 175)
228.32   conceiving] perceiving (II, 167) [*treated as a typographical error in this edition*]
229.3   figure. These] figure. [*paragraph*] These (II, 168)
229.5–6 discussion". . . . "And] discussion. And (II, 168)
230.32–3 "It is not," . . . "all] And here you will observe, it is not all (II, 160)
251n.13 "Those] This law may be thus enounced,—Those (II, 238)
252.1   "whether] Of these ["the vital interests of philosophy"] the first that I shall touch
         upon, is the problem;—Whether (II, 144)
252.34   one into] into one (II, 147) [*treated as a typographical error in this edition*]
253.18   into mind] into the mind (II, 148) [*treated as a typographical error in this edition*]
253.42   "ingenious" . . . "has] [*paragraph*] the same conclusion is attained, through a
         somewhat different process, by Mr James Mill, in his ingenious *Analysis of the
         Phœnomena of the Human Mind*. This author, following Hartley and Priestley, has (II,
         146)
254.3–5 laws," . . . "account . . . principle."] laws. According to Mr Mill, the necessity
         under which we lie of thinking that one contradictory excludes another,—that a thing
         cannot at once be and not be, is only the result of association and custom.^β [*footnote:*]
         ^βChap. iii. p. 75.—ED. [*text:*] It is not, therefore, to be marvelled at, that he should account
         . . . principle; and this he accordingly does.^γ [*footnote:*] ^γChap. iii. p. 68.—ED. (II, 146)
256.4   "in] [*paragraph*] Now in opposition to this doctrine [James Mill's law of association],
         nothing appears to me clearer than the first alternative,—and that, in (II, 149)
256.7–8 "If . . . doctrine" . . . "were] [*no paragraph*] If . . . doctrine were (II, 149)
256.15   perception] perceptions (II, 149) [*treated as a typographical error in this edition*]
256.23   results] result (II, 149) [*treated as a typographical error in this edition*]
256.28   constituted] constituent (II, 150) [*treated as a typographical error in this edition*]
260.18   experience."] experience; our whole empirical knowledge is, therefore, a merely
         accidental possession of the mind. (IV, 74)
272.4   "Whether] The question I refer to is, Whether (I, 338)
272.7–9 "the . . . absurd;"] This is the most general expression of a problem which has
         hardly been mentioned, far less mooted, in this country; and when it has attracted a passing
         notice, the . . . absurd. (I, 338)
272n.2   "Every act . . . consciousness"] You will recollect that, when treating of Conscious-
         ness in general, I stated to you that consciousness necessarily involves a judgment; and as
         every act . . . consciousness, every act of mind, consequently, involves a judgment.^α
         [*footnote omitted*] (II, 277)
272n.7–8 "We must . . . it" . . . "can] We may say of the mental state of perception too, in his
         [Reid's] own language, as indeed we must . . . it can (II, 73)
273n.5   "This is certainly," . . . "an] That, in the interval, when out of consciousness, these
         cognitions do continue to subsist in the mind, is certainly an (II, 209)
273n.10–11 "an . . . self-active powers] But the mental activity, the act of knowledge, of
         which I now speak, is more than this; it is an . . . self-active power (II, 211–12) [*Hamilton is
         quoting from Schmid*]
274n.3   "Every . . . can be neither] To explain, therefore, the disappearance of our mental
         activities, it is only requisite to explain their weakening or enfeeblement,—which may be
         attempted in the following way:—Every . . . can neither be (II, 213) [*Hamilton is quoting
         from Schmid*]
274n.15–16 "Mind, howbeit . . . independence."] Nor can it be argued, that the limitations
         to which the Retentive, or rather the Reproductive, Faculty is subjected in its energies, in
         consequence of its bodily relations, prove the absolute dependence of memory on organi-
         sation, and legitimate the explanation of this faculty by corporeal agencies; for the
         incompetency of this inference can be shown from the contradiction in which it stands to
         the general laws of mind, which, howbeit . . . independence."^α [*footnote:*] ^αH. Schmid,
         Versuch einer Metaphysik [p. 235–6.—ED.] (II, 217–18) [*conclusion of Hamilton's quo-
         tation from Schmid*]

274.1 contains systems] contains certain systems (I, 339)

274.9–13 extinguished." . . . "in . . . of actually] extinguished. For example, there are cases in . . . of accurately (I, 340)

275.4 "mental] [*paragraph*] The problem, then, in regard to this class is,—Are there, in ordinary, mental (I, 347)

275.7–8 "that . . . of;"] [*paragraph*] In the question proposed, I am not only strongly inclined to the affirmative,—nay, I do not hesitate to maintain, that . . . of,—that our whole knowledge, in fact, is made up of the unknown and incognisable. (I, 348)

275.9 "the] And without dealing in any general speculation, I shall at once descend to the special evidence which appears to me, not merely to warrant, but to necessitate the conclusion, that the (I, 349)

275.15–18 "they are . . . zero." . . . "must . . . unperceived," . . . "When] They are . . . zero. But it is evident, that each half must . . . unperceived; for as the perceived whole is nothing but the union of the unperceived halves, so the perception,—the perceived affection itself of which we are conscious,—is only the sum of two modifications, each of which severally eludes our consciousness. When (I, 350)

275.29–31 When . . . sea, "this] When . . . sea,—what are the constituents of the total perception of which we are conscious? This (I, 351)

275.32 something. . . . If] something. The noise of the sea is the complement of the noise of its several waves;—/ποντίων τε κυμάτων/'Ανηριθμον γέλασμα.ª [*footnote:*] ªÆschylus, *Prometheus*, 1. 89.—ED. [*text:*] and if (I, 351)

276n.1 "In] As, to take an example from vision,—in the external perception of a stationary object, a certain space,—an expanse of surface, is necessary to the *minimum visible*, in other words, an object of sight cannot come into consciousness unless it be of a certain size; in like manner, in (I, 369)

276n.4 consciousness."] consciousness; and as time is divisible *ad infinitum*, whatever minimum be taken, there must be admitted to be, beyond the cognisance of consciousness, intervals of time, in which, if mental agencies be performed, these will be latent to consciousness. (I, 369–70)

276n.4–6 "It cannot . . . sensation."] Taking, then, their difference in degree, and supposing that the degree of the impression determines the degree of the sensation, it cannot . . . sensation: but this is undeniable, that, above a certain limit, perception declines, in proportion as sensation rises. (II, 101–2)

277.7 It] [*no paragraph*] Now it (I, 352)

277.28 immediately] mediately (I, 353) [*treated as a typographical error in this edition*]

278.4 "our acquired dexterities and habits."] [*paragraph*] Let us now turn to another class of phænomena, which in like manner are capable of an adequate explanation only on the theory I have advanced;—I mean the operations resulting from our Acquired Dexterities and Habits. (I, 355)

278.21–2 "violates . . . consciousness." "Consciousness] But, in the second place, it [assuming a state of consciousness not remembered] violates . . . consciousness. Consciousness (I, 354)

278.24 "Of] But of (I, 355)

278.26 ideas of A] ideas A (I, 355) [*treated as a typographical error in this edition*]

279.11–12 mind," . . . "that] mind, that (I, 368)

279.13 memory. Vivid] memory. Memory and consciousness are thus in the direct ratio of each other. On the one hand, looking from cause to effect,—vivid (I, 368–9)

279.14 memory."] memory; no consciousness, no memory: and, on the other, looking from effect to cause,—long memory, vivid consciousness; short memory, faint consciousness; no memory, no consciousness. (I, 369)

280.25–31 "would . . . conclusions:" . . . "serious meditation" . . . "without . . . fatigue:" . . . "each . . . process."] In the present instance, its [Stewart's doctrine of real but forgotten consciousness] admission would . . . conclusions. Take the case of a person reading. Now, all of you must have experienced, if ever under the necessity of reading aloud, that, if the matter be uninteresting, your thoughts, while you are going on in the performance of your task, are wholly abstracted from the book and its subject, and you are perhaps deeply occupied in a train of serious meditation. Here the process of reading is performed without interruption, and with the most punctual accuracy; and, at the same time, the process of meditation is carried on without . . . fatigue. Now this, on Mr Stewart's doctrine, would seem impossible, for what does his theory suppose? It supposes that separate acts of concentrated consciousness or attention, are bestowed on each . . . process. (I, 360)

280.37–8 *"concentrated* consciousness or attention,"] *[see entry for* 280.25–31 *above]* (I, 360)

281n.9 restricted] astricted (II, 258) *[treated as a typographical error in this edition]*

281n.14 our nature] their nature (II, 258)

281.12–14 "the . . . each;"] This law is, that the . . . each, and consequently the less vivid and distinct will be the information it obtains of the several objects.[β] *[footnote omitted]* (I, 237)

281.17–18 "the train of serious meditation"] *[see entry for* 280.25–31 *above]* (I, 360)

286.2 "some philosophers who, instead] Nor is this superfluous, for we shall find that some philosophers, instead (II, 376)

286.9–10 "When we . . . aware,". . . "of] [α]When *[footnote:]* [α]Cf. *Discussions,* p. 609.—ED. *[text:]* we . . . aware of (II, 377)

286.10 exist] be (II, 377)

286.11 does this] does the (II, 377)

286.11 that it has a cause] *that it has a cause* (II, 377)

286.20 reverti,"] reverti,"[β] *[footnote:]* [β]Persius, iii. 84. [Cf. Rixner, *Geschichte der Philosophie,* v. i. p. 83, § 62.] (II, 377)

286.24 as] an (II, 377)

286.25 and an alkali] and alkali (II, 377) *[treated as a typographical error in this edition]*

287.1 Put] But (II, 377)

287.2 those] these (II, 377)

287.3 constituents, either] constituents, and these constituents again of simpler elements, either (II, 378)

287.6–7 to the] to their (II, 378) *[treated as a typographical error in this edition]*

287.10 interit,"] interit,"[α] *[footnote:]* [α]Ovid, *Met.* xv. 165.—ED. (II, 378)

287.17–18 "not . . . mind,"] *[paragraph]* The eighth [doctrine regarding the principle of causality] and last opinion is that which regards the judgment of causality as derived; and derives it not . . . mind; in a word, from the principle of the Conditioned. (II, 397)

287.31 "We are . . . construe in] In short, we are . . . construe it in (II, 405)

287.35 the world] a world (II, 405)

287.39–288.1 *Can . . . alone]* *[not in italics]* (II, 406)

288.8 retraction] retractation (II, 406) *[treated as a typographical error in this edition]*

289.34–5 "complement of existence"] *[see* 286 *above]* (II, 377)

290.2–3 "law of the Conditioned,"] The law of mind, that all that is positively inconceivable, lies in the interval between two inconceivable extremes, and which, however palpable when stated, has never been generalised, as far as I know, by any philosopher, I call the Law or Principle of the Conditioned. (II, 404)

291.21–2 "professes . . . explanation evacuates] Brown professes . . . explanation, he evacuates (II, 384)

291.37–8 "concurring . . . effect."] *[paragraph]* But, in the second place, as every effect is only produced by the concurrence of at least two causes, (and by cause, be it observed, I mean everything without which the effect could not be realised), and as these concurring . . . effect, it follows, that the lower we descend in the series of causes, the moe complex will be the product; and that the higher we ascend, it will be the more simple. (I, 59)

291.38–292.2 "an effect" is "nothing . . . which constitutes] *[paragraph]* Considering philosophy, in the first place, in relation to its first end,—the discovery of causes,—we have seen that causes, (taking that term as synonymous for all without which the effect would not be), are only the coefficients of the effect; an effect being nothing . . . which constitute (I, 97)

292.2 "An effect] [*paragraph*] But all the causes or coefficient powers being brought into reciprocal relation, the salt is the result; for an effect (II, 540)

292.3 entities;" "causes] entities,—concauses or coefficient powers. In thought, causes and effects are thus, *pro tanto*, tautological: an effect always pre-existed potentially in its causes; and causes (II, 540)

292.9 "Considering] Now, considering (I, 59)

292.10–11 There are, first . . . secondly . . . thirdly] These are, *first*, . . . *secondly* . . . *thirdly* (I, 59)

292.21 "concause"] [*see entries for* 292.2 *and* 292.3 *above*] (II, 540)

292.22 last," . . . "as] last, as (I, 97)

292.27–8 "as . . . be;"] [*see entry for* 291.38–292.2 *above*] (I, 97)

293.13 "Philosophy] [*paragraph*] Philosophy (I, 60)

293.17–19 view" . . . "and . . . *complete*] view, and . . . complete (I, 60)

293n.1–2 "The lower . . . simple."] [*see entry for* 291.37–8 *above*] (I, 59)

295.13 "attempts] It [the doctrine under discussion] attempts (II, 396)

295.14–16 "Listen," . . . "to] Listen to (II, 397)

295.18 which] that (II, 397)

295.23 consequently we exclude] consequently exclude (II, 397)

295.29–30 opinion," . . . "is] opinion is (II, 397)

295.37 "not] And what is this relation? Not (II, 391)

295.38–9 in volition] in a volition (II, 391)

295.41–296.2 world." [*paragraph*] . . . "This] world. [*paragraph*] αThis [*footnote:*] αSee *Reid's Works*, p. 866. *Discuss.*, p. 612.—ED. (II, 391)

296.12 actually] absolutely (II, 392)

296.14 determination] determinations (II, 392)

296.16–17 the volition] volition (II, 392)

297n.1 "quality of necessity and universality."] Admitting that causation were cognisable, and that perception and self-consciousness were competent to its apprehension, still as these faculties could only take note of individual causations, we should be wholly unable, out of such empirical acts, to evolve the quality of necessity and universality, by which this notion is distinguished. (II, 392)

302.20 "that . . . one."] In the discussion of this question ["whether we can form an adequate idea of that which is denoted by an abstract . . . term"], I shall pursue the following order: first of all, I shall state to you the arguments of the Nominalists,—of those who hold, that we are unable to form an idea corresponding to the abstract and general term; in the second place, I shall state to you the arguments of the Conceptualists,—of those who maintain that we are so competent; and, in the last, I shall show you that . . . one, and that the whole controversy has originated in the imperfection and ambiguity of our philosophical nomenclature. (II, 296)

302.33 "The] [*paragraph*] The (II, 287)

302.38 body." [*paragraph*] . . . "individual abstract notions;" . . . "Abstract General Notions." . . . "when] body. [*no paragraph*] But had we only individual abstract notions, what would be our knowledge? We should be cognisant only of qualities viewed apart from their subjects; (and of separate phænomena there exist none in nature); and as these qualities are also separate from each other, we should have no knowledge of their mutual relations.α [*footnote:*] αWe should also be overwhelmed with their number.—*Jotting*. [*text:*] [*paragraph*] It is necessary, therefore, that we should form Abstract General notions. This is done when (II, 288)

303.7 notion] action (II, 288)

303.25 twofold quantity] twofold kind of quantity (II, 289)

303.34–5 Extension of a notion; the latter, the internal quantity, is called its Comprehension or Intension. . . . The] *Extension* of a notion, (*quantitas ambitus*); the latter, the internal quantity, is called its *Comprehension* or Intension, (*quantitas complexus*). [*ellipsis indicates omission of 3 sentences and lengthy Greek footnote*] The (II, 289–90)

303.37 extension."] extension.β [*footnote omitted*] (II, 290)

303.44 "not only true but self-evident." . . . "irrefragable"] This opinion [that there are no general notions], which, after Hobbes, has been in this country maintained, among others, by Berkeley,[β] Hume,[γ] Adam Smith,[δ] Campbell,[α] and Stewart,[β] [*footnotes identifying specific passages from works of these philosophers omitted*] appears to me not only true but self-evident. [*paragraph*] No one has stated the case of the nominalists more clearly than Bishop Berkeley, and as his whole argument is, as far as it goes, irrefragable, I beg your attention to the following extract from his Introduction to the *Principles of Human Knowledge*.[γ] [*footnote:*] [γ]Sections vii. viii. x. *Works*, i. 5 *et seq.*, 4to edit. Cf. *Encyclopædia Britannica*, art. *Metaphysics*, vol. xiv. p. 622, 7th edit.—ED. (II, 297–8)

304.28   whatever] whatsoever (II, 299)
304.30   abstracting their ideas] *abstracting their ideas* (II, 299)
304.34   part] parts (II, 299)
304.42   whatsoever.] whatsoever.[α] [*footnote:*] [α]This argumentation is employed by Derodon, *Logica*, [pars ii c. vi § 16. *Opera*, p. 236.—ED.], and others. (II, 300)
304.42   am] own (II, 300)
305.15   "point of similarity"] Now it is the points of similarity thus discovered and identified in the unity of consciousness, which constitute Concepts or Notions. (III, 125)
305.16   "is not] It [a concept or notion] is, therefore, not (III, 128)
305.19   expresses. . . . The] expresses. [*ellipsis indicates 1-paragraph omission*] [*paragraph*] But the (III, 128)
305.38–306.1   Presentation . . . Phantasy," that "our] And here I again stated what a Concept or Notion is in itself, and in contrast to a Presentation . . . Phantasy. Our (III, 131)
306.4   mediate, indeterminate] mediate, relative, indeterminate (III, 131)
306.6–7   object. . . . [*paragraph*] Formed by comparison," concepts "express] object. [*ellipsis indicates 2 3/4-page omission*] [*no paragraph*] Formed by comparison, they (III, 131, 134)
306.11   as actually] as so actually (III, 134)
306.30   horse] *horse* (III, 135)
306.35   in] on (III, 135)
307.17   "the employment] This ["that concepts are mere words, and that there is nothing general in thought itself"] is not indeed held in reality by any philosopher; for no philosopher has ever denied that we are capable of apprehending relations, and in particular the relation of similarity and difference; so that the whole controversy between the conceptualist and nominalist originates in the ambiguous employment (III, 136)
307.19–20   relation," . . . "cannot] relation cannot (II, 312)
307.24   given."] given; and accordingly this has been done wherever a philosophical nomenclature of the slightest pretensions to perfection has been formed. (II, 312)
307.28   faculties."] faculties.[α] [*footnote:*] [α]See the Author's note, *Reid's Works*, p. 412; and *Lectures on Metaphysics*, vol. ii. p. 296 *et seq.*—ED. (III, 136)
308.13   "As the . . . comparison," a concept "necessarily] [*entire paragraph indented*] ¶XXII.—2°, A concept or notion, as the . . . comparison, necessarily (III, 128)
308.14–15   "a . . . imagination."] [*see 271 above*] (II, 312)
308.18   "a . . . attributes,"] [*see 305 above*] (III, 129)
308.20   "common circumstance"] [*see 303 above*] (II, 298)
308.25–6   "the . . . objects,"] [*see 307 above*] (II, 312)
309.2–3   "In the formation," . . . "of] This, by way of preface, being understood, I showed that, in the formation of (III, 132)
309.12   the object] its object (III, 132)
309.19   process. But] process; but (III, 132)
310.13   [*paragraph*] The] [*entire paragraph indented*] ¶XXIII. The (III, 137)
311.12   "Language," . . . "is] Language is (III, 138)
311.16–18   it." . . . "is] it. Speech is thus not the mother, but the godmother, of knowledge. But though, in general, we must hold that language, as the product and correlative of thought, must be viewed as posterior to the act of thinking itself; on the other hand, it must be admitted, that we could never have risen above the very lowest degrees in the scale of thought, without the aid of signs. A sign is (III, 138)
311.19   beyond. A] beyond. [*paragraph*] A (III, 138)

312.1 arrested. . . . Admitting] arrested. Thus it is, that the higher exertions of the higher faculty of Understanding,—the classification of the objects presented and represented by the subsidiary powers in the formation of a hierarchy of notions, the connection of these notions into judgments, the inference of one judgment from another, and, in general, all our consciousness of the relations of the universal to the particular, consequently all science strictly so denominated, and every inductive knowledge of the past and future from the laws of nature:—not only these, but all ascent from the sphere of sense to the sphere of moral and religious intelligence, are, as experience proves, if not altogether impossible without a language, at least possible to a very low degree. [*paragraph*] Admitting (II, 139)

315.42–316.1 "realized in thought," . . . "elicited into consciousness."] [*see* 306 *above*] (III, 135, 134)

319.7 "As . . . the fictitious] [*entire paragraph indented*] ¶XXX. As . . . the factitious (III, 171)

319.33–6 "For . . . part, especially . . . thought, to] [*no paragraph*] Speaking of the analysis of complex notions, he [Leibniz] says—"For . . . part, however, especially . . . thought, for the sake of brevity, to (III, 181)

319.38 thousand sides] thousand equal sides (III, 181)

319.39 or thousand] a thousand (III, 181)

320.1 mode] kind (III, 181)

320n.12–14 "the symbolical notions of the understanding," . . . "the . . . Imagination."] consequence of the establishment of this distinction by Leibnitz, that a peculiar expression, (*Begriff, conceptus*), was appropriated to the symbolical notions of the Understanding, in contrast to the . . . Imagination, which last also were furnished with the distinctive appellations of *intuitions,* (*Anschauungen, intuitus*). (III, 183)

321.21 "A Concept," . . . "is] [*paragraph*] The conceiving an object is, therefore, its recognition mediately through a concept; and a Concept is (III, 122)

321.25 "abusive employment"] This abusive employment has, however, not been so frequent in reference to this term [notion] as to the term *conception*; but it must be acknowledged, that nothing can be imagined more vague and vacillating than the meaning attached to *notion* in the writings of all British philosophers, without exception. (III, 121)

321.26 are sometimes] are also sometimes (III, 126)

321.28 general."] general; while the other cognitive modifications to which they are opposed,—perceptions and imaginations,—have, in like manner, their essence in their individuality. (III, 126)

321.29–33 "If I . . . of Sophroniscus, as Athenian, as philosopher, as pugnosed . . . my *notion* or *concept*] If, for example, I . . . of *Sophroniscus*, as *Athenian*, as *philosopher*, as *pugnosed* . . . my notion or concept (III, 78)

321.35 individual.] *individual.*[β] [*footnote:*] [β]Krug, *ibid.* [*Logik*], § 29.—ED. (III, 146)

321.36 "It] Now, it (III, 148)

322.9 here is] is here (III, 148)

322.12–14 "If a . . . is . . . not a proper abstract] [*paragraph*] Thus, it is manifest, that, as Definition is the analysis of a complex concept into its component parts or attributes, if a concept be simple, that is, if it contain in it only a single attribute, it must be indefinable; and again, that as Division is the analysis of a higher or more general concept into others lower and less general, if a . . . is indivisible, is, in fact, not a proper or abstract (III, 152)

323n.20–3 "a concept . . . be clear . . . discriminate" . . . "what . . . notions:"] "A concept . . . be *clear* . . . discriminate what . . . notions; whereas if the degree of consciousness be so remiss that this and other concepts run into each other, in that case, the notion is said to be *obscure.* (III, 160–1) [*Hamilton is quoting from Esser*]

323n.23–5 "notions absolutely clear" are "notions whose *objects*" . . . "possibly . . . unknown."] But, on the other hand, of notions absolutely clear, that is, notions whose objects cannot possibly . . . unknown,—of such notions a limited intelligence is possessed of very few, and, consequently, our human concepts are, properly, only a mixture of the opposite qualities;—*clear* or *obscure* as applied to them, meaning only that the one quality or the other is the preponderant. (III, 161) [*Hamilton is quoting from Esser*]

324.21 "To judge," . . . "is] [*entire paragraph indented*] ¶XLVI. To judge, (κρίνειν,[α]

[*footnote:*] *α*The verb κρίνειν, to *judge*, and still more the substantive, κρίσις, *judgment*, are rarely used by the Greeks,—(never by Aristotle)—as technical terms of Logic or of Psychology. [*text:*] *judicare*) is (III, 225)

324.24–5   a Judgment; considered . . . a Proposition or Predication."] a *Judgment*, (λόγος ἀποφανός, *judicium*); considered . . . a *Proposition* or *Predication*, (ἀπόφανσις, πρότασις,*α* [*footnote omitted*] διάστημα, *propositio, prædicatio, pronunciatum, enunciatio, effatum, profatum, axioma*β). [*footnote:*] β By Stoics and Ramists. (III, 226)

325.1   "Concepts, in] [*entire paragraph indented*] ¶XLII. Considered under their Comprehension, concepts, again, in (III, 213)

325.4–5   notions." . . . "1°.] notions, (τὸ ἀντικεῖσθαι, *oppositio*). This is twofold;—1°, (III, 213)

325.5   Opposition] *Opposition* (III, 214)

325.6   *Repugnance*; and] *Repugnance*, (τὸ ἀντιφατικῶς ἀντικεῖσθαι, ἀντίφασις, *oppositio immediata* sive *contradictoria, repugnantia*); and, (III, 214)

325.6   Opposition. The] *Opposition*, (τὸ ἐναντίως ἀντικεῖσθαι, ἐναντιότης, *oppositio mediata* vel *contraria*). The (III, 214)

325.7   abolishes directly] abolishes, (*tolit*), directly (III, 214)

325.8   establishes; the] establishes, (*ponit*); the (III, 214)

325.10   else."] else.*α* [*footnote:*] *α*[Cf. Drobisch, *Logik*, p. 17, § 25 *seq.*] (III, 214)

325.17   "Identity] [*paragraph*] "Identity (III, 214)

325.21   although themselves] although in themselves (III, 214)

325.22   conflicting] conflictive (III, 214)

325.32   "When] But when (III, 226)

325.39   judgment.] Judgment.*α* [*footnote:*] *α*Cf. Krug, *Logik*, § 61. (III, 227)

326.12   "we] This process, as you remember, is called *Determination*;—a very appropriate expression, inasmuch as by each character or attribute which we add on, we (III, 194)

326.22–9   other." . . . "But if . . . unity; *we judge that polar . . . notion electrical . . . is electrical . . . of polarity.*] other; but if . . . unity, –we judge that *polar . . . notion electrical . . . is electrical . . . of polarity.* (III, 227) [*JSM has added italics except as indicated*]

326.32–3   the . . . other] [*not in italics*] (III, 229)

327.7–8   "capable . . . thought."] [*see* 325 *above*] (III, 227)

328.22   "presentations of phantasy."] [*see entry for* 305.38–306.1 *above*] (III, 131)

329.33   "individual things"] [*see* 324 *above*] (III, 226)

329.36–8   "the . . . other."] [*see* 326 *above*] (III, 229)

330.20   another. It] another. This fourth condition is in truth only a necessary consequence of the third,—for it is impossible to discriminate without judging,—discrimination, or contradistinction, being in fact only the denying one thing of another. It (I, 204)

330.22–3   general" . . . "have] general have (I, 204)

330.26   object?] object?*α* [*footnote:*] *α*See *Reid's Works*, pp. 243, 414, with the Editor's Notes.—ED. (I, 205)

330.32   judgment.] judgment.*α* [*footnote omitted*] (II, 277)

330.39   so and . . . so and] so or . . . so or (II, 278)

331.3   judgment and] judgment or (II, 278)

331.3–6   *so . . . process*] [*not in italics*] (II, 278)

331.6   *process.*"] process itself. (II, 278)

331.17   "Both] These three degrees [Concepts, Judgments, Reasonings] are all in fact, strictly, only modifications of the second, as both (III, 117)

331.19   expressed. A] expressed. By anticipation:—A (III, 117)

331.20–1   *it . . . word*] [*not in italics*] (III, 117)

331.23–4   *a . . . judgment*] [*not in italics*] (III, 117)

332.10   "Water rusts iron:"] [*see* 325 *above*] (III, 227)

335.20–1   "The exposition . . . its Definition:"] [*paragraph*] Again; you will observe the two following distinctions: the first,—the exposition . . . its *Definition*; (a simple notion cannot, therefore, be defined); the second,—the exposition of the Extension of a notion is called its *Division*; (an individual notion cannot be divided.) (III, 143)

335.21–3   "Definition is . . . attributes."] [*paragraph*] Thus, it is manifest, that, as Definition is . . . attributes, if a concept be simple, that is, if it contain in it only a single attribute, it must be indefinable; and again, that as Division is the analysis of a higher or more general concept into others lower and less general, if a concept be an individual, that is, only a bundle of individual qualities, it is indivisible, is, in fact, not a proper or abstract concept at all, but only a concrete representation of Imagination. (III, 151–2)

336n.7 "which] The essential qualities of a thing are those aptitudes, those manners of existence and action, which (I, 150)

338.3–5 "two . . . and predicate," . . . "the . . . other," . . . "either] We may, therefore, articulately define a judgment or proposition to be the product of that act in which we pronounce, that, of two . . . and as predicate, the . . . other, either (III, 229)

338.7 If] [no paragraph] If (III, 231)

338.9 proposition. . . . The] proposition. [paragraph] This distinction of propositions is founded on the distinction of the two quantities of concepts,—their Comprehension and their Extension. The (III, 232)

338.20 or] as (III, 232)

338.22 or] [not in italics] (III, 232)

338.32–3 syllogisms] syllogism (III, 233)

342.7 "Reasoning] [entire paragraph indented] ¶LIII.—Reasoning (III, 274)

342.10 those] these (III, 274) [treated as a typographical error in this edition]

342.11–12 "the self-evident . . . whole."] Let ABC denote the three circles [diagram of circles omitted]. Now, ex hypothesi, we know, and only know, that A contains B, and that B contains C; but as it is a self-evident . . . whole, we cannot, with our knowledge that B contains C, and is contained in A, avoid recognising that C is contained in A. (III, 271)

342.12 "Without] [paragraph] But to speak of the process in general:—without the power of reasoning we should have been limited in our knowledge, (if knowledge of such a limitation would deserve the name of knowledge at all), I say without (III, 277)

346.3 "given . . . intuition."] [see 342 above] (III, 277)

348.7 "the] [paragraph indented] ¶III. What is Logic? Answer—Logic is the (III, 4)

348.18 "the discrimination of] But in the third place, the discrimination itself of (III, 11)

348.21 Politics, and] Politics, Religion, and (III, 11)

348.22 wrong.] wrong.α [footnote:] αCompare Lectures on Metaphysics, vol. i. p. 115 et seq.—ED. (III, 11)

348.23 But . . . were] But in the fourth place, were (III, 11)

349.10–13 "apparently . . . applied," . . . "the . . . usage," . . . "rational . . . trace."] [paragraph] The question, therefore, still remains, Is this restriction of the term art to certain of the practical sciences the . . . usage, or is it founded on any rational . . . trace? The former alternative seems to be the common belief; for no one, in so far as I know, has endeavoured to account for the apparently . . . applied. (I, 116) [JSM has reversed sentence order]

349.16–17 "a habit productive," . . . "a habit practical,"] [paragraph] Now Aristotle, in formally defining art, defines it as a habit productive, and not as a habit practical, ἕξις ποιητικὴ μετὰ λόγου;—and, though he has not always himself adhered strictly to this limitation, his definition was adopted by his followers, and the term in its application to the practical sciences, (the term practical being here used in its generic meaning), came to be exclusively confined to those whose end did not result in mere action or energy. (I, 118)

349.17–19 "not . . . criticism:" . . . "vindicate,"] This distinction [see entry directly above] is not . . . criticism, and I am not here to vindicate its correctness. (I, 118)

349.20–1 "mechanical" . . . "beneath their notice,"] The mechanical dexterities were beneath their notice; and these were accordingly left to receive their appellations from those who knew nothing of the Aristotelic proprieties. (I, 119)

349n.5 "In] [paragraph] In (I, 117)

349n.16 energy. Now] energy.α [Greek footnote omitted] [paragraph] Now (I, 118)

349n.21 genuine] generic (I, 118)

350.5 "incongruity] But that they ["art and practical science"] are not employed as synonymous expressions is, as we have seen, shown by the incongruity (I, 116)

they . . . is, they . . . class."] [*entire paragraph indented*] ¶CVIII. If we have uniformly observed, that a . . . class (genus or species) . . . attribute, we are disposed to conclude that this . . . class. This conclusion is properly called an *Inference of Induction.* Again, if we have observed that two . . . characters, we are disposed to conclude that they . . . is, that they . . . class (genus or species). (IV, 165–6)

372.7–12 "the Law of Reason and Consequent,". . . "Principle of Sufficient Reason." . . . "The Conditions of the Thinkable:"] [*entire paragraph indented*] ¶XIII. The Fundamental Laws of Thought or the conditions of the thinkable, as commonly received, are four:—1. The Law of Identity; 2. The Law of Contradiction; 3. The Law of Exclusion or of Excluded Middle; and, 4. The Law of Reason and Consequent, or of Sufficient Reason. (III, 79)

372n.6 "the laws of Thinking in a strict sense."] [*paragraph*] Laws of Thought are of two kinds:—1°. The laws of the Thinkable,—Identity, Contradiction, &c. 2°. The laws of Thinking in a strict sense—viz. laws of Conception, Judgment, and Reasoning. (IV, App. iv, 244–5)

373.27 "principle of all logical affirmation"] [*paragraph*] The logical importance of the law of Identity lies in this,—that it is the principle of all logical affirmation and definition. (III, 80)

374.2 "expressed . . . *A*,"] It is expressed . . . *A*; and by *A* is denoted every logical thing, every product of our thinking faculty,—concept, judgment, reasoning, &c.ᵃ [*footnote:*] ᵃ[Schulze, *Logik*, §17. Gerlach, *Logik*, §37.] Cf. Krug, *Logik*, §17.—ED. (III, 79–80)

375.4 "The] [*entire paragraph indented*] ¶XVIII. The (III, 114)

376.27–8 "This law," . . . "is the . . . distinction,"] [*paragraph*] The logical import of this law lies in its being the . . . distinction. (III, 82)

376.28 "is] This law is (III, 81)

376.30 not] *not* (III, 81)

376.30 or] *or* (III, 81)

376.30 o:"] O. (III, 81)

376.33–6 "as . . . *non-repugnantia.*"] [*paragraph*] Now, in the first place, in regard to the name of this law, it may be observed that, as . . . *non-repugnantia.*ᵃ [*footnote:*] ᵃCompare Krug, *Logik*, §18.—ED. (III, 82)

379.7–8 "the principle of disjunctive judgments."] [*paragraph*] The law of Excluded Middle is the principle of Disjunctive Judgments, that is, of judgments in which a plurality of judgments are contained, and which stand in such a reciprocal relation that the affirmation of one is the denial of the other. (III, 84)

379.17 "D is either B, or C, or A."] [*Hamilton is quoting from Krug*] [*paragraph*] "Disjunctive judgments are those in which the condition qualifying the relation between the subject and predicate, lies proximately in the predicate, as in the proposition, D *is either* B, *or* C, *or* A. (III, 239)

380.23–4 "Whatever," . . . "violates] The difference in their result [that of the laws of Identity, Contradiction, and Excluded Middle as opposed to that of the law of Reason and Consequent] consists in this,—Whatever violates (III, 98)

380.32 those] these (IV, 65)

380.36–7 "which we are able to violate:"] By *law of thought*, or by *logical necessity*, we do not, therefore, mean a physical law, such as the law of gravitation, but a general precept which we are able certainly to violate, but which if we do not obey, our whole process of thinking is suicidal or absolutely null. (III, 78–9)

382.15 the three] the first three (III, 99)

382.17 itself. When] itself. [*paragraph*] When (III, 99)

382.20–3 done." . . . "But] done. But (III, 99)

382.24 does it] does this (III, 99)

383n.6–9 "If I," . . . "have . . . restricted."] If I have . . . restricted; and that within those bounds, (the Conditioned), natural thought is neither fallible nor mendacious— /"Neque decipitur, nec decipit umquam." (I, App. i, 402)

383n.9–10 "In generating . . . laws. . . . Reason] On the contrary, I have endeavoured to show that Reason,—that Consciousness within its legitimate limits, is always veracious,—that in generating . . . laws,—that Consciousness, in fact, is never spontaneously false, and that Reason (II, App. iv, 543)

383n.12–13   "It is . . . result. . . . The] [*paragraph*] On the contrary, my doctrine holds, 1°, That Space and Time, as given, are real forms of thought and conditions of things; 2°, That Intelligence,—Reason,—within its legitimate limits, is legitimate; within this sphere it never deceives; and it is . . . results;—"Ne sapiamus ultra facultates." The (I, App. i, 403)

384.8   "I] When I say that a thing may be, of which I cannot conceive the possibility, (that is, by conceiving it as the consequent of a certain reason), I (III, 100)

384.10   "solely] It is not, therefore, in any absolute harmony of mere thought that truth consists, but solely (III, 107) [*Hamilton is quoting from Esser*]

385.10   "with the doubtful exception of Aristotle,"] But as all logicians, with the doubtful exception of Aristotle, have limited their consideration to that process of reasoning given in the quantity of extension, to the exclusion of that given in the quantity of comprehension, it will be proper, in order to avoid misapprehension, to place some of the distinctions expressed in this paragraph in a still more explicit contrast. (III, 297)

385.10–11   "have . . . Comprehension"] But as logicians have . . . Comprehension, they have, consequently, not perceived the proper application of the former canon ["Prædicatum prædicati est etiam prædicatum subjecti"]; which, therefore, remained in their systems either a mere *hors d'œuvre*, or else was only forced into an unnatural connection with the principle of the syllogism of extension. (III, 303–4)

385.11–13   "have marvellously . . . comprehension:"] I further showed that logicians had in simple syllogisms marvellously . . . comprehension: and that all their rules were exclusively relative to the reasoning which proceeds in the quantity of extension. (III, 378)

385.14   "relieved] Thus is relieved (IV, App. v, 250)

391.18–392.1   "every . . . quantity."] [*paragraph*] After what I have already stated in regard to the nature of these opposite quantities, under the doctrine of Concepts and Judgments,[α] [*footnote:*] [α]See above, p. 140 *et seq.*—ED. [*text:*] and after the illustrations I have given you of the possibility of conducting any reasoning in either of these quantities at will,[β] [*footnote:*] [β]See above, p. 272 *et seq.*—ED. [*text:*]—every . . . quantity,—it will be here needless to enlarge upon the nature of this distinction in general. (III, 287)

392.5–7   "Every . . . agent,"] *Every . . . agent.* (III, 270)

392.10–12   "Man . . . agent,"] *Man . . . agent.* (III, 273)

392.15   "the] [*paragraph*] It is thus manifest, that, though worthy of notice in a system of Logic, the (III, 399)

392.19–21   "can . . . order,"] They [logicians] ought at least to have made the student of Logic aware, that a syllogism can . . . order. (III, 397)

392.21   "a] [*paragraph*] This is the regular succession of sumption, subsumption, and conclusion, in a syllogism of extension; and as all that can be said, on the present question, of the one quantity, is appilcable, *mutatis mutandis*, to the other, it will be needless to show articulately that a (III, 397)

393.1   "In] [*paragraph*] It is only necessary further to observe, that in (III, 274)

393n.2–3   "altogether . . . Extension"] [*paragraph*] Now, if in the case of simple syllogisms, it be marvellous that logicians should have altogether overlooked the possibility of a reasoning in comprehension, it is doubly marvellous that, with this their prepossession, they should, in the case of the Sorites, have altogether . . . extension. (III, 378–9)

393n.5–6   "a monster undeserving of toleration,"] In fact, the logicians, in consequence of their exclusive recognition of the reasoning in extension, were not in possession of the means of showing, that this figure is a monster undeserving of toleration, far less of countenance and favour. (III, 424)

399n.16–17   "all triangles are trilateral" . . . "All triangles are all trilateral:"] [*paragraph*] For example; if I think that the notion *triangle* contains the notion *trilateral*, and again that the notion *trilateral* contains the notion *triangle*; in other words, if I think that each of these is inclusively and exclusively applicable to the other; I formally say, and, if I speak as I think, must say—*All triangle is all trilateral*. On the other hand,—if I only think that all triangles are trilateral, but do not think all trilaterals to be triangular, and yet say,—*All triangle is all trilateral*, the proposition, though materially true, is formally false. (IV, App. v, 292)

400n.16 "ordinary . . . Predicate as] [*paragraph*] 2°, But, in fact, ordinary . . . Predicate so (IV, App. v, 259)

400n.18 "Virtue is the *only* nobility;"] [*paragraph*] For example, by the limitative designations, *alone* or *only*, we say,—*God alone is good*, which is equivalent to saying,—*God is all good*, that is, *God is all that is good*; *Virtue is the only nobility*, that is, *Virtue is all noble*, that is, all that is noble.*ᵝ* [*footnote omitted*] (IV, App. v, 260)

400n.18 "Of animals man alone is rational,"] [*paragraph*] *Of animals man alone is rational*; that is, *Man is all rational animal*. (IV, App. v, 261)

403.28–30 "taken . . . of words."] The result [of Hamilton's reconsideration of De Morgan's syllogism] was the opinion, that these two quantifications should be taken . . . of moods.*ᵅ* [*footnote:*] *ᵅ*Extract from *A Letter to A. de Morgan, Esq., from Sir W. Hamilton*, p. 41.—ED. (IV, App. vi, 355)

404.29 [*paragraph*] "Logic] [*no paragraph*] I have frequently inculcated on you that Logic (III, 450)

405.9 its] the (III, 450)

405.11 have given] have seen given (III, 451)

405.12–14 Aristotle . . . European] *Aristotle . . . European* (III, 451)

405.25 than as a] than a (III, 451)

405.25–6 certain hypothetical] certain given (III, 451) [*probably JSM's eye skipped down several lines to where the other wording appears*]

405.32 expressions."] expressions.*ᵅ* [*footnote:*] *ᵅ*Cf. Esser, *Logik*, §109.—ED. (III, 451)

407.10 "the] [*paragraph*] The other genus of truth,—(the end which the Real Sciences propose),—is the (IV, 66)

407.12 "harmony] Logical truth is the harmony (IV, 65)

407.16–17 "evolved out of" . . . "Logical] I do not mean by this, that the antecedent should be necessarily true, or that the consequent be really contained in it; it is sufficient that the antecedent be assumed as true, and that the consequent be, in conformity to the laws of thought, evolved out of it as its part or equation. This last is called Logical (II, 343)

407.33 "One . . . philosophers," . . . "defining] [*no paragraph*] "One party of philosophers defining (III, 106) [*Hamilton is quoting from Esser*]

407.36 knowledge.] knowledge.*ᵅ* [*footnote:*] *ᵅ*See Kant, *Logik*, Einleitung, vii.; Krug, *Logik*, §22; Fries, *Logik*, §42.—ED. (III, 106)

408.18 existence."] existence."*ᵅ* [*footnote:*]*ᵅ* Esser, *Logik*, p. 65–6.—ED. (III, 107)

408.23–5 "Two opposite doctrines," . . . "have . . . Logic;"] Yet among modern, nay recent, philosophers, two opposite doctrines have . . . Logic. (III, 106)

408.26 "inaccuracy"] [*paragraph*] The preceding inaccuracy is, however, of little moment compared with the heresy of another class of philosophers, to whose observations on this point I can, however, only allude. (III, 107)

410.17 "is not always possible."] In the second place, this conversion is not always possible, and, therefore, it is never necessary. (III, 342)

411.36–7 "Opposition of Notions," . . . "is] The confliction constitutes the *Opposition* of notions, (τὸ ἀντικεῖσϑαι, *oppositio*). This is (III, 213)

411.40 *media*] *mediata* (III, 214)

412.2 else.] else.*ᵅ* [*footnote:*] *ᵅ*[Cf. Drobisch, *Logik*, p. 17, §25 *seq*.] (III, 214)

412.5 "To] [*paragraph*] "To (III, 214) [*Hamilton is quoting from Krug*]

416.19 "stands . . . unrefutable."] [*paragraph*] 4°, On this [Synthetic] order the objection of *petitio principii* stands . . . unrefutable, against Logic.*ᵅ* [*footnote omitted*] (IV, App. x, 401)

421.13 "a] According to these laws [of matter], things related,—connected, must act and be acted on; but a (II, App. i, 522)

421.18 "the] Therefore the (II, App. i, 522)

421.22–3 Democritus. According . . . erroneous to . . . distant objects] Democritus. [*paragraph*] According . . . erroneous, in the first place, to . . . distant, &c. objects (II, App. i, 522)

422.6–7 "There is . . . any part] [*paragraph*] Now, in the first place, there is . . . any one part (II, 127)

437.22–5   God." . . . [*paragraph*] "The Deity," . . . "is] God. [*no paragraph*] The Deity is (I, 25)

438.30   "Now] [*paragraph*] Now (I, 32)

438.33   agents. . . . But] agents. This being undeniable, it is further evident, that, should we ever be convinced that we are not moral agents, we should likewise be convinced that there exists no moral order in the universe, and no supreme intelligence by which that moral order is established, sustained, and regulated. [*paragraph*] Theology is thus again wholly dependent on Psychology; for, with the proof of the moral nature of man, stands or falls the proof of the existence of a Deity. [*paragraph*] But (I, 32–3)

440.19   "brute necessity"] For if, as the materialist maintains, the only intelligence of which we have any experience be a consequent of matter,—on this hypothesis, he not only cannot assume this order to be reversed in the relations of an intelligence beyond his observation, but, if he argue logically, he must positively conclude, that, as in man, so in the universe, the phænomena of intelligence or design are only in their last analysis the products of a brute necessity. (I, 31)

440n.1–2   "The atheist who holds *matter* or *necessity* . . . is.] Neither is this notion [of a God] completed by adding to a first cause the attribute of Omnipotence, for the atheist who holds matter or necessity . . . is, does not convert his blind force into a God, by merely affirming it to be all-powerful. (I, 26–7)

440n.2   "Those who] Those, accordingly, who (I, 133)

440n.4   fate."] fate—must regard the application of the terms Physiology and Physics to the doctrine of the mind as either singularly inappropriate, or as significant of a false hypothesis in regard to the character of the thinking principle. (I, 133)

445.1   "every] For though an unconquerable feeling compels us to recognise ourselves as accountable, and therefore free, agents, still, when we attempt to realise in thought how the fact of our liberty can be, we soon find that this altogether transcends our understanding, and that every (I, 33–4)

445.3   necessity,"] necessity. (I, 34)

445n.3   "Voluntary] On the other hand, however, we cannot possibly conceive the existence of a voluntary activity independently of all feeling; for voluntary (I, 188)

464.3   "the] [*paragraph*] In the world of sense, illusive appearances hover around us like evil spirits; unreal dreams mingle themselves with real knowledge; the accustomed assumes the character of certainty; and the (III, 47)

487.11   philosophy;"] philosophy:"ᵅ [*footnote:*] ᵅ*Metaphysics*, book i.2, 9. Compare Plato, *Theætetus*, p. 155.—ED. (I, 37)

487.25   heavens."] heavens."ᵝ [*footnote:*] ᵝJacobi, *Werke*, vol. ii p. 52–54. Quoted in *Discussions*, p. 312.—ED. (I, 37)

490n.4–6   "attend . . . time," . . . "that . . . impossible."] [*paragraph*] The doctrine that the mind can attend . . . time, would, in fact, involve the conclusion that . . . impossible; but comparison and discrimination being possible, this possibility disproves the truth of the counter proposition. (I, 252)

491n.2–3   "past . . . perceived;"] We must, therefore, compare the past . . . perceived. (I, 244)

491n.16–17   "instead . . . masses."] On the contrary, I showed that, instead . . . masses; that, though our capacity of attention be very limited in regard to the number of objects on which a faculty can be simultaneously directed, yet that these objects may be large or small. (II, 327)

491n.18–19   "an act of will or desire,"] This remark ["that attention is a voluntary act"] might have led him [Reid] to the observation, that attention is not a separate faculty, or a faculty of intelligence at all, but merely an act of will or desire, subordinate to a certain law of intelligence. (I, 237)

491n.19–20   "a mere vital and irresistible act."] The first [degree of attention], a mere vital and irresistible act; the second, an act determined by desire, which, though involuntary, may be resisted by our will; the third, an act determined by a deliberate volition. (I, 248)

494n.1–2   "Ontology, or Metaphysics Proper;" "the science conversant about inferences . . . manifestations;"] Now, the science conversant about all such inferences . . . manifestations, is called ONTOLOGY, or METAPHYSICS PROPER. (I, 125)

494n.11–12 "a concept . . . be clear when . . . as to enable us . . . it" . . . "as . . . others:"] *[entire paragraph indented]* A concept . . . be *clear*, (*clara*), when . . . as enables us . . . it as . . . others; and *obscure*, (*obscura*), when the degree of consciousness is insufficient to accomplish this. (III, 158)

496n.10–11 "Synthesis without . . . all. . . . A] On the other [hand], synthesis without . . . all. Both [synthesis and analysis], therefore, are absolutely necessary to philosophy, and both are, in philosophy, as much parts of the same method as, in the animal body, inspiration and expiration are of the same vital function. But though these operations are each requisite to the other, yet were we to distinguish and compare what ought to be considered as conjoined, it is to analysis that the preference must be accorded. An analysis is always valuable; for though now without a synthesis, this synthesis may at any time be added; whereas a (I, 99)

496n.28 "reconstruction"] This mental reconstruction is, therefore, the final, the consummative procedure of philosophy, and it is familiarly known by the Greek term *Synthesis*. (I, 98)

499.15–16 "its . . . regarded it more] *[paragraph]* It is needless to attempt a refutation of this hypothesis [of the pre-established harmony], which its . . . regarded more (I, 304)

501.33 "a] You degrade the Divinity, he [Leibniz] subjoined; you [the Cartesians] make him act like a (I, 303) *[Hamilton is quoting Leibniz]*

503.12.13 "The intellect is . . . activity."] *[paragraph]* "The intellect," says Aristotle, in one passage, "is . . . activity;"γ *[footnote:]* γ Said of moral knowledge, *Eth. Nic.* i. 3: Τέλος οὐ γνῶσις, ἀλλὰ πρᾶξις. Cf. *ibid.* i.7, 13; i.8, 9; ix.7, 4; xi.9, 7, 1. *Met.*, xi.7: Ἡ νοῦ ἐνέργεια ζωή.—ED. *[text:]* and in another, "The arts and sciences are powers, but every power exists only for the sake of action; the end of philosophy, therefore, is not knowledge, but the energy conversant about knowledge."⁸ *[footnote omitted]* (I, 12) *[cf.* 503n]

503n.1–2 "Speculative truth . . . and held . . . activity"] *[paragraph]* In speculative knowledge, on the other hand, there may indeed, at first sight, seem greater difficulty; but further reflection will prove that speculative truth . . . and is only held . . . activity: "Sordet cognita veritas" is a shrewd aphorism of Seneca. (I, 10)

503n.2–3 "speculative truth" . . . "only . . . activity."] *[paragraph]* But if speculative truth itself be only . . . activity, those studies which determine the faculties to a more vigorous exertion, will, in every liberal sense, be better entitled, absolutely, to the name of useful, than those which, with a greater complement of more certain facts, awaken them to a less intense, and consequently to a less improving exercise. (I, 13)

——— "Notes to the Above Letter," *Edinburgh Review*, LXIII (April, 1836), 272–5.
NOTE: this is Hamilton's reply to Whewell's letter, "To the Editor of the *Edinburgh Review*" (*q.v.*), which was prompted by Hamilton's "Study of Mathematics—University of Cambridge" (*q.v.*); all three reprinted in Hamilton's *Discussions* at 263–325, 326–8, 329–40.
REFERRED TO: 477

——— "Study of Mathematics—University of Cambridge," *Edinburgh Review*, LXII (Jan., 1836), 409–55.
NOTE: see also Hamilton, "Notes to the Above Letter," and Whewell's letter, "To the Editor of the *Edinburgh Review*"; all three reprinted in Hamilton's *Discussions* at 263–325, 326–8, 329–40.
REFERRED TO: 470–1, 477, 482

HARTLEY, DAVID. Referred to: 9, 17, 250, 487, 493n

——— *Observations on Man, his Frame, his Duty, and his Expectations.* 2 pts. Bath: Leake and Frederick; London: Hitch and Austen, 1749.
NOTE: this ed. in JSM's library, Somerville College. Concerning the reference at 283, where

JSM says that Hartley had cited the colour-wheel experiment before James Mill or Hamilton, it may be noted that Hartley is actually quoting Newton's *Optics*.
REFERRED TO: 278, 278n, 283, 363

HAYWOOD, FRANCIS, trans. *Critick of Pure Reason translated from the original of Immanuel Kant*. 2nd ed., with notes and explanation of terms. London: Pickering, 1848.
NOTE: JSM's page references are to this ed., which is in his library, Somerville College. See also Kant.
REFERRED TO: 154n

HEGEL, GEORG WILHELM FRIEDRICH.
NOTE: the reference at 152 is in a quotation from Hamilton.
REFERRED TO: 19, 33n, 65, 68, 95, 98, 152, 486

———— *Vorlesungen über die Geschichte der Philosophie*. Ed. Carl Ludwig Michelet, in *Werke*. 20 vols. Berlin: Duncker and Humblot, 1834–54, XIII–XV.
NOTE: the quotation is of Mansel's translation of Hegel.
QUOTED: 47

HEUCK, A. "Bemerkungen über ein vierzehnjähriges Mädchen ohne Extremitäten," *Neue Notizen aus dem Gebiete der Natur- und Heilkunde*, VII.1 (July, 1838), cols. 1–5.
NOTE: the periodical was edited by Ludwig Friedrich von Froriep and Dr. Robert Froriep. JSM, who takes the reference from McCosh (who translates from Schopenhauer, where the original is cited), refers, following McCosh, to "Frorieps" rather than Heuck. Eva Lauk is the fourteen-year-old quadraplegic described.
REFERRED TO: 248

HOBBES, THOMAS. "Of Liberty and Necessity," Discourse III of *Tripos*, in *The English Works of Thomas Hobbes*. Ed. William Molesworth. 11 vols. London: Bohn, 1839–45, IV, 229–78.
REFERRED TO: 441n

———— "Physics, or the Phenomena of Nature," Part IV of *Elements of Philosophy: The First Section, Concerning Body*, in *ibid*., I, 387–532.
REFERRED TO: 51

HOOKE, ROBERT. *Micrographia*. London: Martyn and Allestry, 1665.
NOTE: the quotations are simply uses of the term "*experimentum crucis*," which Mill, like most other philosophers (including Hume, and following Newton), attributes elsewhere to Bacon, whose parallel term is actually "*instantia crucis*"; see Bacon, *Novum Organum*, 294.
QUOTED: 222, 237

HUME, DAVID.
NOTE: the reference at 151 is in a quotation from, and that at 448 derives from, Hamilton.
REFERRED TO: cvii, 1, 6, 134, 151, 183, 217n, 294, 296, 297, 448, 493n, 498n

———— *An Inquiry concerning Human Understanding*, in *Essays and Treatises on Several Subjects*. 2 vols. Edinburgh: Cadell, 1793, II, 17–183.
NOTE: in JSM's library, Somerville College. Until 1758 entitled *Philosophical Essays Concerning Human Understanding*. The quotations at 135 are from, and the second reference at 498n–9n is to, "Of the Academical or Sceptical Philosophy" (Section xii of the *Inquiry*); the first quotation at 165n is from "Sceptical Doubts concerning the Operations of the Understanding" (Section iv); the second quotation at 166n is from "Sceptical Solution of these Doubts" (Section v); the reference at 299 is to "Of the Idea of Necessary Connection" (Section vii); and the first reference at 498n–9n is to the work as a whole.
QUOTED: 135, 165n–6n

REFERRED TO: 299, 498n–9n

135.8–11 "universal . . . men." . . . "is soon . . . philosophy."] But this universal . . . men is soon . . . philosophy, which teaches us, that nothing can ever be present to the mind but an image or perception, and that the senses are only the inlets, through which these images are conveyed, without being able to produce any immediate intercourse between the mind and the object. (169)

135.24–5 "blind . . . nature."] It seems also evident, that, when men follow this blind . . . nature, they always suppose the very images, presented by the senses, to be the external objects, and never entertain any suspicion, that the one are nothing but representations of the other. (169)

165n.41 "It may be a subject worthy curiosity] It may therefore be a subject worthy of curiosity (39)

166n.1 *or the records of our memory.*"] [*not in italics*] (39)

166n.1–2 "all reasonings] All reasonings (39)

166n.3 alone can we go] alone, we can go (39)

166n.4 *memory*] memory (39)

166n.8 "where . . . *memory* and senses"] Now, I assert, that this belief, where . . . memory or senses, is one of a similar nature, and arises from similar causes, with the transition of thought and vivacity of conception here explained. (68)

"INQUIRER, AN." See Phillipps, Lucy March.

JACOBI, FRIEDRICH HEINRICH. *David Hume über den Glauben, oder Idealismus und Realismus. Ein Gespräch*, in *Werke*. 6 vols. Leipzig: Fleischer, 1812–25, II, 1–310.
NOTE: the quotation is in a quotation from Hamilton.
QUOTED: 487
REFERRED TO: 488

JOHNSON, SAMUEL. *London, A Poem: in Imitation of the Third Satire of Juvenal*, in *The Works of Samuel Johnson*. 14 vols. London: Buckland, Rivington, *et al.*, 1787–88, I, 319–30.
NOTE: the reference, which is based only on a linguistic resemblance, is given because Bain, in his *John Stuart Mill* (122n), says: "Grote thought that the phrase ["to hell I will go"] was an echo of something occurring in Ben Jonson; when a military captain's implicit obedience is crowned by the illustration—'Tell him to go to hell, to hell he will go'. I have never got any clue to the place." Bain's "Ben Jonson" may be a mistaken echo of Grote; in any case, the context in Samuel Johnson is not appropriate: "No gainful trade their industry can 'scape, / They sing, they dance, clean shoes, or cure a clap: / All sciences a fasting Monsieur knows, / And, bid him go to hell, to hell he goes." (324; 113–16)
REFERRED TO: 103

———— See also Boswell, *Life of Johnson*.

JOUFFROY, THÉODORE. *Mélanges philosophiques*. 2nd ed. Paris: Ladrange, 1838.
NOTE: the reference is to Hamilton's reliance on Jouffroy's "Du sommeil" (Part IV of "Psychologie"), in *Mélanges*, 290–312 (of which Hamilton quotes 290–302); Mansel and Veitch (*Lectures*, I, 324n) give the reference to the 2nd ed.
REFERRED TO: 491

KANT, IMMANUEL.
NOTE: the references at 41, 175 are in quotations from Hamilton; that at 88n is in a self-quotation; those at 208n, 241 are in quotations from Mahaffy.
REFERRED TO: 1, 9, 10, 23, 25, 27, 29, 29n, 39n, 41, 56, 66, 88n, 143, 143n, 147n–8n, 154, 175, 179, 207, 207n–8n, 241, 313n, 320n, 334, 355, 364, 449n, 466n, 485, 493n

—— *Kritik der Praktischen Vernunft*, in *Sämmtliche Werke*. Ed. Karl Rosenkranz and Friedrich Schubert. 14 vols. in 12. Leipzig: Voss, 1838–40, VIII, 105–318.
NOTE: this ed. used because JSM refers to it at 154n.
REFERRED TO: 488

—— *Kritik der Reinen Vernunft*, in *ibid.*, II.
NOTE: see also Haywood.
REFERRED TO: 27n, 135, 154n, 260, 360, 374n

—— *Logic*, in *Prolegomena zu einer jeden künftigen Metaphysik, die als Wissenschaft wird auftreten können und Logic*, in *ibid.*, III.
REFERRED TO: 356, 369n

—— *Metaphysik der Sitten*, in *ibid.*, IX, ix–366.
REFERRED TO: 467

KECKERMANNUS, BARTHOLOMÆUS. *Systema Logicae, Tribus Libris Adornatum*. Geneva: de la Rouiere, 1611.
NOTE: JSM's spelling is Keckermann. A copy of this ed. is in the London Library, and may have been part of the donation by JSM of his father's books.
REFERRED TO: 415

KEPLER, JOHANNES.
NOTE: the reference at 487 is in a quotation from Hamilton.
REFERRED TO: 474, 487

KINGHAN, JOHN.
NOTE: the reference derives from McCosh.
REFERRED TO: 225n

KRUG, WILHELM TRAUGOTT. Referred to: 175, 327, 415

—— *Logik*. 2nd ed. 2 vols. Königsberg: Unzer, 1819.
NOTE: the quotations and references derive from Hamilton's *Lectures*, the editors of which use this ed. of Krug's *Logik*.
QUOTED: 325, 412
REFERRED TO: 286n, 337n, 356, 379, 410, 494, 494n

LAPLACE, PIERRE SIMON DE.
NOTE: the reference is in a quotation from Hamilton.
REFERRED TO: 487

LAUK, EVA. Referred to· 248–9; see also Heuck.

LEIBNIZ, GOTTFRIED WILHELM VON. Referred to: cvii, 152, 295, 320, 440, 485, 499

—— *Essais de théodicée sur la bonté de Dieu, la liberté de l'homme et l'origine du mal*. Amsterdam: Troyel, 1710.
QUOTED: 500
REFERRED TO: 372, 419, 499–500, 502
500.32–3 *par la nature des créatures*] Et elles ont cela par leur nature & par la nature des créatures raisonnables; avant que Dieu décerne de les créer. (347)

—— *Meditationes de Cognitione, Veritate et Ideis*, in *Opera Philosophica*. Ed. Johann Eduard Erdmann. Berlin: Eichler, 1840, 79–81.
NOTE: the quotation is in a quotation from Hamilton.
QUOTED: 319
REFERRED TO: 320, 320n
319.34 (non simul intuemur)] Plerumque autem, præsertim in analysi longiore, non totam simul naturam rei intuemur, sed rerum loco signis utimur, quorum explicationem in

præsenti aliqua cogitatione compendii causa solemus prætermittere, scientes, aut credentes nos eam habere in potestate: ita cum chiliogonum, seu polygonum mille æqualium laterum cogito, non semper naturam lateris, et æqualitatis, et millenarii (seu cubi a denario) considero, sed vocabulis istis (quorum sensus obscure saltem, atque imperfecte menti obversatur) in animo utor loco idearum, quas de iis habeo, quoniam memini me significationem istorum vocabulorum habere, explicationem autem nunc judicio necessariam non esse; qualem cogitationem cæcam, vel etiam symbolicam appellare soleo, qua et in Algebra, et in Arithmetica utimur, imo fere ubique. (79–80)

———— *La Monadologie*, in *ibid.*, 705–12.
REFERRED TO: 500, 502

———— *Troisième Éclaircissement*, in *ibid.*, 134–6.
NOTE: the indirect quotation is in a quotation from Hamilton, who cites this edition.
QUOTED: 501

LEWES, GEORGE HENRY. *Aristotle: A Chapter from the History of Science, including analyses of Aristotle's scientific writings*. London: Smith, Elder, 1864.
QUOTED: 489n

LOCKE, JOHN.
NOTE: the references at 14, 152 and the second reference at 28n are in quotations from Hamilton; that at 169 is in a quotation from Reid.
REFERRED TO: 1, 14, 15, 28n, 110, 139, 152, 155, 169, 362, 449n, 493n

———— *Essay Concerning Human Understanding*, in *Works*. New ed. 10 vols. London: Tegg, Sharpe, Offor, Robinson, and Evans, 1823, I–III.
NOTE: the indirect quotation at 28n is in a quotation from Mansel; the quotation at 141 is summary (Locke uses "original," not "origin"), and so is not collated; the reference at 201 is in a quotation from McCosh.
QUOTED: 141, 448n
REFERRED TO: 28n, 201, 302, 324, 373
448n.1   "Does it not require" . . . "some] For example, does it not require some (III, 27)

LUCRETIUS CARUS, TITUS.
NOTE: the notion of *species sensibiles* is mistakenly attributed to Lucretius; it originated in Artistotle's *On the Soul* (*q.v.*).
REFERRED TO: 15

LUTHER, MARTIN. Referred to: 440

MCCOSH, JAMES. *An Examination of Mr. J. S. Mill's Philosophy, being a Defence of Fundamental Truth*. London: Macmillan, 1866.
QUOTED: 63n–4n, 72n–3n, 73n, 146n, 201, 216n, 225n, 231n–2n, 237n, 246, 246n, 261n, 284n, 317n, 338n, 391n
REFERRED TO: ciii, 72n, 75n, 166n, 208n–9n, 217n, 240, 242n, 244, 247, 262n, 269, 337n, 374n–5n
63n.9–10   word belief," . . . "is] word "belief" is (36)
64n.2   distinguish primitive faith from primitive knowledge,] distinguish "primitive faith" from "primitive knowledge," (36–7)
73n.17   "I] Now I (210)
73n.28   each other] another (211)
73n.29   further] farther (211)
73n.29–30   than another.] than another (see *supra*, pp. 160–8). (211)
146n.30   "the alleged] Not because of any supposed intuition or necessary truth,—I am not aware that they ever appealed to such; not even because of a strong association: but because the alleged (240)
146n.32   downwards."] downwards, and thus, and not on any *a priori* grounds, did they

argue that there could not be antipodes, as persons so situated would fall away into a lower space. (240–1)

201.18 powers by] powers (specially mentioned by Locke, *Essay*, B. II. c. ii. §23) by (118)

201.18 thus] "thus (118) [*McCosh is quoting from JSM*]

216n.18 "elaborated] At this point Mr. Mill hands us over to his friend Professor Bain, who, in *The Senses and the Intellect*, has elaborated (121)

216n.19 Mill's Logic;"] Mill's *Logic*. (121)

216n.29–31 "as . . . things,"] But he was led by the influence of this teacher to regard it as . . . things; and to adopt his favourite method of procedure, which is by deduction from an hypothesis, which he endeavours to show explains all the phenomena. (8)

216n.31 "the influence"] [*see entry above*]

225n.24 "a] Those born blind cannot have the visual idea of space, but they have, he says, a (143n)

231n.3–4 case," . . . "is] case is (163)

231n.5–6 (Phil. Trans. of Roy. Soc. 1841). The] (*Phil. Trans. of Roy. Soc.* 1841), and I shall quote from it at considerable length. The (163)

231n.9 light, a sheet] light, "a sheet (163) [*McCosh is quoting from Franz*]

231n.12–13 denominations," . . . vertical. "'The] denominations." "The (164) [*McCosh is quoting from Franz*]

231n.16 cube . . . sphere] *cube . . . sphere* (164)

231n.17 was] were (164)

231n.18 quadrangular . . . circular] *quadrangular . . . circular* (164)

231n.19 square . . . disc] *square . . . disc* (164)

231n.25 quadrates." . . . "A] quadrates. A (164)

231n.26 plain" . . . "triangle] plain triangle (164)

231n.30–1 it; in fact, said he, I must give it up.] it, 'in fact,' said he, 'I must give it up.' (165)

232n.5–6 the object." . . . "When] the objects. When (165)

237n.10 "This case] The case (151n)

246.6 "if] From a very early age, and long before they give any evidence of knowing distance beyond their bodies, or having any other acquired perceptions, children will indicate that they know at least vaguely the seat of the pain felt by them—if (150)

246.7–8 "any acquired perceptions"] [*see entry above*]

246.14–15 "Müller," . . . "has collected . . . cases,"] Müller has collected . . . cases (*Ib.*, pp. 746, 747). (148) ["Ib." *refers to Müller's* Physiology]

246.16 "a student] "A student (148) [*McCosh is quoting from Müller*]

261n.24–5 "that . . . judgment"] Association may help us to form a reasonable judgment— and it is a happy circumstance when it does so; but whether we are or are not so aided, we should be taught that . . . judgment, in which we look to the nature of things as the same can be discovered by us. (214)

261n.25 "to] But it is a still higher end of the highest education to raise us above all hereditary and casual association of times or circumstances, and to constrain us to (214–15)

284n.10 discover," . . . "no] discover no (185)

284n.11 sensations."] sensations, or that two remembered sensations will ever be anything else than two remembered sensations. (185–6)

317n.1 "I think] I also think (276)

338n.1 "mere] This cannot be said of the second class, or those in which we compare mere (294)

338n.4 "has] I urge, further, in opposition to the doctrine, that in those propositions in which the terms are abstract, the predicate, properly speaking, has (333)

391n.2 "in] In (292)

391n.4 "the] In not a few propositions the (293)

391n.5 the crocodile is a reptile,] 'the crocodile is a reptile,' (293)

391n.9 "the] The (293)

391n.16 "proceed . . . things;"] The "tendency" to do this must surely proceed . . . things;

and the possibility of doing it surely implies an intimate relation between the Comprehension and the Extension. (293)

391n.20–1   "so . . . Comprehension,"] I have granted that, so . . . Comprehension. (303)

391n.21–2   "different . . . Extension,"] But it seems to me to be different . . . Extension. (303)

———— "Mill's Reply to his Critics," *The British and Foreign Evangelical Review*, XVII (April, 1868), 332–62.

QUOTED: 209n, 247, 248, 284n, 285n

REFERRED TO: cvii, 74n, 75n, 208n, 248n–9n, 262n

209n.5–6   "power . . . idea," . . . "empirical theory;"] If he take the other alternative, then he is giving to the mind the power . . . idea—a view utterly inconsistent with his own empirical theory, and the very view of Leibnitz, who makes *intellectus ipse* a source of ideas. (343–4)

209n.16   "mental laws, say the] Do they come in obedience to mental laws, say, to the (345)

209n.22   "obliged"] He is now replying to me (p. 248), is obliged to talk of one group of possibilities of sensations, "destroying or modifying another such group;" and this certainly not by laws acting independently of any discoverable cause in the series which constitutes mind. (346–7)

247.17   "normally"] According to that illustrious physiologist, we localise our affections received by the senses; and the law of our nature is, that in touch or feeling, we place the sensation at the spot where the nerve normally terminates. (350)

248.8–10   "should . . . this," . . . "might] According to the association theory, the affection should . . . this, according to Mr Mill, might (351)

248.20   "Eva] According to this theory, a person born without arms or legs could have no idea of space; but Schopenhauer has brought forward the case of Eva (352)

248.25   as they."] as they.* [*footnote:*]* My attention was called to this case by Mr Bleeck, in his *Mr J. S. Mill's Psychological Theory*. It is quoted by Schopenhauer in his *Die Welt als Wille*, vol. ii. c. 4, and is taken from *Frorieps Neue Notizen aus dem Gebiete der Natur*, July 1838. (353)

248.27–8   "that . . . extension,"] In my *Examination of Mill*, I endeavoured to meet this by psychological considerations, and shewed that . . . extension, could not give us the idea of extension. (352)

284n.21   "a wheel] Now, it so happens that I had produced the ring when a boy, by a lighted piece of paper; in my college days, I had seen the experiment of the seven colours; and, in my mature life, I have seen a wheel (354)

285n.5–6   "the power . . . belief."] It relates to the power . . . belief,—in fact, to take the place of judgment or the comparison of things. (353)

MAHAFFY, JOHN PENTLAND, intro. and trans. Kuno Fischer. *A Commentary on Kant's Critick of Pure Reason*. London: Longmans, Green, 1866.

NOTE: the reference at 27n is to the Introduction, Pt. IV, "The Variations between the First and Second Editions of the Critick, and the Idealism of Kant," and to Appendix C, which includes commentary on those variations.

QUOTED: 145n, 146n, 207n–8n, 225n, 240–1, 244, 266n

REFERRED TO: civ, 27n, 242, 243, 263n

145n.7   "There] Yet there (viii)

145n.8   kind. We] kind. [*1-paragraph omission*] We (viii)

207n.17   you," . . . "conscious] you conscious (lvi)

225n.5   originally] *originally* (xxi)

240.21   passage" . . . "will] passage (pp. 222, *seq.*) which follows will (xviii)

240.33–5   Abbott. (*Sight and Touch*, chap. v.) More] Abbott; "Sight and Touch," chap. v. More (xviii)

241.1   space . . . time] *space . . . time* (xviii–xix)

241.16–17   that . . . time.] *that . . . time.** [*footnote omitted*] (xix)

241.23   passage . . . "We] passage in p. 225: "we (xix)

241.28   changes] *changes* (xx)

241.28   move] *move* (xx)
241.31   Mill."] Mill himself (p. 230.). (xx)
266n.11   child," . . . "who] child who (xxvii)
266n.13   result. . . . Most] [*ellipsis indicates 6-sentence omission*] (xxvii–xxviii)

MAINE DE BIRAN, MARIE FRANÇOIS PIERRE GONTHIER. *Nouvelles Considérations sur les rapports du physique et du moral de l'homme*. Ed. Victor Cousin. Paris: Ladrange, 1834.
NOTE: the reference derives from Hamilton.
REFERRED TO: 237

MALEBRANCHE, NICHOLAS DE. Referred to: 152

―――― *Recherche de la vérité*, in *Œuvres*. Ed. Jules Simon. 2 vols. Paris: Charpentier, 1842, II.
REFERRED TO: 204n

MALTHUS, THOMAS ROBERT. Referred to: 110n

MANSEL, HENRY LONGUEVILLE. Referred to: 30n, 52, 57, 89–90, 207, 262, 465–6

―――― *The Limits of Religious Thought*. 4th ed. London: Murray, 1859.
NOTE: this is the ed. cited by JSM.
QUOTED: 47, 91, 91n, 92, 92n–3n, 93, 93n, 94n–5n, 95, 95–6, 96, 97n–8n, 98, 101, 103
REFERRED TO: 34n, 35n, 45n, 94, 97, 99n, 100, 102, 107n–8n, 383n
47.5   that," asked Hegel, "which] that," says Hegel, "which (30)
91.7   "such . . . Nature"] At present I am concerned only with its pretensions to such . . . Nature as can constitute the foundation of a Rational Theology. (29)
91.8–9   "to conceive . . . is." . . . "conceive] To conceive . . . is, we must conceive (30)
91.17   Absolute] *Absolute* (30)
91.18   Being."] Being [*note omitted*]. (30)
92.10   "a] A (31)
92.14   involves] implies (31)
92.14   relation."] relation [*note omitted*]. (31)
93.1–2   "supposing the . . . cause,"] Supposing the . . . cause, it will follow that it operates by means of free will and consciousness. (32)
93.3   "volition] The act of causation must therefore be voluntary; and volition (32)
93.8   "conscious of itself,"] The Absolute, it may be said, may possibly be conscious, provided it is only conscious of itself [*note omitted*]. (32)
93n.25   as . . . existence] *as . . . existence* (200)
94n.19   "if] If (34)
95n.1   *perfect*] [*not in italics*] (35)
95n.2   *its original perfection."*] [*not in italics; note omitted*] (35)
95n.5   *exhausting . . . being*] [*not in italics*] (38)
95n.7   Absolute."] Absolute; and we are involved in the self-contradictory assumption of a limited universe, which yet can neither contain a limit in itself, nor be limited by anything beyond itself. (38)
95.3   "nothing . . . reality,"] The metaphysical representation of the Deity, as absolute and infinite, must necessarily, as the profoundest metaphysicians have acknowledged, amount to nothing . . . reality [*note omitted*]. (30)
95.6   "all . . . included."] "What kind of an Absolute Being is that," says Hegel, "which does not contain in itself all . . . included?" [*note omitted*] (30)
95.7   infinite," . . . "must] infinite must (31)
95.15–16   "a whole composed of parts," or "a . . . attributes," or a "conscious . . . object.] Not only is the Absolute, as conceived, incapable of a necessary relation to anything else; but it is also incapable of containing, by the constitution of its own nature, an essential relation within itself; as a whole, for instance, composed of parts, or as a . . . attributes, or as a conscious . . . object [*note omitted*]. (33)
95.19   relatives.] relatives [*note omitted*]. (33)

95.22 matter.] matter [*note omitted*]. (33)
96.2 multiplicity."] multiplicity [*note omitted*]. (33)
96.19–20 "that . . . inconceivable," it "consequently] By the *Infinite* is meant that which is free from all possible limitation; that . . . inconceivable; and which consequently (30)
96.23 "cannot] [*paragraph*] The *Infinite*, as contemplated by this philosophy, cannot (30)
96.32 "the] But the (48)
96.33 anything general] anything in general (48)
96.37 limitation.] limitation [*note omitted*]. (48)
97n.25 infinite. . . . And] infinite. We cannot, therefore, start from any abstract assumption of the divine infinity, to reason downwards to any object of human thought. And (60)
98n.1 thoughts] thought (60)
98.4 "the . . . Absolute" . . . "in . . . only" . . . "our] [*paragraph*] What we have hitherto been examining, be it remembered, is not the . . . Absolute in . . . only our (39)
98.7 Being."] Being,—a belief which appears forced upon us, as the complement of our consciousness of the relative and the finite. (45)
101.24 "that] We may suppose the existence in man of a special faculty of knowledge, of which God is the immediate object,—a kind of religious sense or reason, by which the Divine attributes are apprehended in their own nature [*note omitted*]: or we may maintain that (26)
101.27 God,"] God [*note omitted*]. (26)
101.29 "the] The latter [notion concerning means to convey a knowledge of God] is the method of the (26)
101.33 "all the excellences of] On the other hand, we meet with an opposite style of criticism, which reasons somewhat as follows: All the excellences, it contends, of (28)
101.38 character."] character [*note omitted*]. (28)
103.12–13 "the . . . conceiving"] [*see* 101 *above*] (xiii)

——— *The Philosophy of the Conditioned: comprising some remarks on Sir William Hamilton's Philosophy and on Mr. J. S. Mill's Examination of that Philosophy.* London and New York: Strahan, 1866.
NOTE: first published as: "The Philosophy of the Conditioned: Sir William Hamilton and John Stuart Mill," *Contemporary Review*, I (Jan. and Feb., 1866), 31–49, 185–219.
QUOTED: 24, 27, 28n, 29, 34n, 40, 45n, 46n, 50n, 52n, 57n, 58n, 64n, 76n, 77n, 85n, 93n–4n, 94n, 97n, 98n–9n, 99n, 104n–5n, 106n, 107n, 123n, 493n
REFERRED TO: ciii, cv, cvi, cvii, 22n, 25, 26, 28, 30, 30n, 32n, 38n, 49n, 56, 92n, 124n
24.28–30 "reacts . . . recipient,"] The assertion that all our knowledge is relative,—in other words, that we know things only under such conditions as the laws of our cognitive faculties impose upon us,—is a statement which looks at first sight like a truism, but which really contains an answer to a very important question,—Have we reason to believe that the laws of our cognitive faculties impose any conditions at all?—that the mind in any way reacts . . . recipient? (63–4)
27.4 "objects" . . . "things in themselves."] Having thus quietly assumed that "things in themselves" are identical with "objects," and "relations" with "impressions on the human mind," Mr. Mill bases his whole criticism on this tacit *petitio principii*. (79n) [*JSM reverses phrasal order; the quotation derives from Hamilton*]
27.4–7 "Objective existence" . . . "does . . . and a phenomenon . . . as an object] It is simply that *objective existence* does . . . and that a *phenomenon . . . as an object* (82–3)
28n.2–7 "If, indeed," . . . "Hamilton . . . no, he . . . possunt.'"] If, indeed, Hamilton . . . no,* [*footnote:*] *Essay*, ii. 8, §23. [*text:*] he . . . possunt."* [*footnote:*] *Reid's Works*, p. 839. (83–4)
29.5 "out . . . time"] "A direct intuition of things in themselves," according to Kant and Hamilton, is an intuition of things out . . . time." (77–8)
34n.10 "pseudo-concept . . . Infinite,"] Hence it is not to be wondered at—nay, it is a natural consequence of this doctrine,—that our positive conception of God as a Person cannot be included under this pseudo-concept . . . Infinite. (93)
40.21–2 "Out . . . completed" . . . "self-existent] If meant as a statement of Hamilton's use of

the term, it is incorrect: *absolute*, in Hamilton's philosophy, does not mean simply "completed," but "out . . . completed;" *i.e.*, self-existent. (104)

46n.4 Apparent."] Apparent.* [*footnote:*] *Republic*, Book v, p. 479. (109)

50n.1 "indefinitely increasable."] Can any man suppose that, when the Divine attributes are spoken of as infinite, it is meant that they are indefinitely increasable?* [*footnote omitted*] (114)

52n.4 "pseudo-infinite."] Whereas Mr. Mill, by laying down the maxim that the meaning of the abstract must be sought in the concrete, quietly assumes that this pseudo-infinite is a proper predicate of God, to be tested by its applicability to the subject, and that what Hamilton says of *this* infinite cannot be true unless it is also true of God. (93)

52n.17–18 "the unconditionally limited,"] Can Mr. Mill possibly be ignorant that all these attributes are relations; that the Absolute in Hamilton's sense, "the unconditionally limited," is not predicable of God at all; and that when divines and philosophers speak of the absolute nature of God, they mean a nature in which there is no distinction of attributes at all? (106)

57n.2 unconditioned" . . . "God] unconditioned, God (17)

57n.8–9 "one . . . depends,"] This is *Materialism*, which has then to address itself to the further problem, to reduce the various phenomena of matter to some one . . . depends. (7)

58n.9–10 "Hamilton . . . maintains . . . absolute and infinite . . . relative and finite."] Hamilton maintains . . . "absolute" and "infinite" . . . "relative" and "finite;" for "correlatives suggest each other," and the "knowledge of contradictories is one;" but he denies that a concrete thing or object can be positively conceived as absolute or infinite. (110)

64n.18 intuition."] intuition; but to show this in the various instances would require a longer dissertation than our present limits will allow. (126n)

64n.22 "When] But when (126n)

77n.6–7 "To . . . possible," . . . "we . . . possible; but we] It must be remembered that, to . . . possible, we . . . possible but that we (36n)

85n.1–2 "exhaust any finite number, by] Simply because of a conventional arrangement, by which a single digit, according to its position, can express, by one mark, tens, hundreds, thousands, &c., of units; and thus can exhaust the sum by (134)

85n.3 "exhaust the infinite."] But how can such a process exhaust the infinite? (134)

93n.37–94n.1 relation" . . . "and] relation, and (117)

94n.7–10 with undertaking . . . impossibility of conceiving a . . . wise (*i.e.* . . . . existence out . . . relation."] with "undertaking . . . impossibility" of conceiving "a . . . wise"* [*footnote:*] *Examination*, p. 95. [*text:*] (*i.e.* . . . . existence "out . . . relation." (153–4)

97n.3 "Is . . . higher perfection?"] To the first part of this objection we reply by simply asking, "Is . . . 'higher perfection?' " (158)

99n.13–15 saying, I . . . existence?"] saying, "I . . . existence?" (163)

99n.34–5 "the . . . itself," . . . "simple, . . . itself,"] It must therefore be conceivable as the . . . itself; and as simple, . . . itself. (100)

99n.36–40 "we . . . that" . . . "own . . . subject," . . . "only . . . other,"] We . . . that His own . . . subject; but we can conceive Him only . . . other.* [*footnote omitted*] (28)

104n.3 "Mr. Mansel asserts] Mr. Mansel, as we have said, asserts (164)

105n.15 child. . . . We] child. [*ellipsis indicates 1-page omission*] We will not pause to comment on the temper and taste of this declamation; we (167–8)

105n.16–17 it certainly is, . . . fellow creatures] it constantly is, . . . "fellow creatures," (168)

105n.20–1 a good father . . . a good son? . . . as good,] a *good father* . . . a *good son?* . . . as *good*, (169)

106n.32 "We] But as regards the former part, we (172)

107n.26 "The . . . Rationalist] Now the . . . "Rationalist" (175)

123n.1–2 "Hamilton," . . . "maintains] Hamilton maintains (129n)

493n.1–3 "Sir W. Hamilton . . . paper."] Either Sir W. Hamilton . . . paper, or the blunders are Mr. Mill's own. (181)

—————— *Prolegomena Logica. An Inquiry into the Psychological Character of Logical Processes*. Oxford: Graham; London: Whittaker, 1851.

314.8   *sight? . . . All] sight? [ellipsis indicates 9-page omission]* To clear up the point at issue, it will be necessary to bear in mind two facts which have just been noticed; viz. firstly, that in every complete act of conception, the attributes forming the concept are contemplated as coexisting in a possible object of intuition; and, secondly, that all (29)

314.9   only. . . . Similarities] *[ellipsis indicates 5-sentence omission]* (30)

314.10   differences:] differences*; *[footnote omitted]* (31)

318.26–7   "We can," . . . "and] On the other hand, throughout Berkeley's dissertation, too little notice is taken of the important fact, that we can, and (31)

318.28   individualization. . . . I] individualization. But this is done, not in any mere act of conception, but only in the more complex operations of thought in which such act is presupposed. I (31)

318.31–2   *The . . . signified] [not in italics]* (31–2)

322.21–2   "the . . . concepts."] The . . . concepts: the true singular proposition in Logic is not one in which the concept is *materially* limited to an individual by extralogical considerations, but one in which it is *formally* so limited by a sign of individuality. (63)

322.22–3   "The man" .h. . "as] But the man, as (62)

322.25   Cæsar . . . Pompey,] "Cæsar . . . Pompey," (62)

332n.23–4   "may . . . This is here."] The result of every such act may . . . "this is here." (53)

332n.27   "But] Every operation of thought is a judgment, in the psychological sense of the term: but (54)

332n.30   other. . . . The] other. The former cannot be distinguished as true or false, inasmuch as the object is thereby only judged to be present at the moment when we are conscious of it as affecting us in a certain manner; and this consciousness is necessarily true. The latter is true or false, according as the relations thought as existing between certain concepts are actually found in the objects represented by those concepts or not. The (54–5)

337n.20   other is] other set is (59)

337n.33   "must . . . attributes"] Every notion, that is to say, as a condition of its conceivability, must . . . attributes, in consequence of which it is capable of subordination to a higher notion: and it must contain a limited number only of attributes, in consequence of which lower notions may be subordinated to it. (184–5)

337n.34   "for] For (185)

337n.36–7   are never] are thus never (185)

337n.37   object;"] object. (185)

355.7   distinction between] distinction adopted between (226)

355.9   Matter] *Matter* (226)

355.11   Form] *Form* (226)

355.14   it."] it*. *[footnote omitted]* (226)

366.29   "accepts] Thus it accepts (265) *[see next entry]*

366.32   themselves . . . leaving] *[ellipsis indicates that JSM has altered the order of the sentences; see previous entry]* It is competent to test the validity of all such products, in so far as they comply or not with the conditions of pure thought; leaving (265)

448n.16   "In] In this sense, motives addressed to the will are not causes; for, in (152)

465.12   "by] But if they would consider that by (298)

465.12   necessarily] *necessarily* (298)

465.14   does] *does* (299)

465.16   case. No] case; they probably would not find this doctrine either contrary to their experience or revolting to their feelings. And no (299)

465.18   this" . . . "is] this, we might add, is (299)

468.22   "but] The strongest motive prevails; but (302)

——— "Supplementary Remarks on Mr. Mill's Criticism of Sir William Hamilton," *Contemporary Review*, VI (Sept., 1867), 18–31.

QUOTED: 77n, 103n, 107n

REFERRED TO: cvi–cvii, 29n, 35n, 50n, 74n, 85n, 93n

77n.10   "mentally] When I say, "to conceive a thing as possible," I mean mentally (27)

103n.3   "the phenomena] Mr Mill, on the other hand, declares that he will call no being good who is not what he means when he applies the epithet to his fellow creatures; and as his only means of judging are by the phenomena through which such a being is manifested, the declaration can only mean that he will call no being good, the phenomena (30)

107n.8   "if power] For if *power* (30n)

MASSON, DAVID. *Recent British Philosophy: A review, with criticisms; including some comments on Mr. Mill's answer to Sir William Hamilton.* London and Cambridge: Macmillan, 1865.

NOTE: the "substance" of the work was delivered as lectures at the Royal Institution, 21, 23, and 28 March, 1865. A second ed. appeared in 1867. The quotation at 207 is indirect.

QUOTED: 207, 492n

REFERRED TO: vi, 30, 498n

207.14   organic union] It [the notion of Mind or Self] includes an organic *union* somehow of the present with the non-present, the identity somehow, in one conscious organism, of the *was*, the *is*, and the *is to be*. (335)

492n.7   "Try him] Throw that [his strength, nerve, and felicity of style] aside, and try him (308)

492n.12   discussion? . . . Let] discussion. Throw this aside too, and let (308)

492n.12   W.] William (309)

MERSENNE, MARIN.

NOTE: the reference, in a quotation from Hamilton, derives from Baillet.

REFERRED TO: 483

MERVOYER, PIERRE MAURICE. *Etude sur l'association des idées.* Paris: Durand, 1864.

REFERRED TO: 250n

MILL, JAMES. Referred to: 9, 116, 217n, 299, 493n

────── *Analysis of the Phenomena of the Human Mind.* 2 vols. London: Baldwin and Cradock, 1829.

NOTE: at 252–3 JSM would appear to be quoting directly from his father, although Hamilton quotes the same passage; one of the references at 256 is in a quotation from Hamilton.

QUOTED: 115–16, 252–3, 282

REFERRED TO: 67, 199, 253–4, 255, 256, 257, 259, 283

116.2   say that I] say I (I, 170)

116.31   Generical marks] GENERICAL *marks* (I, 172)

252.24–5   "Where . . . ideas," . . . "have] 8. [Mill's eighth observation on the law of association] Where . . . ideas have (I, 68)

252.32   single] simple (I, 68)

252.36–7   compounded. . . . [*paragraph*] It] [*ellipsis indicates 5-paragraph omission*] (I, 69–70)

253.2   is, of concomitance] is, concomitance (I, 71)

253.11   Some] 9. [Mill's ninth observation on the law of association] Some (I, 71)

253.13   we may make] we make (I, 72)

253.33–4   "The . . . another, or] [*paragraph*] The . . . another idea, or (I, 75)

282.12   "under an . . . to:"] That this is no argument against the existence of those feelings, will be made apparent, by the subsequent explanation of other phenomena, in which the existence of certain feelings, and an . . . to them, are out of dispute. (33)

MILL, JOHN STUART. *Auguste Compte and Positivism* (1865). In *Essays on Ethics, Religion, and Society, Collected Works*, X, 261–368.

NOTE: the reference is, more specifically, to 265–9.

REFERRED TO: 217n

———— "Bailey on Berkeley's Theory of Vision," in *Essays on Philosophy and the Classics, Collected Works*, XI, 245–69.

NOTE: reprinted from *Dissertations and Discussions*, II, 84–114; originally in *Westminster Review*, XXXVIII (Oct., 1842), 318–36.

REFERRED TO: 256n

———— "Coleridge," in *Collected Works*, X, 117–63.

NOTE: reprinted from *Dissertations and Discussions*, I, 393–466; originally in *London and Westminster Review*, XXXIII (March, 1840), 257–302.

REFERRED TO: 208n–9n

———— "Grote's Plato," in *Essays on Philosophy and the Classics, Collected Works*, XI, 375–440.

NOTE: reprinted from *Dissertations and Discussions*, III, 275–379; originally in *Edinburgh Review*, CXXIII (April, 1866), 297–364.

REFERRED TO: 46n

———— *On Liberty* (1859). In *Essays on Politics and Society, Collected Works*, XVIII, 213–310.

REFERRED TO: 459n

———— *A System of Logic: Ratiocinative and Inductive* (1848; 8th ed., 1872). *Collected Works*, VII and VIII.

NOTE: though the references generally predate the 8th ed. (the copy-text for the *Collected Works*), most of them are to arguments contained in all editions, and so the version in *Collected Works* (which gives all variant readings) is cited; the reference at 75n is specifically to the 6th ed. (1865). The quotations at 450n are taken from Alexander, *q.v.*; that at 465 is taken from Mansel. The reference at 324 is editorial, calling attention to a parallel passage.

QUOTED: 450n, 465

REFERRED TO: cviii, 68, 75n, 216n, 216n–17n, 262n, 271, 300, 324, 369n, 390, 416, 439n

450n.26   "practical feeling of Free Will"] The metaphysical theory of free will, as held by philosophers, (for the practical feeling of it, common in a greater or less degree to all mankind, is in no way inconsistent with the contrary theory,) was invented because the supposed alternative of admitting human actions to be *necessary*, was deemed inconsistent with every one's instinctive consciousness, as well as humiliating to the pride and even degrading to the moral nature of man. (VIII, 836)

450n.26–7   "a feeling . . . of,"] [*paragraph*] And indeed, if we examine closely, we shall find that this feeling, of our being able to modify our own character *if we wish*, is itself the feeling . . . of. (VIII, 841)

———— *Utilitarianism* (1861). In *Collected Works*, X, 203–59.

REFERRED TO: 460n

MILTON, JOHN. *Paradise Lost*, in *The Poetical Works of Mr. John Milton*. London: Tonson, 1695, 1–343.

NOTE: the quotation at 42 is in a quotation from Hamilton.

QUOTED: 42, 198, 488

42.16   "Won from the cold and formless *Infinite*."] Or hear'st thou rather pure Ethereal Stream, / Whose Fountain who shall tell? before the Sun, / Before the Heav'ns thou wert, and at the voice / Of God as with a Mantle didst invest / The rising world of waters dark and deep, / Won from the void and formless infinite. (62; III, 7–12)

198.23   "hanging self-balanced" on its own "centre"] Thus God the Heav'n created, thus the Earth, / Matter unform'd and void: Darkness profound / Cover'd th' Abyss: but on the watry calm / His brooding wings the Spirit of God outspread, / And vital virtue infus'd, and vital warmth / Throughout the fluid Mass, but downward purg'd / The black tartareous cold infernal dregs / Adverse to life: then founded, then conglob'd / Like things to like, the rest to several place / Disparted, and between spun out the Air, / And Earth self-balanc'd on her Centre hung. (186; VII, 232–42)

488.18–19 "cycle on epicycle, orb on orb?"] To ask or search I blame thee not, for Heav'n /
Is as the Book of God before thee set, / Wherein to reade his wondrous Works and learn /
His Seasons, Hours, or Days, or Months, or Years: / This to attain, whether Heav'n move
or Earth, / Imports not, if thou reck'n right, the rest / From Man or Angel the great
Architect / Did wisely to conceal, and not divulge / His secrets to be scann'd by them who
ought / Rather admire; or if they list to try / Conjecture, he his Fabrick of the Heav'ns /
Hath left to their disputes, perhaps to move / His laughter at their quaint Opinions wide /
Hereafter, when they come to model Heav'n / And calculate the Stars, how they will wield
/ The mighty frame, how build, unbuild, contrive / To save appearances, how gird the
Sphere / With Centrick and Eccentrick scribl'd o'er, / Cycle and Epicycle, Orb in Orb:
(201–2; VIII, 66–84)

MONTESQUIEU, CHARLES-LOUIS DE SECONDAT, BARON DE LA BRÈDE ET DE.
Referred to: 358n

MÜLLER, JOHANNES PETER. *Elements of Physiology.* Trans. with notes, William
Baly. London: Taylor and Walton, 1837.
NOTE: JSM takes the quotations and the reference (which is to a section added by Baly) from
McCosh.
QUOTED: 246, 246–7
246.16 "a student] [*paragraph*] d. [4th of 9 cases cited] A student

NEFFTZER, AUGUSTE. "*La Vie de Jésus* par M. Ernest Renan," *Revue Germanique et
Française*, XXVII (Sept., 1863), 181–4.
QUOTED: 136n

NEWTON, ISAAC.
NOTE: the reference at 152 is in a quotation from Hamilton; that at 297 in a quotation from
Mansel.
REFERRED TO: 92, 152, 297, 434, 449n, 487, 488

——— *Philosophiæ Naturalis Principia Mathematica*, in *Opera quae exstant
omnia.* Ed. Samuel Horsley. 5 vols. London: Nichols, 1779–85, II–III.
NOTE: this ed. is used for ease of reference. The so-called "Jesuit's Edition" (Geneva:
Barillot, 1739–42) is in JSM's library, Somerville College. The references at 191, 420 are to
Newton's theory of gravity; that at 476 is in a quotation from Hamilton.
QUOTED: 421n
REFERRED TO: 191, 420, 476
421n.1–3 "Causas rerum naturalium non plures admitti debere quam quæ *et veræ sint*, et
earum phænomenis explicandis sufficiant."] *Causas rerum naturalium non plures admitti
debere, quàm quæ & veræ sint, & earum phænomenis explicandis sufficiant. [Regula I of*
Regulæ Philosophandi] (III, 2)

NICOLE, PIERRE. See Arnauld, and Baynes.

NUNNELEY, THOMAS. *On the Organs of Vision: Their Anatomy and Physiology.*
London: Churchill, 1858.
NOTE: the quotations are taken by JSM from Fraser, *q.v.* Fraser also reprints the relevant
passage in his ed. of Berkeley's *Works*, I, 446–8. Nunneley identifies his subject only as "a
fine and most intelligent boy, nine years of age," who lived in "a very large manufacturing
village, about sixteen miles from Leeds." (31)
QUOTED: 232n–3n, 236n–7n
232n.32 "at] He could at (32)
232n.33–4 in the shapes of objects," . . . "were . . . same visible figure," . . . "it was] in their
shapes; though he could not in the least say which was the cube, and which the sphere, he
saw they were . . . same figure. It was (32)
232n.34–5 till they had been many times] until they had many times been (32)
232n.35 by sight] by the eye (32)
232n.37 judgments] perception (32)
232n.38 could tell] could or would tell (32)

232n.38   eye] eyes (32)
232n.39   in] into (32)
232n.39   hands. Even] hands; even (32)
236n.17   "said] The boy said (32)
237n.1   walked carefully] walked most carefully (32)
237n.1   up] out (32)

OCCAM. See Ockham, William of.

OCKHAM, WILLIAM OF.
NOTE: the quotation is mistakenly attributed by Hamilton to Ockham. See Ponce.
QUOTED: 418

O'HANLON, HUGH FRANCIS. *A Criticism of John Stuart Mill's Pure Idealism; and an attempt to shew that, if logically carried out, it is pure nihilism.* Oxford and London: Parker, 1866.
NOTE: the passages quoted on 203n, 203n–4n are from an intended letter to Mill (dated 5 Dec., 1866), printed on pp. 12–15 of the pamphlet, in reply to a letter (not extant? O'Hanlon says received 5/12/66) in which Mill asked whether O'Hanlon had published his views, as given in a letter to Mill of Nov., 1865.
QUOTED: 203n, 203n–4n, 205n, 206n–7n
REFERRED TO: civ, 204n
203n.4   absence. . . . If the] absence. [*ellipsis indicates 1¼-page omission*] But if so, if the (12, 14)
203n.5   any] my (14)
203n.7   ground. If] ground. [*paragraph*] If (14)
203n.7   the fire] "the fire" (14)
203n.8   any] my (14)
203n.9–10   modifications . . . absent."] "modifications . . . absent." [*i.e., the quotation marks occur because O'Hanlon is quoting JSM*] (14)
203n.21   "Conceding the] [*paragraph*] Again, conceding the (14)
205n.5   "the] In drawing this conclusion, in extending to C [the group of permanent possibilities of sensation I call my friend Smith], which so closely resembles B [the group of sensations and of permanent possibilities of sensation I call my body], my experience of B, I, according to Mr. Mill, do but extend the (7)
205n.7   "The] [*paragraph*] I. [of four points] The (7)
205n.7   (a)] [*paragraph*](a.) (7)
205n.8   (b)] [*paragraph*] (b.) (8)
206n.33   "A] [*paragraph*] A (8)
206n.39   me, combined] me, or rather in a greater degree, combined (9)
206n.39–40   manner. Yet] manner. [*paragraph*] Yet (9)

OVID. *Metamorphoses* (Latin and English). Trans. Frank Justus Miller. 2 vols. London: Heinemann; New York: Putnam's Sons, 1916.
NOTE: this ed. used for ease of reference. The quotation is in a quotation from Hamilton.
QUOTED: 287
287.10   "Omnia mutantur; nihil interit,"] omnia mutantur, nihil interit: errat et illinc / huc venit, hinc illuc, et quoslibet occupat artus / spiritus eque feris humana in corpora transit / inque feras noster, nec tempore deperit ullo, / utque novis facilis signatur cera figurio / nec manet ut fuerat nec formas servat easdem, / sed tamen ipsa eadem est, animam sic semper eandem / esse, sed in varias doceo migrare figuras. (II, 376; XV, 165–72)

OWEN, ROBERT. Referred to: 453

PALEY, WILLIAM. *Natural Theology: or, Evidences of the Existence and Attributes of the Deity, collected from the Appearances of Nature.* London: Faulder, 1802.
REFERRED TO: 192

—— *A View of the Evidences of Christianity in Three Parts.* 3 vols. London: Faulder, 1794.
REFERRED TO: 192

PASTEUR, LOUIS. Referred to: 280

PERSIUS (Aulus Persius Flaccus). *Satires*, in *Juvenal and Persius* (Latin and English). Trans. G. G. Ramsay. London: Heinemann; New York: Putnam's Sons, 1920, 310–400.
NOTE: this ed. used for ease of reference. The quotation is in a quotation from Hamilton.
QUOTED: 286
286.20 "Ex nihilo nihil, in . . . reverti,"] non ego curo / esse quod Arcesilas aerumnosique Solones / obstipo capite et figentes lumine terram / murmura cum secum et rabiosa silentia rodunt / atque exporrecto trutinantur verba labello, / aegroti veteris meditantes somnia, gigni / de nihilo nihilum, in . . . reverti. (350–2; III, 78–84)

PHILLIPPS, LUCY F. MARCH ("An Inquirer"). *The Battle of the Two Philosophies. By an Inquirer.* London: Longmans, Green, 1866.
NOTE: Lucy F. March Phillipps is identified as the author of the *Battle of the Two Philosophies, inter alia*, on the title page of her Lectures on the *Cumulative Evidences of Divine Revelation* (Cambridge: Deighton Bell; London: Bell and Sons, 1883).
QUOTED: 46n–7n, 124, 141n, 147n, 447n, 451–2, 452n, 458n–9n, 466n, 492n
REFERRED TO: ciii, 38n, 49n, 441n, 493n
124n.3–4 "a very intricate point;"] The charge then is, that in examining the phenomena of knowledge and belief, Sir W. Hamilton ascertained a real distinction existing between them; that in working out the consequences of this distinction he met with a difficulty he had not at first noted; that he had occasion in the course of a lecture on logic to point out this difficulty, but could not then go into it, because his pupils were unprepared for its investigation, and a lecture on logic was not the proper place for an irrelevant discussion on a very intricate point. (32–3)
124n.15–16 "continual . . . discrepancies,"] So also when Mr. Mill charges Sir W. Hamilton with, indeed proves against him continual . . . discrepancies, it would not be difficult to show, both from history and reason, that all sound philosophy, whilst thus incomplete, must be liable to the objection of inconsistency. (7)
141n.5–6 "contrary to all analogy" . . . "that consciousness . . . education."] It is wholly contrary to all analogy, and therefore to all *primâ facie* probability, that consciousness . . . education. (52)
147n.3–5 "at the root of all experience;" . . . "that no experience . . . us."] Lastly, we must show "that it lies at the root of all experience," i.e. that no experience . . . us.* [*footnote:*] *Lectures on Metaphysics*, vol. i. pp. 268–270. (54)
447n.1–2 "gratuitously . . . foreknowledge."] The fourth vice is gratuitously . . . foreknowledge; or even with our being able to judge what men will do, and with there being any such uniformity of volitions as may suffice for statistical averages. (45)
451.25–452.1 "if the temptation . . . made:"] Afterwards, I am as distinctly conscious of having made an effort; and if the temptation . . . made. (43)
452.2 is wholly] is necessarily, or in fact, wholly (44)
452.3 effort. . . . When] effort: if these desires are equally balanced, they mutually destroy each other, and then no effort is possible; if one is ever so little stronger than the other, no effort is necessary. When (44)
452.4 up, no . . . scales.] up—it is Mr. Mill's own illustration—no . . . scales, and any such effort would be that factor in the result, which Mr. Mill is bound to exclude. (44)
458n.7–459n.2 "well . . . opinion, because . . . subject,"] But we cannot but think it a pity, when a well . . . opinion is thrown aside, not from its internal failure, but because . . . subject. (50)
459n.15–19 "If . . . right.' . . . And] Again: if . . . right." By increasing its attractions, you necessarily increase my desire for it. And (49)
459n.20 deserve. . . . For children] deserve; the stronger my evil desire is, the greater the

reward that is to counterbalance it must be; if your first reward is insufficient, you must increase it till its attractions exceed those of the unlawful pleasure. In the case of offenders against society, it might not be prudent thus to strengthen their too feeble virtue by rewards. But it would be quite just; and for children (49)

466n.6–7 "how . . . circumstances."] How . . . circumstances, Mr. Mill omits to say. (46n)

492n.20–3 "that . . . think."] One great ground of censure is, that Sir W. Hamilton has done so little, and left that little so incomplete; but Mr. Mill wholly ignores that . . . think; a work which Plato considered the only work worthy to be called philosophical. (6–7)

PINDAR. *Olympian Odes*, in *The Odes of Pindar Including Principal Fragments* (Greek and English). Trans. John Sandys. London: Heinemann; Cambridge, Mass.: Harvard University Press, 1946, 1–149.
NOTE: this ed. used for ease of reference.
QUOTED: 499n

PLATNER, ERNST. *Philosophische Aphorismen nebst einigen Anleitungen zur philosophischen Geschichte*. 2 vols. Leipzig: Schwickertschen Verlage, 1793, 1800.
NOTE: the quotation at 223–4 (partly repeated at 236) is from Hamilton's translation of the passage in *Lectures* (*q.v.* for the collation); all the references derive from Hamilton, including those that include reference to Mahaffy and McCosh. Platner does not identify the blind person described.
QUOTED: 223–4
REFERRED TO: 224–5, 225n, 227, 229, 237, 238

PLATO. Referred to: 502

——— *Apology*, in *Euthyphro, Apology, Crito, Phædo, Phædrus* (Greek and English). Trans. H. N. Fowler. London: Heinemann; Cambridge, Mass.: Harvard University Press, 1917, 68–144.
NOTE: this ed. used for ease of reference.
REFERRED TO: 129–30

——— *Phædrus*, in *ibid.*, 412–578.
NOTE: this ed. used for ease of reference.
REFERRED TO: 2–3

——— *Republic* (Greek and English). Trans. Paul Shorey. 2 vols. London: Heinemann; Cambridge, Mass.: Harvard University Press, 1946.
NOTE: this ed. used for ease of reference. The reference at 45n derives from Mansel; that at 46n is in a quotation from Mansel.
REFERRED TO: 45n, 46n, 457n

——— *Sophist*, in *Theætetus, Sophist* (Greek and English). Trans. H. N. Fowler. London: Heinemann; Cambridge, Mass.: Harvard University Press, 1921, 264–458.
NOTE: this ed. used for ease of reference.
QUOTED: 44n

——— *Timæus*, in *Timæus, Critias, Cleitophon, Menexenus, Epistles* (Greek and English). Trans. R. G. Bury. London: Heinemann; New York: Putnam's Sons, 1929, 16–252.
NOTE: this ed. used for ease of reference.
REFERRED TO: 419

PLOTINUS. *Operum philosophicorum omnium libri LIV. in sex enneades distributi*. Basel: Lecythus, 1580.
REFERRED TO: 39–40

PLUTARCH. *Life of Cæsar*, in *Lives* (Greek and English). Trans. Bernadotte Perin.

11 vols. London: Heinemann; Cambridge, Mass.: Harvard University Press, 1914–26, VII, 442–608.
NOTE: this ed. used for ease of reference.
REFERRED TO: 281

POIRET, PETER. Referred to: 151

PONCE, JOHN. Annotation in Duns Scotus, *Opera Omnia*. Ed. Luke Wadding, John Ponce, *et al*. 12 vols. Lyons: Durand, 1639, VII, 723.
NOTE: Mill, following Hamilton (who apparently originated the error), attributes the phrase to William of Ockham; for a full, spirited, and apparently still authoritative discussion of the matter, including the attribution to Ponce, see W. M. Thorburn, "The Myth of Occam's Razor," *Mind*, XXVII (July, 1918), 345–53.
QUOTED: 418

PTOLEMY. Referred to: 333

RAVAILLAC, FRANÇOIS. Referred to: 461, 462n

RÉGIS, REY. See CAZILLAC.

REID, THOMAS.
NOTE: the references at 151, 153n, and the last at 168, are in quotations from Hamilton.
REFERRED TO: 1, 62, 109, 110, 111, 113, 119, 123, 128, 137, 137n, 138, 143, 151, 153n, 155, 157, 168, 169, 175, 183, 196, 197, 216, 239, 250, 257, 493n

———— *The Works of Thomas Reid, Collected, with Selections from his Unpublished Letters. Preface, Notes, and Supplementary Dissertations by Sir William Hamilton. Prefixed, Stewart's Account of the Life and Writings of Reid, with Notes by the Editor*. Edinburgh: Maclachlan and Stewart; London: Longman, Brown, Green, and Longmans, 1846.
NOTE: see Hamilton, "Dissertations on Reid" and "Foot-notes to Reid"; and individual works by Reid, below.

———— *Essays on the Active Powers of the Human Mind*, in *ibid*., 509–679.
NOTE: in this ed., Hamilton includes the original page numbers, which we have omitted in the collations.
QUOTED: 356n, 440, 444
REFERRED TO: 468
356n.8   theologians."] Theologians; but Mr. Hume seems not to have attended to it, or to have thought it to be words without any meaning. (650)
440.2–3   "far . . . inference," "can . . . from"] [*paragraph*] Those, therefore, who reason justly from this system of materialism, will easily perceive that the doctrine of necessity is so far . . . inference, that it can . . . from it. (635)
444.21   "Is] [*paragraph*] Is (610)

———— *Essays on the Intellectual Powers of Man*, in *ibid*., 215–508.
NOTE: in this edition, Hamilton includes the original page numbers, which we have omitted in the collations.
QUOTED: 69n, 111, 112, 137n, 172, 172–3, 173, 174, 323, 328
REFERRED TO: 75, 113, 162, 190, 257, 498n
69n.1   "To conceive, to imagine, to apprehend] Let it be observed, therefore, that to *conceive*, to *imagine*, to *apprehend* (223)
69n.4   false. But] false. [*paragraph*] But (223)
69n.4   these] those (223)
69n.5   cannot be] cannot easily be (223)
69n.6   ambiguity. . . . When] ambiguity. Politeness and good-breeding lead men, on most occasions, to express their opinions with modesty, especially when they differ from others whom they ought to respect. Therefore, when (223)

69n.11–12   it. Thus] it. [*paragraph*] Thus (223)

69n.15   opinion. . . . When] opinion. This ambiguity ought to be attended to, that we may not impose upon ourselves or others in the use of them. The ambiguity is indeed remedied, in a great measure, by their construction. When (223)

69n.16   accusative case] *accusative case* (223)

69n.18   infinitive mood] *infinitive mood* (223)

69n.20   they] the words (223)

111.37–8   "immediate knowledge of the past,"] [*paragraph*] It is by memory that we have an immediate knowledge of things past. (339)

112.24–5   "when . . . object,"] But the difficulty is to make his [Berkeley's] opinion coincide with the notions of the vulgar, who are firmly persuaded that the very identical objects which they perceive, continue to exist when they do not perceive them; and who are no less firmly persuaded that, when . . . object. (284)

137n.4–6   "The vulgar . . . and are] [*see collation at* 112.24–5 *above*] (284)

172.31–2   *The one is the sign*] [*not in italics*] (312)

172.34   *perceive them by means*] [*not in italics*] (311)

172.37   *conclude*] [*not in italics*] (310)

173.7–8   *the . . . it*] [*not in italics*] (315)

173.8   forgot. . . . The] [*ellipsis indicates 4-sentence omission*] (315)

173.8–9   The sensations . . . qualities . . . carry] [*paragraph*] Let him again touch the pointed body gently, so as to give him no pain; and now you can hardly persuade him that he feels anything but the figure and hardness of the body: so difficult it is to attend to the sensations . . . qualities, when they are neither pleasant nor painful. They carry (315)

173.10   *Nature . . . signs*] [*not in italics*] (315)

173.12–13   *If . . . follows*] [*not in italics*] (320)

173.16   *the sign*] [*not in italics*] (332)

173.16–17   *brought . . . sign*] [*not in italics*] (332)

173.17   *sign*. In] sign. [*paragraph*] In (332)

173.17   *the . . . sensations*] [*not in italics*] (332)

173.18–19   *The . . . perceived*] [*not in italics*] (332)

173.20   nature. Thus] nature. [*paragraph*] Thus (332)

173.22   *it . . . followed*] [*not in italics*] (332)

174.16   "If we] [*paragraph*] If, therefore, we (258)

174.18   First] *First* (258)

174.19   Secondly] *Secondly* (258)

174.20   Thirdly] *Thirdly* (258)

174.25   "This] [*paragraph*] I observed, *Thirdly*, That this (259)

174.27   perceive."] perceive; we ask no argument for the existence of the object, but that we perceive it; perception commands our belief upon its own authority, and disdains to rest its authority upon any reasoning whatsoever. (259)

323.5   "Most] [*paragraph*] It will be true that most (404)

328.7   "I give] That I may avoid disputes about the meaning of words, I wish the reader to understand, that I give (415)

328.8   *what is true . . . what is false*] [*not in italics*] (415)

———— *Inquiry into the Human Mind*, in *ibid.*, 93–211.

QUOTED: 72n, 169, 170, 171

REFERRED TO: 74n, 172, 175, 234n, 257, 356, 421

72n.24   "every] [*paragraph*] *Prop.* 1. Every (148)

72n.24–5   itself," . . . "any] itself. [*3-paragraph (each 1-sentence long) omission*] [*paragraph*] 5. Any (148)

72n.25   points."] points, and mutually bisect each other. (148)

72n.27–9   "that . . . place." . . . "have . . . sense," . . . "no . . . all, since they would often] [*paragraph*] "It is to be observed, that every Idomenian firmly believes, that . . . place. For this they have . . . sense, and they can no . . . all. They often (151)

169.23   "class of natural signs which . . . though] A third class of natural signs comprehends those which, though (122)

169.26   "I] [*paragraph*] I (122)
169.29   our] any (122)
169.31   "when] When (137)
170.4   "I] But I (111)
170.6   exist. . . . And] exist; that memory suggests the notion of past existence, and the belief that what we remember did exist in time past; and that our sensations and thoughts do also suggest the notion of a mind, and the belief of its existence, and of its relation to our thoughts. By a like natural principle it is, that a beginning of existence, or any change in nature, suggests to us the notion of a cause, and compels our belief of its existence. And (111)
170.6   manner, certain] manner, as shall be shewn when we come to the sense of touch, certain (111)
170.8   motion."] motion, which are nowise like to sensations, although they have been hitherto confounded with them. (111)
170.9   "By] I see nothing left, but to conclude, that, by (121)
170.11   words, this] words, that this (121)
170.19   "Extension] [*paragraph*] Extension (123)
170.19–20 us . . . by] us, by (123)
170.29   "The feelings] [*paragraph*] What hath imposed upon philosophers in this matter is, that the feelings (124)
171.1   he feels it hard] *he feels it hard* (125)
171.5   force. There] force. [*paragraph*] There (125)
171.6   it. . . . The hardness] it. In order to compare these, we must view them separately, and then consider by what tie they are connected, and wherein they resemble one another. The hardness (125)
171.15   "There] [*paragraph*] Now, there (188)
171.16–17 original . . . constitution] *original . . . constitution* (188)
171.17   custom] *custom* (188)
171.17   reasoning. Our] *reasoning.* [*paragraph*] Our (188)
171.18   ways. . . . In] ways, our acquired perceptions in the second, and all that reason discovers of the course of nature, in the third. In (188)
171.20   placed.] placed—as hath been already explained in the fifth chapter of this inquiry. (188)
171.21   "In] [*paragraph*] In (194)
171.24   signified. . . . The] signified. [*paragraph*] We have distinguished our perceptions into original and acquired; and language, into natural and artificial. Between acquired perception and artificial language, there is a great analogy; but still a greater between original perception and natural language. [*paragraph*] The (194–5)
171.24   perceptions] perception (195)
171.28   sign] signs (195)
171.29   creates] create (195)
171.30   "It] Thus, it (195)

RÉVILLE, ALBERT. "De la liberté et du progrès à propos des anciens et des modernes," *Revue Germanique et Française*, XXVII (Sept., 1863), 5–37.
QUOTED: 458n
458n.1   "La liberté] J'entends par là que la liberté (21)

RICARDO, DAVID. Referred to: 110n

ST. ANSELM. *Proslogion seu Alloquium de Dei Existentia*, in *Opera Omnia*, Vols. CLVIII–CLIX of Jacques Paul Migné, ed., *Patrologiæ cursus completus, Series latina*. Paris: Migné, 1853–54, CLVIII, cols. 223–42.
NOTE: this ed. used for ease of reference. The quotation is in a quotation from Hamilton. See also St. Augustine.
QUOTED: 61
61.18   Crede ut intelligas] Neque enim quæro intelligere, ut credam; sed credo, ut intelligam. (227)

ST. AUGUSTINE.
NOTE: the quotation, which is in a quotation from Hamilton, is mistakenly attributed by him to St. Augustine, whom he calls St. Austin.
QUOTED: 42

—— *De Utilitate credendi ad Honoratum liber unus*, in *Opera Omnia*, Vols. XXXII–XLVII of Jacques Paul Migné, ed., *Patrologiæ cursus completus, Series latina*. Paris: Migné, 1841–49, XLII, cols. 65–92.
NOTE: this ed. used for ease of reference. The quotation at 61 appears also in *Retractiones, ibid.*, XXXII, col. 607 (Lib. I, Cap. xiv). As Mill quotes Hamilton's translation of this passage, no collation is given. In conjunction with this passage, Hamilton also cites passages from Abelard (mistakenly) and St. Anselm; in fact, both passages are to be found together in St. Augustine, *Sermo* XLIII, *ibid.*, XXXVIII, col. 258 (Cap. vii).
QUOTED: 61

ST. AUSTIN. See St. Augustine.

SANCHEZ, FRANCISCO. *Minerva, sive De Causis Latinæ linguæ commentarius, cui accedunt animadversiones & notæ*. Ed. Caspar Schoppe and Jacobus Perizonius. Franeker: Strickius, 1687.
NOTE: in JSM's library, Somerville College. The reference is in a quotation from Hamilton.
REFERRED TO: 476

SANCTIUS. See Sanchez.

SANDERSON, ROBERT. *Logicæ Artis Compendium*. 2nd ed. Oxford: Lichfield and Short, 1618.
NOTE: this ed. in JSM's library, Somerville College. JSM's spelling is Saunderson.
QUOTED: 414
414.5   contraria] *Contraria*, (52)
414.7   susceptibili."] susceptibili: ut *Calor & Frigus*. (52)

SAUNDERSON. See Sanderson.

SCHEIBLER, CHRISTOPH. *Opera Philosophica*. 2 vols. Frankfurt: Wustii, 1665.
NOTE: JSM's spelling, Schiebler, is treated as a typographical error.
REFERRED TO: 400n

SCHELLING, FRIEDRICH WILHELM JOSEPH VON.
NOTE: the reference at 52n is in a quotation from Bolton; that at 152 is in a quotation from Hamilton.
REFERRED TO: 19, 33n, 42, 52n, 56n, 68, 152, 486, 495

SCHMID, HEINRICH. *Versuch einer Metaphysik der inneren Natur*. Leipzig: Brockhaus, 1834.
NOTE: JSM quotes from Hamilton's translation in *Lectures*, *q.v.* for the collation.
QUOTED: 273n, 274n
REFFERED TO: 251n

SCHMIDTS.
NOTE: identified by Müller (the authority quoted by McCosh, from whom JSM quotes) only as a student from Aix.
REFERRED TO: 246

SCHOPENHAUER, ARTHUR. *Die Welt als Wille und Vorstellung*. 2 vols. in 1. Leipzig: Brockhaus, 1844.
NOTE: JSM uses McCosh's translation of the passage (though he may have located it himself; see his comment following the quotation; McCosh gives the reference only as Vol. II, Chap. iv), which Schopenhauer takes from Dr. A. Heuck, *q.v.*
QUOTED: 248

SEXTUS EMPIRICUS. *Against the Logicians II*, in *Sextus Empiricus* (Greek and English). Trans. R. G. Bury. 4 vols. London: Heinemann; New York: Putnam's Sons, 1933–49, II, 240–488.
NOTE: this work is often referred to as *Against the Mathematicians VIII*.
REFERRED TO: 39–40

——— *Outlines of Pyrrhonism*, in *ibid.*, I.
QUOTED: 383n

SHAKESPEARE, WILLIAM. *Macbeth*.
NOTE: since the reference is simply to characters in the play, no ed. is cited.
REFERRED TO: 408–9

——— *Twelfth Night*.
NOTE: the quotation is indirect. The comparative passage is taken from the Variorum Edition of Horace H. Furness.
QUOTED: 464
464.8 ginger is hot in the mouth:] Toby. Dost thus think that because thou art vertuous, there / shall be no more cakes and ale? / Clown. Yes, by S. Anne, and Ginger shall be hotte y'th / mouth too. (II, iii, 113–16)

SMITH, HENRY BOYNTON. "Mill's Examination of Hamilton's Philosophy," *American Presbyterian and Theological Review*, IV (Jan., 1866), 126–62.
QUOTED: 58n, 187n
REFERRED TO: civ
58n.20–1 "about . . . entities," . . . "simply] In particular, he justly insists upon it, that the alleged difficulties and contradictions vanish so soon as we cease to talk about . . . entities, and consider them simply (134)
187n.20–2 "an . . . consequence."] [*paragraph*] 6. It is partly implied in what precedes, but is also worthy of distinct notice, that Mr. Mill in all his reasonings on this point assumes an . . . consequence, which he elsewhere as emphatically denies. (157)

SMITH, SAMUEL. *Additus ad Logicam*. 7th ed. Oxford: Hall, 1656.
NOTE: the copy of this ed. in the London Library (bound with Edward Brerewood, *Elementa Logicæ* [Oxford: Hall, 1657]) is autographed "J. Mill" on the title-page, and was presumably given by JSM with other of his father's books.
QUOTED: 414
414.28 "Contraria] [*paragraph*] Contraria (56)
414.30 natura. Ad] naturâ. [*paragraph*] Ad (56)
414.32 positiva."] positiva; tertiò ut se invicem expellant, nisi alterum eorum insit à natura: sic *calor & frigus in aquâ, in pariete albedo & nigredo contrariantur.* (56)

SMITH, WILLIAM HENRY. "J. S. Mill on Our Belief in the External World," *Blackwood's Magazine*, XCIX (Jan., 1866), 20–45.
QUOTED: 201n, 244, 244n
REFERRED TO: civ, 240
201n.2–3 by which they [Things] act upon each other] *by which they act upon each other* (28)
244.18 felt nowhere] *felt nowhere* (26)
244.23 "that . . . will get our pains into our bodies] But we insist on this, that . . . will *get our pains into our bodies* (27)
244.26 other. . . . Many] [*ellipsis indicates 3-sentence omission*] (27)
244.27 acquired perception.] "acquired perception." (27)
244n.1–2 "measure itself"] It follows, therefore, that a muscular sensation, by its greater or less endurance, *measures itself*—measures its own greater or less endurance. (32)

SOCRATES.
NOTE: the reference at 45n derives from Mansel, that at 484 derives from Hamilton.
REFERRED TO: 45n, 129–30, 484, 502

SOPHOCLES. *Œdipus the King, Œdipus at Colonus*.
NOTE: since the reference is general, no ed. is cited.
REFERRED TO: 465

SPENCER, HERBERT. Referred to: 51, 143n, 216n

―――― *First Principles*. London: Williams and Norgate, 1862.
NOTE: in JSM's library, Somerville College. The passages cited are illustrative only.
REFERRED TO: 10

―――― "Mill *versus* Hamilton―The Test of Truth," *Fortnightly Review*, I (15 July,
1865), 531–50.
QUOTED: 144n, 145n, 381n
REFERRED TO: cv, 143n,
144n.5 "the more] The hypothesis that the more (548)
144n.5–6 among" . . . "states] among his states (548)
144n.7 his consciousness:"] his consciousness, furnishes him with solutions of numerous
facts of consciousness: not, however, of all, if he assumes that his adjustment of inner to
outer relations has resulted from his own experiences alone. (548)
144n.24–5 "I find . . . consciousness"] Of this difference I can give no further evidence than
that I am conscious of it, and find . . . consciousness. (538–9)
144n.37–8 "only . . . experiences," . . . "on what] On the other hand, the reply that this truth
is known only . . . experiences, suggests the query―On what (549)
144n.39 memory,"] memory, and its validity is determined solely through the trustworthiness of memory. (549)
144n.39–40 "the . . . memory" . . . "immediate consciousness"] Is it then that the . . .
memory is less open to doubt than the immediate consciousness that two quantities must
be unequal if they differ from a third quantity in unequal degrees? (549)
145n.28 "the net . . . time,"] Considering that I have avowed a general agreement with Mr.
Mill, in the doctrine that all knowledge is from experience, and have defended the test of
inconceivableness on the very ground that it "expresses the net . . . time" (*Principles of
Psychology*, pp. 22, 23)―considering that, so far from asserting the distinction quoted
from Sir W. Hamilton, I have aimed to abolish such distinction―considering that I have
endeavoured to show how all our conceptions, even down to those on Space and Time, are
"acquired"―considering that I have sought to interpret forms of thought (and by implication all intuitions) as products of organized and inherited experiences (*Principles of
Psychology*, p. 579)―I am taken aback at finding myself classed as in the above paragraph.
(536)
145n.36 ice] *ice* (543)
145n.37 cold] *cold* (543)

―――― *Principles of Psychology*. London: Longman, Brown, Green, and
Longmans, 1855.
QUOTED: 227–8
227.40 This symbolic] We have seen that a set of retinal elements may be excited simultaneously, as well as serially; that so, a quasi single state of consciousness becomes the
equivalent of a series of states; that a relation between what we call *coexistent positions*
thus represents a relation of *successive positions*; that this symbolic (224)
227.41 and by] and that, by (224)

SPINOZA, BARUCH. Referred to: 485

STEPHEN, JAMES FITZJAMES. "Mr. Mansel's Metaphysics," in *Essays by a Barrister*. London: Smith, Elder, 1862, 320–35.
NOTE: the essays were reprinted from the *Saturday Review*.
QUOTED: 71n–2n
REFERRED TO: 72n, 266
71n.14 "Consider] Let Mr. Mansel consider (333)
72n.13 he had ever seen] he ever saw (334)

72n.20   exist."] exist; and Mr. Mansel rests his conclusion, that straight lines could not under any circumstances enclose a space, on the impossibility of conceiving that they should do so. (334)

STEWART, DUGALD.
NOTE: the reference at 127 and the second at 256 are in quotations from Hamilton.
REFERRED TO: 110, 119, 127, 143, 155, 183, 196, 197, 216, 250, 252, 255, 256, 278n, 282, 421, 470, 490n, 491n, 493

———— *Elements of the Philosophy of the Human Mind*. 3 vols. Vol. I, London: Strahan and Cadell; Edinburgh: Creech, 1792. Vol. II, Edinburgh: Constable; London: Cadell and Davies, 1814. Vol. III, London: Murray, 1827.
NOTE: all the references are to Vol. I, Chap. ii, "Of Attention"; the quotation is from Vol. I, Chap. v, Part 2, §1, "Of the Influence of Casual Association on our Speculative Conclusions."
QUOTED: 254
REFERRED TO: 278, 280, 281
254.19–20   "In consequence," . . . "of our always] The former of these words expresses (at least in the sense in which we commonly employ it) a sensation in the mind; the latter denotes a quality of an external object; so that there is, in fact, no more connexion between the two notions, than between those of pain and solidity* [*footnote omitted*]; and yet, in consequence of our always (I, 341)
254.23–5   "of very . . . connexion with one another."] I. I formerly had occasion to mention several instances of very . . . connexion with each other. (I, 341)

———— *Philosophical Essays*. Edinburgh: Creech, and Constable; London: Cadell and Davies, Murray, and Constable, Hunter, Park and Hunter, 1810.
NOTE: the references, all to Essay First, Part I, Chap. i, are in a quotation from Hamilton.
REFERRED TO: 127, 128

STIRLING, JAMES HUTCHISON. *Sir William Hamilton, being the Philosophy of Perception; an Analysis*. London: Longmans, Green, 1865.
QUOTED: cv, 27n, 131n
cv.22–3   a . . . disingenuousness"] I seem to myself to have discovered in Hamilton a . . . disingenuousness that, cruelly unjust to individuals, has probably caused the retardation of general British philosophy by, perhaps, a generation; and it is the remaining parts of my deduction that are, after all, the best fitted to demonstrate this, and establish grounds for any indignation which I may have been consequently led to express—though without the slightest ill-will, of which, indeed, however adverse to the mischievous vein concerned, I am entirely unconscious. (vii)
27n.18–19   "the second] I hold the second (30n)
131n.4   "It is] For the truth is even that which is viewed by Hamilton as an absurdity: in very truth there is a consciousness beyond consciousness; and it is (58)

TAINE, HIPPOLYTE. *De l'Intelligence*. 2 vols. Paris: Hachette, 1870.
REFERRED TO: 250n

TUCKER, ABRAHAM.
NOTE: the reference is in a quotation from Hamilton.
REFERRED TO: 152

TURGOT, ANNE ROBERT JACQUES. Referred to: 100

VALENTIN, GABRIEL GUSTAV. "Ueber die subjectiven Gefühle von Personen, welche mit mangelhaften Extremitäten geboren sind," *Repertorium für Anatomie und Physiologie*, I (1836–37), 328–37.
NOTE: the reference derives from McCosh, who takes it from an addition by Baly to Müller's text.
REFERRED TO: 247

VEITCH, JOHN. Referred to: 30n

———— *Memoir of Sir William Hamilton, Bart*. Edinburgh: Blackwood and Sons, 1869.
NOTE: the third Appendix (referred to at 503n) is entitled "Sir William Hamilton on Hume, Leibnitz and Aristotle."
REFERRED TO: cvii–cviii, 503n

VIRGIL (PUBLIUS VERGILIUS MARO). *Aeneid*, in *Works*. Trans. H. Rushton Fairclough. 2 vols. London: Heinemann; New York: Putnam's Sons, 1916, I, 240–570; II, 2–364.
NOTE: this ed. used for ease of reference. The quotation is in a quotation from Hamilton. *Opera*, ed. C. G. Heyne (London: Priestley, 1821), is in JSM's library, Somerville College.
QUOTED: 17
17.26 "Rerumque . . . gaudet."] Talia per clipeum Volcani, dona parentis, / miratur rerumque . . . gaudet, / attollens umero famamque et fata nepotum. (II, 110; VIII, 729–31)

VOLTAIRE, FRANÇOIS MARIE AROUET. *Micromégas, histoire philosophique*, in *Œuvres complètes*. 66 vols. Paris: Renouard, 1817–25, XXXIX, 141–67.
NOTE: this ed. in JSM's library, Somerville College.
REFERRED TO: 17–18

WALLIS, JOHN. *Institutio Logicae, Ad communes usus accommodata*. 3rd ed. Oxford: West, Crosley, Clements, and Peisley, 1702.
NOTE: a copy of this ed., autographed "J. Mill" on the title-page, is in the London Library, presumably part of JSM's donation of his father's books.
QUOTED: 415
415.2 "Contraria] [*paragraph*] *Contraria* (63)
415.2 quæ . . . distant] [*in italics*] (63)
415.2–3 calidum . . . nigrum] [*in italics*] (63)
415.3 contrariæ qualitatis] *contrariæ qualitates* (63)

WALPOLE, HORACE. Referred to: 482

WARD, WILLIAM GEORGE. "Mr. Mill's Denial of Necessary Truth," *Dublin Review*, XVII (Oct., 1871), 285–318.
QUOTED: 165n–6n, 267–8, 269, 269–70, 270, 271
REFERRED TO: cviii, 74n, 166n, 261n
165n.10 "an exception"] Yet here is a most pointed *exception* to the school's general doctrine; and an exception which no phenomenist has made before. (309–10)
165n.14 position" . . . "is] position, his is (310)
165n.16 *ne plus ultra*] [*not in italics*] (310)
165n.23–4 "where the distinction lies between . . . intuitions"] There was an imperative claim on him, then, as he valued his philosophical character, to explain clearly and pointedly *where the distinction lies* between . . . intuitions. (310)
165n.28–9 "more favourably . . . trustworthiness"] To us it seems, that various classes of intuition are *more* favourably . . . trustworthiness, than is that class which Mr. Mill accepts. (310)
267.36 included] *included* (288)
268.3 triangularity . . . then] triangularity,—and if (as we established in our last number) the avouchment of my faculties corresponds infallibly with objective truth,—then (289)
268.6–7 "the . . . truth;"] All these are obvious and undeniable consequences of the fundamental proposition, that, by my very conception of a trilateral figure, I know its triangularity: and to admit therefore this fundamental proposition, is to admit that the . . . truth. (289)
269.6 "a] If, through my constant experience of triangular trilaterals, I am under a practical necessity of fancying that in every possible region of existence all trilaterals are

triangular—much more, through my constant experience of uniformity in phenomenal succession, must I be under a (290)

269.29 "in] Mr. Mill's whole reasoning turns on the phrase, "necessity of thought"; and yet he has used that phrase in (292)

269.29–34 A necessity of thought may . . . mean a . . . judgment. But . . . mean a . . . judgment.] A "necessity of thought" may . . . mean, "a . . . judgment." But . . . mean, "a . . . judgment." (292)

269.35 "that] Now we heartily agree with Mr. Mill, that (292)

269.35 necessity of thought] "necessity of thought" (292)

270.1 necessity of thought] "necessity of thought" (292)

270.2 circumstance. Yet] circumstance: yet (292)

270.3 necessity of thought] "necessity of thought" (292)

270.4 necessity of thought] "necessity of thought" (292)

270.20–1 "mere . . . account for] Most certainly therefore mere . . . account—as Mr. Mill thinks it does—for (299)

270.29–30 Omnipotence can] Omnipotence (if it exist)* [*footnote:*] *We must again remind our readers that, in this early stage of our argument with Mr. Mill, we are not at liberty to assume the *existence* of an Omnipotent Being. [*text:*] can (299)

270.31–2 habitually and unexceptionably] *habitually and unexceptionably* (299)

270.37 "holding] He [JSM] tells me, e.g., to fancy myself holding (298)

271.20–1 "power . . . experience" . . . "one . . . of geometrical forms,"] [*paragraph*] Then (2.) [Ward's second criticism of a passage which he has quoted from JSM's *Logic*]—whereas Mr. Mill purports to account for man's power . . . experience—he based that power on "one . . . of *geometrical* forms." (302) [*the quoted passage is from JSM's* Logic]

———— *On Nature and Grace. A Theological Treatise. Book I: Philosophical Introduction*. London: Burns and Lambert, 1860.

NOTE: only Bk. I was published. JSM's reference might be taken as general, but Chap. i, §1 is specially relevant (JSM's views are discussed, 25–9).

REFERRED TO: 164n–5n

WASHINGTON, GEORGE. Referred to: 100

WEBER, ERNST HEINRICH. "Der Tastsinn und das Gemeingefühl," in Rudolph Wagner, *Handwörterbuch der Physiologie mit Rücksicht auf Physiologische Pathologie*. 4 vols. Braunschweig: Bieweg, 1842–53, III, 481–588.

NOTE: the reference is in a quotation from Mahaffy, who takes his reference from Abbott (who does not give a precise reference).

REFERRED TO: 240

WHATELY, RICHARD. Referred to: 497, 497n–8n

———— *Elements of Logic. Comprising the substance of the article in the Encylopædia Metropolitana: with additions, &c.* London: Mawman, 1826.

NOTE: in JSM's library, Somerville College. Concerning the references at 316n, it may be noted that against the relevant passage (Whately, 56n) JSM has written in the margin "[An] important truth [n]ot sufficiently [e]xplained & [d]eveloped." Against the passage referred to at 354 JSM has pencilled lines in the margin. The quotation is not necessarily from Whately, but the related reference justifies its treatment as such.

QUOTED: 410

REFERRED TO: 316n, 348, 349, 350, 352, 354, 359, 362, 426

410.7 D,"] D; but A is not B, therefore C is D. (113)

WHEWELL, WILLIAM. Referred to: 143, 486

———— *An Elementary Treatise on Mechanics*. Vol. I. Cambridge: Deighton: London: Whittaker, 1819.

NOTE: no further volumes were published, though the volume was expanded and revised in later eds.

REFERRED TO: 496n

—————— *History of the Inductive Sciences, from the Earliest to the Present Time.*
3rd ed. 3 vols. London: Parker and Son, 1857.
NOTE: formerly in JSM's library, Somerville College.
REFERRED TO: 68

—————— *History of Scientific Ideas: being the First Part of the Philosophy of the
Inductive Sciences.* 3rd ed. 2 vols. London: Parker and Son, 1858.
NOTE: in JSM's library, Somerville College. This is the 3rd ed. of the Second Part of the
Philosophy of the Inductive Sciences (i.e., not the 3rd ed. of the *History of Scientific
Ideas*); cf. Whewell's *Novum Organon Renovatum*, which is the 3rd ed. of the First Part of
the *Philosophy of the Inductive Sciences*.
REFERRED TO: 68

—————— *Novum Organon Renovatum: being the Second Part of the Philosophy of
the Inductive Sciences.* 3rd ed. London: Parker and Son, 1858.
NOTE: in JSM's library, Somerville College. This is the 3rd ed. of the Second Part of the
Philosophy of the Inductive Sciences (i.e., not the 3rd ed. of the *Novum Organon
Renovatum*); cf. Whewell's *History of Scientific Ideas*, which is the 3rd ed. of the First Part
of the *Philosophy of the Inductive Sciences*.
REFERRED TO: 68

—————— *On the Philosophy of Discovery, chapters historical and critical; including
the completion of the third edition of the Philosophy of the Inductive Sciences.*
London: Parker and Son, 1860.
NOTE: in JSM's library, Somerville College. Much of this work is an enlargement of Bk. XII
("Review of Opinions on the Nature of Knowledge, and the Means of Seeking it") of the
Philosophy of the Inductive Sciences. Chap. xxii, "Mr. Mill's Logic," is a slightly modified
version of Whewell's *Of Induction, with especial reference to Mr. J. Stuart Mill's System
of Logic* (London: Parker, 1849).
REFERRED TO: 68

—————— *Thoughts on the Study of Mathematics as a Part of a Liberal Education.*
Cambridge: Deighton, 1835.
REFERRED TO: 477

—————— "To the Editor of the *Edinburgh Review*," *Edinburgh Review*, LXIII (April,
1836), 270–2.
NOTE: this is a criticism of Hamilton's "On the Study of Mathematics" (*q.v.*), which promp-
ted Hamilton's "Notes to the Above Letter" (*q.v.*); all three reprinted in Hamilton's
Discussions at 263–325, 326–8, 329–40.
REFERRED TO: 477

WOLFF, CHRISTIAN.
NOTE: the reference derives from Hamilton. Mill, following Hamilton, uses the spelling
Wolf.
REFERRED TO: 295

WORDSWORTH, CHRISTOPHER. *Memoirs of William Wordsworth.* 2 vols. London:
Moxon, 1851.
QUOTED: 488
488.24 [*paragraph*] "Some] [*no paragraph*] Some

WORDSWORTH, WILLIAM.
QUOTED: 488; see Wordsworth, Christopher.

WUNDT, WILHELM. *Beiträge zur Theorie der Sinneswahrnehmung.* Leipzig and
Heidelberg: Winter'sche Verlagshandlung, 1862.
NOTE: the reference derives from McCosh.
REFERRED TO: 247

XENOPHON. *Memorabilia*, in *Memorabilia and Œconomicus* (Greek and English). Trans. E. C. Marchant. London: Heinemann; New York: Putnam's Sons, 1923, 2–358.
NOTE: this ed. used for ease of reference. The reference is in a quotation from Hamilton.
REFERRED TO: 484

ZENO.
NOTE: the references are in quotations, or derive, from Hamilton.
REFERRED TO: 424–6

Index

tion of to object perceived, 111; memory and, 112, 160, 278, 279; every cognitive act comprehended in, 113; knowledge and, 117, 157, 273n, 274; perception and, 119, 150; insight as immediate, 122; character of facts of, 126–8, 147n; reality of and veracity of, 128; doubt and facts of, 129n, 134, 373; Cousin's misinterpretation of, 136; problem of determining what is revealed by, 138–9; condition for recognizing ultimate facts of, 142, 143; authority of, 149; question of duality of, 150–1; Natural Dualists, Cosmothetic Idealists, and testimony of, 152; foundation in of Natural Realism and Absolute Idealism, 153n; and Brown's theory of perception, 158, 158–9, 219–20; and absent or imaginary object, 176; act of mind as act of, 272n; spiritual treasures lying beyond sphere of, 273; production of modifications beyond, 275; minimum of time as condition of, 276n; association and consecution of thoughts in, 277; acquired habits and, 280; concentrated, 280; extension of to consider number of objects, 281; volition and movement as unknown to, 296, 296n; realization of concepts in, 305, 306, 325–6; formation of concepts and, 309; impossibility of eliciting concepts into, 316; judgment and, 330, 330–1; presence of mind and, 422; energy and, 431; freedom of will and testimony of, 443; idea of clearness and degree of, 494n

Mansel on: volition and, 93, 448n; the infinite and modes of, 96; finite character of objects of, 97n; immediate object of belief and, 123n; relation of time to objects of internal, 312; judgment and, 332n

O'Hanlon on: permanent possibilities of sensation and, 203n; intuition of external world in, 203n; principles of inductive evidence and, 205n; difficulty in psychological theory respecting, 206n–7n

Spencer on: relations among one's states of, 144n; inconceivability and states of, 145n; law of excluded middle and modes of, 381n

Consistency: logic of, 370–1; laws of, 373

Contiguity: and association, 177, 251n, 264; question of meaning of, 423

Contradiction: the absolute and law of, 65, 98; and inconceivability, 69–71; and unmeaning propositions, 78–9; Hamilton on law of, 79, 80–1, 295, 376, 377, 380; law of common to all phenomena, 87n; principle

of and Hamilton's law of conditioned, 88n; law of and nature of God's moral attributes, 104; laws of thought and law of, 372; role of logic respecting, 373; character of law of, 376–8; contradictory propositions and law of, 379, 380, 381; law of as law of existence, 382; Esser on truth and principle of, 407; Krug on contrariety and, 412; motion and law of, 424. *See also* Contrariety

Contrariety: Hamilton on relation of, 33n; question of meaning of, 411–16; Krug on contradiction and, 412; Aristotle on meaning of, 413; Ammonius on meaning of, 413; later Aristotelians on, 413–15. *See also* Contradiction

Conversion: Hamilton on simple, 395; and quantification of predicate, 398; Grote on Hamilton's theory of simple, 400n

Cosmothetic Idealism. *See* Idealism, Cosmothetic

Creation: Hamilton's argument concerning, 45n; Mansel on nature of God and, 45n; Hamilton's view of our conception of, 289–90

Hamilton on: nature of our conception of, 286, 287–8; cause of, 290n; inexplicability of ultimate phenomena of, 434

DEDUCTION: applied mathematics and scientific, 480–2; Descartes' abuse of, 485; in French and German thought, 485–6

Definition: and Hamilton's theory of judgment, 328–9; Hamilton on nature of, 335; nature of, 335; Mansel's account of better than Hamilton's, 337n; Hamilton's lecture on, 494n

Design, argument from, 192, 438–9

Determinism: and doctrine of necessity, 439n; as determination of will by motives, 463n. *See also* Necessitarianism, Necessity, Will

Dialectics, Socratic, 484

Difference: as essence of consciousness, 4; as condition of knowledge, 50–1; the absolute and condition of 51–2; Mansel on human attributes conceived under condition of, 97n; source of general notion of, 185

Hamilton on: relation of, 33n; meaning of the absolute and condition of, 43; Cousin's use of term, 55n

Discrimination: Hamilton on attention and, 490n; consciousness and, 490n

Disjunctive, Hamilton's use of word, 408–9

Diversity, Krug on confliction and, 325

thought, 485–6. *See also* Algebra, Arithmetic, Calculus, Geometry of Visibles, Mathematics

Geometry of Visibles, Reid's, 72n, 74n

God: and knowledge of noumena, 8; intuition of, 34, 36, 59; in relation to infinite and absolute, 34n, 35n, 36–9, 49, 52n, 83, 91, 93n, 94–8 *passim*, 441; Cousin on consciousness of, 36; Cousin's conception of, 36, 44, 44n, 45n, 137; meaninglessness of Hamilton's conception of, 45–7; positive conception of, 49, 99n; knowledge of under condition of plurality, 52; absolute cause and knowledge of, 53; necessary conditions of thought and conception of, 57; action of in time, 57n–8n; Mansel's view of our inadequate knowledge of, 89–101 *passim*; nature of attributes of, 102–3; significance of words applied to, 103–4; relation of man's attributes to those of, 105–7, 106n–7n, 108n; conception of moral attributes of, 108; Hamilton's doctrine of consciousness and belief in, 119; testimony of consciousness and veracity of, 132–4; Hamilton's view respecting foundation of our knowledge of, 134; intention of respecting our natural tendencies, 135; determination of mind by special interference of, 164; foundation of morality and arbitrary decree of, 165; psychological theory of ego and existence of, 192–3, 204; veracity of and belief in matter and mind, 193; Malebranche's view of external objects and, 204n; and Hamilton's view of actual and potential existence, 289–90; universe as thought in mind of, 290; mercifulness of, 393; Aristotle on nature and, 418; nature and, 418–19; in Leibniz's philosophy, 419, 500, 501; Hamilton's reasoning respecting inference of existence of, 438; freedom of will and belief in, 439, 441; and doctrine of necessity, 440; infliction of punishment by, 461; Ravaillac motivated by supposed duty to, 462n; predestination and working of, 469

Hamilton on: unknowability of, 34n–5n; Cousin's doctrine concerning, 44n; testimony of consciousness and nature of, 132; creation and, 286, 287–8, 290n; annihilation and, 288; complement of existence and, 289; as first cause, 293; mercifulness of, 393n; metaphysics and knowledge of, 437; nature of our knowledge of, 437–8; as moral governor, 438

Mansel on: creation and, 45n; conception of and action in time, 57n; inconceivability of nature of, 91, 98n–9n; belief in, 98, 98n–9n, 99n, 123n; human morality and, 101, 103; relation of man's attributes to those of, 104n–5n; phenomena produced by will of, 297

Government, art and science of, 350–1

Gravitation: Mansel on, 76n, 297; Hamilton on, 358; mentioned, 264, 422, 434, 474

Greeks: Lower, 39–40, 91; and principle of wholeness, 40n; Mahaffy on view of concerning circular motion, 240; Hamilton's knowledge of, 494

Guilt, and punishment, 458–65

HINDUS, 198

Human nature: Mansel on human attributes and, 104n; and application of word "good," 105n; distance of from divine nature, 108n; and permanent possibilities of sensation, 182; attributes forming subject of treatises on, 336; and science of politics, 350–1; excursion through phenomena of, 435; and man's capability of moral government, 453; and preference for salutary over pernicious, 457n; and wonder, 487

Hydrostatics, and art of navigation, 351

Hypothetical Realism. *See* Idealism, Cosmothetic

IDEALISM: and sensations, 6–7; Kant's socalled refutation of, 27n; basis of, 137n–8n; and belief in matter, 140, 196; with respect to ego and non-ego, 152; O'Hanlon on JSM's pure, 203n

Hamilton on: extremes of materialism and, 23; Fichte's, 151; foundation of Absolute, 153n

Cosmothetic: Hamilton's contempt for, 17n, 153, 153n, 239; Hamilton on, 28n, 152, 153n, 159, 168–9, 175; Hamilton's view of problematical reality of attributes in, 29n; with respect to ego and non-ego, 152; Hamilton's division of, 154–5; Brown and, 159, 171–2, 175–6; and theory of representative knowledge, 161; infers unknown cause from known effect, 162; assumption shared by Hamilton and, 162n, 163n; weak case of against Berkeley, 163n; Reid and, 169, 171–6; and act of perception, 174; and natural beliefs, 239

Ideas: Lockean, 15, 155, 169, 362; Hamilton on Lockean and Cartesian doctrines of, 28n; nature of complex, 48; James Mill on

theory of association, 251n; and laws of obliviscence, 257; signs and, 258; cases of latent, 274; Schmid's argument respecting mind and medium of, 274n; consciousness and, 278–80; sensations and, 282; and recalling of attributes, 310; representation of object in, 352; and perception of harmony, 491n

Hamilton on: consciousness and, 112, 127, 151, 278, 279; contents of act of, 160–1; perception by, 256; restoration of extinct, 274; comparison of past sound as retained in, 491n

Metaphysics: difficulties of at root of all science, 2; Hamilton's place in history of, 4; Comte and, 10, 300; and relativity of knowledge, 11; and doctrine asserting intuitive knowledge of God, 36; Hamilton's introduction of words into English, 39n; Hegel and transcendental, 47; and doctrine of absolute cause, 53; question of terminology in, 63, 69; numerous doctrines of lack substance, 88; Mansel a pupil of Hamilton in, 89; Mansel's mystical, 99n; Hamilton and Scottish school of, 109; and varying significance of difference of names, 115; Hamilton's capacity for, 128; distinction between introspective and psychological methods in, 139, 148; and question of external world, 150; Hamilton a polemical thinker in, 160; Ward as able defender of intuitional, 267; and memory of sensations, 280; and different opinions respecting general names, 301–2; and distinction between analytical and synthetical judgments, 334; and meaning of particles, 354; characteristic doctrine of Kantian, 355; judgments and purposes of abstract, 387; Hamilton on utility of studying, 437; authority in, 449n; mathematics and, 470, and probabilities, 471; and ultimate premises, 474; character of French, 485; Hamilton brings before reader fundamental questions of, 490; Masson on Hamilton and British, 492n; Grote on Hamilton as teacher of, 492n; Kant and constitution of, 493n; incompleteness of Hamilton's treatment of, 494; conflicting systems of in Hamilton's philosophy, 495; Whately's contribution to, 498n. See also Ontology

Meteorology, and art of navigation, 351

Middle Ages, 301, 302, 497

Mind: and relativity of knowledge, 5–12, 17, 19n–20n, 20–1, 31, 188, 208; in Kant's philosophy, 8–9, 23, 27, 27n, 29n, 154, 154n, 355; question of role of original furniture of, 10; and theory admitting capacity of absolute knowledge, 12; contribution of to act of knowledge, 24–6; and representative perception, 27, 29n, 154–5, 175; and doctrine of direct perception, 28, 29n–30n, 30, 32n; and necessary laws of thought, 56–7; and question of inconceivability, 67–70, 73–5, 77n, 78, 79, 82; Stephen on inconceivability and, 71n–2n; laws of, 79, 108, 140, 154, 184, 208n, 209n, 448n; magnitude and duration as forms of, 88n; Mansel and theory of powers and limitations of, 90; and our conception of God's moral attributes, 108; and consciousness, 110–11, 113, 115, 135, 154, 280–1, 448n; memory and, 112, 274; nihilism denies objective existence of, 134; origin of ideas and formation of theory of, 141; belief as original intuition of, 143, 143n; and matter as understood by Cosmothetic Idealists, 152; Hamilton's classification of opinions respecting knowledge of matter and, 153n; in Brown's theory of perception, 156, 158; sensation and, 163n, 165n, 179–81, 184, 187n, 189, 189n–90n, 208n, 209n, 225; modification of and existence of unknown cause, 164; and Hamilton's theory of representative knowledge, 164; and act of perception as understood by some Cosmothetic Idealists, 174; capable of expectation, 177; and psychological theory, 190–4, 196, 198–201, 249; veracity of God as argument for belief in, 193; Mansel's distinction between belief in matter and in, 195n; not perceived or cognized according to Malebranche, 204n; unacceptability of common theory of, 206; reality of, 208; nature of our conception of, 211; Bain's great work on, 216; McCosh on causes and, 216n; and notion of length, 220; Brown on notion of divisibility and, 221n; and idea of extension, 220–3; common opinions of, 239; Schmid's theory of, 251n, 274n; James Mill on association and, 252–3, 253; and necessity, 261, 270; and self-evident necessity, Ward on, 270; unconscious states of, 272; Hamilton's exploration of deeper regions of, 272–3; and stored-up knowledge, 273; Schmid on vital activity of, 274n; perception and unconscious mental modifications of, 275–7; Cardaillac on reminiscence and, 281n; Berkeley on abstract ideas and, 304; and concepts, 317, 321, 327, 328, 330,

332n, 343; and judgments, 330, 386–9;
logic and operation of, 356; phenomenol-
ogy and nomology of, 358n; and forms of
thought, 360, 364; acts of and products of
acts of, 361–2; acts and passive states of,
363–4; laws of thought and structure of,
381; relation of to brain, 422; spirituality
of, 440; free-will, necessity, and, 441; effect of philosophy on, 449n; and associating wrong with punishment, 463;
Hamilton's view of processes of, 470; and
study of mathematics, 470–1, 473, 480;
laws of physical nature and, 486; Jacobi
on physical science and mechanical system of, 487; Hamilton's mode of tunnelling, 495; Leibniz's view of matter and,
501

Hamilton on: our knowledge of, 13, 16–17,
33n, 42, 188–9; perception and, 14, 23, 61,
126–7, 137n, 158, 158–9; and knowledge
of modes, 22; act of knowledge and, 26n,
117; unknowability of the absolute and
the infinite to, 41; conceivability and, 76;
law of conditioned and, 79; consciousness and, 110, 112n, 115, 126, 128, 272n,
279; contrast of known matter and
knowing, 126; absolute co-equality of
matter and, 150; view of nihilists respecting knowledge of, 151; philosophers
who identify matter with, 152; distinction
between Natural Dualists and Cosmothetic Idealists respecting knowledge of,
152; memory and, 112, 160–1, 279; representative knowledge and, 163, 164; and
knowledge of extension, 239; unconscious states of, 272; spiritual treasures
hidden in recesses of, 273; unconscious
possession of whole systems of knowledge by, 274; belief in causality and impotence of, 287; abstract general notions
and, 303; relation of language to, 311–12;
judgment as act of, 330; laws and necessity in world of, 358; forms of thought
and, 361; representation of imagination
and, 362n; action of throughout body,
422; and inconceivability of motion, 424;
energy and modification of, 431; and inference of God's existence, 438; inconceivability of actual phenomena of, 443;
study of mathematics and cultivation of,
475

Mansel on: role of in constitution of
knowledge, 24; meaning of objective
existence and, 27; necessary truths and
constitution of, 262

Reid on: word "conceive" and operations
of, 69n; natural signs and constitution of,
170, 171; perception as act of, 174; judgment as determination of, 328
See also Ego

Minimum visibile, conceivability of, 86

Miracles: intuition and impossibility of,
136n; Nefftzer on impossibility of, 136n

Modifications: Brown's theory of mental, 15,
155–7; consciousness of ego's, 111;
Hamilton's view of consciousness and
mental, 116–17; representative knowledge and mental, 161; unknown cause
and mental, 164; in possibilities of sensation, 181, 197, 203n; notion of mind and
mental, 189; O'Hanlon on in permanent
possibilities of sensation, 203n; antithesis
between ego and ego's, 210n; unconscious mental, 272–3, 275–84; Lockean
ideas as mental, 362

Hamilton on: obtaining of knowledge and
mental, 22, 23; memory and mental, 112,
160–1; consciousness and mental, 117;
mediate perception and mental, 152; unconscious mental, 272, 274, 275, 277

Mohammedans, 469

Momentum, science of dynamics and doctrine of, 358

Monadology: Hamilton on Leibniz's theory
of, 500; Leibniz's theory of, 500, 502

Monists, ego and non-ego as understood by,
152

Monotheism, 300

Morality: psychology as scientific basis of, 2;
Mansel on God and human, 101, 103,
104n–5n; and use of language, 102; God's
attributes and human, 103; intuition and,
165n; art of, 350; Hamilton on liberty and,
438; of philosophic inquiry, 439; Alexander on necessity and, 457n; freedom of
will and, 463n; purpose of Socrates respecting, 484

Motion: Hamilton on phenomena of, 16;
Eleatic argument respecting, 45n, 424–7;
Reid on sensations of touch as suggesting,
170, 171; and resistance, 214–15; Mahaffy
on idea of, 240–1; Berkeley on abstract
idea of, 304; science of dynamics and laws
of, 357; Hamilton on inconceivability of,
424, 424–5, 443

Motives: Reid's view of action and, 444;
Phillipps on balancing of, 452; Alexander
on, 457n, 463n; and legitimacy of punishment, 458–65 *passim*; determination of
will by, 463n, 468–9; in doctrine of moral

ation and idea of, 252; of attributes in our consciousness, 311

Hamilton on: meaning of absolute, 43; Cousin's use of term, 55n; causes and progress towards, 293; when ascribable to any aggregate, 311n

Universals, 301, 302, 306

Universities, influence of Hamilton's articles on English, 492n. *See also* Cambridge University, Oxford University

Utilitarians, 454

VIS VIVA, science of dynamics and doctrine of, 358

Volition. *See* Will

WHOLENESS, as conceived by Greek thinkers, 40n

Will: entirely right, or wrong in different degrees, 37n, 38n; must be either free or caused, 87n; conception of power and conformity of event to, 107n; and possibilities of sensation, 182; and causation, 295–300; religion, morals, and disposition of, 350; and acts of mind, 363; and pleasure and pain, 432; human and divine, 441; power of over action, 450n; Phillipps on, 452; education of, 453; determination of by motives, 463n

Hamilton on: causality and, 295, 296, 296n; and formation of concepts, 309; preor-

dained passions of determined, 463n; attention as act of, 491n

Mansel on: consciousness and, 93, 448n; human and divine, 105n; power and, 107n, 297; strength of motives in relation to, 468

freedom of: law of conditioned applied to, 81–2; Hamilton asserts, 82, 441–8; and unimaginableness of event without cause, 146n; Mansel on, 297; importance to Hamilton of doctrine of, 437, 493; and existence of God, 439; Hamilton on necessity and, 442, 442–3, 444, 445; testimony of consciousness and, 447–53; Phillipps on, 447n, 466n; Alexander on, 449n, 451n, 463n; moral responsibility and, 453–4; moral distinctions and, 454–7; legitimacy of punishment and question of, 458–65; and moral causation, 465–6, 466n–7n; prediction of human actions and, 467; Mansel's arguments respecting, 468–9; study of physics and belief in, 486

See also Liberty

Wonder: Aristotle on as first cause of philosophy, 487; Hamilton on physical science and, 487; Jacobi on physical science and, 487; and knowledge of natural phenomena, 487–8; Faraday on nature and, 489

ZOOLOGY, as concrete science, 472

DATE DUE
